Energy Law

CAROLINA ACADEMIC PRESS

Context and Practice Series

Michael Hunter Schwartz
Series Editor

Administrative Law
Richard Henry Seamon

Advanced Torts
Alex B. Long and Meredith J. Duncan

**An Intersex Athlete's Constitutional Challenge,
Hastings v. USATF, IAAF, and IOC**
Olivia M. Farrar

Civil Procedure for All States
Benjamin V. Madison, III

Constitutional Law
David Schwartz and Lori Ringhand

Contracts
Michael Hunter Schwartz and Denise Riebe

Current Issues in Constitutional Litigation
Sarah E. Ricks, with contributions by Evelyn M. Tenenbaum

Employment Discrimination
SECOND EDITION
Susan Grover, Sandra F. Sperino, and Jarod S. Gonzalez

Energy Law
Joshua P. Fershee

Evidence
Pavel Wonsowicz

International Business Transactions
Amy Deen Westbrook

International Women's Rights, Equality, and Justice
Christine M. Venter

The Lawyer's Practice
Kris Franklin

Professional Responsibility
Barbara Glesner Fines

Sales
Edith R. Warkentine

Torts
Paula J. Manning

Workers' Compensation Law
Michael C. Duff

Energy Law

A Context and Practice Casebook

Joshua P. Fershee
West Virginia University College of Law

Carolina Academic Press
Durham, North Carolina

ISBN 978-1-59460-799-8
LCCN 2014943565

Carolina Academic Press
700 Kent Street
Durham, NC 27701
Telephone (919) 489-7486
Fax (919)493-5668
www.cap-press.com

Printed in the United States of America

Contents

Table of Principal Cases

Series Editor's Preface

Welcome to a new type of casebook. Designed by leading experts in law school teaching and learning, Context and Practice casebooks assist law professors and their students to work together to learn, minimize stress, and prepare for the rigors and joys of practicing law. **Student learning and preparation for law practice are the guiding ethics of these books.**

Why would we depart from the tried and true? Why have we abandoned the legal education model by which we were trained? Because legal education can and must improve.

In Spring 2007, the Carnegie Foundation published *Educating Lawyers: Preparation for the Practice of Law* and the Clinical Legal Education Association published *Best Practices for Legal Education*. Both works reflect in-depth efforts to assess the effectiveness of modern legal education, and both conclude that legal education, as presently practiced, falls quite short of what it can and should be. Both works criticize law professors' rigid adherence to a single teaching technique, the inadequacies of law school assessment mechanisms, and the dearth of law school instruction aimed at teaching law practice skills and inculcating professional values. Finally, the authors of both books express concern that legal education may be harming law students. Recent studies show that law students, in comparison to all other graduate students, have the highest levels of depression, anxiety and substance abuse.

The problems with traditional law school instruction begin with the textbooks law teachers use. Law professors cannot implement *Educating Lawyers* and *Best Practices* using texts designed for the traditional model of legal education. Moreover, even though our understanding of how people learn has grown exponentially in the past 100 years, no law school text to date even purports to have been designed with educational research in mind.

The Context and Practice Series is an effort to offer a genuine alternative. Grounded in learning theory and instructional design and written with *Educating Lawyers* and *Best Practices* in mind, Context and Practice casebooks make it easy for law professors to change.

I welcome reactions, criticisms, and suggestions; my e-mail address is mhschwartz@ualr.edu. Knowing the author(s) of these books, I know they, too, would appreciate your input; we share a common commitment to student learning. In fact, students, if your professor cares enough about your learning to have adopted this book, I bet s/he would welcome your input, too!

Michael Hunter Schwartz, Series Designer and Editor
Co-Director, Institute for Law Teaching and Learning
Dean and Professor of Law, William H. Bowen School of Law,
University of Arkansas at Little Rock

Energy Law

Chapter 1

Introduction to Energy Law

A. Introduction

What is energy law? Over the years, what it means to practice energy law has been an evolving process. In the practice world, even if a lawyer says he or she has an "energy practice," it's not clear what that means. The energy practice group in one law firm might focus on transactions related to mergers and acquisitions for companies in the energy industry. At another firm, it might be a regulatory group that assists clients with state or federal regulators working with electricity or natural gas utilities. Still others might do title work for coal, oil, and gas companies.

Energy law in law schools is similarly difficult to define. In some places, energy law covers everything related to energy: public utilities, natural resources, regulations, environmental impact, and property and mineral leasing issues. In other schools, energy law might mean the law of utilities, such as electricity or natural gas companies for industrial and consumer use.

As with most subjects in legal education, the reality is that energy law is not really a specific area of the law. Energy law is an amalgam of various types of law. This includes traditional core law school courses, such as Property, Torts, Contracts, Constitutional Law, and Criminal Law. In addition, energy law can include issues related to Administrative Law, Business Organizations, Civil Procedure, Environmental Law, Natural Resources, Law, Water Law, Antitrust Law, Climate Law, Indian Law, and International Law. And, of course, Professional Responsibility and Legal Ethics are fundamentally interwoven into any practice area, and energy law is no exception.

Of particular note here is that energy law is related and intertwined with environmental law. Environmental law is necessarily a part of energy law, just as energy policy impacts environmental policy. Similarly, climate law is a part of environmental law, but not all environmental law issues can be said to be climate law issues. These distinctions are discussed in this casebook to help provide context and nuance to these areas, which are often related and consistent, but at times can be conflicting.

B. About This Casebook: Goals and Structure

This casebook is designed to provide insight into the energy law in the broadest sense. As with any broad and new area of the law, learning energy law can sometimes feel like drinking from a fire hose. The goal of this casebook is to help make learning the concepts (and, ultimately, practice) a little more manageable. As such, this casebook does not purport or attempt to be a comprehensive look at energy law. Instead, the book is designed to provide an introduction to the broad and varied legal and policy issues faced by those working in today's energy industry.

Particular focus in the casebook is taken to help facilitate an understanding of basic concepts and terminology, which can be one of the most difficult parts of understanding energy law issues. In fact, even courts can have a hard time clearly explaining, and thus understanding, the concepts before them. Once the basic concepts and terms are understood, finding the answers to difficult questions in energy law becomes more manageable, though never easy.

There are several different ways to organize and structure a course in energy law. This casebook is organized to link concepts and resources in a way in which one might encounter them in legal practice or policy settings, rather than structured by the energy resource itself. Thus, as an example, natural gas is not a specific chapter in this book. Instead, natural gas issues related to mineral leasing are encountered with the similar process for coal and oil. Natural gas used for electricity generation is covered as one of the resources in the electricity resources chapter. And the economic regulation of natural gas as a commodity is covered in the chapter on economic regulation and market structure.

Organizing by resource, e.g., coal or natural gas, has some appeal, because it neatly puts everything (or most everything) about that resource in a single spot. However, those practicing energy law or drafting energy and environmental policy do not always encounter issues that are resource specific. The various legal issues one encounters are likely to be sector, and not resource, specific. That is, those whose primary practice includes a segment of energy law are likely to have a focus, for example, on regulatory issues, perhaps specializing in electricity or natural gas regulations. Others may focus on mineral leasing, which issues have significant overlap among resources whether the resource being sought is coal, oil, or natural gas.

As such, this casebook is organized by industry sector and practice area, rather than by resource. Admittedly, a strong argument can be made for either organizational approach. Ultimately, the current book structure was chosen for two primary reasons. First, consistent with the goals of the Context and Practice Casebook Series, this structure provides the legal context for the cases and materials presented and tries to replicate how one might encounter such issues in a practice setting. Second, no other casebook is structured in this way, and thus this at least provides another option for those involved in teaching and learning energy law.

C. A Brief History of Energy Law

Energy law in some form has likely been an issue as long as laws have existed, but it would not have looked anything like energy law today. Laws dealing with natural resources, such as wood for fires and water for mills, would have been viewed more as property concerns than energy concerns.

The genesis of a more concentrated sense of energy law is (at least arguably) first found in the late 1800s with the advent of electricity as a modern convenience. Thomas Edison's invention was fueled by Samuel Insull's development of electric utilities through the central station model. Insull built his company in part through creation of a private, but regulated, model of utility ownership. As Richard D. Cudahy and William D. Henderson explain, Insull made something of a shocking proposal in response to calls for public ownership:

> In lieu of public ownership, Insull proposed a bargain designed to serve the interests of consumers, taxpayers, and investors:
>
> (1) a single operator should be given an exclusive franchise to provide electricity on the basis of cost plus a reasonable profit, and pricing on this basis would be enforced by state regulation;
>
> (2) to deter monopoly abuse, the public would retain the right to purchase the electric plant;
>
> (3) to protect investors (and thus lower the cost of financing), the public's right to purchase must be exercised only at fair value.

Richard D. Cudahy & William D. Henderson, *From Insull to Enron: Corporate (Re)Regulation After the Rise and Fall of Two Energy Icons*, 26 ENERGY L.J. 35, 46 (2005).

The rise and fall of Insull's Commonwealth Edison led to a host of regulatory measures enacted as part of the New Deal, including the adoption of Public Utilities Holding Company Act of 1935 ("PUHCA"), 15 U.S.C. §79(a)–(z-6) (2000), which was repealed by the Energy Policy Act of 2005. PUHCA was designed to balance protection for consumers and investors, and it provided restrictions on the ownership structure of utilities and geographic restrictions on ownership. (PUHCA is discussed in more detail in Chapter 4.)

The wealthy Clint Murchison, a celebrity oil and gas man who was the Warren Buffett or Bill Gates of his time, in the 1920s and 1930s owned Murchison Oil and started Southern Union Gas Company after a significant discovery of natural gas. He began building a natural gas utility that served customers in Texas and New Mexico, but by 1935, it was clear "[t]he gas utility business was not well suited for Clint Murchinson. Public utility regulation was more a matter for lawyers than for risk takers." Robert Bradley Jr., *Edison to Enron: Energy Markets and Political Strategies* 236 (2011) (providing an excellent history of the political and regulatory history of electricity and natural gas industries). As it did for electric utilities, PUHCA would require Southern Union to divest all of its resources except for those in one state. As such, energy law was a major factor going back to the early 1900s.

Modern energy law came on the scene with the Mideast Oil Crisis in the 1970s, when Arab oil producers implemented an oil embargo on Western consumers. The oil producers issued the boycott of America that was designed to punish Western allies because of support for Israel over Egypt in the Yom Kippur war. The embargo led to crude oil price increases of about 400% between 1973 and 1974, increasing from about $3 per barrel to $12 per barrel.

Throughout this course, consider how this history has provided the framework of U.S. energy law. From market structure to regulatory structure to basic infrastructure, many of our challenges today are in some way connected to this history. At times, this history dictates how we must move forward, but sometimes this history frames our analysis when it doesn't need to. As you analyze problems, try to think about which situation applies to the issue before you.

D. Administrative Law as Energy Law

Energy law is an amalgamation of several different bodies of law, but one thing is clear: administrative law is part of nearly every area. And what is considered perhaps the preeminent administrative law case is also an energy law case. Given that administrative law is taking an increasing role in energy law, and most other areas of the law, it makes sense to start here.

The Environmental Protection Agency provides the following Summary of the Administrative Procedure Act, which is found at 5 U.S.C. §§ 551–559 (1946):

> The Administrative Procedure Act (APA) governs the process by which federal agencies develop and issue regulations. It includes requirements for publishing notices of proposed and final rulemaking in the Federal Register, and provides opportunities for the public to comment on notices of proposed rulemaking. The APA requires most rules to have a 30-day delayed effective date.
>
> In addition to setting forth rulemaking procedures, the APA addresses other agency actions such as issuance of policy statements, licenses, and permits. It also provides standards for judicial review if a person has been adversely affected or aggrieved by an agency action.

U.S. Envt'l Prot. Agency, Summary of the Administrative Procedure Act, http://www2 .epa.gov/laws-regulations/summary-administrative-procedure-act (last visited Aug. 22, 2013).

In a practice or other research setting, it is often beneficial to start with articles or treatises when beginning a new matter or issue, particularly when the area of law is new to us. As we review the scope of the APA, and administrative law generally, consider the following article for an overview of how to challenge agency action. Once you have a sense of how this operates, we review some administrative law cases related to the energy sector.

Terry Fox, *Challenges to Federal Agency Action*

This work has been excerpted from its original form as published in
The Colorado Lawyer at Vol. 38, No. 10, p. 83 (October 2009).

Challenges to federal agency decisions involve final agency action and most often are pursued under the federal Administrative Procedure Act (APA).The type of decisions challenged are almost limitless. Some examples are: (1) the denial of a federal license or permit; (2) changes to grazing activities on federal lands; (3) the granting or withdrawal of environmental protection to various organisms (fish, mammals, birds, and so on); (4) the withdrawal or modification of federal government benefits; and (5) the denial of immigration benefits.

This article describes the key elements of the APA process and provides insight into how to effectively posture the case to secure effective judicial review. The discussion focuses on the court challenge—the appeal—of an agency's action. The article assumes that counsel will have input in the process leading to the agency's decision. If the lawyer has not been involved in the administrative phase of the case, his or her authority to effectively challenge the federal agency's decision may be severely compromised—or even barred.

The Statutory Framework

A critical element of the challenge to the agency's decision is the applicable statutory framework. This framework governs the challenge and may supply the review standard. For example, the Energy Employees Occupational Illness Compensation Program Act (EEOICPA) provides that "a person adversely affected or aggrieved by a final decision of the Secretary under [Part E]" may seek review of that final decision in the appropriate U.S. District Court within sixty days of the date that the final decision was issued. The standard of review contained in the EEOICPA is more deferential to the agency than the APA's standard of review of "arbitrary, capricious, an abuse of discretion or otherwise not in accordance with law." The EEOICPA's review standard requires a plaintiff to prove that a final decision was both "arbitrary *and* capricious" before a court may modify it or set it aside. If the statute does not specify a standard of review, the APA's "arbitrary and capricious" review standard applies.

Most federal statutes, including those that rely on the APA's review provisions, require that the challenging party fully participate in the administrative process and exhaust all available remedies. The rationale for the exhaustion requirement is to give the agency fair notice and an opportunity to reconsider whether it has erred and to fix that error without court intervention. Of course, the agency may disagree that it has erred and may stand by its decision. In this situation—and provided the aggrieved party has taken advantage of the available administrative remedies—the aggrieved party may seek judicial review of the agency's decision.

The Administrative Review Process

A significant difference between traditional civil cases and a case brought pursuant to the state or federal APA is that there is no discovery in APA cases. Rather, the challenge, and the decision, is based on the administrative record. In this sense, an APA case is more akin to an appeal than to standard litigation. Additionally, the APA litigant is not entitled to have a jury decide his or her case. The judge decides the APA challenge. The judge can hold a hearing on the APA challenge, but is not required to do so. It is largely at the judge's discretion whether to schedule argument on an APA challenge.

In APA cases, the court often requires the parties to attend a conference to set a briefing schedule for the case. Before the scheduling conference, the parties must meet and confer about their proposed briefing schedule. At this time, the parties can discuss when the agency's litigation counsel anticipates filing the administrative record. If the record is lengthy, the parties might negotiate additional time to allow litigation counsel to review the proposed administrative record and remove and log any privileged documents contained in the proposed administrative record.

Contents of the Administrative Record

The administrative record should consist of everything that was before the agency pertaining to the merits of its decision. A properly compiled record is the exclusive basis for the court's judicial review, and evidence outside the record may not be cited. If the record is inadequate to support the agency action, the proper remedy is a remand for further proceedings. It is not proper to generate a new record in court. Similarly, if the plaintiff successfully contends that the agency decision is flawed because it failed to take into account evidence erroneously excluded from the record, the proper remedy is to remand the matter to the agency to reconsider in light of the erroneously excluded evidence, not for the reviewing court to reconsider the matter itself.

To avoid potentially protracted battles concerning the contents of the administrative record, the agency's litigation counsel should consider providing the opposing party's counsel (or the party, if it is proceeding *pro se*) an advance copy of the proposed record, or at least an index of the proposed record. If the challenger finds that key documents appear to be missing, the parties can confer about the contents of the record, including whether those missing documents should be made part of the record.

Because the record must contain all materials on which the agency action was based, courts have required the supplementation of a certified record when the agency appears to have relied on documents or materials not included in the administrative record that was filed. The record should not be supplemented, however, with information that was never presented to the agency.

Exceptions to the rule that evidence outside the record may not be relied on by the court are rare. However, a reviewing agency may add information necessary to explain or elaborate on the information already contained in the record.

The reviewing court may consider information supplemental to the record only exceptionally: for instance, if the information is necessary as background "to explain the basis of the agency's action and the factors the agency considered."

Review Standards

The APA authorizes courts to "hold unlawful and set aside agency action" that is:

1) not in accordance with the law;

2) unconstitutional;

3) contrary to a statute; or

4) against the law.

The APA also authorizes the court to "decide all relevant questions of law." Courts generally do not defer to the agency's determination of legal issues.

Arbitrary and Capricious Standard

As noted above, the APA allows the court to set aside final agency action that is "arbitrary, capricious, an abuse of discretion, or otherwise not in accordance with law." The arbitrary and capricious standard "is narrow and a court is not to substitute its judgment for that of the agency." An agency's determinations must be upheld if they "conform to 'certain minimal standards of rationality.'"

The party challenging the agency action bears the heavy burden of proving that the action was arbitrary and capricious. When there is a contemporaneous explanation of the agency decision, the validity of that action "must stand or fall on the propriety of that finding, judged of course, by the appropriate standard of review[.]"

An agency action is arbitrary and capricious only if: the agency has relied on factors which Congress has not intended it to consider, entirely failed to consider an important aspect of the problem, offered an explanation for its decision that runs counter to the evidence before the agency, or is so implausible that it could not be ascribed to a difference in view or the product of agency expertise.

Under this standard, the reviewing court may not set aside agency action merely because the court would have decided the issue differently, as long as the agency has considered the relevant factors and offered a rational explanation for its action. In addition, "[e]ven when an agency explains its decision with 'less than ideal clarity,' a reviewing court will not upset the decision on that account 'if the agency's path may reasonably be discerned.'"

. . . .

Substantial Evidence Standard

Agencies commonly argue that their factual determinations also are entitled to substantial deference. The APA authorizes a court to set aside agency findings that are "unsupported by substantial evidence." The substantial evidence standard of review is employed in cases in which the agency has made factual findings after a formal, trial-type procedure. This standard applies to cases "subject to sections 556 and 557 [of Title 5] or otherwise reviewed on the record of an agency hearing provided by statute."

Section 557 applies to a proceeding "when a hearing is required to be conducted in accordance with section 556," and section 556 applies "to hearings required by section 553 or 554 of this tide to be conducted in accordance with this section." Either way, the agency's factual determinations must be upheld as long as they are supported by the administrative record, even if there are alternative findings that also could be supported by the record. This is especially true with respect to scientific determinations of the agency within its area of expertise. The agency commonly will ask the court to defer to its interpretation of equivocal evidence, as long as it is reasonable.

The challenging party—using all available provisions in the APA or the additional statute that applies in the case—should attempt to demonstrate how the agency's action, including its interpretation of the facts, is neither reasonable nor legal. Sometimes, the administrative record is completely silent regarding why the agency took a particular action. In this case, the opponent can make the argument that the agency cannot now try to supply a *post hoc* rationalization for the convenience of the litigation. The agency's failure to explain its rationale in the earlier proceedings can be used against it.

Advancing the Challenge to the Agency's Action

There are several ways to advance an agency challenge. Challenges may focus on the procedure the agency employed to render its decision, on the actual decision, or both.

Procedural Challenges

An agency's action can be challenged on procedural grounds. The agency's decision is vulnerable if the agency did not follow the required procedure. In fact, if the agency's litigation counsel is made aware of that failure at the outset—even before a lawsuit is filed—the parties may be in a position to negotiate a remand. The remand could result in a favorable decision, thus avoiding the necessity of a court challenge.

Substantive Challenges

In advancing substantive challenges, the parties are well-advised to provide the court with an overview of the governing statutory frameworks. In addition to the APA, a substantive statute often applies to the agency's actions. For example, the Clean Water

Act, the Clean Air Act, or other environmental statutes might apply in an environmental administrative proceeding.

After the legal framework and factual backdrop of the case have been explained, the parties can delve into the legal arguments. The arguments should cite the relevant portions of the administrative record to facilitate the court's review and to persuade the court. If the record contains photographs, maps, or charts, those visuals can be effective in holding the reader's interest. This strategy is especially useful in cases involving access to or the use of federal lands, where it is helpful to orient the court about the area in dispute.

Controlling authority must be cited and applied or distinguished. In addition, it is helpful to find cases—even if they are not controlling—that present similar factual scenarios. Referencing factually similar cases, especially if they contain well-reasoned analyses of the legal issues that are under challenge, can be an effective tack.

Perhaps the most important piece of advice that can be shared with attorneys embarking on challenges to federal agency action is that both sides need to be fair to the administrative record. If one side grossly misconstrues what the record says, opposing counsel—and the court—will check the record and point out the error. The party misconstruing the record will then have damaged its credibility, which could potentially affect the outcome of the case.

Conclusion

Administrative review cases can be challenging. Because the parties are tied to the administrative record, and because the court has a fairly narrow standard of review, effective advocacy is critical. Whether the party is seeking to reverse the denial of a federal license or permit, to enlarge grazing activities on federal lands, to attain environmental protection of a type of fish, or to restore or secure a federal governmental benefit, posturing the case for effective judicial review and advancing compelling arguments supported by the record will go a long way toward a successful appeal of the federal agency's action.

Chevron U.S.A., Inc. v. Natural Resources Defense Council, Inc.

467 U.S. 837 (1984)

JUSTICE STEVENS delivered the opinion of the Court.

In the Clean Air Act Amendments of 1977, Pub.L. 95-95, 91 Stat. 685, Congress enacted certain requirements applicable to States that had not achieved the national air quality standards established by the Environmental Protection Agency (EPA) pursuant to earlier legislation. The amended Clean Air Act required these "nonattainment" States to establish a permit program regulating "new or modified major stationary sources" of air pollution. Generally, a permit may not be issued for a new or modified major stationary source unless several stringent conditions are met. The EPA regulation promulgated to implement this permit requirement allows a State to adopt a plantwide definition of the term "stationary source." Under this definition, an existing plant that contains several pollution-emitting devices may install or modify one piece of equipment without meeting the permit conditions if the alteration will not increase the total emissions from the plant. The question presented by these cases is whether EPA's decision to allow States to treat all of the pollution-emitting devices within the same industrial grouping as though they were encased within a single "bubble" is based on a reasonable construction of the statutory term "stationary source."

I

The EPA regulations containing the plantwide definition of the term stationary source were promulgated on October 14, 1981. 46 Fed.Reg. 50766. Respondents filed a timely petition for review in the United States Court of Appeals for the District of Columbia Circuit pursuant to 42 U.S.C. §7607(b)(1). The Court of Appeals set aside the regulations. *Natural Resources Defense Council, Inc. v. Gorsuch,* 222 U.S.App.D.C. 268, 685 F.2d 718 (1982).

The court observed that the relevant part of the amended Clean Air Act "does not explicitly define what Congress envisioned as a 'stationary source,' to which the permit program … should apply," and further stated that the precise issue was not "squarely addressed in the legislative history." *Id.* at 273, 685 F.2d at 723. In light of its conclusion that the legislative history bearing on the question was "at best contradictory," it reasoned that "the purposes of the nonattainment program should guide our decision here." *Id.*at 276, n. 39, 685 F.2d at 726, n. 39. Based on two of its precedents concerning the applicability of the bubble concept to certain Clean Air Act programs, the court stated that the bubble concept was "mandatory" in programs designed merely to maintain existing air quality, but held that it was "inappropriate" in programs enacted to improve air quality. *Id.* at 276, 685 F.2d at 726. Since the purpose of the permit program—its *"raison d'etre,"* in the court's view—was to improve air quality, the court held that the bubble concept was inapplicable in these cases under its prior precedents. *Ibid.* It therefore set aside the regulations embodying the bubble concept as contrary to law. We granted certiorari to review that judgment, 461 U.S. 956 (1983), and we now reverse.

The basic legal error of the Court of Appeals was to adopt a static judicial definition of the term "stationary source" when it had decided that Congress itself had not commanded that definition. Respondents do not defend the legal reasoning of the Court of Appeals. Nevertheless, since this Court reviews judgments, not opinions, we must determine whether the Court of Appeals' legal error resulted in an erroneous judgment on the validity of the regulations.

II

When a court reviews an agency's construction of the statute which it administers, it is confronted with two questions. First, always, is the question whether Congress has directly spoken to the precise question at issue. If the intent of Congress is clear, that is the end of the matter; for the court, as well as the agency, must give effect to the unambiguously expressed intent of Congress. If, however, the court determines Congress has not directly addressed the precise question at issue, the court does not simply impose its own construction on the statute, as would be necessary in the absence of an administrative interpretation. Rather, if the statute is silent or ambiguous with respect to the specific issue, the question for the court is whether the agency's answer is based on a permissible construction of the statute.

> The power of an administrative agency to administer a congressionally created … program necessarily requires the formulation of policy and the making of rules to fill any gap left, implicitly or explicitly, by Congress.

Morton v. Ruiz, 415 U.S. 199, 231 (1974). If Congress has explicitly left a gap for the agency to fill, there is an express delegation of authority to the agency to elucidate a specific provision of the statute by regulation. Such legislative regulations are given controlling weight unless they are arbitrary, capricious, or manifestly contrary to the statute. Sometimes the legislative delegation to an agency on a particular question is implicit, rather than explicit. In such a case, a court may not substitute its own construction of a statutory provision for a reasonable interpretation made by the administrator of an agency.

We have long recognized that considerable weight should be accorded to an executive department's construction of a statutory scheme it is entrusted to administer, and the principle of deference to administrative interpretations

> has been consistently followed by this Court whenever decision as to the meaning or reach of a statute has involved reconciling conflicting policies, and a full understanding of the force of the statutory policy in the given situation has depended upon more than ordinary knowledge respecting the matters subjected to agency regulations. *See, e.g., National Broadcasting Co. v. United States,* 319 U.S. 190; *Labor Board v. Hearst Publications, Inc.,* 322 U.S. 111; *Republic Aviation Corp. v.* [467 U.S. 845] *Labor Board,* 324 U.S. 793; *Securities & Exchange Comm'n v. Chenery Corp.,* 332 U.S. 194; *Labor Board v. Seven-Up Bottling Co.,* 344 U.S. 344.
>
> ... If this choice represents a reasonable accommodation of conflicting policies that were committed to the agency's care by the statute, we should not disturb it unless it appears from the statute or its legislative history that the accommodation is not one that Congress would have sanctioned.

United States v. Shimer, 367 U.S. 374, 382, 383 (1961). *Accord, Capital Cities Cable, Inc. v. Crisp, ante* at 699–700.

In light of these well-settled principles, it is clear that the Court of Appeals misconceived the nature of its role in reviewing the regulations at issue. Once it determined, after its own examination of the legislation, that Congress did not actually have an intent regarding the applicability of the bubble concept to the permit program, the question before it was not whether, in its view, the concept is "inappropriate" in the general context of a program designed to improve air quality, but whether the Administrator's view that it is appropriate in the context of this particular program is a reasonable one. Based on the examination of the legislation and its history which follows, we agree with the Court of Appeals that Congress did not have a specific intention on the applicability of the bubble concept in these cases, and conclude that the EPA's use of that concept here is a reasonable policy choice for the agency to make.

III

In the 1950's and the 1960's, Congress enacted a series of statutes designed to encourage and to assist the States in curtailing air pollution. *See generally Train v. Natural Resources Defense Council, Inc.,* 421 U.S. 60, 63–64 (1975). The Clean Air Amendments of 1970, Pub.L. 91-604, 84 Stat. 1676, "sharply increased federal authority and responsibility [in the] continuing effort to combat air pollution," 421 U.S. at 64, but continued to assign "primary responsibility for assuring air quality" to the several States, 84 Stat. 1678. Section 109 of the 1970 Amendments directed the EPA to promulgate National Ambient Air Quality Standards (NAAQS's) and § 110 directed the States to develop plans (SIP's) to implement the standards within specified deadlines. In addition, § 111 provided that major new sources of pollution would be required to conform to technology-based performance standards; the EPA was directed to publish a list of categories of sources of pollution and to establish new source performance standards (NSPS) for each. Section 111(e) prohibited the operation of any new source in violation of a performance standard.

Section 111(a) defined the terms that are to be used in setting and enforcing standards of performance for new stationary sources. It provided:

> For purposes of this section:
>
> ....
>
> (3) The term "stationary source" means any building, structure, facility, or installation which emits or may emit any air pollutant.

84 Stat. 1683. In the 1970 Amendments, that definition was not only applicable to the NSPS program required by § 111, but also was made applicable to a requirement of § 110 that each state implementation plan contain a procedure for reviewing the location of any proposed new source and preventing its construction if it would preclude the attainment or maintenance of national air quality standards.

In due course, the EPA promulgated NAAQS's, approved SIP's, and adopted detailed regulations governing NSPS's for various categories of equipment. In one of its programs, the EPA used a plantwide definition of the term "stationary source." In 1974, it issued NSPS's for the nonferrous smelting industry that provided that the standards would not apply to the modification of major smelting units if their increased emissions were offset by reductions in other portions of the same plant.

Nonattainment

The 1970 legislation provided for the attainment of primary NAAQS's by 1975. In many areas of the country, particularly the most industrialized States, the statutory goals were not attained. In 1976, the 94th Congress was confronted with this fundamental problem, as well as many others respecting pollution control. As always in this area, the legislative struggle was basically between interests seeking strict schemes to reduce pollution rapidly to eliminate its social costs and interests advancing the economic concern that strict schemes would retard industrial development with attendant social costs. The 94th Congress, confronting these competing interests, was unable to agree on what response was in the public interest: legislative proposals to deal with nonattainment failed to command the necessary consensus.

In light of this situation, the EPA published an Emissions Offset Interpretative Ruling in December, 1976, *see* 41 Fed.Reg. 55524, to "fill the gap," as respondents put it, until Congress acted. The Ruling stated that it was intended to address

> the issue of whether and to what extent national air quality standards established under the Clean Air Act may restrict or prohibit growth of major new or expanded stationary air pollution sources."

Id. at 55524–55525. In general, the Ruling provided that

> a major new source may locate in an area with air quality worse than a national standard only if stringent conditions can be met.

Id. at 55525. The Ruling gave primary emphasis to the rapid attainment of the statute's environmental goals. Consistent with that emphasis, the construction of every new source in nonattainment areas had to meet the "lowest achievable emission rate" under the current state of the art for that type of facility. *See Ibid.* The 1976 Ruling did not, however, explicitly adopt or reject the "bubble concept."

IV

The Clean Air Act Amendments of 1977 are a lengthy, detailed, technical, complex, and comprehensive response to a major social issue. A small portion of the statute—91 Stat. 745–751 (Part D of Title I of the amended Act, 42 U.S.C. §§ 7501–7508)—expressly deals with nonattainment areas. The focal point of this controversy is one phrase in that portion of the Amendments.

Basically, the statute required each State in a nonattainment area to prepare and obtain approval of a new SIP by July 1, 1979. In the interim, those States were required to comply with the EPA's interpretative Ruling of December 21, 1976. 91 Stat. 745. The deadline for attainment of the primary NAAQS's was extended until December 31, 1982, and in some cases until December 31, 1987, but the SIP's were required to contain a number of provisions designed to achieve the goals as expeditiously as possible.

Most significantly for our purposes, the statute provided that each plan shall

> (6) require permits for the construction and operation of new or modified major stationary sources in accordance with section 173....

Id. at 747. Before issuing a permit, § 173 requires (1) the state agency to determine that there will be sufficient emissions reductions in the region to offset the emissions from the new source and also to allow for reasonable further progress toward attainment, or that the increased emissions will not exceed an allowance for growth established pursuant to § 172(b)(5); (2) the applicant to certify that his other sources in the State are in compliance with the SIP, (3) the agency to determine that the applicable SIP is otherwise being implemented, and (4) the proposed source to comply with the lowest achievable emission rate (LAER).

The 1977 Amendments contain no specific reference to the "bubble concept." Nor do they contain a specific definition of the term "stationary source," though they did not disturb the definition of "stationary source" contained in § 111(a)(3), applicable by the terms of the Act to the NSPS program. Section 302(j), however, defines the term "major stationary source" as follows:

> (j) Except as otherwise expressly provided, the terms "major stationary source" and "major emitting facility" mean any stationary facility or source of air pollutants which directly emits, or has the potential to emit, one hundred tons per year or more of any air pollutant (including any major emitting facility or source of fugitive emissions of any such pollutant, as determined by rule by the Administrator).

91 Stat. 770.

V

The legislative history of the portion of the 1977 Amendments dealing with nonattainment areas does not contain any specific comment on the "bubble concept" or the question whether a plantwide definition of a stationary source is permissible under the permit program. It does, however, plainly disclose that in the permit program Congress sought to accommodate the conflict between the economic interest in permitting capital improvements to continue and the environmental interest in improving air quality. Indeed, the House Committee Report identified the economic interest as one of the "two main purposes" of this section of the bill. It stated:

> Section 117 of the bill, adopted during full committee markup establishes a new section 127 of the Clean Air Act. The section has two main purposes: (1) to allow reasonable economic growth to continue in an area while making reasonable further progress to assure attainment of the standards by a fixed date;

and (2) to allow States greater flexibility for the former purpose than EPA's present interpretative regulations afford.

The new provision allows States with nonattainment areas to pursue one of two options. First, the State may proceed under EPA's present "tradeoff" or "offset" ruling. The Administrator is authorized, moreover, to modify or amend that ruling in accordance with the intent and purposes of this section.

The State's second option would be to revise its implementation plan in accordance with this new provision.

H.R.Rep. No. 95-294, p. 211 (1977).

The portion of the Senate Committee Report dealing with nonattainment areas states generally that it was intended to "supersede the EPA administrative approach," and that expansion should be permitted if a State could "demonstrate that these facilities can be accommodated within its overall plan to provide for attainment of air quality standards." S.Rep. No. 95-127, p. 55 (1977). The Senate Report notes the value of "case-by-case review of each new or modified major source of pollution that seeks to locate in a region exceeding an ambient standard," explaining that such a review

requires matching reductions from existing sources against emissions expected from the new source in order to assure that introduction of the new source will not prevent attainment of the applicable standard by the statutory deadline.

Ibid. This description of a case-by-case approach to plant additions, which emphasizes the net consequences of the construction or modification of a new source as well as its impact on the overall achievement of the national standards, was not, however, addressed to the precise issue raised by these cases.

Senator Muskie made the following remarks:

I should note that the test for determining whether a new or modified source is subject to the EPA interpretative regulation [the Offset Ruling]—and to the permit requirements of the revised implementation plans under the conference bill—is whether the source will emit a pollutant into an area which is exceeding a national ambient air quality standard for that pollutant—or precursor. Thus, a new source is still subject to such requirements as "lowest achievable emission rate" even if it is constructed as a replacement for an older facility resulting in a net reduction from previous emission levels.

A source—including an existing facility ordered to convert to coal—is subject to all the nonattainment requirements as a modified source if it makes any physical change which increases the amount of any air pollutant for which the standards in the area are exceeded.

123 Cong.Rec. 26847 (1977).

VI

As previously noted, prior to the 1977 Amendments, the EPA had adhered to a plantwide definition of the term "source" under a NSPS program. After adoption of the 1977 Amendments, proposals for a plantwide definition were considered in at least three formal proceedings.

In January, 1979, the EPA considered the question whether the same restriction on new construction in nonattainment areas that had been included in its December, 1976, Ruling should be required in the revised SIP's that were scheduled to go into effect in July, 1979.

After noting that the 1976 Ruling was ambiguous on the question "whether a plant with a number of different processes and emission points would be considered a single source," 44 Fed.Reg. 3276 (1979), the EPA, in effect, provided a bifurcated answer to that question. In those areas that did not have a revised SIP in effect by July, 1979, the EPA rejected the plantwide definition; on the other hand, it expressly concluded that the plantwide approach would be permissible in certain circumstances if authorized by an approved SIP. It stated:

> Where a state implementation plan is revised and implemented to satisfy the requirements of Part D, including the reasonable further progress requirement, the plan requirements for major modifications may exempt modifications of existing facilities that are accompanied by intrasource offsets, so that there is no net increase in emissions. The agency endorses such exemptions, which would provide greater flexibility to sources to effectively manage their air emissions at least cost.

Ibid.

In April, and again in September, 1979, the EPA published additional comments in which it indicated that revised SIP's could adopt the plantwide definition of source in nonattainment areas in certain circumstances. *See id.*at 20372, 20379, 51924, 51951, 51958. On the latter occasion, the EPA made a formal rulemaking proposal that would have permitted the use of the "bubble concept" for new installations within a plant as well as for modifications of existing units. It explained:

> "Bubble" Exemption: The use of offsets inside the same source is called the "bubble." EPA proposes use of the definition of "source" (see above) to limit the use of the bubble under nonattainment requirements in the following respects:
>
> i. Part D SIPs that include all requirements needed to assure reasonable further progress and attainment by the deadline under section 172 and that are being carried out need not restrict the use of a plantwide bubble, the same as under the PSD proposal.
>
> ii. Part D SIPs that do not meet the requirements specified must limit use of the bubble by including a definition of "installation" as an identifiable piece of process equipment.

Significantly, the EPA expressly noted that the word "source" might be given a plantwide definition for some purposes and a narrower definition for other purposes. It wrote:

> Source means any building structure, facility, or installation which emits or may emit any regulated pollutant. "Building, structure, facility or installation" means plant in PSD areas and in nonattainment areas except where the growth prohibitions would apply or where no adequate SIP exists or is being carried out.

Id. at 51925. The EPA's summary of its proposed Ruling discloses a flexible, rather than rigid, definition of the term "source" to implement various policies and programs:

> In summary, EPA is proposing two different ways to define source for different kinds of NSR programs:
>
> (1) For PSD and complete Part D SIPs, review would apply only to plants, with an unrestricted plantwide bubble.
>
> (2) For the offset ruling, restrictions on construction, and incomplete Part D SIPs, review would apply to both plants and individual pieces of process equipment, causing the plant-wide bubble not to apply for new and modified major pieces of equipment.

In addition, for the restrictions on construction, EPA is proposing to define "major modification" so as to prohibit the bubble entirely. Finally, an alternative discussed but not favored is to have only pieces of process equipment reviewed, resulting in no plant-wide bubble and allowing minor pieces of equipment to escape NSR regardless of whether they are within a major plant.

Id. at 51934.

In August, 1980, however, the EPA adopted a regulation that, in essence, applied the basic reasoning of the Court of Appeals in these cases. The EPA took particular note of the two then-recent Court of Appeals decisions, which had created the bright-line rule that the "bubble concept" should be employed in a program designed to maintain air quality, but not in one designed to enhance air quality. Relying heavily on those cases, EPA adopted a dual definition of "source" for nonattainment areas that required a permit whenever a change in either the entire plant, or one of its components, would result in a significant increase in emissions even if the increase was completely offset by reductions elsewhere in the plant. The EPA expressed the opinion that this interpretation was "more consistent with congressional intent" than the plantwide definition because it "would bring in more sources or modifications for review," 45 Fed.Reg. 52697 (1980), but its primary legal analysis was predicated on the two Court of Appeals decisions.

In 1981, a new administration took office and initiated a "Government-wide reexamination of regulatory burdens and complexities." 46 Fed.Reg. 16281. In the context of that review, the EPA reevaluated the various arguments that had been advanced in connection with the proper definition of the term "source" and concluded that the term should be given the same definition in both nonattainment areas and PSD areas.

In explaining its conclusion, the EPA first noted that the definitional issue was not squarely addressed in either the statute or its legislative history, and therefore that the issue involved an agency "judgment as how to best carry out the Act." *Ibid.* It then set forth several reasons for concluding that the plantwide definition was more appropriate. It pointed out that the dual definition "can act as a disincentive to new investment and modernization by discouraging modifications to existing facilities" and " can actually retard progress in air pollution control by discouraging replacement of older, dirtier processes or pieces of equipment with new, cleaner ones." *Ibid.* Moreover, the new definition "would simplify EPA's rules by using the same definition of 'source' for PSD, nonattainment new source review, and the construction moratorium. This reduces confusion and inconsistency." *Ibid.* Finally, the agency explained that additional requirements that remained in place would accomplish the fundamental purposes of achieving attainment with NAAQS's as expeditiously as possible. These conclusions were expressed in a proposed rulemaking in August, 1981, that was formally promulgated in October. *See id.* at 50766.

VII

In this Court, respondents expressly reject the basic rationale of the Court of Appeals' decision. That court viewed the statutory definition of the term "source" as sufficiently flexible to cover either a plantwide definition, a narrower definition covering each unit within a plant, or a dual definition that could apply to both the entire "bubble" and its components. It interpreted the policies of the statute, however, to mandate the plantwide definition in programs designed to maintain clean air and to forbid it in programs designed to improve air quality. Respondents place a fundamentally different construction on the statute. They contend that the text of the Act requires the EPA to use a dual definition— if either a component of a plant, or the plant as a whole, emits over 100 tons of pollutant, it is a major stationary source. They thus contend that the EPA rules adopted in 1980, insofar as they apply to the maintenance of the quality of clean air, as well as the 1981 rules which apply to nonattainment areas, violate the statute.

Statutory Language

The definition of the term "stationary source" in § 111(a)(3) refers to "any building, structure, facility, or installation" which emits air pollution. *See supra* at 846. This definition is applicable only to the NSPS program by the express terms of the statute; the text of the statute does not make this definition applicable to the permit program. Petitioners therefore maintain that there is no statutory language even relevant to ascertaining the meaning of stationary source in the permit program aside from § 302(j), which defines the term "major stationary source." *See supra* at 851. We disagree with petitioners on this point.

The definition in § 302(j) tells us what the word "major" means — a source must emit at least 100 tons of pollution to qualify — but it sheds virtually no light on the meaning of the term "stationary source." It does equate a source with a facility — a "major emitting facility" and a "major stationary source" are synonymous under § 302(j). The ordinary meaning of the term "facility" is some collection of integrated elements which has been designed and constructed to achieve some purpose. Moreover, it is certainly no affront to common English usage to take a reference to a major facility or a major source to connote an entire plant, as opposed to its constituent parts. Basically, however, the language of § 302(j) simply does not compel any given interpretation of the term "source."

Respondents recognize that, and hence point to § 111(a)(3). Although the definition in that section is not literally applicable to the permit program, it sheds as much light on the meaning of the word "source" as anything in the statute. As respondents point out, use of the words "building, structure, facility, or installation," as the definition of source, could be read to impose the permit conditions on an individual building that is a part of a plant. A "word may have a character of its own not to be submerged by its association." *Russell Motor Car Co. v. United States,* 261 U.S. 514, 519 (1923). On the other hand, the meaning of a word must be ascertained in the context of achieving particular objectives, and the words associated with it may indicate that the true meaning of the series is to convey a common idea. The language may reasonably be interpreted to impose the requirement on any discrete, but integrated, operation which pollutes. This gives meaning to all of the terms — a single building, not part of a larger operation, would be covered if it emits more than 100 tons of pollution, as would any facility, structure, or installation. Indeed, the language itself implies a "bubble concept" of sorts: each enumerated item would seem to be treated as if it were encased in a bubble. While respondents insist that each of these terms must be given a discrete meaning, they also argue that § 111(a)(3) defines "source" as that term is used in § 302(j). The latter section, however, equates a source with a facility, whereas the former defines "source" as a facility, among other items.

We are not persuaded that parsing of general terms in the text of the statute will reveal an actual intent of Congress. We know full well that this language is not dispositive; the terms are overlapping, and the language is not precisely directed to the question of the applicability of a given term in the context of a larger operation. To the extent any congressional "intent" can be discerned from this language, it would appear that the listing of overlapping, illustrative terms was intended to enlarge, rather than to confine, the scope of the agency's power to regulate particular sources in order to effectuate the policies of the Act.

Legislative History

In addition, respondents argue that the legislative history and policies of the Act foreclose the plantwide definition, and that the EPA's interpretation is not entitled to deference, because it represents a sharp break with prior interpretations of the Act.

Based on our examination of the legislative history, we agree with the Court of Appeals that it is unilluminating. The general remarks pointed to by respondents "were obviously not made with this narrow issue in mind, and they cannot be said to demonstrate a Congressional desire...." *Jewell Ridge Coal Corp. v. Mine Workers*, 325 U.S. 161, 168–169 (1945). Respondents' argument based on the legislative history relies heavily on Senator Muskie's observation that a new source is subject to the LAER requirement. But the full statement is ambiguous, and, like the text of §173 itself, this comment does not tell us what a new source is, much less that it is to have an inflexible definition. We find that the legislative history as a whole is silent on the precise issue before us. It is, however, consistent with the view that the EPA should have broad discretion in implementing the policies of the 1977 Amendments.

More importantly, that history plainly identifies the policy concerns that motivated the enactment; the plantwide definition is fully consistent with one of those concerns— the allowance of reasonable economic growth—and, whether or not we believe it most effectively implements the other, we must recognize that the EPA has advanced a reasonable explanation for its conclusion that the regulations serve the environmental objectives as well. *See supra* at 857–859, and n. 29; *see also supra* at 855, n. 27. Indeed, its reasoning is supported by the public record developed in the rulemaking process, as well as by certain private studies.

Our review of the EPA's varying interpretations of the word "source"—both before and after the 1977 Amendments—convinces us that the agency primarily responsible for administering this important legislation has consistently interpreted it flexibly—not in a sterile textual vacuum, but in the context of implementing policy decisions in a technical and complex arena. The fact that the agency has from time to time changed its interpretation of the term "source" does not, as respondents argue, lead us to conclude that no deference should be accorded the agency's interpretation of the statute. An initial agency interpretation is not instantly carved in stone. On the contrary, the agency, to engage in informed rulemaking, must consider varying interpretations and the wisdom of its policy on a continuing basis. Moreover, the fact that the agency has adopted different definitions in different contexts adds force to the argument that the definition itself is flexible, particularly since Congress has never indicated any disapproval of a flexible reading of the statute.

Significantly, it was not the agency in 1980, but rather the Court of Appeals that read the statute inflexibly to command a plantwide definition for programs designed to maintain clean air and to forbid such a definition for programs designed to improve air quality. The distinction the court drew may well be a sensible one, but our labored review of the problem has surely disclosed that it is not a distinction that Congress ever articulated itself, or one that the EPA found in the statute before the courts began to review the legislative work product. We conclude that it was the Court of Appeals, rather than Congress or any of the decisionmakers who are authorized by Congress to administer this legislation, that was primarily responsible for the 1980 position taken by the agency.

Policy

The arguments over policy that are advanced in the parties' briefs create the impression that respondents are now waging in a judicial forum a specific policy battle which they ultimately lost in the agency and in the 32 jurisdictions opting for the "bubble concept," but one which was never waged in the Congress. Such policy arguments are more properly addressed to legislators or administrators, not to judges.

In these cases, the Administrator's interpretation represents a reasonable accommodation of manifestly competing interests, and is entitled to deference: the regulatory scheme is technical and complex, the agency considered the matter in a detailed and reasoned fashion, and the decision involves reconciling conflicting policies. Congress intended to accommodate both interests, but did not do so itself on the level of specificity presented by these cases. Perhaps that body consciously desired the Administrator to strike the balance at this level, thinking that those with great expertise and charged with responsibility for administering the provision would be in a better position to do so; perhaps it simply did not consider the question at this level; and perhaps Congress was unable to forge a coalition on either side of the question, and those on each side decided to take their chances with the scheme devised by the agency. For judicial purposes, it matters not which of these things occurred.

Judges are not experts in the field, and are not part of either political branch of the Government. Courts must, in some cases, reconcile competing political interests, but not on the basis of the judges' personal policy preferences. In contrast, an agency to which Congress has delegated policymaking responsibilities may, within the limits of that delegation, properly rely upon the incumbent administration's views of wise policy to inform its judgments. While agencies are not directly accountable to the people, the Chief Executive is, and it is entirely appropriate for this political branch of the Government to make such policy choices — resolving the competing interests which Congress itself either inadvertently did not resolve, or intentionally left to be resolved by the agency charged with the administration of the statute in light of everyday realities.

When a challenge to an agency construction of a statutory provision, fairly conceptualized, really centers on the wisdom of the agency's policy, rather than whether it is a reasonable choice within a gap left open by Congress, the challenge must fail. In such a case, federal judges — who have no constituency — have a duty to respect legitimate policy choices made by those who do. The responsibilities for assessing the wisdom of such policy choices and resolving the struggle between competing views of the public interest are not judicial ones: "Our Constitution vests such responsibilities in the political branches." *TVA v. Hill*, 437 U.S. 153, 195 (1978).

We hold that the EPA's definition of the term "source" is a permissible construction of the statute which seeks to accommodate progress in reducing air pollution with economic growth.

> The Regulations which the Administrator has adopted provide what the agency could allowably view as ... [an] effective reconciliation of these twofold ends....

United States v. Shimer, 367 U.S. at 383.

The judgment of the Court of Appeals is reversed.

It is so ordered.

JUSTICE MARSHALL and JUSTICE REHNQUIST took no part in the consideration or decision of these cases.

JUSTICE O'CONNOR took no part in the decision of these cases.

———————

Notes & Questions

1. Legislative history: The Court of Appeals noted that the relevant part of the amended Clean Air Act "does not explicitly define" the term "stationary source," as to the permit program and said that the specific issue was not "squarely addressed in the legislative history." Because of this the court determined that "the purposes of the nonattainment program should guide" their decision. If the statute provided a definition for stationary source, then clearly that should take precedent, but should the same be true of the legislative history, as it is implied here? Is legislative history ever conclusive?

2. Administrative Law, in all contexts, has been known to be something of an alphabet soup (i.e., an acronym-rich environment), and energy and environmental law are no different. We see this in this Clean Air Act (sometimes known as CAA) case and in many other contexts. Note the defined terms in the case:

   a. Environmental Protection Agency (EPA)

   b. National Ambient Air Quality Standards (NAAQS's)

   c. State Implementation Plan (SIP)

   d. New source performance standards (NSPS)

   e. Lowest achievable emission rate (LAER)

   f. Preventing significant deterioration (PSD)

   g. New Source Review (NSR)

Practice Note: Trying to keep up with people who are well versed in the relevant acronyms can be difficult, and it is important to ensure you work to understand what is happening. Often creating a quick guide, like the one above, can be helpful. It is important to also remember your audience when you are in practice. Your clients may know the key acronyms (sometimes better than you do), but others in their company may not. Similarly, judges, juries, policymakers, and the general public may not be aware of the terms or their relevance. Make sure you consider your audience in your advocacy to ensure maximum impact, and remember to carefully define acronyms. As an example of how easy this is to miss: note that both "new source review" and "NSR," listed above, appear in the case, but never together (i.e., NSR is never defined).

3. The Court explains that the Respondents (listed in footnote 3) "filed a timely petition for review [of the EPA decision] in the United States Court of Appeals for the District of Columbia Circuit pursuant to 42 U.S.C. §7607(b)(1)." It may seem odd that such a case skips the United States District Court, but here the agency is the initial finder of fact rather than the District Court. As is the case with administrative agency decisions generally, a petition for review of EPA action is to be taken in the United States Courts of Appeals. EPA decisions generally must be appealed to the United States Court of Appeals for the District of Columbia, but there are provisions for review of certain denials or disapprovals stating that such decisions that are "locally or regionally applicable may be filed only in the United States Court of Appeals for the appropriate circuit."

4. The Court provides citations to both the U.S. Code (U.S.C.) and to the Code of Federal Regulations (C.F.R.). Recognize that the U.S. Code, as passed by Congress, provides federal agencies with their power. This delegation of power comes from what is known as the enabling act, and federal agencies derive both their power and limitations from such acts.

5. Sometimes legislators want to move a bill forward, but doing so requires that the two sides leave something ambiguous for the bill to pass. The Court notes this possibility:

"[P]erhaps Congress was unable to forge a coalition on either side of the question, and those on each side decided to take their chances with the scheme devised by the agency."

Practice Note: Attorneys often end up as policymakers or as counsel to policymakers. As such, it's worth considering: Are the legislators acting rationally if they do so? When might you support or argue against such a strategy? What was the outcome of the decision here? Did it have to be that way?

6. The Court states, "Judges are not experts in the field, and are not part of either political branch of the Government." Although this is accurate, does it necessarily follow that the court must defer to the agency decision here? Certainly judges can make decisions in medical malpractice and products liability cases, areas in which they usually lack general expertise.

Practice Note: Consider how is this situation is arguably different than a medical malpractice and products liability case. (This will give you some sense of the policy arguments you might make to refute or support a court considering such a question.) Try to identify and articulate some differences.

7. Deference to agency decision-making is not unlimited. The United States Supreme Court has explained that *Chevron* deference is appropriate when the agency action satisfies the "force of law" test. *See United States v. Mead Corp.*, 533 U.S. 218, 226–27 (2001). In 2006, the Ninth Circuit explained:

> "*Chevron* deference, however, does not apply to all statutory interpretations issued by agencies." *Miranda Alvarado v. Gonzales,* 449 F.3d 915, 921 (9th Cir.2006). In *United States v. Mead Corp.,* 533 U.S. 218, 226–27, 121 S.Ct. 2164, 150 L.Ed.2d 292 (2001), the Supreme Court elucidated the scope of *Chevron,* holding that *Chevron* deference applies only "when it appears that Congress delegated authority to the agency generally to make rules carrying the force of law, *and* that the agency interpretation claiming deference was promulgated in the exercise of that authority." (emphasis added). *Mead* thus placed crucial "limits [on] *Chevron* deference owed to administrative practice in applying a statute," clarifying that agency interpretations promulgated in a non-precedential manner are "beyond the *Chevron* pale." *Id.* at 226, 234, 121 S.Ct. 2164; *see also Hall v. EPA,* 273 F.3d 1146, 1156 (9th Cir. 2001) ("Interpretations of the Act set forth in such non-precedential documents are not entitled to *Chevron* deference.").

Garcia-Quintero v. Gonzales, 455 F.3d 1006, 1012 (9th Cir. 2006).

BP America Production Co. v. Burton
549 U.S. 84 (2006)

Justice Alito delivered the opinion of the Court.

This case presents the question whether administrative payment orders issued by the Department of the Interior's Minerals Management Service (MMS) for the purpose of assessing royalty underpayments on oil and gas leases fall within 28 U. S. C. §2415(a), which sets out a 6-year statute of limitations for Government contract actions. We hold that this provision does not apply to these administrative payment orders, and we therefore affirm.

A

The Mineral Leasing Act of 1920 (MLA) authorizes the Secretary of the Interior to lease public-domain lands to private parties for the production of oil and gas. 41 Stat. 437, as amended, 30 U. S. C. § 181 *et seq.* MLA lessees are obligated to pay a royalty of at least "12.5 percent in amount or value of the production removed or sold from the lease." § 226(b)(1)(A).

In 1982, Congress enacted the Federal Oil and Gas Royalty Management Act (FOGRMA), 96 Stat. 2447, as amended, 30 U. S. C. § 1701 *et seq.*, to address the concern that the "system of accounting with respect to royalties and other payments due and owing on oil and gas produced from such lease sites [was] archaic and inadequate." § 1701(a)(2). FOGRMA ordered the Secretary of the Interior to "audit and reconcile, to the extent practicable, all current and past lease accounts for leases of oil or gas and take appropriate actions to make additional collections or refunds as warranted." § 1711(c)(1). The Secretary, in turn, has assigned these duties to the MMS. 30 CFR § 201.100 (2006).

Under FOGRMA, lessees are responsible in the first instance for the accurate calculation and payment of royalties. 30 U. S. C. § 1712(a). MMS, in turn, is authorized to audit those payments to determine whether a royalty has been overpaid or underpaid. §§ 1711(a) and (c); 30 CFR §§ 206.150(c), 206.170(d). In the event that an audit suggests an underpayment, it is MMS' practice to send the lessee a letter inquiring about the perceived deficiency. If, after reviewing the lessee's response, MMS concludes that the lessee owes additional royalties, MMS issues an order requiring payment of the amount due. Failure to comply with such an order carries a stiff penalty: "Any person who—(1) knowingly or willfully fails to make any royalty payment by the date as specified by [an] order . . . shall be liable for a penalty of up to $10,000 per violation for each day such violation continues." 30 U. S. C. § 1719(c). The Attorney General may enforce these orders in federal court. § 1722(a).

An MMS payment order may be appealed, first to the Director of MMS and then to the Interior Board of Land Appeals or to an Assistant Secretary. 30 CFR §§ 290.105, 290.108. While filing an appeal does not generally stay the payment order, § 218.50(c), MMS will usually suspend the order's effect after the lessee complies with applicable bonding or financial solvency requirements, § 243.8.

Congress supplemented this scheme by enacting the Federal Oil and Gas Royalty Simplification and Fairness Act of 1996 (FOGRSFA), 110 Stat. 1700, as amended, 30 U. S. C. § 1701 *et seq.* FOGRSFA adopted a prospective 7-year statute of limitations for any "judicial proceeding or demand" for royalties arising under a federal oil or gas lease. § 1724(b)(1). The parties agree that this provision applies both to judicial actions ("judicial proceeding[s]") and to MMS' administrative payment orders ("demand[s]") arising on or after September 1, 1996. *Ibid.* This provision does not, however, apply to judicial proceedings or demands arising from leases of Indian land or underpayments of royalties on pre-September 1, 1996, production. FOGRSFA §§ 9, 11, 110 Stat. 1717, notes following 30 U. S. C. § 1701.

There is no dispute that a lawsuit in court to recover royalties owed to the Government on pre-September 1, 1996, production is covered by 28 U. S. C. § 2415(a), which sets out a general 6-year statute of limitations for Government contract actions. That section, which was enacted in 1966, provides in relevant part:

> "Subject to the provisions of section 2416 of this title, and except as otherwise provided by Congress, every action for money damages brought by the United States or an officer or agency thereof which is founded upon any contract express

or implied in law or fact, shall be barred unless the complaint is filed within six years after the right of action accrues or within one year after final decisions have been rendered in applicable administrative proceedings required by contract or by law, whichever is later." (Emphasis added.)

Whether this general 6-year statute of limitations also governs MMS administrative payment orders concerning pre-September 1, 1996, production is the question that we must decide in this case.

B

Petitioner BP America Production Co. holds gas leases from the Federal Government for lands in New Mexico's San Juan Basin. BP's predecessor, Amoco Production Co., first entered into these leases nearly 50 years ago, and these leases require the payment of the minimum 12.5 percent royalty prescribed by 30 U. S. C. §226(b)(1)(A). For years, Amoco calculated the royalty as a percentage of the value of the gas as of the moment it was produced at the well. In 1996, MMS sent lessees a letter directing that royalties should be calculated based not on the value of the gas at the well, but on the value of the gas after it was treated to meet the quality requirements for introduction into the Nation's mainline pipelines. Consistent with this guidance, MMS in 1997 ordered Amoco to pay additional royalties for the period from January 1989 through December 1996 in order to cover the difference between the value of the treated gas and its lesser value at the well.

Amoco appealed the order, disputing MMS' interpretation of its royalty obligations and arguing that the payment order was in any event barred in part by the 6-year statute of limitations in 28 U. S. C. §2415(a). The Assistant Secretary of the Interior denied the appeal and ruled that the statute of limitations was inapplicable.

Amoco, together with petitioner Atlantic Richfield Co., sought review in the United States District Court for the District of Columbia, which agreed with the Assistant Secretary that §2415(a) did not govern the administrative order. *Amoco Production Co.* v. *Baca,* 300 F. Supp. 2d 1, 21 (2003). The Court of Appeals for the District of Columbia Circuit affirmed, *Amoco Production Co.* v. *Watson,* 410 F. 3d 722, 733 (2005), and we granted certiorari, 547 U. S. ___ (2006), in order to resolve the conflict between that decision and the contrary holding of the United States Court of Appeals for the Tenth Circuit in *OXY USA, Inc.* v. *Babbit,* 268 F. 3d 1001, 1005 (2001) (en banc). We now affirm.

I
A

We start, of course, with the statutory text. *Central Bank of Denver, N. A.* v. *First Interstate Bank of Denver, N. A.,* 511 U. S. 164, 173 (1994). Unless otherwise defined, statutory terms are generally interpreted in accordance with their ordinary meaning. *Perrin* v. *United States,* 444 U. S. 37, 42 (1979). Read in this way, the text of §2415(a) is quite clear.

The statute of limitations imposed by §2415(a) applies when the Government commences any "action for money damages" by filing a "complaint" to enforce a contract, and the statute runs from the point when "the right of action accrues." The key terms in this provision—"action" and "complaint"—are ordinarily used in connection with judicial, not administrative, proceedings. In 1966, when §2415(a) was enacted, a commonly used legal dictionary defined the term "right of action" as "[t]he right to bring suit; a legal right to maintain an action," with "suit" meaning "any proceeding ... in a court of justice."

Black's Law Dictionary 1488, 1603 (4th ed. 1951) (hereinafter Black's). Likewise, "complaint" was defined as "the first or initiatory pleading on the part of the plaintiff in a civil action." *Id.,* at 356. See also *Unexcelled Chemical Corp.* v. *United States,* 345 U. S. 59, 66 (1953) (holding that filing a complaint, in the ordinary sense of the term, means filing a suit in court, not initiating an administrative proceeding; "Commencement of an action by the filing of a complaint has too familiar a history ... for us to assume that Congress did not mean to use the words in their ordinary sense"). The phrase "action for money damages" reinforces this reading because the term "damages" is generally used to mean "pecuniary compensation or indemnity, which may be recovered *in the courts.*" Black's 466 (emphasis added).

Nothing in the language of § 2415(a) suggests that Congress intended these terms to apply more broadly to administrative proceedings. On the contrary, § 2415(a) distinguishes between judicial and administrative proceedings. Section 2415(a) provides that an "action" must commence "within one year after final decisions have been rendered in applicable administrative proceedings." Thus, Congress knew how to identify administrative proceedings and manifestly had two separate concepts in mind when it enacted § 2415(a).

B

In an effort to show that the term "action" is commonly used to refer to administrative, as well as judicial, proceedings, petitioners have cited numerous statutes and regulations that, petitioners claim, document this usage. These examples, however, actually undermine petitioners' argument, since none of them uses the term "action" standing alone to refer to administrative proceedings. Rather, each example includes a modifier of some sort, referring to an "administrative action," a "civil or administrative action," or "administrative enforcement actions." This pattern of usage buttresses the point that the term "action," standing alone, ordinarily refers to a judicial proceeding.

Petitioners contend that their broader interpretation of the statutory term "action" is supported by the reference to "*every* action for money damages" founded upon "*any* contract." 28 U. S. C. § 2415(a) (emphasis added). But the broad terms "every" and "any" do not assist petitioners, as they do not broaden the ordinary meaning of the key term "action."

Petitioners argue that their interpretation is supported by *Pennsylvania* v. *Delaware Valley Citizens' Council for Clean Air,* 478 U. S. 546 (1986), and *West* v. *Gibson,* 527 U. S. 212 (1999), but this reliance is misplaced. In *Delaware Valley Citizens' Council,* we construed the attorney's fee provision of the Clean Water Act (CWA), which authorizes a "court, in issuing any final order in any action brought pursuant to subsection (a) of this section, [to] award costs of litigation ... to any party." 42 U. S. C. § 7604(d). We permitted the recovery of fees both for work done in court and in subsequent administrative proceedings. But the pertinent statutory provision in that case did not employ the key terms that appear in the statute at issue here. Specifically, the CWA provision referred to "litigation," not to an "action" commenced by the filing of a "complaint." Moreover, "the work done by counsel [in the administrative phase of the case] was as necessary to the attainment of adequate relief ... as was all of their earlier work in the courtroom ... obtaining the consent decree." 478 U. S., at 558. And we expressly reserved judgment on the question "whether an award of attorney's fees is appropriate ... when there is no connected court action in which fees are recoverable." *Id.,* at 560, n. 5.

West helps petitioners even less. There, we considered whether the Equal Employment Opportunity Commission (EEOC) could order a federal agency to pay compensatory damages in an administrative proceeding. Section 717(b) of Title VII of the Civil Rights Act of 1964, 42 U. S. C. §2000e-16(b), authorized the EEOC to employ "appropriate remedies," but did not specifically authorize damages, and §717(c) authorized a subsequent court action against an employer agency, 42 U. S. C. §2000e-16(c). In 1991, Congress added Rev. Stat. §1977A(a)(1), 42 U. S. C. §1981a(a)(1), which provided that "[i]n an action brought by a complaining party under section 706 or 717 ... the complaining party may recover compensatory ... damages." In *West*, the defendant agency argued that the enactment of §1981a(a)(1) showed that Congress did not consider compensatory damages to be "appropriate remedies" in an EEOC proceeding, as opposed to an action brought by an aggrieved employee. If Congress had wished to authorize the award of compensatory damages in an EEOC proceeding, the defendant agency reasoned, Congress would have so provided in §1981a(a)(l), by expressly cross-referencing §717(c). We rejected this argument, but in doing so we did not hold that an EEOC proceeding is an "action" under §1981a(a)(1). Rather, we simply concluded that the EEOC's authorization under §717(b) to award "appropriate remedies" was broad enough to encompass compensatory damages. 527 U. S., at 220–221.

For these reasons, we are not persuaded by petitioners' argument that the term "action" in §2415(a) applies to the administrative proceedings that follow the issuance of an MMS payment order.

C

We similarly reject petitioners' suggestion that an MMS letter or payment order constitutes a "complaint" within the meaning of §2415(a). Petitioners point to examples of statutes and regulations that employ the term "complaint" in the administrative context. See, *e.g.,* 15 U. S. C. §45(b) (requiring the Federal Trade Commission to serve a "complaint" on a party suspected of engaging in an unfair method of competition); 29 CFR §102.15 (2006) (a "complaint" initiates unfair labor practice proceedings before the National Labor Relations Board). But the occasional use of the term to describe certain administrative filings does not alter its primary meaning, which concerns the initiation of "a civil action." Black's 356. Moreover, even if the distinction between administrative and judicial proceedings is put aside, an MMS payment order lacks the essential attributes of a complaint. While a complaint is a filing that commences a proceeding that may in the end result in a legally binding order providing relief, an MMS payment order in and of itself imposes a legal obligation on the party to which it is issued. As noted, the failure to comply with such an order can result in fines of up to $10,000 a day. An MMS payment order, therefore, plays an entirely different role from that of a "complaint."

D

To the extent that any doubts remain regarding the meaning of §2415(a), they are erased by the rule that statutes of limitations are construed narrowly against the government. *E. I. DuPont de Nemours & Co.* v. *Davis*, 264 U. S. 456 (1924). This canon is rooted in the traditional rule *quod nullum tempus occurrit regi*—time does not run against the King. *Guaranty Trust Co.* v. *United States*, 304 U. S. 126, 132 (1938). A corollary of this rule is that when the sovereign elects to subject itself to a statute of limitations, the sovereign is given the benefit of the doubt if the scope of the statute is ambiguous.

Bowers v. *New York & Albany Lighterage Co.*, 273 U. S. 346 (1927), cited by petitioners, is not to the contrary. There, as here, the issue was the scope of a statute of limitations. The provision in that case, however, provided that "'[n]o suit or proceeding for the collection of any such taxes'" shall commence more than five years after the filing of the return. *Id.,* at 348–349. The Government argued that the terms "proceeding" and "suit" were coterminous, and urged further that any ambiguity should be resolved in its favor.

The Court recognized the canon, restating it much as we have above. *Id.,* at 349. But the Court concluded that the canon had no application in that case because the text of the relevant statute, unlike § 2415(a), applied clearly and separately to "suits" and "proceedings," and the Court saw no reason to give these different terms the same meaning. *Id.,* at 349–350.

E

We come now to petitioners' argument that interpreting § 2415(a) as applying only to judicial actions would render subsection (i) of the same statute superfluous. Subsection (i) provides as follows:

> "The provisions of this section shall not prevent the United States or an officer or agency thereof from collecting any claim of the United States by means of administrative offset, in accordance with section 3716 of title 31." 28 U. S. C. § 2415(i).

An administrative offset is a mechanism by which the Government withholds payment of a debt that it owes another party in order to recoup a payment that this party owes the Government. 31 U. S. C. § 3701(a)(1). Thus, under subsection (i), the Government may recover a debt via an administrative offset even if the Government would be time barred under subsection (a) from pursuing the debt in court.

Petitioners argue that, if § 2415(a) applies only to judicial proceedings and not to administrative proceedings, there is no need for § 2415(i)'s rule protecting a particular administrative mechanism (*i.e.,* an administrative offset) from the statute of limitations set out in subsection (a). Invoking the canon against reading a statute in a way that makes part of the statute redundant, see, *e.g., TRW Inc.* v. *Andrews,* 534 U. S. 19, 31 (2001), petitioners contend that subsection (i) shows that subsection (a) was meant to apply to administrative, as well as judicial, proceedings. We disagree.

As the Court of Appeals noted, subsection (i) was not enacted at the same time as subsection (a) but rather was added 16 years later by the Debt Collection Act of 1982. 96 Stat. 1749. This enactment followed a dispute between the Office of the Comptroller of the Currency (OCC) and the Department of Justice's Office of Legal Counsel (OLC) over whether an administrative offset could be used to recoup a debt where a judicial recoupment action was already time barred.

In 1978, in response to a question from the United States Civil Service Commission, OLC opined that an administrative offset could not be used to recoup a debt as to which a judicial action was already time barred. OLC reached this conclusion not because it believed that § 2415(a) reached administrative proceedings generally, but rather because of the particular purpose of an administrative offset. "Where [a] debt has not been reduced to judgment," OLC stated, "an administrative offset is merely a pre-judgment attachment device." Memorandum from John M. Harmon, Assistant Attorney General, OLC, to Alan K. Campbell, Chairman, U. S. Civil Service Commission Re: Effect of Statute of Limitations on Administrative Collection of United States Claims 3 (Sept. 29, 1978), Joint Lodging. OLC opined that a prejudgment attachment device such as this exists only to preserve funds to satisfy any judgment the creditor subsequently obtains. *Id.,* at 4 (citing cases). OLC therefore concluded that, where a lawsuit is already foreclosed by § 2415(a), an administrative offset that is the functional equivalent of a pretrial attachment is also unavailable. *Id.,* at 3.

The OCC disagreed. See *In the Matter of Collection of Debts—Statute of Limitations on Administrative Setoff,* 58 Comp. Gen. 501, 504–505 (1979). In its view, the question was answered by

> "[t]he general rule ... that statutes of limitations applicable to suits for debts or money demands bar or run only against the remedy (the right to bring suit) to which they apply and do not discharge the debt or extinguish, or even impair, the right or obligation, either in law or in fact, and the creditor may avail himself of every other lawful means of realizing on the debt or obligation. See *Mascot Oil Co.* v. *United States,* 42 F. 2d 309 (Ct. Cl. 1930), affirmed 282 U. S. 434; and 33 Comp. Gen. 66 (1953). See also *Ready-Mix Concrete Co.* v. *United States,* 130 F. Supp. 390 (Ct. Cl. 1955)." *Ibid.*

That Congress had time-barred the judicial remedy, OCC reasoned, imposed no limit on the administrative remedy.

The OLC-OCC dispute reveals that, even under the interpretation of subsection (a)—the one we are adopting—that considers it applicable only to court proceedings, subsection (i) is not mere surplusage. It clarifies that administrative offsets are not covered by subsection (a) even if they are viewed as an adjunct of a court action.

To accept petitioners' argument, on the other hand, we would have to hold either that § 2415(a) applied to administrative actions when it was enacted in 1966 or that it was extended to reach administrative actions when subsection (i) was added in 1982. The clear meaning of the text of § 2415(a), which has not been amended, refutes the first of these propositions, and accepting the latter would require us to conclude that in 1982 Congress elected to enlarge § 2415 to cover administrative proceedings by inserting text expressly excluding a single administrative vehicle from the statute's reach. It is entirely unrealistic to suggest that Congress would proceed by such an oblique and cryptic route.

III

Petitioners contend that interpreting § 2415(a) as applying only to judicial actions results in a statutory scheme with peculiarities that Congress could not have intended. For example, petitioners note that while they are required by statute to preserve their records regarding royalty obligations for only seven years, 30 U. S. C. § 1724(f), the interpretation of § 2415(a) adopted by the Court of Appeals permits MMS to issue payment orders that reach back much farther.

We are mindful of the fact that a statute should be read where possible as effecting a "'symmetrical and coherent regulatory scheme,'" *FDA* v. *Brown & Williamson Tobacco Corp.,* 529 U. S. 120, 133 (2000), but here petitioners' alternative interpretation of § 2415(a) would itself result in disharmony. For instance, under FOGRSFA, MMS payment orders regarding oil and gas leases are now prospectively subject to a 7-year statute of limitations except with respect to obligations arising out of leases of Indian land. Consequently, if we agreed with petitioners that § 2415(a) applies generally to administrative proceedings, payment orders relating to oil and gas royalties owed under leases of Indian land would be subject to a shorter (*i.e.,* 6-year) statute of limitations than similar payment orders relating to leases of other public-domain lands (which would be governed by FOGRSFA's new 7-year statute). Particularly in light of Congress' exhortation that the Secretary of the Interior "aggressively carry out his trust responsibility in the administration of Indian oil and gas," 30 U. S. C. § 1701(a)(4), it seems unlikely that Congress intended to impose a shorter statute of limitations for payment orders regarding Indian lands.

Petitioners contend, finally, that interpreting § 2415(a) as applying only to judicial actions would frustrate the statute's purposes of providing repose, ensuring that actions are brought while evidence is fresh, lightening recordkeeping burdens, and pressuring federal agencies to assert federal rights promptly. These are certainly cogent policy arguments, but they must be viewed in perspective.

For one thing, petitioners overstate the scope of the problem, since Congress of course can enact and has enacted specific statutes of limitations to govern specific administrative actions. See, *e.g.*, 42 U. S. C. § 5205(a)(1) (statute of limitations for an administrative action to recover payments made to state governments for disaster or emergency assistance). Indeed, in 1996, FOGRSFA imposed just such a limitation prospectively on all non-Indian land, oil, and gas lease claims.

Second, and more fundamentally, the consequences of interpreting § 2415(a) as limited to court actions must be considered in light of the traditional rule exempting proceedings brought by the sovereign from any time bar. There are always policy arguments against affording the sovereign this special treatment, and therefore in a case like this, where the issue is how far Congress meant to go when it enacted a statute of limitations applicable to the Government, arguing that an expansive interpretation would serve the general purposes of statutes of limitations is somewhat beside the point. The relevant inquiry, instead, is simply how far Congress meant to go when it enacted the statute of limitations in question. Here prior to the enactment of § 2415(a) in 1966, contract actions brought by the Government were not subject to any statute of limitations. See *Guaranty Trust Co.*, 304 U. S., at 132. Absent congressional action changing this rule, it remains the law, and the text of § 2415(a) betrays no intent to change this rule as it applies to administrative proceedings.

In the final analysis, while we appreciate petitioners' arguments, they are insufficient to overcome the plain meaning of the statutory text. We therefore hold that the 6-year statute of limitations in § 2415(a) applies only to court actions and not to the administrative proceedings involved in this case.

* * *

For these reasons, the judgment of the Court of Appeals for the District of Columbia Circuit is affirmed.

It is so ordered.

The Chief Justice and Justice Breyer took no part in the consideration or decision of this case.

Notes & Questions

1. A brief bit of history on MMS: BP's Deepwater Horizon oil rig exploded on April 20, 2010, killing eleven people and spilling the first of what would eventually be 4.9 billion gallons of oil into the Gulf of Mexico after the blowout of the Macondo well. The result was what a national commission called "the worst environmental disaster in U.S. history." The event focused more attention on the Minerals Management Service (MMS) in the Department of the Interior (DOI), which was already under scrutiny for a variety of management failures, ethical crises, and other administrative failures. At the time, MMS was the lead regulatory authority offshore oil, gas, and other mineral leasing on the outer continental shelf (OCS).

As a result of these failures, MMS was reorganized as the Bureau of Ocean Energy Management, Regulation and Enforcement (BOEMRE). The duties of BOEMRE were then split into three groups: the Bureau of Ocean Energy Management (OCS leasing for conventional and renewable energy sources), the Bureau of Safety and Environmental Enforcement (permitting, inspections, and other activities related to safety and environmental oversight of offshore energy activities), and the Office of Natural Resources Revenue (collection, disbursement, and verification of Federal and Indian energy and other natural resource revenues).

2. Notice that the court here is unanimous, with two Justices sitting out of the process. Is that surprising? Try to identify points in the opinion that might have gone another way and try to articulate why.

E. Property & Contract Law as Energy Law

Energy generation is resource intensive and often involves companies working with landowners and others to gain access to the needed resources. This is true for fossil fuels, like coal, oil, and gas, as well as renewable resources like wind. As you read the following case, consider the property implications, as well as the practical drafting implications raised.

U.S. Bank v. Koenig

2002 ND 137, 650 N.W.2d 820

Kapsner, Justice.

[¶1] U.S. Bank, as Trustee of the Washburn Trust No. 1, appeals from a summary judgment quieting title to the coal under a quarter section of land to Donald Koenig, Robert Koenig, James Koenig, Eilene Doble, and Joy Person ("Koenigs"). We construe a 1906 warranty deed conveying the land from U.S. Bank's predecessor in interest to the Koenigs' predecessor in interest to reserve the coal to U.S. Bank's predecessor. We reverse and remand for entry of judgment consistent with this opinion.

I

[¶2] In a 1906 warranty deed, William and Lizzie Washburn, U.S. Bank's predecessors in interest, conveyed a quarter section of land to Emil Borchardt, the Koenigs' predecessor in interest. The original 1906 deed is not part of this record, but the county recorder's record for the conveyance identified the Washburns, the grantors, as the "parties of the first part" and Borchardt, the grantee, as the "party of the second part," and provided:

> said second party reserving and excepting therefrom all coal now or hereafter to be found in said land, also the right and title to the use of such surface ground as may be necessary for mining operations, and the right of access to such reserved and excepted coal for the purpose of exploring, developing, working and removal of the same.

[¶3] U.S. Bank commenced this quiet title action against the Koenigs, claiming the reservation clause entitled it to the coal. U.S. Bank alleged the warranty deed contained a "scrivener's error, or an error in transcription of the original deed into the record, in that it states 'said second party reserving and excepting therefrom all coal,' whereas the reservation must necessarily have been to [the Washburns], the parties of the first part, who made the grant." The Koenigs, successors in interest to ninety-five percent of the interest acquired by Borchardt, claimed they owned ninety-five percent of the coal under the land because the warranty deed did not effectively reserve the coal to the Washburns.

[¶ 4] U.S. Bank and the Koenigs both moved for summary judgment. U.S. Bank argued, as a matter of contract interpretation, there was "no question that the parties intended [the reservation] clause to reserve all of the coal to the grantors and that the term 'said second party' at the beginning of the clause was inadvertently substituted for the term 'said first party,' since the party of the second part in a deed, that is the grantee, cannot reserve something which he does not own and cannot except something from the grant being made to him by the grantor." The Koenigs argued that U.S. Bank failed to offer any evidence to clearly and convincingly establish grounds for reformation of the 1906 deed.

[¶ 5] The trial court concluded U.S. Bank failed to establish that the language in the coal reservation constituted a mutual mistake and that the written instrument did not truly express the parties' intent. The court decided U.S. Bank could not sustain the burden of proof necessary for reformation or revision of the warranty deed and granted summary judgment for the Koenigs.

II

[¶ 6] U.S. Bank argues the proper interpretation of the warranty deed establishes its predecessor in interest, the Washburns, reserved and excepted the coal from their conveyance to the Koenigs' predecessor in interest. U.S. Bank argues extrinsic evidence is not necessary to determine the parties' intent because the only possible meaning for the reservation clause is to reserve the coal to the Washburns.

[¶ 7] The issues in this appeal are raised in the posture of summary judgment, which is a procedural device for resolving a controversy on the merits without a trial if the evidence demonstrates there are no genuine issues of material fact, or inferences to be drawn from undisputed facts, and if the evidence shows a party is entitled to judgment as a matter of law. *Bender v. Aviko USA L.L.C.*, 2002 ND 13, ¶ 4, 638 N.W.2d 545.

[¶ 8] Except as otherwise provided in N.D.C.C. ch. 47-09, grants are interpreted in the same manner as contracts. N.D.C.C. § 47-09-11. Contracts are construed to give effect to the parties' mutual intent at the time of contracting. N.D.C.C. § 9-07-03; *Haag v. Noet-zelman*, 1999 ND 157, ¶ 6, 598 N.W.2d 121. The parties' intent must be ascertained from the writing alone if possible. N.D.C.C. § 9-07-04; *Haag*, at ¶ 6. The parties' intent must be ascertained from the entire instrument, and every clause, sentence, and provision should be given effect consistent with the main purpose of the contract. *Haag*, at ¶ 6. Under N.D.C.C. § 9-07-17, "[r]epugnancy in a contract must be reconciled, if possible, by such an interpretation as will give some effect to the repugnant clause subordinate to the general intent and purpose of the whole contract." See *Northwest G.F. Mut. Ins. Co. v. Norgard*, 518 N.W.2d 179, 184 (N.D. 1994). Grants in a contract are interpreted in favor of the grantee, except a reservation in any grant is interpreted in favor of the grantor. N.D.C.C. § 47-09-13. If the parties' intent can be ascertained from the writing alone, the interpretation of the contract is entirely a question of law, and we independently examine and construe the contract to determine if the trial court erred in its interpretation of the contract. *Haag*, at ¶ 6.

[¶ 9] In *Perschke v. Burlington Northern, Inc.*, 311 N.W.2d 564, 565 (N.D. 1981), this Court considered a similar issue regarding the interpretation of a 1906 deed that conveyed a tract of land and "reserved and excepted coal and iron lands." Perschke, the successor in interest of the grantee, argued the reservation reserved the coal and iron lands, surface and all, and not just the coal and iron itself, and thus was void as repugnant to the grant. This Court construed the word "lands" to mean "interests," so the deed reserved the coal and iron interests in the property conveyed without reserving the surface interests:

> In construing the reservation clause of the 1906 deed we must strive to give effect to the mutual intention of the parties as it existed at the time, so far as that intent is ascertainable and lawful. Section 9-07-03, N.D.C.C. Perschke urges us to interpret the clause as reserving coal and iron property, surface and all, with the ultimate effect of voiding the entire reservation for being repugnant to the grant. We are unpersuaded that Perschke's interpretation would give effect to the mutual intention of the parties. Upon examining the reservation it is quite obvious that the grantor was attempting to at least reserve for itself all coal and iron interests in the property granted, but under Perschke's interpretation of the clause the grantor and its successors in interest would have effectively reserved nothing. That interpretation of the clause would also be contrary to the rule that reservations must be interpreted in favor of the grantor. Section 47-09-13, N.D.C.C.; *Gilbertson v. Charlson*, 301 N.W.2d 144 (N.D. 1981).

> In the instant case, as in *Carlson* [*v. Minnesota Land & Colonization Co.*, 129 N.W. 768 (Minn. 1911)], the reservation clause expressly reserves "the use of such surface ground as may be necessary for mining operations." We agree with the Minnesota Supreme Court that if the grantor was attempting to reserve the coal and iron property, surface and all, there would be no reason for it to have reserved the use of the surface for mining operations. In construing a contract or deed we must construe all provisions together and give meaning to every sentence, phrase and word. Section 9-07-06, N.D.C.C.; *Delzer Construction Co. v. New Marian Homes Corp.*, 117 N.W.2d 851 (N.D. 1962). If we were to interpret the reservation as reserving the coal and iron property, surface and all, the phrase "reserving ... the use of such surface ground as may be necessary for mining operations" would be meaningless. Perschke explains that in addition to reserving the coal and iron property the grantor, by reserving the use of the surface ground, was attempting to insure that he had access to the reserved property. We are not convinced that Perschke's explanation gives meaning to the language which reserves use of the surface, because the clause also contains language expressly reserving a *right of access* to the reserved "coal and iron lands."

> In accord with the foregoing analysis we construe the reservation clause of the 1906 deed as reserving the coal and iron interests in the property conveyed without reserving the surface interests of the property. In so construing the clause we have interpreted the term "lands" as meaning "interests." We believe that our construction gives the term "lands" consistency throughout the clause, gives meaning to every sentence and phrase of the clause, and correctly ascertains the intention of the parties to the deed at the time of its execution.

Perschke, at 567.

[¶ 10] Here, the county recorder's records identified the grantee, Borchardt, as the "party of the second part," but the reservation clause said the "second party" reserved and excepted all coal. The reservation clause also said the "second party" reserved and excepted the right and title to the surface for mining operations and for access to the reserved and excepted coal. Under our rules for construing deeds, any uncertainty about the reservation must first be resolved from the four corners of the deed by giving meaning to each word, sentence, and provision in a manner that is consistent with the purpose of the deed. *See Haag*, 1999 ND 157, ¶ 6, 598 N.W.2d 121. Construing the reservation clause to reserve the coal to the grantee would render the reservation clause meaningless. We construe the deed and the reservation clause as a whole in favor of the grantor to give meaning to each word and phrase and to reconcile repugnant words in a manner consistent with the intent and purpose of the deed. *See Perschke*, 311 N.W.2d at 567. Under those rules of construction, we construe the deed to reserve the coal to the grantors, the Washburns. That interpretation construes the reservation in favor of the grantor, see N.D.C.C. § 47-09-13, reconciles repugnant words in a manner that is subordinate to, and consistent with, the general intent and purpose of the deed, see N.D.C.C. § 9-07-17, and gives meaning to every clause, sentence, and provision in the deed. *See Haag*, at ¶ 6; *Perschke*, at 567. We conclude the parties to the 1906 deed intended that the Washburns reserved and excepted the coal from their conveyance to Borchardt. Because we conclude the parties' intent can be ascertained from the document itself, the interpretation of the deed is a question of law for the court to decide, see *Haag*, at ¶ 6, and legal principles regarding reformation are not applicable to our interpretation.

III

[¶ 11] We reverse the summary judgment and remand for entry of judgment consistent with this opinion.

Notes & Questions

1. *Practice Note*: Notice how this case comes to be. It seems clear that the conveyance has a mistake, which could have proven to be a big one. (Based on this case and the cited *Perschke* case, it also appears 1906 was not a good year to draft deeds.) What could the drafter have done to help reduce the chances of such an error? One option is to consider defining the parties as "grantor" and "grantee," rather than "party of the first part" and "party of the second part." Or even "Washburn" and "Borchardt." Not all mistakes can be avoided, but it is a lot easier to keep the parties straight when the defined term reflects some sense of meaning.

2. It seems clear from reading the case that the Washburn intended to reserve the coal, as there would be no need to mention a reservation at all if Washburn intended to convey everything to Borchardt. The state Supreme Court agrees unanimously. Still, don't miss that the court below found for the Koenigs. This may seem like a slam dunk, but two courts found differently. What might lead a court to decide for the Koenigs? Consider the equities of such a decision and the nature of the parties as you think about the options.

Chapter 2

The Business of Energy Law

A. Introduction

The energy industry was a major part of the growth of industry and regulation. As discussed in Chapter 1, the electricity and natural gas industries played major roles in setting up our modern utility structure and heavily influenced securities law. The energy sector remains big business, and understanding the role of business law in energy law is a critical part of learning how to navigate law and policy relating to the energy sector. In short, business law is a foundation of energy law.

This chapter will covers some of the key areas in which energy laws encounter what might otherwise be deemed business-related legal issues. Energy lawyers need to be able to understand entity structure, fiduciary duties, executive compensation, and antitrust law, among other things, to grasp the scope of the potential pitfalls and opportunities presented by clients or policymakers.

1. Vocabulary and Concepts

Board of Directors: The elected body that is charged with management and oversight of a corporations. The board is elected by the shareholders.

Mergers & Acquisitions (M&A): A general term that refers to the consolidation of companies. A merger is a combination of two companies to form a new company. An acquisition is the purchase of one company where the purchasing company absorbs the purchased company.

Redline or Blackline: An electronic document that compares one version of a document with another. Such a document is often requested, and is highly advisable, in contract drafting and negotiating.

Shareholders: A company's equity holders, sometimes thought of as the owners. Shareholders have a residual interest, which is what remains after all creditors are satisfied when a company ceases to operate.

2. Client Issue

Your firm has just taken on a new client who is a large shareholder in many companies. She is particularly concerned about her holdings in Energex, Inc., a publicly traded energy company. Energex was founded in 1977 by a oil and gas man from Louisiana who is still the CEO and a member of the board of directors. The client is concerned that the CEO is taking opportunities for himself that she thinks belong to the Energex. As you read the following sections, think about: (1) What are the potential conflicts of interest the CEO might have? (2) Is it a conflict of interest if the activity is permitted under the CEO's employment contract? (3) What kind of documents might be publicly available for review and where would you find them? (4) If it goes to litigation, what other information might you seek? From whom?

B. Business Organizations & Employment Law as Energy Law

Some energy companies, like Marathon Petroleum and ExxonMobil, have histories dating back more than 150 years. Other companies, like Chesapeake Energy and SandRidge Energy, have their origins in the 1980s. These newer companies grew rapidly and grew from small start-up entities into large, publicly traded companies. The role of the early company investors and executives has, from time to time, proven troublesome. Understanding this interaction requires a basic understanding of how corporations operate.

Corporations are entities that provide investors the ability to invest their capital (usually money), while limiting their liability to that investment. This is something most people understand in the context of large, publicly traded corporations, where one can buy stock (e.g., Broadwind Energy, MidAmerican Energy Holdings Company, Chevron Corporation). The investor can lose all of the money he or she exchanged for the stock, but such investors are not liable for debts beyond that investment.

Corporations are operated under the direction of their board of directors. The board, as a collective body, makes the decisions needed for the company to run. Part of that is choosing (and then delegating authority to) the executive officers of the company, often a Chief Executive Officer (CEO) and/or President, Vice President, and General Counsel. These officers then report to the board of directors and manage the day-to-day operations of the corporation.

Delaware is the dominant state of incorporation for publicly traded companies (such as those traded on the New York Stock Exchange). Under the Delaware General Corporation Law § 141:

> (a) The business and affairs of every corporation organized under this chapter shall be managed by or under the direction of a board of directors, except as may be otherwise provided in this chapter or in its certificate of incorporation. If any such provision is made in the certificate of incorporation, the powers and duties conferred or imposed upon the board of directors by this chapter shall be exercised or performed to such extent and by such person or persons as shall be provided in the certificate of incorporation.

> (b) The board of directors of a corporation shall consist of 1 or more members, each of whom shall be a natural person. The number of directors shall be fixed

by, or in the manner provided in, the bylaws, unless the certificate of incorporation fixes the number of directors, in which case a change in the number of directors shall be made only by amendment of the certificate. Directors need not be stock-holders unless so required by the certificate of incorporation or the bylaws. The certificate of incorporation or bylaws may prescribe other qualifications for directors. Each director shall hold office until such director's successor is elected and qualified or until such director's earlier resignation or removal. Any director may resign at any time upon notice given in writing or by electronic transmission to the corporation. A resignation is effective when the resignation is delivered unless the resignation specifies a later effective date or an effective date determined upon the happening of an event or events....

An officer may also serve as a director, and many boards want to have key officers serve a role on the board. The Securities and Exchange Commission's Rule 16a-1 — Definition of Terms provides the definition of an officer, in that context:

....

(f) Officer:

The term "officer" shall mean an issuer's president, principal financial officer, principal accounting officer (or, if there is no such accounting officer, the controller), any vice-president of the issuer in charge of a principal business unit, division or function (such as sales, administration or finance), any other officer who performs a policy-making function, or any other person who performs similar policy-making functions for the issuer. Officers of the issuer's parent(s) or subsidiaries shall be deemed officers of the issuer if they perform such policy-making functions for the issuer. In addition, when the issuer is a limited partnership, officers or employees of the general partner(s) who perform policy-making functions for the limited partnership are deemed officers of the limited partnership. When the issuer is a trust, officers or employees of the trustee(s) who perform policy-making functions for the trust are deemed officers of the trust.

In the recent past, the CEOs for both Chesapeake Energy and SandRidge Energy were roundly criticized for financial arrangements that raised serious questions about potential conflicts of interest between the CEOs and their companies. Both situations were, in part, related to the fact that each CEO was allowed to make or keep investments that could be potentially competitive with the companies they were running. Reuters reporters brought both situations to the forefront.

In 2012, Reuters issued a special report about personal loan arrangements of Chesapeake co-founder and then-CEO Aubrey McClendon. Part of the concern was that McClendon's biggest lender was also a major investor in parts of Chesapeake, which raised the concern about whether the company's financing terms might be influenced by McClendon's personal loan arrangements. Under some of McClendon's loan arrangements he was also required to take all "commercially reasonable action" to make certain everyone involved with wells related to the loan would "comply with" all "covenants and agreements" in the loans. The clause is a common occurrence, but it is unusual for a CEO to be accountable both personally and on behalf of the entity the CEO runs. The article explained, the arrangement could thus "mean[] McClendon could have an incentive to influence Chesapeake to act in the interest of his lenders, rather than of his shareholders." Anna Driver & Brian Grow, *Special Report: Chesapeake CEO Took $1.1 Billion in Shrouded Personal Loans*, REUTERS, http://www.reuters.com/article/2012/04/18/us-chesapeake-mcclendon-loans-idUSBRE83H0GA 20120418 (Apr. 18, 2012)

In the case of SandRidge, a change to the CEO's executive compensation agreement created some significant concerns: "Giving an executive permission to generate personal income by partnering or competing with the public company he runs is unusual because it could reduce returns for shareholders and create the risk of conflicts of interest, said energy industry attorneys and corporate governance specialists." Michael Erman, et al., *SandRidge gives CEO Wide Scope to Cut His Own Land Deals*, REUTERS, http://www.reuters .com/article/2013/02/06/us-sandridge-contract-idUSBRE9150EM20130206 (Feb. 6, 2013).

The steep drop in natural gas prices (and each company's significant stock price decline) was already creating problems for these CEOs with their shareholders and the possibility that the CEOs were benefiting in ways that might be adverse to their shareholders led both to step down from their posts and resign from their respective boards of directors. Below, we'll first consider the issues raised by Chesapeake's shareholder, then take a look at the SandRidge Energy employment agreement modifications that caused concern.

The following complaint brought by shareholders against Chesapeake and former CEO Aubrey McClendon provides an overview of the kind of duties directors owe to their companies, and the kinds of arrangements that can lead to costly lawsuits and, possibly, liability. Rather than providing a case here, the following complaint is used for two key purposes: (1) to provide an overview of the obligations officers and directors have to their company, and (2) to give a sense of what the complaints that eventually lead to court decisions actually look like.

Amended Shareholder Derivative Complaint for Breach of Fiduciary Duties, Waste of Corporate Assets, Unjust Enrichment, and Violations of the Securities and Exchange Act of 1934

No. 12CV00631
United States District Court, W.D. Oklahoma
June 27, 2102

Derryberry Naifeh, LLP, Darren Derryberry, OBA No., 14542, 4800 N. Lincoln Blvd., Oklahoma City, OK 73105, Telephone: (405) 528-6569, Facsimile: (405) 528-6462.

Johnson & Weaver, LLP, Frank J. Johnson, Brett Weaver, 110 West "A" Street, Suite 750, Telephone: (619) 230-0063, Facsimile: (619) 255-1856.

Robbins Umeda LLP, Brian J. Robbins, George C. Aguilar, Jay N. Razzouk, Lauren N. Ochenduszko, 600 B Street, Suite 1900, San Diego, CA 92101, Telephone: (619) 525-3990, Facsimile: (619) 525-3991.

Holzer Holzer & Fistel, LLC, Michael I. Fistel, JR., Marshall P. Dees, 200 Ashford Center North, Suite 300, Atlanta, GA 30338, Telephone: (770) 392-0090, Facsimile: (770) 392-0029, Counsel for Plaintiff.

* * *

Plaintiff Greg Erickson ("Plaintiff"), by and through his undersigned attorneys, hereby submits this Amended Shareholder Derivative Complaint (the "Complaint") on behalf of nominal defendant Chesapeake Energy Corporation ("Chesapeake" or the "Company") against certain current and former members of its Board of Directors (the "Board") and executive officers seeking to remedy the defendants' misconduct from 2005 to the present (the "Relevant Period"). Plaintiff makes the following allegations based upon individual and personal knowledge as to their own acts, and the investigation undertaken by their undersigned counsel as to other matters, which investigation included, inter alia, an analysis of U.S. Securities and Exchange Commission ("SEC") filings by Chesapeake, as well as securities analysts' reports and advisories about the Company, press releases, and other public statements issued by the Company, and media reports about the Company. Plaintiff believes that substantial additional evidentiary support will exist for the allegations set forth herein after a reasonable opportunity for discovery.

I. NATURE OF THE ACTION

1. Chesapeake's business is the exploration for and production of natural gas. The Company is North America's second-largest producer of natural gas. It owns interests in nearly 40,000 natural gas and oil-producing wells that are currently producing more than 2 billion cubic feet equivalent per day. Chesapeake's strategy is to discover, acquire, and develop conventional and unconventional natural gas reserves.

2. Defendant Aubrey K. McClendon ("McClendon") co-founded the Company in 1989. He has served as Chesapeake's Chief Executive Officer ("CEO") and Chairman of the Board. McClendon has routinely taken advantage of his imperial status at the Company to offload his personal financial risk to Chesapeake and its minority shareholders—all under the guise of purportedly aligning his interests with theirs. This twisted logic is increasingly being exposed for what it is, as investors continue to learn the truth that, between his weight at the Company and his leveraging of other people's money, McClendon can only win while everyone else will lose.

3. Since the Company's initial public offering ("IPO") in 1993, defendant McClendon has participated in a "well participation program" available only to the Company's founders known as the Founder Well Participation Program ("FWPP"). This program has allowed McClendon to personally participate in the Company's exploratory efforts and to seek personal benefits from that participation in addition to the benefits he has obtained by serving as Chesapeake's lead executive. McClendon has participated in almost every single one of the Company's wells since the IPO, thereby obtaining purported ownership interests in gas producing reserves valued at more than $852 million.

4. Defendants' stated purpose of the FWPP, when it was presented to shareholders for approval in 2005, is to retain and motivate defendant McClendon and his co-founder and align their interests with the Company's interests. This has proven—through McClendon and the Board's manipulations—not to be true, as defendants have repeatedly disregarded these justifications of the FWPP and have instead allowed it to simply serve as a vehicle for McClendon to once again leverage himself to the potential peril of the Company.

5. In order to participate in the FWPP during any given "participation period," defendant McClendon was required first to state his intention to do so and to declare "the percentage working interest" that he proposes to participate with during that participation period, not to exceed 2.5% of the total. Thereafter, the Company is supposed to invoice McClendon on a monthly basis for a pro rata portion of certain costs associated with drilling the applicable well. McClendon, however, encountered personal liquidity troubles in 2008 relating to, among other things, his stock ownership in the Company and his personally operated wedge fund, and struggled to fulfill his financial obligations under the FWPP in 2008. More recently, McClendon has been taking out substantial loans totaling ap-

proximately $1 billion to buy into the FWPP, while at the same time using his other FWPP interests as collateral.

6. McClendon's transactions, amounting to approximately $1 billion, were first revealed by *Reuters* on April 18, 2012, in an in-depth investigative report. Amazingly, as part of these transactions, McClendon has assigned the rights to a vast portion of any profits he could hope to make from his FWPP interests, meaning he not only has minimal down side exposure, but also minimal interest in the upside. *Reuters* cites numerous experts, analysts, and investors who expressed surprise and concern regarding the nature and extent of these loans, as well as the threat they pose to the Company.

7. These new loans present a serious conflict of interest between defendant McClendon and the Company, whose interests McClendon is duty bound to put before his own. Some of McClendon's lenders are providing financing to the Company, but at rates that are lucrative to the lenders, while unfair to the Company. For example, while McClendon bought back his map collection at only 2.28% interest (the Company's purported average borrowing cost), one of McClendon's lenders bought preferred stock from the Company that pays an annual dividend of 7%, plus royalty interest from Chesapeake's oil and gas wells. McClendon's massive leveraging of his FWPP interests also runs the serious risk that an imminent default by the CEO could, among other things, ensnare Chesapeake in litigation with McClendon's lenders.

8. Defendant McClendon's use of his FWPP interests presents an additional conflict of interest as he competes with the Company to sell gas. According to Forbes, McClendon has personally collected more than $130 million from Volumetric Production Payment ("VPP") contracts, by which he has promised to deliver certain pre-arranged amounts of gas for a certain period of time, in exchange for an upfront payment. Chesapeake, however, is in no position to be competing with McClendon in the sale of gas. The Company has a debt load of $10 billion and has been scraping for money and liquidating assets to maintain cash flows.

9. The revelations of defendant McClendon's loans and VPP contracts has exposed the FWPP as simply a conduit for McClendon to enrich himself despite the consequences to the Company. He shares very little risk because he is using other people's money to buy into the FWPP, while at the same time he has a low chance of seeing any profits because his lenders will take practically any profits the wells are likely to generate. Defendants' repeated statements to shareholders, year after year, that the FWPP aligns McClendon's interests with those of the Company's, were clearly meant to distract shareholders from discovering the entire slate of McClendon's financial transactions.

10. Indeed, defendants do not hide the fact that the Board was aware of defendant McClendon's financing transactions, and they were quick to partially disclose the deals in the Company's latest Proxy Statement—that is, once the media already broke the news of what had been going on behind the scenes. Defendants' improper and incomplete disclosures are also wrongful because many of them were made in connection with annual Proxy Statements soliciting shareholder votes *for* various compensation proposals that benefitted McClendon and *against* other shareholder-sponsored proposals that sought to limit the extent of McClendon's ability to personally profit at the expense of the best interests of Chesapeake.

11. On top of a reopened investigation by the SEC, the Internal Revenue Service ("IRS") is also investigating potential wrongdoing in connection with the FWPP. A U.S. Senator is also calling for an investigation by the U.S. Department of Justice. These investigations mean the Company may face substantial costs in connection with investigating and

defending itself—and potentially pay steep penalties or fines—as a result of defendants' wrongdoing.

12. Furthermore, Reuters has revealed that between approximately 2004 and 2008, while defendant McClendon was also supposed to be the full time CEO of Chesapeake, he operated a $200 million hedge fund. If the distraction from his duties at Chesapeake (if not potential violation of his employment agreement) was not problematic enough, the CEO's hedging activities involved bets on commodities that Chesapeake produces. Despite the serious conflicts of interest presented by McClendon's hedging activities, the Board amended his employment agreement to make it easier for him to engage in these activities. At the same time, the Board utterly failed to disclose any material facts relating to the hedge fund to shareholders.

13. In light of these facts and the facts alleged below, Plaintiff brings this derivative action on behalf of the Company.

* * *

III. THE PARTIES

A. Shareholder Plaintiff

16. Plaintiff Greg Erickson is a current shareholder of Chesapeake and has continuously held Chesapeake stock since at least October 2005. Plaintiff Erickson is a citizen of Wisconsin.

B. Nominal Defendant

17. Nominal defendant Chesapeake is an Oklahoma corporation headquartered in Oklahoma City, Oklahoma. The Company's principal executive offices are located at 6100 North Western Avenue, Oklahoma City, Oklahoma. Chesapeak's [sic] shares trade on the New York Stock Exchange.

C. Director Defendants

18. Defendant McClendon ("McClendon") has served as CEO of the Company since 1989, when he co-founded the Company. Until recently, he also served as Chairman of the Board of Directors ("Board"). Defendant McClendon is a citizen of Oklahoma.

[Ed.: The other members of the Board of Directors are also named defendants.]

* * *

IV. THE INDIVIDUAL DEFENDANTS' DUTIES

33. By reason of their positions as officers, directors, and fiduciaries of Chesapeake and because of their ability to control the business and corporate affairs of Chesapeake, the Individual Defendants owed and owe Chesapeake fiduciary obligations of good faith, loyalty, and candor, and were and are required to use their utmost ability to control and manage Chesapeake in a fair, just, honest, and equitable manner. The Individual Defendants were and are required to act in furtherance of the best interests of Chesapeake and its shareholders so as to benefit all shareholders equally and not in furtherance of their own personal interest or benefit.

34. Each director and officer of the Company owes to Chesapeake and its shareholders the fiduciary duty to exercise good faith and diligence in the administration of the affairs of the Company and in the use and preservation of its property and assets, and the highest

obligations of fair dealing. In addition, as officers and/or directors of a publicly held company, the Individual Defendants had a duty to promptly disseminate accurate and truthful information with regard to the Company's operations, performance, management, projections, and forecasts so that the market price of the Company's stock would be based on truthful and accurate information. The Individual Defendants are also required to disclose fully and fairly all material information within their control when they seek shareholder action.

35. The directors also have a duty to inform themselves of all material information reasonably available to them prior to making a business decision. Upon receipt of a litigation demand, the directors must investigate and evaluate the charges in order to discharge their duty to the shareholders and the Company. The directors must review all information necessary to objectively and meaningfully evaluate the demand.

36. The Individual Defendants, because of their positions of control and authority as directors and/or officers of Chesapeake, were able to and did, directly and/or indirectly, exercise control over the wrongful acts complained of herein. Because of their advisory, executive, managerial, and directorial positions with Chesapeake, each of the Individual Defendants had knowledge of material, non-public information regarding the Company.

37. To discharge their duties, the officers and directors of Chesapeake were required to exercise reasonable and prudent supervision over the management, policies, practices, and controls of the Company. By virtue of such duties, the officers and directors of Chesapeake were required to, among other things: (i) exercise good faith to ensure that the affairs of the Company were conducted in an efficient, business-like manner and provide the highest quality of performance; (ii) exercise good faith to ensure that the Company was operated in a diligent, honest, and prudent manner and complied with all applicable federal and state laws, rules, and regulations, and all contractual obligations, including acting only within the scope of its legal authority; (iii) ensure that the Company is operated in a diligent, honest, and prudent manner in compliance with all applicable laws, rules, and regulations; (iv) ensure that the purposes and goals of the Company's FWPP are served at all times and are not compromised in order to serve the interests of any of Chesapeake's executive officers; (v) ensure that the Company not waste its corporate assets by conferring personal benefits on its executives or other employees, with no corresponding benefit to the Company; (vi) ensure that the Board and any of its committees, including the Compensation Committee and Audit Committee, fulfill their respective duties, including by ensuring that the Board and its committees become reasonably informed before making any decisions on the Company's behalf; (vii) ensure that the Company's public disclosures do not contain false or misleading statements or omissions of material facts; and (viii) identify and mitigate conflicts of interest and other risks to the Company.

38. Furthermore, Chesapeake's current Code of Business Conduct and Ethics (the "Code") provides that "[a]ll directors, officers and employees of the Company must avoid situations that create a conflict of interest or the appearance or potential for a conflict of interest." The Code defines a conflict of interest as occurring when personal interests are either in conflict with the Company's interest or interfere with one's ability to perform his or her duties to the Company or responsibilities at work. The Individual Defendants are also expected to recognize situations where a conflict of interest has occurred, or has the potential to occur, and take the necessary actions to eliminate or mitigate such conflict, including, if necessary, enlisting the assistance of management. Upon information and belief, the forgoing or its substantial equivalent was required by the Code throughout the Relevant Period.

39. The conduct of the Individual Defendants complained of herein involves a knowing and culpable violation of their obligations as directors and officers of Chesapeake, the absence of good faith on their part, and a disregard for their duties to the Company and its shareholders that the Individual Defendants were aware or should have been aware posed a risk of serious injury to the Company. The Individual Defendants breached their duties of loyalty, care, and good faith by allowing defendants to cause, or by themselves causing, the wrongdoing alleged herein.

* * *

A. Defendant McClendon Borrows over $1 Billion from Chesapeake's Lenders Using His FWPP Interests as Collateral to Continue Participating in the FWPP

61. Contrary to the stated purposes for which shareholders approved the FWPP, from 2009 to 2012, defendant McClendon has borrowed approximately $1.1 billion (and potentially more) to fund his participation in the FWPP, while at the same time using his personal stake in Chesapeake's wells to secure the loans. Most of what is so far publicly known about these loans was revealed by *Reuters* on April 18, 2012, in a special report titled: "The Energy Billionaire's Shrouded Loans."

62. As discussed above, the FWPP is premised on the idea that defendant McClendon's interests will be aligned with Chesapeake's because he will bear his proportionate share of costs (and risks) from drilling new wells in addition to any profits from their success. However, from at least 2009 to 2012, McClendon did not contribute his own cash or assets to pay for his share of the Company's wells. Instead, he used loans secured by his 2.5% interest in others wells that he acquired through the FWPP. McClendon pledged almost his entire interest in these wells as collateral that would be seized if he defaults on the loans.

63. Defendant McClendon obtained approximately $1.1 billion in loans through three companies that he controls: Chesapeake Investments LP, Larchmont Resources LLC, and Jamestown Resources LLC. Each of these companies lists Chesapeake's headquarters as their address.

64. The more than $1 billion in loans consists of three separate loans secured by defendant McClendon's 2.5% interest in Chesapeake's wells. In June 2009, McClendon borrowed $225 million from Union Bank. In December 2010, he borrowed $375 million from TCW Asset Management. Finally, in January 2012, he borrowed at least $500 million from a $1 billion line of credit with EIG Global Energy Partners ("EIG").

	First Quarter 2012	2011	2010	2009
Natural gas and oil revenues	$ 53,103,173	$184,270,948	$ 127,064,861	$ 87,856,431
Lease operating expenditures	(13,203,805)	(42,457,253)	(26,102,787)	(19,481,167)
Net cash flow	39,899,368	141,813,695	100,962,074	68,375,264
Capital expenditures	(127,982,572)	(457,151,007)	(242,839,086)	(184,468,839)
Net after capital expenditures	$ (88,083,204)	(315,337,312)	$(141,877,012)	$(116,093,575)

65. This ever-growing scale of defendant McClendon's borrowing is troubling, especially when taken in context of smaller borrowing in the past. From 1989 to the present, McClendon has frequently borrowed on a much smaller scale. For example, Oklahoma records indicate that Chesapeake Investments took out a $2.9 million loan in 1992. As *Reuters* observes, Chesapeake released a statement indicating that "McClendon's securing of such loans has been 'commonplace' during the past 20 years." With the most recent loan up to or exceeding $500 million, McClendon's increases in borrowing appear dangerously unsustainable. Reflecting this unsustainability, McClendon has even shown willingness on his part to terminate the FWPP before it is set to expire on December 31, 2015.

66. An examination of cash flows from defendant McClendon's FWPP participation confirms that McClendon may not only be cash-poor, but that he is on course to default on his monstrous loans. Since at least 2009, McClendon's FWPP interests have required him to find millions (if not hundreds of millions) of dollars of cash to cover his allotment of expenditures. Meanwhile, McClendon's FWPP interests have generated only nominal revenues. This pattern is illustrated in the following table that the Company published in the Proxy Statement filed with the SEC on April 20, 2012:

67. There is also a grave risk that defendant McClendon's overleveraging of his well interests (like his overleveraging of Company stock in 2008) will negatively impact Chesapeake. According to *Reuters*, these loans required McClendon to "take all commercially reasonable action' to ensure that other owners and operators of the wells — including Chesapeake — 'comply with ... covenants and agreements' of the loans." Thomas O. Gorman, a partner at Dorsey & Whitney in Washington, D.C., commented that, because of this clause, these private loans had the potential to impact Chesapeake. The Individual Defendants rushed to essentially argue that the Company is immune to any claims by McClendon's lenders in connection with his personal loans. Defendants have since admitted that they were not aware of the terms of McClendon's financing transactions. Moreover, their wishful thinking will not prevent the Company from being ensnared in litigation with the lenders who will undoubtedly resort to aggressive tactics to reclaim the vast amounts of money they have lent to McClendon. After all, McClendon's lenders have the capability to bring incredible pressure to bear upon the cash-strapped Company, because these same lenders provide much needed financing to Chesapeake as well. This presents a serious conflict between McClendon and the Company.

68. Defendant McClendon's out-of-control borrowing has also created another serious conflict of interest that has harmed and will continue to harm the Company. McClendon's largest financer, EIG, has provided financing for Chesapeake at a steep price for the Company. Presumably speaking on McClendon's borrowing from EIG, *The Wall Street Journal* reported that McClendon "borrow[ed] up to $1.4 billion from a private-equity firm that has done hundreds of millions of dollars with [Chesapeake] in the past year." In November 2011, EIG was part of a group of investors that bought $1.25 billion worth of "perpetual preferred shares" in Chesapeake Utica LLC, a newly formed entity. Notably, the investment rewarded EIG investors with *an annual dividend of 7% in addition to royalties from oil and gas wells.* On April 9, 2012, the Company announced plans to raise another $1.25 billion from investors including EIG, through CHK Cleaveland Tonkawa, another new subsidiary.

69. EIG has been closely tied to defendant McClendon and Chesapeake for years. In February 2011, EIG met with the New Mexico State Investment Council ("NMSIC"), the state's public investment fund. The fund asked EIG's COO, Randall Wade ("Wade"), about the company's prior investments in McClendon's well interests. Wade told NMSIC that "EIG had known Chesapeake for more than 25 years and 'provided pre-IPO financing for them in the late 1980's.'" He also told the NMSIC that this ongoing relationship

provided opportunities to EIG that were not available to other investors. For example, in 2008 when McClendon did not have the resources to participate in the FWPP, EIG stepped in to provide financing. After negotiations with McClendon, EIG formed a special purpose vehicle, Larchmont Resources, LLC, through which EIG acquired McClendon's well rights for 2009 and 2010. EIG later formed a second special purpose vehicle, Jamestown Resources LLC, which it used to control McClendon's well rights in 2011, with rights to control his interests in 2012 as well.

70. EIG's investments in defendant McClendon and in Chesapeake have been very lucrative. The *7% annual dividends* that are paid by Chesapeake represent very favorable terms to EIG because the dividends on preferred shares get paid first, before the dividends on regular shares. In stark contrast, as part of the proposed settlement, McClendon agreed to buy back his map collection from the Company and pay interest at the paltry rate of 2.28%, which (according to the terms of the proposed settlement) equals Chesapeake's average borrowing rate from approximately January 2009 to July 2011. *Reuters* quoted Mark Hanson, an analyst with Morningstar in Chicago, speaking on preferred shares: "'Basically it's a form of more expensive debt.'" He adds: "'It makes it appear that it's not debt, but it sits on top of obligations to the common shareholder.'"

71. At the same time, EIG's arrangements with defendant McClendon himself are similarly very profitable for EIG and deprive McClendon of substantially all of his future interest in profits from his FWPP participation. Under the deal with McClendon, EIG receives the entirety of the cash flow from the wells McClendon is participating in until EIG recoups its investment, plus a 13% realized return. On top of all that, EIG is entitled to a perpetual 42% share of McClendon's profits from the FWPP. This means that not only is McClendon not exposed to the down-side risks of investing in the FWPP, but he also stands to receive only a small portion of the upside, if any. Without directly sharing the costs and potentially the revenues from his FWPP interests, it is difficult to say that McClendon has much of any remaining interest in the wells. Thus, the FWPP, rather than aligning McClendon's interests with the Company, has provided McClendon with a means to gamble with other peoples' money, a situation strikingly similar to when McClendon gambled (and lost) with bets he made using his shares of Company stock.

72. According to Reuters, citing as its source Henry Hood ("Hood"), the Company's general counsel: "Chesapeake's board of directors is aware that McClendon has borrowed against his share of company wells." In response to the *Reuters* article, the Individual Defendants caused the Company to issue a press release on April 18, 2012 ("April 18 Response"), that quoted Hood making a similar admission that "'[t]he Board of Directors is fully aware of the existence of Mr. McClendon's financing transactions.'" Mr. Hood's comments were immediately met with disbelief. In fact, one analyst said Hood's position is "not only disingenuous, it's borderline delusional." Realizing the seriousness of this admission, the Individual Defendants have backtracked on their earlier statement. They caused the Company to issue a press release on April 26, 2012, to "clarify" their April 18 Response, stating:

> 'The Board of Directors is fully aware of the existence of Mr. McClendon's financing transactions' was intended to convey the fact that the Board of Directors is generally aware that Mr. McClendon used interests acquired through his participation in the FWPP as security in personal financing transactions. The Board of Directors did not review, approve or have knowledge of the specific transactions engaged in by Mr. McClendon or the terms of those transactions.

73. The Board further backtracked from its earlier statements when, on or around April 26, 2012, the Board removed a disingenuous question and answers exchange between

Reuters and defendants (the "Q&A"), described further below, from the Company's website that had originally been posted as the Company's response to the Reuters investigative report.

74. Unlike the Individual Defendants, the public was not aware of the existence of defendant McClendon's loan transactions, let alone the nature and extent of these transactions. To the extent the Individual Defendants may have mentioned the loans at all in their public statements, they did so by issuing, at best, passing references that failed to provide shareholders with adequate information regarding the nature and extent of these transactions and/or their connection to McClendon. In fact, *Reuters* disclosed that even some industry analysts who were experienced with the Company were not aware of the existence of McClendon's loans until they were contacted for the article.

75. Defendants have failed and continue to fail to disclose key aspects of defendant McClendon's loans, which remain hidden from shareholders even despite diligent efforts. A preliminary investigation by Plaintiffs counsel confirms descriptions by Reuters concerning the difficulty involved in following the chain of transactions and business entities, as is required to determine that McClendon has borrowed approximately $1.1 billion to buy into the FWPP using his other FWPP interests as collateral. Even an exhaustive, time-consuming investigation following the trail of various liens, deeds, and other public records can only go so far. Because the loans consist of private promissory notes, the interest rate, the exact amount borrowed, and other details of the transaction remain private. It thus appears difficult, if not virtually impossible, for individuals outside of Chesapeake or McClendon's financiers to determine the exact terms and size of McClendon's loans.

76. Despite the impracticality (if not impossibility) for shareholders to connect the dots on their own, the Individual Defendants refuse to provide adequate disclosure in the Company's Proxy Statements, including disclosures concerning the number, amounts, or terms of defendant McClendon's loans. Granted, to quell growing shareholder furor at the lack of adequate disclosures, on April 26, 2012, McClendon belatedly released aggregated information regarding the amounts of his outstanding debt and the value of his interests in Company wells. But this partial disclosure still falls well short of the material information shareholders require for their investment decisions, including to properly assess material conflicts of interest presented by the loans or the risks associated with a default by McClendon.

77. The Individual Defendants failed to provide adequate disclosures to shareholders. The consensus among the academics, attorneys, and analysts Reuters worked with, who personally reviewed the loan transactions, was that Chesapeake should fully disclose the details of defendant McClendon's loan transactions. David F. Larcker, a professor of accounting at Stanford University's Graduate School of Business, said that given the size, scope, and complicated terms of the loans, the details of these transactions are key information for shareholders to have in evaluating the Company and, thus, they should be fully disclosed. Mike Bread, an oil and gas research analyst at Hodges Capital Management in Dallas, a company that owns Chesapeake shares, agreed that the loans should be disclosed, citing the facts that they are large and related to the oil and gas business. Other analysts seeking disclosure cited the potential conflict created by the fact that McClendon's largest source of loans, EIG, is also an investor in Chesapeake. Joseph Allman, an oil and gas industry analyst at J.P. Morgan in New York, reviewed the loan agreements and concluded that the Company should disclose the details of the loan transactions because of the potential for a conflict with EIG.

78. Notwithstanding the above, the Individual Defendants rushed to defend their concealment of defendant McClendon's leveraged participation in the FWPP. For example,

in the April 18 Response, they claim, among other things, that: (i) they have disclosed the fact that McClendon's financing transactions occurred; (ii) the terms and procedures for the FWPP "are clear and detailed in every proxy for all shareholders to see"; (iii) Mc-Clendon's interests and Chesapeake's are "completely aligned"; and (iv) the "suggestion of any conflict of interest is unfounded." These statements confirm that the Individual Defendants prejudged the appropriateness of McClendon's financing and determined to take no action.

79. In preparation for its article, *Reuters* spoke with over a dozen academics, analysts, and attorneys who were given defendant McClendon's loan agreements to review. Many of these professionals disagreed with McClendon and the Board's view that the loans do not create any possibility of a conflict of interest and need not be disclosed. Joshua Fershee, an associate professor of energy and corporate law at the University of North Dakota, told *Reuters* that McClendon's $1.1 billion in loans through his own companies, which operate in the same industry as Chesapeake, could lead to a high risk for conflicts of interest. Similarly, McClendon's supposed "alignment" of interests was challenged by Mark Hanson, an analyst with Morningstar in Chicago. Hanson noted that because Mc-Clendon has financed his participation in the FWPP without putting up any of his own money, the intended alignment of interests is lacking. Chesapeake's general counsel Hood, speaking on behalf of defendants, has even acknowledged that McClendon's loans with EIG could result in "some theoretical possibility of a conflict of interest," given that the Company is also borrowing from EIG.

80. Also contradicting defendants' assertion that they have properly disclosed defendant McClendon's financing, *Reuters* reported that its April 18, 2012 report "drew swift reaction from investors, who pushed the stock down 5 percent the day it was published." Confirming the seriousness of the Individual Defendants' misconduct, U.S. Senator Bill Nelson ("Nelson") plans to formally request the U.S. Department of Justice (the "DOJ") to investigate potential fraud and price manipulation at Chesapeake.

81. Further demonstrating the inadequacy of the Individual Defendants' earlier public statements, on April 20, 2012, the Individual Defendants issued a preliminary Proxy Statement that added the following new language regarding defendant McClendon's FWPP financing that was not present in earlier Proxy Statements:

> Additionally, over the life of the FWPP, Mr. McClendon has typically mortgaged his interests acquired under the FWPP with one or more lenders, some of which also have lending, investment or advisory relationships with the Company. Mr. McClendon's mortgages with these lenders secure loans used in whole or in part to fund Mr. McClendon's well costs. The Company does not extend loans to Mr. McClendon for participation in the FWPP or any other purposes. The Company does not review or approve financings of Mr. McClendon's personal assets, including his FWPP interests. In addition, the Company has no obligation to repay any loans Mr. McClendon may obtain nor are any of the Company's interests in any assets exposed to such loans or the mortgages securing them.

82. The Board initially took the position that it was not required to look into the loans. Chesapeake's general counsel, Hood, admitted that "the board did not review or approve the transactions." Further, the Board has failed to engage in any analysis of the potential conflicts of interest caused by defendant McClendon's financing. The Board attempted to justify this inaction by claiming that McClendon's financing of his well interests is a personal matter. Instead, the Board took a "wait and see" approach. Hood claimed that "[i]f there were any conflicts of interest … they would have surfaced by now." However,

the Board's (especially that of the 2012 Compensation Committee Defendants) decision to bury its head in the sand is contrary to the terms of the FWPP, which requires the Compensation Committee (if not the whole Board) to administer the program. (As discussed below, the Board has recognized their position to be erroneous, and claims it has begun to investigate McClendon's financing transactions.) This conscious disregard of or, at a minimum, participation in false statements relating to the FWPP and McClendon's participation therewith, further constitutes a breach of the Individual Defendants' fiduciary duties.

83. Contrary to their assertion that they are properly disclosing information regarding the FWPP, the Individual Defendants have historically resisted attempts to get more information regarding defendant McClendon's participation in the FWPP. For example, in 2008 when the SEC requested information regarding McClendon's interests in the FWPP, the request was initially rebuked. As detailed below, after numerous letters between the SEC and Chesapeake and negotiations on the subject, the Company agreed to provide shareholders with a chart showing the costs and revenues for the wells in the program.

* * *

Notes & Questions

1. The purpose of this chapter is to provide an introduction to the various potential issues one might face in the energy law context. This is clearly not a comprehensive introduction to business organizations and corporate governance, and is instead intended to give a brief overview of some of the obligations officers and directors have to their respective companies. Notice the "duties" section does not provide the source of the varying obligations (fiduciary duties), but as a general matter, the statement of officers' and directors' duties is accurate. These duties are defined by state law (usually the state of incorporation), but they are generally similar from state to state.

2. This is only a segment of the total complaint. The overall complaint is nearly fifty pages long, with several sections that were excluded here, including a listing for four specific counts, a prayer for relief, and a demand for a jury trial.

Mergers and acquisitions in the energy sector appear to be especially vulnerable to arrangements that could lead to significant conflicts of interest. Recognizing and understanding potential conflicts of interest is vital in these circumstances. This can be especially difficult for lawyers (and soon-to-be lawyers) who have never seen a compensation agreement.

As noted above, in 2013, it came to light that certain changes were made in 2011 to SandRidge Energy's CEO Tom Ward's 2006 executive compensation agreement. The following provides a comparison of the two agreements, showing the changes to the old language and the new provisions:

EMPLOYMENT AGREEMENT

THIS AGREEMENT is made effective ~~June 8, 2006~~*December 20, 2011* (the "**Effective Date**"), between ~~RIATA~~*SANDRIDGE* ENERGY, INC., a ~~Texas~~*Delaware* corporation (the "**Company**"), and TOM L. WARD, an individual (the "**Executive**").

WITNESSETH:

WHEREAS, the Company and the Executive desire to set forth the terms of their agreements relating to the employment of *the* ~~Executive by the Company; and~~

~~WHEREAS, the Company has adopted the Well Participation Program (the "WP Program") in order to provide for the participation by the Executive in the Company's wells.~~

NOW, THEREFORE, in consideration of the mutual promises herein contained, the Company and the Executive agree as follows:

1. Employment. The Company hereby employs the Executive and the Executive hereby accepts such employment subject to the terms and conditions contained in this Agreement. The Executive is engaged as an employee of the Company, and the Executive and the Company do not intend to create a joint venture, partnership or other relationship that might impose a fiduciary obligation on the Executive or the Company in the performance of this Agreement, other than as an officer and director of the Company~~,~~.

2. Executive's Duties. The Executive is employed on a full-time basis. Throughout the term of this Agreement, the Executive will use ~~the Executive's~~*his* best efforts and due diligence to assist the Company in the objective of achieving the most profitable operation of the Company and the Company's affiliated entities consistent with developing and maintaining a quality business operation *and complying with applicable law. Except as provided in paragraph 3, the Executive shall devote his entire business skill, time and effort diligently to the affairs of the Company in accordance with the duties assigned to the Executive, and the Executive shall perform all such duties, and otherwise conduct himself, in a manner reasonably calculated in good faith by him to promote the best interests of the Company.*

2.1 Specific Duties. During the term of this Agreement, the Executive: (a) will serve as Chief Executive Officer ~~for~~*of* the Company; (b) will be nominated for election or appointed to serve as a director of the Company and will be nominated as Chairman of the ~~Board;~~*Company's Board of Directors (the "Board");* (c) will be appointed as an officer or manager of such of the Company's subsidiaries as the Executive ~~requests~~*deems necessary to execute his duties fully*; and (d) will be nominated for election or appointed to serve as a director of such of the Company's subsidiaries as the Executive ~~requests.~~*deems necessary to execute his duties fully.* The Executive agrees ~~to use the Executive's best efforts to~~*will* perform all of the services required to fully and faithfully execute the ~~offices and positions~~*position* to which the Executive is appointed and ~~elected and~~ such other services as may be ~~reasonably directed~~*assigned* by the Board ~~of Directors of~~*in its sole discretion. In addition, the precise duties to be performed by* the ~~Company in accordance with this Agreement~~*Executive may be changed or curtailed in the sole discretion of the Board.*

~~2.2 Modifications. The precise duties to be performed by the Executive may be extended or curtailed in the discretion of the Board of Directors of the Company. However, except for termination for Cause (as hereinafter defined) under paragraph 6.1.2 of this Agreement, the failure of the Executive to be elected, be reelected or serve as a director of the Company during the term of this Agreement, the removal of the Executive as a member of the Board of Directors of the Company, the failure to reelect or reappoint the Executive as Chairman~~

~~of the Board and Chief Executive Officer of the Company, or the assignment of~~
~~the performance of duties incumbent on the foregoing offices to other persons~~
~~without the prior written consent of the Executive will constitute termination~~
~~without Cause by the Company.~~

~~2.3~~

   2.2 **Rules and Regulations.** From time to time, the Company may issue
policies and procedures applicable to employees and the Executive ~~including~~
~~an Employment Policies Manual.~~.The Executive agrees to comply with such
policies and procedures, ~~except to the extent such policies are inconsistent~~
~~with this Agreement. Such policies and procedures~~*which* may be supplemented,
modified, changed or adopted without notice in the sole discretion of the
Company at any time. In the event of a conflict between such policies and
procedures and this Agreement, this Agreement will control unless compliance
with this Agreement will violate any law or regulation applicable to the
Company or its affiliated entities.

   2.~~4~~3 **Stock Investment.** During the term of this Agreement, the Executive
agrees to hold shares of the Company's common stock having an aggregate
Investment Value (as ~~hereafter~~ defined *below*) greater than~~five hundred percent~~
~~(500%)~~% of the compensation paid to the Executive under paragraphs 4.1
and 4.2 of this Agreement during such calendar year. Any shares of common
stock acquired by the Executive prior to the date of this Agreement and still
owned by the Executive during the term of this Agreement may be used to
satisfy the requirement to own common stock. For purposes of this paragraph,
the **"Investment Value"** of each share of stock will be as follows: (a) for shares
purchased after the date of this Agreement, the price paid by the Executive
for such shares; (b) for shares acquired after the date of this Agreement through
the exercise of stock options, the grant of restricted stock, the conversion of
preferred stock or other than through open market purchases, the fair market
value of the common stock on the date the option was exercised, the *restrictions*
lapsed, the stock was issued, or the stock was acquired through the conversion
of preferred stock, or the date such stock was otherwise acquired; and (c) for
shares acquired on or prior to the date of this Agreement, the price paid by
the Executive. The Company has no obligation to sell or to purchase from
the Executive any of the Company's stock in connection with this paragraph
2.~~4~~3 and has made no representations or warranties regarding the Company's
stock, operations or financial condition.

   3. Other Activities. ~~Except~~*The Executive shall not engage in any business activity*
that, in the judgment of the Board, conflicts with the Executive's duties hereunder,
whether or not such activity is pursued for gain, profit or other pecuniary advantage.
In addition, except for the activities ~~(the "Permitted Activities")~~ permitted under
~~paragraphs~~*paragraph* 3.1~~, 3.2 and 3.3~~ of this Agreement or approved by the Board
~~of Directors, during the period of Executive's employment~~*in writing,* the Executive
will not: (a) engage in activities ~~which~~*that* require such substantial services on
the part of the Executive that the Executive is unable to perform the duties
assigned to the Executive in accordance with this Agreement; (b) serve as an
officer or director of any publicly held entity; or (c) directly or indirectly invest
in, participate in or acquire an interest in any oil and gas business, including,
without limitation, *businesses* (i) producing oil and gas, (ii) drilling, owning or
operating oil and gas leases or wells, (iii) providing services or materials to the

oil and gas industry, *or (iv)* marketing or refining oil or gas~~, or (v) owning any interest in any corporation, partnership, company or entity which conducts any of the foregoing activities~~. The limitations in this paragraph 3 will not prohibit an investment by the Executive in publicly traded securities. ~~The~~ *or the maintenance of investment interests owned prior to the Effective Date. Notwithstanding the foregoing, the* Executive is not restricted from maintaining or making investments, or engaging in other businesses, enterprises or civic, charitable or public service *functions if such activities, investments, businesses or enterprises do not result in a violation of* ~~functions if such activities, investments, businesses or enterprises do not result in a violation of~~ clauses (a) through (c) of this paragraph 3. ~~Notwithstanding the foregoing,~~, *and* the Executive ~~will be~~ *is* permitted to participate in the ~~following~~ activities ~~that will be deemed to be approved by the Company~~ *set forth in paragraph 3.1,* if such activities are undertaken in strict compliance with this Agreement.

3.1 Royalty Interests and Gifts~~.~~, *Outside Oil and Gas Drilling, and Certain Other Drilling Units.* The foregoing restriction in clause (c) will not prohibit, *in areas not being pursued by the Company: (a)* the ownership of royalty interests where the Executive owns ~~or~~, previously owned *or acquires* the surface of the land covered by the royalty interest and the ownership of the royalty interest is incidental to the ownership of the surface estate, or the ownership of royalty, overriding royalty or working interests that are received by gift or inheritance *subject to disclosure by the Executive to the Company in writing; (b) the Executive's participation in outside operated oil and gas drilling; or (c) the Executive's participation as a working interest owner in properties operated by the Company where wells are proposed in drilling units with respect to which the surface or royalty ownership rights are held by TLW Holdings, L.L.C., an Oklahoma limited liability company, 192 Investments, L.L.C., an Oklahoma limited liability company, and entities owned or controlled by the Executive.*

~~**3.2 Existing Interests.** The Executive has in the past conducted oil and gas activities individually and through TLW Investments, Inc., an Oklahoma corporation, and other entities owned or controlled by the Executive (collectively, the "Executive Affiliates"). The Executive also has a pre-existing right to participate in the drilling of oil and gas wells through the Chesapeake Energy Corporation Founder Well Participation Program ("CHK Program") until August 10, 2006. The Executive will be permitted to continue to conduct oil and gas activities (including participation in new wells) through the CHK Program, or otherwise directly or through the Executive Affiliates, but only to the extent such activities are conducted on oil and gas leases or interests which the Executive or Executive Affiliates owned or had the right to acquire as of the date of this Agreement or which Executive or Executive affiliates acquires through the CHK Program (the "Prior Interests").~~

~~**3.3 Company's Activities.** The Executive or the designated Executive Affiliate will be permitted to participate in the WP Program. The WP Program may not be amended or modified without the prior written consent of the Board of Directors and the Executive.~~

These agreements were filed with the SEC:

Riata Energy, Inc., SEC Form S-1, Exhibit 10.11 (Jan. 20, 2008), http://www.sec.gov/Archives/edgar/data/1349436/000095012907005963/h48324a1exv10w11.htm.

SandRidge Energy, Inc., SEC Form 8-K, Exhibit 10.1 (Dec. 27, 2011), http://www.sec.gov/Archives/edgar/data/1349436/000119312511352901/d270965dex101.htm.

Notes & Questions

1. Be sure to look for all the changes and consider what they could mean. The changes are much easier to read this way, but often the two documents will be hard copies that would need to be read side by side. With SEC-filed documents, electronic versions are much easier to obtain.

2. Riata Energy, Inc., changed its name to SandRidge Energy, Inc., in 2006, the same year Tom Ward joined the company. Tom Ward co-founded Chesapeake Energy with Aubrey McClendon.

3. *Practice Note*: What do you think was the goal of the changes to the compensation agreement? Note that boards have an obligation to act in the best interests of the shareholders, but such decisions are protected by what is called the business judgment rule. That rule, in the simple sense, is that courts will not second guess the business judgment of the board unless some form of fraud, illegality, or self-dealing is shown. In this instance, it may seem like self-dealing because of Ward's potential benefit, but he is not the board. If the remaining members of the board were acting without undue influence from Ward and did not benefit from the arrangement, the court will not likely act. Why might a reasonable board of directors choose to make such concessions and allow this kind of change?

C. Antitrust Law as Energy Law

Barak Orbach & D. Daniel Sokol, *Antitrust Energy*

85 S. Cal. L. Rev. 429 (2012) (footnotes omitted)
100 Years of Standard Oil Antitrust Symposium Article
Copyright (c) 2012 University of Southern California;
Barak Orbach; D. Daniel Sokol

I. INTRODUCTION

Antitrust law has been declared a failure, moribund, or possibly just a ghost from the trustbusting era. A quarter of a century ago, Thomas Hazlett declared: "Any responsible historian of American antitrust policy must conclude that, if one takes at face value the assertions that antitrust laws exist to advance competition and protect the consumer, that policy is a failure. The notorious *Berkey Photo* case may be the flagship of that failed policy." Hazlett went as far as suggesting it would be "most effective ... to consider federal enforcement of the antitrust laws to be a per se restraint of trade." Robert Crandall and Clifford Winston examined the question: "Should the United States pursue a vigorous antitrust policy?" They found "little empirical evidence that past interventions have provided much direct benefit to consumers or significantly deterred anticompetitive behavior." Other scholars examined whether antitrust was still alive. Yet, recently some stressed that antitrust is not dead, but while "at one time [it] was skewed toward over-enforcement, ... today if there is any bias it is in the opposite direction." Statistical figures indicate that, since the 1970s, the volume of civil antitrust litigation is low compared to prior decades. For these reasons and others, Jonathan Baker tried to provide "evidence of the necessity and success of antitrust enforcement." The Supreme Court, however, voiced skepticism about antitrust litigation. In the fall of 2007, *Antitrust* therefore posed the question for a special issue: *The End of Antitrust As We Know It?*

Marking the centennial anniversary of *Standard Oil Co. v. United States*, we argue that much of the critique of antitrust enforcement and the skepticism about its social significance suffer from "Nirvana fallacy" — comparing existing and feasible policies to ideal normative policies, and concluding that the existing and feasible ones are inherently inefficient because of their imperfections. Antitrust law and policy have always been and will always be imperfect. However, they are alive and kicking. The antitrust discipline is vibrant, evolving, and global. This essay introduces a number of important innovations in scholarship related to *Standard Oil* and its modern applications and identifies shifts in antitrust that will keep the field energized for some time to come.

Writing for the Court in *Standard Oil*, Chief Justice White expressed the view that Congress passed the Sherman Act because of "the dread of enhancement of prices."Berkey Photo, the alleged flagship of the failed antitrust policy, stands among other things for the proposition that "[s]etting a high price may be a use of monopoly power, but it is not in itself anticompetitive." The transition between these statements was meaningful. The Berkey Photo court unequivocally stated a well-established economic understanding— high prices are not necessarily uncompetitive. Like economic thinking, although perhaps at a slower pace, antitrust evolves.

William Howard Taft, who was President of the United States at the time the Supreme Court handed down the *Standard Oil* decision, described Standard Oil as "the greatest monopoly and combination in restraint of trade in the world[,] ... an octopus that held the trade in its tentacles, and the few actual independent concerns that kept alive were allowed to exist by sufferance merely to maintain an appearance of competition." Standard Oil invented the "corporate trust" and played a central role in the trust movement that motivated Congress to enact the Sherman Act in 1890. More than 130 years after Standard Oil took over almost the entire market for refining of crude oil in the United States, scholars still debate how the company acquired its monopolistic position.

Standard Oil's pricing schemes symbolize traditional and contemporary controversies over potential anticompetitive effects of discounts. *Standard Oil* is iconic because it was the first time antitrust was used to break up a company, and at the time Standard Oil was the largest company in the United States. Structural remedies and choice of remedies have remained controversial ever since.

Standard Oil was involved in numerous legal battles before its dissolution. The lawsuits against Standard Oil illustrate the roles of private and public plaintiffs in Section 2 claims, as well as strategic conduct of such plaintiffs. Contemporary plaintiffs in actions against Microsoft, Intel, Google, and other giants utilize similar strategies and leverage the globalization of competition laws.

Standard Oil is the case in which the Supreme Court embraced reading a reasonableness qualification into the interpretation of Section 1 of the Sherman Act: the rule of reason. For that alone, *Standard Oil* is one of the most significant cases in antitrust jurisprudence. The Supreme Court probably would have endorsed the rule of reason even without *Standard Oil*, and today's rule of reason is rather different from *Standard Oil*'s rule of reason. However, it was still *Standard Oil* that formally contributed the rule of reason to antitrust jurisprudence. By today's standards, the factual and economic analyses of the

Standard Oil Court were crude and imprecise in several ways. Yet, the decision should be judged by the standards of 1911. In retrospect, popular market theories that had been used to criticize antitrust policy were simplistic and socially costly. Today's petroleum markets are very different from the markets Standard dominated, but antitrust remains essential in those markets. Business history shows that antitrust is and has always been needed.

The rise of Standard Oil contributed to the birth of antitrust. The breakup of Standard Oil released enough energy to fuel discussions and disagreements a century later. Despite a somewhat popular (at least outside of the field of antitrust) narrative of the death of antitrust, this Essay introduces several areas of "energy" in antitrust through works authored for the centennial anniversary of *Standard Oil.*

II. ANTITRUST JURISPRUDENCE

A. Uncertainty about the Goals

Writing for the Court in *Standard Oil,* Chief Justice White argued that "it may be with accuracy said that the dread of enhancement of prices and of other wrongs which it was thought would flow from the undue limitation on competitive conditions ... led ... to the prohibition [of] all contracts or acts which were unreasonably restrictive of competitive conditions." That is, Chief Justice White believed that the goals of antitrust could be defined precisely. One hundred years later, the goals of antitrust law are still defined with clarity: protection of consumer welfare. Both definitions are vague and undesirable from the economic perspective.

Chief Justice White's focus on the "dread of enhancement of prices" supposedly suggests that a successful firm could violate antitrust laws only for the capacity to increase prices. In essence, this principle means no-fault liability for monopolists.

The modern stated goal of antitrust laws supposedly reflects the legislative intent of the Sherman Act. In Reiter v. Sonotone Corp., the Supreme Court quoted Robert Bork's argument that Congress passed the Sherman Act as a "consumer welfare prescription." Perhaps the only thing that "may be said with accuracy" is that, since then, courts have been treating the protection of consumer welfare as the goal of antitrust law. Nevertheless, lawyers and economists do not know or agree about the meaning of the term "consumer welfare" in antitrust, although it has a defined meaning in economics.

In *The Antitrust Curse of Bigness,* Barak Orbach and Grace Campbell Rebling point out that Robert Bork introduced his definition in response to antitrust policies that were size oriented and protected small businesses. They note that Bork reconstructed antitrust history to argue that Congress passed the Sherman Act as a "consumer welfare prescription."

In *Standard Oil as Lochner's Trojan Horse,* Alan Meese addresses one aspect of the present controversy over the meaning of the term "consumer welfare." Meese points out that courts are inconsistent with the application of the term. For the purpose of Section 2, courts tend to embrace interpretations that appear to be related to the "total surplus" standard. Under Section 1, because of the rule of reason that Chief Justice White introduced in *Standard Oil,* courts endorse interpretations that focus on consumer interests. Meese goes further and argues that "courts have apparently structured the Rule of Reason analysis in a manner that equates 'consumer welfare' with the welfare of purchasers in the relevant market." Meese argues that the modern "consumer welfare" goal should be interpreted in the spirit of Chief Justice White's Lochnerian idea of the rule of reason. Such interpretation may be closer to the total surplus standard. One concern that comes to mind is that if we defer to the view of Chief Justice White in *Standard Oil* in searching for the goals of antitrust laws, we may end up with the focus on "dread of enhancement of prices and of other wrongs."

Since *Standard Oil* considerable energy has been spent on the discussion of the goals of antitrust laws. And commentators still find energy to debate the topic. Considering the frequent use of the term "consumer welfare" in antitrust, this topic may be one of the most important unsettled areas.

B. The Rule of Reason

In *Standard Oil*, Chief Justice White declared that courts should use the rule of reason to construe the Sherman Act: The "standard of reason which had been applied at the common law" should guide interpretation of the phrase "restraint of trade" in Section 1 of the Sherman Act. In adding a reasonableness qualification to the ban on "[e]very contract, combination in the form of trust or otherwise, or conspiracy, in restraint of trade or commerce," Chief Justice White closed a circle. In 1897, fourteen years earlier, the Supreme Court rejected his approach in a five-to-four decision in Trans-Missouri Freight Ass'n. Justice Peckham wrote the decision for the Court, declaring that the inquiry into whether a restraint of trade was reasonable or unreasonable was unimportant because the Sherman Act denounced all restraints. Justice White wrote the dissent and argued that "a brief consideration of the history and development of the law on the subject will ... demonstrate that the words 'restraint of trade' embrace only contracts which unreasonably restrain trade, and, therefore, that reasonable contracts, although they, in some measure, 'restrain trade,' are not within the meaning of the words."

Two weeks after delivering the *Standard Oil* decision, Chief Justice White delivered another important antitrust decision. In United States v. American Tobacco Co., Chief Justice White clarified his view of the reasonableness qualification:

> [I]n the *Standard Oil* Case [it was held] that, giving to the [Sherman Act] a reasonable construction, the words "restraint of trade" did not embrace all those normal and usual contracts essential to individual freedom and the right to make which were necessary in order that the course of trade might be free.

Justice Peckham, who rejected the reasonableness qualification in Trans-Missouri Freight Ass'n, was inconsistent in applying his own strict interpretation of Section 1. Already in Trans-Missouri he identified a category of contracts that should be excluded from the coverage of Section 1. Similarly, in Joint-Traffic Ass'n, Justice Peckham reiterated the rejection of the reasonableness qualification, but exempted from the Sherman Act restraints of trade he described as "incidental" or "indirect."

In *Standard Oil as Lochner's Trojan Horse*, Alan Meese argues that "*Standard Oil* was simply an application of Lochner to antitrust policy." He reasons that "[a]n unduly broad reading of the statute, then, would infringe the liberty of contract that Lochner and its progeny so jealously protected." Meese points out that today's rule of reason serves as a device to narrow, or "define," the Sherman Act's coverage "so as not to ban contracts and other conduct protected by the due process clause, but instead to reach only those contracts and conduct susceptible to regulation under Lochner's regulatory paradigm." He, thus, concludes that "one of constitutional law's most maligned decisions [Lochner] and its progeny live on, at least nominally [through the rule of reason], with no sign of mortality."

Justice Peckham, who rejected the application of the rule of reason in Trans-Missouri Freight Ass'n, authored *Lochner*. Meese stresses Justice Peckham's approach to the liberty of contract, as reflected in *Lochner* and other decisions, including his antitrust decisions. The endorsement of the rule of reason in *Standard Oil* reflects the general sentiments of the Court as expressed in *Lochner*.

Lochner and *Standard Oil* are landmark cases in which the Supreme Court created rules that narrowed the power of the state to interfere with the liberty of contract. However, there is at least one significant distinction between the *Lochner* jurisprudence and the antitrust restraint of trade jurisprudence. *Lochner* is about Section 1 of the New York Bakeshop Act that intervened in employment agreements for paternalistic concerns to one of the parties to the agreement. The antitrust restraint of trade jurisprudence is mostly about harm to others that restraint of trade (the agreement) may cause. As such, the antitrust restraint of trade jurisprudence seems more like an ordinary application of the police powers at turns of the century.

The incorporation of the reasonableness qualification in *Standard Oil* ended one debate over the proper application of antitrust laws, but marked only the beginning of many other debates and controversies. More than a century later, courts, lawyers, and scholars still have energy to criticize the antitrust rule of reason and debate its scope and meaning of its application. In his article, *Moving Beyond Caricature and Characterization: The Modern Rule of Reason in Practice*, Andrew Gavil evaluates the level of uncertainty under the modern rule of reason one hundred years after the Supreme Court delivered its *Standard Oil* decision. He chronicles the historical journey of the rule of reason from an undefined reasonableness qualification to the ban on restraints of trade to a structured approach that relies on economic analysis. Gavil further illustrates how judicial misunderstanding of the evolution of the rule of reason impedes its progression and adds uncertainty to the application of antitrust laws.

Gavil's analysis of the evolution of the rule of reason also stresses the methodological transition in antitrust analysis. Chief Justice White's view that antitrust laws had something to do with "the dread of enhancement of prices" was an intuitive approach that was grounded in economic analysis. Today, economics guides antitrust policy.

A few weeks after the Supreme Court handed down its *Standard Oil* decision, it delivered another landmark antitrust decision: *Dr. Miles Medical Co. v. John D. Park & Sons Co.* In *Dr. Miles*, adopting a certain liberty of contract theory, the Supreme Court announced that resale price maintenance (RPM) was illegal per se. It took the Court ninety-six years to overrule *Dr. Miles*. In 2007, in *Leegin Creative Leather Products, Inc. v. PSKS, Inc.*, the Supreme Court delivered a five-to-four landmark decision holding that RPM agreements should be assessed under the rule of reason. Three years later, in *American Needle, Inc. v. National Football League*, the Supreme Court took a look into the contractual arrangements of sports leagues and pointed out that when the NFL's contractual activities for its teams with third parties may violate Section 1 of the Sherman Act they should be judged under the rule of reason. The Court rejected the contractual theory that the NFL and its teams are a "single economic enterprise." Both decisions left industries and antitrust practitioners with some uncertainty about how courts would apply the rule of reason.

In some respects, *Dr. Miles* may be antitrust's *Lochner*: A controversial decision that was adopted on some theory of liberty of contract, which the Supreme Court did not apply coherently, ultimately abandoned, and that probably will remain controversial. The rule of reason was a concept present in antitrust before *Standard Oil*, but it was officially embraced by Chief Justice White in *Standard Oil*. As such, *Standard Oil* contributed to the jurisprudence of reasoning in antitrust but left the field with unsolved uncertainties, and energized debates over many doctrinal and economic theories.

* * *

III. MARKET STRUCTURE AND REMEDIES

A. Market Definition

John D. Rockefeller took control over almost the entire market for refining of crude oil in the United States. Controversies still exist as to how he did that. The *Standard Oil* Court, however, did not use the word "market" even once, but the concept of "market" has guided antitrust thinking thus far. "Market definition" has been a core element in structural antitrust analysis. The significance of the antitrust utilization of the term "market" cannot be overstated. Antitrust drove many, if not most, of the methodological developments in definition and understanding of the term. Antitrust critics, who believe that free markets function well without antitrust enforcement, could not have conceptualized the "markets" in which they believe without methodological contributions driven by antitrust enforcement. To a large extent, the modern understanding of markets relies on traditional tools developed for antitrust analysis.

Market definition is also one of the areas that stresses the myopia of the requiem for antitrust. The use of these concepts in antitrust analysis has defined their use and perception in all other areas. The concept of "market" in antitrust analysis is at the verge of methodological transformation. For quite some time, economists have been developing and experimenting with alternative methodologies that would relax the reliance on market analysis and could be used in legal institutions. Once established in antitrust, the applications of these methodologies to other legal fields and thinking of markets in general may be vast.

Traditional market definition methodologies are not helpful in many instances. Simulation models introduced several challenges, but generally they could not withstand scrutiny in court. The 2010 Merger Guidelines relax the reliance on market definition by adopting the upward pricing pressure ("UPP") test for analyzing unilateral competitive effects of horizontal mergers on differentiated products.

Merger analysis is the first area of attack against market definition. Reliance on market definition has been under fire from a number of different directions. One is the increased use of simulation models in differentiated product markets that has not advanced sufficiently. Two additional and relatively new methodologies are now in use: Compensating Marginal-Cost Reductions (CMCRs), which look at prices, quantities and demand elasticities, and Upward Pricing Pressure (UPP), which measures the "strength of the merged firm's incentive to increase price above pre-merger levels."

Other attacks on market definition have come from professors while yet a further set of attacks are based on changes within recent Horizontal Merger Guidelines that seem to embrace UPP. In the merger context, the lessening importance of market definition will play out in the courts in interesting ways, as the courts seem to hold with some level of suspicion the abandonment of the market definition. Yet, if courts over time embrace the current 2010 Horizontal Merger Guidelines as they did the 1992 Merger Guidelines, this may have profound effects across antitrust. The changes in the understanding of market definition with regard to merger law will ultimately impact how courts view issues of market definition in monopolization cases.

B. Monopolization

Enforcement regimes in antitrust law change, but the role of dominant firms in antitrust continues to be hotly debated. In this sense, *Standard Oil* has been a preview to the present and future, not merely a blip in antitrust's past. D. Daniel Sokol shows that the strategic use of private and public litigation against *Standard Oil* share the general characteristics of contemporary strategic use of litigation.

A number of hearings in recent years have addressed various costs of antitrust and their impact on dominant firms. For example, the Department of Justice's Antitrust Division and the Federal Trade Commission held hearings on Single Firm Conduct in 2006. A congressionally created Antitrust Modernization Commission released a report on the future of antitrust in 2007. In February 2008, the Federal Trade Commission organized a workshop to evaluate the welfare effects of unilateral effects analysis, while the Department of Justice authored a report on Section 2 of the Sherman Act (since withdrawn). Across the Atlantic, the European Commission released a White Paper in 2008 on the feasibility of private rights of action for antitrust in the European Union and a 2010 paper on Collective Redress.

The *Standard Oil* case stands for the greatest victory of the U.S. government in a monopolization case. Legal battles, whether via public or private enforcement, are costly. The alternative may be costly as well. In *Antitrust and Business History*, Margaret Levenstein reviewed the recent concentration trend in the United States and summarized: "Large businesses require a large state, a state capacity that we are not willing to create. But there is an alternative, and that is effective antitrust policy which is empowered to promote competitive markets."

C. Mergers

Before the Sherman Act was enacted, Standard Oil acquired its competitors, threatening to drive them out of business. In *Standard Oil and U.S. Steel*, Bill Page examines how the Supreme Court addressed the rise of the next giant that supposedly employed similar strategies: U.S. Steel.

Merger control in the United States owes its existence in part to *Standard Oil*. While the Sherman Act was enacted in 1890, the Clayton Act, which governs mergers, was not enacted until 1914 (and initially for only stock acquisitions), and a systematic premerger notification regime was not adopted until 1976. The origins of the Clayton Act were a function of debate in the 1912 presidential race and the sense that the antitrust laws needed to be strengthened in light of the conduct of Standard Oil and other firms. Had a merger regime been in place when Standard Oil was making its acquisitions, Standard Oil would most likely not have been able to achieve the monopolization it did.

Merger control remains a very important part of antitrust. Today, by volume, most antitrust resources are dedicated to merger control. Competition-directed merger control under antitrust law is generally intended to prevent the formation of combined entities that could use their market power—unilaterally or jointly with other firms—to charge prices above the competitive level. The use of merger control is a more regulatory form of antitrust than conduct cases, but offers certain advantages. Particularly, merger control tools can be refined to the specifics of mergers better than other antitrust tools such as collusion or dominance provisions. It is often easier, for example, to address the issue of dominant firms ex ante with merger law than ex post with monopolization law. Antitrust history provides some examples of the problems of anticompetitive mergers and their economic impact. As Page documents, the mergers that created U.S. Steel and Standard Oil are often viewed as having had a significant negative effect on U.S. consumers. Indeed, emerging empirical scholarship on the merger wave of the 1890s suggests a revisionist interpretation to its welfare impact—these mergers hurt economic development. The current economics of merger control are mixed with regard to the impact of concentration on social welfare.

A merger control statute is often not sufficient for effective merger control. One of the core developments in merger control in many jurisdictions has been the development of merger guidelines. Transparent guidelines present core concepts and explain how both legal and economic analytics are applied to these concepts. When successful, guidelines also provide merging parties with some predictability as to how an agency may respond to their proposed merger.

Over time, antitrust authorities have moved to a more economic based approach in their merger analysis. The Horizontal Merger Guidelines have evolved along with economic thinking, having been created in 1968, and revised in 1982, 1984, 1992, 1997, and again in 2010. European merger law also has gone through increased economic rigor as a result of its 2004 reform, case law developments, and the creation of the chief economist position at the Directorate General for Competition. Developments in the application of the economics embodied in the 2010 Horizontal Merger Guidelines will provide quite a bit of "antitrust energy" for scholarship.

The changes in merger control in the United States and Europe impact merger control globally. After a period of divergence as to economic analysis of important cases across the Atlantic, there has been convergence of the major antitrust merger regimes in recent years. Given the importance of the European and U.S. merger control regimes, anecdotal evidence (though not tested empirically) suggests a similar convergence of both developed and developing world merger control regimes as to substance ("best practices") over time. The convergence is reinforced by numerous factors—capacity building and technical assistance by the United States and European Commission, other agencies, and other technical assistance providers; imitation by younger antitrust regimes; advanced degrees from Europe and the United States in both competition law and economics; secondment in agencies and law firms in major jurisdictions; and recommendations of soft law antitrust organizations. Also relevant have been advances in antitrust merger economics such as the increased use of models for unilateral effects, coordinated effects, merger simulation, efficiencies, and upward pricing pressure.

Supranational solutions to merger control (other than at the European-wide level) have not been adopted to any measurable effect. Their absence largely reflects the lack of any effective international merger review institution. An obvious contender for such an institution, the World Trade Organization, lacks the substantive knowledge of antitrust as well as the legitimacy to undertake such review. In no region other than Europe have regional merger institutions been effectively implemented, although the potential for effective regional merger control includes a reduction in resource and capability constraints. Thus, for the majority of the world, merger review remains a national rather than regional or global endeavor.

Given the lack of supranational protections, merger control may be necessary even for developing economies when other jurisdictions cannot remedy the conduct that will have country-specific effects, when there is sufficient nexus to the transaction, and when economic analysis is sufficiently sound to avert most false positives. Antitrust matters more now because countries regularly use competition and the market where the market did not exist before. The legal framework has also impacted the study of mergers as well as the practice of mergers.

Yet, at what point in the development of a nation's competition regime should the law be expanded to include merger control? The preconditions seem to include (1) that there are enough resources within an agency, (2) that the agency has enough experience with the easier issues of competition law, such as hard core cartel enforcement, and (3) that there has been consolidation via merger with unilateral or coordinated conduct infractions that ex post competition enforcement has been unable to remedy.

D. Remedies

Standard Oil stands for the most dramatic remedy in antitrust: dissolution. Remedies vary in antitrust. Peter Carstensen examines the available remedies for monopolization and changing approaches toward such remedies. The goal of structural remedies is to restore the competition that would have existed but for the monopolization. This was the remedy that was put into place in the *Standard Oil* context. Such remedies may create a new source of competition through divestiture or strengthen an existing competitor who purchases the divested asset(s). Overall, most jurisdictions around the world prefer the use of structural remedies, at least for horizontal mergers. In the conduct context, structural remedies, as Carstensen notes, are rare.

IV. CONCLUSION

One hundred years after the Supreme Court delivered its decision in *Standard Oil*, the case still introduces nuances to the discipline and fuels debates. Antitrust history and the present are rich with many other significant and important judicial decisions and developments. Contrary to some rumors, the field has never lacked energy.

Standard Oil is today's ExxonMobil—the second largest corporation in the United States these days. On the one hundredth anniversary of *Standard Oil*, ExxonMobil was the largest corporation and lost its position to Apple only a few months later. One may argue that *Standard Oil* made no difference, since the octopus regrouped; *Standard Oil* is still with us. Studying the history of antitrust in the petroleum industry, Timothy Muris and Bilal Sayyed explain the rationale for the competition policy in the industry and show that, unlike Standard, ExxonMobil faces competition.

Some debates regarding *Standard Oil* will probably never be settled. The economics of the rebates and drawbacks Standard Oil received from railroads is an example of one of these debates. Dan Crane explores whether they were cost justified and concludes that "there is little or no evidence that the rebates were proportional to the magnitude of the savings." The riddle of how John D. Rockefeller acquired power and made Standard Oil a formidable monopoly is still debated. In 1996, Benjamin Klein and Elizabeth Granitz introduced the most comprehensive explanation thus far: Standard Oil stabilized the cartel among the railroads and used this position to raise its rivals' costs. For this tribute to the centennial anniversary of *Standard Oil*, Klein further elaborates his classic explanation. As *Standard Oil* demands, Klein's classic explanation is contested. George Priest argues that the facts do not support the raising rivals' theory; Rockefeller, he argues bought up his competitors in a merger to monopoly that years later became illegal under antitrust law.

Overall, the opportunity to reflect upon one hundred years of *Standard Oil* provides a window into the past, present and future of antitrust law scholarship. This scholarship has had a significant impact upon the analysis of law overall, as a vanguard of the law and economics movement. Antitrust legal scholarship will continue to provide insights not merely within antitrust but more generally within law, such as the analysis of contractual relations, the interplay of standards versus rules, private versus public enforcement, common law versus administrative law, and globalization of law, mergers, and remedies.

Texaco Inc. v. Dagher
547 U.S. 1 (2006)

Justice Thomas delivered the opinion of the Court.

From 1998 until 2002, petitioners Texaco Inc. and Shell Oil Co. collaborated in a joint venture, Equilon Enterprises, to refine and sell gasoline in the western United States under the original Texaco and Shell Oil brand names. Respondents, a class of Texaco and Shell Oil service station owners, allege that petitioners engaged in unlawful price fixing when Equilon set a single price for both Texaco and Shell Oil brand gasoline. We granted certiorari to determine whether it is *per se* illegal under § 1 of the Sherman Act, 15 U. S. C. § 1, for a lawful, economically integrated joint venture to set the prices at which the joint venture sells its products. We conclude that it is not, and accordingly we reverse the contrary judgment of the Court of Appeals.

I

Historically, Texaco and Shell Oil have competed with one another in the national and international oil and gasoline markets. Their business activities include refining crude oil into gasoline, as well as marketing gasoline to downstream purchasers, such as the service stations represented in respondents' class action.

In 1998, Texaco and Shell Oil formed a joint venture, Equilon, to consolidate their operations in the western United States, thereby ending competition between the two companies in the domestic refining and marketing of gasoline. Under the joint venture agreement, Texaco and Shell Oil agreed to pool their resources and share the risks of and profits from Equilon's activities. Equilon's board of directors would comprise representatives of Texaco and Shell Oil, and Equilon gasoline would be sold to downstream purchasers under the original Texaco and Shell Oil brand names. The formation of Equilon was approved by consent decree, subject to certain divestments and other modifications, by the Federal Trade Commission, see *In re Shell Oil Co.*, 125 F. T. C. 769 (1998), as well as by the state attorneys general of California, Hawaii, Oregon, and Washington. Notably, the decrees imposed no restrictions on the pricing of Equilon gasoline.

After the joint venture began to operate, respondents brought suit in district court, alleging that, by unifying gasoline prices under the two brands, petitioners had violated the *per se* rule against price fixing that this Court has long recognized under § 1 of the Sherman Act, ch. 647, 26 Stat.209, as amended, 15 U. S. C. § 1. See, *e.g.*, *Catalano, Inc. v. Target Sales, Inc.*, 446 U. S. 643, 647 (1980) *(per curiam)*. The District Court awarded summary judgment to Texaco and Shell Oil. It determined that the rule of reason, rather than a *per se* rule or the quick look doctrine, governs respondents' claim, and that, by eschewing rule of reason analysis, respondents had failed to raise a triable issue of fact. The Ninth Circuit reversed, characterizing petitioners' position as a request for an "exception to the *per se* prohibition on price fixing," and rejecting that request. *Dagher v. Saudi Refining, Inc.*, 369 F. 3d 1108, 1116 (2004). We consolidated Texaco's and Shell Oil's separate petitions and granted certiorari to determine the extent to which the *per se* rule against price fixing applies to an important and increasingly popular form of business organization, the joint venture. 545 U. S. ___ (2005).

II

Section 1 of the Sherman Act prohibits "[e]very contract, combination in the form of trust or otherwise, or conspiracy, in restraint of trade or commerce among the several

States." 15 U. S. C. § 1. This Court has not taken a literal approach to this language, however. See, *e.g.*, *State Oil Co. v. Khan*, 522 U. S. 3, 10 (1997) ("[T]his Court has long recognized that Congress intended to outlaw only *unreasonable* restraints" (emphasis added)). Instead, this Court presumptively applies rule of reason analysis, under which antitrust plaintiffs must demonstrate that a particular contract or combination is in fact unreasonable and anticompetitive before it will be found unlawful. See, *e.g.*, *id.*, at 10–19 (concluding that vertical price-fixing arrangements are subject to the rule of reason, not *per se* liability). *Per se* liability is reserved for only those agreements that are "so plainly anticompetitive that no elaborate study of the industry is needed to establish their illegality." *National Soc. of Professional Engineers v. United States*, 435 U. S. 679, 692 (1978). Accordingly, "we have expressed reluctance to adopt *per se* rules 'where the economic impact of certain practices is not immediately obvious.'" *State Oil, supra*, at 10 (quoting *FTC v. Indiana Federation of Dentists*, 476 U. S. 447, 458–459 (1986)).

Price-fixing agreements between two or more competitors, otherwise known as horizontal price-fixing agreements, fall into the category of arrangements that are *per se* unlawful. See, *e.g.*, *Catalano, supra*, at 647. These cases do not present such an agreement, however, because Texaco and Shell Oil did not compete with one another in the relevant market—namely, the sale of gasoline to service stations in the western United States— but instead participated in that market jointly through their investments in Equilon. In other words, the pricing policy challenged here amounts to little more than price setting by a single entity—albeit within the context of a joint venture—and not a pricing agreement between competing entities with respect to their competing products. Throughout Equilon's existence, Texaco and Shell Oil shared in the profits of Equilon's activities in their role as investors, not competitors. When "persons who would otherwise be competitors pool their capital and share the risks of loss as well as the opportunities for profit U such joint ventures [are] regarded as a single firm competing with other sellers in the market." *Arizona v. Maricopa County Medical Soc.*, 457 U. S. 332, 356 (1982) . As such, though Equilon's pricing policy may be price fixing in a literal sense, it is not price fixing in the antitrust sense. See *Broadcast Music, Inc. v. Columbia Broadcasting System, Inc.*, 441 U. S. 1, 9 (1979) ("When two partners set the price of their goods or services they are literally 'price fixing,' but they are not *per se* in violation of the Sherman Act").

This conclusion is confirmed by respondents' apparent concession that there would be no *per se* liability had Equilon simply chosen to sell its gasoline under a single brand. See Tr. of Oral Arg. 34. We see no reason to treat Equilon differently just because it chose to sell gasoline under two distinct brands at a single price. As a single entity, a joint venture, like any other firm, must have the discretion to determine the prices of the products that it sells, including the discretion to sell a product under two different brands at a single, unified price. If Equilon's price unification policy is anticompetitive, then respondents should have challenged it pursuant to the rule of reason. But it would be inconsistent with this Court's antitrust precedents to condemn the internal pricing decisions of a legitimate joint venture as *per se* unlawful.

The court below reached the opposite conclusion by invoking the ancillary restraints doctrine. 369 F. 3d, at 1118–1124. That doctrine governs the validity of restrictions imposed by a legitimate business collaboration, such as a business association or joint venture, on nonventure activities. See, *e.g.*, *National Collegiate Athletic Assn. v. Board of Regents of Univ. of Okla.*, 468 U. S. 85, 113–115 (1984) ; *Citizen Publishing Co. v. United States*,394 U. S. 131, 135–136 (1969). Under the doctrine, courts must determine whether the nonventure restriction is a naked restraint on trade, and thus invalid, or one that is ancillary to the legitimate and competitive purposes of the business association, and thus valid. We agree with petitioners that the ancillary restraints doctrine has no application here, where the business practice being challenged involves the core activity of the joint venture itself—namely, the pricing of the very goods produced and sold by Equilon. And even if we were to invoke the doctrine in these cases, Equilon's pricing policy is clearly ancillary to the sale of its own products. Judge Fernandez, dissenting from the ruling of the court below, put it well:

> "In this case, nothing more radical is afoot than the fact that an entity, which now owns all of the production, transportation, research, storage, sales and distribution facilities for engaging in the gasoline business, also prices its own products. It decided to price them the same, as any other entity could. What could be more integral to the running of a business than setting a price for its goods and services?" 369 F. 3d, at 1127.

See also *Broadcast Music, supra,* at 23 ("Joint ventures and other cooperative arrangements are U not usually unlawful, at least not as price-fixing schemes, where the agreement on price is necessary to market the product at all").

* * *

Because the pricing decisions of a legitimate joint venture do not fall within the narrow category of activity that is *per se* unlawful under § 1 of the Sherman Act, respondents' antitrust claim cannot prevail. Accordingly, the judgment of the Court of Appeals is reversed.

It is so ordered.

Justice Alito took no part in the consideration or decision of these cases.

Notes & Questions

1. What are the concerns that prompt the need for antirust law? Consider the balance between anticompetitive actions and competitive actions. That is, when a company tries to be the biggest and best, aren't they trying to beat the competition?

2. Section 1 of the Sherman Act prohibits "[e]very contract, combination in the form of trust or otherwise, or conspiracy, in restraint of trade or commerce among the several States." 15 U. S. C. § 1. *Texaco* explains, though, that this is not literally true, and that the limit is whether the restraint is "unreasonable." In essence, that has to be true, doesn't it? Don't some contracts need to have restraints to be valuable?

3. *Practice Note*: Here we also see business organizations issues related to the Texaco and Shell Oil joint venture, Equilon. A joint venture is a limited scope business organizations set up for a specific purpose. Such a venture might be entered between two typically competing entities, as we see here. Other notable joint ventures include GM and Toyota's New United Motor Manufacturing, Inc. (NUMMI) automobile manufacturing plant, which was closed in 2010 and re-opened later that year as Tesla Motors' factory, where they build the company's all-electric cars. Also in the auto industry, Global Hybrid Cooperation (initially known as Advanced Hybrid System 2) was developed by General Motors and Daimler/Chrysler. BMW later joined the group. Why would these companies want to work together? Why might we want them to? What do you think their primary concerns would be, and how might they work around them?

D. Mergers and Acquisitions

A subset of antitrust law is the law of mergers and acquisitions. In highly regulated industries, mergers and acquisitions—when two companies join together or when one company buys another—such combinations have several levels of oversight. For electric utilities, for example, at the federal level, the Department of Justice or Federal Trade Commission will review the proposed merger.

> Both the FTC and the U.S. Department of Justice (DOJ) Antitrust Division enforce the federal antitrust laws. In some respects their authorities overlap, but in practice the two agencies complement each other. Over the years, the agencies have developed expertise in particular industries or markets. For example, the FTC devotes most of its resources to certain segments of the economy, including those where consumer spending is high: health care, pharmaceuticals, professional services, food, energy, and certain high-tech industries like computer technology and Internet services. Before opening an investigation, the agencies consult with one another to avoid duplicating efforts. In this guide, "the agency" means either the FTC or DOJ, whichever is conducting the antitrust investigation.

Federal Trade Commission, The Enforcers, http://www.ftc.gov/tips-advice/competition-guidance/guide-antitrust-laws/enforcers.

In addition, the Federal Energy Regulatory Commission (FERC) has review authority for entities under its jurisdiction, and state level authorities have review authority as well. All are critical for the success of the merger. In 2005, a major merger of Exelon Corporation (Exelon) and Public Service Enterprise Group Incorporated (PSEG Holdings) to form Exelon Electric & Gas Corporation (EE&G) obtained the necessary federal approvals, but failed at the state level because the companies could not reach a suitable agreement with the New Jersey Board of Public Utilities. The merger was a $17.7 billion deal that would have created the nation's largest utility. The proposed merger is thus instructive. Consider first FERC's press release announcing its approval of the proposal.

Commission Approves Exelon-PSEG Merger Transaction
News Release: June 30, 2005
Docket Number: EC05-43-000

The Federal Energy Regulatory Commission today approved the proposed merger of Chicago-based Exelon Corp. with Public Service Enterprise Group Inc. (PSEG) of New Jersey, a transaction that would result in the largest U.S. utility with assets of nearly $80 billion. The merged company, to be known as Exelon Electric & Gas Corp., would serve 7 million electric customers and 2 million natural gas customers in Illinois, New Jersey and Pennsylvania.

Under the Federal Power Act and the standards set under the Commission's 1996 merger policy guidelines (Order No.592), the Commission reviews public utility mergers to evaluate the transaction's effect on competition, rates and regulation. The Commission must approve a merger if it finds it is consistent with the public interest.

The companies have committed to divest 4,000 megawatts of intermediate and peaking generation facilities located primarily in eastern PJM Interconnection, and to sell energy from 2,600 megawatts of nuclear capacity, which they characterize a "virtual divestiture". With this proposed mitigation, the merger will not harm competition, the Commission concluded. Further, the Commission said Exelon and PSEG responded to all issues raised by protestors to the merger.

"We have recognized that operational control of generation resources is a key element of market power analysis and mitigation," the Commission said, noting that "the virtual divestiture effectively transfers control of the output of 2,600 MW of nuclear capacity from the merged firm to the purchasers." An independent auction monitor will oversee the companies' compliance with the virtual divesture commitment. In addition, the applicants will set up a public compliance website that will show how they are complying with the virtual divestiture and other mitigation requirements.

The Commission accepted Exelon's and PSEG's identification of a pool of generation available for divestiture rather than specific generating plants. This addresses the concern that Exelon might divest its least efficient units, the Commission said. "Establishing a pool of generation eligible for divestiture allows the potential buyers of the plants to bid on the ones that they most highly value."

Because the applicants identified the general location and cost characteristics of the generation facilities to be divested, the Commission determined that, based on reasonable assumptions about the buyers of the assets, there would be no harm to competition. In addition, the Commission relied upon the commitment to provide an updated analysis of the merger's effect on competition, based on the actual acquirers of the actual divested assets, once they are known. If subsequent analysis shows that the merger's harm to competition has not been sufficiently mitigated, the Commission said it would require additional mitigation at that time.

The Commission further found the applicants' combination of generation and transmission facilities will not harm competition, noting that both companies have transferred control of their transmission systems to the PJM regional transmission organization. Such transfer "mitigates the ability to use control of transmission assets to harm competition in wholesale markets," the Commission concluded.

Exelon, a registered public utility holding company, distributes electricity through its subsidiaries, mainly Commonwealth Edison and PECO Energy. Exelon Generation Company owns or controls approximately 33,000 megawatts of generation capacity, including ownership interests in 11 nuclear generating plants. PSEG Holdings is an exempt public utility holding company with four major subsidiaries, including Public Service Electric and Gas Co.

The Commission's approval is the first of a number of regulatory reviews pending for the Exelon-PSEG merger. Among others, the transaction must be approved by utility regulators in New Jersey and Pennsylvania, as well as by federal agencies including the Nuclear Regulatory Commission, the Securities and Exchange Commission and the Department of Justice.

For more information, go to the Commission's website at www.ferc.gov.

R-05-40

New Jersey's Office of the Public Advocate provided a guide to help explain the role of the New Jersey Board of Public Utilities (BPU) in a piece designed for the general public.

Department of the Public Advocate,
A Citizen's Guide to the Proposed Merger Between Exelon and PSEG
April 26, 2006

Public Service Electric and Gas and Public Service Enterprise Group

Public Service Electric and Gas (PSE&G) is a New Jersey-based and operated company that has been providing electric and gas utility service to New Jersey families and businesses for over 100 years. The company serves more than 2 million electric customers and 1.7 million natural gas customers, covering a 2,600-square mile service territory from Bergen to Gloucester counties.

Headquartered in Newark, PSE&G is recognized as one of the best utilities in the nation, providing reliable and high-quality electric and gas utility service to millions of New Jerseyans. PSE&G is owned by its New Jersey-based parent company, Public Service Enterprise Group (PSEG), which also owns energy generation plants and other energy-related businesses.

Exelon Corporation

Exelon is a Chicago-based company that owns and operates utilities serving 5.2 million electric customers in Illinois and Pennsylvania and 460,000 natural gas customers in the Philadelphia area. Exelon is one of the country's largest utilities. Exelon also has a vast holding of energy generation plants, including the largest fleet of nuclear power plants in the country.

The Proposed Merger between Exelon and PSEG

In December 2004, PSEG and Exelon announced their intention to merge their two companies. If this merger is approved, it would create the largest utility in America and one of the largest in the world.

This merger is of great importance to all New Jersey ratepayers. For PSE&G customers, it could impact their utility rates, the reliability of their service, and the quality of customer service provided by the company.

The impact of this merger, however, is not limited to PSE&G customers. This merger could impact every single family, business and government entity in New Jersey because it has the potential to dramatically increase statewide energy costs and have a profoundly negative impact on New Jersey's statewide economy.

The Department of the Public Advocate believes that the citizens of New Jersey should understand what this merger could mean to them and their families, and why our Department opposes it, as proposed. The issues being debated are technical and complex, but their potential impacts are simple and straightforward, and could affect the quality of life of all New Jerseyans.

In an effort to explain these issues in plain language, the Department of the Public Advocate, working with its Division of Rate Counsel, offers the following question and answer document about what is at stake with the proposed Exelon-PSEG merger.

Q: What state agency decides whether Exelon can merge with PSEG?

A number of regulatory bodies must approve this merger before it can take effect. In New Jersey, the merger is under review by the New Jersey Board of Public Utilities (BPU).

The BPU consists of five commissioners who will vote on whether or not to approve the merger.

The BPU has also asked an Administrative Law Judge (ALJ) to review the case. Once the ALJ makes his decision, the BPU can choose to accept, reject or modify that decision; in other words, the ultimate decision of whether or not to approve this merger still lies with the BPU. Other parties, however, including the Division of Rate Counsel, do have the right to appeal the BPU's decision to the courts.

Q: How will the New Jersey BPU decide whether or not to approve this merger?

The BPU will review the potential impact this merger will have on utility rates, safety and reliability, employees, and competition in New Jersey's energy markets. The BPU has adopted a 'positive benefits' standard of review, meaning that in order to approve the merger the BPU must determine that it will have a positive benefit for the citizens of New Jersey. If the BPU does not find that the companies have demonstrated that this merger will have positive benefits for New Jersey, then they will reject it and PSEG will remain a New Jersey-based and operated company.

Q: What is the role of the Department of the Public Advocate and its Division of Rate Counsel?

The Department of the Public Advocate's Division of Rate Counsel is a party in the merger proceeding before the Administrative Law Judge and BPU, representing the interests of all utility customers throughout New Jersey. In that capacity, we have hired experts to examine the potential impact of the merger, provided testimony, and cross examined Exelon and PSEG's experts before the ALJ.

Q: When will the BPU make its decision?

The BPU is waiting for the ALJ to issue his opinion on the case, which will likely happen at the end of June 2006. The BPU will then consider the recommendation of the ALJ and issue its final ruling, likely in mid-August 2006. Of course, any time between now and then the companies could reach a settlement agreement with the BPU and other interested parties. If a settlement is reached, the BPU could adopt that settlement and approve the merger.

Q: If I am not a PSE&G customer, why should this merger matter to me?

This merger could substantially increase the cost of energy for every single New Jersey family, business and government entity, regardless of whether you are a PSE&G customer or a customer of another utility. If energy prices rise, it would not only burden New Jersey families and businesses who are already paying expensive utility bills, it would also cause a damaging ripple effect throughout New Jersey's economy—everything from running a business to operating a school would become more expensive, and consumers and taxpayers would feel the impact.

Q: How could a merger involving PSE&G increase my energy rates if I get my service from another utility?

To explain how this could happen requires a bit of background on how you pay for utility service in New Jersey. Utility customers' bills are split into two portions—the energy distribution charge and the energy supply charge.

The energy distribution charge is essentially what you pay for someone to deliver electricity or natural gas from the power plant or from the natural gas wellhead to your home. This includes the cost required to build and maintain all of the pipes, wires and other necessary infrastructure, as well as the cost of providing support services, such as reading your meter or processing your bills.

The energy distribution charge is based on the costs incurred by your local utility. This means that if you are not a PSE&G customer, this merger will not directly impact your energy distribution charges.

The energy supply charge is essentially the cost you pay for the actual electricity or natural gas that you use. Electricity is generated from a variety of sources, such as coal power plants, nuclear power plants or renewable sources like solar power. When you pay the energy supply portion of your electric bill, you are buying the electricity generated from these sources.

Your energy supply charges are based on the market price of electricity and natural gas in New Jersey and the surrounding region, which is independent of what utility serves you. The concern about the Exelon-PSEG merger is that the merged company would be so big, and would own so many energy generating plants, that it could drive up the market cost of energy in New Jersey and the region by manipulating the market. This so-called "market power" could mean higher energy costs for everyone in New Jersey, no matter what utility serves you.

Q: What is market power?

Market power is the ability to manipulate a market in order to charge a higher price than would be possible if the market were fully competitive.

A simple illustration might help explain what this means. Let's say a family needs energy to light its home and there are five different power plants from which it could buy power. If those power plants were all owned by different companies, they would compete against each other for the family's business and the family would eventually choose to buy from the company that offered the lowest price. But what if all five of those power plants were owned by the same company? The family would not have different companies competing for its business. Instead, the company that owned all the power plants could greatly increase its price, and the family would have no choice but to buy the power at that inflated price.

In reality, energy markets are much more complex than this example, but the general concept holds true: if one company has too much power in the energy market it can manipulate the market to drive up prices.

Q: Could this merger give Exelon-PSEG market power?

The Division of Rate Counsel has hired experts and done extensive research on this issue, and we have concluded that the merger as currently proposed would give Exelon-PSEG the potential to exercise market power in both the electricity and natural gas markets.

Q: If Exelon-PSEG did exercise market power, what would happen?

The simple answer is that the cost of energy in New Jersey would become even more expensive. Exactly how expensive it could become is hard to determine, but it is very possible that market power could increase costs dramatically. Several experts testified before the ALJ that if Exelon exercised market power even to a small degree it could increase statewide energy costs by hundreds of millions of dollars each year. The potential negative impacts of market power would dwarf any benefits New Jersey citizens would possibly gain in this merger.

Q: How do we prevent Exelon-PSEG from gaining market power?

Exelon and PSEG must commit to selling some of their power plants to ensure that the company cannot exercise market power. In addition, the companies must specify exactly which power plants they intend to sell. Without these specific commitments from Exelon and PSEG, we cannot know whether or not the market power problem has been addressed. Approving the merger without these commitments poses a huge risk that New Jersey could face a dramatic increase in energy prices. This is a risk the Department of the Public Advocate does not believe New Jersey should take.

Q: What promises have Exelon and PSEG made to prevent this problem?

Thus far, Exelon and PSEG have not committed to selling enough power plants, nor have they agreed to specify which plants they will sell.

In fact, rather than selling power plants, the companies have proposed to address the issue of market power almost exclusively through "virtual divestiture." Virtual divestiture means that instead of selling power plants, the companies would simply sell some of the energy generated by those plants for a period of time. Virtual divestiture is an untested idea that has never been used before as a method of addressing market power concerns.

The Department of the Public Advocate opposes virtual divestiture because it believes that if Exelon-PSEG continues to own the power plants in question then there is still too great a risk that the company can exercise market power. The company must sell the plants to eliminate the potential for market manipulation. In addition, the Department does not believe New Jersey should be experimenting with a new way of addressing market power. There is too much at stake for such experimentation when the potential consequence is that New Jersey families and businesses will end up with dramatically higher energy costs.

Q: Will New Jersey citizens and businesses receive any rate relief or direct economic benefit as a result of this merger?

Exelon-PSEG has offered to provide PSE&G customers roughly $30 million per year in rate credits for four years. That would mean a savings of approximately $1 per month to the average PSE&G customer. The Public Advocate believes this offer is unreasonably low by any standard. A number of different reference points will help illustrate why we believe this offer is so low.

For example, several years ago Ohio-based First Energy merged with the New Jersey utility Jersey Central Power and Light (JCP&L). Despite the fact that JCP&L is roughly half the size of PSE&G and there were no concerns about market power, First Energy provided approximately $300 million in savings to New Jersey ratepayers.

Another point of reference is the money Exelon-PSEG will save just by cutting the 950 New Jersey jobs that they have said they will eliminate. The savings the company will gain each year from those job cuts alone will likely be more than double the $30 million per year the companies have offered to New Jersey ratepayers for just four years.

Yet another point of reference is that the companies are asking ratepayers to pay approximately $71 million in severance payments for 35 senior executives, an average of more than $2 million per executive. Under this scenario, PSE&G customers would be paying more than twice as much for lucrative severance packages for 35 executives than all PSE&G customers combined would be getting in rate relief.

Finally, one should consider that over the next several years ratepayers will still be paying almost $2 billion in 'stranded costs' for power plants that PSE&G sold during energy deregulation in the late 1990s. While the procedural and legal background to these transactions is complex, the broader point is that ratepayers are still paying for the cost of building power plants that Exelon-PSEG would be profiting from if this merger were approved. The Department of the Public Advocate believes ratepayers should share in some of the benefits that Exelon-PSEG realizes from running these power plants.

All of these figures help put into context the fact that Exelon-PSEG's offer of rate relief is shockingly low. But it is also important to note that while rate relief is important, this merger is about far more than just temporary rate relief. The negative impacts of market power could instantly wipe out any potential gains from a temporary rate reduction. The main issues at stake here are about statewide energy costs, New Jersey's economy, and the ownership and operation of one of New Jersey's most important businesses for decades to come. These are issues that can only be addressed by firm commitments from Exelon-PSEG, and cannot simply be patched over with offers of short-term rate relief.

Q: What is Exelon's record of reliability and customer service in the states where it does business? How does it compare to PSE&G?

When customers lose utility power, it is more than a minor inconvenience; losing heat, air conditioning or power to run medical equipment can be life threatening. For businesses, from manufacturers to supermarkets, losing power can cause devastating financial losses.

PSE&G has a very strong record of reliability and customer service, and recently received a national award recognizing their superior electric service and reliability. Exelon's utilities have a considerably worse record than PSE&G. For example, Exelon's Illinois utility Commonwealth Edison had power outages that, on average, were more than twice as long as outages experienced by PSE&G customers. Customers of Exelon's Pennsylvania utility PECO experienced power outages about 50 percent more frequently than PSE&G customers, and they lasted an average of twice as long.

The Public Advocate is concerned that after the merger PSE&G will not maintain the high standards and staffing levels that have led to their strong record of customer service and reliability. The Division of Rate Counsel has asked Exelon and PSEG to amend their merger plan with assurances that service and reliability will be maintained after the merger. Exelon and PSEG have so far refused those recommendations.

Q: How will this merger impact low and moderate income customers?

PSE&G serves a great number of low-income customers, many of whom live in New Jersey's largest cities. The Public Advocate is concerned that service to these customers will be diminished if this merger is approved.

For example, PSE&G runs 16 neighborhood walk-in service centers, which are particularly important to customers who want to pay bills in cash, establish creditworthiness, request residential credit assessments and make arrangements for deferring bill payments. Exelon has so far not committed to keeping these walk-in service centers open.

For many years, PSE&G has also supported and funded programs that help low-income customers. This includes New Jersey SHARES, which provides one-time assistance to customers who are facing a sudden financial crisis who are unable to pay their utility bills. Rate Counsel has proposed that as a condition for the merger Exelon-PSEG shareholders should be required to continue to contribute $8 million to New Jersey SHARES over four years so that families facing a serious crisis can get the emergency help they need. Exelon-PSEG have not agreed to this and other proposals to ensure that low and moderate income ratepayers benefit from this merger.

Q: How will this merger impact jobs in New Jersey and our local economy?

Exelon has already said it will eliminate roughly 950 jobs in New Jersey. Because Exelon is headquartered in Chicago and its natural gas operations are centered in Pennsylvania, many additional New Jersey jobs could be moved to another state.

When jobs are lost in New Jersey, it not only hurts the families directly impacted by those job losses, but there is a multiplier effect throughout New Jersey's economy. Rate Counsel has offered the conservative estimate that the elimination of these 950 jobs would cost New Jersey's economy $143 million per year.

Q: What will it mean to New Jersey citizens that PSE&G will no longer be a New Jersey-based company?

This merger would mean that one of the most important businesses in the state would now be controlled and operated by a company in Illinois, potentially for generations to come. Loss of local ownership of a utility can lead to problems such as decreased investment in basic infrastructure, decreased charitable giving and community involvement, deteriorating labor-management relations, and a poorer working relationship between the utility and the BPU, which regulates utility rates.

PSE&G has a long history of quality service, charitable giving, and being involved in partnerships with New Jersey communities. Exelon has not made adequate assurances that this good corporate citizenship would continue long after the merger is approved.

Q: Why does the Department of the Public Advocate oppose this merger?

The Department of the Public Advocate believes the merger, as currently proposed, would do more harm than good to New Jersey citizens.

With PSE&G, New Jersey citizens have a known quantity—a New Jersey-based company that provides safe and reliable energy utility service with strong customer service, and is invested in and involved with New Jersey's communities.

The merger, as proposed, opens New Jersey's families and businesses up to tremendous risk. It would expose families and businesses to the risk of dramatic increases in energy prices. It would expose New Jerseyans to the risk that the new utility would allow reliability and customer service to deteriorate. And it would expose New Jersey to the risk that Exelon will not continue PSE&G's record of good corporate citizenship, environmental stewardship, charitable giving and community involvement.

Given the limited benefits it would offer New Jersey citizens, the Department of the Public Advocate does not believe this merger, as proposed, comes close to justifying such risks.

Q: How can I find out more about this proposed merger? What if I have additional questions?

We encourage people to visit our website at www.state.nj.us/publicadvocate where we've added links to additional information.

If you have additional questions, please email us at info@advocate.state.nj.us.

———————

Notes & Questions

1. Consider how many regulatory bodies must be satisfied for this merger to proceed. The likelihood of success in satisfying regulators is a major concern for large entities

seeking to pursue such combinations. Note the concerns about market power, as well as the other stakeholder concerns raised, especially at the state level. Why should it matter if the jobs are lost or if the resulting utility will be a New Jersey company?

2. In the Energy Policy Act of 2005, Congress lowered the threshold of FERC's authority over mergers and acquisition in the electricity area, but increased it in others. The changes were designed to facilitate investment in infrastructure, but it does not appear the changes had much, if any, effect.

E. Entity Structure and Fiduciary Duties

Energy companies, especially international energy companies, often use complicated and diverse entity structures to carry out their business. As such, it is important to understand the concepts of parents and subsidiaries, and the roles each entity has as related to the others. The following is a classic case taught in many corporations and business organizations courses to explain fiduciary duties. The case also provides a nice example of how such companies can be structured. As you read the case, think about why this structure might be used.

Sinclair Oil Corporation, Defendant Below, Appellant,
v.
Francis S. Levien, Plaintiff Below, Appellee
280 A.2d 717
Supreme Court of Delaware
June 18, 1971
Appeal from the Court of Chancery in and for New Castle County.

WOLCOTT, Chief Justice.

This is an appeal by the defendant, Sinclair Oil Corporation (hereafter Sinclair), from an order of the Court of Chancery, 261 A.2d 911 in a derivative action requiring Sinclair to account for damages sustained by its subsidiary, Sinclair Venezuelan Oil Company (hereafter Sinven), organized by Sinclair for the purpose of operating in Venezuela, as a result of dividends paid by Sinven, the denial to Sinven of industrial development, and a breach of contract between Sinclair's wholly-owned subsidiary, Sinclair International Oil Company, and Sinven.

Sinclair, operating primarily as a holding company, is in the business of exploring for oil and of producing and marketing crude oil and oil products. At all times relevant to this litigation, it owned about 97% Of Sinven's stock. The plaintiff owns about 3000 of 120,000 publicly held shares of Sinven. Sinven, incorporated in 1922, has been engaged in petroleum operations primarily in Venezuela and since 1959 has operated exclusively in Venezuela.

Sinclair nominates all members of Sinven's board of directors. The Chancellor found as a fact that the directors were not independent of Sinclair. Almost without exception, they were officers, directors, or employees of corporations in the Sinclair complex. By reason of Sinclair's domination, it is clear that Sinclair owed Sinven a fiduciary duty. Getty Oil Company v. Skelly Oil Co., 267 A.2d 883 (Del.Supr.1970); Cottrell v. Pawcatuck Co., 35 Del.Ch. 309, 116 A.2d 787 (1955). Sinclair concedes this.

The Chancellor held that because of Sinclair's fiduciary duty and its control over Sinven, its relationship with Sinven must meet the test of intrinsic fairness. The *720 standard of intrinsic fairness involves both a high degree of fairness and a shift in the burden of proof. Under this standard the burden is on Sinclair to prove, subject to careful judicial scrutiny, that its transactions with Sinven were objectively fair. Guth v. Loft, Inc., 23 Del.Ch. 255, 5 A.2d 503 (1939); Sterling v. Mayflower Hotel Corp., 33 Del.Ch. 293, 93 A.2d 107, 38 A.L.R.2d 425 (Del.Supr.1952); Getty Oil Co. v. Skelly Oil Co., supra.

Sinclair argues that the transactions between it and Sinven should be tested, not by the test of intrinsic fairness with the accompanying shift of the burden of proof, but by the business judgment rule under which a court will not interfere with the judgment of a board of directors unless there is a showing of gross and palpable overreaching. Meyerson v. El Paso Natural Gas Co., 246 A.2d 789 (Del.Ch.1967). A board of directors enjoys a presumption of sound business judgment, and its decisions will not be disturbed if they can be attributed to any rational business purpose. A court under such circumstances will not substitute its own notions of what is or is not sound business judgment.

We think, however, that Sinclair's argument in this respect is misconceived. When the situation involves a parent and a subsidiary, with the parent controlling the transaction and fixing the terms, the test of intrinsic fairness, with its resulting shifting of the burden of proof, is applied. Sterling v. Mayflower Hotel Corp., supra; David J. Greene & Co. v. Dunhill International, Inc., 249 A.2d 427 (Del.Ch.1968); Bastian v. Bourns, Inc., 256 A.2d 680 (Del.Ch.1969) aff'd. Per Curiam (unreported) (Del.Supr.1970). The basic situation for the application of the rule is the one in which the parent has received a benefit to the exclusion and at the expense of the subsidiary.

Recently, this court dealt with the question of fairness in parent-subsidiary dealings in Getty Oil Co. v. Skelly Oil Co., supra. In that case, both parent and subsidiary were in the business of refining and marketing crude oil and crude oil products. The Oil Import Board ruled that the subsidiary, because it was controlled by the parent, was no longer entitled to a separate allocation of imported crude oil. The subsidiary then contended that it had a right to share the quota of crude oil allotted to the parent. We ruled that the business judgment standard should be applied to determine this contention. Although the subsidiary suffered a loss through the administration of the oil import quotas, the parent gained nothing. The parent's quota was derived solely from its own past use. The past use of the subsidiary did not cause an increase in the parent's quota. Nor did the parent usurp a quota of the subsidiary. Since the parent received nothing from the subsidiary to the exclusion of the minority stockholders of the subsidiary, there was no self-dealing. Therefore, the business judgment standard was properly applied.

A parent does indeed owe a fiduciary duty to its subsidiary when there are parent-subsidiary dealings. However, this alone will not evoke the intrinsic fairness standard. This standard will be applied only when the fiduciary duty is accompanied by self-dealing—the situation when a parent is on both sides of a transaction with its subsidiary. Self-dealing occurs when the parent, by virtue of its domination of the subsidiary, causes the subsidiary to act in such a way that the parent receives something from the subsidiary to the exclusion of, and detriment to, the minority stockholders of the subsidiary.

We turn now to the facts. The plaintiff argues that, from 1960 through 1966, Sinclair caused Sinven to pay out such excessive dividends that the industrial development of Sinven was effectively prevented, and it became in reality a corporation in dissolution.

From 1960 through 1966, Sinven paid out $108,000,000 in dividends ($38,000,000 in excess of Sinven's earnings during the same period). The Chancellor held that Sinclair caused these dividends to be paid during a period when it had a need for large amounts of cash. Although the dividends paid exceeded earnings, the plaintiff concedes that the payments were made in compliance with 8 Del.C. § 170, authorizing payment of dividends out of surplus or net profits. However, the plaintiff attacks these dividends on the ground that they resulted from an improper motive—Sinclair's need for cash. The Chancellor, applying the intrinsic fairness standard, held that Sinclair did not sustain its burden of proving that these dividends were intrinsically fair to the minority stockholders of Sinven.

Since it is admitted that the dividends were paid in strict compliance with 8 Del.C. § 170, the alleged excessiveness of the payments alone would not state a cause of action. Nevertheless, compliance with the applicable statute may not, under all circumstances, justify all dividend payments. If a plaintiff can meet his burden of proving that a dividend cannot be grounded on any reasonable business objective, then the courts can and will interfere with the board's decision to pay the dividend.

Sinclair contends that it is improper to apply the intrinsic fairness standard to dividend payments even when the board which voted for the dividends is completely dominated. In support of this contention, Sinclair relies heavily on American District Telegraph Co. (ADT) v. Grinnell Corp., (N.Y.Sup.Ct.1969) aff'd. 33 A.D.2d 769, 306 N.Y.S.2d 209 (1969). Plaintiffs were minority stockholders of ADT, a subsidiary of Grinnell. The plaintiffs alleged that Grinnell, realizing that it would soon have to sell its ADT stock because of a pending anti-trust action, caused ADT to pay excessive dividends. Because the dividend payments conformed with applicable statutory law, and the plaintiffs could not prove an abuse of discretion, the court ruled that the complaint did not state a cause of action. Other decisions seem to support Sinclair's contention. In Metropolitan Casualty Ins. Co. v. First State Bank of Temple, 54 S.W.2d 358 (Tex.Civ.App.1932), rev'd. on other grounds, 79 S.W.2d 835 (Sup.Ct.1935), the court held that a majority of interested directors does not void a declaration of dividends because all directors, by necessity, are interested in and benefited by a dividend declaration. See, also, Schwartz v. Kahn, 183 Misc. 252, 50 N.Y.S.2d 931 (1944); Weinberger v. Quinn, 264 A.D. 405, 35 N.Y.S.2d 567 (1942).

We do not accept the argument that the intrinsic fairness test can never be applied to a dividend declaration by a dominated board, although a dividend declaration by a dominated board will not inevitably demand the application of the intrinsic fairness standard. Moskowitz v. Bantrell, 41 Del.Ch. 177, 190 A.2d 749 (Del.Supr.1963). If such a dividend is in essence self-dealing by the parent, then the intrinsic fairness standard is the proper standard. For example, suppose a parent dominates a subsidiary and its board of directors. The subsidiary has outstanding two classes of stock, X and Y. Class X is owned by the parent and Class Y is owned by minority stockholders of the subsidiary. If the subsidiary, at the direction of the parent, declares a dividend on its Class X stock only, this might well be self-dealing by the parent. It would be receiving something from the subsidiary to the exclusion of and detrimental to its minority stockholders. This self-dealing, coupled with the parent's fiduciary duty, would make intrinsic fairness the proper standard by which to evaluate the dividend payments.

Consequently it must be determined whether the dividend payments by Sinven were, in essence, self-dealing by Sinclair. The dividends resulted in great sums of money being transferred from Sinven to Sinclair. However, a proportionate share of this money was received by the minority shareholders of Sinven. Sinclair received nothing from Sinven to the exclusion of its minority stockholders. As such, these dividends were not self-dealing. We hold therefore that the Chancellor erred in applying the intrinsic fairness test as to these dividend payments. The business judgment standard should have been applied.

We conclude that the facts demonstrate that the dividend payments complied with the business judgment standard and with 8 Del.C. § 170. The motives for causing the declaration of dividends are immaterial unless the plaintiff can show that the dividend payments resulted from improper motives and amounted to waste. The plaintiff contends only that the dividend payments drained Sinven of cash to such an extent that it was prevented from expanding.

The plaintiff proved no business opportunities which came to Sinven independently and which Sinclair either took to itself or denied to Sinven. As a matter of fact, with two minor exceptions which resulted in losses, all of Sinven's operations have been conducted in Venezuela, and Sinclair had a policy of exploiting its oil properties located in different countries by subsidiaries located in the particular countries.

From 1960 to 1966 Sinclair purchased or developed oil fields in Alaska, Canada, Paraguay, and other places around the world. The plaintiff contends that these were all opportunities which could have been taken by Sinven. The Chancellor concluded that Sinclair had not proved that its denial of expansion opportunities to Sinven was intrinsically fair. He based this conclusion on the following findings of fact. Sinclair made no real effort to expand Sinven. The excessive dividends paid by Sinven resulted in so great a cash drain as to effectively deny to Sinven any ability to expand. During this same period Sinclair actively pursued a company-wide policy of developing through its subsidiaries new sources of revenue, but Sinven was not permitted to participate and was confined in its activities to Venezuela.

However, the plaintiff could point to no opportunities which came to Sinven. Therefore, Sinclair usurped no business opportunity belonging to Sinven. Since Sinclair received nothing from Sinven to the exclusion of and detriment to Sinven's minority stockholders, there was no self-dealing. Therefore, business judgment is the proper standard by which to evaluate Sinclair's expansion policies.

Since there is no proof of self-dealing on the part of Sinclair, it follows that the expansion policy of Sinclair and the methods used to achieve the desired result must, as far as Sinclair's treatment of Sinven is concerned, be tested by the standards of the business judgment rule. Accordingly, Sinclair's decision, absent fraud or gross overreaching, to achieve expansion through the medium of its subsidiaries, other than Sinven, must be upheld.

Even if Sinclair was wrong in developing these opportunities as it did, the question arises, with which subsidiaries should these opportunities have been shared? No evidence indicates a unique need or ability of Sinven to develop these opportunities. The decision of which subsidiaries would be used to implement Sinclair's expansion policy was one of business judgment with which a court will not interfere absent a showing of gross and palpable overreaching. Meyerson v. El Paso Natural Gas Co., 246 A.2d 789 (Del.Ch.1967). No such showing has been made here.

Next, Sinclair argues that the Chancellor committed error when he held it liable to Sinven for breach of contract.

In 1961 Sinclair created Sinclair International Oil Company (hereafter International), a wholly owned subsidiary used for the purpose of coordinating all of Sinclair's foreign operations. All crude purchases by Sinclair were made thereafter through International.

On September 28, 1961, Sinclair caused Sinven to contract with International whereby Sinven agreed to sell all of its crude oil and refined products to International at specified prices. The contract provided for minimum and maximum quantities and prices. The plaintiff contends that Sinclair caused this contract to be breached in two respects. Although the contract called for payment on receipt, International's payments lagged as much as 30 days after receipt. Also, the contract required International to purchase at least a fixed minimum amount of crude and refined products from Sinven. International did not comply with this requirement.

Clearly, Sinclair's act of contracting with its dominated subsidiary was self-dealing. Under the contract Sinclair received the products produced by Sinven, and of course the minority shareholders of Sinven were not able to share in the receipt of these products. If the contract was breached, then Sinclair received these products to the detriment of Sinven's minority shareholders. We agree with the Chancellor's finding that the contract was breached by Sinclair, both as to the time of payments and the amounts purchased.

Although a parent need not bind itself by a contract with its dominated subsidiary, Sinclair chose to operate in this manner. As Sinclair has received the benefits of this contract, so must it comply with the contractual duties.

Under the intrinsic fairness standard, Sinclair must prove that its causing Sinven not to enforce the contract was intrinsically fair to the minority shareholders of Sinven. Sinclair has failed to meet this burden. Late payments were clearly breaches for which Sinven should have sought and received adequate damages. As to the quantities purchased, Sinclair argues that it purchased all the products produced by Sinven. This, however, does not satisfy the standard of intrinsic fairness. Sinclair has failed to prove that Sinven could not possibly have produced or someway have obtained the contract minimums. As such, Sinclair must account on this claim.

Finally, Sinclair argues that the Chancellor committed error in refusing to allow it a credit or setoff of all benefits provided by it to Sinven with respect to all the alleged damages. The Chancellor held that setoff should be allowed on specific transactions, e.g., benefits to Sinven under the contract with International, but denied an over all setoff against all damages claimed. We agree with the Chancellor, although the point may well be moot in view of our holding that Sinclair is not required to account for the alleged excessiveness of the dividend payments.

We will therefore reverse that part of the Chancellor's order that requires Sinclair to account to Sinven for damages sustained as a result of dividends paid between 1960 and 1966, and by reason of the denial to Sinven of expansion during that period. We will affirm the remaining portion of that order and remand the cause for further proceedings.

Notes & Questions

1. A derivative action is an action brought by a shareholder on behalf of the entity. A derivative suit provides shareholders, usually with a minimum amount of stock holdings (e.g., 5%), with a mechanism to force a company's board of directors to account for harm to the entity. The claim, in essence, is that the board of directors should have acted to protect the company, and because they didn't, the court should compel them to do so.

In this case, for example, the claim was that the parent company, Sinclar, allowed its subsidiary, Sinven, to suffer harm that lowered the value of the company. Note that the shareholder's harm here is indirect and shared with all other shareholders. That is, the actual harm—for example the lost revenues from not holding International to its contractual obligations—is to Sinven, which would have earned the lost revenues. If Sinven were able to recover the lost revenue, those revenues would be paid to Sinven, not to shareholders (thus, the claim is derivative).

2. Although all states have laws regarding incorporation, Delaware is the nation's leading state of incorporation. There is no one reason why this is the case, and the issue has been studied, and debated, at length. Professor Roberta Romano, a leading scholar in the area, determined that the main reason companies seek to form in Delaware is "not just the guarantee of being located in a state that is responsive to corporate desires but also access to a legal system that reduces uncertainty concerning the consequences of actions and hence the transaction costs of doing business." Roberta Romano, *Law as a Product: Some Pieces of the Incorporation Puzzle*, 1 J.L. Econ. & Org. 225, 227 (1985). Delaware law explains fiduciary duties this way:

> Directors of a Delaware corporation have a triad of fiduciary duties to uphold: the duties of care, loyalty, and good faith. These fiduciary responsibilities do not operate intermittently and are "one of the most important methods of regulating the internal affairs of corporations, as these cases articulate the equitable boundaries that cabin directors' exercise of their capacious statutory authority." *In re Topps Co. Shareholders Litig.*, 924 A.2d 951, 960 (Del.Ch.2007).

In re Midway Games Inc., 428 B.R. 303, 313 (Bankr. D. Del. 2010).

3. *Practice Note*: Sinclar had several subsidiaries, e.g., Sinclair Alaska, Sinclair Venezuela, Sinclair International. This is common in many large businesses, especially in the energy sector. Separating the entities can serve several functions. The separate nature of the corporation serves to protect both shareholders and creditors.

Each properly formed corporation creates, in essence, a separate fictional person, which allows the corporation to operate in perpetuity. This separate legal personality of the corporation acts to partition the business assets of the entity from the assets of the shareholders. Stephen M. Bainbridge, *Corporate Law* § 1.1(B) (2d ed. 2009). This separate corporate "person" takes on the legal rights and obligations of an individual. Those doing business with corporations have the option of seeking personal guarantees from those working on behalf of the corporation.

Absent such a guarantee, however, investors' losses are capped at the level of their investment in the corporation. That is, shareholders have limited liability for actions of the corporation, unless the corporation's formation documents expressly state otherwise. In exchange for this limited liability, shareholders give up their individual rights to corporate property and instead become residual claimants having rights only to the corporate property remaining at liquidation after all other debts and obligations of the corporation have been satisfied.

Beyond limited liability protection, the asset partition corporate formation creates serves an additional purpose: to protect those doing business with the corporation. The asset partition creates a separate and clear set of assets that belong to the firm upon which the firm's creditors have a claim that is superior to any claims by personal creditors of any of the corporation's shareholders. Thus, using separate entities can make it easier for creditors of each entity to monitor the assets and operations of the entity with which they are doing business. In addition, the separate entity can make managing taxes, registering assets, maintaining permits, and other regulatory obligations easier.

4. The separate nature of the different Sinclair subsidiaries makes some sense. Notice also that Sinven had 3% outside shareholders, and Sinclar owned the rest of the company. Why structure it this way?

Chapter 3

Minerals and Mineral Rights: Coal, Oil, & Gas

A. Introduction

The history behind mining for coal, oil, and gas has several similarities and some overlapping principles. In this chapter, we begin with a review of a brief history of some key principles related to extraction of these resources. The chapter begins with some vocabulary and concepts that may be new, and is followed by a client issue for you to consider as you read the materials.

1. Vocabulary and Concepts

Coal Seam: A coal bed that is thick enough to be mined for potential profit.

Coalbed Methane (CBM): Methane (CH_4) that is found in coal seams. Also known as coalbed gas, coal-seam gas (CSG), or coal-mine methane.

Dominant Estate: A parcel of real property that has an easement over another estate (the servient estate). Mineral rights, such as those to extract coal, oil, and gas, are generally dominant to the surface estate, with an express or implied easement to reasonable use of the surface and subsurface to access the minerals.

Hydrofracturing or hydraulic fracturing: A process used after an oil or gas well is drilled. The process involves the use of fluids and other materials to create or restore small fractures in a formation to stimulate oil and gas production from new and existing wells. The process has been used since the 1940s, but the modern version that dominates today's landscape is combined with horizontal drilling (well is drilled down vertically, then turned horizontally). Also known as **fracking or fracing.**

Reservation: When an estate is severed, if the grantor keeps some or all of the mineral rights, such rights are called a reservation.

Severed Estate: Land ownership initially (usually) includes both the surface and minerals estates. If one separates the estates, for example, by selling the surface rights but keeping the mineral right, the result is a severed estate.

79

Subsidence: The gradual sinking of land to a lower level because of earth movements, mining operations, and other activities.

Surface Estate: Land ownership that grants the owner the rights to develop the surface. This estate is subordinate to mineral estate.

2. Client Issue

You have a client interested in acquiring mineral rights to all natural gas on a property. You have looked at the deeds and found that the seller has an estate subject to 1994 and 1995 deeds from Grantor that conveyed Grantor's interest in coal and coal mining rights to the Land Owner, and reserved his interest in all gas. The deed conveys "all the coal" and connected mining rights owned by the Grantor, but specifically reserves the Grantor's rights to "all of the gas" on the property. The question before you is: Does this reservation reserve to the Grantor all of the gas in any form, or is the coalbed methane gas excepted?

As you read the following materials, think about what is needed for a grantor to convey separate estates in coal and coalbed methane gas? How might you draft such a provision? What other research might you need to do? What else do you need to know from your client? Would you advise your client to acquire these rights? What are the risks?

The deed in question provides the following:

> The undersigned Grantor specifically reserves all interest which he may have in said land other than the above-described interests in coal and mining rights held in connection with said interests in said coal, and without limiting the generality of the foregoing, the undersigned Grantor specifically reserves all of the oil, gas, petroleum and sulphur in, on and under and that may be produced from any part thereof, together with the full right of ingress and egress to and from said lands and with the full and exclusive right at all times to enter upon said lands to explore, develop, operate and occupy said lands for the purpose of exploring, mining, drilling and developing the said lands and holdings for the production of oil, gas, petroleum and sulphur, or any one or more of them, and for removing the same therefrom, and for the storing, handling, transporting and marketing of the same, and together with the full use of such amount of the surface of said lands as is necessary or useful to explore, produce, store, refine, extract, absorb, treat, transport and remove such oil, gas, petroleum and sulphur and to conduct all operations therefor, and to erect and use thereon all buildings, derricks, tanks, structures, machinery and equipment as may be necessary or proper for such purposes, and together with the right to lay and operate thereon pipelines, telephone and telegraph lines, and to repair and remove from said land any of the Grantor's property thereon at any time, including the right to inject or return gas, water, brine or other substances in the subsurface strata in and under said lands or any part thereof, including the right to drill input wells or shafts for those purposes and, in addition and without limiting the foregoing, each and every other right and privilege necessary and proper for the full enjoyment of the ownership of all such oil, gas, petroleum and sulphur in, on, under and that may be produced from said lands, and each and every right incident to Grantor's full ownership thereof.

Deed language excerpted from: *NCNB Texas Nat. Bank, N.A. v. West,* 631 So. 2d 212, 216–217 (Ala. 1993).

B. Coal

J. Thomas Lane, *Fire in the Hole to Longwall Shears: Old Law Applied to New Technology and Other Longwall Mining Issues*
96 W. Va. L. Rev. 577 (1994)
Copyright © 1993 by the West Virginia Law Review; J. Thomas Lane

* * *

A. Mining Rights Generally

In the eastern states, severances of ownership of minerals with the surface began in the mid-1800s. Such severances soon followed in the western states. Universally, the courts of all states adopted the rule that when severed title exists, the owner of the mineral estate will be deemed to have all rights that are reasonable and necessary to mine and enjoy the separate mineral estate, even if express rights to mine the minerals are absent. Such rights are implied, and together with any rights which are expressed in a severance deed or other grant, are appurtenant to the mineral ownership.

Included are the rights to use the surface for access to the minerals, to mine, to process, to transport, and to exercise any other rights that qualify as reasonable and necessary. Such rights do not include, however, the right to damage or destroy the surface in an unreasonable or unnecessary way.

Debate exists over the basis for such rights. However, it seems most logical that implied rights are akin to ways of necessity. Whatever the basis, however, it is clear that in the absence of express mining rights in a severance deed, or perhaps in addition to those which are expressed, a mineral owner is deemed to have implied rights.

What is implied in a given situation requires further examination of the simple rule that the rights sought to be exercised must be both necessary and reasonable—a two-prong analysis. Looking first to what is "necessary," cases such as *Squires v. Lafferty* establish that the question is not one of absolute necessity because in that case, and others like it, the right that the mineral owner sought to exercise was the ability to prospect for minerals. Clearly, the exercise of this right was not absolutely necessary to extract the minerals. Rather, this right was, as the court stated, "reasonably necessary," and as such, the right to prospect was held to be implied. As to the second prong of the test—"reasonableness"—the inquiry focuses on the owner of the affected land and the question becomes whether the exercise of the right will cause a substantial injury or burden. For example, in *Buffalo Mining Co. v. Martin,* the question was whether the mineral owner could construct power lines over the surface to serve ventilation equipment. According to the court, in order for an implied right to exist "it must be demonstrated not only that the right is reasonably necessary for the extraction of the mineral, but also that the right can be exercised without any substantial burden to the surface owner." In the *Buffalo Mining* case, the severance deed included broad mining rights, although not explicitly providing for electric power lines, and the court emphasized that where an effort is made to express broad rights in the severance deed, "courts will be inclined to imply compatible surface uses that are necessary to the underground mining activity."

Obviously, the reasonable and necessary rule is somewhat imprecise, and in close cases, will require a balance between the need of the mineral owner (is it "necessary") against the burden on the surface owner (is it "substantial").

The rules relating to implied mining rights are complicated by introduction of a relatively new rule of accommodation or alternate means. By whatever name, this rule dictates that each owner of property must exercise "due regard" for other owners in the same property. Under this rule, the exercise of a right, which clearly passes in the abstract the 'reasonable and necessary' test, becomes unreasonable under the particular facts. The decision most frequently cited for this rule, *Getty Oil Co. v. Jones*, exemplifies the problem. In that case, a farmer's irrigation system employed a series of pipes and mechanisms which moved across the surface at approximately seven feet above the surface. Getty, in the exercise of its clear right to drill and produce oil, installed two pumping jacks, one protruding 17 feet and the other 34 feet above the surface. The pump jacks interfered with the irrigation system, and the court considered the fact that other operators constructed their pump jacks below the surface so that no interference occurred and that they did so at a modest increased cost. Upon these facts, the *Getty* court adopted the rule that when the exercise of a right by one owner will interfere with another owner's use in the same land, and a reasonable alternative exists which will not interfere, then in such case a duty arises to use the "alternative." Expressed another way, a duty arises to "accommodate" or exercise "due regard."

These rules, perhaps concisely stated, constitute the common law principles on implied mining rights. While not employed in the same words in every case, it is submitted that most situations are and can be tested within this basic framework.

B. Principles of Subsidence

With respect to subsidence, the early cases established that the surface and upper strata owners have the absolute right to have their property supported, unless such right is waived, either expressly or by necessary implication in a severance deed or other instrument. This principle is considered to be based upon one of two propositions: (1) an implied reservation to the surface owner of enough coal for support; or (2) the principle expressed in the maxim: "Sic utere tuo ut alienum non laedas," meaning, use your property so as not to injure the property of another. The West Virginia court has held that the latter doctrine is the basis for the right of support in West Virginia. Under this doctrine, it seems that a surface owner does not have an unqualified right to have the surface supported in its natural state, but rather, he has the right not to be unreasonably damaged. The right of support is viewed as being absolute from the standpoint that if material damage results, and no waiver exists, there is absolute or strict liability if the damage proximately results from the removal of support.

Whatever the basis, the general rule of support is universally recognized. While not employed in so many words in the cases, the reasonable and necessary test would reach the same result. Thus, if the question were raised of whether a coal owner has an implied right to remove support and subside, the answer would lie in an analysis whether the right is both necessary and reasonable. The question of necessity is probably met by the fact that removal of support is necessary in order to mine all of the coal. The question whether it is "reasonable" depends on whether the surface owner, as stated by the court in *Buffalo Mining Co.*, would be "substantially" burdened or injured. An affirmative answer would indicate that the right does not exist, and conversely, a negative answer should indicate that the right does exist. Indeed, this is the result reached by the Virginia court in *Large v. Clinchfield Coal Co.*, where a determination was made that subsidence would not cause appreciable damage to the surface, and thus, the ability to mine without leaving support was held to be implied.

C. The Surface Mining Cases

The early cases on mining rarely dealt with particular mining methods or technology, but rather the effect or burden of the mining, particularly on the surface. With the advent of the surface mining cases, however, mining methodology became the focal point. In practically all cases involving surface mining, the decisions of the courts are based on the finding that this mining method virtually destroys the surface affected. Upon this finding, the courts generally have ruled that the surface mining method cannot be employed unless expressly granted. In practically all of these cases, the argument was advanced and often adopted by the courts that parties to severance deeds before the advent of surface mining could not have contemplated the surface mining method, ergo such mining method was not implied with the mineral ownership.

D. Contemplation of the Parties

It may be tempting to conclude from the surface mining cases that a new principle emerged whereby use of new methodology, indeed even new technology, is measured by the contemplation of the parties at the time of contracting or executing severance deeds. Indeed, great emphasis can be placed upon language in cases such as *West Virginia-Pittsburgh Coal Co. v. Strong*, where the court held, among other points, that because surface mining was not a known mining method in Brooke County, West Virginia, in 1904, it was not within the contemplation of the parties when they drafted the severance deed in question.

Stopping the analysis at this point, and concluding that the right to surface mine or exercise any other mining right does not exist because not contemplated, misses the real reason and justification for these decisions. The underlying basis for the *Strong* case, and others like it, starts with the fact that the mining right in question (surface mining) was not expressly created, and the issue was whether it would be deemed implied with mineral ownership. The real basis for the decision that it is not an implied right is that the exercise of this right substantially injures the surface.

In one of the most recent cases on this subject, the Kentucky court in *Ward v. Harding* [860 S.W.2d 280 (1993)] considered a 1988 constitutional amendment on this topic, and held with respect to surface mining under Kentucky broad form deeds that

> [p]roperly framed, the question here is not what the parties actually intended, but what they would have intended if significant surface destruction had been contemplated. In circumstances where there is no actual intent, a court should presume a reasonable intent.

The court properly held that the inquiry was not the mining technology and whether the parties could have contemplated surface mining, but rather, whether the parties contemplated a substantial destruction of the surface.

Perhaps without so stating, the courts in all of the surface mining cases have employed the reasonable and necessary test and balanced the "need" of the mineral owner against the "burden" on the surface owner. Thus, while it may be absolutely "necessary" for a mineral owner to use surface mining to extract surface coal, the universal conclusion has been that the substantial injury it would impose on the surface owner makes surface mining unreasonable, and therefore, not an implied right.

An important extension of the surface mining cases is the ultimate question whether surface mining can take place. On this point, the cases vary—even within states. In states such as West Virginia, Ohio, and Pennsylvania, surface mining, if not deemed to exist, may not be employed. Indeed, in some cases the courts adopted a more radical approach in holding that minerals, which could only be mined by surface mining, were not owned by the "mineral" owner but rather the surface owner. In other cases, the courts have held that surface mining is not an implied right in the sense that it can be employed without payment of damages. In these cases, the mineral owner has been allowed to proceed with surface mining but must pay damages. Some states have even adopted several of these approaches.

* * *

U.S. Steel v. Hoge

503 Pa. 140, 468 A.2d 1380 (1983)
Supreme Court of Pennsylvania

ZAPPALA, Justice.

The question presented by this appeal is which of the parties to a coal severance deed, or more precisely which of their successors in interest, is to be recognized as owner of coalbed gas. The Superior Court affirmed a final decree of the Court of Common Pleas of Greene County and quieted title to the gas in favor of the surface owners, permitting them to lease rights to drill into the coal seam to extract the coalbed gas contained therein, subject to restrictions imposed to prevent unreasonable damage to the coal owner's property. *U.S. Steel v. Hoge*, 304 Pa.Super. 182, 450 A.2d 162 (1982).

The Appellant, United States Steel Corporation (hereinafter "coal owner"), is owner of the "Pittsburgh" or "River" Vein of coal underlying certain tracts of land in Greene County owned by Appellees Hoge, Cowan, and Murdock (hereinafter "surface owners"). This coal seam is located approximately 800 feet beneath the earth's surface. Appellant's predecessor in title acquired rights to the coal from Appellees' predecessors in title via a severance deed dated July 23, 1920.

The deed, which contained language common to most coal severance deeds executed in 1920 and in later years, read in pertinent part as follows, conveying

> *All the coal* of the Pittsburgh or River Vein underlying all that certain tract of land ...

> *Together with all the rights and privileges necessary and useful in the mining and removing of said coal, including* the right of mining without leaving any support..., *the right of ventilation* and drainage and of access to the mines for men and materials ...

> The parties of the first part [surface owners] hereby *reserve the right to drill and operate through said coal for oil and gas* without being held liable for any damages.

> Together with all and singular the improvements, ways, waters, water courses, rights, liberties, privileges, hereditaments and appurtenances ... (Emphasis added)

In 1976 and 1977, Appellee Cunningham (hereinafter "gas lessee") acquired all of the foregoing reserved gas and oil rights from the surface owners. In 1978, the gas lessee began drilling wells for the purpose of recovering coalbed gas from the "Pittsburgh" coal seam. Upon learning of the drilling operations and the gas lessee's intention to stimulate recovery of coalbed gas through a process known as hydrofracturing, the Appellant coal owner initiated actions in equity to terminate the intrusion upon its coal seam and to determine the ownership of, and right to develop, the coalbed gas. The chancellor entered a decree permitting the drilling for such gas in Appellant's coal seam, but prohibiting the use of hydrofracturing methods to stimulate gas recovery. Superior Court affirmed.

Hydrofracturing is the forcing of fluids under pressure into the well so as to cause a fracturing of the target stratum. When applied to coal seams, the process creates fractures in the coal which serve as conduits through which gas can flow through the seam to the well's shaft. Developed by the drilling industry in the late 1940's, hydrofracturing was initially utilized to recover natural gases from strata other than coal veins, and has more regularly been so used.

The ownership of, and right to develop, coalbed gas are questions of first impression. Consideration of the characteristics, origins, and history of development of gas is necessary to a determination of the issues presented. The following factual background is condensed from the chancellor's findings. Coalbed gas is found in and around coal veins, having long been recognized by the mining industry as a highly combustible and deadly poisonous gas which must be, at all times during the active coal mining process, ventilated to prevent explosion or inhalation; hence, the gas has traditionally been wasted into the atmosphere. Coalbed gas is always present in coal seams; its molecules are absorbed in micropores of coal, and even the smallest particle of coal always contains, and when exposed emits, some coalbed gas. Coal and coalbed gas are, nevertheless, separate physical entities.

The gas which has commonly been referred to as "natural gas" is generally found in strata deeper than coal veins, though it shares many of the characteristics of coalbed gas. Both gases evolved, through natural processes, from carbonaceous material beneath the earth's surface, and both contain mixtures of various hydrocarbons, including methane, ethane, propane, butane, carbon dioxide, carbon monoxide, and hydrogen sulfide. Both are, as are all gases, migratory, thus being capable of escaping their natural habitats to enter other strata, and both are found in the same geographic areas of Pennsylvania. Due to its fugacious character, natural gas is capable, under certain circumstances, of commingling with coalbed gas in the upper strata.

Natural gas and coalbed gas have value as energy sources, the latter having approximately a 90 percent heating value as compared to the former. The energy value of the coalbed gas is far less, however, than that of the coal itself; the value of the coalbed gas is only one percent of the b.t.u. value of the coal.

Extensive and costly drilling operations are required in order to extract coalbed gas or natural gas from strata where they are found. As early as the year 1900, certain wells were drilled in Greene County into the subject Pittsburgh Vein of coal, and not deeper, and some of these wells produced coalbed gas in paying quantities. Commercial exploitation of coalbed gas, however, has remained very limited and sporadic until recently. As a result of our nation's high energy demands and shortage of energy supplies, conditions which gained much attention during the past decade, both the gas industry and the mining industry have come to regard coalbed gas as having sound market potential. There has recently developed an industrial capacity to drill into coal seams both horizontally and vertically to recover coalbed gas. With either drilling approach, the process of hydrofracturing facilitates recovery of coalbed gas in greater volumes and over longer periods of time. Nevertheless, in some areas coalbed gas can be recovered in paying quantities without any artificial stimulation of the coal seam. As noted previously, certain gas companies have through the years produced coalbed gas from wells in Greene County and in other portions of western Pennsylvania. More recently certain coal owners, including Appellant, have drilled into and in some cases hydrofractured their own coal seams in various regions—as experimental determinations of coalbed gas production capacities and as a means of alleviating the presence of the gas in areas soon to be mined. Against this background, we examine the ownership and development rights to coalbed gas.

The fact that gas is of a fugacious character does not prevent ownership in it from being granted prior to its being reduced to possession. We have long recognized that gas may be owned prior to being recovered from its natural underground habitat. *Hamilton v. Foster*, 272 Pa. 95, 102, 116 A. 50, 52–53 (1922). Gas is a mineral, though not commonly spoken of as such, and while in place it is part of the property in which it is contained, as is the case with other minerals within the bounds of a freehold estate. *Id.* Gas necessarily belongs to the owner in fee, so long as it remains part of the property; ownership in it will be lost only upon grant or upon the gas leaving the property through migration. *Id.* In *Westmoreland & Cambria Natural Gas Co. v. DeWitt*, 130 Pa. 235, 249, 18 A. 724, 725 (1889), the governing principle of gas ownership was stated as follows:

> Water and oil, and still more strongly gas, may be classed by themselves, if the analogy be not too fanciful, as minerals *ferae naturae*. In common with animals, and unlike other minerals, they have a power and a tendency to escape without the volition of the owner ... They *belong to the owner of the land* and are part of it, *so long as they are on or in it*, and are subject to his control; but when they escape and go to other land, or come under another's control, the title of the former owner is gone. (Emphasis added)

Thus, as a general rule, subterranean gas is owned by whoever has title to the property in which the gas is resting. Cf. *Kier v. Peterson*, 41 Pa. 357 (1862) (owner of subterranean salt entitled to oil commingled with it). But cf. *Erwin's Appeal*, 7 Sad. 477, 12 A. 149 (Pa.1887). When a landowner conveys a portion of his property, in this instance coal, to another, it cannot thereafter be said that the property conveyed remains as part of the former's land, since title to the severed property rests solely in the grantee. In accordance with the foregoing principles governing gas ownership, therefore, *such gas as is present in coal must necessarily belong to the owner of the coal,* so long as it remains within his property and subject to his exclusive dominion and control. The landowner, of course, has title to the property surrounding the coal, and owns such of the coalbed gas as migrates into the surrounding property.

We do not regard as inconsistent with this analysis the fact that the coal owner's interest in the situs occupied by the coal may be less than perpetual. In addressing questions of title to coal, and of rights of access to and through coal to secure its removal, this Court has not construed the conveyance of coal alone as a grant of a fee simple estate in the situs where the coal is located. Rather, the coal owner's interest in that situs has been regarded as being in the nature of an estate determinable, which reverts to the surface landowner by operation of law at some time subsequent to removal of the coal. *Webber v. Vogel*, 189 Pa. 156, 160, 42 A. 4, 5 (1899); *Chartiers Block Coal Co. v. Mellon*, 152 Pa. 286, 296–297, 25 A. 597, 599 (1893). The potential for reversion of the situs, however, does not diminish the character of the coal as property of its grantee, or of the gas contained therein as a mineral *ferae naturae* resting inside the coal owner's property and falling within the dominion and control of the coal estate. The owner of coal may, as may any property owner, exercise dominion over his property so as to maximize his right of enjoyment thereover, within bounds limiting impingement upon the rights of other property owners. *Chartiers Block Coal Co. v. Mellon,* 152 Pa. at 295, 25 A. at 598. Hence, the coal owner may mine his coal, extract the gas from it, or both. If he chooses to extract the gas, drilling as well as hydrofracturing are available means, so long as their utilization does not impinge upon the rights of owners of the surrounding property, since the damage to coal inflicted by these processes is within his dominion to inflict.

Although coalbed gas contained in coal is, *ab initio,* property of the coal owner, that owner may allow others certain rights respecting the gas. In the present case, the grantor of the coal severance deed reserved therein the "right to drill and operate through said coal for oil and gas without being held liable for any damages." In construing the extent of the rights thereby reserved, effect should be given to the intentions of the parties to the instrument. *In re Conveyance of Land Belonging to City of Dubois,* 461 Pa. 161, 169–170, 335 A.2d 352, 357 (1975); *Dunham & Shortt v. Kirkpatrick,* 101 Pa. 36, 43–44 (1882) (severance of mineral rights). The language of the deed should be considered in its entirety, giving effect to all its terms and provisions, and construing the language in light of conditions existing at the time of its execution. *In re Conveyance of Land Belonging to the City of Dubois,* 461 Pa. at 169; 335 A.2d at 357; *St. Michael & Archangel Russian Orthodox Greek Catholic Church v. Uhniat,* 451 Pa. 176, 186, 301 A.2d 655, 660 (1973). The plain meaning, in the common understanding, of the provisions in a severance deed has been utilized as the best construction, where it may safely be assumed that such was the understanding which the parties themselves accorded the terms. *Dunham & Shortt v. Kirkpatrick,* 101 Pa. at 44. In accordance with these rules of construction, and in light of the chancellor's findings of fact as to the circumstances surrounding the deed's execution, the instant severance deed in question may be examined for evidence of the parties' intent.

As found by the chancellor, at the time this coal severance deed was entered into, although commercial exploitation of coalbed gas was known such operations were very limited and sporadic. Indeed for the most part coalbed gas was a dangerous waste product which had to be vented from the coal seam to allow for safe mining of the coal. This common practice is attested to by the presence in the deed under consideration of a "right of ventilation", permitting the grantee of the coal severance deed the right of reasonable encroachment on the estate retained by the grantor for the purpose of ventilating the gas from the coal seam.

The reservation to the grantor of the right to drill through the coal seam deeded away for oil and gas is stated generally. Although the unrestricted term "gas" was used in the reservation clause, in light of the conditions existing at the time of its execution we find it inconceivable that the parties intended a reservation of all types of gas. In so finding, we are unable to overlook a basic question: Why would a party retain the right to something which is only a waste product with well-known dangerous propensities? Case law is replete with examples of terms coming to have recognized meanings either more or less inclusive than they have in common parlance, usually through usage of the particular parties involved or the attendant business or industry. We find implicit in the reservation of the right to drill through the severed coal seam for "oil and gas" a recognition of the parties that the gas was that which was generally known to be commercially exploitable. It strains credulity to think that the grantor intended to reserve the right to extract a valueless waste product with the attendant potential responsibility for damages resulting from its dangerous nature. *See* McGinley, *Legal Problems Relating to Ownership of Gas Found in Coal Deposits,* 80 W.Va.L.Rev. 369, 391 (1978). We find more logical and reasonable the interpretation offered by the Appellant that the reservation intended only a right to drill through the seam to reach the unconveyed oil and natural gas generally found in strata deeper than the coal.

The order of the Superior Court is reversed, and the case is remanded to the Court of Common Pleas of Greene County for entry of a final decree quieting title in the Plaintiff-Appellant, United States Steel Corporation.

FLAHERTY, J., filed a dissenting opinion in which HUTCHINSON, J., joined.

FLAHERTY, Justice, dissenting.

This case was originally assigned to this writer, and the following opinion was prepared as a proposed majority opinion, but it received insufficient votes. It is now submitted for publication as a dissent. Thus, in accordance with the opinion which follows, the order of the Superior Court, insofar as it affirmed the final decree of the chancellor which dissolved a preliminary injunction against drilling operations and prohibited utilization of the hydrofracturing process by the gas lessee, should be affirmed, and, to the extent that the order quieted title to the gas in coal in favor of the surface owners, it should be modified.

This is an appeal from an order of the Superior Court which affirmed a final decree of the Court of Common Pleas of Greene County dissolving a preliminary injunction against drilling operations directed at recovering coalbed gas from a certain coal seam, and quieting title to that gas in favor of the surface owners so as to permit their lessee of gas rights to drill into the coal seam to extract the coalbed gas contained therein, subject to restrictions imposed to prevent unreasonable damage to the coal owner's property.

The appellant, United States Steel Corporation (hereinafter "coal owner"), is owner of the "Pittsburgh" or "River" Vein of coal underlying certain tracts of land in Greene County owned by appellees Hoge, Cowan, and Murdock (hereinafter "surface owners"), such coal seam being located approximately 800 feet beneath the earth's surface. Appellant's predecessor in title acquired rights to the coal from appellees' predecessors in title via a severance deed dated July 23, 1920. The deed reserved to the surface owners "the right to drill and operate through said coal for oil and gas without being held liable for any damages."[2] In 1976 and 1977, appellee Cunningham (hereinafter "gas lessee") acquired all of the foregoing reserved gas and oil rights from the surface owners. In 1978, the gas lessee began drilling wells for the purpose of recovering coalbed gas from the "Pittsburgh" coal seam. Upon learning of the drilling operations and the gas lessee's intention to stimulate recovery of coalbed gas through a process known as hydrofracturing, the appellant coal owner initiated actions in equity to terminate the intrusion upon its coal seam and to determine the ownership of, and right to develop, coalbed gas. The chancellor entered a decree permitting the drilling for such gas in appellant's coal seam, but prohibiting the use of hydrofracturing methods to stimulate gas recovery. Superior Court affirmed.

_____

2. The deed, which contained language common to most coal severance deeds executed in 1920 and in later years, read in pertinent part as follows:

"All the coal of the Pittsburgh or River Vein underlying all that certain tract of land situate in ...

Together with all the rights and privileges necessary and useful in the mining and removing of said coal, including the right of mining without leaving any support..., the right of ventilation and drainage and of access to the mines for men and materials ...

The parties of the first part hereby reserve the right to drill and operate through said coal for oil and gas without being held liable for any damages.

Together with all and singular the improvements, ways, waters, water courses, rights, liberties, privileges, hereditaments and appurtenances ..."

Hydrofracturing is the forcing of fluids under pressure into the well so as to cause a fracturing of the target stratum. When applied to coal seams, the process creates fractures in the coal which serve as conduits through which gas can flow through the seam to the well's shaft.

The ownership of, and right to develop, coalbed gas are questions of first impression. Consideration of the characteristics, origins, and history of development of gas is necessary to a determination of the issues presented. Hence, the following factual background, condensed from the chancellor's findings, pertains. Coalbed gas, often called methane, is found in and around coal veins, having long been recognized by the mining industry as a highly combustible and deadly poisonous gas which must be, at all times during the active coal mining process, ventilated to prevent explosion or inhalation; hence, the gas has traditionally been wasted into the atmosphere. Coalbed gas is always present in coal seams; its molecules are adsorbed in micropores of coal, and even the smallest particle of coal always contains and emits, when exposed, some coalbed gas. Coal and coalbed gas are, nevertheless, separate physical entities.

The gas which has commonly been referred to as "natural gas" is generally found in strata deeper than coal veins, though it shares many of the characteristics of coalbed gas. Both gases evolved, through natural processes, from carbonaceous material beneath the earth's surface, and both contain mixtures of various hydrocarbons, including methane, ethane, propane, butane, carbon dioxide, carbon monoxide, and hydrogen sulfide. Both are, as are all gases, migratory, thus being capable of escaping their natural habitats to enter other strata, and both are found in mainly the same geographic areas of Pennsylvania. Due to its fugacious character, natural gas is capable, under certain circumstances, of commingling with coalbed gas in the upper strata. Natural gas and coalbed gas have value as energy sources, the latter having approximately a 90% heating value as compared to the former. The energy value of coalbed gas in the relevant geographic area is far less, however, than that of coal itself; the coalbed gas has an energy equivalent value of only 1% of the b.t.u. value of the coal.

Extensive and costly drilling operations are required in order to extract coalbed gas or natural gas from strata where they are found. As early as the year 1900, however, certain wells were drilled in Greene County into the subject Pittsburgh vein of coal, and not deeper, and some of these wells produced coalbed gas in paying quantities. More recently there has developed an industrial capacity to drill into coal seams both horizontally and vertically to recover coalbed gas. With either drilling approach, the process known as hydrofracturing, see fn. 3, supra, facilitates recovery of coalbed gas in greater volumes and over longer periods of time. Nevertheless, coalbed gas can, in some areas, be recovered in paying quantities without any artificial stimulation of the coal seam. Developed by the drilling industry in the late 1940's, hydrofracturing was initially and has more regularly been utilized to recover natural gases from strata other than coal veins. When applied to coal seams, however, the process is highly efficient and desirable from the standpoint of the gas developer, but it presents serious threats to the interests of the owner of the coal estate.

When a coal seam is penetrated by a high frequency of gas well bore holes, and particularly when such holes are then hydrofractured, there is a distinct possibility of interference with coal mining processes, even when there is a careful exchange of information between the coal operator and the gas developer. Harm to the mining potential of coal arises from the fact that the inherently uncontrollable lesions caused by hydrofracturing permanently damage the coal seams, rendering any future mining operation slower in production, less safe, and more expensive. Even where hydrofracturing is not employed, but where gas wells are drilled with high frequency through the coal seam, the coal owner's estate is damaged, since as a safety precaution there must be left in place by the coal operator a barrier of coal surrounding each well hole. Such barriers, of course, interfere with full development of the coal, and cause considerable additional costs to the coal operator.

As a result of our nation's high energy demands and shortage of energy supplies, conditions which gained much attention during the past decade, the gas industry and the mining industry have come to regard coalbed gas as having sound market potential. Certain gas companies have, to a very limited and sporadic extent through the years dating back to at least 1918, produced coalbed gas from wells in Greene County and in other portions of western Pennsylvania. More recently certain coal owners, including appellant, have drilled and in some cases hydrofractured their own coal seams in various regions as experimental determinations of coalbed gas production capacities, and as a means of alleviating the presence of the gas in areas soon to be mined. Against this background, we examine the ownership and development rights to coalbed gas.

The fact that gas is of a fugacious character does not prevent ownership in it from being granted prior to its being reduced to possession, for we have long recognized that gas may be owned prior to being recovered from its natural underground habitat. *Hamilton v. Foster,* 272 Pa. 95, 102, 116 A. 50, 52–53 (1922). Gas is a mineral, though not commonly spoken of as such, and, while in place, it is part of the property in which it is contained, as is the case with other minerals within the bounds of a freehold estate, which extends to the center of the earth. *Id.* (In the words of an old maxim, "Cujus est solum, ejus est usque ad coelum et ad inferos," or, "To whomsoever the soil belongs, he owns also to the sky and to the depths.") Gas necessarily belongs to the owner in fee, *so long as* it remains part of the property; ownership in it will be lost only upon grant or upon the gas leaving the property through migration. *Id.* In *Westmoreland & Cambria Natural Gas Co. v. DeWitt,* 130 Pa. 235, 249, 18 A. 724, 725 (1889) (emphasis added), the governing principle of gas ownership was stated as follows:

> Water and oil, and still more strongly gas, may be classed by themselves, if the analogy be not too fanciful, as minerals *ferae naturae.* In common with animals, and unlike other minerals, they have a power and a tendency to escape without the volition of the owner ... They *belong to the owner of the land* and are part of it, *so long as they are on or in it,* and are subject to his control; but when they escape and go to other land, or come under another's control, the title of the former owner is gone.

Thus, as a general rule, subterranean gas is owned by whoever has title to the property in which the gas is resting. When a landowner conveys a portion of his property, in this instance coal, to another, it cannot thereafter be said that the property conveyed remains as part of the former's land, since title to the severed property rests solely in the grantee. In accordance with the foregoing principles governing gas ownership, therefore, such gas as is present in coal must necessarily belong to the owner of the coal, so long as it remains within his property and subject to his exclusive dominion and control. The landowner, of course, has title to the property surrounding the coal, and owns such of the coalbed gas as migrates into that surrounding property.

We do not regard as inconsistent with this analysis the fact that the coal owner's interest in the situs occupied by the coal may be less than perpetual. In addressing questions of title to coal, and of rights of access to and through coal to secure its removal, this Court has not construed the conveyance of coal alone as a grant of a fee simple estate in the situs where the coal is located. Rather, the coal owner's interest in that situs has been regarded as being in the nature of an estate determinable, which reverts to the surface landowner by operation of law at some time subsequent to removal of the coal. *Webber v. Vogel*, 189 Pa. 156, 160, 42 A. 4, 5 (1899); *Chartiers Block Coal Co. v. Mellon*, 152 Pa. 286, 296–297, 25 A. 597, 599 (1893). The potential for reversion of the situs, however, does not diminish the character of the coal as property of its grantee, or of the gas contained therein as a mineral *ferae naturae* resting inside the coal owner's property and falling within the dominion and control of the coal estate. The owner of coal may, as is the right of any property owner, exercise dominion over his property so as to maximize his right of enjoyment thereover, within bounds limiting impingement upon the rights of other property owners. *Chartiers Block Coal Co. v. Mellon*, 152 Pa. at 295, 25 A. at 598. Hence, the coal owner may mine his coal, extract the gas from it, or both. If he chooses to extract the gas, drilling as well as hydrofracturing are available means, so long as their utilization does not impinge upon the rights of owners of the surrounding property, since the damage to coal inflicted by these processes is within his dominion to inflict.

Although coalbed gas contained in coal is, ab initio, property of the coal owner, that owner may allow others certain rights respecting the gas. In the present case, the grantor of the coal severance deed reserved therein the "right to drill and operate through said coal for oil and gas without being held liable for any damages." In construing the extent of the rights thereby reserved, effect should be given to the intentions of the parties to the instrument. *In re Conveyance of Land Belonging to City of Dubois*, 461 Pa. 161, 169–170, 335 A.2d 352, 357 (1975); *Dunham & Shortt v. Kirkpatrick*, 101 Pa. 36, 43–44 (1882) (severance of mineral rights). The language of the deed should be considered in its entirety, giving effect to all its terms and provisions, and construing the language in light of conditions existing at the time of its execution. *In re Conveyance of Land Belonging to the City of Dubois*, supra; *St. Michael & Archangel Russian Orthodox Greek Catholic Church v. Uhniat*, 451 Pa. 176, 186, 301 A.2d 655, 660 (1973). The plain meaning, in the common understanding, of the provisions in a severance deed has been utilized as the best construction, where it may safely be assumed that such was the understanding which the parties themselves accorded the terms. *Dunham & Shortt v. Kirkpatrick*, supra. In accordance with these rules of construction, the instant severance deed may be examined for evidence of the parties' intent, in light of the chancellor's findings of fact as to the circumstances surrounding the deed's execution.

In plain terms, the deed reserves to the grantor the right to drill for "gas", without any express qualification limiting the types of gas that may be extracted. It is argued by appellant that the term "gas", as it was used in the deed, should be construed narrowly as a reference to what has traditionally been called "natural gas", the characteristics of which have heretofore been described, rather than as a reference to all gases. The chancellor found, however, that in the year 1920 it was well known that coal mines always contained coalbed gas; thus, it cannot be asserted that the parties were unaware of the existence of the particular gas now in dispute, though they may or may not have been aware of the few wells in Greene County and elsewhere that produced coalbed gas in paying quantities. Given their awareness of the presence of coalbed gas in the stratum, the earlier described similarities between coalbed gas and what has commonly been referred to as "natural gas", and the fact that the unrestricted term "gas" was employed in the reservation clause, we believe the plain meaning of the term "gas" would be too far subverted were we to exclude coalbed gas as a recoverable gas.

Granted, the parties may not have foreseen that gas generally, or coalbed gas in particular, would one day be such a highly valued resource as it has become, and, as a corollary, they may not have expected that extensive operations would ever be warranted to recover coalbed gas. In the year 1920, coalbed gas was primarily regarded as a lethal substance to be removed from mines and wasted into the atmosphere, to wit a gas that the mine owner would have preferred that the coalbed did not contain, as is evidenced by the clause in the instant deed providing access through the surface tract to ventilate gas from the mine. Thus, while the parties intended what the deed states, to allow drilling for gas generally, without specification as to its type, the broad reservation of gas rights may not have been motivated to any extent by an expectation of profitably developing coalbed gas within the future as foreseen from the year 1920.

Our determination that the grantor of the coal severance deed retained a right to drill through the coal and extract coalbed gas does not foreclose the appellant coal owner from proceeding to extract the same gas, for the right retained by the grantor does not, by the language employed in the deed, purport to be an *exclusive* one to all gas in the coalbed;[7] rather it is a right to remove only so much of the gas as is present and extractable through drilling efforts, whenever drilling is conducted. While the previously discussed methods available to the coal owner for extraction of the gas include those, such as hydrofracturing or intensive drilling, which may inflict substantial damage to the coal, the methods reserved to the coal grantor are less extensive, for they are bounded by the necessarily implied constraint that the coal estate granted will not be rendered useless, or unreasonably impaired, by the actions of one who has surrendered ownership of, and dominion over, the coal. Cf. *Chartiers Block Coal Co. v. Mellon*, 152 Pa. at 295, 25 A. at 598.

Hence, the reserved drilling right must not be interpreted as authority for there to be drilled into the coal so many wells that the coal's potential for being mined would be unreasonably impaired. Similarly, the hydrofracturing process, which had not even been suggested, let alone employed, in the year 1920, could not have been contemplated by the parties to the deed as an authorized form of "drilling and operating through" the coal; its potential for substantially damaging the coal exceeds what could have been intended as falling within the range of acceptable risk to the coal estate accruing from normal drilling operations. Thus, absent the express consent of the coal owner, such methods of extracting coalbed gas cannot be utilized by the holder of gas drilling rights.

The parties to this case, and amicus curiae, have offered various policy arguments regarding who, as between coal operators and gas developers, *should* own coalbed gas. Such arguments focus upon the ease and efficiency with which the gas can be recovered by the competing industries, as well as their respective motives to develop the resource. The issue before us, however, is not properly to be characterized as who *should* own and develop coalbed gas, but rather as who *does* own and have the right to develop the resource under the provisions of a particular coal severance deed. Whether coal and gas rights were in fact allocated by that deed in a manner that, in retrospect, would appear most desirable, has not been the focus of our inquiry. Nevertheless, we note that allowing development of coalbed gas under the subject tracts by both the coal owner and the holder of gas drilling rights will facilitate development of that resource.

HUTCHINSON, J., joins this dissenting opinion.

––––––––––

7. The appellee gas lessee agreed to pay the owners of the surface tracts one-eighth of all of the methane gas extracted. Although the surface owners purported to convey to the gas lessee all of the gas under their tracts, they clearly could not convey any interest in gas that had been previously forfeited via the coal severance deed. The terms of the gas lease are not, therefore, relevant to construction of the coal severance deed.

Notes & Questions

1. *Practice Note*: Title examination. This chapter introduces the importance of determining the correct ownership of mineral estates and surface estates before the extraction of natural resources. Additionally, *U.S. Steel v. Hogue* and other cases and articles in this chapter are good examples of what is at stake when the establishment of ownership is not accurate before extraction of resources takes place on a given property. Below are some of the steps that are necessary to take to establish accurate ownership in a title examination:

a. Identify the parcel of land

b. Identify current owner of land

c. Track ownership using grantor/grantee indices

d. Search for adverse conveyances

e. Search for encumbrances (e.g., mortgages, tax liens, court judgments, etc....)

For traditional, residential title searches, tracking ownership back 40 to 60 years has generally been a sufficient timeframe to examine title history. This is a product of the typical type of encumbrances that would interfere with flawless ownership of a residential property. For example, statutes typically limit the effectiveness of mortgage liens and other encumbrances that could affect a residential property.

Alternatively, when examining title ownership for property that has the presence of a valuable, underlying mineral estate, it is generally the practice to track ownership anywhere from 100 years to a timeframe that takes the ownership records of the given land parcel all the way back to patent conveyance from the government. The necessity to track ownership this far into the past exists because many mineral estates were severed from surface estates in the late 1800s and early 1900s.

2. Some states, like Ohio and North Dakota, have dormant mineral rights. Ohio's Dormant Minerals Act (Ohio Rev. Code Ann. § 5301.56) returns the mineral rights to a surface owner after twenty years where the minerals are deemed abandoned and the surface owner takes proper steps to join title. The North Dakota Century Code similarly provides:

38-18.1-02. Statement of claims — Recording — Reversion.

Any mineral interest is, if unused for a period of twenty years immediately preceding the first publication of the notice required by section 38-18.1-06, deemed to be abandoned, unless a statement of claim is recorded in accordance with section 38-18.1-04. Title to the abandoned mineral interest vests in the owner or owners of the surface estate in the land in or under which the mineral interest is located on the date of abandonment. The owner of the surface estate in the land in or under which the mineral interest is located on the date of abandonment may record a statement of succession in interest indicating that the owner has succeeded to ownership of the minerals under this chapter.

Several other states have dormant mineral statutes, too, many of which are based on the 1986 Uniform Minerals Act.

3. Draft an example clause for your client issue raised at the beginning of the chapter. After you draft that clause, be sure you can explain why you used the language you did. What did you reject? What might counsel for the other side object to? What concerns do you have?

4. Suppose, in your investigation, you find out that the Land Owner's attorney told the Grantor that coalbed methane would be included in the reservation. Land Owner's

attorney told you he "pulled one over" on the Grantor by telling him, "All gas means all gas. That's clearly the law, but you don't need a lawyer to tell you that. It's obvious. What more do you want?" How does this impact your client? How does it impact you? Suppose your client needs this lease to keep their business viable. How do you proceed?

C. Oil and Gas

1. Vocabulary

Rule of Capture: The general rule, originating in English Common Law, which states that the first person to capture resources like groundwater, oil, or natural gas, owns that resource. A landowner who extracts oil, for example, from a well that bottoms within the landowner's boundaries acquires absolute ownership of the oil, even if it is actually being drained from the subsurface of another owners' land.

Correlative Rights: A corollary to the rule of capture, this provides that a landowner's right to capture oil and gas from their property is limited by a duty to extract without waste or negligence. Pennsylvania defines this as: "The rights of each owner of oil and gas interest in a common pool or source of supply of oil or gas to have a fair and reasonable opportunity to obtain and produce his just and equitable share of the oil and gas in the pool or sources of supply without being required to drill unnecessary wells or incur other unnecessary expense to recover or receive the oil or gas or its equivalent." 25 Pa. Code §79.1.

Pooling: The joining together or combining of small tracts or portions of tracts for the purpose of having enough acreage to obtain a well drilling permit under the state laws and regulations. This is also done to share production by interest owners in the pooled unit.

Mandatory Pooling: In some states, an operator can request this when it is not able to acquire the leases needed to meet the necessary acreage or spacing requirements when applying for a drilling permit. Approximately 38 states have some version of this concept. Operators often have to hold a certain percentage of the proposed pool to make the request, ranging broadly, e.g., from 65% to 90%.

Unitization: A method through which ownership interests in a drilling unit are consolidated to share the drilling revenues. Usually, sharing is based on each owner's percentage of the drilling unit's surface area. This is broader than pooling, as it is targeted at a specific reservoir or geologic formation.

2. Basic Concepts

David E. Pierce, *Minimizing the Environmental Impact of Oil and Gas Development by Maximizing Production Conservation*

85 N.D. L. Rev. 759 (2009) (footnotes omitted)

I. INTRODUCTION

American property law has conspired against the oil and gas industry since the first wells were drilled and courts were called upon to define rights in the oil and gas resource. The "rule of capture" was initially a rule of necessity that quickly became the foundational principle for defining rights in oil and gas. The rule simply provides that in order to perfect ownership in oil and gas, you must associate yourself with a well that extracts the oil and gas from beneath your land. Unfortunately, the venerable rule of capture continues as the foundation of property in oil and gas.

Although the rule of capture spawned the oil and gas production conservation movement, the promise of production conservation has never been fully realized. Today, every state's system of oil and gas conservation regulation, including that of North Dakota, has the rule of capture at its core. Until this is changed, waste in the form of unnecessary drilling, and the associated environmental degradation, will continue; the inability to maximize recovery of the available oil and gas resource will continue. The capture regime will also haunt technological advances that require cooperation instead of competition in the subsurface porous and permeable rock structures where oil and gas reside. Whether contemplating hydraulic fracturing or carbon sequestration, a capture-based property regime will continue to create conceptual, practical, and artificial hurdles for developers.

The quick-fix common law solution to the historical capture-based property regime is to embrace the connected nature of the common reservoir instead of competing with it. This can be done by elevating "correlative rights" principles to the position now held by the rule of capture. Elevating correlative rights to this position can be accomplished by motivated oil and gas conservation commissions and a public that demands more from the commissions than the commissions have been willing to deliver to date. Perhaps the Sierra Club and other environmental groups can pick up where Henry Doherty left off by moving the industry the next mile toward true production conservation. It is ironic that it may take, at this late date, outside environmental forces to accomplish what the visionaries of the oil and gas industry have been unable to accomplish during its 150 years of existence.

II. RULE OF CAPTURE AND "WASTE"

Regardless of the conceptual ownership regime a state adopts to define rights in oil and gas, oil and gas ownership and development in all states is ultimately governed by the rule of capture. Under the rule of capture, you must have rights in a well to secure your opportunity to perfect a property interest in oil and gas; no well means no property rights in the in oil and gas. Extraction of oil and gas is the defining event when inchoate ownership becomes property. The more you can extract, the more you convert from conceptual ownership to actual ownership. More wells, operated at their maximum rates of production, yield more real ownership of oil and gas. Although this may result in unnecessary damage to the environment, excessive occupancy and use of surface resources, and tremendous waste of the oil and gas resource itself, it is all justified by a simple common law reality: if you do not produce the oil and gas and reduce it to property, someone else will.

All of the losses associated with the rule of capture are measured against the alternative measure of zero, which is what you get if you do not associate with a well and engage in capture of the resource. Because the negative aspects of the rule are shared with others in the reservoir and society at large, seldom will the negatives of engaging in the practice yourself be less than zero. This means that so long as the projected volume and value of captured oil and gas exceed the cost of drilling wells and the required return on investment, wells will be drilled even though the "cost" to others in the reservoir and society at large may far exceed any one individual's return on investment. This is the oil and gas industry's "tragedy of the commons."

The industry has been cognizant of this tragedy and has fought to mitigate it since the inception of the industry. Major strides had been made by 1960, but even today the promise of oil and gas conservation has not been realized. The failure of conservation regulation is simple: the statutes in every state operate on a capture-based property model.

A. The Failure of State Conservation Laws

All states unnecessarily tolerate environmental degradation, excessive surface use, and other forms of "waste" of the oil and gas resource. This is because all state oil and gas "conservation" statutes have the rule of capture as their foundation. To protect your "correlative rights" in the oil and gas in place, you need a well. The oil and gas conservation authority will issue a drilling permit if the applicant can show compliance with, among other requirements, "spacing" regulations. Spacing regulations are premised on either a state-wide rule or a special rule that seeks to define the maximum area that can be efficiently drained by a single well. This is a capture model. To perfect ownership in the oil and gas beneath your property, you need to be associated with a well. Spacing requirements merely specify that the rule of capture must be played using squares and rectangles. Pooling adds nothing to the mix, except to provide a mechanism to combine separate properties within the designated square or rectangle with which the capture game must be played. Although no one would deny that conservation laws have averted a substantial amount of waste, they have done so by tacitly accepting a substantial amount of waste through the preservation of a capture-based regulatory regime.

* * *

III. CORRELATIVE RIGHTS: THE FORGOTTEN CORNERSTONE OF OIL AND GAS PROPERTY LAW

Correlative rights recognize that each owner overlying an oil and gas reservoir has rights and duties with regard to other owners above the reservoir. The connected nature of the reservoir rock structure makes it possible for any owner conducting operations within the reservoir to impact other owners. Conceptually, this initially appears to be a nuisance-based right: one owner cannot use its land so as to unreasonably interfere with the use of surrounding lands. At the surface, the common medium being fouled is often air, water, or land. Beneath the surface, the common medium, regarding oil and gas, is the porous and permeable rock structure where the oil and gas reside. Correlative rights, however, are more "property" than "tort." Nuisance is a tort remedy to protect property; it does not define the property itself. Therefore, ownership of the oil and gas gives rise to the associated correlative rights that define what can and cannot be done in the reservoir. Correlative rights are part of the bundle of sticks comprising ownership of the oil and gas, much like the rights to lateral and subjacent support are part of the bundle of sticks comprising land ownership.

The most important aspect of correlative rights are the extra-territorial rights created in each owner in the reservoir. For example, if A is engaging in acts totally within the boundaries of A's property, but the activity negatively impacts the reservoir in some way, B and others owning rights in the reservoir may be able to enjoin A to protect their property interests in the reservoir. Similarly, B may have the *affirmative right* to impact A's property to the extent it *positively impacts* the reservoir in some way. This second observation may appear to be a bit radical, but it is the logical corollary of the first principle. Parties owning property in a reservoir must be cognizant of the rights of all parties to effectively maximize their rights in the reservoir, so long as they do not injure the reservoir. This prevents parties from trying to artificially fence off their connected tract when they do not agree with what is best for the collective owners of the reservoir.

Individual rights and collective rights must be evaluated to define each party's precise rights and duties under a given set of circumstances. Correlative rights have been a recognized adjunct to oil and gas ownership for over 100 years. When courts were tentative regarding a state's right to control oil and gas development to protect the public against "waste," courts relied primarily on a private basis for state action: the protection of correlative rights. Once state action for the prevention of waste became ensconced in American jurisprudence, the protection of correlative rights became a secondary basis for state action. Too often courts have failed to recognize the important correlative rights component of oil and gas ownership, focusing instead on ill-fitting concepts such as the rule of capture. This seemingly "unseen" nature of correlative rights was recently illustrated by the Texas Supreme Court, which used the rule of capture to try to solve a problem that was, in essence, a correlative rights problem.

The rule of capture was used in *Coastal Oil & Gas Corp. v. Garza Energy Trust* to avoid liability for hydraulic fracturing operations that sent a fracture through the reservoir underlying the operator's property and into a portion of the reservoir underlying the land of an adjacent landowner. Instead of evaluating the nature of the physical intrusion into the adjacent landowner's portion of the reservoir, the court held liability did not exist because the only injury alleged was the loss of hydrocarbons through drainage. The court concluded that because the drainage was encompassed by the rule of capture, no damage existed and, therefore, no liability resulted. The obvious flaw in this analysis was the failure to address the lawfulness of the event giving rise to the drainage. If the event was lawful, the drainage would have been legitimate under the rule of capture. If the event was not lawful, the drainage would not have been legitimate and, therefore, the draining party would not have been exempt from liability. The legitimacy of the drainage depends upon whether the fracture crossing a boundary line is more like slant drilling, as opposed to legitimate completion operations of a well properly bottomed on the developer's property.

Addressing the issue in a surface-oriented context suggests that any entry into the adjacent lands is a trespass. But addressing the issue in a correlative rights context requires that the conduct itself be evaluated to determine whether it is appropriate behavior within the reservoir community. Under a correlative rights analysis, if the hydraulic fracturing is held to be "appropriate behavior within the reservoir community," the resulting drainage will be protected by the rule of capture. On the other hand, if the hydraulic fracturing is held to violate correlative rights of others within the reservoir community, drainage will not be protected by the rule of capture.

Using a correlative rights analysis requires that the true nature of all owners' rights in the reservoir be defined before the conduct at issue is evaluated. It is not a simple trespass issue because each owner overlying the reservoir in fact has rights in the reservoir beneath every other owners' land. This creates a sort of cotenant-like relationship throughout the common reservoir, where no single owner has exclusive rights or an absolute say as to what can or cannot take place within the reservoir. When it is recognized that each owner possesses certain undivided rights within the reservoir, it becomes apparent that intra-reservoir issues lack the basic exclusivity required for the application of trespass concepts. This is what the court missed in Coastal. Although the court purported to depart from traditional *ad coelum* concepts, a departure was not necessary because the exclusivity con-templated by *ad coelum* concepts simply does not exist regarding issues among owners within a common reservoir. Similarly, the rule of capture does not come into play until the underlying property rights of the parties are defined. The property model the court operated under was a single landowner that had total dominance over his or her prop-erty—another classic *ad coelum* concept. However, this was not an accurate model because no single landowner has total dominance over a common reservoir that underlies lands owned by others. Instead, an owner's rights are correlative.

Correlative rights are the essence of oil and gas ownership in a common reservoir. An owner's capture rights are limited by the correlative rights of other owners that impose reciprocal duties on each owner not to exercise their capture rights, or any other rights, that could impair maximum efficient recovery of the oil and gas resource from the reservoir. Correlative rights, consistent with the public interest in preventing waste, focus on maximizing the resource benefits for all reservoir co-owners as opposed to merely maximizing an individual owner's capture rights. Once conservation statutes and oil and gas ownership are properly oriented around correlative rights as opposed to capture rights, courts and administrative agencies can, for the first time, truly approach the effective prevention of waste and protection of correlative rights.

Notes & Questions

1. How does the Rule of Capture lead to the less than optimal economic extraction of oil and/or natural gas?

2. Correlative Rights. Where else does the legal principle of "correlative rights" come into play? How are these other correlative rights issues significantly implicated by evolving oil and natural gas production technologies?

D. Extraction & Production

1. Underground Mining

Citizens Coal Council v. Norton

330 F.3d 478 (D.C. Cir. 2003)

Before: SENTELLE and ROGERS, Circuit Judges, and SILBERMAN, Senior Circuit Judge.

This is an appeal by the Secretary of the Interior and intervenor National Mining Association ("NMA") from a judgment of the District Court. The District Court held that the Secretary's interpretation of the Surface Mining Control and Reclamation Act's ("SMCRA") section 701(28), 30 U.S.C. § 1291(28) (2000), to exclude subsidence from the definition of "surface coal mining operations" regulated under section 522(e) of the Act, 30 U.S.C. § 1272(e), was contrary to the law and therefore invalid. Because we find that Congress did not speak un-ambiguously on this precise issue in the SMCRA and because we find the Secretary's interpretation to be reasonable, we defer to the Secretary and reverse the District Court.

I. Background

A. The Litigation

This case began with Citizens Coal Council's ("CCC") challenge to the Secretary of the Interior's final rulemaking action by which she promulgated the regulation contained in 30 C.F.R. § 761.200 (2003). The challenged regulation is an interpretive rule, based on sections 701(28) and 522(e) of the SMCRA, 30 U.S.C. § 1201, et seq. The regulation states:

> 761.200 Interpretive rule related to subsidence due to underground coal mining in areas designated by Act of Congress. OSM has adopted the following interpretation of rules promulgated in part 761.
>
> (a) Interpretation of § 761.11—Areas where mining is prohibited or limited. Subsidence due to underground coal mining is not included in the definition of surface coal mining operations under section 701(28) of the Act and § 700.5 of this chapter and therefore is not prohibited in areas protected under section 522(e) of the Act.

30 C.F.R. § 761.200. CCC sought review of this rulemaking in District Court, after exhausting its administrative remedies. It claimed that the Secretary's interpretation of the cited provisions of the SMCRA was contrary to the clear law, and therefore, unworthy of any deference by the courts. As a remedy, CCC requested that the court vacate the regulation and instruct the Secretary to impose instead, a regulation stating that subsidence was included within 701(28)'s definition. The District Court granted CCC's motion for summary judgment holding that "Congress has expressed its intent clearly on the precise point at issue here and that the Secretary's interpretation of § [701(28)] and § [522(e)] is contrary to law." *Citizens Coal Council v. Norton*, 193 F.Supp.2d 159, 165 (D.D.C.2002). The District Court then remanded the regulation to the Secretary without instruction.

CCC filed a notice of appeal on April 11, 2002, and intervenor NMA filed its notice the following day. On June 5, 2002, the District Court granted the appellant's motion to stay the remand order, but vacated the regulation and stayed its judgment pending appeal.

See Citizens Coal Council v. Babbitt, No. 00-0274 (June 5, 2002). On June 6, 2002, the Secretary filed a notice of appeal of both rulings. In the present case, the Secretary and NMA appeal the District Court's ruling that the regulation was invalid and its subsequent vacation of the regulation, and CCC appeals the District Court's refusal to grant the full relief it requested.

B. The Statutory Scheme

We recognize from the outset that the SMCRA is a complex and often puzzling statute, in many cases raising a variety of questions as to its correct interpretation. SMCRA was enacted in an effort by Congress to both "protect society and the environment from the adverse effects of surface coal mining operations" and to "assure that the coal supply essential to the Nation's energy requirements, and to its economic and social well-being is provided and strike a balance between protection of the environment and agricultural activity and the Nation's need for coal as an essential source of energy." 30 U.S.C. § 1202(a), (f). As the District Court recognized and the parties do not dispute, the focus of the regulation in SMCRA was primarily on the surface mining techniques, such as strip-mining, and one of its goals was to encourage the development and application of underground mining technologies as an alternative less likely to disturb lands used for other activities. *See Citizens Coal*, 193 F.Supp.2d at 161 (citing 30 U.S.C. §§ 1201, 1202(k)).

To this purpose, SMCRA section 522(e) prohibits "surface coal mining operations" with certain exceptions, in a number of protected areas, particularly within the boundaries of the national parks system, national forests, and public parks and historic sites. In addition, these operations are also prohibited "within [100] feet of the outside right-of-way line of any public road"; "within [300] feet from any occupied dwelling, unless waived by the owner thereof"; and "within [300] feet of any public building, school, church, community, or institutional building, public park, or within [100] feet of a cemetery." 30 U.S.C. § 1272(e)(4), (5).

SMCRA section 701(28) defines "surface coal mining operations" as follows:

> (A) activities conducted on the surface of lands in connection with a surface coal mine or subject to the requirements of section 1266 of this title surface operations and surface impacts incident to an underground coal mine, the products of which enter commerce or the operations of which directly or indirectly affect interstate commerce. Such activities include excavation for the purpose of obtaining coal including such common methods as contour, strip, auger, mountaintop removal, box cut, open pit, and area mining, the uses of explosives and blasting, and in situ distillation or retorting, leaching or other chemical or physical processing, and the cleaning, concentrating, or other processing or preparation, loading of coal for interstate commerce at or near the mine site ... and

> (B) the areas upon which such activities occur or where such activities disturb the natural land surface. Such areas shall also include any adjacent land the use of which is incidental to any such activities, all lands affected by the construction of new roads or the improvement or use of existing roads to gain access to the site of such activities and for haulage, and excavations, workings, impoundments, dams, ventilation shafts, entryways, refuse banks, dumps, stockpiles, overburden piles, spoil banks, culm banks, tailings, holes or depressions, repair areas, storage areas, processing areas, shipping areas and other areas which are sited structures, facilities, or other property or materials on the surface, resulting from or incident to such activities[.]

30 U.S.C. § 1291(28). SMCRA section 516(a) requires the Secretary to promulgate rules and regulations directed toward "the surface effects of underground coal mining operations" embodying the requirements of section 516(b), but instructs the Secretary, in adopting such rules, to "consider the distinct difference between surface coal mining and underground coal mining." 30 U.S.C. § 1266(a). The permit requirement of section 516(b) mentions subsidence specifically, in contrast to sections 522 and 701(28).

516(b): Permit requirements

Each permit issued under any approved State or Federal program pursuant to this chapter and relating to underground coal mining shall require the operator to—

(1) adopt measures consistent with known technology in order to prevent subsidence causing material damage to the extent technologically and economically feasible, maximize mine stability, and maintain the value and reasonably foreseeable use of such surface lands, except in those instances where the mining technology used requires planned subsidence in a predictable and controlled manner: *Provided*, That nothing in this subsection shall be construed to prohibit the standard method of room and pillar mining;

30 U.S.C. § 1266(b)(1). Section 516(c) extends the Secretary's authority to regulate underground coal mining if it creates a danger to inhabitants.

c) Suspension of underground coal mining operations in urbanized areas

In order to protect the stability of the land, the regulatory authority shall suspend underground coal mining under urbanized areas, cities, towns, and communities and adjacent to industrial or commercial buildings, major impoundments, or permanent streams if he finds imminent danger to inhabitants of the urbanized areas, cities, towns, and communities.

30 U.S.C. § 1266(c). Section 516(d) extends the subchapter to cover "surface operations and surface impacts incident to underground coal mining operations."

The provisions of this subchapter relating to State and Federal programs, permits, bonds, inspections and enforcement, public review, and administrative and judicial review shall be applicable to surface operations and surface impacts incident to an underground coal mine with such modifications to the permit application requirements, permit approval or denial procedures, and bond requirements as are necessary to accommodate the distinct difference between surface and underground coal mining.

30 U.S.C. § 1266(d).

II. Analysis

We review the Secretary's interpretation of the provisions of the SMCRA, a statute she administers, under the analysis articulated in *Chevron, U.S.A. Inc. v. Natural Res. Def. Council, Inc.*, 467 U.S. 837, 104 S.Ct. 2778, 81 L.Ed.2d 694 (1984). The two-step test of *Chevron* requires, first, that both the agency and the courts give effect to Congress's unambiguously expressed intent if the underlying statute speaks directly to the precise question at issue. *Chevron*, 467 U.S. at 842–43, 104 S.Ct. at 2781–82. In this first analytical step, the courts use "traditional tools of statutory interpretation—text, structure, purpose, and legislative history." *Pharm. Research & Mfrs. of Am. v. Thompson*, 251 F.3d 219, 224 (D.C.Cir.2001). If, however, the statute is "silent or ambiguous with respect to the specific issue" the court must defer to the agency's interpretation if it is reasonable. *Chevron*, 467

U.S. at 843, 104 S.Ct. at 2782. Because we find that the term "surface impacts incident to an underground coal mine" as it appears in section 701(28) does not unambiguously include subsidence, the second step of *Chevron* requires that we defer to the Secretary's reasonable interpretation of the statute and reverse the District Court. See *NMA v. Dep't of the Interior*, 105 F.3d 691, 694 (D.C.Cir.1997).

We begin, as always, with the plain language of the statute in question. The Secretary interprets the definition of "surface coal mining operations" contained in 701(28), and thereby prohibited in 522(e), to exclude subsidence. The Secretary first argues that the plain meaning of the word "operations" suggests a reference to some human activity, and not to a possible effect of underground mining, like subsidence. *See Webster's Third New International Dictionary* 1581 (1971) (defining "operation" as "doing or performing"). If 701(28)'s definition ended after its first phrase, "activities conducted on the surface of lands in connection with a surface coal mine or subject to the requirements of section 516 surface operations," this interpretation might be more clearly compelled. However, as CCC points out, the phrase which follows: "surface operations and surface impacts incident to an underground coal mine" could add significantly to the scope of the term "operations" as used in this context.

As the District Court noted, the Secretary essentially parses the definition to read "activities conducted on the surface of lands in connection with [1] a surface coal mine or [2] subject to the requirements of section 1266 of this title[,] surface operations and surface impacts incident to an underground coal mine ...". *Citizens Coal*, 193 F.Supp.2d at 163 (citing 30 U.S.C. § 1291(28)(A)). The Secretary supports this interpretation with the definition's next sentence which begins with the phrase "[s]uch activities." This phrase is repeated throughout the remainder of the definition, and is defined within the provision by the examples of activities listed, *e.g.*, excavation; physical or chemical processing; and loading for interstate transport. *See* 30 U.S.C. § 1291(28)(A). The Secretary therefore concludes that the opening sentence refers to these "activities" only. The District Court held that this reading was not "the most natural" one, in light of the legislative history and the overall purpose of the Act. *See Citizens Coal*, 193 F.Supp.2d at 163–64. The reading advanced as the "most natural" by CCC and accepted by the District Court "becomes apparent with the addition of three commas" as follows: "'surface coal mining operations' means—(A) activities conducted on the surface of lands in connection with a surface coal mine[,] or [,] subject to the requirements of section 1266 of this title [,] surface operations and surface impacts incident to an underground coal mine...." *Id.* at 163. The District Court and CCC therefore read 701(28) to mean the surface coal mining operations—prohibited in areas specified by 522(e)—to include as a separate matter "surface impacts" incident to an underground mine, which must then include subsidence.

We need not disavow the District Court's determination that CCC's tendered interpretation is the more natural one in order to reverse the District Court and uphold the Secretary. As noted by the District Court we have, on a previous occasion, observed that "[t]he most natural reading of the [SMCRA] as a whole, and the definition in [§ 1291(28)] in particular ... then suggests that 'surface coal mining operations' encompasses both surface coal mines and the surface effects of underground mines." *Citizens Coal*, 193 F.Supp.2d at 163 (quoting *Nat'l Wildlife Fed'n v. Hodel*, 839 F.2d 694, 753 (D.C.Cir.1988)). Even assuming the correctness of our reasoning and that of the District Court, the ambiguity of the statute in combination with the *Chevron* doctrine eclipses the ability of the courts to substitute their preferred interpretation for an agency's reasonable interpretation when that agency is the entity authorized to administer the statute in question. See, e.g., *NMA v. Babbitt*, 172 F.3d 906, 916 (D.C.Cir.1999) ("If we were interpreting the statute de novo, we might well agree that appellant has the better argument. But we are not. And although the government's reading is a bit of a stretch, we think it passes the *Chevron* test"). While we do not find that the language of the definition of "surface coal mining operations" compels the exclusion of subsidence from its scope, neither do we find that the definition compels its inclusion. Therefore, we endeavor to resolve this issue under the second analytical step of *Chevron* because Congress has not spoken unambiguously on this precise question. We find the Secretary's interpretation, while not necessarily the most natural one, is reasonable, and therefore we defer to it. *Cf. Young v. Cmty. Nutrition Inst.*, 476 U.S. 974, 980–81, 106 S.Ct. 2360, 2364–65, 90 L.Ed.2d 959 (1986). (Upholding the FDA's interpretation of an ambiguous statutory provision, finding that although the lower court's "reading of the statute may seem to be the more natural interpretation ... the phrasing ... admits of either respondents' or petitioners' reading of the statute.... We find the FDA's interpretation ... to be sufficiently rational to preclude a court from substituting its judgment for that of the FDA.").

Both parties argue that the legislative history of the SMCRA supports its interpretation. CCC relies on several statements in the Senate and House reports relating to SMCRA's promulgation. According to CCC, the Senate report indicates that SMCRA was addressed to "surface coal mining operations—including exploration activities and the surface effects of underground mining." S.Rep. No. 95-128, at 49 (1977). CCC contends that the report clarifies that those effects include subsidence, quoting a discussion in the report on the environmental hazards posed by coal mining: "Similar hazards also occur from the surface effects of underground coal mining, including the dumping of coal waste piles, subsidence and mine fires." *Id.* at 50. Additionally, the report states that the Act's initial regulatory requirements extended to "[a]ll surface coal mining operations, which include, by definition surface impacts incident to underground coal mines." *Id.* at 71. The District Court relied on this passage from the report to support its position that section 522(e) applied to subsidence.

> 'Surface coal mining operations' is so defined to include not only traditionally regarded coal surface mining activities but also surface operations incident to underground coal mining, and exploration activities. The effect of this definition is that coal surface mining and surface impacts of underground coal mining are subject to regulation under this Act.

Id. at 98. The court found that the references in the reports to "surface effects" of underground coal mining, and "surface impacts" of underground coal mining must include subsidence. *See Citizens Coal*, 193 F.Supp.2d at 163–64. Finally, CCC contends that the House report also supports its position in a discussion entitled "Surface Impacts of Underground Mines," stating:

> The environmental problems associated with underground mining for coal which are directly manifested on the land surface are addressed in section [516] and other such sections which may have application. These problems include surface subsidence.

H.R.Rep. No. 95-218, at 125–26 (1977). Essentially, the CCC interprets the legislative history's use of the phrase "surface impacts" which appears in 701(28) to necessarily include subsidence.

The Secretary counters with the argument that the legislative history does show that Congress had an intention to regulate subsidence within the SMCRA, but intended to limit that regulation to section 516. More importantly, this interpretation is consistent with the language of the statute. Section 516 is the only section in the statute in which subsidence is specifically mentioned. This demonstrates that Congress specifically stated that subsidence was being dealt with in a provision when its intention was to include subsidence under that section of the SMCRA. The Secretary argues that the House report on section 516 illustrates Congress's intention to authorize the Secretary to regulate subsidence in that section, rather than prohibit it entirely by way of section 522(e).

> Surface subsidence has a different effect on different land uses. Generally, no appreciable impact is realized on agricultural land and similar types of land and productivity is not affected. On the other hand when subsidence occurs under developed land such as an urbanized area, substantial damage results to surface improvements be they private homes, commercial buildings or public roads and schools· It is the intent of this section to provide the Secretary with the authority to require the design and conduct of underground mining methods to control subsidence to the extent technologically and economically feasible in order to protect the value and use of surface lands.

H.R.Rep. No. 95-218, at 126 (1977). The Secretary reiterates that Congress did not discuss subsidence as being among the "impacts" of underground mining that are prohibited in section 522(e) areas. The Secretary also noted that she had concluded during the promulgation of the regulation at issue that the passage from the Senate report on which the District Court specifically relied was "imprecise" and of questionable precedential value because it states that exploration activities are included in the definition of "surface coal mining operations" even though the statute expressly provides to the contrary. See 64 Fed.Reg. 70,844-45 (citing 30 U.S.C. § 1291(28)(A)). Furthermore, the Secretary points out that the Senate report on section 522(e) notes that "surface coal mining" is prohibited within the specified distances of public roads, occupied buildings, and active underground mines "for reasons of public health and safety." S.Rep. No. 95-128, at 55. The Secretary posits that to accomplish that purpose, 522(e) need not prohibit subsidence, because underground mines must already meet the requirements of section 516, which prevents almost all risks to public health and safety.

Taken together, as is so often the case, legislative history on which both parties rely is at best inconclusive as to either interpretation. As Judge Leventhal once observed, reviewing legislative history is like "looking over a crowd and picking out your friends." Patricia M. Wald, *Some Observations on the Use of Legislative History in the 1981 Supreme Court Term*, 68 Iowa L. Rev. 195, 214 (1983). This inconclusiveness underscores our conclusion that the statute is ambiguous on the question of whether subsidence is included within the prohibitions in 522(e). In addition, one amendment to the statute since its promulgation bolsters the reasonableness of the Secretary's interpretation. In 1992, Congress added section 720 to the SMCRA, an amendment entitled "Subsidence," which provides compensation for property owners who suffer material damage caused by subsidence to "occupied residential dwelling and structures related thereto, or non-commercial building due to underground coal mining operations." 30 U.S.C. § 1309a(a)(1). Intervenor NMA argues that the passage of this section demonstrates that Congress was aware that SMCRA does not prohibit subsidence in section 522(e) areas and therefore added the section to provide a remedy for property owners damaged by this result of an underground mining operation. CCC argues that the addition of this provision does not foreclose their interpretation because section 522(e)'s alleged prohibition of subsidence does not apply to mines operating pursuant to valid existing rights as of August 3, 1977, and section 720 offers compensation to property owners damaged by these mines, as well as to those who have waived 522(e)'s protections, or where subsidence damage occurs from a mine more than 300 feet away from protected structures, and thereby outside 522(e)'s buffer zone. Nothing in the statute or in section 720 supports CCC's arguments, and a far more plausible explanation for the provision is that it provides a remedy for subsidence damage, because subsidence was not already prohibited by section 522(e), as the Secretary argues. While this section does not, in combination with the others, resolve all ambiguity on the precise issue in question, it supports the reasonableness of the Secretary's interpretation.

Finally, we do not find compelling the argument drawn by CCC from a footnote in the District Court's opinion. At the end of its opinion, the court added the note, which reads in pertinent part: "[s]ection [522] also falls within § [516(d)]'s mandate that SMCRA provisions 'relating to State and Federal programs [and] permits ... shall be applicable to surface operations and surface impacts incident to an underground coal mine,' since it imposes requirements on federal and state regulators...." *Citizens Coal*, 193 F.Supp.2d at 165 n. 3. The District Court offered no further reasoning or explanation in support of this conclusion. CCC argues that this footnote is an alternative holding meaning that section 516(d), by referencing provisions "relating to ... permits" unambiguously requires the Secretary to apply section 522(e) to protect against subsidence, simply because of the use of the word "permitted" in that later section. We disagree.

There is certainly a colorable difference between the noun "permit" and the verb "permitted." The SMCRA contains a number of provisions which do deal directly and specifically with "Permits." For example, section 506, 30 U.S.C. § 1256, is entitled "Permits" and provides for the terms, termination, and renewal of permits. The following section 30 U.S.C. § 1257 is entitled "Application requirements" and provides for the fee and content requirements of the permits. These sections stand in contrast to section 522(e) which provides for a number of prohibitions, and uses the verb "permitted" simply to describe the geographical limitations to which the Secretary is bound when "[d]esignating areas unsuitable for surface coal mining," as the title of the section instructs. *See* 30 U.S.C. § 1272(e) (no surface coal mining operations ... shall be permitted—(1) on any lands within the boundaries of units of the National Park System ... (2) on any Federal lands within the boundaries of any national forest ... (3) which will adversely affect any publicly owned park ... (4) within 100 feet of the outside right-of-way line of any public road ... (5) within 300 feet from any occupied dwelling....). Thus, the "permit" argument based on section 516(d) has no compelling force on the interpretation of section 522(e).

III. Conclusion

For the reasons explained above, we find that the definition of "surface coal mining operations" in SMCRA section 701(28) is ambiguous as to whether Congress intended it to include subsidence, and therefore, whether subsidence is among the prohibitions contained in section 522(e) is likewise ambiguous. We conclude that the Secretary's interpretation, albeit perhaps not the "most natural" reading, is a reasonable one, and therefore we defer to that interpretation in accordance with the requirements of *Chevron*. We reverse the decision of the District Court and uphold the validity of the regulation.

SENTELLE, Circuit Judge

2. Mining: Surface & Mineral Rights

Dave Fredley, *Surface and Mineral Rights and the Weeks Act*

32 Forest History Today, Spring/Fall 2011*

One oft-overlooked aspect of the Weeks Act has to do with who owns the subsurface mineral rights of land purchased under the act. This issue, recently the focus of a federal lawsuit, reminds us that the Weeks Act will have an impact on land management for years to come. It also serves as a reminder that the eastern national forests have management issues rarely encountered on the western national forests established from the public domain.

The Weeks Act of 1911 and the establishment of the eastern national forests may seem like ancient history, but the U.S. Forest Service has recently been reminded that the wording of the act is just as important today as it was 100 years ago.

On September 20, 2011, the U.S. Court of Appeals for the Third Circuit determined that the Forest Service was misinterpreting its authority over development of private mineral rights beneath the surface of lands acquired by purchase under the Weeks Act. The Forest Service had argued that the Organic Act of 1897 gave the Forest Service the authority to require mineral owners to get approval prior to development. The court disagreed and confirmed earlier decisions that the Organic Act applied to lands reserved from the public domain (mainly western national forests) and not to lands acquired by purchase pursuant to the Weeks Act.

When the Weeks Act was written, the purchase of surface rights only, with the mineral estate remaining in private ownership, was an issue that needed to be addressed. Many of the lands in the East were either known to have oil, gas, coal, and stone or had high potential for mineral development. Parcels were sold to the Forest Service under different arrangements. The seller (the fee owner) might convey both the land and the minerals beneath ("surface and mineral estate"), or he might convey only the surface, having reserved the subsurface rights to himself or having sold them to a third party ("reserved mineral rights"). Section 9 of the Weeks Act specifically allowed "reservation" of the mineral estate and mandated that any rules regarding the removal of those minerals be expressed in the deed. However, in some cases, the surface was sold with no contractual relationship between a third-party mineral estate owner and the new surface owner ("out-standing mineral rights").

Whether the mineral rights were reserved or outstanding, prior to purchase of the surface, the Forest Service and the National Forest Reservation Commission, which approved all purchases, had to determine that the exercise of private mineral rights would not substantially impair the value of the surface estate for national forest purposes. Congress specifically stated in a 1913 amendment to the Weeks Act that "acquisition by the United States shall in no case be defeated because of located or defined rights-of-way, easements, and reservations, which, from their nature will, in the opinion of the National Forest Reservation Commission and the secretary of Agriculture, in no manner interfere with the use of the lands so encumbered, for the purposes of the Act."

* Dave Fredley is a federally certified mineral examiner and a former assistant director of Minerals and Geology for the U.S. Forest Service. The author [Fredley] expresses appreciation to Craig Mayer, General Counsel, Pennsylvania General Energy, for his contributions to and review of this paper.

PUBLIC LANDS VERSUS PRIVATE RIGHTS

Over the past century, the Forest Service acquired approximately 21 million acres under the Weeks Act in the eastern United States. Owners reserved minerals in about 13 percent of the area, and minerals are outstanding in about 20 percent more. This divided ownership arrangement has created management challenges for the Forest Service. One example is the Allegheny National Forest, in northwestern Pennsylvania. It contains two designated wilderness areas, a national recreation area, and two Wild and Scenic Rivers on its 517,000 acres. But oil was being produced on or near the lands acquired for the Allegheny for a half-century before the Weeks Act passed. The national forest is so oil-rich that 93 percent of the acquired surface is underlain by private mineral estate, and roughly 8,000 oil wells are currently operating. Minard Oil Company, the oldest continuously operating oil driller in the world and the first to drill in America, is just one of the many companies, and it was also the lead appellant in the September 2011 circuit court case.

For decades the Allegheny managers dealt with private mineral owners almost on a handshake, a cooperative approach that goes back to the instructions in the Forest Service's first *Use Book*, published in 1905. Because drilling or mining activity might involve clearing timber or building roads, private mineral owners would provide at least 60 days' notice of intent, and the agency would issue a notice to proceed. As a result of a settlement with environmental groups in 2009, however, the Forest Service changed its policy and postponed issuance of the go-ahead notices until a forest-wide environmental impact study, which might take several years, could be completed. The moratorium, the appellants said, caused irreparable injury to owners by depriving them of "unique oil and gas extraction opportunities." Forest Service employees who testified stated that individualized assessment of drilling and mining applications had "hindered forest management, resulting in duplicative roads or development facilities for adjoining pieces of land, and unnecessary clearing of the forest." The environmental groups that were party to the suit asserted that the natural beauty of the Allegheny had been impaired. The district court issued a preliminary injunction against the Forest Service; the Third Circuit required the agency to return to its prior process. Both courts ruled that the agency's approval was not required for surface access.

Private mineral estate also exists in wilderness areas where the surface was acquired pursuant to the Weeks Act. According to a 1984 report of the General Accounting Office (GAO), the Boundary Waters Canoe Area Wilderness on the Superior National Forest has 640,000 acres of private mineral estate; in the Otter Creek Wilderness on the Monongahela National Forest, 96 percent of the mineral estate is privately owned; and in the Cranberry Wilderness on the Monongahela, 90 percent of the mineral estate is privately owned. Moreover, Congress designated the Beaver Creek Wilderness on the Daniel Boone National Forest even though 99 percent of the mineral estate was privately owned and evidence of previous uses included several abandoned deep coal mines, a cemetery, a bridge, and roads. Thus the Forest Service faces a quandary in management of wilderness areas. Does the agency allow the mineral owners development of their constitutionally protected property rights, or does it purchase those mineral rights? GAO found that 23 eastern wilderness areas contained private mineral rights and estimated it would cost hundreds of millions of dollars to purchase them.

DEVELOPMENT OF FEDERALLY OWNED MINERALS

The majority of Weeks Act lands were acquired in fee, with the mineral estate acquired by the federal government. In 1916 Congress authorized the secretary of Agriculture to permit the prospecting, development, and utilization of those acquired mineral resources. The first Forest Service regulations provided for prospecting permits, preference rights upon the discovery of a valuable mineral deposit, and mining permits. An annual fee for rental was required. Both the preamble to the 1917 regulations and their 1932 revision specifically excluded their application to "mineral rights reserved by the grantors." This exclusion applied as well to outstanding mineral rights, those owned by third parties. Since 1917, nothing has changed in the law to suggest that Forest Service regulations regarding prospecting permits and leases for mineral resources acquired by the federal government have any applicability to reserved or outstanding mineral estates. Private mineral rights remain regulated and governed, as they have since the Weeks Act was passed, by state law. A recent controversy concerned whether common sandstone was a reserved mineral estate subject to development by a private mineral owner and whether the Forest Service regulations and instructions applied to the reserved or outstanding mineral estates. The court determined that sandstone was a mineral that could be developed by the subsurface owner, and that the Forest Service regulations were not applicable.

Further complicating management of the Weeks Act national forests is the sharing of authority with the Department of the Interior. The authority to allow the development of federal oil and gas, coal, oil shale, and other resources was modified in 1947 by the Mineral Leasing Act for Acquired Lands, which gave the secretary of the Interior the responsibility to develop regulations to lease minerals acquired pursuant to the Weeks Act. Today there are 2,517 leases on 1.6 million acres of Weeks Act-acquired minerals on eastern national forests. Authority to lease hardrock minerals (gold, copper, nickel, lead) was transferred from the secretary of Agriculture to the secretary of the Interior in 1946.

Mineral exploration and development on Weeks Act lands have been continuous for the 100 years since the act was passed. Because Weeks Act lands provide the nation with oil, gas, coal, stone, and other valuable minerals, the Forest Service will, as it did on the Allegheny National Forest, have to find a way to balance public opinion and forest management goals with private rights, and do so within the existing historical and legal framework.

Respect for the private property rights of subsurface mineral was part of the Weeks Act, as was direction to the Forest Service to cooperate with forest users. Soon after the act took effect, Congress gave authority to the Forest Service to allow development of the mineral estate that had been acquired, and that authority was later transferred to the secretary of the Interior. Active mineral leasing, exploration, and development continue today on those federally acquired minerals.

Language penned 100 years ago still speaks loud and clear to us today. On April 15, 1910, while reviewing the final version of the Weeks Act, the House Committee on Agriculture noted: "It will be observed from this review of the provisions of the bill that the interests of the people are carefully safeguarded at every point beyond any possibility of invasion, except by collusion of highest officials of the legislative, executive, and administrative branches of the Government."

———————

Hobbs v. Hutson

733 S.W.2d 269 (Tex. App. 1987)

CORNELIUS, Chief Justice.

This is a suit to determine ownership of royalty in lignite produced from fifty-three acres of land in Titus County. The dispute centers around the proper construction of a mineral reservation.

Marshall Hobbs and others, herein called "Hobbs," owned the land prior to 1956. They sold it to O.L. Hale in September of 1956 by deed containing this reservation:

> SUBJECT, however, to one-sixteenth (1/16th) non-participating royalty interest heretofore reserved in the deed from Marshall Hobbs et ux Ruth and Inez Young et vir Mitchell, to Ernest Milton Hobbs, dated March 15, 1954, recorded in volume 207, page 303 of the Deed Records of Titus County, Texas.

> SAVE AND EXCEPT, However, that the grantors herein reserve unto themselves, their heirs, executors and administrators, a one-sixteenth (1/16th) non-participating royalty interest (the same being a one-half (1/2) of the usual one-eighth (1/8th) royalty in and to eleven-twelfths (11/12ths) of all of the oil, gas and minerals, on and under and that may be produced from the above described land herein conveyed, for the period of twenty-five (25) years from the date hereof and as long thereafter as oil, gas or other minerals or either of them is produced or mined from the lands described herein, in paying or commercial quantities. If, at the expiration of said term, oil, gas or otherminerals (sic), or either of them is not produced or mined from said land or any portion thereof, in paying or commercial quantities this contract shall be null and void, and the grantors' rights herein reserved shall terminate.

By mesne conveyances, C.W. Hutson and Helen Hutson, in 1966 acquired title to the land subject to the quoted reservation. The Hutsons later sold the surface to Paul Boggs, reserving one-half of the coal. Boggs in turn sold the land to L.D. Cross, reserving and excepting all of the coal and lignite.

In February of 1956, the Hobbses sold to J.W. Caviness, trustee, a mineral lease on the land in question which specifically covered "clay, coal, lignite and other minerals" but did not cover oil and gas. The lease was ratified by the Hutsons on December 19, 1968. Lignite is being mined from the land by strip mining within 200 feet of the surface. The royalties in dispute are being paid into the registry of the court for disposition according to the decision as to their ownership.

The Hobbses contend that the lignite was included in their mineral reservation. The Hutsons contend that the lignite, under the holdings of *Acker v. Guinn*, 464 S.W.2d 348 (Tex.1971), and *Reed v. Wylie*, 597 S.W.2d 743 (Tex.1980), is part of the surface and was not included in the reservation, and that they own the lignite by virtue of their reservation when they sold the land to Boggs. The Hobbses counter that if the reservation did not as a matter of law include lignite, the conveyance from them to Hale should be reformed to include it specifically because the parties to the conveyance intended lignite to be included and were mutually mistaken in believing that the effect of the words they used in the reservation had that legal effect.

Both parties sought judgment in the trial court declaring that they owned the lignite. The Hobbses also filed a counterclaim designated a "cross-action," seeking reformation of the conveyance and reservation. Both parties moved for summary judgment. The trial court denied the Hobbs motion and granted the Hutson motion, thereby ruling against the Hobbses as a matter of law on both their claim for declaratory judgment and their claim for reformation. We have concluded that the trial court was correct in ruling that the lignite was not included in the reservation, but that summary judgment against the claim for reformation should not have been granted because the summary judgment proof failed to conclusively defeat the Hobbses' claim in that regard.

Texas has adopted the rule that a reservation between private parties covering oil, gas and other minerals does not include near surface lignite unless the reservation specifically or expressly includes lignite. *Schwarz v. State*, 703 S.W.2d 187 (Tex.1986); *Moser v. U.S. Steel Corp.*, 676 S.W.2d 99 (Tex.1984); *Reed v. Wylie*, supra; *Acker v. Guinn*, supra. Lignite within 200 feet of the surface is "near surface" as a matter of law. *Reed v. Wylie*, supra. The rule is based on a presumed general intent that a surface owner would not consent to the reservation of a substance when the surface must be destroyed to mine it, unless a specific intent to the contrary is expressed in the instrument. No such specific intent is expressed in the reservation in question here, so lignite is not included.

The Hobbses argue that the quoted rule applies only to disputes between surface owners and mineral owners, and that a specific intent rule should apply when the dispute is between only royalty or mineral claimants, as here. Be that as it may, when the estate here was created by the reservation, the parties to the transaction were surface owners and mineral owners. Thus, the presumed general intent rule applied and is binding on subsequent owners absent the presence of overriding equitable claims or considerations. The trial court correctly concluded that, by the terms of the reservation, lignite was not included.

We find, however, that summary judgment should not have been granted to the Hutsons against the Hobbses' claim for reformation.

Reformation may be granted in disputes of this kind on the basis of a mutual mistake of the parties as to the legal effect of the language used in the reservation, i.e., when the parties believed and intended that the legal effect of a reservation of "oil, gas and minerals" would include lignite. *Reed v. Wylie*, supra. The Hobbses pleaded such a state of facts and supported their claim by summary judgment evidence that all parties to the reservation in question intended, believed and were told by their lawyer that the reservation as a matter of law included lignite.

One of the Hutsons' defenses against reformation was that they were innocent purchasers without notice of any mutual mistake. If they sustain that position it will defeat the Hobbses' right to reformation, *Reed v. Wylie*, supra at 749; *Miles v. Martin*, 159 Tex. 336, 321 S.W.2d 62 (1959), but to be entitled to summary judgment on that basis, their summary judgment proof must have *conclusively demonstrated* that the claim for reformation cannot prevail. They attempted to demonstrate that by the affidavit of C.W. Hutson in which he stated that "[a]t the time of purchase of said property, I was not advised by anyone that there was a mistake in the reservations ... nor was I ever advised that the coal and lignite was to be considered part of the reservations...."

The Hobbses' summary judgment proof included, among other things, the mineral lease they executed in 1956 which specifically excluded oil and gas, described lignite and coal as minerals, and expressly provided for the mining of lignite by strip mining the surface of the land.

A summary judgment proceeding should not amount to a trial by affidavits or by weighing the relative strength of conflicting facts and inferences, and summary judgment is particularly inappropriate when there are ultimate issues such as notice, intent, uncertainty and the like. *Gaines v. Hamman*, 163 Tex. 618, 358 S.W.2d 557 (1962); *Gulbenkian v.*

Penn, 151 Tex. 412, 252 S.W.2d 929 (1952); *Kolb v. Texas Employers' Insurance Association,* 585 S.W.2d 870 (Tex.Civ.App.—Texarkana 1979, writ ref'd n.r.e.); 4 R. McDonald, *Texas Civil Practice in District and County Courts* § 17.26.12 (rev. 1984). Unless a defendant movant's summary judgment evidence conclusively negates one or more of the essential elements of the plaintiff's case, summary judgment should not be granted against the plaintiff.

C.W. Hutson's affidavit only stated that he was not *advised* that lignite was intended to be reserved, and there is no summary judgment evidence that Helen Hutson was lacking in knowledge. Moreover, a land purchaser has constructive notice of every provision and recital that appears in any instrument in his chain of title. *Cooksey v. Sinder,* 682 S.W.2d 252 (Tex.1984); *Westland Oil Development Corp. v. Gulf Oil Corp.,* 637 S.W.2d 903 (Tex.1982). Thus, the Hutsons were charged with knowledge of every provision and recital in the lease, and if any fact or recital therein would put a reasonable man upon inquiry, they were also charged with notice of whatever such an inquiry would have revealed. *Miles v. Martin,* supra; *Gulf Production Co. v. Continental Oil Co.,* 139 Tex. 183, 164 S.W.2d 488 (1942); *Texas Osage Co-operative Royalty Pool v. Clark,* 314 S.W.2d 109 (Tex.Civ.App.—Amarillo 1958), *writ ref'd n.r.e. per curiam,* 159 Tex. 441, 322 S.W.2d 506 (1959); *Wessels v. Rio Bravo Oil Co.,* 250 S.W.2d 668 (Tex.Civ.App.—Eastland 1952, writ ref'd); *Blocker v. Davis,* 241 S.W.2d 698 (Tex.Civ.App.—Fort Worth 1951, writ ref'd n.r.e.); *Myers v. Crenshaw,* 116 S.W.2d 1125 (Tex.Civ.App.—Texarkana 1938), *aff'd,* 134 Tex. 500, 137 S.W.2d 7 (1940); *Wilkerson v. Ward,* 137 S.W. 158 (Tex.Civ.App.1911, writ ref'd). The lease's description of lignite as a mineral might or might not be sufficient, depending upon all of the circumstances, to apprise a reasonable person that the previous owners intended to include lignite in a reservation of "other minerals," or to put them to further inquiry to determine the facts. But the characterization of lignite as a mineral, as said with reference to an analogous situation in *Miles v. Martin,* supra, 321 S.W.2d at 69:

> [m]ight well suggest to a prudent purchaser that the provisions and legal effect of the deed were not in accordance with the agreement and understanding of the parties. Whether a person of ordinary prudence with knowledge of this recital would have been put on inquiry and whether a diligent search would have led to a discovery of the mistake are issues to be determined by the trier of fact under all the evidence.

In view of the recorded mineral lease which specifically described lignite as a mineral and the incomplete nature of C.W. Hutson's summary judgment proof, a lack of notice was not conclusively established, and the issue of notice is one of fact to be determined upon a trial. *See Rio Bravo Oil Co. v. Hunt Petroleum Corp.,* 455 S.W.2d 722 (Tex.1970).

The district court correctly denied the Hobbses' motion for summary judgment. Since there is only one judgment, however, and we find it incorrectly granted summary judgment on the claim for reformation, we reverse the judgment and remand the cause for trial on the claim for reformation. *See Reed v. Wylie,* supra at 749.

Notes & Questions

1. The Weeks Act: The implications of private mineral ownership under U.S. National Forests. As explored in the article *Surface and Mineral Rights and the Weeks Act* above, a significant portion of mineral interests underlying some National Forests are privately owned. Consider some of the following questions:

a. What is the ownership in national forests close to you? Consider the Monongahela National Forest in West Virginia; the Pisgah National Forest in North Carolina; the George Washington National Forest in Virginia; etc....

b. Is this an issue that is primarily faced in eastern National Forests? Are National Forests in the western states plagued with split ownership issues?

c. The article *Surface and Mineral Rights and the Weeks Act* suggests that private mineral holders will likely be permitted to continue to develop their mineral estates underlying National Forest lands. If this is correct, what steps can be taken to minimize the impacts of drilling on these lands?

2. What exactly is "unconventional production" or production from "unconventional formations or sources"?

3. Strip Mining

Bragg v. West Virginia Coal Ass'n
248 F.3d 275 (4th Cir. 2001)

Niemeyer, J. (before Luttig and Williams, JJ.):

This case, which is of great importance to the citizens of West Virginia, was commenced by some of its citizens and an environmental group against the Director of the West Virginia Division of Environmental Protection to challenge his issuance of permits for mountain-top-removal coal mining in the State. The complaint alleged that the Director "has routinely approved surface coal mining permits which decapitate the State's mountains and dump the resulting waste in nearby valleys, burying hundreds of miles of headwaters of West Virginia's streams," and it requested an injunction prohibiting the further issuance of such permits.

The public concern over this issue is demonstrated by the remarkably broad spectrum of interests represented in these proceedings, as well as by their unusual alliances, in both the political and legal arenas. On one side of the dispute are plaintiffs, consisting of a group of private citizens and environmental groups who oppose West Virginia's current permitting practices, and they enjoy the support of the U.S. Environmental Protection Agency. On the other side are the coal mining companies, who are allied with the United Mine Workers of America and the West Virginia State political establishment, all of whom favor current mining practices. And, until this litigation was commenced, these practices had the approval of the U.S. Army Corps of Engineers, although the United States' interests are now aligned with the position taken by the U.S. Environmental Protection Agency.

Following extensive and careful consideration of motions for summary judgment on the substantive issues presented and cross-motions to dismiss, the district court denied the motions to dismiss, found that West Virginia's approval of mountaintop mining practices violated both federal and State law, and enjoined the State from issuing further permits that authorize dumping of mountain rock within 100 feet of intermittent and perennial streams.

Because we conclude that the doctrine of sovereign immunity bars the citizens from bringing their claims against an official of West Virginia in federal court, we vacate the district court's injunction and remand with instructions to dismiss the citizens' complaint without prejudice so that they may present their claims in the proper forum. We affirm, however, the district court's earlier consent decree approving a settlement of some of the claims asserted. The reasons for our rulings follow.

I

Mountaintop-removal coal mining, while not new, only became widespread in West Virginia in the 1990s. Under this method, to reach horizontal seams of coal layered in mountains, the mountaintop rock above the seam is removed and placed in adjacent valleys; the coal is extracted; and the removed rock is then replaced in an effort to achieve the original contour of the mountain. But because rock taken from its natural state and broken up naturally "swells," perhaps by as much as 15 to 25%, the excess rock not returned to the mountain—the "overburden"—remains in the valleys, creating "valley fills." Many valley fills bury intermittent and perennial streams and drainage areas that are near the mountaintop. Over the years, the West Virginia Director of Environmental Protection (the "Director" or "State Director"), as well as the U.S. Army Corps of Engineers, has approved this method of coal mining in West Virginia.

The disruption to the immediate environment created by mountaintop mining is considerable and has provoked sharp differences of opinion between environmentalists and industry players. *See, e.g.*, Penny Loeb, *Shear Madness*, U.S. News & World Rept., Aug. 11, 1997. As Loeb reported these differences of opinion, environmentalists decry the "startling" change in the topography, which leaves the land more subject to floods, results in the pollution of streams and rivers, and has an "incalculable" impact on wildlife. The environmentalists also criticize the mining process itself, which cracks foundations of nearby houses, causes fires, creates dust and noise, and disrupts private wells. The coal companies concede that the process changes the landscape, but note on the positive side that land is reclaimed, that grass, small shrubs, and trees are planted, and that waterfowl ponds are added. Moreover, the companies observe that mining is critical to the West Virginia economy and creates high-paying jobs in the State.

In July 1998, Patricia Bragg, along with eight other West Virginia citizens and the West Virginia Highlands Conservancy (collectively "Bragg"), commenced this action against officials of the U.S. Army Corps of Engineers and the State Director. Bragg alleged that the State Director, in granting surface coal mining permits, "engaged in an ongoing pattern and practice of violating his non-discretionary duties under the Surface Mining Control and Reclamation Act [of 1977, 30 U.S.C. § 1201 et seq.] and the West Virginia state program approved under that statute." More particularly, she alleged that the Director consistently issued permits to mining operations, without making requisite findings, that (1) authorized valley fills, (2) failed to assure the restoration of original mountain contours, and (3) violated other environmental protection laws. She asserted that the Director violated his federal- and State-law duty to "withhold approval of permit applications that are not complete and accurate and in compliance with all requirements of the state program." She also alleged that the Corps of Engineers breached its duties under federal law.

The Director moved to dismiss the complaint, asserting that Bragg's claims were barred by the Eleventh Amendment and that the court, in any case, lacked subject matter jurisdiction. He argued that although only injunctive relief and declaratory judgments against him in his official capacity were sought, the *Ex parte Young* exception to Eleventh Amendment immunity did not apply because Bragg's claims arose under State law. The district court disagreed and permitted Bragg's suit to proceed against the Director.

All but two counts of the complaint were settled,[1] and the court resolved Counts 2 and 3 on motions for summary judgment. Both of these counts addressed a West Virginia regulation, enacted to conform with a federal regulation, that established 100-foot "buffer zones" around "perennial" and "intermittent" streams, within which surface mining activities may not disturb the land, unless the State agency "specifically authorizes" such activities after making certain findings. W. Va. Code St. R. tit. 38 §2-5.2; *see also* 30 C.F.R. §816.57 (the federal counterpart).2 Count 2 alleged that the Director engaged in a pattern and practice of approving mountaintop removal operations without even attempting to make the required findings, and Count 3 alleged that because valley fills inherently have an adverse effect upon stream ecology and cause violations of water quality standards, the findings required by the State regulation could never be made, at least not accurately, for valley fill permits. In entering summary judgment in favor of Bragg, the district court ruled (1) that "the Director has a nondiscretionary duty to make the findings required under the buffer zone rule before authorizing any incursions, including valley fills, within one hundred feet of an intermittent or perennial stream." *Bragg v. Robertson*, 72 F. Supp. 2d 642, 661 (S.D. W. Va. 1999); and (2) that "the Director has a nondiscretionary duty under the buffer zone rule to deny variances for valley fills in intermittent and perennial streams because they necessarily adversely affect stream flow, stream gradient, fish migration, related environmental values, water quality and quantity, and violate state and federal water quality standards," id. at 663. Based on these rulings, the court enjoined the Director "from approving any further surface mining permits under current law that would authorize placement of excess spoil in intermittent and perennial streams for the primary purpose of waste disposal." Id. The district court stayed its injunction, however, pending appeal to this court. See *Bragg v. Robertson*, 190 F.R.D. 194, 196 (S.D. W. Va. 1999).

The State Director appealed, challenging not only the district court's substantive rulings on Counts 2 and 3, but also its rulings that the Eleventh Amendment did not bar this suit against him and that the federal court had jurisdiction to consider Bragg's claims. Coal mining companies and coal associations, that had intervened in the case, also appealed, again contesting the district court's substantive rulings on Counts 2 and 3 and challenging the district court's jurisdiction both to enter the injunction and to enter the February 17, 2000 consent decree approving the settlement of the other claims against the Director. Finally, the United States appealed, challenging the breadth of the district court's injunction.

II

The Surface Mining Control and Reclamation Act of 1977 ("SMCRA") was enacted to strike a balance between the nation's interests in protecting the environment from the adverse effects of surface coal mining and in assuring the coal supply essential to the nation's energy requirements. *See* 30 U.S.C. § 1202(a), (d), (f); *see also Hodel v. Va. Mining & Reclamation Ass'n*, 452 U.S. 264, 268–69 (1981). The Act accomplishes these purposes through a "cooperative federalism," in which responsibility for the regulation of surface coal mining in the United States is shared between the U.S. Secretary of the Interior and State regulatory authorities. *See* H.R. Rep. No. 95-218, at 57 (1977) (hereinafter "Legislative History"), *reprinted in* 1977 U.S.C.C.A.N. 593, 595. Under this scheme, Congress established in SMCRA "minimum national standards" for regulating surface coal mining and encouraged the States, through an offer of exclusive regulatory jurisdiction, to enact their own laws incorporating these minimum standards, as well as any more stringent, but not inconsistent, standards that they might choose. See Legislative History, at 167, reprinted in 1977 U.S.C.C.A.N. at 698; 30 U.S.C. § 1255(b).

To implement this cooperative federalism, SMCRA directs the U.S. Secretary of the Interior to develop a "federal program" of regulation that embodies the minimum national standards and to consider for approval any "State programs" that are submitted to it for approval. To obtain approval of its program, a State must pass a law that provides for the minimum national standards established as "requirements" in SMCRA and must also demonstrate that it has the capability of enforcing its law. *See* 30 U.S.C. § 1253(a). Once the Secretary is satisfiedthat a State program meets these requirements and approves the program, the State's laws and regulations implementing the program become operative for the regulation of surface coal mining, and the State officials administer the program, *see id.* § 1252(e), giving the State "exclusive jurisdiction over the regulation of surface coal mining" within its borders, *id.* § 1253(a). If, however, a State fails to submit a program for approval, or a program that it submits is not approved, or approval of a State's program is withdrawn because of ineffective enforcement, then the federal program becomes applicable for the State, and the Secretary becomes vested with "exclusive jurisdiction for the regulation and control of surface coal mining and reclamation operations taking place [in the] State." Id. § 1254(a); *see also* Legislative History, at 85–86, reprinted in 1977 U.S.C.C.A.N. at 622.

Thus, SMCRA provides for *either* State regulation of surface coal mining within its borders or federal regulation, but not both. The Act expressly provides that one or the other is exclusive, *see* 30 U.S.C. §§ 1253(a), 1254(a), with the exception that an approved State program is always subject to revocation when a State fails to enforce it, *see id.* §§ 1253(a); 1271(b). Federal oversight of an approved State program is provided by the Secretary's obligation to inspect and monitor the operations of State programs. *See id.* §§ 1267, 1271. Only if an approved State program is revoked, as provided in § 1271, however, does the federal program become the operative regulation for surface coal mining in any State that has previously had its program approved. *See id.* §§ 1254(a), 1271.

In sum, because the regulation is mutually exclusive, either federal law or State law regulates coal mining activity in a State, but not both simultaneously. Thus, after a State enacts statutes and regulations that are approved by the Secretary, these statutes and regulations become operative, and the federal law and regulations, while continuing to provide the "blueprint" against which to evaluate the State's program, "drop out" as operative provisions. They are reengaged only following the instigation of a § 1271 enforcement proceeding by the Secretary of the Interior.

In the case before us, West Virginia submitted a program to the Secretary in 1980 for approval, and the Secretary approved the program in 1981, thus granting West Virginia "primacy" status—a status under which its law exclusively regulates coal mining in the State. *See* 30 C.F.R. § 948.10 (noting the Secretary's approval of West Virginia's plan). As part of this program, the West Virginia legislature enacted its own statute entitled the "Surface Coal Mining and Reclamation Act" (the "West Virginia Coal Mining Act"). *See* W. Va. Code § 22-3-1 *et seq.* As amended, the West Virginia Coal Mining Act vests the Director of the State Division of Environmental Protection with the authority to administer the Act and otherwise to provide for the regulation of surface coal mining within the State. *See* W. Va. Code § 22-3-4. The West Virginia Act sets out minimum performance standards that mirror those found in SMCRA, and the State Director has exercised his statutorily granted power to promulgate State regulations that parallel those issued by the Secretary of the Interior pursuant to the federal Act. *See* 38 W. Va. Code St. R. § 2-1 *et seq.* Thus, since the Secretary's approval of the West Virginia program in 1981, the Director has served as the exclusive permitting authority in the State, and West Virginia has maintained "exclusive jurisdiction," with certain exceptions inherent in the federal oversight provisions, over surface mining regulation within its borders.

III

Bragg brought this action against the State Director under the "citizen suit" provision of SMCRA, which provides in relevant part:

Any person having an interest which is or may be adversely affected may commence a civil action on his own behalf to compel compliance with this chapter—

* * *

(2) against the Secretary or the appropriate State regulatory authority to the extent permitted by the eleventh amendment to the Constitution where there is alleged a failure of the Secretary or the appropriate State regulatory authority to perform any act or duty under this chapter which is not discretionary with the Secretary or with the appropriate State regulatory authority.

The district courts shall have jurisdiction, without regard to the amount in controversy or the citizenship of the parties.

30 U.S.C. § 1270(a)(2).

The State Director asserted below and now contends that, as an official of West Virginia who has been sued in his official capacity, he is immune from suit in federal court under the doctrine of sovereign immunity guaranteed by the Eleventh Amendment. In response to the district court's reliance on *Ex parte Young*, 209 U.S. 123 (1908), to overcome the Eleventh Amendment bar, the Director argues that the *Ex parte Young* exception does not apply because the issues in this case involve enforcement of West Virginia law, not federal law. Acknowledging that Bragg nominally asserts violations of both federal and State law, the Director argues that Bragg actually seeks to compel the Director "to comply with the approved West Virginia surface mining program" because once a State program is approved by the Secretary of the Interior, it is State law, not federal law, that governs. Thus, the Director concludes that the *Ex parte Young* exception for ongoing federal violations does not apply; rather, *Pennhurst State School & Hospital v. Halderman*, 465 U.S. 89 (1984), controls. In *Pennhurst*, the Supreme Court held the *Ex parte Young* doctrine inapplicable to a suit brought against a State official to compel his compliance with State law. *See* 465 U.S. at 106. Bragg, on the other hand, contends that the *Ex parte Young* exception permits suit against the State Director. She argues first that Congress, by enacting 30 U.S.C. § 1270(a)(2), "authorized citizens to bring *Ex parte Young* suits against State officials who have the responsibility to comply with SMCRA and federally-approved State programs under that Act." Second, she asserts that her suit seeks to enforce federal, not State, law because (1) States with federally approved programs are still bound by federal statutory mandates that govern their activities, and (2) the buffer zone regulation promulgated by West Virginia is federal law. Finally, she maintains that West Virginia, in choosing "to submit a state program for federal approval, accepted the federal government's invitation to act as regulators of surface coal mining in the state." She asserts that West Virginia, by participating in the federal program, agreed to submit to federal jurisdiction under 30 U.S.C. § 1270(a)(2), thereby waiving its Eleventh Amendment immunity.

The district court ruled that SMCRA's grant to citizens to bring suits against State regulatory authorities "to the extent permitted by the eleventh amendment," 30 U.S.C. § 1270(a)(2), amounts to an "implicit authorization" to citizens to bring *Ex parte Young* actions against State officials, and cited *Natural Resources Defense Council v. California Department of Transportation*, 96 F.3d 420, 423–24 (9th Cir. 1996), for support. The court also rejected the Director's argument that State law, not federal law, is being enforced because the State law is incorporated into federal law, and cited *Arkansas v. Oklahoma*, 503 U.S. 91, 110 (1992), for support. See *Bragg v. Robertson*, No. 2:98-0636, slip op. at 8 (S.D. W. Va. Oct. 9, 1998).

* * *

B

As we have noted, under SMCRA Congress intended to divide responsibility for the regulation of surface coal mining between the federal government and the States. But characterizing the regulatory structure of SMCRA as "cooperative" federalism is not entirely accurate, as the statute does not provide for shared regulation of coal mining. Rather, the Act provides for enforcement of either a federal program or a State program, but not both. Thus, in contrast to other "cooperative federalism" statutes, SMCRA exhibits extraordinary deference to the States. *See* Mark Squillace, *Cooperative Federalism Under the Surface Mining Control and Reclamation Act: Is This Any Way to Run a Government?*, 15 Envtl. L. Rep. 10039 (1985) (calling SMCRA's "broad delegation" to States "unparalleled"); *cf. Bell Atl. Md.*, 240 F.3d at 300 (describing analogously how the Telecommunications Act of 1996 "partially flooded the existing statutory landscape with specific preempting federal requirements, deliberately leaving numerous islands of State responsibility"). The statutory federalism of SMCRA is quite unlike the cooperative regime under the Clean Water Act, 33 U.S.C. § 1251 *et seq.*, which was construed in *Arkansas v. Oklahoma*, 503 U.S. 91(1992). As the Supreme Court noted there, one of the Clean Water Act's regulations "*effectively incorporate[d]*" State law into the unitary federal enforcement scheme, making State law, in certain circumstances, federal law. *Id.* at 110 (emphasis added). Under SMCRA, in contrast, Congress designed a scheme of mutually exclusive regulation by either the U.S. Secretary of the Interior or the State regulatory authority, depending on whether the State elects to regulate itself or to submit to federal regulation. Because West Virginia isa primacy state, its regulation of surface coal mining on nonfederal lands within its borders is "exclusive." *See* 30 U.S.C. § 1253(a); 30 C.F.R. § 948.10. This federal policy of encouraging "exclusive" State regulation was careful and deliberate. The Act's preliminary findings explain that "because of the diversity in terrain, climate, biologic, chemical, and other physical conditions in areas subject to mining operations, the primary governmental responsibility for developing, authorizing, issuing, and enforcing regulations for surface mining and reclamation operations subject to this chapter should rest with the States." 30 U.S.C. § 1201(f). According to the Act, it is the States, not the federal government, that are to "develop[] and implement[] a program to achieve the purposes of this chapter." *Id.* § 1202(g). To make this point absolutely clear, SMCRA provides explicitly that when States regulate, they do so exclusively, *see id.* § 1253(a), and when the Secretary regulates, he does so exclusively, *see id.* § 1254(a).

Even so, SMCRA does manifest an ongoing federal interest in assuring that minimum national standards for surface coal mining are enforced. But when a State fails to enforce these minimum national standards, it does not automatically forfeit the right of exclusive regulation. SMCRA vindicates its national-standards policy through a limited and ordered federal oversight, grounded in a process that can lead ultimately to the withdrawal of the State's exclusive control. *See* 30 U.S.C. §§ 1271, 1267; *see also In re Permanent Surface Mining Regulation Litig.*, 653 F.2d 514, 520 (D.C. Cir. 1981) (en banc) (hereinafter "*Regulation Litig.*") (describing the oversight process). Until that withdrawal occurs, because an approved State program must include "a *State law* which provides for the regulation of surface coal mining and reclamation operations in accordance with the requirements of this chapter," 30 U.S.C. § 1253(a)(1) (emphasis added), the minimum national standards are attained by State enforcement of its own law. "It is with an approved state law and with state regulations ... that mine operators must comply." *Regulation Litig.*, 653 F.2d at 519; *see also* Background, Surface Coal Mining and Reclamation Operations Final Rule, 53 Fed. Reg. 26728, 26728 (July 24, 1988) (quoting Regulation Litig.).

In sum, even though the States ultimately remain subject to SMCRA, the Act grants "exclusive jurisdiction" to a primacy State (one with an approved program), thereby conditionally divesting the federal government of direct regulatory authority. *See Regulation Litig.*, 653 F.2d at 519; *see also* 30 U.S.C. § 1253(a) (requiring a would-be primacy State to demonstrate that it has "the capability of carrying out the provisions of this chapter"). Therefore, when a State's program has been approved by the Secretary of the Interior, we can look only to State law on matters involving the enforcement of the minimum national standards; whereas, on matters relating to the good standing of a State program, SMCRA remains directly applicable. See *Regulation Litig.*, 653 F.2d at 519 (observing that "judicial appeals of permit decisions are matters of State jurisdiction in which the Secretary plays no role"); *see also* 30 U.S.C. § 1276(e).

* * *

In sum, rather than asking the States to enforce the federal law, Congress through SMCRA invited the States to create their own laws, which would be of "exclusive" force in the regulation of surface mining within their borders. *See Hodel*, 452 U.S. at 289 (noting that under SMCRA, states "enact and administer their own regulatory programs"). An order from an Article III court instructing an officer of such a State to conform his conduct with a duly enacted State law would create an affront to that State's dignity similar to that created by the orders at issue in *Pennhurst*. And particularly when that State's law specifically provides for its own enforcement in a State forum, the concerns that gave rise to the exception of *Ex parte Young* evaporate.

Accordingly, we conclude that Bragg's claims filed against the State Director in federal court are not authorized by the *Ex parte Young* exception to the Eleventh Amendment.

C

Alternatively, Bragg contends that West Virginia waived its sovereign immunity in federal court when it elected to submit its program to the Secretary for approval and thereby accepted the federal government's invitation to act as the regulator of surface coal mining in the State. She argues that in exchange for giving the State the right to regulate surface coal mining, "Congress required the states to agree to submit to federal jurisdiction under [30 U.S.C.] § 1270(a)(2) to review their non-discretionary actions for conformity with federal law" and therefore that the State "waived its immunity." We cannot agree.

"If Congress is not unmistakably clear and unequivocal in its intent to condition a gift or gratuity on a State's waiver of its sovereign immunity, we cannot presume that a State, by accepting Congress' proffer, knowingly and voluntarily assented to such a condition." *Bell Atl. Md.*, 240 F.3d at 292. Congress provided no "unequivocal" warning that States which submit a program for approval by the Secretary thereby waive their immunity. To the contrary, the citizen-suit provision explicitly authorizes a compliance action "against … the appropriate State regulatory authority," but only "to the extent permitted by the eleventh amendment to the Constitution." 30 U.S.C. § 1270(a)(2) (emphasis added). Far from expressing Congress' clear intent that participating States waive Eleventh Amendment immunity, this language actually preserves a State's sovereign immunity. See *Burnette v. Carothers*, 192 F.3d 52, 57 (2d Cir. 1999) (concluding that similar language in the Clean Water Act, the Resource Conservation and Recovery Act, and the Comprehensive Environmental Response, Compensation and Liability Act did not evidence Congress' intent to abrogate state immunity). Accordingly, we reject Bragg's argument that West Virginia waived its sovereign immunity in federal court when it accepted Congress' invitation to assume "exclusive jurisdiction" over the regulation of surface mining within its borders.

* * *

V

For the reasons given, the consent decree of February 17, 2000, is affirmed, but the judgment of the district court enjoining the State Director is vacated, and the case is remanded to the district court with instructions to dismiss Bragg's unsettled claims asserted in Counts 2 and 3 without prejudice to any suit she may wish to pursue in West Virginia State court.

AFFIRMED IN PART, VACATED IN PART, AND REMANDED WITH INSTRUCTION

---

4. Drilling for Oil & Gas

Kent Holsinger and Peter Lemke, *Water, Oil, and Gas: A Legal and Technical Framework*

16 U. Denv. Water L. Rev. 1 (2012)[footnotes omitted]

I. INTRODUCTION

The economic impact of oil and gas operations is tremendous. In 2011, oil and gas generated nearly 10% of all new jobs in the United States. The University of Colorado Leeds School of Business reported $3.1 billion in direct labor income—supporting over 107,000 jobs and $32 billion of economic activity—from oil and gas in Colorado. Remarkable technologies are breathing new life into old oil and gas fields. With hydraulic fracturing and directional drilling, the Rocky Mountain West could produce as much oil and natural gas as the United States currently imports from countries like Saudi Arabia and Venezuela. But hydraulic fracturing requires water. Both the source water used for the process and the water produced subsequent to drilling are heavily regulated under various state and federal laws.

Water demands for hydraulic fracturing are less than a proverbial drop in the bucket. According to the Colorado Department of Natural Resources, water required for hydraulic fracturing will be less than 20,000 acre-feet annually for the next several years. This amounts to less than one tenth of one percent of Colorado's annual water use. By comparison, releases for environmental purposes at a single Colorado reservoir (the Aspinall Unit) exceeded 35,000 acre-feet last year in 2011. And the Platte River Recovery Implementation Program requires Colorado, Wyoming, and Nebraska to provide 130,000 to 150,000 acre-feet per year for the federally listed least turn, pallid sturgeon, and piping plover.

Many water professionals may not realize severance taxes from oil and gas help fund water projects throughout Colorado. Industry contributes over $600 million of severance taxes and annual ad valorem taxes to state and local governments. These taxes help finance water projects through the Colorado Water Conservation Board's ("CWCB") construction loan program. By statute, the first priority for those funds is putting Colorado's compact waters to beneficial use. Other priorities include repair and rehabilitation of existing water storage and delivery systems, maintenance, satellite monitoring, management, and studies. Severance taxes also support Colorado's Species Conservation Trust Fund, which helps provide Endangered Species Act compliance for water right owners around the state.

This Article discusses the integration of oil and gas into the western water law system as well as the legal and technical framework related to water produced from oil and gas operations in Colorado.

II. TECHNICAL ASPECTS OF PRODUCED WATER MANAGEMENT AND TREATMENT

Exploration and production of energy resources like oil and gas are inextricably linked with technical challenges relating to water. Freshwater sources required to start a well and begin production ("source water") may be in short supply or may require treatment prior to use. On the other end of development, the flow of produced water from production wells may require treatment prior to reuse, discharge, or disposal. This section first provides an overview of production methods. Second, it explains the water issues related to various production methods. Third, it explains how the Clean Water Act and Safe Drinking Water Act govern these water issues. Last, it describes water management and treatment alternatives required by law in the state of Colorado, and includes cost estimates for their implementation.

A. OVERVIEW OF PRODUCTION METHODS

Oil and gas production is a multi-step process and involves the use of water at every step. The first step is exploration. During the exploration phase, geologists perform extensive surveys of a potential formation, including drilling test wells. Second, producers drill a vertical well into the target formation. Water is required to facilitate the drilling process. For conventional production, after the initial well is drilled and cased, oil or gas can flow up the well shaft and little else is required. Unconventional production requires more complicated techniques. For example, in coalbed methane ("CBM") extraction, a coal seam must be completely dewatered before production can occur, which results in the extraction of large quantities of "produced water." With other forms of production like hydraulic fracturing ("fraccing"), producers may need to drill horizontal wells and inject fluid (mostly water) at high pressure to create micro-fractures, allowing oil or gas to flow freely to the production well. As conventional and non-CBM unconventional wells approach the end of their life spans, the wells start to produce significantly less quantities of oil and gas and increasing amounts of water. This produced water is highly regulated and must be dealt with in very specific ways.

On a macro scale, economics and an emphasis on energy independence have led to an increase in production activity from unconventional resources in the United States. Geographically, unconventional resources are widespread, from the Rocky Mountain West to North Dakota, Texas, and the northeast United States. The abundance or scarcity of surface water and groundwater, competing demand for that water, and a variety of state and local regulations across diverse regions all play into the technical challenges associated with the management and treatment of produced water.

It is important to note that water issues in oil and gas exploration and production are highly site-specific. There is no typical characterization for produced water. The water quality characteristics can vary greatly within a production basin or even within a pro-duction-well field. Nor is there a single most economically or technically effective process for treating produced water. Produced water characterization before treatment (influent) and quality requirements for water in its post-treatment disposition (effluent) are the key drivers in the water management/treatment decision-making process.

On the broadest level, oil and gas production methods are either conventional or un-conventional. Conventional production refers to resources that are relatively easy to develop. This type of production often occurs in highly permeable formations like limestone or dolomite formations with interconnected pore spaces. Drilling into a conventional oil or gas reservoir will result in the relatively free flow of product to the surface. In contrast, resources that are more tightly bound in the formation, requiring additional steps beyond simply drilling vertical wells, define unconventional production. Examples of unconventional resources include low permeability formations that have to be fractured to allow production flow, or CMB, which is typically bound in coal seams near the presence of groundwater.

1. Conventional Production

Early in conventional production, the resource-bearing formations allow for the relatively free flow of the resource to the production well. As the readily recoverable resource becomes increasingly difficult to access, enhanced oil recovery ("EOR") techniques may be required for continued production. EOR methods include chemical flooding, miscible displacement, and thermal recovery, pressurization, steam flooding or hot water flooding.

2. Unconventional Production

Resource-bearing formations that cannot be economically exploited through conventional methods require the use of unconventional production techniques. Tight shale formations and coal beds are examples of unconventional resources. The label "unconventional production" applies to the resource formation rather than just the individual well. Unconventional production techniques are not necessarily innovative or new. For example, unconventional production in tight shales may utilize hydraulic fracturing, a technique that dates back to the 1960s.

Fraccing can involve both vertical and horizontal drilling into formations situated thousands of feet below surface. The primary advantage of horizontal drilling is the ability to reach a greater area of the formation from a single surface well location, in comparison to the multiple vertical wells required to achieve the same areal coverage. This means that with horizontal drilling, there is minimal surface impact *and* maximum production from a single well. The vertical portion of the horizontal well is cased and cemented in order to isolate the producing formation from contact with other formations. Therefore, horizontal drilling and effective well casings cause more gas and/or oil to reach the surface while protecting groundwater resources from contamination by fraccing fluid, gas, or produced water.

In areas where groundwater is relied upon for potable or other beneficial uses, the groundwater formation is typically found at a depth of no more than several hundred feet, while the gas-bearing shale formation may be at a depth of over seven thousand feet. This means a properly executed well casing and cementing will provide minimal probability for contamination of the groundwater resource by fraccing fluid or produced gas. See Figure 1 below for a visual representation of the casing and depth of a horizontal well, and isolation of the gas bearing formation from drinking water aquifer resources.

The fraccing process follows horizontal drilling. Fraccing creates micro-fissures in the producing formation. Fraccing fluid is over ninety-eight percent water, and includes sand, which acts as a "proppant" to hold the micro-fissures open after the fraccing process is complete, and allows for maximum gas flow. In addition to sand, a completed frac requires multiple injections with a variety of chemistries (for example, high viscosity to carry the sand, low viscosity to release the sand, friction reducers, corrosion preventers, and biocides). Completion of a single frac can require between five hundred thou sand and five million gallons of water. This is largely a one-time use, with fifty to ninety percent of the injected fluid remaining below ground. Between ten and forty percent of the flowback that returns up the wellbore after fraccing is frac fluid. The majority of this flowback occurs in the first several weeks after production begins. However, produced water may continue to flow throughout the productive life of the well. In total, fraccing water constitutes a miniscule percentage of the Colorado's total water use; and oil and gas development accounts for just one tenth of one percent of the total water use in the state.

3. Coalbed Methane

CBM resources typically do not require the use of hydraulic fracturing or horizontal drilling to optimize gas production. Coal beds are shallower formations, relative to tight shales, so they are closer to groundwater formations and water wells and are relatively porous and naturally fractured. CBM is considered an unconventional resource because the coal is both the source and storage reservoir for the gas. Because the gas is often held in coal seams by the presence of water, dewatering of a CBM formation is necessary to allow for gas flow. And because of its relatively shallow depths, the produced water from CBM development can be of good quality, even very near potable standards. The primary issue related to CBM production may be finding a use or disposal method for the water produced during dewatering of the formation and dealing with affected landowners.

B. WATER QUALITY ISSUES AND RELATED PRECAUTIONS

1. Water Quality Risks

There are a variety of pathways that could potentially result in adverse impacts to surface or groundwater quality as a result of oil and gas production. Wells that are improperly cased or cemented in shallow aquifer zones could provide a contamination route for oil, gas, or production fluids to reach drinking water wells. Surface impoundments that are frequently used to temporarily store produced water near drilling pads prior to reuse or disposal could allow for contamination of shallow aquifers if leaks develop in liner materials. Moreover, breaching or overtopping of surface impoundments may result in the release of produced water or drilling fluids into the surrounding environment. Fencing and bird repellant devices are frequently used, but even when properly maintained and contained, surface impoundments can present environmental risks to wildlife.

In a produced water treatment scenario, unexpected changes in the treatment process may result in the release of inadequately treated effluent. Spikes in contaminant loads or surges in flow are potential causes of process excursions. Failures of treatment process equipment or controls could also result in release of inadequately treated effluent.

In an evaporation pond disposal scenario, the risks to groundwater, environmental release, and wildlife exposure are similar to those described for well pad surface impoundments. Deep injection well disposal also presents risks of contamination due to well failure or surface spill. When produced water is hauled by tanker truck from a production site to a distant disposal site, as is common in the Marcellus shale formation, transportation hazards may also pose environmental risks. These risks include traffic accidents, leaks, spills associated with loading and unloading the tankers, and the resulting impacts on human health or the environment. Along with environmental risks are the "nuisances" of truck traffic such as noise, traffic congestion, and dust kicked up on unpaved roads. A 5,000,000-gallon frac could require transport of 500 to 1,000 truckloads of water.

All of the environmental release scenarios just described would only occur due to a failure of industry standards and regulations. As noted above, the production and disposal wells are cased and cemented to provide an isolation barrier between the well and any aquifers that the well passes through. For pond leakage to reach groundwater would usually require the simultaneous failures of a double liner system and leak detection instrumentation. Pond overflow would only occur where a storm overfilled the pond in excess of its capacity. Produced water treatment systems normally include an influent equalization basin to buffer the treatment process from influent "spikes," and real-time monitoring of critical-process control parameters, allowing system operators to take corrective actions.

2. Federal and State Laws Regulating Water Quality

Both federal and state laws govern water quality issues associated with produced water. The federal regulatory scheme includes the Clean Water Act ("CWA") and Safe Drinking Water Act ("SDWA").

i. The Clean Water Act

In 1972, Congress enacted the Federal Water Pollution Control Act, also known as the Clean Water Act. The CWA imposes national, technology-based standards on individual sources to make the nation's water fishable, swimmable, and to eliminate pollutant discharge into navigable waters. The two main programs under the CWA are its point source and nonpoint source programs. The point source program monitors the discharge of pollutants from a specific conveyance. Direct discharges into water systems are permit-controlled through the National Pollutant Discharge Elimination System ("NPDES"). The nonpoint source program governs pollution from nonspecific areas, but regulation of these areas has produced little actual control and is not discussed in this Article.

Either the Environmental Protection Agency ("EPA") or states with EPA-approved programs (called "primacy states") can issue NPDES permits to dischargers meeting "Effluent Limitation Guidelines" in order to regulate "point sources." EPA works with other federal agencies, state and local governments, and Indian Country governments to develop and enforce regulations under existing environmental laws. A point source is "any discernible, confined and discrete conveyance ... from which pollutants are or may be discharged." NPDES grants permits that control the amount and concentration of pollutants discharged directly into streams, lakes, or the ocean by industrial and municipal facilities. All private industrial facilities discharging pollutants into waters of the United States may only discharge subject to stringent technology-based standards. In Colorado, these permits are required for discharges into tributary groundwater.

Section 302 of the CWA authorizes EPA to monitor the overall water quality of a body of water. EPA and states do this by issuing Total Maximum Daily Loads ("TMDLs") that establish the minimum requirements of the CWA for each body of water. All NPDES permits issued by the state or EPA must be in keeping with the TMDLs for the relevant body of water. If existing water quality is better than the minimum requirement, the CWA imposes an "antidegradation" requirement to enforce the status quo. EPA rules clarify sediment from oil and gas construction activities will not trigger NPDES requirements unless the sediment carries oil, pollutants or other hazardous substances.

ii. The Safe Drinking Water Act

The SDWA, also enacted in 1972, is the major federal law that ensures the quality of America's drinking water both above and below ground. Under the SDWA, EPA sets health-based standards for drinking water quality and oversees the states, localities, and water suppliers who implement those standards. EPA regulates these water systems by specifying contaminants and setting limits for them called maximum contaminant levels. EPA also specifies treatment techniques on a "best available technology" standard.

EPA sets two types of standards for roughly ninety total contaminants. The first type of standard is the primary standard, which applies to biological contamination, disinfectants, organic and inorganic chemicals, and radionuclides. The primary standard sets the limit of these contaminants at a point to which their presence in drinking water will result in no known or expected risk to health. The second type of standard is the secondary standard, which creates non-enforceable guidelines regulating contaminants that may cause cosmetic effects or aesthetic effects.

The SDWA also legally defines underground sources of drinking water. Groundwater is considered clean enough for use as drinking water if it has less than 10,000 mg/l of total dissolved solids ("TDS") and currently supplies or contains a sufficient quantity of groundwater to supply a public water system.

Finally, the SDWA has an underground injection control ("UIC") program. This program regulates deep well injection of waste into "dry" wells, thereby assuring underground injection will not endanger drinking water sources. The extent of the regulation depends upon which of five regulatory categories the well encompasses. See Table 1 on the next page for a breakdown of the five regulatory categories.

As evidenced by Table 1, the majority of wells used by the oil and gas industry are either Class II or Class V. As also noted in the chart, Class II wells are deep injection wells. These wells are used in areas where surface impoundments and discharge are technically and economically unfeasible. Class II wells are also used to safely store hydrocarbons once they are produced. These wells must inject into a geologically isolated formation in order to protect USDWs. In order to ensure the integrity of these wells, injection pressure and the geology of the injection zone are carefully examined to ensure beneficial groundwater sources are not contaminated.

The type of Class V wells used by the oil and gas industry are shallow aquifer storage and recovery wells. These wells are most commonly used in CMB production because they inject produced water of sufficient quality, with or without treatment, into relatively shallow wells or back into the coalbed aquifer itself.

Permits for Class II or V wells can be written for a single well or for an area served by multiple wells. Typically, the state oil and gas agency has primacy for issuing permits for Class II wells, as is the case in Colorado where the Colorado Oil and Gas Conservation Commission ("COGCC") issues permits. Conversely, a water quality agency, public health agency, or EPA primarily issues permits for Class V wells.

Certain aquifers are exempted from the SDWA. Exempt aquifers include aquifers that are not and will not be suitable for water supply purposes, aquifers that are "mineral, hydrocarbon or geothermal energy producing," aquifers that are capable of becoming commercially mineral or hydrocarbon energy producing, aquifers that are already contaminated, or aquifers that are located over a Class III mining area subject to collapse.

As a result, water that meets federal drinking water standards is generally considered to be high quality. It is therefore common for permits under a variety of environmental regulatory programs to reference federal drinking water standards.

C. CHEMISTRY OF PRODUCED WATER

Oil- and gas-bearing formations are often encased in briny, non-potable groundwater. When drilling a well, this water will often flow up the well bore to the surface and is sub-

Table 1: Types of Wells Under the UIC Program

Class	Basic Description	Level of Monitoring Required	No. of wells Nationwide
Class I	Class I wells inject hazardous and nonhazardous wastes into deep, isolated rock formations that are thousands of feet below the lowermost USDW	The construction, permitting, operating, and monitoring requirements are more stringent for Class I hazardous wells than for the other types of injection wells.	Approximately 550
Class II	Class II wells inject fluids associated with oil and natural gas production. Most of the injected fluid is salt water (brine), which is brought to the surface in the process of producing oil and gas. In addition, brine and other fluids are injected to enhance (improve) oil and gas production.	A state has the option of requesting primacy for Class II wells under either § 1422 or 1425 of the SDWA:	Approximately 1440,000
Class III	Class III wells inject fluids to dissolve and extract minerals such as uranium, salt, copper, and sulfur. More than 50 percent of the salt and 80 percent of the uranium extraction in the United States involves the use of Class III injection wells.	All Class III wells are operated under individual or area permits. Contamination from mining wells is prevented by implementing requirements for mining well operators before commencing injection, during operation, and when injection is complete.	Approximately 18,500
Class IV	Class IV wells are shallow wells used to inject hazardous or radioactive wastes into or above a geologic formation that contains a USDW.	In 1984, EPA banned the use of Class IV injection wells for disposal of hazardous or radioactive waste. Now, these wells may only be operated as part of an EPA- or state-authorized groundwater cleanup action.	There are about 32 waste clean-up sites with Class IV wells
Class V	Most Class V wells are shallow disposal systems that depend on gravity to drain fluids directly in the ground. There are over 20 well subtypes that fall into the Class V category and these wells are used by individuals and businesses to inject a variety of nonhazardous fluids underground. Most of these Class V wells are unsophisticated shallow disposal systems that include storm water drainage wells, cesspools, and septic system leach fields. However, the Class V well category also includes more complex wells that are typically deeper and often used at commercial or industrial facilities.	EPA established minimum requirements to prevent injection wells from contaminating underground sources of drinking water (USDWs). Operators must:— Submit inventory information to their permitting authority and verify that they are authorized to inject. The permitting authority will review the information to be sure that the well will not endanger a USDW.—Operate the wells in a way that does not endanger USDWs.—Properly close their Class V well when it is no longer being used. The well should be closed in a way that prevents movement of any contaminated fluids into USDWs.	More than 650,000 Class V wells

sequently called "produced water." Produced water may be present throughout the life of a well. In addition to groundwater, produced water can include "frac flowback." Frac flowback is an initially high flow of produced water from a fraced well. Enhanced oil recovery methods, including the use of steam or hot water flooding, also contribute to the flow of produced water in long-term production.

The chemistry of produced water is extremely variable from site to site. Produced water contaminants may include free oils; gritty solids; finely emulsified oil and other suspended solids; water-soluble organic compounds; and dissolved inorganics including: salts, metals, and naturally occurring radioactive materials. Microbiological components (bacteria) may also be present. Combinations, proportions, and concentrations of contaminants present site-specific challenges in water management.

Further complicating the characterization of produced water is the potential for changes in water quality and quantity over time. Changes in water quality or quantity may occur naturally or may result from enhanced recovery techniques, such as hot water flooding. Understanding the complexities of water chemistry is vital to the decision-making process over the disposition of produced water. The variability in chemical characterization of produced waters is illustrated in Table 2. The complexity and costs of treatment increase when there is a greater variety of contaminants, and/or contaminants at higher concentrations.

Along with the variability in chemical characterization of produced water, there are also a variety of potential end uses. Producers may consider economics, legal requirements, and sustainability when deciding what to do with produced water. Regional environmental conditions, including climate and the abundance or scarcity of surface water and groundwater, also factor into the final disposition of produced water.

1. Economics of Water Management and Treatment

The handling, management, and treatment of produced water fall into operating expenses for oil and gas production ("OPEX"). For Industry, minimizing OPEX results in higher profitability. If ongoing production activities require water resources, such as fraccing or steam flooding, on-site treatment of produced water allows for immediate

Table 2: Chemical Characterization of Produced Waters

Parameter (mg/L)	Wind River, WY	Rifle, CO	Vernal, UT	Trinidad, WI
Total dissolved solids	6,500	14,000	29,000	9,900
Chloride	2,000	8,500	28,500	3,200
Total suspended solids	150	330	150	189
Oil & grease	120	30		200 to 1,900
Gasoline range organics	78	350	55	
Diesel range organics	14	150	100	240
Chemical oxygen demand				4,700

reuse. The economic advantages associated with this type of treatment are twofold: there is reduced demand for fresh water supply and there is reduced volume of wastewater to dispose.

When produced water is not needed on-site for continuing production activities, disposal by deep well injection is typically the most economical choice. Alternatively, hauling water to offsite commercial deep well injection facilities remains an option. In arid and semi-arid regions, disposal by solar evaporation is also an option. However, some states regulate solar evaporation ponds for air emissions. The presence of volatile organic compounds in produced water that may potentially be released into the air may preclude evaporation as a disposal option.

There is a preference for on-site treatment for immediate reuse in fraccing operations. Removal of suspended solids may be the only treatment step required prior to reusing produced water as frac fluid. If the produced water requires more intensive treatment, hauling water offsite to a commercial treatment or disposal facility will likely prove more economical.

Oil and gas prices further complicate the economics of produced water treatment. When the natural gas commodity price is low, gas fields may temporarily shut down only to be put back into production when the price allows for profitable operation. Fields from which it is easier to produce natural gas with less water, or simpler water chemistry, will receive preference.

2. Legal Requirements

Legal drivers for produced water treatment come into play when the best option for final disposition is discharge to the environment, or to a regulated form of reuse. Discharges may be to surface water, groundwater, or land application. Crop irrigation and livestock watering are examples of typical state-regulated reuses. Each of these discharge and reuse options have their own sets of water quality standards, permitting, and long-term monitoring requirements. The range of standards is illustrated in Table 3 on the next page. The viability of any particular discharge or reuse option is dependent on the complexity and cost of treatment required to produce effluent that is compliant with discharge standards. Where multiple discharge options are available, cost usually determines the preferred option.

Municipal wastewater treatment plants may also treat produced water in accordance with a pretreatment permit. Pretreatment permits typically require that produced water will not result in toxicity to microbiological processes in the wastewater treatment plant, and will not pass through the plant untreated. However, this discharge option is used infrequently; municipal treatment facilities may not be in close proximity to production sites, and generally are not designed to remove the contaminants potentially present in produced water.

In Colorado, produced water also affects water rights (as discussed in more detail below). The determination of whether produced water is tributary or nontributary, or whether a vested water right is potentially injured by the flow of produced water from aquifer to the surface, may figure into the level of treatment and how the treated water is reintroduced to the stream.

III. WHAT DO WE DO WITH PRODUCED WATER?

Variability in the chemistry of produced water, variety of potential dispositions, and economic factors provide for an abundance of treatment and management alternatives. Direct disposal, including deep well or evaporation ponds, may be the most expeditious

Table 3: Regulatory and industry standards for discharge and reuse options for produced water, post-treatment. All constituent target values are reported as mg/L, except as noted.

Constituent	NPDES (permitted surface water outfall)	Land application (surface disposal or irrigation use)	Industrial re-use
Total suspended solids	20–30		<50
pH (standard units)	6.5–9	4.5–9	9.8–10.2
Oil and grease	10		1.4
Biological oxygen demand	30–45		30
Chemical oxygen demand			250
Coliform (count/100 mL)	6,000		0
Residual chlorine	2.2–3.6		0.25
Total dissolved solids		480	
Sulfate			192
Chloride	230	250	45–55
Trace metals	<1	<1	<1

of alternatives. If economic disposal options are not available, treatment to an appropriate quality level for onsite reuse is the next logical step. And, while every instance of produced water is different, there are some common characteristics that allow for a "roadmapped" approach to treatment and management planning.

Treatment stages include removal of free oils, fine suspended solids, emulsified oils, dissolved organic compounds, and dissolved inorganic compounds (salts, metals and in some cases naturally occurring radioactive materials). Each stage produces secondary waste by-products, which need to be managed or disposed of. Thus, the general producer's preference is for the simplest treatment process that results in reusable water.

Web-based software programs are used to assist in the decision-making process for treatment of produced water, or to answer the question "how clean is clean?" The U.S. Department of Energy's National Energy Technology Laboratory developed a "Produced Water Management Information Sys tem." This tool provides information for treatment and disposal of produced water subject to EPA regulations for both onshore and offshore production. Figure 2 is an illustration of the framework.

Another useful tool, targeting CBM development in the Mountain West, is the "CBM Produced Water Management Tool." This tool steps through four modules, allowing user input to water quality, treatment selection, beneficial use screening, and economics. The resulting output can be a guide to balanced optimization of treatment efficiency, cost and sustainability—a triple bottom line evaluation.

Because the OPEX costs associated with produced water management can vary drastically, these logic flow diagrams are useful to sort through issues such as regional variability, production methods, reuse, treatment, and disposal options. Regional availability of commercial treatment facilities, mobile treatment equipment available for leased use, or the production company's willingness to make a capital investment in water treatment all figure into the cost of produced water management and treatment.

As a result, it is difficult to quantify the cost to treat produced water. As illustrated above, the relevant considerations include the chemical characterization of produced water; discharge or reuse water quality standards; hauling distance to treatment or disposal; availability of mobile equipment; generation and disposal or secondary waste products; and the potential to offset treatment cost through reducing demand for source water. Reported costs for treatment of produced water range from $0.08 to $12.00 per barrel. NETL reports a more moderate range of treatment costs from $3.00 to $5.00 per barrel. More accurate costs associated with management and treatment of produced water can only be developed on a site-specific basis.

* * *

V. INTEGRATING OIL AND GAS WITH WATER LAWS

A. PRODUCED WATER

Historically, oil and gas wells were regulated at the state level exclusively by the Colorado Oil and Gas Conservation Commission ("COGCC"). In 2009, the Colorado Supreme Court held that water produced during the CMB extraction process constituted a "beneficial use" of the water, subject to administration by the Colorado SEO. Following the Vance decision, the SEO faced the staggering reality that thousands of oil and gas wells in the state could require individual permitting determinations. There was also significant concern on the part of the industry that the SEO could curtail the production of oil and gas in order to protect vested water rights.

To address these issues, the Colorado General Assembly authorized the SEO to undertake an orderly process integrating CBM wells and, where necessary, conventional oil and gas wells into the priority system. These bills amended the GWMA, and specifically section 37-90-137(7), to help provide certainty to water users, oil and gas, and the SEO without jeopardizing vested water rights. Under that authority, the SEO then promulgated "Rules and Regulations for the Determination of the Nontributary Nature of Ground Water Produced Through Wells in Conjunction with the Mining of Minerals" ("Rules").

Over a three-year period, the Colorado General Assembly passed three amendments to section 37-90-137(7) of the GWMA. Colorado House Bill 09-1303 ("HB 09-1303") created specific timelines for compliance and granted the SEO authority to promulgate rules to administer the withdrawal of nontributary groundwater for oil and gas development. Furthermore, HB 09-1303 clarified that (i) nontributary water was not subject to the priority system; (ii) interested parties would have the right to conduct cross-examinations during the rule making; and (iii) judicial review of the rules would be in water court under an Administrative Procedure Act standard of review.

Senate Bill 10-165 extended certain deadlines and provided further permitting guidelines for the SEO. For example, nontributary groundwater produced in oil and gas development does not require a permit, with the exception of CBM development, if the water is not beneficially used. Generally, under these circumstances, water is not deemed beneficially used if it is extracted for the purpose of facilitating oil and gas production and it is disposed of in the same geologic basin from which it was removed. The legislation also exempted non-tributary wells from the landowner consent and the six hundred foot spacing requirement.

These bills created a framework for the SEO to administer groundwater produced during oil and gas development that recognizes the differences between CBM extraction

Table 4: Permit Requirements

Type of Well	Well Permit Required?	Required to Replace Depletions via SEO Substitute Water Supply Plan?	Required to Replace Depletions via Water Court Augmentation Plan?
Conventional Nontributary	NO (unless water put to beneficial use)	NO	NO
Conventional Tributary	YES	YES	YES
CBM Nontributary	YES	NO	NO
CBM Tributary	YES	YES	YES

and other forms of oil and gas development and allows for the integration of oil and gas into the priority system (refer to Table 4 for a chart that explains this framework).

Much of the groundwater associated with oil and gas development is generally very deep and trapped in isolated geologic formations. The Rules include basin-specific rules that define boundaries delineating large areas of land where wells are deemed to be nontributary to any surface stream. The Rules also provided a process for subsequent identification of other such areas.

For those oil and gas wells that the SEO deemed to be tributary, operators in over-appropriated basins must replace their depletions to prevent material injury to vested water rights. Because nontributary groundwater is not administered within Colorado's water rights priority system, a party need not replace depletions for nontributary wells to prevent injury to vested water rights. The rulemaking was an extensive effort that took nearly a year of the SEO's staff's time and a three million-dollar industry investment.

In 2010, many of the same plaintiffs from the Vance case challenged the SEO's authority to promulgate the Rules in lawsuits filed throughout the majority of Colorado's water divisions. Those cases were consolidated case in Division 1 Water Court in Greeley, Colorado. In 2011, the Colorado General Assembly passed legislation to clarify and confirm the SEO's authority for the rulemaking and subsequent adjudications; that appeals and facial challenges to the Rules and nontributary determinations thereunder be held to an APA standard; and the creation of a rebuttable presumption in favor of the SEO's determinations where allege injury in water court as a result of oil and gas development.

Challenges to the SEO Rules. The SEO adopted the Final Rules in December 2009 and the Basin-Specific Rules were incorporated in early 2010. On March 1, 2010, a group of water users and water right holders, including the plaintiffs in Vance, filed complaints in Water Divisions 1, 2, 4, 6, and 7, which were consolidated into one proceeding in Division One Water Court in Greeley, captioned *Pawnee Well Users v. Wolfe.* In their complaint, the plaintiffs challenged the Final Rules and the Basin-Specific Rules, claiming that the SEO exceeded its statutory authority and that there was insufficient public notice of the rulemaking and related procedures. The water court ruled in favor of the SEO and industry intervenor defendants on nearly every claim. Among other things, the court ruled that the SEO had the authority to make nontributary determinations in section 37-90-137(7) of the Colorado Revised Statutes through rulemakings or adjudicatory proceedings.

However, the water court did set aside the SEO's rule for the Fruitland Formation within and outside of the Southern Ute Reservation on grounds that the SEO lacks jurisdiction on tribal lands. Both the SEO and the Southern Ute Tribe filed motions for reconsideration on this issue, and the Colorado Supreme Court heard the issue on November 7, 2012.

Currently, the SEO has issued CBM permits for over 5,000 wells in Colorado. Thousands of wells can now operate without the need for permits or administration where they are within nontributary geologic basins. Where the wells are tributary, producers need to file SWSPs with the SEO and/or augmentation plans in water court. The Rules strike a reasonable balance. They recognize the importance of oil and gas to Colorado while protecting vested water rights.

B. LOCAL REGULATION OF WATER SOURCES

Local regulation may also impact water used for oil and gas operations. For example, on June 1, 2012, the Northern Colorado Water Conservancy District ("Northern") adopted Rules Governing the Use of Colorado-Big Thompson Project Water and Windy Gap Project Water for the Development of Oil, and Gas Wells ("Northern Rules"). The Northern Rules require that all Colorado-Big Thompson Project water and the first use of all Windy Gap water used for oil and gas must be within the boundaries of the Northern District and its municipal sub-district. This significantly restricts water used for oil and gas in the northern Front Range.

Congress approved the Colorado-Big Thompson Project ("C-BT") in 1937 to bring water from the western slop, across the continental divide, and to the eastern slope of Colorado via a thirteen-mile tunnel under Rock Mountain National Park. Northern and its municipal sub-district administer the projects that irrigate some 640,000 acres and serve roughly 850,000 people. Northern enacted these rules because its key governing documents require that C-BT Project water, and the first use of Windy Gap Project water, be within the boundaries of Northern or its municipal subdistrict. Northern cited the terms of its 1938 Contract with the United States, the Conservancy Act, and its allotment contracts as authority.

The Northern Rules impact many municipalities that earn significant revenues selling water for oil and gas purposes. Service providers and companies were particularly affected in Weld County. Local regulation of facets of oil and gas development has become a significant issue in Colorado. For example, residents of the City of Longmont voted to ban fraccing in the November 2012 election. While such actions are likely preempted by state law, additional local regulations related to water and oil and gas may be forthcoming.

VI. CONCLUSION

Oil and gas has a tremendous economic impact on Colorado and the West. While the industry's demands on water are comparatively small, the need for dependable water supplies in hydraulic fracturing is great. Accordingly, water rights and water quality are increasingly important for source water as well as produced water. We hope this article provides a general understanding of applicable state and federal laws that may help operators make key compliance decisions.

———————

Notes & Questions

1. How is "cooperative federalism" effective under federal environmental statues like the Clean Water Act? State Implementation Plans give the states the ability to implement

plans that meet the unique characteristics of their local industry and environmental needs while meeting minimum standards of effluent—or net pollution limits—set by the federal government.

2. The Safe Drinking Water Act: What is the Halliburton Loophole? How has the loophole been effective for industry? How has it potentially been detrimental to industry?

5. Hydraulic Fracturing

Before reading this section, consider Appendix B. This appendix includes the West Virginia Horizontal Drilling law, as well as all the permits necessary to drill a well. As you will see, it is quite comprehensive. Consider, though, what might be missing. If you worked for an environmental protection organization, what else might you want to see? If you worked for a drilling company, what is your biggest challenge?

Joshua P. Fershee, *The Oil and Gas Evolution: Learning from the Hydraulic Fracturing Experiences in North Dakota and West Virginia*
19 Tex. Wes. L. Rev. 23 (2012)

I. Introduction

Hydraulic fracturing, the method used to recover most new oil and gas in the United States, marks the next evolution in fossil fuel extraction. The world has moved from what is deemed (relatively) easy oil and gas extraction to more complex, more expensive means of extraction. What was traditionally known as tight oil and tight gas is now flowing freely in many parts of the United States thanks to new technologies and higher prices. The technologies for extraction oil and gas are similar, but despite many similarities, the respective commodities have some significant differences that warrant consideration.

This extraction method has created significant excitement coupled with equally high levels of concern. The economic benefits of hydraulic fracturing are well recognized, but the environmental risks remain a point of contention. Risks related to possible groundwater contamination, earthquakes, and other potential harms have raised serious questions about the hydraulic fracturing process, as well as regulatory oversight of the oil and gas industry.

Two of the country's major shale plays are the Bakken Shale, which is located primarily in North Dakota and Montana, and the Marcellus Shale, which is largely in West Virginia and Pennsylvania. While similar, these formations also have some key differences. The main similarity between the Bakken and Marcellus is that advanced hydraulic fracturing techniques have made the minerals found in both formations accessible and cost effective under current market conditions. The main difference is the commodity that comes from each of the respective formations. The Bakken Shale formation is an "oil play," and the Marcellus Shale, on the other hand, is a "natural gas play."

This Article will thus consider major differences and similarities in U.S. oil and gas extraction via hydraulic fracturing through a comparison of the experiences in North Dakota and West Virginia. Although there are other parts of the country experiencing growth in oil and gas extraction, Pennsylvania and Texas as but two examples, North

Dakota and West Virginia are particularly apt for comparison. Both states have relatively small populations, meaning that the impact of large-scale energy extraction in each state is likely to have a large impact on the state, economically, environmentally, and socially.

There are three main areas worth considering in this comparison. In Part II, this Article will discuss the impact of the oil industry in North Dakota and the gas industry in West Virginia. This Part will consider some of the financial, environmental, and social impacts of the hydraulic fracturing boom. Part III will then consider the legislative and regulatory landscape of both states and how each state's approach to enforcement and planning can and is likely to impact development in the state. Finally, the Article concludes that the North Dakota and West Virginia experiences can and should inform state and federal policy with regard to hydraulic fracturing and energy policy generally, and provides some suggestions how best to maximize the value of the lessons already learned.

II. All About the Economy: Financial, Environmental, and Social Impacts

North Dakota and West Virginia are both states in which the energy industry has had a significant economic impact. Over the years, both states have followed boom-and-bust economic cycles related to the energy industry, and in the recent years, both states have fared better than much of the country because of their oil and gas reserves. In some ways, the two states seemed to be running on parallel tracks, but there are some key differences, as well.

A. An Oil Play: The North Dakota Impact

North Dakota passed California in oil production early in December 2011, making the state the third largest U.S. oil producer. Then, in March 2012, North Dakota passed Alaska to become the second largest oil producing state, behind Texas. The heavy oil extraction has allowed North Dakota maintain a budget surplus of more than $1 billion, and the surplus is expected to continue into the foreseeable future.

According to a North Dakota State University study on the economic impact of the petroleum industry in North Dakota, the industry-wide, oil-and-gas industry impact for 2009 was approximately $12.663 billion. This includes estimated direct impacts of $4.9 billion and $7.7 billion in estimated indirect impacts.

Employment figures are similarly impressive for such a low population state. In the 2010 U.S. Census, North Dakota had a population of 672,591 people. The NDSU study estimated that the petroleum industry directly accounted for 18,328 full-time jobs, which provided $4.9 billion in economy-wide personal income, retail sales of $3.3 billion statewide, and $822 in state and local tax revenues. The study also estimated secondary employment of 46,800 people in "full-time equivalent jobs." This means that nearly 10% of the state's total population worked directly or indirectly in petroleum-related jobs (this number climbs to 12.4% if you only consider the population over the age of 18).

The rapidly increasing rate of activity has been, and remains, remarkable. Between 2005 and 2009, expenditures for exploration activities, such as mineral leasing and drilling wells, increase by 482%, as controlled for inflation. Overall economic activity over the same time period increased 117%, and the overall gross business volume almost tripled, increasing from $4.231 billion to $12.663 billion in those four years.

This activity does not come without social costs. The schools in western North Dakota are working to keep pace with the rapid population increase, housing shortages abound, and inflation has skyrocketed. The heavy truck traffic related to the oil boom has taken a great toll on the roads and will require hundreds of millions of dollars for repair and expansion. The increased traffic has also led to numerous accidents and deaths, to the point that some believe traffic is "[t]he most dangerous aspect of working in the North Dakota oil patch." The traffic issues and other public safety concerns have swamped courts and police departments and changed a once quiet part of the state into a series of boomtowns.

Finally, the increased oil-related activity has led to numerous environmental problems and concerns. The natural gas that is extracted along with oil is currently being flared. With low natural gas prices and the lack of existing pipelines to move the gas, it's simply cheaper to burn off the associated natural gas that accompanies the oil being extracted. Although flaring gas is environmentally preferable to simply venting the gas, the process still raises significant air quality concerns that have prompted the Environmental Protection Agency to put new air quality standards in place for fractured wells.

Additionally, some research indicates that hydraulic fracturing may pose risks to safe water supplies and that the process could cause earthquakes. There is also research that suggests that hydraulic fracturing that is done correctly poses little risk to drinking water supplies and that other similar risks can be minimized and/or mitigated. There are clearly some environmental risks involved, as there are in every mineral extraction. The key issues that need to be addressed next are the degree of risk, the efforts being taken to avoid the possible negative impacts raised by such risk, and the best method of enforcement or oversight to ensure risks are minimized as much as possible.

B. A Gas Play: The West Virginia Impact

In contrast to North Dakota, West Virginia's shale play provides primarily natural gas, not oil. The Marcellus Shale has massive gas reserves, and the ability to access those reserves via hydraulic fracturing has, according on 2009 study conducted by West Virginia University (WVU) researchers, provided a boost to the state's economy and created thousands of job opportunities.

The WVU study concluded that the oil and gas industry led to more than $4.5 billion in direct impact and directly employed 9,869 people, leading to more than $551.9 million in wages. That activity, in turn, generated $12 billion in business volume impact, and created roughly 24,400 jobs. Those jobs led to $1.1 billion in employee compensation. The Marcellus Shale alone was determined to account for 7,600 jobs in 2009 and had a business volume impact of $2.35 billion. The state has benefitted from the oil and natural gas industry, too, receiving direct payments of $65.9 million in severance 2009, with an additional $44.5 million in other state taxes generated by the industry's economic activity.

As one might expect, not all the impacts of hydraulic fracturing in West Virginia have been positive. The process has led to environmental concerns in West Virginia, as it has everywhere else it is occurring. For example, a recent study conducted by researchers at the United States Forest Service determined that more research is needed to determine how to safely dispose of hydraulic fracturing wastewater, which often contains chemicals that could pose a risk.

The study found that more than half of the trees in a section of the Fernow Experimental Forest (part of the Monongahela National Forest) were dead two years after the wastewater was legally disposed of in the forest. Approximately 303,000 liters of the wastewater was applied over two days to less than half an acre of forest "to minimize the area of forest potentially affected by the fluid application." The study noted that high concentration of the fluid in such a small area likely contributed to that damage, and that using more land would likely have led to less environmental damage.

Still, the researchers explained, "the application met the terms of the permit issued by the West Virginia Division of Environmental Protection, Office of Oil and Gas, which is a concentration-based standard." Thus, "a dose-based standard might be considered as a means to provide more protection to vegetation and that research to develop such a standard is a high priority."

West Virginia has had reason to be concerned about potential harms to drinking water from hydraulic fracturing since at least 1987. At that time, the EPA issued a report related to the drinking water on James Parsons' property in Jackson County, West Virginia, finding that "fracture fluid, along with natural gas was present..., render[ed] it unusable." The case appears to have been one in which the responsible parties were unaware of the aquifer; still, the case shows that even if such damage should be avoidable, damage can occur if proper steps are not taken in the drilling process.

Similar to western North Dakota, the gas boom in West Virginia has created traffic problems in affected areas. Traffic jams have become a regular occurrence as trucks move drilling equipment to new sites. In addition to traffic concerns, there are worries that the benefit of the gas boom will not benefit the state. The Affiliated Construction Trades Foundation, a group affiliated with 20,000 West Virginia-based union construction workers, has complained the gas companies are hiring out-of-state contractors.

This concern has been raised around the state. As one commentator stated, "[M]ost of the wealth generated by gas won't go to West Virginians. As with coal, almost all of West Virginia's gas will be extracted by out-of-state companies that will repatriate the profits elsewhere." In addition, there are additional concerns that the tax revenues generated by the gas industry activity will be offset by the increased infrastructure needs of those doing the drilling.

Despite the challenges, West Virginia may be better prepared than other states in the gas boom because of the state's history as an energy state. All of the long-time oil states, like Texas, Oklahoma, Alaska, and North Dakota, have significant taxes on their energy resources. According to one report, however, "[a]mong the new boom states, only West Virginia has a substantial tax — an old natural resources levy, a little above 5%, that applies to oil, gas and coal." New York and Pennsylvania, in contrast, have no severance tax, and Ohio has a very modest tax designed only to cover regulatory costs.

III. North Dakota and West Virginia Embrace State-Based Regulation

Hydraulic fracturing process is still a relatively new technology, at least at the scale in which it is happening today. Some have deemed this new and expansive use of hydraulic fracturing an energy "revolution." Whether this industry "game changer" is more of an evolution than a revolution really depends on the perspective.

There is no doubt that hydraulic fracturing has helped trigger a resurgence of U.S. oil and gas production not seen for years. However, the oil and gas boom of today is not unlike some of the oil and gas booms of the past. Although the processes used to extract oil and gas have changed, the business models and the commodities being sold have not. In this sense, at least, the resurgence of U.S. oil and gas is more evolutionary than revolutionary.

In other ways, this new age of oil and gas is revolutionary. The newly (economically) accessible oil in North Dakota may create some market stability prior oil booms did not have. Similarly, the massive natural gas reserves available in West Virginia (and other places around the country) have extended the expected availability of natural gas by decades, creating potential longer-term stability for natural gas markets.

Whether hydraulic fracturing is viewed as evolutionary or revolutionary seems to be driving much of the debate about proper regulation of the industry. Industry has largely advocated that the process is old and established and is thus an evolution of long-standing processes. This camp seeks to keep regulatory models for hydraulic fracturing within the traditional oil and gas framework, which is primarily at the state level.

In contrast, many environmental groups and some regulators have argued that the process is revolutionary and requires a fundamental change in the regulatory process. These groups tend to advocate for federally mandated rules and disclosures, or, absent that, a more fundamental (and different) set of state regulations for hydraulic fracturing.

Traditionally, oil and gas regulation was handled at the state level, and most regulation related to hydraulic fracturing remains at the state level. This state legislation varies widely. From a regulatory perspective, legislators and executives from both North Dakota and West Virginia seem to view hydraulic fracturing from primarily an evolutionary perspective, aggressively advocating state oversight.

Some states, like New York, plainly view hydraulic fracturing as revolutionary. The New York governor's office place moratorium on all hydraulic fracturing, opting for additional time to study the potential implications before the state developed regulations. Similarly, Vermont's legislature is considering legislation that would ban the practice for three years (as the House of Representatives proposed) or longer. North Dakota, on the other hand, took another tack.

The North Dakota Legislature made clear it viewed hydraulic fracturing as positive for the state when it passed House Bill No. 1216, which provides:

Hydraulic fracturing—Designated as acceptable recovery process.

Notwithstanding any other provision of law, the legislative assembly designates hydraulic fracturing, a mechanical method of increasing the permeability of rock to increase the amount of oil and gas produced from the rock, an acceptable recovery process in this state.

In addition, in November 2011 during a special session, the North Dakota legislature set aside $1 million to fund expenses to fight possible U.S. Environmental Protection Agency efforts to regulate hydraulic fracturing. At the legislative level, at least, there is very little dissent on this issue.

North Dakota has not completely ignored the possible need for new regulations because of the dramatic increase in hydraulic fracturing in the state. The North Dakota Industrial Commission in January 2012 sought to improve transparency for the drilling process and improve environmental protections. The new regulations have a particular focus on reducing the use of open wastewater pits, requiring chemical disclosures, and increased well bonds. These regulations are an improvement to the prior regulations, but are relatively modest steps forward.

Similarly, West Virginia's governor requested that the state's Department of Environmental Protection use it ability to issue emergency rules "to promulgate additional regulations to ensure the responsible development of the Marcellus Shale in West Virginia." The West Virginia DEP filed the emergency rule on August 22, 2011, and it provided a number of new requirements related specifically to "horizontal well development in the state."

Under the rule, operators must estimate the amount of water they will use in drilling and fracturing their wells and disclose those estimated to DEP. Operators must submit water management plans for any wells expected to use more than 210,000 gallons of water in any one-month period. Among several provisions designed to protect water supplies, the operator must the state the type and location their water source, and state the expected amount of water to be withdrawn and when they plan to do so.

The rule also creates disclosure requirements related to the fracturing fluid additives; requires tracking of the amounts and disposal of flowback water and mandates (for areas larger than three acres) proper disposal of drill cuttings and drill mud and erosion and sediment control plans. The rule further provides for public notice of at least 30 days before issuance of a drill permit for the first well on a well pad within a municipality's boundary. This final provision originally required notice of "drilling inside municipal limits or within a mile of those boundaries"; however, at the last minute, the one-mile provision was dropped and another change was made reducing oversight, leading to some to claims that industry groups had influenced the changes.

Nonetheless, several important regulations were passed as part of the emergency measure. Perhaps the most important of these regulations provides: "All casing installed in the well must be new, with a pressure rating that exceeds the anticipated maximum pressure to which the casing will be exposed and meet the appropriate American Petroleum Institute (API) standards." As API explains:

Maintaining well integrity is a key design principle and design feature of all oil and gas production wells. Maintaining well integrity is essential for the two following reasons.

1) To isolate the internal conduit of the well from the surface and subsurface environment. This is critical in protecting the environment, including the groundwater, and in enabling well drilling and production.

2) To isolate and contain the well's produced fluid to a production conduit within the well.

Adopting the API best practices as part of the emergency rule is a strong first step toward in helping avoid well casing disasters, ideally with the goal of making such disasters "never events" in hydraulic fracturing. Adoption of the API standards also helps put industry at the forefront of the safety movement in an area where industry technical expertise is critical to understanding, and thus mitigating (and hopefully avoiding) risks related to these highly specialized processes.

IV. Conclusion: Avoiding a Revolution During the Evolution of Hydraulic Fracturing

Hydraulic fracturing has already contributed tremendously to the U.S. economy, and North Dakota and West Virginia have benefitted greatly. Despite the massive exploration and production projects underway, the industry surrounding hydraulic fracturing is very much developing. And the debates about the risks, rewards, and proper regulation of the process are only beginning.

Once of the key battlegrounds in the area is whether the EPA will take a role in regulating hydraulic fracturing. Environmental groups and some academics have advocated for a strong EPA role in hydraulic fracturing. Others, including many from industry and state government officials, have called for the EPA to stay out of the regulatory structure.

Government officials in both North Dakota and West Virginia have both been vocal about their opposition to EPA regulation in the energy industry. As noted earlier, the North Dakota legislature strongly supported a $1 million fund to fight potential U.S. EPA efforts to regulate hydraulic fracturing.

West Virginia's governor has been similarly outspoken in opposition of EPA regulation. In his inaugural address, Governor Earl Ray Tomblin took aim at the EPA's role in regulating the coal industry: "I will fight for our state's coal industry, the backbone of our economy. We will continue to take on the federal government and oppose efforts by the EPA and others to stop production of the most efficient fuel our country knows."

Although both North Dakota and West Virginia have traditionally been opposed to EPA involvement in energy regulation, there is an opportunity for both states to take a leadership role in proper energy regulation, if they can work with the EPA (and the EPA is willing to do so) to develop baseline standards for hydraulic fracturing. As states active in the early part of the hydraulic fracturing explosion, regulators and industry operators in North Dakota and West Virginia have information and expertise that could should be put to use in other areas undertaking hydraulic fracturing.

The EPA would be well served to pursue option to require West Virginia's model of requiring compliance with the API's best practices for hydraulic fracturing. Although the EPA is considering other, and possibly more stringent, requirements, the industry's own best practices should be an absolute minimum for any well drilled in the United States. This makes sense for all involved.

A massive hydraulic fracturing accident could cause broad-reaching harm to the environment, landowners, drinking water, industry employees, and consumers. As witnessed when BP's Deepwater Horizon oil platform suffered a blowout in the Gulf of Mexico, everyone can suffer when an industry actor errs. In that circumstance, one industry leader stated, "It certainly appears that not all the standards that we would recommend or that we would employ were in place." Nonetheless, all of the companies in the industry were negatively impacted by the moratorium placed on offshore drilling put in place following the disaster.

Although companies need latitude to determine their own course on many business decisions, API and industry leaders seem to agree that there are some parts of the drilling process that must be followed. Industry leaders, trade associations, environmental leaders, engineers, scientists, and state and federal regulators should working together to ensure that there are baseline standards in place to create a list of, and then avoid, "never events" for oil and gas drilling.

All involved need to avoid allowing the enemy of their version of "the perfect" to be the enemy of the overall good. Instead, we need to learn from the BP disaster and we need to learn from the experiences of those drilling, regulating, and studying hydraulic fracturing. As Laurence J. Peter, once said, "There's only one thing more painful than learning from experience, and that is not learning from experience." Looking to the experiences of those in North Dakota and West Virginia—economically, environmentally, and socially—would be a good place to start learning.

Notes & Questions

1. How do demographics lead to varying experiences from county to county, state to state, and nation to nation, in relation to energy development? Compare Pennsylvania to Texas; West Virginia to North Dakota; the United States to Poland.

2. How might state and local governments appropriately tax the extraction of oil and natural gas? What are the risks associated with taxation? With not taxing? How can this potential revenue source benefit the citizens of those given areas?

3. What do recent booms in oil and gas development mean for the legal profession? Have these changes been noticeable in your state or region?

4. The oil boom has been great for lawyers, but it has made life difficult for many in the boom areas. Rents are high and inflation has made everything more expensive. Legal advice in rural areas was already a challenge, and now many of the attorneys in boom areas are so busy they are turning away clients. Think about how legal services might be made available for underserved populations in these areas. What can be done? What is a lawyer's obligation? What should the obligation be?

Chapter 4

Electricity & Related Resources

A. Introduction

As discussed in Chapter 1, Thomas Edison and Samuel Insull laid the foundation for our national electricity model. Part of that model involved providing access to electricity for the entire nation. The process set in motion our national energy grid and our national markets for electricity. One of the most critical elements to our functioning electricity system is infrastructure — the physical facilities that deliver electricity. The process of developing that infrastructure was not simple, and maintaining it and expanding it for increasing demand remains a major challenge.

1. Vocabulary and Concepts

Sometimes when lawyers encounter new areas of the law, or new issues in an old area, it is necessary to seek help for terms and definitions. One great source for energy information is the Federal Energy Regulatory Commission's (FERC) website. Following are some definitions and concepts to assist in reading this chapter from FERC's Glossary, available at http://www.ferc.gov/help/glossary.asp.

BTU: A British Thermal Unit (BTU) is a measure of the heating value of a fuel. It is the amount of heat energy required to raise the temperature of one pound of water one degree Fahrenheit.

Cogenerator: A generating facility that produces electricity and another form of useful thermal energy (such as heat or steam), that is used for industrial, commercial, heating, or cooling purposes.

Cost-Based Rates: A ratemaking concept used for the design and development of rate schedules to ensure that the filed rate schedules recover only the cost of providing the service.

Distribution: For electric—the act of distributing electric power using low voltage transmission lines that deliver power to retail customers.

Electric Utilities: All enterprises engaged in the production and/or distribution of electricity for use by the public, including investor-owned electric utility companies; cooperatively-owned electric utilities; government-owned electric utilities (municipal systems, federal agencies, state projects, and public power districts).

Federal Rates: Rates that apply to the marketing of wholesale power and transmission services provided by government owned or leased facilities to non-Federal customers. This is done through FERC-approved rate schedules or contracts at revenue levels sufficient to repay the Federal charges incurred in providing these services.

Generation: The act of producing electrical energy from other forms of energy (such as thermal, mechanical, chemical or nuclear); also, the amount of electric energy produced, usually expressed in kilowatthours (Kwh) or megawatthours (MWh).

Independent System Operator: An independent, Federally regulated entity established to coordinate regional transmission in a non-discriminatory manner and ensure the safety and reliability of the electric system.

Independent Power Producer: A corporation, person, agency, authority, or other legal entity or instrumentality that owns or operates facilities for the generation of electricity for use primarily by the public, and that is not an electric utility.

Interstate: Sales where transportation of natural gas, oil, or electricity crosses state boundaries. Interstate sales are subject to Commission jurisdiction.

Intervenor: An intervenor formally participates in a Commission proceeding by filing a request to intervene. Intervenors are able to file briefs, appear at hearings, and be heard by the courts if they choose to appeal the Commission's final ruling.

Intrastate: Sales where transportation of natural gas, oil, or electricity occur within a single state and do not cross state boundaries. Intrastate sales are not subject to Commission jurisdiction.

Local Distribution Company: Any firm, other than a natural gas pipeline, engaged in the transportation or local distribution of natural gas and its sale to customers that will consume the gas.

Negotiated Rate: An alternative to traditional cost-of-service rates, where a rate for a service varies from a pipeline's otherwise applicable tariff and is mutually agreed upon by a pipeline and its customer. At the time a customer is considering a negotiated rate, a recourse rate that is on file in the pipeline's tariff must also be available to that customer. Also known as negotiated/recourse rates.

Open Access: Order No. 888 requires utilities to allow others to use their transmission and distribution facilities, to move bulk power from one point to another on a nondiscriminatory basis for a cost-based fee.

Tariff: A compilation of all effective rate schedules of a particular company or utility. Tariffs include General Terms and Conditions along with a copy of each form of service agreement.

Transmission: Moving bulk energy products from where they are produced or generated to distribution lines that carry the energy products to consumers.

Wheeling: The transmission of electricity by an entity that does not own or directly use the power it is transmitting.

Wholesale Sales: Sales for resale in bulk power markets, natural gas, and oil.

Following are some additional terms and concepts, as well as some alternate definitions, as provided by the ISO New England, http://www.iso-ne.com/support/training/glossary/:

Combined Cycle (CC): A technology that produces electricity from otherwise lost waste heat from a combustion turbine, which increases the unit's efficiency for generating electricity.

Congestion: A condition that arises on the transmission system when one or more restrictions prevents the economic dispatch of electric energy from serving load.

Demand: Load; the amount of electrical power used; the level of electricity consumption at a particular time measured in megawatts.

Demand Resource, Demand-Side Resource: A source of capacity whereby a customer reduces the demand for electricity from the bulk power system, such as by using energy-efficient equipment, shutting off equipment, and using electricity generated on site.

Dispatch: When a control room operator issues electronic or verbal instructions to generators, transmission facilities, and other market participants to start up, shut down, raise or lower generation, change interchange schedules, or change the status of a dispatchable load in accordance with applicable contracts or demand bid parameters.

Distributed Generation (DG): Generation provided by relatively small installations directly connected to distribution facilities or retail customer facilities. A small (24 kilowatt) solar photovoltaic system installed by a retail customer is an example of distributed generation.

Distribution: The delivery of electricity to end users via low-voltage electric power lines (typically <69 kV) (see **Transmission**); the transfer of electricity from high-voltage lines to lower-voltage lines.

Off-Peak Hours: In New England, weekday hours between 11:00 p.m. and 7:00 a.m. and all day Saturdays, Sundays, and holidays. See peak hours.

On-Peak Hours: From 7:00 a.m. through 11:00 p.m. on all nonholiday weekdays; same as peak hours.

Peak Hours: In New England, the hours between 7:00 a.m. and 11:00 pm on nonholiday weekdays; same as on-peak hours.

Peak-Load Generating Unit: A generating unit that is used to meet system requirements during peak-load periods when the demand on the system is the greatest. These units typically operate at a relatively high cost and run when the price of electric energy is high.

Transmission: The transporting of electricity through high-voltage lines to distribution lines (see distribution).

Transmission Line: Any line with a voltage greater than or equal to 69 kV that carries bulk power over long distances. Typical industry voltages are 69 kV, 115 kV, 138 kV, 230 kV, and 345 kV.

2. Client Issue

Your client is a utility that is in a state that has not required an integrated resource plan (IRP) to date, but state legislation is pending that would require one. In addition, some analysts and shareholder groups have been asking the utility to create one, regardless of commission requirements, as part of the prudent planning process. An IRP is a comprehensive plan designed to facilitate a utility in meeting the company's objective, which is to provide reliable and lowest-cost electric service to all customers. As part of the IRP, the objectives also must include a plan to deal with the substantial risks and uncertainties that are part of every electric utility's business.

The IRP will require input from a variety of stakeholders, including state regulators, ratepayer groups, industry groups, and others. The IRP must include: (1) a plan to deliver the needed electricity over the next 10 years, (2) a 20-year overall plan, and (3) a preferred set of resources that will provide the electricity (including the anticipated fuel and facilities to do so).

Based on the following readings, consider what concerns the utility will likely need to address as part of this process. Seek to identify the economic, environmental, and social concerns, as well as the reliability concerns, that should be part of the IRP. In addition, think about why an IRP would make prudent business sense. What are the downsides to doing an IRP? What are the downsides to not doing an IRP? Keep track of the issues you see as you read the chapter.

B. Electricity Market Overview

The Energy Market Competition Task Force, *Report to Congress on Competition on Wholesale and Retail Markets for Electric Energy Pursuant to Section 1815 of the Energy Policy Act of 2005*

* * *

INDUSTRY STRUCTURE, LEGAL AND REGULATORY BACKGROUND, TRENDS AND DEVELOPMENTS
(footnotes omitted)

For almost all of the 20th Century, the electric power industry was dominated by regulated monopoly utilities. Beginning in the late 1960s, a number of technological, economic, regulatory, and political developments led to fundamental changes in the structure of the industry.

In the 1970s, vertically integrated utility companies (investor-owned, municipal, or cooperative) controlled over 95 percent of the electric generation in the United States. Typically, a single local utility sold and delivered electricity to retail customers under an exclusive franchise regulated under state law. Today, the electric power industry includes both utility and nonutility entities, including many new companies that produce, market and deliver electric energy in wholesale and retail markets. As a result of industry changes, by 2004 electric utilities owned less than 60 percent of electric generating capacity. Increasingly, decisions affecting retail customers and electricity rates are split among federal, state, and new private, regional entities. This chapter highlights structural changes in the industry since the late 1960s. It provides an overview of the important legislative and regulatory changes, as well as trends that have contributed to increased competition.

A. Industry Structure and Regulation

Participants in the electric power sector in the United States include investor-owned utilities and electric cooperatives; federal, state, and municipal utilities, public utility

districts and irrigation districts; cogenerators and onsite generators; and nonutility independent power producers (IPPs), affiliated power producers, power marketers, and independent transmission companies that generate, distribute, transmit, or sell electricity
at wholesale or retail.

In 2004, 3,276 regulated retail electric providers supplied electricity to over 136 million
customers, with retail sales totaling almost $270 billion. Retail customers purchased more
than 3.5 billion megawatt hours (MWhs) of electricity. Active retail electric providers
include utilities, federal agencies, and power marketers selling directly to retail customers.
These entities differ greatly in size, ownership, regulation, customer load characteristics,
and regional conditions. These differences are reflected in policy and regulation....

1. Investor-Owned Utilities

Investor-owned utility operating companies (IOUs) are private, shareholder-owned
companies ranging from small local operations serving a retail customer base of a few
thousand to giant multi-state holding companies serving millions of customers. Most
IOUs are or are part of a vertically integrated system that owns or controls generation,
transmission, and distribution facilities/resources to meet the needs of retail customers
in their franchise service areas. Many IOUs have undergone significant restructuring and
reorganization under state retail competition plans over the past decade. As a result, many
IOUs no longer own generation, but those that sell electric power to retail customers
must procure electricity from wholesale markets. See Chapter 4 and Appendix D of this
document for details on state experience with retail competition. IOUs continue to be a
major presence. In 2004 there were 220 IOUs serving approximately 94 million retail distribution customers, accounting for 68.9 percent of all retail customers and 60.8 percent
of retail electricity sales. IOUs directly owned about 39.6 percent of total electric generating
capacity and accounted for 44.8 percent of generation for retail and wholesale sales in
2004. IOUs provide service to retail customers under state regulation of territories,
finances, operations, services, and rates. States that have not restructured retail service
generally regulate retail rates under traditional bundled cost-of-service rate methods. In
states that have restructured IOUs, distribution services continue to be provided under
monopoly cost-of-service rates, and retail customers obtain generation service either at
market rates from alternative competitive providers or at regulated "provider of last resort"
(POLR) rates from the distribution utility or another designated POLR service provider.
IOUs serve retail customers in every state but Nebraska. Under the Federal Power Act
(FPA) [16 U.S.C. §§ 791a et seq. (2000)], the Federal Energy Regulatory Commission
(FERC) regulates wholesale electricity transactions (sales for resale) and unbundled transmission activities of IOUs as "public utilities" engaged in interstate commerce. The
exceptions are IOUs that do not have direct interconnections with utilities in other states
that allow unimpeded flow of electricity across systems. Thus, IOUs in Alaska, Hawaii,
and the Electric Reliability Council of Texas (ERCOT) region of Texas generally are not
subject to FERC jurisdiction.

2. Public Power Systems

The more than 2,000 publicly owned power systems include local, municipal, state,
and regional public power systems. These providers range from tiny municipal distribution
companies to large systems such as the Los Angeles Department of Water and Power.
Publicly owned systems operate in every state but Hawaii. About 1,840 of these systems
are cities and municipal governments that own and control the day-to-day operation of
their electric utilities. Public power systems served over 19.6 million retail customers in

2004, or about 14.4 percent of all customers. Together, they generated 10.3 percent of the nation's power in 2004, accounted for 16.7 percent of total electricity sales and owned about 9.6 percent of total generating capacity. Many public systems are distribution-only utilities that purchase, rather than generate, power. According to the American Public Power Association, about 70 percent of public power retail sales were met from wholesale power purchases, including purchases from municipal joint action agencies by the agencies' member systems. Only about 30 percent of the electricity for public power retail sales comes from power generated by a utility to service its own native load. Publicly owned utilities, thus, depend overwhelmingly on transmission and the wholesale market to bring electricity to their retail customers.

Regulation of public power systems varies among states. In some, the public utility commission exercises jurisdiction in whole or part over operations and rates of publicly-owned systems. In most states, public power systems are regulated by local governments or are self-regulated. Municipal systems usually are governed by a local city council or an independent board elected by voters or appointed by city officials. Other public power systems are operated by public utility districts, irrigation districts, or special state authorities.

On the whole, state retail restructuring initiatives did not affect retail services in public systems. However, some states allow public systems to adopt retail choice alternatives voluntarily.

3. Electric Cooperatives

Electric cooperatives are privately-owned, non-profit electric systems owned and controlled by the members they serve. Members vote directly for the board of directors. In 2004, 884 electric distribution cooperatives provided retail electric service to almost 16.6 million customers. In addition, another 65 generation and transmission cooperatives (G&Ts) own and operate generation and transmission and secure wholesale power and transmission services from others to meet the needs of their distribution cooperative members' retail customers and other rural native load customers. G&T systems and their members engage in joint planning and power supply operations to achieve some of the savings available under a vertically integrated utility structure. Electric cooperatives operate in 47 states. Most were originally organized and financed under the federal rural electrification program and operate in primarily rural areas. Cooperatives provide electric service in all or parts of 83 percent of the counties in the United States.

In 2004, electric cooperatives sold more than 345 million MWhs, served 12.2 percent of retail customers, and accounted for 9.7 percent of electricity sold at retail. Nationwide electric cooperatives generate about 4.7 percent of total electric generation and own approximately 4.2 percent of generating capacity.

While some cooperative systems generate their own power and sell power in excess of their members' needs, most G&Ts and distribution cooperatives are net buyers. Cooperatives nationwide generated only about half of the power needed by their retail customers. They secured approximately half of their power needs from other wholesale suppliers in 2004. Although cooperatives own and operate transmission facilities, almost all rely to some extent on transmission owned by others to deliver power to their customers.

Regulatory jurisdiction over cooperatives varies among states. Some states exercise considerable authority over rates and operations, while others exempt cooperatives from state regulation. In addition to state regulation, cooperatives with outstanding loans under the Rural Electrification Act of 1936 [7 U.S.C. 901 *et seq.*] are subject to financial and operating requirements of the Rural Utilities Service (RUS), Department of Agriculture.

RUS must approve borrowers' long-term wholesale power contracts, operating agreements, and transfers of assets. Cooperatives that have repaid their RUS loans and that engage in wholesale sales or provide transmission services to others have been regulated by FERC as public utilities under the FPA. EPAct 2005 gave FERC additional discretionary jurisdiction over transmission services provided by larger electric cooperatives.

4. Federal Power Systems

Federally-owned or chartered power systems include the federal power marketing administrations (PMAs), the Tennessee Valley Authority (TVA), and facilities operated by the U.S. Army Corps of Engineers, the Bureau of Reclamation, the Bureau of Indian Affairs, and the International Water and Boundary Commission. Wholesale power from federal facilities (primarily hydroelectric dams) is marketed through four federal power marketing agencies: Bonneville Power Administration, Western Area Power Administration, Southeastern Power Administration, and Southwestern Power Administration. The PMAs own and control transmission to deliver power to wholesale and direct service customers. They also may purchase power from others to meet contractual needs and may sell surplus power as available to wholesale markets. Existing legislation requires that the PMAs and TVA give preference in selling their generation to public power systems and to rural electric cooperatives.

Together, federal systems have an installed generating capacity of approximately 71.4 gigawatts (GW) or about 6.9 percent of total capacity. Federal systems provided 7.2 percent of the nation's power generation in 2004. Although most federal power sales are at the wholesale level, some are made to end users. Federal systems nationwide directly served 39,845 retail customers in 2004, mostly industrial customers and about 1.2 percent of retail load.

5. Nonutilities

Nonutilities are entities that generate, transmit, or sell electric power but do not operate regulated retail distribution franchises. ["Nonutilities"—as that term is defined for EIA reporting purposes and as used here—may still be characterized as "utilities" and subject to public service regulation under state law and regulated as "public utilities" by FERC.] They include wholesale nonutility affiliates of regulated utilities, merchant generators, and qualifying facilities (QFs). [QFs are small power producers using eligible alternative electric generating technologies and industrial and commercial cogenerators (combined heat and power producers) that have special status under PURPA.] They also include power marketers that buy and sell power at wholesale or retail but that do not own generation, transmission, or distribution facilities. Independent transmission companies that own and operate transmission facilities but do not own generation or retail distribution facilities or sell electricity to retail customers are also included in this category for EIA reporting purposes.

Non-QF wholesale generators engaged in wholesale power sales in interstate commerce are subject to FERC regulation under the FPA. Power marketers selling at wholesale are also subject to FERC oversight. Power marketers selling only at retail are subject to state jurisdiction and oversight in states where they operate. FERC regulates interstate transmission services of independent transmission companies under the FPA. Such companies also may be organized and regulated as utilities where they are located for planning, siting, permitting, and other purposes.

As retail electric providers, 152 power marketers reporting to EIA served about 6 million retail customers or about 4.4 percent of all retail customers and reported revenues of over $28 billion, on about 11.6 percent of retail electricity sold.

Nonutilities are a growing presence in the industry. In 2004, nonutilities owned or controlled approximately 408,699 megawatts (MWs) or 39.6 percent of all electric generation capacity, compared to about 8 percent in 1993. About half of nonutility generation capacity is owned by nonutility affiliates or subsidiaries of holding companies that also own a regulated electric utility. Nonutilities accounted for about 33 percent of generation in 2004. [See] Table 1-1....

B. Growth of the Electric Power Industry

For a variety of legal, economic, and technological reasons, the electric utility industry in the United States developed as a collection of separate, mostly vertically-integrated

Table 1-1. U.S. Retail Electric Providers, 2004

Ownership	Number of Electricity Providers	Percent of Total	Number of Customers			Percent of Total
			Full-Service	Delivery Only	Total	
Publicly-owned utilities	2,011	61.4	19,628,710	6,125	19,634,835	14.4
Investor-owned utilities	220	6.7	90,970,557	2,879,114	93,849,671	68.9
Cooperatives	884	27	16,564,780	12,170	16,576,950	12.2
Federal Power Agencies	9	0.3	39,843	2	39,845	0.03
Power Marketers	152	4.6	6,017,611	0	6,017,611	4.4
Total	3,276	100	133,221,501	2,897,411	136,118,912	100

Notes:

 * Delivery-only customers represent the number of customers in a utility's service territory that purchase energy from an alternative supplier.

** Ninety-eight percent of all power marketers' full-service customers are in Texas. Investor-owned utilities in the ERCOT region of Texas no longer report ultimate customers. Their customers are counted as full-service customers of retail electric providers (REPs), which are classified by the Energy Information Administration as power marketers. The REPs bill customers for full-service and then pay the IOU for the delivery portion. REPs include the regulated distribution utility's successor affiliated retail electric provider that assumed service for all retail customers that did not select an alternative provider. Does not include U.S. territories.

Source: American Public Power Association, 2006-07 Annual Directory & Statistical Report, from Energy Information Administration Form EIA-861, 2004, data.

monopoly franchises with wholesale and retail prices and services extensively regulated under state and federal law. Many states have elected to maintain this model. The legacy of this vertically-integrated monopoly structure creates substantial challenges for state and federal efforts to restructure the industry and to create new institutional arrangements to facilitate increased reliance on competitive market prices. This section provides a brief overview of the evolutionary changes in the electric power industry.

1. The Rise of Electric Utility Monopolies and Public Utility Regulation

In the late 19th Century, electric utilities developed as small central station power plants with limited local distribution networks. Franchise rights granted by manufacturers and by municipal governments allowed use of public streets and rights of ways. These franchises were often exclusive, but in some cities there was head-to-head competition among competing electric lighting companies. In addition, because lighting, electric motors, and traction were the major uses of electricity, customers could turn to alternatives—natural gas lighting or self-generation in the case of street railway, commercial, and industrial customers. Many municipalities elected to create and operate their own electric utility systems.

Certain characteristics of providing electric service were recognized early on. Utility systems incurred high fixed costs for investments in generating plants needed to meet peak load and to extend the delivery system. Because they had relatively low operating costs, their profits were determined by the percent of time the power plant was in use. Complementary load diversity—such as balancing daytime traction and electric motor loads with evening lighting loads—could raise generating plant use and revenues to offset fixed costs and boost profits. The high capital costs of electric generating plants made investments risky. Steady gains in generation, transmission, and distribution economies of scale provided incentives to expand the electric networks. Larger plants produced cheaper electricity than many smaller plants. The substantial investment required for electric utility plants also spurred creation of long-term financing structures and the corresponding interest in providing assurances to investors that the entity would be profitable and would remain financially viable long enough to repay the debt.

These characteristics led some to suggest that a single monopoly provider of integrated generation, transmission and distribution service could provide electric service most economically and safely. To avoid abuses of this monopoly power, it was suggested that impartial state agencies should be created to award franchises and establish rates and service standards. An early associate of Thomas Edison, Samuel Insull of Chicago Edison was among them and proposed state regulation of private utilities in a speech before the National Electric Light Association in 1898. Insull characterized electricity production as a "natural monopoly." Initially, the proposal for state regulation was poorly received, but as private electric companies began to grow and consolidate and concerns were raised over trusts in many industries, the concept began to gain support. In 1907, Wisconsin adopted legislation regulating electric utilities and was quickly joined by two other states. By 1916, 33 states had established state agencies to oversee private electric utilities.

Generally, under this approach, the state regulatory commission granted exclusive retail electric franchises to private companies within specified territories, protecting the utility from competition. In return, the utility assumed an obligation to provide safe and adequate service to all retail customers within its territory under just and reasonable rates, terms and conditions overseen by the state. Often the utility was authorized to use public rights of way and eminent domain for electric facilities. To meet this obligation to serve, most private utilities built and controlled the generation, transmission, and distribution facilities needed to provide service to customers. Rates were set to cover the companies' reasonable costs plus a fair return on shareholders' investment. The utility could expect a right to reasonable compensation for its services, although a specific rate of return was not guaranteed. Retail rates (price) were based on the average historical system cost of production (including the investors' fair return on investment).

In the early 20th Century, private electric utilities continued to expand under this system of state regulation. Most continued to build their own generation plants and transmission systems, primarily due to the cost and technological limitations of transmitting electricity over distances. Initially, there was little wholesale trade among utilities. As the industry grew, continued improvements in technology allowed expansion beyond central cities, and prices for electricity fell at the same time that demand increased substantially.

Over the same period, electric utility holding companies were created and began to acquire local private and municipal utilities. While a holding company's local utility operating companies were regulated by the state, the holding company and its other affiliates and subsidiaries were not, and often did business in several states. The proliferation, consolidation, and complexity of such companies coincided with a number of financial and securities abuses that were documented in an investigation by the Federal Trade Commission (FTC). These holding companies often became the sole providers of various services and products to their affiliated utilities, and their sometimes inflated costs were passed through to the retail customers. By 1932, the eight largest utility holding companies controlled 73 percent of the investor-owned electric industry.

This pattern of consolidated ownership and holding company abuses led to calls for federal involvement in the electric power industry. As a result of the FTC findings, Congress passed the Public Utility Holding Company Act of 1935 (PUHCA 1935), which required the breakup and stringent federal oversight of the large utility holding companies. The FPA expanded the Federal Power Commission's authority to include oversight and regulation of interstate sales of wholesale power (e.g., sales of power between utility systems) and interstate electricity transmission at wholesale by "public utilities" (i.e., investor-owned utilities). FPA jurisdiction over interstate sales closed a gap in electric industry regulation that the Supreme Court had identified in 1927.

When the FPA was enacted, wholesale and interstate sales of electricity were limited. Most wholesale transactions were long-term power supply contracts by investor-owned utilities to sell and deliver power to neighboring public power and cooperative utilities. Over time, utilities became more interconnected via high-voltage transmission networks. Constructed primarily for reliability, these networks also facilitated more opportunities for interstate trade. However, wholesale trade was slow to develop.

Until the late 1960s, the vertically integrated monopoly utility model appeared to work reasonably well. Utilities were able to meet increasing demand for electricity at decreasing prices as advances in generation technology and transmission provided increased economies of scale with larger units and decreased costs.

2. The Energy Crisis of the 1970s, PURPA, and the Expansion of Nonutility Generation and Wholesale Power Markets

The shift toward a more competitive marketplace for electricity was precipitated by industry changes that began in the late 1960s and accelerated throughout the 1970s. Resulting financial stresses challenged the continued profitability of the large vertically integrated utility model. They also provoked criticisms of the traditional cost-of-service regulatory model that allowed the pass-through of higher costs and risks of construction to consumers.

By the end of the 1960s, electricity demand and generation were increasing at an annual rate of 7.5 percent, and residential rates were declining at an average annual rate of 1.5 percent. At the same time, the new large nuclear and coal plants built in the 1970s did not yield the dramatic improvements in economies of scale that earlier technological advances in generating plant size had produced. The industry's characterization as a long-term decreasing cost industry came into question. Periods of rapid inflation and higher interest rates substantially increased the completion costs of large, base load generating plants. New environmental and safety regulations required addition of pollution controls and design features that added to costs and construction time. Moreover, once in operation, many of the new, larger units required more maintenance and longer downtimes than expected. Thus, by the late 1970s, a newer, larger, generation facility no longer could be assumed to be more cost-efficient than a smaller plant.

This experience stimulated interest in smaller, modular, more energy-efficient generating units. One expression of this interest resulted in commercialization of aeroderivative gas turbine technology. This technology allowed smaller generation units to be constructed at lower costs, more quickly, and at less financial risk than large base-load coal and nuclear plants. Thus, construction of low-cost generation became an option for utilities that were formerly captive to high-cost generators and emerged as a viable path for new nonutility generators to enter the market.

As the difficulties plaguing utilities' generation construction programs were playing out, utility fuel prices were escalating rapidly in response to the Arab oil embargo of 1973-1974 and subsequent world oil market disruptions. Significantly higher energy prices added to inflation and increased electric rates. Other developments also substantially contributed to the growing interest in electric utility reforms. First, the 1965 Northeast power blackout raised concerns about the reliability of weakly coordinated bulk power system operating arrangements among utilities. The nuclear accident at the Three Mile Island plant in Pennsylvania on March 28, 1979, heightened concerns over safety and led to stringent new regulatory requirements for nuclear plants.

Criticism of the traditional cost-of-service utility regulation model by economists and policy analysts also increased during the 1970s with suggestions for alternate approaches to regulation and changes in industry structure. Critics of cost-based regulation argued that the industry structure limited opportunities for more efficient suppliers to expand, placed insufficient pressure on less efficient suppliers to improve performance, and insulated customers from the cost impacts of energy use.

Congress enacted the Public Utility Regulatory Policies Act (PURPA) as a response to the energy crises of the 1970s. PURPA's major goal was to promote energy conservation and alternative energy technologies and to reduce oil and gas consumption through use of improved technology and regulatory reforms. A perhaps unanticipated side effect was that PURPA prompted a number of parties to see potential profits in developing competitive generating plants, creating an opportunity for nonutilities to emerge as important electric power producers.

PURPA required electric utilities to interconnect with and purchase power from co-generation facilities and small power producers that met statutory criteria for a qualifying facility (QF). A utility had to pay the QF at the utility's incremental cost of production. In a departure from cost-based rate approaches, FERC defined this as the utility's avoided cost of power.

Box 1-1 on the next page discusses how implementation of PURPA encouraged nonutility generation suppliers by guaranteeing a market for the electricity produced. PURPA changed

---

Box 1-1. State Implementation of PURPA

PURPA required states to determine each utility's avoided costs of production. This cost was used to set the price for purchasing a QF's power. To encourage renewable and alternative energy generation, several states, including California, New York, Massachusetts, Maine, and New Jersey, required utilities to sign long-term contracts with QFs at prices that eventually ended up being much higher than the utilities' actual marginal savings of not producing the power itself (avoided costs). As a result, many utilities in these states entered into long-term purchase contracts at prices higher than those available in the competitive wholesale markets. The costs of these QF contracts were reflected in retail rates as cost pass-throughs. The experience added to the dissatisfaction with retail rate regulation.

---

prevailing views that vertically integrated public utilities were the only reliable sources of power and showed that nonutilities could build and operate generation facilities effectively and without disrupting the reliability of the electric grid. PURPA contributed substantially, both directly and indirectly, to the creation of an independent competitive generation sector.

Before passage of PURPA, nonutility generation was confined primarily to commercial and industrial facilities that generated heat and power for onsite use where it was advantageous to do so. Although nonutility generation facilities were located across the country, development was heavily concentrated geographically, with about two-thirds of such facilities located in California and Texas. Nonutility generation development advanced in states where avoided costs were high enough to attract interest and where natural gas supplies were available. Federal law largely precluded electric utilities from constructing new natural gas plants during the decade following enactment of PURPA, but nonutility generators faced no such restriction and quickly turned to the new smaller gas turbines as the preferred generating technology.

The response to PURPA was dramatic. Annual QF filings at FERC rose from 29 applications covering 704 MW in 1980 to 979 in 1986 totaling over 18,000 MW. From 1980 to 1990, FERC received a total of 4,610 QF applications for a total of 86,612 MW of generating capacity.

Following PURPA, continued improvement in generating technology lowered costs and further contributed to an influx of new entrants in wholesale markets. They could sell electric power profitably with smaller scale generators, including renewable energy technologies and more efficient, modular gas turbines. Other nonutilities that could not meet QF criteria began building new capacity to compete in bulk power markets to meet the needs of utilities. These new entities were known as merchant generators or independent power producers (IPPs). By 1991, nonutilities (QFs and IPPs) owned about 6 percent of the electric generating capacity and produced about 9 percent of the total electricity generated in the United States. Nonutility facilities accounted for one-fifth of all additions to generating capacity in the 1980s. Beginning in the 1980s, FERC allowed many new utility and nonutility generators to sell electricity at rates negotiated in wholesale markets, rather than established under cost-of-service formulas.

In 1988, FERC solicited public comments on three notices of proposed rulemaking (NOPRs) dealing with electricity pricing in wholesale transactions. These NOPRs addressed the following issues: (1) competitive bidding for new power requirements; (2) treatment of independent power producers; and (3) determination of avoided costs under PURPA.

These proposals would have moved FERC towards greater use of a "non-traditional" market-based pricing approach in ratemaking as opposed to the agency's "traditional" cost-based approach. The NOPRs, however, proved controversial, and efforts to establish formal rules or policies were abandoned. However, the overall policy goals were still pursued on a case-by-case basis.

Between 1983 and 1991, FERC was asked to approve more than 30 non-traditional market-based rate proposals. These proposals were brought by IPPs, power brokers/marketers, utility-affiliated power producers, and traditional franchised utilities. FERC approved all but four. In explaining its approach, FERC staff wrote: "The Commission has accepted non-traditional rates where the seller or its affiliate lacked or had mitigated market power over the buyer, and there was no potential abuse of affiliate relationships which might directly or indirectly influence the market price and no potential abuse of reciprocal dealing between the buyer and seller." In determining whether the seller could exercise market power over the buyer, FERC considered whether the seller or its affiliates owned or controlled transmission that might prevent the buyer from accessing other power sources. A seller with transmission control might be able to force the buyer to purchase from the seller, thus limiting competition and significantly influencing price. The FPA does not allow rates to reflect an exercise of such market power.

FERC recognized the potential for control of transmission to create market power and the challenge such control created in moving to greater reliance on market-based rates. FERC staff told Congress, "Because the Commission's very premise of finding market-based rates just and reasonable under the FPA is the absence or mitigation of market power, or the existence of a workably competitive market, and because the FPA mandates that the Commission prevent undue preference and undue discrimination, we believe the Commission is legally required to prevent abuse of transmission control and affiliate or any other relationships which may influence the price charged a ratepayer."

Despite these developments, two limitations at that time were perceived to discourage competitive wholesale generation markets. First, IPPs and other generators of cheaper electric power could not easily access the transmission grid to reach potential customers. Under the FPA as then written, FERC had limited authority to order access. FERC would subsequently find that "intervening" transmitting utilities would deny or limit transmission service to competing suppliers of generation to protect demand for wholesale power supplied by their own facilities. Second, unlike QFs that enjoyed a statutory exemption under PURPA, IPPs were subject to PUHCA 1935, which discouraged nonutilities from entering the generation business.

* * *

Joshua P. Fershee, *Atomic Power, Fossil Fuels, and the Environment: Lessons Learned and the Lasting Impact of the Kennedy Energy Policies*
39 Texas Environmental Law Journal 131 (2009)

...

President Kennedy's time was not so different from our own in terms of a vast need for energy infrastructure. In addition to nuclear power and coal slurry lines, there was a continuing need for electricity infrastructure.

President Kennedy often touted the success of the Rural Electrification Act (REA), provided the long-term financing and technical expertise needed to expand the availability of electricity to rural customers. President Kennedy's prepared remarks for a September 1963 speech at the University of North Dakota stated that, since the REA passed in 1936, more than 900 cooperative rural electrification systems had been built with the assistance of federal financing.

The REA's financial undertaking was enormous. "More than $5 billion has been advanced to 1,000 borrowers. Over 1,500,000 miles of power lines—enough to criss-cross the nation 500 times—have been built, serving 20 million American people." The investment, President Kennedy noted, was remarkably sound: "Out of roughly 1,000 borrowers, only one is delinquent in payment; and the total losses on the $5 billion advanced are less than $50,000." This low level of default is especially striking in today's financial times.

Few investors were willing to invest in the rural electrification project without federal financing, yet few private businesses could cite such a successful record. In 1963, North Dakota-based REA-funded cooperatives served on average around one metered farm per mile of line, compared to the average urban-area utility system of 33 electric meters per mile of line. North Dakota, at a remarkable 97%, was the state with the highest percentage of people being served by REA-funded utilities.

In addition to the financing issues, President Kennedy argued that the REA raised the standard of living, strengthened the U.S. economy, and even improved national security by providing the power necessary to increase industrial activity when needed. In the State of North Dakota, the President noted in his address, prior to the REA, 3% of farms were powered by electricity; by 1963, nearly every farm in the state had power. "What was 30 years ago a life of affluence, in a sense today is a life of poverty."

President Kennedy recognized, though, that despite the success of the REA, the task of rural electrification was not complete. The President sought continuation of the REA to ensure that rural residents had access to power at competitive costs. Today, continued construction is necessary, but this time the need is not related to demand. U.S. energy infrastructure has not kept up with the increasing needs of a growing population that uses more per capita power than ever before. Construction of energy infrastructure continued through the 1960s, but investment in electric transmission lines (the high-voltage lines moving wholesale electric energy), declined (in real dollars) for the twenty-three consecutive years between 1975 and 1998. Since 1998, investment has slowly increased, but is still below 1975 levels. In 2004, this failure of infrastructure investment translated into a 0.6% increase in circuit miles on the U.S. interstate transmission system.

The capital needed to improve the U.S. energy infrastructure investment remains significant. Estimates from $56 billion to $100 billion, are uncommon, and others have argued that as much as $450 billion is needed to appropriately address electricity infrastructure needs. And these investment estimates do not account for all of the additional investments that would be need to address climate change concerns.

Notes & Questions

1. Appendix C provides the Federal Power Act. The Federal Power Act is what gives FERC its authority. FERC has exclusive jurisdiction over the "transmission of electric energy in interstate commerce," and over the "sale of electric energy at wholesale in interstate commerce," and over "all facilities for such transmission or sale of electric energy." *See* 16 U.S.C. § 824(b).

2. Appendix C also gives a glimpse into the transmission grid. Note how much of the country is covered (and how much is not). Think about the benefits that come from having federal authority over wholesale sales on the transmission grid. Does it make sense to have siting for transmission lines remain a local and regional authority when sales over such lines are federally regulated? As you continue through the chapter, think about the various reasons this might make sense. Is it a states' rights issue? Local control? Cooperative federalism?

The Energy Market Competition Task Force,
Part II: Report to Congress on Competition on Wholesale and Retail Markets for Electric Energy Pursuant to Section 1815 of the Energy Policy Act of 2005
April 5, 2007

* * *

3. The Energy Policy Act of 1992 and FERC Orders Nos. 888 and 889

EPAct 1992 amended the FPA and PUHCA 1935 to address what were then seen as the two major limitations to the development of a competitive generation sector.

First, EPAct 1992 created a new category of power producers, called exempt wholesale generators (EWGs). An EWG is an entity that directly, or indirectly through one or more affiliates, owns or operates facilities dedicated exclusively to producing electric power for sale in wholesale markets. EWGs are exempted from PUHCA 1935 regulations, thus eliminating a major barrier for utility-affiliated and nonaffiliated power producers that wanted to build or acquire new non-rate-based power plants to sell electricity at wholesale.

Second, EPAct 1992 expanded FERC's authority to order transmitting utilities to provide transmission service for wholesale power sales to any electric utility, federal power marketing agency, or any person generating electric energy. It provided for orders to be issued on a case-by-case basis following a hearing if certain protective conditions were met. Although FERC implemented this new mandatory wheeling authority, it ultimately concluded that procedural limitations restricted its reach and a broader remedy was needed to eliminate pervasive undue discrimination in transmission service that hindered competition in wholesale markets.

In April 1996, FERC adopted Order No. 888 in exercise of its statutory obligation under the FPA to remedy undue transmission discrimination. The goal was to ensure that transmission owners do not use their transmission facility monopoly to unduly discriminate against IPPs and other sellers of electric power in wholesale markets. In Order No. 888, FERC found that undue discrimination and anti-competitive practices existed in transmission service provided by public utilities in interstate commerce. FERC determined that non-discriminatory open access transmission service was an appropriate remedy and one of the most critical components of a successful transition to competitive wholesale electricity markets. Accordingly, FERC required all public utilities that own, control or operate facilities used for transmitting electric energy in interstate commerce to file open access transmission tariffs (OATTs) containing certain non-price terms and conditions.

They also were required to "functionally unbundle" wholesale power services from transmission services. This meant that a public utility was required to: (1) take wholesale transmission services under the same tariff of general applicability as it offered its customers; (2) define separate rates for wholesale generation, transmission and ancillary services; and (3) rely on the same electronic information network that its transmission customers rely on to obtain information about the utility's transmission system.

Concurrent with Order No. 888, FERC issued Order No. 88959 that imposed standards of conduct governing communications between a utility's transmission and wholesale power functions to prevent the utility from giving its power marketing arm preferential access to transmission information. Order No. 889 requires each public utility that owns, controls, or operates facilities used for the transmission of electric energy in interstate commerce to create or participate in an Open Access Same-Time Information System (OASIS). OASIS must provide information regarding available transmission capacity, prices, and other information that will enable transmission customers to obtain open access to non-discriminatory transmission service.

In Order No. 888, FERC also encouraged grid regionalization through the formation of independent system operators (ISOs). Participating utilities would voluntarily transfer operating control of their transmission facilities to the ISO to ensure independent operation of the transmission grid. The expectation was that ISO regional control would lead to improved coordination, reliability, and efficient operation. However, ISO participation was voluntary and was not embraced in all regions. Together, Order Nos. 888 and 889 serve as the primary federal regulatory foundation for providing nondiscriminatory transmission service and information about the availability of transmission service.

4. Retail Electricity Competition and State Electric Restructuring Initiatives

In the early 1990s, several states with high electricity prices began exploring opening retail electric service to competition. While customers would choose their supplier, the delivery of electricity would still be done by the local distribution utility. Retail competition was expected to result in lower retail prices, innovative services and pricing options. It also was expected to shift the risks of new generation construction from ratepayers to competitive market providers. The substantial rate disparity among and between utilities in different states spurred state interest in retail competition. For example, in 1998, customers in New York paid more than two and one-half times the rates paid by customers in Kentucky. Rates in California were well over twice the rates in Washington. Some of this disparity can be attributed to different natural resource endowments across regions, such as the availability of hydroelectric resources in the Northwest and of abundant coal reserves in Kentucky and Wyoming—which were reflected in the low cost of electricity in these states. In contrast, in more urban states without these resources, utilities invested heavily in large, new nuclear and coal plants, which often turned out to be more expensive than anticipated, adding to retail rates. Some utilities in high-cost states also had entered into long-term PURPA contracts that subsequently resulted in higher prices than in the wholesale power market. These QF contract costs were ultimately reflected in the regulated retail rates.

Many large industrial customers viewed these rate disparities among states as a competitive disadvantage and looked to retail competition as a way to secure lower cost electricity supplies. Many industrial customers had long objected that they subsidized lower rates for residential customers under state regulated rates. For example, a survey by the Electricity Consumers Resource Council in 1986 contended that industrial electricity consumers paid more than $2.5 billion annually in subsidies to other electricity customers (e.g., commercial and residential customers). It was presumed that allowing industrial customers to choose a new supplier would avoid these subsidies, thereby resulting in lower electricity prices for such customers.

Thus, it was not surprising that many states adopting plans to restructure retail electric service were those with higher prices.... States with high electricity rates, such as California and those in New England and the mid-Atlantic region, were among the most aggressive in adopting retail competition and restructuring electric service in the hope of lowering retail rates. As of 2004, the disparity in retail prices among the states persisted, as illustrated in Figure 1-1.

Most states considered the merits and implications of competition and industry re-structuring, but not all adopted retail competition plans. As of July 2000, 24 states and the District of Columbia had enacted legislation or passed regulatory orders to restructure their electric power industries. Two states had legislation or regulatory orders pending, while 16 states had ongoing legislative or regulatory investigations. Only eight states did not formally initiate restructuring studies

The meltdown of California's electricity markets and the ensuing Western Energy market crisis of 2000-2001 are widely perceived to have halted interest by states in restructuring retail markets. Since 2000, no additional states have announced plans to implement retail competition programs, and several states that had introduced such programs have delayed, scaled back, or repealed their programs entirely....

In 2006, retail customers in 30 states continue to receive service almost exclusively under a traditional regulated monopoly utility service franchise. These states include 44

Figure 1-1. U.S. Electric Power Industry, Average Retail Price of Electricity, by State, 2004

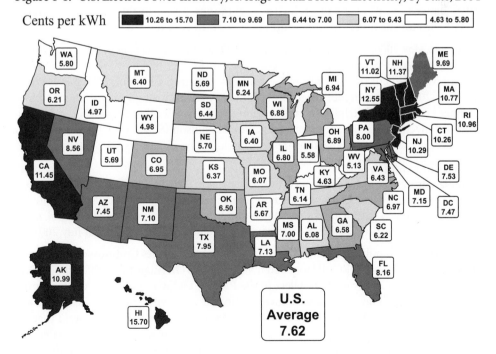

Cents per kWh | 10.26 to 15.70 | 7.10 to 9.69 | 6.44 to 7.00 | 6.07 to 6.43 | 4.63 to 5.80 |

Source: EIA, *Electric Power Annual 2004*, Figure 7.4

percent of all U.S. retail customers, representing 49 percent of electricity demand. However, 20 states and the District of Columbia have state restructuring plans in force that allow competitive retail providers to provide service to some if not all retail customers at prices set in the market.

State retail restructuring plans often involved divestiture of generating assets by local vertically integrated utilities. As a result, the distribution utilities that sell electricity to retail customers must procure power from wholesale markets under long- or short-term bilateral contracts and from wholesale spot markets. These jurisdictions include many of the most populous states, accounting for over half of all retail customers and loads. With some exceptions, retail competition has been slow to develop in many of these states, particularly for residential customers. Without a competitive provider option, most customers continue service under regulated "provider of last resort" (POLR) rates. In some states, freezes and caps on POLR rates approved by state regulators under retail restructuring cases are expiring, and POLR rates are being revised sharply upward to reflect higher market-based wholesale electricity costs....

5. The Western Energy Market Crisis 2000-2001.

California opened its retail markets to competition and started spot markets for wholesale electricity in 1998. In response to the state plan, the three major investor-owned utilities divested most of their non-nuclear generation and turned over operation of transmission facilities to the new California Independent System Operator (CAISO). The IOUs were required to sell into and purchase power through the new California Power Exchange (CalPX) and the CAISO. Retail rates were reduced but remained well above the national average. Rates were then frozen until the utilities recovered their stranded costs. At that point, competitive markets were expected to drive prices lower. San Diego Gas and Electric (SDG&E) fully recovered its stranded costs by summer of 1999, and its retail rates were then allowed to reflect the utility's cost of obtaining power in the wholesale markets. Retail rates for the other two major utilities remained frozen.

In late May 2000, the CAISO called its first Stage 2 power alert as system reserves fell below 5 percent. PX prices that had averaged about $27 per MWh in April spiked to over $50 in May and continued upwards, eventually reaching a high of $450 per MWh in January 2001. These higher prices were quickly passed through in San Diego, where average customer bills tripled by mid-summer. California's other major utilities, Pacific Gas and Electric (PG&E) and Southern California Edison (SCE), were forced to pay the unexpectedly higher PX wholesale prices, but could not pass increases on to retail customers as they were still under a rate freeze.

Price spikes were not California's only problems. On June 14, 2000, the CAISO imposed rolling blackouts in PG&E's San Francisco service area because of shortages attributed to the maintenance shutdown of several generating plants. These were the first of many power emergencies and blackouts affecting the state that did not end until July 2001.

Responding to public concern, the California Public Utilities Commission, the state's attorney general, and FERC all launched investigations. On August 2, 2000, SDG&E filed a complaint at FERC against all sellers in the PX and ISO markets and asked for a price cap of $250. FERC opened a formal investigation of wholesale pricing in California and the West in general. A preliminary FERC staff report in November 2000 found that the market rules and structure were "seriously flawed" and, coupled with supply and demand imbalance, could result in rates that were not "just and reasonable." The staff report concluded that the state's market structure created the potential for abuse of market power when supplies were tight. FERC proposed interim emergency remedies that were instituted in December 2000.

As the state's market problems continued and spread, price spikes affected electricity pricing hubs and utilities across the West, including states that had not adopted retail competition and that were not included in the CAISO. The region's increased power costs were estimated in the tens of billions and led to retail rate increases in many Western states. California declared multiple power emergencies in December 2000, followed by blackouts in January and March 2001. High wholesale market prices that utilities were not allowed to recover through retail rates threatened the solvency of the state's three major IOUs. California sought to end the procurement difficulties faced by IOUs in the state by entering into long-term contracts to secure power on behalf of the utilities and to preserve service to retail customers. Contract prices were set at some of the highest prices prevailing over this period. As a condition of assuming responsibility for power procurement, the state suspended retail competition for all but large customers that already had contracts with competitive suppliers. In April, PG&E's retail electric utility subsidiary, one of the largest in the nation, filed for bankruptcy protection, later joined by a number of wholesale seller-creditors, because the financially distressed distribution utilities did not make timely payments to these generators. Power prices did not return to "normal" ranges until fall of 2001.

Over this period, FERC issued a number of orders setting and lowering price caps, establishing market monitoring requirements, and opening an investigation of possible market manipulation in the run-up of natural gas prices in the West. State, federal, and private investigations ultimately uncovered a number of market abuses and regulatory gaps. Many FERC and other proceedings arising out of the dysfunctional California markets continue today. A number of energy traders eventually faced criminal charges. The 2000-2001 Western Energy Crisis had wide repercussions as other regions adapted their market rules and structures to avoid the problems encountered in the West.

6. Development of Regional Transmission Organizations and Regional Wholesale Markets

After issuing Order Nos. 888 and 889, FERC continued to receive complaints about transmission owners discriminating against independent generating companies. Transmission customers remained concerned that implementation of functional unbundling did not produce complete separation between operating the transmission system and marketing and selling electric power in wholesale markets. There were also concerns that Order No. 888 made some discriminatory behavior in transmission access more subtle and difficult to identify and document.

After FERC issued Order Nos. 888 and 889, the electric industry continued to evolve in response to competitive pressures and state retail restructuring initiatives. Utilities today purchase more wholesale power to meet load than in the past and are relying more on availability of other utility transmission facilities to deliver power. Retail competition increased significantly, and state initiatives brought about the divestiture of generation plants by traditional electric utilities. In addition, there were a number of mergers among traditional electric utilities and among electric utilities and gas pipeline companies. The number of power marketers and independent generation developers increased dramatically, and ISOs were established to manage large parts of the transmission system. Trade in wholesale power markets has increased significantly, and the nation's transmission grid is now used more heavily and in new ways.

In December 1999, responding to continuing complaints of discrimination and lack of transmission availability, FERC issued Order No. 2000. This order recognized that

Order No. 888 set up the foundation for competitive electric markets, but did not eliminate the potential to engage in undue discrimination and preference in providing transmission service. FERC concluded that regional transmission organizations (RTOs) could eliminate transmission rate pancaking, increase region-wide reliability, and eliminate any residual discrimination in transmission services where operation of the transmission system remains in the control of a vertically integrated utility. Accordingly, FERC encouraged voluntary formation of RTOs.

RTOs are entities set up in response to FERC Order Nos. 888 and 2000 encouraging utilities to voluntarily enter into arrangements to operate and plan regional transmission systems on a nondiscriminatory open access basis. RTOs are independent entities that control and operate regional electric transmission grids for the purpose of promoting efficiency and reliability in the operation and planning of the transmission grid and for ensuring non-discrimination in the provision of electric transmission services. RTOs currently do not own transmission.

FERC has approved RTOs or ISOs in several regions including the Northeast (PJM, New York ISO, ISO-New England), California, the Midwest (MISO) and the Southwest (SPP), as shown in Figure 1-3. By the end of 2004, regions accounting for 68 percent of all economic activity in the United States had chosen the RTO option. In 2004 and 2005, the PJM RTO grid expanded substantially to include several additional service territories in the Midwest. In 2004, the territories served by Commonwealth Edison (ComEd), American Electric Power (AEP), and Dayton Power and Light joined PJM. The expansion continued in 2005 with the addition of Duquesne Light and Dominion Resources. PJM now covers about 18 percent of total electricity consumption in the United States and includes utility service territories in the Mid-Atlantic, Midwest, and parts of the Southeast.

In most cases, RTOs have assumed responsibility to calculate the amount of available transfer capability (ATC) for wholesale trades for member systems across the footprint of the RTO. RTOs also are responsible for coordinating regional planning, at least for facilities necessary for reliability above a certain voltage. As of 2004, all RTOs coordinate dispatch of generators in their systems and provide transmission services under a single RTO open access tariff. In addition to operating the regional transmission grid, RTOs operate regional organized energy markets, including a short-term market which prices energy, congestion, and losses. RTOs in the East offer day-ahead and real-time markets, while California and Texas offer real-time markets alone. All current RTOs use or plan to use some form of locational pricing to manage transmission congestion and have independent market monitors that assess and report on market activities.

The RTO model and regional organized wholesale markets have been voluntarily adopted by utilities and market participants in the Northeast, Mid-Atlantic, California, and parts of the Midwest and Southwest. Some states required RTO participation as part of restructuring under the state retail competition plan. RTO members include utilities in states that have not adopted retail competition. State regulators often serve on RTO advisory bodies and have been active in FERC proceedings involving RTOs. Although RTOs enjoy broad participation by utilities and competitive power suppliers, some comments filed with the Task Force86 raised concerns over perceived high costs of RTO implementation and operations and oversight of RTO markets.

In other regions, including most of the Southeast, the West outside of California, and other parts of the Midwest, RTOs have been considered, but formation has stalled. State regulators and utilities in these regions have found it difficult to assess the potential benefits

Figure 1-3. RTO Configurations in 2006

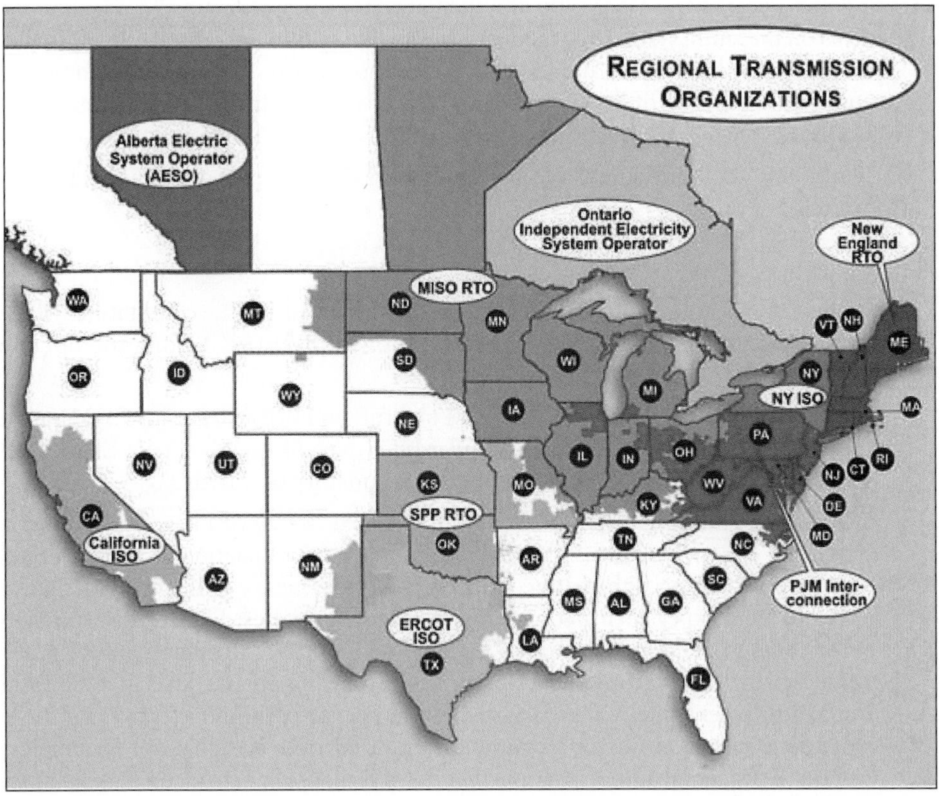

Note: This map shows the general location of approved RTOs. Not all transmitting utilities within the shaded area of an RTO are necessarily members of the RTO and some RTO members are not shown in this map.

Source: FERC RTO Regional Map, 2006, created using Platts POWERmap, *available at* http://www.ferc .gov/industries/electric/indusact/rto/rto-map.asp

and costs of establishing RTOs. They have been reluctant to create new institutional arrangements that could diminish local control over transmission facilities and could impose additional costs on retail customers.

7. August 2003 Blackout

On August 14, 2003, an electrical outage in Ohio precipitated a cascading blackout across seven other states and as far north as Ontario, Canada, leaving more than 50 million people without power. The August 2003 blackout was the largest in United States history, leaving some parts of the nation without power for up to four days and costing between $4 billion and $10 billion. It affected large portions of the Midwest and Northeast United States and Ontario and an estimated 61,800 MWs of load. It was the eighth major blackout in North America since the 1965 Northeast Blackout. A Joint U.S.-Canada Power System Outage Task Force issued a final Blackout Report in April 2004. The report identified factors that were common to some of the eight major outages from 1965 through the 2003, as shown below:

(1) conductor contact with trees; (2) overestimation of dynamic reactive output of system generators; (3) inability of system operators or coordinators to visualize events on the entire system; (4) failure to ensure that system operation was within safe limits; (5) lack of coordination on system protection; (6) ineffective communication; (7) lack of "safety nets;" and (8) inadequate training of operating personnel.

In addition to the Joint Study, affected states and NERC carried out their own investigations.

8. The Energy Policy Act of 2005

In August 2005, Congress passed EPAct 2005, which amended the core statutes (FPA, PURPA, PUHCA 1935) governing the electric power industry. Among the notable provisions of EPAct 2005 are the following:

- Reliability: Section 1211 authorizes FERC to certify an Electric Reliability Organization to propose and enforce reliability standards for the bulk power system. EPAct 2005 authorized penalties for violation of these mandatory standards.

- Transmission Siting: Section 1221 requires the Secretary of Energy to conduct a study of electricity congestion within one year of the enactment of EPAct 2005 and every three years thereafter. It authorizes the Secretary of Energy to designate certain areas experiencing congestion as "National Interest Electric Transmission Corridors" based on these studies. In certain limited circumstances, FERC is authorized to approve construction permits for transmission facilities in designated corridors when states either lack such authority, or withhold approval for more than one year after filing of an application or corridor designation. Proponents of this new federal authority argue that it will facilitate construction of new transmission and help alleviate transmission congestion that can impair competition in electric markets.

- *Transmission Investment Incentives*: Section 1241 requires FERC to establish incentive-based rate treatments for public utilities' transmission infrastructure to promote capital investment in transmission infrastructure, attract new investment with an attractive return on equity, encourage improvement in transmission technology, and allow for recovery of prudently incurred costs related to reliability and improved transmission infrastructure. Proponents contend this will encourage the expansion of transmission capacity and, thus, help foster greater competition in electric markets.

- *PURPA Reform*: Section 1253 permits FERC to terminate, prospectively, the obligation of electric utilities to buy power from QFs, such as industrial cogenerators. FERC may do so when the QFs in the relevant area have adequate opportunities to make competitive sales, as defined by EPAct 2005. The premise is that growth in competitive opportunities in electric markets negates the need for PURPA's "forced sale" requirements.

- *PUHCA 1935 Repeal*: Title XVII, subtitle F repeals PUHCA 1935 and replaces it with new PUHCA 2005. It provides FERC and state access to books and records of holding companies and their members. It also provides that certain holding companies or states may obtain FERC-authorized cost allocations for non-power goods or services provided by an associate company to public utility members in the holding company. PUHCA 2005 also contains a mandatory exemption from the federal books and records access provisions for entities that are holding companies solely with respect to EWGs, QFs or foreign utility companies. The goal is to reduce legal obstacles to investment in the electric utility industry and, thereby, help facilitate the construction of adequate infrastructure.

C. Recent Trends Related to Competition in the Electric Energy Industry

This section discusses several more recent electric industry policy developments and characteristics.

1. Increases in Generation and Growth of Nonutility Generation Suppliers

Electric power industry restructuring has been sustained largely by technological improvements in gas turbines. It is no longer necessary to build a larger generating plant to gain operating efficiencies. Combined-cycle gas turbines reach maximum efficiency at 400 MW, while aero-derivative gas turbines can be efficient at sizes as low as 10 MW. These new gas-fired combined cycle plants can be more energy efficient and less costly than the older oil and gas-fired plants.91 Because of their smaller footprint and low emissions, gas turbine generators can often be located close to load, avoiding the need for additional transmission. Coupled with greater transmission access as a result of Order No. 888, it became feasible for generating plants hundreds of miles apart to compete with each other, giving customers more choices in electricity suppliers.

The market participation of utilities and other generation suppliers began changing in response to increases in energy costs in the 1970-1990s and the passage of PURPA, which facilitated entry of nonutility QFs as energy-efficient, environmentally-friendly, alternative sources of electric power. The change continued through Order No. 888, which opened up the transmission grid to competing wholesale electricity suppliers.93 Until the early 1980s, electric utilities' share of electric power production increased steadily, reaching 97 percent in 1979. By 1991, however, the trend had reversed itself, and the utilities' share declined to 91 percent. By 2004, regulated electric utilities' share of total generation continued to decline (63.1 percent in 2004 versus 63.4 percent in 2003) as nonutilities' share increased (28.2 percent versus 27.4 percent in 2003).

… While most of the existing capacity and most of the additions to capacity through the late 1980s were built by electric utilities, their share of capacity additions declined in the 1990s. Between 1996 and 2004, roughly 74 percent of electricity capacity additions were made by nonutility power producers.

However, the pattern of merchant generation investment outpacing utility investment may be shifting. Traditional regulated utilities, including public power and cooperative utilities, accounted for about 60 percent of capacity additions from 2005 through May 2006. In California, six new power plants began operations, including four owned by public utilities and two owned by IOUs.

2. Transmission Investment

Despite these increased investments in new generation, the Edison Electric Institute (EEI) reports that IOU investment in transmission declined from 1975 through 1999. Over that period, electricity demand more than doubled, resulting in a significant decrease in transmission capacity relative to demand. Box 1-2 on the next page suggests reasons for this trend. Since 1999, according to EEI surveys, transmission investment has increased annually. From 1999 to 2003, IOU investment increased 12 percent annually. For 2004 to 2008, IOUs expect to invest about $28 billion in transmission, an almost 60 percent increase over the prior five-year period.

Box 1-2. Decline in Transmission Investment

Transmission is the physical link between electricity supply and demand. Without adequate transmission capacity, wholesale competition cannot function effectively.

Some reasons suggested for the decline in transmission investment between 1975 and 1997 are a decline in investment in large base-load generating plants requiring associated new large transmission additions, an overbuilt system prior to 1975, lack of available capital due to other investment activities by vertically integrated utilities, the protection of vertically integrated utility generation from competition, and regulatory uncertainty over recovery of new transmission investment.

Another explanation for the decline in investment is the difficulty of siting new transmission lines. Siting can bring long delays and negative publicity. Local opposition can be significant. Also, some states may require a showing of benefits to the state for approval of a transmission line. This creates challenges for interstate transmission facilities proposed to primarily benefit interstate commerce.

---

3. Retail Prices of Residential Electricity

As seen in Figure 1-6, between 1970 and 1985, national average residential electricity prices more than tripled in nominal terms and increased by 25 percent in real terms

Figure 1-6. National Average Retail Prices of Electricity for Residential Customers, 1960–2005

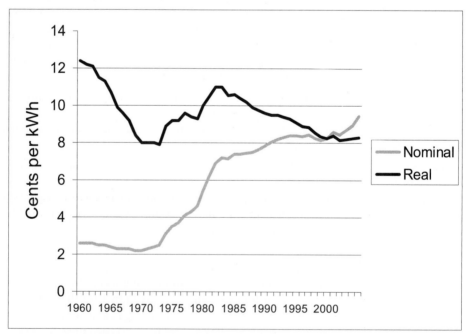

Note: Real prices are shown in chained (2000) dollars, calculated by using gross domestic product implicit price deflators.

Source: EIA, *Annual Energy Review 2004*, Table 8.10 Average Retail Prices of Electricity, 1960-2004, and EIA, Monthly Energy Review, July 2006, Table 5-3.

(adjusting for inflation). U.S. real retail electricity prices began to fall after the mid-1980s until 2000-2001 as fossil fuel prices and interest rates declined and inflation moderated significantly. Real retail prices stayed flat through 2004, but have begun to increase in all regions reflecting higher fuel prices and operating costs.

According to the latest information from EIA, residential electric prices in 2005 averaged 9.43 cents per kilowatthour (kWh), an increase of about 5 percent from 2004. Retail electric prices continue to increase, and the national average price for residential customers in April 2006 was 10.31 cents per kWh, up 12 percent from a year earlier. These increases reflect substantially higher fuel and purchased power costs.

4. Changing Patterns of Fuel Use for Generation—Reaction to Increased Oil Prices and Clean-Air Environmental Regulations

For many years, coal was the fuel most commonly used to generate electricity, providing 46 percent of utilities' generation in 1970 and more than 50 percent since 1980. As world oil prices escalated in the 1970s, oil-fired and gasoline-fired generation's share of electricity supply began decreasing and utilities' use of oil and gas for new generation was restricted by federal law.

Hydroelectric power also has played a large role in the supply of electric power, but its share has declined relative to other major fuels mainly because there are a limited number of suitable sites for hydroelectric projects. Nuclear power emerged as the second largest fuel source in 1991 but was not expected to increase.

For nonutilities, natural gas has been the major fuel for new plant additions. Indeed, in recent years, new capacity additions reflect the prevalence of natural gas.... The Clean Air Act Amendments of 1990 (CAA) and state clean air requirements also contributed to increased use of natural gas. The CAA sought to address the most widespread and persistent pollution problems caused by hydrocarbons and nitrogen oxides, both of which are prevalent with traditional coal and petroleum-based generation. The CAA fundamentally changed the generation business because emission of air pollutants would no longer be cost-free. As a result, many generation owners and new plant developers turned to cleaner-burning natural gas as the fuel source for new generation plants. California has depended heavily on gas-fired generation because of its specific air quality standards.

The result of these plant additions through December 2005 is that 49.9 percent of the nation's electric power was generated at coal-fired plants. Nuclear plants contributed 19.3 percent; 18.6 percent was generated by natural gas-fired plants, and 2.5 percent was generated at petroleum liquid-fired plants. Conventional hydroelectric power provided 6.6 percent of the total, while other renewables (primarily biomass, but also geothermal, solar, and wind) and other miscellaneous energy sources generated the remaining electric power.

The trend toward gas-fueled capacity additions may be changing. There is renewed interest in coal-fired generation as reflected in utilities' and nonutilities' announcements of new coal plant construction projects. Two major reasons may explain coal's resurgence: (1) the relative price of natural gas compared to coal has increased substantially and (2) the cost of environmental equipment for coal plants, such as scrubbers, has decreased. "Over the past decade, many merchant combined-cycle gas-fired units were built on the assumption that natural gas would be relatively inexpensive and that cleaning technology for coal plants would drive the price of coal plants significantly higher. Sharp increases in natural gas prices in recent years have challenged these assumptions." DOE's EIA estimated that 573 MWs of new coal generation would be added nationally in 2005, which compares with an estimate of 15,216 MWs of gas-fired additions for the same year. For

2009, however, predicted trends shift; the EIA projects that 8,122 MWs of new coal generation will be added that year, whereas only 5,451 MWs of gas-fired generation additions are predicted. DOE predicts a resurgence of coal-fired generation as far into the future as 2025.

Higher gas prices and environmental concerns have also spurred renewed interest in nuclear generation. EPAct 2005 includes a number of provisions intended to encourage and facilitate a new and improved generation of nuclear power plants.

5. Fuel Price Trends

Natural gas prices have been increasing in recent years, due in part to historically high petroleum prices. Natural gas prices increased 51.5 percent between 2002 and 2003, 10.5 percent between 2003 and 2004, and 37.6 percent between 2004 and 2005. Strong demand for natural gas, as well as natural gas production disruptions in the Gulf of Mexico, contributed to these increases.... [F]or December 2005 the overall price of fossil fuels was influenced by the price increases in natural gas. In December 2005, the average price for fossil fuels was $3.71 per million Btu (MMBtu), 10.1 percent higher than for November 2005, and 44.4 percent higher than in December 2004. As natural gas prices increase relative to coal prices, the change may make development of clean-burning coal plants more economically attractive than they were when natural gas fuel prices were lower.

6. Mergers, Acquisitions, and Power Plant Divestitures of Investor-Owned Electric Utilities

Many IOUs have fundamentally reassessed their corporate strategies to function more like competitive, market-driven entities than in their more regulated past. One result is that there was a wave of mergers and acquisitions in the late 1980s through the late 1990s between traditional electric utilities and between electric utilities and gas pipeline companies.

IOUs also have divested a substantial number of generation assets to IPPs or transferred them to an unregulated nonutility subsidiary within the company. Even though FERC-regulated IOUs have functionally unbundled generation from transmission, and some have formed RTOs and ISOs, many utilities have divested their power plants because of state requirements. Some states that opened the electric market to retail competition view the separation of power generation ownership from power transmission and distribution ownership as a prerequisite for retail competition. For example, California, Connecticut, Maine, New Hampshire, and Rhode Island enacted laws requiring utilities to divest their power plants. In other states, the state public utility commission may encourage divestiture to arrive at a quantifiable level of stranded costs for purposes of recovery during the transition to competition.

Since 1997, IOUs have divested power generation assets at unprecedented levels, and these power plant divestitures have also reduced the total number of IOUs that own generation capacity. A few utilities have decided to sell their power plants, as a business strategy, deciding that they cannot compete in a competitive power market. In a few instances, an IOU has divested power generation capacity to mitigate potential market power resulting from a merger.... [B]etween 1998 and 2001, over 300 plants, representing nearly 20 percent of U.S. installed generating capacity, changed ownership.

Since 2001 the merger trends have shifted slightly, as financial difficulties of the merchant generating sector have prompted the sale or transfer of a substantial share of the merchant fleet. Some purchasers have been traditional utilities, including public power and cooperative utilities.

There were no significant electric power company mergers from 2001 to 2004, but in 2004 utilities and financial institutions exhibited growing interest in mergers and acquisitions, prompting many analysts to herald 2004 as a new round of consolidation in the power sector. One utility-to-utility acquisition closed, and three were announced. Most electric acquisitions in 2004 involved the purchase of specific generation assets. Many companies strove to stabilize financial profiles through asset sales. In aggregate, almost 36 GW of generation, or nearly 6 percent of installed capacity, changed hands in 2004.

* * *

The Influence of Price on Generation

As explained in the above report, electricity is generated from a variety of resources, with the majority of the nation's electricity coming from natural gas, coal, nuclear, and water (hydropower). Water and nuclear require massive infrastructure investments (both time and financial). Investments in coal and natural gas generating facilities are significant, as well, but they are more price sensitive. With nuclear and hydropower, once the investment is made, the incremental costs of generation are nominal. With coal and natural gas facilities, the cost of the fuel needed to keep the facilities operating is critical.

Natural gas, in particular, has been subject to massive price fluctuations. In the past forty to fifty years, natural gas prices have periodically dropped to levels where the price and available supplies seemed to indicate massive fuel switching was both prudent and wise. Virtually every time this has happened, though, supplies have dropped and costs have risen, making natural gas a problematic fuel source. You can see these concerns reflected in the 2007 report.

However, since 2007, the massive increase in potential natural gas supplies by virtue of horizontal drilling and hydraulic fracturing in U.S. shale formations may have changed that trend for the foreseeable future. In 2012, for the first time since the Energy Information Administration (EIA) began collecting the data, natural gas-fired plants moved into a virtual tie with generation from coal-fired plants, with both fuels accounting for about 32% of total electricity generation.

Still, some price volatility remains. In March 2013, EIA data showed that coal has generated 40% or more of the nation's electricity each month since November 2012, with natural gas handling about 25% of electricity generation over that time. Since May 2012, a combination of higher prices for natural gas and increased demand for electricity during the summer months led electric systems across much of the country to increase their use of coal-fired units. Coal-fired units generated a little more than 130,000 megawatt-hours of electricity in March 2013; natural gas was used to generate nearly 85,000 megawatt-hours.

EIA, *Future Power Market Shares of Coal, Natural Gas Generators Depend on Relative Fuel Prices*

April 23, 201
http://www.eia.gov/todayinenergy/detail.cfm?id=10951

Heading into the 2013 spring shoulder season (between winter and summer), when demand for electricity typically falls, higher prices for natural gas reduced the fuel's share of total generation below the record levels of last April.

Nonetheless, the coal share of total generation remained well below its typical range prior to 2009. Between 2001 and 2008, the coal share (on an annual basis) ranged from 48% to 51%. Coal last achieved a 50% share in 2005 and is expected to be 40% in 2013, according to the most recent Short-Term Energy Outlook.

Recent statistics on electricity generation and the consumption, prices, and quantity of fuels used to produce electricity through March 2013 were released in the Electric Power Monthly, and regional trends in the use of these resources were discussed in the Electricity Monthly Update.

In recent years, natural gas competed more effectively with coal as a fuel for electricity generation as the cost of operating natural gas-fired generators fell below the cost of operating coal-fired generators in some regions, changing the least-cost dispatch ordering of available units. EIA's most recent outlook shows how generation market shares respond to changing fuel prices.

In 2012, the national average per-megawatt hour costs for producing electricity from coal steam plants and natural gas combined-cycle plants were nearly equal. In the Reference case forecast (shown in the graph above), natural gas plants begin to lose competitive advantage over time as natural gas prices increase relative to coal prices. Because fuel prices vary by region and because considerable variation in efficiencies exists across the fleets of both coal-fired plants and combined-cycle plants, continued competition for dispatch between coal and natural gas is expected, even in the Reference case.

The coal and natural gas shares of total electricity generation vary widely across the alternative cases. The coal share of total generation varies from 28% to 40% in 2040, and the natural gas share varies from 18% to 42% (see graph below). In the High Oil and Gas Resource case, natural gas becomes the dominant generation fuel after 2015, and its share of total generation is 42% in 2040.

There is significant uncertainty about future coal and natural gas prices. Higher coal prices or lower natural gas prices give natural gas combined-cycle plants more opportunities to displace coal-fired generators. In Annual Energy Outlook (AEO2013), for both the High Coal Cost case and the High Oil and Gas Resource case (characterized by low natural gas prices), average natural gas combined-cycle units are close to or more economical than average coal steam turbines.

Fuel costs for power generation

At any point in time, short-term competition between existing coal- and gas-fired generators—i.e., the economic decisions determining which generators will be dispatched to generate electricity—is largely dependent on the relative operating costs of each technology. Fuel costs represent a major portion of the total operating costs. The fuel cost ratio in the chart above illustrates the relative competitiveness of dispatching coal steam turbines versus natural gas combined-cycle plants. A second aspect of competition occurs over the longer term, as developers choose which fuels and technologies to use for new capacity, and whether to make mandated or optional upgrades to existing plants. The natural gas or coal share of total generation depends both on the available capacity of each fuel type (affected by the latter type of competition) and on how intensively the capacity is operated.

Notes & Questions

1. What are stranded costs? How do stranded costs relate to electricity generation infrastructure?

2. Investment: How do well established, clear regulations help facilitate an economic environment that encourages investment? Particularly, how does regulation relate to incentivize the construction or alterations of power generating facilities?

C. Generation Resources

1. Coal

As you begin this part of the chapter, take a look at Appendix A, which shows how coal consumption has fluctuated over time. If you worked for a coal company, how might these changes influence your thinking? How about if you worked for an environmental organization that is committed to fuel-switching away from coal?

Current State and Future Direction of Coal-Fired Power in the Eastern Interconnection

ICF Incorporated White Paper For EISPC and NARU
Funded by the U.S. Department of Energy
June 2013

1 Introduction

The Eastern Interconnection States' Planning Council (EISPC) represents the 39 states, the District of Columbia, the City of New Orleans, and the eight Canadian provinces located within the Eastern Interconnection electric transmission grid. One of EISPC's goals is to evaluate transmission development options within the Interconnection, and as part of that effort ICF International (ICF) was commissioned to conduct a study for EISPC focused on the present state and future direction of coal-fired electricity generating capacity in the U.S. portion of the Eastern Interconnection (hereafter simply referred to as the EI).

This Whitepaper is a summary of ICF's research exploring the challenges and opportunities faced by coal-fired generating resources. Coal capacity in the US is concentrated in the Eastern part of the country, with 84% of national coal-fired capacity within the EI. Due to a combination of existing and proposed environmental regulations and low gas prices, existing coal-fired generating facilities are facing a choice of whether to retire or to spend the necessary capital to comply with the regulations. Future development of coal-fired resources is also challenged by increasingly stringent environmental regulations. Additionally, the future for new coal-fired generating resources will continue to be impacted by uncertainties around the commercial availability of carbon capture and storage (CCS) technologies and the costs of building new coal-fired units.

The Whitepaper is organized into five sections. Following the Introduction, the next section describes the state of coal-fired capacity in the Eastern Interconnection, including geographic distribution of coal-fired capacity in the EI. The subsequent section outlines five major challenges to both existing and future coal power plants: current and anticipated environmental regulations and their associated impacts; development of shale gas resources and the impact of low natural gas prices; current state of development of CCS technologies; comparisons of levelized costs of electricity of various types generating resources (including CCS); and impact of electricity markets and regional planning authorities. The next section describes potential opportunities for coal power based on state level incentives for coal-fired power generation and the coal mining industry, followed by the concluding section.

Where appropriate, material presented here references specific sections of ICF's Final Study Report that contains all six of the Task reports developed throughout this study.

2 Coal-fired Capacity and Generation in the Eastern Interconnection

The vast majority of coal-fired units in the U.S. are located within the EI, and coal still serves as the most common fuel source for power generation in the EI and in the U.S. as a whole. In 2010, within the EI there were approximately 269 GW of coal-fired capacity comprised of 1,099 individual coal units, which accounted for 84% of U.S. coal capacity and 87% of coal units in the U.S.2 Of the 269 GW of capacity in the EI, roughly one-third are located in the following five states: Illinois, Indiana, Ohio, Pennsylvania, and West Virginia. These units heavily rely on bituminous and sub-bituminous coal. Geographically, the EI covers the following six NERC regions: Northeast Power Coordinating Council (NPCC), ReliabilityFirst Corporation (RFC), Midwest Reliability Organization (MRO), Sothern Power Pool (SPP), Southeastern Electric Reliability Council (SERC), and Florida Reliability Coordinating Council (FRCC). In 2010, 204 GW (75% of total coal capacity in the EI) was located in RFC and SERC.

In terms of generation of electricity, coal accounts for the largest percentage of total US generation. In 1985 coal provided 53% of U.S. generation but over the past 30 years, the national fuel mix has undergone a gradual shift to a more diverse mix of fuels as illustrated in Exhibit 1. Coal-based power generation grew during the 1990s but began to hit a plateau at around 2 TWh in the 2000s. With the economic crisis in 2009, coal-

Exhibit 1. Historical Generation Fuel Mix in the U.S.

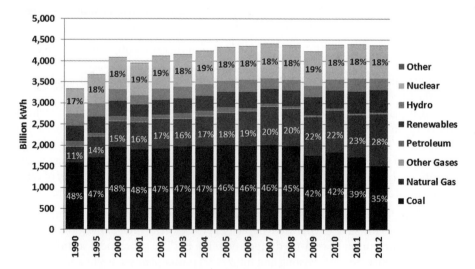

Source: EIA, Annual Energy Review; EIA Electric Power Monthly

based generation (as well as the overall power demand) dropped. Although there was some recovery in 2010, coal-based generation has continued to drop in 2011 and 2012. Nationally, coal generation reduced to about 35% of total generation in 2012. However, based on data from the first quarter of 2013 from the EIA, recent rise in natural gas prices has led coal to regain some market share. According to Form EIA-923 detailed data, coal-fired generation contributed to 40% of total electricity generation in the United States. At the same time, from 1990 to 2012, the share of generation from natural gas-fired units nationally has increased from 11% to 28%, and the total generation from gas continues to increase on an annual basis. Total nuclear generation in the region has continued to increase due to uprates at existing facilities, even though the last nuclear units came online in the 1980s. Although total generation from nuclear units has increased in recent years, it has not kept pace with demand growth, and the share of nuclear power as part of the generation mix has begun to erode.

Similar to the national trend, demand for coal-based electricity in the EI has stayed relatively flat in most of 2000s, followed by a drop due to the economic crisis in 2009, as illustrated in Exhibit 2. There is also an evident switch from coal-fired to gas-fired resources in terms of generation levels with the gas-based generation increasing from 11% of power demand in 2001 to about 28% in 2012. Furthermore, overall demand for electricity as also decreased slightly in the EI over the last few years, with increased energy efficiency and demand resources making up for the difference.

The coal plants in the EI are relatively old, with significant amount of coal units in RFC and SERC being older than 50 years, as indicated in Exhibit 3. By 2015, roughly half of the coal-fired units in the Eastern Interconnection will be 50 years of age or older, and on a state level, the average age of all coal units in the five states of Illinois, Indiana, Ohio, Pennsylvania, and West Virginia will be nearly 50 years by 2015. Hence, it is likely that these regions have the greatest potential for retirements and subsequent transmission related changes.

Furthermore, … the older units tend to be smaller in terms of capacity (although, they altogether still represent 25% of total capacity), and these older units also tend to be the ones

Exhibit 2. Electricity Generation Mix in the Eastern Interconnect

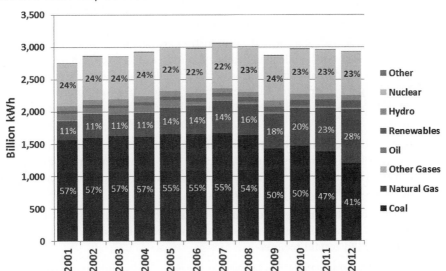

Source: EIA, Annual Energy Review; EIA Electric Power Monthly

without emission controls. These units that have been operating for 50 years and longer—and uncontrolled for SO_2—represent the subset of units with the highest risk of retirement.

2. Natural Gas

Gas-Power Interdependence: Knock-On Effects of the Dash to Gas

ScottMadden Management Consultants, Copyright © 2013

INTRODUCTION

The energy industry has recently been turned on its head as natural gas prices have held below $4 per MMBTU for several years. This is driven by significantly greater supply as natural gas producers begin to exploit and extract as much as 300 trillion cubic feet of estimated reserves, including those accessible through unconventional drilling, especially hydraulic-fracturing techniques.

The combination of evolving environmental regulations limiting reliance on coal generation and low gas prices has led to a significant increase in the amount of gas-fired generation in the United States. Low gas prices and significant financial hurdles are limiting the prospects for new nuclear. Renewables are not economical without subsidies, and when they are a significant part of the generation mix, they require quick response grid support that gas-fired generation can provide.

The current assumption in the energy industry is that these trends will continue and could lead to an unprecedented reliance on natural gas generation. A recent Energy Information Administration estimate found that gas could account for 25% of power generation by 2020, up from 20% in 2010. As such, it is worth considering the degree to which the electric and gas industries have become dependent upon one another and the implications of that interdependence.

ScottMadden believes there are five characteristics of interdependence that may threaten the reliability of the grid in certain circumstances.

- **"Co-dependence":** Electric and gas industries are becoming more "co-dependent." The reliability of the electric industry is increasingly dependent on gas-fired generation and its associated infrastructure. Much gas infrastructure is dependent on electricity to operate. Failure in either sector now has potential reliability impacts or cascading effects on the other. The risk of common mode failures is increasing.

- **Increased volumetric requirements:** The gas-fired plants being built today are different from earlier generations, because they require higher gas pressure and consume larger amounts of gas on a daily basis than previous ones, placing greater demands on the existing infrastructure.

- **Reliance on interruptible contracting:** The current balance of firm and interruptible contracts to meet the needs of gas-fired generation may not align with the needs of the grid in certain regions.

- **Operational mismatches:** As far back as the early 2000s, industry participants and standards makers, like North American Energy Standards Board, identified the lack of alignment between the trading days for gas and electricity as a potential systemic weakness and an important area of coordination. Further, the planning horizons for the two industries are significantly different, which may result in building the infrastructure most easily (or quickly) deployed while not considering the optimal reliability solution for the region.

- **System design vs. emerging usage patterns:** The gas pipeline system was designed to do one thing—move gas from supply centers to demand centers primarily for retail use—and now we are asking it to do something quite different in locations served, pressures required, and reserve capacity maintained. This introduces system constraints. In some cases, the gas pipeline infrastructure may be insufficient to handle coincident heating load and electric load peaks, especially if any tipping point factors are present, such as the loss of significant coal generation. This was demonstrated by rolling blackouts in the Southwest in February 2011, as coal units failed during a cold snap, heating load peaked, and many generators needed a five-fold increase in gas supply and could not obtain it.

These issues are surfacing across the country, most acutely in regions with the highest dependence on gas-fired generation. Some regions, driven by the proverbial wolf at the door, have been very proactive in attempting to resolve these challenges. Others have been less proactive and less organized in their responses.

What are the Possible Impacts of Expanded Power Generation on Gas Infrastructure?

Gas-fired generation now makes up 22% of the generation mix in the United States, and it comprises more than 40% of that mix in New England and Texas. However, these are not the only regions that must consider the risks attendant with gas-power interdependence.

Table 1 shows that nine of the ten largest (by volume) generating companies in the United States reduced their use of coal in generation from 2010 to 2011. Of these nine, eight concurrently increased gas-fired generation.

This increased power generation demand will place significant strain on natural gas pipelines. For example, the Midwest Independent Transmission System Operator (MISO) recently performed an analysis which concluded that replacing 12 GW of coal generation with gas-fired generation would lead to gas deliverability problems. These problems occur as the existing pipeline system simply does not have enough capacity to take on this additional power generation.

Consider the Northern Border Pipeline (NBP), which runs from Montana to Indiana. Current throughput capacity on the NBP is approximately 2 BCF per day and has annual capacity utilization of about 65%. In the worst case scenario, MISO found that the effect of an extra 12 GW leaning on the NBP due to coal plant retirements would mean the pipeline's gas-fired combined-cycle generators could face insufficient pipeline capacity of up to almost half the days in the year. MISO found that up to 102 days in summer and up to 78 days in winter would be underserved by NBP.[]

Common Mode Failures and the Gas-Electric Negative Feedback Loop

As more gas-fired generation is added to the grid, the electric industry faces increased risk associated with common mode failure. Common mode failure occurs when multiple failures are caused by a single fault. To the extent that multiple gas-fired generators are dependent upon a single gas pipeline, if that pipeline fails or has insufficient capacity for a coincident heating and generation peak, several generating facilities may also go down.

Table 1: Fuel Mix of Top 10 U.S. Generators

Fuel Mix of Top 10 U. S. Generators	Coal Share of Total Generation		Gas Share of Total Generation	
	2010	2011	2010	2011
Southern Co.	57%	51%	25%	30%
NextEra Energy	4%	3%	51%	57%
American Electric Power	81%	77%	8%	11%
Exelon	5%	3%	1%	1%
TVA	49%	47%	7%	8%
Duke Energy	60%	57%	7%	10%
Entergy	13%	12%	23%	25%
First Energy	64%	70%	0%	0%
Dominion Resources	38%	32%	14%	19%
Progress Energy	45%	36%	29%	32%

Source: FERC Data; ScottMadden analysis

Transmission planning criteria require planning for the single or two worst contingencies on the system (including the loss of generating units). However, they do not plan for these more extreme eventualities such as loss of pipeline capacity. Importantly, this loss of pipeline capacity could be due to physical failure of the facility (though rare) or due to lack of contracted capacity for gas.

When a generating unit is built, it is assumed (for transmission planning purposes) to be available to address system contingencies. The reality is that may not be the case if issues around gas supply are not addressed. For instance, loss of a single generator could cause multiple gas-fired units to be called up; sudden demand could cause pipeline pressures to drop and reduce quality of service to other customers including generators. This could potentially lead to another common mode failure.

Because grid stability depends on the network of generators available and running, a common mode failure in generation of sufficient scope and immediacy could also lead to grid instability, rolling blackouts, or collapse.

Electric transmission service interruptions can affect service to motor-driven gas compressor stations. On peak days, just as electricity is most needed to power gas compressors so gas can serve peak heating and electric loads, it may not be available because the interruptible gas is no longer available to fuel the generators needed to provide energy or support the grid—and thereby power the compressors. To the extent that compromised electric service causes a failure at a compressor station, this could have follow-on effects: the gas-fired plants and other customers dependent on that pipeline may not have access to the gas they need. The risk of however, this type of follow-on effect due to electric-gas interdependence is not.

Moreover, cold weather not only drives gas demand, but it can also lead to unexpected generator failures (as seen during the rolling blackouts in Texas in February 2011). So, during cold weather peaks, the need for marginal gas units on interruptible contracts may increase, exacerbating this common mode failure risk.

Increased Volumetric Demand of Newer Gas-Fired Power Generation

The types of generating stations being built today require more gas at higher pressures. A 1,270 MW combustion turbine operating at a 70% capacity factor requires almost 400 million cubic feet per day. That volume is more than the amount delivered to nearly 650,000 Boston Gas Company customers on a typical day in 2011—about 300 million cubic feet.

Moreover, the gas pressure required for gas combustion turbines (CTs) built today is 450 to 475 pounds per square inch (psi). Plants built in the 1990s required approximately 270 psi, 40% less than today's gas CTs. This means these plants have the ability to exhaust gas pipeline line pack (pressure built up overnight and intended to be exhausted during the day) significantly faster than their predecessors. This limits the ability of the grid as a whole to react to unexpected or abrupt changes in load, such as storms or loss of another generator, especially where they are coincident with high retail gas demand.

Winter's Not Just for End-Users Anymore

Historically, winter gas demand by generators has not been extraordinary. But as the percentage of gas-fired capacity has increased, demand for fuel for gas generation is increasingly a year-round phenomenon, especially as gas is now supplanting coal in many cases for base load duty.

For example, in 2000, gas-fired capacity constituted less than 20% of New England's generation capacity; by May 2012, that percentage exceeded 40%. Coinciding peaks (i.e., high winter-heating days) will put a strain on both the gas distribution utilities meeting residential loads, which have and will likely continue to have priority access to gas, and the gas-fired generation meeting electricity requirements. This has led to price spikes and could ultimately lead to reliability challenges....

CONCLUSION

The evolving interdependence between the gas and electric industries is presenting new and potentially critical reliability challenges. This has become acute in the regions most dependent upon gas-fired generation. The challenges are as follows:

 * Emerging electric-gas "co-dependence"
 * Increased volumetric requirements
 * Reliance on interruptible contracting
 * Operational mismatches
 * System design vs. developing usage patterns

Fortunately, in those regions of the country most critically impacted, ISOs, RTOs, and industry groups have begun to study and address the issues described in this paper, as summarized in *Table 2* below. ScottMadden strongly believes these industry-led initiatives should continue, as regional approaches appear much more likely to succeed in addressing reliability concerns.

However, we believe the magnitude of the risks and opportunities is not yet matched by the responses of many companies and public policy makers. There are significant opportunities for many players to increase reliability for all and to make money from the sea changes occurring in both markets.

ScottMadden believes there are holistic policy-level considerations which must accompany these technical solutions to ensure that the two industries build a framework within which to cooperate for the foreseeable future. Some feel this holistic approach, by definition, requires federal (read FERC) intervention. While FERC should continue

Table 2: Various Approaches to Bridging Gas-Power "Seams" Issues

Approach	Description	Issues and Considerations
Infrastructure Enhancement		
Enhanced gas pipeline capacity	Development, expansion, or extension of pipelines into gas-constrained power generation demand centers	• Gas pipeline industry already considering expansion of capacity. • Increasing number of projects transport gas. • Increasingly a grid, not a one-way flow from the Gulf and Canada. • Industry does not, however, build to include a pipeline "reserve margin." • Pipelines require long-term capacity subscriptions and firm commitments, precisely what power generators are not offering.
Enhanced gas storage	Development of storage near power generation demand centers	• Geological potential varies by region and may not provide desired rapid withdrawal. • Above-ground storage is limited in scale and would require public acceptance (NB: similar issues regarding siting LNG terminals). • Market pricing of storage may make it more attractive with peak pricing. • Like pipelines, currently requires capacity subscriptions and "anchor tenants."
Expanded power transmission	Increasing electric transmission expansion in at-risk gas-dependent but pipeline-constrained regions	• Expanding electric transmission is a lengthy process, more so than gas. • Stakeholders and constituents for electric transmission differ from those of gas transmission. • Cost allocation and socialization issues are similar for electric transmission as for gas. • Power transmission also requires "anchor tenants."
Operational Enhancements		
Improved communication	Increased communication between gas pipeline and power grid operators on power grid and gas transportation situation and contingencies	• Concerns about proprietary information being improperly shared. • Currently regulatory "code-of-conduct" limitations on information sharing may need to be relaxed. • Some regions establishing coordination mechanisms, especially where weather events may warrant.
Additional intraday nomination opportunities	Increasing the frequency of opportunities within the gas day to nominate additional volumes	• Some regions are contemplating adding additional intraday gas nomination. • Capacity release programs are already in place for market participants to procure, if available, gas transportation. • Intraday nominations help adjust volumes for those with firm transportation, but may provide little aid to firms with interruptible capacity on peak days.

Table 2: Various Approaches to Bridging Gas-Power "Seams" Issues, *continued*

Approach	Description	Issues and Considerations
Contracting		
Cost recovery for firm gas contracts	Increased firm contracting and mechanism for cost recovery	• As more gas-fired generation serves base load duty, willingness of those power generators to enter into firm transportation agreements may increase. • For load following and peaking capacity, the issue is how to socialize costs without putting gas-fired generators "out of the market." • Could ISOs or RTOs play a role in gas transportation as quasi-capacity product/service, either directly or through a market-based structure? • One key issue: mismatch of gas transportation contracts (5 to 10 years) versus, in some bid-based markets and restructured retail markets, triennial provider of last resort and capacity bidding. • ISOs and RTOs are reluctant to craft fuel-specific rules or structures, as the perceived mandate is fuel neutrality.

to provide leadership in this area and undertake select rulemakings to address those issues to which a common standard would be beneficial, by and large, ScottMadden's view is that regional approaches are much more likely to succeed in a timely manner. We propose that, due to the regional nature of the issues, the solutions should also be regional.

Many factors are driving the dash to gas (e.g., low gas prices, environmental regulation, etc.). This industry shift is not without consequences and, as a result, the gas and electric industries must continue to evaluate the nature and gravity of this convergence and take steps to ensure that reliability across all customers is preserved, business models are adjusted, and public policy is far-sighted and constructive.

* * *

Notes & Questions

1. As noted above, the price of fuels used in base-load electricity generation can greatly affect the economics of producing electricity. Particularly noted were the sensitivities associated with the price of natural gas. What major market factors affect the price of natural gas?

2. What is convergence in the natural gas market? How should that impact electricity policy? Do vast increases in potential natural gas supplies change anything? Why or why not?

3. Return to the client issue raised at the beginning of the chapter. Keep working on your outline of the key issues and topics that an IRP should cover, and keep that list going as you continue through the chapter. What new issues do new fuel resources raise? How does each sector change your view of the prior sector? Also, think about who your primary audience is for an IRP? Who else can or should be part of your analysis?

3. Nuclear

Sharon Squassoni, *Nuclear Power in the Global Energy Portfolio*
From *The Future of Nuclear Power in the United States*,
edited by Dr. Charles D. Ferguson and Dr. Frank A. Settle
Federation of American Scientists (FAS) and
Washington and Lee University*

Nuclear energy has generated commercial electricity for more than half a century. Although advocates had high hopes for its widespread use, nuclear energy growth in the last twenty years faltered on lower costs for alternatives like natural gas and a steep drop in public support after the reactor accidents at three Mile Island and Chernobyl. In the United States, escalating costs and a nascent environmental movement halted virtually all new construction after 1978. Some countries, such as Japan, France and the Republic of Korea, however, embraced nuclear energy enthusiastically.

Today, nuclear power plants produce about 14 percent of global electricity. Without sustained and aggressive government support, this percentage is expected to decline to about 10 percent by 2030, according to the International Energy Agency. At least two factors will make it difficult for nuclear energy to gain a larger market share—overall electricity demand is projected to double, and older reactors will need to be retired.

It is this rising electricity demand, along with concerns about improving energy security and mitigating climate change that led many more countries to consider nuclear energy as a viable option. At least 27 nations since 2005 have declared they will install nuclear power for the first time and a total of 65 countries have expressed interest to the International Atomic Energy Agency (IAEA). This contrasts with the thirty countries plus Taiwan that are already operating nuclear power plants. The Organization for Economic Cooperation and Development's (OECD) Nuclear Energy Agency suggested in its 2008 Nuclear Energy Outlook that the world could be building 54 reactors per year in the coming decades to meet all these challenges. For many reasons, an expansion of nuclear energy of this magnitude will be difficult to achieve. The current industrial base for nuclear reactors has supported just ten reactors coming on-line per year for the past two decades. The nuclear industry is scaling up its capacity but this could take some time. In some cases, the lack of a price on carbon dioxide emissions means that new nuclear power plant construction will remain relatively more expensive than coal, oil or natural gas, although this varies from country to country, depending on existing resources. Significant shale oil and

---

* About FAS: Founded in 1945 by many of the scientists who built the first atomic bombs, the Federation of American Scientists (FAS) is devoted to the belief that scientists, engineers, and other technically trained people have the ethical obligation to ensure that the technological fruits of their intellect and labor are applied to the benefit of humankind. The founding mission was to prevent nuclear war. While nuclear security remains a major objective of FAS today, the organization has expanded its critical work to issues at the intersection of science and security.

FAS publications are produced to increase the understanding of policymakers, the public, and the press about urgent issues in science and security policy. Individual authors who may be FAS staff or acknowledged experts from outside the institution write these reports. Thus, these reports do not represent an FAS institutional position on policy issues. All statements of fact and expressions of opinion contained in this and other FAS Special Reports are the sole responsibility of the author or authors.

shale gas discoveries have made utilities, at least in the United States, less enthusiastic about nuclear energy as a competitive source of electricity generation.

In response to mitigating climate change, many countries will find that nuclear power is neither the least-cost nor the quickest approach to reducing carbon dioxide emissions.1 Until nuclear energy is able to produce hydrogen or process heat, or until transportation sectors are electrified, nuclear energy's potential contribution to reducing carbon dioxide emissions will be somewhat limited.

Perhaps most importantly, the March 2011 accident at Japan's Fukushima Daiichi Nuclear Power Plant shook the confidence of the public not just in Japan but also abroad. The devastating earthquake and tsunami that killed tens of thousands of people eliminated off-site and backup electricity for four of six reactors and their spent fuel pools at Fukushima Daiichi. Hydrogen explosions destroyed secondary containments, exposing spent fuel pools, and three of the reactors had partial core meltdowns.

The Japanese government evacuated some of the population immediately. The clean-up effort at Fukushima will drag on for years and the cost will likely range in the billions of dollars.

Other countries with operating nuclear power plants, including the United States, announced safety reviews, and some halted construction and even operation of existing power reactors. Several countries that had been considering nuclear power may face a significant challenge in overcoming public mistrust. Still, the long-term impact of the Fukushima accident on nuclear power in Japan and worldwide is unknowable. Although many countries regard the possibility of another event combining a magnitude 9.0 earthquake and tsunami to be very low, the difficulties Japan—a highly sophisticated and technologically competent country—experienced because of the lack of electricity is raising questions about the costs and risks of nuclear power.

Nuclear Energy in the United States: Promises of the Past

The 104 reactors operating in the United States constitute about 25 percent of world capacity. Commercial nuclear power in the United States was a direct spin-off from the military's nuclear programs. General Electric and Westinghouse leveraged their military nuclear contracts with the U.S. Navy and emerged as the two dominant reactor vendors not just in the United States but in the world for many years. GE's introduction of the "turnkey" contract, which offered fully constructed power plants at a fixed price, provided significant momentum to construction in the mid-1960s. Westinghouse followed suit to remain competitive. By 1967, American utilities had ordered more than 50 power reactors and in the next seven years, they placed an additional 196 orders. By 1973, 40 units were operating.These first- and second-generation reactors were built primarily by Westinghouse and GE, whose pressurized water (PWR) and boiling water (BWR) designs, respectively, were adopted worldwide. Two-thirds (69) of U.S. reactors are PWRs, and the remaining (35) are BWRs.... .

Along with construction of nuclear power plants, the Atomic Energy Commission (AEC) also encouraged spent fuel reprocessing and the development of plutonium breeder reactors, primarily in response to concerns about scarce uranium. In 1966, the AEC granted a license to Nuclear Fuel Services (NFS) to operate a commercial reprocessing plant at West Valley, New York, which reprocessed both defense related material and commercial spent fuel until 1972. A temporary shutdown became permanent and NFS abandoned the plant to the State of New York. Legislation in 1980 committed the federal government to take on 90 percent of the cleanup costs, which have totaled $2 billion so far.

Two other reprocessing plants under construction never managed to operate: GE's Morris, Illinois plant, and Allied-General Nuclear Services' plant in Barnwell, South Carolina. Declared inoperable in 1974, the GE plant eventually stored spent fuel; the Barnwell plant was neither complete nor ready for licensing when the Carter Administration decided in 1977 no longer to support reprocessing and recycling, even domestically, because of proliferation concerns. By the time the Reagan administration reversed that decision in 1981, Allied-General decided the Barnwell project was commercially unviable.

Long before Three Mile Island, regulations on nuclear power in the United States began to tighten. In the early 1970s, critics of the AEC argued that its regulation was "insufficiently rigorous in several important areas, including radiation protection standards, reactor safety, plant siting, and environmental protection." A 1974 reorganization of the AEC created the Energy Research and Development Administration (ERDA, now the Department of Energy) and the Nuclear Regulatory Commission (NRC). Creation of the Environmental Protection Agency, the Council on Environmental Quality and new requirements for environmental impact statements also had a significant impact, as did growing public interest in environmental issues. More than half the challenges to almost 100 construction permits for nuclear power plants between 1962 and 1971 came from environmentalists concerned about the impact of waste heat from power plants on the local waterways. the creation of the Critical Mass Energy Program (which reportedly had 200,000 members) by Public Citizen founder Ralph Nader in 1974 to lobby against nuclear power further increased the pressure.

The changed licensing environment began to affect new reactor orders by 1975. In the early licensing scheme, less than 50 percent of the engineering designs were generally completed before construction, requiring field engineering and backfitting based on operating experience in other plants. These designs were released too early to engineering, procurement and construction. Slowdowns also came from utilities, because high finance costs and falling demand made it very difficult to borrow money to build plants no longer needed by the original dates. "Cost-plus" construction contracts also contributed to spiraling costs.

Cost overruns became more transparent and egregious, sometimes ten times above industry estimates. For the 75 reactors built between 1966 and 1977, cost overruns averaged 207 percent. In the end, more than 100 reactor orders were cancelled, including all those ordered after 1973. Regulatory hurdles increased in the wake of Three Mile Island, which may partly account for even greater cost overruns for the 40 plants constructed after 1979, which averaged 250 percent.

By 1985, popular magazines such as Fortune and Time had pronounced the death of nuclear power in the United States; Forbes magazine called it "the largest managerial disaster in history." The $2.25 billion municipal bond default of the Washington Public Power Supply System (WPPSS) plants in 1983 certainly contributed to that popular sentiment. The closing in 1989 of the Shoreham plant—fully constructed for $5.4 billion and never operated—was the final nail in the coffin. The initial cost estimate for Shoreham had been $350 million.... .

Relaunching Nuclear Energy in the United States

Many of the Bush-era initiatives on nuclear power focused on new plant construction, but also on returning to a policy of promoting recycling of spent fuel. Although the Obama administration may have wished to avoid these debates altogether, its decision to cancel the Yucca Mountain repository in 2009 brought all these difficult issues to the fore as did the March 2011 accident at the Fukushima-Daiichi reactors, which especially highlighted safety concerns with spent nuclear fuel pools.

New Nuclear Power Plants

With the hiatus in building new plants, the nuclear industry has focused on improving operating efficiencies and refitting plants. The 1992 Energy Policy Act created a "onestep" licensing procedure for new nuclear reactors, combining construction and operation licenses, and limiting kinds of interventions but did not lead to any new license applications. Since 2000, however, a panoply of policies, laws, and programs to help jump-start new nuclear power plant construction has produced applications, if no real construction yet. A few of the highlights are listed below:

- 2001: the National Energy Policy Development Group recommends supporting "the expansion of nuclear energy in the United States as a major component of our national energy policy," including research and development for spent fuel recycling with the aim of reducing waste streams and enhancing proliferation resistance.

- 2002: Nuclear Power 2010 spends $550 million to help jump-start new power reactor construction. Includes shared costs with industry for regulatory approval of new reactor sites, applying for licenses and preparing detailed plant designs. Also includes development of early site permits separate from reactor design reviews to facilitate licensing process.

- 2001-2009: DOE R&D budget triples for nuclear energy. Programs included Generation IV program, the Nuclear Hydrogen Initiative Program (NHI), and the Advanced Fuel Cycle Initiative (AFCI).

- 2005: Energy Policy Act of 2005 includes incentives such as production tax credits, energy facility loan guarantees, cost-sharing, limited liability and delay insurance.

- 2010: Additional loan guarantees announced.

Of all these, the Energy Policy Act (EPACT) of 2005 and the issue of loan guarantees deserve more description. Under EPACT 2005, a production tax credit would provide 1.8 cents/kWh during the first eight years of operation of qualified new nuclear power plants. To put this in context, the average wholesale price of electricity in 2005 was 5 cents/kWh. The credit has a limit of $7.5 billion, or the first 6,000 MW of capacity (equivalent to about five plants). Only those projects that have applied for a combined construction-operating license by December 2008, and that begin construction by January 2014 and operation by 2021 are eligible for the credit.

The U.S. nuclear industry has singled out government loan guarantees as essential because the private market finds loans for nuclear power plants to be too risky, and U.S. utilities are too small to take on a bigger equity to debt ratio, which would lower the cost of capital, a key element in the cost of the new plants. Under the loan guarantee program, the U.S. Treasury will guarantee 100 percent of a loan which is limited to 80 percent of the construction costs. This effectively transfers the risk of cost overruns due to lengthier construction times from project owners to the taxpayer.

Congress appropriated $18.5 billion in loan guarantees for nuclear power facilities, and President Obama has recommended tripling this to $54 billion. This still falls far short of the $122 billion in requests. Industry sources suggest DOE will be able to support no more than 2-4 reactors, given costs of $5 billion to $12 billion per reactor. The

Department of Energy awarded the first loan guarantee to the Vogtle reactor project in Georgia (over $8 billion) in 2010.

The DOE also committed to sharing design and licensing costs for the "first of a kind" reactor, with its share estimated at $281 million. EPACT also extended Price-Anderson limits on liability through 2025, capping new plants' liability in case of accidents at $10.6 billion. Finally, delay insurance would apply to the first six new licensed reactors delayed by the regulatory process; some $500 million would be available for each of the first two reactors and $250 million for each of the next four reactors. This was intended to compensate for delays in implementing the new combined construction and operating license process by the NRC.

Spent Fuel Recycling

As noted above, the Bush administration sought to close the nuclear fuel cycle in the United States by promoting the development of fast reactors to burn up plutonium and "recycling" waste for that purpose. The basic idea was to reduce the volume of nuclear waste by reusing the fuel in fast reactors, which can burn more of the material. The Global Nuclear Energy Partnership (GNEP), the Advanced Fuel Cycle Initiative, and other related programs have all sought to implement that goal. Thus far, the U.S. Congress has taken a "go slow" approach, delaying demonstrations of advanced recycling technologies until more research can be completed. A National Academy of Sciences report in 2008, which reviewed DOE's nuclear energy R&D, suggested that DOE reconsider reactor technologies under the Gen IV program that would support both advanced fuel cycles and the production of process heat, instead of pursuing two reactor technologies — very high temperature reactors and sodium-cooled fast reactors — for those tasks. It also recommended that DOE continue research on advanced recycling techniques, rather than move toward a technology demonstration plant. The Obama administration has advocated research into a modified open fuel cycle in which some research would be conducted on conditioning spent fuel.

Current Status

The nuclear industry in the United States responded quickly to the incentives package provided in EPACT 2005. Three designs for pressurized water reactors and two boiling water reactor designs are now under consideration for this next round of nuclear power plants. These include Westinghouse's Advanced Passive Reactor (AP-1000), AREVA's European Pressurized Water Reactor (EPR); and Mitsubishi's Advanced Pressure Water Reactor (APWR). In addition, designs for GE/Hitachi/Toshiba's Advanced Boiling Water Reactor (ABWR) and GE/Hitachi's Economic Simplified Boiling Water Reactor (ESBWR) have also been submitted.

These are described in greater detail in later chapters. It should be noted that the hoped-for standardization of designs has not happened, that not all the reactors have yet been certified and that a few of these designs have submitted modifications to their applications. For example, the designs for both the AP-1000 and the ABWR have been certified by the NRC, but planned changes will require additional certification and in the case of the ABWR, design certification renewal. Only one project envisions building an ABWR. The design certification applications for the other reactors were submitted several years ago: the EPR and APWR in December 2007 and the ESBWR in 2005....

Four considerations affect the attractiveness of these designs for U.S. utilities: capital cost, time to market, evolutionary versus revolutionary technologies, and active versus passive safety design features. For the most part, unregulated electricity generators—such as Constellation Energy Group, NRG Energy Inc. and PPL Corp.—have chosen active safety designs, presumably because they rely on the market for cost recovery and therefore want the most proven technologies. Regulated utilities have so far valued the lower life-cycle costs of passive designs, choosing the AP-1000 and ESBWR. Although Exelon Corporation initially chose the ESBWR, it appears that in the wake of Fukushima, Exelon will focus on building natural gas plants as opposed to nuclear power plants, citing their overwhelming costs.

New License Applications for Nuclear Power Plants

As of December 2010, 17 licenses for constructing and operating 26 new reactors were filed with the NRC. By type of reactor, these include: fourteen AP-1000 (Westinghouse-Toshiba) at seven sites; three ESBWR (GE-Hitachi) at three sites; four EPR (AREVA) at four sites; two ABWR (GE-Hitachi) at a single site; and three APWR (Mitsubishi) at two sites. Several of the license applications have been suspended by request of the proect managers, including Entergy for River Bend and Grand Gulf, and Exelon for Victoria County. NRG decided in April 2011 to terminate its involvement in the South Texas Project, and Constellation Energy decided in late 2010 to pull out of its deal with Electricite de France for the EPR project at Calvert Cliffs. EDF would like to go forward, but requires an American partner to do so. The map below shows the locations of sites for new COLs.

* * *

Waste Management

The history of nuclear waste management in the United States reflects a lot of study and research, punctuated by a few decisions every few decades. In 1956, a National Academy of Sciences study group concluded that a deep geologic repository was the best solution to dispose of high-level waste from nuclear reactors. The Nuclear Waste Policy Act, however, was not passed until 1982. It appears now, almost thirty years later, that some parts of the law may need revision.

Nuclear power reactors in the United States each year generate about 2,000 metric tons of fuel. So far, the United States has accumulated about 57,700 metric tons of spent fuel, which is stored in spent fuel ponds and in dry storage casks at 121 sites in 39 states. According to the 1982 Nuclear Waste Policy Act (NWPA), nuclear power plant operators are required to pay into the Nuclear Waste Fund (now estimated at $20 billion) in return for DOE waste disposal services—that is, eventual disposal in a geologic waste repository. That repository, designated as the Yucca Mountain site in 1987, was supposed to have opened in 1998. Beginning in 1997, nuclear power plant operators filed 56 lawsuits against the DOE for costs incurred in the absence of shipments to Yucca Mountain. DOE estimates that its liabilities under the current law will total $11 billion if shipments begin by 2020, and a lot more if they do not. The NWPA did not provide for another method of disposing waste, such as reprocessing, and the Nuclear Waste Fund may not be used for anything other than legislated purposes. Further delays are ahead, since the Obama administration decided to cancel construction funds for the Yucca Mountain program in early 2009, while continuing the licensing process at the NRC. This raises the question of whether the funding decision could be reversed in the future. If so, advocates of Yucca Mountain would still need to address storage capacity and geology issues. The NWPA set an arbitrary limit of 70,000 tons for Yucca Mountain, but it presupposed a second waste site would be authorized. By

2020, the level of waste is expected to reach 81,000 metric tons. Including defense waste and shipments by U.S. reactors through 2066, the expected accumulated waste is estimated to reach 122,100 metric tons. Geologic issues include the risk of transporting radioactive wastes in a porous environment, because fractures in volcanic tuff can transport water, and the location of the Bow Ridge fault line underneath a facility, rather than a few hundred feet away.

* * *

Notes & Questions

1. Consider the major national and international nuclear disasters. How many can you think of? What might that tell you about nuclear power? Consider the outcomes of each. Think about the different experiences in the United States and elsewhere.

2. Make a list of the benefits and risks of nuclear power. How does this impact public perception? Is that perception accurate? There are plainly differing opinions about nuclear power. Try to assess the different arguments and see where you agree or disagree.

3. Some have claimed that the biggest problem for nuclear power is not siting or permitting. Instead, the argument is that financing (or lack of) is the real problem. Why might lenders want to avoid nuclear power? Is that rational? Consider the idea from the 1950s and 1960s that nuclear power might be "too cheap to meter." Does that impact your thinking?

4. Hydropower

The History of Hydropower Development in the United States

U.S. Department of Interior/ Bureau of Reclamation
http://www.usbr.gov/power/edu/history.html

By using water for power generation, people have worked with nature to achieve a better lifestyle. The mechanical power of falling water is an age-old tool. It was used by the Greeks to turn water wheels for grinding wheat into flour, more than 2,000 years ago. In the 1700's mechanical hydropower was used extensively for milling and pumping. By the early 1900's, hydroelectric power accounted for more than 40 percent of the United States' supply of electricity. In the 1940's hydropower provided about 75 percent of all the electricity consumed in the West and Pacific Northwest, and about one third of the total United States' electrical energy. With the increase in development of other forms of electric power generation, hydropower's percentage has slowly declined and today provides about one tenth of the United States' electricity.

Niagra Falls was the first of the American hydroelectric power sites developed for major generation and is still a source of electric power today. The early hydroelectric plants were direct current stations built to power arc and incandescent lighting during the period from about 1880 to 1895. When the electric motor came into being the demand for new electrical energy started its upward spiral. The years 1895 through 1915 saw rapid changes occur in hydroelectric design and a wide variety of plant styles built. Hydroelectric plant design became fairly well standardized after World War I with most development in the 1920's and 1930's being related to thermal plants and transmission and distribution

The Bureau of Reclamation became involved in hydropower production because of its commitment to water resource management in the arid West. The waterfalls of the Reclamation dams make them significant producers of electricity. Hydroelectric power generation has long been an integral part of Reclamation's operations while it is actually a byproduct of water development. In the early days, newly created projects lacked many of the modern conveniences, one of these being electrical power. This made it desirable to take advantage of the potential power source in water.

Power plants were installed at the dam sites to carry on construction camp activities. Hydropower was put to work lifting, moving, and processing materials to build the dams and dig canals. Power plants ran sawmills, concrete plants, cableways, giant shovels, and draglines. Night operations were possible because of the lights fed by hydroelectric power. When construction was complete, hydropower drove pumps that provided drainage of conveyed water to lands at higher elevations than could be served by gravity-flow canals.

Surplus power was sold to existing power distribution systems in the area. Local industries, towns and farm consumers benefitted from the low-cost electricity. Much of the construction and operating costs of dams and related facilities were paid for by this sale of surplus power, rather than by the water users alone. This proved to be a great savings to irrigators struggling to survive in the West.

Reclamation's first hydroelectric powerplant was built to aid construction of the Theodore Roosevelt Dam on the Salt River about 75 miles northeast of Phoenix, Arizona. Small hydroelectric generators, installed prior to construction, provided energy for construction and for equipment to lift stone blocks into place. Surplus power was sold to the community, and citizens were quick to support expansion of the dam's hydroelectric capacity. A 4,500 kilowatt powerplant was constructed and, in 1909, five generators were in operation, supplying power for pumping irrigation water and furnishing electricity to the Phoenix area.

Power development, a byproduct of water development, had a tremendous impact on the area's economy and living conditions. Power was sold to farms, cities, and industries. Wells pumped by electricity meant more irrigated land for agriculture, and pumping also lower water tables in those areas with water logging and alkaline soil problems. By 1916, nine pumping plants were in operation irrigating more than 10,000 acres. In addition Reclamation supplied all of the residential and commercial power needs of Phoenix. Cheap hydropower, in abundant supply, attracted industrial development as well. A private company was able to build a large smelter and mill nearby to process low-grade copper ore, using hydroelectric power.

The Theodore Roosevelt Powerplant was one of the first large power facilities constructed by the Federal Government. Its capacity has since been increased from 4,500 kW to over 36,000 kW.

Power, first developed for building Theodore Roosevelt Dam and for pumping irrigation water, also helped pay for construction, enhanced the lives of farmers and city dwellers, and attracted new industry to the Phoenix area.

During World War I, Reclamation projects continued to provide water and hydroelectric power to Western farms and ranches. This helped to feed and clothe the Nation, and the power revenues were a welcome source of income to the Federal Government.

The Depression of the 1930's, coupled with widespread floods and drought in the West, spurred the building of great multipurpose Reclamation projects such as Grand Coulee Dam on the Columbia River, Hoover Dam on the lower Colorado River, and the

Central Valley Project in California. This was the "big dam" period, and the low-cost hydropower produced by those dams had a profound effect on urban and industrial growth.

With the advent of World War II the Nation's need for hydroelectric power soared. At the outbreak of the war, the Axis Nations had three times more available power than the United States. The demand for power was identified in this 1942 statement on "The War Program of the Department of the Interior:"

"The war budget of $56 billion will require 154 billion kWh of electric energy annually for the manufacture of airplanes, tanks, guns, warships, and fighting material, and to equip and serve the men of the Army, Navy and Marine Corps."

Each dollar spent for wartime industry required about 2-3/4 kWh of electric power. The demand exceeded the total production capacity of all existing electric utilities in the United States. To produce enough aluminum to meet the President's goal of 60,000 new planes in 1942 alone required 8.5 billion kWh of electric power.

Hydropower provided one of the best ways for rapidly expanding the country's energy output. Addition of more powerplant units at dams throughout the West made it possible to expand energy production, and construction pushed ahead to speed up the availability of power. In 1941, Reclamation produced more than 5 billion kWh, resulting in a 25 percent increase in aluminum production. By 1944 Reclamation quadrupled its hydroelectric power output.

From 1940 through 1945, Reclamation powerplants produced 47 billion kWh of electricity, enough to make:

69,000 airplanes	79,000 machine guns
5,000 ships	7,000,000 aircraft bombs, and
5,000 tanks	31,000,000 shells

During the war, Reclamation was the major producer of power in the West where needed resources were located. The supply of low-cost electricity attracted large defense industries to the area. Shipyards, steel mills, chemical companies, oil refineries, and automotive and aircraft factories all needed vast amounts of electrical power. Atomic energy installations were located at Hanford, Washington, to make use of hydropower from Grand Coulee.

While power output of Reclamation projects energized the war industry, it was also used to process food, light military posts, and meet needs of the civilian population in many areas.

With the end of the war, powerplants were put to use in rapidly developing peacetime industries. Hydropower has been vital for the West's industries which use mineral resources or farm products as raw materials. Many industries have depended wholly on Federal hydropower. In fact, periodic low flows on the Columbia River have disrupted manufacturing in that region.

Farming was tremendously important to America during the war and continues to be today. Reclamation delivers 10 trillion gallons of water delivered to more than 31 million people each year and provides 1 out of 5 Western farmers (140,000) with irrigation water for 10 million farmland acres that produce 60% of the nation's vegetables and 25% of the its fruits and nuts

Hydropower directly benefits rural areas in three ways:

- It produces revenue which contributes toward repayment of irrigation facilities, easing the water user's financial burden.

- It makes irrigation of lands at higher elevations possible through pumping facilities.
- It makes power available for use on the farm for domestic purposes.

Reclamation is second only to the Corps of Engineers in the operation of hydroelectric powerplants in the United States. Reclamation uses some of the power it produces to run its facilities, such as pumping plants. Excess hydropower is sold first to preferred customers, such as rural electric power co-ops, public utility districts, municipalities, and state and Federal agencies. Any remaining power may be sold to private electric utilities. Reclamation generates enough hydropower to meet the needs of millions of people, and power revenues exceed $900 million a year. Power revenues are returned to the Federal Treasury to repay the cost of constructing, operating, and maintaining projects.

An excellent book detailing the history of hydroelectricity is the two volume set of "Hydroelectric Development in the United States 1880–1940" prepared for the Task Force on Cultural Resource Management, Edison Electric Institute, Duncan Hay, New York State Museum, 1991. This book details American hydroelectric development from the first use of hydroelectric power around 1880 up to 1940. The following timeline includes data from the above referenced book highlighting a chronology of American hydroelectric development.

1879	First commercial arc lighting system installed, Cleveland, Ohio.
1879	Thomas Edison demonstrates incandescent lamp, Menlo Park, New Jersey.
1880	Grand Rapids Michigan: Brush arc light dynamo driven by water turbine used to provide theater and storefront illumination.
1881	Niagra Falls, New York; Brush dynamo, connected to turbine in Quigley's flour mill lights city street lamps.
1882	Appleton, Wisconsin; Vulcan Street Plant, first hydroelectric station to use Edison system.
1883	Edison introduces "three-wire" transmission system.
1886	Westinghouse Electric Company organized.
1886	Frank Sprague builds first American transformer and demonstrates use of step up and step down transformers for long distance AC power transmission in Great Barrington, Massachusetts.
1886	40 to 50 water powered electric plants reported on line or under construction in the U.S. and Canada.
1887	San Bernadino, California; High Grove Station, first hydroelectric plant in the West.
1888	Rotating field AC alternator invented.
1889	American Electrical Directory lists 200 electric companies that use waterpower for some or all of their generation.
1889	Oregon City Oregon, Willamette Falls station, first AC hydroelectric plant. Single phase power transmitted 13 miles to Portland at 4,000 volts, stepped down to 50 volts for distribution.
1891	Ames, Colorado; Westinghouse alternator driven by Pelton waterwheel, 320 foot head. Single phase, 3000 volt, 133 cycle power transmitted 2.6 miles to drive ore stamps at Gold King Mine.
1891	Frankfort on Main, Germany; First three-phase hydroelectric system used for 175 km, 25,000 volt demonstration line from plant at Lauffen.
1891	60 cycle AC system introduced in U.S.
1892	Bodie, California; 12.5 mile, 2,500 AC line carried power from hydroelectric plant to ore mill of Standard Consolidated Mining Co.

1892	San Antonio Creek, California; Single phase 120 kW plant, power carried to Pomona over 13 mile 5,000 volt line. Voltage increased to 10,000 and line extended 42 miles to San Bernadino within a year. First use of step up and step down transformers in hydroelectric project.
1892	General Electric Company formed by the merger of Thomson-Houston and Edison General Electric.
1893	Mill Creek, California; First American three-phase hydroelectric plant. Power carried 8 miles to Redlands on 2,400 volt line.
1893	Westinghouse demonstrates "universal system" of generation and distribution at Chicago exposition.
1893	Folsom, California; Three-phase, 60 cycle, 11,000 volt alternators installed at plant on American River. Power transmitted 20 miles to Sacramento.
1889–93	Austin, Texas; First dam designed specifically for hydroelectric power built across Colorado River.
1895	Niagra Falls, New York; 5,000 horsepower, 60 cycle, three-phase generators go into operation.
1897	Mechanicville, New York; Hudson River Power Transmission Company completes 5,250 kW, 38 cycle plant and 17 mile line to Schenectady.
1897	Minneapolis, Minnesota; Lower Dam hydroelectric plant completed at St. Anthony's Falls on the Mississippi.
1898	Los Angeles, California; 83 mile line built from Santa Anna River No. 1 hydroelectric plant.
1899	Nevada City, California; power from Nevada City, Yuba, and Colgate hydroelectric plants sold to Sacramento Power & Light Co. over 62 mile line to Folsom.
1899	Kalamazoo, Michigan; 24-mile, 22,000 volt line built from Trowbridge Dam hydroelectric plant.
1901	Oakland, California; 142 mile line built from Colgate hydroelectric plant by Bay Counties Power Company.
1901	First Federal Water Power Act
1901	Trenton Falls, New York; First installation of high head reaction turbines designed and built in the U. S.
1889–1902	Massena, New York; Dam and powerhouse built at confluence of St. Lawrence & Grasse Rivers. Power primarily used for smelting by Aluminum Corporation of America (ALCOA)
1902	Reclamation Act of 1902 establishes the Reclamation Service which later becomes the U.S. Bureau of Reclamation. Included in the act is the authority to develop the hydropower potential of Reclamation projects.
1897–1903	Sault Ste. Marie, Michigan; Michigan, Lake Superior Power Company Plant, 80 horizontal shaft units delivered 40,000 horsepower.
1905	Sault Ste. Marie, Michigan; First low head plant with direct connected vertical shaft turbines and generators.
1906	Ilchester, Maryland; Fully submerged hydroelectric plant built inside Ambursen Dam.
1906	Town Sites and Power Development Act—Authorized Secretary of the Interior to lease surplus power or power privileges.
1907	Hauser Lake, Montana: Short lived steel dam built across Missouri River by Wisconsin Bridge & Iron Co. for Helena Power & Transmission Co.
1910	Federal Water Power Act revised.

1910	Big Creek, California; Construction begins on a hydroelectric system that would eventually include eight powerhouses, over a 6,200 foot fall, rated at 685,000 kW.
1905–1911	Roosevelt Dam, Salt River, Arizona; Largest, and last, masonry dam ever built by U.S. Bureau of Reclamation. Mixed use irrigation/hydroelectric project.
1911	R. D. Johnson invents differential surge tank and Johnson hydrostatic penstock valve.
1912	Holtwood, Pennsylvania; First commercial installation of Kingsbury vertical thrust bearing in hydroelectric plant.
1910–1913	Keokuk, Iowa; Mississippi River Power Transmission Plant.
1913	Tallulah Falls, Georgia; Highest head hydroelectric plant in the East.
1913	Nolenchucky, Tennessee; First use of W. M. White's plate steel spiral turbine case.
1914	S. J. Zowski develops high specific speed reaction (Francis) turbine runner for low head applications.
1914	Argo, Michigan; Streamline draft tube introduced.
1916	First commercial installation of fixed-blade propeller turbine designed by Forrest Nagler.
1917	Hydracone draft tube patented by W. M. White.
1917	National Defense Act authorizes construction of government dam and powerplant at Muscle Shoals, Alabama.
1919	Viktor Kaplan demonstrates adjustable blade propeller turbine runner at Podebrady, Czechoslovakia.
1920	Federal Power Act establishes Federal Power Commission with authority to issue licenses for hydroelectric development on public lands.
1922	First hydroelectric plant built specifically for peaking power.
1922	Organization representing the power industry and manufacturers met to standardize voltages
1924	First World Power Conference, London.
1929	Del Rio, Texas; First Kaplan turbines installed in the U.S.—Lake Walk plant.
1929	Rocky River Plant, New Milford, Connecticut; First major pumped storage hydroelectric plant.
1930	Federal Power Act revised, independent full-time Federal Power Commission established.
1931	Construction begins, Boulder (later Hoover) Dam, Colorado River, Arizona-Nevada.
1933	Tennessee Valley Authority Act.
1933	Construction begins, Grand Coulee Dam, Columbia River, Washington.
1935	Federal Power Commission authority extended to all hydroelectric projects built by utilities engaged in interstate commerce.
1933–1937	Bonneville Dam, Columbia River, Washington/Oregon.
1937	First power generated at Hoover Dam, Arizona/Nevada.
1937	Bonneville Project Act—Created BPA (Bonneville Power Administration)
1940	Over 1500 hydroelectric facilities produce about one third of the United States' electrical energy.
1941	First power generated at Grand Coulee Powerplant, Washington—Presently the third largest hydroelectric plant in the world at 6,800 megawatts installed capacity.
1944	First power generated at Shasta Dam in California.
1964	First power generated at Glen Canyon Dam in Arizona.

1968   Wild and Scenic Rivers Act—Protects rivers in their natural state by excluding them from consideration as hydroelectric power sites.

1969   National Environmental Policy Act—Ensures that environmental considerations are systematically taken into account by Federal agencies.

1974   Fish and Wildlife Coordination Act—Ensures equal consideration of fish and wildlife protection in the activities of Federal agencies.

1978   Public Utility Regulatory Policies Act—Encourages small-scale power production facilities; exempted certain hydroelectric projects from Federal licensing requirements, and required utilities to purchase—at "avoided cost" rates—power from small production facilities that use renewable resources

1979   First power generated at New Melones Dam in California. Built by the Corps of Engineers and turned over to the Bureau of Reclamation, this is the last of the larger powerplants (over 30 megawatts) in the Bureau of Reclamation's power program.

1980   Energy Security Act—Exempted small-scale hydroelectric power from some licensing requirements.

1980   Crude Oil Windfall Profit Tax—Provided tax incentives to small-scale hydropower producers.

1983   First power generated at Itaipú powerplant, Brazil/Paraguay—Presently the largest hydroelectric powerplant in the world at 12,600 megawatts installed capacity.

1986   Electric Consumers Protection Act—Amended the Federal Power Act to remove public preference for relicensing actions; gives equal consideration to non-power values (e.g., energy conservation, fish, wildlife, recreation, etc.) as well as to power values when making license decisions.

1986   First power generated at Guri (Raul Leoni) powerplant, Venezuela—Presently the second largest hydroelectric powerplant in the world at 10,300 megawatts installed capacity.

1992   The top five electric generating countries in order are Canada, the United States, Brazil, Russia, and China.

1992   Energy Policy Act of 1992—An act to provide for improved energy efficiency. Includes provisions to allow for greater competition in energy sales and amendments to section 211 of the Federal Power Act.

1994   National Hydropower Association establishes the Hydropower Research Foundation to facilitate research and to promote educational opportunities on the value of hydropower.

1994   The Federal Energy Regulatory Commission has authorized, through its licensing authority under the Federal Power Act, almost 1,700 hydroelectric projects. These projects include about 2,300 dams and multi-purpose water resource developments that provide about 55,000 MW of hydroelectric generating capacity (about one-half of the nation's hydro capacity).

2005   Energy Policy Act, Public Law 109-58

2008   Hydroelectric generation provides about six percent of the United States' electricity.

Hydropower: Environmental Issues

U.S. Fish & Wildlife Service
http://www.fws.gov/habitatconservation/hydro_issues.pdf

Hydropower projects convert the energy of flowing water into electricity. A dam holds back water, creating a reservoir of potential power. On the upper side of the dam, a gate is opened to let water surge through a tunnel leading to turbines. The water turns the turbines which in turn spins generators to create electricity. Transmission lines carry the electricity to wherever it is needed. From an electricity production standpoint, one of the leading benefits of hydropower is its unique ability to load follow, or to almost instantaneously produce electricity as consumers require it. When demand is up, more water is released from above the dam, through the turbines and into the river downstream. As demand wanes, water flow is reduced. The resulting modifications in streamflow can have both immediate and long-term impacts on aquatic life and on basic components of water quality (e.g., temperature, dissolved oxygen, dissolved nitrogen).

Dams also have an affect on fish passage. They can fragment a river system, impede or block fish movement, and kill or injure fish. The viability and mobility of fish species that would otherwise move to and from different habitats within a river system may diminish substantially, if not completely, due to a hydropower project. In addition to their direct benefits to society, these fish may also be important components of food webs that support populations of other commercially and recreationally important species.

Water impoundments and flow changes affect not just the river itself, but the associated streamside (riparian) and wetland habitats. Load following exacerbates riverbank erosion and harms fish, invertebrates, amphibians, another aquatic life and reservoirs may flood land used by avian and terrestrial species. Corridors needed for transmission lines may also fragment habitats and create flight hazards to migratory birds, and maintaining corridors with herbicides may cause adverse effects to plants and wildlife.

Summary: National Wildlife Federation v. National Marine Fisheries Service

422 F.3d 782 (9th Cir. 2005)
First publication in Environmental Law, 36 Envtl. L. 985 (2006)
Lewis & Clark Law School's Environmental Law Online,
http://www.elawreview.org/summaries/natural_resources/endangered_
species_act/national_wildlife_federation_v.html

Defendants National Marine Fisheries Service (NMFS) and the Army Corps of Engineers petitioned the Ninth Circuit to review a U.S. District Court for the District of Oregon decision to grant a preliminary injunction to plaintiffs National Wildlife Federation (NWF) requiring federal dam operators to spill water over five dams on the Columbia and Snake rivers during summer 2005 to facilitate the survival of salmon migrating to the Pacific Ocean. The Ninth Circuit affirmed the preliminary injunction, but remanded the question of whether the injunction should be modified to the district court.

Snake River fall chinook salmon were listed as a threatened species under the Endangered

Species Act (ESA)[1] in 1992. As required by section 7 of the ESA,[2] the Federal Columbia River Power System, which operates 14 sets of dams on the Columbia River system, consulted with National Marine Fisheries Service (NMFS) to prepare a Biological Opinion (BiOp) on whether dam operations would "jeopardize the continued existence of a listed species or result in the destruction or adverse modification of critical habitat...."[3] In 2000, NMFS issued a BiOp which found the effects of continued dam operations to jeopardize salmon, but concluded that off-site mitigation activities unrelated to the dam operations would avoid jeopardy for the salmon. NWF challenged the BiOp, and a district court found it to be invalid because the agency had reached its no-jeopardy conclusion by relying on off-site federal mitigation actions which were not included in the environmental baseline of its analysis, as well as on non-federal mitigation actions not reasonably certain to occur.

The court remanded to give the agency the opportunity to correct the 2000 BiOp, but the agency instead issued a new BiOp in 2004. The 2004 BiOp classified the existing dams, nondiscretionary dam operations, and all past and present impacts from those operations as part of the environmental baseline in its jeopardy analysis. By evaluating only the discretionary operation of the dams, NMFS determined the dam operations would not jeopardize the continued existence of any listed species or threaten critical habitat. The district court found the 2004 BiOp to be invalid. It held the BiOp was both procedurally and substantively flawed under the ESA because the jeopardy analysis failed to include all the elements of the proposed action; it failed to consider the impacts of the dam operations, the environmental baseline, and the cumulative impacts as the basis for the jeopardy analysis; the critical habitat determination was flawed because it failed to make a separate determination of whether the dam operations would destroy or adversely modify critical habitat for both the survival and the recovery of listed species; and it failed to address the recovery and survival of listed species. After declaring the BiOp invalid, the district court granted NWF's request for a preliminary injunction requiring spills at five of the dams. The Ninth Circuit denied NMFS's motion for an emergency stay of the injunction pending the appeal, but it ordered this expedited hearing of the appeal.

A district court's decision to grant a preliminary injunction is reversible on appeal only if it was an abuse of discretion or if it was based on "an erroneous legal standard or on clearly erroneous findings of fact."[4] When a preliminary injunction is issued pursuant to the ESA, Congress has mandated courts should strike a balance in favor of the endangered species, rather than apply a traditional balancing of the competing interests of the parties.[5] The Ninth Circuit determined the district court had thus applied the correct legal standard in issuing the injunction.

The Ninth Circuit held the preliminary injunction was not based on clearly erroneous findings of fact. An appellate court will consider factual findings to be "clearly erroneous if it is implausible in light of the record, viewed in its entirety."[6] The district court's finding that the federal dam operations contributed to the salmon's endangerment was hotly contested at trial. NMFS disputed the district court's finding that dam operations were

1. Endangered Species Act of 1973, 16 U.S.C. §§ 1531-1544 (2000).
2. Id. § 1536(a)(2).
3. 50 C.F.R. § 402.14(h) (2005).
4. United States v. Peninsula Commc'ns, Inc., 287 F.3d 832, 839 (9th Cir. 2002).
5. Tenn. Valley Auth. v. Hill, 437 U.S. 153, 194 (1978).
6. Serv. Employees Int'l Union v. Fair Political Practices Comm'n, 955 F.2d 1312, 1317 n.7 (9th Cir. 1992).

detrimental to the salmon, and cited data indicating that salmon return runs had increased. NWF argued that the increased returns were the result of large releases of hatchery fish, and that the federal agencies' own data showed high levels of fish kills from the dams. The Ninth Circuit noted, however, that it was undisputed that fall chinook salmon were endangered species under the ESA, and that it was not the appellate court's place to resolve contested facts. The court concluded the district court's factual finding of irreparable harm to salmon was not clearly erroneous.

The Ninth Circuit next determined the district court did not abuse its discretion in granting the preliminary injunction. The test for determining whether an injunction was appropriate when the ESA has been violated is whether an injunction is necessary to "effectuate the congressional purpose behind the statute" by requiring both substantive and procedural compliance with the ESA.[7] The court determined the district court's rejection of the BiOp the dam's operations were premised upon and its conclusion that continued operations would result in irreparable harm to salmon were "precisely the circumstances" under which issuing an injunction was appropriate.[8] The Ninth Circuit distinguished this case from one of its own recent decisions, in which it concluded the district court had misread the governing statute, and that the agency had acted in conformity with the statute.[9] In contrast, in this case the district court had statutory support, was faced with an agency that had altered its own interpretation of the statute, and the record contained a long history of dam operations. In addition, the Ninth Circuit concluded when balancing the equities in review of an injunction issued under the ESA "the balance has been struck in favor of affording Endangered Species the highest of priorities."[10] Thus, the Ninth Circuit concluded the district court's grant of a preliminary injunction was not a reversible error.

The court next examined the nature and scope of relief granted by the district court. Because the dam operations were ongoing, the district court had to decide between allowing the continued operation of the dams at the status quo, which it determined would cause irreparable harm to species, or order modifications in the operations. In deciding to order spills, the district court took into consideration expert testimony regarding the effectiveness of spills for fish passage, the results of previous spills, and NMFS conclusions in the 2000 BiOp that salmon survival was highest through spills when compared to alternative passage methods. While NMFS offered evidence which raised "significant and serious concerns"[11] regarding effectiveness of spills on fish passage survival rates, the existence of this evidence alone did not rise to the level of a "clear error of judgment"[12] necessary to constitute a reversible abuse of discretion.

NMFS argued the district court was required to defer to agency expertise as to the best course of action. However, the court had already invalidated the 2004 BiOp, the agency's basis for the dam operations, because its conclusions were based on flawed analysis, and it was premised on a statutory interpretation of environmental baseline which was a complete reversal from the agency's own earlier interpretation. Agency interpretations of a statute conflicting with the agency's own earlier interpretations are "entitled to considerably less

---

7. Biodiversity Legal Found. v. Badgley, 309 F.3d 1166, 1177 (9th Cir. 2002) (citing Tenn. Valley Auth., 437 U.S. at 194).

8. Nat'l Wildlife Fed'n v. Nat'l Marine Fisheries Serv., 422 F.3d 782, 796 (9th Cir. 2005).

9. Ranchers Cattlemen Action Legal Fund United Stockgrowers of Am. v. U.S. Dep't of Agric., 415 F.3d 1078, 1090 (9th Cir. 2005).

10. Tenn. Valley Auth., 437 U.S. at 194.

11. Nat'l Wildlife Fed'n, 422 F.3d at 798.

12. Secs. & Exch. Comm'n v. Coldicutt, 258 F.3d 939, 941 (9th Cir. 2001).

deference" than consistent agency interpretations.[13] In light of NMFS conclusions in its 2000 BiOp that continued operations would jeopardize salmon, and in the absence of a valid BiOp, the Ninth Circuit found there to be "a more than sufficient basis" for the district court to order spills.[14] Therefore, the district court had not abused its discretion in ordering the spills.

The Ninth Circuit finally addressed NMFS argument that the injunction was not narrowly tailored and thus should be vacated, although the agency did not indicate how the injunction should be narrowed. The court refused to vacate injunction. However, it noted issues raised after the injunction was ordered may require the district court to modify its order. The Ninth Circuit denied both parties' motions to supplement the record, noting it was inappropriate to decide issues of fact for the first time on appeal. It remanded the question of whether the injunction should be modified back to the district court. In addition, intervener BPA Customer Group argued the injunction should be vacated on the grounds it "insufficiently relates the remedy to the alleged ESA violation."[15] Because the district court did not address this issue when it ordered the preliminary injunction, the Ninth Circuit remanded the question to the district court as well.

In conclusion, the Ninth Circuit affirmed the district court's preliminary injunction ordering spills at several dams on the Columbia and Snake rivers, and remanded the question of whether the injunction should be modified.

Notes & Questions

1. Why might hydropower be considered different than what we think of as a "renewable" energy source? Consider the lifecycle of construction and operation of a hydro project. What must happen for hydropower to come on line? Is that a good thing? For whom?

2. Consider the effects hydropower can have on fisheries. Can they be dealt with effectively? There is at least some argument that it is possible. Consider the National Oceanic and Atmospheric Administration's article: Multitasking the Nation's Rivers: http://www.habitat.noaa.gov/protection/hydro/bakerlakess.html. The article provides a brief case study of the Baker Lake salmon experience in the Pacific Northwest.

5. Renewables

This section discusses the main types of renewable energy and how they fit into the energy mix. The mechanisms used to increase the use of renewable energy will be discussed in Chapter 5 as part of the renewable mandates used for electricity generation via renewable electricity standards.

In practical terms, renewable energy is whatever the applicable statute or regulation says it is. The Texas Renewable Energy Industries Association uses the following definition:

> Renewable energy: Any energy resource that is naturally regenerated over a short time scale and derived directly from the sun (such as thermal, photochemical, and photoelectric), indirectly from the sun (such as wind, hydropower, and pho-

13. Watt v. Alaska, 451 U.S. 259, 273 (1981).
14. Nat'l Wildlife Fed'n, 422 F.3d at 797.
15. Id. at 800.

tosynthetic energy stored in biomass), or from other natural movements and mechanisms of the environment (such as geothermal and tidal energy). Renewable energy does not include energy resources derived from fossil fuels, waste products from fossil sources, or waste products from inorganic sources.

Over time, renewable energy has had its challenges, mostly financial, but there are other environmental challenges, as well. The debates about the values of renewable energy usually occur in discussions about renewable mandates, tax credits, and subsidies. Some of the challenges, and how they might be addressed, were the subject of a recent study conducted for the National Renewable Energy Laboratory

Renewable Electricity Futures Study: Executive Summary

Mai, T.; Sandor, D.; Wiser, R.; Schneider, T (2012). Renewable Electricity Futures Study: Executive Summary. NREL/TP-6A20-52409-ES. Golden, CO: National Renewable Energy Laboratory, *available at* http://www.nrel.gov/docs/fy13osti/52409-ES.pdf (footnotes & figures omitted)

Perspective

The Renewable Electricity Futures Study (RE Futures) provides an analysis of the grid integration opportunities, challenges, and implications of high levels of renewable electricity generation for the U.S. electric system. The study is not a market or policy assessment. Rather, RE Futures examines renewable energy resources and many technical issues related to the operability of the U.S. electricity grid, and provides initial answers to important questions about the integration of high penetrations of renewable electricity technologies from a national perspective. RE Futures results indicate that a future U.S. electricity system that is largely powered by renewable sources is possible and that further work is warranted to investigate this clean generation pathway. The central conclusion of the analysis is that renewable electricity generation from technologies that are commercially available today, in combination with a more flexible electric system, is more than adequate to supply 80% of total U.S. electricity generation in 2050 while meeting electricity demand on an hourly basis in every region of the United States.

The renewable technologies explored in this study are components of a diverse set of clean energy solutions that also includes nuclear, efficient natural gas, clean coal, and energy efficiency. Understanding all of these technology pathways and their potential contributions to the future U.S. electric power system can inform the development of integrated portfolio scenarios. RE Futures focuses on the extent to which U.S. electricity needs can be supplied by renewable energy sources, including biomass, geothermal, hydropower, solar, and wind.

The study explores grid integration issues using models with unprecedented geographic and time resolution for the contiguous United States. The analysis (1) assesses a variety of scenarios with prescribed levels of renewable electricity generation in 2050, from 30% to 90%, with a focus on 80% (with nearly 50% from variable wind and solar photovoltaic generation); (2) identifies the characteristics of a U.S. electricity system that would be needed to accommodate such levels; and (3) describes some of the associated challenges and implications of realizing such a future.

In addition to the central conclusion noted above, RE Futures finds that increased electric system flexibility, needed to enable electricity supply-demand balance with high levels of renewable generation, can come from a portfolio of supply- and demand-side options, including flexible conventional generation, grid storage, new transmission, more responsive loads, and changes in power system operations. The analysis also finds that the abundance and diversity of U.S. renewable energy resources can support multiple combinations of renewable technologies that result in deep reductions in electric sector greenhouse gas emissions and water use. The study finds that the direct incremental cost associated with high renewable generation is comparable to published cost estimates of other clean energy scenarios. Of the sensitivities examined, improvement in the cost and performance of renewable technologies is the most impactful lever for reducing this incremental cost. Assumptions reflecting the extent of this improvement are based on incremental or evolutionary improvements to currently commercial technologies and do not reflect U.S. Department of Energy activities to further lower renewable technology costs so that they achieve parity with conventional technologies.

    . . .

    The Renewable Electricity Futures Study (RE Futures) is an initial investigation of the extent to which renewable energy supply can meet the electricity demands of the contiguous United States over the next several decades. This study includes geographic and electric system operation resolution that is unprecedented for long-term studies of the U.S. electric sector. The analysis examines the implications and challenges of renewable electricity generation levels—from 30% up to 90%, with a focus on 80%, of all U.S. electricity generation from renewable technologies—in 2050. At such high levels of renewable electricity penetration, the unique characteristics of some renewable resources, specifically geographical distribution and variability and uncertainty in output, pose challenges to the operability of the U.S. electric system. The study focuses on some key technical implications of this environment, exploring whether the U.S. power system can supply electricity to meet customer demand with high levels of renewable electricity, including variable wind and solar generation. The study also begins to address the potential economic, environmental, and social implications of deploying and integrating high levels of renewable electricity in the United States.

    RE Futures was framed with a few important questions:

- The United States has diverse and abundant renewable energy resources that are available to contribute higher levels of electricity generation over the next decades. Future renewable electricity generation will be driven in part by federal incentives and renewable portfolio standards mandated in many states. Practically, how much can renewable energy technologies, in aggregate, contribute to future U.S. electricity supply?

- In recent years, variable renewable electricity generation capacity in the United States has increased considerably. Wind capacity, for example, has increased from 2.6 GW in 2000 to 40 GW in 2010, while solar capacity has also begun to grow rapidly. Can the U.S. electric power system accommodate higher levels of variable generation from wind or solar photovoltaics (PV)?

- Overall, renewable energy contributed about 10% of total power-sector U.S. electricity supply in 2010 (6.4% from hydropower, 2.4% from wind energy, 0.7% from biopower, 0.4% from geothermal energy, and 0.05% from solar energy). Are there synergies that can be realized through combining these diverse sources, and to what extent can aggregating their output over larger areas help enable their integration into the power system?

    Multiple international studies have explored the possibility of achieving high levels of renewable electricity penetration, primarily as a greenhouse gas (GHG) mitigation measure.

RE Futures presents systematic analysis of a broad range of potential renewable electricity futures for the contiguous United States based on unprecedented consideration of geographic, temporal, and electric system operation aspects.

RE Futures explores a number of scenarios using a range of assumptions for generation technology improvement, electric system operational constraints, and electricity demand to project the mix of renewable technologies — including wind, PV, concentrating solar power (CSP), hydropower, geothermal, and biomass — that meet various prescribed levels of renewable generation, from 30% to 90%. Additional sensitivity cases are focused on an 80%-by-2050 scenario. At this 80% renewable generation level, variable generation from wind and solar technologies accounts for almost 50% of the total generation.

Within the limits of the tools used and scenarios assessed, hourly simulation analysis indicates that estimated U.S. electricity demand in 2050 could be met with 80% of generation from renewable electricity technologies with varying degrees of dispatchability, together with a mix of flexible conventional generation and grid storage, additions of transmission, more responsive loads, and changes in power system operations. Further, these results were consistent for a wide range of assumed conditions that constrained transmission expansion, grid flexibility, and renewable resource availability. The analysis also finds that the abundance and diversity of U.S. renewable energy resources can support multiple combinations of renewable technologies that result in deep reductions in electric sector greenhouse gas emissions and water use. Further, the study finds that the incremental cost associated with high renewable generation is comparable to published cost estimates of other clean energy scenarios. Of the sensitivities examined, improvement in the cost and performance of renewable technologies is the most impactful level for reducing this incremental cost.

While this analysis suggests such a high renewable generation future is possible, a transformation of the electricity system would need to occur to make this future a reality. This transformation, involving every element of the grid, from system planning through operation, would need to ensure adequate planning and operating reserves, increased flexibility of the electric system, and expanded multi-state transmission infrastructure, and would likely rely on the development and adoption of technology advances, new operating procedures, evolved business models, and new market rules.

Key results of this study include the following:

- Deployment of Renewable Energy Technologies
    - Renewable energy resources, accessed with commercially available generation technologies, could adequately supply 80% of total U.S. electricity generation in 2050 while balancing supply and demand at the hourly level.
    - All regions of the United States could contribute substantial renewable electricity supply in 2050, consistent with their local renewable resource base.
    - Multiple technology pathways exist to achieve a high renewable electricity future. Assumed constraints that limit power transmission infrastructure, grid flexibility, or the use of particular types of resources can be compensated for through the use of other resources, technologies, and approaches.
    - Annual renewable capacity additions that enable high renewable generation are consistent with current global production capacities but are significantly higher than recent U.S. annual capacity additions for the technologies considered. No insurmountable long-term constraints to renewable electricity technology manufacturing capacity, materials supply, or labor availability were identified.

- Grid Operability and Hourly Resource Adequacy
  - Electricity supply and demand can be balanced in every hour of the year in each region with nearly 80% electricity from renewable resources, including nearly 50% from variable renewable generation, according to simulations of 2050 power system operations.
  - Additional challenges to power system planning and operation would arise in a high renewable electricity future, including management of low-demand periods and curtailment of excess electricity generation.
  - Electric sector modeling shows that a more flexible system is needed to accommodate increasing levels of renewable generation. System flexibility can be increased using a broad portfolio of supply- and demand-side options, and will likely require technology advances, new operating procedures, evolved business models, and new market rules.
- Transmission Expansion
  - As renewable electricity generation increases, additional transmission infrastructure is required to deliver generation from cost-effective remote renewable resources to load centers, enable reserve sharing over greater distances, and smooth output profiles of variable resources by enabling greater geospatial diversity.
- Cost and Environmental Implications of High Renewable Electricity Futures
  - High renewable electricity futures can result in deep reductions in electric sector greenhouse gas emissions and water use.
  - The direct incremental cost associated with high renewable generation is comparable to published cost estimates of other clean energy scenarios. Improvement in the cost and performance of renewable technologies is the most impactful lever for reducing this incremental cost.
- Effects of Demand Growth
  - With higher demand growth, high levels of renewable generation present increased resource and grid integration challenges.

This report presents the analysis of some of the technical challenges and opportunities associated with high levels of renewable generation in the U.S. electric system. However, the analysis presented in this report represents only an initial set of inquiries on a national scale. Additional studies are required to more fully assess the technical, operational, reliability, economic, environmental, social, and institutional implications of high levels of renewable electricity generation, and further explore the nature of the electricity system transformation required to enable such a future.

RE Futures is an initial analysis of scenarios for high levels of renewable electricity in the United States; additional research is needed to comprehensively investigate other facets of high renewable or other clean energy futures in the U.S. power system. First, this study focuses on renewable-specific technology pathways and does not explore the full portfolio of clean technologies that could contribute to future electricity supply. Second, the analysis does not attempt a full reliability analysis of the power system that includes addressing sub-hourly, transient, and distribution system requirements. Third, although RE Futures describes the system characteristics needed to accommodate high levels of renewable generation, it does not address the institutional, market, and regulatory changes that may be needed to facilitate such a transformation. Fourth, a full cost-benefit analysis was not conducted to comprehensively evaluate the relative impacts of renewable and non-renewable electricity generation options.

Lastly, as a long-term analysis, uncertainties associated with assumptions and data, along with limitations of the modeling capabilities, contribute to significant uncertainty in the implications reported. Most of the scenario assessment was conducted in 2010 with assumptions concerning technology cost and performance and fossil energy prices generally based on data available in 2009 and early 2010. Significant changes in electricity and related markets have already occurred since the analysis was conducted, and the implications of these changes may not have been fully reflected in the study assumptions and results. For example, both the rapid development of domestic unconventional natural gas resources that has contributed to historically low natural gas prices, and the significant price declines for some renewable technologies (e.g., photovoltaics) since 2010, were not reflected in the study assumptions.

Nonetheless, as the most comprehensive analysis of U.S. high-penetration renewable electricity conducted to date, this study can inform broader discussion of the evolution of the electric system and electricity markets toward clean systems.

* * *

Analysis Approach

Scenario Framework

Given the inherent uncertainties involved with analyzing alternative long-term energy futures, and given the variety of pathways that might lead to higher levels of renewable electricity supply, multiple future scenarios were modeled and analyzed. The scenarios examined included the following considerations:

- **Energy Efficiency:** Most of the scenarios assumed adoption of energy efficiency (including electricity) measures in the residential, commercial, and industrial sectors that resulted in flat demand growth over the 40-year study period.

- **Transportation:** Most of the scenarios assumed a shift of some transportation energy away from petroleum and toward electricity in the form of electric and plug-in hybrid electric vehicles, partially offsetting the electricity efficiency advances that were considered.

- **Grid Flexibility:** Most scenarios assumed improvements in electric system operations to enhance flexibility in both electricity generation and end-use demand, helping to enable more efficient integration of variable-output renewable electricity generation.

- **Transmission:** Most scenarios expand the transmission infrastructure and access to existing transmission capacity to support renewable energy deployment. Distribution- level upgrades were not considered.

- **Siting and Permitting:** Most scenarios assumed project siting and permitting regimes that allow renewable electricity development and transmission expansion subject to standard land-use exclusions.

In all the scenarios analyzed, only currently commercially available technologies (as of 2010) were considered, together with their incremental or evolutionary improvements despite the long-term (2050) timeframe, because the focus of this study was on grid integration and not on the potential advances of any individual technologies. Technologies such as enhanced geothermal systems; ocean energy technologies (e.g., wave, tidal, current or ocean thermal); floating offshore wind technology; and others that are currently under development and pilot testing—and which show significant promise but are not yet generally commercially available—were not included.

More than two dozen scenarios were modeled and analyzed in this study.... The number and diversity of scenarios allowed an assessment of multiple pathways that depended on highly uncertain future technological, institutional, and market choices. The framework included scenarios with specific renewable electricity generation levels to enable exploration of some of the technical issues associated with the operation of the U.S. electricity grid at these levels. This scenario framework does not prescribe a set of policy recommendations for renewable electricity generation in the United States, nor does it present a vision of what the total mix of energy sources should look like in the future. Further, the framework does not intend to imply that one future is more likely than another.

* * *

Low-Demand Baseline Scenario

A Low-Demand Baseline scenario was designed to reflect a largely conventional generation system as a point of comparison, or reference, for the high-penetration renewable electricity scenarios. The Low-Demand Baseline scenario assumes that a combination of emerging trends—including policies and legislation dealing with codes and standards, innovation in energy efficiency, and the green building and supply chain movements—drive the adoption of energy efficiency measures in the residential, commercial, and industrial sectors (see Volume 3 for details). Substantial adoption of electric and plug-in hybrid electric vehicles was also assumed. In aggregate, these low-demand assumptions resulted in overall electricity consumption that exhibits little growth from 2010 to 2050. Existing state policies (e.g., renewable portfolio standards) and existing federal policies (e.g., investment tax credits, production tax credits, tax depreciation rules) were assumed to continue only as allowed under existing law, with no extensions. Expiration dates for existing federal policies vary, but generally are 2017 or earlier.

In combination with incremental technology improvements, these assumptions result in low levels of renewable electricity generation in the Low-Demand Baseline scenario.

Exploratory Scenarios

A series of "exploratory scenarios," in which the proportion of renewable electricity in 2050 increased in 10% increments from 30% to 90%, was evaluated. The primary purpose of these exploratory scenarios was to assess how increased levels of renewable electricity might impact the generation mix of renewable and non-renewable resources, the extent of transmission expansion in these cases, and the use of various forms of supply- and demand-side flexibility to enable a match between electricity supply and demand. These exploratory scenarios were evaluated under two distinct sets of renewable electricity technology advancement assumptions: Incremental Technology Improvement (ITI) and Evolutionary Technology Improvement (ETI).

Core 80% RE Scenarios

Further analysis was performed on six core 80% RE scenarios, each of which met the same 80%- by-2050 renewable electricity penetration level and each of which was designed to elucidate the possible implications of certain technological, institutional, and market drivers. Three scenarios explored the impacts of future renewable energy technology advancements of currently commercial technologies and the resulting deployment of different combinations of renewable energy technologies:

- The RE—No Technology Improvement (80% RE-NTI) scenario simply assumed that the performance of each renewable technology was maintained at 2010 levels for all years in the study period (2010–2050).

- The RE—Incremental Technology Improvement (80% RE-ITI) scenario reflected only partial achievement of the future technical advancements that may be possible (Black & Veatch 2012).

- The RE—Evolutionary Technology Improvement (80% RE-ETI) scenario reflected a more-complete achievement of possible future technical advancements (Volume 2). The RE-ETI scenario is not designed to be a lower bound and does not span the full range of possible futures; further technical advancements beyond the RE-ETI are possible.

Three additional scenarios explored the impacts of different electricity system constraints based on assumptions that limited the building of new transmission, reduced system flexibility to manage the variability of wind and solar resources, and decreased renewable resource availability:

- The Constrained Transmission scenario evaluated how limits to building new transmission might impact the location and mix of renewable resources used to meet an 80%-by-2050 future.

- The Constrained Flexibility scenario sought to understand how institutional constraints to and concerns about managing the variability of wind and solar resources, in particular, might impact the resource mix of achieving an 80%-by-2050 future.

- The Constrained Resources scenario posited that environmental or other concerns may reduce the developable potential for many of the renewable technologies in question, and evaluated how such constraints could impact the resource mix of renewable energy supply.

High-Demand Scenarios

The scenarios described above—the Low-Demand Baseline scenario, the exploratory scenarios, and the six core 80% RE scenarios—were based on the low-demand assumptions, with overall electricity consumption that exhibits little growth from 2010 to 2050. To test the impacts of a higher-demand future, a scenario with the 80%-by-2050 renewable electricity generation but a *higher end-use electricity demand* was evaluated, with demand in 2050 30% higher than in the low-demand scenarios. A corresponding reference scenario, the High-Demand Baseline scenario, with the same higher demand was also evaluated.

Alternative Fossil Scenarios

Finally, given uncertainties in the *future cost of fossil energy sources*, the analysis included 80%- by-2050 RE scenarios in which: (1) the price of fossil energy (coal and natural gas) was both higher and lower than otherwise assumed in the other scenarios and (2) fossil energy technologies experienced greater technology improvements over time than assumed in the other scenarios. Corresponding reference scenarios with these alternate fossil energy projections were also evaluated.

Renewable Resources Characterization

The United States has diverse and abundant renewable resources, including biomass, geothermal, hydropower, ocean, solar, and wind resources. Solar and wind are the most abundant of these resources. These renewable resources are geographically constrained but widespread — most are distributed across all or most of the contiguous states.... Within these broad resource types, a variety of commercially available renewable electricity generation technologies have been deployed in the United States and other countries, including stand-alone biopower, co-fired biopower (in coal plants), hydrothermal geothermal, hydropower, distributed PV, utility-scale PV, CSP, onshore wind, and fixed-bottom offshore wind.

* * *

While only commercially available biomass, geothermal, hydropower, solar PV, CSP, and wind-powered systems were considered in the modeling analysis — only incremental and evolutionary advances in renewable technologies were assumed — the study describes a broad range of commercial and emerging renewable energy technologies in Volume 2, including the following:

- **Biomass power** ... is generated by collecting and combusting plant matter and using the heat to drive a steam turbine. Biomass resources from agricultural and forest residues, although concentrated primarily in the Midwest and Southeast, are available throughout the United States. While biomass supply is currently limited, increased supply is possible in the future from increased production from energy crops and advanced harvesting technologies. DOE (2011) provides an estimate of 696–1,184 million annual dry tonnes of biomass inventory potential (of which 52%–61% represents dedicated biomass crops) in 2030. The estimated biomass feedstocks correspond to roughly 100 GW of dedicated biopower capacity. Biopower can be generated from stand- alone plants, or biomass can be co-fired in traditional pulverized coal plants.

- **Geothermal power** ... is generated by water that is heated by hot underground rocks to drive a steam turbine. Geothermal resources are generally concentrated in the western United States, and they are relatively limited for hydrothermal technologies (36 GW of new technical resource potential), which rely on natural hot water or steam reservoirs with appropriate flow characteristics. Only commercially available hydrothermal technologies were included in the modeling analysis. Although not modeled, emerging technologies, including enhanced geothermal systems, engineered hydrothermal reservoirs, geopressured resources, low temperature resources, or co-production from oil and gas wells, could expand the geothermal resource potential in the United States by more than 500 GW.

- **Hydropower** ... is generated by using water — from a reservoir or run-of-river — to drive a hydropower turbine. Run-of-river technology could produce electricity without creating large inundated areas, and many existing dams could be equipped to generate electricity. The future technical potential of run-of-river hydropower from within the contiguous United States is estimated at 152–228 GW. Only new run-of-river hydropower capacity was considered in RE Futures modeling, and existing hydropower plants were assumed to continue operation. Other hydropower technologies, such as new generation at non-powered dams and constructed waterways, have the potential to contribute to future electricity supply, but they were not modeled in this study.

- **Ocean technologies** … are not broadly commercially available at this time, and therefore were not modeled in this study, but both U.S. and international research and development programs are working to reduce the cost of the technologies. Ocean current resources are best on the U.S. Gulf and South Atlantic Coasts; wave energy resources are strongest on the West Coast. All resources are uncertain; preliminary estimates indicate that the U.S. wave energy technical potential is on the order of 2,500 TWh/yr. Other ocean technologies, including ocean thermal energy conversion technologies and tidal technologies, may also contribute to future electricity supply.

- **Solar resources** … are the most abundant renewable resources. They extend across the entire United States, with the highest quality resources concentrated in the Southwest. The technical potential of utility-scale PV and CSP technologies is estimated to be approximately 80,000 GW and 37,000 GW, respectively, in the United States. Distributed rooftop PV technologies are more limited, with approximately 700 GW available. PV technologies convert sunlight directly to electricity while CSP technologies collect high temperature heat to drive a steam turbine.

- **Wind resources** … on land are abundant, extending throughout the United States, and offshore resources provide additional options for coastal and Great Lakes regions. Onshore and fixed-bottom offshore technologies are currently commercially available. Floating platform offshore wind technologies that could access high-quality wind resources in deeper waters are less mature and were not considered in the modeling. Wind technical resource estimates exceed 10,000 GW in the contiguous United States.

Renewable resource supply varies by location and, in most cases, by the time of day and season. The electricity output characteristics of some renewable energy technologies also vary substantially, potentially introducing electric system operation challenges. A key performance characteristic of generators in general is their degree of dispatchability, specifically the ability of operators to control power plant output over a range of specified output generation levels. Conventional fossil plants are considered dispatchable, to varying degrees. Several renewable generator types, including biopower, geothermal, and hydropower plants with reservoir storage, are also considered dispatchable technologies in that system operators have some ability to specify generator output, if needed. Concentrating solar power with thermal storage can similarly be considered a dispatchable technology but is limited by the amount of storage. The output from run-of-river hydropower is generally constant over short time periods (minutes to hours) but varies over longer periods (days to seasons). Several emerging ocean technologies, such as ocean-current, may also provide fairly constant output and, in some cases, may be able to offer some level of dispatchability.

Wind and solar PV have little dispatchability—the output from these sources can be reduced, but not increased on demand. An additional challenge is the variability and uncertainty in the output profile of these resources, with wind and solar having limited predictability over various time scales. High levels of deployment of these generation types can therefore introduce new challenges to the task of ensuring reliable grid operation. However, it deserves note that the requirement for balanced supply and demand must be met on an *aggregate* basis—the variability and uncertainty of any individual plant or load entity does not ultimately define the integration challenge associated with high levels of variable renewable generation.

The analysis presented here focuses on electricity generation technology deployment, system operational challenges, and implications associated with specified levels of renewable generation, which represent the total annual renewable electricity generation from commercially available biomass, geothermal, hydropower, solar, and wind electricity generating technologies.

Climate Change 1995: The IPCC
Second Assessment Report

Editors: Robert T. Watson, M.C. Zinyowera, and Richard H. Moss
http://www.ipcc-wg2.gov/publications/SAR/SAR_Chapter%20B.pdf

Part I.B. Energy Primer

* * *

B.3.3.2. Renewable Energy Potentials and Natural Flows

In contrast to fossil energy sources, renewable energy forms such as solar, wind, and hydro can be either carbon-free or carbon-neutral. The sustainable use of biomass, for example, is carbon-neutral. Solar photovoltaic electricity generation is carbon-free. One must be careful, of course, to examine the full life cycle of the system when comparing the GHG implications of different energy systems because, for example, all energy systems currently rely on fossil fuels to construct devices, transport material, and dispose of waste.

Figure B-10 provides a schematic illustration of annual global energy flows without anthropogenic interference (Sørensen, 1979), and Table B-4 gives a summary of the annual (global) natural flows of renewable energy worldwide and their technical recovery potentials, as well as estimates for more practical potentials that could be achieved by 2020–2025 with current and near- to medium-term technologies and cost structures. The concept of technical potential can be used in a similar fashion as the concept of energy resources, and potentials by 2020 as the concept of energy reserves. The fundamental difference, of course, is that renewable potentials represent annual flows available, in principle, on a sustainable basis indefinitely, whereas fossil energy reserves and resources, although expanding in time, are fundamentally finite quantities. Lifecycle analyses remain important because although the energy flows are sustainable they still require materials like concrete and copper and the commitment of land and other resources.

The renewable energy potentials identified in Table B-4 are theoretically large enough to provide the current primary energy needs for the world, and the technical potentials are large enough to cover most of the conceivable future growth of global energy demand.

Hydropower is currently the most-developed modern renewable energy source worldwide. Table B-4 shows that the maximum technical potential is almost as large as the total final electricity consumption in 1990 as given in Table B-2 [omitted] (WEC, 1993b; Moreira and Poole, 1993). The technology to harness geothermal resources is established. Its current total use is about 0.2 EJ of electricity (Arai,1993; Häfele et al., 1981). There are four types of geothermal occurrences: hydrothermal sources, hot dry rock, magma, and geopressurized sources. The total accessible resource base of geothermal energy to a depth of 5 km is more than 126 million EJ (Palmerini, 1993), but occurrences within easily accessible layers of the crust reduce the technical potential. The annual flow from Earth is estimated at about 800 EJ/yr (Sørensen, 1979). The long-term technical

Figure B-10.

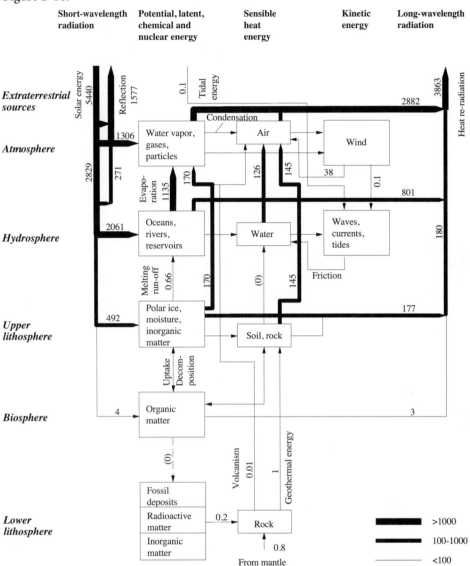

	Short-wavelength radiation	Potential, latent, chemical and nuclear energy	Sensible heat energy	Kinetic energy	Long-wavelength radiation

potential could be greater than 20 EJ—especially if deep drilling costs can be reduced, as these are a major limitation to this energy source.

The energy flux of the atmosphere corresponds to about 200,000 EJ/yr of wind energy. The height limitations of wind converters, the distance of offshore sites, and insufficient wind velocities and land use all limit the practical potential. The ultimate potential of wind-generated electricity worldwide could indeed be very large: Some estimates place it at 50 times current global final electricity consumption (Grubb and Meyer, 1993; WEC, 1993b; Cavallo et al., 1993; Gipe, 1991; Häfele et al., 1981). Wind electricity is produced at many sites, and it is often also an economic option for electricity generation. The conversion efficiency is not the real barrier to the successful operation of wind-powered electricity generators. The technological challenge is that wind velocity is not constant in

Table B-4: Global renewable energy potentials by 2020–2025, maximum technical potentials, and annual natural flows, in EJ thermal equivalent.[a]

	Consumption[b]		Potential by 2020–2025[c]	Long-Term Technical Potentials[d]	Annual Flows
	1860-1990	1990			
Hydro	560	21	35–55	>130	>400
Geothermal	–	<1	4	>20	>800
Wind	–	–	7–10	>130	>200000
Ocean	–	–	2	>20	>300
Solar	–	–	16–22	>2600	>3000000
Biomass	1150	55	72–137	>1300	
Total	1710	76	130–230	>4200	>3000000

Sources: Hall et al., 1993; Moreira and Poole, 1993; Grubb and Meyer, 1993; Johansson et al., 1993; Swisher and Wilson, 1993; WEC, 1993b, 1994; Dessus et al., 1992; Grübler and Nakicenovic, 1992; Hall, 1991; IPCC, 1992; Jensen and Sørensen, 1984; Sørensen, 1979.

Notes: All totals have been rounded; – = negligible amounts; blanks = data not available.

[a] All estimates have been converted into thermal equivalent with an average factor of 38.5%.
[b] Grübler and Nakicenovic, 1992.
[c] Range estimated from the literature. Survey includes the following sources: Johansson et al., 1993; WEC, 1993b; Dessus et al., 1992; EPA, 1990. It represents renewable potentials by 2020–2025, in scenarios with assumed policies for enhanced exploitation of renewable potentials.
[d] Long-term technical potentials are based on the Working Group II evaluation of the literature sources given in this table. This evaluation is intended to correspond to the concept of fossil energy resources, conventional and unconventional.

magnitude and direction. To utilize much higher windspeeds offshore, one option is to install floating windmills and to transport the electricity generated directly to the location of consumption or to use it for on-board hydrogen production.

Ocean energy flows include thermal energy, waves, tides, and the sea-freshwater interfaces as rivers flow into oceans. The low temperature gradients and low wave heights lead to an annual flow up to 300 EJ/yr of electricity. The technical potential is about 10 to 100 times smaller (Cavanagh et al., 1993; WEC, 1993b; Baker, 1991; Sørensen, 1979).

All conceivable human energy needs could be provided for by diverting only a small fraction of the solar influx to energy use, assuming that a significantly large area could be devoted to solar energy gathering because of low spatial energy densities. Solar thermal and photovoltaic demonstration power plants are operating in a number of countries. Many gigawatts (GW) of installed electric capacity could be constructed after a few years of development. The main challenge is to reduce capital costs. Other proposals also have been made—for instance, placing solar power satellites in space.

Four general categories of biomass energy resources are used for fuels: fuelwood, wastes, forests, and energy plantations. Biomass wastes originate from farm crops, animals, forestry wastes, wood-processing byproducts, and municipal waste and sewage. The potential of biomass energy crops and plantations depends on the land area available, the harvestable yield, its energy content, and the conversion efficiency. Biomass potentials by 2020–2025 in Table B-4 are based on a literature survey of estimates and scenarios (Johansson et al., 1993; WEC, 1993b; Hall, 1991). The technical potential of biomass energy crops and plantations is especially difficult to estimate. Based on land-use capacity studies, estimates of the land available for tropical plantations range between 580 and 620 million ha (Houghton et al., 1991; Grainger, 1990).

Notes & Questions

1. Renewable Portfolio Standards (RPSs), discussed in Chapter 6, require covered electricity providers to provide a certain percentage of power sold from renewable resources (as defined by statute or regulation). State governments have been responsible for establishing RPSs, though there have been federal proposals. How does this state-level action impact our national fuel mix for electricity generation? Why might that make sense? What problems might that cause?

2. *Practice Note*: When considering the environmental benefits of renewable resources, it is important to consider not just the lack of fossil fuel that is necessary to generate power, but the amount of fossil fuel it took to produce and mine raw minerals to make steel for a windmill or build the technical components of a solar panel. This is true of all resources, and is called a life-cycle analysis. Consider the various resources discussed in this chapter. What might we tend to overlook for each resource? Consider shipping costs, extraction costs, emissions, etc. What else might be wise to consider?

3. Going back to the initial client question, think about the IRP issues you have been compiling over the course of the chapter. Where do renewable energy sources fit in an IRP? In considering renewable resources, is the analysis any different than those for conventional resources? Is there a moral or ethical difference between such resources? Does that matter?

4. Utilities in West Virginia are dealing with the client issue raised at the outset of the chapter right now. The State of West Virginia recently passed a law requiring an IRP. It is not as detailed as some other state IRP requirements, but it is now a requirement. Returning to the client issue above regarding a utility IRP, read the West Virginia statute below and think about how well your list of issues would address the requirements of the West Virginia statute. Are there issues you missed? Are there issues the statute should have included? What is in the statute your client might have tried to keep out of the law?

Enrolled Committee Substitute for H. B. 2803

[Passed March 7, 2014; in effect ninety days from passage.]

AN ACT to amend the Code of West Virginia, 1931, as amended, by adding thereto a new section, designated § 24-2-19, relating to requiring electric utilities to develop integrated resource plans; requiring the Public Service Commission to order development of integrated resource plans; specifying certain deadlines for the plans; requiring commission review; authorizing commission to request additional information from the utilities; and providing considerations for commission when developing requirements for integrated resource plans.

Be it enacted by the Legislature of West Virginia:

That the Code of West Virginia, 1931, as amended, be amended by adding thereto a new section, designated § 24-2-19, to read as follows:

ARTICLE 2. POWERS AND DUTIES OF PUBLIC SERVICE COMMISSION.
§ 24-2-19. Integrated Resource Planning Required.

(a) Not later than March 31, 2015, the Public Service Commission shall issue an order directing any electric utility that does not have an existing requirement approved by the Public Service Commission that provides for the future review of both supply side and demand side resources to develop an initial integrated resource plan to be filed not later than January 1, 2016, in conjunction with other similar deadlines required by other states or entities of the electric utilities. This order may include guidelines for developing an integrated resource plan.

(b)(1) Any electric utility that has an existing requirement approved by the Public Service Commission that provides for the future review of both supply side and demand side resources is exempt from this initial integrated resource plan filing until such time as that existing requirement has been satisfied. Thereafter, such electric utility is required to file an integrated resource plan pursuant to subsection (a) of this section.

(2) Each electric utility that has filed the initial integrated resource plan shall file an updated plan at least every five years after the initial integrated resource plan has been filed. Any electric utility that was exempt from filing an initial integrated resource plan shall file an integrated resource plan within five years of satisfying any existing requirement and at least every five years thereafter. All integrated resource plans shall comply with the provisions of any relevant order of the Public Service Commission establishing guidelines for the format and contents of updated and revised integrated resource plans.

(c) The Public Service Commission shall analyze and review an integrated resource plan. The Public Service Commission may request further information from the utility, as necessary. Nothing in this section affects the obligations of utilities to obtain otherwise applicable commission approvals.

(d) The Commission may consider both supply-side and demand-side resources when developing the requirements for the integrated resource plans. The plan shall compare projected peak demands with current and planned capacity resources in order to develop a portfolio of resources that represents a reasonable balance of cost and risk for the utility and its customers in meeting future demand for the provision of adequate and reliable service to its electric customers as specified by the Public Service Commission.

Chapter 5

Economic Regulation and Market Structure

A. Introduction

1. Vocabulary and Concepts

Cost of Service Formula: $R = O + B(r)$, which is used to determined unit prices
  R = Revenue requirement (amount utility needs to recover)
  O = Operating expenses and maintenance (passed through/no return)
  B = Rate Base (capital investments that are permitted to earn a return)
  r = Rate of Return

Cost of Service Ratemaking: Rates that are determined from a utility's cost of providing service including an opportunity for the utility to earn a reasonable rate of return on its investment.

Investor-Owned Utility (IOU): A business entity providing service deemed to be a utility (often called a "public utility" even if privately owned). The entity is managed privately rather than as a division of government or a utility cooperative.

Market-Based Rates: Rate authority (instead of cost-of-service rates) granted by the Federal Energy Regulatory Commission (FERC) authorizing wholesale sales of electric energy, capacity, and ancillary services. Such authority will only be granted to sellers that can show that they and their affiliates do not have, or have adequately mitigated, market power (both horizontal and vertical).

Motions to Intervene: Individuals are given the option to intervene in Federal Energy Regulatory Commission (FERC) proceedings, as well as in most similar state proceedings. **Intervenors** (individuals or entities filing such a motion) become participants in the proceeding. Those intervening before FERC have the right to request rehearing of FERC orders and can seek appeal final agency actions in the U.S. Circuit Courts of Appeal.

Natural Monopoly: A natural monopoly occurs in an industry where it is most efficient to concentrate production in a single firm. The electricity sector was widely considered a natural monopoly, but as you will see in this chapter, some portions of the sector may benefit from competition.

Rate Case: The formal process governments use to determine the rates to charge customers for electricity, natural gas, and other regulated utility services.

Rate of Return: The return (or profit) a regulated utility is allowed to earn on investments, which is determined as a percentage of the utility's rate base.

Ratepayer Advocate: A government office that actively represents ratepayers in utility proceedings related to service, including cost allocation, utility infrastructure, and fuel costs (including hedging).

Ratepayers: Utility customers often meaning those paying for electricity or natural gas according to established rates.

Stranded Cost Issues: Costs that utilities were permitted to recover through their cost-of-service rates that may not be recoverable (in whole or in part) because of the regulatory change. This is a side effect of reduced utility regulation, which is usually done to increase competition for the impacted sector.

Test Year: The twelve-month period chosen to calculate the revenue requirement for the utility. The chosen period should reflect conditions that the utility is expected during the period when the rates will be applied. This means the most recent twelve months may not be used, especially when there are, for example, extreme events such as unusually hot summers or cold winters.

Unit Price Formula: $P = R/u$, which determines ratepayer unit prices
  P = Price per unit
  R = Total Revenue
  u = Units expected to be sold

Used and Useful Property: The concept in utility regulation that, for a utility to recover costs of its capital investments, those costs must related to property that us physically used and useful to the utility's current ratepayers.

2. Client Issue

You work for a law firm that represents a major natural gas utility. A partner with whom you work has just informed you that the utility will be intervening in a rate case to dispute the rate-of-return issue. (They will want to keep the return as low as possible.) As you read this chapter, think about what items would be relevant to the rate-of-return issue (and what would not). Keep a running list of search terms to help you in your research.

You also know that your utility client has its own rate case pending in two years. Consider the implication of arguing for a lower rate of return as an intervenor, then asking for a higher rate of return later in the utility's own rate case. Are there ethical problems with doing that as their counsel? What might the concern be? Or is this more of a practical concern than an ethical one?

3. Ratemaking

John S. Moot, *Economic Theories of Regulation and Electricity Restructuring*

25 Energy L.J. 273 (2004)
Copyright (c) 2004 Energy Bar Association; John S. Moot

I. Introduction

The regulation of American industry has fascinated social scientists for many years. There was a time when political scientists and economists presumed regulation beneficial in remedying market failures. That view began to change in the 1960s when empirical studies suggested regulation often did more harm than good, creating producer rents rather than efficiency. According to one of the most influential thinkers of this period, Nobel laureate economist George Stigler, the reason was that regulation was a public good being allocated by politicians to the highest bidder, and producers were more likely than not to prevail over consumers in that political marketplace. Many forms of regulation thereafter became suspect as creating barriers to entry and regulating price as a means of providing supracompetitive rents to producers, rather than correcting market failures. Economic theories of regulation also exposed other warts, such as regulation's tendency to cross-subsidize high cost consumers by imposing higher rates to low-cost consumers. Political scientists also began to take a closer look at government regulation and bureaucracy.

Almost as quickly as these theories of regulation took hold, however, the U.S. Congress and certain federal regulatory commissions began dismantling entry and price regulation of many industries. This deregulatory movement included the airline, trucking, railroad, telecommunications, natural gas, and banking industries. This trend surprised social scientists, causing them to reevaluate their previously pessimistic views of government. Derthick and Quirk, political scientists, concluded that this deregulatory wave restored confidence in the American system of government. Sam Peltzman, the economist who formalized Stigler's theory of regulation, offered a different perspective. In his view, deregulation had occurred in most cases because regulation had ceased to provide supracompetitive rents to producers, thereby leading them to abandon their support for regulation. Regulatory outcomes, in his view, continued to reflect the central hypothesis of an economic theory of regulation.

The deregulatory wave of the 1970s and 1980s, and the debate over how to explain it, left one major industry largely untouched—the electric utility industry. At the close of the 1980s, the electric utility industry looked much as it had fifty years before: vertically integrated with traditional price and entry regulation. However, it was becoming apparent that one sector of the industry, the generation sector, would likely emerge as competitive. In 1978, a regulatory initiative, the Public Utilities Regulatory Policy Act (PURPA), had reduced barriers to entry in generation for certain technologies. Perhaps its more significant legacy, however, was that government-set prices designed to induce this new entry turned out to be billions of dollars in excess of market prices. The PURPA was not alone in creating over-market costs. A fleet of nuclear plants with enormous cost overruns were added during the 1980s, and many states burdened electric rates further with programs designed to benefit environmental and other constituencies. Yet, as the embedded cost of regulated supply additions was rising dramatically, the marginal cost of producing electricity was falling rapidly in the short-run due to excess capacity, and in the long-run due to new combined-cycle gas turbine technology. Then, in 1992, Congress lowered barriers to entry for all generation technologies when it passed the Energy Policy Act of 1992. When the economy fell into recession during the early 1990s, this combination of events—high regulated electric rates, low market prices, ease of entry, and an economic recession—created enormous pressure on traditional regulation of the generation sector.

The dam finally broke in 1994 when the California Public Utilities Commission (CPUC) announced that it would deregulate the generation sector of the California electric industry. The CPUC's action initiated a wave of reform, with twenty-four states following California's lead by enacting "retail restructuring" legislation over the next several years. The Federal Energy Regulatory Commission (FERC) also began developing pro-competitive policies during the late 1980s. Then, in 1996, the FERC facilitated greater competition in the generation sector by ordering all utilities to provide open and nondiscriminatory access to their transmission grids. The FERC then followed this landmark rulemaking with two more rulemakings in 1999 and 2002, which fostered the creation of regional transmission organizations (RTOs) and regional energy markets, with the purpose being to increase efficiency and lower barriers to entry for independent generators.

However, as quickly as this wave of reform took hold, it abruptly halted. In 2000-2001, the California electricity industry "melted down" with skyrocketing prices, blackouts, and the largest utility bankruptcy in history. Other regions also experienced significant increases in market prices during 2000-2001 as natural gas prices surged and supply and demand tightened. In the wake of the California crisis and rising wholesale market prices, not a single state adopted retail access legislation after 2000, and eight states delayed, suspended, or repealed their retail access programs. The federal regulatory reform effort stalled as well. Only one regional grid operator has been created since June 2000, and the FERC's third rulemaking, the standard market design (SMD) rulemaking, was thwarted by opposition in Congress and the states.

Is there a theory of regulation that can explain the uneven course of electricity restructuring? The purpose of this article is to explore this question. The article's focus is on positive theories of regulation that seek to explain when and in what form regulation (or deregulation) will occur, not normative theories of when and in what form regulation (or deregulation) should occur. Electricity restructuring is a good test of the former, because it involves a mix of both deregulation and increased regulation and has been marked by tremendous swings in policy direction. Deregulation of the generation sector swept the nation and then contracted. Increased regulation of other portions of the industry—particularly the transmission business and the creation of quasi-governmental entities to operate regional markets—grew steadily, but has since faltered as well.

This article concludes that many aspects of electricity restructuring are broadly consistent with an economic theory of regulation. This is particularly true of Peltzman's hypotheses that: (i) regulation will tend to dampen swings in commodity prices, protecting consumers against severe price increases and producers against economic downturns; (ii) regulation will tend to distribute public goods across various interest groups according to marginal utility, rather than awarding them to a single winning group; and (iii) regulation will tend toward average cost prices, causing low-cost customers to subsidize high-cost customers, a conclusion also reached by Posner. The California electricity crisis is a good example of the first hypothesis; retail access legislation and the FERC's Order No. 2000 are good examples of the second hypothesis; and many of the rate-setting practices of both state commissions and the FERC are good examples of the third hypothesis.

This article also concludes that information costs are central to understanding the ongoing struggle between producer and consumer interests in the electric industry. Both informational and organizational transaction costs generate the hypothesis that small, cohesive groups, such as producers, will tend to prevail over large, diffuse interests, such as consumers. Producers will tend to prevail because their potential gains from regulation are greater than the transaction costs of influencing government policy (including the cost of organizing and supplying campaign contributions). By contrast, the transaction costs incurred by consumers generally will exceed their gains from influencing government action. This is true for several reasons, not the least of which is that consumers face significant information costs in uncovering regulatory failures that harm them. The costs incurred by any single consumer to uncover such failures will exceed the benefits of her doing so, and the cost of organizing collectively to uncover regulatory failures is generally prohibitive due to the free rider problem, among others.

The importance of information costs is revealed in the many facets of electricity restructuring. Consider, for example, retail restructuring. Twenty-four states adopted retail access legislation in the late 1990s, allowing competitors to compete for the once-captive retail customers of vertically integrated utilities. This movement is explainable, in some measure, through an economic theory of regulation because reduced barriers to entry had dampened the prospects for rents from the utilities' construction of new generation. But this conclusion is, at best, a heavily qualified one. Utilities still faced huge losses from deregulation because their sunken investment was far above the market value of that investment, which is why most utilities initially opposed deregulation. Moreover, an explanation rooted in new entry and declining rents cannot easily overcome the fact that new entry continues to be relatively easy, has occurred in significant amounts in many regions, and is placing downward pressure on future utility profits from regulation. Yet, the retail access movement has all but stopped.

Only closer examination of information costs can supply the answer. In the 1990s, a combination of the visible and costly failures of regulation such as qualifying facilities (QFs) and nuclear plants, and the seemingly large benefits of deregulation due to new entry and low market prices, fostered the conclusion that regulation was a failure. Deregulation sheltered utilities from market efficiencies, and promised to both increase efficiency and cause prices to fall dramatically. Importantly, this confluence of events supplied not only a normative basis for deregulation, but the political impetus as well. Politicians could promise consumers (voters) an immediate price cut through retail access by pointing to the large price gap between market and regulated rates. The consumer interest was therefore at its zenith because (i) information costs (both as to regulatory failures and deregulatory benefits) were low; (ii) the expected per capita gains to consumers through deregulation were high; and (iii) the number of consumers (voters) affected was at its peak (since virtually every voter consumes electricity). It was therefore not surprising that utility opposition was not effective in stopping retail access (although it was, as discussed below, effective in moderating its financial impact).

The same factors also explain the demise of retail access. Retail access died at precisely the time (2001) when utility support for it should have been, and indeed was, at its zenith—with stranded cost recovery assured, a shrinking price gap, and Wall Street rewarding deregulated generation companies with high price/earnings ratios. Without a closer examination of the role of information and its impact on the strength of the consumer interest, one would have expected retail access to continue spreading, spurred on by utility support as well as the support of other groups (e.g., independent producers and industrial customers). But the factors present in the 1990s had entirely reversed by

2001. The California meltdown sent political shockwaves across the nation, providing a concrete, if extreme, example of the political risks of supporting retail access initiatives. Equally important, the regulated-market price gap had all but disappeared in most regions due to rising natural gas prices and tightening of supply and demand conditions. Retail access had gone from providing a tax cut to the average consumer (voter) to a regulatory reform effort that posed few consumer benefits and significant political risks. Thus, it is not surprising that the movement so quickly died.

By offering this perspective on electricity restructuring, I am not suggesting that regulation (or deregulation) is governed entirely by political forces. Not all politicians seek continued re-election or re-appointment. Not all their decisions are determined by external pressure groups. It is for this reason, among others, that the predictive power of an economic theory of regulation is admittedly modest. This does not, however, deprive the theory of its usefulness. Individuals do matter, but they are not impervious to pressure groups. There are many obvious examples. CPUC Chairman Fessler had a critical influence on the California restructuring—and is perhaps the reason California was first in the nation—yet pressure groups significantly changed his blueprint for restructuring. FERC Chairman Wood was the principal reason why the FERC proposed the SMD rulemaking; yet, here again, pressure groups were successful in modifying and, perhaps, ultimately defeating that reform effort. Both Fessler and Wood had strong visions, and their internal normative compasses surely cannot be explained by an economic theory of regulation. However, an economic theory of regulation can help to explain why their visions were not ultimately enacted into law as proposed.

This article is organized as follows: Section I provides an overview of economic theories of regulation. Section II analyzes whether these theories can help to explain some of the major policy initiatives associated with electric restructuring. Section II.A discusses the spread of retail access and its later demise. Section II.B considers the California crisis. Section II.C evaluates the FERC's major rulemakings respecting wholesale market reform. Section II.D examines the continuing tendency of regulation to subsidize high cost consumers.

This article concludes with a normative comment. If, as this article suggests, public policy will tend toward the consumer interest as information costs decline, then it should also be true that government policy should encourage information collection and dissemination. The payoff from better information should be particularly significant, in the case of electricity restructuring, given the huge sums of money (and associated resource allocations) involved. In particular, better information might help push the industry off its current precipice—teetering between deregulation and traditional regulation. It is often said today that regulation protects consumers by guaranteeing "predictable and equitable" prices, whereas deregulation tends to exploit them. This is a normative debate that is beyond the scope of this article. I would suggest, however, that better information would provide for a more balanced debate. The "failures" of deregulation, e.g., market dysfunction and manipulation, price spikes, and supply shortages, are, by their nature, far more visible than any recognizable failures of regulation itself. This is despite the fact that regulation itself shoulders some of the blame for the ills of deregulation. The absence of time-of-use pricing inhibits demand response, which in turn impairs the competitiveness of wholesale energy markets. There also are significant regulatory barriers to constructing new transmission, including a politicized siting process and rate practices that discourage new investment, which, in turn, impair reliability and interstate trade and increase transmission congestion. Alfred Kahn reminds us that the choice is not between perfect competition and perfect regulation, but rather between an imperfect version of each. The current view, however, seems unduly weighted toward a belief that deregulation is primarily flawed and regulation largely benign. Perhaps better information would somewhat level the playing field.

II. An Economic Theory of Regulation

An economic theory of regulation cannot be discussed without first considering its primary alternative: a public interest theory of regulation. A public interest theory starts from the uncontroversial normative proposition that regulation should occur when necessary to address "market failures" such as natural monopoly and externality (social costs). However, can a public interest theory of regulation function as a positive theory by determining whether regulation does occur under those, and only those, circumstances? The "normative-positive" theory of regulation posits that it will. As summarized by Viscusi, et al.:

> According to the public interest theory, if a market is a natural monopoly, the public will demand industry regulation because the best solution is not achievable in the absence of regulation. Unfettered competition will result in excessive pricing and/or too many firms producing, thus exceeding a socially optimal level. Net welfare gains result by industry regulation, and this potential for welfare gains generates the public's demand for regulation.

In order for this to occur in anything other than a textbook scenario, however, one must assume low or zero transaction costs, as Noll describes:

> In a limited but complex sense, normative welfare economics constitutes a positive theory of government if the conditions of the Coase Theorem are true: information is perfect and costless, and the political process is free of its counterparts to transaction costs.... [I]mperfect information and transactions costs provide an entering wedge for political theories as to why regulation can be inefficient: capture by interest groups for the purpose of acquiring monopoly rents, or otherwise redistributing wealth to themselves in ways that also create inefficiency. Transaction costs are not, of course, zero. It is for this reason that although the public interest theory is not without some successes, it cannot explain the myriad of regulatory failures documented by economists.

Recognizing that transaction costs are not zero, George Stigler developed a positive theory of regulation that sought "to explain who will receive the benefits or burdens of regulation, what form regulation will take, and the effects of regulation upon the allocation of resources." Typically referred to as the "economic theory of regulation" (ET), Stigler's theorem posits that: 1) All individuals will act rationally in their self-interest; 2) Politicians and regulators will act to further their own careers by maximizing political support through the allocation of public goods among affected interest groups; 3) Interest groups will use their resources to compete for these public goods, providing political support through campaign contributions and other vote-getting measures; 4) Producers of goods and services will seek to increase their profits by lobbying for entry barriers, price supports, tariff quotas and the like; and 5) Consumers will defend their interests by opposing this rent-seeking behavior by producers, but more often than not will lose the political competition because consumers are too large and diffuse an interest group to lobby the government effectively. Thus, under Stigler's theory, "[t]he prototypical result ... is the triumph of the cohesive producer interest over the diffuse consumer interest" in a "political equilibrium ... in which cohesive minorities tax diffuse majorities." This was the basis for Stigler's conclusion that "as a rule, regulation is acquired by the industry and is designed and operated primarily for its benefit."

A few years later, Stigler's colleague, Sam Peltzman, formalized Stigler's theory. Peltzman's model retained the assumption that the political effectiveness of an interest group is a function of its net per capita gains from lobbying, but cautioned that this did not guarantee a single winning group. Rather, Peltzman concluded that "regulators will allocate benefits across consumer and producer groups so that total political utility is maximized." Although Peltzman's model did not allow one to predict "whether the producers, the consumers, or neither group typically gets the lion's share of the rents[,]" it did contain two important hypotheses. First, regulation would act to "offset the effect of market forces on the division of rents between producers and consumers" such that, for example, "[r]egulation will tend to be more heavily weighted toward 'producer protection' in depressions and toward 'consumer protection' in expansions." Second, regulation would tend to cross subsidize high cost consumers because of "the lack of any general connection between the cost differences and the political importance of [high and low cost consumers]." Peltzman's finding was consistent with Richard Posner's earlier conclusions.

Peltzman later applied this economic theory of regulation to the deregulation of the railroad, trucking, airline, financial services, and long-distance telecommunications industries. He acknowledged that "[n]ot one economist in a hundred practicing in the early 1970s predicted the sweeping changes that were soon to happen[,]" but nonetheless concluded that many, albeit not all, of the cases of deregulation were broadly consistent with an economic theory of regulation. In most of these industries the rents gained by producers through regulation dissipated due to reductions in demand, changes in technology, or new entry. Consequently, the marginal cost of expending resources in support of continued regulation exceeded the benefits of doing so, thereby eliminating the incentive for producers to support regulation and reducing the rents available for regulators to distribute across groups. For example, continued regulation of the railroad industry was undercut by competition from other carriers (particularly trucking), and as a result "[t]he organized producer interest ultimately favored and got deregulation." Rents also had dissipated in the airline industry, albeit due to quality competition or service rather than new entry, so that costs were increased without increasing marginal rates. Although, some carriers, nonetheless continued to support regulation, the largest airline, United, supported deregulation. Peltzman acknowledged, however, that deregulation of the trucking and telecommunications industries did not fit neatly into an economic theory of regulation.

Numerous economists also contributed to an economic theory of regulation. Gary Becker provided a more uplifting hypothesis, positing that regulation would tend toward efficient outcomes. This hypothesis rested on the premise that regulation does not transfer wealth efficiently, i.e., for every dollar taken from consumers to subsidize producers, producers will receive less than a dollar, resulting in dead weight loss. The loss increases with the level of subsidy being sought and, because of this, consumers' incentive to oppose inefficient regulation increases as the subsidy increases. This effect did not, as Becker acknowledged, eliminate inefficient regulation, but nonetheless imposed an important counterweight to its excesses.

Richard Posner's work focused on a different phenomenon—the tendency of regulation to transfer wealth from the low-cost to the high-cost consumer. Dubbing this "taxation by regulation," he concluded that "one of the functions of regulation is to perform distributive and allocative chores usually associated with the taxing or financial branch of government[,]" resulting in "the deliberate and continued provision of many services at lower rates and in larger quantities than would be offered in an unregulated competitive market...."

Economists readily acknowledged the limits of their theories, however. Posner noted the limitation of economic theories of regulation, as did Peltzman in examining the cases of deregulation. Joskow and Noll also concluded that "the [economic] theory of regulation serves as a convenient way of organizing historical material, but not one that is particularly rich in predictive value." Not surprisingly, political scientists were even more skeptical of economic theories of regulation.

One distinct limitation of an economic theory of regulation is that, as Peltzman acknowledged, it does not allow one to predict, a priori, whether "the producers, the consumers, or neither group typically gets the lion's share of the rents." This is due, in part, to the variability of transaction costs across different industries and the difficulty of estimating those costs for purposes of testing a positive theory of regulation.

A simple example illustrates this problem. Assume there are three producers operating in a single state. The producers employ 100,000 workers, have 5,000 in-state shareholders, and sell a product used by three million consumers. In this example, the three producers will form a more effective political organization than the diffuse group of three million consumers, but the consumers will have a distinct numerical voting advantage (three million consumers compared to 105,000 workers and shareholders). Consequently, the producers in this example must be efficient in their political influence by translating money and other support into votes in order to overcome their substantial disadvantage in terms of voting strength.

The presence of information costs gives these three producers an advantage over the three million consumers. The producers will know what form of regulation increases their profits, but the consumers often will not know they are being harmed by pro-producer regulation. Consumers may even be misled into thinking that pro-producer regulation actually benefits them through political advertising. It was for this reason that Becker discounted the role of voting in his interest group model.

An even more fundamental limitation on consumer voting strength is that inefficient regulation often has such a small effect on consumers that it does not influence their voting behavior. Consumers are likely to be more concerned with larger issues in the voting booth, such as national defense and macroeconomic policy. Peltzman noted this truism and suggested it may help explain why public policy is broadly responsive to the public, but not necessarily in the regulation of particular industries.

If Peltzman is correct, it should follow that the organizational advantages of producers will vary not only with group size and structure, e.g., free-rider problems, but also on the nature of the product they provide. The greater the number of those consuming the product, and the more important it is to them, the more likely that public policy will tend toward the consumer interest. For example, if an industry provides an essential service that affects the entire population, such as telephone and electric service, the organizational advantages of producers should be at their lowest because the consumer voting pool is the greatest and the product's importance to their daily lives is also at its highest. The caveat, of course, is whether those consumers have the necessary information to understand that their essential product costs more than it should (or is supplied in less than optimal quantities) due to producer subsidies.

Although consumers are unlikely to procure that information on their own, political entrepreneurs often have the incentive to do it for them, as Noll describes:

> [P]olitical entrepreneurs can play the role of market perfectors, identifying failures and reporting them to those harmed.... [I]nformation pertinent to identifying market failures is most cheaply acquired and disseminated by government. Government alone can compel private parties to provide it, and relevant information is a byproduct of other government activities. Moreover, government officials,

because of their importance and recognizability, can readily access the public through the media to announce the information they acquire. Wilson, Bonbright, and others have offered similar observations.

Politicians therefore need not be viewed as primarily reactive, awarding public goods only to those who are effectively organized or those having acquired sufficient non-free information on their own account. Rather, politicians should have an incentive to pursue regulatory reform as a means of obtaining votes even when consumers have not organized effectively and are not aware of the need for reform. However, for there to be such a political incentive, the benefits of reform must be both material and transparent to the public. The latter is particularly important because voters will not reward a politician for a public policy benefit that is unknown.

The difficulty of quantifying organization and information costs—including the cost (benefit) that political entrepreneurs incur (receive) in formulating and communicating particular pro-consumer policies to the public—undermines the testability of positive theories of regulation. This does not mean that such theories cannot, in a broader sense, explain or predict the general course of regulatory policy or its reform. As discussed in section III, there is little doubt that, when information costs were at their lowest regarding the failures of regulation or deregulation, regulatory policy tended toward the consumer interest, rather than well organized producer groups such as utilities and independent producers.

People ex rel. Madigan v. Illinois Commerce Comm'n
988 N.E.2d 146 (Ill. App. 2d 2013)

Justice HUTCHINSON delivered the judgment of the court, with opinion.

¶ 1 In this consolidated appeal, petitioners, Attorney General Lisa Madigan and the Citizens Utility Board (CUB), challenge the decision of the Illinois Commerce Commission (the Commission) approving a volume-balancing-adjustment rider with respect to the delivery of natural gas to residences and businesses in and around Chicago by respondents Peoples Gas Light & Coke Company (Peoples Gas) and North Shore Gas Company (North Shore) (collectively, the Utilities). Specifically, petitioners challenge the Commission's authority to impose revenue decoupling on the consumers of respondents' product, natural gas.

¶ 2 In March 2007, the Utilities petitioned the Commission to approve a new "tracker" rider, the volume-balancing-adjustment rider, called "Rider VBA." See *In re North Shore Gas Co.*, Nos. 07–0241, 07–0242, 2008 WL 631214, at *1. The Commission stated, "[i]n simplest form, Rider VBA would adjust customer prices * * * in a way that the Utilities['] revenues are held constant despite changes in customer consumption." *Id.* at *127. The Commission reasoned:

> "Such changes in consumption are brought about by rising natural gas prices, the call for conservation measures, warming weather trends, the involvement of the Utilities in gas efficiency programs, and other events. The proposed monthly adjustments under Rider VBA are symmetrical meaning that they are based on both the over-recovery as well as the under-recovery of target revenues. Implementing Rider VBA imposes some additional administrative expenses and, among other things called for by Staff, there would be annual internal audits." *Id.*

Following an evidentiary hearing and a review of the materials, in 2008 the Commission approved Rider VBA as a four-year pilot program. *Id.* at * 141.

¶ 3 The Attorney General appealed the Commission's decision; however, the Appellate Court, First District, determined that it lacked jurisdiction to consider the appeal and transferred the case to the Second District. See *People ex rel. Madigan v. Illinois Commerce Comm'n,* 407 Ill.App.3d 207, 224, 347 Ill.Dec. 78, 941 N.E.2d 947 (2010). On January 10, 2012, and during the pendency of the appeal in the Second District, the Commission issued an order approving Rider VBA on a permanent basis. Thereafter, the parties moved to dismiss the appeal as moot, and this court allowed the motion. See *People ex rel. Madigan v. Illinois Commerce Comm'n,* No. 2–11–0380 (2012) (minute order).

¶ 4 In its January 2012 decision, the Commission set out the positions of the Utilities, the Commission's staff, and the Attorney General, and the response of the Utilities to the Attorney General's position. It then set out its analysis and conclusions. The Commission reflected that among the problems that Rider VBA was originally intended to protect the Utilities from were the revenue losses attributable to a diminishing customer base and to the implementation of aggressive energy efficiency programs. The Commission next expounded on the reasons to continue Rider VBA: it was "a symmetrical and transparent formula for collecting the approved distribution revenue requirement"; it would reduce reliance on forecasting, which was predictive and "inevitably incorrect"; and it would influence the Utilities to pursue fewer rate cases, because Rider VBA would make under-recovery of their revenue requirement less likely. The Commission addressed the criticism that questioned whether decoupling would prompt the Utilities to spend more on energy efficiency programs. It responded that its original approval of Rider VBA as a pilot program was not centered on energy efficiency factors and that energy efficiency was not the only reason it approved the decoupling mechanism. The Commission explained:

> "[O]ur rationale then and now is appropriately multi-faceted to address the many components that such a mechanism seeks to resolve. For example, weather affects customer usage and decoupling means that customers do not overpay when weather is colder than normal or underpay when weather is warmer than normal. Decoupling also addresses load changes, including declining load attributable to energy efficiency. Whether Rider VBA prompts the [Utilities] to spend more on energy efficiency is immaterial. The [Utilities'] forecast showed declining load on their systems. Section 8–104 of the Act requires them to offer energy efficiency programs to meet ever-increasing load reductions through energy efficiency measures. Decoupling will take the effects of efficiency into account together with other factors, notably weather, that affects load and promote distribution rate stability for customers and the [Utilities]."

¶ 5 The Commission concluded that the benefits of "distribution rate stability for customers and the [Utilities]" justified approving the Rider VBA on a permanent basis. The Attorney General and CUB timely filed their notices of appeal.

¶ 6 Petitioners challenge the validity of Rider VBA and the Commission's discretion in authorizing it. Petitioners argue that the deferential standard that generally applies to the Commission's exercise of its discretion does not apply here because it "expressly departed from past practice" and it "necessarily abused its discretion if it made an error of law by approving a rider absent 'exceptional circumstances.'" In support of their argument, petitioners assert that (1) Rider VBA violates fundamental ratemaking principles by retroactively modifying consumer charges to meet revenue forecasts, and (2) Rider VBA violates the prohibition against single-issue ratemaking.

¶ 7 Contrary to petitioners' request for a more stringent review, our scope of review is governed by section 10–201 of the Public Utilities Act (the Act) (see 220 ILCS 5/10–201 (West 2010)). Section 10–201 provides in relevant part that a reviewing court shall reverse a Commission's order or decision, in whole or in part, if it finds that (a) the findings of the Commission were not supported by substantial evidence based on the entire record of evidence presented to or before the Commission for and against such order or decision; (b) the order or decision was without the jurisdiction of the Commission; (c) the order or decision was in violation of the state or federal constitution or laws; or (d) the proceedings or manner by which the Commission considered and entered its order or decision were in violation of the state or federal constitution or laws, to the prejudice of the appellant. 220 ILCS 5/10–201(e)(iv) (West 2010). This court gives " substantial deference to the decisions of the Commission, in light of its expertise and experience in this area." *Commonwealth Edison Co. v. Illinois Commerce Comm'n*, 405 Ill.App.3d 389, 397, 344 Ill.Dec. 662, 937 N.E.2d 685 (2010) (*ComEd*). "Accordingly, on appeal, the Commission's findings of fact are considered *prima facie* true; its orders are considered *prima facie* reasonable; and the appellant bears the burden of proof on all issues raised." *ComEd*, 405 Ill.App.3d at 397, 344 Ill.Dec. 662, 937 N.E.2d 685.

¶ 8 " 'In making adequate findings, the Commission is not required to provide findings on each evidentiary claim; its findings are sufficient if they are specific enough to enable the court to make an informed and intelligent review of its order.' " *People ex rel. Madigan v. Illinois Commerce Comm'n*, 2012 IL App (2d) 100024, ¶ 39, 359 Ill.Dec. 833, 967 N.E.2d 863 (quoting *ComEd*, 405 Ill.App.3d at 398, 344 Ill.Dec. 662, 937 N.E.2d 685). " 'In other words, it must state the facts essential to its ruling so that the court can properly review the basis for the decision.' " *Id.* (quoting *ComEd*, 405 Ill.App.3d at 398, 344 Ill.Dec. 662, 937 N.E.2d 685). "On review, this court can neither reevaluate the credibility or weight of the evidence nor substitute its judgment for that of the Commission." *Id.* ¶ 40 (quoting *ComEd*, 405 Ill.App.3d at 398, 344 Ill.Dec. 662, 937 N.E.2d 685).

¶ 9 Section 9–101 of the Act requires the Commission to establish "just and reasonable" rates for consumers. 220 ILCS 5/9–101 (West 2010). In so doing, the Commission must also ensure that all of its rules and regulations affecting or pertaining to its rates are "just and reasonable." *Id.* With respect to ratemaking, at least two types are prohibited: those that constitute retroactive ratemaking and those that constitute single-issue ratemaking. See, *e.g.*, *Illinois Bell Telephone Co. v. Illinois Commerce Comm'n*, 203 Ill.App.3d 424, 149 Ill.Dec. 148, 561 N.E.2d 426 (1990) (retroactive ratemaking); *Citizens Utility Board v. Illinois Commerce Comm'n*, 166 Ill.2d 111, 209 Ill.Dec. 641, 651 N.E.2d 1089 (1995) (single-issue ratemaking). Retroactive ratemaking occurs when a utility establishes a scheme whereby it provides refunds to its consumers when its rates are too high and surcharges when its rates are too low. See *Illinois Bell Telephone Co.*, 203 Ill.App.3d at 435, 149 Ill.Dec. 148, 561 N.E.2d 426 (citing *Citizens Utilities Co. of Illinois v. Illinois Commerce Comm'n*, 124 Ill.2d 195, 207, 124 Ill.Dec. 529, 529 N.E.2d 510 (1988)). Single-issue ratemaking occurs when a utility considers changes to components of its revenue requirement in isolation in setting rates; this type of ratemaking is prohibited because considering any one item in a revenue formula in isolation risks understating or overstating the revenue requirement. See *Citizens Utility Board*, 166 Ill.2d at 137, 209 Ill.Dec. 641, 651 N.E.2d 1089. Petitioners assert that Rider VBA constitutes both retroactive ratemaking and single-issue ratemaking and that therefore the Commission's order should be reversed.

¶ 10 In the analysis and decision section of its 2008 decision, the Commission noted that the Rider VBA was "fundamentally different from any other rider that the Commission has authorized thus far and which the courts have approved." *In re North Shore Gas Co.*, 2008

WL 631214, at *128. Accordingly, prior to reaching the arguments, and relying on information from United States Department of Energy research reports and the testimony from the Commission's hearing, we provide a brief overview of natural gas revenue decoupling.

¶ 11 Some of a natural gas utility's expenses are for its "assets," such as distribution pipelines, mains, facilities, and equipment to maintain the utility's physical presence. See, e.g., *People ex rel. Madigan v. Illinois Commerce Comm'n*, 2011 IL App (1st) 100654, ¶ 5, 354 Ill.Dec. 662, 958 N.E.2d 405 (describing infrastructure in relation to an "'Infra-structure Cost Recovery Rider'"). Using our own hypothetical, we will say that this is 75% of its expenses. Then the remaining 25% of its expenses is the actual cost of preparing and distributing gas to its customers. Citizen "A" should not have to pay as much for natural gas to maintain the house at 65 degrees as Citizen "B," who maintains the house at 75 degrees. See, e.g., 220 ILCS 5/1–102(d)(iii) (West 2010) (finding equitable that "the cost of supplying public utility services is allocated to those who cause the costs to be in-curred"). For this policy reason, among others, rates traditionally have been structured so that citizens are paying a lesser fixed fee and a higher rate for their consumption of natural gas. However, if everyone in the service area suddenly uses only a fraction of the natural gas they used to use, the utility still has 75% of its expenses. Therefore, to continue to operate and profit, the utility must necessarily raise rates.

¶ 12 Ideally, the variable cost for citizens should equal the utility's cost to prepare and distribute the natural gas they consume, while the fixed cost should equal the total main-tenance costs for the entire infrastructure divided equally among its customer base. Thanks to conservation and energy efficiency programs, the variable cost should be falling. As citizens become more energy conscious, consumption declines. In turn, the utility requests a rate change. See, e.g., 220 ILCS 5/9–201 (West 2010) (procedures relating to changing rates and hearings). In this hypothetical, the Commission approves the change, which effectively increases the fixed charge and lowers the variable consumption charge. Un-derstandably then, the citizens are paying for infrastructure, not the consumption of natural gas. Legislative policies allowing this reaction to less demand essentially created little incentive for utility companies to shift their business model to invest in more energy efficient technology or programs to deal with less demand for their conventional service. To summarize then, revenue decoupling has not happened despite supply and demand; it has happened *because* of supply and demand.

¶ 13 In enacting section 8–104 of the Act, our legislature implemented a policy requiring natural gas utilities to use cost-effective energy efficiency measures to reduce direct and indirect costs to consumers. See 220 ILCS 5/8–104 (West 2010). Under traditional ratemaking, utilities are told to do one thing (promote energy efficiency) while they typically make more money when they do the opposite (increase sales). With traditional ratemaking, therefore, utilities experience a financial conflict of sorts when their efforts to reduce energy consumption are successful.

¶ 14 Revenue decoupling is a type of rate design that public utility commissions use to delink a utility's revenues from the volume of gas distributed (sales). With this type of regulation, a utility's revenues are essentially fixed by the public utility commission. If a utility's actual revenues are above the fixed level due to a larger volume of sales than expected, customers receive a credit from the utility for the difference; if actual revenues are below the fixed level due to a smaller volume of sales than expected, the utility issues a customer surcharge for the difference. Thus, a utility's revenues are decoupled from its volume of sales because its revenues are fixed as sales fluctuate. In other words, revenue decoupling is a regulatory mechanism that separates a utility's revenues from its level of sales by ensuring that the utility earns a reasonable and fixed level of revenues, even as sales fluctuate. See Sandy Glatt & Myka Dunkle, United States Department of Energy, Natural Gas Revenue Decoupling Regulation: Impacts on Industry (July 2010).

¶ 15 We, therefore, have two primary concepts. First, a traditional rate case uses a forecast of sales to set a rate, whereas revenue decoupling uses actual sales to set a rate. Because actual sales can be known only after the fact, revenue decoupling calculates an adjustment at a later date (called a "true-up calculation"). Second, a traditional rate case allows revenues to fluctuate around a fixed rate, whereas revenue decoupling allows a rate to fluctuate around a fixed level of revenues.

¶ 16 Decoupling was first introduced in 1978 in California to relieve the natural gas utilities of reduced revenues. To date, more than half of the states use or are considering natural gas revenue decoupling legislation. Each state and utility implements decoupling differently; however, the most common features used are as follows: both surcharges and credits issued; adjustments calculated and issued separately for different customer classes; adjustments based on the difference between actual and authorized revenues on a revenue-per-customer basis; a separate adjustment mechanism for weather; adjustments calculated annually; or surcharges and credits shown as a separate tariff page on a customer's bill.

¶ 17 In 2007, the Public Utility Commission of Ohio implemented revenue decoupling for Vectren Ohio. However, a few years later, the policy was replaced with another type of rate design called a straight fixed-variable (SFV) mechanism. See *Ohio Consumers' Counsel v. Public Utilities Comm'n of Ohio,* 127 Ohio St.3d 524, 2010–Ohio–6239, 941 N.E.2d 757. An SFV mechanism is a nonvolumetric rate design that charges a flat monthly fee regardless of the volume of gas delivered. In the present case, the Commission considered, and then rejected, the SFV design in favor of Rider VBA.

¶ 18 Revenue decoupling has its advantages and disadvantages, and the Commission in the present case took evidence from the parties, which is reflected in detail in its 2008 and 2012 decisions. As it pertains to customers and utilities, revenue decoupling offers reduced volatility in the utility's revenues and in customers' bills; it provides more equity between customers and the utility because decoupling is based on actual revenues rather than estimates, thereby helping to remove the zero-sum game between customers and the utility; and significant energy conservation has the potential to cause a gradual decline in gas commodity prices as the overall demand is reduced. Disadvantages include customers' lack of understanding how decoupling serves their long-term interests when they experience surcharges in the short term; the delays in surcharges and credits on bills can dilute customers' perceived risk reduction from fluctuating energy bills; and volatility in utility revenues can be perceived as being in the rate payers' best interest—in other words, rate payers should benefit when weather is mild or they adopt energy conservation measures. As stated earlier, the Commission's 2012 findings and conclusions explained that Rider VBA was beneficial because, *inter alia,* it was "a symmetrical and transparent formula for collecting the approved distribution revenue requirement"; it would reduce reliance on forecasting, which was predictive and "inevitably incorrect"; and it would influence the utility companies to pursue fewer rate cases, because Rider VBA would make underrecovery of their revenue requirement less likely.

¶ 19 As noted, more than half of the states use or are considering natural gas revenue decoupling regulations. See Ralph Cavanagh, *Report: "Decoupling" Is Transforming the Utility Industry,* Switchboard, Natural Resources Defense Council Staff Blog, http://switchboard.nrdc.org/blogs/rcavanagh/report_ decoupling_is_transform.html (last visited Mar. 14, 2013). Moreover, nearly every state has implemented some form of adjustment clauses or riders for its various utilities. For example, in April 2007, the New York State Public Service Commission determined that utility revenue decoupling mechanisms were needed, and it requested proposals to implement such regulations. See *In re the Investigation of Potential Gas Delivery Rate Disincentives Against the Promotion of Energy Efficiency, Renewable Technologies and Distributed Generation,* Case No. 06–G–0746.

¶ 20 Turning to the merits, petitioners first argue that Rider VBA violates the prohibition against retroactive ratemaking. Petitioners explain that all businesses must predict customer demand for their products; this is "fundamental to establishing price and thus fundamental to establishing just and reasonable rates that mimic market incentives." Petitioners claim that, under Rider VBA, "if customer gas usage differs from test-year projections, the Utilities add a monthly surcharge or credit to customer bills *the following year* to eliminate any deficiency or surplus from the initial charge." Petitioners conclude that the surcharge or credit customers receive during the recovery period constitutes retroactive ratemaking.

¶ 21 Initially, the Utilities and the Commission (collectively, respondents) counter that petitioners' argument is forfeited because "nowhere in these documents * * * did either the Attorney General or CUB raise a retroactive ratemaking argument before the Commission." First, we note that forfeiture is a limitation on the parties and not on the jurisdiction of this court. See *Central Illinois Light Co. v. Home Insurance Co.,* 213 Ill.2d 141, 152, 290 Ill.Dec. 155, 821 N.E.2d 206 (2004). Second, the Commission's 2008 decision included a discussion of its staff's view of Rider VBA. See *In re North Shore Gas Co.,* 2008 WL 631214, at * 116 ("According to Staff, Rider VBA takes the revenues that the rates approved in a base rate proceeding were intended to recover (which includes the Company's authorized return on rate base), and provides a surcharge if those rates produced insufficient revenues or a credit if those rates produced surplus revenues. In Staff's view, this is clearly contrary to the rule against retroactive ratemaking."). Third, the Commission rejected the argument. *In re North Shore Gas Co.,* 2008 WL 631214, at *133. Fourth, the Commission's 2012 order reflected the Attorney General's position that "Revenue Decoupling is Illegal Under Illinois Law" and addressed the "over- or under-recovery" of "costs being refunded or recovered through monthly adjustments." Despite the lack of the descriptive term "retroactive ratemaking," we believe that the argument was sufficiently raised to withstand forfeiture. For these reasons and in the interest of preserving a sound and uniform body of precedent, we choose to address petitioners' argument.

¶ 22 In *Mandel Brothers, Inc. v. Chicago Tunnel Terminal Co.,* 2 Ill.2d 205, 117 N.E.2d 774 (1954), our supreme court first enunciated the rule against retroactive ratemaking. It determined that rates approved by the Commission as just and reasonable could not be "excessive or unjustly discriminatory" for the purposes of awarding reparations even if those rates were later reversed by a reviewing court. *Id.* at 208, 117 N.E.2d 774. The court's holding was based on the Act's requirement that a utility charge rates approved by the Commission throughout the appellate process unless the reviewing court stayed or suspended the new rates. *Id.* at 211, 117 N.E.2d 774. The court reasoned that, because the utility was required to charge rates set by the Commission, these rates could not be deemed to be excessive as a basis of a claim for reparations. *Id.* at 212, 117 N.E.2d 774. The court's holding was subsequently reaffirmed in *Independent Voters of Illinois v. Illinois Commerce Comm'n,* 117 Ill.2d 90, 109 Ill.Dec. 782, 510 N.E.2d 850 (1987), *Citizens Utilities Co. of Illinois,* 124 Ill.2d 195, 124 Ill.Dec. 529, 529 N.E.2d 510, and *People ex rel. Hartigan v. Illinois Commerce Comm'n,* 148 Ill.2d 348, 170 Ill.Dec. 386, 592 N.E.2d 1066 (1992).

¶ 23 The supreme court later described the concept of retroactive ratemaking: "Once the Commission establishes rates, the Act does not permit refunds if the established rates are too high, or surcharges if the rates are too low." *Business & Professional People for the Public Interest v. Illinois Commerce Comm'n,* 146 Ill.2d 175, 243, 166 Ill.Dec. 10, 585 N.E.2d 1032 (1991) (*BPI II*) (citing *Business & Professional People for the Public Interest v. Illinois Commerce Comm'n,* 136 Ill.2d 192, 209, 144 Ill.Dec. 334, 555 N.E.2d 693 (1989) (*BPI I*)). The rule against retroactive ratemaking is consistent with the prospective nature of the Commission's ratemaking function and promotes stability in the ratemaking process. *Id.*

¶ 24 Although revenue decoupling is a different rate design from traditional ratemaking, the legal principles remain the same, *i.e.,* once the Commission approves a ratemaking plan, it cannot later modify that plan to correct an error. In the present case, the Commission approved Rider VBA, which included a ratemaking plan of revenue decoupling. In approving Rider VBA, the Commission has not acted to correct any error. Rather, the Commission approved a design, which involved fixed and reasonable amounts of revenues for the Utilities and which involved a later true-up calculation based on actual sales. This two-tiered design was approved only once by the Commission and was not later modified. The Utilities' proposal of revenue decoupling through Rider VBA and the Commission's approval of it has not created a surcharge to compensate for low rates. Rider VBA provides the Utilities with a fixed level of revenue, not based on sales, that the Commission determined was just and reasonable. See 220 ILCS 5/9–101 (West 2010). This rate methodology was approved by the Commission and not added retroactively to cure a mistake. Accordingly, we conclude that the Commission's acceptance and adoption of revenue decoupling does not constitute retroactive ratemaking.

¶ 25 Next, petitioners argue that Rider VBA violates the prohibition against single-issue ratemaking. Petitioners assert that the rider is an "automatic adjustment" to existing rates that can change a rate without requiring the utility to delay recovery until it files a general rate case, thus distorting the ratemaking process. Petitioners argue that the sole purpose of Rider VBA is "to alter the Utilities' actual rate of return so that it matches forecasts from the test year." Petitioners continue, "[w]hen the Utilities' residential and small business revenues decline due to reduced gas usage, Rider VBA provides a monthly surcharge to improve the Utilities' bottom line" and "[w]hen income exceeds expectations, Rider VBA imposes a refund to reduce profits to those justified by test year projections." Petitioners conclude that, under Rider VBA, "consumer rates and company profits fluctuate based on a single strand in the overall revenue requirement, which is exactly what the rule against single[-]issue ratemaking seeks to prevent."

¶ 26 "The rule against single-issue ratemaking makes it improper to consider in isolation changes in particular portions of a utility's revenue requirement." *ComEd,* 405 Ill.App.3d at 410, 344 Ill.Dec. 662, 937 N.E.2d 685 (citing *BPI II,* 146 Ill.2d at 244, 166 Ill.Dec. 10, 585 N.E.2d 1032). "The rule ensures that the utility's revenue requirement is based on the utility's aggregate costs and the demand on the utility, rather than on certain specific costs related to a component of its operation." (Emphasis omitted.) *Id.* "Often a change in one item of the revenue-requirement formula is offset by a corresponding change in another component of the formula. For instance, certain expenses for one aspect of a utility's business may be offset by savings in another area, thus removing the need for greater revenue." *Id.* "If rates are increased based solely on one factor, the ratemaking structure becomes distorted because there is no consideration of the changes to the other elements of the revenue formula, such as the operational savings from the improvements." *Id.* "Single-issue ratemaking is prohibited because it considers changes in isolation, thereby ignoring potentially offsetting considerations and risking understatement or overstatement of the overall revenue requirement." *Id.* at 411,

344 Ill.Dec. 662, 937 N.E.2d 685 (citing *Citizens Utility Board,* 166 Ill.2d at 137, 209 Ill.Dec. 641, 651 N.E.2d 1089).

¶ 27 In *ComEd,* this court recognized that because a rider, by nature, was a method of single-issue ratemaking, it was not allowed absent a showing of exceptional circumstances. *Id.* at 415, 344 Ill.Dec. 662, 937 N.E.2d 685 (citing *A. Finkl & Sons Co. v. Illinois Commerce Comm'n,* 250 Ill.App.3d 317, 327, 189 Ill.Dec. 824, 620 N.E.2d 1141 (1993)). After analyzing prior decisions, this court gleaned a guiding principle for testing a rider's validity:

> "[T]he Commission has discretion to approve a utility's proposed rider mechanism to recover a particular cost if (1) the cost is imposed upon the utility by an external circumstance over which the utility has no control and (2) the cost does not affect the utility's revenue requirement. In other words, a rider is appropriate only if the utility cannot influence the cost [citation] and the expense is a pass-through item that does not change other expenses or increase income [citation]."
> *Id.* at 414, 344 Ill.Dec. 662, 937 N.E.2d 685 (citing *Citizens Utility Board,* 166 Ill.2d at 138, 209 Ill.Dec. 641, 651 N.E.2d 1089).

¶ 28 Again, because revenue decoupling is a different rate design from traditional ratemaking, none of the cases that the parties cite is analogous to the present case. Therefore, Rider VBA is unlike other riders discussed generally in *ComEd;* that is, we decline to categorically find that Rider VBA is a method of single-issue ratemaking. Rider VBA does not provide for the recovery of any specific cost and it does not isolate any particular cost. *Cf. id.* at 409–15, 344 Ill.Dec. 662, 937 N.E.2d 685 (rejecting as single-issue ratemaking ComEd's proposed Rider SMP, a " 'system modernization project' " charge to customers, to immediately recoup the costs of modernizing its delivery system toward a " 'smart grid' "). Petitioners' conclusion that "consumer rates and company profits fluctuate based on a single strand in the overall revenue requirement" is inaccurate because, as we stated earlier, revenue decoupling is a rate design that a public utility commission uses to delink a utility's revenues from its sales, thereby fixing the utility's revenues. By approving Rider VBA in the present case, the Commission has determined the reasonable and fixed level of revenue for the Utilities, no matter how much or how little natural gas their customers use. Under Rider VBA, the Utilities' profits are part of the fixed revenue components that the Commission approved. Finally, unlike the types of riders discussed in *ComEd,* Rider VBA takes into account only those costs associated with the fixed revenue requirements that the Commission approved. Because Rider VBA is distinct from the types of riders discussed in *ComEd,* it is therefore not subject to *ComEd*'s requirements to establish its validity. See *id.* at 414, 344 Ill.Dec. 662, 937 N.E.2d 685.

¶ 29 The Utilities invested significant resources into the critical infrastructure necessary to distribute natural gas to customers' homes and businesses. This investment was approved long ago by the Commission. We conclude that the revenue decoupling mechanism known as Rider VBA was approved by the Commission to guarantee that the Utilities recoup the costs for the infrastructure in which they prudently invested, not to ensure profits but to satisfy the distribution needs of their customers.

¶ 30 We hold that Rider VBA did not violate either the rule against retroactive ratemaking or the rule against single-issue ratemaking. We further hold that the findings of the Commission were supported by substantial evidence. See 220 ILCS 5/10–201(e)(iv) (West 2010). Therefore, for the foregoing reasons, we affirm the order of the Commission.

¶ 31 Affirmed.

Justices BIRKETT and SPENCE concurred in the judgment and opinion.

B. Electricity

Michael Keegan, *Bargaining for Power: Resolving Open Questions from* NRG Power Marketing, LLC v. Maine Public Utilities Commission

65 Me. L. Rev. 99 (2012)

Introduction

Many industries are subject to regulation, whether by the federal government, the state, or both. Electric utility companies' retail rates are subject to regulation by the states, and their wholesale rates charged among enterprises involved in providing the electric power to retail sellers are regulated by the federal government. Under the Federal Power Act of 1935 ("FPA"), the Federal Energy Regulatory Commission ("FERC") is responsible for ensuring that rates for wholesale electric power sales and electric transmission are "just and reasonable."

The "classic scheme" of administrative rate setting called for rates to be established unilaterally by the regulated companies and set forth in rate schedules of general applicability (i.e., "tariffs"), subject to oversight by the relevant administrative agency. However, the federal government has regulated rates for goods and services transferred *between businesses* differently from the way rates *between businesses and the public* are regulated. The Supreme Court has noted that "[i]n wholesale markets, the party charging the rate and the party charged were often sophisticated businesses enjoying presumptively equal bargaining power, who could be expected to negotiate a 'just and reasonable' rate as between the two of them." With the FPA, Congress departed from a strict scheme of tariff-only rate regulation, permitting wholesale arrangements between the parties to be established through individually-negotiated contracts, subject to FERC oversight.

Over the years, the number of FERC-regulated transactions has grown, and FERC and electric utilities have developed new contractual vehicles under which to transact. Among other innovations, FERC has established organized markets, instituted a market-based rate program, and ordered electric industry restructuring (i.e., unbundling of power and transmission transactions). In addition, FERC has required electric utilities offering transmission service to do so pursuant to a standardized tariff of general applicability, with rates established under the "classic scheme" of administrative rate setting mentioned above.

* * *

II. Rate Regulation Under the Federal Power Act and the *Mobile-Sierra* Doctrine

A. The Federal Power Act

Part II of the FPA vests FERC with jurisdiction over the electric utility industry, including over the transmission of electric energy in interstate commerce, the sale of electric energy at wholesale in interstate commerce, and facilities for such sales or transmission. "[A]ny person who owns or operates facilities subject to the jurisdiction of [FERC] under [Part II of the FPA]" is a "public utility."

Sections 205 and 206 of the FPA, which provide for the regulation by FERC of rates for the sale and transmission of electric power, are the "bread and butter" of the FPA. Sections 205 and 206 of the FPA are substantially identical to sections 4 and 5 of the Natural Gas Act ("NGA"), and decisions construing the analogous provisions of the two statutes are interchangeable. The fundamental command of these sections is that all rates charged must be "just and reasonable." This standard is modeled on the Interstate Commerce Act ("ICA"), which has required that charges for services rendered by common carriers be "just and reasonable" and has prohibited "every unjust and unreasonable charge" for such services.

Public utilities generally have been subject to rate regulation due to their position as natural monopolies. The paradigm that developed included regulation over both retail rates charged directly to the public and wholesale rates charged among enterprises involved in providing the goods or services offered by the retail seller. Retail rates were generally regulated by the states or municipal governments, and the regulation of wholesale rates was taken up by the federal government, since the transmission or transportation involved was generally deemed to be interstate in nature.

The "classic scheme" of administrative rate setting called for rates to be set forth by the regulated utility company in rate schedules of general applicability (i.e., "tariffs"), based on the model applied to railroad carriers under the ICA. This system was adopted by the federal government because the innumerable "retail transactions of railroads made the policing of individual transactions administratively impossible; effective regulation could be accomplished only by requiring compliance with a single schedule of rates applicable to all shippers."

However, the federal government has regulated rates for goods and services transferred between businesses differently from the way states and municipalities have regulated rates between businesses and the public. The Supreme Court has noted that "[i]n wholesale markets, the party charging the rate and the party charged were often sophisticated business enjoying presumptively equal bargaining power, who could be expected to negotiate a 'just and reasonable' rate as between the two of them." With the FPA and the NGA, Congress departed from a strict scheme of tariff-only rate regulation. Under the FPA and NGA, Congress permitted wholesale arrangements between the parties to be established initially through individually-negotiated contracts. Protection of the public interest would be achieved through supervision by FERC of the individual contracts.

To that end, the FPA requires public utilities to file their individual contracts with FERC and grants to FERC the power to review rates subject to its jurisdiction that have been set initially by public utilities. The relevant subsections here are FPA sections 205I, 205(d), 205(e), and 206(a). Section 205(c) requires public utilities to file all rates and contracts with FERC. Under section 205(d), changes in previously-filed rates or contracts generally must be filed with FERC at least sixty days before they go into effect. However, FERC may under section 205(e) suspend the operation of a new rate for up to five months, pending a determination of the new rate's reasonableness. If FERC has not reached a decision before the suspension period has expired, the filed rate shall go into effect, subject to a refund or adjustment to be made retroactive to that date. Section 206(a) authorizes FERC to modify any rate or contract which it determines to be "unjust, unreasonable, unduly discriminatory or preferential."

In 1956, in *United Gas Pipe Line Co. v. Mobile Gas Serv. Corp.* ("*Mobile*"), the Supreme Court explained that sections 205 and 206 are part of a "statutory scheme under which all rates are established initially by the [public utilities], by contract or otherwise, and all rates are subject to being modified by [FERC] upon a finding that they are unlawful."

However, FPA section 205 "purports neither to grant nor to define the initial rate-setting powers of [public utilities]." Instead, the FPA (1) defines FERC's review powers, and (2) imposes duties on public utilities as are necessary for FERC to effectuate its powers.

FERC's powers are defined by sections 205(e) and 206(a). Under section 206(a), FERC may set aside and modify any rate or contract which it determines to be "unjust, unreasonable, unduly discriminatory, or preferential." The Court in *Mobile* stated that this was "neither a 'rate-making' nor a 'rate-changing' procedure. It is simply the power to review rates and contracts made in the first instance by [public utilities] and, if they are determined to be unlawful, to remedy them." Section 205(e) only adds to this basic power the "further powers (1) to preserve the status quo pending review of [a] new rate by suspending its operation for a limited period, and (2) thereafter to make its order retroactive, by means of the refund procedure, to the date the change became effective."

The limitations on public utilities are set forth in section 205I and 205(d). Section 205I requires rate schedules and contracts in force to be filed with the Commission. Section 205(d) requires all changes in such schedules and contracts to be filed with FERC at least sixty days before they go into effect. The *Mobile* Court explained that section 205(d) was a prohibition, *not* a grant of power. Otherwise valid changes to a contract *cannot* be put into effect without giving the required notice to FERC. However, the FPA does not say under what circumstances a public utility can make such a change.

In *Mobile*, the Court concluded that FPA sections 205 and 206 do not establish a rate-changing procedure or constitute a mechanism for initiating rate "proceedings." Section 205 does not provide for the filing of rate "proposals"; it provides only for *notice* to FERC of the rates established by the public utility and for *review* by FERC of those rates. If a public utility has the power to make a change to a rate schedule or contract, then the change is effectuated upon compliance with section 205(d)'s notice requirement.

B. The *Mobile-Sierra* Doctrine

1. *Mobile, Sierra*, and *Memphis*

In twin cases decided on February 27, 1956, *Mobile* (discussed above) and *Federal Power Commission v. Sierra Pacific Power Co.* ("*Sierra*"), the Supreme Court addressed the authority of FERC to modify rates that had been negotiated bilaterally and set forth in contracts. In *Mobile*, the Court rejected a natural gas pipeline's argument that NGA section 4's requirement that all new rates must be filed with FERC authorized such pipelines to unilaterally change existing contracts. As explained above, the NGA did not grant extra-contractual power to jurisdictional pipelines. If a contract does not grant either party the unilateral right to make changes to the contract, no such right exists.

However, the Court in *Mobile* noted that NGA section 5 authorizes FERC to investigate rates "upon complaint," as well as on its own initiative. The Court reasoned that although the jurisdictional natural gas pipelines were not enumerated among the list of entities that might file a complaint with FERC seeking the commencement of an investigation, "there is nothing to prevent them from furnishing to [FERC] any relevant information and requesting it to initiate an investigation on its own motions." If FERC concludes after an investigation and hearing that the rate in a natural gas pipeline's contract is "so low as to conflict with the *public interest*, [FERC] may under [NGA] § 5(a) authorize the natural gas company to file a schedule increasing the rate."

In *Sierra*, the Supreme Court applied the holding from *Mobile* to the analogous provision of the FPA-section 205. The Court concluded that a public utility could not unilaterally file a new rate under FPA section 205(d) that was contrary to the terms of an effective contract. However, *Sierra* involved an issue not present in *Mobile*—when FERC, under FPA section 206(a), was authorized to find that an existing contract rate was unlawful and to fix a new lawful rate. The Court explained that FERC could not find that an existing contract rate was "unreasonable solely because it yields the public utility less than a fair return on net invested capital." Faced with the question of how FERC must evaluate whether an existing contract rate is just and reasonable, the Court explained:

> [FERC's] conclusion appears on its face to be based on an erroneous standard.... [W]hile it may be that [FERC] may not normally impose upon a public utility a rate which would produce less than a fair return, it does not follow that the public utility may not itself agree by contract to a rate affording less than a fair return or that, if it does so, it is entitled to be relieved of its improvident bargain.... In such circumstances the sole concern of [FERC] would seem to be whether the rate is so low as to adversely affect the public interest-as where it might impair the financial ability of the public utility to continue its service, cast upon other consumers an excessive burden, or be unduly discriminatory.

From these two cases, the eponymous "*Mobile-Sierra* doctrine" was born. The doctrine acts as a presumption when such rates are investigated pursuant to FPA section 206(a). As the Court has subsequently explained, under the *Mobile-Sierra* doctrine, FERC "must presume that the rate set out in a freely negotiated wholesale-energy contract meets the 'just and reasonable' requirement imposed" by the FPA. The presumption is only overcome if the contract seriously harms the public interest; that is, where the contract might (1) impair the financial ability of the public utility to continue its service, (2) cast upon other consumers an excessive burden, or (3) be unduly discriminatory. Indeed, "[t]he regulatory system created by the [FPA] is premised on contractual agreements voluntarily devised by the regulated companies; it contemplates abrogation of these agreements only in circumstances of unequivocal public necessity." In neither case did the Court find that the public interest required the existing rates to be reformed.

Both *Mobile* and *Sierra* involved attempts by sellers to change rates set forth in existing bilateral contracts negotiated by the parties, and where the contracts did not otherwise permit such changes. In subsequent cases, the Supreme Court addressed whether the *Mobile-Sierra* presumption applies where rates are set forth in instruments other than individually negotiated bilateral contracts, or contracts that specifically permit rate changes.

In *United Gas Pipe Line Co. v. Memphis Light, Gas and Water Division* ("*Memphis*"), the Court held that parties could include in contracts the right to unilaterally change rates at will. The Court distinguished the case from *Mobile*, noting that in *Mobile*, the natural gas pipeline had contractually bound itself to furnish gas throughout the contract term at a particular price and had "bargained away by contract the right to change its rates unilaterally." However, the agreement at issue in *Memphis* did not state a single fixed rate, but included a rate provision that amounted to the pipeline's "'going' rate," reserving to the pipeline the power to make rate changes subject to the procedures and limitations of the NGA. The Court found that the pipeline, when filing a new rate with FERC, simply sought to assert, in accordance with the notice procedures in the NGA, its rights expressly reserved to it by contract. In a subsequent case, the Supreme Court referred to the rule from *Memphis* as permitting parties to "contract out of the *Mobile-Sierra* presumption" by including in their contracts a provision that would permit one or both parties to unilaterally establish a new rate that would supersede the existing contract rate. The Supreme Court has stated that *Memphis* is consistent with the lead role of contracts in the FPA's regulatory scheme. However, absent the presence of a "*Memphis* clause," the *Mobile-Sierra* presumption remains the default rule.

Although the Court in *Memphis* did not, for purposes of its analysis, draw a distinction between rates set by bilateral contract and rates set forth in a tariff of general applicability, the arrangements at issue in *Memphis* involved such tariffs. The Court noted that FERC had promulgated regulations requiring natural gas pipeline companies to convert from using individual bilateral agreements to a "tariff-and-service-agreement" system. Under the tariff-and-service-agreement system, natural gas pipelines must adopt system-wide "tariffs" that establish terms and conditions of service for their customers and rates for different classes of customers. The tariff is not itself an agreement or contract between the pipeline and any customer. Customers must execute their own agreements with the pipeline. Instead of individually tailored contracts between pipelines and their customers, pipelines and customers execute "service agreements" containing references to rates set forth in the tariff's rate schedules of general applicability and incorporating the tariff's general terms and conditions. In *Memphis*, the Court was satisfied that the parties to such arrangements could permissibly reserve for natural gas pipelines the right to change their rates. The Court believed that it was not unlikely that customers would have agreed to be charged a "going rate" that could be changed consistent with the notice provisions under NGA section 4(d).

The innovation of *Memphis* clauses and the introduction of the tariff-and-service agreement regime for natural gas pipelines resulted in fewer *Mobile-Sierra* doctrine issues for the natural gas industry. However, the electric utility industry did not convert to a tariff-and-service agreement system for electric transmission service until FERC issued Order No. 888 in 1996. Until then, electric utilities had entered into numerous bilateral and multiparty arrangements for the sale of bundled power-that is, power together with transmission. Public utilities continue to enter into bilateral and multiparty arrangements for the sale of electric power and capacity. Thus, *Mobile-Sierra* issues continue to arise in the electric industry.

2. *Morgan Stanley*

The next chapter in the story of the *Mobile-Sierra* doctrine came in the Supreme Court's 2008 case, *Morgan Stanley Capital Group Inc. v. Public Utility District No. 1 of Snohomish County* ("*Morgan Stanley*"). The cases on review in *Morgan Stanley* presented the Court with two issues for review: (1) whether the *Mobile-Sierra* presumption applies only if FERC has had an initial opportunity to review a contract rate without the presumption; and (2) whether the *Mobile-Sierra* presumption imposes as high a bar to challenges by *purchasers* of wholesale electricity as it does to challenges by *sellers*. The Court answered no to the first question and yes to the second.

Under FERC's market-based rate regime, a wholesale electricity seller that has demonstrated that it lacks (or has adequately mitigated) market power may enter into freely negotiated contracts with purchasers. Those contracts are not filed with FERC before they go into effect; instead, market-based rate sellers must file quarterly reports summarizing each of the contracts into which they have entered. In 2000 and 2001, prices for electricity in the western United States rose dramatically. As a result, retail utilities entered into long-term contracts with market-based rate sellers that locked in rates that were very high by historical standards. After prices began to return to normal levels, many retail utility-purchasers asked FERC to modify the contracts, contending that the contracts should be reviewed without *Mobile-Sierra*'s public interest presumption that the rates are just and reasonable. FERC disagreed, applied the public interest presumption to its review of the contracts, and determined that the purchasers could not overcome the presumption. On appeal, the Ninth Circuit reversed, finding that because the market-based rate agreements had not been initially reviewed by FERC, the public interest presumption did not apply to the challenges. In addition, the Ninth Circuit found that even if the presumption applied, the standard for overcoming the presumption is different when a purchaser challenges a high rate. The Supreme Court granted certiorari.

On its way to resolving the questions presented, the Court in *Morgan Stanley* reiterated and clarified several points about the *Mobile-Sierra* presumption that are relevant here. First, the Court noted, as it had in *Mobile* and *Memphis*, that the FPA permits public utilities to set jurisdictional rates with electric power customers through individually-negotiated bilateral contracts as well as through tariffs of general applicability. For tariffs, as opposed to individually-negotiated contracts, FERC traditionally reviewed rates under the "cost of service" method, ensuring that a public utility covers its costs plus a rate of return sufficient to attract investment. Both individual contracts and tariffs of general applicability are subject to the FPA's notice and filing requirements.

The Court next addressed how application of the *Mobile-Sierra* presumption fits within the FPA's requirement that jurisdictional rates be "just and reasonable." The Court noted that since 1956, FERC and the courts of appeals referred to two differing modes of review: one with the *Mobile-Sierra* presumption, i.e., the "public interest standard"; and the other without, i.e., the "just and reasonable standard." The Supreme Court explained that, notwithstanding this nomenclature, the "public interest standard" was not a different standard from the statutory "just and reasonable standard." Instead, the Court concluded, the "public interest standard" refers to the differing application of the just-and-reasonable standard to freely negotiated rates.

Thus, FERC's review of rates under the FPA's just and reasonable standard must begin with a threshold inquiry: whether the rate at issue is the result of bilateral (or multi-party) negotiations and bargaining. If so, FERC must apply the *Mobile-Sierra* presumption and can only make a finding that the existing rate is unjust or unreasonable-and, thereby, fix a new rate-where the existing rate seriously harms the public interest. Application of the presumption is appropriate because, "[i]n wholesale markets, the party charging the rate and the party charged are often sophisticated businesses enjoying presumptively equal bargaining power, who could be expected to negotiate a 'just and reasonable' rate as between the two of them." The Court in *Morgan Stanley* explained that *Sierra* provided "a definition of what it means for a rate to satisfy the just-and-reasonable standard in the contract context." However, if the rate under review is not the result of bilateral (or multi-party) negotiations-or if the parties to the arrangement state that the *Mobile-Sierra* presumption does not apply-FERC would perform its review without applying the presumption and review the rate under cost of service (or other) principles.

Establishing that the *Mobile-Sierra* presumption should be applied when rates are set through a negotiated agreement, the Court in *Morgan Stanley* answered the first question presented for review, holding that the FPA's just and reasonable standard is not applied differently depending on when a rate is challenged. If a rate is one to which the *Mobile-Sierra* presumption should apply, the presumption applies each time the rate is reviewed by FERC. The FPA does not require FERC to review the rate under cost of service principles before the rate can be reviewed subject to the *Mobile-Sierra* presumption. The Court stated that it was proper in a regulatory scheme to review rates set by negotiated contracts by evaluating whether the rates seriously harm the public interest, not whether the rates are unfair to one of the parties that voluntarily entered into the contract. Thus, FERC may abrogate a valid contract only if that contract harms the public interest.

Turning to the second question presented for review, FERC found that the *Mobile-Sierra* presumption applies equally regardless of whether the rate is challenged by purchasers of wholesale electricity rather than by sellers (as had been the case in *Mobile* and *Sierra*). The Court noted that the three factors identified in *Sierra*—where a rate might (1) impair the financial ability of the public utility to continue its service, (2) cast upon other consumers an excessive burden, or (3) be unduly discriminatory-were not all directly applicable to a challenge brought by a purchaser, and that the three factors from *Sierra* were not an exclusive list. Where the challenge is brought by a purchaser, the primary concern is likely whether the rate imposes an excessive burden on that customer, not other customers (as in *Sierra*'s second prong). However, the fact that the customer is the challenger does not transform the "excessive burden" prong into an inquiry as to whether the customer pays a cost above the public utility's marginal cost, in effect reverting to a form of cost-based analysis. The Court concluded that the FPA intended to reserve FERC's power to abrogate negotiated contract rates only for those extraordinary circumstances where the public would be severely harmed.

NRG Power Mktg., LLC v. Maine Pub. Utilities Comm'n

558 U.S. 165, 130 S. Ct. 693, 694, 175 L. Ed. 2d 642 (2010)

Justice GINSBURG delivered the opinion of the Court.

The Federal Power Act (FPA or Act), 41 Stat. 1063, as amended, 16 U.S.C. §791a *et seq.,* authorizes the Federal Energy Regulatory Commission (FERC or Commission) to superintend the sale of electricity in interstate commerce and provides that all wholesale-electricity rates must be "just and reasonable," §824d(a). Under this Court's *Mobile–Sierra* doctrine, FERC must presume that a rate set by "a freely negotiated wholesale-energy contract" meets the statutory "just and reasonable" requirement. *Morgan Stanley Capital Group Inc. v. Public Util. Dist. No. 1 of Snohomish Cty.,* 554 U.S. 527, ___, 128 S.Ct. 2733, 2734, 171 L.Ed.2d 607 (2008). "The presumption may be overcome only if FERC concludes that the contract seriously harms the public interest." *Ibid.*

This case stems from New England's difficulties in maintaining the reliability of its energy grid. In 2006, after several attempts by the Commission and concerned parties to address the problems, FERC approved a comprehensive settlement agreement (hereinafter Settlement Agreement or Agreement). Most relevant here, the Agreement established rate-setting mechanisms for sales of energy capacity, and provided that the *Mobile–sierra* public interest standard would govern rate challenges. Parties who opposed the settlement petitioned for review in the United States Court of Appeals for the D.C. Circuit. Among multiple objections to FERC's order approving the Agreement, the settlement opponents urged that the rate challenges of nonsettling parties should not be controlled by the restrictive *Mobile–Sierra* public interest standard. The Court of Appeals agreed, holding that "when a rate challenge is brought by a non-contracting third party, the *Mobile–Sierra* doctrine simply does not apply." *Maine Pub. Util. Comm'n v. FERC,* 520 F.3d 464, 478 (2008) *(per curiam).*

We reverse the D.C. Circuit's judgment to the extent that it rejects the application of *Mobile–Sierra* to noncontracting parties. Our decision in *Morgan Stanley,* announced three months after the D.C. Circuit's disposition, made clear that the *Mobile–Sierra* public interest standard is not an exception to the statutory just-and-reasonable standard; it is an application of that standard in the context of rates set by contract. The "venerable *Mo-*

bile–Sierra doctrine" rests on "the stabilizing force of contracts." *Morgan Stanley,* 554 U.S., at ___, 128 S.Ct. at 2747; see *id.,* at ___, 128 S.Ct. at 2749 (describing contract rates as "a key source of stability"). To retain vitality, the doctrine must control FERC itself, and, we hold, challenges to contract rates brought by noncontracting as well as contracting parties.

I

In a capacity market, in contrast to a wholesale energy market, an electricity provider purchases from a generator an option to buy a quantity of energy, rather than purchasing the energy itself. To maintain the reliability of the grid, electricity providers generally purchase more capacity, *i.e.,* rights to acquire energy, than necessary to meet their customers' anticipated demand. For many years in New England, the supply of capacity was barely sufficient to meet the region's demand. FERC and New England's generators, electricity providers, and power customers made several attempts to address this problem. This case stems from the latest effort to design a solution.

In 2003, a group of generators sought to enter into "reliability must-run" agreements with the New England Independent System Operator (ISO), which operates the region's transmission system. In its orders addressing those agreements, FERC directed the ISO to develop a new market mechanism that would set prices separately for various geographical sub-regions. *Devon Power LLC,* 103 FERC ¶ 61,082, pp. 61,266, 61,271 (2003).

In March 2004, the ISO proposed a market structure responsive to FERC's directions. See *Devon Power LLC,* 107 FERC ¶ 61,240, p. 62,020 (2004). FERC set the matter for hearing before an Administrative Law Judge (ALJ), who issued a 177–page order largely accepting the ISO's proposal. *Devon Power LLC,* 111 FERC ¶ 63,063, p. 65,205 (2005). Several parties filed exceptions to the ALJ's order; on September 20, 2005, the full Commission heard arguments on the proposed market structure, and thereafter established settlement procedures. *Devon Power LLC,* 113 FERC ¶ 61,075, p. 61,271 (2005).

After four months of negotiations, on March 6, 2006, a settlement was reached. Of the 115 negotiating parties, only 8 opposed the settlement.

The Settlement Agreement installed a "forward capacity market" under which annual auctions would set capacity prices; auctions would be conducted three years in advance of the time when the capacity would be needed. *Devon Power LLC,* 115 FERC ¶ 61,340, pp. 62,304, 62,306–62,308 (2006). Each energy provider would be required to purchase enough capacity to meet its share of the "installed capacity requirement," *i.e.,* the minimum level of capacity needed to maintain reliability on the grid, as determined by the ISO. *Id.,* at 62,307. For the three-year gap between the first auction and the time when the capacity procured in that auction would be provided, the Agreement prescribed a series of fixed, transition-period payments to capacity-supplying generators. *Id.,* at 62,308–62,309.

The issue before us centers on § 4.C of the Agreement (hereinafter *Mobile–Sierra* provision). Under that provision, challenges to both transition-period payments and auction-clearing prices would be adjudicated under "the 'public interest' standard of review set forth in *United Gas Pipe Line Co. v. Mobile Gas Service Corp.,* 350 U.S. 332, 76 S.Ct. 373, 100 L.Ed. 373 (1956)[,] and [*FPC*] *v. Sierra Pacific Power Co.,* 350 U.S. 348, 76 S.Ct. 368, 100 L.Ed. 388 (1956) (the '*Mobile–Sierra*' doctrine)." App. 95. *Mobile–Sierra* applies, § 4.C instructs, "whether the [price is challenged] by a Settling Party, a non-Settling Party, or [by] the FERC acting *sua sponte.*" *Ibid.*

FERC approved the Settlement Agreement, "finding that as a package, it presents a just and reasonable outcome for this proceeding consistent with the public interest." 115

FERC, at 62,304. The *Mobile–Sierra* provision, FERC explicitly determined, "appropriately balances the need for rate stability and the interests of the diverse entities who will be subject to the [forward capacity market's auction system]." *Id.,* at 62,335.

Six of the eight objectors to the settlement sought review in the D.C. Circuit. For the most part, the Court of Appeals rejected the objectors' efforts to overturn FERC's order approving the settlement. 520 F.3d, at 467. But the objectors prevailed on the *Mobile–Sierra* issue: The D.C. Circuit held that *Mobile–Sierra* applies only to contracting parties. *Id.,* at 478. In this Court, the parties have switched places. Defenders of the settlement, including the *Mobile–sierra* provision, are petitioners; objectors to the settlement, victorious in the Court of Appeals only on the *Mobile–Sierra* issue, are respondents.

Because of the importance of the issue, and in light of our recent decision in *Morgan Stanley,* we granted certiorari, 556 U.S. ___, 129 S.Ct. 2050, 173 L.Ed.2d 1132 (2009), to resolve this question: "[Does] *Mobile–Sierra*'s public-interest standard appl[y] when a contract rate is challenged by an entity that was not a party to the contract[?]" Brief for Petitioners i. Satisfied that the answer to that question is yes, we reverse the D.C. Circuit's judgment insofar as it rejected application of *Mobile–Sierra* to noncontracting parties.

II

The FPA gives FERC authority to regulate the "sale of electric energy at wholesale in interstate commerce." See 16 U.S.C. §824(b)(1). The Act allows regulated utilities to set rates unilaterally by tariff; alternatively, sellers and buyers may agree on rates by contract. See §824d(c), (d). Whether set by tariff or contract, however, all rates must be "just and reasonable." §824d(a). Rates may be examined by the Commission, upon complaint or on its own initiative, when a new or altered tariff or contract is filed or after a rate goes into effect. §§824d(e), 824e(a). Following a hearing, the Commission may set aside any rate found "unjust, unreasonable, unduly discriminatory or preferential," and replace it with a just and reasonable rate. §824e(a).

The *Mobile–Sierra* doctrine originated in twin decisions announced on the same day in 1956: *United Gas Pipe Line Co. v. Mobile Gas Service Corp.,* 350 U.S. 332, 76 S.Ct. 373, 100 L.Ed. 373, and *FPC v. Sierra Pacific Power Co.,* 350 U.S. 348, 76 S.Ct. 368, 100 L.Ed. 388. Both concerned rates set by contract rather than by tariff. *Mobile* involved the Natural Gas Act, which, like the FPA, requires utilities to file all new rates with the regulatory commission. 15 U.S.C. §717cI. In *Mobile,* we rejected a gas utility's argument that the file-all-new-rates requirement authorized the utility to abrogate a lawful contract with a purchaser simply by filing a new tariff. 350 U.S., at 336–337, 76 S.Ct. 373. Filing, we explained, was a *precondition* to changing a rate, not an *authorization* to do so in violation of a lawful contract. *Id.,* at 339–344, 76 S.Ct. 373; see *Morgan Stanley,* 554 U.S., at ___, 128 S.Ct. at 2739.

The *Sierra* case involved a further issue. Not only had the Commission erroneously concluded that a newly filed tariff superseded a contract rate. In addition, the Commission had suggested that, in any event, the contract rate, which the utility sought to escape, was itself unjust and unreasonable. The Commission thought that was so "solely because [the contract rate] yield[ed] less than a fair return on the [utility's] net invested capital." 350 U.S., at 355, 76 S.Ct. 368.

The Commission's suggestion prompted this Court to home in on "the question of how the Commission may evaluate whether a contract rate is just and reasonable." *Morgan Stanley,* 554 U.S., at ___, 128 S.Ct. at 2739. The *Sierra* Court answered the question this way:

"[T]he Commission's conclusion appears on its face to be based on an erroneous standard.... [W]hile it may be that the Commission may not normally *impose* upon a public utility a rate which would produce less than a fair return, it does not follow that the public utility may not itself agree by contract to a rate affording less than a fair return or that, if it does so, it is entitled to be relieved of its improvident bargain.... In such circumstances *the sole concern of the Commission would seem to be whether the rate is so low as to adversely affect the public interest*— as where it might impair the financial ability of the public utility to continue its service, cast upon other consumers an excessive burden, or be unduly discriminatory." 350 U.S., at 354–355, 76 S.Ct. 368 (some emphasis added).

In a later case, we similarly explained: "The regulatory system created by the [FPA] is premised on contractual agreements voluntarily devised by the regulated companies; it contemplates abrogation of these agreements only in circumstances of unequivocal public necessity." *Permian Basin Area Rate Cases,* 390 U.S. 747, 822, 88 S.Ct. 1344, 20 L.Ed.2d 312 (1968).

Two Terms ago, in *Morgan Stanley,* 554 U.S. 527, 128 S.Ct. 2733, the Court reaffirmed and clarified the *Mobile–Sierra* doctrine. That case presented two questions: First, does the *Mobile–Sierra* presumption (that contract rates freely negotiated between sophisticated parties meet the just and reasonable standard imposed by 16 U.S.C. §824d(a)) "apply only when FERC has had an initial opportunity to review a contract rate without the presumption?" 554 U.S., at ___, 128 S.Ct. at 2737. "Second, does the presumption [generally] impose as high a bar to challenges by purchasers of wholesale electricity as it does to challenges by sellers?" *Id.,* at ___, 128 S.Ct. at 2737; see *id.,* at ___, ___, 128 S.Ct. at 2747–48. Answering no to the first question and yes to the second, the Court emphasized the essential role of contracts as a key factor fostering stability in the electricity market, to the longrun benefit of consumers. *Id.,* at ___, ___, 128 S.Ct. at 2747, 2749; see, *e.g.,* Market–Based Rates ¶6, 72 Fed.Reg. 39906 (2007) (noting chilling effect on investments caused by "uncertainties regarding rate stability and contract sanctity"); *Nevada Power Co. v. Duke Energy Trading & Marketing, L.L. C.,* 99 FERC ¶61,047, pp. 61,184, 61,190 (2002) ("Competitive power markets simply cannot attract the capital needed to build adequate generating infrastructure without regulatory certainty, including certainty that the Commission will not modify market-based contracts unless there are *extraordinary* circumstances.").

Morgan Stanley did not reach the question presented here: Does *Mobile–Sierra*'s public interest standard apply to challenges to contract rates brought by noncontracting parties? But *Morgan Stanley*'s reasoning strongly suggests that the D.C. Circuit's negative answer misperceives the aim, and diminishes the force, of the *Mobile–Sierra* doctrine.

In unmistakably plain language, *Morgan Stanley* restated *Mobile–Sierra*'s instruction to the Commission: FERC "must presume that the rate set out in a freely negotiated wholesale-energy contract meets the 'just and reasonable' requirement imposed by law. The presumption may be overcome only if FERC concludes that the contract seriously harms the public interest." 554 U.S., at ___, 128 S.Ct. at 2734. As our instruction to FERC in *Morgan Stanley* conveys, the public interest standard is not, as the D.C. Circuit presented it, a standard independent of, and sometimes at odds with, the "just and reasonable" standard, see 520 F.3d, at 478; rather, the public interest standard defines "what it means for a rate to satisfy the just-and-reasonable standard in the contract context." *Morgan Stanley,* 554 U.S., at ___, 128 S.Ct. at 2746. And if FERC itself must presume just and reasonable a contract rate resulting from fair, arms-length negotiations, how can it be maintained that noncontracting parties nevertheless may escape that presumption?

Moreover, the *Mobile–Sierra* doctrine does not overlook third-party interests; it is framed with a view to their protection. The doctrine directs the Commission to reject a contract rate that "seriously harms the consuming public." *Morgan Stanley,* 554 U.S., at ___, 128 S.Ct. at 2746; see *Verizon Communications Inc. v. FCC,* 535 U.S. 467, 479, 122 S.Ct. 1646, 152 L.Ed.2d 701 (2002) (When a buyer and a seller agree upon a rate, "the principal regulatory responsibility [i]s not to relieve a contracting party of an unreasonable rate, ... but to protect against potential discrimination by favorable contract rates between allied businesses to the detriment of *other* wholesale customers." (Emphasis added.)).

Finally, as earlier indicated, see *supra,* at 699–700, the D.C. Circuit's confinement of *Mobile–Sierra* to rate challenges by contracting parties diminishes the animating purpose of the doctrine: promotion of "the stability of supply arrangements which all agree is essential to the health of the [energy] industry." *Mobile,* 350 U.S., at 344, 76 S.Ct. 373. That dominant concern was expressed by FERC in the order on review: "Stability is particularly important in this case, which was initiated in part because of the unstable nature of [installed capacity] revenues and the effect that has on generating units, particularly those ... critical to maintaining reliability." 115 FERC, at 62,335. A presumption applicable to contracting parties only, and inoperative as to everyone else—consumers, advocacy groups, state utility commissions, elected officials acting *parens patriae*—could scarcely provide the stability *Mobile–Sierra* aimed to secure.

We therefore hold that the *Mobile–Sierra* presumption does not depend on the identity of the complainant who seeks FERC investigation. The presumption is not limited to challenges to contract rates brought by contracting parties. It applies, as well, to challenges initiated by third parties.

III

The objectors to the settlement appearing before us maintain that the rates at issue in this case—the auction rates and the transition payments—are prescriptions of general applicability rather than "contractually negotiated rates," hence *Mobile–Sierra* is inapplicable. See Brief for Respondents 15–17, and n. 1 (internal quotation marks omitted). FERC agrees that the rates covered by the settlement "are not themselves contract rates to which the Commission was *required* to apply *Mobile–Sierra.*" Brief for FERC 15. But, FERC urges, "the Commission had discretion to do so," *id.,* at 28; furthermore, "[t]he court of appeals' error in creating a third-party exception to the *Mobile–Sierra* presumption is a sufficient basis for reversing its judgment," *id.,* at 22. Whether the rates at issue qualify as "contract rates," and, if not, whether FERC had discretion to treat them analogously are questions raised before, but not ruled upon by, the Court of Appeals. They remain open for that court's consideration on remand. See Tr. Of Oral Arg. 16.

* * *

For the reasons stated, the judgment of the Court of Appeals for the D.C. Circuit is reversed to the extent that it rejects the application of *Mobile– Sierra* to noncontracting parties, and the case is remanded for further proceedings consistent with this opinion.

It is so ordered.

Justice STEVENS, dissenting.

The opinion that the Court announces today is the third chapter in a story about how a reasonable principle, extended beyond its foundation, becomes bad law.

In the first chapter the Court wisely and correctly held that a seller who is a party to a long-term contract to provide energy to a wholesaler could not unilaterally repudiate its contract obligations in response to changes in market conditions by simply filing a new rate schedule with the regulatory commission. Only if the rate was so low that the seller might be unable to stay in business, thereby impairing the public interest, could the seller be excused from performing its contract. That is what the Court held in *United Gas Pipe Line Co. v. Mobile Gas Service Corp.,* 350 U.S. 332, 76 S.Ct. 373, 100 L.Ed. 373 (1956), and *FPC v. Sierra Pacific Power Co.,* 350 U.S. 348, 76 S.Ct. 368, 100 L.Ed. 388 (1956).

In the second chapter the Court unwisely and incorrectly held that the same rule should apply to a buyer who had been forced by unprecedented market conditions to enter into a long-term contract to buy energy at abnormally high prices. The Court held the Federal Energy Regulatory Commission (FERC) could not set aside such a contract as unjust and unreasonable, even though it saddled consumers with a duty to pay prices that would be considered unjust and unreasonable under normal market conditions, unless the purchaser could also prove that "the contract seriously harms the public interest." *Morgan Stanley Capital Group Inc. v. Public Util. Dist. No. 1 of Snohomish Cty.,* 554 U.S. 527, ___, 128 S.Ct. 2733, 2734, 171 L.Ed.2d 607 (2008).

The Court held in *Morgan Stanley* that *Mobile–sierra* established a presumption: ferc "must presume that the rate SET out in a freely negotiated wholesale-energy contract meets the 'just and reasonable' requirement imposed by law." 554 U.S., at ___, 128 S.Ct. at 2734. And that presumption, according to the Court, is a simple application of the just-and-reasonable standard to contract rates, not a different standard of review. *Id.,* at ___, 128 S.Ct. at 2740 (rejecting the "obviously indefensible proposition that a standard different from the statutory just-and-reasonable standard applies to contract rates"). But applying the presumption nonetheless sets a higher bar for a rate challenge. FERC may abrogate the rate only if the public interest is *seriously* harmed. *Id.,* at ___, 128 S.Ct. at 2735 ("[U]nder the *Mobile–Sierra* presumption, setting aside a contract rate requires a finding of 'unequivocal public necessity,'" *Permian Basin Area Rate Cases,* 390 U.S. 747, 822, 88 S.Ct. 1344, 20 L.Ed.2d 312 (1968), "or 'extraordinary circumstances,' *Arkansas Louisiana Gas Co. v. Hall,* 453 U.S. 571, 582, 101 S.Ct. 2925, 69 L.Ed.2d 856 (1981)").

As I explained in my dissent in *Morgan Stanley,* the imposition of this additional burden on purchasers challenging rates was not authorized by the governing statute. Under the Federal Power Act (FPA), all wholesale electricity rates must be "just and reasonable." 16 U.S.C. § 824d(a). "[N]othing in the statute mandates differing application of the statutory standard to rates set by contract." *Morgan Stanley,* 554 U.S., at ___, 128 S.Ct. at 2735 (STEVENS, J., dissenting) (internal quotation marks omitted; emphasis deleted). And the *Mobile–Sierra* line of cases did not "mandate a 'serious harm' standard of review," much less "require any assumption that high rates and low rates impose symmetric burdens on the public interest." *Morgan Stanley,* 554 U.S., at ___, 128 S.Ct. at 2755 (STEVENS, J., dissenting). Instead, "the statement in *Permian Basin* about 'unequivocal public necessity,' 390 U.S., at 822, 88 S.Ct. 1344, speaks to the difficulty of establishing injury to the public interest in the context of a low-rate challenge," *i.e.,* one brought by sellers of electricity. *Id.,* at ___, 128 S.Ct. at 2747. It does not establish a new standard that applies as well to a "high-rate challenge" brought by purchasers. *Ibid.*

But even accepting *Morgan Stanley* as the law, the Court unwisely goes further today. In this third chapter of the *Mobile–Sierra* story, the Court applies a rule — one designed initially to protect the enforceability of freely negotiated contracts against parties who seek a release from their obligations — to impose a special burden on third parties exercising their statutory right to object to unjust and unreasonable rates. This application of the rule represents a quantum leap from the modest origin set forth in the first chapter of this tale. As the Court of Appeals correctly concluded in the opinion that the Court sets aside today: "This case is clearly outside the scope of the *Mobile–Sierra* doctrine." *Maine Pub. Util. Comm'n v. FERC,* 520 F.3d 464, 477 (C.A.D.C.2008) (*per curiam*).

As the D.C. Circuit noted, "[c]ourts have rarely mentioned the *Mobile–Sierra* doctrine without reiterating that it is premised on the existence of a voluntary contract between the parties." *Ibid*. But, the Court asks, "[I]f FERC itself must presume just and reasonable a contract rate resulting from fair, arms-length negotiations, how can it be maintained that noncontracting parties nevertheless may escape that presumption?" *Ante,* at 700. This Court's understanding of *Sierra* provides an answer. "*Sierra* was grounded in the commonsense notion that '[i]n wholesale markets, the party charging the rate and the party charged [are] often sophisticated businesses enjoying presumptively equal bargaining power, who could be expected to negotiate a "just and reasonable" rate *as between the two of them.*'" *Morgan Stanley,* 554 U.S., at ___, 128 S.Ct. at 2746 (quoting *Verizon Communications Inc. v. FCC,* 535 U.S. 467, 479, 122 S.Ct. 1646, 152 L.Ed.2d 701 (2002); emphasis added). This "commonsense notion" supports the rule requiring FERC to apply a presumption against letting a party out of its own contract, as the D.C. Circuit recognized. 520 F.3d, at 478 ("The *Mobile– Sierra* doctrine applies a more deferential standard of review to preserve the terms of the bargain as between the contracting parties"). It does not, however, support a rule requiring FERC to apply a presumption against abrogating any rate set by contract, even when, as in this case, a noncontracting party may be required in practice to pay a rate it did not agree to.

The Court further reasons that "confinement of *Mobile–Sierra* to rate challenges by contracting parties diminishes the animating purpose of the doctrine," which is ensuring the stability of contract-based supply arrangements. *Ante,* at 700–01. Maybe so, but applying *Mobile–Sierra* to rate challenges by noncontracting parties loses sight of the animating purpose of the FPA, which is "the protection of the public interest." *Sierra,* 350 U.S., at 355, 76 S.Ct. 368. That interest is "the interest of consumers in paying '"the lowest possible reasonable rate consistent with the maintenance of adequate service in the public interest."'" *Morgan Stanley,* 554 U.S., at ___, 128 S.Ct. at 2755 (STEVENS, J., dissenting) (quoting *Permian Basin,* 390 U.S., at 793, 88 S.Ct. 1344). I do not doubt that stable energy markets are important to the public interest, but "under the FPA, Congress has charged FERC, not the courts, with balancing the short-term and long-term interests of consumers" under the just-and-reasonable standard of review. *Morgan Stanley,* 554 U.S., at ___, 128 S.Ct. at 2756 (STEVENS, J., dissenting). The Court today imposes additional limits upon FERC's ability to protect that interest. If a third-party wholesale buyer can show a rate harms the public interest (perhaps because it is too high to be just and reasonable under normal review), but cannot show it *seriously* harms the public, FERC may do nothing about it.

The Court assures respondents that the "public interest standard" does not "overlook third-party interests" and is "framed with a view to their protection." *Ante,* at 700, 700–01. Perhaps in practice the *Mobile–Sierra* doctrine will protect third parties' interests, and the public interest, just as well as the so-called "ordinary" just-and-reasonable standard. But respondents are rightly skeptical. The *Mobile–Sierra* doctrine, as interpreted by the Court in *Morgan Stanley,* must pose a higher bar to respondents' rate challenge—that is, it requires them to show greater harm to the public. Otherwise, it would hardly serve to protect contract stability better than the plain vanilla just-and-reasonable standard and the Court's decision in *Morgan Stanley* would have little effect. Furthermore, the Court today reiterates that the doctrine poses a high bar. See *ante,* at 699–700.

It was sensible to require a contracting party to show something more than its own desire to get out of what proved to be a bad bargain before FERC could abrogate the parties' bargain. It is not sensible, nor authorized by the statute, for the Court to change the *de facto* standard of review whenever a rate is set by private contract, based solely on the Court's view that contract stability should be preserved unless there is extraordinary harm to the public interest.

For these reasons, I respectfully dissent.

Notes & Questions

1. The Keegan article, above, argues that FERC was wrong and that the Supreme Court was not very helpful in resolving the open questions of when the *Mobile-Sierra* doctrine should apply. Part of the reason Keegan is concerned is that so many rate disputes are solved via settlement. Why does that matter?

2. As you read additional cases (in this course and others), consider the implications the case might have beyond the litigation context. For example, does the *NRG Power Marketing* case change how you might draft certain transactional documents? Should it? Does the case shift the balance of power in negotiations? Does the case change how prior contracts will be interpreted?

3. The next article discusses some attempts to increase investment in energy infrastructure, in part by removing decades old restrictions on ownership. Again, we see business-related issues coming back to fore. How do mergers and acquisitions restrictions impact energy investment? As you read the article, try to come up with your own rationale for each law or proposal you encounter. Try also to differentiate between the value of a law when passed and when it might be repealed. For example, even if you disagree with the idea of the 70-year-old law restricting public utility holding companies, be sure you see that the rationale against repealing it may be different than the reasons put forth to oppose it in the first place.

Joshua P. Fershee, *Misguided Energy: Why Recent Legislative, Regulatory, and Market Initiatives Are Insufficient to Improve the U.S. Energy Infrastructure*

44 Harv. J. on Legis. 327 (2007)
Copyright © 2007 by the President and Fellows of Harvard College;
Joshua P. Fershee

I. INTRODUCTION

Soaring energy prices, natural gas supply shortages, and blackouts in major areas of the United States have led to a flurry of legislative and regulatory activity. Through this activity, lawmakers and regulators purport to resolve problems regarding natural gas and electricity supplies and service reliability. A major goal of these actions has been to address the overall energy crisis by increasing investment in the U.S. energy infrastructure. However, as is often the case with political remedies for difficult problems, what is being done and what legislators and policy-makers claim is being done are two entirely different things. Recent legislative and regulatory policies are simply ill-equipped to have any substantial impact on the nation's energy infrastructure in the foreseeable future. Although some of the policies provide long-term hope for increasing the amount and sources of capital available for investment, they are not adequate solutions to a current, and progressing, energy crisis.

The goal of increasing investment in U.S. energy infrastructure is well-founded. The most notable recent infrastructure failure was the blackout of August 2003, which left more than fifty million people in Canada and the Great Lakes, New England, and mid-Atlantic regions without power and reportedly caused $10 billion in damage in the United States alone. More recently, an unexpected 101-degree April day in Texas led to rolling blackouts affecting approximately 210,000 homes. Such failures cause a "ripple effect of disruption and damage far beyond the energy industry's own domain" because of the substantial economic investments that are based on electricity being available at predicted levels and costs.

And the crisis likely will only get worse. The current energy infrastructure is insufficient in light of current demand, and the demand for energy in the United States is projected to increase at an average annual rate of 1.5% per year. In 2005, the volume of electricity generation rose 2.1% and electricity sales increased by 3.2% from 2004 levels.

Unfortunately, such failures are not shocking. A dearth of investment in electricity transmission infrastructure is a significant part of the problem. Electric transmission investment, in real dollars, declined for the twenty-three years between 1975 and 1998. Investment increased after 1998 but remains below 1975 levels. In the same time period, demand for electricity has more than doubled. Perhaps more illustrative of the lack of infrastructure investment is that "the interstate transmission system expanded [merely] by a total of 0.6 percent in circuit miles" in 2004. There are indications that transmission investment has been growing considerably since 1999, but additional transmission investment remains necessary because current investment is not necessarily increasing efficiency.

Rather than establishing an effective transportation grid, developers currently tend to invest in electricity transmission only where it is clearly necessary for reliability or where it lowers local costs. Both of these are good reasons for investment, but new investment is also needed to create an effective nationwide transportation network that will facilitate long-distance electricity transportation. Such a network would provide economic benefit and improve reliability, and would facilitate a better energy market through increased energy source options.

The amount of capital needed for infrastructure investment is staggering: "Energy industry spokespeople have called for grid investments of $56 billion, $100 billion, and even as much as $450 billion in total electricity infrastructure investments." And these infrastructure investments are needed now. Congress, regulators, and other leaders should address the problem directly because a failing infrastructure truly is a crisis. Yet, despite political rhetoric to the contrary, these actors are apparently reluctant to wage a more full-scale, direct attack on the problem, perhaps in part because it is not clear that appropriate short-term measures are readily available. Assertive measures, more expansive than the "emergency measures" taken by the Federal Energy Regulatory Commission ("FERC" or "Commission") in response to the California energy crisis of 2000 to 2001 ("2000-2001 California Energy Crisis") and Hurricanes Katrina and Rita, are necessary on a sustained, national scale.

There are strong indications that infrastructure investment is key to alleviating many of the energy issues affecting the United States. The 2003 blackout affecting much of the United States and the New York metropolitan area demonstrated that the current energy infrastructure cannot always satisfy peak demand and lacks important redundancies that would improve reliability. The chaos that accompanied these mass power outages — the result of both infrastructure and operational failures — indicates that the United States could be especially vulnerable to targeted and deliberate attacks on its power supplies. This risk is yet another reason to support improvements in the U.S. energy infrastructure. Improved energy infrastructure would not, of course, prevent terrorist attacks. But an improved infrastructure would help mitigate the damages and difficulties stemming from power outages, regardless of the cause.

The most high-profile portion of the Energy Policy Act of 2005 ("EPAct 2005") represents a response to the complaints of business and corporate leaders that restrictions on corporate structures and other regulatory hurdles have limited the number of available sources of capital for investment in utilities. Prior to the enactment of EPAct 2005, business leaders continually argued that regulatory changes (that is, relaxed regulation) were essential to increase investment. In response to the current and continuing "energy crisis," Congress took action to remove several long-standing restrictions on the corporate structure and governance of U.S. utilities, and thereby improve, at least in theory, the U.S. energy infrastructure. Politicians, regulators, and corporate leaders have all lauded these recent activities as crucial steps that will increase capital investment and "help modernize our aging energy infrastructure."

Other less prominent portions of EPAct 2005 could increase investment more directly if the new or modified grants of power are actively and aggressively used. In one of the provisions providing the most promise, FERC was granted "backstop authority" for siting interstate electric trasmission facilities. This limited authority is available only in areas the Department of Energy ("DOE") identifies as a "national interest electric transmission corridor" ("NIETC"). DOE will issue a report in which it will "designate any geographic area experiencing electric energy transmission capacity constraints or congestion that adversely affects consumers as a [NIETC]." In addition, EPAct 2005 grants FERC exclusive jurisdiction over siting, construction, expansion, and operation of liquefied natural gas ("LNG") terminals. However, despite the promise of these provisions, similar past initiatives have failed to produce significant results.

EPAct 2005 was passed, in part, because the United States faces both short- and long-term energy issues, and while the recent high-profile activities may provide some long-term benefit, they do not offer much promise for remedying the very real short-term problems. As a sponsor of EPAct 2005, Senator Pete Domenici (R-N.M.) admitted: "It's not a bill for today or necessarily tomorrow — it's for the future." The suggestion that EPAct 2005 may not be especially effective is not a unique proposition. It is, after all, the same bill that Senator John McCain (R-Ariz.), among others, dubbed "the No Lobbyist Left Behind Act of 2005."

Given the political rhetoric regarding both public safety issues and energy prices, it would seem that the nation's leaders would be eager to incentivize significant and immediate infrastructure investment. However, recent legislative and regulatory actions provide, at best, long-term promise rather than reasonably quick fixes to what is an imminent concern. The political claims that EPAct 2005 comprehensively addresses the looming "energy crisis" simply do not accurately describe the actions taken. Certainly, it partly addresses the energy crisis, but for all the discussion about the major problems, the proposed fixes are either small in scope or do not address the infrastructure problems.

There are three primary ways in which legislators and regulators have attempted to increase investment in energy infrastructure. First, with the hope of increasing utilities' access to capital, they have removed or relaxed several barriers to capital investment.

Second, they have permitted incentive pricing policies, including market-based rates (as opposed to traditional, cost-based rates) and favorable tax treatment for new investments in certain circumstances for both natural gas and electricity. Third, the regulatory approval processes for mergers and acquisitions and for construction of new facilities have been streamlined, at least in theory.

The present programs designed to address major infrastructure are too vague and ill-defined to initiate major construction projects. Conversely, recent short-term efforts are so limited that vast infrastructure needs remain even in the targeted areas. To address a large-scale energy crisis, a coherent and comprehensive federal energy program is needed. A major program must be designed to identify energy infrastructure needs quickly and accurately, provide attractive financial incentives, and provide aggressive yet feasible deadlines to motivate investors. The authority of the federal government must be expanded and exercised to ensure that regulatory delays do not impede the process.

This article reviews recent federal legislative and regulatory activity seeking to improve energy infrastructure and analyzes the ability of each action to achieve this goal efficiently and effectively. In Part II, the Article reviews the current federal statutory scheme and related developments in market rates and pricing. Part II first briefly reviews EPAct 2005, which includes the historic repeal of the Public Utilities Holding Company Act of 1935 ("PUHCA"). This discussion considers the events leading to the passage of PUHCA and its subsequent repeal and assesses the likely impact (both positive and negative) that the repeal of PUHCA will have on timely investment in energy infrastructure. Part II next describes the use of pricing incentives and the advent of market-based rates in wholesale energy markets, and elucidates the apparent economic and political rationales behind such incentives and rates. This Part then summarizes recent and expected developments related to these incentive pricing programs. Part II concludes by looking at recent legislation and the subsequent regulatory actions related to approval of mergers and acquisitions under the Federal Power Act ("FPA").

Part III explains that while significant legislative and regulatory activities abound, the actions to date provide little reason to expect significant changes in the near future. This Part considers recent FERC action in response to certain "emergencies" related to the 2000-2001 California Energy Crisis and Hurricanes Rita and Katrina and argues that these emergency actions provide yet another example of plans that fail to effectively improve the nation's energy infrastructure in a timely way. This Part argues that more aggressive action is necessary to implement the programs effectively.

Finally, Part IV concludes that it is time for an aggressive and innovative plan that will lead to immediate and sustained energy infrastructure enhancements. Even with financial incentives tied to specific deadlines for putting new facilities in service, such as those used in FERC's emergency orders, improvements in energy infrastructure under current policies are insufficient to effectuate real change. A targeted and comprehensive program is needed to ensure new facilities are built in a timely and effective manner.

II. Indirect Market-Based Energy Policies: High Hopes, Unrealistic Expectations

A. The Impact of PUHCA Repeal: New Investment or Just New Investors?

Of all the laws regulating utilities today, PUHCA may well be the most antiquated. Its detailed provisions continue to inhibit the market discovery process and to ward off hobgoblins that have long ceased to exist.

—R. Richard Geddes

Closing the barn door after the horses have fled is a futile act. Public-utility holding companies and their subsidiary companies are affected with a national public interest, and consumers and investors are harmed by the lack of effective public regulation to prevent abuses similar to those that gave rise to the enactment of PUHCA.

—Rep. John D. Dingell (D-Mich.)

When President Bush signed EPAct 2005 on August 8, 2005, it signaled the removal of one of the longest standing and most significant regulatory hurdles facing investors in the U.S. energy industry: PUHCA. Enacted in 1935, PUHCA was passed as part of President Franklin Delano Roosevelt's New Deal. The goal of PUHCA was to regulate "for the equal benefit of the consumer and the investor." PUHCA was created to protect investors and consumers—who had lost billions of dollars in the crash of Samuel Insull's utility holding company empire—"by authorizing the SEC to regulate the financial and corporate transactions of registered holding companies that owned utility subsidiaries in more than one state."

As of 1930, Insull controlled nearly ten percent of the electricity in the United States, and was a monopoly service provider in the Chicago area. Insull built his conglomerate, Commonwealth Edison, through a series of holding companies in a sort of a pyramid scheme, which created enormous profits until just after the market crashed following the Great Depression. The collapse of the "Insull monstrosity" led to the passage of PUHCA and the resulting restrictions on the corporate structures of public utility holding companies would last for more than seventy years.

PUHCA allowed utility holding companies to own electricity distribution systems in only a single state or region and prevented them from owning businesses that were not functionally or otherwise related to their energy business. Each utility was to operate as a solitary, integrated system, and thus, PUHCA significantly discouraged ownership of U.S. electric and natural gas utilities by domestic industrial and financial institutions and by foreign institutions.

PUHCA also required that any holding company register with the Securities and Exchange Commission ("SEC") if it owned subsidiaries that operated utilities in more than one U.S. state. The business structures and operations of these registered holding companies were severely restricted. Such companies were required to maintain a specified capital structure, their relationships with affiliates were limited, and potential diversification activities were constrained. Furthermore, registered holding companies faced additional potential liabilities that could be imposed by federal and state rate regulators.

Without PUHCA's restrictions, widely dispersed utility companies can now be owned without regard to where each utility is located or whether the resulting entity can be operated as a single system following a merger or acquisition. This change will likely accelerate consolidation in the energy sector and presents increasing opportunities for foreign investors interested in acquiring U.S. utilities. Prior to passage of EPAct 2005, some acquisitions were apparently negotiated and proposed with the full expectation that PUHCA repeal was imminent. For example, MidAmerican-Pacifi-Corp, approved by FERC in December 2005, would not have been permitted under PUHCA because of restrictions on "cross-country" transactions—transactions that would merge geographically remote electric utilities.

The repeal of PUHCA provides diverse and ample investment opportunities for non-U.S. investors because it allows new kinds of nonutility investors to enter the market without these restrictions. Additionally, PUHCA's repeal could significantly impact the overall business structure of utilities in the United States, potentially leading to additional consolidation among U.S. utilities and diversification by utility companies and their affiliates, especially in light of the removal of the structural and geographic restrictions PUHCA imposed.

However, PUHCA's repeal does not eliminate all regulatory obstacles to utility-related mergers and acquisitions. FERC and state regulatory commissions will continue to review mergers and acquisitions in the energy industry. EPAct 2005 requires that public utility holding companies and their affiliates and subsidiaries maintain "books and records" and make them available to FERC to ensure that consumers are protected with respect to jurisdictional rates (that is, the rates over which FERC already has jurisdiction under the FPA and the Natural Gas Act). EPAct 2005 also extended FERC's merger approval authority over electric utilities to mergers and acquisitions, including stock acquisitions, by holding companies.

In particular, now that PUHCA no longer serves as an initial defense in preserving local control over utility operations, state regulators are expected to scrutinize acquisitions of electric and gas distribution utilities by geographically distant companies, whether such companies are utility or nonutility in nature. Under EPAct 2005, to the extent necessary to discharge their duties, state commissions have access to books and records comparable to those possessed by FERC. It is not clear whether these changes will lead to additional (or reduced) investment by current utility owners; additional mergers or acquisitions being attempted and completed; or a rise in the number of new investors.

In addition to this change in the regulation of mergers and acquisitions, the repeal of PUHCA might increase the amount of capital available for investment by increasing the number of potential investors. Upon signing EPAct 2005, President Bush stated that "[t]he bill removes out-dated obstacles to investment in electricity transmission lines in generating facilities" and that it would "modernize the electricity grid." However, it is not clear that removing barriers to investment will actually increase investment in new facilities. Given the relaxed regulation of consolidation, PUHCA's repeal could simply trigger a wave of consolidation through mergers and acquisitions, particularly in the near term. This might result in mere change in the ownership of current facilities rather than the planning and construction of new facilities by new investors.

Ultimately, to the extent industry consolidation is furthered by the repeal of PUHCA, the resulting mergers could conceivably lead to the exercise of market power and, thus, to increased prices. The repeal of PUHCA may lead to this power shift because, at least to some degree, PUHCA protected consumers from anticompetitive behavior by large utilities. Without PUHCA, merged utilities can inappropriately maintain and use increased market power largely because competitors are unable to enter the market following a merger-induced price spike. If competitors could easily enter the market they would (relatively) quickly drive prices back down, but the long timeline for most energy projects makes this an impossible outcome. Furthermore, a merged utility would be less inclined to invest in new infrastructure because, without PUHCA's restrictions on nonutility investment, it may pursue higher-risk, higher reward investments first, because utility mergers themselves can be risky investments, and "in turn both stockholders and customers feel the pinch as the utility seeks to compensate for its overvalued investment."

Several legislators believe that consolidated market power is at least one reason current oil and gas prices are so high. In an interesting move, several members of the Senate Judiciary Committee recently introduced the Oil and Gas Industry Antitrust Act of 2006 ("Oil and Gas Act"), which is designed "to improve competition in the oil and gas industry" and strengthen antitrust enforcement of energy industry mergers. The Oil and Gas Act is targeted primarily at "the escalating price of gasoline," which have risen more than seventy percent between January 2001 and March 2007. Other targets include the increased prices for other petroleum products, such as heating oil and natural gas. Senator Specter, for one, has claimed that energy industry price increases are linked primarily to "rapid consolidation in the oil and gas industry," which created a "collusive environment" and gave market power to the remaining entities. This, according to Senator Specter, created the opportunity to increase prices for oil and gas supplies beyond the proper market price.

Beyond the effects of consolidation, recent history provides another indicator that deregulation, at least in the energy sector, does not lead directly to new infrastructure investment. The 2000-01 California Energy Crisis followed massive deregulation in the form of Assembly Bill 1890 ("AB 1890") in 1996, and the investment in new power plants that was predicted to follow never came to fruition. Some commentators have argued that deregulation is a major hurdle to the success of the market, including increased infrastructure investment, when, as in California, it creates redundant regulation by both the federal and state government. This potential hurdle may be particularly worrisome against the backdrop of the newly created state access to books and records that will coincide with FERC's review.

Indeed, redundant regulation may have recently affected the success of two proposed mega-mergers. The merger of PSEG with Exelon and of Constellation Energy with FPL Group, failed despite, and perhaps in part due to, PUHCA's repeal. The PSEG-Exelon merger was a deal valued at about $17.7 billion that would have resulted in the United States' largest utility. Exelon and PSEG obtained approvals from FERC, the U.S. Department of Justice, and Pennsylvania state regulators before getting bogged down by "insurmountable obstacles, chiefly rate concessions and power-plant divestitures sought by public officials and consumer advocates in New Jersey, where PSEG is based." The companies' offer of $600 million in rate concessions proved insufficient to satisfy New Jersey regulators and overcome concerns regarding the resulting market power of the merged entities. The failure was costly: Exelon spent more than $100 million in pursuit of the doomed merger. Similarly, Constellation Energy and FPL Group called off their $12.5 billion merger in the face of "continued uncertainty over regulatory and judicial matters in Maryland and the potential for a protracted and open-ended merger review process." These failures have dampened the enthusiasm of many industry executives and analysts, who once believed that PUHCA's repeal would lead to a friendlier merger environment. It now appears that PUHCA's repeal may have initially created excitement and incentives for additional mergers and acquisitions, yet the resulting regulatory redundancies have limited the likelihood such transactions would be completed.

Finally, even if PUHCA's repeal is actually successful in bringing new investors into the arena, such a "success" could, in fact, slow the actual development of new infrastructure that already was planned by a pre-PUHCA entity. Investors not familiar with the energy arena and its political and regulatory landscape may not be as effective in moving projects forward as current industry participants. In addition, state and federal legislators may be skeptical of new market participants, which could delay their review and approval of much needed new construction. Over time, the increased numbers of capital sources may very well translate into infrastructure enhancements. But any such benefits are years from leading to even applications for initial construction, let alone putting new facilities into service.

B. Incentive Pricing and Market Forces: A Waiting Game

Transmission congestion has been rising steadily since 1998. Transmission underinvestment is a national problem. We need a national solution. Transmission pricing reform can be an important part of the solution.

FERC has long used incentive-based pricing policies, including the use of market-based rates, in wholesale energy markets (i.e., those regulated by FERC) in order to increase efficiencies in the energy industry. FERC started harnessing market forces in the 1980s as a means to reduce wholesale power prices, permitting certain public utilities to move from traditional cost-based rates to market-based rates for wholesale power sales. The goal of this policy shift was "to create competitive pressures that would improve efficiency and lower wholesale power prices." The Commission's policy was based on the concept that a competitive market leads to a reasonable exchange and that prices will lead a seller to obtain a "normal return on its investment." This policy assumes that no participant in a Commission-approved transaction will have excessive market power and that there is sufficient competition in the market.

The Commission moved to market-based rates because it believed that traditional cost-of-service "rate regulation does not encourage the regulated utility to be efficient and provide service at a low cost." Current FERC chairman Joseph T. Kelliher has stated that the Commission's market-based rate "policy was never intended to deregulate wholesale power markets." FERC merely shifted its focus, according to Chairman Kelliher, and FERC now regulates energy markets instead of only regulating energy prices. In limited circumstances, FERC's market rules have been used in establishing price caps to prevent FERC-jurisdictional power sellers (wholesale energy sellers) from exacting monopoly rents, but such rules are clearly not the norm.

Courts have upheld market-based rates as adequate to assure just and reasonable rates for both electricity and natural gas. A recent case in the Ninth Circuit similarly upheld this market-based rate authority; however, in upholding the market-based rate policy as just and reasonable, the court also stated that FERC cannot use market-based rates alone in carrying out its duties under the FPA. That is, a mere finding that a seller lacks market power is not sufficient oversight to ensure just and reasonable rates. Additional oversight, such as FERC's reporting requirement, is necessary.

FERC continues to view pricing policies as a key way in which to improve the U.S. energy infrastructure. FERC's first goal in its Fiscal Year 2007 Congressional Performance Budget Request is to "Promote Development of a Robust Energy Infrastructure." Admittedly, part of the reason FERC has focused on pricing programs to reach the goal of developing energy infrastructure is because, beyond hydroelectric power, FERC does not have direct jurisdiction over the development of electric generation capacity and natural gas reserves. As discussed above, FERC's jurisdiction extends to the wholesale markets in which such products operate.

Beyond granting market-based rate authority, FERC's ability to impact these areas was increased in EPAct 2005, which expanded the Commission's role in electric transmission siting and mandated a rulemaking proceeding to establish "incentive-based rates for the transmission of electric energy in interstate commerce." EPAct 2005 included a section entitled Transmission Infrastructure Investment. FERC accordingly amended its regulations to establish "incentive-based (including performance-based) rate treatments" for electric energy transmission "for the purpose of benefiting consumers by ensuring reliability and reducing the cost of delivered power by reducing transmission congestion." FERC's proposed rules provide for a variety of incentives for transmission investment. These include:

- a rate of return on equity sufficient to attract new investment in transmission facilities;
- 100 percent of prudently incurred Construction Work in Progress (CWIP) in rate base;

- recovery of prudently incurred pre-commercial operations costs;
- hypothetical capital structure;
- accelerated regulatory book depreciation;
- recovery of 100 percent of prudently incurred costs of transmission facilities that are cancelled or abandoned due to factors beyond the control of the public utility;
- deferred cost recovery; and
- any other incentives approved by the Commission, pursuant to the requirements of this paragraph, that are determined to be just and reasonable and not unduly discriminatory or preferential.

However, FERC's rules are another example of initiatives with long-term potential but little short-term value. As discussed in more detail in Part IV, without clear authority to ensure a place to build the necessary infrastructure, these incentives are, at best, only half-measures.

These rules do demonstrate that FERC has recognized the infrastructure problem. There remains, however, what seems to be a misplaced faith in the abilities of the current market—one that implies that the market is providing correct infrastructure investment cues right now. For example, FERC Commissioner Nora Brownell recently stated:

> I think it is important to recognize that scarcity pricing is the market response to a supply/demand imbalance that appropriately signals the need for infrastructure. For example, the high prices of 2000-2001 that reflected supply/demand fundamentals resulted in the first new power plants being constructed in California in ten years; price risk being hedged through the use of long-term contracting; and renewed efforts to correct a flawed market design.

Such an assessment is accurate if massive blackouts and power shortages are merely considered "appropriate signals" for initiating long-term construction projects, but it is becoming more apparent that this type of reactive policy comes with significant costs.

C. Mergers and Acquisitions: New Rules, New Process, New Investment?

The recent enactment of EPAct 2005 and the subsequent regulatory actions related to approval of mergers and acquisitions under the FPA have the potential to trigger improvements to the U.S. energy infrastructure, but not in the near term. Section 1289 of EPAct 2005, "Merger Review Reform," amended section 203 of the FPA to restrict certain elements of FERC authority while expanding others. The amendment restricted FERC authority by raising the monetary threshold for FERC review of several types of transactions from $50,000 to $10 million. Similarly, it limited FERC's review of public utility acquisitions of the securities of other public utilities to transactions valued at more than $10 million, whereas there was no such monetary limitation before. On the other hand, the amendment expanded FERC authority to include some previously exempt transactions involving the transfer of generation facilities and certain other holding company transactions that have a value in excess of $10 million. Amended section 203 further requires FERC to examine cross-subsidization and pledges and encumbrances of utility assets when considering a transaction subject to section 203 review. Finally, FERC was ordered to adopt procedures to expedite review of applications for section 203 approval of dispositions, consolidations, and acquisitions. Even if these changes will make merger review more efficient in the long term, by simultaneously expanding and contracting FERC authority in these ways Congress has also created a new set of rules for energy companies to decipher before entering potential mergers.

Following a notice of proposed rulemaking, FERC issued an order, Order No. 669, adopting a final rule on the new mergers and acquisitions authority granted by EPAct 2005. In addition to implementing the rules related to FERC's authority under section 203 described above, the final rule granted "blanket authorizations for certain types of transactions, including foreign utility acquisitions by holding companies, intra-holding company system financing and cash management arrangements, certain internal corporate reorganizations, and certain investments in transmitting utilities and electric utility companies." The rule also provides for the "expeditious consideration of completed applications for the approval of transactions that are not contested, do not involve mergers, and are consistent with Commission precedent."

FERC stated that the goal of Order No. 669 was to ensure that all transactions subject to FPA section 203 were "consistent with the public interest and at the same time ensure that our rules do not impede day-to-day business transactions or *stifle timely investment in transmission and generation infrastructure*." FERC noted that it believed it had accomplished that result but that it would be addressing additional issues, such as the "appropriateness of blanket authorizations" and whether "additional steps are needed to protect against cross-subsidization and pledges or encumbrance of utility assets," in a technical conference announced in the PUHCA 2005 Final Rule.

The U.S. energy industry is likely to face a new wave of mergers and acquisitions activity following the recent legislative and regulatory changes. Of course, even before the repeal of PUHCA, the energy industry was experiencing significant merger activity, which started in the mid-1990s. This trend toward consolidation has not led to adequate, if any, infrastructure improvements. Given that this trend has been in place for nearly ten years, there is little reason to believe that making the mergers and acquisitions process easier or open to more potential investors would have any direct impact on the state of the U.S. energy infrastructure, particularly in the near term.

III. Market-Based Hope and Limited Scope: Long-Term Market Evolution and Emergency Orders Are Not Adequate Solutions

Critics of U.S. energy policies often focus on decisions to implement short-term gap-filling policies instead of developing comprehensive long-term programs. However, federal energy policies have actually "evolved" to the point of including equally inadequate long-term and short-term gap-filling policies. In fact, the majority of recent legislative and regulatory actions are intended to provide long-term solutions by increasing energy infrastructure through various types of market evolution. Unfortunately, such indirect, long-term "solutions" have not worked over the past thirty years, and there is little to indicate that the new proposals will, on their own, fare any better.

Market-based rates, for one, without additional support, will not provide the necessary incentives to trigger infrastructure improvements in an efficient and acceptable manner. Barring almost complete deregulation, there is little indication that market-based rates can be successful at all. Social, political, and environmental costs, as well as safety and reliability concerns, make full deregulation imprudent and impractical. Additionally, although an open market might lead to better rates for those in high-demand areas, rural and other isolated locations could suffer without mandatory service obligations. Given the limited impact of recent market-based efforts, and the risks associated with any broader implementation, there is little reason to expect significant impact from such policies in the near future.

What is obvious is that the current energy infrastructure is insufficient for the current and ever-growing U.S. demand. Recent FERC emergency orders tried incentives tied to specific deadlines to put new facilities in service. These FERC actions, in response to energy emergencies caused by the 2000-2001 California energy crisis and Hurricanes Rita and Katrina, would seem to warrant consideration as a possible larger-scale solution. The EPAct 2005 legislation enacted some provisions similar to these emergency actions, and should provide some promise as well. But more is needed to effectively and immediately improve the nation's energy infrastructure, because even investment incentives tied to deadlines have not proven especially effective.

A. Market-Based Rates Come Up Short

Market-based rates are wholly inadequate as a short-term solution to the infrastructure problem. Because infrastructure construction itself is so time consuming, consumers necessarily suffer during the lag between market signals of infrastructure problems and the completion of infrastructure improvements prompted by such signals.

More fundamentally, it is unclear what the market is expected to provide in the first place. That is, most politicians and many court cases seem to imply that Pareto-optimal improvements will result from allowing market forces to work. Certainly, this kind of economic outcome is what most consumers would expect from a "market system." However, it seems more likely that any benefits would, at best, represent a Kaldor-Hicks improvement, providing lower costs to industrial and other large users while raising individual rates for many consumers. To the extent consumers understand or believe that this is what is occurring, the result would be politically untenable.

Such problems are inherent in a market system. The market may eventually provide an infrastructure that will provide sufficient transmission capacity. Most likely, the market would actually provide excess capacity in certain parts of the United States at some point because investors will be clamoring to get in on the action once energy prices rise high enough. Once the capacity exceeds demand, prices will drop. It is this principle that leads many to argue for deregulation as a trigger for investment.

Commentators have discussed the "market effect" deregulation had in the telecommunications industry in great detail. In the wake of the recent failures of many telecommunications companies, some commentators have argued that there was not really any deregulation of the industry at all and that the present regulatory scheme negatively impacts the telecommunications market. Regardless, it seems clear that the telecommunications market participants had some degree of freedom to build their systems, which they did at their own peril. Whether the trigger was deregulation or simply the changes in the subject markets (e.g., the Internet boom), when demand for telecommunications took off and prices soared, companies like Tyco, WorldCom, and Global Crossing put billions of dollars into communications infrastructure around the world. As the prices of the telecommunications services plummeted, along with corresponding stock valuations, many companies in the sector went bankrupt, the infrastructure was sold off, and consumers finally reaped the benefits with lower prices. Of course, these benefits were of little solace to stockholders and creditors of their dramatically devalued holdings.

This demonstrates how, over the long term, markets might be able to provide adequate infrastructure and proper pricing (i.e., producers being able to set prices that recover their total cost over a cycle) but can impose undesirable, and perhaps unacceptable, societal costs over short-term cycles. This is perhaps particularly true of energy markets. For instance, people often require a minimum amount of energy for survival, and extremely high costs over significant periods of time can have disastrous effects for consumers. A low average cost over time does not assist paycheck-to-paycheck consumers needing heat or air conditioning to survive during times of crisis. Concerning overinvestment, there are potential environmental concerns as well: building unnecessary infrastructure can cause significant harms to wetlands and increased emissions without related net price or efficiency gains.

B. Limited Small-Scale Success of Emergency "Remedies"

In March 2001, FERC issued an order announcing actions within its regulatory authorities under the Federal Power Act, the Natural Gas Act, the Natural Gas Policy Act, the Public Utility Regulatory Policies Act, and the Interstate Commerce Act to help increase electric generation supply and delivery in the Western United States, in order to protect consumers from supply disruptions.

Despite the lofty goals, FERC recognized its own limitations: "The Commission recognizes that the actions announced here, by themselves, will not solve the electricity crisis facing California and other areas of the West and will not prevent electricity blackouts in the summer of 2001." Nonetheless, FERC initiated a plan to help alleviate energy supply concerns in the short term while attempting to provide "medium and longer term solutions, including new infrastructure that [could] help avert future recurrences of the current electric supply shortage in the West."

To boost electric supply, FERC planned to provide premium returns on equity and a favorable depreciable life for facilities that could be placed in service quickly. This effectively raised the available return on equity from 11.5% to as high as 14.5%. FERC also provided similar incentives for electric transmission system upgrades that required new rights of way (providing a return on equity of 12.5% and a 15-year depreciable life if in service by November 1, 2001) and for new "facilities needed to interconnect new supply to the grid" (providing a return on equity of 13.5% if in service by November 1, 2001 and 12.5% if in service by November 1, 2002).

FERC subsequently approved a similar 200-basis point return-on-equity adder for a Pacific Gas & Electric ("PG&E") expansion project ("Path 15 Project") that would not be completed until late 2004. The Path 15 Project was designed to reduce congestion on an eighty-four-mile segment of high-voltage transmission lines that connects southern and northern California. Despite protests by the California Public Utilities Commission ("CPUC") that FERC had "unlawfully extended the dead-line" in the Removing Obstacles Order, the D.C. Circuit found that FERC had appropriately approved the incentive "on a case-by-case basis."

FERC's approval of the Path 15 Project is an isolated example of aggressive and appropriate action that helped ensure needed infrastructure was built where it was most needed. Despite fervent (and expected) challenges, FERC recognized that construction was needed to alleviate congestion and also knew "that unless it approved the PG&E incentives, the project would likely not be built in the near future." This represented an uncharacteristically bold step through which FERC exercised its limited authority "to foster 'the installation of critical transmission investment,' by offering incentives to increase the supply of energy." In doing so, FERC demonstrated the aggressive action that is appropriate in responding to a "crisis," albeit on far too small of a scale.

More recently, in response to Hurricanes Katrina and Rita, FERC issued an order on November 18, 2005, temporarily waiving its regulations and raising the limitations on the costs for projects that natural gas pipe-lines may construct without prior specific authorization under their Part 157, Subpart F blanket certificates. The Commission stated that it was acting to help more natural gas reach the market to mitigate the cost impact on consumers. To expedite the construction of infrastructure that might provide access to additional natural gas supplies, the Commission increased the costs of projects that can be constructed under the automatic provisions of blanket certificates from $8 million to $16 million and under the "prior-notice" provisions from $22 million to $50 million, thus eliminating several regulatory hurdles to infrastructure construction for larger scale projects.

Importantly, FERC provided that these temporary waivers would apply only to those projects constructed and placed in service by October 31, 2006. Recognizing "that projects which cannot be completed in time to provide service at the start of the heating season might still deliver the benefits associated with additional gas supply if they are placed into service before the end of the heating season," the Commission extended the waivers to include projects built and placed into service by February 28, 2007.

The Commission also expanded the definition of "eligible facilities" to include mainline facilities for this purpose. Specifically, the Commission temporarily waived several of its regulatory provisions to include the following as "eligible facility[ies]:" main lines; extensions of main lines; facilities, including compression and looping, that alter the capacity of main lines; and temporary compression that raises the capacity of main lines. The cost-limit waivers described above were also permitted to apply to newly eligible facilities, and these temporary waivers were also put in effect through October 31, 2006. The waivers are still, however, capped at $50 million. As such, any eligible facilities built under these provisions would still be significantly limited in size and scope.

As FERC perhaps recognized, the emergency orders have not been especially effective. At the time the Commission issued the deadline extension, there had not been a single filing of a prior-notice application. That is not to say that the program was not helpful at all. However, while some smaller-scale projects ($16 million or less) may have been undertaken, not a single large-scale project ($16 million to $50 million) related to the emergency order had been announced five months after the order became effective. Of course, this is not especially shocking: one year is a short time frame to plan and complete construction projects with costs approaching $50 million.

Incentives of the type used in FERC's emergency orders should be effective in increasing energy infrastructure, but often even those with strict in-service dates can fail to incentivize the appropriate investment in a timely manner. As the D.C. Circuit noted in *California Public Utilities Commission*: "Although it was well-known that Path 15 was constrained and although this suggested a ready market if new transmission lines were built, no party stepped forward to construct upgrades." Participants for the expansion project were found only after specific requests for proposals were issued, "and then only [after] incentives were offered" and the deadline was extended.

The limited success of the Path 15 Project and the Katrina relief orders indicate that more is needed to trigger additional infrastructure investment, even for smaller scale projects. In addition to aggressive pricing incentives, realistic in-service deadlines (i.e., deadlines tied to the size and scope of a proposed project) and targeted outreach to current and potential industry participants are needed to promote much-needed infrastructure investment.

C. Small Solutions Are Inadequate for a Large Energy Crisis

Energy industry professionals are aware and agree that infrastructure needs exist all over the United States similar to those in California and the areas affected by Hurricanes Katrina and Rita, yet persuading utility companies to make the needed infrastructure investments remains difficult. Motivating utilities to make the necessary infrastructure investments is imperative if reliable energy is to remain available in the fastest-growing regions of the country.

EPAct 2005 in fact includes several provisions that are similar to FERC's recent emergency orders. The provisions requiring DOE to identify and report NIETCs are very similar to those used to combat the California issues in 2000 to 2001. The NIETC provision identifies key areas in need of investment and provides a clear deadline for both federal and state action. This provision provides for federal intervention (via FERC) to ensure that transmission lines are built if a state cannot or will not act to move forward a project in the areas targeted by DOE. The purpose of this provision is, in part, to address the not-in-my-back-yard ("NIMBY") problem, which often stops much-needed infrastructure development. Even with the changes, though, it has been recognized that NIMBY issues could mean that necessary energy projects will not be built. As FEC Commissioner Nora Brownell recently stated: "Nobody wants anything in their backyard. I don't want anything in my backyard either, but I want to turn the lights on when I flip a switch."

EPAct 2005 also purportedly provided FERC with "exclusive" jurisdiction over onshore LNG siting. Construction of new LNG terminals unquestionably faces a NIMBY problem, and proposed new construction has been vociferously opposed. Congress acted to provide this "exclusive" jurisdiction in response to a dispute in California over a proposed LNG terminal in Long Beach. The CPUC had asserted that California, not FERC, had the power to approve or deny the siting of an LNG terminal. The case was dropped following the passage of EPAct 2005.

However, while it is technically accurate that LNG siting is now solely a federal issue, the legislative history is replete with contradictory statements concerning the scope of FERC's exclusivity. The House and Senate committee reports assert that LNG siting is now completely under FERC's authority, while acknowledging that a significant state role remains.

Statements by members of Congress indicate an even more nuanced sharing of authority with the states. For example, several representatives from California warned Governor Arnold Schwarzenegger: "The bill will hand over exclusive jurisdiction for the siting of [LNG] facilities to [FERC], preventing the states from having a role in approving the location of LNG terminals and the conditions under which these terminals must operate." Yet the states still have a role in the process of bringing an LNG facility online, which could ultimately dilute the effectiveness of FERC's exclusivity:

> States retain their authority to issue or deny permits under federal statutes such as the Coastal Zone Management Act and the Clean Water Act. This bill takes away no state authority, as long as state permitting agencies issue timely decisions. Let me repeat: State permitting authority remains in place under [EPAct 2005]. States can still deny LNG facilities on their coasts. But they need a reason — Clean Air Act, Clean Water Act, or the Coastal Zone Management Act.

As such, states cannot choose or deny a particular site, but they still retain significant authority over an LNG terminal at a given site. The scope of potential dilatory tactics has simply been reduced.

Additionally, EPAct 2005 created a new section of the FPA, which requires FERC to "establish, by rule, incentive-based (including performance-based) rate treatments for the transmission of electric energy in interstate commerce by public utilities for the purpose of benefitting [sic] consumers by ensuring reliability and reducing the cost of delivered power by reducing transmission congestion." The rules must include provisions to: (1) promote capital investment in efficient and reliable generation and transmission; (2) provide an attractive return on equity to attract new investment; (3) encourage increases in the capacity of current facilities; and (4) permit the recovery of all prudent costs related to reliability and infrastructure investment.

As discussed above, the incentives found in FERC's emergency orders have worked in some smaller-scale circumstances, but it is clear from these instances that the market required additional prodding and concessions to achieve the investment goals. As the Path 15 Project indicated, specific requests for action may be necessary to motivate investors to act. In contrast, the repeal of PUHCA simply removes impediments to certain types of investors. But there is no indication that these investors will actually initiate new construction. In fact, history has shown that market participants have failed to act until expressly asked (and then motivated through additional incentives), even when the market seemed to be sending appropriate investment signals.

The introduction of market forces, the repeal of PUHCA, and other recent policy changes might assist in the process of enhancing infrastructure, but a more comprehensive and focused approach is needed. The availability of financial resources (i.e., investment capital) is clearly a pre-requisite to infrastructure enhancement. Thus, Congress has made construction of new infrastructure more feasible by making new funding sources available through such measures as the PUHCA repeal. But this is only a small first step. Providing availability of new funding sources without providing direct incentives and specific locations for new infrastructure construction is like oiling a hamster wheel: the wheel will spin faster, but it still won't go anywhere. Bringing in new funding sources is unlikely to be effective in a market where the current funding sources are not willing to invest in an industry that already represents solid and stable investment.

IV. Conclusion

To improve the U.S. energy infrastructure effectively, additional measures are necessary. These measures must include the aggressive implementation of processes for identifying necessary infrastructure enhancements, such as those related to NIETCs, and the use of incentives combined with realistic in-service deadlines so that investors will invest and initiate construction quickly.

Despite the touted "comprehensive" nature of EPAct 2005, there remains a need for action. A few recent proposals provide examples of the types of aggressive, innovative approaches that should be applied to improving energy infrastructure.

In the natural gas sector, for instance, a "unique alliance" of five CEOs representing natural gas consumers and producers in the United States has outlined an "immediate" proposal to increase U.S. natural gas supply. The proposal calls for Congress to "[r]educe the permitting back-log and accelerate the processes for applications to work on onshore federal non-park, non-wilderness lands," open up certain lands in the Gulf of Mexico, and "push to lift the exploration moratoria on the East Coast, West Coast and offshore Alaska." Although the wisdom of these proposals might be debatable, they are at least the kind of proposals that *could* have a direct and immediate impact on the U.S. energy supply.

In the electricity area, Congress could have taken a bold move toward improving the U.S. energy infrastructure but instead stopped short of implementing a proven and much-needed measure: granting FERC exclusive siting authority for transmission lines. Although Congress granted limited backstop authority to approve federal electric transmission line siting in a few specific circumstances, the process is protracted and inefficient. Congress should have granted FERC exclusive jurisdiction over transmission siting, making the FPA mirror the Natural Gas Act ("NGA").

Historically, electricity was believed to be a local commodity: one better generated and monitored locally. When it comes to electricity transmission, transactions (buying and selling capacity on transmission lines) are inherently "interstate" in nature, and are exclusively federally regulated under the FPA. However, when it comes time to site and build the transmission lines upon which that federally regulated capacity will be bought and sold, the states have authority to restrict the construction. Thus, the competitive wholesale market concept is being advanced by federal regulators who lack siting jurisdiction, and the states with the siting authority may lack the statutory authority (if they were to have the inclination) to promote that market concept. Exclusive federal transmission siting is the surest way to change course and initiate new interstate transmission infrastructure where it is desperately needed.

EPAct 2005, current market-based rate programs, and FERC's limited emergency orders all lack the scope and focus needed to trigger significant infrastructure investment. Even where such initiatives show promise, recent programs have been too fragmented and isolated to lead to significant change. The current large-scale programs are too long-term and speculative to be an adequate response to an energy crisis; recent short-term emergency solutions are so limited in time and scope that vast infrastructure needs remain even in the targeted areas. A large-scale, coherent, and comprehensive federal energy program is needed. This program must quickly and clearly identify energy infrastructure needs, provide significant financial incentives and realistic deadlines to entice and enable investors, and expand and exercise all available federal authorities to ensure that regulatory delays do not impede the process.

Despite the political battles that might lie ahead, the nation needs programs and plans that directly address the nation's energy crisis by improving the U.S. energy infrastructure. Given the unquestioned need for additional generation facilities and transmission lines and increased access to natural gas supplies to avert potentially drastic energy outages, it is time for FERC, Congress, and the Administration to put forth an innovative plan, building upon EPAct 2005, which will lead to immediate and sustained energy infrastructure enhancements. The need for energy is too significant, and the time line for construction too long, to tolerate additional misguided policies.

Southwest Power Pool, Inc. v. Federal Energy Regulatory Commission

736 F.3d 994 (D.C. Cir. 2013)

WILLIAMS, Senior Circuit Judge:

This dispute between two regional transmission organizations ("RTOs") turns on the interpretation of a single contract provision. The Federal Energy Regulatory Commission resolved the conflict against petitioner Southwest Power Pool ("SPP"). Applying both the Administrative Procedure Act and the "*Chevron*-like analysis" that governs review of such an interpretation, *Colorado Interstate Gas Co. v. FERC*, 599 F.3d 698, 701 (D.C.Cir.2010), we find that the Commission failed to provide a reasoned explanation for its decision. It leapt to an interpretation of one item of evidence without explaining its implicit rejection of alternative interpretations, and, equally without explanation (or at least adequate explanation), it disregarded evidence that the applicable law required it to consider. See Order on Petition for Declaratory Order, 136 FERC ¶ 61,010 (2011) ("Order"), rehearing denied,

Order on Rehearing, 138 FERC ¶ 61,055 (2012) ("Order on Rehearing"). Accordingly, its decision was arbitrary and capricious, and we vacate and remand the orders.

* * *

SPP is an RTO adjacent to another RTO, the Midwest Independent Transmission System Operator ("MISO"), recently renamed Midcontinent Independent System Operator, evidently to reflect its continuing expansion to the south. Entergy Arkansas, an operating subsidiary of Entergy Corporation and at the time of the petition not part of any RTO, abuts both SPP and MISO.

In 2011 Entergy Arkansas made a regulatory filing addressing the possibilities of joining MISO or SPP, and indicating a preference for MISO. Order, 136 FERC ¶ 61,010 at p. 7. That preference rested at least in part on the considerable savings in production costs that joining MISO would yield relative to joining SPP. Entergy Corp., *RTO Path for Entergy Operating Companies* 4, 9; Joint Appendix ("J.A.") 225, 230. To realize those savings, however, MISO must be able to move to Entergy Arkansas electricity generated elsewhere in MISO. Although Entergy Arkansas has transmission connections to both SPP and MISO, its connection to MISO is relatively limited compared to those to SPP and others. MISO would therefore need to rely on these other, non-MISO transmission providers. MISO believes that its Joint Operating Agreement ("JOA") with SPP gives it the *right* to rely on SPP's transmission facilities to do so, *even after Entergy Arkansas becomes part of* MISO itself, an event that appears imminent—Entergy Arkansas has received multiple regulatory approvals to join MISO. See Press Release, Entergy Corp., *APSC Issues Final Conditional Order on Entergy Arkansas' MISO Integration* (Apr. 11, 2013). Section 5.2 of the JOA, the provision invoked by MISO, provides:

> **Sharing Contract Path Capacity.** If the Parties have contract paths to the same entity, the combined contract path capacity will be made available for use by both Parties. This will not create new contract paths for either Party that did not previously exist. SPP will not be able to deal directly with companies with which it does not physically or contractually interconnect and the [MISO] will not be able to deal directly with companies with which it does not physically or contractually interconnect.

The parties agree that at the time of FERC's decision, with Entergy Arkansas distinct from MISO, both RTOs had "contract paths to the same entity," to wit Entergy Arkansas. Thus Section 5.2 allowed one RTO to use the other's transmission network to move electricity to Entergy Arkansas. That is where agreement ends.

The alternative readings of Section 5.2 are these: MISO understands "contract path to the same entity" to include any physical or contractual interconnection and to apply regardless of whether the "entity" is a part of either RTO. So, even if Entergy Arkansas becomes part of MISO, Entergy Arkansas will (under MISO's view) be an "entity" to which both RTOs have contract paths. SPP argues that an RTO cannot have a "contract path to" itself or to part of itself. Thus, once Entergy Arkansas joins MISO, Section 5.2 will no longer (under SPP's view) apply, despite the existence of a "physical or contractual" interconnection between the part of MISO made up of Entergy Arkansas and the other parts of MISO.

After the parties negotiated for some time in vain, MISO petitioned FERC for a declaratory judgment on the interpretation of Section 5.2. FERC adopted MISO's reading, finding that the term "contract path" was broad enough to encompass any physical or contractual interconnection, and that "entity" could include any operating entity, whether or not it was part of one of the RTOs. Order, 136 FERC ¶ 61,010 at pp. 61–62; Order on

Rehearing, 138 FERC ¶ 61,055 at p. 19. We discuss the details of the Commission's decision as they become relevant.

* * *

Before reaching the merits of SPP's arguments, we must first address FERC's assertions that SPP lacks standing and that, in any case, its claims are unripe.

On standing, FERC contends that SPP's interest in the interpretation of Section 5.2 is too attenuated to create an injury that is "actual or imminent." *Lujan v. Defenders of Wildlife*, 504 U.S. 555, 560–61, 112 S.Ct. 2130, 119 L.Ed.2d 351 (1992). It says that no harm will ensue for SPP unless Entergy Arkansas elects to join MISO and secures the necessary state and federal approval, and MISO then seeks to use Section 5.2 to transmit electricity to Entergy Arkansas. Thus FERC characterizes SPP's injury as "too speculative."

We have held that an agency interpretation that defines contractual rights and obligations may itself create enough of an injury to confer standing on a party to that contract. See *Dominion Transmission, Inc. v. FERC*, 533 F.3d 845, 852 (D.C.Cir.2008). We need not explore the scope of that decision, because the Commission's decision here cast a very present shadow over the three-way maneuvering between SPP, MISO and Entergy Arkansas. The latter's parent corporation (Entergy) proclaimed in its 2011 presentation on joinder with MISO that "[r]esolution of the JOA issue in MISO's favor would increase the potential production cost savings and further tip the benefit ratio in MISO's favor." Entergy Corp., *RTO Path for Entergy Operating Companies* 9; J.A. 230. It is surprising that FERC should think that standing rules require SPP to remain in limbo while its competitor MISO woos Entergy Arkansas with FERC's assurance of access to SPP's infrastructure—an assurance that SPP believes is unlawful.

FERC's ripeness argument fares no better. Ripeness of course typically involves an inquiry into the fitness of the issues for judicial review and the hardship to the parties of withholding that review. *Abbott Labs. v. Gardner*, 387 U.S. 136, 149, 87 S.Ct. 1507, 18 L.Ed.2d 681 (1967). But a showing of hardship is ordinarily unnecessary where the agency "has suggested no institutional interests in postponing review..., and adjudication will not benefit from additional facts." *Pub. Serv. Elec. & Gas Co. v. FERC*, 485 F.3d 1164, 1168 (D.C.Cir.2007).

Neither SPP nor FERC has suggested a need for further factual development. And although FERC insists that it may address "implementation" issues in a subsequent proceeding, it nowhere suggests that its interpretation of Section 5.2 has not crystallized enough for this court's review. *Burlington N.R. Co. v. Surface Transp. Bd.*, 75 F.3d 685, 691 (D.C.Cir.1996). Instead, the Commission repackages its standing argument, asserting that many "contingencies" lie between the order under review and any harm to SPP, rendering the order unripe. Our discussion of standing of course dooms that argument.

* * *

Our review of the Commission's decision in the end does not call on us to answer the "*Chevron*-like" question whether FERC has adopted a "reasonable interpretation" of the contract—"not necessarily the only possible interpretation, nor even the interpretation deemed most reasonable by the courts." *Entergy Corp. v. Riverkeeper, Inc.*, 556 U.S. 208, 218, 129 S.Ct. 1498, 173 L.Ed.2d 369 (2009); *Am. Elec. Power Serv. Corp. v. FCC*, 708 F.3d 183, 186 (D.C.Cir.2013). Here FERC's treatment of the issue founders on APA principles—the requirements that it "examine the relevant data and articulate a satisfactory explanation for its action including a 'rational connection between the facts found and the choice made.'" *Motor Vehicle Mfrs. Ass'n of U.S., Inc. v. State Farm Mut. Auto. Ins. Co.*, 463 U.S. 29, 43, 103 S.Ct. 2856, 77 L.Ed.2d 443 (1983) (quoting *Burlington Truck Lines*

Inc. v. United States, 371 U.S. 156, 168, 83 S.Ct. 239, 9 L.Ed.2d 207 (1962)). Agency action that fails either requirement is arbitrary and capricious. *Id.*

Neither SPP nor FERC contends that Section 5.2's meaning is unambiguous. Although FERC attempts to draw meaning from a couple of terms, its theme is only that they do not preclude MISO's preferred interpretation. Only Intervenor MISO contends that the text is in fact unambiguous. But its argument consists largely of declarations that if the parties intended SPP's interpretation, they could have made that clear. Of course; the parties' potential ability to make a provision clear is a universal characteristic of ambiguity. But it hardly establishes that the parties affirmatively made MISO's preferred reading clear. Agreeing with SPP and the Commission that Section 5.2 is ambiguous on the relevant issue, we turn to the process by which the Commission sought to resolve that ambiguity.

SPP raises two principal complaints about FERC's decisionmaking, first, that the Commission misinterpreted the evidence on which it relied and, second, that it erred in refusing to consider relevant evidence before it.

FERC relied heavily on what it termed "course of performance" evidence, to wit the only prior use of Section 5.2—a transaction between MISO, SPP, and a third party, coincidentally, Entergy Arkansas. The particular circumstances of the transaction are critical.

It is undisputed that both SPP and MISO have (or at least had at the relevant times) contract paths to Entergy Arkansas within the meaning of Section 5.2. MISO's is an interchange agreement between MISO (in the form of a MISO transmission owner, Ameren Company), Entergy Arkansas and a third party. Order, 136 FERC ¶ 61,010 at p. 3; Affidavit of Carl A. Monroe on behalf of SPP ¶ 12; Affidavit of Thomas J. Mallinger on behalf of MISO ¶ 13. During a period when that contract path was out of order, MISO used SPP's path to Entergy Arkansas in order to "allow Ameren to continue to serve its radial load on the Entergy transmission system." Mallinger Aff. ¶ 13; Order on Rehearing, 138 FERC ¶ 61,055 at p. 20.

The Commission regarded this episode as supporting MISO's view of Section 5.2. Though acknowledging that it was a "use of SPP's path to Ameren through SPP and across Entergy Arkansas," the Commission seemed to find decisive the fact that the path in question "was still used to provide transmission service to Ameren, an internal MISO operating member." Order on Rehearing, 138 FERC ¶ 61,055 at p. 20.

Thus, so far as we can see, FERC acknowledges that the only service provided by SPP under Section 5.2 was between MISO and a third party, Entergy Arkansas. Why it is important that the MISO member using this service then went on to reach its own operating area via Entergy Arkansas is never explained. The service SPP provided appears consistent both with its view of Section 5.2 and with MISO's broader view (though not in any way *relying on* that broader view). Given the episode's apparent complete consistency with both parties' competing views, we are at a loss to see why FERC regarded the episode as decisive in favor of MISO. Its unexplained leap from neutral evidence to a decision in favor of one side rendered its order arbitrary and capricious.

FERC's confident reading of the single use of Section 5.2 led it to dismiss additional types of evidence offered by SPP. First, SPP introduced an affidavit by Carl Monroe, SPP's chief negotiator for the JOA, stating that at the time of the negotiations, SPP understood that Section 5.2 would apply only when the electricity was transmitted to a third party, not when it was delivered to part of the originating RTO. Monroe Aff. ¶ 15. Second, SPP pointed to definitions of "contract path" used by the North American Electric Reliability Corporation and the North American Energy Standards Board. It urged the relevance of these by pointing to our statement that "[r]elying on the trade usage of [a] term is appropriate, as construing terms in light of their commonly understood meaning is a hallmark of reasonable interpretation." *Colorado Interstate Gas Co. v. FERC*, 599 F.3d at 703 (quoted in SPP's Request for Rehearing at 10 n. 27, J.A. 333). The trade materials SPP cited are replete with words of art, and without the Commission's having explored them at all we are in no position to assess their force in support of SPP's contention.

FERC, however, "decline[d] to consider" these materials. It observed, correctly, that the Restatement (Second) of Contracts § 203(b) and Delaware law (agreed by the parties to be controlling) accord "greater weight" to course of performance evidence than to evidence based on usage of trade or course of dealing (as FERC characterized the Monroe Affidavit). In a literal sense, of course, FERC afforded "greater weight" to course of performance evidence, as it accorded no weight at all to any other. See Order on Rehearing, 138 FERC ¶ 61,055 at pp. 21–22 ("declin[ing]" to consider either type of evidence). But FERC points to nothing in Delaware law or the Restatement supporting total disregard of either type of extrinsic evidence. We may assume arguendo that in some instances course of performance evidence would be so overwhelming as to justify disregard of other evidence, but the seemingly neutral impact of the single episode of Section 5.2's use makes any such assumption irrelevant. Thus, together with its unexplained reading of that episode, the Commission's complete failure to consider the evidence proffered renders its orders arbitrary and capricious.

* * *

The orders are therefore

Vacated and remanded.

Notes & Questions

1. The electricity restructuring process continues to be a challenge, which is largely related to the long history of electric regulations. Companies built their systems on a differently regulated market, and adjusting to the changed structure has moved from utility to utility to RTO to RTO. Who has the better argument: SPP or FERC?

2. Whose fault is the ambiguity in the contract at issue? How could it have been fixed? Does that give you some insight to how the FERC should analyze the contract on remand?

3. FERC has a dilemma here. FERC has to try to promote transmission development while also maximizing the effective use of the current grid infrastructure. What's the solution? Is that an option for FERC?

C. Natural Gas

United Distribution Companies v. F.E.R.C.
88 F.3d 1105 (D.C. Cir. 1996)

I. Introduction

In Order No. 636, the Federal Energy Regulatory Commission ("Commission" or "FERC") took the latest step in its decade-long restructuring of the natural gas industry, in which the Commission has gradually withdrawn from direct regulation of certain industry sectors in favor of a policy of "light-handed regulation" when market forces make that possible. We review briefly the regulatory background for natural gas.

A. Background: Natural Gas Industry Structure

The natural gas industry is functionally separated into production, transportation, and distribution. Traditionally, before the move to open-access transportation, a producer extracted the gas and sold it at the wellhead to a pipeline company. The pipeline company then transported the gas through high-pressure pipelines and re-sold it to a local distribution company (LDC). The LDC in turn distributed the gas through its local mains to residential and industrial users. *See generally* EDWARD C. GALLICK, COMPETITION IN THE NATURAL GAS INDUSTRY 9–12 (1993).

The Natural Gas Act (NGA), ch. 556, 52 Stat. 821 (1938) (codified as amended at 15 U.S.C. §§ 717–717w (1994)), enacted in 1938, gave the Commission jurisdiction over sales for resale in interstate commerce and over the interstate transportation of gas, but left the regulation of local distribution to the states. NGA § 1(b), 15 U.S.C. § 717(b). The NGA was intended to fill the regulatory gap left by a series of Supreme Court decisions that interpreted the dormant Commerce Clause to preclude state regulation of interstate transportation and of wholesale gas sales. *See Arkansas Elec. Coop. Corp. v. Arkansas Pub. Serv. Comm'n*, 461 U.S. 375, 377–80, 103 S.Ct. 1905, 1908–10, 76 L.Ed.2d 1 (1983). The overriding purpose of the NGA is "'to protect consumers against exploitation at the hands of natural gas companies.'" *FPC v. Louisiana Power & Light Co.*, 406 U.S. 621, 631, 92 S.Ct. 1827, 1833, 32 L.Ed.2d 369 (1972) (quoting *FPC v. Hope Natural Gas Co.*, 320 U.S. 591, 610, 64 S.Ct. 281, 291, 88 L.Ed. 333 (1944)). Federal regulation of the natural gas industry is thus designed to curb pipelines' potential monopoly power over gas transportation. The enormous economies of scale involved in the construction of natural gas pipelines tend to make the transportation of gas a natural monopoly. Indeed, even with the expansion of the national pipeline grid, or network, in recent decades, many "captive" customers remain served by a single pipeline. Order No. 436, ¶ 30,665, at 31,473.

Even though the market function potentially subject to monopoly power is the transportation of gas, for many years the Commission also regulated the price and terms of sales by producers to interstate pipelines. *See Phillips Petroleum Co. v. Wisconsin*, 347 U.S. 672, 677–84, 74 S.Ct. 794, 796–800, 98 L.Ed. 1035 (1954). Producer price regulation was widely regarded as a failure, introducing severe distortions into what otherwise would have been a well-functioning producer sales market. *See* STEPHEN G. BREYER & PAUL W. MACAVOY, ENERGY REGULATION BY THE FEDERAL POWER COMMISSION 56–88 (1974). When a severe gas shortage developed in the 1970s, Congress enacted the Natural Gas Policy Act of 1978 (NGPA), Pub.L. No. 95-621, 92 Stat. 3351 (codified as amended at 15 U.S.C. §§ 3301–3432 (1994)), which gradually phased out producer price regulation. Under the NGPA's partially regulated producer-price system, many pipelines entered into long-term contractual obligations, in what were known as "take-or-pay" provisions, to purchase minimum quantities of gas from producers at costs that proved to be well above current market prices of gas. *See* Richard J. Pierce, Jr., *Reconstituting the Natural Gas Industry from Wellhead to Burnertip*, 9 ENERGY L.J. 1, 11–16 (1988).

The problem of pipelines' take-or-pay settlement costs has plagued the industry and the Commission over the last fifteen years. The Commission's initial response to escalating pipeline take-or-pay liabilities was to authorize pipelines to offer less expensive sales of third-party (non-pipeline-owned) gas to non-captive customers while still offering only higher-priced pipeline gas to captive customers. The court struck down these measures because the Commission "ha[d] not adequately attended to the agency's prime constituency," captive customers vulnerable to pipelines' market power. *Maryland People's Counsel v. FERC*, 761 F.2d 780, 781 (D.C.Cir.1985) (*MPC II*); *see also Maryland People's Counsel v. FERC*, 761 F.2d 768, 776 (D.C.Cir.1985) (*MPC I*). In response to the court's decisions in *MPC I* and *MPC II*, the Commission embarked on its landmark Order No. 436 rulemaking. *See* Order No. 436, ¶ 30,665, at 31,467.

B. Order No. 436: Open-Access Transportation

In Order No. 436, the Commission began the transition toward removing pipelines from the gas-sales business and confining them to a more limited role as gas transporters. Under a new Part 284 of its regulations, the Commission conditioned receipt of a blanket certificate for firm transportation of third-party gas on the pipeline's acceptance of non-discrimination requirements guaranteeing equal access for all customers to the new service. Order No. 436, ¶ 30,665, at 31,497–518. In effect, the Commission for the first time imposed the duties of common carriers upon interstate pipelines. *See Associated Gas Distributors v. FERC*, 824 F.2d 981, 997 (D.C.Cir.1987) (*AGD I*), *cert. denied*, 485 U.S. 1006, 108 S.Ct. 1468, 1469, 99 L.Ed.2d 698 (1988). By recognizing that anti-competitive conditions in the industry arose from pipeline control over access to transportation capacity, the equal-access requirements of Order No. 436 regulated the natural-monopoly conditions directly. In addition, every open-access pipeline was required to allow its existing bundled firm-sales customers to convert to firm-transportation service and, at the customer's option, to reduce its firm-transportation entitlement (its "contract demand"). Order No. 436, ¶ 30,665, at 31,518–33. Moreover, the Commission established a flexible rate structure under which transportation charges were limited to the maximum approved rate (based on fully allocated costs) but pipelines could selectively discount down to the minimum approved rate (based on average variable cost). *Id.* at 31,533–49.

The court largely approved Order No. 436, but the principal stumbling-block was the unresolved problem of uneconomical pipeline-producer contracts in the transition to the unbundled environment. The Commission had decided not to provide pipelines with relief from their take-or-pay liabilities, even though the introduction of open-access transportation in Order No. 436 would likely exacerbate the problem by reducing pipeline sales *AGD I*, 824 F.2d at 1021–23. After the court remanded the case on the ground that the Commission's inaction on take-or-pay did not exhibit reasoned decision making in light of open access, *id.* at 1030, the Commission adopted various interim measures in Order No. 500. First, it instituted a "crediting mechanism," under which a pipeline could apply any third-party gas that it transported toward the pipeline's minimum-purchase obligation from that particular producer. Order No. 500, ¶ 30,761, at 30,779–84. Second, the Commission adopted two alternative cost-recovery mechanisms. As customary, a pipeline could recover all of its prudently incurred costs in its commodity (sales) charges, although that could prove difficult for pipelines with shrinking sales-customer bases. In the alternative, under the equitable-sharing approach, a pipeline offering open-access transportation could, if it voluntarily absorbed between twenty-five and fifty percent of the costs, recover an equal share of the costs through a "fixed charge" and recover the remaining amount (up to fifty percent) through a volumetric surcharge based on total throughput (and thus borne by both sales and transportation customers alike). *Id.* at 30,784–92; 18 C.F.R. §2.104. Third, the Commission authorized pipelines not recovering take-or-pay costs in any other manner to impose a "gas inventory charge" (GIC), a fixed charge for "standing ready" to deliver gas—the sales analogue to a reservation charge. Order No. 500, ¶ 30,761, at 30,792–94; 18 C.F.R. §2.105.

The Commission's alternative solutions to the problem of take-or-pay settlement costs in Order No. 500 fared poorly on judicial review. First, the court remanded the crediting mechanism for an explanation of whether the Commission had the requisite authority under §7 of the NGA. *American Gas Ass'n v. FERC*, 888 F.2d 136, 148–49 (D.C.Cir.1989) (*AGA I*). After the Commission explained its §7 authority for the crediting mechanism in Order No. 500-H, the court upheld the crediting mechanism. *American Gas Ass'n v. FERC*, 912 F.2d 1496, 1509–13 (D.C.Cir.1990) (*AGA II*). Second, the court struck down the equitable-sharing cost-recovery mechanism on the ground that the Commission's "purchase deficiency" method for calculating the "fixed charge," which assigned costs to each customer based on how much its purchases had declined over the relevant preceding period, violated the filed-rate doctrine. *Associated Gas Distributors v. FERC*, 893 F.2d 349, 354–57 (D.C.Cir.1989) (*AGD II*), *reh'g en banc denied*, 898 F.2d 809 (D.C.Cir.),*cert. denied*, 498 U.S. 907, 111 S.Ct. 277, 278, 112 L.Ed.2d 233 (1990). The Commission responded to the invalidation of the "purchase deficiency" method in *AGD II* by adopting Order No. 528, which allowed pipelines, in the "fixed charge," to pass through a portion of costs to customers based on any of several measures of current (rather than past) demand or usage, with the intent of avoiding the filed-rate problem. Order No. 528, ¶61,163, at 61,597–98. Finally, the court struck down the Commission's approval of a GIC on a particular pipeline because it had given undue weight to the pipeline's customers' having agreed to the GIC and failed adequately to consider the interests of end-users. *Tejas Power Corp. v. FERC*, 908 F.2d 998, 1003–05 (D.C.Cir.1990).

Congress completed the process of deregulating the producer sales market by enacting the Natural Gas Wellhead Decontrol Act of 1989, Pub.L. No. 101-60, 103 Stat. 157 (codified in scattered sections of 15 U.S.C.). As the House Committee on Energy and Commerce emphasized, the Commission's creation of open-access transportation was "essential" to Congress' decision completely to deregulate wellhead sales. H.R.REP. NO. 29, 101st Cong., 1st Sess. 6 (1989), U.S.Code Cong. & Admin.News 1989, pp. 51, 56. The committee report declared also that "[b]oth the FERC and the courts are strongly urged to retain and improve this competitive structure in order to maximize the benefits of decontrol." *Id.* The committee expected that, by ensuring that "[a]ll buyers [are] free to reach the lowest-selling producer," *id.*, open-access transportation would allow the more efficient producers to emerge, leading to lower prices for consumers, *id.* at 3, 7.

C. Order No. 636: Mandatory Unbundling

In Order No. 636, the Commission declared the open-access requirements of Order No. 436 a partial success. The Commission found that pipeline firm sales, which in 1984 had been over 90 percent of deliveries to market, had declined by 1990 to 21 percent. Order No. 636, ¶30,939, at 30,399 tbl. 1. On the other hand, only 28 percent of deliveries to market in 1990 were firm transportation, whereas 51 percent of deliveries used interruptible transportation. *Id.* at 30,399 & n. 61. The Commission concluded that many customers had not taken advantage of Order No. 436's option to convert from firm-sales to firm-transportation service because the firm-transportation component of bundled firm-sales service was "superior in quality" to stand-alone firm-transportation service. *Id.* at 30,402. In particular, the Commission found that stand-alone firm-transportation service was often subject to daily scheduling and balancing requirements, as well as to penalties for variances from projected purchases in excess of ten percent. Moreover, pipelines usually did not offer storage capacity on a contractual basis to stand-alone firm-transportation shippers. *Id.* The result was that many of the non-converted customers used the pipelines' firm-sales service during times of peak demand but in non-peak periods bought third-party gas and transported it with interruptible transportation. The Commission found that "[i]t is often cheaper for pipeline sales customers to buy gas on the spot market, and pay the pipeline's demand charge plus the interruptible rate, than to purchase the pipeline's gas." *Id.* at 30,400. Because of the distortions in the sales market, these customers often paid twice for transportation services and still received an inferior form of transportation (interruptible rather than firm). *Id.* Because of the anti-competitive effect on the industry, the Commission found that pipelines' bundled firm-sales service violated §§ 4(b) and 5(a) of the NGA. *Id.* at 30,405.

The Commission's remedy for these anti-competitive conditions, and the principal innovation of Order No. 636, was mandatory unbundling of pipelines' sales and transportation services. By making the separation of the two functions mandatory, the Commission expects that pipelines' monopoly power over transportation will no longer distort the sales market. Order No. 636, ¶ 30,939, at 30,406–13; Order No. 636-A, ¶ 30,950, at 30,527–46; Order No. 636-B, ¶ 61,272, at 61,988–92. To replace the firm-transportation component of bundled firm-sales service, the Commission introduced the concept of "no-notice firm transportation," stand-alone firm transportation without penalties. Those customers who receive bundled firm-sales service have the right, during the restructuring process, to switch to no-notice firm-transportation service. Pipelines that did not offer bundled firm-sales service are not required to offer no-notice transportation; but if they do, they must offer no-notice transportation on a non-discriminatory basis. Order No. 636, ¶ 30,939, at 30,421–25; Order No. 636-A, ¶ 30,950, at 30,570–77; Order No. 636-B, ¶ 61,272, at 62,006–10; *see* 18 C.F.R. § 284.8(a)(4).

In contrast to the continued regulation of the transportation market, the Commission essentially deregulated the pipeline sales market. The Commission issued every Part 284 pipeline a blanket certificate authorizing gas sales. Although acknowledging that "only Congress can 'deregulate,'" the Commission "institut[ed] light-handed regulation, relying upon market forces at the wellhead or in the field to constrain unbundled pipeline sale for resale gas prices within the NGA's 'just and reasonable' standard." Order No. 636, ¶ 30,939, at 30,440. The Commission reasoned that open-access transportation, combined with its finding that "adequate divertible gas supplies exist in all pipeline markets," would ensure that the free market for gas sales would keep rates within the zone of reasonableness. *Id.* at 30,437–43; Order No. 636-A, ¶ 30,950, at 30,609–24; Order No. 636-B, ¶ 61,272, at 62,024–25; *see* 18 C.F.R. §§ 284.281–284.288.

The Commission also undertook several measures to ensure that the pipeline grid, or network, functions as a whole in a more competitive fashion. First, open-access pipelines may not inhibit the development of "market centers," which are pipeline intersections that allow customers to take advantage of many more transportation routes and choose between sellers from different natural gas production areas. Similarly, open-access pipelines may not interfere with the development of "pooling areas," which allow the aggregation of gas supplies at a production area. Order No. 636, ¶ 30,939, at 30,427–28; Order No. 636-A, ¶ 30,950, at 30,581–82; Order No. 636-B, ¶ 61,272, at 62,011–12; *see* 18 C.F.R. §§ 284.8(b)(6), 284.9(b)(5). Finally, as part of the move toward open-access transportation, the Commission required Part 284 pipelines to allow shippers to deliver gas at any delivery point without penalty and to allow customers to receive gas at any receipt point without penalty. Order No. 636, ¶ 30,939, at 30,428–29; Order No. 636-A, ¶ 30,950, at 30,582–86; Order No. 636-B, ¶ 61,272, at 62,012–13; *see* 18 C.F.R. § 284.221(g)-(h).

Even though this is the court's first occasion to address Order No. 636, which was enacted in 1992, we do not write on a clean slate. Beginning with *MPC I* and *MPC II*, the court has consistently required the Commission to protect consumers against pipelines' monopoly power. No longer reluctantly engaged in the unbundling enterprise, the Commission has responded by initiating sweeping changes with Order No. 636. Accordingly, we review the Commission's exercise of its authority under the NGA in light of the principles that the court has already applied in this area.

. . . .

II. Open-Access Firm Transportation

A. Unbundling

The petitioners challenge four aspects of the Commission's unbundling remedy: the rule that customers must retain contractual firm-transportation capacity for which the pipeline receives no other offer; the Commission's policy on pipelines' ability to modify existing storage contracts without abandonment proceedings; the rule that transportation-only pipelines may not acquire capacity on other pipelines; and the eligibility date for no-notice transportation service.

1. Prohibition on unilateral customer release of transportation capacity

When the Commission concluded that the pipelines' bundled firm-sales service violated §§ 4(b) and 5(a) of the NGA, Order No. 636, ¶ 30,939, at 30,405, the Commission found also that "the continued enforcement of a pipeline sales customer's purchase obligations, agreed to before implementation of unbundling under this rule, is unjust and unreasonable, and unduly discriminatory." *Id.* at 30,453. Accordingly, all existing bundled firm-sales customers were given the option to reduce or terminate their contractual purchase obligations during the pipeline's restructuring proceedings. 18 C.F.R. § 284.14(d)(1). By contrast, those customers were not relieved of their contractual transportation obligations unless either an alternative, creditworthy shipper offered to assume the capacity at the same or a higher rate (up to the maximum approved rate), or the pipeline agreed to reduce or terminate the transportation obligation. *Id.* § 284.14(e)(2). If a customer wished to reduce or terminate its transportation obligation, and either a replacement shipper assumed the capacity or the pipeline agreed, then the pipeline was authorized to abandon the service under the prior contract. *Id.* § 284.14(e)(3). In effect, existing bundled firm-sales customers remained contractually bound to receive firm-transportation service on the pipeline.

On rehearing, Northern Indiana Public Service Company (NIPSCO) maintained that the Commission's actions entirely abrogated the existing pipeline-customer bundled firm-sales contracts, and that the Commission could not require the LDCs to enter into new transportation contracts. The Commission denied that it had abrogated the contracts: the pipelines remained contractually obligated to provide separate sales and transportation services. "[T]he fact that LDCs have an opportunity to revise their sales entitlements under existing contracts with their pipeline suppliers does not mean they should also have an unqualified right to terminate their obligations for the costs of transportation capacity under those contracts." Order No. 636-A, ¶ 30,950, at 30,638. The Commission also explained that if it released former bundled-sales customers from transportation obligations, "these capacity costs could be shifted from the customer who has contracted for the capacity to the pipeline or other customers that have no need for the capacity." *Id.* at 30,637.

NIPSCO, joined by other LDC petitioners, contends that, by holding pipeline customers to the transportation component of bundled firm-sales contracts, the Commission essentially imposed a new contract upon the customers, which is beyond the Commission's § 5 authority. Section 5(a) provides that, whenever the Commission has found that an existing contract is "unjust, unreasonable, unduly discriminatory, or preferential," it "shall determine the just and reasonable contract to be thereafter observed and in force, and shall fix the same by order." 15 U.S.C. § 717d(a). NIPSCO contests not the Commission's underlying finding that the bundled firm-sales contracts violated §§ 4(b) and 5(a), but only the remedy imposed under § 5. Our review is limited to whether the Commission's reading of § 5 to authorize it to hold LDCs to the remaining terms of a modified pipeline-customer contract is a reasonable construction of its statutory authority. *See AGD I,* 824 F.2d at 1001.

The bundled firm-sales contracts between pipelines and LDCs were subject to the Commission's § 5 authority. The regulatory structure of the Natural Gas Act is contract-based: it "permits the relations between the parties to be established initially by contract, the protection of the public interest being afforded by supervision of the individual contracts." *United Gas Pipe Line Co. v. Mobile Gas Serv. Corp.,* 350 U.S. 332, 339, 76 S.Ct. 373, 378, 100 L.Ed. 373 (1956). Under § 5, "the Commission has plenary authority to limit or to proscribe contractual arrangements that contravene the relevant public interests." *Permian Basin Area Rate Cases,* 390 U.S. 747, 784, 88 S.Ct. 1344, 1369, 20 L.Ed.2d 312 (1968). For example, in *Wisconsin Gas Co. v. FERC,* 770 F.2d 1144 (D.C.Cir.1985), *cert. denied,* 476 U.S. 1114, 106 S.Ct. 1968, 1969, 90 L.Ed.2d 653 (1986), the court affirmed the Commission's decision in Order No. 380 that "minimum bill" provisions in existing contracts were "unjust and unreasonable" under § 5. The court upheld the Commission's remedy, eliminating the minimum bill from the contracts, against the claim that such a remedy "unlawfully alter[ed] the terms of existing contracts," on the ground that "section 5 gives the Commission authority to alter terms of any existing contract found to be 'unjust' or 'unreasonable.'" *Id.* at 1153 n. 9.

NIPSCO also maintains that the Commission has construed its § 5 authority to extend beyond the limits in § 1(b) on the Commission's jurisdiction. Regardless of the Commission's authority to impose modified contractual obligations on pipelines, NIPSCO contends that the Commission lacks such authority over LDCs because LDCs are "non-jurisdictional" entities. Under § 1(b), the Commission's jurisdiction over "the transportation of natural gas in interstate commerce" does not apply to "the local distribution of natural gas or to the facilities used for such distribution." 15 U.S.C. § 717(b). But the local-distribution exception applies only to the movement of gas within an LDC's local mains and not to the movement of gas in high-pressure interstate pipelines. *FPC v. East Ohio Gas Co.,* 338 U.S. 464, 470–71, 70 S.Ct. 266, 269–70, 94 L.Ed. 268 (1950); *see also Louisiana Power & Light,* 406 U.S. at 636 & n. 13, 92 S.Ct. at 1836 & n. 13. Thus, for the same reasons that the Commission has jurisdiction over the re-sale of interstate capacity rights by LDCs to local end-users, *see infra* Part III.B.2, it also has jurisdiction over an LDC's ability to reduce or terminate its contractual interstate-transportation obligation. The pipeline-LDC contracts for transportation through interstate pipelines do not fall within the local-distribution exception to the Commission's jurisdiction.

The Commission cannot use the pipeline-LDC contracts as a jurisdictional hook for non-jurisdictional measures that do not relate to the Commission's § 5 remedial authority over the contracts. As the court has held in a different context, the Commission may not assert its jurisdiction over a party merely because it is "involved in a contractual relationship with a jurisdictional pipeline." *ARCO Oil & Gas Co. v. FERC,* 932 F.2d 1501, 1503 (D.C.Cir.1991). NIPSCO maintains that the Commission has done just that by replacing the agreed-upon contractual terms with entirely new terms of the Commission's own devising, when it would otherwise be without jurisdiction to compel the LDC to receive service in the first instance. But we do not agree that the Commission has overstepped the bounds of its § 5 authority in the first place. First, an LDC may maintain its original bargain by choosing not to exercise its unilateral right to terminate the purchase obligation. The resulting combination of sales service and no-notice firm-transportation service replicates its prior contractual entitlement. Thus, it is somewhat difficult to see the purported compulsion against LDCs in the Commission's decision not to grant them the right to terminate their transportation obligations. Second, the Commission's remedy was appropriately confined to the underlying violation. Because the Commission found the sales component of the bundled contracts to be unjust and unreasonable, Order No. 636, ¶ 30,939, at 30,453, it interfered with existing contracts only to the extent necessary to remedy the effects of pipelines' market power. The Commission has the authority under § 5 to adopt a remedy proportionate to the problem being addressed. *AGD I*, 824 F.2d at 1019. Finally, § 5 instructs that "the Commission shall determine the just and reasonable ... contract to be thereafter observedand in force, and shall fix the same by order." 15 U.S.C. § 717d(a). The limits of the Commission's authority to modify pipeline-LDC contracts under § 5 lie in the requirement that, given the original contract and the Commission's findings of unlawfulness, the resulting contract be "just and reasonable." NIPSCO does not contend that the result of unbundling the firm-sales contracts was unjust or unreasonable. We therefore uphold the Commission's § 5 authority to hold LDCs to the transportation component of the modified bundled firm-sales contracts.

NIPSCO contends in the alternative that, even if the Commission's action was within its § 5 authority, the Commission acted arbitrarily and capriciously. In NIPSCO's view, the limited nature of the remedy allows pipelines to continue to exercise market power over customers in the transportation contracts, in contravention of the overall goals of Order No. 636. We reject this challenge as well because the Commission has provided a reasonable basis for its decision not to allow customers unilaterally to reduce their contractual transportation obligations. *Cf. ARCO*, 932 F.2d at 1502.

The Commission found in Order No. 636 that "the amount of capacity reserved for pipeline firm sales still far exceeds the pipelines' actual sales so that capacity is not available for firm transportation and, as a result, interruptible transportation maintains a significant share of peak period transportation." Order No. 636, ¶ 30,939, at 30,406. In other words, because many firm-sales customers decided to purchase third-party gas and transport it using interruptible service, those customers ended up holding excess reserved capacity. NIPSCO asserts that the effect of the Commission's decision not to allow LDCs unilaterally to reduce their contractual transportation obligations is to perpetuate customers' excessive capacity holdings. NIPSCO is correct insofar as the effect of any contract is to lock in current conditions, and the existence of a long-term contract necessarily slows the transition of a market to a new equilibrium when some underlying condition changes. Moreover, the capacity-release mechanism is an imperfect solution for the LDCs because the existing pipeline customer is unlikely to receive full compensation for released capacity in an excess-capacity market situation. Yet the problem of capacity excess that the Commission identified was that customers held more capacity in bundled-sales contracts than they purchased gas from the pipeline, not that customers held more firm-transportation capacity than needed for their peak demand. Contrary to NIPSCO's contention, there is no contradiction between the general goal in Order No. 636 of encouraging more efficient use of reserved capacity and the challenged rule that customers may not unilaterally release contractual transportation obligations: the Commission never found that the natural gas industry after mandatory unbundling would be characterized by excess reserved capacity.

Moreover, the Commission provided in Order No. 636-A a coherent rationale for its decision. Because a pipeline's rate structure is predicated upon levels of reserved capacity, providing customers with the unilateral option to reduce those levels would either reduce the pipeline's cost recovery or force the pipeline to increase rates for the remaining customers. Order No. 636-A, ¶ 30,950, at 30,637. Because someone has to bear the costs of unfavorable contractual capacity obligations, the Commission reasoned that the customer who voluntarily assumed those obligations by entering into the contract should bear those costs rather than spreading them over all of the pipeline's customers.

The Commission decided to modify the set of contracts that forms the structure of the natural gas industry only as much as necessary to alleviate the anti-competitive sales component of the bundled contracts. The Commission is not required to exercise its § 5 authority beyond the limits of the problem it has identified, *see AGD I,* 824 F.2d at 1019, and its cost-shifting rationale was a well-reasoned justification for its decision not to go further. We therefore uphold this portion of the rules.

2. Pipeline modification of contract-storage rights

Because the Commission found that "pipelines' superior rights with respect to access and control provide them with several advantages over other gas merchants with no access to storage for their gas," it required pipelines to offer access to their storage capacity on an open-access basis. Order No. 636, ¶ 30,939, at 30,425–26. By defining "transportation" to include "storage," 18 C.F.R. § 284.1(a), the Commission made storage subject to the same non-discrimination requirements as capacity rights. *Id.* §§ 284.8(b), 284.9(b). Although pipelines were allowed to retain storage capacity for system management and in order to ensure the delivery of no-notice service, they were required to offer remaining storage capacity on an open-access contractual basis for customer-owned gas. Order No. 636, ¶ 30,939, at 30,426–27. The Commission granted former bundled firm-sales customers a priority right to that storage capacity. Order No. 636-A, ¶ 30,950, at 30,578.

In its request for rehearing of Order No. 636, CNG Transmission Corporation, a pipeline company, explained that the changes involving open-access storage would create difficulties for it in providing the contractual levels of service to its existing contract-storage customers. Because "current contract storage injection and withdrawal schedules, and other related operational protocols, are based upon current levels of contract storage service," CNG requested the ability to modify existing storage customers' contractual rights to inject or withdraw gas. The Commission responded that its

> intent was that current contract storage customers retain their full right to capacity as specified in their contracts. The Commission did not mean to infer [*sic*] that the terms and conditions associated with their rights could not be changed if they proved unreasonable in light of Order No. 636's requirements of no-notice transportation and open access contract storage. This, of course, is a pipeline specific matter and must be addressed in the restructuring proceeding.

Order No. 636-A, ¶ 30,950, at 30,579. Upon further rehearing, however, the Commission went further, stating that,

> while it has authorized pipelines to propose to change existing storage arrangements, if necessary, to provide no-notice transportation service, the pipeline must still show that the changes are necessary and reasonable. This includes an impact of a change on current contract storage customers. The Commission has not authorized any reduction in contract storage capacity. The Commission views changes to injection and withdrawal schedules as changes to terms and conditions, rather than to the level of certificated service. Hence, the Com-

mission concludes that changes to existing contract storage terms and conditions
will not need action under NGA section 7(b).

Order No. 636-B, ¶ 61,272, at 62,011.

A group of LDC petitioners challenges the Commission's statement that changes to
contract-storage withdrawal and injection schedules do not require a § 7(b) abandonment
proceeding. We agree with the petitioners that it is difficult to discern exactly what the
Commission's position is on this issue, and we grant the petitioners relief insofar as the
Commission stated in Order No. 636-B that any change to injection and withdrawal
schedules can be effected without a § 7(b) abandonment proceeding.

If the Commission has permitted the pipelines to "abandon" a "service rendered by
means of … facilities" certificated by the Commission, then it has failed to comply with
§ 7(b), which requires a "due hearing" and a Commission finding that "the present or
future public convenience or necessity permit such abandonment." 15 U.S.C. § 717f(b).
In general, the test for § 7 abandonment is whether the certificate-holder "permanently
reduces a significant portion of a particular service." *Reynolds Metals Co. v. FPC*, 534 F.2d
379, 384 (D.C.Cir.1976); *see also Kansas Power & Light Co. v. FERC*, 851 F.2d 1479, 1481
(D.C.Cir.1988). By comparison, the withholding of gas delivery to an interruptible-trans-
portation customer is not an "abandonment," because the customer has no right to
guaranteed delivery under its contract or the certificate of service. *Cerro Wire & Cable
Co. v. FERC*, 677 F.2d 124, 129–30 (D.C.Cir.1982). Although the court has reserved the
issue whether a § 7(b) abandonment occurs when only the identity of the customer
changes, an abandonment does take place "when there is a reduction or alteration in
overall service." *Tennessee Gas Pipeline Co. v. FERC*, 972 F.2d 376, 384 (D.C.Cir.1992).

According to the submissions by the Associated Gas Distributors in the administrative
record, a customer who contracts for storage is concerned with two elements: capacity
(how much gas can be stored) and deliverability (how much gas can be withdrawn on a
given day). The AGD attached affidavits from six member LDCs who stated that changes
to injection and withdrawal schedules could reduce deliverability, with adverse consequences
on their ability to meet residential customers' demands. Elizabethtown Gas Company, in
its opposition to CNG's compliance filing in its restructuring proceeding, objected to
CNG's specific proposals to reduce withdrawal amounts when contract-storage customers
had low gas inventories in storage, to maintain elevated minimum inventory levels during
the early winter months, to limit monthly withdrawal amounts to less than the total of
the daily amounts, to reduce firm withdrawal rights to best-efforts rights, and to impose
minimum inventory turnovers.

It is impossible, on the current record, to determine on a generic basis what changes
to injection and withdrawal schedules would "permanently reduce[ ] a significant portion"
of contract-storage service. *Reynolds Metals*, 534 F.2d at 384. Because contractual
deliverability entitlements are an integral part of the customer's contract-storage rights,
modifications that affect those rights could in some instances constitute a § 7 abandonment.
On the other hand, under other circumstances an adjustment to an injection or withdrawal
schedule could be sufficiently minor or temporary that no abandonment would occur.
Whether an abandonment proceeding is necessary depends on the individual customer's
storage contract and on the pipeline's proposed modifications, none of which are before
us now.

To the extent that the Commission issued in Order No. 636-B a sweeping statement
that no modifications to injection and withdrawal schedules for a contract-storage customer
require an abandonment proceeding, such a statement is inconsistent with § 7. In its brief,

however, the Commission denies that it has taken any such steps to degrade contract-storage rights. Instead, the Commission maintains that it has merely allowed pipelines to propose "necessary and reasonable" changes in the restructuring proceedings, Order No. 636-B, ¶ 61,272, at 62,011, for which the Commission has authority under § 5. In the restructuring proceedings, the Commission has followed this approach, approving proposed modifications to withdrawal and injection schedules if the pipeline can prove that the changes are "necessary and reasonable.

The Commission's theory that it has the authority to proceed in the restructuring proceedings under § 5 rather than in abandonment proceedings under § 7(b) is explained nowhere in the Order No. 636 series. *See* Order No. 636-A, ¶ 30,950, at 30,579; Order No. 636-B, ¶ 61,272, at 62,011. Under § 7(b), the Commission must hold a "due hearing" and must make a finding that "the present or future public convenience or necessity permit such abandonment." 15 U.S.C. § 717f(b). By contrast, under § 5 the Commission need hold only a "hearing" and must find that an existing contract is "unjust, unreasonable, unduly discriminatory, or preferential." *Id.* § 717d(a). We need not decide whether compliance with the procedures in § 5 could in certain circumstances satisfy the applicable statutory requirement in § 7(b). The Commission has assured us in its brief that its approach under § 5 will be "consistent" with the § 7 requirements. But without any explanation in the Order No. 636 decisions for why the Commission's procedures satisfy § 7(b), we cannot accept the Commission's suggestion that its exercise of its § 5 authority in the restructuring proceeding would obviate the need for abandonment hearings.

On the other hand, any claim that a particular pipeline's modification to contract-storage withdrawal and injection schedules requires a § 7(b) abandonment proceeding is premature and should be raised, if at all, in the review of individual restructuring proceedings.

3. Capacity retention by transportation-only pipelines

A central part of the Commission's unbundling program is the requirement that all pipelines assign to their firm-transportation customers the firm-transportation capacity that the pipelines held on upstream pipelines. 18 C.F.R. § 284.242. Now that customers can buy gas directly from the producers, they may bear the responsibility of reserving capacity both on "upstream" and "downstream" pipelines. If the downstream pipeline were allowed to retain the capacity on the upstream pipeline, the Commission reasoned, it would inhibit the formation of a competitive gas-sales market by preventing downstream customers from gaining access to the new opportunity to purchase gas directly from the producers. Order No. 636, ¶ 30,939, at 30,417–18.

Two pipeline petitioners, ANR Pipeline Company and Colorado Interstate Pipeline Company, urge the Commission to carve out an exception for "transportation-only pipelines"—pipelines that do not offer any gas sales. For example, a downstream pipeline may wish to offer a customer a package of firm-transportation capacity on its pipeline as well as on a connecting upstream pipeline; the customer may well prefer not to have to contract separately with the upstream pipeline.

This petition for review has been rendered moot by an intervening declaratory order. In *Texas Eastern Transmission Corp.,* 74 F.E.R.C. ¶ 61,074, at 61,220 (1996), *reh'g pending,* Docket No. CP 95-218, the Commission declared that the successful completion of unbundling under Order No. 636, with the separation of pipelines' merchant and transportation functions, had alleviated the Commission's former concerns that pipelines would obstruct access to production areas to favor their merchant functions. Accordingly, the Commission announced that it would "decide whether to allow pipelines to acquire upstream or downstream capacity on a case-by-case basis." *Id.* The Commission's intervening action appears to have provided the pipeline petitioners with the relief that they had sought; any further relief is available in review of the declaratory-order proceeding.

4. Eligibility date for no-notice transportation

In its new regulation, the Commission requires interstate pipelines "that provided a firm sales service on May 18, 1992" to offer no-notice transportation service. 18 C.F.R. § 284.8(a)(4). In Order No. 636-A, the Commission clarified that "[t]he pipelines are required to offer no-notice transportation service only to customers that were entitled to receive a no-notice firm, city-gate, sales service on May 18, 1992." Order No. 636-A, ¶ 30,950, at 30,573. Although several commentators requested the Commission to require pipelines to extend no-notice transportation service to customers who had already converted from bundled firm-sales service under Order No. 436 and consequently no longer received such service on May 18, 1992, the Commission denied rehearing. The Commission offered three reasons: first, that it was prudent to begin the experiment with no-notice transportation on a limited basis; second, that customers who were not receiving bundled firm-sales service on May 18, 1992, "were not relying on that service"; and third, that such customers "could not reasonably expect to receive no-notice transportation in the future" because neither Order No. 436 nor the Notice of Proposed Rulemaking for Order No. 636 had contemplated it. Order No. 636-B, ¶ 61,272, at 62,007.

The National Association of Gas Consumers (NAGC) contends that the ineligibility of former bundled firm-sales customers who converted to open-access transportation under Order No. 436 to receive no-notice transportation is unduly discriminatory. NAGC relies on the Commission's own regulation, promulgated by Order No. 436, which requires an open-access pipeline to offer service "without undue discrimination." 18 C.F.R. § 284.8(b)(1). And as NAGC points out, the Commission found in Order No. 636 that the pipelines' open-access firm-transportation service under Order No. 436 was unlawfully discriminatory because it did not provide the same quality of transportation service as was available with bundled firm-sales service. Order No. 636, ¶ 30,939, at 30,402. Now, customers who converted under Order No. 436 remain limited to stand-alone firm-transportation service subject to scheduling and balancing requirements and other penalties. Thus, NAGC maintains that the Commission must extend eligibility for no-notice transportation service to customers who converted before Order No. 636 in reliance on the non-discrimination provisions.

We find the Commission's justifications in Order No. 636-B unconvincing. The Commission's desire to proceed cautiously with no-notice transportation, rather than require pipelines to offer it to all customers, cannot explain the disadvantaging of former bundled firm-sales customers who converted under Order No. 436. Although those customers had no right to expect to receive no-notice transportation service under Order No. 636, neither did customers who did receive bundled firm-sales service on May 18, 1992. Finally, the Commission has not provided substantial evidence to support its assumption that bundled firm-sales customers who retained bundled service relied more heavily on reliability of transportation service than did customers who switched to open-access transportation. We therefore remand this issue to the Commission for further explanation of which customers should be eligible for no-notice transportation service.

B. Right of First Refusal

Section 7(b) of the Natural Gas Act prohibits pipelines from abandoning certificated firm-transportation service until the Commission makes a finding that "the present or future public convenience or necessity permit such abandonment." 15 U.S.C. §717f(b). In its original adoption of open-access transportation in Order No. 436, the Commission provided automatic "pre-granted abandonment" for all firm-transportation service provided under a Part 284 blanket certificate. 18 C.F.R. §284.221(d) (1989). After the order was twice vacated on other grounds, the Commission re-promulgated the automatic pre-granted abandonment rule in Order No. 500-H, ¶30,867, at 31,583–85. In its review of Order No. 500-H, the court remanded automatic pre-granted abandonment because "the Commission has not yet adequately explained how pregranted abandonment trumps another basic precept of natural gas regulation—protection of gas customers from pipeline exercise of monopoly power through refusal of service at the end of a contract period." *AGA II,* 912 F.2d at 1518. In *AGA II,* the court concluded that the Commission's reliance on various market alternatives available to LDCs—namely interruptible transportation, stand-by gas service and gas from alternative suppliers—provided inadequate protection for LDCs. *Id.* at 1517. The court similarly rejected the Commission's contention that it was furthering purposes other than the protection of existing customers because "the Commission's response seems to entail an enormous qualification of its basic purpose." *Id.* On remand from *AGA II,* the Commission decided to hold the issue of pre-granted abandonment in abeyance until Order No. 636. *See* Order No. 500-J, [Current] F.E.R.C. Stats. & Regs. (CCH) ¶30,915 (1991).

In Order No. 636, the Commission responded to *AGA II* by amending its regulations to provide that an existing customer of long-term firm-transportation service could avoid pre-granted abandonment if it abided by a new right-of-first-refusal (ROFR) mechanism. 18 C.F.R. §284.221(d). No petitioner challenges the Commission's rule that interruptible transportation, and firm transportation with a contract term of less than one year, are subject to automatic pre-granted abandonment even without the right of first refusal. Order No. 636, ¶30,939, at 30,446; Order No. 636-A, ¶30,950, at 30,625–26. But the petitioners do challenge pre-granted abandonment for long-term firm transportation. In essence, the issue is whether the right-of-first-refusal mechanism provides the protection for pipeline customers that *AGA II* requires.

The right-of-first-refusal mechanism consists principally of two matching requirements: rate and contract term. *See* 18 C.F.R. §284.221(d)(2)(ii). Near the end of a long-term firm-transportation contract, the existing customer may notify the pipeline that it intends to exercise its right of first refusal. The pipeline must post the availability of that capacity on its electronic bulletin board and, in accordance with the criteria set forth in its tariff, identify the "best bid" offered by any competing shippers. Order No. 636, ¶30,939, at 30,451; Order No. 636-A, ¶30,950, at 30,634. The customer then has the right to match the competing bid's rate, up to the maximum "just and reasonable" rate that the Commission has approved for that service, and the competing bid's contract term. Competing shippers may choose to bid for only a portion of the capacity in the expiring contract. Order No. 636, ¶30,939, at 30,451–52; Order No. 636-A, ¶30,950, at 30,634–35. The Commission promised that it would scrutinize competing bids from pipelines' marketing affiliates to ensure that they did not collude to increase the bidding level. Order No. 636, ¶30,939, at 30,451; Order No. 636-A, ¶30,950, at 30,634.

Originally, the Commission contemplated that competing bids could be for any contract length. According to the Commission, "[o]ther things being equal, the satisfaction of long-term transportation needs should have priority over the satisfaction of shorter-term needs." Order No. 636, ¶30,939, at 30,450. In Order No. 636-A, the Commission reconsidered that decision and found

> that capping the contract term that must be matched by a customer exercising
> its right of first refusal at a period of 20 years strikes an appropriate balance

between the pipeline's need for stability, the customer's need for flexibility, and the Commission's overall goal in Order No. 636 to foster long-term, market driven arrangements in the gas industry. This cap, in the Commission's judgement, ensures that the customer obtaining the service values the service sufficiently to commit to using it for a reasonable period and provides the pipeline with a reasonable level of stability. Twenty years has been the traditional length of long-term contracts in the natural gas industry and a number of recent contracts for new capacity are for a twenty year term.

Order No. 636-A, ¶ 30,950, at 30,631. Commissioner Moler, dissenting in part, characterized the twenty-year period as "a blatantly anti-LDC rule," given that LDCs typically have existing contractual relationships jeopardized by pre-granted abandonment, and urged the adoption of a shorter contract-term cap. *Id.* at 30,678–79.

1. Pre-granted abandonment generally

Many of the petitioners contend that the Commission's pre-granted abandonment of firm-transportation service violates § 7. The petitioners maintain that the right-of-first-refusal mechanism provides inadequate protection to existing pipeline customers from the pipelines' market power.

The Commission may satisfy its § 7 obligations by making generic findings of public convenience and necessity. In *Mobil Oil Exploration & Producing Southeast Inc. v. United Distribution Cos.,* 498 U.S. 211, 227, 111 S.Ct. 615, 625, 112 L.Ed.2d 636 (1991), the Supreme Court upheld a pre-granted abandonment scheme under the Commission's Order No. 451, even though the Commission's "approval is not specific to any single abandonment but is instead general, prospective, and conditional." *See also FPC v. Moss,* 424 U.S. 494, 499–502, 96 S.Ct. 1003, 1007–08, 47 L.Ed.2d 186 (1976). The Court approved the Commission's findings that, under its good-faith negotiation procedures for the pre-granted abandonment of producers' sale of "old gas" under the NGPA to pipelines, pipelines would be protected "by allowing them to buy at market rates elsewhere if contracting producers insisted on the new ceiling price." *Mobil Oil,* 498 U.S. at 227, 111 S.Ct. at 626. In *AGA II,* by contrast, the court held that the Commission had not adequately explained why pre-granted abandonment of firm-transportation in Order No. 500-H would not "allow pipelines indirectly to extract monopoly profits from their customers." 912 F.2d at 1516. Most important, the Commission's proposed alternatives to existing firm-transportation service, such as interruptible transportation and standby service, failed to provide the existing customer with an adequate level of protection. *Id.* at 1517. From *Mobil Oil* and *AGA II,* we conclude that, for a finding of public convenience and necessity for pre-granted abandonment under § 7, the Commission must make appropriate findings that existing market conditions and regulatory structures protect customers from pipeline market power.

The Commission's initial protective measures—contractual "evergreen" or "roll-over" clauses—are by themselves inadequate. The Commission allows the pipeline and the customer to negotiate such a contractual provision allowing the parties to extend the contract before termination and thereby avoid the abandonment issue. Moreover, the Commission requires pipelines that offer evergreen or roll-over clauses to do so on a non-discriminatory basis. Order No. 636-A, ¶ 30,950, at 30,628. Yet the Commission declined to mandate the inclusion of contract-extension clauses. *Id.* As the petitioners note, the voluntary nature of evergreen and roll-over clauses means that those pipelines that do enjoy market power will likely refuse to offer such clauses to their customers. Thus, voluntary contract-extension clauses alone do not provide sufficient protection to existing pipeline customers.

The mandatory right-of-first-refusal mechanism, however, provides substantially more protection to existing customers. First, shippers bid against one another for capacity, which in the Commission's view will prevent the pipeline from using the right-of-first-refusal mechanism to push the rate above the competitive market price. Second, under the right-of-first-refusal mechanism the competing bid is capped at the maximum "just and reasonable" rate, which protects the existing shipper from having to match a bid higher than the Commission-approved rate. If the existing customer is willing to pay the maximum approved rate, then the right-of-first-refusal mechanism ensures that the pipeline may not abandon the certificated service. In this way, even a captive customer served by a single pipeline can exercise its right of first refusal and retain its long-term firm-transportation service against rival bidders. Hence, the basic structure of the right-of-first-refusal mechanism provides the protections from pipeline market power required for pre-granted abandonment under § 7.

2. The twenty-year contract term

The petitioners also contend that the contract term-matching condition allows pipelines to exercise market power inconsonant with pre-granted abandonment. Thus, oncapacity-constrained pipelines existing customers may be forced to match competing bids for twenty years' duration, which would not be the outcome in a competitive market without pipelines' natural monopoly. Competing bidders who come up against the rate ceiling for this scarce resource—capacity on constrained pipelines—may bid up the length of the contract term to try to win the auction. In effect, bidding for a longer contract term becomes a surrogate for bidding beyond the maximum rate level. Especially with the new capacity-release mechanism, a competing bidder could bid for a longer contract term than it would contract for in a competitive market, release the excess capacity at a discount, and absorb the loss just as though it had bid an above-maximum rate for a shorter term.

The Commission acknowledged the reality that contract duration is a measure of value when it declared that its policy was "for the capacity to go to the person who values it the most, as evidenced by its willingness to bid the highest price for the longest reasonable time." Order No. 636-A, ¶ 30,950, at 30,630. As a general matter, in a perfectly competitive market, a long-term contract incorporates a premium for stability, and a pipeline naturally values a longer-term transportation contract more highly, *ceteris paribus.* Order No. 636, ¶ 30,939, at 30,450. Thus, the contract term-matching condition is a rational means of emulating a competitive market for allocating firm-transportation capacity. There are obvious drawbacks—the industrial petitioners provide the example of a factory owner with a productive asset that has only a short useful life. Order No. 636-A, ¶ 30,950, at 30,629–30. But industrial end-users are also far more likely to have ready access to alternative fuels than do the residential consumers served by LDCs. *See AGD I,* 824 F.2d at 995.

For purposes of pre-granted abandonment, however, the issue is whether the Commission has shown that its choice of a twenty-year term-matching cap protects consumers against the exercise of pipeline market power. The petitioners note that longer-term contracts lock in customers and serve as a barrier to entry into the pipeline market by potential competitors. Rival pipelines will not build extensions to their system if the market for additional capacity has been foreclosed by long-term contracts with the existing pipeline. The Commission responds only that the pipeline plays no role in the competitive bidding process and thus cannot exercise market power. In the Commission's view, its choice of a twenty-year period reflects a reasonable weighing of the relative interests in preventing market constraint and encouraging market stability. None of these explanations, however, supports a finding that the twenty-year term-matching cap adequately protects against pipelines' pre-existing market power, which they enjoy by virtue of natural-monopoly conditions. The Commission has not explained why the twenty-year cap will prevent bidders on capacity-constrained pipelines from using long contract duration as a price surrogate to bid beyond the maximum approved rate, to the detriment of captive customers. If the maximum approved rate artificially limits a rival shipper's ability to outbid the existing shipper, the rival shipper may offer a higher-value contract by bidding up the contract duration instead.

A further concern with the Commission's choice of a twenty-year cap is the Commission's reasoning in selecting twenty years. Most of the commentators before the agency had proposed much shorter contract-term caps, such as five years. The Commission relied on the fact that twenty-year contracts have been "traditional" in the natural-gas industry. Order No. 636-A, ¶ 30,950, at 30,631 n.437. However, numerous commentators on rehearing of Order No. 636-A, as well as Commissioner Moler, *id.* at 30,679, pointed out that twenty-year contracts have been traditional only for contracts involving the construction of new facilities, where the pipeline requires a long-term contract to secure financing for the project, but not for contracts for the continuation of service after contract expiration. Indeed, both of the decisions that the Commission cited for the proposition that twenty-year contracts are customary were for new facilities. Also, renewal contracts appear more similar to the situation in the right-of-first-refusal mechanism. The Commission in its brief responds that the term-matching cap was designed "not to determine the length of typical gas contracts, but to establish a reasonable outer boundary for contract length, within which the ROFR might reasonably function." The petitioners' claim, however, is that because the Commission looked to the wrong type of contract to determine the typical contract length it may have selected an outer boundary that is longer than it would have been if the Commission had examined the duration of renewal contracts. The Commission failed to respond to this objection in the Order No. 636 series.

Both of these reasons—the Commission's failure to explain why the twenty-year cap will protect against pipelines' market power, and the failure to explain why it looked at new-construction contracts in arriving at the twenty-year figure—persuade us to remand the length of the contract term-matching condition to the Commission for further consideration. The right-of-first-refusal mechanism, incorporating the twin matching conditions of rate and contract term, is sufficiently justified. We remand only as to the Commission's reasons for adopting a twenty-year cap.

3. Requirement to discount

Petitioner Meridian Oil Inc., joined by the American Public Gas Association, challenges a different aspect of the right-of-first-refusal mechanism. The Commission declared that a pipeline need not accept a competing bid for a rate less than the maximum approved rate; in other words, "pipelines are not required to discount under the rule." Order No. 636-A, ¶ 30,950, at 30,629. The result is that a pipeline can choose between providing service to the highest bidder at a discounted rate and not providing service at all unless a shipper is willing to pay the maximum approved rate. In its comments to the Commission, Meridian urged that pipelines be required to accept the "best bid," which on pipelines on which capacity was not constrained would likely be less than the maximum approved rate. The Commission responded that it would

> not require pipelines to discount transportation rates. However, if a pipeline
> fails to attempt to maximize throughput, there is no guarantee that it will be

able to recover all the costs of its underutilized capacity from its firm customers
when it files its next rate case. Evidence that a pipeline refused to accept the
highest valued bid for capacity below the maximum rate will be given significant
weight during its next rate case.

Order No. 636-B, ¶ 61,272, at 62,028 (footnote omitted).

Meridian contends first that the Commission violated § 7(b) by authorizing pre-granted
abandonment without requiring the pipeline to discount. In Meridian's view, by forcing
the existing customer to pay the maximum approved rate to ensure continuity of service,
even if the competitive outcome as determined by the bidding process is a below-maximum
rate, the Commission has failed to protect customers against pipelines' market power. *See
Mobil Oil,* 498 U.S. at 227, 111 S.Ct. at 625; *AGA II,* 912 F.2d at 1517. However, as we held
above, the Commission has already protected against pipelines' market power by removing
the pipeline's ability to influence the bidding and by limiting the maximum rate that the
pipeline may charge. *See supra* at 76. The Commission first authorized selective discounting
by pipelines providing transportation under a Part 284 blanket certificate in Order No.
436, ¶ 30,665, at 31,540–48. *See* 18 C.F.R. § 284.7(d)(5); *AGD I,* 824 F.2d at 1007–13; *see
also Mississippi Valley Gas Co.,* 68 F.3d at 507. Given that the purpose of selective discounting
is to increase throughput by allowing pipelines to engage in price discrimination in favor
of demand-elastic customers, *AGD I,* 824 F.2d at 1011, Meridian's proposal that pipelines
be required to discount in favor of demand-inelastic, captive customers would render
meaningless pipelines' ability to charge up to the maximum approved rate. The § 7(b)
abandonment provisions protect customers against loss of service only if the customer is
willing to pay the maximum rate approved in a rate proceeding.

Meridian's second contention is that the Commission acted in an arbitrary and capricious
manner by not responding to Meridian's comments that the lack of a requirement to
discount would prevent the right-of-first-refusal mechanism from reflecting competitive
market forces on pipelines with excess capacity. The Commission responded to Meridian's
objection by assuring that a pipeline is not entitled to full cost recovery in its next rate
proceeding when it forgoes the opportunity to recover some of its fixed costs from a bid
rate between the minimum and maximum filed rates. Order No. 636-B, ¶ 61,272, at
62,028. Meridian has offered no reason why the Commission's rate scrutiny will not
provide sufficient incentives for pipelines to discount in appropriate circumstances. Accordingly, we affirm the Commission's decision not to require pipelines to discount in
the right-of-first-refusal process.

C. Curtailment

When supply shortages arose in the natural gas industry during the 1970s, the
Commission adopted end-use curtailment plans to protect high-priority customers from
an interruption of supply. *See generally Consolidated Edison Co. v. FERC,* 676 F.2d 763,
765–67 (D.C.Cir.1982); *North Carolina v. FERC,* 584 F.2d 1003, 1006–08 (D.C.Cir.1978).
In 1973, the Commission found itself "'impelled to direct curtailment on the basis of end
use rather than on the basis of contract simply because contracts do not necessarily serve
the public interest requirement of efficient allocation of this wasting resource.'" Order No.
467, 49 F.P.C. 85, 86 (quoting *Arkansas Louisiana Gas Co.,* 49 F.P.C. 53, 66 (1973)), *order
on reh'g,* 49 F.P.C. 217, *order on reh'g,* 49 F.P.C. 583 (1973), *petitions for review dismissed
sub nom. Pacific Gas & Elec. Co. v. FPC,* 506 F.2d 33 (D.C.Cir.1974). The Commission's
end-use curtailment schemes were essentially enacted into law by title IV of the Natural
Gas Policy Act of 1978 (NGPA), which establishes the following priority system:

Whenever there is an insufficient supply, under the Act first in line to receive gas are schools, small business, residences, hospitals, and all others for whom a curtailment of natural gas could endanger life, health, or the maintenance of physical property. After these "high-priority" users have been satisfied, next in line are those who will put the gas to "essential agricultural uses," followed by those who will use the gas for "essential industrial process or feedstock uses," followed by everyone else.

Process Gas Consumers Group v. United States Dep't of Agric., 657 F.2d 459, 460 (D.C.Cir.1981) (*Process Gas I*); *see also* 18 C.F.R. §§ 281.201–281.215 (the Commission's regulations implementing NGPA § 401).

With the introduction of stand-alone firm-transportation service in Order No. 436, the Commission distinguished for the first time between supply curtailment and capacity curtailment. Transportation service can suffer from a capacity interruption (such as a *force majeure* loss of capacity due to pipeline system failure or a pipeline's overbooking of capacity), whereas sales service can suffer from a shortage in the supply of gas. *See* Order No. 436, ¶ 30,665, at 31,515; Order No. 436-A, ¶ 30,675, at 31,652. The Commission's subsequent approach was to allow pipelines to adopt *pro rata* capacity curtailment (allocation proportional to the amount reserved, without regard to end use), *see, e.g., Texas Eastern Transmission Corp.*, 37 F.E.R.C. ¶ 61,260, at 61,692–93, 1986 WL 215099 (1986), *order on reh'g*, 41 F.E.R.C. ¶ 61,015 (1987), *aff'd sub nom. Texaco, Inc. v. FERC*, 886 F.2d 749 (5th Cir.1989), unless the parties agreed to end-use capacity curtailment on a particular pipeline, *see, e.g., Florida Gas Transmission Co.*, 51 F.E.R.C. ¶ 61,309, at 62,010–11, *order on reh'g*, 53 F.E.R.C. ¶ 61,396 (1990).

In *City of Mesa v. FERC*, 993 F.2d 888 (D.C.Cir.1993), the court reviewed a proceeding in which the Commission had approved end-use curtailment for supply shortages but *pro rata* curtailment for capacity interruption. *El Paso Natural Gas Co.*, 54 F.E.R.C. ¶ 61,316, at 61,928–29, *order on reh'g*, 56 F.E.R.C. ¶ 61,290, at 62,153–54 (1991). First, the court upheld the Commission's interpretation of the word "deliveries" in § 401(a) of the NGPA to refer only to pipelines' sale of gas, so that the statutory end-use curtailment scheme in title IV applied only to supply curtailment. 993 F.2d at 892–94; *see also Atlanta Gas Light Co. v. FERC*, 756 F.2d 191, 196–97 (D.C.Cir.1985). The court found that different treatment of supply and capacity curtailment was reasonable because high-priority users can "generally 'fend for themselves'" to protect against capacity interruption:

> Supply shortages usually lead to prolonged periods in which there is simply too little gas to serve the needs of all users. In contrast, capacity constraints occur when there is enough gas in the market but an unexpected event has caused a brief interruption in the movement of the gas to consumers. Additionally, capacity constraints, unlike supply shortages, may only affect the movement of gas on *part* of a pipeline, thereby allowing customers to receive their quota of gas by using alternate routes that skirt the pipeline bottleneck. These differences mean that pipeline customers can more easily adopt self-help measures to protect their high-priority end-users against the harmful effects of capacity curtailments than supply shortages.

City of Mesa, 993 F.2d at 894–95.

Although *City of Mesa* upheld the limitation of title IV of the NGPA to supply shortages, the court acknowledged that the NGA provided protections for capacity shortages. The court stated that "implicit in th[e] consumer protection mandate [of NGA §§ 4 and 7(e)] is a duty to assure that consumers, especially high-priority consumers, have continuous access to needed supplies of natural gas." 993 F.2d at 895. This duty arises because "'[n]o single factor in the Commission's duty to protect the public can be more important to the public than the continuity of service provided.'" *Id.* (quoting *Sunray Mid-Continent Oil Co. v. FPC*, 239 F.2d 97, 101 (10th Cir.1956), *rev'd on other grounds*, 353 U.S. 944, 77 S.Ct. 792, 1 L.Ed.2d 794 (1957)). The court emphasized that "since the NGA gives the FERC no specific guidance as to how to apply its broad mandates in a particular case, our review of the FERC's actions here is, again, quite limited." *Id.* In *City of Mesa,* the court concluded that the Commission had failed to engage in reasoned decision making when it approved a curtailment plan that protected "most" high-priority users rather than all such users. *Id.* at 896–97. The court noted that in Order No. 636-A the Commission had held that "self-help strategies were generally sufficient to assure protection of end-users and thus to meet NGA mandates" but did not further examine whether self-help measures were adequate to protect against capacity curtailment. *Id.* at 897.

In Order No. 636, which was issued before the court's decision in *City of Mesa,* the Commission continued without change its curtailment policies since Order No. 436. First, the Commission acknowledged that, as a policy matter, it chafed at the title IV end-use curtailment scheme for supply shortages but stated that it was bound by the statute. Order No. 636, ¶ 30,939, at 30,430; *see also Transcontinental Gas Pipe Line Corp.,* 57 F.E.R.C. ¶ 61,345, at 62,117 (1991). The Commission reiterated its reading of § 401(a) that limited its scope to pipelines' sale of gas. Order No. 636-A, ¶ 30,950, at 30,586–89. Second, the Commission maintained that self-help measures would allow the consumer-protection mandate of the NGA to be satisfied by *pro rata* capacity curtailment:

> The Commission believes that with deregulated wellhead sales and a growing menu of options for unbundled pipeline service, customers should rely on prudent planning, private contracts, and the marketplace to the maximum extent practicable to secure both their capacity and supply needs. In today's environment, LDC's [*sic*] and end-users no longer need to rely exclusively on their traditional pipeline supplier. Rather, to an ever-increasing degree they rely on private contracts with gas sellers, storage providers, and others; a more diverse portfolio of pipeline suppliers, where possible; local self-help measures (*e.g.,* local production, peak shaving and storage); and their own gas supply planning through choosing between an increasing array of unbundled service options.

Id. at 30,590.

The Commission's curtailment policies are challenged from both sides. Elizabethtown Gas Company contends that the Commission should have adopted *pro rata* curtailment for shortages in the supply of pipeline gas, and a group of small distributors contends that the Commission should have adopted end-use curtailment for capacity interruption and for shortages in the supply of third-party gas.

1. Supply curtailment of pipeline gas

Elizabethtown contends that because § 402(a) of the NGPA requires end-use curtailment only "to the maximum extent practicable," 15 U.S.C. § 3392(a), the declining role of pipelines as gas merchants renders end-use curtailment for shortages of pipeline gas no longer "practicable." The court recently rejected this argument, made by the same petitioner, in *Elizabethtown Gas Co. v. FERC,* 10 F.3d 866 (D.C.Cir.1993) (*Elizabethtown III*):

> This argument makes no sense to us. Even if [the pipeline] supplies a smaller share of the gas bought by each of the LDCs, the gas it does deliver to them could

still in times of shortage go first to "high-priority users." Accordingly, it seems entirely "practicable" to increase the level of protection for high priority users above that provided by the pro rata plan.

Id. at 874; *see also Process Gas Consumers Group v. United States,* 694 F.2d 778, 787–92 (D.C.Cir.1982) (en banc) (*Process Gas II*) (holding that the phrase "to the maximum extent practicable" gives the Commission broad powers). Although Elizabethtown contends that the near-elimination of pipelines as gas merchants following Order No. 636 requires us to reconsider our holding in *Elizabethtown III,* this change in the industry does not affect our reasoning that end-use curtailment remains "practicable" no matter how small the pipelines' share of the gas-sales market. The Commission recognized that the limitation of title IV of the NGPA to pipelines' sale of gas means that pipelines are disadvantaged vis-à-vis other gas merchants, but explained that it remained bound by the statute. Order No. 636, ¶ 30,929, at 30,430. Because we have already decided this question in *Elizabethtown III,* we affirm the Commission's decision that title IV of the NGPA mandates end-use curtailment for shortages in the supply of pipeline gas.

Elizabethtown also maintains that the Commission acted arbitrarily in not requiring high-priority users to compensate pipeline customers who lose gas supply under end-use curtailment. In *Elizabethtown III,* the court "held that a compensation provision is not necessarily inconsistent with § 401(a)." 10 F.3d at 875. Indeed, this court has long held that the Commission retains the authority under title IV of the NGPA to adopt a compensation scheme. *See Consolidated Edison Co. v. FERC,* 676 F.2d 763, 767 (D.C.Cir.1982); *cf. Elizabethtown Gas Co. v. FERC,* 575 F.2d 885, 887–89 (D.C.Cir.1978) (*Elizabethtown I*) (holding that the Commission has authority under the NGA to adopt a curtailment compensation plan). In *Elizabethtown III,* the court remanded with instructions for the Commission to consider Elizabethtown's "request for a curtailment compensation scheme." *Id.* In the Order No. 636 series, decided before the court's decision in *Elizabethtown III,* the Commission stated that its

> position on curtailment compensation plans is that the parties in the individual restructuring proceedings must explore the development of such schemes ... in the context of developing their individual curtailment plans and in the development of voluntary emergency contractual arrangements between shippers. However, the Commission believes that it would be contrary to the concept of the restructuring proceeding process and the negotiation and development of individually tailored curtailment allocation procedures and emergency mechanisms for it to mandate a generic compensation scheme.

Order No. 636-A, ¶ 30,950, at 30,592; *see also* Order No. 636, ¶ 30,929, at 30,430. The comments by the Commission in the Order No. 636 series continue the Commission's pattern of avoiding the question of curtailment compensation and do not exhibit the reasoned consideration of curtailment compensation that the court subsequently requested in *Elizabethtown III.*

The Commission has reconsidered the issue of curtailment compensation, however, on remand from *Elizabethtown III. See Transcontinental Pipe Line Corp.,* 72 F.E.R.C. ¶ 61,037, *reh'g denied,* 73 F.E.R.C. ¶ 61,357 (1995). In those proceedings, the Commission

> conclude[d] that compensation is needed to render Transco's gas supply curtailment plan just and reasonable. The priority curtailment plan affects the contractual rights of Transco's customers by altering the *pro rata* allocation of curtailed supplies so that higher priority customers can obtain gas that would otherwise go to lower priority customers.

72 F.E.R.C. ¶ The Commission rejected Elizabethtown's proposed compensation scheme, however, in favor of requiring the higher-priority customer to pay: (1) 150% of the spot market price for gas if the lower-priority customer was unable to cover (locate replacement gas on the spot market), or (2) the difference between the cover price and the original contract price if the lower-priority customer was able to cover. *Id.* at 61,237–38.

In light of the Commission's *Transcontinental* decision, the issue of curtailment compensation is not ripe for review. The Commission enjoys broad discretion whether to adopt a compensation scheme on a generic basis or in pipeline-specific proceedings. *See Mobil Oil,* 498 U.S. at 230, 111 S.Ct. at 627. If Elizabethtown remains aggrieved by the Commission's decision to accept its general argument but fashion a different compensation mechanism, then it may seek relief in review of the *Transcontinental* decision. We therefore express no opinion on the appropriateness of any particular curtailment compensation plan.

2. Capacity curtailment

The small distributor petitioner group, on the other hand, contends that *pro rata* capacity curtailment violates the consumer-protection mandate of the NGA. We review the Commission's policy on *pro rata* curtailment to determine whether it is "just and reasonable" under § 4 and whether it serves the "present or future public convenience and necessity" under § 7(e). *See City of Mesa,* 993 F.2d at 895. The Commission decided that the consumer-protection mandate of the NGA did not require it to adopt end-use capacity curtailment across the board and promised to address the issue in each pipeline restructuring proceeding. Order No. 636-A, ¶ 30,950, at 30,591–92. Indeed, the Commission has broad latitude on whether to effectuate its policies in generic rulemakings or in individual-pipeline adjudications. *Mobil Oil,* 498 U.S. at 230, 111 S.Ct. at 627. The issue presented to us, then, is whether the Commission's decision that the NGA does not require end-use curtailment in all circumstances is " 'reasoned, principled, and based upon the record.' " *Great Lakes Gas Transmission Ltd. Partnership v. FERC,* 984 F.2d 426, 432 (D.C.Cir.1993) (quoting *Columbia Gas Transmission Corp. v. FERC,* 628 F.2d 578, 593 (D.C.Cir.1979)).

The Commission explained that Order No. 636 had allowed the development of market structures that would enable customers to take independent, market-based steps to avoid the need for Commission-mandated end-use curtailment. Order No. 636-A, ¶ 30,950, at 30,590. Moreover, the Commission found that since the enactment of the NGPA in 1978 "the industry has not experienced shortages beyond isolated, short-lived dislocation," *id.* at 30,591, and "gas has always flowed according to the dictate of the market, *i.e.,* to the heat sensitive users who need it most and who are thus willing to pay the prevailing market price for it." *Id.* at 30,592. This experience with the industry provides substantial evidence for the Commission's conclusion that end-use curtailment is not required in all circumstances.

We are unpersuaded, particularly in light of the Commission's own actions in the restructuring proceedings, that *pro rata* capacity curtailment would adequately protect all high-priority customers on all pipelines. *Cf. City of Mesa,* 993 F.2d at 896–97. The Commission's market-based alternatives for customers to avoid curtailment fall into the following categories: (1) arrangements with other pipelines; (2) arrangements with other gas sellers; (3) arrangements for gas storage; (4) arrangements with other customers (including the capacity-release mechanism); and (5) "peak shaving." First, arrangements with other pipelines are more widely available after Order No. 636, such as by using different pipelines that connect to one "market center," but a capacity constraint on a pipeline will still cut off delivery to any "captive customers," no matter how many transportation options some other customers may have. Second, arrangements with other gas sellers are by definition relevant only to supply curtailment, not to capacity curtailment. Third, arrangements for gas storage are unhelpful if the capacity interruption occurs at a point between the contract-storage area and the customer's receipt point. Fourth, obtaining gas from other customers, whether through the capacity-release mechanism or otherwise, depends upon the willingness of lower-priority customers to forgo deliveries. Fifth, practices such as "peak shaving" (letting a little gas go a longer way) can temporarily help to alleviate curtailment problems but cannot ensure continuous service if the interruption lasts too long. None of these market-based solutions, therefore, can guarantee continuous service to all high-priority customers in cases of capacity interruptions. Many of the market-based solutions fail to acknowledge that many customers have far less control over access to pipeline capacity than they do over gas supply. In addition, some of the self-help mechanisms will be more readily available to larger pipeline customers. *City of Mesa*, 993 F.2d at 897 n. 7.

Yet the Commission has not applied Order No. 636 in the restructuring proceedings to preclude the development of curtailment plans that provide more protection to higher-priority users. For example, on remand from *City of Mesa*, the Commission reiterated its general policy that "customers can, and should, avail themselves of self-help methods to obtain their needed supplies" but, in light of the decision in *City of Mesa*, ordered El Paso to "includ[e] provisions giving relief to any high priority shipper when that shipper has exercised all other self-help remedies in times of *bona fide* emergencies." *El Paso Natural Gas Co.*, 69 F.E.R.C.¶ 61,164, at 61,624 (1994), *order on reh'g*, 72 F.E.R.C.¶ 61,042, *reh'g denied*, 73 F.E.R.C. ¶ 61,074 (1995). In another restructuring proceeding, the Commission approved a settlement and found its curtailment plan consistent with *City of Mesa* because it "provides an exemption from *pro rata* curtailment whenever necessary to avoid irreparable injury to life or property." *Florida Gas Transmission Co.*, 70 F.E.R.C. ¶ 61,017, at 61,061 (1995). On occasions, the Commission has suggested that "there may be extraordinary circumstances when reasonable self-help efforts are insufficient, even for large customers," such that some emergency protections may always be required for certain *force majeure* capacity interruptions. *El Paso*, 69 F.E.R.C. ¶ 61,164, at 61,624; *see also United Gas Pipe Line Co.*, 65 F.E.R.C. ¶ 61,006, at 61,092, *reh'g denied sub nom. Koch Gateway Pipeline Co.*, 65 F.E.R.C. ¶ 61,338, at 62,630–31 (1993).

We need not reach the issue whether the adoption of a pure *pro rata* capacity-curtailment scheme on a generic basis would comply with the Commission's duty under the NGA to ensure that "high-priority consumers[ ] have continuous access to needed supplies of natural gas." *City of Mesa*, 993 F.2d at 895. All the Commission did in Order No. 636 was to decide not to require end-use capacity curtailment for all pipelines. Because the Commission expressly declared that it would re-examine the suitability of pure *pro rata* capacity curtailment for customers on each pipeline, Order No. 636-A, ¶ 30,950, at 30,591–92, we construe any indications that *pro rata* curtailment will be the default as unreviewable policy statements under § 4(b)(A) of the Administrative Procedure Act, 5 U.S.C. § 553(b)(A). *See Pacific Gas & Elec. Co. v. FPC*, 506 F.2d 33, 39 (D.C.Cir.1974). The manner in which the Commission has applied its curtailment policy in the restructuring proceedings supports our conclusion that any preference for *pro rata* schemes is not suitable for review. *See Public Citizen, Inc. v. NRC*, 940 F.2d 679, 682–83 (D.C.Cir.1991). Accordingly, the compliance of specific curtailment plans with the NGA's consumer-protection mandate remains open on review of the restructuring proceedings.

We uphold the Commission's decision not to require end-use curtailment on a generic basis for capacity curtailment but to proceed instead on a case-by-case basis.

3. Supply curtailment of third-party gas

Finally, the small distributor petitioners contend that the consumer-protection mandate of the NGA requires the Commission to adopt end-use curtailment for shortages in the supply of third-party gas. The petitioners concede that title IV of the NGPA applies only to pipelines' sale of gas, but urge that §§ 4 and 7(e) of the NGA require some form of end-use curtailment for the sale of gas by producers and other third parties. The Commission declined to "impos[e] ... the industry-wide, end-use supply curtailment scheme envisioned by the petitioners" because "the best protection against, and remedy for, supply shortages [i]s to allow the market to establish the price for gas." Order No. 636-A, ¶ 30,950, at 30,591.

As an initial matter, a group of intervenors in support of the Commission maintains that the Commission lacks jurisdiction under § 1(b) to enact a curtailment plan for third-party gas. But the Supreme Court has held expressly that "curtailment plans are aspects of [the Commission's] 'transportation' and not its 'sales' jurisdiction." *Louisiana Power & Light,* 406 U.S. at 641, 92 S.Ct. at 1839 (citing *Panhandle Eastern Pipe Line Co. v. Public Serv. Comm'n,* 332 U.S. 507, 523, 68 S.Ct. 190, 198, 92 L.Ed. 128 (1947)). The intervenors rely on a Fifth Circuit case, *Sebring Utilities Commission v. FERC,* 591 F.2d 1003 (5th Cir.), *cert. denied,* 444 U.S. 879, 100 S.Ct. 167, 62 L.Ed.2d 109 (1979), in which the court indicated that the Commission would not have jurisdiction to order curtailment of gas not owned by a statutory "natural-gas company." *Id.* at 1016–19. However, the ownership of the gas is not relevant to the Commission's transportation jurisdiction because in adopting a curtailment scheme the Commission exercises its jurisdiction over the pipeline, iwhich incorporates any curtailment plan into its tariff. If we were to follow *Sebring,* then the Commission would also lack jurisdiction to regulate capacity curtailment of third-party gas—a proposition implicitly rejected by the *City of Mesa* court, which in remanding on the capacity-curtailment issue assumed that the Commission had jurisdiction over curtailment plans for third-party gas. 993 F.2d at 895–98. Moreover, *Sebring* was decided before the unbundling of sales from transportation, at a time when virtually all gas was pipeline-owned. Under the principles of *Louisiana Power & Light,* the Commission's transportation jurisdiction extends to supply curtailment of third-party gas.

The Commission decided that an end-use supply curtailment plan for third-party gas was not required to ensure high-priority customers "continuous access to needed supplies of natural gas." *City of Mesa,* 993 F.2d at 895. As discussed with respect to capacity curtailment, *see supra* at 83–84, the Commission provided a list of market-based alternatives to secure the continuous supply of gas that is convincing in the context of supply curtailment. Although the petitioners posit a *force majeure* supply shortage that the market-based protections would not cover, namely a "freeze-off" of wells that would prevent all producers from producing sufficient quantities of gas during cold weather, the petitioners have provided no evidence that such an event has ever occurred or is likely to occur in the future. The Commission's decision that such an occurrence is unlikely "given foreseeable supply conditions" is reasonable. Order No. 636-A, ¶ 30,950, at 30,591. In addition, the Commission noted that title III of the NGPA, 15 U.S.C. §§ 3361–3364, authorizes the President to "declare a natural gas supply emergency" in the event of "a severe natural gas shortage, endangering the supply of natural gas for high-priority uses." *Id.* § 3361(a); *see* Order No. 636-A, ¶ 30,950, at 30,591.

Thus, the Commission has complied with the continuity-of-service guarantee of the NGA, as articulated in *City of Mesa,* with respect to supply shortages of third-party gas.

     ....

Notes & Questions

1. How are the natural gas markets and electricity markets similar after FERC Order No. 636 and FERC Order No. 888? How are they different? Note that both orders are good examples of what some people consider deregulation of the market, when in fact it is really modified regulation. That is, some restrictions on the market are being changed, but it is not as though FERC is eliminating its role in the market.

2. Notice the court's discussion of the NGPA and other natural gas law. Pull those laws out and try to discern what the policy goals were for those laws. How effective were they? What do you think was Congress trying to do?

3. *Practice Note*: Interstate pipelines are regulated by FERC. Intrastate pipelines are different. For example, Hinshaw pipelines are local distribution pipelines that served by interstate pipelines. Hinshaw pipelines are not under FERC's jurisdiction, as set forth in section 1(c) of the Natural Gas Act. Hinshaw pipelines can seek a "Blanket Certificate" to transport natural gas for (1) any interstate pipeline or (2) any local distribution company that is served by an interstate pipeline. To do so, though, the pipeline with the Blanket Certificate must file rates, charges, and operating conditions with FERC as required in section 284.224 of FERC's regulations. Non-Hinshaw intrastate pipelines are regulated under section 311 of the Natural Gas Policy Act (NGPA).

Chapter 6

Energy and Environmental Regulation and Policies

A. Introduction

Environmental regulation came about, in major part, because of energy use for industrial and residential consumers. Still, environmental law and energy law often operate in separate silos, which can lead to bad policy and a poor understanding of the full scope of legal, regulatory, and business issues in the energy sector. As Professor Lincoln Davies explains:

> It is well-documented that energy and environmental law operate in separate worlds that rarely overlap, despite the fact that their subject matters are intrinsically intertwined. Energy and the environment are two sides of the same problem. Energy law dictates our resource use; environmental law controls the effects of that use. Energy use drives our ecological problems; those problems cause us to question how we use energy.

Lincoln L. Davies, *Power Forward: The Argument for a National RPS*, 42 Conn. L. Rev. 1339, 1391-92 (2010) (footnotes omitted).

This chapter begins with an overview of some of the key environmental laws impacting the energy sector and is followed by key energy policies including renewable resource mandates and incentives for traditional and renewables energy sources.

1. Vocabulary and Concepts

One of the great challenges in energy law is the host of "alphabet soup" that accompanies so much of the area. U.S. environmental law is similarly challenging. From the Clean Air Act (CAA) to the Clean Water Act (CWA), acronyms and abbreviations abound. Below are some of the key terms that you will encounter in this book (and in practice in this area). The terms are described in more detail in the readings, but it's worth having an easy reference for just the full terms. As you read through this chapter, consider adding definitions to these terms to help you learn them.

Key Environmental Law Terms

> **EA:** Environmental Assessment
>
> **EIS:** Environmental Impact Statement
>
> **FONSI:** Finding of No Significant Impact
>
> **NAA:** Non-attainment Area
>
> **NAAQS:** National Ambient Air Quality Standards
>
> **NEPA:** National Environmental Policy Act of 1969
>
> **NESHAPs:** National Emissions Standards for Hazardous Air Pollutants
>
> **NSPS:** New Source Performance Standards
>
> **PSD:** Prevention of Significant Deterioration
>
> **SIPs:** State Implementation Plans

Renewable Energy Terms and Concepts

Renewable Portfolio Standard (RPS): A legislative or regulatory mandate, present in 29 states and the District of Columbia, that requires a utility to procure a certain amount of electricity from renewable resources (as defined in the mandate). The amount can be self-generated or the utility can pay for it (using RECs, see below). Also known as a **Renewable Electricity Standard (RES).**

Renewable Energy Credits (RECs): The "green" or renewable component of electricity that is generated from renewable resources. RECs can be sold with the electricity generated or as a separate commodity.

Renewable Portfolio Goal (RPG): Similar to an RPS, the RPG is styled in the same manner, but it does not have penalties for failures to comply.

Public Utility Regulatory Policies Act of 1978 (PURPA): A federal law that required utilities to purchase renewable energy from **Qualifying Facilities (QFs)**, at avoided cost (see below).

Avoided Cost: Often defined as the cost a public utility would incur to produce one more unit of power or purchase from another source if it were not buying from a QF.

2. Client Issue

You have an investment company client who is looking into a major purchase. The client is considering the purchase of a company that owns a coal-fired electricity generating facility. The client is running the numbers for the sales costs, but has asked you to compile a list of risks and potential risks under the Clean Air Act and Clean Water Act so that they can develop a list of due diligence issues for their team to consider. (Due diligence is the investigation or audit of a potential acquisition or other investment. The process is used to confirm the material facts of the transaction.) As you read this chapter, develop your list of possible items of question and concern.

B. Environmental Laws

1. Clean Air Act

Understanding the Clean Air Act

available at http://www.epa.gov/air/caa/peg/understand.html

Brief History of the Clean Air Act

In October 1948, a thick cloud of air pollution formed above the industrial town of Donora, Pennsylvania. The cloud, which lingered for five days, killed 20 people and caused sickness in 6,000 of the town's 14,000 people. In 1952, over 3,000 people died in what became known as London's "Killer Fog." The smog was so thick that buses could not run without guides walking ahead of them carrying lanterns.

Events like these alerted us to the dangers that air pollution poses to public health. Several federal and state laws were passed, including the original Clean Air Act of 1963, which established funding for the study and the cleanup of air pollution. But there was no comprehensive federal response to address air pollution until Congress passed a much stronger Clean Air Act in 1970. That same year Congress created the EPA and gave it the primary role in carrying out the law. Since 1970, EPA has been responsible for a variety of Clean Air Act programs to reduce air pollution nationwide.

In 1990, Congress dramatically revised and expanded the Clean Air Act, providing EPA even broader authority to implement and enforce regulations reducing air pollutant emissions. The 1990 Amendments also placed an increased emphasis on more cost-effective approaches to reduce air pollution.

Clean Air Act Roles and Responsibilities

The Clean Air Act is a federal law covering the entire country. However, states, tribes and local governments do a lot of the work to meet the Act's requirements. For example, representatives from these agencies work with companies to reduce air pollution. They also review and approve permit applications for industries or chemical processes.

EPA's Role

Under the Clean Air Act, EPA sets limits on certain air pollutants, including setting limits on how much can be in the air anywhere in the United States. This helps to ensure basic health and environmental protection from air pollution for all Americans. The Clean Air Act also gives EPA the authority to limit emissions of air pollutants coming from sources like chemical plants, utilities, and steel mills. Individual states or tribes may have stronger air pollution laws, but they may not have weaker pollution limits than those set by EPA.

EPA must approve state, tribal, and local agency plans for reducing air pollution. If a plan does not meet the necessary requirements, EPA can issue sanctions against the state and, if necessary, take over enforcing the Clean Air Act in that area.

EPA assists state, tribal, and local agencies by providing research, expert studies, engineering designs, and funding to support clean air progress. Since 1970, Congress and the EPA have provided several billion dollars to the states, local agencies, and tribal nations to accomplish this.

State and Local Governments' Role

It makes sense for state and local air pollution agencies to take the lead in carrying out the Clean Air Act. They are able to develop solutions for pollution problems that require special understanding of local industries, geography, housing, and travel patterns, as well as other factors.

State, local, and tribal governments also monitor air quality, inspect facilities under their jurisdictions and enforce Clean Air Act regulations.

States have to develop State Implementation Plans (SIPs) that outline how each state will control air pollution under the Clean Air Act. A SIP is a collection of the regulations, programs and policies that a state will use to clean up polluted areas. The states must involve the public and industries through hearings and opportunities to comment on the development of each state plan.

Tribal Nations' Role

In its 1990 revision of the Clean Air Act, Congress recognized that Indian Tribes have the authority to implement air pollution control programs.

EPA's Tribal Authority Rule gives Tribes the ability to develop air quality management programs, write rules to reduce air pollution and implement and enforce their rules in Indian Country. While state and local agencies are responsible for all Clean Air Act requirements, Tribes may develop and implement only those parts of the Clean Air Act that are appropriate for their lands.

––––––––––

Key Elements of the Clean Air Act http://www.epa.gov/air/caa/peg/elements.html

EPA's mission is to protect human health and the environment. To achieve this mission, EPA implements a variety of programs under the Clean Air Act that focus on:

- reducing outdoor, or ambient, concentrations of air pollutants that cause smog, haze, acid rain, and other problems;
- reducing emissions of toxic air pollutants that are known to, or are suspected of, causing cancer or other serious health effects; and
- phasing out production and use of chemicals that destroy stratospheric ozone.

These pollutants come from stationary sources (like chemical plants, gas stations, and power plants) and mobile sources (like cars, trucks, and planes).

2. Clean Water Act

Summary of the Clean Water Act
33 U.S.C. § 1251 et seq. (1972)
http://www2.epa.gov/laws-regulations/summary-clean-water-act

The Clean Water Act (CWA) establishes the basic structure for regulating discharges of pollutants into the waters of the United States and regulating quality standards for surface waters. The basis of the CWA was enacted in 1948 and was called the Federal Water Pollution Control Act, but the Act was significantly reorganized and expanded in 1972. "Clean Water Act" became the Act's common name with amendments in 1972.

Under the CWA, EPA has implemented pollution control programs such as setting wastewater standards for industry. We have also set water quality standards for all contaminants in surface waters.

The CWA made it unlawful to discharge any pollutant from a point source into navigable waters, unless a permit was obtained. EPA's National Pollutant Discharge Elimination System (NPDES) permit program controls discharges. Point sources are discrete conveyances such as pipes or man-made ditches. Individual homes that are connected to a municipal system, use a septic system, or do not have a surface discharge do not need an NPDES permit; however, industrial, municipal, and other facilities must obtain permits if their discharges go directly to surface waters.

EPA, *History of the Clean Water Act*

http://www2.epa.gov/laws-regulations/history-clean-water-act

The Federal Water Pollution Control Act of 1948 was the first major U.S. law to address water pollution. Growing public awareness and concern for controlling water pollution led to sweeping amendments in 1972. As amended in 1972, the law became commonly known as the Clean Water Act (CWA).

The 1972 amendments:

- Established the basic structure for regulating pollutants discharges into the waters of the United States.

- Gave EPA the authority to implement pollution control programs such as setting wastewater standards for industry.

- Maintained existing requirements to set water quality standards for all contaminants in surface waters.

- Made it unlawful for any person to discharge any pollutant from a point source into navigable waters, unless a permit was obtained under its provisions.

- Funded the construction of sewage treatment plants under the construction grants program.

- Recognized the need for planning to address the critical problems posed by nonpoint source pollution.

Subsequent amendments modified some of the earlier CWA provisions. Revisions in 1981 streamlined the municipal construction grants process, improving the capabilities of treatment plants built under the program. Changes in 1987 phased out the construction grants program, replacing it with the State Water Pollution Control Revolving Fund, more commonly known as the Clean Water State Revolving Fund. This new funding strategy addressed water quality needs by building on EPA-state partnerships.

Over the years, many other laws have changed parts of the Clean Water Act. Title I of the Great Lakes Critical Programs Act of 1990, for example, put into place parts of the Great Lakes Water Quality Agreement of 1978, signed by the U.S. and Canada, where the two nations agreed to reduce certain toxic pollutants in the Great Lakes. That law required EPA to establish water quality criteria for the Great Lakes addressing 29 toxic pollutants with maximum levels that are safe for humans, wildlife, and aquatic life. It also required EPA to help the States implement the criteria on a specific schedule.

The Clean Water Act: Protecting and Restoring Our Nation's Waters

http://water.epa.gov/action/cleanwater40/cwa101.cfm

Forty years ago, in the midst of a national concern about untreated sewage, industrial and toxic discharges, destruction of wetlands, and contaminated runoff, the principal law to protect the nation's waters was passed. Originally enacted in 1948 to control water pollution primarily based on state and local efforts, the Federal Water Pollution Control Act, or Clean Water Act (CWA), was totally revised in 1972 to give the Act its current shape. The CWA set a new national goal "to restore and maintain the chemical, physical, and biological integrity of the Nation's waters", with interim goals that all waters be fishable and swimmable where possible. The Act embodied a new federal-state partnership, where federal guidelines, objectives and limits were to be set under the authority of the U.S. Environmental Protection Agency, while states, territories and authorized tribes would largely administer and enforce the CWA programs, with significant federal technical and financial assistance. The Act also gave citizens a strong role to play in protecting and restoring waters.

The CWA specifies that all discharges into the nation's waters are unlawful unless authorized by a permit and sets baseline, across-the-board technology-based controls for municipalities and industry. It requires all dischargers to meet additional, stricter pollutant controls where needed to meet water quality targets and requires federal approval of these standards. It also protects wetlands by requiring "dredge and fill" permits. The CWA authorizes federal financial assistance to states and municipalities to help achieve these national water goals. The Act has robust enforcement provisions and gives citizens a strong role to play in watershed protection. Congress has revised the Act, most notably in 1987, where it established a comprehensive program for controlling toxic pollutants and stormwater discharges, directed states to develop and implement voluntary nonpoint pollution management programs, and encouraged states to pursue groundwater protection. Notwithstanding these improvements, the 1972 statute, its regulatory provisions and the institutions that were created 40 years ago, still make up the bulk of the framework for protecting and restoring the nation's rivers, streams, lakes, wetlands and coastal waters.

EPA, *Core Programs to Protect and Restore the Nation's Waters*

http://water.epa.gov/action/cleanwater40/cwa101.cfm

Establishing the Standards to Measure Success

Water quality standards are the regulatory and scientific foundation of the CWA's water protection programs. Under the Act, states and authorized tribes establish water quality targets that define the goals and limits for waters within their jurisdictions. These standards are then used to determine which waters must be cleaned up, how much pollution can be discharged, and what is needed for protection. To help achieve these targets, EPA reviews and approves state and tribal standards; develops replacement standards where needed, and provides technical and scientific support for development of standards.

Identifying Polluted Waters and Developing Plans to Restore Them

Every two years states are required to assess the condition of surface waters and submit lists of those that are too polluted to meet water quality standards (called impaired waters). The Act requires that states establish priorities to address these impaired waters by developing water restoration plans (also known as Total Maximum Daily Loads or TMDLs). TMDLs identify pollutant load limits necessary to clean up the water to meet water quality standards and then quantify a pollutant "budget" for different sources of pollutants. This water restoration plan is then implemented via permit requirements and through a variety of other local, state or federal water protection programs.

Permitting Discharges of Pollutants from Point Sources

The National Pollutant Discharge Elimination System (NPDES) is one of the key regulatory tools available in the CWA to protect and restore the nation's waters. The law requires that any point source facility that discharges polluted wastewater into a body of water must first obtain a permit from the EPA or their designated representative (46 States and 1 Territory are delegated). Permits are issued once the operator of the facility shows that they are using the best available technology to reduce pollutants from their discharges. In addition, water quality standards have been established under the CWA as targets for individual bodies of water. These may also be used to require additional mitigation measures before issuing a permit if water quality targets have not been met. NPDES permitted sources include municipal and industrial wastewater, wet weather discharges including stormwater sources, combined sewer and sanitary sewer overflows, and large concentrated animal feeding operations.

Addressing diffuse, nonpoint sources of pollution

Prior to 1987, CWA programs were primarily directed at point source pollution. CWA Section 319 changed that by creating a new federal program that provides money to states, tribes, and territories for the development of programs to reduce pollution from unregulated, diffuse sources, such as agriculture. EPA grants are used to identify waters impaired by nonpoint sources, help stakeholders implement best management practices to reduce runoff, and monitor and evaluate progress to restore waters.

Protecting Wetlands

The CWA regulates the discharge of dredged or fill material into waters of the U.S., including wetlands. Activities regulated include fill for development, water resource projects (such as dams and levees), infrastructure development (such as highways and airports) and mining projects. The Act requires the issuance of a permit before dredged or fill material may be discharged into waters of the U.S., unless the activity is exempt (e.g., certain farming and forestry activities).

Protecting Coastal Waters through the National Estuary Program

The National Estuary Program (NEP) is a unique community-based program designed to restore and maintain the water quality and ecological integrity of 28 estuaries of national significance. The NEP uses an effective watershed-based ecosystem planning approach to connect upstream pollution sources with downstream impacts. The program operates through partnerships among federal, state and local agencies; nonprofit organizations; industry; academia; environmental and business groups; and community residents.

Protecting Large Aquatic Ecosystems

The CWA authorizes EPA to administer programs for 10 large aquatic ecosystems, such as South Florida, Gulf of Mexico and the Pacific Islands. These geographic-based programs involve private and public stakeholders to address specific problems, such as loss of habitat, polluted runoff and invasive species. Their activities include water quality monitoring, working with states to negotiate pollution controls, and educating citizens regarding the causes and cures for these environmental problems. EPA provides funding, guidance and technical support that builds the capacity of these programs to restore and protect their ecosystems with input from local partners.

Enforcement

The NPDES permit is the CWA's principal enforcement tool. EPA may issue a compliance order or bring a civil suit in U.S. district court when there are violations of the terms of a permit. Further, the CWA provides for substantial penalties for permit violators. The CWA also allows individuals to bring a citizen suit in U.S. district court against persons who violate a permit limit or standard. Individuals may also bring citizen suits against EPA's Administrator (or equivalent state official) for failure to carry out their duties as specified under the CWA.

The Watershed Approach

Evolution of CWA programs during the last 40 years has also included a shift from a program-by-program, source-by-source, pollutant-by-pollutant approach to a more integrated, place-based watershed protection strategy. Under the watershed approach, equal emphasis is placed on protecting healthy waters and restoring impaired ones, and a full array of issues are addressed, not just those subject to CWA regulatory authority. Involving multiple stakeholders at the state, tribal and local level to develop and implement strategies for achieving and maintaining state water quality and other environmental goals is another hallmark of this approach.

Financial Assistance

Federal law has authorized grants for planning, design and construction of municipal sewage treatment facilities since 1956, but Congress greatly expanded this Construction Grants Program in 1972 to help cities meet the CWA's new pollution control requirements. In 1987, Congress voted to phase out this direct grant program and replace it with the Clean Water State Revolving Fund. Under this financial approach, EPA provides annual capitalization grants to states, who in turn provide low interest loans for a wide variety of water quality improvement projects. States must match the federal funds. Some funds are also provided to territories and tribes to be used as grants for municipal wastewater treatment projects. Since its inception, in excess of $84 billion has been provided via more than 28,000 agreements related to wastewater treatment, nonpoint source runoff, and watershed and estuary management. The CWA section 106 also authorizes additional federal grants to states, tries and territories to support the development and operation of core CWA programs such as monitoring, developing water quality standards, wetlands and watershed planning.

3. NEPA

Under National Environmental Policy Act of 1969, 42 U.S.C. §§ 4321-4370 (2012), federal actions require an environmental assessment (EA), unless an agency decides to jump past the EA and move directly to an environmental impact statement (EIS). 40 C.F.R. § 1501.3 (a) The relevant regulation provides: "Agencies shall prepare an environmental assessment (§ 1508.9) when necessary under the procedures adopted by individual agencies to supplement these regulations as described in § 1507.3. An assessment is not necessary if the agency has decided to prepare an environmental impact statement."

After an agency decides to proceed with an EA, the agency (based on the EA) may decide that further review is needed. In that case, the agency must then create an environmental impact statement. 42 U.S.C. § 4332(C) (2000). The other option is that the EA could lead to a finding of no significant impact (FONSI). 40 C.F.R. § 1501.4. If the EA leads to a FONSI, it is not does not mean that the EA found no impact (or effect) from the proposed action, simply that that the impact was not deemed significant. The relevant regulation, 40 C.F.R. § 1508.13 explains: "Finding of no significant impact means a document by a Federal agency briefly presenting the reasons why an action, not otherwise excluded (§ 1508.4), will not have a significant effect on the human environment and for which an environmental impact statement therefore will not be prepared."

The EPA explains the "NEPA Basics" at http://www.epa.gov/compliance/basics/nepa.html, (last updated 6/25/2012):

EPA, *National Environmental Policy Act (NEPA)*

...

Basic Information

...

NEPA Requirements

Title I of NEPA contains a Declaration of National Environmental Policy which requires the federal government to use all practicable means to create and maintain conditions under which man and nature can exist in productive harmony. Section 102 requires federal agencies to incorporate environmental considerations in their planning and decision-making through a systematic interdisciplinary approach. Specifically, all federal agencies are to prepare detailed statements assessing the environmental impact of and alternatives to major federal actions significantly affecting the environment. These statements are commonly referred to as environmental impact statements (EISs).

Title II of NEPA establishes the Council on Environmental Quality (CEQ).

Oversight Of NEPA

The Council on Environmental Quality, which is headed by a fulltime Chair, oversees NEPA. A staff assists the Council. The duties and functions of the Council are listed in Title II, Section 204 of NEPA and include:

- Gathering information on the conditions and trends in environmental quality
- Evaluating federal programs in light of the goals established in Title I of the Act
- Developing and promoting national policies to improve environmental quality
- Conducting studies, surveys, research, and analyses relating to ecosystems and environmental quality.

Implementation

In 1978, CEQ promulgated regulations [40 CFR Parts 1500-15081] implementing NEPA which are binding on all federal agencies. The regulations address the procedural provisions of NEPA and the administration of the NEPA process, including preparation of EISs. To date, the only change in the NEPA regulations occurred on May 27, 1986, when CEQ amended Section 1502.22 of its regulations to clarify how agencies are to carry out their environmental evaluations in situations where information is incomplete or unavailable.

CEQ has also issued guidance on various aspects of the regulations including: an information document on "Forty Most Asked Questions Concerning CEQ's National Environmental Policy Act," Scoping Guidance, and Guidance Regarding NEPA Regulations. Additionally, most federal agencies have promulgated their own NEPA regulations and guidance which generally follow the CEQ procedures but are tailored for the specific mission and activities of the agency.

The NEPA Process

The NEPA process consists of an evaluation of the environmental effects of a federal undertaking including its alternatives. There are three levels of analysis: categorical exclusion determination; preparation of an environmental assessment/finding of no significant impact (EA/FONSI); and preparation of an environmental impact statement (EIS).

Categorical Exclusion: At the first level, an undertaking may be categorically excluded from a detailed environmental analysis if it meets certain criteria which a federal agency has previously determined as having no significant environmental impact. A number of agencies have developed lists of actions which are normally categorically excluded from environmental evaluation under their NEPA regulations.

EA/FONSI: At the second level of analysis, a federal agency prepares a written environmental assessment (EA) to determine whether or not a federal undertaking would significantly affect the environment. If the answer is no, the agency issues a finding of no significant impact (FONSI). The FONSI may address measures which an agency will take to mitigate potentially significant impacts.

EIS: If the EA determines that the environmental consequences of a proposed federal undertaking may be significant, an EIS is prepared. An EIS is a more detailed evaluation of the proposed action and alternatives. The public, other federal agencies and outside parties may provide input into the preparation of an EIS and then comment on the draft EIS when it is completed.

If a federal agency anticipates that an undertaking may significantly impact the environment, or if a project is environmentally controversial, a federal agency may choose to prepare an EIS without having to first prepare an EA.

After a final EIS is prepared and at the time of its decision, a federal agency will prepare a public record of its decision addressing how the findings of the EIS, including consideration of alternatives, were incorporated into the agency's decision-making process.

EA And EIS Components

An EA is described in Section 1508.9 of the CEQ NEPA regulations. Generally, an EA includes brief discussions of the following:

- The need for the proposal

- Alternatives (when there is an unresolved conflict concerning alternative uses of available resources)
- The environmental impacts of the proposed action and alternatives
- A listing of agencies and persons consulted.

An EIS, which is described in Part 1502 of the regulations, should include:

- Discussions of the purpose of and need for the action
- Alternatives
- The affected environment
- The environmental consequences of the proposed action
- Lists of preparers, agencies, organizations and persons to whom the statement is sent
- An index
- An appendix (if any)

Federal Agency Role

The role of a federal agency in the NEPA process depends on the agency's expertise and relationship to the proposed undertaking. The agency carrying out the federal action is responsible for complying with the requirements of NEPA.

Lead Agency: In some cases, there may be more than one federal agency involved in an undertaking. In this situation, a lead agency is designated to supervise preparation of the environmental analysis. Federal agencies, together with state, tribal or local agencies, may act as joint lead agencies.

Cooperating Agency: A federal, state, tribal or local agency having special expertise with respect to an environmental issue or jurisdiction by law may be a cooperating agency in the NEPA process. A cooperating agency has the responsibility to assist the lead agency by participating in the NEPA process at the earliest possible time; by participating in the scoping process; in developing information and preparing environmental analyses including portions of the environmental impact statement concerning which the cooperating agency has special expertise; and in making available staff support at the lead agency's request to enhance the lead agency's interdisciplinary capabilities.

Council of Environmental Quality (CEQ): Under Section 1504 of CEQ's NEPA regulations, federal agencies may refer to CEQ on interagency disagreements concerning proposed federal actions that might cause unsatisfactory environmental effects. CEQ's role, when it accepts a referral, is generally to develop findings and recommendations, consistent with the policy goals of Section 101 of NEPA.

EPA's Role

The Environmental Protection Agency (EPA), like other federal agencies, prepares and reviews NEPA documents. However, EPA has a unique responsibility in the NEPA review process. Under Section 309 of the Clean Air Act, EPA is required to review and publicly comment on the environmental impacts of major federal actions, including actions which are the subject of EISs. If EPA determines that the action is environmentally unsatisfactory, it is required by Section 309 to refer the matter to CEQ.

In accordance with a Memorandum of Agreement between EPA and CEQ, EPA carries out the operational duties associated with the administrative aspects of the EIS filing process. The Office of Federal Activities in EPA has been designated the official recipient in EPA of all EISs prepared by federal agencies.

The Public's Role

The public has an important role in the NEPA process, particularly during scoping, in providing input on what issues should be addressed in an EIS and in commenting on the findings in an agency's NEPA documents. The public can participate in the NEPA process by attending NEPA-related hearings or public meetings and by submitting comments directly to the lead agency. The lead agency must take into consideration all comments received from the public and other parties on NEPA documents during the comment period.

The following case provides a look at NEPA and the Clean Water Act in action.

National Wildlife Federation, et al., Petitioners,

v.

Federal Energy Regulatory Commission, Respondent, The City of Fort Smith, Arkansas, Intervenor.

912 F.2d 1471, 286 U.S.App.D.C. 117, 115 P.U.R.4 278, 20 Envtl. L. Rep. 21,098

No. 88-1697.

United States Court of Appeals, District of Columbia Circuit.
Decided July 31, 1990.

PER CURIAM:

The National Wildlife Federation, et al. ("NWF") petitions for review of orders of the Federal Energy Regulatory Commission ("FERC" or "the Commission") granting to the City of Fort Smith, Arkansas, ("Fort Smith") a license for the construction and operation of a dam on Lee Creek, near the Arkansas-Oklahoma border. Because a small hydroelectric powerhouse was to be built along the dam, FERC jurisdiction attached to the project which was undertaken primarily to satisfy the water-supply needs of Fort Smith. The questions presented for review are whether FERC, in granting the license, failed to comply with certain requirements, involving the consideration of the projected environmental impact of the proposed dam, of the Federal Power Act ("FPA"), 16 U.S.C. Secs. 797(e), 803(a), and 803(j), the Clean Water Act ("CWA"), 33 U.S.C. Sec. 1341, and the National Environmental Policy Act ("NEPA"), 42 U.S.C. Sec. 4332(2)(C). We find no reason to disturb FERC's actions and accordingly deny the petition for review.

I. BACKGROUND

In the late 1970s, Fort Smith, aware that its municipal water supply would not be able to meet the demands of its growing populace, decided to create a reservoir by building a dam on Lee Creek. Lee Creek flows south from Oklahoma into Arkansas, and the proposed dam was to be built in Crawford County, Arkansas, just south of the Oklahoma-Arkansas border. The proposed dam was to enable Fort Smith to construct a reservoir in Arkansas, but it was also going to flood parts of Oklahoma. In November 1983, Fort Smith sought from FERC a license to construct, operate and maintain a small hydroelectric generator at the proposed Lee Creek site.

As envisioned by Fort Smith, the proposed project was to be implemented in two phases. The initial phase ("Phase I") was to allow for an approximately 10 million-gallon-per-day water supply. "Phase II," the eventual extension of Phase I envisioned by Fort Smith, was further to increase substantially Fort Smith's water supply. Phase II was to entail environmental costs over and above those of Phase I because the rise in the height of the dam would increase the total area of lands flooded, and would eliminate part of Lee Creek in Oklahoma, including several miles of an Oklahoma state-designated scenic river.

Because approval of the proposed project would constitute a major federal action "significantly affecting the quality of the human environment" within the meaning of NEPA, 42 U.S.C. Sec. 4332(2)(C), FERC directed its staff to prepare an environmental impact statement ("EIS") relating to the proposed dam. After a public hearing and a meeting with interested parties concerning the projected environmental impact of the proposed dam, FERC issued a draft EIS and solicited comments from interested parties and the public. In February 1987, FERC issued a final EIS in which it addressed many of the comments received in response to its draft EIS.

In March of 1988, although numerous objections to the proposed dam project remained, FERC granted Fort Smith's license application with a few conditions and modifications. Order Issuing License (Minor), 42 FERC p 61,361 (1988). FERC subsequently denied various requests for rehearing and upheld its grant to Fort Smith of a license to undertake the Lee Creek dam project. Order on Rehearing, 44 FERC p 61,160 (1988). The State of Oklahoma and the Oklahoma Water Resources Board (collectively "Oklahoma") petitioned this Court for review of FERC's grant of the license, arguing that FERC had failed to comply with certain FPA and CWA requirements involving consideration of the environmental impact of the dam. NWF also petitioned this Court, raising most of Oklahoma's FPA and CWA contentions, as well as other challenges based on the FPA and NEPA.

During the pendency of this litigation, Oklahoma and Arkansas agreed to a settlement which addressed many of Oklahoma's concerns. Pursuant to Oklahoma's request, this Court dismissed Oklahoma's petition with prejudice. NWF's petition remains, however, and that petition raises substantially the same arguments as did Oklahoma's petition.

First, NWF contends that FERC failed to consider adequately the potential environmental effects of Phase II of the dam project in deciding whether to approve Phase I of that project. FERC's failure to take into account the environmental impacts of Phase II, according to NWF, violated both the FPA and NEPA. Second, NWF argues that FERC violated several other provisions of the FPA by failing to consider adequately and follow the recommendations of various relevant federal and state agencies and by including the water-supply gains from the dam as a benefit of the dam project to be weighed against the costs. Third, NWF argues that FERC violated section 401(a)(2) of the CWA by granting the Fort Smith license without requiring the city to obtain a water-quality certification from Oklahoma. Finally, NWF argues that FERC's EIS did not comply with NEPA because the EIS failed to explore reasonable alternatives to the project and because the EIS was based in part on data compiled by a concededly interested party.

. . . .

B. FERC's Failure to Consider Phase II and NEPA

NEPA, like the FPA, requires that an agency of the federal government, when reviewing proposals requesting federal action, include an EIS in every recommendation or report on proposals for major federal actions that significantly affect the quality of the human environment. 42 U.S.C. Sec. 4332(2)(C). The EIS should detail:

(i) the environmental impact of the proposed action,

(ii) any adverse environmental effects which cannot be avoided should the proposal be implemented,

(iii) alternatives to the proposed action,

(iv) the relationship between local short-term uses of [the] environment and the maintenance and enhancement of long-term productivity, and

(v) any irreversible and irretrievable commitments of resources which would be involved in the proposed action should it be implemented.

Id.

The regulations implementing NEPA provide that where proposed actions are connected or cumulative they should be "discussed in the same impact statement." 40 C.F.R. Sec. 1508.25(a)(1) & (2) (1989). Actions are connected if they:

(i) Automatically trigger other actions which may require environmental impact statements.

(ii) Cannot or will not proceed unless other actions are taken previously or simultaneously.

(iii) Are interdependent parts of a larger action and depend on the larger action for their justification.

Id. at Sec. 1508.25(a)(1). Actions are cumulative if, when viewed with other proposed actions, they have "cumulatively significant impacts." *Id.* at Sec. 1508.25(a)(2). The statutory and regulatory scheme requires comprehensive analysis of the impact of connected or cumulative proposed actions in order to "prevent agencies from dividing one project into multiple individual actions 'each of which individually has an insignificant environmental impact, but which collectively have a substantial impact.'" *Natural Resources Defense Council, Inc. v. Hodel*, 865 F.2d 288, 297-98 (D.C.Cir.1988) (quoting *Thomas v. Peterson*, 753 F.2d 754, 758 (9 Cir.1985)).

NWF argues that FERC should have prepared a comprehensive EIS covering both Phases I and II of the Lee Creek Project. NWF cites *Scientists' Inst. For Public Information, Inc. v. Atomic Energy Comm'n*, 481 F.2d 1079, 1090 (D.C.Cir.1973), and *Swain v. Brinegar*, 542 F.2d 364, 369 (7 Cir.1976) (en banc), for the proposition that if a commitment of resources to one action is likely to restrict later alternatives, an EIS should address all of the environmental issues raised by the entire project. The question, according to NWF, is not whether granting a license for Phase I makes Phase II inevitable, but is whether granting the Phase I license limits future alternative uses of the resource too restrictively. Because Phase II would become a cheaper and thus more attractive alternative for a future expansion of Fort Smith's water supply once Phase I was completed, NWF argues that FERC, in preparing its EIS, should have taken into account not only the impact of Phase I of the project, but also the potential effects of Phase II. NWF fears that by granting the license for Phase I the Commission irretrievably committed resources, thereby severely limiting FERC review should the Commission later consid er the best alternatives to a licensing request for Phase II.

NWF further argues that although Fort Smith may not have formally sought a license for Phase II, the Commission nonetheless reviewed the benefits of Phase II when considering the alternatives to Fort Smith's proposal. Specifically, NWF argues that FERC compared the water capacity available under Phase II of the dam project with the alternative supplies available through other plans. In essence, the petitioners believe that FERC engaged in a sleight of hand by comparing the water supply available upon completion of Phase II — and the corresponding benefit of alleviating Fort Smith's anticipated water needs — against the detriment associated with Phase I.

Responding to NWF's first argument, the Commission maintains, again, that Phase II will by no means inevitably follow from Phase I. The Commission cites *Kleppe v. Sierra Club*, 427 U.S. 390, 410, 96 S.Ct. 2718, 2730, 49 L.Ed.2d 576 (1976), and argues that NEPA does not require an agency to consider the possible environmental impacts of speculative or hypothetical actions when preparing an impact statement on proposed actions. Rather, contends the Commission, NEPA merely requires an agency to consider all other proposed actions that may, along with the proposed action in issue, have a cumulative or synergistic impact on an environment. According to the Commission, in this case Phase II was not proposed at all, and the grant of a Phase I license in no way restricted future alternatives. In fact, in its Order on Rehearing the Commission explicitly noted that enlargement of the Lee Creek reservoir pursuant to Phase II plans would likely have a number of highly significant adverse impacts to water quality, fisheries, and recreation and thus might not be approved in a later proceeding. 44 FERC p 61,160 at 61,515. See also Order Issuing License (Minor), 42 FERC p 61,362 at 62,052.

The Commission further denies that it improperly considered the benefits from Phase II in evaluating the Phase I license application. The Commission argues that it merely examined, as one factor in its calculus, possible future expansions of the various alternatives to Fort Smith's proposal. Order on Rehearing, 44 FERC p 61,160 at 61,514-15.

We conclude that the Commission was not required more thoroughly to evaluate the possible effects of Phase II in its EIS. In *Kleppe v. Sierra Club* the Court held that the Department of the Interior need not execute a regional EIS regarding a proposal seeking approval for private development of certain coal reserves on federal land. The Sierra Club had argued that because the Department of the Interior "contemplated" regional development when it evaluated the proposal, NEPA required the Department's EIS to take into account the regional effects of the otherwise limited proposal. The Supreme Court rejected this contention, arguing that an agency must prepare an EIS concerning an action at " 'the time at which it makes a recommendation or report on a proposal for federal action.' " 427 U.S. at 406, 96 S.Ct. at 2728 (quoting *Aberdeen & Rockfish R.R. Co. v. SCRAP*, 422 U.S. 289, 320, 95 S.Ct. 2336, 2356, 45 L.Ed.2d 191 (1975)) (emphasis in *SCRAP*). Because "the contemplation of a project and the accompanying study thereof do not necessarily result in a proposal for major federal action," an EIS regarding a project that had not yet reached the proposal stage would be unnecessary. Id. The Court thus concluded that section 102(2)(C) of NEPA requires only that an EIS be conducted in regards to the proposed action.

The Court conceded that "when several proposals for [related] actions that will have cumulative or synergistic environmental impact upon a region are pending concurrently before an agency, their environmental consequences must be considered together," *id.* 427 U.S. at 410, 96 S.Ct. at 2730, but the Court explicitly limited the application of this requirement to existing, presently proposed actions that might have cumulative or synergistic effects. The Court wrote:

> At some points in their brief respondents appear to seek a comprehensive impact statement covering contemplated projects in the region as well as those that already have been proposed. The statute, however, speaks solely in terms of

proposed actions; it does not require an agency to consider the possible environmental impacts of less imminent actions when preparing the impact statement on proposed actions. Should contemplated actions later reach the stage of actual proposals, impact statements on them will take into account the effect of their approval upon the existing environment; and the condition of that environment presumably will reflect earlier proposed actions and their effects.

Id. at 410 n. 20, 96 S.Ct. at 2730 n. 20 (emphasis in original). *Kleppe* thus clearly establishes that an EIS need not delve into the possible effects of a hypothetical project, but need only focus on the impact of the particular proposal at issue and other pending or recently approved proposals that might be connected to or act cumulatively with the proposal at issue. In this case, the Commission did not ignore any relevant proposals involving Lee Creek. Fort Smith withdrew its proposals with respect to Phase II, as we have already noted, and any claim that it would reintroduce its Phase II proposal was merely speculative and hypothetical.

NWF's reliance on *Scientists' Inst. For Public Information, Inc. v. Atomic Energy Comm'n*, 481 F.2d 1079 (D.C.Cir.1973), wherein this Court ruled that future, yet unproposed projects should be considered in the EIS analyzing a proposal if the envisioned future projects would impact the relevant environment, is misplaced. We seriously doubt that the relevant reasoning in *Scientists' Institute* survives the Supreme Court's *Kleppe* decision. Moreover, given that, by approving Phase I, the Commission did not in any way bind itself to approve Phase II, *Scientists' Institute* may not even support NWF's claim.

We further conclude that the Commission did not improperly consider the benefits of the possible Phase II expansion in evaluating the Phase I application. In reviewing Fort Smith's application FERC compared and analyzed the various alternatives to the proposed project not only with reference to their relative abilities to satisfy Fort Smith's present water demands, but with an eye to their relative potentials to satisfy Fort Smith's future water needs. In doing so, the Commission did take into account factors relating to Phase II of the Lee Creek project. FERC did not, though, compare the 70 million-gallon-per-day yield of Phase II to the present yields of the alternatives to the project. Rather, FERC weighed each alternative against Fort Smith's application, weighing, among other things, the potential for expansion of the available alternatives against the potential for expansion of the proposed Lee Creek dam project.

The mere fact that it considered possible future expansion as one factor in its evaluation of the present project does not bind FERC to consider the future harms and benefits of a proposal not before it. Moreover, FERC is by no means bound to later approve Phase II merely because it considered the possibility of later expansion in approving Phase I. When comparing present alternatives, the Commission should consider potential future expansion to accommodate future needs. By doing so the Commission neither automatically brings Phase II under Commission review nor binds itself to later approve Phase II. In fact, Fort Smith would take a risk if it implemented Phase I at great initial expense, relying on a belief that Phase II would ultimately be approved by the Commission and would render its initial action profitable. Fort Smith may later be forced to rely on numerous smaller and arguably more expensive water-supply sources to meet its future water needs. We cannot hold that FERC acted arbitrarily by analyzing potential future development.

The Commission did not have before it a proposal for a license as to Phase II and, although the Commission in reviewing the future ramifications of granting Fort Smith's application did consider benefits that might ensue from the implementation of Phase II of the Lee Creek dam project, the Commission in no way approved Phase II. The

Commission was thus not required to consider the potential environmental impact of Phase II of the project in its EIS regarding Fort Smith's application.

...

IV. FERC'S COMPLIANCE WITH THE CLEAN WATER ACT

The Clean Water Act provides:

> (1) Any applicant for a Federal license or permit to conduct any activity ... which may result in any discharge into the navigable waters, shall provide the licensing or permitting agency a certification from the State in which the discharge originates or will originate ... that any such discharge will comply with the applicable provisions [of certain listed sections] of this title.

33 U.S.C. Sec. 1341(a)(1). The Act further provides that whenever such a discharge might affect the quality of the waters of any other state so as to violate any water quality requirement in that state, that state must be notified of the application and afforded an opportunity for a hearing. Id. Sec. 1341(a)(2).

NWF argues that the Lee Creek dam project would result in a discharge originating in Oklahoma. The dam would back up the waters flowing in from Oklahoma, and would cause severe soil erosion within Oklahoma, according to NWF. Because the project would result in a discharge that would originate in Oklahoma, NWF contends that FERC was required to obtain the requisite certification from the Oklahoma Water Resources Board ("OWRB") before approving the project. FERC was unable to obtain such certification, and its approval of the Lee Creek dam project, NWF asserts, thus violated the CWA.

The Commission responds that a certification is only required under the CWA from the state in which a discharge originates. Other states, even if they are affected by a discharge, have only an advisory role in regulating the discharge, and they do not have the authority to block the issuance of permits if they are dissatisfied with the proposed standards. The Commission contends that in this case the discharge would occur at the dam, several miles within the Arkansas border.

We conclude that the Commission acted properly in approving the project without certification from the OWRB. The Commission is clearly only required to obtain a certification from the state where the discharge originates. As the Supreme Court explained in *International Paper Co. v. Ouellette*, 479 U.S. 481, 490, 107 S.Ct. 805, 810-11, 93 L.Ed.2d 883 (1987),

> While source States have a strong voice in regulating their own pollution, the CWA contemplates a much lesser role for States that share an interstate waterway with the source.... Even though it may be harmed by the discharges, an affected State only has an advisory role in regulating pollution that originates beyond its borders.... [and] does not have the authority to block the issuance of the permit if it is dissatisfied with the proposed standards.

Moreover, the Commission did not abuse its discretion in determining that in this case the discharge would originate by the dam — in Arkansas, not Oklahoma. Common sense supports FERC's conclusion that the discharge in this case would occur at the dam, where the flow of water would be blocked and consequently the water would be backed up, rather than at some point upstream where the water ended up or where the soil eroded as a result of the blockage downstream.

Further, Oklahoma withdrew all objections to the project as a result of the Settlement Agreement and it amended its water-quality standards to provide explicitly that the changes in water quality caused by the impoundment of water by the hydroelectric project to be constructed on Lee Creek would not constitute a violation of those standards. Thus, even if the discharge in question did originate in Oklahoma, we doubt that the CWA would pose a genuine barrier to FERC's approval of the Lee Creek dam project.

V. THE ADEQUACY OF FERC'S EIS UNDER NEPA

In addition to arguing that the Commission's EIS regarding the Lee Creek dam project should have examined the projected impact from Phase II, NWF contends that the Commission's EIS was deficient for two other reasons. First, NWF argues that the Commission failed adequately to consider alternatives to the Fort Smith proposal. Second, NWF contends that the Commission's EIS rests in part on data compiled by a party with a conceded conflict of interest, rendering the EIS suspect.

A. The Commission's Consideration of Alternatives

NEPA requires that reasonable alternatives to a proposed project be evaluated in the EIS. 40 C.F.R. Sec. 1502.14 (1989). NWF argues first that the Commission failed to consider any alternatives to the hydropower portion of the Lee Creek dam project. Although the Commission did consider some alternatives to satisfy the water-supply purposes of the project, it did not really explore other means of satisfying the power-production purposes of the project. According to NWF, the Commission's EIS is therefore deficient. Second, NWF argues that FERC neglected to examine in its EIS alternatives that would satisfy the water-supply purposes of the project. Specifically, NWF charges that the Commission improperly declined to consider the possibility of reallocating some waters from Tenkiller Ferry Lake, in Oklahoma, on the grounds that interstate transfer of waters requires legislative approval in Oklahoma and is discouraged in Arkansas. NWF explains that the Tenkiller Lake water could be allocated to those communities within Oklahoma currently supplied by Fort Smith, thus leaving Fort Smith more water from its already existing supply. NWF further contends that the Commission improperly rejected the alternative of water conservation.

The Commission responds that it did not consider in depth alternatives to the hydropower portion of Fort Smith's proposal because the dam was proposed to satisfy water-supply needs, not power needs. Moreover, the Commission argues that it did adequately consider alternatives to the water-supply portion of the Fort Smith proposal but that, in the end, it rejected those alternatives.

We conclude that the Commission's EIS did adequately evaluate alternatives to the Lee Creek dam project. The Fort Smith proposal was designed to satisfy Fort Smith's water-supply needs. The production of hydroelectric power was merely incidental to the project. Any alternative that would facilitate the production of the same amount of power without satisfying Fort Smith's water-supply needs would not satisfy the central goal of the proposed project and thus would not constitute a reasonable alternative to the Lee Creek dam project. The Commission thus properly concluded that "reasonable alternatives are those that address [Fort Smith's] need for water." Order on Rehearing, 44 FERC p 61,160 at 61,515.

Further, the Commission did consider various alternatives that would satisfy the water-supply goals of the Fort Smith proposal. The final EIS contains an analysis of the conservation alternative, but concludes that even with a conservation plan, eventually Fort Smith's water demand will exceed system limits. Lee Creek Project, Final Environmental Impact Statement Sec. 2.3 (Feb. 1987) (J.A. 86-87). The EIS also extensively examined various aspects of the Lake Shepherd Springs alternative, the Blue Mountain Lake alternative, the Pine Mountain alternative, the Cedar Creek alternative, the Lee Creek-Cedar Creek alternative, the Arkansas River alternative, and the Arkansas River alluvium alternative.

The Commission did not explore the Tenkiller Reservoir option more thoroughly because it concluded that Oklahoma and Arkansas law and policy disfavored interstate transfer of water, and that the amount of water that could be reallocated from Tenkiller Reservoir to the Oklahoma communities served by Fort Smith was so small that it would free up only negligible quantities of water for Fort Smith's use. Order on Rehearing, 44 FERC p 61,160 at 61,515-16. The Commission's decision not to explore the alternative of transferring water interstate was justified because NEPA does not require detailed discussion of the environmental effects of remote and speculative alternatives. *Natural Resources Defense Council, Inc. v. Morton*, 458 F.2d 827, 837-38 (D.C.Cir.1972). FERC's conclusion that only negligible gains could be realized from the reallocation of water from the Tenkiller Reservoir to Oklahoma communities served by Fort Smith was supported by substantial evidence in the record.

NEPA does not require the Commission to consider every conceivable alternative in its EIS. Rather, the statute requires agencies to consider all reasonable alternatives to proposed actions. We conclude that the Commission satisfied this requirement.

B. Commission's Use of Data from a "Biased" Party

When the Commission analyzed the costs of the Lee Creek project it used data prepared by an engineering firm employed by Fort Smith. This firm held interests in real estate within the project area which would increase in value if the project were approved. The Commission, aware of this situation, nonetheless used the data in making its licensing determination.

NWF argues that FERC could not properly rely on the information provided by the firm in question without first investigating the accuracy of that information. Because the Commission's approval of the Lee Creek dam project was granted in reliance on this questionable data, NWF argues that FERC's decision should be vacated and that FERC should investigate the validity of the information.

The Commission responds that agency reliance upon information submitted by applicants and other interested parties is inherent in the regulatory process. The Commission argued that it could properly rely on information from a party as long as the information was independently confirmed. The Commission asserts that it has independently confirmed the data in issue.

We reject NWF's contention and find the Commission's use of the evidence in question reasonable. The Commission noted that it was aware of the inherent bias in party-submitted information, but explained that it had independently confirmed the reasonableness of the analyses of the capacities of the project and the estimated construction costs for the project and alternatives. Order on Rehearing, 44 FERC p 61,160 at 61,517. NWF has not pointed to any inaccuracies in the disputed data, but has merely speculated that the data are unreliable due to the interests of the proponents of the evidence. Such a speculation, without more, is insufficient to undermine the Commission's independent determination that the data were reliable.

VI. CONCLUSION

For the foregoing reasons, we conclude that the Commission's orders issuing Fort Smith a license to undertake the Lee Creek dam project were reasonable and lawful under the FPA, the CWA, and NEPA. We thus deny NWF's petition for review of these orders.

Notes & Questions

1. This case is a good example of a court confusing the difference between actions and impacts. That is, the court conflates the requirement to consider all connected or cumulative actions in the same comprehensive EIS with the need to assess the cumulative impacts of the proposal and other reasonably foreseeable actions to follow. In *Fritiofson v. Alexander*, 772 F.2d 1225 (5th Cir. 1985), that court explains that only actual proposals must be considered together in a single EIS. When the scope of the EIS has been determined, though, the agency must consider all of the cumulative impacts of future actions, regardless of who (or what) will take such actions.

2. *Practice Note*: Consider the "biased" party claim that NWF tried to use. If an agency is never permitted to consider data from a party with an interest in the issue before it, where would the data come from? Would that be reasonable? Consider cases where the data must come from a party. Isn't this something courts consider and analyze all the time? Where possible, it's best to use neutral parties for data and other expertise, but it is not always possible. Minimizing the appearance of bias is worth the effort, as long as the effort is honest and transparent. That is, getting caught trying to hide possible connections between parties can be counterproductive and potentially devastating.

C. Energy Incentives and Mandates: Traditional and Renewable Resources

Joshua P. Fershee, *Promoting an All of the Above Approach or Pushing (Oil) Addiction and Abuse?: The Curious Role of Energy Subsidies and Mandates in U.S. Energy Policy*

7 Envtl. & Energy L. & Pol'y J. 125 (2012) (footnotes omitted)

Much has been made about the role of U.S. energy policy and the need for an "all of the above approach" to pursue "energy independence," improved environmental conditions, and keep costs reasonable. Governments thus often seek policies to support development of energy resources deemed important. This Part explains some of the key programs implemented to support energy development and considers some examples of each program.

Government-funded energy subsidies have been used in virtually every country to increase access to energy resources and output. At some point, virtually every possible energy resource has received government subsidies or similar support. Governments also sometimes use fuel mandates to encourage the use of specific energy sources, or groups of energy sources, as in the case of a renewable portfolio standard (or renewable electricity standards) and renewable fuels standards. Subsidies and mandates share the same goal: increase the use of the targeted energy source or sources.

Energy subsidies play a major role in global energy policies, especially U.S. energy policies, and are likely to continue to do so. Subsidies and other mechanisms of support remain available for traditional resources, including hydropower, corn-based ethanol, coal, oil, natural gas, and nuclear, as well as renewable and emerging sources such as "clean coal," wind, solar, biomass, and next generation transportation fuels. Although subsidies vary depending on location, motivation, and political ideology, subsidy programs have been a part of virtually all government energy policies used to expand access to energy or increase energy production.

A. The Many Types of Energy Subsidies

There are four primary types of energy subsidies. These government-initiated programs usually take one of the following forms: (1) direct spending, (2) tax reduction, (3) support for research and development (R&D), and (4) government-run programs facilitating access. These forms are not necessarily exclusive, and some energy policies use combinations of these to support the targeted energy source.

1. Direct Spending Subsidies

Direct spending subsidy programs are programs in which payments are provide (by the government) directly to energy producers or end users (consumers). Some such payments are made for production of a certain amount of the supported source or they could take the form of direct payments to consumers. Direct subsidy programs might, for example, be designed to facilitate renewable energy resources or combat climate change. Some recent legislative proposals have suggested that proceeds from a cap-and-trade program or a carbon tax could be used to fund subsidies to those investing in renewable and sustainable energy projects.

Some direct subsidy programs are not motivated directly by the desire to increase energy use, but have that effect. One such program is the Low Income Home Energy Assistance Program (LIHEAP), which is a federal program designed to support the energy needs of low-income households. Although this program is designed as a public assistance program, it directly facilitates the consumption of energy by ensuring that low-income households can pay their energy bills. In either case, the government is directly funding energy consumption.

2. Tax Reduction Subsidies

Another popular type of subsidies are tax reduction programs, which can take the forms of tax deductions (that reduce the taxable income upon which taxes would be calculated) and tax credits (that reduce an overall tax obligation). The reductions are typically linked to investment in energy infrastructure or energy production, but can be used in other parts of energy use (e.g., tax credits or deductions for electric vehicles).

a. Production Tax Credits

The production tax credit (PTC) is one common option. This credit is calculated by multiplying the credit amount (e.g., 2.1 cents per kilowatt hour) by the amount of output (e.g., 80 kilowatt hours of electricity generated). The PTC is paid each year for the length of the specified credit period. This period, along with the credit amount and type or types of resources covered, is set by law and can vary widely. A PTC often has restrictions on who takes the energy out, such as a requirement that the generated electricity be sold to an unaffiliated entity. Finally, because the PTC is usually used to support a new or developing energy source that costs more than other market competitors, most PTCs will have a price cap that phases out the credit as the market price of the power created rises.

b. Investment Tax Credits

Another oft-used energy subsidy is the investment tax credit (ITC). At least recently, this type of credit has been used primarily to support renewable energy projects, but it can work for any type of energy project. Instead of basing the credit on energy production like the PTC, an ITC is based on the cost of the energy facility or the property costs for the covered facility. Again, eligible facilities are determined by the operative statute, and often include projects with high start-up costs. Projects for geothermal technologies, solar power, and non-utility scale wind projects are typical examples. ITCs the project owner a percentage of the project costs, and those costs typically vest over a certain time frame. As an example, an ITC of 25% of the total project cost might be captured by the developer at 20% of the credit per year for five years.

c. End-User Energy Credits and Tax-Free Grants

Consumer-side (or end-user) grants and credits can also be used to promote energy projects, and these are especially common to promote the use of renewable energy or encourage improved efficiency. Theses subsidies can be tax credits (reducing the amount of tax owed dollar for dollar) or tax deductions (reducing the taxable income of the recipient, which thus reduces the tax owed). Examples of consumer-side tax credits or deductions include home energy efficiency credits (such as insulating an attic), residential renewable energy credits (such as a solar water heater), and credits for renewable or alternative fuel vehicles. Finally, some governments use tax-free grants to encourage energy efficiency projects. For instance, Canada has provided as much as $5,000 in tax-free grants for residents who have an energy-efficiency audit before they begin a renovation.

3. Research and Development (R&D) Subsidies

Research and development (R&D) subsidies are designed to increase energy supplies and to support new energy production technologies or increase efficiency. R&D subsidies are designed to lead to useful technologies and processes they can impact future prices and rates of production, but they are not expenditures that are likely to impact energy output or prices in the relatively short term.

These subsidies sometimes take the form of government-sponsored grants that are used to reduce the initial risks related to the development or installation of new energy projects. R&D subsidies are also used to fund (or fund portions of) projects for promising, but unproven, technologies. Such grants can take the form of a public-private partnership, where the governmental subsidy might be matched with funds from other private companies interested in the technology. A recent program funded by the U.S. Department of Energy, for example, offered $338 million dollars in government grant money for geothermal research and development. Private and other non-Federal funding sources provided the additional funds required for the projects to occur.

4. Government Programs to Facilitate Access to Energy

Government programs to increase access to energy are often targeted at remote or low-income regions that are not developing as quickly as other areas. A common use of this kind of subsidy program includes government-funded programs that help develop large electricity projects for market in the targeted region. Indirect subsidies, via loans and loan guarantees, can also help facilitate construction of infrastructure needed to make energy accessible in the targeted region.

At some point, virtually all governments have used these kinds of subsidies to increase access to energy, either by location or amount. A classic example of an early such program in the United State is the Rural Electrification Act (REA), passed in 1936. The highly successful REA provided the long-term financing and technical expertise needed to develop access to electricity for rural customers. By 1963, more than 900 cooperative rural electrification systems had been built using the government-subsidized financing made available by the REA.

The risk related to the enormous financial undertaking needed to electrify rural America was enormous and needed subsidization to become near-term reality. Despite the financial risk, and the amount of capital needed, it was believed that the REA would raise the standard of living, strengthen the country's economy, and improve national security by creating the option of increasing industrial activity through increased access to power.

The REA subsidy program made more than $5 billion available to roughly 1,000 borrowers This funding facilitated construction of more than 1,500,000 miles of power lines that served 20 million American people by the 1960s. Despite the enormous size of the project (and the related risk) the government's investment was sound. By 1963, only one of the approximately 1000 borrowers had been reported as making a delinquent payment. Of the $5 billion of financial assistance provided, losses were expected to be less than $50,000, a remarkably low rate of loss.

B. Traditional Fuel Subsidies Versus Renewable Source Subsidies

As noted above, most governments use energy subsidies in some way as part of their overall energy policy, though the type and level of government intervention varies greatly. Such subsidies have been traditionally used to support energy production and development, increase consumer and industrial access to energy, and improve economic productivity. Despite the mature nature of the markets, many developed countries continue to subsidize coal, oil, and natural gas extraction, and some of the major oil exporting nations have continued to subsidize petroleum consumption.

Today's government subsidies often target the same goals as those of past, but the use of subsidies has evolved beyond output and access to include environmental goals and provide incentives for sustainable energy development. With the goal of supporting or creating sustainable energy markets, many governments use subsidies and mandates to promote the use of sustainable energy sources. These subsidies are not universally appreciated. Such subsidies are often criticized, with opponents claiming that renewable energy sources are unfairly and unwisely subsidized when more traditional forms of energy are "cheaper."

These criticisms usually ignore the reality that many traditional energy sources (mainly fossil fuel sources) have costs that are not fully internalized, thus making the market price lower (or "cheaper"), while the actual cost is higher. For example, some costs of traditional sources, such as greenhouse gas emissions that can contribute to climate concerns, are not part of the cost of consumption. These costs are often not part of—they are not internalized in—the price consumers of fossil fuels pay

Many people criticize the use of subsidies for renewable or sustainable energy and complain that a "free-market" (i.e., one without renewable subsidies) would provide more efficient markets. However, removing these types of incentives to ensure free markets implies that there are no other incentives related to energy sources. It is simply not the case that renewable energy sources are the only sources receiving subsidies.

If the free market were truly the goal, the only way to understand what "the market" wants would be to eliminate *all* energy subsidies. Unfortunately, many people fail to acknowledge that subsidies exist for traditional as well as renewable and next generation energy resources. This opens the door for those supporting traditional fuels to argue a reduction or elimination of subsidies only for renewable energy sources. When this occurs, the argument results in a market-based argument that is really a veiled source-based argument. That is, on can veil a preference for fossil fuels over renewable sources by arguing that renewable subsidies distort the market. The reality is that a true "free market" argument would acknowledge the vast reach of subsidies for traditional fuels and would seek the repeal of all subsidies, not just those for renewable energy.

Despite some claims to the contrary, incentives for traditional energy sources are similar to renewable industry incentives in many spots. One of the main arguments against renewable energy subsidies is that renewable subsidies are far higher than they are for traditional fuels per unit of output. For example, they argue that the amount of subsidies per megawatt hour received to support fossil fuels is far less than the subsidies received to support each megawatt hour of renewable energy. However, these subsidies can indicate different things depending upon how issue is framed.

Most calculations of subsidies per energy source do not consider the full range of the energy subsidies and the impact of the subsidies on energy markets. For example, negative externalities related to some fossil fuel energy sources are completely ignored in the analysis of the resource receiving the subsidies. Often, those complaining about renewable subsidies make a per-unit comparison, considering a strict per-unit-of-output comparison of subsidies. Such a comparison, does not, of course, consider the total market impact of the subsidies.

For example, suppose the U.S. government provides a subsidy to a small car company that amounts to $15,000 per auto produced, while the government makes a similar subsidy to a major automaker that is only $500 per auto produced. The per-unit subsidy is very high for the small automaker, but if the small automaker is only making 1,000 vehicles, and the large automaker is making 1 million autos, the subsidy to the large automaker would be a much larger—and more market-significant—subsidy ($15 million versus $500 million). In such cases, looking only at the per-auto dollar amount of the subsidy would not provide an accurate view of the market impact of the subsidies.

A look at recent U.S. energy subsidies helps further explain this analysis. According to the Energy Information Administration (EIA), federal energy-specific subsidies and support to all forms of energy for 2010 were estimated at $27.16 billion for fiscal year (FY) 2010, up from $17.895 billion in FY 2007. In FY 2010, the U.S government provided $11.873 billion in electricity production and support subsidies. This means that 55.3% of the subsidies were used to support renewable energy generation and 44.7% were used to support traditional fuels (e.g., coal, nuclear, natural gas) and transmission and distribution.

Wind receives, by far, the largest subsidy, taking 42% of all electricity sector subsidies. These subsidies have also lead to the largest increase in percentage of generation between 2000 and 2010. Wind energy production grew from 0.2% of generation in 2000 to 2.3% of production, an increase of 31.8% During the same time frame, only natural gas increased generation by more than 2%, increasing 3.6% (from 19.1% of total generation to 25%).

Subsidies for fuels used outside the electricity sector grew even more substantially. In FY 2007, such fuels received $6.2 billion in subsidies; this grew to $10.448 billion in FY 2010. Biomass and biofuels took the vast majority of these subsidies, claiming 73.2% of all non-electricity-related subsidies, while leading to 10.9% of the fuel production in that category. By comparison, natural gas and petroleum liquids received 20.7% of the subsidies and produced 80.3% of such fuel.

For both electricity generation and other fuels production, it is clear that the majority of U.S. subsidies have provided support for renewable fuel use and production. However, it is also clear that significant subsidies exist for traditional fossil fuels sources, providing support for well-established fuel sources in their respective markets. It can at least be argued that the total dollars spent on traditional energy resources provide a greater market distortion than dollars spent on renewables because the subsidies are supporting long-established market participants that already have established consumer bases and distribution systems.

Furthermore, until very recently, support for traditional fuels sources out paced those for renewable generation sources. In 2007, U.S. subsidies for renewables were 29% of total subsidies and support, an increase from 17% in 1999. In total 2007 dollars, renewables accounted for $4.875 billion of the $16.581 in FY 2007 energy subsidies. Thus, $11.706 billion of FY 2007 subsidies went to non-renewable-related energy projects. As such, as recently as 2007, the overall impact of dollars spent on traditional U.S. fuel subsidies was more than two times greater than that spent on renewable subsidies.

Although subsidies for renewables increased in the three years between 2007 and 2010, subsidies for well-established, traditional fuel sources have also continued. The goal of subsidies, regardless of what they support, is to get the market to produced more of whatever is being subsidized. Therefore, subsidies for renewables will (or should) lead to more renewables, and subsidies for fossil fuels, even if less than those provided for renewables, will also lead to production of more fossil fuels than a subsidy-free market would have produced. Fossil fuel subsidies thus serve to undermine, or at least limit, the effectiveness of the subsidies for renewable and sustainable energy sources because the benefits of the renewable source subsidies are being offset by the parallel subsidies provided to traditional energy sources.

It is also worth noting that subsidies over longer periods of time, as opposed to short-term support, can impact the market for many years. As such, year-to-year comparisons are often misleading. For example, the federal government subsidized nuclear power for many years, with especially large investments in R&D starting in 1950s and 1960s. The investments (at least arguably) paid off, but those subsidy dollars spent years ago are not reflected in today's subsidy analysis. Nuclear power, then, may appear significantly cheaper in a snapshot look at today as compared to looking at a total cost perspective. Furthermore, non-production-subsidy-related clean-up costs are significant costs not usually added into today's costs.

History suggests that energy subsidies will continue to play a major role in U.S. energy policy, as well as policies around the world. These tensions between the competing goals of current subsidies create difficulty for policymakers who try to balance the needs and desires of various constituent groups. These decisions are by no means an easy balance.

Continued subsidies for traditional fossil fuel sources can impede progress on renewable and sustainable development, but such subsidies may be essential to provide low (or lower) cost, near-term access to energy. This is especially true in developing nations. Similarly, subsidies for renewable and sustainable sources can provide incentives and opportunities for resources that are more sustainable and have less environmental impact. However, incentives for both types of projects can improperly support projects that are not, and never will be, economically viable. Such subsidies are a waste of funding and can served to impede progress for toward more efficient and sustainable markets.

C. Mandates

Like subsidies, goals and mandates can be powerful ways to encourage the construction of new generating facilities and production techniques. Goals and mandates have traditionally been used in the electricity sector, although recent support for renewable fuels has seen similar mandates in the transportation fuel sector.

1. Electricity Goals and Mandates

a. The First Modern Mandate: PURPA

Perhaps the most significant renewable energy mandate is the Public Utility Regulatory Policies Act of 1978 ("PURPA"), which was passed following the 1970s oil crisis. Although PURPA's role has largely been supplanted by state renewable electricity mandates, PURPA serves as critical example of a U.S. energy mandate.

Under PURPA, utilities were required to buy the renewable energy generated by certain qualified facilities (QFs). QFs include "small power producers," which are typically generators of 80 MW or facilities less that generate power using at least 75% renewable sources. To help promote competition, electric utilities (or their holding companies) were limited to ownership 50% of a QF. Federal Energy Regulatory Commission (FERC) regulations provided that that utilities buy electricity from QFs at "avoided cost" rates. Under PURPA, the amount a utility can be forced to pay a QF is capped at "incremental cost," also known as "full avoided cost." FERC decided that the statutory cap would be the amount utilities must pay for all QF purchases. Avoided cost is determined by a complex process that considers a variety of issues, including reliability, availability, and "usefulness." This creates a scenario under which FERC's avoided cost rates interpretation often grants a QF a higher price for sales to a utility than the price the utility could charge the QF if the QF purchased power from the utility.

PURPA has a two-tiered regulatory structure. At the federal level, the initial implementing body was FERC, which determined which facilities were QFs. Next, the avoided cost rates that were to be charged to utilities were determined by the appropriate state-level agency.

At the start, PURPA proved to be a reasonably effective mechanism for bringing new renewable power generation online. PURPA did not have a specific renewable energy development goal, but PURPA was still credited with being the primary reason for wind energy development between 1978 and into the 1990s. PURPA's rate structure and ownership requirements created a market where QFs could compete with the vertically integrated utilities.

In fact, the ability of small power generators to succeed under PURPA indicated that large monopoly power producers were not necessarily the best model for power generation, and certainly showed that was not the only model that could be successful. PURPA created a freer market for electricity by introducing competition to markets that were previously served by vertically integrated electrical utilities. To do so, PURPA limited ownership and provided purchase obligations that helped QFs compete.

The success of this new market spurred further restructuring in the industry, leading in part to the National Energy Policy Act of 1992, which sought to increase competition further and trigger restructuring of electricity sector. This act, too, proved to be a success as it increased competition by adding exemptions for some power producers under the Public Utility Holding Company Act and laying the groundwork for FERC's orders creating an open access transmission tariff for those seeking access to the electric transmission grid, w by unbundling (separating) electricity generation and transmission.

Shortly thereafter, states also began deregulating the wholesale and retail markets in the electricity sector. Utilities, along with state and federal regulators, began forming "independent, unbiased transmission operators to ensure equal access to the power grid for new, non-utility competitors." This led to today's state and regional organizations called Independent System Operators (ISOs) or Regional Transmission Organizations (RTOs), which now serve two-thirds of the electricity consumers in the United States (and more than half of Canada's consumers).

In more recent years, after deregulation and the decline of available credit markets for financing (among other things) QFs began to have a hard time staying competitive. The market became even more difficult for many QFs when FERC in compliance with a mandate in the Energy Policy Act of 2005, repealed PURPA's must-purchase option where a QFs has "nondiscriminatory access" to wholesale markets for electricity sales. PURPA, despite its major role in the current structure of the industry, is no longer an effective or efficient mechanism for inducing renewable power generation. In response, the regulators and policymakers have moved to mechanisms and mandates better suited to the new market.

b. Renewable Portfolio Standards

Renewable energy mandates are often known as renewable portfolio standards (RPSs) or renewable electricity standards (RESs). (RPS and RES, for purposes of this article, can be used interchangeably.) Today, the RPS is the most common renewable fuel source mandate. Comparable programs for the transportation sector have been imposed through renewable fuel standards, which are discussed below. Note that what counts as "renewable" under the RPS is determined solely by the statute or regulation at issue. Thus, a statute could choose to define anything as renewable, from wind and solar to coal and nuclear.

An RPS requires all covered electricity suppliers to obtain a certain percentage of their electricity from renewable resource generation or purchase renewable energy credits from others using renewable sources to meet the statutory (or regulatory) mandate. RPS plans usually set a mid- to long-range goal and phase in the mandate. For example, an RPS might have a first-year 2.75% renewable energy mandate that increases gradually (but significantly) over ten or twenty years to 20%. Some such programs will allow covered utilities use efficiency programs to reach some or all of the RPS mandate. To secure compliance, an RPS will typically use sanctions (such as fines or penalties) and/or waivers (permission for temporary noncompliance) for failures to meet the RPS requirements.

When state RPS programs were first implemented, there was some concern the state RPS might run conflict with PURPA. As explained above, both PURPA and RPS programs were created to encourage renewable resource development. In 1997, FERC decided that PURPA preempted state agencies from requiring utilities to purchase power generated by QFs at any rate that was above avoided cost. However, state mandates that required utilities to use, or obtain electricity generated by, renewable resources did not violate PURPA merely by having such a mandate.

c. An Emerging Option: The Feed-in Tariff

Another example of fuel source mandate is the use of a feed-in tariff to promote renewable electricity generation. A feed-in tariff provides a specific price that will be paid for the output from covered energy generators deemed renewable, states how long that price will be available for such energy, and has a requirement that utilities buy the generated renewable energy. The feed-in tariff has been popular in Europe and other countries, while the RPS has been the primary choice of U.S. states. The potential appeal of a feed-in tariff is that is provides market participants a price guarantee for their output (at least as long as the law is active).

2. Transportation Fuels

The clearest U.S. policy initiative designed to reduce oil consumption through the support of new fuel sources is the renewable fuel standard (RFS), which was initially passed as part of the Energy Policy Act of 2005. As oil prices continued to rise, along with a the goal of achieving energy independence, the RFS mandate increased in the Energy Independence and Security Act of 2007 (EISA). The RFS provides that "transportation fuel sold or introduced into commerce in the United States (except in noncontiguous States or territories)" must include a minimum of 9 billion gallons of renewable fuel in 2008, increasing to 36 billion gallons per year by 2022. The RFS thus dramatically mandated the increased use of ethanol as part of the U.S. fuel mix. Initial RFS compliance can be obtained through the use of ethanol from any source (which is usually corn). As the RFS evolves, the later year mandate shifts to a requirement that additional gallons of alternative fuels be from next generation ethanol sources, such as prairie grass, corn stalks, or algae.

The appeal of ethanol and other biofuels as an alternative to oil-based gasoline makes sense. Ethanol is grown from the earth, rather than extracted from it, making biofuels seem like an almost perfect solution. Furthermore, ethanol and other biofuels work in combustion engines, meaning that the current installed base of vehicles, with some minor modifications, can use the fuel.

The most common biofuel is ethanol, which can be made from corn, soy, and other plant materials. Alternative fuel production varies greatly in its efficiency from depending on the energy source. For example, prairie switchgrass, which is highly resistant to drought, uses a lot less water and less petroleum-based fertilizers than corn. As would be expected, the varied fuel sources also impact the economic and environmental impact of the resulting fuel. Although not yet available for large-scale production, researchers are also working using algae to generate ethanol. To date, though, only corn-based ethanol has any significant U.S. market share.

Notes & Questions

1. *Practice Note*: Be sure to consider the program you are analyzing carefully. RPSs are often thought of as environmental policies or climate change policies, but neither description is quite right. RPS programs are designed to incentivize the use of renewable fuels sources, again, as defined in the RPS, to generate electricity. This can have the effect of reducing greenhouse gas emissions or other toxic emissions, but the RPS does not monitor such things. The RPS solely tracks the source of the resource used to create electricity. Any other benefit from increasing the amount of renewable-sourced electricity via an RPS is a tangential benefit.

2. Why do you think so many states have been supportive of RPS plans? The states in the southeastern United States are by far the least supportive of RPSs. Why might that be?

3. Several states have viewed RPS programs as jobs bills. There has been some success on that front, but it remains limited. Competition from overseas is one impediment, as was the lack of financing following the financial crisis of 2008.

4. Why subsidize or provide other incentives to promote oil drilling in the United States? Remember that the point of subsidies is to encourage producers to produce more

of the subsidized good or behavior. But is that necessary for oil? That is, do the subsidies actually lead to more oil production in the United States or would oil companies do what they are doing anyway? Subsidies may lower the market price of oil, but there is a reasonable argument that is not a benefit because then all taxpayers pay to lower the price, when the consumer of the product should be the one paying for the full price of the good consumed. This is a policy question, and reasonable minds can differ, but consider the implications.

5. What do you think is the best of the subsidies? That is, what subsidies will most likely lead to an increase in something we want that would not occur without the incentive?

New Mexico Industrial Energy Consumers v. New Mexico Public Regulation Commission
168 P.3d 105 (N.M. 2007)

SERNA, Justice.

{1} Pursuant to the Renewable Energy Act ("REA"), NMSA 1978, §§ 62-16-1 to -10 (2004, prior to 2007 amendment), El Paso Electric Company ("EPE") purchased Renewable Energy Certificates ("RECs") representing renewable energy generated by Public Service Company of New Mexico ("PNM"); however, EPE did not purchase the actual renewable energy represented by the RECs. Pursuant to the REA, Section 62-16-6(A), EPE sought recovery of the REC costs through its automatic adjustment clause, see NMSA 1978, § 62-8-7(E) (2003). The Public Regulation Commission ("Commission") approved this form of cost recovery in a Final Order on Recommended Decision ("Order"). NMPRC Case No. 05-00231-UT. New Mexico Industrial Energy Consumers ("NMIEC") appealed the Order directly to this Court. See NMSA 1978, § 62-11-1 (1993).

{2} For the following reasons, we hold that EPE's REC costs are not eligible for automatic adjustment clause recovery. Accordingly, the Commission's Order is unlawful and hereby vacated. We remand to the Commission for proceedings in accordance with this Opinion.

I. RENEWABLE ENERGY ACT

{3} The Renewable Energy Act entered into effect on May 19, 2004. Section 62-16-1, note. Pursuant to Section 62-16-7, the Commission adopted Rule 572, implementing the REA. See 17.9.572 NMAC. The REA requires public utilities1 to include renewable energy as part of their electric energy supply portfolios. Section 62-16-4(A). Beginning January 1, 2006, renewable energy must comprise "no less than five percent of each public utility's total retail sales to New Mexico customers." Section 62-16-4(A)(1). This requirement is called the Renewable Portfolio Standard ("RPS"), and it increases by one percent each year until January 1, 2011, when it will reach ten percent of each public utility's annual retail sales in New Mexico. Section 62-16-4(A)(2).

{4} Utilities must establish their compliance with the Renewable Portfolio Standard by filing Renewable Energy Certificates with the Commission. Section 62-16-5(A) (directing the Commission to establish a system of RECs); 17.9.572.13 NMAC (stating that utilities must establish their annual compliance with the Renewable Portfolio Standard "through the filing of [R]enewable [E]nergy [C]ertificates with the [C]ommission"). Rule 572 defines a Renewable Energy Certificate as "a document evidencing that the enumerated renewable energy kilowatt-hours have been generated from a renewable energy generating facility." 17.9.572.7(E) NMAC. Each REC must have "a minimum value of one kilowatt-hour of renewable energy represented by the certificate for purposes of compliance with the [R]enewable [P]ortfolio [S]tandard." Section 62-16-5(A). RECs

> may be traded, sold or otherwise transferred by their owner to any other party; provided that the transfers and use of the certificate by a public utility for compliance with the renewable energy portfolio standard shall require the electric energy represented by the certificate to be contracted for delivery in New Mexico.

Section 62-16-5(B)(1)(b). Rule 572 adds that "transfers and use of the [Renewable Energy] [C]ertificate by a public utility for compliance with the [R]enewable ... [P]ortfolio [S]tandard do not require physical delivery of the electric energy represented by the certificate to a public utility." 17.9.572.13(B)(2) NMAC. Thus, compliance with the RPS provision of the REA can be established through RECs representing renewable energy the utility itself has generated; renewable energy the utility has purchased from another source; or renewable energy generated and contracted for delivery in New Mexico without the utility itself purchasing the energy. To ensure that compliance costs are reasonable, the REA requires that each year until 2012, and if necessary thereafter, public utilities file for the Commission's approval a report on their purchases of renewable energy during the prior calendar year as well as a procurement plan. Section 62-16-4(D)-(E).

{5} The REA authorizes public utilities to recover the reasonable costs of compliance with the REA "through the rate-making process." Section 62-16-6(A) states:

> A public utility that procures or generates renewable energy shall recover, through the rate-making process, the reasonable costs of complying with the renewable portfolio standard. Costs that are consistent with commission approval of procurement plans or transitional procurement plans shall be deemed to be reasonable.

The REA does not define the "rate-making process."

{6} A related statute, the Public Utility Act ("PUA"), NMSA 1978, §62-13-1 (1993), grants the Commission "general and exclusive power and jurisdiction to regulate and supervise every public utility in respect to its rates and service regulations." NMSA 1978, §62-6-4(A) (2003). In order to change or increase rates, a utility normally must go through a notice, hearing, and approval process. Section 62-8-7(A)-(E). However, utilities can recover certain costs—"taxes or cost of fuel, gas or purchased power"—automatically through an automatic adjustment clause. Section 62-8-7(E). The Commission adopted Rule 550, 17.9.550 NMAC, regarding the implementation, oversight, and maintenance of automatic adjustment clauses, pursuant to Section 62-8-7(E).

II. FACTS AND PROCEDURAL BACKGROUND

{7} In 2004, El Paso Electric Company obtained Commission approval of its 2004 renewable energy transitional procurement plan ("2004 Plan"), pursuant to Section 62-16-4(D)-(E) and Rule 572. EPE sought to comply with the Renewable Portfolio Standard by purchasing Renewable Energy Certificates, without taking physical delivery of the associated energy, from Public Service Company of New Mexico. In its 2004 Plan, EPE proposed to recover the costs of complying with the REA through its automatic adjustment clause. See §62-8-7(E). The Commission approved EPE's 2004 Plan; however, the Commission deferred the issue of the appropriate mechanism for cost recovery to this case. Final Order, NMPRC Case No. 04-00306-UT.

{8} On September 1, 2005, EPE filed its 2005 renewable energy procurement plan ("2005 Plan"), which contained the specific REC contract with PNM as well as the costs

EPE sought to recover through the automatic adjustment clause. NMPRC Case No. 05-00355-UT. In the instant proceeding, EPE sought Commission approval, on a permanent basis, of the automatic adjustment clause as the mechanism for recovering all costs of the purchased RECs under its approved Plan. In support, EPE filed testimony of its witness Steven P. Busser, contending that automatic adjustment clause recovery is appropriate under the REA, the PUA, and Commission Rules 572 and 550, and is the most reasonable mechanism for recovery of REA compliance costs. According to Busser, automatic adjustment clause recovery (i) would allow EPE to recover costs on a per kilowatt-hour basis; (ii) would be the least costly recovery mechanism, resulting in the lowest costs to EPE customers; (iii) would most timely allow one hundred percent of net proceeds from the sale of any excess RECs to be credited back to customers (although EPE does not intend to purchase RECs in excess of its REA compliance requirements); and (iv) was authorized by EPE's Stipulation and Final Order in its last rate case. The Commission also filed testimony, which staff witness Charles W. Gunter, a Utility Economist for the Utility Division of the Commission, adopted, in support of EPE's proposed automatic adjustment clause recovery, concluding that it (i) is the most appropriate method of cost recovery; (ii) is authorized by the REA and PUA; and (iii) will result in the lowest cost to EPE customers. NMIEC, Western Water and Power Production Limited, the Coalition for Clean Affordable Energy, and New Mexico State University ("NMSU") filed motions to intervene in the proceeding.

{9} The Commission held a public hearing on October 26, 2005, at which EPE witness Busser and Commission witness Gunter testified in favor of automatic adjustment clause recovery of EPE's REC costs. NMIEC and NMSU cross-examined the witnesses to establish that RECs are not "purchased power" under the PUA, and thus their costs cannot be recovered automatically through the automatic adjustment clause.

{10} On December 8, 2005, the Commission issued a Final Order, which concluded that automatic adjustment clause recovery is the appropriate method for recovery of EPE's REC costs. In reaching its decision, the Commission first determined that automatic adjustment clauses are part of the "rate-making process," contemplated in Section 62-16-6(A), based on (i) a previous Commission determination that they are (NMPRC Case No. 04-00334-UT) and (ii) Commission Rule 572, which "expressly recognizes the [automatic adjustment clause] may be used as part of a utility's rates for renewable cost recovery." Next, the Commission explained that it has "wide latitude to determine that the cost of purchasing or acquiring RECs are purchased power costs" because the PUA "grants the Commission 'latitude' and 'discretion' to include costs closely related to the broad categories of purchased power." See § 62-8-7. The Commission noted that it has previously allowed automatic recovery of gas hedging costs, "which demonstrate[s] the breadth of the Commission's authority to determine which costs to include in the adjustment clauses." The Commission agreed with EPE that "[b]ecause RECs are a requirement of EPE's energy supply mix, their cost is a purchased power cost." Thus, "[c]haracterizing RECs in this way, as 'part of the overall cost' of energy, is consistent with Commission precedent and with the express provisions and REC requirements of the REA."

{11} The Commission went on to determine that, as a policy matter, it should not treat cost recovery differently for RECs with delivered energy and RECs without delivered energy because both require generation of renewable energy which must be contracted for delivery in New Mexico. The Commission reasoned that "[a] utility should not be adversely affected through the ratemaking process for its renewable energy procurement decisions," especially in this case because EPE (i) chose to comply with the REA by purchasing RECs without the accompanying energy because they were "the lowest cost option for its customers" and (ii) sought automatic adjustment clause recovery of the REC costs as "the most economical means to recover the cost of compliance with the Act." The Commission stated that cost recovery of RECs through the automatic adjustment clause "makes a great deal of sense" because "RECs are an integral part of purchased power and are created and come about because renewable power is generated ... [and] do not exist without actual renewable energy generation that is contracted for delivery in New Mexico."

{12} Finally, the Commission determined, after examining the two other cost recovery alternatives, a separate rate rider or deferral of REC costs with carrying charges, that automatic adjustment clause recovery is the "proper and most efficient method of rate recovery." The Commission concluded that automatic adjustment clause recovery "will best assure that costs are recovered concurrently with their expenditure, on an equitable [kilowatt-hour] basis, and it will avoid additional costs associated with other collection alternatives. Recovery through the [automatic adjustment clause] results in the lowest cost collection from customers." The Commission found these to be "compelling" reasons for automatic adjustment clause recovery of REC costs. While NMIEC contended that automatic adjustment clause recovery of REC costs would compromise the Commission's ability to address the prudence of EPE's REC procurement, the Commission found numerous safeguards exist to address such concerns, including monthly and annual reporting as well as automatic adjustment clause reconciliation and continuation filings. As part of the Order, the Commission granted a variance that would add separate line items to EPE's monthly Rule 550 Reports "to separately track REC costs and potential credits" recovered through the automatic adjustment clause.

III. STANDARD OF REVIEW

{13} We review administrative orders to determine whether "the [Commission]'s decision is arbitrary and capricious, not supported by substantial evidence, outside the scope of the agency's authority, or otherwise inconsistent with law," *Dona Ana Mut. Domestic Water Consumers Ass'n v. N.M. Pub. Regulation Comm'n*, 2006-NMSC-032, ¶ 9, 140 N.M. 6, 139 P.3d 166, with the burden on the appellant to make this showing, see NMSA 1978, § 62-11-4 (1965). In reviewing the Commission's decision, we "begin by looking at two interconnected factors: whether the decision presents a question of law, a question of fact, or some combination of the two; and whether the matter is within the agency's specialized field of expertise." *Morningstar Water Users Ass'n v. N.M. Pub. Util. Comm'n*, 120 N.M. 579, 582, 904 P.2d 28, 31 (1995).

IV. DISCUSSION

{14} NMIEC appeals the Final Order of the Commission directly to this Court, pursuant to Section 62-11-1. NMIEC argues that the Final Order should be vacated on the ground that it is unlawful because it allows for recovery of EPE's REC costs through EPE's automatic adjustment clause, even though RECs do not constitute "purchased power" or any of the other specific costs which Section 62-8-7(E) authorizes for automatic cost recovery. NMIEC goes on to argue that the Commission exceeded its authority by finding that RECs are "closely related to" purchased power, when EPE purchased only the RECs and not the associated power that they represent, and are thus inappropriate for automatic adjustment clause recovery. The Commission's logic, according to NMIEC, renders the limitation language in Section 62-8-7(E) — "taxes or cost of fuel, gas or purchased power" — meaningless and would lead to the unreasonable result of "virtually any utility cost [being] 'related to' purchased power and therefore eligible for [automatic adjustment] clause recovery."

{15} The Commission and EPE, on the other hand, argue that this appeal centers on the question of substantial evidence in the record to support the Commission's Order, which they contend is within the Commission's broad rate-setting authority and discretion. The Commission advocates a two-step review. According to the Commission, we must first decide "whether the Commission's determination that RECs are closely related to purchased power costs in the context of the [REA] was supported by substantial evidence in the record and was within the Commission's authority." Next, we "must establish whether, after the Commission determined that RECs are closely related to purchased power costs in the context of the REA, it acted within its authority and ratemaking discretion by deciding that those costs are properly recoverable through a[n] [automatic] adjustment clause."

{16} The Commission begins by explaining that the exclusive method of complying with the REA is through the filing of RECs with the Commission, and that the REA does not require utilities to purchase the accompanying power in order to comply. The REA provides for recovery of the reasonable costs of compliance through the "rate-making process," and the Commission contends that it has broad discretion in setting rates, and that it has already determined that automatic adjustment clauses are part of the rate-making process. Therefore, since the Commission has determined that RECs, even without the purchase of energy, are "closely related to purchased power," in its discretion, the Commission can allow for REC cost recovery through EPE's automatic adjustment clause, in the same way it has previously allowed for such recovery of costs like gas hedging agreements, which likewise are not specifically enumerated in Section 62-8-7(E). El Paso Electric, the Real Party in Interest, also submitted a brief in which it makes essentially the same argument as the Commission.

{17} We view this case as involving two related questions. First, we are confronted with a matter of pure statutory interpretation, wherein we must determine the "rate-making process" contemplated in Section 62-16-6(A) of the REA. Based on the following analysis, we conclude that the "rate-making process" includes both rate cases and automatic adjustment clauses. Second, we review whether substantial evidence supports a finding that EPE's REC costs constitute "purchased power" or, in the alternative, whether the Commission had the authority to allow for automatic recovery of EPE's REC costs by determining that they are "closely related to purchased power."

A. THE "RATE-MAKING PROCESS" CONTEMPLATED BY THE REA INCLUDES BOTH GENERAL RATE CASES AND AUTOMATIC ADJUSTMENT CLAUSE RECOVERY, DEPENDING ON THE TYPE OF COST INVOLVED

{18} The REA authorizes public utilities to recover the reasonable costs of compliance thereto through "the rate-making process." Section 62-16-6(A). As a threshold matter, we note that EPE's REA compliance costs are presumed reasonable, as the Commission approved EPE's 2004 and 2005 Plans. Thus, we must determine what constitutes "the rate-making process" referred to in Section 62-16-6(A).

{19} Statutory interpretation is an issue of law, which we review de novo. *Pub. Serv. Co. of N.M. v. N.M. Pub. Util. Comm'n*, 1999-NMSC-040, ¶ 14, 128 N.M. 309, 992 P.2d 860 (quoting *State v. Rowell*, 121 N.M. 111, 114, 908 P.2d 1379, 1382 (1995)). We will reverse the agency's interpretation of a law if it is unreasonable or unlawful. NMSA 1978, § 62-11-5 (1982); *Morningstar Water Users Ass'n*, 120 N.M. at 583, 904 P.2d at 32. Where as here an agency is construing the same statutes by which it is governed, we accord some deference to the agency's interpretation. *Morningstar Water Users Ass'n*, 120 N.M. at 583, 904 P.2d at 32. The deference we accord the agency's interpretation depends on the legal question involved. As we have explained in the past,

> [t]he court will confer a heightened degree of deference to legal questions that implicate special agency expertise or the determination of fundamental policies within the scope of the agency's statutory function. However, the court is not bound by the agency's interpretation and may substitute its own independent judgment for that of the agency because it is the function of the courts to interpret the law.

Id. (internal citations and quotations marks omitted). Because statutory construction itself is not a matter within the purview of the Commission's expertise, "we afford little, if any, deference to the Commission on this matter." *Pub. Serv. Co. of N.M.*, 1999-NMSC-040, ¶ 14. Indeed, we are troubled by the multiple references, at the Commission hearing, in the Commission's and EPE's briefing, and at oral argument, to the legal conclusions of Commission staff with respect to matters of statutory construction as well as the Commission's apparent reliance on those legal conclusions in its Final Order.

{20} When construing statutes, our guiding principle is to determine and give effect to legislative intent. *Id.* ¶ 18. In ascertaining the Legislature's intent, we are aided by classic canons of statutory construction. *Id.* We look first to the plain language of the statute, giving the words their ordinary meaning, unless the Legislature indicates a different one was intended. *Id.* In addition, we strive to read related statutes in harmony so as to give effect to all provisions:

> In ascertaining legislative intent, the provisions of a statute must be read together with other statutes in pari materia under the presumption that the legislature acted with full knowledge of relevant statutory and common law.... Thus, two statutes covering the same subject matter should be harmonized and construed together when possible, in a way that facilitates their operation and the achievement of their goals.

Id. ¶ 23 (quoting *State ex rel. Quintana v. Schnedar*, 115 N.M. 573, 575-76, 855 P.2d 562, 564-65 (1993)).

{21} We thus begin with the plain language of Section 62-16-6(A) to ascertain the legislative intent. The Legislature did not define or specify "the rate-making process" in the REA, so we look to a related statute, the PUA, to inform the meaning of Section 62-16-6(A). The Legislature, through the PUA, has granted the Commission "general and exclusive power and jurisdiction to regulate and supervise every public utility in respect to its rates and service regulations." Section 62-6-4(A). In Section 62-8-7 of the PUA, entitled "Change in rates," the Legislature set forth the framework for setting and changing utility rates. See *Otero County Elec. Coop., Inc. v. N.M. Pub. Serv. Comm'n*, 108 N.M. 462, 464, 774 P.2d 1050, 1052 (1989). Section 62-8-7(E) states, in pertinent part: "Except as otherwise provided by law, any increase in rates or charges for the utility commodity based upon cost factors other than taxes or cost of fuel, gas or purchased power ... shall be permitted only after notice and hearing as provided by this section." Thus, the normal process a utility must follow for setting or changing its rates includes a notice, hearing, and approval process. However, utilities can recover specifically enumerated costs automatically through an automatic adjustment clause.

{22} Reading the related provisions of the REA and the PUA together, we agree with the Commission and conclude that by "rate-making process" in Section 62-16-6(A) of the REA, the Legislature meant the process set forth in Section 62-8-7 of the PUA, i.e., both general rate cases involving a Commission notice, hearing, and approval process as well as automatic adjustment clauses, depending on the type of cost involved.

B. EPE's REC COSTS CANNOT BE RECOVERED THROUGH ITS AUTOMATIC ADJUSTMENT CLAUSE

1. SUBSTANTIAL EVIDENCE DOES NOT SUPPORT A FINDING THAT RECs, UNACCOMPANIED BY THE PURCHASE OF THE RENEWABLE ENERGY THEY REPRESENT, ARE "PURCHASED POWER"

{23} Having determined that the "rate-making process" includes both general rate cases and automatic adjustment clauses, see Section 62-8-7, we must determine the proper method of cost recovery for EPE's REC costs. EPE sought automatic adjustment clause recovery of its REC costs, which the Commission approved. Section 62-8-7(E) of the PUA allows for automatic adjustment clause recovery of "taxes or cost of fuel, gas or purchased power." It is undisputed that EPE's REC costs do not constitute taxes or fuel or gas costs. However, the parties disagree as to whether EPE's REC costs constitute "purchased power." The Commission and EPE contend that they are; while NMIEC argues that they are not.

{24} With respect to questions of fact, we look to the whole record to determine whether substantial evidence supports the Commission's decision. *Att'y Gen. of N.M. v. N.M. Pub. Util. Comm'n* (*In re Comm'n's Investigation of the Rates for Gas Serv. of PNM's Gas Servs.*), 2000-NMSC-008, ¶ 4, 128 N.M. 747, 998 P.2d 1198. In reviewing the whole record,

> the court must be satisfied that the evidence demonstrates the reasonableness of the decision. No part of the evidence may be exclusively relied upon if it would be unreasonable to do so. The reviewing court needs to find evidence that is credible in light of the whole record and that is sufficient for a reasonable mind to accept as adequate to support the conclusion reached by the agency.

Id. (quoting *Nat'l Council on Comp. Ins. v. N.M. State Corp. Comm'n*, 107 N.M. 278, 282, 756 P.2d 558, 562 (1988)). We view the evidence in the light most favorable to the Commission's decision, *N.M. Indus. Energy Consumers v. N.M. Pub. Serv. Comm'n*, 104 N.M. 565, 570, 725 P.2d 244, 249 (1986) (quoting *Att'y Gen. of N.M. v. N.M. Pub. Serv. Comm'n*, 101 N.M. 549, 553, 685 P.2d 957, 961 (1984)), and draw every inference in support of the Commission's decision, but we will not uphold the decision if it is not supported by substantial evidence. *Pub. Serv. Co. of N.M. v. N.M. Pub. Serv. Comm'n*, 92 N.M. 721, 722, 594 P.2d 1177, 1178 (1979). In analyzing the nature of EPE's REC costs, we hold that substantial evidence does not support a conclusion that they constitute "purchased power."

{25} Commission Rule 572 defines a REC as "a document evidencing that the enumerated renewable energy kilowatt-hours have been generated from a renewable energy generating facility." 17.9.572.7(E) NMAC. Utilities are required to file RECs with the Commission to establish their compliance with the RPS of the REA. Section 62-16-5(A); 17.9.572.13 NMAC. However, utilities need not purchase the actual renewable energy represented by the REC. 17.9.572.13(B)(2) NMAC. Rather, as explained previously, the RECs can represent renewable energy the utility itself has generated; renewable energy the utility has purchased from another source; or renewable energy generated and contracted for delivery in New Mexico without the utility itself purchasing the energy.

{26} In the instant case, EPE purchased RECs representing a certain quantity of kilowatt-hours of renewable energy that had been generated by PNM and contracted for delivery in New Mexico. EPE did not, however, purchase the generated renewable energy represented by the RECs. In other words, EPE took credit for renewable energy generated by another source, in this case PNM, to fulfill its compliance requirements under the REA.2 In addition to the fact that EPE did not purchase any actual power when it incurred the REC costs, the record is replete with admissions by the Commission and EPE that EPE's RECs, indeed, do not constitute "purchased power." The first set of admissions came at the Commission hearing. EPE witness Busser stated, "When you are purchasing a REC you are not purchasing power, correct, in our situation." Commission witness Gunter stated, "A REC is not purchased electric power, that's correct." With specific respect to EPEs RECs, Gunter stated, "EPE is not purchasing renewable electric power but the REC itself comes about in connection with that generation of renewable energy." Gunter also stated that EPE's RECs are "not electric power strictly speaking." Then, at oral argument, the Commission's counsel stated, in reference to EPE's RECs, "I don't think that the Commission can contend that it is literally purchased power."

{27} Beyond these admissions, allowing for automatic adjustment clause recovery of EPE's REC costs would directly contradict the stated purpose of automatic adjustment clauses set forth in the Commission's own Rule 550. The rule states that the purpose of an automatic adjustment clause "is to flow through to the users of electricity the increases or decreases in Applicable Fuel and Purchased Power costs per kilowatt-hour of delivered energy above or below a Base Cost." 17.9.550.6(D) NMAC (emphasis added). The Base Cost is "the cost of fuel and purchased power upon which the applicable rate schedule was based stated on a [dollar] per [kilowatt-hour] basis." 17.9.550.7(F) NMAC. Through an automatic adjustment clause, a public utility can increase or decrease the Base Cost on a dollar per kilowatt-hour basis, calculating that cost adjustment based on the required format and data calculations set forth in the Appendix to Rule 550. 17.9.550.7(C), (I) NMAC; 17.9.550.13 NMAC; 17.9.550.13 NMAC app. at 1-2 (Rule 550 Form I for Investor Owned Utilities and Generation and Transmission Cooperatives). We acknowledge that RECs are enumerated on a per kilowatt-hour basis and that the Commission requires that RECs contain some of the same data3 used to calculate the purchased power automatic cost adjustment pursuant to Rule 550 Form I. In addition, we acknowledge that the RECs EPE purchased represent renewable energy that was generated, a fact upon which the Commission and EPE both focus. However, the fact of generation is not part of the statutory inquiry. Indeed, EPE did not purchase that renewable energy, and it was never delivered to EPE's customers. Therefore, we would create a legal fiction if we allowed EPE to recover its REC costs through its automatic adjustment clause because EPE would not be "flow[ing] through to the users of electricity the increases or decreases in Applicable Fuel and Purchased Power costs per kilowatt-hour of delivered energy above or below a Base Cost." 17.9.550.6(D) NMAC (emphasis added).

{28} "'Substantial evidence is more than a mere scintilla. It means such relevant evidence as a reasonable mind might accept as adequate to support a conclusion.'" *In re Comm'n's Investigation of the Rates for Gas Serv. of PNM's Gas Servs.*, 2000-NMSC-008, ¶ 11, (quoting *Consol. Edison Co. v. N.L.R.B.*, 305 U.S. 197, 229 (1938)). The evidence of record does not support a conclusion that EPE's REC costs are "purchased power." Indeed, the record supports the opposite conclusion.

2. THE COMMISSION EXCEEDED ITS AUTHORITY BY CHARACTERIZING EPE'S REC COSTS AS "CLOSELY RELATED TO PURCHASED POWER" AND THUS RECOVERABLE THROUGH EPE'S AUTOMATIC ADJUSTMENT CLAUSE

{29} The Commission determined that EPE's REC costs were "so closely related to purchased power" so as to constitute "purchased power" and thus be automatically recoverable. Both the Commission and EPE rested on the argument that REC costs are "so closely related to" and "an integral part" of "purchased power" because (i) RECs represent renewable energy; (ii) RECs would not exist unless renewable energy were generated; and (iii) the Commission has "wide latitude" to determine what constitutes "purchased power" and what is appropriate for automatic adjustment clause recovery. At oral argument, Commission counsel stated the Commission's reasoning as follows: EPE's REC costs are "in fact closely enough related to literally energy or literally power that [they] w[ere] appropriately included in that clause." Having concluded that EPE's REC costs do not constitute "purchased power," we review the Commission's decision that it has the authority and discretion to determine that EPE's REC costs are "closely related to purchased power" and thus recoverable through EPE's automatic adjustment clause.

{30} At the outset, we note this Court's long recognition of the broad authority of the Commission in setting utility rates. *N.M. Indus. Energy Consumers v. N.M. Pub. Serv. Comm'n (In re Ratemaking Methodology)*, 111 N.M. 622, 635, 808 P.2d 592, 605 (1991) ("The Commission is vested with broad discretion to pursue its statutory mandate to set just and reasonable rate or rates." (internal quotation marks and quoted authority omitted)); *Att'y Gen. of N.M. v. N.M. Pub. Serv. Comm'n.*, 101 N.M. at 553-54, 685 P.2d at 961-62 ("The Legislature has vested exclusive rate-making authority in the Commission. Furthermore, in a rate case, the Commission is vested with considerable discretion in de-termining the justness and reasonableness of utility rates.... Thus, the Commission is statutorily and constitutionally free to use any ratemaking formula it chooses." (quoted authority and internal citations omitted)). The Commission's broad rate-making authority "involves the making of pragmatic adjustments." *Hobbs Gas Co. v. N.M. Pub. Serv. Comm'n*, 94 N.M. 731, 733-34, 616 P.2d 1116, 1118-19 (1980) (quoted authority omitted). Indeed, "the result reached, not the method employed" is what controls. *Id.* at 734, 616 P.2d at 1119; *see also N.M. Indus. Energy Consumers*, 104 N.M. at 569-70, 725 P.2d at 248-49 (noting that the Court has "consistently construed the [PUA] broadly rather than to limit the Commission to any one particular method; the touchstone is the reasonableness of the ultimate decision"). However, the instant case does not implicate the Commission's expertise and discretion in setting utility rates, as both the Commission and EPE paint the issue. Rather, our inquiry centers on the Commission's construction of the related provisions of the REA and the PUA, a matter not within the Commission's expertise and to which we accord little deference.

{31} The language of Section 62-8-7(E) is plain and unambiguous: only "taxes or cost of fuel, gas or purchased power" may be recovered automatically. In addition, the Com-mission's own Rule 550 and Rule 550 Form I for calculating the automatic cost adjustment factor specifically enumerate only these four costs for automatic recovery. The Legislature authorized automatic cost recovery for only limited types of costs in order to regulate the use of automatic adjustment clauses and to avoid the massive abuses of the past. Commission rate cases involving notice, hearing, and approval remain the general rule for cost recovery, while automatic adjustment clause recovery is a narrow exception.

{32} The Legislature never amended the PUA provisions regarding automatic adjustment clauses when it approved the REA, nor did it create any exceptions in the REA itself to the limitations on automatic adjustment clause recovery. Indeed, the Commission has not amended its own Rule 550 to make special provision for REA compliance costs. We acknowledge that the Commission has the authority to promulgate rules regarding "which costs should be included in an adjustment clause, procedures to avoid the inclusion of costs in an adjustment clause that should not be included and methods by which the propriety of costs that are included may be determined by the commission in a timely manner." Section 62-8-7(E)(3). However, this provision does not authorize the Commission to expand the list of costs eligible for automatic adjustment clause recovery. Otherwise, the limitation language of Section 62-8-7(E) would be rendered meaningless, and the abuses that the Legislature was concerned about could come to fruition. Rather, we read Section 62-8-7(E)(3) as granting the Commission the authority to promulgate rules that safeguard against abuses and thus fulfill the intent of the Legislature that automatic cost recovery be limited to the specifically enumerated costs set forth in Section 62-8-7(E). Likewise, the fact that the Commission has in the past allowed automatic recovery of gas hedging agreements and other costs not enumerated in Section 62-8-7(E) does not mean that we will sanction such a practice in the instant case.

{33} In light of its plainly exclusive language, we interpret Section 62-8-7(E) narrowly and decline to read into it " 'language which is not there, particularly if it makes sense as written.' " *Pub. Serv. Co. of N.M.*, 1999-NMSC-040, ¶ 18 (quoting *Burroughs v. Bd. of County Comm'rs*, 88 N.M. 303, 306, 540 P.2d 233, 236 (1975)). Based on the fact that EPE did not purchase the renewable energy associated with the RECs as well as the admissions of both the Commission and EPE that EPE's REC costs are not, in fact, "purchased power," we conclude that the Commission exceeded its authority by allowing EPE to recover its REC costs through its automatic adjustment clause by categorizing them as "closely related to purchased power." Consequently, the Commission's Order is unlawful. Because EPE did not purchase the renewable energy represented by the RECs, we do not pass on the propriety of automatic adjustment clause recovery for the costs of RECs which represent actual renewable energy purchased by the utility.

{34} In closing, we note that the Commission and EPE focused, in part, on the efficiency and cost-effectiveness of automatic adjustment clause recovery of EPE's REC costs, particularly in light of the mandatory nature of REA compliance. The Commission determined that automatic adjustment clause recovery would be the most efficient and cost-effective method for recovering EPE's REC costs, both for EPE and for consumers. While cost-effectiveness and efficiency are important goals, they are not the standard for automatic adjustment clause recovery which the Legislature has set forth in the PUA. In the final analysis, EPE may recover the reasonable costs of complying with the REA through a general rate case. Nevertheless, this case highlights the need for the Legislature to harmonize the antecedent PUA with the related provisions of the REA. However, until the Legislature does so, we will continue to read the PUA as written and allow for automatic recovery only of the costs specifically enumerated in Section 62-8-7(E), "taxes or cost of fuel, gas or purchased power."

V. CONCLUSION

{35} The REA allows utilities to recover reasonable compliance costs though the "rate-making process." Section 62-16-6(A). We read this provision together with Section 62-8-7(E) of the PUA and hold that the "rate-making process" refers to both general rate cases and automatic adjustment clauses, depending on the type of cost involved. Automatic adjustment clauses may be used to recover only "taxes or cost of fuel, gas or purchased power." Section 62-8-7(E). Substantial evidence does not support the conclusion that EPE's REC costs are "purchased power." Morever, the Commission exceeded its authority in declaring these costs "closely related to purchased power" and thus recoverable through EPE's automatic adjustment clause. Consequently, the Commission's Order is unlawful and is hereby vacated. We remand to the Commission for proceedings in accordance with this Opinion.

{36} IT IS SO ORDERED.

Notes & Questions

1. *Practice Note*: The purpose of the automatic adjustment clause was to "flow through" the increases or decreases in costs of "delivered energy" to electricity consumers. The court found that RECs were not "delivered" energy because the RECs were not sold with the electricity that generated the RECs. The court admitted that recovery under the automatic adjustment clause would be the "most efficient and cost-effective method" for recovering costs, but still determined that state law simply did not allow it. Just the fact that you are right on policy (or even substance) doesn't ensure you'll win, and you want to make sure your clients understand that, too.

2. Was the court's analysis the only possible outcome? While reasonable, there is a counterargument that, because of the RPS mandate, purchased RECs (at least up to the state mandated percentage) are actually a cost of "delivered energy." The argument is thus that RECs represent an increase in the cost of delivered energy because state law requires a certain number of RECs be part of the electricity delivery process. Essentially, RECs convert the utility's purchased power (or a part of it) into energy that meets the RPS mandate. With a requirement that a certain percentage of purchased power come from renewable resources, RECs are arguably a cost of any purchased power. Which is the better argument? Why?

Chapter 7

Climate Change Law & Policy

A. Introduction

Greenhouse gas (GHG) emissions are a byproduct of almost every human activity and are a leading cause of climate change (or "global warming"). More recently, some have turned to the phrase "climate disruption" because the specific impacts related to increased GHGs in the atmosphere can lead to unpredictable results.

Climate impacts can include droughts, heat waves, hurricanes, heavy storms, and floods. GHG emissions reduction policies started to emerge in the late 1980s, and have notably increased in the past fifteen years. Claims to the contrary notwithstanding, there is a scientific consensus that increased GHGs in the atmosphere will lead to climate disruptions. The real debate is not (or should not be) about the threat, but rather about how to deal with GHG emissions. Resource allocation, funding, and scope all are major concerns with no clear answers.

Still, municipalities, state and federal governments, and international organizations have contemplated, and in some cases implemented, programs to reduce GHG emissions. Following are some of the leading programs and proposals.

1. Vocabulary and Concepts

The U.S. Environmental Protection Agency provides the following Climate Change Vocabulary, available at http://epa.gov/r5climatechange/posters/climate-change-vocab-list.pdf:

Arctic: The Arctic is a vast, ice-covered ocean, surrounded by treeless, frozen ground. This habitat is home to organisms living in and on the ice including fish, marine mammals, birds, land animals, and human societies.

Atmosphere: The mixture of gases and aerosols — the air — that surrounds the Earth in layers protecting us from the sun's powerful ultraviolet (UV) radiation, and even from meteors. The atmosphere extends up to 20 miles above the Earth.

Carbon Dioxide (CO_2): A heavy, colorless atmospheric gas. It is emitted during respiration by plants and by all animals, fungi, and microorganisms that depend either directly or indirectly on plants for food. CO_2 is also generated as a byproduct of the burning of fossil fuels or vegetable matter. CO_2 is absorbed from the air by plants during their growth process. It is one of the greenhouse gases.

Climate: The average weather for a particular region over an extended time period. In other words, climate is the weather you would expect to have in a particular region.

Climate Change: Major changes in temperature, rainfall, snow, or wind patterns lasting for decades or longer. Climate change may result from both natural processes and/or human activities.

Emissions: The act or instance of discharging (emitting) something into the air, such as exhaust that comes out of the tail pipe of a car or a smokestack.

Fossil Fuels: Fossil fuels are natural substances made deep within the Earth from the remains of ancient plants and animals. Over time, heat and pressure turned the decomposing remains into substances that act as fuel to release energy when burned. Coal, oil, and natural gas are the three main fossil fuels.

Global Warming: An increase in the Earth's average temperature, which in turn causes changes in climate. This increase in temperature is caused mainly by an increase in greenhouse gases like carbon dioxide and methane in the atmosphere.

Greenhouse Effect: The effect produced by greenhouse gases allowing incoming solar energy to pass through the Earth's atmosphere, but preventing most of the outgoing heat from escaping into space. The natural greenhouse effect is necessary to maintain life on earth, as it keeps the Earth 60°F warmer than it would be without the presence of these gases.

Greenhouse Gases: Gases such as water vapor, carbon dioxide, methane, and nitrous oxide that allow incoming solar radiation to pass through the Earth's atmosphere, but prevent most of the outgoing infrared (heat) radiation from the surface and lower atmosphere from escaping into outer space. Greenhouse gases are present in the atmosphere from both natural processes and human activities such as burning fossil fuels and driving cars.

Solar Radiation: The energy emitted by the sun. This energy can be seen and felt as heat in the sun's rays.

Weather: The specific condition of the atmosphere at a particular place and time. It is measured in terms of such things as wind, temperature, humidity, atmospheric pressure, cloudiness, and precipitation. In most places, weather can change from hour-to-hour, day-to-day, and season-to-season.

2. Client Issue

Your firm has just had a request from a large retail client to look for ways to offset costs through many efficiency measures they are considering. The company plans to improve energy efficiency company-wide, including their trucking fleet and in heating, cooling, and lighting efficiency in their retail stores. They plan to consider options for reducing carbon emissions in all of these cases, and they have asked you to figure out opportunities to maximize the corporate benefit of doing so. That is, are there states or other levels of government that they should be lobbying? Are there regulations that will reward these activities? Are there other areas they should be considering? As you read this chapter, look for possible opportunities or hurdles, and think about other areas they may want to pursue. Use Appendix E as an additional resource that may help you tailor your responses. In practice, you will find that the statute and/or regulations can provide both business and legal challenges and opportunities.

3. The Regional Greenhouse Gas Initiative (RGGI)

Regional Greenhouse Gas Initiative

Welcome, http://www.rggi.org/

The Regional Greenhouse Gas Initiative (RGGI) is the first market-based regulatory program in the United States to reduce greenhouse gas emissions. RGGI is a cooperative effort among the states of Connecticut, Delaware, Maine, Maryland, Massachusetts, New Hampshire, New York, Rhode Island, and Vermont to cap and reduce CO_2 emissions from the power sector.

Following a comprehensive 2012 Program Review, the RGGI states implemented a new 2014 RGGI cap of 91 million short tons. The RGGI CO_2 cap then declines 2.5 percent each year from 2015 to 2020. The RGGI CO_2 cap represents a regional budget for CO_2 emissions from the power sector.

States sell nearly all emission allowances through auctions and invest proceeds in energy efficiency, renewable energy, and other consumer benefit programs. These programs are spurring innovation in the clean energy economy and creating green jobs in the RGGI states.

3. The Western Climate Initiative (WCI)

The Western Climate Initiative, Design Summary

(excerpt), July 27, 2010, *available at* http://www.westernclimateinitiative.org/ document-archives/func-download/281/chk,6ef3df0d56ecf191eb4 abc3d426c33e3/no_html,1/

The Western Climate Initiative (WCI) is a collaboration of seven U.S. states and four Canadian provinces that have been working together since 2007 to identify, evaluate, and implement policies to address climate change.

The WCI Partner jurisdictions reflect diverse geographies, climates, populations, industries, and energy and transportation infrastructures.... Nevertheless, the Partners share a commitment to tackling the economic, energy, and environmental challenges associated with greenhouse gas (GHG) emissions, recognizing that:

- Adverse impacts of climate change are already being experienced in our states and provinces.

- Acting now reduces the risk of far more significant adverse climate change impacts and associated unacceptable economic harm.

- Acting now reduces costs for future generations and provides substantial economic opportunities for the residents of our jurisdictions, contributing to job growth and economic recovery, and reducing reliance on imported fossil fuels.

A Comprehensive Initiative

The WCI Partner jurisdictions have developed a comprehensive strategy to reduce regional GHG emissions to 15 percent below 2005 levels by 2020. This goal is based on the individual GHG emission reduction goals of the Partner jurisdictions. Our strategy will also spur investment in and development of clean-energy technologies, create green jobs, and protect public health. The WCI Partner jurisdictions' plan includes the following elements:

- **Using the power of the market.** A market-based approach that caps GHG emissions and uses tradable permits will provide incentives for companies and inventors to create new technologies that increase efficiency, promote greater use of renewable or lower-polluting fuels, and foster process improvements that reduce dependence on fossil fuels.

- **Encouraging reductions throughout the economy.** To reduce compliance costs and encourage emissions reductions, offset certificates will reward emissions reductions in sectors such as forestry and agriculture that are not covered by emissions caps.

- **Advancing core policies and programs to speed the transition to a clean energy economy** by targeting cost-effective emissions reductions, including:
  - Expanding energy efficiency programs that reduce customer utility bills;
  - Encouraging additional renewable energy sources that diversify supply resources and reduce air and water pollution;
  - Tackling transportation emissions through vehicle emissions standards, fuel standards, and incentives for improved community and transportation planning;
  - Establishing performance benchmarks and standards for high-emitting industries to spur innovation and improve competitiveness; and
  - Identifying best practices in workforce and community programs to help individuals transition to new jobs in the clean energy economy.

The WCI Partner jurisdictions' comprehensive strategy is good for the environment and good for the economy. It encourages the lowest cost reductions in GHG emissions and improved energy efficiency. Economic modeling conducted by the Partner jurisdictions indicates that the program will result in modest cost savings between 2012 and 2020. The strategy balances the principles adopted by the WCI Partner jurisdictions to maximize total benefits throughout the region, including reducing air pollutants, diversifying energy sources, and advancing economic, environmental, and public health objectives, while also avoiding localized or disproportionate environmental or economic impacts.

From the beginning, the Partner jurisdictions' strategy for addressing climate change has recognized the need for broad collaborative action to reduce GHG emissions. All of the WCI Partner jurisdictions have adopted climate action plans, and are taking steps to reduce emissions. We also are in discussions with other regional greenhouse gas initiatives—the Regional Greenhouse Gas Initiative (RGGI) and the Midwestern Greenhouse Gas Reduction Accord—to further broaden the collaboration on mitigation activities. In addition, WCI Partner jurisdictions are working closely with our federal governments to promote national and international action, and to ensure coordination among state, provincial, regional, and national programs.

The WCI Partner jurisdictions understand that even if it were possible to substantially reduce or even eliminate GHG emissions today, our jurisdictions would still feel the impacts of climate change due to emissions that have already occurred. Scientific research continues to confirm that our water resources, natural ecosystems, air quality, and environment-dependent industries like agriculture and tourism will be significantly impacted by changes in climate. Consequently, in addition to limiting GHG emissions, efforts are needed to address the impacts of climate change. The WCI Partner jurisdictions are therefore also committed to undertaking preparation and adaptation efforts.

. . . .

How the WCI Cap-and-Trade Program Works

The WCI Cap-and-Trade Program will be composed of the individual jurisdictions' cap-and-trade programs implemented through state and provincial regulations. Each WCI Partner jurisdiction implementing the cap- and-trade program design will issue "emission allowances" to meet its jurisdiction-specific emissions goal. The total number of available allowances serves as the "cap" on emissions. The allowances can be bought and sold ("traded"). A regional allowance market is created by the Partner jurisdictions recognizing one another's allowances for compliance. Through this recognition, the emissions allowances issued by each jurisdiction will be usable throughout the jurisdictions for compliance purposes.

The WCI Cap-and-Trade Program includes rigorous emissions reporting requirements that ensure accurate and timely measurement and recording of GHG emissions by the entities included in the program. At least once each three years, covered entities are required to turn into the state or province one "emission allowance" for each metric ton of carbon dioxide equivalent (CO_2e) emissions they emit and report. To reduce the total amount of emissions, the number of allowances issued will be reduced over time.

There is no restriction on who can own emission allowances—they can be sold between and among covered entities or third parties. Entities that reduce their emissions below the number of allowances they hold can sell their excess allowances or hold them for later use. Selling excess allowances allows entities to recoup some of their emissions reduction costs, while holding allowances for later use will lessen future compliance costs. This "trading" of emission allowances keeps compliance costs lower than would otherwise be the case because it provides flexibility in how and when reductions are made. It also puts a price on the emissions, which provides an incentive to innovate and find new ways to reduce emissions.

The WCI program design includes important features to ensure that the participating jurisdictions achieve their emissions goals affordably and cost-effectively. Emission offsets, representing emissions reductions from sources not covered by the program, can be used for compliance in limited quantity along with allowances from other trading programs that have been recognized by the WCI Partner jurisdictions. There is no limitation on how long an emission allowance may be held for future use. Allowing entities to turn in allowances in three-year periods provides flexibility as to when emissions reductions are made.

4. The Kyoto Protocol

United Nations Framework Convention on Climate Change

http://unfccc.int/kyoto_protocol/items/2830.php

Kyoto Protocol

The Kyoto Protocol is an international agreement linked to the United Nations Framework Convention on Climate Change, which commits its Parties by setting internationally binding emission reduction targets.

Recognizing that developed countries are principally responsible for the current high levels of GHG emissions in the atmosphere as a result of more than 150 years of industrial activity, the Protocol places a heavier burden on developed nations under the principle of "common but differentiated responsibilities."

The Kyoto Protocol was adopted in Kyoto, Japan, on 11 December 1997 and entered into force on 16 February 2005. The detailed rules for the implementation of the Protocol were adopted at COP 7 in Marrakesh, Morocco, in 2001, and are referred to as the "Marrakesh Accords." Its first commitment period started in 2008 and ended in 2012.

Doha Amendment

In Doha, Qatar, on 8 December 2012, the "Doha Amendment to the Kyoto Protocol" was adopted. The amendment includes:

- New commitments for Annex I Parties to the Kyoto Protocol who agreed to take on commitments in a second commitment period from 1 January 2013 to 31 December 2020;

- A revised list of greenhouse gases (GHG) to be reported on by Parties in the second commitment period; and

- Amendments to several articles of the Kyoto Protocol which specifically referenced issues pertaining to the first commitment period and which needed to be updated for the second commitment period.

On 21 December 2012, the amendment was circulated by the Secretary-General of the United Nations, acting in his capacity as Depositary, to all Parties to the Kyoto Protocol in accordance with Articles 20 and 21 of the Protocol.

During the first commitment period, 37 industrialized countries and the European Community committed to reduce GHG emissions to an average of five percent against 1990 levels. During the second commitment period, Parties committed to reduce GHG emissions by at least 18 percent below 1990 levels in the eight-year period from 2013 to 2020; however, the composition of Parties in the second commitment period is different from the first.

The Kyoto mechanisms

Under the Protocol, countries must meet their targets primarily through national measures. However, the Protocol also offers them an additional means to meet their targets by way of three market-based mechanisms.

The Kyoto mechanisms are:

- International Emissions Trading
- Clean Development Mechanism (CDM)
- Joint implementation (JI)

The mechanisms help to stimulate green investment and help Parties meet their emission targets in a cost-effective way.

Monitoring emission targets

Under the Protocol, countries' actual emissions have to be monitored and precise records have to be kept of the trades carried out.

Registry systems track and record transactions by Parties under the mechanisms. The UN Climate Change Secretariat, based in Bonn, Germany, keeps an international transaction log to verify that transactions are consistent with the rules of the Protocol.

Reporting is done by Parties by submitting annual emission inventories and national reports under the Protocol at regular intervals.

A compliance system ensures that Parties are meeting their commitments and helps them to meet their commitments if they have problems doing so.

Adaptation

The Kyoto Protocol, like the Convention, is also designed to assist countries in adapting to the adverse effects of climate change. It facilitates the development and deployment of technologies that can help increase resilience to the impacts of climate change.

The Adaptation Fund was established to finance adaptation projects and programmes in developing countries that are Parties to the Kyoto Protocol. In the first commitment period, the Fund was financed mainly with a share of proceeds from CDM project activities. In Doha, in 2012, it was decided that for the second commitment period, international emissions trading and joint implementation would also provide the Adaptation Fund with a 2 percent share of proceeds.

The road ahead

The Kyoto Protocol is seen as an important first step towards a truly global emission reduction regime that will stabilize GHG emissions, and can provide the architecture for the future international agreement on climate change.

In Durban, the Ad Hoc Working Group on the Durban Platform for Enhanced Action (ADP) was established to develop a protocol, another legal instrument or an agreed outcome with legal force under the Convention, applicable to all Parties. The ADP is to complete its work as early as possible, but no later than 2015, in order to adopt this protocol, legal instrument or agreed outcome with legal force at the twenty-first session of the Conference of the Parties and for it to come into effect and be implemented from 2020.

Notes & Questions

1. The United States has not signed on to the Kyoto Protocol, in part because of objections that other large emitters, like China and India, were not part of the protocol. The process used for the protocol, the Clean Development Mechanism (CDM), has had its share of problems, including allegations of fraud and abuse.

2. *Practice Note*: Sometimes good things happen, even without regulation or legislation. Despite not signing on to the treaty, between 2007 and 2012 the United States beat Europe's emissions reductions targets. This is primarily because electricity generators engaged in large amounts of fuel switching to natural gas (from coal) due to the low U.S. natural gas prices. Those prices are largely related to the massive increase in available supply because of hydraulic fracturing in the Barnett Shale and Marcellus Shale formations. Consider what that might mean for the future. Is enough being done? Can this gas-driven market change create new and expanded opportunities for GHG emissions reductions?

B. U.S. Climate Law and Regulation

Massachusetts v. EPA

549 U.S. 497 (2007) (footnotes omitted)

Justice Stevens delivered the opinion of the Court.

A well-documented rise in global temperatures has coincided with a significant increase in the concentration of carbon dioxide in the atmosphere. Respected scientists believe the two trends are related. For when carbon dioxide is released into the atmosphere, it acts like the ceiling of a greenhouse, trapping solar energy and retarding the escape of reflected heat. It is therefore a species — the most important species — of a "greenhouse gas."

Calling global warming "the most pressing environmental challenge of our time," a group of States, local governments, and private organizations, alleged in a petition for certiorari that the Environmental Protection Agency (EPA) has abdicated its responsibility under the Clean Air Act to regulate the emissions of four greenhouse gases, including carbon dioxide. Specifically, petitioners asked us to answer two questions concerning the meaning of § 202(a)(1) of the Act: whether EPA has the statutory authority to regulate greenhouse gas emissions from new motor vehicles; and if so, whether its stated reasons for refusing to do so are consistent with the statute.

In response, EPA, supported by 10 intervening States and six trade associations, correctly argued that we may not address those two questions unless at least one petitioner has standing to invoke our jurisdiction under Article III of the Constitution. Notwithstanding the serious character of that jurisdictional argument and the absence of any conflicting decisions construing § 202(a)(1), the unusual importance of the underlying issue persuaded us to grant the writ. 548 U.S. __ (2006).

I

Section 202(a)(1) of the Clean Air Act, as added by Pub. L. 89–272, § 101(8), 79 Stat. 992, and as amended by, inter alia, 84 Stat. 1690 and 91 Stat. 791, 42 U.S.C. § 7521(a)(1), provides:

> "The [EPA] Administrator shall by regulation prescribe (and from time to time revise) in accordance with the provisions of this section, standards applicable to the emission of any air pollutant from any class or classes of new motor vehicles or new motor vehicle engines, which in his judgment cause, or contribute to, air pollution which may reasonably be anticipated to endanger public health or welfare...."

The Act defines "air pollutant" to include "any air pollution agent or combination of such agents, including any physical, chemical, biological, radioactive ... substance or matter which is emitted into or otherwise enters the ambient air." § 7602(g). "Welfare" is also defined broadly: among other things, it includes "effects on ... weather ... and climate." § 7602(h).

When Congress enacted these provisions, the study of climate change was in its infancy. In 1959, shortly after the U.S. Weather Bureau began monitoring atmospheric carbon dioxide levels, an observatory in Mauna Loa, Hawaii, recorded a mean level of 316 parts per million. This was well above the highest carbon dioxide concentration — no more than 300 parts per million—revealed in the 420,000-year-old ice-core record. By the time Congress drafted §202(a)(1) in 1970, carbon dioxide levels had reached 325 parts per million.

In the late 1970's, the Federal Government began devoting serious attention to the possibility that carbon dioxide emissions associated with human activity could provoke climate change. In 1978, Congress enacted the National Climate Program Act, 92 Stat. 601, which required the President to establish a program to "assist the Nation and the world to understand and respond to natural and man-induced climate processes and their implications," *id.*, §3. President Carter, in turn, asked the National Research Council, the working arm of the National Academy of Sciences, to investigate the subject. The Council's response was unequivocal: "If carbon dioxide continues to increase, the study group finds no reason to doubt that climate changes will result and no reason to believe that these changes will be negligible.... A wait-and-see policy may mean waiting until it is too late."

Congress next addressed the issue in 1987, when it enacted the Global Climate Protection Act, Title XI of Pub. L. 100–204, 101 Stat. 1407, note following 15 U.S.C. §2901. Finding that "manmade pollution—the release of carbon dioxide, chlorofluorocarbons, methane, and other trace gases into the atmosphere—may be producing a long-term and substantial increase in the average temperature on Earth," §1102(1), 101 Stat. 1408, Congress directed EPA to propose to Congress a "coordinated national policy on global climate change," §1103(b), and ordered the Secretary of State to work "through the channels of multilateral diplomacy" and coordinate diplomatic efforts to combat global warming, §1103(c). Congress emphasized that "ongoing pollution and deforestation may be contributing now to an irreversible process" and that "[n]ecessary actions must be identified and implemented in time to protect the climate." §1102(4).

Meanwhile, the scientific understanding of climate change progressed. In 1990, the Intergovernmental Panel on Climate Change (IPCC), a multinational scientific body organized under the auspices of the United Nations, published its first comprehensive report on the topic. Drawing on expert opinions from across the globe, the IPCC concluded that "emissions resulting from human activities are substantially increasing the atmospheric concentrations of ... greenhouse gases [which] will enhance the greenhouse effect, resulting on average in an additional warming of the Earth's surface."

Responding to the IPCC report, the United Nations convened the "Earth Summit" in 1992 in Rio de Janeiro. The first President Bush attended and signed the United Nations Framework Convention on Climate Change (UNFCCC), a nonbinding agreement among 154 nations to reduce atmospheric concentrations of carbon dioxide and other greenhouse gases for the purpose of "prevent[ing] dangerous anthropogenic [*i.e.*, human-induced] interference with the [Earth's] climate system." S. Treaty Doc. No. 102–38, Art. 2, p. 5 (1992). The Senate unanimously ratified the treaty.

Some five years later—after the IPCC issued a second comprehensive report in 1995 concluding that "[t]he balance of evidence suggests there is a discernible human influence on global climate"—the UNFCCC signatories met in Kyoto, Japan, and adopted a protocol that assigned mandatory targets for industrialized nations to reduce greenhouse gas emissions. Because those targets did not apply to developing and heavily polluting nations such as China and India, the Senate unanimously passed a resolution expressing its sense that the United States should not enter into the Kyoto Protocol. See S. Res. 98, 105th Cong., 1st Sess. (July 25, 1997) (as passed). President Clinton did not submit the protocol to the Senate for ratification.

II

On October 20, 1999, a group of 19 private organizations filed a rulemaking petition asking EPA to regulate "greenhouse gas emissions from new motor vehicles under § 202 of the Clean Air Act." App. 5. Petitioners maintained that 1998 was the "warmest year on record"; that carbon dioxide, methane, nitrous oxide, and hydrofluorocarbons are "heat trapping greenhouse gases"; that greenhouse gas emissions have significantly accelerated climate change; and that the IPCC's 1995 report warned that "carbon dioxide remains the most important contributor to [man-made] forcing of climate change." *Id.*, at 13 (internal quotation marks omitted). The petition further alleged that climate change will have serious adverse effects on human health and the environment. *Id.*, at 22–35. As to EPA's statutory authority, the petition observed that the agency itself had already confirmed that it had the power to regulate carbon dioxide. See *id.*, at 18, n. 21. In 1998, Jonathan Z. Cannon, then EPA's General Counsel, prepared a legal opinion concluding that "CO_2 emissions are within the scope of EPA's authority to regulate," even as he recognized that EPA had so far declined to exercise that authority. *Id.*, at 54 (memorandum to Carol M. Browner, Administrator (Apr. 10, 1998) (hereinafter Cannon memorandum)). Cannon's successor, Gary S. Guzy, reiterated that opinion before a congressional committee just two weeks before the rulemaking petition was filed. See *id.*, at 61.

Fifteen months after the petition's submission, EPA requested public comment on "all the issues raised in [the] petition," adding a "particular" request for comments on "any scientific, technical, legal, economic or other aspect of these issues that may be relevant to EPA's consideration of this petition." 66 Fed. Reg. 7486, 7487 (2001). EPA received more than 50,000 comments over the next five months. See 68 Fed. Reg. 52924 (2003).

Before the close of the comment period, the White House sought "assistance in identifying the areas in the science of climate change where there are the greatest certainties and uncertainties" from the National Research Council, asking for a response "as soon as possible." App. 213. The result was a 2001 report titled Climate Change: An Analysis of Some Key Questions (NRC Report), which, drawing heavily on the 1995 IPCC report, concluded that "[g]reenhouse gases are accumulating in Earth's atmosphere as a result of human activities, causing surface air temperatures and subsurface ocean temperatures to rise. Temperatures are, in fact, rising." NRC Report 1.

On September 8, 2003, EPA entered an order denying the rulemaking petition. 68 Fed. Reg. 52922. The agency gave two reasons for its decision: (1) that contrary to the opinions of its former general counsels, the Clean Air Act does not authorize EPA to issue mandatory regulations to address global climate change, see *id.*, at 52925–52929; and (2) that even if the agency had the authority to set greenhouse gas emission standards, it would be unwise to do so at this time, *id.*, at 52929–52931.

In concluding that it lacked statutory authority over greenhouse gases, EPA observed that Congress "was well aware of the global climate change issue when it last comprehensively amended the [Clean Air Act] in 1990," yet it declined to adopt a proposed amendment establishing binding emissions limitations. *Id.*, at 52926. Congress instead chose to authorize further investigation into climate change. *Ibid.* (citing §§ 103(g) and 602(e) of the Clean Air Act Amendments of 1990, 104 Stat. 2652, 2703, 42 U.S.C. §§ 7403(g)(1) and 7671a(e)). EPA further reasoned that Congress' "specially tailored solutions to global atmospheric issues," 68 Fed. Reg. 52926 — in particular, its 1990 enactment of a comprehensive scheme to regulate pollutants that depleted the ozone layer, see Title VI, 104 Stat. 2649, 42 U.S.C. §§ 7671–7671q — counseled against reading the general authorization of § 202(a)(1) to confer regulatory authority over greenhouse gases.

EPA stated that it was "urged on in this view" by this Court's decision in *FDA v. Brown & Williamson Tobacco Corp.*, 529 U.S. 120 (2000). In that case, relying on "tobacco['s] unique political history," *id.*, at 159, we invalidated the Food and Drug Administration's reliance on its general authority to regulate drugs as a basis for asserting jurisdiction over an "industry constituting a significant portion of the American economy," *ibid.*

EPA reasoned that climate change had its own "political history": Congress designed the original Clean Air Act to address *local* air pollutants rather than a substance that "is fairly consistent in its concentration throughout the *world's* atmosphere," 68 Fed. Reg. 52927 (emphasis added); declined in 1990 to enact proposed amendments to force EPA to set carbon dioxide emission standards for motor vehicles, *ibid.* (citing H. R. 5966, 101st Cong., 2d Sess. (1990)); and addressed global climate change in other legislation, 68 Fed. Reg. 52927. Because of this political history, and because imposing emission limitations on greenhouse gases would have even greater economic and political repercussions than regulating tobacco, EPA was persuaded that it lacked the power to do so. *Id.*, at 52928. In essence, EPA concluded that climate change was so important that unless Congress spoke with exacting specificity, it could not have meant the agency to address it.

Having reached that conclusion, EPA believed it followed that greenhouse gases cannot be "air pollutants" within the meaning of the Act. See *ibid.* ("It follows from this conclusion, that [greenhouse gases], as such, are not air pollutants under the [Clean Air Act's] regulatory provisions …"). The agency bolstered this conclusion by explaining that if carbon dioxide were an air pollutant, the only feasible method of reducing tailpipe emissions would be to improve fuel economy. But because Congress has already created detailed mandatory fuel economy standards subject to Department of Transportation (DOT) administration, the agency concluded that EPA regulation would either conflict with those standards or be superfluous. *Id.*, at 52929.

Even assuming that it had authority over greenhouse gases, EPA explained in detail why it would refuse to exercise that authority. The agency began by recognizing that the concentration of greenhouse gases has dramatically increased as a result of human activities, and acknowledged the attendant increase in global surface air temperatures. *Id.*, at 52930. EPA nevertheless gave controlling importance to the NRC Report's statement that a causal link between the two "'cannot be unequivocally established.'" *Ibid.* (quoting NRC Report 17). Given that residual uncertainty, EPA concluded that regulating greenhouse gas emissions would be unwise. 68 Fed. Reg. 52930.

The agency furthermore characterized any EPA regulation of motor-vehicle emissions as a "piecemeal approach" to climate change, *id.*, at 52931, and stated that such regulation would conflict with the President's "comprehensive approach" to the problem, *id.*, at 52932. That approach involves additional support for technological innovation, the creation of nonregulatory programs to encourage voluntary private-sector reductions in greenhouse gas emissions, and further research on climate change—not actual regulation. *Id.*, at 52932–52933. According to EPA, unilateral EPA regulation of motor-vehicle greenhouse gas emissions might also hamper the President's ability to persuade key developing countries to reduce greenhouse gas emissions. *Id.*, at 52931.

III

Petitioners, now joined by intervenor States and local governments, sought review of EPA's order in the United States Court of Appeals for the District of Columbia Circuit. Although each of the three judges on the panel wrote a separate opinion, two judges agreed "that the EPA Administrator properly exercised his discretion under §202(a)(1) in denying the petition for rule making." 415 F. 3d 50, 58 (2005). The court therefore denied the petition for review.

In his opinion announcing the court's judgment, Judge Randolph avoided a definitive ruling as to petitioners' standing, *id.*, at 56, reasoning that it was permissible to proceed to the merits because the standing and the merits inquiries "overlap[ped]," *ibid.* Assuming without deciding that the statute authorized the EPA Administrator to regulate greenhouse gas emissions that "in his judgment" may "reasonably be anticipated to endanger public health or welfare," 42 U.S.C. § 7521(a)(1), Judge Randolph concluded that the exercise of that judgment need not be based solely on scientific evidence, but may also be informed by the sort of policy judgments that motivate congressional action. 415 F. 3d, at 58. Given that framework, it was reasonable for EPA to base its decision on scientific uncertainty as well as on other factors, including the concern that unilateral regulation of U.S. motor-vehicle emissions could weaken efforts to reduce greenhouse gas emissions from other countries. *Ibid.*

Judge Sentelle wrote separately because he believed petitioners failed to "demonstrat[e] the element of injury necessary to establish standing under Article III." *Id.*, at 59 (opinion dissenting in part and concurring in judgment). In his view, they had alleged that global warming is "harmful to humanity at large," but could not allege "particularized injuries" to themselves. *Id.*, at 60 (citing *Lujan v. Defenders of Wildlife*, 504 U.S. 555, 562 (1992)). While he dissented on standing, however, he accepted the contrary view as the law of the case and joined Judge Randolph's judgment on the merits as the closest to that which he preferred. 415 F. 3d, at 60–61.

Judge Tatel dissented. Emphasizing that EPA nowhere challenged the factual basis of petitioners' affidavits, *id.*, at 66, he concluded that at least Massachusetts had "satisfied each element of Article III standing—injury, causation, and redressability," *id.*, at 64. In Judge Tatel's view, the "'substantial probability,'" *id.*, at 66, that projected rises in sea level would lead to serious loss of coastal property was a "far cry" from the kind of generalized harm insufficient to ground Article III jurisdiction. *Id.*, at 65. He found that petitioners' affidavits more than adequately supported the conclusion that EPA's failure to curb greenhouse gas emissions contributed to the sea level changes that threatened Massachusetts' coastal property. *Ibid.* As to redressability, he observed that one of petitioners' experts, a former EPA climatologist, stated that "'[a]chievable reductions in emissions of CO_2 and other [greenhouse gases] from U.S. motor vehicles would ... delay and moderate many of the adverse impacts of global warming.'" *Ibid.* (quoting declaration of Michael MacCracken, former Executive Director, U.S. Global Change Research Program ¶ 5(e) (hereinafter MacCracken Decl.), available in 2 Petitioners' Standing Appendix in No. 03–1361, etc., (CADC), p. 209 (Stdg. App.)). He further noted that the one-time director of EPA's motor-vehicle pollution control efforts stated in an affidavit that enforceable emission standards would lead to the development of new technologies that "'would gradually be mandated by other countries around the world.'" 415 F. 3d, at 66 (quoting declaration of Michael Walsh ¶¶ 7–8, 10, Stdg. App. 309–310, 311). On the merits, Judge Tatel explained at length why he believed the text of the statute provided EPA with authority to regulate greenhouse gas emissions, and why its policy concerns did not justify its refusal to exercise that authority. 415 F. 3d, at 67–82.

IV

Article III of the Constitution limits federal-court jurisdiction to "Cases" and "Controversies." Those two words confine "the business of federal courts to questions presented in an adversary context and in a form historically viewed as capable of resolution through the judicial process." *Flast v. Cohen*, 392 U.S. 83, 95 (1968). It is therefore familiar learning that no justiciable "controversy" exists when parties seek adjudication of a political question, *Luther v. Borden*, 7 How. 1 (1849), when they ask for an advisory opinion, *Hayburn's Case*, 2 Dall. 409 (1792), see also *Clinton v. Jones*, 520 U.S. 681, 700, n. 33 (1997), or when the question sought to be adjudicated has been mooted by subsequent developments, *California v. San Pablo & Tulare R. Co.*, 149 U.S. 308 (1893). This case suffers from none of these defects.

The parties' dispute turns on the proper construction of a congressional statute, a question eminently suitable to resolution in federal court. Congress has moreover authorized this type of challenge to EPA action. See 42 U.S.C. § 7607(b)(1). That authorization is of critical importance to the standing inquiry: "Congress has the power to define injuries and articulate chains of causation that will give rise to a case or controversy where none existed before." *Lujan*, 504 U.S., at 580 (Kennedy, J., concurring in part and concurring in judgment). "In exercising this power, however, Congress must at the very least identify the injury it seeks to vindicate and relate the injury to the class of persons entitled to bring suit." *Ibid.* We will not, therefore, "entertain citizen suits to vindicate the public's nonconcrete interest in the proper administration of the laws." *Id.*, at 581.

EPA maintains that because greenhouse gas emissions inflict widespread harm, the doctrine of standing presents an insuperable jurisdictional obstacle. We do not agree. At bottom, "the gist of the question of standing" is whether petitioners have "such a personal stake in the outcome of the controversy as to assure that concrete adverseness which sharpens the presentation of issues upon which the court so largely depends for illumination." *Baker v. Carr*, 369 U.S. 186, 204 (1962). As Justice Kennedy explained in his *Lujan* concurrence:

> "While it does not matter how many persons have been injured by the challenged action, the party bringing suit must show that the action injures him in a concrete and personal way. This requirement is not just an empty formality. It preserves the vitality of the adversarial process by assuring both that the parties before the court have an actual, as opposed to professed, stake in the outcome, and that the legal questions presented ... will be resolved, not in the rarified atmosphere of a debating society, but in a concrete factual context conducive to a realistic appreciation of the consequences of judicial action." 504 U.S., at 581 (internal quotation marks omitted).

To ensure the proper adversarial presentation, *Lujan* holds that a litigant must demonstrate that it has suffered a concrete and particularized injury that is either actual or imminent, that the injury is fairly traceable to the defendant, and that it is likely that a favorable decision will redress that injury. See *id.*, at 560–561. However, a litigant to whom Congress has "accorded a procedural right to protect his concrete interests," *id.*, at 572, n. 7—here, the right to challenge agency action unlawfully withheld, § 7607(b)(1)— "can assert that right without meeting all the normal standards for redressability and immediacy," *ibid.* When a litigant is vested with a procedural right, that litigant has standing if there is some possibility that the requested relief will prompt the injury-causing party to reconsider the decision that allegedly harmed the litigant. *Ibid.*; see also *Sugar Cane Growers Cooperative of Fla. v. Veneman*, 289 F. 3d 89, 94–95 (CADC 2002) ("A [litigant] who alleges a deprivation of a procedural protection to which he is entitled never has to prove that if he had received the procedure the substantive result would have been altered. All that is necessary is to show that the procedural step was connected to the substantive result").

Only one of the petitioners needs to have standing to permit us to consider the petition for review. See *Rumsfeld v. Forum for Academic and Institutional Rights, Inc.*, 547 U.S. 47, n. 2 (2006). We stress here, as did Judge Tatel below, the special position and interest of Massachusetts. It is of considerable relevance that the party seeking review here is a sovereign State and not, as it was in *Lujan*, a private individual.

Well before the creation of the modern administrative state, we recognized that States are not normal litigants for the purposes of invoking federal jurisdiction. As Justice Holmes explained in *Georgia v. Tennessee Copper Co.*, 206 U.S. 230, 237 (1907), a case in which Georgia sought to protect its citizens from air pollution originating outside its borders:

> "The case has been argued largely as if it were one between two private parties; but it is not. The very elements that would be relied upon in a suit between fellow-citizens as a ground for equitable relief are wanting here. The State owns very little of the territory alleged to be affected, and the damage to it capable of estimate in money, possibly, at least, is small. This is a suit by a State for an injury to it in its capacity of quasi-sovereign. In that capacity the State has an interest independent of and behind the titles of its citizens, in all the earth and air within its domain. It has the last word as to whether its mountains shall be stripped of their forests and its inhabitants shall breathe pure air."

Just as Georgia's "independent interest ... in all the earth and air within its domain" supported federal jurisdiction a century ago, so too does Massachusetts' well-founded desire to preserve its sovereign territory today. Cf. *Alden v. Maine*, 527 U.S. 706, 715 (1999) (observing that in the federal system, the States "are not relegated to the role of mere provinces or political corporations, but retain the dignity, though not the full authority, of sovereignty"). That Massachusetts does in fact own a great deal of the "territory alleged to be affected" only reinforces the conclusion that its stake in the outcome of this case is sufficiently concrete to warrant the exercise of federal judicial power.

When a State enters the Union, it surrenders certain sovereign prerogatives. Massachusetts cannot invade Rhode Island to force reductions in greenhouse gas emissions, it cannot negotiate an emissions treaty with China or India, and in some circumstances the exercise of its police powers to reduce in-state motor-vehicle emissions might well be pre-empted. See *Alfred L. Snapp & Son, Inc. v. Puerto Rico ex rel. Barez*, 458 U.S. 592, 607 (1982) ("One helpful indication in determining whether an alleged injury to the health and welfare of its citizens suffices to give the State standing to sue parens patriae is whether the injury is one that the State, if it could, would likely attempt to address through its sovereign lawmaking powers").

These sovereign prerogatives are now lodged in the Federal Government, and Congress has ordered EPA to protect Massachusetts (among others) by prescribing standards applicable to the "emission of any air pollutant from any class or classes of new motor vehicle engines, which in [the Administrator's] judgment cause, or contribute to, air pollution which may reasonably be anticipated to endanger public health or welfare." 42 U.S.C. §7521(a)(1). Congress has moreover recognized a concomitant procedural right to challenge the rejection of its rulemaking petition as arbitrary and capricious. §7607(b)(1). Given that procedural right and Massachusetts' stake in protecting its quasi-sovereign interests, the Commonwealth is entitled to special solicitude in our standing analysis.

With that in mind, it is clear that petitioners' submissions as they pertain to Massachusetts have satisfied the most demanding standards of the adversarial process. EPA's steadfast refusal to regulate greenhouse gas emissions presents a risk of harm to Massachusetts that is both "actual" and "imminent." *Lujan*, 504 U.S., at 560 (internal quotation marks omitted).

There is, moreover, a "substantial likelihood that the judicial relief requested" will prompt EPA to take steps to reduce that risk. *Duke Power Co. v. Carolina Environmental Study Group, Inc.*, 438 U.S. 59, 79 (1978).

The Injury

The harms associated with climate change are serious and well recognized. Indeed, the NRC Report itself—which EPA regards as an "objective and independent assessment of the relevant science," 68 Fed. Reg. 52930—identifies a number of environmental changes that have already inflicted significant harms, including "the global retreat of mountain glaciers, reduction in snow-cover extent, the earlier spring melting of rivers and lakes, [and] the accelerated rate of rise of sea levels during the 20th century relative to the past few thousand years...." NRC Report 16.

Petitioners allege that this only hints at the environmental damage yet to come. According to the climate scientist Michael MacCracken, "qualified scientific experts involved in climate change research" have reached a "strong consensus" that global warming threatens (among other things) a precipitate rise in sea levels by the end of the century, MacCracken Decl. ¶ 15, Stdg. App. 207, "severe and irreversible changes to natural ecosystems," *id.*, ¶ 5(d), at 209, a "significant reduction in water storage in winter snowpack in mountainous regions with direct and important economic consequences," *ibid.*, and an increase in the spread of disease, *id.*, ¶ 28, at 218–219. He also observes that rising ocean temperatures may contribute to the ferocity of hurricanes. *Id.*, ¶¶ 23–25, at 216–217.

That these climate-change risks are "widely shared" does not minimize Massachusetts' interest in the outcome of this litigation. See *Federal Election Comm'n v. Akins*, 524 U.S. 11, 24 (1998) ("[W]here a harm is concrete, though widely shared, the Court has found 'injury in fact'"). According to petitioners' unchallenged affidavits, global sea levels rose somewhere between 10 and 20 centimeters over the 20th century as a result of global warming. MacCracken Decl. ¶ 5(c), Stdg. App. 208. These rising seas have already begun to swallow Massachusetts' coastal land. *Id.*, at 196 (declaration of Paul H. Kirshen ¶ 5), 216 (MacCracken Decl. ¶ 23). Because the Commonwealth "owns a substantial portion of the state's coastal property," *id.*, at 171 (declaration of Karst R. Hoogeboom ¶ 4), it has alleged a particularized injury in its capacity as a landowner. The severity of that injury will only increase over the course of the next century: If sea levels continue to rise as predicted, one Massachusetts official believes that a significant fraction of coastal property will be "either permanently lost through inundation or temporarily lost through periodic storm surge and flooding events." *Id.*, ¶ 6, at 172. Remediation costs alone, petitioners allege, could run well into the hundreds of millions of dollars. *Id.*, ¶ 7, at 172; see also Kirshen Decl. ¶ 12, at 198.

Causation

EPA does not dispute the existence of a causal connection between man-made greenhouse gas emissions and global warming. At a minimum, therefore, EPA's refusal to regulate such emissions "contributes" to Massachusetts' injuries.

EPA nevertheless maintains that its decision not to regulate greenhouse gas emissions from new motor vehicles contributes so insignificantly to petitioners' injuries that the agency cannot be haled into federal court to answer for them. For the same reason, EPA does not believe that any realistic possibility exists that the relief petitioners seek would mitigate global climate change and remedy their injuries. That is especially so because predicted increases in greenhouse gas emissions from developing nations, particularly China and India, are likely to offset any marginal domestic decrease.

But EPA overstates its case. Its argument rests on the erroneous assumption that a small incremental step, because it is incremental, can never be attacked in a federal judicial forum. Yet accepting that premise would doom most challenges to regulatory action. Agencies, like legislatures, do not generally resolve massive problems in one fell regulatory swoop. See *Williamson v. Lee Optical of Okla., Inc.*, 348 U.S. 483, 489 (1955) ("[A] reform may take one step at a time, addressing itself to the phase of the problem which seems most acute to the legislative mind"). They instead whittle away at them over time, refining their preferred approach as circumstances change and as they develop a more-nuanced understanding of how best to proceed. Cf. *SEC v. Chenery Corp.*, 332 U.S. 194, 202 (1947) ("Some principles must await their own development, while others must be adjusted to meet particular, unforeseeable situations"). That a first step might be tentative does not by itself support the notion that federal courts lack jurisdiction to determine whether that step conforms to law.

And reducing domestic automobile emissions is hardly a tentative step. Even leaving aside the other greenhouse gases, the United States transportation sector emits an enormous quantity of carbon dioxide into the atmosphere—according to the MacCracken affidavit, more than 1.7 billion metric tons in 1999 alone. ¶ 30, Stdg. App. 219. That accounts for more than 6% of worldwide carbon dioxide emissions. *Id.*, at 232 (Oppenheimer Decl. ¶ 3); see also MacCracken Decl. ¶ 31, at 220. To put this in perspective: Considering just emissions from the transportation sector, which represent less than one-third of this country's total carbon dioxide emissions, the United States would still rank as the third-largest emitter of carbon dioxide in the world, outpaced only by the European Union and China. Judged by any standard, U.S. motor-vehicle emissions make a meaningful contribution to greenhouse gas concentrations and hence, according to petitioners, to global warming.

The Remedy

While it may be true that regulating motor-vehicle emissions will not by itself reverse global warming, it by no means follows that we lack jurisdiction to decide whether EPA has a duty to take steps to *slow* or *reduce* it. See also *Larson v. Valente*, 456 U.S. 228 , n. 15 (1982) ("[A] plaintiff satisfies the redressability requirement when he shows that a favorable decision will relieve a discrete injury to himself. He need not show that a favorable decision will relieve his *every* injury"). Because of the enormity of the potential consequences associated with man-made climate change, the fact that the effectiveness of a remedy might be delayed during the (relatively short) time it takes for a new motor-vehicle fleet to replace an older one is essentially irrelevant. Nor is it dispositive that developing countries such as China and India are poised to increase greenhouse gas emissions substantially over the next century: A reduction in domestic emissions would slow the pace of global emissions increases, no matter what happens elsewhere.

We moreover attach considerable significance to EPA's "agree[ment] with the President that 'we must address the issue of global climate change,'" 68 Fed. Reg. 52929 (quoting remarks announcing Clear Skies and Global Climate Initiatives, 2002 Public Papers of George W. Bush, Vol. 1, Feb. 14, p. 227 (2004)), and to EPA's ardent support for various voluntary emission-reduction programs, 68 Fed. Reg. 52932. As Judge Tatel observed in dissent below, "EPA would presumably not bother with such efforts if it thought emissions reductions would have no discernable impact on future global warming." 415 F. 3d, at 66.

In sum—at least according to petitioners' uncontested affidavits—the rise in sea levels associated with global warming has already harmed and will continue to harm Massachusetts. The risk of catastrophic harm, though remote, is nevertheless real. That risk would be reduced to some extent if petitioners received the relief they seek. We therefore hold that petitioners have standing to challenge the EPA's denial of their rulemaking petition.

V

The scope of our review of the merits of the statutory issues is narrow. As we have repeated time and again, an agency has broad discretion to choose how best to marshal its limited resources and personnel to carry out its delegated responsibilities. See *Chevron U.S.A. Inc. v. Natural Resources Defense Council, Inc.*, 467 U.S. 837, 842–845 (1984). That discretion is at its height when the agency decides not to bring an enforcement action. Therefore, in *Heckler v. Chaney*, 470 U.S. 821 (1985), we held that an agency's refusal to initiate enforcement proceedings is not ordinarily subject to judicial review. Some debate remains, however, as to the rigor with which we review an agency's denial of a petition for rulemaking.

There are key differences between a denial of a petition for rulemaking and an agency's decision not to initiate an enforcement action. See *American Horse Protection Assn., Inc. v. Lyng*, 812 F. 2d 1, 3–4 (CADC 1987). In contrast to nonenforcement decisions, agency refusals to initiate rulemaking "are less frequent, more apt to involve legal as opposed to factual analysis, and subject to special formalities, including a public explanation." *Id.*, at 4; see also 5 U.S.C. §555(e). They moreover arise out of denials of petitions for rulemaking which (at least in the circumstances here) the affected party had an undoubted procedural right to file in the first instance. Refusals to promulgate rules are thus susceptible to judicial review, though such review is "extremely limited" and "highly deferential." *National Customs Brokers & Forwarders Assn of America, Inc. v. United States*, 883 F. 2d 93, 96 (CADC 1989).

EPA concluded in its denial of the petition for rulemaking that it lacked authority under 42 U.S.C. §7521(a)(1) to regulate new vehicle emissions because carbon dioxide is not an "air pollutant" as that term is defined in §7602. In the alternative, it concluded that even if it possessed authority, it would decline to do so because regulation would conflict with other administration priorities. As discussed earlier, the Clean Air Act expressly permits review of such an action. §7607(b)(1). We therefore "may reverse any such action found to be ... arbitrary, capricious, an abuse of discretion, or otherwise not in accordance with law." §7607(d)(9).

VI

On the merits, the first question is whether §202(a)(1) of the Clean Air Act authorizes EPA to regulate greenhouse gas emissions from new motor vehicles in the event that it forms a "judgment" that such emissions contribute to climate change. We have little trouble concluding that it does. In relevant part, §202(a)(1) provides that EPA "shall by regulation prescribe ... standards applicable to the emission of any air pollutant from any class or classes of new motor vehicles or new motor vehicle engines, which in [the Administrator's] judgment cause, or contribute to, air pollution which may reasonably be anticipated to endanger public health or welfare." 42 U.S.C. §7521(a)(1). Because EPA believes that Congress did not intend it to regulate substances that contribute to climate change, the agency maintains that carbon dioxide is not an "air pollutant" within the meaning of the provision.

The statutory text forecloses EPA's reading. The Clean Air Act's sweeping definition of "air pollutant" includes "*any* air pollution agent or combination of such agents, including any physical, chemical ... substance or matter which is emitted into or otherwise enters the ambient air...." § 7602(g) (emphasis added). On its face, the definition embraces all airborne compounds of whatever stripe, and underscores that intent through the repeated use of the word "any." Carbon dioxide, methane, nitrous oxide, and hydrofluorocarbons are without a doubt "physical [and] chemical ... substance[s] which [are] emitted into ... the ambient air." The statute is unambiguous.

Rather than relying on statutory text, EPA invokes postenactment congressional actions and deliberations it views as tantamount to a congressional command to refrain from regulating greenhouse gas emissions. Even if such postenactment legislative history could shed light on the meaning of an otherwise-unambiguous statute, EPA never identifies any action remotely suggesting that Congress meant to curtail its power to treat greenhouse gases as air pollutants. That subsequent Congresses have eschewed enacting binding emissions limitations to combat global warming tells us nothing about what Congress meant when it amended § 202(a)(1) in 1970 and 1977. And unlike EPA, we have no difficulty reconciling Congress' various efforts to promote interagency collaboration and research to better understand climate change with the agency's pre-existing mandate to regulate "any air pollutant" that may endanger the public welfare. See 42 U.S.C. § 7601(a)(1). Collaboration and research do not conflict with any thoughtful regulatory effort; they complement it.

EPA's reliance on *Brown & Williamson Tobacco Corp.*, 529 U.S. 120, is similarly misplaced. In holding that tobacco products are not "drugs" or "devices" subject to Food and Drug Administration (FDA) regulation pursuant to the Food, Drug and Cosmetic Act (FDCA), see 529 U.S., at 133, we found critical at least two considerations that have no counterpart in this case.

First, we thought it unlikely that Congress meant to ban tobacco products, which the FDCA would have required had such products been classified as "drugs" or "devices." *Id.*, at 135–137. Here, in contrast, EPA jurisdiction would lead to no such extreme measures. EPA would only *regulate* emissions, and even then, it would have to delay any action "to permit the development and application of the requisite technology, giving appropriate consideration to the cost of compliance," § 7521(a)(2). However much a ban on tobacco products clashed with the "common sense" intuition that Congress never meant to remove those products from circulation, *Brown & Williamson*, 529 U.S., at 133, there is nothing counterintuitive to the notion that EPA can curtail the emission of substances that are putting the global climate out of kilter.

Second, in *Brown & Williamson* we pointed to an unbroken series of congressional enactments that made sense only if adopted "against the backdrop of the FDA's consistent and repeated statements that it lacked authority under the FDCA to regulate tobacco." *Id.*, at 144. We can point to no such enactments here: EPA has not identified any congressional action that conflicts in any way with the regulation of greenhouse gases from new motor vehicles. Even if it had, Congress could not have acted against a regulatory "backdrop" of disclaimers of regulatory authority. Prior to the order that provoked this litigation, EPA had never disavowed the authority to regulate greenhouse gases, and in 1998 it in fact affirmed that it *had* such authority. See App. 54 (Cannon memorandum). There is no reason, much less a compelling reason, to accept EPA's invitation to read ambiguity into a clear statute.

EPA finally argues that it cannot regulate carbon dioxide emissions from motor vehicles because doing so would require it to tighten mileage standards, a job (according to EPA) that Congress has assigned to DOT. See 68 Fed. Reg. 52929. But that DOT sets mileage standards in no way licenses EPA to shirk its environmental responsibilities. EPA has been charged with protecting the public's "health" and "welfare," 42 U.S.C. §7521(a)(1), a statutory obligation wholly independent of DOT's mandate to promote energy efficiency. See Energy Policy and Conservation Act, §2(5), 89 Stat. 874, 42 U.S.C. §6201(5). The two obligations may overlap, but there is no reason to think the two agencies cannot both administer their obligations and yet avoid inconsistency.

While the Congresses that drafted §202(a)(1) might not have appreciated the possibility that burning fossil fuels could lead to global warming, they did understand that without regulatory flexibility, changing circumstances and scientific developments would soon render the Clean Air Act obsolete. The broad language of §202(a)(1) reflects an intentional effort to confer the flexibility necessary to forestall such obsolescence. See *Pennsylvania Dept. of Corrections v. Yeskey*, 524 U.S. 206, 212 (1998) ("[T]he fact that a statute can be applied in situations not expressly anticipated by Congress does not demonstrate ambiguity. It demonstrates breadth" (internal quotation marks omitted)). Because greenhouse gases fit well within the Clean Air Act's capacious definition of "air pollutant," we hold that EPA has the statutory authority to regulate the emission of such gases from new motor vehicles.

VII

The alternative basis for EPA's decision—that even if it does have statutory authority to regulate greenhouse gases, it would be unwise to do so at this time—rests on reasoning divorced from the statutory text. While the statute does condition the exercise of EPA's authority on its formation of a "judgment," 42 U.S.C. §7521(a)(1), that judgment must relate to whether an air pollutant "cause[s], or contribute[s] to, air pollution which may reasonably be anticipated to endanger public health or welfare," *ibid.* Put another way, the use of the word "judgment" is not a roving license to ignore the statutory text. It is but a direction to exercise discretion within defined statutory limits.

If EPA makes a finding of endangerment, the Clean Air Act requires the agency to regulate emissions of the deleterious pollutant from new motor vehicles. *Ibid.* (stating that "[EPA] shall by regulation prescribe ... standards applicable to the emission of any air pollutant from any class of new motor vehicles"). EPA no doubt has significant latitude as to the manner, timing, content, and coordination of its regulations with those of other agencies. But once EPA has responded to a petition for rulemaking, its reasons for action or inaction must conform to the authorizing statute. Under the clear terms of the Clean Air Act, EPA can avoid taking further action only if it determines that greenhouse gases do not contribute to climate change or if it provides some reasonable explanation as to why it cannot or will not exercise its discretion to determine whether they do. *Ibid.* To the extent that this constrains agency discretion to pursue other priorities of the Administrator or the President, this is the congressional design.

EPA has refused to comply with this clear statutory command. Instead, it has offered a laundry list of reasons not to regulate. For example, EPA said that a number of voluntary executive branch programs already provide an effective response to the threat of global warming, 68 Fed. Reg. 52932, that regulating greenhouse gases might impair the President's ability to negotiate with "key developing nations" to reduce emissions, *id.*, at 52931, and that curtailing motor-vehicle emissions would reflect "an inefficient, piecemeal approach to address the climate change issue," *ibid.*

Although we have neither the expertise nor the authority to evaluate these policy judgments, it is evident they have nothing to do with whether greenhouse gas emissions contribute to climate change. Still less do they amount to a reasoned justification for declining to form a scientific judgment. In particular, while the President has broad authority in foreign affairs, that authority does not extend to the refusal to execute domestic laws. In the Global Climate Protection Act of 1987, Congress authorized the State Department—not EPA—to formulate United States foreign policy with reference to environmental matters relating to climate. See § 1103(c), 101 Stat. 1409. EPA has made no showing that it issued the ruling in question here after consultation with the State Department. Congress did direct EPA to consult with other agencies in the formulation of its policies and rules, but the State Department is absent from that list. § 1103(b).

Nor can EPA avoid its statutory obligation by noting the uncertainty surrounding various features of climate change and concluding that it would therefore be better not to regulate at this time. See 68 Fed. Reg. 52930–52931. If the scientific uncertainty is so profound that it precludes EPA from making a reasoned judgment as to whether greenhouse gases contribute to global warming, EPA must say so. That EPA would prefer not to regulate greenhouse gases because of some residual uncertainty—which, contrary to Justice Scalia's apparent belief, post, at 5–8, is in fact all that it said, see 68 Fed. Reg. 52929 ("We do not believe ... that it would be either effective or appropriate for EPA *to establish [greenhouse gas] standards for motor vehicles* at this time" (emphasis added))—is irrelevant. The statutory question is whether sufficient information exists to make an endangerment finding.

In short, EPA has offered no reasoned explanation for its refusal to decide whether greenhouse gases cause or contribute to climate change. Its action was therefore "arbitrary, capricious, ... or otherwise not in accordance with law." 42 U.S.C. § 7607(d)(9)(A). We need not and do not reach the question whether on remand EPA must make an endangerment finding, or whether policy concerns can inform EPA's actions in the event that it makes such a finding. Cf. *Chevron U.S.A. Inc. v. Natural Resources Defense Council, Inc.*, 467 U.S. 837, 843–844 (1984). We hold only that EPA must ground its reasons for action or inaction in the statute.

VIII

The judgment of the Court of Appeals is reversed, and the case is remanded for further proceedings consistent with this opinion.

It is so ordered.

Notes & Questions

1. Justice Roberts dissented, arguing that standing was inappropriate for Massachusetts. He also argued that the claimed climate-change injuries were too hard to quantify and lacked scientific certainty. Justice Roberts next stated that the perceived harm and the cause were not closely linked (there was a lack of "causal connection"). Further, regarding the fact that emissions from other countries, like India and China, also contributed to global warming, Justice Roberts stated that "[r]edressability is even more problematic."

2. Justice Scalia also dissented. He, too, would not have found standing, and would have ended the case there. Justice Scalia continued, though, because the majority did, primarily arguing that the Court should have deferred to the reasoned judgment of the EPA, applying *Chevron* deference, as discussed in Chapter 1.

3. The EPA has started down the road of dealing with greenhouse gas emission with proposals under the Clean Air Act section 111(d), 42 U.S.C. § 7411, which is a state-based program for existing emissions sources. EPA establishes the guidelines so that states can

then design programs that will achieve the required reductions consistent with the state's mix of sources and existing programs. The EPA proposal for existing emissions sources was released in June 2014.

4. In 2013, the EPA proposed emissions rules under section 111(b) for new sources. In a report, *Regulatory Impact Analysis for the Proposed Standards of Performance for Greenhouse Gas Emissions for New Stationary Sources: Electric Utility Generating Units* (Sept. 2013), the EPA described the proposal as follows:

> ...

> Summary of the Proposed Rule

> This rule proposes emission standards for affected fossil fuel-fired units within existing subparts—natural gas-fired stationary combustion turbines and fossil fuel-fired electric utility steam generating units (boilers and IGCC). All affected new fossil fuel-fired EGUs would be required to meet an output-based emission rate of a specific mass of CO_2 per MWh of electricity generated energy output on a gross basis. These standards would be met on a 12-operating-month rolling average basis. The EPA is proposing standards of performance for affected sources within the following subcategories: (1) natural gas-fired stationary combustion turbines with a heat input rating to the turbine engine that is greater than 850 million British Thermal units per hour (MMBtu/hr); (2) natural gas-fired stationary combustion turbines with a heat input rating to the turbine engine that is less than or equal to 850 MMBtu/hr; and (3) all fossil fuel-fired boilers and IGCC units. The respective emission limits are shown in Table 1-1.

Table 1-1. Proposed Emission Limits

Source	Emission Limit (lb CO_2/MWh Gross Basis)
Stationary natural gas-fired combustion turbine EGUs with a heat input rating greater than 850 MMBtu/hr	1,000
Stationary natural gas-fired combustion turbine EGUs with a heat input rating less than or equal to 850 MMBtu/hr	1,100
Fossil fuel-fired boilers and IGCCs	1,100

This action also proposes an alternative emission limit, available only to new fossil-fuel fired boilers and IGCCs, which can be met over an 84-operating month rolling average basis. The alternative emission limit will be between 1,000 and 1,050 lb CO_2/MWh of gross energy output.

C. Adaptation & Mitigation

Re California Institute for Climate Solutions
Rulemaking Proceeding 07-09-008
California Public Utilities Commission
2007 WL 2872466 (Cal.P.U.C.)
PUR Slip Copy
(September 20, 2007)

BY THE COMMISSION:

ORDER INSTITUTING RULEMAKING TO CONSIDER ESTABLISHING
CALIFORNIA INSTITUTE FOR CLIMATE SOLUTIONS

1. Summary

This order initiates a rulemaking as part of the California Public Utilities Commission's (Commission) continuing effort to aggressively pursue creative and cost effective ways to reduce greenhouse gas (GHG) emissions within California.

Attached to this order is a proposal submitted to the Commission on August 1, 2007 by the University of California (UC) for establishing an institute dedicated to supporting California's public research institutions and policymakers in developing and implementing innovative solutions to the challenges posed by global climate change. The proposal describes the mission, organizational structure, priority program and research areas, and annual budget for the proposed California Institute for Climate Solutions (CICS or Institute). The Commission notes that the proposal is only a preliminary one. It is not a complete or exhaustive description of how the institute should be structured, but should serve as a good starting point from which we can develop a far more detailed final decision that is specifically tailored to best meet ratepayer needs. We respectfully request that UC supplement and augment the proposal as needed. The Commission invites comments from the respondents and other interested parties on this proposal.

This rulemaking will:

- Consider and approve, if appropriate, an organizational and governance structure for the proposed institute;

- Consider and establish, if appropriate, program and research priorities for the proposed institute that should result in public policies, research and technology development that will be beneficial to utility ratepayers by reducing GHG emissions; and

- Establish a funding mechanism for the proposed institute's programs and research that will be cost effective for ratepayers.

2. Introduction

Climate change is the pre-eminent environmental challenge of our time. The problem is global in scope, but will lead to significant local impacts. Among the grave threats to Californians' health and economic well-being are rising sea-levels, a shrinking snow-pack, higher temperatures and deteriorating air quality. Indeed, California is already experiencing the effects of climate change. As the primary regulator of California's largest energy utilities, the Commission is considering this proposal submitted by UC, which among its many public charges is responsible for promoting education, and undertaking research and technology development in ways that will provide benefits to all Californians.

Slowing and ultimately stopping GHG emissions will require a monumental and coordinated effort at the global, national, regional, state, and local levels. California's elected leaders have recognized the need for immediate action on an unprecedented scale by enacting a series of groundbreaking laws and policies aimed at reducing our state's GHG emissions. Most notably, Assembly Bill (AB) 32 requires that California reduce GHG emissions to 1990 levels by 2020, 25% below projected business-as-usual levels. In addition, Governor Schwarzenegger's June 1, 2005 Executive Order (#S-3-05) targets a reduction of 80% below 1990 levels by 2050. These aggressive goals require not only the development of new technologies and public policies, but also the formation of new partnerships which will create institutional channels through which they can be deployed, implemented, and otherwise disseminated.

The problem of devising and then implementing climate change solutions is substantially one of organization. Even where GHG reduction tools are widely recognized and accepted— like reducing consumption of water, constructing energy efficient buildings, and capturing and destroying methane gas—turning them into public policies that can be implemented effectively and efficiently requires a level of coordination and cooperation between state agencies, corporations, academic institutions, and individuals that has yet to be achieved.

California must continue to be on the vanguard of solving the problem of climate change if we are to accomplish our goals. Our policies have impacts beyond our borders and effect change regionally, nationally, and globally. The time to act is now. Each year California's population grows by close to a half million people. This means that by 2009 the state's population could top 40 million. This growth will put additional strains on the state's physical and environmental infrastructure, including unprecedented demands on the energy sector, transportation systems, and water-delivery systems. We must ensure that we have committed the resources and established the institutions that will enable us to incorporate future growth and the attendant demands on our infrastructure in a way that does not compromise our climate policies.

The level of societal effort needed to successfully combat the challenge of climate change has been likened to a new industrial revolution. To realize this wholesale transformation of our economy and lifestyle, California must draw on our collective financial and intellectual capital. We must fully engage not only the public and private sectors, but in particular the academic community. Recognizing this, the Commission President requested that the University of California, as the public university research institution in California, formulate a proposal for an institute that could develop and implement the necessary mission-based research that is needed. The Commission's intent is to engage not only the UC system, but also the major private research universities, Cal Tech, Stanford and USC, and the California State University and Community College systems as well. Other research and academic institutions within the state may be able to make valuable contributions to this effort as well and will encourage their contributions. To the degree that the attached UC proposal is inconsistent with this intent, the OIR controls.

The proposed CICS could support achievement of California's GHG reduction goals in three key ways:

- Conduct mission-oriented, applied research that results in practical technological solutions and policy recommendations;

- Train the next generation of researchers and professionals; and

- Disseminate knowledge widely to practicing public and private sector professionals.

Establishing the CICS could be the critical next step in the State's effort to develop a long range strategy for reducing GHG emissions and thereby slowing the impacts of climate change.

Finally, the Commission recognizes that there may be overlap between the scope of research outlined in the CICS proposal and existing research projects conducted by individual utilities or programs administered by other state agencies. It is not the Commission's intent to fund redundant programs. This rulemaking, therefore, should consider how to structure the CICS so that it complements and augments existing efforts in a cost effective manner instead of replicating them.

3. Funding

The UC proposal includes an estimated budget of $600 million to be spread evenly over a decade, $60 million each year. As a preliminary matter this proceeding will consider whether funding on this scale for researching and developing climate solutions is needed. If so, the final decision will consider and adopt, if appropriate, the governance framework and procedural safeguards to ensure that ratepayer funds will maximize ratepayer benefits.

Because climate change is a global problem, caused in significant part by the generation and consumption of electricity and natural gas, we ask for comments on the proposal that the annual cost of funding the Institute be paid equally by all ratepayers on an equal cents per kilowatt-hour basis and an equal cents per therm basis through utility bills. Because much of California's energy is produced by natural gas fueled generation, we invite comments as to whether or not natural gas delivered to power generators by California utilities should be exempt from these payments.

        ....

California Institute for Climate Solutions

1. Executive Summary
1.a. Introduction

The University of California (UC) proposes to establish the California Institute for Climate Solutions (CICS) to address the impacts of climate change with new and innovative cross-cutting strategies and programs in energy and environmental research, technology development and deployment, climate economics, infrastructure design, socioeconomic impacts and responses, education, public services, and policy action. Research and education are critical components in identifying, developing and implementing solutions to climate change, and the UC can serve as a key partner supporting the efforts of business and government. The UC is prepared to make a major personnel, infrastructure, and public-engagement commitment to this Institute and to the study and design of strategies for addressing climate change as a state, national, and global issue.

In the face of unprecedented social and economic challenges, California has embarked on the most aggressive climate change policy initiatives in the country. The Governor and the Legislature have set forth ambitious greenhouse gas emissions reduction goals for 2020 and 2050 (including AB1493, AB32 SB1368), which will profoundly change the state's electricity and transportation sectors. Furthermore, the consequences of climate change will force California to adapt its transportation, energy, and water infrastructure, as well as many public services, such as health and disaster relief. With a rapidly growing population—a 75% increase is projected in the next 50 years—California will have to address climate challenges while fostering the economic growth needed to support over 70 million people. The very nature of this economic growth will impact greenhouse gas emissions on a global scale.

While California has set forth bold goals to address both the causes and consequences of climate change, many fundamental challenges remain regarding how to best achieve these goals. The CICS will address these critical challenges by identifying and helping to design a broad set of policies that target critical carbon-intensive sectors of California economy. Policies must be crafted to induce the development and widespread adoption of new climate-friendly systems and the economic, legal, and policy instruments to bring new technologies into the mainstream. State and local agencies must adapt to the consequences of climate change, especially in the areas of water resources, disaster pre- paredness (e.g., wildfires), and new threats to human health. One of the major legal issues for the state is whether and how new federal legislation will pre-empt California's new policies. How should new policies be financed? How should policies be optimally monitored and enforced? In what way and how frequently should energy and climate-related policies be evaluated to ensure they adapt to future environment changes and refinements of scientific knowledge?

Another challenge is to evaluate the cost effectiveness and efficacy of the various strategies necessary to motivate individual people to change their behavior in ways that will lead to lower greenhouse gas emissions. These strategies include regulations, taxes and markets, incentives (for example, time-of-day pricing for electrical use), informing consumer behavior through carbon footprint and carbon content analysis, labeling, or pricing, public education, and access to new technologies. There is a great need to develop ways to evaluate how public choices are made, the degree to which education about energy and climate issues actually influences them, and how they are distributed demographically.

A third challenge is to rapidly conduct research and move into practice sustainable ways for people to live while maintaining quality of life, healthy ecosystems, and preventing disruptive effects of climate change. This requires a focused effort that is unusual for both government and research universities and persuading innovative and productive researchers to alter the direction of their research and contribute to achieving the vision of a sustainable future. A particular challenge will be to develop practices that safeguard and in fact address from the outset issues of social and environmental justice for disadvantaged communities.

A fourth challenge is responding to the need for a changing workforce. Enacting the kinds of technological and societal changes needed to reduce greenhouse gas emissions requires increased training of both students and the public in a range of areas. The UC system has exceptionally strong undergraduate, graduate, and postdoctoral training programs, as well as nationally recognized K-12 science outreach programs. Many campuses also host technology transfer offices and offer extension services that bridge university research and industry,

Each of these challenges requires sustainability as a solution. Sustainability will be the primary criterion for successful climatic and environmental impacts mitigation, and adap- tation policies and practices.

1.b. Mission of the California Institute for Climate Solutions (CICS)

To address the consequences of climate changes on infrastructure, public services, and policies that will mitigate the effect of climate change, the CICS will have three missions:

- Identify and support researchers at all of the UC campuses and laboratories who can make a contribution to solving real problems related to energy, climate change, and quality of life
- Establish a system for accelerating research and analysis on specific issues relating to climate change (see Table 1) and its causes and consequences in California
- Educate and train a new generation of researchers and public officials to alter the direction of their research and contribute to achieving a vision of a sustainable future.

The CICS will bring together UC researchers to assist the Public Utility Commission (PUC) and other state agencies in resolving critical problems, conducting research, developing new modeling and planning analysis tools, analyzing and commenting on policy issues, and responding to informational requests from other agencies, municipalities and the general public. It will host active basic and applied research and education programs aimed at advancing the understanding of the relationship between climate, energy, and sustainable quality of life. As designed, the CICS will be responsive to ongoing policy issues and support high-risk, high-benefit efforts, as well as longer-term collaborations, and be a platform to leverage opportunities in federal, state, industrial, and venture capital markets.

The Institute will be an active partner, designing and implementing short-term and long-term solutions to the diverse impacts of global climate change on California rate-payers, businesses, municipalities, and community groups, as well as in assisting the state in meeting regional and global challenges raised by the changing climate. This partnership will serve as a model program for engaging university resources to provide mission-oriented research, education, and policy support to public agencies that bridges the gap between research and application.

. . . .

2. Organizational Structure and Governance
2.a. Governance and Administration

The CICS will be a dynamic research and educational partnership between the University of California, the PUC, and other stakeholders. Working together, this group will strategically develop and pursue a research and educational agenda that transcends individual interests and priorities. This necessarily requires an organizational structure that is able to (1) seamlessly integrate policy, science, and technology; (2) sustain efforts over an extended period; and (3) maintain a nimbleness that allows it to shift emphasis to immediate or critical problems as they arise.

A master agreement between the UC and PUC will allow for the efficient deployment of both short- and long-term task orders to undertake specific projects or respond to policy analysis requests. Task orders have been used successfully on several campuses and facilitate inter-campus agreements, allow expedited processing of time sensitive topics and provide an on-going mechanism in support of a regular consultative process. In general, task orders will be issued for projects identified and supported through the proposal process and headed by researchers with expertise in the principal area required by the individual task orders; project durations will range from a short period (e.g., a few months for expert reviews or analysis) to as long as several years. The structure of the CICS will also allow for periodic external peer review and reassessment of overall priorities and goals.

The task-order mechanism will also fund, through cost-sharing agreements, the CICS's engagement with state municipalities, agencies, and the private sector in part through a parallel program of internship opportunities and visiting staff periods. In this way, the mission-oriented efforts of the Institute will support not only industry, government, and university professionals, but also researchers at all levels of the UC, from undergraduate to post-doctoral. These exchanges will serve several goals: (1) provide educational instruction or mentoring in the CICS's areas of active work; (2) engage professionals from the public or private sector in specific program areas, or in the design or implementation of programmatic aspects of the mission of the Institute; and (3) provide opportunities for officials from agencies or industries outside California to participate in the development of technologies, programs, and policies to address climate change.

. . . .

3. Research and Education Themes
3.a. Background

California is facing the difficult challenge of attempting to meet its long-term energy needs while reducing and stabilizing greenhouse gas emissions to levels far below today's emissions rate. The Governor and Legislature have adopted goals for 2020 and 2050 commensurate with the future emission pathways considered necessary to avoid dangerous climate change, while still allowing for global economic growth and development (Wigley, Richels et al. 1996; Baer, Harte et al. 2000; Hayhoe, Cayan et al. 2004; Intergovernmental Panel on Climate Change 2007). Achieving greenhouse gas stabilization by 2050 will not be easy. The 2020 climate-stabilization target requires a reversal of historical trends (Figure 3), while the 2050 target calls for a profound change in energy supply and other parts of the economy. With the 2020 goal only slightly more than a decade away, and because energy technologies tend to be large, complex, and slow to change, to achieve the short-term goal California will need to rely on (1) mature technologies that are already in the market but are under-used; (2) technologies that can be commercialized within the next several years; and (3) a variety of non-technological solutions. The more distant, and far more ambitious, 2050 climate-stabilization goal requires a very different approach. The products needed to achieve the 2050 goal, such as vehicles and fuels, are not available today, so technological innovation will be required. Attaining the 2050 climate-stabilization goal therefore translates to major innovations and investments in new technologies, as well as changes in behavior. Government action is not only appropriate but necessary to bring these changes about because climate change is a market externality and, like most environmental protection, a public good. Without government intervention, markets ignore externalities and provide fewer products and services that cater to public good than is socially and economically optimal. In addition, innovation designed to achieve public good also requires government action (Arrow, Bolin et al. 1995; Norberg-Bohm 1999).

. . . .

In general, any effort to mitigate greenhouse gas emissions will affect climate and quality of life (health, air and water quality) through a wide range of changes to the atmosphere, as well as to natural and managed (built) systems and how we live in them. An end-to-end analysis of particular strategies, which incorporates the significant predicted growth in California's population, will need to encompass all of these potential impacts. Some aspects of climate-change mitigation will rely on voluntary choices made by the people of California. In addition to projecting the changes in personal choices required to achieve certain mitigation solutions, there is a need to educate citizens about these choices and evaluate the rate at which they are adopted.

Climate change, whether at the lower or higher end of projected levels, will produce substantial environmental and health impacts, and these impacts are inextricably linked to energy production and demand. In recognition of the interrelationships, we have adopted the following principles in developing the priority program areas for research, innovation, and education:

- Encouraging investment in and improvement of current and near-term knowledge, education, and advanced technologies that will help meet the 2050 goal, while supporting progress toward the 2020 goal.

- Stimulating innovation and development of new knowledge, education, and technologies that can dramatically lower greenhouse gas emissions at minimum cost and be deployed ideally by 2020 or soon thereafter, but clearly get the state on track for meeting the 2050 goal.

- Contributing to the attainment of the state's objectives while ensuring economic growth, public health protection, air quality and other environmental protection goals, affordable energy prices, environmental justice, and diverse and reliable energy sources.

3.b. Priority Program Areas

The CICS will initially focus on five primary research areas to address the causes and consequences of climate change in California as well as supporting two key cross-cutting themes that clearly underpin efforts in each of the primary research areas: measurement and informatics and education and technology transfer. It is important to note that all of these program areas should not be considered lists of projects, but rather those topics, concepts, and areas in which the greatest intellectual and public/private innovative capacity must be brought to bear. There are numerous situations in which these five areas overlap; cross-cutting impacts are ubiquitous throughout the program areas. This intentional redundancy ensures that the program as a whole will be greater than the sum of its parts, that a multifaceted approach is taken to address each area, and that the entire UC system knowledge base is leveraged. Finally, we have made certain that policy analysis has been built into each focus area so that social scientists will work alongside natural and physical scientists, and together they will partner with policymakers and consumer groups to inform each other and the general public.

3.b.i. Buildings and Homes: Energy Efficiency and Conservation

Buildings currently use approximately 68% of all electricity and 34% of all natural gas consumed in California, thus California cannot succeed in addressing energy challenges without an aggressive program focused on building-energy performance. With a projected state population of 59 million people in 2050, this program area will focus not only on making efficiency and conservation improvements to existing structures, but also planning and designing more-efficient urban and suburban development where new residents will live and work. The location, demography, and forms of urban growth will impact greenhouse gas emissions from virtually all major energy sectors, including transportation, residential, and electrical-energy generation. Plans for new urban growth seldom incorporate measures to assess and reduce greenhouse gas emissions, despite the potential for land use and planning policy to help California meet its regulatory goals.

Energy efficiency innovations, for example, new or improved technologies, residential and commercial practices, pricing strategies, and innovative policies such as the decoupling of electricity sales and revenues, have transformed the California economy. While California is as much as 40% more-efficient per capita than the U.S. as whole, there still exist tremendous opportunities for continuing and even accelerating efficiency gains. Total emissions per capita must decrease if greenhouse gas emissions are to decline in an era with continued rapid population increase. Enhancing building codes; installing cool roofs; benchmarking industrial energy use; integrating new energy and environmental sensing technologies into building and houses; prototyping, developing and applying lower-cost and higher functionality 'smart' meters; and advancing battery technology, solid state lighting, power storage, and energy-oriented nano-technology all offer the potential for a 'second revolution' of energy efficiency. New approaches to designing the urban and suburban landscapes in ways that minimize transportation-related emissions and take advantage of landscaping to enhance local climate and environmental quality will also be required to extend emission reductions while sustaining growth in new communities.

As reflected in AB32 and SB1493, the regulatory burden of addressing climate change will fall most heavily on the transportation and electric-power sectors. The state currently faces a wide array of policy approaches for mitigating greenhouse gas emissions within these two critical sectors of the California economy. Policymakers will need to analyze the likely impacts of alternative policy approaches; within the electricity-supply sectors, candidate policies include renewable portfolio standards, an emissions cap and trade program, mandated best available technologies, tax breaks and rebates for renewable energy sources, and subsidies for research and development of new technologies through the energy supply chain.

The critical challenge for improving energy efficiency and conservation in buildings is recognizing that knowledge in public, private, and university spheres must be integrated. Energy science and technology research must be coupled with robust policy and economic analysis, ultimately leading to aggressive implementation efforts. Widespread implementation of new technologies and behaviors will depend on the modification of building codes and other regulations, consumer expectations and behaviors, financial incentives, and product availability, among others. UC programs can partner productively with local and regional NGOs in nascent efforts to influence governments, industries, and the public by offering substantive information and credibility. While maintaining academic objectivity, UC faculty, students, and research staff can actively participate on the advisory and governing boards that are responsible for developing and implementing programs to increase energy efficiency and conservation.

BUILDINGS AND HOMES

Opportunities and Impacts

- Improved building codes will reduce energy use and enhance development
- Advanced end-use technologies will improve energy efficiency
- Real-time monitoring will enhance user conservation practices

3.b.ii. Energy Supply, Sources, and Technologies

As described in the previous section, increased population and changes in climate will clearly impact energy demand. Meeting those increased demands without increasing greenhouse gas emissions will require not only energy efficiency and conservation but also the development of new energy sources and technologies. UC researchers are currently participating in the development and innovation of numerous low-carbon renewable-energy technologies that are the subject of increasing state and national interest, including wind energy, solar photovoltaics, solar thermal energy, ocean energy, geothermal energy, and interactions of biology and nanotechnology with energy systems design.

In this program area, research and education will focus on developing new and innovative approaches to standard and renewable energy sources and technology. More research is needed to identify sustainable resources suitable for providing fuel and energy, for making those resources cost-effective and competitive, and for assuring that they do not bring unintended consequences that create new problems or exacerbate old ones (e.g., air pollution).

Climate warming is expected to shift the state's hydroclimate toward a more flood-prone regime. This, coupled with the risk of catastrophic fire, has serious implications on a reliable supply of hydropower, which currently provides more than 15% of California's energy, and is especially important during periods of peak demand. There is great potential to develop new solar energy sources, which fall into three categories according to their primary energy product: solar electricity, solar fuels, and solar thermal systems. Each of the three generic approaches to exploiting the solar resource has untapped capability well beyond its present usage. All three categories can benefit by the development of new materials to efficiently absorb sunlight, new techniques to harness the full spectrum of wavelengths in solar radiation, and new approaches, based on nanostructured architectures, that can revolutionize the technology used to produce solar electricity. Basic research is needed to develop approaches and systems to bridge the gap between the scientific frontier and practical technology. Across all solar technologies, the current rate of scientific discovery is simply too slow to match the rate at which technological advances are needed to bring new products to bear on the state's urgent energy needs.

As wind and solar power become more cost-effective, issues of intermittency and energy storage must be addressed. We must advance the capabilities to efficiently produce and store energy during peak production times so it can be used during peak consumption periods. Electromechanical and electrochemical technologies for energy storage must be advanced for use in large-scale renewable energy systems; they are also required for large-scale deployment of hybrids and plug-in hybrids, as well as a huge market in consumer goods. Furthermore, integrating all energy production and storage systems requires a reliable and secure transmission grid system. California needs to begin to strategically invest in an intelligent grid-system that spans all regions of the state.

Finally, the technologies for removing greenhouse gases (especially CO_2) from the atmosphere require careful consideration. A number of potentially promising technologies (e.g., biosequestration, gas and liquid trapping, sorption to mineral phases) will require careful cost-analysis in the short and long term. California has an enormous sequestration resource, estimated between 180 and more than 800 Gt CO_2. This resource can hold emissions from large point sources, including natural gas power plants, refineries, ethanol plants, and cement manufacturing plants. In short, carbon capture and sequestration (CCS) has the potential to dramatically reduce net carbon dioxide emissions within and outside the state. The principal issues surrounding CCS are the stability and accessibility of geologic storage sites, investment in the needed infrastructure, cost, and risk. There is a need to sustain biosequestration by better understanding the carbon dynamics of forests, agricultural sources and sinks, and wildland accumulation. For example, many current agricultural and production forestry practices actually reduce carbon storage in comparison to wildland preservation and minimum tillage approaches. If found to be a cost-effective method for providing stable, long-term storage, sequestration could permit fossil-fuel baseload power plants to operate while still achieving the state emission-reduction targets outlined in AB32 and SB1368. Research and development is needed to both reduce costs for these CCS technologies and to develop new technologies beyond these options.

Large-scale state-wide application of CCS to reduce CO_2 emissions will depend on demonstration projects at a scale that tests our knowledge of site characterization, capture and sequestration processes, and operations. California is a centerpiece of large-scale demonstration projects, such as the WestCarb activities and the large, industrially-based project at Carson, CA. Through demonstrations like these, the CICS partners will develop protocols for risk assessments and regulations, as well as monitoring plans, that will allow safe and efficient operation of large-scale CCS projects. These protocols and regulatory frameworks need to be developed and, when completed, could serve as national standards.

ENERGY SUPPLY, SOURCES, AND TECHNOLOGIES

Opportunities and Impacts

- Deploy next-generation solar, wind, biofuel, geothermal, and environmentally sensitive hydro power to achieve California's emission targets
- Reduce costs of carbon capture and sequestration and ensure permanence of storage
- Next-generation biofuels and distribution networks will expand energy sources

3.b.iii. Governance, Policy, and Management

Effective mitigation policy in support of AB32 and SB 1368 must be based on current scientific knowledge of the full range of activities that alter climate. Transforming the economies of California, the U.S., and the world to operate under climate-change constraints, all while ensuring economic growth, will necessarily involve a number of in-terrelated policies. This transformation must be based on knowledge of the efficacy and reliability of various energy sources, as well as address the economic and security risks inherent in the energy sector. Success in mitigating climate change will require the har-monization of efforts among several regulatory agencies, as well as private and public sectors, and the combining of innovative governance approaches, attention to environmental justice concerns, and sophisticated legal crafting with a systemic view. The primary mission of this program area is to translate science into policy recommendations and to harness ongoing social science research to support policy analysis.

Efforts in this program area will focus on short-term and long-term regulatory policy analysis of market options, the ways in which environmental governance can be implemented, and the efficacy of mitigation strategies. Studies of innovative environmental governance will assist policymakers and regulators in developing and testing new and in-novative alternatives for the variety of sector-based concerns raised by the economy-wide climate challenge. These activities are also intended to support the development and im-plement of new approaches being developed by business, and government.

Over the past 15 years, the United States has invested heavily in scientific research, monitoring, data management, and assessment for climate-change analyses to build a foundation of knowledge for decision-making. Formal assessments, that involve exploring the uses and identifying the limits of evolving knowledge to manage risks and opportunities, are a key component of both policy-making and decision-making. The CICS will sponsor an ongoing synthesis and assessment program, with key products timed to support a range of actions in support of AB32.

The Institute will also explore the use of advanced modeling in decision support for adaptive management and a range of options that go well beyond what is currently in place in applications. Analyses will be built around projections of future California energy requirements, consumer behavior, energy production technologies, and projections of the costs, availability, and environmental impact of resources. The future system structure depends on technology developments, the cost and availability of resources in California, and the required level of greenhouse gas reductions. The CICS will identify practical options for the future California system, identify the key decision points and alternatives along the way, and identify the key information about technologies and resources that are needed to make those decisions.

GOVERNANCE, POLICY, AND MANAGEMENT

Opportunities and Impacts

- Project California's energy future to identify technology, resource, and policy needs; integrate risk assessment methods
- Conduct short- and long-term regulatory and economic analysis toward efficient energy and other resource markets
- Use new life-cycle methods for greenhouse gas, water, and consumer product assessments, and product accounting and labeling

3.b.iv. Climate Forecasts and Analysis

With the passage of AB32 and SB 1368, California has taken decisive steps to moderate global warming through reductions in greenhouse gas emissions. Observations demonstrate that climate is already changing and projections indicate that climate in California will change substantially, despite having in place the most-aggressive greenhouse gas mitigation policies in the country. Thus, progress in meeting California's emission targets will be affected by the continual evolution of the water, transportation, and energy sectors in response to the changing environment. We know that climate change will produce a cascade of effects: warming will alter the hydrologic cycle in the form of more rain and less snow, increased evaporation, and likely acceleration in the rise of sea level. This, in turn, will change energy demands for transporting water around the state, influence people's choices about where to live and work, and potentially affect food security, due to impacts on the agricultural sector. It is crucial for California to have the capacity to understand these cascading effects in regional and local detail, because these changes will likely have profound impacts on not only the supply and demand of energy in the state, but also water supply, water and air quality, agriculture productivity, human health, ecosystems, and many other vital resources.

In this program area, the CICS will provide detailed and robust forecasts of climate change to help safeguard the state's social and natural infrastructure and its vital economic sectors, and provide a better understanding of the conditions that drive energy supply and demand in California. Research in this program area will generate state-of-the-art regional and local predictions of climate changes and their downstream impacts on energy, water, and other sectors so that California can continuously update its approach for managing supplies of water and energy, and adapt its infrastructure for transportation and industry. This program area will develop an interactive analysis and modeling system that links global climate, regional climate and weather, and local impacts, such as those described by hydrology, airsheds, coastal zones, and other applications models. California's location on the border of the Pacific basin, which modulates current climate and will certainly affect climate change in the state, requires that regional modeling will need to include an interactive coastal ocean component. Thus, the modeling system will be designed to encompass a hierarchy of models that simulate and predict climate and its impacts.

The modeling system developed in this program area will be tailored to address public policy needs in conducting risk assessment, and exploring options for adaptation/mitigation at the state and local levels. Models forecasting climate change at the level of the State of California are rapidly improving; an aspect of producing better climate forecasts must involve a high-level analysis capacity to test and improve models in the context of a range of historical and real-time observations. To be most effective, this effort will be carried out in concert with intensive monitoring of state climate and climate indicators. Because climate forecasts will always carry substantial uncertainty, a crucial element of the modeling and analysis effort will consist of developing an ensemble of possible climate-change scenarios that can be used to assess climate and climate impacts probabilistically, and to provide this in sufficient detail that decision makers can evaluate possible outcomes. This interlinked climate modeling and analysis system will also allow an assessment of vulnerabilities, extreme events, and possible tipping points. In particular, the modeling and analysis conducted in this program area would aim to understand and predict heat waves, floods, drought, and hazardous-air-quality episodes.

CLIMATE FORECASTS AND ANALYSIS

Opportunities and Impacts

- Produce predictions of climate-change impacts to California's water system, air quality, and ecosystems

- Deploy intensive monitoring system to examine state climate and climate-change indicators

- Develop regional/local analysis and modeling system

3.b.v. Quality of Life: Health and the Environment

This program area will conduct research and education that focuses on determining the direction, magnitude, and frequency of health and environmental change in California. Efforts will focus on characterizing and understanding the effects of climate change on our natural and human surroundings, and will bring forward new and innovative methods to minimize or eliminate these effects in conjunction with state and local agencies. Understanding who and what is at greatest risk from current patterns, and how impacted segments will be affected by different policy choices are critical to targeting resources and building consensus.

The vitality of California's society and economy are inextricably linked to the health of its population and its environment. Health is affected by a variety of exposures that occur indoors and outdoors (e.g., to pollutants and extreme temperatures) and many of these exposures will be modified by climate change, by adaptations to climate change (e.g., more air conditioning), and by efforts to mitigate climate change.

One focus of this program area is the impact of climate change and energy policy on (1) exposure and health effects in marginalized communities, and (2) the environment. This includes heat-related exposures, air quality changes, water quality, and indirect effects, e.g. soil moisture effects on disease vectors. It is expected that this research will make use of existing health data, direct measurements of air and water, modeling, and social science data. Climate change, and the climatic and environmental impacts of changes in energy use strategies, will impact California's diverse communities and natural resources to different degrees. Aspects of mitigation that rely on voluntary choices need to be enhanced through education and outreach to all communities, and impacts on natural resources must be minimized. Equally important will be to project the change in personal choices needed to achieve certain mitigation levels, and then evaluate the rate at which California is moving toward those choices.

This program area will combine research and education on issues related to environmental justice and equity with a unique new social extension and partnership program. In this program, we will provide energy and society extension services; offer short courses and yearlong fellowships to underserved communities, labor, and communities involved in environmental justice issues; and create convening mechanisms to bring together key stakeholders in business, government, and environmental justice communities to discuss issues and policies.

Another focus of this program area is to sustain California's environmental quality and ecological diversity despite the challenges posed by climate change. The health of the state's environment is directly linked to the availability and quality of California's water, air, land, and ecological resources. Through careful management of its natural environment, the state has ensured reliable supplies of water; however, the provision of adequate water could be seriously affected by the environmental impacts of climate change. These impacts include significant reductions in snowpack in a warmer California climate; a loss of forest vitality, which mitigates the effects of flooding and erosion; reductions in commercial and sport fishing industries; and rising sea level changes coupled with biological disturbances, such as harmful algal blooms and waste-disposal conditions. Researchers at the CICS will actively partner with state agencies to monitor, predict, and mitigate the impacts of climate change on these vital ecosystem services.

California has some of the worst air quality regions in the country in terms of ozone and particulate matter concentrations. The local, state, and federal governments and agencies are concerned that climate change will exacerbate California's already severe air quality problems. Particulates and ozone formed by photochemical smog contribute directly to climate change regionally and globally, and indirect effects of pollution include changes in the lifetimes of greenhouse gases. Air quality is important to climatic, human, and ecosystem sustainability. Finally, with climate and hydrologic modeling, and the new measurements needed to drive these models, CICS researchers will provide needed understanding of forest management and climate-change effects on mountain precipitation and runoff, help to identify sustainable watershed and forest management practices, investigate impacts of changes in land cover and land use in source-water areas, and explore the effects of increased demand to optimize production for agriculture and urban needs. In short, research conducted in this program area will help us better understand watershed management practices (to increase the efficiency of water use and harness for energy generation), the tradeoffs of transporting water versus desalinization, the effect of climate change on air quality, and how actions taken to mitigate greenhouse gas increases will impact air quality at a range of spatial scales.

QUALITY OF LIFE: HEALTH AND THE ENVIRONMENT

Opportunities and Impacts

- Identify potential health issues from climate change (e.g. heat waves, droughts, changes in disease vectors)
- Improve air quality through monitoring, modeling, and reductions in particulate- and ozone-causing emissions
- Deploy observational network for ecosystem impacts and monitor feedback from climate change

3.b.vi. Measurement, Informatics, and Analytical Infrastructure

The CICS will construct and maintain a multifaceted, longitudinal, and shared database to be used by all CICS participants. This database will be in the form of an internet server—easily accessible to all participants—that has the computing power to run the kinds of complex analyses required to understand the intricacies of climate change. It will leverage the vast computing power of existing data centers at the UC campuses and our partners (e.g., LLNL). The information and analysis system will harvest multi-source data, multi-scale data, and generating data products to address key policy issues using the best available observations and model results. The scope of information sources will encompass observing networks and existing local, state, and federal sources, and will allow for the integration of future sources through an open standards approach. Data libraries will be routinely updated to document the expected changes in future climate and their associated uncertainties. This digital library will be available to all impact planners, giving them a quantitative description of the expected future changes upon which to build policy directions.

The first step to building the kind of databases necessary for both short-term progress and long-term sustainability is identifying the range and scope of climate-change effects, and the types of informed decisions that must be made about mitigation activities. These questions drive the need for continuous, current information, ranging from observations of climate, air quality, and energy use to health-related factors. These data allow us to build and test better predictive models and to better understand the interrelationships between climate and its impacts (e.g., forecasting the relationship of energy demand to temperature, the relationship of snowpack to water and hydroelectric energy supply, or the impact of locally-sourced goods versus those transported over long distances on air quality and health).

Among the types of measurements that will be made and existing data that will be captured for portal availability are: temporally disaggregated electricity demand information for representative classes of consumers across the state; spatially, temporally and functionally resolved energy use information from sensors placed in representative buildings; energy use patterns across a range of consumer categories; energy supply characteristics at sufficient detail to resolve patterns and provide a basis for optimal use; environmental data, such as precipitation, snowpack, soil moisture, evapotranspiration, and runoff measurements from source-water catchments in support of hydropower and watershed management research; information on the demand for and use of energy and climate information by various categories of stakeholders; and water use patterns in relation to pumping and other popatwer uses.

Reliable data from a variety of user groups, from research to mitigation to adaptation, is a vital resource that California and its partners need in order to deal with the energy-related impacts of climate change. This program area will collect and verify both real-time and snapshot data, and act as a clearinghouse and data verification resource for the UC, the state, its partners, cities, utilities, and other businesses and communities involved in climate-change mitigation and adaptation.

. . . .

Notes & Questions

1. The Public Utilities Commission of the State of California issued an Opinion establishing the California Institute for Climate Solutions in September 2007. Note the

scope of the project. The project looks beyond causes of climate change to also consider the broad range of impacts and methods for adapting and mitigating such harms. How effective can a state-based program be? Why do you think California focused on this?

2. *Practice Note*: Failing to plan can be devastating for communities, and this is true for climate change harms, as well as hurricanes, floods, and other natural disasters, whether they are linked to climate change or not. The risk need to be recognized and managed. In 1997, Grand Forks, North Dakota, suffered a devastating flood that caused millions of dollars of damage (as well as lost productivity and tremendous heartache) that could have been managed by a dike system or other proper planning. The same is true for many of the losses in New Orleans in the aftermath of Hurricane Katrina. But planning ahead is not always easy, even when there are examples to follow as this excerpt explains. From Joshua P. Fershee, *The Rising Tide of Climate Change: What America's Flood Cities Can Teach Us About Green Energy Policy, and Why We Should Be Worried*, 39 Environmental Law 1109 (2009):

> Decisions to make expensive capital investments in the present are difficult when the potential future savings are uncertain in both timing and amount, even when the need for action is compelling. Expensive investments are always difficult because such decisions always mean that some other project will be delayed or eliminated completely. Furthermore, preventative investments, such as dikes and levees, rarely, if ever, lead to additional growth (i.e., they do not generate income). Instead, they are subject to the classic "lawyer's dilemma": the investment requires a significant expenditure to keep what is already in hand, which in essence feels like a loss. What is often missed is that the loss would be even more significant, and usually far more painful, without the upfront expenditure.

> The Red River Valley itself has a proximate and particularly apt example of how difficult the process can be. In Winnipeg, Manitoba, 144 miles north of Grand Forks (and just across the border into Canada), efforts to control flooding of the Red River of the North in the 1960s led to significant ridicule. Following massive flooding in 1950, which destroyed more than 10,000 homes, Manitoban Premier Duff Roblin required the construction of an enormous diversion system to re-route water around the city. The expensive project was initially dubbed "Duff's Ditch" or "Duff's Folly," but since then, the construction has saved billions of government dollars and "is now accepted as a brilliant idea that has saved the City of Winnipeg from severe floods."

> Of course, no system is perfect, and follow-on impacts of any plan need to be considered. Although the diversion system has kept Winnipeg largely safe from flooding, areas to the north and south of the city are vulnerable to flooding that is caused, at least in part, by the raised gates of the diversion project. As time passes, and communities evolve, more and more is learned about the consequences of past actions. However, the fact that early measures to help mitigate a problem are not perfect—whether it is flooding in Winnipeg or climate change—does not mean that no action is the best option.

> To the contrary, once a serious problem is clearly recognized, action is warranted because the costs, financially and psychologically, become even more severe over time. Winnipeg's diversion canal cost about $63 million dollars, a "price tag ... considered by some to be astronomical." However, the cost of doing the same project today would be between (roughly) $390,000,000 and $990,000,000 in today's dollars (depending on the type of comparison), not including the "literally billions of dollars" saved over the years by the project.

As Grand Forks learned in 1997, the ability to predict potential losses is of limited value if action is not taken. In Grand Forks, there was "enormous lead time," yet the predictions were not able to avoid major losses. Building a flood protection system that eventually cost more than $400 million dollars would have saved billions of dollars. Instead, those millions were paid out on top of the billions of washed away in the flood.

3. What areas are ripe for adaptation and mitigation plans? What are the biggest risk areas in the country? In the world? In 2012, Congress passed a law to increase flood-insurance rates for high-risk areas. The law is still in place but has received significant push back, and proposals for repeal (or rollback) have been put forth. Recall the discussion of subsidies in Chapter 6. Flood insurance rates that are lower than the market would bear because of government intervention are subsidized rates. Subsidies lead to more of what is being subsidized, in this case, owning property in high-risk areas. Consider the implications of these types of subsidies. What is the effect of this program? What's fair? To whom?

Chapter 8

The Unique Nature of the Transportation Sector

A. Introduction

Transportations fuels are among the most high-profile energy sources. This is likely because most Americans have a regular and repeated connection to gasoline: when they fill up their car or truck. We (usually) pump the gas (unless we live in New Jersey), we pay for the gas, and we start the car and drive away. In other energy forms, at least most of the time, there is a less tactile and more distant relationship. We turn on the lights, but we don't see a coal-fired plant or wind turbine. Even if we do, we aren't connected to it. We are sent a bill or get one via email. It's different. We notice home heating and electricity when we get the bill, or when it is suddenly unavailable. Otherwise, we tend to ignore it. We have a much closer relationship with our transportation fuels.

1. Vocabulary and Concepts

Alternative Fuels: The U.S. Department of Transportation, Center for Climate Change and Environmental Forecasting lists the following: "Methanol, denatured ethanol, and other alcohols, mixtures containing 85 percent or more (or such other percentage, but not less than 70 percent) by volume of methanol, denatured ethanol, and other alcohols with gasoline or other fuels; natural gas; liquefied petroleum gas; hydrogen; coal-derived liquid fuels; fuels (other than alcohol) derived from biological materials; and electricity, including electricity from solar energy."

The Energy Information Administration's Energy Glossary defines alternative fuels as:

> "[A]ny other fuel the Secretary determines, by rule, is substantially not petroleum and would yield substantial energy security benefits and substantial environmental benefits." The term "alternative fuel" does not include alcohol or other blended portions of primarily petroleum-based fuels used as oxygenates or extenders, i.e. MTBE, ETBE, other ethers, and the 10-percent ethanol portion of gasohol.

361

Compressed Natural Gas (CNG): Methane stored at high pressure that can be used in place of liquid fuels in transporation vehicles.

Corporate Average Fuel Economy (CAFE) Standards: A federal requirement that vehicle manufacturers comply with the gas mileage standards set by the U.S. Department of Transportation (DOT).

Crude Oil Refining: Crude oil has four primary, profitable components that come from the erfining process: (1) gasoline; (2) kerosene (jet fuel); (3) diesel; and (4) fuel oil. The different carbon chain lengths in petroleum have progressively higher boiling points, so they can be separated out by distillation.

Freight Modes: This includes truck, air, marine, rail, and pipeline freight modes, but not gas and water pipelines.

Hydrogen Fuel Cell: A device that converts the chemical energy from hydrogen into electricity through a chemical reaction with oxygen or another oxidizing agent. Other fuels can be used as well.

Light-Duty Vehicles: This includes cars, motorcycles, and light trucks.

Light Rail: A light volume electric railway with lower traffic capacity compared to heavy rail. Light rail includes streetcars and other trams, and includes those with exclusive or shared rights of way.

Light Trucks: Single unit two-axle, four-tire trucks. This includes pickup trucks, sports utility vehicles (SUVs), vans, motor homes, and similar vehicles. EIA defines light truck as all trucks weighing 8,500 pounds or less.

Transportation Sector: The U.S. Department of Transportation, Center for Climate Change and Environmental Forecasting definiton: "An energy-consuming sector that consists of all vehicles whose primary purpose is transporting people and/or goods from one physical location to another. Included are automobiles; trucks; buses; motorcycles; trains, subways, and other rail vehicles; aircraft; and ships, barges, and other waterborne vehicles. Vehicles whose primary purpose is not transportation (e.g., construction cranes and bulldozers, farming vehicles, and warehouse tractors and forklifts) are classified in the sector of their primary use."

2. Client Issue

Your client is considering the acquisition of an electric sports car company (Insull Motors). The client has its business advisors considering the economics of the deal, but they need to know assess the regulatory risks for such an acquisition. Your client is especially interested in knowing what legal and regulatory changes pose risks and opportunities for electric vehicles generally. That is, what changes could make electric vehicles more attractive, and what changes would make the market more difficult? As part of the analysis, your client would also like a similar summary for potential competitors, such as gasoline vehicles, diesel vehicles, natural gas vehicles, and hydrogen fuel-cell vehicles. As you read this chapter, think about where laws and regulations could be modified, repealed, or created to help or hinder each type of vehicle.

B. Promoting Efficiency

Center for Biological Diversity v. National Hwy. Traffic Safety Administration

538 F.3d 1172 (9th Cir. 2008)

BETTY B. FLETCHER, Circuit Judge:

Eleven states, the District of Columbia, the City of New York, and four public interest organizations petition for review of a rule issued by the National Highway Traffic Safety Administration (NHTSA) entitled "Average Fuel Economy Standards for Light Trucks, Model Years 20082011," 71 Fed.Reg. 17,566 (Apr. 6, 2006) ("Final Rule") (codified at 49 C.F.R. pt. 533). Pursuant to the Energy Policy and Conservation Act of 1975 (EPCA), 49 U.S.C. §§ 32901–32919 (2007), the Final Rule sets corporate average fuel economy (CAFE) standards for light trucks, defined by NHTSA to include many Sport Utility Vehicles (SUVs), minivans, and pickup trucks, for Model Years (MYs) 2008–2011. For MYs 2008–2010, the Final Rule sets new CAFE standards using its traditional method, fleet-wide average (Unreformed CAFE). For MY 2011 and beyond, the Final Rule creates a new CAFE structure that sets varying fuel economy targets depending on vehicle size and requires manufacturers to meet different fuel economy levels depending on their vehicle fleet mix (Reformed CAFE).

Petitioners challenge the Final Rule under the EPCA and the National Environmental Policy Act of 1969 (NEPA), 42 U.S.C. §§ 4321–4347 (2007). First, they argue that the Final Rule is arbitrary, capricious, and contrary to the EPCA because (a) the agency's cost-benefit analysis does not set the CAFE standard at the "maximum feasible" level and fails to give due consideration to the need of the nation to conserve energy; (b) its calculation of the costs and benefits of alternative fuel economy standards assigns zero value to the benefit of carbon dioxide (CO_2) emissions reduction; (c) its calculation of costs and benefits of alternative fuel economy standards fails to evaluate properly the benefit of vehicle weight reduction; (d) Reformed CAFE standards will depend on manufacturer fleet mix and not guarantee a minimum average fuel economy or "backstop"; (e) the transition period during which manufacturers may choose to comply with either Unreformed or Reformed CAFE is contrary to the "maximum feasible" requirement and unnecessary; (f) it perpetuates the "SUV loophole," which allows SUVs, minivans, and pickup trucks to satisfy a lower fuel economy standard than cars; and (g) it excludes most vehicles rated between 8,500 and 10,000 pounds gross vehicle weight (comprised mostly of large pickup trucks) from any fuel economy regulation, even though these vehicles satisfy the statutory criteria for regulation.

Second, Petitioners argue that NHTSA's Environmental Assessment is inadequate under NEPA because it fails to take a "hard look" at the greenhouse gas implications of its rulemaking and fails to analyze a reasonable range of alternatives or examine the rule's cumulative impact. Petitioners also argue that NEPA requires NHTSA to prepare an Environmental Impact Statement.

NHTSA argues that the Final Rule is not arbitrary and capricious or contrary to the EPCA, the Environmental Assessment's evaluation of the environmental consequences of its action is adequate, and an Environmental Impact Statement is not required.

We have jurisdiction under 49 U.S.C. § 32909(a) to review the Final Rule issued by NHTSA. We hold that the Final Rule is arbitrary and capricious, contrary to the EPCA in its failure to monetize the value of carbon emissions, failure to set a backstop, failure to close the SUV loophole, and failure to set fuel economy standards for all vehicles in the 8,500 to 10,000 gross vehicle weight rating ("GVWR") class. We also hold that the Environmental Assessment was inadequate and that Petitioners have raised a substantial question as to whether the Final Rule may have a significant impact on the environment. Therefore, we remand to NHTSA to promulgate new standards as expeditiously as possible and to prepare either a revised Environmental Assessment or an Environmental Impact Statement.

I. FACTUAL AND PROCEDURAL BACKGROUND

A. CAFE Regulation Under the Energy Policy and Conservation Act

In the aftermath of the energy crisis created by the 1973 Mideast oil embargo, Congress enacted the Energy Policy and Conservation Act of 1975, Pub.L. No. 94–163, 89 Stat. 871, 901–16. *See* H.R.Rep. No. 94–340 at 1–3 (1975), *as reprinted in* 1975 U.S.C.C.A.N. 1762, 1763–65. Congress observed that "[t]he fundamental reality is that this nation has entered a new era in which energy resources previously abundant, will remain in short supply, retarding our economic growth and necessitating an alteration in our life's habits and expectations." *Id.* at 1763. The goals of the EPCA are to "decrease dependence on foreign imports, enhance national security, achieve the efficient utilization of scarce resources, and guarantee the availability of domestic energy supplies at prices consumers can afford." S.Rep. No. 94–516 (1975) (Conf. Rep.), *as reprinted in* 1975 U.S.C.C.A.N. 1956, 1957. These goals are more pressing today than they were thirty years ago: since 1975, American consumption of oil has risen from 16.3 million barrels per day to over 20 million barrels per day, and the percentage of U.S. oil that is imported has risen from 35.8 to 56 percent. NRDC Cmt. at 11; *see also* 71 Fed.Reg. at 17,644.

In furtherance of the goal of energy conservation, Title V of the EPCA establishes automobile fuel economy standards. An "average fuel economy standard" (often referred to as a CAFE standard) is "a performance standard specifying a minimum level of average fuel economy applicable to a manufacturer in a model year." 49 U.S.C. § 32901(a)(6) (2007). Only "automobiles" are subject to fuel economy regulation, and passenger automobiles must meet a statutory standard of 27.5 mpg, 49 U.S.C. § 32902(b), whereas non-passenger automobiles must meet standards set by the Secretary of Transportation, *id.* § 32902(a). Congress directs the Secretary to set fuel economy standards at "the maximum feasible average fuel economy level that the Secretary decides the manufacturers can achieve in that model year." *Id.* § 32902(a). Under this subsection, the Secretary is authorized to "prescribe separate standards for different classes of automobiles." *Id.* Congress also provides that "[w]hen deciding maximum feasible average fuel economy under this section, the Secretary of Transportation shall consider technological feasibility, economic practicability, the effect of other motor vehicle standards of the Government on fuel economy, and the need of the United States to conserve energy." *Id.* § 32902(f).

Under the EPCA's definitional scheme, vehicles not manufactured primarily for highway use and vehicles rated at 10,000 lbs. gross vehicle weight or more are excluded from fuel economy regulation altogether because they are not "automobiles." An "automobile" is defined as:

> a 4–wheeled vehicle that is propelled by fuel, or by alternative fuel, manufactured primarily for use on public streets, roads, and highways..., and rated at—
>
> (A) not more than 6,000 pounds gross vehicle weight; or

(B) more than 6,000, but less than 10,000, pounds gross vehicle weight, if the Secretary decides by regulation that —

(i) an average fuel economy standard under this chapter for the vehicle is feasible; and

(ii) an average fuel economy standard under this chapter for the vehicle will result in significant energy conservation or the vehicle is substantially used for the same purposes as a vehicle rated at not more than 6,000 pounds gross vehicle weight.

49 U.S.C. § 32901(a)(3). Although NHTSA has the authority to regulate the fuel economy of vehicles up to 10,000 lbs. GVWR, *see id.* § 32901(a)(3)(B), the agency has excluded vehicles exceeding 8,500 lbs. (other than medium-duty passenger vehicles manufactured during MY 2011 or thereafter) from its definition of "automobile," *see* 49 C.F.R. § 523.3(b).

The CAFE standards NHTSA sets for non-passenger automobiles or "light trucks," as referred to by the agency in its regulations, are lower than the standards for passenger automobiles. *Compare* 49 C.F.R. § 533.5(a) (2007) *with* 49 C.F.R. § 531.5(a) (2007). A "passenger automobile" is defined as:

an automobile that the Secretary decides by regulation is manufactured primarily for transporting not more than 10 individuals, but does not include an automobile capable of off-highway operation that the Secretary decides by regulation —

(A) has a significant feature (except 4–wheel drive) designed for off-highway operation; and

(B) is a 4–wheel drive automobile or is rated at more than 6,000 pounds gross vehicle weight.

49 U.S.C. § 32901(a)(16).

The Final Rule sets CAFE standards for "light trucks," defined by NHTSA to include many SUVs, vans, and pickup trucks, for MYs 2008–2011. *See* 71 Fed.Reg. at 17,568; 49 C.F.R. § 533.5(a), (g), (h). A "light truck" is:

an automobile other than a passenger automobile which is either designed for off-highway operation, as described in paragraph (b) of this section, or designed to perform at least one of the following functions: (1) Transport more than 10 persons; (2) Provide temporary living quarters; (3) Transport property on an open bed; (4) Provide greater cargo-carrying than passenger-carrying volume; or (5) Permit expanded use of the automobile for cargo-carrying purposes or other non-passenger-carrying purposes through [removable or foldable, stowable seats to create a flat floor].

49 C.F.R. § 523.5(a) (2007).

For MYs 1996 to 2004, Congress froze the light truck CAFE standard at 20.7 mpg. *See* 71 Fed.Reg. at 17,568. After the legislative restrictions were lifted, NHTSA set new light truck CAFE standards in April 2003: 21.0 mpg for MY 2005, 21.6 mpg for MY 2006, and 22.2 mpg for MY 2007. Light Truck Average Fuel Economy Standards Model Years 2005–2007, 68 Fed.Reg. 16,868, 16,871 (Apr. 7, 2003) (codified at 49 C.F.R. pt. 533).

In response to a request from Congress, the National Academy of Sciences (NAS) published in 2002 a report entitled "Effectiveness and Impact of Corporate Average Fuel Economy (CAFE) Standards." The NAS committee made several findings and recommendations. It found that from 1970 to 1982, CAFE standards helped contribute to a 50 percent increase in fuel economy for new light trucks. *Id.* at 14. In the subsequent decades, however, light trucks became more popular since domestic manufacturers faced less competition in the light truck category and could generate greater profits. *Id.* at 18–19. The "less stringent CAFE standards for trucks ... provide[d] incentives for manufacturers to invest in minivans and SUVs and to promote them to consumers in place of large cars and station wagons." *Id.* at 18. When the CAFE regulations were originally promulgated in the 1970s, "light truck sales accounted for about 20 percent of the new vehicle market," but now they account for about half. *Id.* at 88. This shift has had a "pronounced" effect on overall fuel economy. *Id.* at 19. As the market share of light trucks has increased, the overall average fuel economy of the new light duty vehicle fleet (light trucks and passenger automobiles) has declined "from a peak of 25.9 MPG in 1987 to 24.0 MPG in 2000." *Id.* Vehicle miles traveled (VMT) by light trucks has also been growing more rapidly than passenger automobile travel. *Id.*

The NAS committee found that the CAFE program has increased fuel economy, but that certain aspects of the program "have not functioned as intended," including "[t]he distinction between a car for personal use and a truck for work use/cargo transport," which "has been stretched well beyond the original purpose." *Id.* at 3. The committee also found that technologies exist to "significantly reduce fuel consumption," for cars and light trucks and that raising CAFE standards would reduce fuel consumption. *Id.* at 3–4. Significantly, the committee found that of the many reasons for improving fuel economy, "[t]he most important ... is concern about the accumulation in the atmosphere of so-called greenhouse gases, principally carbon dioxide. Continued increases in carbon dioxide emissions are likely to further global warming." *Id.* at 2. In addition, the committee found "externalities of about $0.30/gal of gasoline associated with the combined impacts of fuel consumption on greenhouse gas emissions and on world oil market conditions" that "are not necessarily taken into account when consumers purchase new vehicles." *Id.* at 4.

    ....

D. The Final Rule: CAFE Standards for Light Trucks MYs 2008–2011

NHTSA issued the Final Rule on April 6, 2006. 71 Fed.Reg. at 17,566. NHTSA set the CAFE standards for MY 2008–2010 (Unreformed CAFE) at the same levels as proposed in the NPRM. Unreformed CAFE sets a fleet-wide average fuel economy standard "with particular regard to the 'least capable manufacturer with a significant share of the market.'" 71 Fed.Reg. at 17,580. NHTSA has reformed the structure of the CAFE program for light trucks, effective MY 2011 (Reformed CAFE). Under Reformed CAFE, fuel economy standards are based on a truck's footprint, with larger footprint trucks subject to a lower standard and smaller footprint trucks subject to higher standards. 71 Fed.Reg. at 17,566. Instead of six footprint categories (a step function) as proposed in the NPRM, Reformed CAFE would be based on a continuous function, meaning a separate fuel economy target for each vehicle of a different footprint. *See id.* at 17,595–96. "A particular manufacturer's compliance obligation for a model year will be calculated as the harmonic average of the fuel economy targets for the manufacturer's vehicles, weighted by the distribution of manufacturer's production volumes among the footprint increments." *Id.* at 17,566. A manufacturer's CAFE compliance obligation will vary with its fleet mix. A manufacturer that produces more large footprint light trucks will have a lower required CAFE standard than one that produces more small footprint light trucks.

During MYs 2008–2010, manufacturers may choose to comply with Unreformed CAFE or Reformed CAFE. *See id.* at 17,593–94.

NHTSA used the manufacturers' preexisting product plans as the baseline for its analyses of technical and economic feasibility under both Unreformed and Reformed CAFE. *Id.* at 17,579. NHTSA made adjustments to the product plans by applying additional technologies in a "cost-minimizing fashion," *id.* at 17,582, and stopping at the point where marginal costs equaled marginal benefits, *id.* at 17,597. NHTSA considered the cost of new technologies and the benefits of fuel savings over the lifetime of the vehicle as the costs and benefits of higher fuel economy standards. *Id.* at 17,585–87, 17,622–23. NHTSA monetized some externalities such as emission of criteria pollutants during gasoline refining and distribution and crash and noise costs associated with driving. *See* Final Regulatory Impact Analysis, Corporate Average Fuel Economy and CAFE Reform for MY 2008–2011 Light Trucks at VIII–60, VIII–74–80 (March 2006) (FRIA). However, NHTSA did not monetize the benefit of reducing carbon dioxide emissions, which it recognized was the "the main greenhouse gas emitted as a result of refining, distribution, and use of transportation fuels." FRIA at VIII–61 to 62. NHTSA acknowledged the estimates suggested in the scientific literature, *see* 71 Fed.Reg. at 17,638; FRIA at VIII–63, but concluded:

> [T]he value of reducing emissions of CO_2 and other greenhouse gases [is] too uncertain to support their explicit valuation and inclusion among the savings in environmental externalities from reducing gasoline production and use. There is extremely wide variation in published estimates of damage costs from greenhouse gas emissions, costs for controlling or avoiding their emissions, and costs of sequestering emissions that do occur, the three major sources for developing estimates of economic benefits from reducing emissions of greenhouse gases.

71 Fed.Reg. at 17,638; *see also* FRIA at VIII–64 to 65.

In its cost-benefit analysis, NHTSA also excluded weight reduction for vehicles between 4,000 and 5,000 lbs. curb weight as a potential measure that manufacturers could use to increase fuel economy. 71 Fed.Reg. at 17,627. NHTSA accepted the possibility of weight reduction for vehicles over 5,000 lbs. curb weight as a cost-effective technology that would not reduce overall safety. *Id.* NHTSA relied on a study by Dr. Charles Kahane for this 5,000 lb. figure:

> [T]he net safety effect of removing 100 pounds from a light truck is zero for light trucks with a curb weight greater than 3,900 lbs. However, given the significant statistical uncertainty around that figure, we assumed a confidence bound of approximately 1,000 lbs. and used 5,000 lbs. as the threshold for considering weight reduction.

Id. (footnotes omitted). By "net safety effect," NHTSA means that 3,900 lbs. is the breakeven point: "the point where the total effect of reducing all vehicles heavier than the breakeven weight by an equal amount is zero." *Id.* at 17,628. In the FRIA, NHTSA explained that it chose the approximately 1,000 lb. confidence bound based on additional empirical work found in Kahane's study:

> Kahane estimated a crossover weight of 5,085 lbs. if manufacturers changed both weight and footprint, and the interval estimated ranged from 4,224 lbs. to 6,121 lbs[.], i.e., an interval +/–1000 lbs[.] around the point estimate. Although the crossover weight differs from the point of zero net impact, they would both tend to have similar sampling errors. We applied this interval to the 3,900 lbs. point of zero net impact (which is based on the assumption that footprint is held constant); therefore, the agency felt it would be prudent to limit weight reductions to those vehicles above 5,000 lbs. curb weight.

FRIA at V–15 (internal citation omitted).

NHTSA rejected the idea of a "backstop" under Reformed CAFE. 71 Fed.Reg. at 17,592; *id.* at 17,617. NHTSA stated that a backstop, or a required fuel economy level applicable to a manufacturer if its required level under Reformed CAFE fell below a certain minimum, "would essentially be the same as an Unreformed CAFE standard." *Id.* at 17,592. NHTSA argued that "EPCA permits the agency to consider consumer demand and the resulting market shifts in setting fuel economy standards," *id.* at 17,593, and that a backstop "would essentially limit the ability of manufacturers to respond to market shifts arising from changes in consumer demand. If consumer demand shifted towards larger vehicles, a manufacturer potentially could be faced with a situation in which it must choose between limiting its production of the demanded vehicles, and failing to comply with the CAFE light truck standard." *Id.*

Finally, NHTSA declined to change the regulatory definition of cars and light trucks to close the SUV loophole and refused to regulate vehicles between 8,500 and 10,000 lbs. GWVR, other than MDPVs. *See id.* at 17,574.

. . . .

III. DISCUSSION

A. Energy Policy and Conservation Act Issues

1. NHTSA's use of marginal cost-benefit analysis to determine "maximum feasible average fuel economy level"

With respect to non-passenger automobiles (i.e., light trucks), the fuel economy standard "shall be the maximum feasible average fuel economy level that the Secretary decides the manufacturers can achieve in that model year." 49 U.S.C. § 32902(a). "Maximum feasible" is not defined in the EPCA. However, the EPCA provides that "[w]hen deciding maximum feasible average fuel economy under this section, the Secretary of Transportation shall consider technological feasibility, economic practicability, the effect of other motor vehicle standards of the Government on fuel economy, and the need of the United States to conserve energy." *Id.* § 32902(f).

Petitioners argue that the meaning of "maximum feasible" is plain, and that NHTSA's decision to maximize economic benefits is contrary to the plain language of the EPCA because "feasible" means " 'capable of being done,' " not economically optimal. But even if "feasible" means " 'capable of being done,' " technological feasibility, economic practicability, the effect of other motor vehicle standards, and the need of the nation to conserve energy must be considered in determining the "maximum feasible" standard. *American Textile Manufacturers Institute v. Donovan* does not support Petitioners' interpretation of "feasible." 452 U.S. 490, 101 S.Ct. 2478, 69 L.Ed.2d 185 (1981). In that case, no other language in the statute modified the phrase at issue: "to the extent feasible." *Id.,* 452 U.S. at 508–11, 101 S.Ct. 2478. Here, "maximum feasible" standards are to be determined in light of technological feasibility, economic practicability, the effect of other motor vehicle standards, and the need of the nation to conserve energy.

The EPCA clearly requires the agency to consider these four factors, but it gives NHTSA discretion to decide how to balance the statutory factors—as long as NHTSA's balancing does not undermine the fundamental purpose of the EPCA: energy conservation. In *Center for Auto Safety v. NHTSA,* the D.C. Circuit considered whether NHTSA gave "impermissible weight to shifts in consumer demand" in setting the MY 1985 and 1986 standards for light trucks. 793 F.2d 1322, 1338 (D.C.Cir.1986). Petitioners in that case challenged NHTSA's rule that revised the standards downward. *Id.* at 1323–24. The court held that since Congress had not directly spoken to the issue of consumer demand, the court must determine whether the agency's interpretation represented a " 'reasonable accommodation of conflicting policies that were committed to the agency's care by the statute.' " *Id.* at 1338 (quoting *Chevron,* 467 U.S. at 845, 104 S.Ct. 2778). The court reasoned that:

> Congress intended energy conservation to be a long term effort that would continue through temporary improvements in energy availability. Thus, it would clearly be impermissible for NHTSA to rely on consumer demand to such an extent that it ignored the overarching goal of fuel conservation. At the other extreme, a standard with harsh economic consequences for the auto industry also would represent an unreasonable balancing of EPCA's policies.

Id. at 1340 (footnote omitted). The court concluded that NHTSA's consideration of consumer demand was permissible because Congress did not speak to the precise issue, and "it specifically delegated the process of setting light truck fuel economy standards with *broad* guidelines concerning the factors that the agency must consider. NHTSA has remained within the reasonable range permitted by those factors." *Id.* at 1341; *see also Pub. Citizen v. NHTSA,* 848 F.2d 256, 265 (D.C.Cir.1988) (R. Ginsburg, J.).

In *Public Citizen,* the petitioners challenged the NHTSA's lowering of the fuel economy standard for passenger cars for MY 1986. 848 F.2d at 259. They argued that NHTSA's determination that the statutory 27.5 mpg standard was not economically practicable improperly elevated consumer demand and market forces, subordinated the statute's technology–forcing design, and ignored the need of the nation to conserve energy. *Id.* at 264. The court held that NHTSA's "consideration of the likelihood of economic hardship within its assessment of 'economic practicability[ ]' must be accorded due weight." *Id.* at 264–65. Based on economic analyses supplied by other governmental agencies, "NHTSA concluded that the industry-wide economic effects of the higher CAFE standard would be severe," *id.* at 265, "including sales losses well into the hundreds of thousands, and job losses well into the tens of thousands," *id.* at 264; *see also* 49 Fed.Reg. 41,250, 41,252 (Oct. 22, 1984).

Petitioners cite *Public Citizen* for the proposition that consideration of "economic practicability" allows lowering fuel economy standards *only if* a higher standard would cause substantial economic hardship to a manufacturer with a substantial share of the market. But that is not precisely what *Public Citizen* held. Rather, that court concluded that given the extensive evidence in the record showing that severe economic hardship would result from a higher standard, NHTSA's decision to lower the standard under those circumstances was not devoid of rational support. *Pub. Citizen,* 848 F.2d at 265.

The *Public Citizen* court held that NHTSA's balancing of the statutory factors in 49 U.S.C. § 32902(f) was reasonable given that the possible energy savings from the higher standard *did not outweigh* the severe economic costs, *id.* at 265, since "the maximum potential increase in annual fuel consumption attributable to th[e] rule would amount to less than 0.1 percent of current consumption," *id.* at 268. The court observed, "NHTSA found the *maximum* yearly impact of the lower (26.0 mpg) standard on U.S. gasoline consumption to be 210 million gallons, 0.3% of annual U.S. gasoline consumption and 0.09% of annual U.S. petroleum consumption. That savings, NHTSA stated, was not commensurate with 'potential sales losses to the industry in the hundreds of thousands, job losses in the tens of thousands, or the unreasonable restriction of consumer choices.' "

Pub. Citizen, 848 F.2d at 260–61 (citation omitted). In sum, Congress did not "offer[ ] a more precise balancing formula for the agency to apply to the four ... factors," and "[i]n the absence of a sharper congressional delineation," the court could not conclude that, under the circumstances presented there, NHTSA's decision was not a reasonable accommodation of conflicting statutory policies. *Id.* at 265.

In this rulemaking, NHTSA does not set forth its interpretation of the four factors in 49 U.S.C. § 32902(f). It simply states that in determining the "maximum feasible" fuel economy level, NHTSA "assesses what is technologically feasible for manufacturers to achieve without leading to adverse economic consequences, such as a significant loss of jobs or the unreasonable elimination of consumer choice." 70 Fed.Reg. at 51,425; 71 Fed.Reg. at 17,585 (citing *Pub. Citizen,* 848 F.2d at 264). NHTSA "balance[s]" the four factors in § 32902(f), "along with other factors such as safety," in determining the CAFE standards. 71 Fed.Reg. at 17,588, 17,655. In earlier rulemakings, NHTSA interpreted "technological feasibility" to mean "whether particular methods of improving fuel economy will be available for commercial application in the model year for which a standard is being established," "economic practicability" to mean "whether the implementation of projected fuel economy improvements is within the economic capability of the industry," "effect of other Federal motor vehicle standards on fuel economy" to mean "an analysis of the unavoidable adverse effects on fuel economy of compliance with emission, safety, noise, or damageability standards," and "the need of the Nation to conserve energy" to mean "the consumer cost, national balance of payments, *environmental, and foreign policy implications* of our need for large quantities of petroleum, especially imported petroleum." 42 Fed.Reg. 63,184, 63,188 (Dec. 15, 1977) (emphasis added); *see also Ctr. for Auto Safety,* 793 F.2d at 1325 n. 12.

NHTSA "recognize[s] that [it] in the past has expressed its belief that the statutory consideration of economic practicability differs from, but does not preclude consideration of, cost/ benefit analysis." 70 Fed.Reg. at 51,435. In its final rule establishing passenger automobile CAFE standards for MYs 1981–1984, NHTSA stated, "not equating cost-benefit considerations with economic practicability is consistent with the goal of achieving maximum feasible fuel economy by allowing economically and technologically possible standards which will improve fuel economy but which an analysis, subject to many practical limitations, might indicate are not cost-beneficial." *See* 42 Fed.Reg. 33,534, 33,536 (1977). The agency further opined, "A cost-benefit analysis would be useful in considering [economic practicability], but sole reliance on such an analysis would be contrary to the mandate of the Act." *Id.* at 33,537. In this rulemaking, however, NHTSA states that "the cost/benefit analyses conducted today ... are substantially more robust than those conducted in decades past and provide a more substantial basis for consideration of economic practicability." 70 Fed.Reg. at 51,435.

We agree with NHTSA that "EPCA neither requires nor prohibits the setting of standards at the level at which net benefits are maximized." *Id.* at 51,435. The statute is silent on the precise question of whether a marginal cost-benefit analysis may be used. *See Chevron,* 467 U.S. at 843, 104 S.Ct. 2778. *Public Citizen* and *Center for Auto Safety* persuade us that NHTSA has discretion to balance the oft-conflicting factors in 49 U.S.C. § 32902(f) when determining "maximum feasible" CAFE standards under 49 U.S.C. § 32902(a).

To be clear, we reject only Petitioners' contention that EPCA *prohibits* NHTSA's use of marginal cost-benefit analysis to set CAFE standards. Whatever method it uses, NHTSA cannot set fuel economy standards that are contrary to Congress's purpose in enacting the EPCA — energy conservation. We must still review whether NHTSA's balancing of the statutory factors is arbitrary and capricious. Additionally, the persuasiveness of the analysis in *Public Citizen* and *Center for Auto Safety* is limited by the fact that they were decided two decades ago, when scientific knowledge of climate change and its causes were not as advanced as they are today. The need of the nation to conserve energy is even more pressing today than it was at the time of EPCA's enactment. *See, e.g.,* NRDC Cmt. at 4, 11 ("When fuel economy legislation was first enacted, America consumed 16.3 million barrels of oil per day and 35.8 percent of U.S. oil came from imports. In the nearly 30 years since then, oil consumption has risen to over 20 million barrels per day and 56 percent of U.S. oil is imported. If fuel economy standards are not strengthened, these trends are only expected to get worse, with transportation oil use driving 80 percent of U.S. oil demand growth through 2025 and imports rising to 68 percent of U.S. oil demand. The light duty vehicle fleet currently consumes 8.3 million barrels per day, and in the absence of stronger standards, that is projected to grow to 12.45 million barrels by 2025."); NAS Report at 13–14, 20. What was a reasonable balancing of competing statutory priorities twenty years ago may not be a reasonable balancing of those priorities today.

2. Failure to monetize benefits of greenhouse gas emissions reduction

Even if NHTSA may use a cost-benefit analysis to determine the "maximum feasible" fuel economy standard, it cannot put a thumb on the scale by undervaluing the benefits and overvaluing the costs of more stringent standards. NHTSA fails to include in its analysis the benefit of carbon emissions reduction in either quantitative or qualitative form. It did, however, include an analysis of the employment and sales impacts of more stringent standards on manufacturers. *See* 71 Fed.Reg. at 17,590–91.

To determine the "maximum feasible" CAFE standards, NHTSA began with the fuel economy baselines for each of the seven largest manufacturers—that is, "the fuel economy levels that manufacturers were planning to achieve in those years." *Id.* at 17,581. NHTSA then "add[ed] fuel saving technologies to each manufacturer's fleet until the incremental cost of improving its fuel economy further just equal[ed] the incremental value of fuel savings and other benefits from doing so." *Id.* at 17,596. The standard is further adjusted "until industry-wide net benefits are maximized. Maximization occurs when the incremental change in industry-wide compliance costs from adjusting it further would be exactly offset by the resulting incremental change in benefits." *Id.* NHTSA claims that this "cost-benefit analysis carefully considers and weighs all of the benefits of improved fuel savings," and that "there is no compelling evidence that the unmonetized benefits would alter our assessment of the level of the standard for MY 2011." *Id.* at 17,592.

Under this methodology, the values that NHTSA assigns to benefits are critical. Yet, NHTSA assigned no value to the most significant benefit of more stringent CAFE standards: reduction in carbon emissions. Petitioners strongly urged NHTSA to include this value in its analysis, and they cited peer-reviewed scientific literature in support. NRDC cited figures for the benefit of carbon emissions reduction ranging from $8 to $26.50 per ton CO_2, based on values assigned by the California Public Utilities Commission, the Idaho Power Company, and the European Union (EU) carbon trading program. NRDC Cmt. at 8. NRDC also cited a study published by the National Commission on Energy Policy, which "found that measures mitigating climate change emissions have estimated benefits of $3–19 per ton of carbon dioxide equivalent. The Commission recommends a price of $7 per ton beginning in 2010 and then rising 5 percent each year." *Id.* at 23 (footnote omitted). Environmental Defense and the Union of Concerned Scientists recommended a minimum value of $50 per ton carbon (or $13.60 per ton CO_2), which reflects a mean marginal damage cost developed in 28 peer-reviewed studies. Environmental Defense Cmt. at 6, A–4; UCS Cmt. at 16. Valuing carbon emissions at $50 per ton carbon translates into approximately $0.15 per gallon of gasoline saved. UCS Cmt. at 16. The NAS committee, on which NHTSA relies for other aspects of its analysis, also valued the benefit of carbon emissions reduction at $50 per ton carbon. NAS Report at 85.

NHTSA acknowledged that "[c]onserving energy, especially reducing the nation's dependence on petroleum, benefits the U.S. in several ways. [It] has benefits for economic growth and the environment, as well as other benefits, such as reducing pollution and improving security of energy supply." 71 Fed.Reg. at 17,644. NHTSA also acknowledged the comments it received that recommended values for the benefit of carbon emissions reduction; however, the agency refused to place a value on this benefit. *See id.* at 17,638. NHTSA stated:

> The agency continues to view the value of reducing emissions of CO_2 and other greenhouse gases as too uncertain to support their explicit valuation and inclusion among the savings in environmental externalities from reducing gasoline production and use. There is extremely wide variation in published estimates of damage costs from greenhouse gas emissions, costs for controlling or avoiding their emissions, and costs of sequestering emissions that do occur, the three major sources for developing estimates of economic benefits from reducing emissions of greenhouse gases. Moreover, ... commenters did not reliably demonstrate that the unmonetized benefits, which include CO_2, and costs, taken together, would alter the agency's assessment of the level of the standard for MY 2011. Thus, the agency determined the stringency of that standard on the basis of monetized net benefits.

Id.; *see also* FRIA, at VIII–64 to 65.

NHTSA's reasoning is arbitrary and capricious for several reasons. First, while the record shows that there is a range of values, the value of carbon emissions reduction is certainly not zero. NHTSA conceded as much during oral argument when, in response to questioning, counsel for NHTSA admitted that the range of values begins at $3 per ton carbon. NHTSA insisted at argument that it placed no value on carbon emissions reduction rather than zero value. We fail to see the difference. The value of carbon emissions reduction is nowhere accounted for in the agency's analysis, whether quantitatively or qualitatively. This position also contradicts NHTSA's own explanation in the Final Rule that "the agency determined the stringency of [the MY 2011] standard *on the basis of monetized net benefits.*" 71 Fed.Reg. at 17,638 (emphasis added). By presenting a scientifically-supported range of values that does not begin at zero, Petitioners have shown that it is possible to monetize the benefit of carbon emissions reduction.

Second, NHTSA gave no reasons why it believed the range of values presented to it was "extremely wide"; in fact, several commenters and the NAS committee recommended the *same* value: $50 per ton carbon. The NAS committee selected the value of $50 per ton carbon although it acknowledged the wide range of values in the literature and the potential controversy in selecting a particular value. NAS Report at 85. NHTSA argues that the problem was not simply "the ultimate value to be assigned, but the wide variation in published estimates of the three major underlying costs of carbon dioxide emissions — the cost of damages caused by such emissions, the costs of avoiding or controlling such emissions, and the costs of sequestering resulting emissions." NHTSA Br. at 49. But NHTSA fails to explain why those three "underlying costs" are relevant to the question of how carbon emissions should be valued. We are convinced by Petitioners' response:

> To monetize the benefits of reducing CO_2 emissions from automobiles, NHTSA did not need to calculate the "costs of sequestering emissions." Carbon capture

and sequestration, though a feasible means of reducing emissions from large stationary sources such as coal-fired power plants, was not within the range of actions at issue in this automobile fuel economy rulemaking. Nor were "costs for controlling or avoiding [CO_2] emissions" a genuine methodological barrier here: NHTSA already performed an elaborate analysis of the costs of mandating increases in fuel economy. For purposes of this rulemaking, that was the relevant category of control costs.

EPCA Reply Br. at 10–11. In sum, there is no evidence to support NHTSA's conclusion that the appropriate course was not to monetize or quantify the value of carbon emissions reduction at all.

Citizens for Clean Air v. EPA, 959 F.2d 839 (9th Cir.1992), which NHTSA cites to support its contention that agencies may decline to adopt a "particular monetary value" when the "costs and benefits are too uncertain," NHTSA Br. at 48, is inapposite. In *Citizens for Clean Air,* petitioners filed for administrative review of a state agency's grant of a permit for construction of a solid waste incinerator. *Citizens for Clean Air,* 959 F.2d at 841. EPA denied the petitions, and this court held that the decision of the EPA not to consider recycling as a possible "best available control technology" under the Clean Air Act was not arbitrary or capricious. *Id.* at 841–42. The EPA noted in its proposed rule that "it was 'unable to reliably quantify the emission reductions attributable to materials separation when a[ ] [waste incinerator] is equipped with highly efficient at-the-stack air pollution control devices.'" *Id.* at 844 (citation omitted). Petitioners submitted "no hard evidence" that recycling would reduce air pollution when the waste incinerators are already equipped with "state-of-the-art pollution control equipment" (e.g., scrubbers). *Id.* at 847–48. In addition, the Clean Air Act required "that the proposed technology [i.e., recycling] be the *best available* control technology, and in the absence of anything specific or quantifiable in support ... we conclude that EPA's decision not to consider recycling in permitting Spokane's incinerator was not arbitrary or capricious." *Id.* at 848. The petitioners in *Citizens for Clean Air* had to satisfy such a high statutory threshold ("best available control technology"), and they could not satisfy that threshold without hard evidence. By contrast, Petitioners here provided substantial evidence of the value of carbon emissions reduction, and they do not have to satisfy a high statutory threshold.

Third, NHTSA's reasoning is arbitrary and capricious because it has monetized other uncertain benefits, such as the reduction of criteria pollutants, crash, noise, and congestion costs, *see* FRIA at VIII–73 to 80, and "the value of increased energy security," 71 Fed.Reg. at 17,592. Dr. Michael Wang of the Center for Transportation Research at Argonne National Laboratory stated in his peer review of the CAFE compliance and effect model used by NHTSA in its rulemaking that the wide range of dollar values per ton of CO_2 "is not a good reason that CO[2] dollar values are not included.... The same can be said [of] dollar values for criteria pollutants. Yet, monetary values for criteria pollutant emissions are included in the model." Wang Cmt. at 6.

Fourth, NHTSA's conclusion that commenters did not "reliably demonstrate" that monetizing the value of carbon reduction would have affected the stringency of the CAFE standard "'runs counter to the evidence'" before it. *NRDC v. U.S. Forest Serv.,* 421 F.3d 797, 806 (9th Cir.2005) (citation omitted). The Union of Concerned Scientists concluded that "including [a $50/tC value] in the determination of cost–efficient fuel economy could increase the 2011 targets by an average of 0.4–1.1 mpg." UCS Cmt. at 16. Given that the CAFE standards set by NHTSA increase only 1.5 mpg from MY 2008 to 2011, an additional 0.4 to 1.1 mpg increase by MY 2011 is significant. In addition, Environmental Defense "calculate[d] the benefits of the cumulative reductions at $50/tC and 3% discount rate at $19.7 billion by 2020 and $28.4 billion by 2030 (current dollars)." Environmental Defense Cmt. at 6.

We agree with Petitioners that the values they suggest, 10–22 cents per gallon of gasoline in NHTSA's estimation, would not be a small benefit. Under NHTSA's own calculation that Reformed CAFE will save 2.8 billion gallons of gasoline for MY 2011 light trucks, *see* 71 Fed.Reg. at 17,619, 10–22 cents a gallon of carbon benefits "would yield hundreds of millions of dollars in benefits even after discounting—benefits that by themselves would be substantial in relation to the net benefits that NHTSA calculated for the rule." EPCA Reply Br. at 12 (citing 71 Fed.Reg. at 17,623 (showing net benefits of $461 million for MY 2011 under Reformed CAFE)). NHTSA simply did not " 'examine the relevant data and articulate a satisfactory explanation for its action including a rational connection between the facts found and the choice made.' " *Motor Vehicle Mfrs. Ass'n*, 463 U.S. at 43, 103 S.Ct. 2856 (quoting *Burlington Truck Lines v. United States*, 371 U.S. 156, 168, 83 S.Ct. 239, 9 L.Ed.2d 207 (1962)).

Finally, there is no merit to NHTSA's unfounded assertion that if it had accounted for the benefit of carbon emissions reduction, it would have had to account for the adverse safety effects of downweighting, and the two would have balanced out, resulting in no change to the final CAFE standards. No evidence supports this assertion. The assertion is also based on the controversial assumption that higher fuel economy standards for light trucks causes adverse safety effects from downweighting.

Thus, NHTSA's decision not to monetize the benefit of carbon emissions reduction was arbitrary and capricious, and we remand to NHTSA for it to include a monetized value for this benefit in its analysis of the proper CAFE standards.

. . . .

6. Changing the definition of passenger and non-passenger automobiles in order to close the SUV loophole

Petitioners challenge NHTSA's decision not to reform the SUV loophole. They argue that this decision is arbitrary and capricious because it runs counter to the evidence showing that the majority of SUVs, minivans, and pickup trucks function solely or primarily as passenger vehicles, and because NHTSA has not provided a reasoned explanation for why the transition to Reformed CAFE could not be accomplished at the same time as a revision in the definitions.

The EPCA defines "passenger automobile" as "an automobile that the Secretary decides by regulation is manufactured primarily for transporting not more than 10 individuals," excluding "an automobile capable of off-highway operation that the Secretary decides ... has a significant feature except 4–wheel drive designed for off-highway operation" and is 4–wheel drive or more than 6,000 lbs. GVWR. 49 U.S.C. § 32901(a)(16). "Non-passenger automobiles" are thus defined by exclusion. NHTSA defines an automobile other than a passenger automobile as a "light truck," a term not used in the statute. 49 C.F.R. § 523.5 (2007). Under 49 U.S.C. § 32901(a)(16), the Secretary has discretion to decide what constitutes a "passenger automobile" within the confines of the listed criteria.

NHTSA initially sought input on ways to revise the regulatory distinction because the passenger automobile/light truck distinction had become obsolete: "The application of the regulation to the current vehicle fleet (designed with the regulatory distinctions in mind) less clearly differentiates between passenger cars and light trucks than it did in the 1970s." 68 Fed.Reg. at 74,927 (ANPRM). However, in the NPRM, NHTSA decided not to:

chang[e] those classification regulations at this time in part because [NHTSA] believe[s] an orderly transition to Reformed CAFE could not be accomplished if [NHTSA] simultaneously change[s] which vehicles are included in the light truck program and because, as applied in MY 2011, Reformed CAFE is likely to reduce the incentive to produce vehicles classified as light trucks instead of as passenger cars.

70 Fed.Reg. at 51,422. Ultimately, NHTSA did not change the light truck definition other than by expanding the flat floor provision to include vehicles with folding seats, if the vehicles have at least three rows of designated seating. *See* 49 C.F.R. § 523.5(a)(5); 71 Fed.Reg. at 17,650–52.

We conclude that NHTSA's decision not to otherwise revise the passenger automobile/light truck definitions is arbitrary and capricious. First, NHTSA has not provided a reasoned explanation of why an orderly transition to Reformed CAFE could not be accomplished at the same time that the passenger automobile/light truck definitions are revised.

Second, NHTSA asserts that it reasonably decided to look to the purpose for which a vehicle is manufactured instead of consumers' use of a vehicle because it is a more objective way of differentiating between passenger and non-passenger automobiles. But this overlooks the fact that many light trucks today *are* manufactured primarily for transporting passengers, as NHTSA itself has acknowledged: "Many vehicles produced today, while smaller than many other passenger cars, qualify as light trucks because they have been *designed* so that their seats can be easily removed and their cargo carrying capacity significantly enhanced." 68 Fed.Reg. at 74,927 (emphasis added); *see also* 71 Fed.Reg. at 17,621 n. 102 ("NAS Report ... noted that [the passenger automobile/light truck fuel economy] gap created an incentive to design vehicles as light trucks instead of cars."). Today's design differences, which capitalize on the lower light truck CAFE standard, are the very reason that NHTSA sought input on ways to revise the regulatory distinction "in light of the current and emerging motor vehicle fleet." *See* 68 Fed.Reg. at 74,927.

In addition, NHTSA's new focus on the purpose for which automobiles are manufactured conflicts with its earlier assertion that "Congress intended that passenger automobiles be defined as those *used primarily* for the transport of individuals." *Id.* at 74,926 (emphasis added); *see also id.* at 74,913 ("The market suggests that while some light trucks may be *used primarily* to transport passengers, their 'peak use or value' capability (towing boats, hauling heavy loads, etc.) may be a critical factor in the purchase decision." (emphasis added)).

Third, NHTSA's decision runs counter to the evidence showing that SUVs, vans, and pickup trucks are manufactured primarily for the purpose of transporting passengers and are generally not used for off-highway operation. The NAS committee found that:

> The less stringent CAFE standards for trucks did provide incentives for manufacturers to invest in minivans and SUVs *and to promote them to consumers in place of large cars and station wagons....* By shifting their product development and investment focus to trucks, they created more desirable trucks with more carlike features: quiet, luxurious interiors with leather upholstery, top-of-the-line audio systems, extra rows of seats, and extra doors.

NAS Report at 18 (emphasis added); *see also id.* at 23 (noting the exploding demand for light trucks such as minivans and "four-door SUVs and pickup trucks with passenger-friendly features such as extra rows of seats"). Consumers use light trucks primarily for passenger-carrying purposes in large part because that is precisely the purpose for which manufacturers have manufactured and marketed them. *See, e.g.,* App. A to Public Citizen Cmt. (Kathleen Kerwin, "You Call This the Family Car? Pickups with Roomy Cabs Become a Status Accessory," *Business Week,* Apr. 26, 1999.). A pickup truck usage study conducted by R.L. Polk & Co. showed that 73% of light pickup users use their trucks to carry passengers on a daily or weekly basis, 68% use them for personal trips on a daily or weekly basis, 58% use them for commuting on a daily or weekly basis, 59% *never* use them for towing, and 69% *never* use them for driving off-road. Polk Study at 11. Seventy-three percent of medium pickup users use them for carrying passengers on a daily or weekly basis, 65% use them for commuting on a daily or weekly basis (61% daily), and 64% *never* use them for driving off-road. Polk Study at 12. Even among heavy pickup users, 76% use them for carrying passengers on a daily or weekly basis, and 52% never use them for driving off-road. Polk Study at 13. The NAS Committee further found:

> When CAFE regulations were originally formulated, different standards were set for passenger vehicles and for work/cargo vehicles.... because [work/cargo vehicles] needed extra power, different gearing, and less aerodynamic body configurations to carry out their utilitarian, load-carrying functions.... [But this] working definition distinction between a car for personal use and a truck for work use/cargo transport[ ] has broken down, initially with minivans, and more recently with sport utility vehicles and other "cross-over" vehicles that may be designed for peak use but which are actually used almost exclusively for personal transport.... The car/truck distinction has been stretched well beyond its original purpose.

NAS Report at 88 (internal quotation marks and citation omitted). One of the changes the NAS committee recommended to alleviate this problem was to "tighten" the definition of a light truck, a step the EPA has already taken for emissions standards purposes. *Id.* We agree with Petitioners that NHTSA's decision not to do the same was arbitrary and capricious, especially in light of EPCA's overarching goal of energy conservation. Thus, we remand to NHTSA to revise its regulatory definitions of passenger automobile and light truck or provide a valid reason for not doing so.

7. Exclusion of 8,500–10,000 lb. pickup trucks from CAFE regulation

Petitioners argue that NHTSA's decision not to regulate the fuel economy of vehicles between 8,500 and 10,000 lbs. GVWR (generally referred to as Class 2b trucks), other than MDPVs, is arbitrary and capricious because fuel economy standards for these vehicles are feasible and will result in significant energy conservation. *See* 49 U.S.C. § 32901(a)(3). We agree.

All 4–wheeled, fuel and alternative fuel-propelled vehicles manufactured for use on roads and highways that are 6,000 lbs. gross vehicle weight or less are automobiles. *See* 49 U.S.C. § 32901(a)(3)(A). Vehicles more than 6,000 but less than 10,000 lbs. gross vehicle weight are "automobile[s]" for the purpose of fuel economy regulation "if the Secretary decides by regulation that—(i) an average fuel economy standard under this chapter for the vehicle is feasible; and (ii) an average fuel economy standard ... for the vehicle will result in significant energy conservation or the vehicle is substantially used for the same purposes as a vehicle rated at not more than 6,000 pounds gross vehicle weight." *Id.* § 32901(a)(3)(B). Since 1978, NHTSA has defined vehicles 8,500 lbs. GVWR or less as automobiles. *See* 49 C.F.R. § 523.3(b)(2)(iii).

The ANPRM presented two options under which the fuel economy of vehicles with a GWVR of up to 10,000 lbs. could be regulated. *See* 68 Fed.Reg. at 74,930. One option was to include MDPVs, vehicles with a GVWR of greater than 8,500 but less than 10,000 lbs. that are designed primarily for the transportation of persons. NHTSA explained that "[t]his definition would essentially make SUVs between 8,500 and 10,000 lbs. GVWR subject to CAFE, while continuing to exclude most medium and heavy-duty pickups and most medium and heavy-duty cargo vans that are primarily used for agricultural and commercial purposes." *Id.* Another option was to make all vehicles between 8,500 and 10,000 lbs. GVWR subject to CAFE standards. *Id.* NHTSA invited comments on these and any other proposals to regulate vehicles between 8,500 and 10,000 lbs. GVWR. *Id.* The NPRM discussed the inclusion of MDPVs, but it did not address the proposal to regulate all vehicles between 8,500 and 10,000 lbs. GVWR. *See* 70 Fed.Reg. at 51,455–56.

The Final Rule incorporates MDPVs into the definition of "automobile" such that these vehicles would be regulated as light trucks beginning in MY 2011. 49 C.F.R. § 523.3(b)(3); 71 Fed.Reg. at 17,648. NHTSA declined to regulate other vehicles between 8,500 and 10,000 lbs. because unlike MDPVs, they:

> are not subject to EPA testing that provides the data necessary to determine compliance with the CAFE program. Inclusion of the heavier-rated-non-MDPVs would increase the test burden for manufacturers. These vehicles would be subject to a whole new testing regime. Moreover, because these vehicles are not subject to comparable testing requirements, there is not sufficient data to estimate a fuel economy baseline. Without a reliable baseline, the agency is unable to determine fuel economy targets that would result in required fuel economy levels that are economically practicable and technologically feasible.

71 Fed.Reg. at 17,650.

We conclude that this is not a reasoned explanation for excluding Class 2b trucks from CAFE regulation. First, Petitioners presented compelling evidence that setting fuel economy standards for Class 2b trucks is feasible. For example, a Department of Energy research planning study included estimates:

> based on detailed simulation modeling of both the city and highway driving cycles working from a baseline Class 2b truck; baseline estimates were 21.1 mpg city, 15.4 mpg highway, and 13.6 mpg combined.... [The study] identified technology options capable of yielding substantial improvements, including 50% higher fuel economy with technologies available over a 7–year horizon and, with use of hybrid engines in diesel versions of the vehicles, a near doubling of the fuel economy of a baseline gasoline Class 2b pickup would be a feasible "stretch goal."

App. F to Environmental Defense Cmt. at 1. An Argonne National Laboratory study identified numerous technological improvements that could be applied to Class 2b trucks, including "aerodynamic improvements," "lower tire rolling resistance," "improved transmissions," "turbo–charging for diesel engines," "other engine refinements," "integrated starter-generator," and "hybrid-electric powertrains." *Id.* Another study, published by the American Council for an Energy–Efficient Economy, found that the potential fuel economy improvement was "37% ... over a baseline full-size pickup." *Id.* at 2. Overall, while Class 2b trucks are "designed with heavier frames and higher capacities, and therefore larger powertrains and other components, [they] (primarily heavy-duty pickups) entail substantially the same engineering as vehicles under 8500 lbs GVWR, and in many cases share components." *Id.* at 1; *see also* UCS Cmt. at 34.

Second, Petitioners presented substantial evidence that setting CAFE standards for Class 2b trucks would result in significant energy conservation and that these vehicles are substantially used for the same purposes as a vehicle 6,000 lbs. GVWR or less. Class 2b trucks constitute the majority of vehicles in the 8,500 to 10,000 lb. GVWR class. *See* ACEEE Cmt. to ANPRM at 10 ("[P]ickups constitute about 85% of vehicles in the 8,500–10,000 lb. weight range."). One of the Petitioners argued:

> EPA estimates sales of class 2b trucks at 931,000 per year. Given higher per vehicle oil consumption, we estimate that 2b trucks consume 13% of overall demand from trucks under 10,000 pounds GVWR.
>
> …
>
> If class 2b trucks were to improve their fuel economy by 4% per year … over MY 2008–2011, it would save 47,000 barrels of gasoline and diesel fuel per day by 2020 and reduce GHG emissions by a cumulative 16 mmtC over that time frame. Even at comparable fuel economy improvements to those NHTSA proposes for the largest class 2a trucks regulated under the Reformed system—roughly 2% per year, the country would save 24,000 barrels of gasoline and diesel fuel per day by 2020. These amounts are significant: A 24,000 barrel per day (bpd) saving would be equivalent to $700 million of annual savings at a relatively modest shadow price of $1.90/gallon. This far exceeds the $100 million threshold for a "significant energy action" under [Executive Order] 13211.

Environmental Defense Cmt. at 10; *see also* UCS Cmt. at 34 (estimating that "[i]f these vehicles had been held to the same fuel economy standard as other light-duty trucks, the total fuel consumption by trucks under 10,000 lbs GVWR would be approximately 890 million gallons less in 2005, for a savings of nearly 60,000 barrels of oil per day. This corresponds to about 18% of Class 2b fuel use.").

The evidence also shows that Class 2b trucks are "substantially used for the same purposes" as vehicles not more than 6,000 lbs. GVWR. The Polk Study showed that 76% of heavy pickup truck owners use them for carrying passengers on a daily or weekly basis, 57% use them for personal trips on a daily or weekly basis, 49% use them for commuting on a daily basis, and 52% *never* use them for driving off-road. Polk Study at 13; *see also* Environmental Defense Cmt. at 10 (citing a 2002 vehicle inventory and use survey conducted by the U.S. Census Bureau for the argument that "[i]n the intervening decades [since NHTSA revised its definition of 'automobile' to include Class 2a trucks but exclude Class 2b trucks], trucks of all sizes have increasingly shifted from commercial uses to personal uses.").

NHTSA did not address any of this evidence in the Final Rule, and it does not argue that setting CAFE standards for Class 2b trucks would not be feasible, that it would not result in significant energy conservation, or that Class 2b trucks are not substantially used for the same purposes as smaller trucks. *See* 71 Fed.Reg. at 17,649–50; NHTSA Br. at 77–81. Instead, NHTSA makes the bold assertion that "the agency is not obliged to justify exclusion of such very large vehicles, as the statute has already excluded them, subject to NHTSA's discretionary decision to *include* such vehicles." NHTSA Br. at 79 (emphasis in original). This is clearly wrong. The statute gives NHTSA some discretion in deciding whether the 49 U.S.C. § 32901(a)(3) factors are met for Class 2b trucks, but if these factors are satisfied, then they are "automobiles" for which NHTSA must set fuel economy standards.

NHTSA asserts that without EPA testing data, it cannot set CAFE standards for Class 2b trucks. 71 Fed.Reg. at 17,650. But EPA already subjects most Class 2b trucks to the city and highway fuel economy tests (i.e., city and highway chassis dynamometer testing) that NHTSA asserts are needed for it to determine CAFE standards. *See* 40 C.F.R. § 86.101 (2007) (applying test procedures to gasoline-fueled trucks above 8,500 lbs. GVWR ("Otto-cycle complete heavy-duty vehicles")). NHTSA does not dispute this fact.

Moreover, NHTSA has given no explanation of why it would be infeasible to set standards for Class 2b trucks without EPA's tests. Instead, NHTSA's position is merely that imposing one set of tests "minimize[s]" the "test burden to manufacturers." *See* 71 Fed.Reg. at 17,649. This concern has no relevance to any of the statutory factors under 49 U.S.C. § 32901(a)(3)(B).

Finally, NHTSA's reasoning is arbitrary because it decided that it is feasible to set CAFE standards for MDPVs even though they are not currently subject to EPA testing. *See id.* ("MDPVs are not currently required to undergo chassis dynamometer testing."). EPA will begin phasing in city chassis dynamometer testing for MDPVs in MY 2008, but MDPVs are exempted from highway chassis dynamometer testing. *Id.* Yet, having "determined that this additional testing will not be burdensome for the manufacturers," NHTSA required highway tests as a result of including MDPVs in its "automobile" definition. *Id.*

In sum, NHTSA's decision not to set average fuel economy standards for all vehicles between 8,500 and 10,000 lbs. GVWR is arbitrary and capricious. That Class 2b trucks have never been regulated by NHTSA is not a reason for not regulating them now. We remand to NHTSA to revisit this issue and promulgate average fuel economy standards for these vehicles, or to provide a validly reasoned basis for continuing to exclude them from the regulation.

. . . .

IV. CONCLUSION

NHTSA's failure to monetize the value of carbon emissions in its determination of the MY 2008–2011 light truck CAFE standards, failure to set a backstop, failure to revise the passenger automobile/light truck classifications, and failure to set fuel economy standards for all vehicles in the 8,500 to 10,000 lb. GVWR class, was arbitrary and capricious and contrary to the EPCA. We therefore remand to NHTSA to promulgate new standards consistent with this opinion as expeditiously as possible and for the earliest model year practicable.

. . . .

REVERSED AND REMANDED.

Notes & Questions

1. The preceding case is often viewed as an environmental law case (the significant NEPA section of the case is mostly redacted), but obviously this is also an energy law case. Note here the impacts of the "SUV loophole" and how that has led to increased fuel consumption. Can you clearly identify the SUV loophole, how it came to be, and why? Consider also what happened to the auto industry (especially American automakers) in 2008. Can you make an energy-related, market-based argument that the SUV loophole ultimately harmed those it was designed to help? This is arguably an example of how regulations can send market signals and create market incentives, but the regulations still do not always set the market. Do you see how?

2. This case provides a good introduction to the concept of CAFE standards, which have helped increase gas mileage in vehicles over time. There has been much debate about whether the fuel standards have been raised quickly enough—many people suspect not— as the standards were not raised for about 30 years. Following is an explanation of how

CAFE standards were implemented in 2006. As you read the explanation, consider: What are the flaws? How were car companies likely to react? What does this mean for consumers? Does your car get the mileage the sticker says it will?

Environmental Protection Agency, Office of Transportation and Air Quality, *EPA Issues New Test Methods for Fuel Economy Window Stickers*
(Dec. 2006)

Background

Existing Tests and Methods

Fuel economy estimates have been provided to consumers since the 1970s as a tool to help shoppers compare the fuel economy of different vehicles. Currently, EPA relies on data from two laboratory tests to determine the city and highway fuel economy estimates. The test methods for calculating these estimates were last revised in 1984, when the fuel economy derived from the two tests were adjusted downward—10 percent for city and 22 percent for highway—to more accurately reflect driving styles and conditions.

The city and highway tests are currently performed under mild climate conditions (75 degrees F) and include acceleration rates and driving speeds that EPA believes are generally lower than those used by drivers in the real world. Neither test is run while using accessories, such as air conditioning. The highway test has a top speed of 60 miles per hour, and an average speed of only 48 miles per hour.

Since the mid-1990s, EPA's emissions certification program has required the use of three additional tests which capture a much broader range of real-world driving conditions, including high-speed, fast-acceleration driving, the use of air conditioning, and colder temperature operation (20 degrees F). These conditions affect not only the amount of air pollutants a vehicle emits, but also a vehicle's fuel economy. However, these tests were not required to measure fuel economy.

The New Methods to Determine Fuel Economy Estimates

For the first time, the EPA fuel economy estimates will use vehicle-specific data from tests designed to replicate three real-world conditions, which can significantly affect fuel economy: high speed/rapid acceleration driving, use of air conditioning, and cold temperature operation. Previously, these conditions were accounted for by across-the-board adjustments, rather than by vehicle-specific testing.

EPA's new fuel economy estimates will also reflect other conditions that influence fuel economy, like road grade, wind, tire pressure, load, and the effects of different fuel properties. The fuel economy for each vehicle model will continue to be presented to consumers on the label as city and highway MPG estimates.

In 2011, manufacturers will need to perform additional cold temperature, air conditioning, and/or high speed/rapid acceleration driving tests for those vehicles most sensitive to these conditions. However, in order to provide consumers with better fuel economy estimates sooner, EPA will use new calculation methods that capture these driving conditions. These estimates will begin with model year 2008 vehicles. The interim period from model year 2008 to model year 2011 will give manufacturers enough time to plan for this additional testing, while providing consumers with estimates that capture more realistic driving conditions.

How the New Test Methods Will Affect Fuel Economy Estimates

Under EPA's new methods, the new fuel economy estimates for most vehicles will be lower. This is not because auto makers have designed the same vehicles to be less fuel efficient — it is because our new test methods take into account factors that have been missing or not fully accounted for in the current tests. Because some vehicles are more sensitive to these factors than others, the impact of the changes will vary from vehicle to vehicle.

Compared to today's estimates, the city mpg estimates for the manufacturers of most vehicles will drop by about 12 percent on average, and by as much as 30 percent for some vehicles. The highway mpg estimates will drop on average by about 8 percent, and by as much as 25 percent for some vehicles.

In vehicles that achieve generally better fuel economy, such as gasoline-electric hybrid vehicles, new city estimates will be about 20 to 30 percent lower than today's labels, and new highway estimates will be 10 to 20 percent lower. The nature of current hybrid technology — the addition of a battery as a second source of on-board power, sophisticated control systems, and sometimes a smaller engine — makes a hybrid's fuel economy more sensitive to certain factors, such as colder weather and air conditioning use. However, many hybrid models will remain among the most fuel-efficient vehicles on the market.

Since driving behaviors and conditions vary, there is no test that can perfectly predict the fuel economy that every driver will get. With any estimate, there will always be times when a driver's actual fuel economy will be higher or lower. However, EPA's new test methods will do a better job of bringing the estimates on the window sticker closer to people's real-world fuel economy experience.

Laboratory Tests Reflect Real-World Conditions

It is essential that EPA's fuel economy estimates continue to be derived from controlled, repeatable laboratory tests to enable a standardized or "level playing field," comparison between all vehicle models. However, the underlying calculations to determine the estimates are based on data from real-world driving behavior and conditions. Laboratory testing also preserves EPA's ability to confirm the results of manufacturers' testing.

Auto makers will continue to be responsible for performing the fuel economy testing and calculating the label mpg estimates. EPA will continue to confirm the manufacturers' test results by performing audit testing at its National Vehicle and Fuel Emissions Laboratory in Ann Arbor, Michigan.

C. Influencing U.S. Gas Prices

High gas prices are not well tolerated by American consumers, and recent price fluctuations have caused concern about collusion among oil companies, price manipulation by oil speculators, and other conspiracy theories. In response to such concerns, the U.S. Federal Trade Commission prepared a report to address this and other concerns. The report explains how the gasoline market tends to operate.

Gasoline Price Changes: The Dynamic of Supply, Demand, and Competition

Federal Trade Commission (2005)

EXECUTIVE SUMMARY

Many people who purchased gasoline in the U.S. in the past week likely could report the price paid per gallon. Consumers closely follow gasoline prices, and with good reason. U.S. consumers have experienced dramatic increases and wide fluctuations in gasoline prices over the past several years. During 2004 and 2005, U.S. consumers spent millions of dollars more on gasoline than they had anticipated. In the spring of 2005, the national weekly average price of gasoline at the pump, including taxes, rose as high as $2.28 per gallon. Steep, but temporary, gasoline price spikes have occurred in various areas throughout the U.S. Since the mid-1990s, consumers on the West Coast, especially in California, have observed that their gasoline prices are usually higher than elsewhere in the U.S.

Rising average gasoline prices and gasoline price spikes command our attention. What causes high gasoline prices like those of 2004 and 2005? What causes gasoline price spikes? These important questions require a thorough and accurate analysis of the factors— supply, demand, and competition, as well as federal, state, and local regulations—that drive gasoline prices, so that policymakers can evaluate and choose strategies likely to succeed in addressing high gasoline prices.

This Report provides such an analysis, drawing upon what the Federal Trade Commission (FTC) has learned about the factors that can influence average gasoline prices or cause gasoline price spikes. Over the past 30 years, the FTC has investigated nearly all oil-related antitrust matters and has held public hearings, undertaken empirical economic studies, and prepared extensive reports on oil-related issues, such as the Midwest gasoline price spike in June 2000. Since 2002, the staff of the FTC has monitored weekly average retail gasoline and diesel prices in 360 cities nationwide to find and, if necessary, recommend appropriate action on pricing anomalies that might indicate anticompetitive conduct.

Some observers suggest that oil company collusion, anticompetitive mergers, or other anticompetitive conduct—not market forces—may be the primary cause of higher gasoline prices. Anticompetitive conduct is always a possibility, of course. That is the reason for the antitrust laws. The FTC has been and remains vigilant regarding anticompetitive conduct in this industry. The FTC has taken action against proposed mergers in this industry at concentration levels lower than in other industries. Since 1981, the FTC has investigated 16 large petroleum mergers. In 12 of these cases, the FTC obtained significant divestitures and in the four other cases, the parties abandoned the transactions altogether after antitrust challenge. In 2004, the FTC staff published a study reviewing the petroleum industry's mergers and structural changes as well as the antitrust enforcement actions the FTC has taken. In no other industry does the FTC maintain a price monitoring project such as its project to monitor retail gasoline and diesel prices. Most recently, on June 10, 2005, the FTC announced the acceptance of two consent orders that resolved the competitive concerns relating to Chevron's acquisition of Unocal and settled the FTC's 2003 monopolization complaint against Unocal. The Unocal settlement alone has the potential of saving consumers nationwide billions of dollars in future years.

The vast majority of the FTC's investigations have revealed market factors to be the primary drivers of both price increases and price spikes. This Report describes the complex landscape of market forces that affect gasoline prices in the U.S.

The Report does not suggest or evaluate strategies for addressing high gasoline prices. Rather, the Report provides an empirical analysis to help policymakers evaluate different proposals to address high gasoline prices and consumers understand the reasons for gasoline price changes.

I. A CASE EXAMPLE TEACHES THREE BASIC LESSONS.

In August 2003, the FTC staff observed anomalous retail gasoline prices in Phoenix, Arizona. At the beginning of August 2003, the average price of gasoline in Phoenix was $1.52 per gallon. By the third week of August, however, it had peaked at $2.11 per gallon. Over the next few weeks, the price dropped, falling to $1.80 per gallon by the end of September.

The price spike was caused by a pipeline rupture on July 30, and the failure of temporary repairs, which had reduced the volume of gasoline supplies to Phoenix by 30 percent from August 8 through August 23. Arizona has no refineries. It obtains gasoline primarily through two pipelines, one traveling from west Texas and the other from the West Coast. The rupture closed the portion of the Texas line between Tucson and Phoenix.

The shortage of gasoline supplies in Phoenix caused gasoline prices to increase sharply. To obtain additional supply, Phoenix gas stations had to pay higher prices to West Coast refineries than West Coast gas stations were paying. West Coast refineries responded by selling more of their supplies to the Phoenix market.

Phoenix consumers did not respond to significantly increased gasoline prices with substantial reductions in the amount of gasoline they purchased. In theory, to prevent a gasoline price hike, Phoenix consumers could have reduced their gasoline purchases by 30 percent. Without price increases, however, consumers do not have incentives to change the amount of gasoline they buy. Moreover, even with price increases, most consumers do not respond to short-term supply disruptions such as a pipeline break by making the types of major changes—the car they drive, their driving habits, where they live, or where they work—that could substantially reduce the amount of gasoline they consume.

At some point, gasoline prices can become high enough that consumers will make substantial reductions in their gasoline purchases. *How much* prices need to increase depends on how easily consumers can adopt substitutes for gasoline—such as taking public transportation. Empirical studies indicate that consumers do not easily find substitutes for gasoline, and that prices must increase significantly to cause even a relatively small decrease in the quantity of gasoline consumers want. In the short run, a gasoline price increase of 10 percent would reduce consumer demand by just 2 percent, according to these studies. This suggests that gasoline prices in Phoenix would have had to increase by a large amount to reduce the quantity of consumers' purchases by 30 percent, the amount of lost supply. Extrapolating from above, prices would have to increase by 150 percent. Phoenix prices did increase substantially—by 40 percent—but remained far below a 150 percent price increase, because Phoenix gas stations had succeeded in obtaining some additional gasoline supplies from the West Coast. This new supply of gasoline dampened price increases to some extent.

On August 24, the pipeline owner restarted gasoline flow on the Tucson-Phoenix line, although at a reduced capacity. Retail gasoline prices in Phoenix declined by about $0.31 per gallon between the last week in August and the end of September. Phoenix gas stations, however, still had to obtain significant quantities of gasoline from West Coast refineries by pipeline or from other terminals by truck—both at higher cost.

Three basic lessons emerge from this example.

First, in general, the price of a commodity, such as gasoline, reflects producers' costs and consumers' willingness to pay. Gasoline prices rise if it costs more to produce and supply gasoline, or if people wish to buy more gasoline at the current price—that is, when demand is greater than supply. Gasoline prices fall if it costs less to produce and supply gasoline, or if people wish to buy less gasoline at the current price—that is, when supply is greater than demand. Gasoline prices will stop rising or falling when they reach the price at which the quantity consumers demand matches the quantity that producers will supply. In Phoenix, prices rose primarily because there was not enough gasoline to supply the quantity demanded at the prices that prevailed before the pipeline broke.

Second, how consumers respond to price changes will affect how high prices rise and how low they fall. Limited substitutes for gasoline restrict the options available to consumers to respond to price increases. That gasoline consumers typically do not reduce their purchases substantially in response to price increases makes them vulnerable to substantial price increases, such as the 40 percent price increase in Phoenix.

Third, how producers respond to price changes will affect how high prices rise and how low they fall. In general, when there is not enough of a product to meet consumers' demands at current prices, higher prices will signal a potential profit opportunity and may bring additional supply into the market. How high prices have to be to bring in additional supply will depend on how costly it is for producers to expand output. Phoenix gas stations' offers to pay prices to West Coast refiners that were higher than they had been receiving from West Coast gas stations were sufficient to bring additional supplies into Phoenix.

II. WORLDWIDE SUPPLY, DEMAND, AND COMPETITION FOR CRUDE OIL ARE THE MOST IMPORTANT FACTORS IN THE NATIONAL AVERAGE PRICE OF GASOLINE IN THE U.S.

To understand U.S. gasoline prices over the past three decades, including why gasoline prices rose so high and so sharply in 2004 and 2005, we must begin with crude oil.

- *The World Price of Crude Oil Is the Most Important Factor in the Price of Gasoline. Over the Last 20 Years, Changes in Crude Oil Prices Have Explained 85 Percent of the Changes in the Price of Gasoline in the U.S.*

U.S. refiners compete with refiners all around the world to obtain crude oil. Refiners in the U.S. now import more than 60 percent of their crude from foreign sources, up from 43 percent in 1978. The prices of crude oil produced and sold domestically also are linked to world crude prices.

If world crude prices rise, then U.S. refiners must offer and pay higher prices for crude they buy. Facing higher input costs from crude, refiners charge more for the gasoline they sell at wholesale. This requires gas stations to pay more for their gasoline. In turn, gas stations, facing higher input costs, charge consumers more at the pump. To illustrate this relationship, Figure 2-1 compares the U.S. annual average price of gasoline (excluding taxes) with the annual average price of a recognized crude oil benchmark, West Texas Intermediate (WTI), from 1984 to January 2005. When crude oil prices rise, gasoline prices rise because gasoline becomes more costly to produce.

...

- *Since 1973, Production Decisions by OPEC Have Been a Very Significant Factor in the Prices That Refiners Pay for Crude Oil.*

The Organization of Petroleum Exporting Countries (OPEC) is a cartel designed specifically to coordinate output decisions and to affect world crude oil prices. Beginning with OPEC's first successful assertion of market power in 1973-1974, market forces no longer were the sole determinant of the world price of crude oil. At that time, OPEC members agreed to limit how much crude oil they would produce and to embargo the sale of crude oil to the U.S. OPEC members adhered to the production limits and, when OPEC lifted the embargo six months later, crude oil prices had tripled from $4 to $12 per barrel.

The degree of OPEC's success in raising crude oil prices has varied over time. OPEC members can be tempted to "cheat" and sometimes sell more crude oil than specified by OPEC limits. Higher world crude prices due to OPEC's actions increased the incentives to search for oil in other areas, and crude supplies from non-OPEC members such as Canada, the United Kingdom, and Norway have increased significantly. In 2003, almost 30 years after the first oil embargo, OPEC's total crude production was about the same as in 1974, but accounted for only 38 percent of world crude production, as compared to 52 percent of world crude oil production in 1974. Another countervailing force against higher crude prices has been new technologies that aid in finding new oil fields and lowering extraction costs.

Nonetheless, OPEC still produces a large enough share of world crude oil to exert market power and strongly influence the price of crude oil when OPEC members adhere to their assigned production quotas. Especially when demand surges unexpectedly, as in 2004, OPEC decisions on whether to increase supply to meet demand can have a significant impact on world crude oil prices.

- *Over the Past Two Decades, the Demand for Crude Oil Has Grown Significantly.*

The demand for crude oil depends on the demand for refined products, such as gasoline, diesel fuel, jet fuel, and heating oil. Since 1982, gasoline has accounted for 49 to 53 percent of the daily consumption of all petroleum products. Crude oil consumption has fallen during some periods over the past 30 years, partially in reaction to higher prices and federal laws such as requirements to increase the fuel efficiency of cars. Gasoline consumption in the U.S. fell significantly between 1978 and 1982, and remained lower during the 1980s than it had been at the beginning of 1978. *See* Figure 3-6, *supra.*

Overall, however, the long-run trend is toward significantly increased demand for crude oil. Over the last 20 years, average daily U.S. consumption of all refined petroleum products increased on average by 1.5 percent per year, leading to a total increase of 30 percent. As a result, worldwide demand for crude increased by 27 percent between 1988 and 2004. One would expect increased demand for crude oil at current prices to produce crude oil price increases. Throughout most of the 1990s, however, crude prices remained relatively stable, suggesting that crude producers increased production to meet increased demand. *See* Figure 3-6, *supra.*

- *In 2004, Crude Producers Were Unprepared to Produce Enough Crude Oil to Meet Larger-than-Predicted Increases in World Demand. Crude Oil Prices Increased Because There Was Not Enough Crude Supply to Meet Increasing Demand at Previous Price Levels. Steep Increases in World Prices for Crude Oil Caused Steep Increases in Gasoline Prices.*

Crude oil producers had set 2004 production levels based on much lower projections for demand growth than actually occurred. Projections had placed likely growth in world demand for crude oil at 1.5 percent. In fact, the 2004 rate of growth in crude demand was more than double the projections: 3.3 percent. *See* Figure 2-6. Large demand increases from rapidly industrializing countries, particularly China and India, made supplies much tighter than expected. This phenomenon was not limited to crude oil. Other commodities that form the basis for expanded growth in developing economies, such as steel and lumber, also saw unexpectedly rapid growth in demand, along with higher prices.

. . .

In addition, unexpected production difficulties reduced some producers' crude output, putting upward pressure on prices. Finally, the 2004 political outlook in certain regions, including prospects for terrorist incidents or civil unrest, appeared to threaten the production capacity of some major oil producers. For the most part, production actually did not decrease significantly in any of the areas of concern. However, even incidents that do not directly affect current crude oil production can create concerns and fears about potential crude supply disruptions and thus contribute to increases in crude spot and futures prices.

III. GASOLINE SUPPLY, DEMAND, AND COMPETITION PRODUCED RELATIVELY LOW AND STABLE ANNUAL AVERAGE REAL U.S. GASOLINE PRICES FROM 1984 UNTIL 2004, DESPITE SUBSTANTIAL INCREASES IN U.S. GASOLINE CONSUMPTION.

A review of annual average U.S. gasoline prices in real terms over the past decades reveals surprisingly low prices. Despite ever-growing gasoline consumption in the U.S., increased gasoline supply from U.S. refiners and imports, as well as relatively stable crude oil prices, kept U.S. gasoline prices in check throughout the 1990s. These prices reflect national averages that do not capture regional differences, to be discussed in the succeeding section. Yet they provide an important historical perspective on gasoline prices over the past 20 years.

• *U.S. Consumer Demand for Gasoline Has Risen Substantially, Especially Since 1990.*

In 1978, U.S. gasoline consumption was about 7.4 million barrels per day. By 1981, in the face of sharply escalating crude oil and gasoline prices and a recession, U.S. gasoline consumption had fallen by roughly a million barrels per day, averaging about 6.5 million barrels per day. As gasoline prices began to fall in the 1980s, U.S. consumption of gasoline began to rise once again. In 1993, U.S. gasoline consumption rose above 1978 levels; it has continued to increase at a fairly steady rate since then. In 2004, U.S. gasoline consumption averaged about 9 million barrels per day. U.S. gasoline consumption continues to rise, with the U.S. Energy Information Administration (EIA) forecasting 2005 demand at an average of 9.2 million barrels per day.

• *Increased Gasoline Supply from U.S. Refineries and Imports Helped to Meet Increased U.S. Demand for Gasoline and Keep Gasoline Prices Relatively Steady.*

A comparison of "real" average annual retail gasoline prices and average annual retail gasoline consumption in the U.S. from 1978 through 2004 shows that, in general, gasoline prices remained relatively stable despite significantly increased demand. *See* Figure 3-6. "Real" prices are adjusted for inflation and therefore reflect the different values of a dollar at different times; they provide more accurate comparisons of prices in different time periods. "Nominal" prices are the literal prices shown at the time of purchase.

. . .

• *For Most of the Past 20 Years, Real Annual Average Retail Gasoline Prices in the U.S., Including Taxes, Have Been Lower than at Any Time Since 1919.*

This analysis examines real annual average retail gasoline prices in the U.S., including taxes, from 1919 to 2004. The data show that, from 1986 through 2003, using 2004 dollars, real national annual average retail prices for gasoline, including taxes, generally have been below $2.00 per gallon. By contrast, between 1919 and 1985, real national annual average retail gasoline prices were above $2.00 per gallon more often than not.

Data from 1978 forward allow us to exclude taxes from the analysis. Prices that exclude taxes give a better sense of market dynamics, because gasoline taxes vary from state to state, are not set by market forces, and represent a large proportion of the annual average U.S. retail price for a gallon of gasoline. For example, from 1991 through 2004, taxes contributed on average 30.3 percent of the U.S. annual average retail price of gasoline.

If taxes are excluded, the data show that real annual average retail gasoline prices in the U.S. did not rise above $1.20 per gallon between 1986 and 2003, and generally ranged between $0.80 and $1.05 per gallon. *See* Figure 3-2. In 2004, however, those prices rose sharply to $1.44. This is the highest real national annual average retail price per gallon since 1984, but it remains well below the 1981 high of $2.10 per gallon.

...

Average U.S. retail prices, including taxes, have been increasing since 2003, from an average of $1.56 in 2003 to an average of $2.04 in the first five months of 2005, but it is difficult to predict whether these increases represent the beginning of a longer term trend.

- *To Meet Increased U.S. Demand for Gasoline, U.S. Refiners Have Taken Advantage of Economies of Scale and Adopted More Efficient Technologies and Business Strategies.*

U.S. refinery production meets more than 90 percent of U.S. demand for gasoline, on average. Between 1985 and 2004, U.S. refineries increased their total capacity to refine crude oil into various refined petroleum products by 7.8 percent, moving from 15.7 million barrels per day in 1985 to 16.9 million barrels per day as of May 2004. This increase—approximately one million barrels per day—is roughly equivalent to adding 10 average-sized refineries to industry supply. This increase occurred even though U.S. refiners did not build any new refineries during this time and, as refineries were closed, the number of overall refineries declined. Rather, they added this capacity through the expansion of existing refineries, enabling them to take advantage of economies of scale. All else equal, scale economies make larger refineries more efficient than small refineries. U.S. refiners also have adopted processing methods that broaden the range of crude oil that they can process and allow them to produce more refined product for each barrel of crude they process. In addition, they have lowered inventory holdings, thereby lowering inventory costs. Lower inventory holdings may, however, make an area more susceptible to short-term price spikes when there is a disruption in supply.

- *Increased Environmental Requirements Since 1992 Likely Have Raised the Retail Price of a Gallon of Gasoline by a Few Cents in Some Areas.*

Even though many U.S. refineries have become more efficient and have adopted processing methods that allow them to produce more refined product for each barrel of crude they process, some regulations likely have raised retail gasoline prices in some areas. For example, gasoline use is a major factor in air pollution in the United States. Under the Clean Air Act, the U.S. Environmental Protection Agency (EPA) requires various gasoline blends for particular geographic areas that have not met certain air quality standards. The air quality in the U.S. has improved due to the Clean Air Act. As with any regulatory program, however, costs come with the benefits. Environmental laws and regulations have required substantial and expensive refinery upgrades, particularly over the past 15 years. It costs more to produce cleaner gasoline than to produce conventional gasoline. Estimates of the increased costs of environmentally mandated gasoline range from $0.03 to $0.11 per gallon and affect some areas of the country more than others.

- *Profits Play Necessary and Important Roles in a Well-Functioning Market Economy. Recent Oil Company Profits Are High but Have Varied Widely over Time, over Industry Segments, and Among Firms.*

Profits compensate owners of capital for the use of the funds they have invested in a firm. Profits also compensate firms for taking risks, such as the risks in the oil industry that war or terrorism may destroy crude production assets or that new environmental requirements may require substantial new refinery capital investments. EIA's Financial Reporting System (FRS) tracks the financial performance of the 28 major energy producers currently operating in the U.S. In 2003, these firms had a return on capital employed of 12.8 percent as compared to the return on capital employed for the overall S&P Industrials, which was 10.0 percent. Between 1973 and 2003, the annual average return on equity for FRS companies was 12.6 percent, while it was 13.1 percent for the S&P Industrials.

The rates of return on equity for FRS companies have varied widely over the years, ranging from 1.1 percent to 21.1 percent between 1974 and 2003. Returns on equity vary across firms as well. Crude oil exploration and production operations typically generate much higher returns than refining and marketing. In essence, companies with exploration and production operations now find themselves in a position analogous to that of a homeowner who bought a house in a popular area just before increased demand for housing caused real estate prices to escalate. Like the homeowner, crude oil producers can charge higher prices due to increased demand. If high prices and high profits are expected to continue, they may draw greater investments over time into the oil industry, in particular to crude exploration and production. Over the long run, such investments may elicit more crude supply, which could reduce high prices.

IV. REGIONAL DIFFERENCES IN ACCESS TO GASOLINE SUPPLIES AND ENVIRONMENTAL REQUIREMENTS FOR GASOLINE AFFECT AVERAGE REGIONAL PRICES AND THE VARIABILITY OF REGIONAL PRICES.

Different regions of the country differ in their access to gasoline supplies. Some regions have large local refining capacity or ready access to multiple sources of more distant refining supply through pipeline, barge, or tanker. Other regions have more limited supply options. These differences can affect gasoline prices.

Differences in requirements for environmentally mandated fuel also can affect gasoline prices. The EPA requires particular gasoline blends for certain geographic areas, but it sometimes allows variations on those blends. Differing fuel specifications in different areas can limit the ability of gasoline wholesalers to find adequate substitutes in the event of a supply shortage.

- *Different Regions Have Different Access to Gasoline Supplies.*

The **Gulf Coast** has plentiful access to gasoline from its own refineries, which produce far more gasoline than the Gulf Coast consumes. As a result, the Gulf Coast supplies a large proportion of the gasoline sold in the U.S. Most of the gasoline supplies are transported through a large system of refined product pipelines that connects the Gulf Coast with all other regions—except portions of the West Coast.

The **East Coast** produces some gasoline, but also relies heavily on deliveries from the Gulf Coast and, to a lesser extent, imports from Canada, the Caribbean, Europe, and

South America. Large parts of the East Coast are within easy reach of gasoline supplies; however, New England and some areas of the southeast, such as Florida, lack refineries or pipeline connections and therefore depend heavily on water shipments.

The **Midwest** relies primarily on its own refineries and on gasoline supplies from the Gulf Coast. Pipeline capacity for gasoline deliveries from the Gulf Coast to the Midwest has increased in recent years.

The **Rocky Mountain** states rely largely on their own refineries, which produce about the same amount of gasoline as consumed there. This region has limited refined product pipeline connections to surrounding areas and therefore remains vulnerable to supply shortages resulting from unanticipated refinery outages.

The **West Coast** relies primarily on its own refineries and water shipments and has very limited pipeline connections to obtain supply from other regions. California is particularly isolated from other regions, in part because it lacks pipeline connections and in part because the state requires the use of unique, environmentally mandated fuel.

- *Since 1992, Annual Average Real Retail Gasoline Prices, Excluding Taxes, Have Risen up to $0.14 Higher in the Rocky Mountain States, and up to $0.25 Higher on the West Coast, than in the Gulf Coast, the East Coast, and the Midwest Regions, Where Prices Tend to Be Within a Few Cents of Each Other.*

The timing of the price changes—*see* Figure 4-11—suggests they may bear some relationship to the introduction of Phase I (1992) and Phase II (1996) of the stringent and specialized CARB requirements for gasoline sold in California. CARB has required cleaner and more expensive gasoline than in other states, so increased gasoline prices on the West Coast may reflect increased production costs, to some extent. In addition, only a limited number of refineries outside California produce CARB gasoline, which limits substitute gasoline supplies, and thus raises costs in the event of a supply shortage.

The same trend toward higher prices appears in the Rocky Mountain states, however, where environmental requirements are less restrictive, and therefore suggests other possible sources of higher prices. The Rocky Mountain states' limited access to pipeline connections to alternate sources of gasoline contrast with the extensive pipeline connections of the Midwest and East Coast and therefore may contribute to these price differences.

. . .

Boutique fuels and differential access to gasoline supplies also can contribute to the variability of gasoline prices—that is, the fluctuation of gasoline prices—in particular circumstances.

To address concerns about the variability in gasoline prices, FTC staff analyzed the impact of boutique fuel requirements, access to pipelines, substitutable gasoline supplies and local refinery capacity on gasoline price variability. The FTC staff economic analysis reports the following results:

- **Gulf Coast boutique fuel gasoline prices are not more variable than conventional gasoline prices on the Gulf Coast.** Thus, boutique fuel requirements do not, in and of themselves, cause greater price variability.

- **CARB gasoline prices in California are significantly more variable than conventional gasoline prices on the Gulf Coast.** Boutique fuels may exacerbate price variability in areas, such as California, that are not interconnected with large refining centers in other areas. Among other things, California's inability to substitute gasoline from other refinery regions in the U.S. or to obtain gasoline imports without significant delay makes it vulnerable to the types of unforeseen circumstances, such as pipeline or refinery outages, that can cause price variability.

- **Gasoline prices in the East Coast, the Midwest, and the Rocky Mountain states are significantly more variable than Gulf Coast gasoline prices.** The importance of excess local refining capacity in reducing local gasoline price variability appears in the significantly lower gasoline price variability in the Gulf Coast. The Gulf Coast has a large refining base that produces much more gasoline than is used locally, in contrast to the East Coast, the Midwest, and the Rocky Mountain states.

- **Pipeline access to gasoline supplies can significantly reduce price variability, particularly when adjacent areas along the pipeline are using the same type of fuel**. To have adjacent areas using the same type of fuel may reduce the time it takes to reallocate supplies in case of a supply disruption.

V. STATE AND LOCAL FACTORS, AS WELL AS THE EXTENT OF VERTICAL INTEGRATION AMONG FIRMS, CAN AFFECT RETAIL GASOLINE PRICES.

- *Other Things Being Equal, Retail Gasoline Prices Are Likely to Be Lower When Consumers Can Choose, and Switch Purchases, among a Greater Number of Gas Stations.*

A small number of empirical studies have examined gasoline station density in relation to prices. One study found that stations in southern California that imposed a 1 percent price increase lost different amounts of sales, depending on how many competitors were close to it. Those with a large number of nearby competitors (27 or more within 2 miles) lost 4.4 percent of sales in response to a 1 percent price increase; those with a small number of nearby competitors (fewer than 19 within 2 miles) lost only 1.5 percent of sales. All else equal, stations that face greater lost sales from raising prices will likely have lower retail prices than stations that lose fewer sales from raising prices.

- *The Density of Gas Stations in a Particular Area Will Depend on Cost Conditions.*

The size and density of a market will influence how many stations can operate and cover their fixed costs. Fixed costs will depend on the cost of land and building a station. Zoning regulations may limit the number of stations in an area below what market conditions would indicate the area could profitably sustain. Studies suggest that entry by new gasoline competitors tends to be more difficult in areas with high land prices and strict zoning regulations.

- *Over the Past Three Decades, the Format of Retail Gas Stations Has Changed to Include Convenience Stores and to Increase Sales Volumes per Station. Examples Suggest That the Largest-volume Stations, So-Called "Hypermarkets," Lower Local Retail Gasoline Prices.*

Differences in local retail prices may result from differences in the types of retailers selling gasoline in particular areas. The number of traditional gasoline-pump-and-repair-bay outlets has dwindled for a number of years as brand-name gasoline retailers have moved toward a convenience store format. Independent gasoline/convenience stores—such as RaceTrac, Sheetz, QuikTrip, and Wawa—typically feature large convenience stores with multiple fuel islands and multi-product dispensers. They are sometimes called "pumpers" because of their large-volume fuel sales. By 1999, the latest year for which data are available, brand-name and independent convenience store and pumper stations accounted for almost 67 percent of the volume of U.S. retail gasoline sales.

In addition, hypermarkets are large retailers of general merchandise and grocery items, such as Wal-Mart and Safeway, that have begun to sell gasoline. Hypermarket sites typically sell even larger—sometimes, 4 to 8 times larger—volumes of gasoline than pumper stations. Hypermarkets' substantial economies of scale generally enable them to sell significantly greater volumes of gasoline at lower prices.

- *State and Local Taxes Can Be Significant Factors in the Retail Price of Gasoline.*

Higher gasoline taxes drive up the final price of gasoline. In 2004, the average state sales tax was $0.225 per gallon, with the highest state tax at $0.334 per gallon (New York). In some states, local governments also impose gasoline taxes.

- *Bans on Self-Service Sales Appear to Raise Gasoline Prices.*

New Jersey and Oregon ban self-service sales, thus requiring consumers to buy gasoline bundled with services that may increase costs—that is, having staff available to pump the gasoline. Some experts have estimated that self-service bans alone cost consumers between $0.02 to $0.05 per gallon.

- *Bans on Below-Cost Sales Appear to Raise Gasoline Prices.*

About 11 states have a type of below-cost sales or minimum mark-up laws, which typically either prohibit a gas station from making sales below a certain defined cost or require a gas station to charge a minimum amount above its wholesale gasoline cost. These laws are likely to harm consumers by depriving them of the lower prices that more efficient (*e.g.*, high volume) gas stations can charge.

- *Differences in Vertical Relationships Influence How Gasoline Arrives and Is Sold at Retail Stations. The Relative Importance of Different Distribution Systems Varies from Region to Region Across the Country, with the West Coast Showing a Relatively High Degree of Integration Between Refining and Marketing as Compared to Other Regions.*

The degree to which one company will perform all or only some of the steps involved in refining and marketing gasoline varies among companies. A refiner that is integrated with its own distribution system may set up a *direct* distribution system under which it supplies gasoline to (1) retail sites that it owns and operates, also known as "company-owned-and-operated stations;" (2) retail outlets that are owned by the refiner, but operated by independent lessee-dealers; and (3) retail outlets that are owned and operated by independent "open" dealers that sell company-branded product. An integrated refiner's wholesale price for company-owned-and-operated stations is a non-public, internal transfer price. When an integrated refiner supplies retail outlets owned by the refiner but operated by independent lessee-dealers, or owned and operated by independent "open" dealers, it charges the "dealer tank wagon" (DTW) price to the dealer.

Alternatively, an integrated or independent refiner may use a *jobber* distribution system. A jobber, which may be brand-name, unbranded, or both, buys gasoline at the terminal rack and then delivers the gasoline to (1) stations that it owns and operates; (2) stations that it owns but leases to third parties; and (3) stations that are independently owned and operated. Jobbers pay a "wholesale rack price" for their gasoline purchases, although other contractual terms may also affect the net price. Jobbers may switch brands if alternatives are available.

Compared to the nation as a whole, the Midwest, the Gulf Coast, and the Rocky Mountain states distribute more wholesale gasoline at the rack through jobbers than through DTW sales or internal transfers. The East Coast also distributes the majority of its wholesale gasoline at the rack through jobbers, although DTW sales have more importance in the New England and mid-Atlantic states. By contrast, on the West Coast, the percentage of DTW distribution is significantly higher than rack sales. The relatively high degree of integration between refining and marketing on the West Coast dates back to at least 1994, predating the wave of petroleum mergers affecting the West Coast that began in 1997.

  • *Most Empirical Studies Indicate That Vertical Integration Between Refining and Marketing Can Save Costs and Lower Gasoline Prices. However, Two Studies Suggest That Instances of Vertical Integration Between Refining and Marketing in California Were Associated with Higher Wholesale or Retail Gasoline Prices.*

A 2003 report concluded that the available empirical evidence generally supports the proposition that retail prices at vertically integrated gas stations can be from $0.015 to $0.05 per gallon lower than at leased or independent stations, all else equal. Two studies assessed in the 2003 report found that divorcement statutes—which prohibit refiners from maintaining or acquiring retail gas stations—tend to lead to higher, rather than lower, average retail gasoline prices. Two other studies assessed in the 2003 report examining the West Coast, however, found higher wholesale gasoline prices appear to have resulted from increased vertical integration between refining and marketing.

  • *Since 1990, the Degree of Vertical Integration Between Different Levels in the U.S. Gasoline Industry Has Lessened.*

The extent of common ownership of different stages of exploration and production, refining, distribution, and marketing is generally termed the "degree of vertical integration." Recent moves toward less vertical integration in the oil industry—especially between exploration/production and refining—suggest some decrease in the benefits of vertical integration between upstream and downstream levels. The increased ability of U.S. refiners to switch economically among different types of crude oil, and the maturation of spot and futures markets, are among the factors that may explain why incentives for integration between upstream and downstream levels appear to have diminished over time.

  • *Refiner Marketing Practices Such as Zone Pricing and Territorial Restrictions Can Have Pro-and Anti-competitive Effects. The Commission Will Remain Watchful of these Practices.*

Through zone pricing, a brand-name refiner may charge different prices to lessee dealer stations located in different geographic zones. A brand-name refiner also may impose territorial restrictions on jobbers—that is, independent jobbers may supply brand-name gasoline to their own gas stations or open dealers in some areas, but not in others.

———————

Notes & Questions

1. Consider worldwide prices for gasoline. The United States has lower prices than Europe, for example, and we see cars in Europe with different priorities, such as higher gas mileage. Diesel fuel is also far more popular in Europe, and smaller cars are the norm.

2. In some towns, virtually of the gas prices are the same. Other towns have wide variances. Why might that be? Are gas stations with the same prices in the same area colluding? Are they artificially high or has the market brought the price down? How could you tell?

3. When gas prices first hit $4 per gallon, the country reacted strongly, with a significant drop in consumption. Since then, gas has fluctuated and returned briefly to that range without a major reaction. Why might that be?

4. Should the United States be working to keep gas prices low? How might the country do that? What are the benefits and harms from policies designed at keeping prices lower than the market would otherwise bear?

5. For gasoline and diesel fuel, as of January 1, 2013, the U.S. federal excise taxes on retail sales in cents per gallon, were 18.40 for gasoline and 24.40 for diesel. The average for all states was 23.47 (gasoline) and 24.00 (diesel). Does this seem high or low? Consider how a change to tax based on a percentage of the fuel cost might impact the market. Would this be good or bad? Why?

D. Beyond Gasoline

Over the years there has been speculation that some new fuel would take over for gasoline. That fuel switch has been exceedingly modest for a variety of reasons, including significant influence from U.S. energy law and policy. The following article discusses the possible options for fuel switching away from gasoline and the challenges facing the various options.

Note also that the article was written before the scope of the natural gas from U.S. shale formations was fully appreciated. As such, the article likely overestimated the potential costs of natural gas as a vehicle fuel source, at least in the near term.

Joshua P. Fershee, *Struggling Past Oil: The Infrastructure Impediments to Adopting Next-Generation Transportation Fuel Sources*
40 Cumb. L. Rev. 87 (2010) (footnotes omitted)

I. INTRODUCTION

Since at least the 1970s, Americans have known that reliance on gasoline is a risky proposition. Low gas prices and largely effective policies designed to incentivize the sale of large cars and trucks for most of the 1990s and early 2000s, however, further entrenched and intertwined the American economy with the price of gasoline. In 2008, when crude oil spot prices topped $130 per barrel and the average per gallon gasoline price rose to over $4.00 per gallon, U.S. consumers slowed their gas consumption (finally) and began to look for other options. Over the years, many reasons to reduce oil consumption have emerged.

The utilization of oil as the primary energy source for transportation raises a wide range of policy concerns, from Peak Oil to climate change and national security to market manipulation. Despite several compelling reasons to move beyond oil to a cleaner, more sustainable fuel source, petroleum-derived fuels remain the predominate choice for transportation needs. There have been numerous policies seeking to reduce Americans' dependence on oil, especially foreign-sourced oil, but none have made a significant impact on the transportation fuel mix.

There are a variety of reasons for the staying power of gasoline and diesel fuel as the primary transportation fuels, but ultimately all reasons come back to one common theme:

infrastructure. When one thinks of infrastructure, typically one thinks of it in the physical sense, as in equipment or construction projects. For example, bridges and roads are a major part of transportation infrastructure, and although less directly, so too are gas stations and oilrigs. But beyond the brick-and-mortar infrastructure, transportation has other, less tangible types of infrastructure, which can be viewed as a psychological infrastructure. Both physical and psychological infrastructures raise significant impediments to moving away from oil and on to other fuel sources, but distinguishing between the two infrastructures could have a great impact on the tactics used to pursue transportation's next wide-scale fuel source(s).

In the past decade, there has been more fervent interest in significantly reducing U.S. oil consumption. A variety of world events sparked interest in some key areas, leading to new or renewed interest in national security concerns, an expanded understanding and appreciation of the potential impacts of climate change, and a fear of the potentially dramatic economic effects of high gasoline prices. In just the past five years, Congress has passed multiple major energy bills designed to address these concerns. All of the policies seeking to change the U.S. fuel mix, however, have run headlong into major physical and psychological infrastructure roadblocks. Whether the hurdle is overcoming the institutional inertia (i.e., objections of stakeholders who own existing infrastructure) or cultivating a willingness to absorb the costs of the major financial investments needed, there is little indication that a dramatic shift away from current transportation fuel sources is imminent.

Many people consider the hybrid vehicle—a car that is powered by gasoline and electricity—a signal that change is already moving toward a new transportation fuel source. And while the hybrid is probably the most significant mass-market vehicle innovation in the last twenty-five years, the hybrid car is powered primarily by gasoline or electricity generated by motion that originated with gasoline. The electricity a traditional hybrid uses at various points is generated by the gasoline engine and creates electricity through regenerative braking, which is only possible if the vehicle is already at a speed obtained by the use of gasoline.

The dependence on gasoline is not to say that some of the hybrid automobiles are not an impressive achievement; many of them are. For example, the most popular hybrid, the Toyota Prius, averages approximately fifty miles per gallon. When compared model to model, the best hybrid cars can use significantly less gasoline than their traditional counterparts, which is a step in the right direction. The point is simply that the widely available hybrid vehicles still run only on gasoline. As discussed in Part III of this Article, there are some fully electric cars on the horizon, but none have yet to reach the mass market.

There are four major options to replace fossil fuels as the primary transportation energy source: alternative fuels, including ethanol, biofuels, and synthetic fuels; electricity; natural gas; and hydrogen. All options have significant physical and psychological infrastructure hurdles to overcome. In Part II, this Article first considers alternative fuels, focusing primarily on the U.S. Renewable Fuel Standard (RFS) and discusses the related economic and environmental problems, including a discussion of the problems created by the food-fuel link created by corn-based ethanol. Part III then discusses the infrastructure problems and the potential raised by electricity, natural gas, and hydrogen as transportation energy sources. Part IV concludes that, in most cases, when new transportation fuel sources are pursued, physical infrastructure problems are often ignored, allowing policies that promote sources with strong psychological infrastructure to lead the way, even when the sources are less feasible or sensible.

II. AN IMPERFECT SUBSTITUTE: THE PROBLEMS WITH
AND POTENTIAL OF ALTERNATIVE FUELS

The most overt U.S. policy initiative designed to reduce oil consumption is the RFS, which was initially passed as part of the Energy Policy Act of 2005 (EP Act 2005). With oil prices rising and a desire to reduce the threat from foreign fuel sources, Congress significantly expanded the RFS in the Energy Independence and Security Act of 2007 (EISA), which was signed into law on December 19, 2007. The RFS requires that "transportation fuel sold or introduced into commerce in the United States (except in noncontiguous States or territories)" include a minimum of 9 billion gallons of renewable fuel in 2008, rising to 36 billion gallons per year by 2022. As such, the RFS mandate has dramatically increased the use of ethanol in the fuel mix since its passage. In the early years of the RFS, ethanol could come from any source (meaning primarily corn); in later years, the mandate shifts, requiring that additional gallons of alternative fuels come from next generation sources, such as prairie grass, corn stalks, or algae.

At times, ethanol and other biofuels have seemed like a panacea for the oil problem. Grown from the earth, rather than extracted from it, biofuels appeared to be an almost perfect solution. Need more fuel? Just grow more. Furthermore, ethanol and other biofuels work in combustion engines and add to the psychological benefit of the alternative fuels as an alternative to petroleum-based fuels. Rather than a psychological infrastructure impediment, biofuels seemed to have a major psychological infrastructure benefit.

The most prevalent biofuel is ethanol, which can be derived from corn, soy, and other plant materials. The efficiency of alternative fuel production varies greatly from source to source. For example, prairie switchgrass, which is highly resistant to drought, uses considerably less water and uses less petroleum-based fertilizers than corn. As would be expected, the varied fuel sources also impact the economic and environmental impact of the resulting fuel. Researchers are also working to use algae to generate ethanol, although this use is not yet available for large-scale production. To date, only corn-based ethanol has had any significant U.S. market share.

A. Economic Problems: When the Math Doesn't Work

When the spot price of oil was hovering around $100 per barrel, the RFS seemed, at least to some, like it could be a promising (meaning economical) step toward reducing domestic consumption of foreign oil. After further review, however, researchers discovered that ethanol, at least derived from traditional sources, has costs that may outweigh its benefits. For example, renewable fuels on the level mandated by the RFS require expensive new processing facilities and distribution channels and rely heavily on multiple-use commodities, most notably corn. To help facilitate the production process, the EP Act of 2005 included significant subsidies for industrial fuel producers to facilitate the production of ethanol and other advanced biofuels. These subsidies work to hide the real costs of this energy policy.

To ensure the pipeline for these renewable fuels in the long term, many market contingencies must be managed. In 2008, shortly after the RFS mandate was increased, a number of ethanol plants in North Dakota and Minnesota delayed opening production because the high price of market inputs (i.e., corn) made operations too expensive. High oil prices, however, could motivate the plants to restart operations. At the same time, a significant drought, even with the RFS requirements, could push renewable fuel production costs well out of the profitable range year to year. Over the long term, a fuel policy that relies on corn in any significant part will have problems. First, the amount of corn needed to have any significant impact on oil consumption is staggering. Even if all U.S. corn and soybean crops were diverted to produce fuel, the crops would still only satisfy 18% of the current fuel demanded for vehicles. Another way to think about the futility of corn ethanol as a replacement for gasoline is to consider that for the United States to power every vehicle on ethanol, as much as 97% of U.S. soil could be needed to grow enough corn to produce sufficient amounts of fuel.

Energy and food became inextricably linked in December 2007, when the U.S. Congress passed, and President Bush signed, the current RFS. Food and energy, both essential to human life, have long been closely linked. Energy, particularly energy from petroleum-based fuel, became an essential part of food production and delivery as modern society evolved from an agrarian society into an industrial one, and machines, pesticides, and fertilizers facilitated large-scale farming. With the advent of the RFS, food and energy have become even more intertwined as ethanol and other biofuel production—motivated by new technology, government subsidies, and government mandates—has dramatically increased. This increased link between food and fuel has, among other things, significantly increased food and fuel production costs.

This new—or better stated, more significant—link between food and fuel has some ominous overtones. When two markets become "inextricably linked," the effect can have economy-wide impacts. This is true whether it is food and crude oil, electricity and natural gas, or steel and coal.

There is a basic economic problem when corn used in the food chain (i.e., as food for people or animals) is also used for fuel: increased demand and lower supply equals increased costs. The Congressional Budget Office recently issued a report which found that "expanded production of ethanol contributed between 0.5 and 0.8 percentage points of the 5.1 percent increase in food prices measured by the consumer price index (CPI)." Even without ethanol mandates, the report further indicated the link between food and fuel, finding that, "[o]ver the same period, certain other factors—for example, higher energy costs—had a greater effect on food prices than did the use of ethanol as a motor fuel."

The market felt the impact of the increased ethanol mandates almost immediately. Shortly after the ethanol increases took effect, several political leaders, including Texas Governor Rick Perry, sought to have the ethanol mandates cut in half because the overall dramatically increased demand for corn was driving the corn prices too high, especially for livestock feed. Governor Perry's coalition of food, livestock, and environmental groups sought an emergency waiver that would have cut the ethanol mandate to 4.5 billion gallons from the 2008 mandate of 9 billion gallons and the 2009 mandate of 10.5 billion gallons. The EPA denied the request, but the more than 15,000 comments filed in response to Governor Perry's request clearly indicate that the debate about the mandate is far from over.

B. Environmental Issues: It Isn't Green Just Because You Grow It

As awareness about climate change and other environmental concerns has increased, the initial appeal of ethanol and other biofuels is hardly surprising. "It makes intuitive sense: cars emit carbon no matter what fuel they burn, but the process of growing plants for fuel sucks some of that carbon out of the atmosphere." So the reasoning goes, corn-based ethanol should be green, or at least greener than oil. Unfortunately, it is more complicated than that.

Some initial studies indicated that bio-based fuels were more environmentally friendly than petroleum-based fuels. The studies that led to calculations deeming ethanol greener than petroleum-based fuels were based on the added carbon sequestration that would take place because of the crops planted for fuel. But there appears to be (at least) one flaw: those studies failed to consider whether the fuel crops would be replacing rangelands or forestlands that were already sequestering carbon, without concomitant carbon outputs related to crop growth, such as those from tractors and other farm equipment.

Not all biofuels come from food or feedstock. There are indications that cellulosic-source ethanol could be a much more environmentally friendly alternative to traditional fuels. Recognizing this, the RFS gradually phases in a mandate for fuel from other biofuel sources, rather than from corn-based ethanol. In the near term, however, there is nothing requiring that the RFS be met with only ethanol from cellulosic sources. Despite some claims of "green" motivations, the current biofuel-promotion policies are simply predicated on producing additional biofuel stores and not on addressing or even considering the environmental and human impacts of such policies. As it stands, between now and 2022, ethanol from corn will be expected to comprise 15 billion gallons of fuel's annual sales.

In addition, the RFS requires replacement of gasoline and diesel fuel, yet there is no similar requirement for jet fuel. The oil refining process produces more than just gasoline, however. Crude oil has four primary, profitable components: (1) gasoline; (2) kerosene (jet fuel); (3) diesel; and (4) fuel oil. Without non-crude oil sources of jet fuel, reduced refinement of crude for gasoline will lead to increased demand and price for jet fuel and will require purchases of the refined product from other sources. One option to alleviate this problem would be to use coal-to-liquids, a technology used to replace jet fuel, but the process is dirty and inefficient. The other option would be to use crop oils to create jet fuels. The technology exists, and if there is going to be an RFS, it would make more sense to impose a parallel requirement on jet fuel.

As such, ethanol has significant hurdles to overcome, all of which are nearly insurmountable unless solved by technological advances. Unfortunately, current technology cannot make a significant dent in the amount of foreign oil needed to satisfy U.S. demand. Also, as corn prices fluctuate, the impact on food and oil are likely to prove untenable for many Americans.

III. THE OTHER TRANSPORTATION FUEL OPTIONS: ELECTRICITY, NATURAL GAS, AND HYDROGEN

Although renewable fuels are the most widely used non-fossil-based transportation fuel by consumers, other options exist for the next generation transportation fuel source. Each has positive and negative consequences, and all have significant infrastructure hurdles to overcome before becoming the next fuel of choice.

A. Electricity: Back to the Future

Interestingly, one of the first automotive fuels is once again worthy of consideration: electricity. The very first electric car was developed in 1839 by Robert Anderson in Aberdeen, Scotland. There were those who believed that electric cars were the "future of the automobile business" because "[y]ou can't get people to sit over an explosion...." The lack of a battery that could store power, however, led to the triumph of the gasoline-powered internal combustion engine.

Today, the technology exists to power passenger cars with electricity stored onboard the vehicle. In 1996, prompted by California's zero emissions mandates, General Motors (GM) introduced the EV1, a plug-in, electric-only car, in a California test project. The two-seat car had a range of sixty to eighty miles and had to be charged for approximately eight hours. Chronicled in the popular documentary, *Who Killed the Electric Car?*, was the story of how the EV1 was loved by its owners, but deemed too costly by GM. GM pulled all the cars off the road in 2003, "inciting conspiracy rumors" that provided the documentary's primary storyline.

More recently, the upscale, all-electric Tesla Roadster and the in-development, plug-in hybrid Chevy Volt are the next possible options. The Tesla vehicle is designed as a two-seat sports car, with a cost of $109,000. The Tesla fully charges in approximately 314 hours, accelerates from zero to sixty miles per hour in 3.9 seconds, and has a top speed of 125 miles per hour. The cruising range is approximately 244 miles. Depending on the success of the Roadster, Tesla plans to also introduce an all-electric sedan, which will be priced just under $60,000.

The Chevy Volt, priced around $40,000, is another much anticipated hybrid. The Volt promises a plug-in motor with a forty-mile range, plus a small gas-powered engine to increase the driving range. The Volt is not expected to make money, but the hope is that the vehicle will help turn around the stodgy image of Chevy's parent, GM, which is emerging from bankruptcy. Another hope is that GM will be able to quickly move the plug-in technology across its line of vehicles and reverse the company's fortunes. GM will need to act quickly, as competitors like Toyota and Nissan are planning plug-in hybrids for 2010, and Mitsubishi has a $47,000 electric car that the company claims has a 100-mile range on a single charge.

1. The Positive Side of Electricity as a Transportation Fuel Source

Electricity is used regularly and consistently by virtually every American. The Rural Electrification Project, made possible by the Rural Electrification Act (REA), provided the long-term financing and technical expertise needed to expand the availability of electricity beyond the cities to rural customers. The REA's financial undertaking was enormous. With the REA providing funding to more than 1,000 borrowers, more than 1,500,000 miles of power lines were built and 20 million American people obtained power.

Today, virtually all Americans have access to electricity. Short-term electricity demand fluctuates relative to business cycles, fuel prices, weather conditions, and other factors. Over the longterm, however, electricity demand growth has generally slowed year to year since the 1950s. In recent years, electricity-demand increases have slowed to an average increase of 1.1% per year, and the slowdown is expected to continue as energy prices increase and products become more efficient.

As such, there is tremendous physical infrastructure already available in the electricity sector. Other fuel sources, such as ethanol and hydrogen, face significant infrastructure hurdles related to providing widespread access to the fuel source. As a plugin option, electricity is readily available and accessible. Again, almost every home and business in the United States already has access to electricity. This means that the backbone infrastructure is already available for access to the fuel source, even if relatively minor modifications are needed to provide plug in fueling locations. In fact, people in some of the coldest parts of the United States are already familiar with plugging in their car at night and using engine block heaters to ensure their cars will start in the morning.

In addition, because of the broad market penetration, electricity already has a full-scale regulatory and financial structure in place. This too provides the necessary infrastructure that would, for the most part, need to be expanded, rather than overhauled. This is not to say that if electricity were to become the primary transportation fuel source, major changes would not be needed. The most important changes to provide increased energy access, however, are already being discussed as necessary, regardless of electricity in the transportation sector.

Smart-grid and smart-metering technologies, both of which would be extremely helpful in providing broader access to electricity for transportation consumers, are also important for increasing overall efficiency. These technologies would lower net costs, reduce the strain on the existing transmission system, and provide for lower greenhouse gas emissions (where sources creating such emissions generate the electricity).

There is no doubt that a dramatic increase in electricity demand caused by adding the transportation sector to the list of consumers would require significant expansion of generation capacity, and there are methods to meet this demand. Furthermore, much of the demand could be generated from cleaner resources, such as wind and solar power. One of the major criticisms of wind and solar power for electricity generation is that neither are "on" all the time. That is, the wind is not always blowing and the sun is not always shining. Unlike gasoline, natural gas, and other fuel sources, electricity cannot be stored in large quantities, and for traditional electricity use, this can pose a significant problem.

On the other hand, large-scale electric-powered transportation would provide a currently non-existent storage option. Vehicles powered by electricity would need to have batteries capable of holding significant charges to provide adequate driving range. As the market for plug-in cars grew, there would be many cars plugged-in and charged, such as vehicles charged overnight or while at work. Each car could draw electricity up to a full charge. If the grid needed additional electricity during these times and generation capacity was not available from intermittent sources (e.g., wind or solar), the grid could call small amounts of power from each of the plugged-in cars to provide additional electricity where needed. Although this process could present something of a chicken-or-egg problem, it could in many cases be solved by using wind or solar resources as parallels to fossil-fuel or other base-load sources in the near term, with a planned phase-out as more electric vehicles became part of the infrastructure.

2. The Negative Side of Electricity as a Transportation Fuel Source

One of the major hurdles to switching to electric vehicles is a physical infrastructure issue, at least in the sense that a lack of physical infrastructure—batteries sufficient to provide adequate driving range—impacts the ability to choose this fuel source. This technological problem, as discussed above, however, is diminishing rather quickly.

There is no question that the lack of long-range, quick-charging batteries impacts the ability of electricity to replace gasoline immediately because drivers often need the ability to drive long distances without long refueling stops. Thus, even a high-end car like the Tesla is limited in its ability to be used for long road trips. This hurdle, however, currently impacts natural gas and hydrogen as well. But to the extent there is a real problem, there are already options that can diminish these issues.

The concern with physical infrastructure also underscores the essence of a psychological infrastructure problem. A common complaint about electric cars is the limited range. Going back to the EV1, the range was limited as compared to a gasoline-powered car. At full charge, the EV1 initially had a range of about eighty miles and was later able to get nearly 150 miles in charge, which is significantly less than gasoline-powered cars. Most gasoline cars have the advantage of providing a cruising range in the area of 350-450 miles. The average commute for most Americans, however, is currently less than forty miles round trip, meaning that, even without a charge at work, most users would have far more driving range than they would ever need in a given day. In fact, many people currently have a car for driving to work (perhaps a normal passenger car) and another "trip" or "family" car, such as a mini-van. Thus, because many people may have already made the decision to have cars that serve differing needs, making that "work car" an electric vehicle should not provide much difficulty in concept or practice.

Furthermore, there are companies working to address directly the issue of limited range by providing a way for drivers to refuel "on the go" as they do today. The company Better Place proposes developing removable batteries that drivers could simply swap at "charging stations," which is an intriguing solution. For one thing, gas stations could be transitioned into "charging stations" where people could still buy snacks or use the restroom while refueling, thus potentially using the infrastructure already in place for traditional motor vehicles.

The process of swapping fuel containers is also familiar to many people. Blue Rhino and Amerigas are propane companies that allow people to exchange empty propane tanks, used for gas grills among other things, for full tanks. People buy their first propane tank and then, rather than filling that tank, they simply exchange it for another tank at an authorized site. Familiarity with this process may help ease consumer concerns about the new process, as long as the charging stations maintain high-quality exchanges.

Another problem with electric-powered vehicles is the staggering cost related to updating and expanding electricity infrastructure. This physical infrastructure problem already exists for the current aging transmission system, and some may argue that adding demand would make this problem an even bigger concern. But because system upgrades already need to be made, the infra-structure issue can be addressed just as the infrastructure will need to be addressed for any transportation fuel switch.

Similarly, demand for gasoline will continue to increase if no changes are made to our current system. Gasoline already has a potential infrastructure problem in the refining area. No new oil refineries have been built since 1976, and the system is, at times, running at or near capacity. As seen following Hurricanes Rita and Katrina, the gasoline market is highly vulnerable to shortages in the event any refining capacity is reduced or eliminated. Thus, even though a lack of physical infrastructure exists in the electricity sector, the concern is not limited to that type of energy.

B. Natural Gas: Almost Too Easy?

Natural gas is an appealing option as the next-generation transportation fuel because natural gas vehicles (NGVs) operate in essentially the same manner as gasoline-powered vehicles. The fuel mixes with air and is fed into a cylinder where a spark plug ignites the fuel, which then moves a piston up and down. One of the major advantages of natural gas is that the fuel can be used in all the same vehicles currently using gasoline and diesel. Nevertheless, some modifications are needed to make an NGV run efficiently because unlike gasoline and diesel fuel, natural gas is not a liquid at standard pressure and temperature.

A main concern about natural gas is the price of the fuel, which has fluctuated severely over the past decade. One impact on prices is that natural gas has been one of the primary fuels of choice for electric generating facilities because it is a cleaner burning energy source than coal. Before the 1990s, natural gas demand was generally seasonal because it was used primarily for winter home heating. Today, however, natural gas demand has become more constant on a year-round basis as use for power generation has increased, thereby increasing the need in the summer months.

The consideration of natural gas as a transportation fuel recently received a significant push from oil billionaire T. Boone Pickens, whose "Pickens Plan" calls for a revised U.S. energy policy that promotes expanded wind generation for electricity use and seeks to use "America's natural gas to replace imported oil as a transportation fuel." Pickens has pushed for a rapid transition to natural gas use in heavy-duty trucking and in municipal fleets as a way of reducing oil imports.

Although natural gas supplies were expected to be much lower even two years ago, new drilling techniques have significantly increased supply estimates for natural gas. A recent report from the Potential Gas Committee indicated a 35% increase in domestic natural gas estimates over its last biennial report. Increased supplies of natural gas are expected to lower prices, making increased natural gas use a viable alternative.

An increased supply would seem like it should raise the odds that natural gas would be the next transportation fuel, despite competing markets that could make the move unwise. As the United States prepares to address climate change concerns, natural gas for electricity generation is going to have renewed appeal. Natural gas has about half the greenhouse gas emissions of coal, and there are currently several natural gas plants not operating because fuel costs have been too high. Reduced gas prices, combined with a likely price increase of other fossil fuels if a federal cap-and-trade or other carbon-reduction program is enacted, are likely to signal increased demand for natural gas in the electric power arena. In fact, there are those who believe that the increased natural gas supply could mean that emissions reduction targets of current draft legislation "may even be too weak" because the ample supply should keep cost reasonable.

The competing markets for natural gas raise perhaps the most complex infrastructure issues of all the possible alternative transportation fuels. On one hand, natural gas already has a broad and expansive infrastructure with a well-established pipeline system throughout the country. And although not as pervasive as electricity, more than 61% of homes use natural gas. As such, people are familiar with natural gas as a fuel and most people already have access to a supply.

Furthermore, many vehicles that are currently on the road can run on compressed natural gas (CNG) if equipped with a conversion system. The cost to convert to CNG runs from approximately $12,500 to $22,500, depending on the vehicle and who completes the conversion. CNG tanks are the most expensive part of the conversion process, and often it can take many miles or many years to recoup the cost of the conversion.

Access to fuel can be limited, but would obviously improve as more commercial sites opened. There are currently 772 CNG stations in the United States, in forty-five states; New York, California, Utah, and Oklahoma are the leaders in available CNG stations. There are also home refueling appliances available, which range from $4,500 to just under $10,000 plus installation costs.

From a psychological infrastructure perspective, the use of natural gas for consumer transportation has some hurdles, including the concerns about access to fuel, which is a concern that is shared by all alternative-fuel vehicles that cannot also run on gasoline. For instance, there are some safety concerns because natural gas is easily flammable. CNG tanks are thick, however, and are put through rigorous testing. In addition, unlike gasoline, which pools when it leaks and can create major fire and explosion hazards, CNG is lighter than air and will rise and dissipate relatively quickly. Thus, although CNG is not a risk-free fuel, there is no indication the safety concerns are any different than those already existing for gasoline vehicles. The advantage of gasoline is that people have already internalized the risks to the point that such risks are no longer a daily concern.

Natural gas, when used in motor vehicles, is also recognized as more environmentally friendly than gasoline. Vehicles using CNG "produce significantly lower amounts of harmful emissions such as nitrogen oxides, particulate matter, and toxic and carcinogenic pollutants as well as the greenhouse gas carbon dioxide." The only commercially available production vehicle on the market is the Honda Civic GX, which the U.S. Environmental Protection Agency called "the cleanest internal-combustion vehicle on Earth."

Natural gas vehicles are also appealing because the general operating principle is the same for CNG-powered vehicles and traditional-fuel vehicles. Therefore, it is possible to have dual-fuel vehicles, which permit drivers to use gasoline or diesel when CNG is not available. The availability of gasoline or diesel could further promote CNG by helping to offset the psychological concern about lack of access to fuel. The downside to this type of dual-fuel vehicle is that passenger or cargo space will be less than a singlefuel vehicle because CNG requires a separate fueling system.

The biggest concern about widespread use of natural gas for transportation is the risk of dramatic price spikes, such as those seen in the natural gas industry after the last major new market expansion: natural gas for electricity generation. One of the reasons for the fuel switch to natural gas in the 1990s was the abundant availability and reasonable cost of natural gas. When costs dramatically increase, however, as they did in 2000 and 2001, consumers suffer.

There is legitimate concern this could happen again if more and more CNG vehicles are put into the market. Furthermore, although additional natural gas supplies are available because of new drilling techniques, supplies are also high because of the economic downturn. Demand for natural gas is expected to fall by 2.2% in 2009, with an 8% reduction by industrial users as automobile and steel makers scale back production. If the economy were to turn around and demand were to increase dramatically, there would likely be at least a short-term price spike that could slow or halt the transition to natural gas vehicles. Even if the fear was largely unfounded, memories are long and cost risks could be a psychological barrier that could impair a transition to natural gas as a major transportation fuel.

In addition, although natural gas is generally considered a better environmental alternative than gasoline and diesel fuel, it is not without impact. The major new drilling process to extract natural gas from shale is called hydraulic fracturing, which uses chemicals as part of the process. Currently, such drilling is exempted from regulation under the Safe Water Drinking Act through EP Act 2005, but there are some legislative efforts aimed at removing that exemption. Proponents of the legislation argue that more oversight and disclosure are necessary to ensure public health as the new process becomes more prevalent. The natural gas industry is concerned, however, that new regulations will slow extraction, thus raising prices and reducing opportunities.

Natural gas faces many of the same hurdles as other options in the quest to be the next generation transportation fuel. It also appears to be the most readily available option, technologically, and politically. Beyond economic uncertainties, the biggest hurdle may be the commitment, or lack thereof, to making a change in fuels at all.

C. Hydrogen: The First Element, But Is It the Best?

In the film *Who Killed the Electric Car?*, the California Air Resources Board (CARB) is shown as one of the reasons the EV1 was put to rest. Filmmaker Chris Paine portrays CARB's changed emissions mandates, which had helped support electric vehicles like the EV1, as a move to help expand options for hydrogen vehicles. Paine sets forth several theories for the demise of the EV1, including:

- The Bush administration, which the film accuses of pulling a bait-and-switch by pushing hydrogen fuel cell cars, while ignoring electric ones. Paine presents a daunting list of reasons why hydrogen-powered cars won't be coming any time soon, and why they'll be impossibly expensive to operate.

- The California Air Resources Board, which by any reading of the record, folded in the face of auto industry complaints.

Regardless, in 2003, CARB made "major amendments to the California Zero Emission Vehicle (ZEV) program regulations, which had previously been amended in a 2001 rule-making." The new amendments delay "the start of the percentage ZEV requirements from the 2003 model year (MY) to the 2005 MY." The amendments also "establish [ed] a new mechanism allowing large-volume auto manufacturers to choose one of two compliance paths."

Under the first path, large-volume manufacturers could satisfy ZEV obligations by meeting requirements that were essentially the same as the 2001 regulations. The 2001 amendments created a formula that "allows a mix of credits from three categories of vehicles—2 percent from 'gold' pure ZEVs, 2 percent from 'silver' advanced technology partial ZEV allowance vehicles (AT PZEVs), and 6 percent from 'bronze' partial ZEV allowance vehicles (PZEVs)."

Under the second compliance path, large-volume manufacturers could instead "meet part of its ZEV requirement by producing its sales-weighted market share of approximately 250 fuel cell ZEVs by the 2008 MY; the remainder of the manufacturer's ZEV obligations could initially be achieved with a credit mix of 4 percent from AT PZEVs and 6 percent from PZEVs." Therefore, this change allowed a manufacturer to maintain compliance via fuel cell vehicles and eliminated any requirement for a true zero emission vehicle. Whether CARB was right to make these changes remains a contentious issue, but either way, the world's largest automakers are pursuing hydrogen vehicles.

The Hydrogen Road Tour, an initiative created by the California Fuel Cell Partnership, allowed the public "to see—and drive—the Chevy Equinox Fuel Cell, Honda FCX Clarity, Hyundai Tucson FCEV, Kia Borrego FCEV, Mercedes F-Cell, Nissan X-Trail FCV, Toyota FCHV-adv Highlander and Volkswagen HyMotion." Honda already offers leases on its FCX Clarity in Los Angeles, which has enough hydrogen fueling stations available to support consumers. The FCX Clarity lease is offered for $600 per month.

It remains to be seen how hydrogen vehicles do in real-world conditions, but there are reasons to be excited about hydrogen vehicles. At least some Hydrogen vehicles can "get two to three times the mileage of a conventional car." In addition, "Toyota[] has developed a fuel-cell car that can travel nearly 500 miles on a single tank." Of course, the current hydrogen vehicles are mostly million-dollar prototypes, which will need to drop significantly in price, probably in the $30,000 to $40,000 range, to be commercially viable.

From a psychological infrastructure perspective, the appeal is quite clear. Hydrogen vehicles have tanks that need to be filled, just like gasoline tanks, and the process is comfortable and familiar. Also, gas station owners are more apt to like the concept because if a new fuel is to be embraced, this process retains the outside vendor as the access point for fuel.

But from a physical infrastructure perspective, there are real questions with hydrogen. First, pure hydrogen, at least in the quantities needed, must be produced somewhere; it cannot be found in nature. This is not necessarily insurmountable, but it raises real concerns because it is costly and requires new infrastructure. One option is to use excess electricity capacity and to produce hydrogen. Wind turbines and nuclear plants raise the most promising opportunities because both tend to have excess power available during non-peak times. As the country considers ways to provide additional electricity generation or replace older, environmentally hazardous generating plants, adding hydrogen production facilities along with the new generating plant is possible. Hydrogen is available in most energy sources, including "water, natural gas, gasoline or even coal." The trick is separating the hydrogen into a useful form, which also takes energy.

Nevertheless, simply generating hydrogen is not the only hurdle. There must also be a way to get the fuel. This would most likely be at a commercial service station, like a traditional gas station, that sells hydrogen. The service station option is conceivable, but it is also an expensive infrastructure upgrade due to the current limited hydrogen infrastructure. There are only sixty-two hydrogen-fueling stations in the United States, and nine more in Canada. One major reason for the slow rollout is the expensive nature of these commercial projects. For example, Shell recently opened a hydrogen filling station near Washington, D.C., which was built at a cost of $2 million. This is an especially expensive project when there are so few potential customers currently on the road.

Hydrogen home fueling stations are also an option, although this does not solve the problem also seen with electric cars when it comes to traveling away from home. Honda announced that it would be providing a home fueling station with its partner, Plug Power. The home fueling station, although expected to be costly, could offset some of the costs via "the station's byproducts: electricity, heat and hot water for the home." Other home fueling stations are designed to extract hydrogen from natural gas, thus using one fossil fuel to get away from another fossil fuel. As such, the driver would still contribute greenhouse gas emissions to the atmosphere, although the carbon footprint would be about 30% less than a typical driver. As discussed in Part III.B, new supplies of natural gas may make the hydrogen option more promising than it seemed only a few years ago, but the process may lead to infrastructure needs, at least in the near term, for both natural gas and hydrogen.

There are some who believe that manufacturers are stymieing their hydrogen, and perhaps other non-gasoline, vehicles because the carmakers are concerned that a successful new-fuel vehicle would significantly harm their other vehicle sales. One ardent promoter of this theory in the hydrogen market is author Edwin Black. In his book, *The Plan: How to Rescue Society the Day the Oil Stops—or the Day Before,* he argues that Honda "understood that if it mass produces the Clarity and Home Energy Station, the public will flock to it as fast as they have been fleeing from Honda SUVs and similar gas guzzlers." Helping "the world out of its financially wracking oil addiction," he argues, "would hamstring overall profits for the Japanese carmakers."

According to Black, Honda may have slowed access to its best alternative-fuel vehicles "for no reason other than the preservation of profits on gas guzzling vehicles well into the third decade of the 21st century." Furthermore, he explains that with gasoline as the primary fuel source, when U.S. consumers look for more fuel-efficient vehicles, they are likely to avoid the U.S. automakers and look to the more efficient Honda models, allowing Honda to dominate the gasoline-based auto industry.

Black's theories are, of course, highly speculative, and it is not entirely clear why Honda could not gain market share in the fuel-efficient gasoline market while taking the lead in the hydrogen market. Nonetheless, there are many who believe that gasoline is so entrenched as a fuel source that all of the major stakeholders are committed to preserving the status quo. The fact that there are no mass-market alternative-fuel vehicles that do not run without some gasoline lends some validity to the claim.

IV. CONCLUSION

Alternative liquid fuels, electricity, natural gas, and hydrogen all have the ability, in theory, to take over for gasoline as the primary transportation fuel. As discussed above, however, all the alternatives have significant limitations that are hard to overlook.

Sometimes it is the policies designed to promote alternative fuel sources that are the problem, not the fuel source itself. As an example, instead of providing a well-reasoned approach to U.S. fuel concerns, the RFS reflects Merton's "imperious immediacy of interest" problem. That is, as Congress sought to do something, anything, to address rising fuel costs and allay national security concerns regarding oil imports, ethanol proponents were willing to ignore any unintended effects, such as higher food and feedstock costs, the potential for lost rangelands and forestlands, and dramatic increases in jet fuel costs. This problem could impact policies related to all of the alternative fuels sources for transportation.

Ultimately, there are two related steps that would prove especially helpful in providing an option to gasoline and diesel fuels as the primary transportation fuels. First, policymakers and consumers should stop looking for *the* replacement fuel and start considering *a* replacement fuel. That is, rather than trying to make a single, wholesale change in the nation's transportation fuel choice and then waiting, there should be a greater focus on considering more local transitions to a variety of fuel sources. Instead of a one-size-fits-all approach, there is no reason that different cities or regions of the country should not choose different fuel source vehicles that serve their communities needs. For example, Los Angeles and San Diego might choose to build an infrastructure to support hydrogen vehicles and New Orleans and Houston might choose an infrastructure to provide support for natural gas vehicles. Certainly, there are very small test cases occurring around the country, but policy-makers should be more aggressive in pursuing options to promote large-scale changes in more local markets.

Second, on a broader scale, policymakers need to allow markets to work. That means internalizing the costs related to continued use of oil as the primary source of transportation fuel. To help transition away from gasoline as the primary transportation fuel, there should be a hefty, federal per-gallon tax added to all end-use gasoline sales. A portion of the additional revenues generated should be set aside for state or local projects to pursue alternative, non-oil-based transportation fuel options.

The tax should be based on a percentage of the sales price, as is done with other sales taxes, with a floor tax. For example, the tax could be set at 20%, with a floor price of fifty cents per gallon (the current federal gas tax, last adjusted in 2003, is 18.4 cents per gallon). Thus, the minimum would be triggered for gasoline priced below $2.50 per gallon before taxes. States and municipalities should follow suit with their own taxes. Ideally, there would also be a reduction in taxes elsewhere, such as lower payroll taxes, so that most consumers would have incentives to adjust their transportation choices, even though their disposable (or at least accessible) income remained roughly the same.

By using a percentage, tax collectors would share in the revenues when prices go up significantly. When gasoline prices went past $4 per gallon in 2008, oil companies were posting record profits because their percentage of the revenues went up with the prices. Tax collections, however, dropped significantly with the declining consumption because it was only the number of gallons sold (unadjusted for inflation) that generated revenue. A proposal for a per gallon carbon tax is, of course, nothing new. It is just unappealing to many people.

When considering the current options for alternative transportation fuels, it becomes abundantly clear that without significant policy changes, the status quo is simply too strong to overcome. Until consumers are able to understand the financial costs of their decisions at the pump and at the auto dealership, consumers will not change. And they shouldn't, from an economic perspective. Most consumers are making decisions that align directly with incentives put before them in the form of both physical and psychological infrastructure: they (we) drive gasoline-fueled vehicles because, in the foreseeable future, such vehicles are the most cost-effective option.

Notes & Questions

1. With the enormous amounts of natural gas deposits in U.S. shale plays, there has been a push to promote natural gas as a large vehicle source to replace diesel fuel in over-the-road trucks and fleet vehicles. As discussed above, Texas oil and gas magnate T. Boone Pickens proposed a plan that would initially promote wind energy for electricity generation and shift the natural gas to fleet vehicle use. That plan has evolved from a green energy plan into a plan to further the goal of reducing dependence on foreign and unfriendly sourced oil-based fuels. One recent proposal is a bill to provide tax credits of up to $64,000 per truck or vehicle to incentivize large trucks and corporate and government fleets to convert to compressed natural gas (CNG). The size of the tax credit will likely determine whether the program will gain any traction. Fleet vehicles are the most likely to be early adopters because they usually fuel at bulk stations, which are more easily converted to provide the fuel (and natural gas companies would likely pay for such a conversion).

2. What about the idea of moving to electric vehicles as much as possible? Battery technology is still evolving and there are questions about vehicle range, as most electric vehicles cannot be quickly recharged and have limited range. Plug-in hybrid cars (that can run on electricity from an outlet or run on gasoline) solve that problem, other than the higher vehicle costs. Electricity, though, can be generated from a variety of sources, from wind to solar to coal to nuclear, and the resulting electricity operates the same, regardless of the source. Thus, rather than switching vehicles from gasoline to natural gas to hydrogen to electricity, going straight to electricity would allow the electric generators to be the spot for all fuel switching without impacting consumers directly. What problems do you foresee with this proposal? What kind of programs and incentives would you use to pursue such a goal? How would you fund it?

3. *Practice Note*: It is sometimes easy to miss that one goal will impact another important consideration. (This is sometimes called the Law of Unintended Consequences.) Gasoline taxes are how much of our transportation infrastructure, especially roads, is funded. If vehicles don't run on gasoline, they don't pay gas taxes. More efficient vehicles use less gasoline, which means less revenue. Both will mean less money for building and maintaining roads. How might you address that problem? What other options are there for funding roads? Who should pay?

Appendix A

Coal

A. Coal Production Map

Coal production by region in million short tons, 2012
(percent change from 2011)

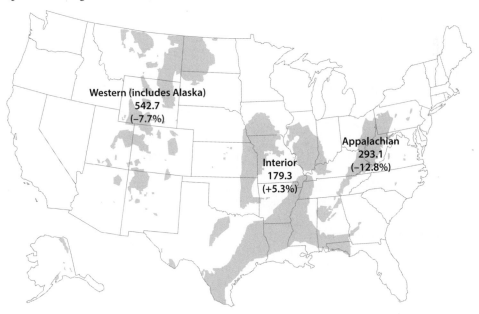

Western (includes Alaska)
542.7
(−7.7%)

Interior
179.3
(+5.3%)

Appalachian
293.1
(−12.8%)

Data Source: U.S. Energy Information Administration, *Quarterly Coal Report*, October–December 2012 (March 2013), preliminary 2012 data. Production does not include refuse recovery.

B. Coal Production, Consumption, & Exports

U.S. coal production, consumption, and net exports (1950–2012)
million short tons

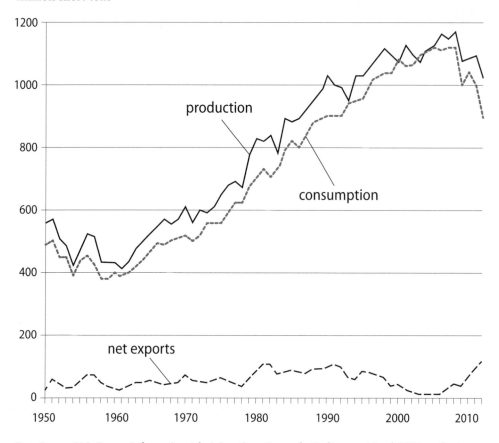

Data Source: U.S. Energy Information Administration, *Quarterly Coal Report*, March 2013, preliminary 2012 data, and Annual Energy Review (August 2012).

Appendix B

Oil & Gas (Hydraulic Fracturing)

A. West Virginia Horizontal Drilling Laws

State of West Virginia
TITLE 35
LEGISLATIVE RULE
DEPARTMENT OF ENVIRONMENTAL PROTECTION OIL AND GAS
SERIES 8
RULES GOVERNING HORIZONTAL WELL DEVELOPMENT

§ 35-8-1. General

1.1. Scope. — This rule shall govern and apply to permit application requirements, operational rules to protect water quantity and quality, and public notice procedures for oil or natural gas operators developing horizontal wells, which wells are also regulated by W. Va. Code § 22-6-1, et seq. and the Legislative Rules promulgated in Title 35 of West Virginia's Code of State Rules and entitled *Oil and Gas*.

1.2. Authority. — W. Va. Code §§ 22-1-3, 22-6-2, and 22-11-4(a)(16)

1.3. Filing Date. —

1.4. Effective Date. —

1.5. Applicability. — Applications submitted after the effective date of this rule shall be subject to the provisions of this rule.

§ 35-8-2. Definitions

2.1 Unless the context in which the term is used clearly requires a different meaning, the definitions set forth in W. Va. Code §§ 22-6-1 and 22-11-3 and in 35 C.S.R. 4 § 2 shall apply to this Rule.

2.2. "Horizontal well" means any well that is drilled initially on a vertical plane but eventually curved to become horizontal, or nearly horizontal, to parallel or intersect a particular geologic formation or formations, for the purpose of maximizing the length and contact of the wellbore that is exposed to the formation or formations.

§ 35-8-3. Permit Application Requirements for Operators Developing Horizontal Wells

3.1. Erosion and Sediment Control Plan.—Erosion and sediment control plans submitted in conjunction with applications for well work permits involving well sites that disturb three acres or more of surface, excluding pipelines, gathering lines, and roads, shall be certified by, and constructed in accordance with plans certified by, a West Virginia registered professional engineer and in compliance with best management practices (BMPs) established by the Office of Oil and Gas (Office) and contain both a narrative and a set of drawings. The plans shall be considered conditions of the permit and be enforceable as such.

3.1.a. The narrative components of the plan shall include:

3.1.a.1. A general sequence of events that describe in relative terms how and when each construction phase (i.e. clearing and grubbing, mass grading, stabilization) will occur and when each erosion and sediment control BMP will be installed;

3.1.a.2. A description of the stabilization methods to be used, including the application rates for temporary and permanent seeding and mulching, and provide the timeframes for establishing stabilization; and

3.1.a.3. Details or specifications for the erosion and sediment control BMPs employed on the project.

3.1.b. The drawings submitted with the plan shall include:

3.1.b.1. A vicinity map locating the site in relation to the surrounding area and roads;

3.1.b.2. A plan view site map at a scale of one inch equal to one hundred feet (1" = 100') or greater, showing appropriate detail of all site features, including the identification of site access that provides for a stabilized construction entrance and exit to reduce tracking of sediment onto public or private roads; and

3.1.b.3. The location of all proposed erosion and sediment control BMPs.

3.2. Site Construction Plan.—All applications for well work permits involving well sites that will disturb three acres or more of surface, excluding pipelines, gathering lines, and roads, shall be accompanied by a site construction plan certified by, and constructed in accordance with plans certified by, a West Virginia registered professional engineer. The plan should describe the nature and purpose of the construction project and identify the procedures for construction that will be used to achieve site stability. The plan shall be considered conditions of the permit and be enforceable as such.

3.2.a. The site construction plan shall contain the following information:

3.2.a.1. A vicinity map locating the site in relation to the surrounding area and roads;

3.2.a.2. A plan view site map at a scale of one inch equal to one hundred feet (1" = 100') or greater that shows appropriate detail of all site features and:

3.2.a.2.A. Clearly identifies the limit of disturbance for the project;

3.2.a.2.B. Provides existing topographic information on a contour interval that affords sufficient detail to illustrate site terrain conditions;

3.2.a.2.C. Identifies proposed cut and fill areas with grading contours at an interval that provides sufficient detail to accurately depict slope ratios, indicating top and bottom of slopes; and

3.2.a.2.D. Identifies any existing structures, roads, water bodies, and other critical areas within the area that would most likely be affected by the construction.

3.2.a.3. A cross-section of the length and width of the location, providing cut and fill volumes; and the project.

3.2.a.4. Any other engineering designs or drawings necessary to construct

3.2.b. At a minimum, site construction shall be conducted in accordance with the following criteria:

3.2.b.1. All woody material, brush, and trees shall be cleared from the site area and kept to the minimum necessary for proper construction, including the installation of necessary sediment controls. Trees six inches in diameter and larger shall be cut and logs stacked;

3.2.b.2. Topsoil shall be removed from construction areas and stockpiled for reuse during reclamation. In woodland areas, tree stumps, large roots, large rocks, tree and leaf debris, and ground vegetation shall be removed prior to actual site construction;

3.2.b.3. No embankment fill shall be placed on frozen material;

3.2.b.4. The fill material shall be clean mineral soil, free of roots, woody vegetation, stumps, sod, large rocks, frozen soil or other objectionable material;

3.2.b.5. Embankment material shall exhibit adequate soil strength and contain the proper amount of moisture to ensure that compaction will be achieved;

3.2.b.6. Earthen fill slopes should be constructed with slopes no steeper than a ratio of two-to-one (2:1);

3.2.b.7. Fill material will be placed in lifts or layers over the length of the fill. Lift thickness of the soil shall be as thin as the suitable random excavated material will permit, typically from six to twelve (12) inches; and

3.2.b.8. The size of rock lifts shall not exceed thirty-six (36) inches. The rock shall not be greater in any dimension than thirty-six (36) inches;

3.2.b.9. Compaction shall be obtained by compaction equipment or by routing the hauling equipment over the fill so that the entire surface of each fill lift is compacted by at least one wheel or tread track of equipment or by a compactor. Each lift shall be compacted before beginning the next lift;

3.2.b.10. Surface water diversion ditches shall be constructed above the disturbed area to intercept water and to divert surface water runoff around the site; and

3.2.b.11. In areas of steep terrain, a terraced bench shall be constructed at the base of the slope where fill is to be placed, creating a toe foundation and aid in holding fill material. Additional terracing shall be constructed for each additional fifty (50) vertical feet of slope and shall be a minimum of ten (10) feet wide.

3.3. Water Management Plan. — All applications for well work permits shall include an estimation of the volume of water that will be used in conjunction with drilling, fracturing or stimulating the well for which the permit is sought and, if the drilling, fracturing or stimulating of such well will require water withdrawals from the waters of this State in amounts of two hundred ten thousand (210,000) gallons or more during any one-month period, then the applicant shall file with the Office a water management plan as part of the application for the well work permit.[1] It shall be considered conditions of

---

1. This Rule in no way abrogates the statutory requirement that water withdrawals in excess of seven hundred fifty thousand (750,000) gallons per calendar month be registered with the Division of Water and Waste Management. *See,* W. Va. Code § 22-26-1, et seq.

the permit and be enforceable as such. The water management plan, which may be submitted either on an individual well basis or on a watershed basis, shall include the following information:

3.3.a. The type of water source, such as surface or ground water, the county in which each water source to be used for water withdrawals is located, and the latitude and longitude of each anticipated withdrawal location;

3.3.b. The anticipated volume of each water withdrawal;

3.3.c. The anticipated months when water withdrawals will be made;

3.3.d. The planned management and disposition of wastewater from fracturing, stimulation, and production activities;

3.3.e. A listing of the anticipated additives that may be used in the water used for fracturing or stimulating the well, and, upon well completion, a listing of the additives that were actually used in the fracturing or stimulating of the well shall be submitted as part of the completion report required by W. Va. Code § 22-6-22;

3.3.f. For all surface water withdrawals, the water management plan shall include the following, in addition to the information required in subdivisions 3.3.a. through 3.3.e. above:

3.3.f.1. Identification of the current designated and existing water uses, including any public water intakes within one mile downstream of the withdrawal location;

3.3.f.2. A demonstration, using methods acceptable to the Secretary, that sufficient in-stream flow will be available immediately downstream of the point of withdrawal. Sufficient in-stream flow is maintained when pass-by flow that is protective of the identified use of the stream is preserved immediately downstream of the point of withdrawal; and

3.3.f.3. Identification of the methods to be used to minimize significant adverse impact to aquatic life.

3.4. Well Site Safety Plan. — All applications for well work permits involving well sites that will disturb three acres or more of surface, excluding pipelines, gathering lines, and roads, shall be accompanied by a well site safety plan to address measures to be employed by the operator for the protection of persons on the site, as well as the general public and the environment. The plan shall encompass all aspects of the operation, including the actual well work for which the permit is sought, completion activities, and production activities, and shall provide an emergency point of contact and twenty-four (24)-hour contact information for the well operator. The well operator shall provide a copy of the well site safety plan to the local emergency planning committee for the emergency planning district in which the well work will occur or to the county office of emergency services at least seven days before commencement of well work or site preparation work that involves any disturbance of land. It may be modified only upon approval by the Office and shall be considered conditions of the permit and be enforceable as such.

3.4.a. The well site safety plan shall be drafted in accordance with standards developed by the Office and include, at a minimum, the following:

3.4.a.1. A plan view map showing the well location, access road, pits, flare lines, dwellings, and noting the north and prevailing wind directions;

3.4.a.2. An area topographical map showing the well site location;

3.4.a.3. An evacuation plan for the removal of personnel and residents in the surrounding area who have the potential to be affected by an emergency;

3.4.a.4. A list of telephone numbers, including twenty-four (24)-hour contact information, for the following entities (which shall also be posted at the well site): the operator, any contractors of the operator, the Department, the local oil and gas inspector, and local emergency response units;

3.4.a.5. A list of all schools and public facilities within a one-mile radius of the proposed well, including telephone numbers for the same;

3.4.a.6. Material Safety Data Sheets (MSDS) for all materials and chemicals on the well site shall be readily available and maintained at the well site; and

3.4.b. Well site safety meetings. — Safety meetings shall be held on-site weekly, at a minimum, and specifically prior to the beginning of drilling, completion, and work-over operations. Meeting attendance shall be logged, and the log shall be maintained on site. A check-in and check-out list of all personnel shall be maintained during the drilling and completion phases of the operation.

§ 35-8-4. Operational Rules to Protect Water Quality and Quantity

4.1. All operators are required to protect the quality and quantity of water in surface and ground water systems both during and after drilling operations and during reclamation by:

4.1.a. Withdrawing water from surface waters of the State using methods deemed appropriate by the Secretary so as to maintain sufficient in-stream flow immediately downstream of the withdrawal location;

4.1.b. Casing, sealing or otherwise managing wells to keep fluids or natural gas from entering ground or surface waters;

4.1.c. Conducting oil and gas operations using BMPs so as to prevent, to the extent practicable, additional contributions of suspended or dissolved solids to stream flow or runoff outside the permit area, but in no event shall the contributions be in excess of requirements set by applicable State or federal law; and

4.1.d. Registering all water supply wells with the Office and constructing and plugging all such wells in accordance with applicable laws governing water well construction.

4.2. All operators who withdraw two hundred ten thousand (210,000) gallons or more of water from waters of this State during any one-month period shall adhere to the following operational and reporting requirements:

4.2.a. Within forty-eight (48) hours, but no less than twenty-four (24) hours, prior to the withdrawal of water, the operator shall identify the location of withdrawal by latitude and longitude; verify, using methods deemed acceptable by the Secretary, that sufficient flow exists to protect designated uses of the stream; and provide notice to the Office as prescribed by the Secretary;

4.2.b. All surface water withdrawal locations and facilities identified in the water management plan set forth in subsection 3.3 above shall be identified with a sign that discloses that the location is a water withdrawal point and the name and telephone number of the operator for which the water withdrawn will be utilized. When the withdrawal location is no longer being utilized, or at the direction of the Secretary, the operator shall notify the Office and remove all signage; and

4.2.c. For all water used in connection with hydraulic fracturing activities and for all produced water from production activities, operators shall comply with the following record- keeping requirements:

4.2.c.1. For production activities, the following information shall be recorded and retained by the operator:

4.2.c.1.A. The quantity of flowback water from hydraulic fracturing of the well;

4.2.c.1.B. The quantity of produced water from the well; and

4.2.c.1.C. The method of management or disposal of the flowback and produced water.

4.2.c.2. For transportation activities, the following information shall be recorded and retained by the operator:

4.2.c.2.A. The quantity of water transported;

4.2.c.2.B. The collection and delivery or disposal location(s) of the water; and

4.2.c.2.C. The name(s) of the water hauling company(ies).

4.3. All drill cuttings and associated drilling mud generated from well sites that disturb three acres or more of surface, excluding pipelines, gathering lines, and roads, or that use two hundred ten thousand (210,000) gallons or more of water during any one-month period shall be disposed of in an approved solid waste facility or managed on-site in a manner otherwise approved by the Secretary.

4.4. Casing and cementing standards. — The operator shall prudently drill through fresh groundwater zones so as to minimize any disturbance of such zones. Further, the operator shall construct the well and conduct casing and cementing activities of all horizontal wells in accordance with standards developed by the Office and in a manner that will provide for control of the well at all times, prevent the migration of gas and other fluids into the fresh groundwater and coal seams, and prevent pollution of or diminution of fresh groundwater. At a minimum, the following standards shall apply:

4.4.a. Casing standards.

4.4.a.1. All casing installed in the well must be new, with a pressure rating that exceeds the anticipated maximum pressure to which the casing will be exposed and meet the appropriate American Petroleum Institute (API) standards;

4.4.a.2. The casing must be of sufficient quality and condition to withstand the effects of tension and maintain its structural integrity during installation, cementing, and subsequent drilling and production operations;

4.4.a.3. Centralizers must be used, with the proper spacing, during the casing installation to ensure that the casing is centered in the hole;

4.4.a.4. Casing shall not be disturbed for a period of at least eight hours after the completion of cementing operations; and

4.4.a.5. No gas or oil production or pressure shall exist on the surface casing or the coal protection casing.

4.4.b. Cement standards.

4.4.b.1. All cement used in the well must meet the appropriate API standards and secure the casing to the wellbore, isolate the wellbore from all fluids, contain all pressures during all phases of drilling and operation of the well, and protect the casing from corrosion and degradation;

4.4.b.2. Cement used in conjunction with surface and coal protection casing must prevent gas flow in the casing annulus;

4.4.b.3. The operator shall provide notice to the Office at least twenty-four (24) hours prior to the commencement of any cementing operations and maintain a copy of the cementing log at the well site during the drilling and completion of the well.

§ 35-8-5. Public Notice Procedures

5.1. Applicants for well work permits seeking to drill the first horizontal Marcellus Shale well on any particular well pad located in an area within the boundaries of any municipality, as that term is defined in W. Va. Code § 8-1-2, shall publish public notice of the filing of such well work permit application as follows: At the time that a well work permit application is filed, the applicant shall also place a Class I legal advertisement in a newspaper of general circulation in the area where the well is proposed to be located. No well work permit shall be issued to any applicant until at least thirty (30) days' notice has been provided to the public. The advertisement shall contain, at a minimum, the name of the applicant, the proposed location of the well, the proposed date on which site preparation for the proposed well will begin, and a contact telephone number for more information.

B. West Virginia Horizontal Well Permit Packet

WW-6B
(9/13)

STATE OF WEST VIRGINIA
DEPARTMENT OF ENVIRONMENTAL PROTECTION, OFFICE OF OIL AND GAS
WELL WORK PERMIT APPLICATION

1) Well Operator: _____

Operator ID	County	District	Quadrangle

2) Operator's Well Number: _____   Well Pad Name: _____

3) Farm Name/Surface Owner: _____   Public Road Access: _____

4) Elevation, current ground: _____ Elevation, proposed post-construction: _____

5) Well Type   (a) Gas _____ Oil _____ Underground Storage _____

           Other _____

        (b)If Gas   Shallow _____ Deep _____

           Horizontal _____

6) Existing Pad: Yes or No _____

7) Proposed Target Formation(s), Depth(s), Anticipated Thickness and Associated Pressure(s):

_____

8) Proposed Total Vertical Depth: _____

9) Formation at Total Vertical Depth: _____

10) Proposed Total Measured Depth: _____

11) Proposed Horizontal Leg Length: _____

12) Approximate Fresh Water Strata Depths: _____

13) Method to Determine Fresh Water Depths: _____

14) Approximate Saltwater Depths: _____

15) Approximate Coal Seam Depths: _____

16) Approximate Depth to Possible Void (coal mine, karst, other): _____

17) Does Proposed well location contain coal seams
directly overlying or adjacent to an active mine?   Yes _____   No _____

  (a) If Yes, provide Mine Info: Name: _____

                     Depth: _____

                     Seam: _____

                     Owner: _____

WW-6B
(9/13)

18)   **CASING AND TUBING PROGRAM**

TYPE	Size	New or Used	Grade	Weight per ft. (lb/ft)	FOOTAGE: For Drilling	INTERVALS: Left in Well	CEMENT: Fill-up (Cu. Ft.)
Conductor							
Fresh Water							
Coal							
Intermediate							
Production							
Tubing							
Liners							

TYPE	Size	Wellbore Diameter	Wall Thickness	Burst Pressure	Cement Type	Cement Yield (cu. ft./k)
Conductor						
Fresh Water						
Coal						
Intermediate						
Production						
Tubing						
Liners						

PACKERS

Kind:				
Sizes:				
Depths Set:				

WW-6B
(9/13)

19) Describe proposed well work, including the drilling and plugging back of any pilot hole:

20) Describe fracturing/stimulating methods in detail, including anticipated max pressure and max rate:

21) Total Area to be disturbed, including roads, stockpile area, pits, etc., (acres): _____

22) Area to be disturbed for well pad only, less access road (acres): _____

23) Describe centralizer placement for each casing string:

24) Describe all cement additives associated with each cement type:

25) Proposed borehole conditioning procedures:

*Note: Attach additional sheets as needed.

WW-PN
(5-04-2012)

Horizontal Natural Gas Well Work Permit
Application Notice By Publication

Notice is hereby given:
Pursuant to West Virginia Code 22-6A-10(e) prior to filing an application for a permit for a horizontal well the applicant shall publish in the county in which the well is located or is proposed to be located a Class II legal advertisement.

Paper: _____

Public Notice Date: _____

The following applicant intends to apply for a horizontal natural well work permit which disturbs three acres or more of surface excluding pipelines, gathering lines and roads **or** utilizes more than two hundred ten thousand gallons of water in any thirty day period.

Applicant: _____   **Well Number:** _____

Address: _____

_____

Business Conducted: Natural gas production.

Location –

State:	_____	County:	_____
District:	_____	Quadrangle:	_____

UTM Coordinate NAD83 Northing: _____

UTM coordinate NAD83 Easting: _____
Watershed: _____

Coordinate Conversion:
To convert the coordinates above into longitude and latitude, visit: http://tagis.dep.wv.gov/convert/llutm_conus.php

Electronic notification:
To receive an email when applications have been received or issued by the Office of Oil and Gas, visit http://www.dep.wv.gov/insidedep/Pages/DEPMailingLists.aspx to sign up.

Reviewing Applications:
Copies of the proposed permit application may be reviewed at the WV Department of Environmental Protection headquarters, located at 601 57th Street, SE Charleston, WV 25304 (304-926-0450). Full copies or scans of the proposed permit application will cost $15, whether mailed or obtained at DEP headquarters. Copies may be requested by calling the office or by sending an email to DEP.oog@wv.gov.

Submitting Comments:
Comments may be submitted online at https://apps.dep.wv.gov/oog/comments/comments.cfm, or by letter to Permit Review, Office of Oil and Gas, 601 57th Street, SE Charleston, WV 25304. Please reference the county, well number, and operator when using this option.

Regardless of format for comment submissions, they must be received no later than thirty days after the permit application is received by the Office of Oil and Gas.

For information related to horizontal drilling visit: www.dep.wv.gov/oil-and-gas/pages/default.aspx

WW-6A
(9-13)

API NO. 47-_____-_____
OPERATOR WELL NO. _____
Well Pad Name: _____

STATE OF WEST VIRGINIA
DEPARTMENT OF ENVIRONMENTAL PROTECTION, OFFICE OF OIL AND GAS
NOTICE OF APPLICATION

Notice Time Requirement: notice shall be provided no later than the **filing date of permit application.**

Date of Notice: _____   **Date Permit Application Filed**: _____
Notice of:

☐ PERMIT FOR ANY   ☐ CERTIFICATE OF APPROVAL FOR THE
   WELL WORK   CONSTRUCTION OF AN IMPOUNDMENT OR PIT

Delivery method pursuant to West Virginia Code § 22-6A-10(b)

☐ PERSONAL   ☐ REGISTERED   ☐ METHOD OF DELIVERY THAT REQUIRES A
   SERVICE   MAIL   RECEIPT OR SIGNATURE CONFIRMATION

Pursuant to W. Va. Code § 22-6A-10(b) no later than the filing date of the application, the applicant for a permit for any well work or for a certificate of approval for the construction of an impoundment or pit as required by this article shall deliver, by personal service or by registered mail or by any method of delivery that requires a receipt or signature confirmation, copies of the application, the erosion and sediment control plan required by section seven of this article, and the well plat to each of the following persons: (1) The owners of record of the surface of the tract on which the well is or is proposed to be located; (2) The owners of record of the surface tract or tracts overlying the oil and gas leasehold being developed by the proposed well work, if the surface tract is to be used for roads or other land disturbance as described in the erosion and sediment control plan submitted pursuant to subsection (c), section seven of this article; (3) The coal owner, operator or lessee, in the event the tract of land on which the well proposed to be drilled is located [sic] is known to be underlain by one or more coal seams; (4) The owners of record of the surface tract or tracts overlying the oil and gas leasehold being developed by the proposed well work, if the surface tract is to be used for the placement, construction, enlargement, alteration, repair, removal or abandonment of any impoundment or pit as described in section nine of this article; (5) Any surface owner or water purveyor who is known to the applicant to have a water well, spring or water supply source located within one thousand five hundred feet of the center of the well pad which is used to provide water for consumption by humans or domestic animals; and (6) The operator of any natural gas storage field within which the proposed well work activity is to take place. (c)(1) If more than three tenants in common or other co-owners of interests described in subsection (b) of this section hold interests in the lands, the applicant may serve the documents required upon the person described in the records of the sheriff required to be maintained pursuant to section eight, article one, chapter eleven-a of this code. (2) Notwithstanding any provision of this article to the contrary, notice to a lien holder is not notice to a landowner, unless the lien holder is the landowner. W. Va. Code R. § 35-8-5.7.a requires, in part, that the operator shall also provide the Well Site Safety Plan ("WSSP") to the surface owner and any water purveyor or surface owner subject to notice and water testing as provided in section 15 of this rule.

☐ Application Notice ☐ WSSP Notice ☐ E&S Plan Notice ☐ Well Plat Notice   is hereby provided to:

☐ SURFACE OWNER(s)
Name: _____
Address: _____
_____

Name: _____
Address: _____
_____

☐ SURFACE OWNER(s) (Road and/or Other Disturbance)
Name: _____
Address: _____
_____

Name: _____
Address: _____
_____

☐ SURFACE OWNER(s) (Impoundments or Pits)
Name: _____
Address: _____
_____

☐ COAL OWNER OR LESSEE
Name: _____
Address: _____
_____

☐ COAL OPERATOR
Name: _____
Address: _____

☐ SURFACE OWNER OF WATER WELL
AND/OR WATER PURVEYOR(s)
Name: _____
Address: _____

☐ OPERATOR OF ANY NATURAL GAS STORAGE FIELD
Name: _____
Address: _____
_____
*Please attach additional forms if necessary

WW-6A
(8-13)

API NO. 47-_____-_____
OPERATOR WELL NO. _____
Well Pad Name: _____

Notice is hereby given:
Pursuant to West Virginia Code § 22-6A-10(b), notice is hereby given that the undersigned well operator has applied for a permit for well work or for a certificate of approval for the construction of an impoundment or pit.

This Notice Shall Include:
Pursuant to W. Va. Code § 22-6A-10(b), this notice shall include: (1) copies of the application; (2) the erosion and sediment control plan required by section seven of this article; and (3) the well plat.

Pursuant to W. Va. Code § 22-6A-10(f), this notice shall include: (1) a statement of the time limits for filing written comments; (2) who may file written comments; (3) the name and address of the secretary for the purpose of filing the comments and obtaining additional information; and (4) a statement that the persons may request, at the time of submitting written comments, notice of the permit decision and a list of persons qualified to test water.

Pursuant to W. Va. Code R. § 35-8-5.7.a, the operator shall provide the Well Site Safety Plan to the surface owner and any water purveyor or surface owner subject to notice and water testing as provided in section 15 of this rule.

Pursuant to W. Va. Code R. § 35-8-15.2.c, this notice shall: (1) contain a statement of the surface owner's and water purveyor's right to request sampling and analysis; (2) advise the surface owner and water purveyor of the rebuttable presumption for contamination or deprivation of a fresh water source or supply; advise the surface owner and water purveyor that refusal to allow the operator to conduct a pre-drilling water well test constitutes a method to rebut the presumption of liability; (3) advise the surface owner and water purveyor of his or her independent right to sample and analyze any water supply at his or her own expense; advise the surface owner and water purveyor whether or not the operator will utilize an independent laboratory to analyze any sample; and (4) advise the surface owner and or water purveyor that he or she can obtain from the Chief a list of water testing laboratories in the subject area capable of and qualified to test water supplies in accordance with standard acceptable methods.

Additional information related to horizontal drilling may be obtained from the Secretary, at the WV Department of Environmental Protection headquarters, located at 601 57th Street, SE, Charleston, WV 25304 (304-926-0450) or by visiting www.dep.wv.gov/oil-and-gas/pages/default.aspx.

Well Location Restrictions
Pursuant to W. Va. Code § 22-6A-12, Wells may not be drilled within two hundred fifty feet measured horizontally from any existing water well or developed spring used for human or domestic animal consumption. The center of well pads may not be located within six hundred twenty-five feet of an occupied dwelling structure, or a building two thousand five hundred square feet or larger used to house or shelter dairy cattle or poultry husbandry. This limitation is applicable to those wells, developed springs, dwellings or agricultural buildings that existed on the date a notice to the surface owner of planned entry for surveying or staking as provided in section ten of this article or a notice of intent to drill a horizontal well as provided in subsection (b), section sixteen of this article was provided, whichever occurs first, and to any dwelling under construction prior to that date. This limitation may be waived by written consent of the surface owner transmitted to the department and recorded in the real property records maintained by the clerk of the county commission for the county in which such property is located. Furthermore, the well operator may be granted a variance by the secretary from these distance restrictions upon submission of a plan which identifies the sufficient measures, facilities or practices to be employed during well site construction, drilling and operations. The variance, if granted, shall include terms and conditions the department requires to ensure the safety and protection of affected persons and property. The terms and conditions may include insurance, bonding and indemnification, as well as technical requirements. (b) No well pad may be prepared or well drilled within one hundred feet measured horizontally from any perennial stream, natural or artificial lake, pond or reservoir, or a wetland, or within three hundred feet of a naturally reproducing trout stream. No well pad may be located within one thousand feet of a surface or ground water intake of a public water supply. The distance from the public water supply as identified by the department shall be measured as follows: (1) For a surface water intake on a lake or reservoir, the distance shall be measured from the boundary of the lake or reservoir. (2) For a surface water intake on a flowing stream, the distance shall be measured from a semicircular radius extending upstream of the surface water intake. (3) For a groundwater source, the distance shall be measured from the wellhead or spring. The department may, in its discretion, waive these distance restrictions upon submission of a plan identifying sufficient measures, facilities or practices to be employed during well site construction, drilling and operations to protect the waters of the state. A waiver, if granted, shall impose any permit conditions as the secretary considers necessary. (c) Notwithstanding the foregoing provisions of this section, nothing contained in this section prevents an operator from conducting the activities permitted or authorized by a Clean Water Act Section 404 permit or other approval from the United States Army Corps of Engineers within any waters of the state or within the restricted areas referenced in this section. (d) The well location restrictions set forth in this section shall not apply to any well on a multiple well pad if at least one of the wells was permitted prior to the effective date of this article. (e) The secretary shall, by December 31, 2012, report to the Legislature on the noise, light, dust and volatile organic compounds generated by the drilling of horizontal wells as they relate to the well location restrictions regarding occupied dwelling structures pursuant to this section. Upon a finding, if any, by the secretary that the well location restrictions regarding occupied dwelling structures are inadequate or otherwise require alteration to address the items

WW-6A

(8-13)

examined in the study required by this subsection, the secretary shall have the authority to propose for promulgation legislative rules establishing guidelines and procedures regarding reasonable levels of noise, light, dust and volatile organic compounds relating to drilling horizontal wells, including reasonable means of mitigating such factors, if necessary.

Water Well Testing:

Pursuant to West Virginia Code § 22-6A-10(d), notification shall be made, with respect to surface landowners identified in subsection (b) or water purveyors identified in subdivision (5), subsection (b) of this section, of the opportunity for testing their water well. The operator shall provide an analysis to such surface landowner or water purveyor at their request.

Water Testing Laboratories:

Pursuant to West Virginia Code § 22-6A-10(i), persons entitled to notice pursuant to subsection (b) of this section may contact the department to ascertain the names and locations of water testing laboratories in the subject area capable and qualified to test water supplies in accordance with standard accepted methods. In compiling that list of names the department shall consult with the state Bureau for Public Health and local health departments. A surface owner and water purveyor has an independent right to sample and analyze any water supply at his or her own expense. The laboratory utilized by the operator shall be approved by the agency as being certified and capable of performing sample analyses in accordance with this section.

Rebuttable Presumption for Contamination or Deprivation of a Fresh Water Source or Supply:

W. Va. Code § 22-6A-18 requires that (b) unless rebutted by one of the defenses established in subsection (c) of this section, in any action for contamination or deprivation of a fresh water source or supply within one thousand five hundred feet of the center of the well pad for horizontal well, there is a rebuttable presumption that the drilling and the oil or gas well or either was the proximate cause of the contamination or deprivation of the fresh water source or supply. (c) In order to rebut the presumption of liability established in subsection (b) of this section, the operator must prove by a preponderance of the evidence one of the following defenses: (1) The pollution existed prior to the drilling or alteration activity as determined by a predrilling or prealteration water well test. (2) The landowner or water purveyor refused to allow the operator access to the property to conduct a predrilling or prealteration water well test. (3) The water supply is not within one thousand five hundred feet of the well. (4) The pollution occurred more than six months after completion of drilling or alteration activities. (5) The pollution occurred as the result of some cause other than the drilling or alteration activity. (d) Any operator electing to preserve its defenses under subdivision (1), subsection (c) of this section shall retain the services of an independent certified laboratory to conduct the predrilling or prealteration water well test. A copy of the results of the test shall be submitted to the department and the surface owner or water purveyor in a manner prescribed by the secretary. (e) Any operator shall replace the water supply of an owner of interest in real property who obtains all or part of that owner's supply of water for domestic, agricultural, industrial or other legitimate use from an underground or surface source with a comparable water supply where the secretary determines that the water supply has been affected by contamination, diminution or interruption proximately caused by the oil or gas operation, unless waived in writing by that owner. (f) The secretary may order the operator conducting the oil or gas operation to: (1) Provide an emergency drinking water supply within twenty-four hours; (2) Provide temporary water supply within seventy-two hours; (3) Within thirty days begin activities to establish a permanent water supply or submit a proposal to the secretary outlining the measures and timetables to be used in establishing a permanent supply. The total time in providing a permanent water supply may not exceed two years. If the operator demonstrates that providing a permanent replacement water supply cannot be completed within two years, the secretary may extend the time frame on case-by-case basis; and (4) Pay all reasonable costs incurred by the real property owner in securing a water supply. (g) A person as described in subsection (b) of this section aggrieved under the provisions of subsections (b), (e) or (f) of this section may seek relief in court... (i) Notwithstanding the denial of the operator of responsibility for the damage to the real property owner's water supply or the status of any appeal on determination of liability for the damage to the real property owner's water supply, the operator may not discontinue providing the required water service until authorized to do so by the secretary or a court of competent jurisdiction.

Written Comment:

Pursuant to West Virginia Code § 22-6A-11(a), all persons described in subsection (b), section ten of this article may file written comments with the secretary as to the location or construction of the applicant's proposed well work within thirty days after the application is filed with the secretary. All persons described in West Virginia Code § 22-6A-10(b) may file written comments as to the location or construction of the applicant's proposed well work to the Secretary at:

Chief, Office of Oil and Gas

Department of Environmental Protection

601 57th St. SE

Charleston, WV 25304

(304) 926-0450

Such persons may request, at the time of submitting written comments, notice of the permit decision and a list of persons qualified to test water. **NOTE: YOU ARE NOT REQUIRED TO FILE ANY COMMENT.**

WW-6A

(8-13)

API NO. 47-_____-_____
OPERATOR WELL NO. _____
Well Pad Name: _____

Time Limits and Methods for Filing Comments.

The law requires these materials to be served on or before the date the operator files its Application. You have **THIRTY (30) DAYS** after the filing date to file your comments. Comments must be filed in person or received in the mail by the Chief's office by the time stated above. You may call the Chief's office to be sure of the date. Check with your postmaster to ensure adequate delivery time or to arrange special expedited handling. If you have been contacted by the well operator and you have signed a "voluntary statement of no objection" to the planned work described in these materials, then the permit may be issued at any time.

Pursuant to West Virginia Code § 22-6A-11(c)(2), Any objections of the affected coal operators and coal seam owners and lessees shall be addressed through the processes and procedures that exist under sections fifteen, seventeen and forty, article six of this chapter, as applicable and as incorporated into this article by section five of this article. The written comments filed by the parties entitled to notice under subdivisions (1), (2), (4), (5) and (6), subsection (b), section ten of this article shall be considered by the secretary in the permit issuance process, but the parties are not entitled to participate in the processes and proceedings that exist under sections fifteen, seventeen or forty, article six of this chapter, as applicable and as incorporated into this article by section five of this article.

Comment Requirements

Your comments must be in writing and include your name, address and telephone number, the well operator's name and well number and the approximate location of the proposed well site including district and county from the application. You may add other documents, such as sketches, maps or photographs to support your comments.

Disclaimer: All comments received will be placed on our web site http://www.dep.wv.gov/oil-and-gas/Horizontal-Permits/Pages/default.aspx and the applicant will automatically be forwarded an email notice that such comments have been submitted. The applicant will be expected to provide a response to comments submitted by any surface owner, water purveyor or natural gas storage operator noticed within the application.

Permit Denial or Condition

The Chief has the power to deny or condition a well work permit. Pursuant to West Virginia Code § 22-6A-8(d), the permit may not be issued or be conditioned, including conditions with respect to the location of the well and access roads prior to issuance if the director determines that:

      (1) The proposed well work will constitute a hazard to the safety of persons;

      (2) The plan for soil erosion and sediment control is not adequate or effective;

      (3) Damage would occur to publicly owned lands or resources; or

      (4) The proposed well work fails to protect fresh water sources or supplies.

A permit may also be denied under West Virginia Code § 22-6A-7(k), the secretary shall deny the issuance of a permit if the secretary determines that the applicant has committed a substantial violation of a previously issued permit for a horizontal well, including the applicable erosion and sediment control plan associated with the previously issued permit, or a substantial violation of one or more of the rules promulgated under this article, and in each instance has failed to abate or seek review of the violation within the time prescribed by the secretary pursuant to the provisions of subdivisions (1) and (2), subsection (a), section five of this article and the rules promulgated hereunder, which time may not be unreasonable.

Pursuant to West Virginia Code § 22-6A-10(g), any person entitled to submit written comments to the secretary pursuant to subsection (a), section eleven of this article, shall also be entitled to receive from the secretary a copy of the permit as issued or a copy of the order modifying or denying the permit if the person requests receipt of them as a part of the written comments submitted concerning the permit application. Such persons may request, at the time of submitting written comments, notice of the permit decision and a list of persons qualified to test water.

WW-6A
(8-13)

API NO. 47-_____-_____
OPERATOR WELL NO. _____
Well Pad Name: _____

Notice is hereby given by:

Well Operator:_____   Address:_____

Telephone: _____   _____

Email: _____   Facsimile: _____

Oil and Gas Privacy Notice:

The Office of Oil and Gas processes your personal information, such as name, address and telephone number, as part of our regulatory duties. Your personal information may be disclosed to other State agencies or third parties in the normal course of business or as needed to comply with statutory or regulatory requirements, including Freedom of Information Act requests. Our office will appropriately secure your personal information. If you have any questions about our use or your personal information, please contact DEP's Chief Privacy Officer at depprivacyofficer@wv.gov.

Subscribed and sworn before me this _____ day of _____,_____.

_____ Notary Public

My Commission Expires_____

WW-6AW
(1-12)

API NO. 47-_____-_____
OPERATOR WELL NO. _____
Well Pad Name: _____

STATE OF WEST VIRGINIA
DEPARTMENT OF ENVIRONMENTAL PROTECTION, OFFICE OF OIL AND GAS
VOLUNTARY STATEMENT OF NO OBJECTION

Instructions to Persons Named on Page WW-6A
The well operator named on page WW-6A is applying for a permit from the State of West Virginia to conduct oil or gas well work. Well work permits are valid for twenty-four (24) months. Please contact the listed well operator and the Office of Oil and Gas if you do not own any interest in the listed surface tract.

Comment and Waiver Provisions
Pursuant to West Virginia Code § 22-6A-11(a), all persons described in subsection (b), section ten of this article may file written comments with the secretary as to the location or construction of the applicant's proposed well work within thirty days after the application is filed with the secretary.

Pursuant to West Virginia Code § 22-6A-8(b) No permit may be issued less than thirty days after the filing date of the application for any well work except plugging or replugging; and no permit for plugging or replugging may be issued less than five days after the filing date of the application except a permit for plugging or replugging a dry hole: *Provided,* That if the applicant certifies that all persons entitled to notice of the application under the provisions of subsection (b), section ten of this article have been served in person or by certified mail, return receipt requested, with a copy of the well work application, including the erosion and sediment control plan, if required, and the well plat, and further files written statements of no objection by all such persons, the secretary may issue the well work permit at any time.

VOLUNTARY STATEMENT OF NO OBJECTION

I, _____, hereby state that I have read the Instructions to Persons Named on Page WW-6A and the associated provisions listed above, and that I have received copies of a Notice of Application, an Application for a Well Work Permit on Form WW-6A and attachments consisting of pages one (1) through _____, including the erosion and sediment control plan, if required, and the well plat, all for proposed well work on the tract of land as follows:

State: _____   UTM NAD 83 Easting: _____
County: _____   Northing: _____
District: _____   Public Road Access: _____
Quadrangle: _____ Generally used farm name: _____
Watershed: _____

I further state that I have no objection to the planned work described in these materials, and I have no objection to a permit being issued on those materials.

*Please check the box that applies	FOR EXECUTION BY A NATURAL PERSON
☐ SURFACE OWNER	Signature: _____
☐ SURFACE OWNER (Road and/or Other Disturbance)	Print Name: _____ Date: _____
☐ SURFACE OWNER (Impoundments/Pits)	
☐ COAL OWNER OR LESSEE	FOR EXECUTION BY A CORPORATION, ETC. Company: _____
☐ COAL OPERATOR	By: _____ Its: _____
☐ WATER PURVEYOR	Signature: _____
☐ OPERATOR OF ANY NATURAL GAS STORAGE FIELD	Date: _____

Oil and Gas Privacy Notice:
The Office of Oil and Gas processes your personal information, such as name, address and telephone number, as part of our regulatory duties. Your personal information may be disclosed to other State agencies or third parties in the normal course of business or as needed to comply with statutory or regulatory requirements, including Freedom of Information Act requests. Our office will appropriately secure your personal information. If you have any questions about our use or your personal information, please contact DEP's Chief Privacy Officer at depprivacyofficer@wv.gov.

WW-6AC
(1/12)

STATE OF WEST VIRGINIA
DEPARTMENT OF ENVIRONMENTAL PROTECTION, OFFICE OF OIL AND GAS
<u>**NOTICE CERTIFICATION**</u>

Date of Notice Certification: _____

API No. 47-_____-_____
Operator's Well No._____
Well Pad Name: _____

Notice has been given:
Pursuant to the provisions in West Virginia Code § 22-6A, the Operator has provided the required parties with the Notice Forms listed below for the tract of land as follows:

State: _____   UTM NAD 83   Easting: _____
County: _____   Northing: _____
District: _____   Public Road Access: _____
Quadrangle: _____   Generally used farm name: _____
Watershed: _____

Pursuant to West Virginia Code § 22-6A-7(b), every permit application filed under this section shall be on a form as may be prescribed by the secretary, shall be verified and shall contain the following information: (14) A certification from the operator that (i) it has provided the owners of the surface described in subdivisions (1), (2) and (4), subsection (b), section ten of this article, the information required by subsections (b) and (c), section sixteen of this article; (ii) that the requirement was deemed satisfied as a result of giving the surface owner notice of entry to survey pursuant to subsection (a), section ten of this article six-a; or (iii) the notice requirements of subsection (b), section sixteen of this article were waived in writing by the surface owner; and Pursuant to West Virginia Code § 22-6A-11(b), the applicant shall tender proof of and certify to the secretary that the notice requirements of section ten of this article have been completed by the applicant.

Pursuant to West Virginia Code § 22-6A, the Operator has attached proof to this Notice Certification that the Operator has properly served the required parties with the following: *PLEASE CHECK ALL THAT APPLY	**OOG OFFICE USE ONLY**
☐ 1. NOTICE OF SEISMIC ACTIVITY or ☐ NOTICE NOT REQUIRED BECAUSE NO SEISMIC ACTIVITY WAS CONDUCTED	☐ **RECEIVED/ NOT REQUIRED**
☐ 2. NOTICE OF ENTRY FOR PLAT SURVEY or ☐ NO PLAT SURVEY WAS CONDUCTED	☐ **RECEIVED**
☐ 3. NOTICE OF INTENT TO DRILL or ☐ NOTICE NOT REQUIRED BECAUSE NOTICE OF ENTRY FOR PLAT SURVEY WAS CONDUCTED or ☐ WRITTEN WAIVER BY SURFACE OWNER (PLEASE ATTACH)	☐ **RECEIVED/ NOT REQUIRED**
☐ 4. NOTICE OF PLANNED OPERATION	☐ **RECEIVED**
☐ 5. PUBLIC NOTICE	☐ **RECEIVED**
☐ 6. NOTICE OF APPLICATION	☐ **RECEIVED**

Required Attachments:
The Operator shall attach to this Notice Certification Form all Notice Forms and Certifications of Notice that have been provided to the required parties and/or any associated written waivers. For the Public Notice, the operator shall attach a copy of the Class II Legal Advertisement with publication date verification or the associated Affidavit of Publication. The attached Notice Forms and Certifications of Notice shall serve as proof that the required parties have been noticed as required under West Virginia Code § 22-6A. Pursuant to West Virginia Code § 22-6A-11(b), the Certification of Notice to the person may be made by affidavit of personal service, the return receipt card or other postal receipt for certified mailing.

WW-6AC
(1/12)

Certification of Notice is hereby given:

THEREFORE, I _____ , have read and understand the notice requirements within West Virginia Code § 22-6A. I certify that as required under West Virginia Code § 22-6A, I have served the attached copies of the Notice Forms, identified above, to the required parties through personal service, by registered mail or by any method of delivery that requires a receipt or signature confirmation. I certify under penalty of law that I have personally examined and am familiar with the information submitted in this Notice Certification and all attachments, and that based on my inquiry of those individuals immediately responsible for obtaining the information, I believe that the information is true, accurate and complete. I am aware that there are significant penalties for submitting false information, including the possibility of fine and imprisonment.

Well Operator: _____   Address: _____
By: _____
Its: _____   Facsimile: _____
Telephone: _____   Email: _____

NOTARY SEAL	Subscribed and sworn before me this _____ day of _____.
	_____ Notary Public
	My Commission Expires_____

Oil and Gas Privacy Notice:
The Office of Oil and Gas processes your personal information, such as name, address and telephone number, as part of our regulatory duties. Your personal information may be disclosed to other State agencies or third parties in the normal course of business or as needed to comply with statutory or regulatory requirements, including Freedom of Information Act requests. Our office will appropriately secure your personal information. If you have any questions about our use or your personal information, please contact DEP's Chief Privacy Officer at depprivacyofficer@wv.gov.

WW-6A2
(1/12)

STATE OF WEST VIRGINIA
DEPARTMENT OF ENVIRONMENTAL PROTECTION, OFFICE OF OIL AND GAS
NOTICE OF SEISMIC ACTIVITY

Notice Time Requirement: The notice shall be provided at least **THREE (3) DAYS** prior to commencement of the seismic activity.
Date of Notice: _____ **Date of Seismic Activity:** _____

Delivery method pursuant to West Virginia Code § 22-6A-10a

☐ PERSONAL   ☐ REGISTERED   ☐ METHOD OF DELIVERY THAT REQUIRES A
SERVICE   MAIL   RECEIPT OR SIGNATURE CONFIRMATION

Pursuant to West Virginia Code § 22-6A-10(j), (1) Prior to conducting any seismic activity for seismic exploration for natural gas to be extracted using horizontal drilling methods, the company or person performing the activity shall provide notice to Miss Utility of West Virginia Inc. and to all surface owners, coal owners and lessees, and natural gas storage field operators on whose property blasting, percussion or other seismic-related activities will occur. (2) The notice shall be provided at least three days prior to commencement of the seismic activity. (3) The notice shall also include a reclamation plan in accordance with the erosion and sediment control manual that provides for the reclamation of any areas disturbed as a result of the seismic activity, including filling of shotholes used for blasting. (4) Nothing in this subsection decides questions as to whether seismic activity may be secured by mineral owners, surface owners or other ownership interests.

Notice is hereby provided to:

☐ MISS UTILITY OF WEST VIRGINIA INC.   ☐ COAL OWNER OR LESSEE
Address: _____   Name: _____
_____   Address: _____
                                                     _____

☐ SURFACE OWNER(s)   ☐ NATURAL GAS STORAGE FIELD OPERATOR
Name: _____   Name: _____
Address: _____   Address: _____
_____   _____
Name: _____
Address: _____
_____

Notice is hereby given:
Pursuant to West Virginia Code § 22-6A-10(j), notice is hereby given that the undersigned well operator will be conducting seismic related activities for seismic exploration for natural gas to be extracted using horizontal drilling methods on the tract of land as follows:
State:_____;   UTM Coordinate NAD83 Northing:_____;
County:_____;   UTM Coordinate NAD83 Easting: _____;
District:_____;   Public Road Access: _____;
Quadrangle: _____;   Watershed: _____;
                                         Generally used farm name: _____;

This Notice Shall Include:
Pursuant to West Virginia Code § 22-6A-10(j)(3), this notice shall include a reclamation plan in accordance with the erosion and sediment control manual that provides for the reclamation of any areas disturbed as a result of the seismic activity, including filling of shotholes used for blasting. Additional information related to horizontal drilling may be obtained from the Secretary, at the WV Department of Environmental Protection headquarters, located at 601 57th Street, SE, Charleston, WV 25304 (304-926-0450) or by visiting www.dep.wv.gov/oil-and-gas/pages/default.aspx.

Notice is hereby given by:
Well Operator:_____   Address:_____
Telephone: _____   _____
Email:_____   Facsimile: _____

Oil and Gas Privacy Notice:
The Office of Oil and Gas processes your personal information, such as name, address and telephone number, as part of our regulatory duties. Your personal information may be disclosed to other State agencies or third parties in the normal course of business or as needed to comply with statutory or regulatory requirements, including Freedom of Information Act requests. Our office will appropriately secure your personal information. If you have any questions about our use or your personal information, please contact DEP's Chief Privacy Officer at depprivacyofficer@wv.gov.

Page 1 of _____

WW-6A3
(1/12)

Operator Well No. _____

STATE OF WEST VIRGINIA
DEPARTMENT OF ENVIRONMENTAL PROTECTION, OFFICE OF OIL AND GAS
NOTICE OF ENTRY FOR PLAT SURVEY

Notice Time Requirement: Notice shall be provided at least **SEVEN (7)** days but no more than **FORTY-FIVE (45)** days prior to entry

Date of Notice: _____   **Date of Planned Entry**: _____

Delivery method pursuant to West Virginia Code § 22-6A-10a

☐ PERSONAL   ☐ REGISTERED   ☐ METHOD OF DELIVERY THAT REQUIRES A
   SERVICE   MAIL   RECEIPT OR SIGNATURE CONFIRMATION

Pursuant to West Virginia Code § 22-6A-10(a), Prior to filing a permit application, the operator shall provide notice of planned entry on to the surface tract to conduct any plat surveys required pursuant to this article. Such notice shall be provided at least seven days but no more than forty-five days prior to such entry to: (1) The surface owner of such tract; (2) to any owner or lessee of coal seams beneath such tract that has filed a declaration pursuant to section thirty-six, article six, chapter twenty-two of this code; and (3) any owner of minerals underlying such tract in the county tax records. The notice shall include a statement that copies of the state Erosion and Sediment Control Manual and the statutes and rules related to oil and gas exploration and production may be obtained from the Secretary, which statement shall include contact information, including the address for a web page on the Secretary's web site, to enable the surface owner to obtain copies from the secretary.

Notice is hereby provided to:

☐ SURFACE OWNER(s)   ☐ COAL OWNER OR LESSEE
Name: _____   Name: _____
Address: _____   Address: _____
_____   _____
Name: _____
Address: _____   ☐ MINERAL OWNER(s)
_____   Name: _____
Name: _____   Address: _____
Address: _____   _____
_____   *please attach additional forms if necessary

Notice is hereby given:
Pursuant to West Virginia Code § 22-6A-10(a), notice is hereby given that the undersigned well operator is planning entry to conduct a plat survey on the tract of land as follows:
State: _____   Approx. Latitude & Longitude: _____
County: _____   Public Road Access: _____
District: _____   Watershed: _____
Quadrangle: _____   Generally used farm name: _____

Copies of the state Erosion and Sediment Control Manual and the statutes and rules related to oil and gas exploration and production may be obtained from the Secretary, at the WV Department of Environmental Protection headquarters, located at 601 57th Street, SE, Charleston, WV 25304 (304-926-0450). Copies of such documents or additional information related to horizontal drilling may be obtained from the Secretary by visiting www.dep.wv.gov/oil-and-gas/pages/default.aspx.

Notice is hereby given by:
Well Operator: _____   Address: _____
Telephone: _____   _____
Email: _____   Facsimile: _____

Oil and Gas Privacy Notice:
The Office of Oil and Gas processes your personal information, such as name, address and telephone number, as part of our regulatory duties. Your personal information may be disclosed to other State agencies or third parties in the normal course of business or as needed to comply with statutory or regulatory requirements, including Freedom of Information Act requests. Our office will appropriately secure your personal information. If you have any questions about our use or your personal information, please contact DEP's Chief Privacy Officer at depprivacyofficer@wv.gov.

WW-6A4
(1/12)

Operator Well No. _____

STATE OF WEST VIRGINIA
DEPARTMENT OF ENVIRONMENTAL PROTECTION, OFFICE OF OIL AND GAS
NOTICE OF INTENT TO DRILL

Pursuant to W. Va. Code § 22-6A-16(b), the Notice of Intent to Drill is only required if the notice requirements of W. Va. Code § 22-6A-10(a) have NOT been met or if the Notice of Intent to Drill requirement has NOT been waived in writing by the surface owner.

Notice Time Requirement: Notice shall be provided at least **TEN (10)** days prior to filing a permit application.
Date of Notice: _____   **Date Permit Application Filed**: _____

Delivery method pursuant to West Virginia Code § 22-6A-16(b)

☐ HAND   ☐ CERTIFIED MAIL
    DELIVERY   RETURN RECEIPT REQUESTED

Pursuant to W. Va. Code § 22-6A-16(b), at least ten days prior to filing a permit application, an operator shall, by certified mail return receipt requested or hand delivery, give the surface owner notice of its intent to enter upon the surface owner's land for the purpose of drilling a horizontal well: *Provided,* That notice given pursuant to subsection (a), section ten of this article satisfies the requirements of this subsection as of the date the notice was provided to the surface owner: *Provided, however,* That the notice requirements of this subsection may be waived in writing by the surface owner. The notice, if required, shall include the name, address, telephone number, and if available, facsimile number and electronic mail address of the operator and the operator's authorized representative.

Notice is hereby provided to the SURFACE OWNER(s):
Name: _____   Name: _____
Address: _____   Address: _____
_____   _____

Notice is hereby given:
Pursuant to West Virginia Code § 22-6A-16(b), notice is hereby given that the undersigned well operator has an intent to enter upon the surface owner's land for the purpose of drilling a horizontal well on the tract of land as follows:
State: _____   UTM NAD 83   Easting: _____
County: _____   Northing: _____
District: _____   Public Road Access: _____
Quadrangle: _____   Generally used farm name: _____
Watershed: _____

This Notice Shall Include:
Pursuant to West Virginia Code § 22-6A-16(b), this notice shall include the name, address, telephone number, and if available, facsimile number and electronic mail address of the operator and the operator's authorized representative. Additional information related to horizontal drilling may be obtained from the Secretary, at the WV Department of Environmental Protection headquarters, located at 601 57th Street, SE, Charleston, WV 25304 (304-926-0450) or by visiting www.dep.wv.gov/oil-and-gas/pages/default.aspx.

Notice is hereby given by:
Well Operator: _____   Authorized Representative: _____
Address: _____   Address: _____
_____   _____
Telephone: _____   Telephone: _____
Email: _____   Email: _____
Facsimile: _____   Facsimile: _____

Oil and Gas Privacy Notice:
The Office of Oil and Gas processes your personal information, such as name, address and telephone number, as part of our regulatory duties. Your personal information may be disclosed to other State agencies or third parties in the normal course of business or as needed to comply with statutory or regulatory requirements, including Freedom of Information Act requests. Our office will appropriately secure your personal information. If you have any questions about our use or your personal information, please contact DEP's Chief Privacy Officer at depprivacyofficer@wv.gov.

WW-6A4W
(1/12)

Operator Well No. _____

STATE OF WEST VIRGINIA
DEPARTMENT OF ENVIRONMENTAL PROTECTION, OFFICE OF OIL AND GAS
NOTICE OF INTENT TO DRILL

WAIVER

Pursuant to W. Va. Code § 22-6A-16(b), at least ten days prior to filing a permit application, an operator shall, by certified mail return receipt requested or hand delivery, give the surface owner notice of its intent to enter upon the surface owner's land for the purpose of drilling a horizontal well: *Provided,* That notice given pursuant to subsection (a), section ten of this article satisfies the requirements of this subsection as of the date the notice was provided to the surface owner: *Provided, however,* That the notice requirements of this subsection may be waived in writing by the surface owner. The notice, if required, shall include the name, address, telephone number, and if available, facsimile number and electronic mail address of the operator and the operator's authorized representative.

Surface Owner Waiver:
I, _____, hereby state that I have read the notice provisions listed above and hereby waive the notice requirements under West Virginia Code § 22-6A-16(b) for the tract of land as follows:

State:	_____	UTM NAD 83 Easting:	_____
County:	_____	Northing:	_____
District:	_____	Public Road Access:	_____
Quadrangle:	_____	Generally used farm name:	_____
Watershed:	_____		

Name: _____   Signature: _____
Address: _____
_____   Date: _____

Oil and Gas Privacy Notice:
The Office of Oil and Gas processes your personal information, such as name, address and telephone number, as part of our regulatory duties. Your personal information may be disclosed to other State agencies or third parties in the normal course of business or as needed to comply with statutory or regulatory requirements, including Freedom of Information Act requests. Our office will appropriately secure your personal information. If you have any questions about our use or your personal information, please contact DEP's Chief Privacy Officer at depprivacyofficer@wv.gov.

WW-6A5
(1/12)

Operator Well No. _____

STATE OF WEST VIRGINIA
DEPARTMENT OF ENVIRONMENTAL PROTECTION, OFFICE OF OIL AND GAS
NOTICE OF PLANNED OPERATION

Notice Time Requirement: notice shall be provided no later than the **filing date of permit application.**
Date of Notice: _____   **Date Permit Application Filed:** _____

Delivery method pursuant to West Virginia Code § 22-6A-16(c)

☐ CERTIFIED MAIL   ☐ HAND
   RETURN RECEIPT REQUESTED   DELIVERY

Pursuant to W. Va. Code § 22-6A-16(c), no later than the date for filing the permit application, an operator shall, by certified mail return receipt requested or hand delivery, give the surface owner whose land will be used for the drilling of a horizontal well notice of the planned operation. The notice required by this subsection shall include: (1) A copy of this code section; (2) The information required to be provided by subsection (b), section ten of this article to a surface owner whose land will be used in conjunction with the drilling of a horizontal well; and (3) A proposed surface use and compensation agreement containing an offer of compensation for damages to the surface affected by oil and gas operations to the extent the damages are compensable under article six-b of this chapter. (d) The notices required by this section shall be given to the surface owner at the address listed in the records of the sheriff at the time of notice.

Notice is hereby provided to the SURFACE OWNER(s)
(at the address listed in the records of the sheriff at the time of notice):
Name: _____   Name: _____
Address: _____   Address: _____
_____   _____

Notice is hereby given:
Pursuant to West Virginia Code § 22-6A-16(c), notice is hereby given that the undersigned well operator has developed a planned operation on the surface owner's land for the purpose of drilling a horizontal well on the tract of land as follows:

State: _____   UTM NAD 83   Easting: _____
County: _____   Northing: _____
District: _____   Public Road Access: _____
Quadrangle: _____   Generally used farm name: _____
Watershed: _____

This Notice Shall Include:
Pursuant to West Virginia Code § 22-6A-16(c), this notice shall include: (1)A copy of this code section; (2) The information required to be provided by **W. Va. Code § 22-6A-10(b)** to a surface owner whose land will be used in conjunction with the drilling of a horizontal well; and (3) A proposed surface use and compensation agreement containing an offer of compensation for damages to the surface affected by oil and gas operations to the extent the damages are compensable under article six-b of this chapter. Additional information related to horizontal drilling may be obtained from the Secretary, at the WV Department of Environmental Protection headquarters, located at 601 57th Street, SE, Charleston, WV 25304 (304-926-0450) or by visiting www.dep.wv.gov/oil-and-gas/pages/default.aspx.

Well Operator: _____   Address: _____
Telephone: _____
Email: _____   Facsimile: _____

Oil and Gas Privacy Notice:
The Office of Oil and Gas processes your personal information, such as name, address and telephone number, as part of our regulatory duties. Your personal information may be disclosed to other State agencies or third parties in the normal course of business or as needed to comply with statutory or regulatory requirements, including Freedom of Information Act requests. Our office will appropriately secure your personal information. If you have any questions about our use or your personal information, please contact DEP's Chief Privacy Officer at depprivacyofficer@wv.gov.

WW-6RW
(1-12)

API NO. 47-_____-_____
OPERATOR WELL NO. _____
Well Pad Name: _____

STATE OF WEST VIRGINIA
DEPARTMENT OF ENVIRONMENTAL PROTECTION, OFFICE OF OIL AND GAS
WELL LOCATION RESTRICTION WAIVER

The well operator, _____ is applying for a permit from the State of West Virginia to conduct oil or gas well work. Please be advised that well work permits are valid for twenty-four (24) months.

Well Location Restrictions
Pursuant to West Virginia Code § 22-6A-12(a), Wells may not be drilled within two hundred fifty feet measured horizontally from any existing water well or developed spring used for human or domestic animal consumption. The center of well pads may not be located within six hundred twenty-five feet of an occupied dwelling structure, or a building two thousand five hundred square feet or larger used to house or shelter dairy cattle or poultry husbandry. This limitation is applicable to those wells, developed springs, dwellings or agricultural buildings that existed on the date a notice to the surface owner of planned entry for surveying or staking as provided in section ten of this article or a notice of intent to drill a horizontal well as provided in subsection (b), section sixteen of this article was provided, whichever occurs first, and to any dwelling under construction prior to that date. This limitation may be waived by written consent of the surface owner transmitted to the department and recorded in the real property records maintained by the clerk of the county commission for the county in which such property is located. Furthermore, the well operator may be granted a variance by the secretary from these distance restrictions upon submission of a plan which identifies the sufficient measures, facilities or practices to be employed during well site construction, drilling and operations. The variance, if granted, shall include terms and conditions the department requires to ensure the safety and protection of affected persons and property. The terms and conditions may include insurance, bonding and indemnification, as well as technical requirements.

WAIVER

I, _____, hereby state that I have read the Instructions to Persons Named on Page WW-6A and the associated provisions listed above, and that I have received copies of a Notice of Application, an Application for a Well Work Permit on Form WW-6A and attachments consisting of pages one (1) through _____, including the erosion and sediment control plan, if required, and the well plat, all for proposed well work on the tract of land as follows:

State: _____   UTM NAD 83 Easting: _____
County: _____   UTM NAD 83 Northing: _____
District: _____   Public Road Access: _____
Quadrangle: _____   Generally used farm name: _____
Watershed: _____

I further state that I have no objection to the planned work described in these materials, and I have no objection to a permit being issued on those materials and I therefore waive all well site restrictions listed under West Virginia Code § 22-6A-12(a).

WELL SITE RESTRICTIONS BEING WAIVED	FOR EXECUTION BY A NATURAL PERSON
*Please check all that apply	Signature: _____
	Print Name: _____
☐ EXISTING WATER WELLS	Date: _____
	FOR EXECUTION BY A CORPORATION, ETC.
☐ DEVELOPED SPRINGS	Company: _____
	By: _____
☐ DWELLINGS	Its: _____
	Signature: _____
☐ AGRICULTURAL BUILDINGS	Date: _____

Well Operator: _____   Signature: _____
By: _____   Telephone: _____
Its: _____

NOTARY SEAL	Subscribed and sworn before me this_____day of _____
	_____Notary Public
	My Commission Expires _____

Oil and Gas Privacy Notice:
The Office of Oil and Gas processes your personal information, such as name, address and telephone number, as part of our regulatory duties. Your personal information may be disclosed to other State agencies or third parties in the normal course of business or as needed to comply with statutory or regulatory requirements, including Freedom of Information Act requests. Our office will appropriately secure your personal information. If you have any questions about our use or your personal information, please contact DEP's Chief Privacy Officer at depprivacyofficer@wv.gov.

WW-6A1   Operator's Well No. _____
(5/13)

INFORMATION SUPPLIED UNDER WEST VIRGINIA CODE
Chapter 22, Article 6A, Section 5(a)(5)
IN LIEU OF FILING LEASE(S) AND OTHER CONTINUING CONTRACT(S)

       Under the oath required to make the verification on page 1 of this Notice and Application, I depose and say that I am the person who signed the Notice and Application for the Applicant, and that –

(1) the tract of land is the same tract described in this Application, partly or wholly depicted in the accompanying plat, and described in the Construction and Reclamation Plan;

(2) the parties and recordation data (if recorded) for lease(s) or other continuing contract(s) by which the Applicant claims the right to extract, produce or market the oil or gas are as follows:

Lease Name or Number	Grantor, Lessor, etc.	Grantee, Lessee, etc.	Royalty	Book/Page

Acknowledgement of Possible Permitting/Approval
In Addition to the Office of Oil and Gas

The permit applicant for the proposed well work addressed in this application hereby acknowledges the possibility of the need for permits and/or approvals from local, state, or federal entities in addition to the DEP, Office of Oil and Gas, including but not limited to the following:

- WV Division of Water and Waste Management
- WV Division of Natural Resources WV Division of Highways
- U.S. Army Corps of Engineers
- U.S. Fish and Wildlife Service
- County Floodplain Coordinator

The applicant further acknowledges that any Office of Oil and Gas permit in no way overrides, replaces, or nullifies the need for other permits/approvals that may be necessary and further affirms that all needed permits/approvals should be acquired from the appropriate authority before the affected activity is initiated.

Well Operator: _____

By: _____

Its: _____

Page 1 of _____

WW-9
(9/13)

API Number 47 - _____ - _____
Operator's Well No._____

STATE OF WEST VIRGINIA
DEPARTMENT OF ENVIRONMENTAL PROTECTION
OFFICE OF OIL AND GAS

FLUIDS/ CUTTINGS DISPOSAL & RECLAMATION PLAN

Operator Name_____ OP Code _____

Watershed (HUC 10)_____ Quadrangle _____

Elevation _____ County_____ District_____

Do you anticipate using more than 5,000 bbls of water to complete the proposed well work?   Yes ☐   No ☐

Will a pit be used?   Yes ☐   No ☐

    If so, please describe anticipated pit waste: _____

    Will a synthetic liner be used in the pit? Yes ☐   No ☐   If so, what ml.?_____

    Proposed Disposal Method For Treated Pit Wastes:

        _____ Land Application
        _____ Underground Injection (UIC Permit Number_____)
        _____ Reuse (at API Number_____)
        _____ Off Site Disposal (Supply form WW-9 for disposal location)
        _____ Other (Explain_____

Will closed loop system be used? If so, describe: _____

Drilling medium anticipated for this well (vertical and horizontal)? Air, freshwater, oil based, etc. _____

    -If oil based, what type? Synthetic, petroleum, etc._____

Additives to be used in drilling medium?_____

Drill cuttings disposal method? Leave in pit, landfill, removed offsite, etc._____

    -If left in pit and plan to solidify what medium will be used? (cement, lime, sawdust)_____

    -Landfill or offsite name/permit number? _____

        I certify that I understand and agree to the terms and conditions of the GENERAL WATER POLLUTION PERMIT issued on August 1, 2005, by the Office of Oil and Gas of the West Virginia Department of Environmental Protection. I understand that the provisions of the permit are enforceable by law. Violations of any term or condition of the general permit and/or other applicable law or regulation can lead to enforcement action.

        I certify under penalty of law that I have personally examined and am familiar with the information submitted on this application form and all attachments thereto and that, based on my inquiry of those individuals immediately responsible for obtaining the information, I believe that the information is true, accurate, and complete. I am aware that there are significant penalties for submitting false information, including the possibility of fine or imprisonment.

Company Official Signature_____

Company Official (Typed Name)_____

Company Official Title_____

Subscribed and sworn before me this_____ day of_____, 20_____

_____ Notary Public

My commission expires_____

Form WW-9

Operator's Well No._____

Proposed Revegetation Treatment: Acres Disturbed _____ Prevegetation pH _____

    Lime _____ Tons/acre or to correct to pH _____

    Fertilizer type _____

    Fertilizer amount_____ lbs/acre

    Mulch_____Tons/acre

Seed Mixtures

Temporary		**Permanent**	
Seed Type	lbs/acre	Seed Type	lbs/acre
_____	_____	_____	_____
_____	_____	_____	_____
_____	_____	_____	_____

Attach:
Drawing(s) of road, location, pit and proposed area for land application (unless engineered plans including this info have been provided)

Photocopied section of involved 7.5' topographic sheet.

Plan Approved by:_____

Comments: _____

_____

_____

_____

_____

_____

_____

_____

Title:_____   Date:_____

Field Reviewed?   (_____) Yes   (_____) No

WW-6A7
(6-12)

OPERATOR:_____   WELL NO:_____

PAD NAME:_____

REVIEWED BY: _____   SIGNATURE: _____

WELL RESTRICTIONS CHECKLIST

HORIZONTAL 6A WELL

Well Restrictions

☐ At Least 100 Feet from Pad and LOD (including any E&S Control Feature) to any Perennial Stream, Lake, Pond, Reservoir or Wetland; OR

☐ DEP Waiver and Permit Conditions

☐ At Least 300 Feet from Pad and LOD (including any E&S Control Feature) to any Naturally Producing Trout Stream; OR

☐ DEP Waiver and Permit Conditions

☐ At Least 1000 Feet from Pad and LOD (including any E&S Control Feature) to any Groundwater Intake or Public Water Supply; OR

☐ DEP Waiver and Permit Conditions

☐ At Least 250 Feet from an Existing Water Well or Developed Spring to Well Being Drilled; OR

☐ Surface Owner Waiver and Recorded with County Clerk, OR

☐ DEP Variance and Permit Conditions

☐ At Least 625 Feet from an Occupied Dwelling Structure to Center of the Pad; OR

☐ Surface Owner Waiver and Recorded with County Clerk, OR

☐ DEP Variance and Permit Conditions

☐ At Least 625 Feet from Agricultural Buildings Larger than 2500 Square Feet to the Center of the Pad; OR

☐ Surface Owner Waiver and Recorded with County Clerk, OR

☐ DEP Variance and Permit Conditions

Horizontal 6A Well Permit App. Checklist   Operator Well No. _____

OPERATOR: _____

PAD NAME: _____ WELL: _____

PAD BUILT: ____YES ____NO   DATE REVIEWED: _____INT.____

REVIEWED BY (APPLICANT): _____

CONTACT PHONE: _____ EMAIL: _____

APPLICANT SIGNATURE: _____

CHECKLIST FOR FILING A PERMIT
HORIZONTAL 6A WELL

Please include these required elements in the Horizontal Well 6A applications, in order listed below. Do not use staples.

First Well	Subsequent Well
$10,150.00 ☐	$5,150.00 ☐

_____ Fees

_____Checklist / Cover letter

_____ WW-6B Notice of Application   _____ Field Approved

_____Cement Additives

_____Well Bore Schematic

_____ WW-9 Fluids/Cuttings Disposal and Reclamation Plan   _____ Field Approved

_____ Site Safety Plan   _____ Field Approved

_____ Water Management Plan   _____ DWWM Approval

_____Topographic Map w/water purveyors, showing access road

_____ Mylar Plat (Signed and sealed) (Surface Owner matches WW-6A)

_____ WW-6A1 Lease Information

_____ Road Crossing Letter

_____ WW-PN Application Notice by Publication

_____ Public Notice (dated copy of advertisement or affidavit of publication)

Revised 12/30/13

Horizontal 6A Well Permit App. Checklist   Operator Well No. _____

_____ WW-6AC Notice Certifications, notarized

_____ WW-6A Notice of Application notarized w/ any attachments

_____Topographic Map with labeled surrounding water wells

_____ Certified Mail receipts for WW-6A

_____ WW-6A3 Notice of Entry for Plat Survey

_____ Certified Mail receipts for WW-6A3

_____ WW-6A4 Notice of Intent to Drill

_____ Certified Mail receipts for WW-6A4

_____ WW-6A5 Notice of Planned Operation

_____ Certified Mail receipts for WW-6A5

_____ WW-6RW Well Location Restriction Waiver

_____ WW-6AW Voluntary Statement of No Objection

_____Waiver for Surface Owner at Wellhead

_____Waiver for Surface Owner for Roads or other Disturbances

_____Waiver for Coal Owner, Operator or Lessee

_____Waiver for surface owner for Impoundment or Pit

_____Waiver for Surface Owner or Water Purveyor within 1500 feet of Center of Pad

_____Waiver for Natural gas Storage Field Operator

_____ Road Bonding Agreement / DOH Certification

_____ Frac Additives List of Chemical Names & CAS #s

_____ Site Construction, Reclamation, Erosion & Sediment Control Plans   _____ Field Approved

_____Copy of To Scale Plans

_____Inspector packet mailed to inspector (Plat, Topographic Map, WW-6B, WW-9, All Plans)

_____ Bond ($250,000)

_____Operator is registered with the SOS

Revised 12/30/13

Horizontal 6A Well Permit App. Checklist   Operator Well No. _____

_____Workers Compensation / Unemployment Insurance account is OK

_____ Professional Engineer/Company has COA

_____ Check for Mine Data at proposed coordinates

_____ Check for Floodplain Data at proposed coordinates

_____ IMP-1A Associated Pit or Impoundment

_____ WW-6A7 Well Restrictions Form w/ Signature

   _____ At Least 100 Feet from Pad and LOD (including any E&S Control Feature) to any Perennial Stream, Lake, Pond, Reservoir or Wetland

      _____ DEP Waiver and Permit Conditions

   _____ At Least 300 Feet from Pad and LOD (including any E&S Control Feature) to any Naturally Producing Trout Stream

      _____ DEP Waiver and Permit Conditions

   _____ At Least 1000 Feet from Pad and LOD (including any E&S Control Feature) to any Groundwater Intake or Public Water Supply

      _____ DEP Waiver and Permit Conditions

   _____ At Least 250 Feet from an Existing Water Well or Developed Spring to Well Being Drilled

      _____ Surface Owner Waiver and Recorded with County Clerk, OR

      _____ DEP Variance and Permit Conditions

   _____ At Least 625 Feet from an Occupied Dwelling Structure to the Center of the Pad

      _____ Surface Owner Waiver and Recorded with County Clerk, OR

      _____ DEP Variance and Permit Conditions

   _____ At Least 625 Feet from Agricultural Buildings Larger than 2500 Square Feet to the Center of the Pad

      _____ Surface Owner Waiver and Recorded with County Clerk, OR

      _____ DEP Variance and Permit Conditions

Revised 12/30/13

Appendix C

Electricity

A. U.S. Transmission Grid

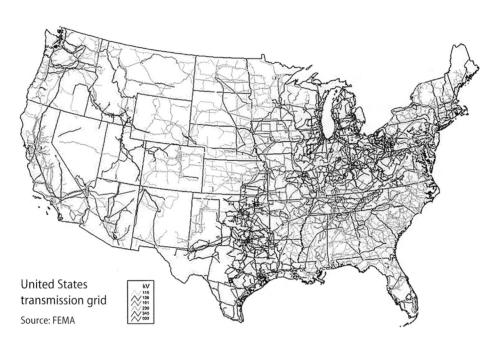

United States
transmission grid

Source: FEMA

| kV |
| 115 |
| 138 |
| 161 |
| 230 |
| 345 |
| 500 |

For the most current view of the energy infrastructure, consult the EIA's interactive U.S. Energy Mapping System, which is available here: http://www.eia.gov/state/maps.cfm.

B. Federal Power Act

SUBCHAPTER II—REGULATION OF ELECTRIC UTILITY COMPANIES ENGAGED IN INTERSTATE COMMERCE

§ 824. Declaration of policy; application of subchapter

(a) Federal regulation of transmission and sale of electric energy

It is declared that the business of transmitting and selling electric energy for ultimate distribution to the public is affected with a public interest, and that Federal regulation of matters relating to generation to the extent provided in this subchapter and subchapter III of this chapter and of that part of such business which consists of the transmission of electric energy in interstate commerce and the sale of such energy at wholesale in interstate commerce is necessary in the public interest, such Federal regulation, however, to extend only to those matters which are not subject to regulation by the States.

(b) Use or sale of electric energy in interstate commerce

(1) The provisions of this subchapter shall apply to the transmission of electric energy in interstate commerce and to the sale of electric energy at wholesale in interstate commerce, but except as provided in paragraph (2) shall not apply to any other sale of electric energy or deprive a State or State commission of its lawful authority now exercised over the exportation of hydroelectric energy which is transmitted across a State line. The Commission shall have jurisdiction over all facilities for such transmission or sale of electric energy, but shall not have jurisdiction, except as specifically provided in this subchapter and subchapter III of this chapter, over facilities used for the generation of electric energy or over facilities used in local distribution or only for the transmission of electric energy in intrastate commerce, or over facilities for the transmission of electric energy consumed wholly by the transmitter.

(2) Notwithstanding subsection (f) of this section, the provisions of sections 824b(a)(2), 824e(e), 824i, 824j, 824j–1, 824k, 824o, 824p, 824q, 824r, 824s, 824t, 824u, and 824v of this title shall apply to the entities described in such provisions, and such entities shall be subject to the jurisdiction of the Commission for purposes of carrying out such provisions and for purposes of applying the enforcement authorities of this chapter with respect to such provisions. Compliance with any order or rule of the Commission under the provisions of section 824b(a)(2), 824e(e), 824i, 824j, 824j–1, 824k, 824o, 824p, 824q, 824r, 824s, 824t, 824u, or 824v of this title, shall not make an electric utility or other entity subject to the jurisdiction of the Commission for any purposes other than the purposes specified in the preceding sentence.

(c) Electric energy in interstate commerce

For the purpose of this subchapter, electric energy shall be held to be transmitted in interstate commerce if transmitted from a State and consumed at any point outside thereof; but only insofar as such transmission takes place within the United States.

(d) "Sale of electric energy at wholesale" defined

The term "sale of electric energy at wholesale" when used in this subchapter, means a sale of electric energy to any person for resale.

(e) "Public utility" defined

The term "public utility" when used in this subchapter and subchapter III of this chapter means any person who owns or operates facilities subject to the jurisdiction of the Commission under this subchapter (other than facilities subject to such jurisdiction solely by reason of section 824e(e), 824e(f),[1] 824i, 824j, 824j–1, 824k, 824o, 824p, 824q, 824r, 824s, 824t, 824u, or 824v of this title).

(f) United States, State, political subdivision of a State, or agency or instrumentality thereof exempt

No provision in this subchapter shall apply to, or be deemed to include, the United States, a State or any political subdivision of a State, an electric cooperative that receives financing under the Rural Electrification Act of 1936 (7 U.S.C. 901 et seq.) or that sells less than 4,000,000 megawatt hours of electricity per year, or any agency, authority, or instrumentality of any one or more of the foregoing, or any corporation which is wholly owned, directly or indirectly, by any one or more of the foregoing, or any officer, agent, or employee of any of the foregoing acting as such in the course of his official duty, unless such provision makes specific reference thereto.

(g) Books and records

(1) Upon written order of a State commission, a State commission may examine the books, accounts, memoranda, contracts, and records of—

(A) an electric utility company subject to its regulatory authority under State law,

(B) any exempt wholesale generator selling energy at wholesale to such electric utility, and

(C) any electric utility company, or holding company thereof, which is an associate company or affiliate of an exempt wholesale generator which sells electric energy to an electric utility company referred to in subparagraph (A),

wherever located, if such examination is required for the effective discharge of the State commission's regulatory responsibilities affecting the provision of electric service.

(2) Where a State commission issues an order pursuant to paragraph (1), the State commission shall not publicly disclose trade secrets or sensitive commercial information.

(3) Any United States district court located in the State in which the State commission referred to in paragraph (1) is located shall have jurisdiction to enforce compliance with this subsection.

(4) Nothing in this section shall—

(A) preempt applicable State law concerning the provision of records and other information; or

(B) in any way limit rights to obtain records and other information under Federal law, contracts, or otherwise.

(5) As used in this subsection the terms "affiliate", "associate company", "electric utility company", "holding company", "subsidiary company", and "exempt wholesale generator" shall have the same meaning as when used in the Public Utility Holding Company Act of 2005 [42 U.S.C. 16451 et seq.].

(June 10, 1920, ch. 285, pt. II, §201, as added Aug. 26, 1935, ch. 687, title II, §213, 49 Stat. 847; amended Pub. L. 95–617, title II, §204(b), Nov. 9, 1978, 92 Stat. 3140; Pub.

---

1. *So in original. Section 824e of this title does not contain a subsec. (f).*

L. 102–486, title VII, § 714, Oct. 24, 1992, 106 Stat. 2911; Pub. L. 109–58, title XII, §§ 1277(b)(1), 1291(c), 1295(a), Aug. 8, 2005, 119 Stat. 978, 985.)

References in Text

The Rural Electrification Act of 1936, referred to in subsec. (f), is act May 20, 1936, ch. 432, 49 Stat. 1363, as amended, which is classified generally to chapter 31 (§ 901 et seq.) of Title 7, Agriculture. For complete classification of this Act to the Code, see section 901 of Title 7 and Tables.

The Public Utility Holding Company Act of 2005, referred to in subsec. (g)(5), is subtitle F of title XII of Pub. L. 109–58, Aug. 8, 2005, 119 Stat. 972, which is classified principally to part D (§ 16451 et seq.) of subchapter XII of chapter 149 of Title 42, The Public Health and Welfare. For complete classification of this Act to the Code, see Short Title note set out under section 15801 of Title 42 and Tables.

Amendments

2005 — Subsec. (b)(2). Pub. L. 109–58, § 1295(a)(1), substituted "Notwithstanding subsection (f) of this section, the provisions of sections 824b(a)(2), 824e(e), 824i, 824j, 824j–1, 824k, 824o, 824p, 824q, 824r, 824s, 824t, 824u, and 824v of this title" for "The provisions of sections 824i, 824j, and 824k of this title" and "Compliance with any order or rule of the Commission under the provisions of section 824b(a)(2), 824e(e), 824i, 824j, 824j–1, 824k, 824o, 824p, 824q, 824r, 824s, 824t, 824u, or 824v of this title" for "Compliance with any order of the Commission under the provisions of section 824i or 824j of this title".

Subsec. (e). Pub. L. 109–58, § 1295(a)(2), substituted "section 824e(e), 824e(f), 824i, 824j, 824j–1, 824k, 824o, 824p, 824q, 824r, 824s, 824t, 824u, or 824v of this title" for "section 824i, 824j, or 824k of this title".

Subsec. (f). Pub. L. 109–58, § 1291(c), which directed amendment of subsec. (f) by substituting "political subdivision of a State, an electric cooperative that receives financing under the Rural Electrification Act of 1936 (7 U.S.C. 901 et seq.) or that sells less than 4,000,000 megawatt hours of electricity per year," for "political subdivision of a state,", was executed by making the substitution for "political subdivision of a State," to reflect the probable intent of Congress.

Subsec. (g)(5). Pub. L. 109–58, § 1277(b)(1), substituted "2005" for "1935".

1992 — Subsec. (g). Pub. L. 102–486 added subsec. (g).

1978 — Subsec. (b). Pub. L. 95–617, § 204(b)(1), designated existing provisions as par. (1), inserted "except as provided in paragraph (2)" after "in interstate commerce, but", and added par. (2).

Subsec. (e). Pub. L. 95–617, § 204(b)(2), inserted "(other than facilities subject to such jurisdiction solely by reason of section 824i, 824j, or 824k of this title)" after "under this subchapter".

Effective Date of 2005 Amendment

Amendment by section 1277(b)(1) of Pub. L. 109–58 effective 6 months after Aug. 8, 2005, with provisions relating to effect of compliance with certain regulations approved and made effective prior to such date, see section 1274 of Pub. L. 109–58, set out as an Effective Date note under section 16451 of Title 42, The Public Health and Welfare.

State Authorities; Construction

Nothing in amendment by Pub. L. 102–486 to be construed as affecting or intending to affect, or in any way to interfere with, authority of any State or local government relating to environmental protection or siting of facilities, see section 731 of Pub. L. 102–486, set out as a note under section 796 of this title.

PRIOR ACTIONS; EFFECT ON OTHER AUTHORITIES

Pub. L. 95–617, title II, §214, Nov. 9, 1978, 92 Stat. 3149, provided that:

"(a) Prior Actions.—No provision of this title [enacting sections 823a, 824i to 824k, 824a–1 to 824a–3 and 825q–1 of this title, amending sections 796, 824, 824a, 824d, and 825d of this title and enacting provisions set out as notes under sections 824a, 824d, and 825d of this title] or of any amendment made by this title shall apply to, or affect, any action taken by the Commission [Federal Energy Regulatory Commission] before the date of the enactment of this Act [Nov. 9, 1978].

"(b) Other Authorities.—No provision of this title [enacting sections 823a, 824i to 824k, 824a–1 to 824a–3 and 825q–1 of this title, amending sections 796, 824, 824a, 824d, and 825d of this title and enacting provisions set out as notes under sections 824a, 824d, and 825d of this title] or of any amendment made by this title shall limit, impair or otherwise affect any authority of the Commission or any other agency or instrumentality of the United States under any other provision of law except as specifically provided in this title."

§ 824a. Interconnection and coordination of facilities; emergencies; transmission to foreign countries

(a) Regional districts; establishment; notice to State commissions

For the purpose of assuring an abundant supply of electric energy throughout the United States with the greatest possible economy and with regard to the proper utilization and conservation of natural resources, the Commission is empowered and directed to divide the country into regional districts for the voluntary interconnection and coordination of facilities for the generation, transmission, and sale of electric energy, and it may at any time thereafter, upon its own motion or upon application, make such modifications thereof as in its judgment will promote the public interest. Each such district shall embrace an area which, in the judgment of the Commission, can economically be served by such interconnection and coordinated electric facilities. It shall be the duty of the Commission to promote and encourage such interconnection and coordination within each such district and between such districts. Before establishing any such district and fixing or modifying the boundaries thereof the Commission shall give notice to the State commission of each State situated wholly or in part within such district, and shall afford each such State commission reasonable opportunity to present its views and recommendations, and shall receive and consider such views and recommendations.

(b) Sale or exchange of energy; establishing physical connections

Whenever the Commission, upon application of any State commission or of any person engaged in the transmission or sale of electric energy, and after notice to each State commission and public utility affected and after opportunity for hearing, finds such action necessary or appropriate in the public interest it may by order direct a public utility (if the Commission finds that no undue burden will be placed upon such public utility thereby) to establish physical connection of its transmission facilities with the facilities of one or more other persons engaged in the transmission or sale of electric energy, to sell energy to or exchange energy with such persons: *Provided,* That the Commission shall have no authority to compel the enlargement of generating facilities for such purposes, nor to compel such public utility to sell or exchange energy when to do so would impair its ability to render adequate service to its customers. The Commission may prescribe the terms and conditions of the arrangement to be made between the persons affected by any such order, including the apportionment of cost between them and the compensation or reimbursement reasonably due to any of them.

(c) Temporary connection and exchange of facilities during emergency

During the continuance of any war in which the United States is engaged, or whenever the Commission determines that an emergency exists by reason of a sudden increase in the demand for electric energy, or a shortage of electric energy or of facilities for the generation or transmission of electric energy, or of fuel or water for generating facilities, or other causes, the Commission shall have authority, either upon its own motion or upon complaint, with or without notice, hearing, or report, to require by order such temporary connections of facilities and such generation, delivery, interchange, or transmission of electric energy as in its judgment will best meet the emergency and serve the public interest. If the parties affected by such order fail to agree upon the terms of any arrangement between them in carrying out such order, the Commission, after hearing held either before or after such order takes effect, may prescribe by supplemental order such terms as it finds to be just and reasonable, including the compensation or reimbursement which should be paid to or by any such party.

(d) Temporary connection during emergency by persons without jurisdiction of Commission

During the continuance of any emergency requiring immediate action, any person engaged in the transmission or sale of electric energy and not otherwise subject to the jurisdiction of the Commission may make such temporary connections with any public utility subject to the jurisdiction of the Commission or may construct such temporary facilities for the transmission of electric energy in interstate commerce as may be necessary or appropriate to meet such emergency, and shall not become subject to the jurisdiction of the Commission by reason of such temporary connection or temporary construction: *Provided*, That such temporary connection shall be discontinued or such temporary construction removed or otherwise disposed of upon the termination of such emergency: *Provided further*, That upon approval of the Commission permanent connections for emergency use only may be made hereunder.

(e) Transmission of electric energy to foreign country

After six months from August 26, 1935, no person shall transmit any electric energy from the United States to a foreign country without first having secured an order of the Commission authorizing it to do so. The Commission shall issue such order upon application unless, after opportunity for hearing, it finds that the proposed transmission would impair the sufficiency of electric supply within the United States or would impede or tend to impede the coordination in the public interest of facilities subject to the jurisdiction of the Commission. The Commission may by its order grant such application in whole or in part, with such modifications and upon such terms and conditions as the Commission may find necessary or appropriate, and may from time to time, after opportunity for hearing and for good cause shown, make such supplemental orders in the premises as it may find necessary or appropriate.

(f) Transmission or sale at wholesale of electric energy; regulation

The ownership or operation of facilities for the transmission or sale at wholesale of electric energy which is (a) generated within a State and transmitted from the State across an international boundary and not thereafter transmitted into any other State, or (b) generated in a foreign country and transmitted across an international boundary into a State and not thereafter transmitted into any other State, shall not make a person a public utility subject to regulation as such under other provisions of this subchapter. The State within which any such facilities are located may regulate any such transaction insofar as such State regulation does not conflict with the exercise of the Commission's powers under or relating to subsection (e) of this section.

(g) Continuance of service

In order to insure continuity of service to customers of public utilities, the Commission shall require, by rule, each public utility to —

(1) report promptly to the Commission and any appropriate State regulatory authorities any anticipated shortage of electric energy or capacity which would affect such utility's capability of serving its wholesale customers,

(2) submit to the Commission, and to any appropriate State regulatory authority, and periodically revise, contingency plans respecting —

(A) shortages of electric energy or capacity, and

(B) circumstances which may result in such shortages, and

(3) accommodate any such shortages or circumstances in a manner which shall —

(A) give due consideration to the public health, safety, and welfare, and

(B) provide that all persons served directly or indirectly by such public utility will be treated, without undue prejudice or disadvantage.

(June 10, 1920, ch. 285, pt. II, § 202, as added Aug. 26, 1935, ch. 687, title II, § 213, 49 Stat. 848; amended Aug. 7, 1953, ch. 343, 67 Stat. 461; Pub. L. 95–617, title II, § 206(a), Nov. 9, 1978, 92 Stat. 3141.)

Amendments

1978 — Subsec. (g). Pub. L. 95–617 added subsec. (g).

1953 — Subsec. (f). Act Aug. 7, 1953, added subsec. (f).

Effective Date of 1978 Amendment

Pub. L. 95–617, title II, § 206(b), Nov. 9, 1978, 92 Stat. 3142, provided that: "The amendment made by subsection (a) [adding subsec. (g) of this section] shall not affect any proceeding of the Commission [Federal Energy Regulatory Commission] pending on the date of the enactment of this Act [Nov. 9, 1978] or any case pending on such date respecting a proceeding of the Commission."

Delegation of Functions

Functions of President respecting certain facilities constructed and maintained on United States borders delegated to Secretary of State, see Ex. Ord. No. 11423, Aug. 16, 1968. 33 F.R. 11741, set out as a note under section 301 of Title 3, The President.

Performance of Functions Respecting Electric Power and Natural Gas Facilities Located on United States Borders

For provisions relating to performance of functions by Secretary of Energy respecting electric power and natural gas facilities located on United States borders, see Ex. Ord. No. 10485, Sept. 8, 1953, 18 F.R. 5397, as amended by Ex. Ord. No. 12038, Feb. 3, 1978, 43 F.R. 4957, set out as a note under section 717b of Title 15, Commerce and Trade.

§ 824a–1. Pooling

(a) State laws

The Commission may, on its own motion, and shall, on application of any person or governmental entity, after public notice and notice to the Governor of the affected State and after affording an opportunity for public hearing, exempt electric utilities, in whole or in part, from any provision of State law, or from any State rule or regulation, which prohibits or prevents the voluntary coordination of electric utilities, including any agreement for central dispatch, if the Commission determines that such voluntary coordination is designed to obtain economical utilization of facilities and resources in any area. No such exemption may be granted if the Commission finds that such provision of State law, or rule or regulation —

(1) is required by any authority of Federal law, or

(2) is designed to protect public health, safety, or welfare, or the environment or conserve energy or is designed to mitigate the effects of emergencies resulting from fuel shortages.

(b) Pooling study

(1) The Commission, in consultation with the reliability councils established under section 202(a) of the Federal Power Act [16 U.S.C. 824a], the Secretary, and the electric utility industry shall study the opportunities for —

(A) conservation of energy,

(B) optimization in the efficiency of use of facilities and resources, and

(C) increased reliability,

through pooling arrangements. Not later than 18 months after November 9, 1978, the Commission shall submit a report containing the results of such study to the President and the Congress.

(2) The Commission may recommend to electric utilities that such utilities should voluntarily enter into negotiations where the opportunities referred to in paragraph (1) exist. The Commission shall report annually to the President and the Congress regarding any such recommendations and subsequent actions taken by electric utilities, by the Commission, and by the Secretary under this Act, the Federal Power Act [16 U.S.C. 791a et seq.], and any other provision of law. Such annual reports shall be included in the Commission's annual report required under the Department of Energy Organization Act [42 U.S.C. 7101 et seq.].

(Pub. L. 95–617, title II, § 205, Nov. 9, 1978, 92 Stat. 3140.)

References in Text

This Act, referred to in subsec. (b)(2), means Pub. L. 95–617, Nov. 9, 1978, 92 Stat. 3117, known as the "Public Utility Regulatory Policies Act of 1978". For complete classification of this Act to the Code, see Short Title note set out under section 2601 of this title and Tables.

The Federal Power Act, referred to in subsec. (b)(2), is act June 10, 1920, ch. 285, 41 Stat. 1063, as amended, which is classified generally to this chapter. For complete classification of this Act to the Code, see section 791a of this title and Tables.

The Department of Energy Organization Act, referred to in subsec. (b)(2), is Pub. L. 95–91, Aug. 4, 1977, 91 Stat. 565, as amended, which is classified principally to chapter 84 (§ 7101 et seq.) of Title 42, The Public Health and Welfare. For complete classification of this Act to the Code, see Short Title note set out under section 7101 of Title 42 and Tables.

Codification

Section was enacted as part of the Public Utility Regulatory Policies Act of 1978, and not as part of the Federal Power Act which generally comprises this chapter.

DEFINITIONS

For definitions of terms used in this section, see section 2602 of this title.

§ 824a–2. Reliability

(a) Study

(1) The Secretary, in consultation with the Commission, shall conduct a study with respect to—

(A) the level of reliability appropriate to adequately serve the needs of electric consumers, taking into account cost effectiveness and the need for energy conservation,

(B) the various methods which could be used in order to achieve such level of reliability and the cost effectiveness of such methods, and

(C) the various procedures that might be used in case of an emergency outage to minimize the public disruption and economic loss that might be caused by such an outage and the cost effectiveness of such procedures.

Such study shall be completed and submitted to the President and the Congress not later than 18 months after November 9, 1978. Before such submittal the Secretary shall provide an opportunity for public comment on the results of such study.

(2) The study under paragraph (1) shall include consideration of the following:

(A) the cost effectiveness of investments in each of the components involved in providing adequate and reliable electric service, including generation, transmission, and distribution facilities, and devices available to the electric consumer;

(B) the environmental and other effects of the investments considered under subparagraph (A);

(C) various types of electric utility systems in terms of generation, transmission, distribution and customer mix, the extent to which differences in reliability levels may be desirable, and the cost-effectiveness of the various methods which could be used to decrease the number and severity of any outages among the various types of systems;

(D) alternatives to adding new generation facilities to achieve such desired levels of reliability (including conservation);

(E) the cost-effectiveness of adding a number of small, decentralized conventional and nonconventional generating units rather than a small number of large generating units with a similar total megawatt capacity for achieving the desired level of reliability; and

(F) any standards for electric utility reliability used by, or suggested for use by, the electric utility industry in terms of cost-effectiveness in achieving the desired level of reliability, including equipment standards, standards for operating procedures and training of personnel, and standards relating the number and severity of outages to periods of time.

(b) Examination of reliability issues by reliability councils

The Secretary, in consultation with the Commission, may, from time to time, request the reliability councils established under section 202(a) of the Federal Power Act [16 U.S.C. 824a(a) of this title] or other appropriate persons (including Federal agencies) to examine and report to him concerning any electric utility reliability issue. The Secretary shall report to the Congress (in its annual report or in the report required under subsection (a) of this section if appropriate) the results of any examination under the preceding sentence.

(c) Department of Energy recommendations

The Secretary, in consultation with the Commission, and after opportunity for public comment, may recommend industry standards for reliability to the electric utility industry, including standards with respect to equipment, operating procedures and training of personnel, and standards relating to the level or levels of reliability appropriate to adequately and reliably serve the needs of electric consumers. The Secretary shall include in his annual report—

(1) any recommendations made under this subsection or any recommendations respecting electric utility reliability problems under any other provision of law, and

(2) a description of actions taken by electric utilities with respect to such recommendations.

(Pub. L. 95–617, title II, § 209, Nov. 9, 1978, 92 Stat. 3143.)

Codification

Section was enacted as part of the Public Utility Regulatory Policies Act of 1978, and not as part of the Federal Power Act which generally comprises this chapter.

Definitions

For definitions of terms used in this section, see section 2602 of this title.

§ 824a–3. Cogeneration and small power production

(a) Cogeneration and small power production rules

Not later than 1 year after November 9, 1978, the Commission shall prescribe, and from time to time thereafter revise, such rules as it determines necessary to encourage cogeneration and small power production, and to encourage geothermal small power production facilities of not more than 80 megawatts capacity, which rules require electric utilities to offer to—

(1) sell electric energy to qualifying cogeneration facilities and qualifying small power production facilities[1] and

(2) purchase electric energy from such facilities.

Such rules shall be prescribed, after consultation with representatives of Federal and State regulatory agencies having ratemaking authority for electric utilities, and after public notice and a reasonable opportunity for interested persons (including State and Federal agencies) to submit oral as well as written data, views, and arguments. Such rules shall include provisions respecting minimum reliability of qualifying cogeneration facilities and qualifying small power production facilities (including reliability of such facilities during emergencies) and rules respecting reliability of electric energy service to be available to such facilities from electric utilities during emergencies. Such rules may not authorize a qualifying cogeneration facility or qualifying small power production facility to make any sale for purposes other than resale.

(b) Rates for purchases by electric utilities

The rules prescribed under subsection (a) of this section shall insure that, in requiring any electric utility to offer to purchase electric energy from any qualifying cogeneration facility or qualifying small power production facility, the rates for such purchase—

---

1. *So in original. Probably should be followed by a comma.*

(1) shall be just and reasonable to the electric consumers of the electric utility and in the public interest, and

(2) shall not discriminate against qualifying cogenerators or qualifying small power producers.

No such rule prescribed under subsection (a) of this section shall provide for a rate which exceeds the incremental cost to the electric utility of alternative electric energy.

(c) Rates for sales by utilities

The rules prescribed under subsection (a) of this section shall insure that, in requiring any electric utility to offer to sell electric energy to any qualifying cogeneration facility or qualifying small power production facility, the rates for such sale—

(1) shall be just and reasonable and in the public interest, and

(2) shall not discriminate against the qualifying cogenerators or qualifying small power producers.

(d) "Incremental cost of alternative electric energy" defined

For purposes of this section, the term "incremental cost of alternative electric energy" means, with respect to electric energy purchased from a qualifying cogenerator or qualifying small power producer, the cost to the electric utility of the electric energy which, but for the purchase from such cogenerator or small power producer, such utility would generate or purchase from another source.

(e) Exemptions

(1) Not later than 1 year after November 9, 1978, and from time to time thereafter, the Commission shall, after consultation with representatives of State regulatory authorities, electric utilities, owners of cogeneration facilities and owners of small power production facilities, and after public notice and a reasonable opportunity for interested persons (including State and Federal agencies) to submit oral as well as written data, views, and arguments, prescribe rules under which geothermal small power production facilities of not more than 80 megawatts capacity, qualifying cogeneration facilities, and qualifying small power production facilities are exempted in whole or part from the Federal Power Act [16 U.S.C. 791a et seq.], from the Public Utility Holding Company Act,[2] from State laws and regulations respecting the rates, or respecting the financial or organizational regulation, of electric utilities, or from any combination of the foregoing, if the Commission determines such exemption is necessary to encourage cogeneration and small power production.

(2) No qualifying small power production facility (other than a qualifying small power production facility which is an eligible solar, wind, waste, or geothermal facility as defined in section 3(17)(E) of the Federal Power Act [16 U.S.C. 796(17)(E)]) which has a power production capacity which, together with any other facilities located at the same site (as determined by the Commission), exceeds 30 megawatts, or 80 megawatts for a qualifying small power production facility using geothermal energy as the primary energy source, may be exempted under rules under paragraph (1) from any provision of law or regulation referred to in paragraph (1), except that any qualifying small power production facility which produces electric energy solely by the use of biomass as a primary energy source, may be exempted by the Commission under such rules from the Public Utility Holding Company Act[3] and from State laws and regulations referred to in such paragraph (1).

2. *See References in Text note below.*
3. *So in original. Probably should be followed by a comma.*

(3) No qualifying small power production facility or qualifying cogeneration facility may be exempted under this subsection from—

> (A) any State law or regulation in effect in a State pursuant to subsection (f) of this section,

> (B) the provisions of section 210, 211, or 212 of the Federal Power Act [16 U.S.C. 824i, 824j, or 824k] or the necessary authorities for enforcement of any such provision under the Federal Power Act [16 U.S.C. 791a et seq.], or

> (C) any license or permit requirement under part I of the Federal Power Act [16 U.S.C. 791a et seq.] any provision under such Act related to such a license or permit requirement, or the necessary authorities for enforcement of any such requirement.

(f) Implementation of rules for qualifying cogeneration and qualifying small power production facilities

(1) Beginning on or before the date one year after any rule is prescribed by the Commission under subsection (a) of this section or revised under such subsection, each State regulatory authority shall, after notice and opportunity for public hearing, implement such rule (or revised rule) for each electric utility for which it has ratemaking authority.

(2) Beginning on or before the date one year after any rule is prescribed by the Commission under subsection (a) of this section or revised under such subsection, each nonregulated electric utility shall, after notice and opportunity for public hearing, implement such rule (or revised rule).

(g) Judicial review and enforcement

(1) Judicial review may be obtained respecting any proceeding conducted by a State regulatory authority or nonregulated electric utility for purposes of implementing any requirement of a rule under subsection (a) of this section in the same manner, and under the same requirements, as judicial review may be obtained under section 2633 of this title in the case of a proceeding to which section 2633 of this title applies.

(2) Any person (including the Secretary) may bring an action against any electric utility, qualifying small power producer, or qualifying cogenerator to enforce any requirement established by a State regulatory authority or nonregulated electric utility pursuant to subsection (f) of this section. Any such action shall be brought only in the manner, and under the requirements, as provided under section 2633 of this title with respect to an action to which section 2633 of this title applies.

(h) Commission enforcement

(1) For purposes of enforcement of any rule prescribed by the Commission under subsection (a) of this section with respect to any operations of an electric utility, a qualifying cogeneration facility or a qualifying small power production facility which are subject to the jurisdiction of the Commission under part II of the Federal Power Act [16 U.S.C. 824 et seq.], such rule shall be treated as a rule under the Federal Power Act [16 U.S.C. 791a et seq.]. Nothing in subsection (g) of this section shall apply to so much of the operations of an electric utility, a qualifying cogeneration facility or a qualifying small power production facility as are subject to the jurisdiction of the Commission under part II of the Federal Power Act.

(2)(A) The Commission may enforce the requirements of subsection (f) of this section against any State regulatory authority or nonregulated electric utility. For purposes of any such enforcement, the requirements of subsection (f)(1) of this section shall be treated as a rule enforceable under the Federal Power Act [16 U.S.C. 791a et seq.]. For purposes of any such action, a State regulatory authority or nonregulated electric utility shall be treated as a person within the meaning of the Federal Power Act. No enforcement action may be brought by the Commission under this section other than—

(i) an action against the State regulatory authority or nonregulated electric utility for failure to comply with the requirements of subsection (f) of this section[3] or

(ii) an action under paragraph (1).

(B) Any electric utility, qualifying cogenerator, or qualifying small power producer may petition the Commission to enforce the requirements of subsection (f) of this section as provided in subparagraph (A) of this paragraph. If the Commission does not initiate an enforcement action under subparagraph (A) against a State regulatory authority or nonregulated electric utility within 60 days following the date on which a petition is filed under this subparagraph with respect to such authority, the petitioner may bring an action in the appropriate United States district court to require such State regulatory authority or nonregulated electric utility to comply with such requirements, and such court may issue such injunctive or other relief as may be appropriate. The Commission may intervene as a matter of right in any such action.

(i) **Federal contracts**

No contract between a Federal agency and any electric utility for the sale of electric energy by such Federal agency for resale which is entered into after November 9, 1978, may contain any provision which will have the effect of preventing the implementation of any rule under this section with respect to such utility. Any provision in any such contract which has such effect shall be null and void.

(j) **New dams and diversions**

Except for a hydroelectric project located at a Government dam (as defined in section 3(10) of the Federal Power Act [16 U.S.C. 796(10)]) at which non-Federal hydroelectric development is permissible, this section shall not apply to any hydroelectric project which impounds or diverts the water of a natural watercourse by means of a new dam or diversion unless the project meets each of the following requirements:

(1) **No substantial adverse effects**

At the time of issuance of the license or exemption for the project, the Commission finds that the project will not have substantial adverse effects on the environment, including recreation and water quality. Such finding shall be made by the Commission after taking into consideration terms and conditions imposed under either paragraph (3) of this subsection or section 10 of the Federal Power Act [16 U.S.C. 803] (whichever is appropriate as required by that Act [16 U.S.C. 791a et seq.] or the Electric Consumers Protection Act of 1986) and compliance with other environmental requirements applicable to the project.

(2) **Protected rivers**

At the time the application for a license or exemption for the project is accepted by the Commission (in accordance with the Commission's regulations and procedures in effect on January 1, 1986, including those relating to environmental consultation), such project is not located on either of the following:

3. *So in original. Probably should be followed by a comma.*

(A) Any segment of a natural watercourse which is included in (or designated for potential inclusion in) a State or national wild and scenic river system.

(B) Any segment of a natural watercourse which the State has determined, in accordance with applicable State law, to possess unique natural, recreational, cultural, or scenic attributes which would be adversely affected by hydroelectric development.

(3) Fish and wildlife terms and conditions

The project meets the terms and conditions set by fish and wildlife agencies under the same procedures as provided for under section 30(c) of the Federal Power Act [16 U.S.C. 823a(c)].

(k) "New dam or diversion" defined

For purposes of this section, the term "new dam or diversion" means a dam or diversion which requires, for purposes of installing any hydroelectric power project, any construction, or enlargement of any impoundment or diversion structure (other than repairs or reconstruction or the addition of flashboards or similar adjustable devices)[4]

(l) Definitions

For purposes of this section, the terms "small power production facility", "qualifying small power production facility", "qualifying small power producer", "primary energy source", "cogeneration facility", "qualifying cogeneration facility", and "qualifying cogenerator" have the respective meanings provided for such terms under section 3(17) and (18) of the Federal Power Act [16 U.S.C. 796(17), (18)].

(m) Termination of mandatory purchase and sale requirements

(1) Obligation to purchase

After August 8, 2005, no electric utility shall be required to enter into a new contract or obligation to purchase electric energy from a qualifying cogeneration facility or a qualifying small power production facility under this section if the Commission finds that the qualifying cogeneration facility or qualifying small power production facility has nondiscriminatory access to —

(A)(i) independently administered, auction-based day ahead and real time wholesale markets for the sale of electric energy; and (ii) wholesale markets for long-term sales of capacity and electric energy; or

(B)(i) transmission and interconnection services that are provided by a Commission-approved regional transmission entity and administered pursuant to an open access transmission tariff that affords nondiscriminatory treatment to all customers; and (ii) competitive wholesale markets that provide a meaningful opportunity to sell capacity, including long-term and short-term sales, and electric energy, including long-term, short-term and real-time sales, to buyers other than the utility to which the qualifying facility is interconnected. In determining whether a meaningful opportunity to sell exists, the Commission shall consider, among other factors, evidence of transactions within the relevant market; or

(C) wholesale markets for the sale of capacity and electric energy that are, at a minimum, of comparable competitive quality as markets described in subparagraphs (A) and (B).

(2) Revised purchase and sale obligation for new facilities

---

4. *So in original. Probably should be followed by a period.*

(A) After August 8, 2005, no electric utility shall be required pursuant to this section to enter into a new contract or obligation to purchase from or sell electric energy to a facility that is not an existing qualifying cogeneration facility unless the facility meets the criteria for qualifying cogeneration facilities established by the Commission pursuant to the rulemaking required by subsection (n) of this section.

(B) For the purposes of this paragraph, the term "existing qualifying cogeneration facility" means a facility that—

(i) was a qualifying cogeneration facility on August 8, 2005; or

(ii) had filed with the Commission a notice of self-certification, self recertification or an application for Commission certification under 18 CFR 292.207 prior to the date on which the Commission issues the final rule required by subsection (n) of this section.

(3) Commission review

Any electric utility may file an application with the Commission for relief from the mandatory purchase obligation pursuant to this subsection on a service territory-wide basis. Such application shall set forth the factual basis upon which relief is requested and describe why the conditions set forth in subparagraph (A), (B), or (C) of paragraph (1) of this subsection have been met. After notice, including sufficient notice to potentially affected qualifying cogeneration facilities and qualifying small power production facilities, and an opportunity for comment, the Commission shall make a final determination within 90 days of such application regarding whether the conditions set forth in subparagraph (A), (B), or (C) of paragraph (1) have been met.

(4) Reinstatement of obligation to purchase

At any time after the Commission makes a finding under paragraph (3) relieving an electric utility of its obligation to purchase electric energy, a qualifying cogeneration facility, a qualifying small power production facility, a State agency, or any other affected person may apply to the Commission for an order reinstating the electric utility's obligation to purchase electric energy under this section. Such application shall set forth the factual basis upon which the application is based and describe why the conditions set forth in subparagraph (A), (B), or (C) of paragraph (1) of this subsection are no longer met. After notice, including sufficient notice to potentially affected utilities, and opportunity for comment, the Commission shall issue an order within 90 days of such application reinstating the electric utility's obligation to purchase electric energy under this section if the Commission finds that the conditions set forth in subparagraphs (A), (B) or (C) of paragraph (1) which relieved the obligation to purchase, are no longer met.

(5) Obligation to sell

After August 8, 2005, no electric utility shall be required to enter into a new contract or obligation to sell electric energy to a qualifying cogeneration facility or a qualifying small power production facility under this section if the Commission finds that—

(A) competing retail electric suppliers are willing and able to sell and deliver electric energy to the qualifying cogeneration facility or qualifying small power production facility; and

(B) the electric utility is not required by State law to sell electric energy in its service territory.

(6) No effect on existing rights and remedies

Nothing in this subsection affects the rights or remedies of any party under any contract or obligation, in effect or pending approval before the appropriate State regulatory authority or non-regulated electric utility on August 8, 2005, to purchase electric energy or capacity from or to sell electric energy or capacity to a qualifying cogeneration facility or qualifying small power production facility under this Act (including the right to recover costs of purchasing electric energy or capacity).

(7) Recovery of costs

(A) The Commission shall issue and enforce such regulations as are necessary to ensure that an electric utility that purchases electric energy or capacity from a qualifying cogeneration facility or qualifying small power production facility in accordance with any legally enforceable obligation entered into or imposed under this section recovers all prudently incurred costs associated with the purchase.

(B) A regulation under subparagraph (A) shall be enforceable in accordance with the provisions of law applicable to enforcement of regulations under the Federal Power Act (16 U.S.C. 791a et seq.).

(n) Rulemaking for new qualifying facilities

(1)(A) Not later than 180 days after August 8, 2005, the Commission shall issue a rule revising the criteria in 18 CFR 292.205 for new qualifying cogeneration facilities seeking to sell electric energy pursuant to this section to ensure—

(i) that the thermal energy output of a new qualifying cogeneration facility is used in a productive and beneficial manner;

(ii) the electrical, thermal, and chemical output of the cogeneration facility is used fundamentally for industrial, commercial, or institutional purposes and is not intended fundamentally for sale to an electric utility, taking into account technological, efficiency, economic, and variable thermal energy requirements, as well as State laws applicable to sales of electric energy from a qualifying facility to its host facility; and

(iii) continuing progress in the development of efficient electric energy generating technology.

(B) The rule issued pursuant to paragraph (1)(A) of this subsection shall be applicable only to facilities that seek to sell electric energy pursuant to this section. For all other purposes, except as specifically provided in subsection (m)(2)(A) of this section, qualifying facility status shall be determined in accordance with the rules and regulations of this Act.

(2) Notwithstanding rule revisions under paragraph (1), the Commission's criteria for qualifying cogeneration facilities in effect prior to the date on which the Commission issues the final rule required by paragraph (1) shall continue to apply to any cogeneration facility that—

(A) was a qualifying cogeneration facility on August 8, 2005, or

(B) had filed with the Commission a notice of self-certification, self-recertification or an application for Commission certification under 18 CFR 292.207 prior to the date on which the Commission issues the final rule required by paragraph (1).

(Pub. L. 95–617, title II, §210, Nov. 9, 1978, 92 Stat. 3144; Pub. L. 96–294, title VI, §643(b), June 30, 1980, 94 Stat. 770; Pub. L. 99–495, §8(a), Oct. 16, 1986, 100 Stat. 1249; Pub. L. 101–575, §2, Nov. 15, 1990, 104 Stat. 2834; Pub. L. 109–58, title XII, §1253(a), Aug. 8, 2005, 119 Stat. 967.)

References in Text

The Federal Power Act, referred to in subsecs. (e), (h), (j)(1), and (m)(7)(B), is act June 10, 1920, ch. 285, 41 Stat. 1063, as amended, which is classified generally to this chapter (§ 791a et seq.). Part I of the Federal Power Act is classified generally to subchapter I (§ 791a et seq.) of this chapter. Part II of the Federal Power Act is classified generally to this subchapter (§ 824 et seq.). For complete classification of this Act to the Code, see section 791a of this title and Tables.

The Public Utility Holding Company Act, referred to in subsec. (e), probably means the Public Utility Holding Company Act of 1935, title I of act Aug. 26, 1935, ch. 687, 49 Stat. 803, as amended, which was classified generally to chapter 2C (§ 79 et seq.) of Title 15, Commerce and Trade, prior to repeal by Pub. L. 109–58, title XII, § 1263, Aug. 8, 2005, 119 Stat. 974. For complete classification of this Act to the Code, see Tables.

The Electric Consumers Protection Act of 1986, referred to in subsec. (j)(1), is Pub. L. 99–495, Oct. 16, 1986, 100 Stat. 1243. For complete classification of this Act to the Code, see Short Title of 1986 Amendment note set out under section 791a of this title and Tables.

This Act, referred to in subsecs. (m)(6) and (n)(1)(B), is Pub. L. 95–617, Nov. 9, 1978, 92 Stat. 3117, as amended, known as the Public Utility Regulatory Policies Act of 1978. For complete classification of this Act to the Code, see Short Title note set out under section 2601 of this title and Tables.

Codification

Section was enacted as part of the Public Utility Regulatory Policies Act of 1978, and not as part of the Federal Power Act which generally comprises this chapter.

August 8, 2005, referred to in subsec. (n)(1)(A), was in the original "the date of enactment of this section", which was translated as meaning the date of enactment of Pub. L. 109–58, which enacted subsecs. (m) and (n) of this section, to reflect the probable intent of Congress.

Amendments

2005 — Subsecs. (m), (n). Pub. L. 109–58 added subsecs. (m) and (n).

1990 — Subsec. (e)(2). Pub. L. 101–575 inserted "(other than a qualifying small power production facility which is an eligible solar, wind, waste, or geothermal facility as defined in section 3(17)(E) of the Federal Power Act)" after first reference to "facility".

1986 — Subsecs. (j) to (l). Pub. L. 99–495 added subsecs. (j) and (k) and redesignated former subsec. (j) as (l).

1980 — Subsec. (a). Pub. L. 96–294, § 643(b)(1), inserted provisions relating to encouragement of geothermal small power production facilities.

Subsec. (e)(1). Pub. L. 96–294, § 643(b)(2), inserted provisions relating to applicability to geothermal small power production facilities.

Subsec. (e)(2). Pub. L. 96–294, § 643(b)(3), inserted provisions respecting a qualifying small power production facility using geothermal energy as the primary energy source.

Effective Date of 1986 Amendment

Pub. L. 99–495, § 8(b), Oct. 16, 1986, 100 Stat. 1250, provided that:

"(1) Subsection (j) of section 210 of the Public Utility Regulatory Policies Act of 1978 (as amended by subsection (a) of this section) [16 U.S.C. 824a–3(j)] shall apply to any project for which benefits under section 210 of the Public Utility Regulatory Policies Act of 1978 are sought and for which a license or exemption is issued by the Federal Energy Regulatory Commission after the enactment of this Act [Oct. 16, 1986], except as otherwise provided in paragraph (2), (3) or (4) of this subsection.

"(2) Subsection (j) shall not apply to the project if the application for license or exemption for the project was filed, and accepted for filing by the Commission, before the enactment of this Act [Oct. 16, 1986].

"(3) Paragraphs (1) and (3) of such subsection (j) shall not apply if the application for the license or exemption for the project was filed before the enactment of this Act [Oct. 16, 1986] and accepted for filing by the Commission (in accordance with the Commission's regulations and procedures in effect on January 1, 1986, including those relating to the requirement for environmental consultation) within 3 years after such enactment.

"(4)(A) Paragraph (3) of subsection (j) shall not apply for projects where the license or exemption application was filed after enactment of this Act [Oct. 16, 1986] if, based on a petition filed by the applicant for such project within 18 months after such enactment, the Commission determines (after public notice and opportunity for public comment of at least 45 days) that the applicant has demonstrated that he had committed (prior to the enactment of this Act) substantial monetary resources directly related to the development of the project and to the diligent and timely completion of all requirements of the Commission for filing an acceptable application for license or exemption. Such petition shall be publicly available and shall be filed in such form as the Commission shall require by rule issued within 120 days after the enactment of this Act. The public notice required under this subparagraph shall include written notice by the petitioner to affected Federal and State agencies.

"(B) In the case of any petition referred to in subparagraph (A), if the applicant had a preliminary permit and had completed environmental consultations (required by Commission regulations and procedures in effect on January 1, 1986) prior to enactment, there shall be a rebuttable presumption that such applicant had committed substantial monetary resources prior to enactment.

"(C) The applicant for a license or exemption for a project described in subparagraph (A) may petition the Commission for an initial determination under paragraph (1) of section 210(j) of the Public Utility Regulatory Policies Act of 1978 [16 U.S.C. 824a–3(j)(1)] prior to the time the license or exemption is issued. If the Commission initially finds that the project will have substantial adverse effects on the environment within the meaning of such paragraph (1), prior to making a final finding under that paragraph the Commission shall afford the applicant a reasonable opportunity to provide for mitigation of such adverse effects. The Commission shall make a final finding under such paragraph (1) at the time the license or exemption is issued. If the Federal Energy Regulatory Commission has notified the State of its initial finding and the State has not taken any action described in paragraph (2) of section 210(j) before such final finding, the failure to take such action shall be the basis for a rebuttable presumption that there is not a substantial adverse effect on the environment related to natural, recreational, cultural, or scenic attributes for purposes of such finding.

"(D) If a petition under subparagraph (A) is denied, all provisions of section 210(j) of the Public Utility Regulatory Policies Act of 1978 [16 U.S.C. 824a–3(j)] shall apply to the project regardless of when the license or exemption is issued."

Amendment by Pub. L. 99–495 effective with respect to each license, permit, or exemption issued under this chapter after Oct. 16, 1986, see section 18 of Pub. L. 99–495, set out as a note under section 797 of this title.

CALCULATION OF AVOIDED COST

Pub. L. 102–486, title XIII, §1335, Oct. 24, 1992, 106 Stat. 2984, provided that: "Nothing in section 210 of the Public Utility Regulatory Policies Act of 1978 (Public Law 95–617) [16 U.S.C. 824a–3] requires a State regulatory authority or nonregulated electric utility to treat a cost reasonably identified to be incurred or to have been incurred in the construction or operation of a facility or a project which has been selected by the Department of Energy and provided Federal funding pursuant to the Clean Coal Program authorized by Public Law 98–473 [see Tables for classification] as an incremental cost of alternative electric energy."

Applicability of 1980 Amendment to Facilities Using Solar Energy as Primary Energy Source

Pub. L. 100–202, § 101(d) [title III, § 310], Dec. 22, 1987, 101 Stat. 1329–104, 1329–126, provided that:

"(a) The amendments made by section 643(b) of the Energy Security Act (Public Law 96–294) [amending this section] and any regulations issued to implement such amendment shall apply to qualifying small power production facilities (as such term is defined in the Federal Power Act [16 U.S.C. 791a et seq.]) using solar energy as the primary energy source to the same extent such amendments and regulations apply to qualifying small power production facilities using geothermal energy as the primary energy source, except that nothing in this Act [see Tables for classification] shall preclude the Federal Energy Regulatory Commission from revising its regulations to limit the availability of exemptions authorized under this Act as it determines to be required in the public interest and consistent with its obligations and duties under section 210 of the Public Utility Regulatory Policies Act of 1978 [this section].

"(b) The provisions of subsection (a) shall apply to a facility using solar energy as the primary energy source only if either of the following is submitted to the Federal Energy Regulatory Commission during the two-year period beginning on the date of enactment of this Act [Dec. 22, 1987]:

"(1) An application for certification of the facility as a qualifying small power production facility.

"(2) Notice that the facility meets the requirements for qualification."

Study and Report to Congressional Committees on Application of Provisions Relating to Cogeneration, Small Power Production, and Interconnection Authority to Hydroelectric Power Facilities

Pub. L. 99–495, § 8(d), Oct. 16, 1986, 100 Stat. 1251, provided that:

"(1) The Commission shall conduct a study (in accordance with section 102(2)(C) of the National Environmental Policy Act of 1969 [42 U.S.C. 4332(2)(C)]) of whether the benefits of section 210 of the Public Utility Regulatory Policies Act of 1978 [16 U.S.C. 824a–3] and section 210 of the Federal Power Act [16 U.S.C. 824i] should be applied to hydroelectric power facilities utilizing new dams or diversions (within the meaning of section 210(k) of the Public Utility Regulatory Policies Act of 1978).

"(2) The study under this subsection shall take into consideration the need for such new dams or diversions for power purposes, the environmental impacts of such new dams and diversions (both with and without the application of the amendments made by this Act to sections 4, 10, and 30 of the Federal Power Act [16 U.S.C. 797, 803, 823a] and section 210 of the Public Utility Regulatory Policies Act of 1978 [16 U.S.C. 824a–3]), the environmental effects of such facilities alone and in combination with other existing or proposed dams or diversions on the same waterway, the intent of Congress to encourage and give priority to the application of section 210 of Public Utility Regulatory Policies Act of 1978 to existing dams and diversions rather than such new dams or diversions, and the impact of such section 210 on the rates paid by electric power consumers.

"(3) The study under this subsection shall be initiated within 3 months after enactment of this Act [Oct. 16, 1986] and completed as promptly as practicable.

"(4) A report containing the results of the study conducted under this subsection shall be submitted to the Committee on Energy and Commerce of the United States House of Representatives and the Committee on Energy and Natural Resources of the United States Senate while both Houses are in session.

"(5) The report submitted under paragraph (4) shall include a determination (and the basis thereof) by the Commission, based on the study and a public hearing and subject to review under section 313(b) of the Federal Power Act [16 U.S.C. 825l(b)], whether any of the benefits referred to in paragraph (1) should be available for such facilities and whether applications for preliminary permits (or licenses where no preliminary permit has been issued) for such small power production facilities utilizing new dams or diversions should be accepted by the Commission after the moratorium period specified in subsection (e). The report shall include such other administrative and legislative recommendations as the Commission deems appropriate.

"(6) If the study under this subsection has not been completed within 18 months after its initiation, the Commission shall notify the Committees referred to in paragraph (4) of the reasons for the delay and specify a date when it will be completed and a report submitted."

Moratorium on Application of This Section to New Dams

Pub. L. 99–495, §8(e), Oct. 16, 1986, 100 Stat. 1251, provided that: "Notwithstanding the amendments made by subsection (a) of this section [amending section 824a–3 of this title], in the case of a project for which a license or exemption is issued after the enactment of this Act [Oct. 16, 1986], section 210 of the Public Utility Regulatory Policies Act of 1978 [16 U.S.C. 824a–3] shall not apply during the moratorium period if the project utilizes a new dam or diversion (as defined in section 210(k) of such Act) unless the project is either—

"(1) a project located at a Government dam (as defined in section 3(10) of the Federal Power Act [16 U.S.C. 796(10)]) at which non-Federal hydroelectric development is permissible, or

"(2) a project described in paragraphs (2), (3), or (4) of subsection (b) [set out as a note above].

For purposes of this subsection, the term 'moratorium period' means the period beginning on the date of the enactment of this Act and ending at the expiration of the first full session of Congress after the session during which the report under subsection (d) [set out as a note above] has been submitted to the Congress."

Definitions

For definitions of terms used in this section, see section 2602 of this title.

§824a–4. Seasonal diversity electricity exchange

(a) Authority

The Secretary may acquire rights-of-way by purchase, including eminent domain, through North Dakota, South Dakota, and Nebraska for transmission facilities for the seasonal diversity exchange of electric power to and from Canada if he determines—

(1) after opportunity for public hearing—

(A) that the exchange is in the public interest and would further the purposes referred to in section 2611(1) and (2) of this title and that the acquisition of such rights-of-way and the construction and operation of such transmission facilities for such purposes is otherwise in the public interest,

(B) that a permit has been issued in accordance with subsection (b) of this section for such construction, operation, maintenance, and connection of the facilities at the border for the transmission of electric energy between the United States and Canada as is necessary for such exchange of electric power, and

(C) that each affected State has approved the portion of the transmission route located in each State in accordance with applicable State law, or if there is no such applicable State law in such State, the Governor has approved such portion; and

(2) after consultation with the Secretary of the Interior and the heads of other affected Federal agencies, that the Secretary of the Interior and the heads of such,[1] other agencies concur in writing in the location of such portion of the transmission facilities as crosses Federal land under the jurisdiction of such Secretary or such other Federal agency, as the case may be.

The Secretary shall provide to any State such cooperation and technical assistance as the State may request and as he determines appropriate in the selection of a transmission route. If the transmission route approved by any State does not appear to be feasible and in the public interest, the Secretary shall encourage such State to review such route and to develop a route that is feasible and in the public interest. Any exercise by the Secretary of the power of eminent domain under this section shall be in accordance with other applicable provisions of Federal law. The Secretary shall provide public notice of his intention to acquire any right-of-way before exercising such power of eminent domain with respect to such right-of-way.

(b) Permit

Notwithstanding any transfer of functions under the first sentence of section 301(b) of the Department of Energy Organization Act [42 U.S.C. 7151(b)], no permit referred to in subsection (a)(1)(B) may be issued unless the Commission has conducted hearings and made the findings required under section 202(e) of the Federal Power Act [16 U.S.C. 824a(e)] and under the applicable execution order respecting the construction, operation, maintenance, or connection at the borders of the United States of facilities for the transmission of electric energy between the United States and a foreign country. Any finding of the Commission under an applicable executive order referred to in this subsection shall be treated for purposes of judicial review as an order issued under section 202(e) of the Federal Power Act.

(c) Timely acquisition by other means

The Secretary may not acquire any rights-of-day[2] under this section unless he determines that the holder or holders of a permit referred to in subsection (a)(1)(B) of this section are unable to acquire such rights-of-way under State condemnation authority, or after reasonable opportunity for negotiation, without unreasonably delaying construction, taking into consideration the impact of such delay on completion of the facilities in a timely fashion.

(d) Payments by permittees

(1) The property interest acquired by the Secretary under this section (whether by eminent domain or other purchase) shall be transferred by the Secretary to the holder of a permit referred to in subsection (b) of this section if such holder has made payment to the Secretary of the entire costs of the acquisition of such property interest, including administrative costs. The Secretary may accept, and expend, for purposes of such acquisition, amounts from any such person before acquiring a property interest to be transferred to such person under this section.

(2) If no payment is made by a permit holder under paragraph (1), within a reasonable time, the Secretary shall offer such rights-of-way to the original owner for reacquisition at the original price paid by the Secretary. If such original owner refuses to reacquire such property after a reasonable period, the Secretary shall dispose of

1. *So in original. The comma probably should not appear.*
2. *So in original. Probably should be "rights-of-way".*

such property in accordance with applicable provisions of law governing disposal of property of the United States.

(e) Federal law governing Federal lands

This section shall not affect any Federal law governing Federal lands.

(Pub. L. 95–617, title VI, § 602, Nov. 9, 1978, 92 Stat. 3164.)

CODIFICATION

Subsection (f), which required the Secretary to report annually to Congress on actions taken pursuant to this section, terminated, effective May 15, 2000, pursuant to section 3003 of Pub. L. 104–66, as amended, set out as a note under section 1113 of Title 31, Money and Finance. See, also, page 90 of House Document No. 103–7.

Section was enacted as part of the Public Utility Regulatory Policies Act of 1978, and not as part of the Federal Power Act which generally comprises this chapter.

DEFINITIONS

For definitions of terms used in this section, see section 2602 of this title.

§ 824b. Disposition of property; consolidations; purchase of securities

(a) Authorization

(1) No public utility shall, without first having secured an order of the Commission authorizing it to do so—

(A) sell, lease, or otherwise dispose of the whole of its facilities subject to the jurisdiction of the Commission, or any part thereof of a value in excess of $10,000,000;

(B) merge or consolidate, directly or indirectly, such facilities or any part thereof with those of any other person, by any means whatsoever;

(C) purchase, acquire, or take any security with a value in excess of $10,000,000 of any other public utility; or

(D) purchase, lease, or otherwise acquire an existing generation facility—

(i) that has a value in excess of $10,000,000; and

(ii) that is used for interstate wholesale sales and over which the Commission has jurisdiction for ratemaking purposes.

(2) No holding company in a holding company system that includes a transmitting utility or an electric utility shall purchase, acquire, or take any security with a value in excess of $10,000,000 of, or, by any means whatsoever, directly or indirectly, merge or consolidate with, a transmitting utility, an electric utility company, or a holding company in a holding company system that includes a transmitting utility, or an electric utility company, with a value in excess of $10,000,000 without first having secured an order of the Commission authorizing it to do so.

(3) Upon receipt of an application for such approval the Commission shall give reasonable notice in writing to the Governor and State commission of each of the States in which the physical property affected, or any part thereof, is situated, and to such other persons as it may deem advisable.

(4) After notice and opportunity for hearing, the Commission shall approve the proposed disposition, consolidation, acquisition, or change in control, if it finds that the proposed transaction will be consistent with the public interest, and will not result

in cross-subsidization of a non-utility associate company or the pledge or encumbrance of utility assets for the benefit of an associate company, unless the Commission determines that the cross-subsidization, pledge, or encumbrance will be consistent with the public interest.

(5) The Commission shall, by rule, adopt procedures for the expeditious consideration of applications for the approval of dispositions, consolidations, or acquisitions, under this section. Such rules shall identify classes of transactions, or specify criteria for transactions, that normally meet the standards established in paragraph (4). The Commission shall provide expedited review for such transactions. The Commission shall grant or deny any other application for approval of a transaction not later than 180 days after the application is filed. If the Commission does not act within 180 days, such application shall be deemed granted unless the Commission finds, based on good cause, that further consideration is required to determine whether the proposed transaction meets the standards of paragraph (4) and issues an order tolling the time for acting on the application for not more than 180 days, at the end of which additional period the Commission shall grant or deny the application.

(6) For purposes of this subsection, the terms "associate company", "holding company", and "holding company system" have the meaning given those terms in the Public Utility Holding Company Act of 2005 [42 U.S.C. 16451 et seq.].

(b) Orders of Commission

The Commission may grant any application for an order under this section in whole or in part and upon such terms and conditions as it finds necessary or appropriate to secure the maintenance of adequate service and the coordination in the public interest of facilities subject to the jurisdiction of the Commission. The Commission may from time to time for good cause shown make such orders supplemental to any order made under this section as it may find necessary or appropriate.

(June 10, 1920, ch. 285, pt. II, §203, as added Aug. 26, 1935, ch. 687, title II, §213, 49 Stat. 849; amended Pub. L. 109–58, title XII, §1289(a), Aug. 8, 2005, 119 Stat. 982.)

References in Text

The Public Utility Holding Company Act of 2005, referred to in subsec. (a)(6), is subtitle F of title XII of Pub. L. 109–58, Aug. 8, 2005, 119 Stat. 972, which is classified principally to part D (§16451 et seq.) of subchapter XII of chapter 149 of Title 42, The Public Health and Welfare. For complete classification of this Act to the Code, see Short Title note set out under section 15801 of Title 42 and Tables.

Amendments

2005 — Subsec. (a). Pub. L. 109–58 amended subsec. (a) generally. Prior to amendment, subsec. (a) read as follows: "No public utility shall sell, lease, or otherwise dispose of the whole of its facilities subject to the jurisdiction of the Commission, or any part thereof of a value in excess of $50,000, or by any means whatsoever, directly or indirectly, merge or consolidate such facilities or any part thereof with those of any other person, or purchase, acquire, or take any security of any other public utility, without first having secured an order of the Commission authorizing it to do so. Upon application for such approval the Commission shall give reasonable notice in writing to the Governor and State commission of each of the States in which the physical property affected, or any part thereof, is situated, and to such other persons as it may deem advisable. After notice and opportunity for hearing, if the Commission finds that the proposed disposition, consolidation, acquisition, or control will be consistent with the public interest, it shall approve the same."

Pub. L. 109–58, title XII, § 1289(b), (c), Aug. 8, 2005, 119 Stat. 983, provided that:

"(b) Effective Date. — The amendments made by this section [amending this section] shall take effect 6 months after the date of enactment of this Act [Aug. 8, 2005].

"(c) Transition Provision. — The amendments made by subsection (a) [amending this section] shall not apply to any application under section 203 of the Federal Power Act (16 U.S.C. 824b) that was filed on or before the date of enactment of this Act [Aug. 8, 2005]."

§ 824c. Issuance of securities; assumption of liabilities

(a) Authorization by Commission

No public utility shall issue any security, or assume any obligation or liability as guarantor, indorser, surety, or otherwise in respect of any security of another person, unless and until, and then only to the extent that, upon application by the public utility, the Commission by order authorizes such issue or assumption of liability. The Commission shall make such order only if it finds that such issue or assumption (a) is for some lawful object, within the corporate purposes of the applicant and compatible with the public interest, which is necessary or appropriate for or consistent with the proper performance by the applicant of service as a public utility and which will not impair its ability to perform that service, and (b) is reasonably necessary or appropriate for such purposes. The provisions of this section shall be effective six months after August 26, 1935.

(b) Application approval or modification; supplemental orders

The Commission, after opportunity for hearing, may grant any application under this section in whole or in part, and with such modifications and upon such terms and conditions as it may find necessary or appropriate, and may from time to time, after opportunity for hearing and for good cause shown, make such supplemental orders in the premises as it may find necessary or appropriate, and may by any such supplemental order modify the provisions of any previous order as to the particular purposes, uses, and extent to which, or the conditions under which, any security so theretofore authorized or the proceeds thereof may be applied, subject always to the requirements of subsection (a) of this section.

(c) Compliance with order of Commission

No public utility shall, without the consent of the Commission, apply any security or any proceeds thereof to any purpose not specified in the Commission's order, or supplemental order, or to any purpose in excess of the amount allowed for such purpose in such order, or otherwise in contravention of such order.

(d) Authorization of capitalization not to exceed amount paid

The Commission shall not authorize the capitalization of the right to be a corporation or of any franchise, permit, or contract for consolidation, merger, or lease in excess of the amount (exclusive of any tax or annual charge) actually paid as the consideration for such right, franchise, permit, or contract.

(e) Notes or drafts maturing less than one year after issuance

Subsection (a) of this section shall not apply to the issue or renewal of, or assumption of liability on, a note or draft maturing not more than one year after the date of such issue, renewal, or assumption of liability, and aggregating (together with all other then outstanding notes and drafts of a maturity of one year or less on which such public utility is primarily or secondarily liable) not more than 5 per centum of the par value of the other securities of the public utility then outstanding. In the case of securities having no par value, the par value for the purpose of this subsection shall be the fair market value as of the date of issue. Within ten days after any such issue, renewal, or assumption of liability, the public utility shall file with the Commission a certificate of notification, in such form as may be prescribed by the Commission, setting forth such matters as the Commission shall by regulation require.

(f) Public utility securities regulated by State not affected

The provisions of this section shall not extend to a public utility organized and operating in a State under the laws of which its security issues are regulated by a State commission.

(g) Guarantee or obligation on part of United States

Nothing in this section shall be construed to imply any guarantee or obligation on the part of the United States in respect of any securities to which the provisions of this section relate.

(h) Filing duplicate reports with the Securities and Exchange Commission

Any public utility whose security issues are approved by the Commission under this section may file with the Securities and Exchange Commission duplicate copies of reports filed with the Federal Power Commission in lieu of the reports, information, and documents required under sections 77g, 78l, and 78m of title 15.

(June 10, 1920, ch. 285, pt. II, § 204, as added Aug. 26, 1935, ch. 687, title II, § 213, 49 Stat. 850.)

Transfer of Functions

Executive and administrative functions of Securities and Exchange Commission, with certain exceptions, transferred to Chairman of such Commission, with authority vested in him to authorize their performance by any officer, employee, or administrative unit under his jurisdiction, by Reorg. Plan No. 10 of 1950, §§ 1, 2, eff. May 24, 1950, 15 F.R. 3175, 64 Stat. 1265, set out in the Appendix to Title 5, Government Organization and Employees.

§ 824d. Rates and charges; schedules; suspension of new rates; automatic adjustment clauses

(a) Just and reasonable rates

All rates and charges made, demanded, or received by any public utility for or in connection with the transmission or sale of electric energy subject to the jurisdiction of the Commission, and all rules and regulations affecting or pertaining to such rates or charges shall be just and reasonable, and any such rate or charge that is not just and reasonable is hereby declared to be unlawful.

(b) Preference or advantage unlawful

No public utility shall, with respect to any transmission or sale subject to the jurisdiction of the Commission, (1) make or grant any undue preference or advantage to any person or subject any person to any undue prejudice or disadvantage, or (2) maintain any unreasonable difference in rates, charges, service, facilities, or in any other respect, either as between localities or as between classes of service.

(c) Schedules

Under such rules and regulations as the Commission may prescribe, every public utility shall file with the Commission, within such time and in such form as the Commission may designate, and shall keep open in convenient form and place for public inspection schedules showing all rates and charges for any transmission or sale subject to the jurisdiction of the Commission, and the classifications, practices, and regulations affecting such rates and charges, together with all contracts which in any manner affect or relate to such rates, charges, classifications, and services.

(d) Notice required for rate changes

Unless the Commission otherwise orders, no change shall be made by any public utility in any such rate, charge, classification, or service, or in any rule, regulation, or contract relating thereto, except after sixty days' notice to the Commission and to the public. Such notice shall be given by filing with the Commission and keeping open for public inspection new schedules stating plainly the change or changes to be made in the schedule or schedules then in force and the time when the change or changes will go into effect. The Commission, for good cause shown, may allow changes to take effect without requiring the sixty days' notice herein provided for by an order specifying the changes so to be made and the time when they shall take effect and the manner in which they shall be filed and published.

(e) Suspension of new rates; hearings; five-month period

Whenever any such new schedule is filed the Commission shall have authority, either uponcomplaint or upon its own initiative without complaint, at once, and, if it so orders, without answer or formal pleading by the public utility, but upon reasonable notice, to enter upon a hearing concerning the lawfulness of such rate, charge, classification, or service; and, pending such hearing and the decision thereon, the Commission, upon filing with such schedules and delivering to the public utility affected thereby a statement in writing of its reasons for such suspension, may suspend the operation of such schedule and defer the use of such rate, charge, classification, or service, but not for a longer period than five months beyond the time when it would otherwise go into effect; and after full hearings, either completed before or after the rate, charge, classification, or service goes into effect, the Commission may make such orders with reference thereto as would be proper in a proceeding initiated after it had become effective. If the proceeding has not been concluded and an order made at the expiration of such five months, the proposed change of rate, charge, classification, or service shall go into effect at the end of such period, but in case of a proposed increased rate or charge, the Commission may by order require the interested public utility or public utilities to keep accurate account in detail of all amounts received by reason of such increase, specifying by whom and in whose behalf such amounts are paid, and upon completion of the hearing and decision may by further order require such public utility or public utilities to refund, with interest, to the persons in whose behalf such amounts were paid, such portion of such increased rates or charges as by its decision shall be found not justified. At any hearing involving a rate or charge sought to be increased, the burden of proof to show that the increased rate or charge is just and reasonable shall be upon the public utility, and the Commission shall give to the hearing and decision of such questions preference over other questions pending before it and decide the same as speedily as possible.

(f) Review of automatic adjustment clauses and public utility practices; action by Commission; "automatic adjustment clause" defined

(1) Not later than 2 years after November 9, 1978, and not less often than every 4 years thereafter, the Commission shall make a thorough review of automatic adjustment clauses in public utility rate schedules to examine —

(A) whether or not each such clause effectively provides incentives for efficient use of resources (including economical purchase and use of fuel and electric energy), and

(B) whether any such clause reflects any costs other than costs which are —

(i) subject to periodic fluctuations and

(ii) not susceptible to precise determinations in rate cases prior to the time such costs are incurred.

Such review may take place in individual rate proceedings or in generic or other separate proceedings applicable to one or more utilities.

(2) Not less frequently than every 2 years, in rate proceedings or in generic or other separate proceedings, the Commission shall review, with respect to each public utility, practices under any automatic adjustment clauses of such utility to insure efficient use of resources (including economical purchase and use of fuel and electric energy) under such clauses.

(3) The Commission may, on its own motion or upon complaint, after an opportunity for an evidentiary hearing, order a public utility to—

(A) modify the terms and provisions of any automatic adjustment clause, or

(B) cease any practice in connection with the clause,

if such clause or practice does not result in the economical purchase and use of fuel, electric energy, or other items, the cost of which is included in any rate schedule under an automatic adjustment clause.

(4) As used in this subsection, the term "automatic adjustment clause" means a provision of a rate schedule which provides for increases or decreases (or both), without prior hearing, in rates reflecting increases or decreases (or both) in costs incurred by an electric utility. Such term does not include any rate which takes effect subject to refund and subject to a later determination of the appropriate amount of such rate.

(June 10, 1920, ch. 285, pt. II, § 205, as added Aug. 26, 1935, ch. 687, title II, § 213, 49 Stat. 851; amended Pub. L. 95–617, title II, §§ 207(a), 208, Nov. 9, 1978, 92 Stat. 3142.)

Amendments

1978—Subsec. (d). Pub. L. 95–617, § 207(a), substituted "sixty" for "thirty" in two places.

Subsec. (f). Pub. L. 95–617, § 208, added subsec. (f).

Study of Electric Rate Increases Under Federal Power Act

Section 207(b) of Pub. L. 95–617 directed chairman of Federal Energy Regulatory Commission, in consultation with Secretary, to conduct a study of legal requirements and administrative procedures involved in consideration and resolution of proposed wholesale electric rate increases under Federal Power Act, section 791a et seq. of this title, for purposes of providing for expeditious handling of hearings consistent with due process, preventing imposition of successive rate increases before they have been determined by Commission to be just and reasonable and otherwise lawful, and improving procedures designed to prohibit anticompetitive or unreasonable differences in wholesale and retail rates, or both, and that chairman report to Congress within nine months from Nov. 9, 1978, on results of study, on administrative actions taken as a result of this study, and on any recommendations for changes in existing law that will aid purposes of this section.

§ 824e. Power of Commission to fix rates and charges; determination of cost of production or transmission

(a) Unjust or preferential rates, etc.; statement of reasons for changes; hearing; specification of issues

Whenever the Commission, after a hearing held upon its own motion or upon complaint, shall find that any rate, charge, or classification, demanded, observed, charged, or collected by any public utility for any transmission or sale subject to the jurisdiction of the Commission, or that any rule, regulation, practice, or contract affecting such rate, charge, or classification is unjust, unreasonable, unduly discriminatory or preferential, the Commission shall determine the just and reasonable rate, charge, classification, rule, regulation, practice, or contract to be thereafter observed and in force, and shall fix the same by order. Any complaint or motion of the Commission to initiate a proceeding under this section shall state the change or changes to be made in the rate, charge, classification, rule, regulation, practice, or contract then in force, and the reasons for any proposed change or changes therein. If, after review of any motion or complaint and answer, the Commission shall decide to hold a hearing, it shall fix by order the time and place of such hearing and shall specify the issues to be adjudicated.

(b) **Refund effective date; preferential proceedings; statement of reasons for delay; burden of proof; scope of refund order; refund orders in cases of dilatory behavior; interest**

Whenever the Commission institutes a proceeding under this section, the Commission shall establish a refund effective date. In the case of a proceeding instituted on complaint, the refund effective date shall not be earlier than the date of the filing of such complaint nor later than 5 months after the filing of such complaint. In the case of a proceeding instituted by the Commission on its own motion, the refund effective date shall not be earlier than the date of the publication by the Commission of notice of its intention to initiate such proceeding nor later than 5 months after the publication date. Upon institution of a proceeding under this section, the Commission shall give to the decision of such proceeding the same preference as provided under section 824d of this title and otherwise act as speedily as possible. If no final decision is rendered by the conclusion of the 180-day period commencing upon initiation of a proceeding pursuant to this section, the Commission shall state the reasons why it has failed to do so and shall state its best estimate as to when it reasonably expects to make such decision. In any proceeding under this section, the burden of proof to show that any rate, charge, classification, rule, regulation, practice, or contract is unjust, unreasonable, unduly discriminatory, or preferential shall be upon the Commission or the complainant. At the conclusion of any proceeding under this section, the Commission may order refunds of any amounts paid, for the period subsequent to the refund effective date through a date fifteen months after such refund effective date, in excess of those which would have been paid under the just and reasonable rate, charge, classification, rule, regulation, practice, or contract which the Commission orders to be thereafter observed and in force: *Provided*, That if the proceeding is not concluded within fifteen months after the refund effective date and if the Commission determines at the conclusion of the proceeding that the proceeding was not resolved within the fifteen-month period primarily because of dilatory behavior by the public utility, the Commission may order refunds of any or all amounts paid for the period subsequent to the refund effective date and prior to the conclusion of the proceeding. The refunds shall be made, with interest, to those persons who have paid those rates or charges which are the subject of the proceeding.

(c) **Refund considerations; shifting costs; reduction in revenues; "electric utility companies" and "registered holding company" defined**

Notwithstanding subsection (b) of this section, in a proceeding commenced under this section involving two or more electric utility companies of a registered holding company, refunds which might otherwise be payable under subsection (b) of this section shall not be ordered to the extent that such refunds would result from any portion of a Commission order that (1) requires a decrease in system production or transmission costs to be paid by one or more of such electric companies; and (2) is based upon a determination that the amount of such decrease should be paid through an increase in the costs to be paid by other electric utility companies of such registered holding company: *Provided,* That refunds, in whole or in part, may be ordered by the Commission if it determines that the registered holding company would not experience any reduction in revenues which results from an inability of an electric utility company of the holding company to recover such increase in costs for the period between the refund effective date and the effective date of the Commission's order. For purposes of this subsection, the terms "electric utility companies" and "registered holding company" shall have the same meanings as provided in the Public Utility Holding Company Act of 1935, as amended.[1]

(d) Investigation of costs

The Commission upon its own motion, or upon the request of any State commission whenever it can do so without prejudice to the efficient and proper conduct of its affairs, may investigate and determine the cost of the production or transmission of electric energy by means of facilities under the jurisdiction of the Commission in cases where the Commission has no authority to establish a rate governing the sale of such energy.

(e) Short-term sales

(1) In this subsection:

(A) The term "short-term sale" means an agreement for the sale of electric energy at wholesale in interstate commerce that is for a period of 31 days or less (excluding monthly contracts subject to automatic renewal).

(B) The term "applicable Commission rule" means a Commission rule applicable to sales at wholesale by public utilities that the Commission determines after notice and comment should also be applicable to entities subject to this subsection.

(2) If an entity described in section 824(f) of this title voluntarily makes a short-term sale of electric energy through an organized market in which the rates for the sale are established by Commission-approved tariff (rather than by contract) and the sale violates the terms of the tariff or applicable Commission rules in effect at the time of the sale, the entity shall be subject to the refund authority of the Commission under this section with respect to the violation.

(3) This section shall not apply to—

(A) any entity that sells in total (including affiliates of the entity) less than 8,000,000 megawatt hours of electricity per year; or

(B) an electric cooperative.

(4)(A) The Commission shall have refund authority under paragraph (2) with respect to a voluntary short term sale of electric energy by the Bonneville Power Administration only if the sale is at an unjust and unreasonable rate.

(B) The Commission may order a refund under subparagraph (A) only for short-term sales made by the Bonneville Power Administration at rates that are higher than the highest just and reasonable rate charged by any other entity for a short-term sale of electric energy in the same geographic market for the same, or most nearly comparable, period as the sale by the Bonneville Power Administration.

(C) In the case of any Federal power marketing agency or the Tennessee Valley Authority, the Commission shall not assert or exercise any regulatory authority or

---

1. *See References in Text note below.*

power under paragraph (2) other than the ordering of refunds to achieve a just and reasonable rate.

(June 10, 1920, ch. 285, pt. II, § 206, as added Aug. 26, 1935, ch. 687, title II, § 213, 49 Stat. 852; amended Pub. L. 100–473, § 2, Oct. 6, 1988, 102 Stat. 2299; Pub. L. 109–58, title XII, §§ 1285, 1286, 1295(b), Aug. 8, 2005, 119 Stat. 980, 981, 985.)

REFERENCES IN TEXT

The Public Utility Holding Company Act of 1935, referred to in subsec. (c), is title I of act Aug. 26, 1935, ch. 687, 49 Stat. 803, as amended, which was classified generally to chapter 2C (§ 79 et seq.) of Title 15, Commerce and Trade, prior to repeal by Pub. L. 109–58, title XII, § 1263, Aug. 8, 2005, 119 Stat. 974. For complete classification of this Act to the Code, see Tables.

AMENDMENTS

2005—Subsec. (a). Pub. L. 109–58, § 1295(b)(1), substituted "hearing held" for "hearing had" in first sentence.

Subsec. (b). Pub. L. 109–58, § 1295(b)(2), struck out "the public utility to make" before "refunds of any amounts paid" in seventh sentence.

Pub. L. 109–58, § 1285, in second sentence, substituted "the date of the filing of such complaint nor later than 5 months after the filing of such complaint" for "the date 60 days after the filing of such complaint nor later than 5 months after the expiration of such 60-day period", in third sentence, substituted "the date of the publication" for "the date 60 days after the publication" and "5 months after the publication date" for "5 months after the expiration of such 60-day period", and in fifth sentence, substituted "If no final decision is rendered by the conclusion of the 180-day period commencing upon initiation of a proceeding pursuant to this section, the Commission shall state the reasons why it has failed to do so and shall state its best estimate as to when it reasonably expects to make such decision" for "If no final decision is rendered by the refund effective date or by the conclusion of the 180-day period commencing upon initiation of a proceeding pursuant to this section, whichever is earlier, the Commission shall state the reasons why it has failed to do so and shall state its best estimate as to when it reasonably expects to make such decision".

Subsec. (e). Pub. L. 109–58, § 1286, added subsec. (e).

1988—Subsec. (a). Pub. L. 100–473, § 2(1), inserted provisions for a statement of reasons for listed changes, hearings, and specification of issues.

Subsecs. (b) to (d). Pub. L. 100–473, § 2(2), added subsecs. (b) and (c) and redesignated former subsec. (b) as (d).

EFFECTIVE DATE OF 1988 AMENDMENT

Pub. L. 100–473, § 4, Oct. 6, 1988, 102 Stat. 2300, provided that: "The amendments made by this Act [amending this section] are not applicable to complaints filed or motions initiated before the date of enactment of this Act [Oct. 6, 1988] pursuant to section 206 of the Federal Power Act [this section]:*Provided, however,* That such complaints may be withdrawn and refiled without prejudice."

LIMITATION ON AUTHORITY PROVIDED

Pub. L. 100–473, § 3, Oct. 6, 1988, 102 Stat. 2300, provided that: "Nothing in subsection (c) of section 206 of the Federal Power Act, as amended (16 U.S.C. 824e(c)) shall be interpreted to confer upon the Federal Energy Regulatory Commission any authority not granted to it elsewhere in such Act [16 U.S.C. 791a et seq.] to issue an order that (1) requires a decrease in system production or transmission costs to be paid by one or more electric utility companies of a registered holding company; and (2) is based upon a determination that the amount of such decrease should be paid through an increase in the costs to be paid by other electric utility companies of such registered holding company. For purposes of this section, the terms 'electric utility companies' and 'registered holding company' shall have the same meanings as provided in the Public Utility Holding Company Act of 1935, as amended [15 U.S.C. 79 et seq.]."

STUDY

Pub. L. 100–473, § 5, Oct. 6, 1988, 102 Stat. 2301, directed that, no earlier than three years and no later than four years after Oct. 6, 1988, Federal Energy Regulatory Commission perform a study of effect of amendments to this section, analyzing (1) impact, if any, of such amendments on cost of capital paid by public utilities, (2) any change in average time taken to resolve proceedings under this section, and (3) such other matters as Commission may deem appropriate in public interest, with study to be sent to Committee on Energy and Natural Resources of Senate and Committee on Energy and Commerce of House of Representatives.

§ 824f. Ordering furnishing of adequate service

Whenever the Commission, upon complaint of a State commission, after notice to each State commission and public utility affected and after opportunity for hearing, shall find that any interstate service of any public utility is inadequate or insufficient, the Commission shall determine the proper, adequate, or sufficient service to be furnished, and shall fix the same by its order, rule, or regulation:*Provided*, That the Commission shall have no authority to compel the enlargement of generating facilities for such purposes, nor to compel the public utility to sell or exchange energy when to do so would impair its ability to render adequate service to its customers.

(June 10, 1920, ch. 285, pt. II, § 207, as added Aug. 26, 1935, ch. 687, title II, § 213, 49 Stat. 853.)

§ 824g. Ascertainment of cost of property and depreciation

(a) Investigation of property costs

The Commission may investigate and ascertain the actual legitimate cost of the property of every public utility, the depreciation therein, and, when found necessary for rate-making purposes, other facts which bear on the determination of such cost or depreciation, and the fair value of such property.

(b) Request for inventory and cost statements

Every public utility upon request shall file with the Commission an inventory of all or any part of its property and a statement of the original cost thereof, and shall keep the Commission informed regarding the cost of all additions, betterments, extensions, and new construction.

(June 10, 1920, ch. 285, pt. II, § 208, as added Aug. 26, 1935, ch. 687, title II, § 213, 49 Stat. 853.)

§ 824h. References to State boards by Commission

(a) Composition of boards; force and effect of proceedings

The Commission may refer any matter arising in the administration of this subchapter to a board to be composed of a member or members, as determined by the Commission, from the State or each of the States affected or to be affected by such matter. Any such board shall be vested with the same power and be subject to the same duties and liabilities as in the case of a member of the Commission when designated by the Commission to hold any hearings. The action of such board shall have such force and effect and its proceedings shall be conducted in such manner as the Commission shall by regulations prescribe. The board shall be appointed by the Commission from persons nominated by the State commission of each State affected or by the Governor of such State if there is no State commission. Each State affected shall be entitled to the same number of representatives on the board unless the nominating power of such State waives such right. The Commission shall have discretion to reject the nominee from any State, but shall thereupon invite a new nomination from that State. The members of a board shall receive such allowances for expenses as the Commission shall provide. The Commission may, when in its discretion sufficient reason exists therefor, revoke any reference to such a board.

(b) Cooperation with State commissions

The Commission may confer with any State commission regarding the relationship between rate structures, costs, accounts, charges, practices, classifications, and regulations of public utilities subject to the jurisdiction of such State commission and of the Commission; and the Commission is authorized, under such rules and regulations as it shall prescribe, to hold joint hearings with any State commission in connection with any matter with respect to which the Commission is authorized to act. The Commission is authorized in the administration of this chapter to avail itself of such cooperation, services, records, and facilities as may be afforded by any State commission.

(c) Availability of information and reports to State commissions; Commission experts

The Commission shall make available to the several State commissions such information and reports as may be of assistance in State regulation of public utilities. Whenever the Commission can do so without prejudice to the efficient and proper conduct of its affairs, it may upon request from a State make available to such State as witnesses any of its trained rate, valuation, or other experts, subject to reimbursement to the Commission by such State of the compensation and traveling expenses of such witnesses. All sums collected hereunder shall be credited to the appropriation from which the amounts were expended in carrying out the provisions of this subsection.

(June 10, 1920, ch. 285, pt. II, § 209, as added Aug. 26, 1935, ch. 687, title II, § 213, 49 Stat. 853.)

§ 824i. Interconnection authority

(a) Powers of Commission; application by State regulatory authority

(1) Upon application of any electric utility, Federal power marketing agency, geothermal power producer (including a producer which is not an electric utility), qualifying cogenerator, or qualifying small power producer, the Commission may issue an order requiring—

(A) the physical connection of any cogeneration facility, any small power production facility, or the transmission facilities of any electric utility, with the facilities of such applicant,

(B) such action as may be necessary to make effective any physical connection described in subparagraph (A), which physical connection is ineffective for any reason, such as inadequate size, poor maintenance, or physical unreliability,

(C) such sale or exchange of electric energy or other coordination, as may be necessary to carry out the purposes of any order under subparagraph (A) or (B), or

(D) such increase in transmission capacity as may be necessary to carry out the purposes of any order under subparagraph (A) or (B).

(2) Any State regulatory authority may apply to the Commission for an order for any action referred to in subparagraph (A), (B), (C), or (D) of paragraph (1). No such order may be issued by the Commission with respect to a Federal power marketing agency upon application of a State regulatory authority.

(b) Notice, hearing and determination by Commission

Upon receipt of an application under subsection (a) of this section, the Commission shall —

(1) issue notice to each affected State regulatory authority, each affected electric utility, each affected Federal power marketing agency, each affected owner or operator of a cogeneration facility or of a small power production facility, and to the public.

(2) afford an opportunity for an evidentiary hearing, and

(3) make a determination with respect to the matters referred to in subsection (c) of this section.

(c) Necessary findings

No order may be issued by the Commission under subsection (a) of this section unless the Commission determines that such order —

(1) is in the public interest,

(2) would —

(A) encourage overall conservation of energy or capital,

(B) optimize the efficiency of use of facilities and resources, or

(C) improve the reliability of any electric utility system or Federal power marketing agency to which the order applies, and

(3) meets the requirements of section 824k of this title.

(d) Motion of Commission

The Commission may, on its own motion, after compliance with the requirements of paragraphs (1) and (2) of subsection (b) of this section, issue an order requiring any action described in subsection (a)(1) of this section if the Commission determines that such order meets the requirements of subsection (c) of this section. No such order may be issued upon the Commission's own motion with respect to a Federal power marketing agency.

(e) Definitions

(1) As used in this section, the term "facilities" means only facilities used for the generation or transmission of electric energy.

(2) With respect to an order issued pursuant to an application of a qualifying cogenerator or qualifying small power producer under subsection (a)(1) of this section, the term "facilities of such applicant" means the qualifying cogeneration facilities or qualifying small power production facilities of the applicant, as specified in the application. With respect to an order issued pursuant to an application under subsection (a)(2) of this section, the term "facilities of such applicant" means the qualifying cogeneration facilities, qualifying small power production facilities, or the transmission facilities of an electric utility, as specified in the application. With respect to an order issued by the Commission on its own motion under subsection (d) of this section, such term means the qualifying cogeneration facilities, qualifying small power production facilities, or the transmission facilities of an electric utility, as specified in the proposed order.

(June 10, 1920, ch. 285, pt. II, §210, as added Pub. L. 95–617, title II, §202, Nov. 9, 1978, 92 Stat. 3135; amended Pub. L. 96–294, title VI, §643(a)(2), June 30, 1980, 94 Stat. 770.)

AMENDMENTS

1980—Subsec. (a)(1). Pub. L. 96–294 added applicability to geothermal power producers.

STUDY AND REPORT TO CONGRESSIONAL COMMITTEES ON APPLICATION OF PROVISIONS RELATING TO COGENERATION, SMALL POWER PRODUCTION, AND INTERCONNECTION AUTHORITY TO HYDROELECTRIC POWER FACILITIES

For provisions requiring the Federal Energy Regulatory Commission to conduct a study and report to Congress on whether the benefits of this section and section 824a–3 of this title should be applied to hydroelectric power facilities utilizing new dams or diversions, within the meaning of section 824a–3(k) of this title, see section 8(d) of Pub. L. 99–495, set out as a note under section 824a–3 of this title.

§824j. Wheeling authority

(a) Transmission service by any electric utility; notice, hearing and findings by Commission

Any electric utility, Federal power marketing agency, or any other person generating electric energy for sale for resale, may apply to the Commission for an order under this subsection requiring a transmitting utility to provide transmission services (including any enlargement of transmission capacity necessary to provide such services) to the applicant. Upon receipt of such application, after public notice and notice to each affected State regulatory authority, each affected electric utility, and each affected Federal power marketing agency, and after affording an opportunity for an evidentiary hearing, the Commission may issue such order if it finds that such order meets the requirements of section 824k of this title, and would otherwise be in the public interest. No order may be issued under this subsection unless the applicant has made a request for transmission services to the transmitting utility that would be the subject of such order at least 60 days prior to its filing of an application for such order.

(b) Reliability of electric service

No order may be issued under this section or section 824i of this title if, after giving consideration to consistently applied regional or national reliability standards, guidelines, or criteria, the Commission finds that such order would unreasonably impair the continued reliability of electric systems affected by the order.

(c) Replacement of electric energy

No order may be issued under subsection (a) or (b) of this section which requires the transmitting utility subject to the order to transmit, during any period, an amount of electric energy which replaces any amount of electric energy—

(1) required to be provided to such applicant pursuant to a contract during such period, or

(2) currently provided to the applicant by the utility subject to the order pursuant to a rate schedule on file during such period with the Commission: *Provided,* That nothing in this subparagraph shall prevent an application for an order hereunder to be filed prior to termination or modification of an existing rate schedule: *Provided,* That such order shall not become effective until termination of such rate schedule or the modification becomes effective.

(d) Termination or modification of order; notice, hearing and findings of Commission; contents of order; inclusion in order of terms and conditions agreed upon by parties

(1) Any transmitting utility ordered under subsection (a) or (b) of this section to provide transmission services may apply to the Commission for an order permitting such transmitting utility to cease providing all, or any portion of, such services. After public notice, notice to each affected State regulatory authority, each affected Federal power marketing agency, each affected transmitting utility, and each affected electric utility, and after an opportunity for an evidentiary hearing, the Commission shall issue an order terminating or modifying the order issued under subsection (a) or (b) of this section, if the transmitting utility providing such transmission services has demonstrated, and the Commission has found, that—

(A) due to changed circumstances, the requirements applicable, under this section and section 824k of this title, to the issuance of an order under subsection (a) or (b) of this section are no longer met, or[1]

(B) any transmission capacity of the utility providing transmission services under such order which was, at the time such order was issued, in excess of the capacity necessary to serve its own customers is no longer in excess of the capacity necessary for such purposes, or

(C) the ordered transmission services require enlargement of transmission capacity and the transmitting utility subject to the order has failed, after making a good faith effort, to obtain the necessary approvals or property rights under applicable Federal, State, and local laws.

No order shall be issued under this subsection pursuant to a finding under subparagraph (A) unless the Commission finds that such order is in the public interest.

(2) Any order issued under this subsection terminating or modifying an order issued under subsection (a) or (b) of this section shall—

(A) provide for any appropriate compensation, and

(B) provide the affected electric utilities adequate opportunity and time to—

(i) make suitable alternative arrangements for any transmission services terminated or modified, and

(ii) insure that the interests of ratepayers of such utilities are adequately protected.

(3) No order may be issued under this subsection terminating or modifying any order issued under subsection (a) or (b) of this section if the order under subsection (a) or (b) of this section includes terms and conditions agreed upon by the parties which—

(A) fix a period during which transmission services are to be provided under the order under subsection (a) or (b) of this section, or

(B) otherwise provide procedures or methods for terminating or modifying such order (including, if appropriate, the return of the transmission capacity when necessary to take into account an increase, after the issuance of such order, in the needs of the transmitting utility subject to such order for transmission capacity).

---

1. *So in original. The word "or" probably should not appear.*

(e) "Facilities" defined

As used in this section, the term "facilities" means only facilities used for the generation or transmission of electric energy.

(June 10, 1920, ch. 285, pt. II, §211, as added Pub. L. 95–617, title II, §203, Nov. 9, 1978, 92 Stat. 3136; amended Pub. L. 96–294, title VI, §643(a)(3), June 30, 1980, 94 Stat. 770; Pub. L. 99–495, §15, Oct. 16, 1986, 100 Stat. 1257; Pub. L. 102–486, title VII, §721, Oct. 24, 1992, 106 Stat. 2915; Pub. L. 109–58, title XII, §1295(c), Aug. 8, 2005, 119 Stat. 985.)

AMENDMENTS

2005 — Subsec. (c). Pub. L. 109–58, §1295(c)(1), struck out par. (2) designation before introductory provisions, redesignated former subpars. (A) and (B) as pars. (1) and (2), respectively, and in par. (2) substituted "termination or modification" for "termination of modification".

Subsec. (d)(1). Pub. L. 109–58, §1295(c)(2), substituted "if the transmitting utility providing" for "if the electric utility providing" in introductory provisions.

1992 — Subsec. (a). Pub. L. 102–486, §721(1), amended first sentence generally. Prior to amendment, first sentence read as follows: "Any electric utility, geothermal power producer (including a producer which is not an electric utility), or Federal power marketing agency may apply to the Commission for an order under this subsection requiring any other electric utility to provide transmission services to the applicant (including any enlargement of transmission capacity necessary to provide such services)."

Pub. L. 102–486, §721(2), in second sentence, substituted "the Commission may issue such order if it finds that such order meets the requirements of section 824k of this title, and would otherwise be in the public interest. No order may be issued under this subsection unless the applicant has made a request for transmission services to the transmitting utility that would be the subject of such order at least 60 days prior to its filing of an application for such order." for "the Commission may issue such order if it finds that such order—

"(1) is in the public interest,

"(2) would—

"(A) conserve a significant amount of energy,

"(B) significantly promote the efficient use of facilities and resources, or

"(C) improve the reliability of any electric utility system to which the order applies, and

"(3) meets the requirements of section 824k of this title."

Subsec. (b). Pub. L. 102–486, §721(3), amended subsec. (b) generally, substituting provisions relating to reliability of electric service for provisions which related to transmission service by sellers of electric energy for resale and notice, hearing, and determinations by Commission.

Subsec. (c). Pub. L. 102–486, §721(4), struck out pars. (1), (3), and (4), and substituted "which requires the transmitting" for "which requires the electric" in introductory provisions of par. (2). Prior to amendment, pars. (1), (3), and (4) read as follows:

"(1) No order may be issued under subsection (a) of this section unless the Commission determines that such order would reasonably preserve existing competitive relationships.

"(3) No order may be issued under the authority of subsection (a) or (b) of this section which is inconsistent with any State law which governs the retail marketing areas of electric utilities.

"(4) No order may be issued under subsection (a) or (b) of this section which provides for the transmission of electric energy directly to an ultimate consumer."

Subsec. (d). Pub. L. 102–486, §721(5), in first sentence substituted "transmitting" for "electric" before "utility" in two places, in second sentence inserted "each affected transmitting utility," before "and each affected electric utility", in par. (1) substituted ", or" for period at end of subpar. (B) and added subpar. (C), and in par. (3)(B) substituted "transmitting" for "electric" before "utility".

1986—Subsec. (c)(2)(B). Pub. L. 99–495 inserted provisions that nothing in this subparagraph shall prevent an application for an order hereunder to be filed prior to termination or modification of an existing rate schedule, provided that such order shall not become effective until termination of such rate schedule or the modification becomes effective.

1980—Subsec. (a). Pub. L. 96–294 added applicability to geothermal power producers.

Effective Date of 1986 Amendment

Amendment by Pub. L. 99–495 effective with respect to each license, permit, or exemption issued under this chapter after Oct. 16, 1986, see section 18 of Pub. L. 99–495, set out as a note under section 797 of this title.

State Authorities; Construction

Nothing in amendment by Pub. L. 102–486 to be construed as affecting or intending to affect, or in any way to interfere with, authority of any State or local government relating to environmental protection or siting of facilities, see section 731 of Pub. L. 102–486, set out as a note under section 796 of this title.

§ 824j–1. Open access by unregulated transmitting utilities

(a) Definition of unregulated transmitting utility

In this section, the term "unregulated transmitting utility" means an entity that—

(1) owns or operates facilities used for the transmission of electric energy in interstate commerce; and

(2) is an entity described in section 824(f) of this title.

(b) Transmission operation services

Subject to section 824k(h) of this title, the Commission may, by rule or order, require an unregulated transmitting utility to provide transmission services—

(1) at rates that are comparable to those that the unregulated transmitting utility charges itself; and

(2) on terms and conditions (not relating to rates) that are comparable to those under which the unregulated transmitting utility provides transmission services to itself and that are not unduly discriminatory or preferential.

(c) Exemption

The Commission shall exempt from any rule or order under this section any unregulated transmitting utility that—

(1) sells not more than 4,000,000 megawatt hours of electricity per year;

(2) does not own or operate any transmission facilities that are necessary for operating an interconnected transmission system (or any portion of the system); or

(3) meets other criteria the Commission determines to be in the public interest.

(d) Local distribution facilities

The requirements of subsection (b) of this section shall not apply to facilities used in local distribution.

(e) Exemption termination

If the Commission, after an evidentiary hearing held on a complaint and after giving consideration to reliability standards established under section 824o of this title, finds on the basis of a preponderance of the evidence that any exemption granted pursuant to subsection (c) of this section unreasonably impairs the continued reliability of an interconnected transmission system, the Commission shall revoke the exemption granted to the transmitting utility.

(f) Application to unregulated transmitting utilities

The rate changing procedures applicable to public utilities under subsections (c) and (d) of section 824d of this title are applicable to unregulated transmitting utilities for purposes of this section.

(g) Remand

In exercising authority under subsection (b)(1) of this section, the Commission may remand transmission rates to an unregulated transmitting utility for review and revision if necessary to meet the requirements of subsection (b) of this section.

(h) Other requests

The provision of transmission services under subsection (b) of this section does not preclude a request for transmission services under section 824j of this title.

(i) Limitation

The Commission may not require a State or municipality to take action under this section that would violate a private activity bond rule for purposes of section 141 of title 26.

(j) Transfer of control of transmitting facilities

Nothing in this section authorizes the Commission to require an unregulated transmitting utility to transfer control or operational control of its transmitting facilities to a Transmission Organization that is designated to provide nondiscriminatory transmission access.

(June 10, 1920, ch. 285, pt. II, § 211A, as added Pub. L. 109–58, title XII, § 1231, Aug. 8, 2005, 119 Stat. 955.)

§ 824k. Orders requiring interconnection or wheeling

(a) Rates, charges, terms, and conditions for wholesale transmission services

An order under section 824j of this title shall require the transmitting utility subject to the order to provide wholesale transmission services at rates, charges, terms, and conditions which permit the recovery by such utility of all the costs incurred in connection with the transmission services and necessary associated services, including, but not limited to, an appropriate share, if any, of legitimate, verifiable and economic costs, including taking into account any benefits to the transmission system of providing the transmission service, and the costs of any enlargement of transmission facilities. Such rates, charges, terms, and conditions shall promote the economically efficient transmission and generation of electricity and shall be just and reasonable, and not unduly discriminatory or preferential. Rates, charges, terms, and conditions for transmission services provided pursuant to an order under section 824j of this title shall ensure that, to the extent practicable, costs incurred in providing the wholesale transmission services, and properly allocable to the provision of such services, are recovered from the applicant for such order and not from a transmitting utility's existing wholesale, retail, and transmission customers. ·

(b) Repealed. Pub. L. 102–486, title VII, § 722(1), Oct. 24, 1992, 106 Stat. 2916

(c) Issuance of proposed order; agreement by parties to terms and conditions of order; approval by Commission; inclusion in final order; failure to agree

(1) Before issuing an order under section 824i of this title or subsection (a) or (b) of section 824j of this title, the Commission shall issue a proposed order and set a reasonable time for parties to the proposed interconnection or transmission order to agree to terms and conditions under which such order is to be carried out, including the apportionment of costs between them and the compensation or reimbursement reasonably due to any of them. Such proposed order shall not be reviewable or enforceable in any court. The time set for such parties to agree to such terms and conditions may be shortened if the Commission determines that delay would jeopardize the attainment of the purposes of any proposed order. Any terms and conditions agreed to by the parties shall be subject to the approval of the Commission.

(2)(A) If the parties agree as provided in paragraph (1) within the time set by the Commission and the Commission approves such agreement, the terms and conditions shall be included in the final order. In the case of an order under section 824i of this title, if the parties fail to agree within the time set by the Commission or if the Commission does not approve any such agreement, the Commission shall prescribe such terms and conditions and include such terms and conditions in the final order.

(B) In the case of any order applied for under section 824j of this title, if the parties fail to agree within the time set by the Commission, the Commission shall prescribe such terms and conditions in the final order.

(d) Statement of reasons for denial

If the Commission does not issue any order applied for under section 824i or 824j of this title, the Commission shall, by order, deny such application and state the reasons for such denial.

(e) Savings provisions

(1) No provision of section 824i, 824j, 824m of this title, or this section shall be treated as requiring any person to utilize the authority of any such section in lieu of any other authority of law. Except as provided in section 824i, 824j, 824m of this title, or this section, such sections shall not be construed as limiting or impairing any authority of the Commission under any other provision of law.

(2) Sections 824i, 824j, 824l, 824m of this title, and this section, shall not be construed to modify, impair, or supersede the antitrust laws. For purposes of this section, the term "antitrust laws" has the meaning given in subsection (a) of the first sentence of section 12 of title 15, except that such term includes section 45 of title 15 to the extent that such section relates to unfair methods of competition.

(f) Effective date of order; hearing; notice; review

(1) No order under section 824i or 824j of this title requiring the Tennessee Valley Authority (hereinafter in this subsection referred to as the "TVA") to take any action shall take effect for 60 days following the date of issuance of the order. Within 60 days following the issuance by the Commission of any order under section 824i or of section 824j of this title requiring the TVA to enter into any contract for the sale or delivery of power, the Commission may on its own motion initiate, or upon petition of any aggrieved person shall initiate, an evidentiary hearing to determine whether or not such sale or delivery would result in violation of the third sentence of section 15d(a)

of the Tennessee Valley Authority Act of 1933 (16 U.S.C. 831n–4), hereinafter in this subsection referred to as the TVA Act [16 U.S.C. 831 et seq.].

(2) Upon initiation of any evidentiary hearing under paragraph (1), the Commission shall give notice thereof to any applicant who applied for and obtained the order from the Commission, to any electric utility or other entity subject to such order, and to the public, and shall promptly make the determination referred to in paragraph (1). Upon initiation of such hearing, the Commission shall stay the effectiveness of the order under section 824i or 824j of this title until whichever of the following dates is applicable—

(A) the date on which there is a final determination (including any judicial review thereof under paragraph (3)) that no such violation would result from such order, or

(B) the date on which a specific authorization of the Congress (within the meaning of the third sentence of section 15d(a) of the TVA Act [16 U.S.C. 831n–4(a)]) takes effect.

(3) Any determination under paragraph (1) shall be reviewable only in the appropriate court of the United States upon petition filed by any aggrieved person or municipality within 60 days after such determination, and such court shall have jurisdiction to grant appropriate relief. Any applicant who applied for and obtained the order under section 824i or 824j of this title, and any electric utility or other entity subject to such order shall have the right to intervene in any such proceeding in such court. Except for review by such court (and any appeal or other review by an appellate court of the United States), no court shall have jurisdiction to consider any action brought by any person to enjoin the carrying out of any order of the Commission under section 824i or section 824j of this title requiring the TVA to take any action on the grounds that such action requires a specific authorization of the Congress pursuant to the third sentence of section 15d(a) of the TVA Act [16 U.S.C. 831n–4(a)].

(g) Prohibition on orders inconsistent with retail marketing areas

No order may be issued under this chapter which is inconsistent with any State law which governs the retail marketing areas of electric utilities.

(h) Prohibition on mandatory retail wheeling and sham wholesale transactions

No order issued under this chapter shall be conditioned upon or require the transmission of electric energy:

(1) directly to an ultimate consumer, or

(2) to, or for the benefit of, an entity if such electric energy would be sold by such entity directly to an ultimate consumer, unless:

(A) such entity is a Federal power marketing agency; the Tennessee Valley Authority; a State or any political subdivision of a State (or an agency, authority, or instrumentality of a State or a political subdivision); a corporation or association that has ever received a loan for the purposes of providing electric service from the Administrator of the Rural Electrification Administration under the Rural Electrification Act of 1936 [7 U.S.C. 901 et seq.]; a person having an obligation arising under State or local law (exclusive of an obligation arising solely from a contract entered into by such person) to provide electric service to the public; or any corporation or association which is wholly owned, directly or indirectly, by any one or more of the foregoing; and

(B) such entity was providing electric service to such ultimate consumer on October 24, 1992, or would utilize transmission or distribution facilities that it owns or controls to deliver all such electric energy to such electric consumer.

Nothing in this subsection shall affect any authority of any State or local government under State law concerning the transmission of electric energy directly to an ultimate consumer.

(i) Laws applicable to Federal Columbia River Transmission System

(1) The Commission shall have authority pursuant to section 824i of this title, section 824j of this title, this section, and section 824l of this title to (A) order the Administrator of the Bonneville Power Administration to provide transmission service and (B) establish the terms and conditions of such service. In applying such sections to the Federal Columbia River Transmission System, the Commission shall assure that—

(i) the provisions of otherwise applicable Federal laws shall continue in full force and effect and shall continue to be applicable to the system; and

(ii) the rates for the transmission of electric power on the system shall be governed only by such otherwise applicable provisions of law and not by any provision of section 824i of this title, section 824j of this title, this section, or section 824l of this title, except that no rate for the transmission of power on the system shall be unjust, unreasonable, or unduly discriminatory or preferential, as determined by the Commission.

(2) Notwithstanding any other provision of this chapter with respect to the procedures for the determination of terms and conditions for transmission service—

(A) when the Administrator of the Bonneville Power Administration either (i) in response to a written request for specific transmission service terms and conditions does not offer the requested terms and conditions, or (ii) proposes to establish terms and conditions of general applicability for transmission service on the Federal Columbia River Transmission System, then the Administrator may provide opportunity for a hearing and, in so doing, shall—

(I) give notice in the Federal Register and state in such notice the written explanation of the reasons why the specific terms and conditions for transmission services are not being offered or are being proposed;

(II) adhere to the procedural requirements of paragraphs (1) through (3) of section 839e(i) of this title, except that the hearing officer shall, unless the hearing officer becomes unavailable to the agency, make a recommended decision to the Administrator that states the hearing officer's findings and conclusions, and the reasons or basis thereof, on all material issues of fact, law, or discretion presented on the record; and

(III) make a determination, setting forth the reasons for reaching any findings and conclusions which may differ from those of the hearing officer, based on the hearing record, consideration of the hearing officer's recommended decision, section 824j of this title and this section, as amended by the Energy Policy Act of 1992, and the provisions of law as preserved in this section; and

(B) if application is made to the Commission under section 824j of this title for transmission service under terms and conditions different than those offered by the Administrator, or following the denial of a request for transmission service by the Administrator, and such application is filed within 60 days of the Administrator's final determination and in accordance with Commission procedures, the Commission shall—

(i) in the event the Administrator has conducted a hearing as herein provided for (I) accord parties to the Administrator's hearing the opportunity to offer for the Commission record materials excluded by the Administrator from the hearing record, (II) accord such parties the opportunity to submit for the Commission record comments on appropriate terms and conditions, (III) afford those parties the opportunity for a hearing if and to the extent that the Commission finds the Administrator's hearing record to be inadequate to support a decision by the Commission, and (IV) establish terms and conditions for or deny transmission service based on the Administrator's hearing record, the Commission record, section 824j of this title and this section, as amended by the Energy Policy Act of 1992, and the provisions of law as preserved in this section, or

(ii) in the event the Administrator has not conducted a hearing as herein provided for, determine whether to issue an order for transmission service in accordance with section 824j of this title and this section, including providing the opportunity for a hearing.

(3) Notwithstanding those provisions of section 825l(b) of this title which designate the court in which review may be obtained, any party to a proceeding concerning transmission service sought to be furnished by the Administrator of the Bonneville Power Administration seeking review of an order issued by the Commission in such proceeding shall obtain a review of such order in the United States Court of Appeals for the Pacific Northwest, as that region is defined by section 839a(14) of this title.

(4) To the extent the Administrator of the Bonneville Power Administration cannot be required under section 824j of this title, as a result of the Administrator's other statutory mandates, either to (A) provide transmission service to an applicant which the Commission would otherwise order, or (B) provide such service under rates, terms, and conditions which the Commission would otherwise require, the applicant shall not be required to provide similar transmission services to the Administrator or to provide such services under similar rates, terms, and conditions.

(5) The Commission shall not issue any order under section 824i of this title, section 824j of this title, this section, or section 824l of this title requiring the Administrator of the Bonneville Power Administration to provide transmission service if such an order would impair the Administrator's ability to provide such transmission service to the Administrator's power and transmission customers in the Pacific Northwest, as that region is defined in section 839a(14) of this title, as is needed to assure adequate and reliable service to loads in that region.

(j) Equitability within territory restricted electric systems

With respect to an electric utility which is prohibited by Federal law from being a source of power supply, either directly or through a distributor of its electric energy, outside an area set forth in such law, no order issued under section 824j of this title may require such electric utility (or a distributor of such electric utility) to provide transmission services to another entity if the electric energy to be transmitted will be consumed within the area set forth in such Federal law, unless the order is in furtherance of a sale of electric energy to that electric utility: *Provided, however,* That the foregoing provision shall not apply to any area served at retail by an electric transmission system which was such a distributor on October 24, 1992, and which before October 1, 1991, gave its notice of termination under its power supply contract with such electric utility.

(k) ERCOT utilities

(1) Rates

Any order under section 824j of this title requiring provision of transmission services in whole or in part within ERCOT shall provide that any ERCOT utility which is not a public utility and the transmission facilities of which are actually used for such transmission service is entitled to receive compensation based, insofar as practicable and consistent with subsection (a) of this section, on the transmission ratemaking methodology used by the Public Utility Commission of Texas.

(2) **Definitions**

For purposes of this subsection—

(A) the term "ERCOT" means the Electric Reliability Council of Texas; and

(B) the term "ERCOT utility" means a transmitting utility which is a member of ERCOT.

(June 10, 1920, ch. 285, pt. II, §212, as added Pub. L. 95–617, title II, §204(a), Nov. 9, 1978, 92 Stat. 3138; amended Pub. L. 102–486, title VII, §722, Oct. 24, 1992, 106 Stat. 2916.)

REFERENCES IN TEXT

The TVA Act, referred to in subsec. (f)(1), means act May 18, 1933, ch. 32, 48 Stat. 58, as amended, known as the Tennessee Valley Authority Act of 1933, which is classified generally to chapter 12A (§831 et seq.) of this title. For complete classification of this Act to the Code, see section 831 of this title and Tables.

The Rural Electrification Act of 1936, referred to in subsec. (h)(2)(A), is act May 20, 1936, ch. 432, 49 Stat. 1363, as amended, which is classified generally to chapter 31 (§901 et seq.) of Title 7, Agriculture. For complete classification of this Act to the Code, see section 901 of Title 7 and Tables.

The Energy Policy Act of 1992, referred to in subsec. (i)(2)(A)(III), (B)(i), is Pub. L. 102–486, Oct. 24, 1992, 106 Stat. 2776. For complete classification of this Act to the Code, see Short Title note set out under section 13201 of Title 42, The Public Health and Welfare and Tables.

AMENDMENTS

1992—Subsec. (a). Pub. L. 102–486, §722(1), added subsec. (a) and struck out former subsec. (a) which related to determinations by Commission.

Subsec. (b). Pub. L. 102–486, §722(1), struck out subsec. (b) which required applicants for orders to be ready, willing, and able to reimburse parties subject to such orders.

Subsec. (e). Pub. L. 102–486, §722(2), amended subsec. (e) generally. Prior to amendment, subsec. (e) related to utilization of interconnection or wheeling authority in lieu of other authority and limitation of Commission authority.

Subsecs. (g) to (k). Pub. L. 102–486, §722(3), added subsecs. (g) to (k).

STATE AUTHORITIES; CONSTRUCTION

Nothing in amendment by Pub. L. 102–486 to be construed as affecting or intending to affect, or in any way to interfere with, authority of any State or local government relating to environmental protection or siting of facilities, see section 731 of Pub. L. 102–486, set out as a note under section 796 of this title.

§824*l*. Information requirements

(a) Requests for wholesale transmission services

Whenever any electric utility, Federal power marketing agency, or any other person generating electric energy for sale for resale makes a good faith request to a transmitting utility to provide wholesale transmission services and requests specific rates and charges, and other terms and conditions, unless the transmitting utility agrees to provide such services at rates, charges, terms and conditions acceptable to such person, the transmitting utility shall, within 60 days of its receipt of the request, or other mutually agreed upon period, provide such person with a detailed written explanation, with specific reference to the facts and circumstances of the request, stating (1) the transmitting utility's basis for the proposed rates, charges, terms, and conditions for such services, and (2) its analysis of any physical or other constraints affecting the provision of such services.

(b) Transmission capacity and constraints

Not later than 1 year after October 24, 1992, the Commission shall promulgate a rule requiring that information be submitted annually to the Commission by transmitting utilities which is adequate to inform potential transmission customers, State regulatory authorities, and the public of potentially available transmission capacity and known constraints.

(June 10, 1920, ch. 285, pt. II, § 213, as added Pub. L. 102–486, title VII, § 723, Oct. 24, 1992, 106 Stat. 2919.)

State Authorities; Construction

Nothing in this section to be construed as affecting or intending to affect, or in any way to interfere with, authority of any State or local government relating to environmental protection or siting of facilities, see section 731 of Pub. L. 102–486, set out as a note under section 796 of this title.

§ 824m. Sales by exempt wholesale generators

No rate or charge received by an exempt wholesale generator for the sale of electric energy shall be lawful under section 824d of this title if, after notice and opportunity for hearing, the Commission finds that such rate or charge results from the receipt of any undue preference or advantage from an electric utility which is an associate company or an affiliate of the exempt wholesale generator. For purposes of this section, the terms "associate company" and "affiliate" shall have the same meaning as provided in section 16451 of title 42.[1]

(June 10, 1920, ch. 285, pt. II, § 214, as added Pub. L. 102–486, title VII, § 724, Oct. 24, 1992, 106 Stat. 2920; amended Pub. L. 109–58, title XII, § 1277(b)(2), Aug. 8, 2005, 119 Stat. 978.)

References in Text

Section 16451 of title 42, referred to in text, was in the original "section 2(a) of the Public Utility Holding Company Act of 2005" and was translated as reading "section 1262" of that Act, meaning section 1262 of subtitle F of title XII of Pub. L. 109–58, to reflect the probable intent of Congress, because subtitle F of title XII of Pub. L. 109–58 does not contain a section 2 and section 1262 of subtitle F of title XII of Pub. L. 109–58 defines terms.

Amendments

2005 — Pub. L. 109–58 substituted "section 16451 of title 42" for "section 79b(a) of title 15".

Effective Date of 2005 Amendment

Amendment by Pub. L. 109–58 effective 6 months after Aug. 8, 2005, with provisions relating to effect of compliance with certain regulations approved and made effective prior to such date,

---

1. *See References in Text note below.*

see section 1274 of Pub. L. 109–58, set out as an Effective Date note under section 16451 of Title 42, The Public Health and Welfare.

Nothing in this section to be construed as affecting or intending to affect, or in any way to interfere with, authority of any State or local government relating to environmental protection or siting of facilities, see section 731 of Pub. L. 102–486, set out as a note under section 796 of this title.

§ 824n. Repealed. Pub. L. 109–58, title XII, § 1232(e)(3), Aug. 8, 2005, 119 Stat. 957

Section, Pub. L. 106–377, § 1(a)(2) [title III, § 311], Oct. 27, 2000, 114 Stat. 1441, 1441A–80, related to authority regarding formation and operation of regional transmission organizations.

§ 824o. Electric reliability

(a) Definitions

For purposes of this section:

(1) The term "bulk-power system" means—

(A) facilities and control systems necessary for operating an interconnected electric energy transmission network (or any portion thereof); and

(B) electric energy from generation facilities needed to maintain transmission system reliability.

The term does not include facilities used in the local distribution of electric energy.

(2) The terms "Electric Reliability Organization" and "ERO" mean the organization certified by the Commission under subsection (c) of this section the purpose of which is to establish and enforce reliability standards for the bulk-power system, subject to Commission review.

(3) The term "reliability standard" means a requirement, approved by the Commission under this section, to provide for reliable operation of the bulk-power system. The term includes requirements for the operation of existing bulk-power system facilities, including cybersecurity protection, and the design of planned additions or modifications to such facilities to the extent necessary to provide for reliable operation of the bulk-power system, but the term does not include any requirement to enlarge such facilities or to construct new transmission capacity or generation capacity.

(4) The term "reliable operation" means operating the elements of the bulk-power system within equipment and electric system thermal, voltage, and stability limits so that instability, uncontrolled separation, or cascading failures of such system will not occur as a result of a sudden disturbance, including a cybersecurity incident, or unanticipated failure of system elements.

(5) The term "Interconnection" means a geographic area in which the operation of bulk-power system components is synchronized such that the failure of one or more of such components may adversely affect the ability of the operators of other components within the system to maintain reliable operation of the facilities within their control.

(6) The term "transmission organization" means a Regional Transmission Organization, Independent System Operator, independent transmission provider, or other transmission organization finally approved by the Commission for the operation of transmission facilities.

(7) The term "regional entity" means an entity having enforcement authority pursuant to subsection (e)(4) of this section.

(8) The term "cybersecurity incident" means a malicious act or suspicious event that disrupts, or was an attempt to disrupt, the operation of those programmable electronic devices and communication networks including hardware, software and data that are essential to the reliable operation of the bulk power system.

(b) Jurisdiction and applicability

(1) The Commission shall have jurisdiction, within the United States, over the ERO certified by the Commission under subsection (c) of this section, any regional entities, and all users, owners and operators of the bulk-power system, including but not limited to the entities described in section 824(f) of this title, for purposes of approving reliability standards established under this section and enforcing compliance with this section. All users, owners and operators of the bulk-power system shall comply with reliability standards that take effect under this section.

(2) The Commission shall issue a final rule to implement the requirements of this section not later than 180 days after August 8, 2005.

(c) Certification

Following the issuance of a Commission rule under subsection (b)(2) of this section, any person may submit an application to the Commission for certification as the Electric Reliability Organization. The Commission may certify one such ERO if the Commission determines that such ERO—

(1) has the ability to develop and enforce, subject to subsection (e)(2) of this section, reliability standards that provide for an adequate level of reliability of the bulk-power system; and

(2) has established rules that—

(A) assure its independence of the users and owners and operators of the bulk-power system, while assuring fair stakeholder representation in the selection of its directors and balanced decisionmaking in any ERO committee or subordinate organizational structure;

(B) allocate equitably reasonable dues, fees, and other charges among end users for all activities under this section;

(C) provide fair and impartial procedures for enforcement of reliability standards through the imposition of penalties in accordance with subsection (e) of this section (including limitations on activities, functions, or operations, or other appropriate sanctions);

(D) provide for reasonable notice and opportunity for public comment, due process, openness, and balance of interests in developing reliability standards and otherwise exercising its duties; and

(E) provide for taking, after certification, appropriate steps to gain recognition in Canada and Mexico.

(d) Reliability standards

(1) The Electric Reliability Organization shall file each reliability standard or modification to a reliability standard that it proposes to be made effective under this section with the Commission.

(2) The Commission may approve, by rule or order, a proposed reliability standard or modification to a reliability standard if it determines that the standard is just, reasonable, not unduly discriminatory or preferential, and in the public interest. The Commission shall give due weight to the technical expertise of the Electric Reliability Organization with respect to the content of a proposed standard or modification to a reliability standard and to the technical expertise of a regional entity organized on an Interconnection-wide basis with respect to a reliability standard to be applicable within that Interconnection, but shall not defer with respect to the effect of a standard on competition. A proposed standard or modification shall take effect upon approval by the Commission.

(3) The Electric Reliability Organization shall rebuttably presume that a proposal from a regional entity organized on an Interconnection-wide basis for a reliability standard or modification to a reliability standard to be applicable on an Interconnection-wide basis is just, reasonable, and not unduly discriminatory or preferential, and in the public interest.

(4) The Commission shall remand to the Electric Reliability Organization for further consideration a proposed reliability standard or a modification to a reliability standard that the Commission disapproves in whole or in part.

(5) The Commission, upon its own motion or upon complaint, may order the Electric Reliability Organization to submit to the Commission a proposed reliability standard or a modification to a reliability standard that addresses a specific matter if the Commission considers such a new or modified reliability standard appropriate to carry out this section.

(6) The final rule adopted under subsection (b)(2) of this section shall include fair processes for the identification and timely resolution of any conflict between a reliability standard and any function, rule, order, tariff, rate schedule, or agreement accepted, approved, or ordered by the Commission applicable to a transmission organization. Such transmission organization shall continue to comply with such function, rule, order, tariff, rate schedule or agreement accepted, approved, or ordered by the Commission until—

(A) the Commission finds a conflict exists between a reliability standard and any such provision;

(B) the Commission orders a change to such provision pursuant to section 824e of this title; and

(C) the ordered change becomes effective under this subchapter.

If the Commission determines that a reliability standard needs to be changed as a result of such a conflict, it shall order the ERO to develop and file with the Commission a modified reliability standard under paragraph (4) or (5) of this subsection.

(e) **Enforcement**

(1) The ERO may impose, subject to paragraph (2), a penalty on a user or owner or operator of the bulk-power system for a violation of a reliability standard approved by the Commission under subsection (d) of this section if the ERO, after notice and an opportunity for a hearing—

(A) finds that the user or owner or operator has violated a reliability standard approved by the Commission under subsection (d) of this section; and

(B) files notice and the record of the proceeding with the Commission.

(2) A penalty imposed under paragraph (1) may take effect not earlier than the 31st day after the ERO files with the Commission notice of the penalty and the record of proceedings. Such penalty shall be subject to review by the Commission, on its own motion or upon application by the user, owner or operator that is the subject of the penalty filed within 30 days after the date such notice is filed with the Commission. Application to the Commission for review, or the initiation of review by the Commission on its own motion, shall not operate as a stay of such penalty unless the Commission otherwise orders upon its own motion or upon application by the user, owner or operator that is the subject of such penalty. In any proceeding to review a penalty imposed under paragraph (1), the Commission, after notice and opportunity for hearing (which hearing may consist solely of the record before the ERO and opportunity for the presentation of supporting reasons to affirm, modify, or set aside the penalty), shall by order affirm, set aside, reinstate, or modify the penalty, and, if appropriate, remand to the ERO for further proceedings. The Commission shall implement expedited procedures for such hearings.

(3) On its own motion or upon complaint, the Commission may order compliance with a reliability standard and may impose a penalty against a user or owner or operator of the bulk-power system if the Commission finds, after notice and opportunity for a hearing, that the user or owner or operator of the bulk-power system has engaged or is about to engage in any acts or practices that constitute or will constitute a violation of a reliability standard.

(4) The Commission shall issue regulations authorizing the ERO to enter into an agreement to delegate authority to a regional entity for the purpose of proposing reliability standards to the ERO and enforcing reliability standards under paragraph (1) if—

(A) the regional entity is governed by—

(i) an independent board;

(ii) a balanced stakeholder board; or

(iii) a combination independent and balanced stakeholder board.

(B) the regional entity otherwise satisfies the provisions of subsection (c)(1) and (2) of this section; and

(C) the agreement promotes effective and efficient administration of bulk-power system reliability.

The Commission may modify such delegation. The ERO and the Commission shall rebuttably presume that a proposal for delegation to a regional entity organized on an Interconnection-wide basis promotes effective and efficient administration of bulk-power system reliability and should be approved. Such regulation may provide that the Commission may assign the ERO's authority to enforce reliability standards under paragraph (1) directly to a regional entity consistent with the requirements of this paragraph.

(5) The Commission may take such action as is necessary or appropriate against the ERO or a regional entity to ensure compliance with a reliability standard or any Commission order affecting the ERO or a regional entity.

(6) Any penalty imposed under this section shall bear a reasonable relation to the seriousness of the violation and shall take into consideration the efforts of such user, owner, or operator to remedy the violation in a timely manner.

(f) Changes in Electric Reliability Organization rules

The Electric Reliability Organization shall file with the Commission for approval any proposed rule or proposed rule change, accompanied by an explanation of its basis and purpose. The Commission, upon its own motion or complaint, may propose a change to the rules of the ERO. A proposed rule or proposed rule change shall take effect upon a finding by the Commission, after notice and opportunity for comment, that the change is just, reasonable, not unduly discriminatory or preferential, is in the public interest, and satisfies the requirements of subsection (c) of this section.

(g) Reliability reports

The ERO shall conduct periodic assessments of the reliability and adequacy of the bulk-power system in North America.

(h) Coordination with Canada and Mexico

The President is urged to negotiate international agreements with the governments of Canada and Mexico to provide for effective compliance with reliability standards and the effectiveness of the ERO in the United States and Canada or Mexico.

(i) Savings provisions

(1) The ERO shall have authority to develop and enforce compliance with reliability standards for only the bulk-power system.

(2) This section does not authorize the ERO or the Commission to order the construction of additional generation or transmission capacity or to set and enforce compliance with standards for adequacy or safety of electric facilities or services.

(3) Nothing in this section shall be construed to preempt any authority of any State to take action to ensure the safety, adequacy, and reliability of electric service within that State, as long as such action is not inconsistent with any reliability standard, except that the State of New York may establish rules that result in greater reliability within that State, as long as such action does not result in lesser reliability outside the State than that provided by the reliability standards.

(4) Within 90 days of the application of the Electric Reliability Organization or other affected party, and after notice and opportunity for comment, the Commission shall issue a final order determining whether a State action is inconsistent with a reliability standard, taking into consideration any recommendation of the ERO.

(5) The Commission, after consultation with the ERO and the State taking action, may stay the effectiveness of any State action, pending the Commission's issuance of a final order.

(j) Regional advisory bodies

The Commission shall establish a regional advisory body on the petition of at least two-thirds of the States within a region that have more than one-half of their electric load served within the region. A regional advisory body shall be composed of one member from each participating State in the region, appointed by the Governor of each State, and may include representatives of agencies, States, and provinces outside the United States. A regional advisory body may provide advice to the Electric Reliability Organization, a regional entity, or the Commission regarding the governance of an existing or proposed regional entity within the same region, whether a standard proposed to apply within the region is just, reasonable, not unduly discriminatory or preferential, and in the public interest, whether fees proposed to be assessed within the region are just, reasonable, not unduly discriminatory or preferential, and in the public interest and any other responsibilities requested by the Commission. The Commission may give deference to the advice of any such regional advisory body if that body is organized on an Interconnection-wide basis.

(k) Alaska and Hawaii

The provisions of this section do not apply to Alaska or Hawaii.

(June 10, 1920, ch. 285, pt. II, § 215, as added Pub. L. 109–58, title XII, § 1211(a), Aug. 8, 2005, 119 Stat. 941.)

STATUS OF ERO

Pub. L. 109–58, title XII, § 1211(b), Aug. 8, 2005, 119 Stat. 946, provided that: "The Electric Reliability Organization certified by the Federal Energy Regulatory Commission under section 215(c) of the Federal Power Act [16 U.S.C. 824o(c)] and any regional entity delegated enforcement authority pursuant to section 215(e)(4) of that Act [16 U.S.C. 824o(e)(4)] are not departments, agencies, or instrumentalities of the United States Government."

ACCESS APPROVALS BY FEDERAL AGENCIES

Pub. L. 109–58, title XII, § 1211(c), Aug. 8, 2005, 119 Stat. 946, provided that: "Federal agencies responsible for approving access to electric transmission or distribution facilities located on lands within the United States shall, in accordance with applicable law, expedite any Federal agency approvals that are necessary to allow the owners or operators of such facilities to comply with any reliability standard, approved by the [Federal Energy Regulatory] Commission under section 215 of the Federal Power Act [16 U.S.C. 824o], that pertains to vegetation management, electric service restoration, or resolution of situations that imminently endanger the reliability or safety of the facilities."

§ 824p. Siting of interstate electric transmission facilities

(a) Designation of national interest electric transmission corridors

(1) Not later than 1 year after August 8, 2005, and every 3 years thereafter, the Secretary of Energy (referred to in this section as the "Secretary"), in consultation with affected States, shall conduct a study of electric transmission congestion.

(2) After considering alternatives and recommendations from interested parties (including an opportunity for comment from affected States), the Secretary shall issue a report, based on the study, which may designate any geographic area experiencing electric energy transmission capacity constraints or congestion that adversely affects consumers as a national interest electric transmission corridor.

(3) The Secretary shall conduct the study and issue the report in consultation with any appropriate regional entity referred to in section 824o of this title.

(4) In determining whether to designate a national interest electric transmission corridor under paragraph (2), the Secretary may consider whether—

(A) the economic vitality and development of the corridor, or the end markets served by the corridor, may be constrained by lack of adequate or reasonably priced electricity;

(B)(i) economic growth in the corridor, or the end markets served by the corridor, may be jeopardized by reliance on limited sources of energy; and

(ii) a diversification of supply is warranted;

(C) the energy independence of the United States would be served by the designation;

(D) the designation would be in the interest of national energy policy; and

(E) the designation would enhance national defense and homeland security.

(b) Construction permit

Except as provided in subsection (i) of this section, the Commission may, after notice and an opportunity for hearing, issue one or more permits for the construction or modification of electric transmission facilities in a national interest electric transmission corridor designated by the Secretary under subsection (a) of this section if the Commission finds that—

(1)(A) a State in which the transmission facilities are to be constructed or modified does not have authority to—

(i) approve the siting of the facilities; or

(ii) consider the interstate benefits expected to be achieved by the proposed construction or modification of transmission facilities in the State;

(B) the applicant for a permit is a transmitting utility under this chapter but does not qualify to apply for a permit or siting approval for the proposed project in a State because the applicant does not serve end-use customers in the State; or

(C) a State commission or other entity that has authority to approve the siting of the facilities has—

(i) withheld approval for more than 1 year after the filing of an application seeking approval pursuant to applicable law or 1 year after the designation of the relevant national interest electric transmission corridor, whichever is later; or

(ii) conditioned its approval in such a manner that the proposed construction or modification will not significantly reduce transmission congestion in interstate commerce or is not economically feasible;

(2) the facilities to be authorized by the permit will be used for the transmission of electric energy in interstate commerce;

(3) the proposed construction or modification is consistent with the public interest;

(4) the proposed construction or modification will significantly reduce transmission congestion in interstate commerce and protects or benefits consumers;

(5) the proposed construction or modification is consistent with sound national energy policy and will enhance energy independence; and

(6) the proposed modification will maximize, to the extent reasonable and economical, the transmission capabilities of existing towers or structures.

(c) Permit applications

(1) Permit applications under subsection (b) of this section shall be made in writing to the Commission.

(2) The Commission shall issue rules specifying—

(A) the form of the application;

(B) the information to be contained in the application; and

(C) the manner of service of notice of the permit application on interested persons.

(d) Comments

In any proceeding before the Commission under subsection (b) of this section, the Commission shall afford each State in which a transmission facility covered by the permit is or will be located, each affected Federal agency and Indian tribe, private property owners, and other interested persons, a reasonable opportunity to present their views and recommendations with respect to the need for and impact of a facility covered by the permit.

(e) Rights-of-way

(1) In the case of a permit under subsection (b) of this section for electric transmission facilities to be located on property other than property owned by the United States or a State, if the permit holder cannot acquire by contract, or is unable to agree with the owner of the property to the compensation to be paid for, the necessary right-of-way to construct or modify the transmission facilities, the permit holder may acquire the right-of-way by the exercise of the right of eminent domain in the district court of the United States for the district in which the property concerned is located, or in the appropriate court of the State in which the property is located.

(2) Any right-of-way acquired under paragraph (1) shall be used exclusively for the construction or modification of electric transmission facilities within a reasonable period of time after the acquisition.

(3) The practice and procedure in any action or proceeding under this subsection in the district court of the United States shall conform as nearly as practicable to the practice and procedure in a similar action or proceeding in the courts of the State in which the property is located.

(4) Nothing in this subsection shall be construed to authorize the use of eminent domain to acquire a right-of-way for any purpose other than the construction, modification, operation, or maintenance of electric transmission facilities and related facilities. The right-of-way cannot be used for any other purpose, and the right-of-way shall terminate upon the termination of the use for which the right-of-way was acquired.

(f) Compensation

(1) Any right-of-way acquired pursuant to subsection (e) of this section shall be considered a taking of private property for which just compensation is due.

(2) Just compensation shall be an amount equal to the fair market value (including applicable severance damages) of the property taken on the date of the exercise of eminent domain authority.

(g) State law

Nothing in this section precludes any person from constructing or modifying any transmission facility in accordance with State law.

(h) Coordination of Federal authorizations for transmission facilities

(1) In this subsection:

(A) The term "Federal authorization" means any authorization required under Federal law in order to site a transmission facility.

(B) The term "Federal authorization" includes such permits, special use authorizations, certifications, opinions, or other approvals as may be required under Federal law in order to site a transmission facility.

(2) The Department of Energy shall act as the lead agency for purposes of coordinating all applicable Federal authorizations and related environmental reviews of the facility.

(3) To the maximum extent practicable under applicable Federal law, the Secretary shall coordinate the Federal authorization and review process under this subsection

with any Indian tribes, multistate entities, and State agencies that are responsible for conducting any separate permitting and environmental reviews of the facility, to ensure timely and efficient review and permit decisions.

(4)(A) As head of the lead agency, the Secretary, in consultation with agencies responsible for Federal authorizations and, as appropriate, with Indian tribes, multistate entities, and State agencies that are willing to coordinate their own separate permitting and environmental reviews with the Federal authorization and environmental reviews, shall establish prompt and binding intermediate milestones and ultimate deadlines for the review of, and Federal authorization decisions relating to, the proposed facility.

(B) The Secretary shall ensure that, once an application has been submitted with such data as the Secretary considers necessary, all permit decisions and related environmental reviews under all applicable Federal laws shall be completed—

(i) within 1 year; or

(ii) if a requirement of another provision of Federal law does not permit compliance with clause (i), as soon thereafter as is practicable.

(C) The Secretary shall provide an expeditious pre-application mechanism for prospective applicants to confer with the agencies involved to have each such agency determine and communicate to the prospective applicant not later than 60 days after the prospective applicant submits a request for such information concerning—

(i) the likelihood of approval for a potential facility; and

(ii) key issues of concern to the agencies and public.

(5)(A) As lead agency head, the Secretary, in consultation with the affected agencies, shall prepare a single environmental review document, which shall be used as the basis for all decisions on the proposed project under Federal law.

(B) The Secretary and the heads of other agencies shall streamline the review and permitting of transmission within corridors designated under section 503 of the Federal Land Policy and Management Act[1] (43 U.S.C. 1763) by fully taking into account prior analyses and decisions relating to the corridors.

(C) The document shall include consideration by the relevant agencies of any applicable criteria or other matters as required under applicable law.

(6)(A) If any agency has denied a Federal authorization required for a transmission facility, or has failed to act by the deadline established by the Secretary pursuant to this section for deciding whether to issue the authorization, the applicant or any State in which the facility would be located may file an appeal with the President, who shall, in consultation with the affected agency, review the denial or failure to take action on the pending application.

(B) Based on the overall record and in consultation with the affected agency, the President may—

(i) issue the necessary authorization with any appropriate conditions; or

(ii) deny the application.

(C) The President shall issue a decision not later than 90 days after the date of the filing of the appeal.

---

1. *So in original. Probably should be followed by "of 1976".*

(D) In making a decision under this paragraph, the President shall comply with applicable requirements of Federal law, including any requirements of—

(i) the National Forest Management Act of 1976 (16 U.S.C. 472a et seq.);

(ii) the Endangered Species Act of 1973 (16 U.S.C. 1531 et seq.);

(iii) the Federal Water Pollution Control Act (33 U.S.C. 1251 et seq.);

(iv) the National Environmental Policy Act of 1969 (42 U.S.C. 4321 et seq.); and

(v) the Federal Land Policy and Management Act of 1976 (43 U.S.C. 1701 et seq.).

(7)(A) Not later than 18 months after August 8, 2005, the Secretary shall issue any regulations necessary to implement this subsection.

(B)(i) Not later than 1 year after August 8, 2005, the Secretary and the heads of all Federal agencies with authority to issue Federal authorizations shall enter into a memorandum of understanding to ensure the timely and coordinated review and permitting of electricity transmission facilities.

(ii) Interested Indian tribes, multistate entities, and State agencies may enter the memorandum of understanding.

(C) The head of each Federal agency with authority to issue a Federal authorization shall designate a senior official responsible for, and dedicate sufficient other staff and resources to ensure, full implementation of the regulations and memorandum required under this paragraph.

(8)(A) Each Federal land use authorization for an electricity transmission facility shall be issued—

(i) for a duration, as determined by the Secretary, commensurate with the anticipated use of the facility; and

(ii) with appropriate authority to manage the right-of-way for reliability and environmental protection.

(B) On the expiration of the authorization (including an authorization issued before August 8, 2005), the authorization shall be reviewed for renewal taking fully into account reliance on such electricity infrastructure, recognizing the importance of the authorization for public health, safety, and economic welfare and as a legitimate use of Federal land.

(9) In exercising the responsibilities under this section, the Secretary shall consult regularly with—

(A) the Federal Energy Regulatory Commission;

(B) electric reliability organizations (including related regional entities) approved by the Commission; and

(C) Transmission Organizations approved by the Commission.

(i) **Interstate compacts**

(1) The consent of Congress is given for three or more contiguous States to enter into an interstate compact, subject to approval by Congress, establishing regional transmission siting agencies to—

(A) facilitate siting of future electric energy transmission facilities within those States; and

(B) carry out the electric energy transmission siting responsibilities of those States.

(2) The Secretary may provide technical assistance to regional transmission siting agencies established under this subsection.

(3) The regional transmission siting agencies shall have the authority to review, certify, and permit siting of transmission facilities, including facilities in national interest electric transmission corridors (other than facilities on property owned by the United States).

(4) The Commission shall have no authority to issue a permit for the construction or modification of an electric transmission facility within a State that is a party to a compact, unless the members of the compact are in disagreement and the Secretary makes, after notice and an opportunity for a hearing, the finding described in subsection (b)(1)(C) of this section.

(j) **Relationship to other laws**

(1) Except as specifically provided, nothing in this section affects any requirement of an environmental law of the United States, including the National Environmental Policy Act of 1969 (42 U.S.C. 4321 et seq.).

(2) Subsection (h)(6) of this section shall not apply to any unit of the National Park System, the National Wildlife Refuge System, the National Wild and Scenic Rivers System, the National Trails System, the National Wilderness Preservation System, or a National Monument.

(k) **ERCOT**

This section shall not apply within the area referred to in section 824k(k)(2)(A) of this title.

(June 10, 1920, ch. 285, pt. II, §216, as added Pub. L. 109–58, title XII, §1221(a), Aug. 8, 2005, 119 Stat. 946.)

REFERENCES IN TEXT

The National Forest Management Act of 1976, referred to in subsec. (h)(6)(D)(i), is Pub. L. 94–588, Oct. 22, 1976, 90 Stat. 2949, as amended, which enacted sections 472a, 521b, 1600, and 1611 to 1614 of this title, amended sections 500, 515, 516, 518, 576b, and 1601 to 1610 of this title, repealed sections 476, 513, and 514 of this title, and enacted provisions set out as notes under sections 476, 513, 528, 594–2, and 1600 of this title. For complete classification of this Act to the Code, see Short Title of 1976 Amendment note set out under section 1600 of this title and Tables.

The Endangered Species Act of 1973, referred to in subsec. (h)(6)(D)(ii), is Pub. L. 93–205, Dec. 28, 1973, 87 Stat. 884, as amended, which is classified principally to chapter 35 (§1531 et seq.) of this title. For complete classification of this Act to the Code, see Short Title note set out under section 1531 of this title and Tables.

The Federal Water Pollution Control Act, referred to in subsec. (h)(6)(D)(iii), is act June 30, 1948, ch. 758, as amended generally by Pub. L. 92–500, §2, Oct. 18, 1972, 86 Stat. 816, which is classified generally to chapter 26 (§1251 et seq.) of Title 33, Navigation and Navigable Waters. For complete classification of this Act to the Code, see Short Title note set out under section 1251 of Title 33 and Tables.

The National Environmental Policy Act of 1969, referred to in subsecs. (h)(6)(D)(iv) and (j), is Pub. L. 91–190, Jan. 1, 1970, 83 Stat. 852, as amended, which is classified generally to chapter 55 (§4321 et seq.) of Title 42, The Public Health and Welfare. For complete classification of this Act to the Code, see Short Title note set out under section 4321 of Title 42 and Tables.

The Federal Land Policy and Management Act of 1976, referred to in subsec. (h)(6)(D)(v), is Pub. L. 94–579, Oct. 21, 1976, 90 Stat. 2743, as amended, which is classified principally to chapter 35 (§ 1701 et seq.) of Title 43, Public Lands. For complete classification of this Act to the Code, see Short Title note set out under section 1701 of Title 43 and Tables.

§ 824q. Native load service obligation

(a) Definitions

In this section:

(1) The term "distribution utility" means an electric utility that has a service obligation to end-users or to a State utility or electric cooperative that, directly or indirectly, through one or more additional State utilities or electric cooperatives, provides electric service to end-users.

(2) The term "load-serving entity" means a distribution utility or an electric utility that has a service obligation.

(3) The term "service obligation" means a requirement applicable to, or the exercise of authority granted to, an electric utility under Federal, State, or local law or under long-term contracts to provide electric service to end-users or to a distribution utility.

(4) The term "State utility" means a State or any political subdivision of a State, or any agency, authority, or instrumentality of any one or more of the foregoing, or a corporation that is wholly owned, directly or indirectly, by any one or more of the foregoing, competent to carry on the business of developing, transmitting, utilizing, or distributing power.

(b) Meeting service obligations

(1) Paragraph (2) applies to any load-serving entity that, as of August 8, 2005 —

(A) owns generation facilities, markets the output of Federal generation facilities, or holds rights under one or more wholesale contracts to purchase electric energy, for the purpose of meeting a service obligation; and

(B) by reason of ownership of transmission facilities, or one or more contracts or service agreements for firm transmission service, holds firm transmission rights for delivery of the output of the generation facilities or the purchased energy to meet the service obligation.

(2) Any load-serving entity described in paragraph (1) is entitled to use the firm transmission rights, or, equivalent tradable or financial transmission rights, in order to deliver the output or purchased energy, or the output of other generating facilities or purchased energy to the extent deliverable using the rights, to the extent required to meet the service obligation of the load-serving entity.

(3)(A) To the extent that all or a portion of the service obligation covered by the firm transmission rights or equivalent tradable or financial transmission rights is transferred to another load-serving entity, the successor load-serving entity shall be entitled to use the firm transmission rights or equivalent tradable or financial transmission rights associated with the transferred service obligation.

(B) Subsequent transfers to another load-serving entity, or back to the original load-serving entity, shall be entitled to the same rights.

(4) The Commission shall exercise the authority of the Commission under this chapter in a manner that facilitates the planning and expansion of transmission facilities to meet the reasonable needs of load-serving entities to satisfy the service obligations of the load-serving entities, and enables load-serving entities to secure firm transmission

rights (or equivalent tradable or financial rights) on a long-term basis for long-term power supply arrangements made, or planned, to meet such needs.

(c) Allocation of transmission rights

Nothing in subsections (b)(1), (b)(2), and (b)(3) of this section shall affect any existing or future methodology employed by a Transmission Organization for allocating or auctioning transmission rights if such Transmission Organization was authorized by the Commission to allocate or auction financial transmission rights on its system as of January 1, 2005, and the Commission determines that any future allocation or auction is just, reasonable and not unduly discriminatory or preferential, provided, however, that if such a Transmission Organization never allocated financial transmission rights on its system that pertained to a period before January 1, 2005, with respect to any application by such Transmission Organization that would change its methodology the Commission shall exercise its authority in a manner consistent with the[1] chapter and that takes into account the policies expressed in subsections (b)(1), (b)(2), and (b)(3) of this section as applied to firm transmission rights held by a load-serving entity as of January 1, 2005, to the extent the associated generation ownership or power purchase arrangements remain in effect.

(d) Certain transmission rights

The Commission may exercise authority under this chapter to make transmission rights not used to meet an obligation covered by subsection (b) of this section available to other entities in a manner determined by the Commission to be just, reasonable, and not unduly discriminatory or preferential.

(e) Obligation to build

Nothing in this chapter relieves a load-serving entity from any obligation under State or local law to build transmission or distribution facilities adequate to meet the service obligations of the load-serving entity.

(f) Contracts

Nothing in this section shall provide a basis for abrogating any contract or service agreement for firm transmission service or rights in effect as of August 8, 2005. If an ISO in the Western Interconnection had allocated financial transmission rights prior to August 8, 2005, but had not done so with respect to one or more load-serving entities' firm transmission rights held under contracts to which the preceding sentence applies (or held by reason of ownership or future ownership of transmission facilities), such load-serving entities may not be required, without their consent, to convert such firm transmission rights to tradable or financial rights, except where the load-serving entity has voluntarily joined the ISO as a participating transmission owner (or its successor) in accordance with the ISO tariff.

(g) Water pumping facilities

The Commission shall ensure that any entity described in section 824(f) of this title that owns transmission facilities used predominately to support its own water pumping facilities shall have, with respect to the facilities, protections for transmission service comparable to those provided to load-serving entities pursuant to this section.

(h) ERCOT

This section shall not apply within the area referred to in section 824k(k)(2)(A) of this title.

---

1. *So in original. Probably should be "this".*

(i) Jurisdiction

This section does not authorize the Commission to take any action not otherwise within the jurisdiction of the Commission.

(j) TVA area

(1) Subject to paragraphs (2) and (3), for purposes of subsection (b)(1)(B) of this section, a load-serving entity that is located within the service area of the Tennessee Valley Authority and that has a firm wholesale power supply contract with the Tennessee Valley Authority shall be considered to hold firm transmission rights for the transmission of the power provided.

(2) Nothing in this subsection affects the requirements of section 824k(j) of this title.

(3) The Commission shall not issue an order on the basis of this subsection that is contrary to the purposes of section 824k(j) of this title.

(k) Effect of exercising rights

An entity that to the extent required to meet its service obligations exercises rights described in subsection (b) of this section shall not be considered by such action as engaging in undue discrimination or preference under this chapter.

(June 10, 1920, ch. 285, pt. II, § 217, as added Pub. L. 109–58, title XII, § 1233(a), Aug. 8, 2005, 119 Stat. 957.)

FERC RULEMAKING ON LONG-TERM TRANSMISSION RIGHTS IN ORGANIZED MARKETS

Pub. L. 109–58, title XII, § 1233(b), Aug. 8, 2005, 119 Stat. 960, provided that: "Within 1 year after the date of enactment of this section [Aug. 8, 2005] and after notice and an opportunity for comment, the [Federal Energy Regulatory] Commission shall by rule or order, implement section 217(b)(4) of the Federal Power Act [16 U.S.C. 824q(b)(4)] in Transmission Organizations, as defined by that Act [16 U.S.C. 791a et seq.] with organized electricity markets."

§ 824r. Protection of transmission contracts in the Pacific Northwest

(a) Definition of electric utility or person

In this section, the term "electric utility or person" means an electric utility or person that—

(1) as of August 8, 2005, holds firm transmission rights pursuant to contract or by reason of ownership of transmission facilities; and

(2) is located—

(A) in the Pacific Northwest, as that region is defined in section 839a of this title; or

(B) in that portion of a State included in the geographic area proposed for a regional transmission organization in Commission Docket Number RT01–35 on the date on which that docket was opened.

(b) Protection of transmission contracts

Nothing in this chapter confers on the Commission the authority to require an electric utility or person to convert to tradable or financial rights—

(1) firm transmission rights described in subsection (a) of this section; or

(2) firm transmission rights obtained by exercising contract or tariff rights associated with the firm transmission rights described in subsection (a) of this section.

(June 10, 1920, ch. 285, pt. II, § 218, as added Pub. L. 109–58, title XII, § 1235, Aug. 8, 2005, 119 Stat. 960.)

§ 824s. Transmission infrastructure investment

(a) Rulemaking requirement

Not later than 1 year after August 8, 2005, the Commission shall establish, by rule, incentive-based (including performance-based) rate treatments for the transmission of electric energy in interstate commerce by public utilities for the purpose of benefitting consumers by ensuring reliability and reducing the cost of delivered power by reducing transmission congestion.

(b) Contents

The rule shall—

(1) promote reliable and economically efficient transmission and generation of electricity by promoting capital investment in the enlargement, improvement, maintenance, and operation of all facilities for the transmission of electric energy in interstate commerce, regardless of the ownership of the facilities;

(2) provide a return on equity that attracts new investment in transmission facilities (including related transmission technologies);

(3) encourage deployment of transmission technologies and other measures to increase the capacity and efficiency of existing transmission facilities and improve the operation of the facilities; and

(4) allow recovery of—

(A) all prudently incurred costs necessary to comply with mandatory reliability standards issued pursuant to section 824o of this title; and

(B) all prudently incurred costs related to transmission infrastructure development pursuant to section 824p of this title.

(c) Incentives

In the rule issued under this section, the Commission shall, to the extent within its jurisdiction, provide for incentives to each transmitting utility or electric utility that joins a Transmission Organization. The Commission shall ensure that any costs recoverable pursuant to this subsection may be recovered by such utility through the transmission rates charged by such utility or through the transmission rates charged by the Transmission Organization that provides transmission service to such utility.

(d) Just and reasonable rates

All rates approved under the rules adopted pursuant to this section, including any revisions to the rules, are subject to the requirements of sections 824d and 824e of this title that all rates, charges, terms, and conditions be just and reasonable and not unduly discriminatory or preferential.

(June 10, 1920, ch. 285, pt. II, § 219, as added Pub. L. 109–58, title XII, § 1241, Aug. 8, 2005, 119 Stat. 961.)

§ 824t. Electricity market transparency rules

(a) In general

(1) The Commission is directed to facilitate price transparency in markets for the sale and transmission of electric energy in interstate commerce, having due regard for

the public interest, the integrity of those markets, fair competition, and the protection of consumers.

(2) The Commission may prescribe such rules as the Commission determines necessary and appropriate to carry out the purposes of this section. The rules shall provide for the dissemination, on a timely basis, of information about the availability and prices of wholesale electric energy and transmission service to the Commission, State commissions, buyers and sellers of wholesale electric energy, users of transmission services, and the public.

(3) The Commission may—

(A) obtain the information described in paragraph (2) from any market participant; and

(B) rely on entities other than the Commission to receive and make public the information, subject to the disclosure rules in subsection (b) of this section.

(4) In carrying out this section, the Commission shall consider the degree of price transparency provided by existing price publishers and providers of trade processing services, and shall rely on such publishers and services to the maximum extent possible. The Commission may establish an electronic information system if it determines that existing price publications are not adequately providing price discovery or market transparency. Nothing in this section, however, shall affect any electronic information filing requirements in effect under this chapter as of August 8, 2005.

(b) Exemption of information from disclosure

(1) Rules described in subsection (a)(2) of this section, if adopted, shall exempt from disclosure information the Commission determines would, if disclosed, be detrimental to the operation of an effective market or jeopardize system security.

(2) In determining the information to be made available under this section and time to make the information available, the Commission shall seek to ensure that consumers and competitive markets are protected from the adverse effects of potential collusion or other anticompetitive behaviors that can be facilitated by untimely public disclosure of transaction-specific information.

(c) Information sharing

(1) Within 180 days of August 8, 2005, the Commission shall conclude a memorandum of understanding with the Commodity Futures Trading Commission relating to information sharing, which shall include, among other things, provisions ensuring that information requests to markets within the respective jurisdiction of each agency are properly coordinated to minimize duplicative information requests, and provisions regarding the treatment of proprietary trading information.

(2) Nothing in this section may be construed to limit or affect the exclusive jurisdiction of the Commodity Futures Trading Commission under the Commodity Exchange Act (7 U.S.C. 1 et seq.).

(d) Exemption from reporting requirements

The Commission shall not require entities who have a de minimis market presence to comply with the reporting requirements of this section.

(e) Penalties for violations occurring before notice

(1) Except as provided in paragraph (2), no person shall be subject to any civil penalty under this section with respect to any violation occurring more than 3 years

before the date on which the person is provided notice of the proposed penalty under section 825o-1 of this title.

(2) Paragraph (1) shall not apply in any case in which the Commission finds that a seller that has entered into a contract for the sale of electric energy at wholesale or transmission service subject to the jurisdiction of the Commission has engaged in fraudulent market manipulation activities materially affecting the contract in violation of section 824v of this title.

(f) ERCOT utilities

This section shall not apply to a transaction for the purchase or sale of wholesale electric energy or transmission services within the area described in section 824k(k)(2)(A) of this title.

(June 10, 1920, ch. 285, pt. II, §220, as added Pub. L. 109–58, title XII, §1281, Aug. 8, 2005, 119 Stat. 978.)

REFERENCES IN TEXT

The Commodity Exchange Act, referred to in subsec. (c)(2), is act Sept. 21, 1922, ch. 369, 42 Stat. 998, as amended, which is classified generally to chapter 1 (§1 et seq.) of Title 7, Agriculture. For complete classification of this Act to the Code, see section 1 of Title 7 and Tables.

§824u. Prohibition on filing false information

No entity (including an entity described in section 824(f) of this title) shall willfully and knowingly report any information relating to the price of electricity sold at wholesale or the availability of transmission capacity, which information the person or any other entity knew to be false at the time of the reporting, to a Federal agency with intent to fraudulently affect the data being compiled by the Federal agency.

(June 10, 1920, ch. 285, pt. II, §221, as added Pub. L. 109–58, title XII, §1282, Aug. 8, 2005, 119 Stat. 979.)

§824v. Prohibition of energy market manipulation

(a) In general

It shall be unlawful for any entity (including an entity described in section 824(f) of this title), directly or indirectly, to use or employ, in connection with the purchase or sale of electric energy or the purchase or sale of transmission services subject to the jurisdiction of the Commission, any manipulative or deceptive device or contrivance (as those terms are used in section 78j(b) of title 15), in contravention of such rules and regulations as the Commission may prescribe as necessary or appropriate in the public interest or for the protection of electric ratepayers.

(b) No private right of action

Nothing in this section shall be construed to create a private right of action.

(June 10, 1920, ch. 285, pt. II, §222, as added Pub. L. 109–58, title XII, §1283, Aug. 8, 2005, 119 Stat. 979.)

§824w. Joint boards on economic dispatch

(a) In general

The Commission shall convene joint boards on a regional basis pursuant to section 824h of this title to study the issue of security constrained economic dispatch for the various market regions. The Commission shall designate the appropriate regions to be covered by each such joint board for purposes of this section.

(b) Membership

The Commission shall request each State to nominate a representative for the appropriate regional joint board, and shall designate a member of the Commission to chair and participate as a member of each such board.

(c) Powers

The sole authority of each joint board convened under this section shall be to consider issues relevant to what constitutes "security constrained economic dispatch" and how such a mode of operating an electric energy system affects or enhances the reliability and affordability of service to customers in the region concerned and to make recommendations to the Commission regarding such issues.

(d) Report to the Congress

Within 1 year after August 8, 2005, the Commission shall issue a report and submit such report to the Congress regarding the recommendations of the joint boards under this section and the Commission may consolidate the recommendations of more than one such regional joint board, including any consensus recommendations for statutory or regulatory reform.

(June 10, 1920, ch. 285, pt. II, § 223, as added Pub. L. 109–58, title XII, § 1298, Aug. 8, 2005, 119 Stat. 986.)

Appendix D

Natural Gas

A. Natural Gas Pipelines Map

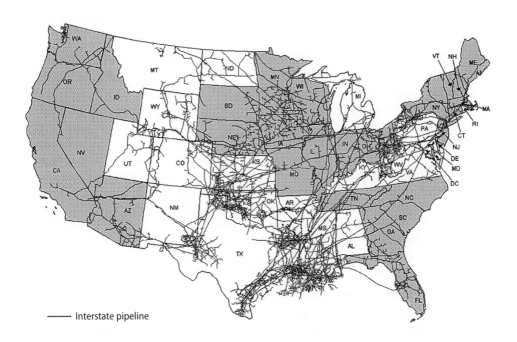

——— Interstate pipeline

Note: A state's relative dependence on the interstate natural gas pipeline network for its supplies was determined by the level of natural consumed within the state in 2007 relative to the amount of natural gas produced within the state. A state with no natural gas production was 100 percent dependent on the interstate natural gas pipeline network for its supplies.

Source: Energy Information Administration, Form EIA176 "Annual Report of Natural Gas and Supplemental Gas Supply and Disposition." http://www.eia.gov/pub/oil_gas/natural_gas/analysis_publications/ngpipeline/dependstates_map.html. For the most current view of the energy infrastructure, consult the EIA's interactive U.S. Energy Mapping System, which is available here: http://www.eia.gov/state/maps.cfm.

B. Natural Gas Act

15 U.S. Code § 717—Regulation of natural gas companies

(a) Necessity of regulation in public interest

As disclosed in reports of the Federal Trade Commission made pursuant to S. Res. 83 (Seventieth Congress, first session) and other reports made pursuant to the authority of Congress, it is declared that the business of transporting and selling natural gas for ultimate distribution to the public is affected with a public interest, and that Federal regulation in matters relating to the transportation of natural gas and the sale thereof in interstate and foreign commerce is necessary in the public interest.

(b) Transactions to which provisions of chapter applicable

The provisions of this chapter shall apply to the transportation of natural gas in interstate commerce, to the sale in interstate commerce of natural gas for resale for ultimate public consumption for domestic, commercial, industrial, or any other use, and to natural-gas companies engaged in such transportation or sale, and to the importation or exportation of natural gas in foreign commerce and to persons engaged in such importation or exportation, but shall not apply to any other transportation or sale of natural gas or to the local distribution of natural gas or to the facilities used for such distribution or to the production or gathering of natural gas.

(c) Intrastate transactions exempt from provisions of chapter; certification from State commission as conclusive evidence

The provisions of this chapter shall not apply to any person engaged in or legally authorized to engage in the transportation in interstate commerce or the sale in interstate commerce for resale, of natural gas received by such person from another person within or at the boundary of a State if all the natural gas so received is ultimately consumed within such State, or to any facilities used by such person for such transportation or sale, provided that the rates and service of such person and facilities be subject to regulation by a State commission. The matters exempted from the provisions of this chapter by this subsection are declared to be matters primarily of local concern and subject to regulation by the several States. A certification from such State commission to the Federal Power Commission that such State commission has regulatory jurisdiction over rates and service of such person and facilities and is exercising such jurisdiction shall constitute conclusive evidence of such regulatory power or jurisdiction.

(d) Vehicular natural gas jurisdiction

The provisions of this chapter shall not apply to any person solely by reason of, or with respect to, any sale or transportation of vehicular natural gas if such person is—

(1) not otherwise a natural-gas company; or

(2) subject primarily to regulation by a State commission, whether or not such State commission has, or is exercising, jurisdiction over the sale, sale for resale, or transportation of vehicular natural gas.

15 U.S. Code § 717a—Definitions

When used in this chapter, unless the context otherwise requires—

(1) "Person" includes an individual or a corporation.

(2) "Corporation" includes any corporation, joint-stock company, partnership, association, business trust, organized group of persons, whether incorporated or not, receiver or receivers, trustee or trustees of any of the foregoing, but shall not include municipalities as hereinafter defined.

(3) "Municipality" means a city, county, or other political subdivision or agency of a State.

(4) "State" means a State admitted to the Union, the District of Columbia, and any organized Territory of the United States.

(5) "Natural gas" means either natural gas unmixed, or any mixture of natural and artificial gas.

(6) "Natural-gas company" means a person engaged in the transportation of natural gas in interstate commerce, or the sale in interstate commerce of such gas for resale.

(7) "Interstate commerce" means commerce between any point in a State and any point outside thereof, or between points within the same State but through any place outside thereof, but only insofar as such commerce takes place within the United States.

(8) "State commission" means the regulatory body of the State or municipality having jurisdiction to regulate rates and charges for the sale of natural gas to consumers within the State or municipality.

(9) "Commission" and "Commissioner" means the Federal Power Commission, and a member thereof, respectively.

(10) "Vehicular natural gas" means natural gas that is ultimately used as a fuel in a self-propelled vehicle.

(11) "LNG terminal" includes all natural gas facilities located onshore or in State waters that are used to receive, unload, load, store, transport, gasify, liquefy, or process natural gas that is imported to the United States from a foreign country, exported to a foreign country from the United States, or transported in interstate commerce by waterborne vessel, but does not include—

(A) waterborne vessels used to deliver natural gas to or from any such facility; or

(B) any pipeline or storage facility subject to the jurisdiction of the Commission under section 717f of this title.

15 U.S. Code § 717b—Exportation or importation of natural gas; LNG terminals

(a) Mandatory authorization order

After six months from June 21, 1938, no person shall export any natural gas from the United States to a foreign country or import any natural gas from a foreign country without first having secured an order of the Commission authorizing it to do so. The Commission shall issue such order upon application, unless, after opportunity for hearing, it finds that the proposed exportation or importation will not be consistent with the public interest. The Commission may by its order grant such application, in whole or in part, with such modification and upon such terms and conditions as the Commission may find necessary or appropriate, and may from time to time, after opportunity for hearing, and for good cause shown, make such supplemental order in the premises as it may find necessary or appropriate.

(b) Free trade agreements

With respect to natural gas which is imported into the United States from a nation with which there is in effect a free trade agreement requiring national treatment for trade in natural gas, and with respect to liquefied natural gas—

(1) the importation of such natural gas shall be treated as a "first sale" within the meaning of section 3301 (21) of this title; and

(2) the Commission shall not, on the basis of national origin, treat any such imported natural gas on an unjust, unreasonable, unduly discriminatory, or preferential basis.

(c) Expedited application and approval process

For purposes of subsection (a) of this section, the importation of the natural gas referred to in subsection (b) of this section, or the exportation of natural gas to a nation with which there is in effect a free trade agreement requiring national treatment for trade in natural gas, shall be deemed to be consistent with the public interest, and applications for such importation or exportation shall be granted without modification or delay.

(d) Construction with other laws

Except as specifically provided in this chapter, nothing in this chapter affects the rights of States under—

(1) the Coastal Zone Management Act of 1972 (16 U.S.C. 1451 et seq.);

(2) the Clean Air Act (42 U.S.C. 7401 et seq.); or

(3) the Federal Water Pollution Control Act (33 U.S.C. 1251 et seq.).

(e) LNG terminals

(1) The Commission shall have the exclusive authority to approve or deny an application for the siting, construction, expansion, or operation of an LNG terminal. Except as specifically provided in this chapter, nothing in this chapter is intended to affect otherwise applicable law related to any Federal agency's authorities or responsibilities related to LNG terminals.

(2) Upon the filing of any application to site, construct, expand, or operate an LNG terminal, the Commission shall—

(A) set the matter for hearing;

(B) give reasonable notice of the hearing to all interested persons, including the State commission of the State in which the LNG terminal is located and, if not the same, the Governor-appointed State agency described in section 717b–1 of this title;

(C) decide the matter in accordance with this subsection; and

(D) issue or deny the appropriate order accordingly.

(3) (A) Except as provided in subparagraph (B), the Commission may approve an application described in paragraph (2), in whole or part, with such modifications and upon such terms and conditions as the Commission find [finds?] necessary or appropriate.

(B) Before January 1, 2015, the Commission shall not—

(i) deny an application solely on the basis that the applicant proposes to use the LNG terminal exclusively or partially for gas that the applicant or an affiliate of the applicant will supply to the facility; or

(ii) condition an order on—

(I) a requirement that the LNG terminal offer service to customers other than the applicant, or any affiliate of the applicant, securing the order;

(II) any regulation of the rates, charges, terms, or conditions of service of the LNG terminal; or

(III) a requirement to file with the Commission schedules or contracts related to the rates, charges, terms, or conditions of service of the LNG terminal.

(C) Subparagraph (B) shall cease to have effect on January 1, 2030.

(4) An order issued for an LNG terminal that also offers service to customers on an open access basis shall not result in subsidization of expansion capacity by existing customers, degradation of service to existing customers, or undue discrimination against existing customers as to their terms or conditions of service at the facility, as all of those terms are defined by the Commission.

(f) **Military installations**

(1) In this subsection, the term "military installation"—

(A) means a base, camp, post, range, station, yard, center, or homeport facility for any ship or other activity under the jurisdiction of the Department of Defense, including any leased facility, that is located within a State, the District of Columbia, or any territory of the United States; and

(B) does not include any facility used primarily for civil works, rivers and harbors projects, or flood control projects, as determined by the Secretary of Defense.

(2) The Commission shall enter into a memorandum of understanding with the Secretary of Defense for the purpose of ensuring that the Commission coordinate and consult ["coordinates and consults"?] with the Secretary of Defense on the siting, construction, expansion, or operation of liquefied natural gas facilities that may affect an active military installation.

(3) The Commission shall obtain the concurrence of the Secretary of Defense before authorizing the siting, construction, expansion, or operation of liquefied natural gas facilities affecting the training or activities of an active military installation.

15 U.S. Code § 717b–1—State and local safety considerations

(a) Promulgation of regulations

The Commission shall promulgate regulations on the National Environmental Policy Act of 1969 (42 U.S.C. 4321 et seq.) pre-filing process within 60 days after August 8, 2005. An applicant shall comply with pre-filing process required under the National Environmental Policy Act of 1969 prior to filing an application with the Commission. The regulations shall require that the pre-filing process commence at least 6 months prior to the filing of an application for authorization to construct an LNG terminal and encourage applicants to cooperate with State and local officials.

(b) State consultation

The Governor of a State in which an LNG terminal is proposed to be located shall designate the appropriate State agency for the purposes of consulting with the Commission regarding an application under section 717b of this title. The Commission shall consult with such State agency regarding State and local safety considerations prior to issuing an order pursuant to section 717b of this title. For the purposes of this section, State and local safety considerations include—

(1) the kind and use of the facility;

(2) the existing and projected population and demographic characteristics of the location;

(3) the existing and proposed land use near the location;

(4) the natural and physical aspects of the location;

(5) the emergency response capabilities near the facility location; and

(6) the need to encourage remote siting.

(c) Advisory report

The State agency may furnish an advisory report on State and local safety considerations to the Commission with respect to an application no later than 30 days after the application was filed with the Commission. Before issuing an order authorizing an applicant to site, construct, expand, or operate an LNG terminal, the Commission shall review and respond specifically to the issues raised by the State agency described in subsection (b) of this section in the advisory report. This subsection shall apply to any application filed after August 8, 2005. A State agency has 30 days after August 8, 2005 to file an advisory report related to any applications pending at the Commission as of August 8, 2005.

(d) Inspections

The State commission of the State in which an LNG terminal is located may, after the terminal is operational, conduct safety inspections in conformance with Federal regulations and guidelines with respect to the LNG terminal upon written notice to the Commission. The State commission may notify the Commission of any alleged safety violations. The Commission shall transmit information regarding such allegations to the appropriate Federal agency, which shall take appropriate action and notify the State commission.

(e) Emergency Response Plan

(1) In any order authorizing an LNG terminal the Commission shall require the LNG terminal operator to develop an Emergency Response Plan. The Emergency Response Plan shall be prepared in consultation with the United States Coast Guard and State and local agencies and be approved by the Commission prior to any final approval to begin construction. The Plan shall include a cost-sharing plan.

(2) A cost-sharing plan developed under paragraph (1) shall include a description of any direct cost reimbursements that the applicant agrees to provide to any State and local agencies with responsibility for security and safety—

(A) at the LNG terminal; and

(B) in proximity to vessels that serve the facility.

15 U.S. Code § 717c—Rates and charges

(a) Just and reasonable rates and charges

All rates and charges made, demanded, or received by any natural-gas company for or in connection with the transportation or sale of natural gas subject to the jurisdiction of the Commission, and all rules and regulations affecting or pertaining to such rates or charges, shall be just and reasonable, and any such rate or charge that is not just and reasonable is declared to be unlawful.

(b) Undue preferences and unreasonable rates and charges prohibited

No natural-gas company shall, with respect to any transportation or sale of natural gas subject to the jurisdiction of the Commission,

(1) make or grant any undue preference or advantage to any person or subject any person to any undue prejudice or disadvantage, or

(2) maintain any unreasonable difference in rates, charges, service, facilities, or in any other respect, either as between localities or as between classes of service.

(c) Filing of rates and charges with Commission; public inspection of schedules

Under such rules and regulations as the Commission may prescribe, every natural-gas company shall file with the Commission, within such time (not less than sixty days from June 21, 1938) and in such form as the Commission may designate, and shall keep open in convenient form and place for public inspection, schedules showing all rates and charges for any transportation or sale subject to the jurisdiction of the Commission, and the classifications, practices, and regulations affecting such rates and charges, together with all contracts which in any manner affect or relate to such rates, charges, classifications, and services.

(d) Changes in rates and charges; notice to Commission

Unless the Commission otherwise orders, no change shall be made by any natural-gas company in any such rate, charge, classification, or service, or in any rule, regulation, or contract relating thereto, except after thirty days' notice to the Commission and to the public. Such notice shall be given by filing with the Commission and keeping open for public inspection new schedules stating plainly the change or changes to be made in the schedule or schedules then in force and the time when the change or changes will go into effect. The Commission, for good cause shown, may allow changes to take effect without requiring the thirty days' notice herein provided for by an order specifying the changes so to be made and the time when they shall take effect and the manner in which they shall be filed and published.

(e) Authority of Commission to hold hearings concerning new schedule of rates

Whenever any such new schedule is filed the Commission shall have authority, either upon complaint of any State, municipality, State commission, or gas distributing company, or upon its own initiative without complaint, at once, and if it so orders, without answer or formal pleading by the natural-gas company, but upon reasonable notice, to enter upon a hearing concerning the lawfulness of such rate, charge, classification, or service; and, pending such hearing and the decision thereon, the Commission, upon filing with such schedules and delivering to the natural-gas company affected thereby a statement in writing of its reasons for such suspension, may suspend the operation of such schedule and defer the use of such rate, charge, classification, or service, but not for a longer period than five months beyond the time when it would otherwise go into effect; and after full hearings, either completed before or after the rate, charge, classification, or service goes into effect, the Commission may make such orders with reference thereto as would be proper in a proceeding initiated after it had become effective. If the proceeding has not been concluded and an order made at the expiration of the suspension period, on motion of the natural-gas company making the filing, the proposed change of rate, charge, classification, or service shall go into effect. Where increased rates or charges are thus made effective, the Commission may, by order, require the natural-gas company to furnish a bond, to be approved by the Commission, to refund any amounts ordered by the Commission, to keep accurate accounts in detail of all amounts received by reason of such increase, specifying by whom and in whose behalf such amounts were paid, and, upon completion of the hearing and decision, to order such natural-gas company to refund, with interest, the portion of such increased rates or charges by its decision found not justified. At any hearing involving a rate or charge sought to be increased, the burden of proof to show that the increased rate or charge is just and reasonable shall be upon the natural-gas company, and the Commission shall give to the hearing and decision of such questions preference over other questions pending before it and decide the same as speedily as possible.

(f) Storage services

(1) In exercising its authority under this chapter or the Natural Gas Policy Act of 1978 (15 U.S.C. 3301 et seq.), the Commission may authorize a natural gas company (or any person that will be a natural gas company on completion of any proposed construction) to provide storage and storage-related services at market-based rates for new storage capacity related to a specific facility placed in service after August 8, 2005, notwithstanding the fact that the company is unable to demonstrate that the company lacks market power, if the Commission determines that—

(A) market-based rates are in the public interest and necessary to encourage the construction of the storage capacity in the area needing storage services; and

(B) customers are adequately protected.

(2) The Commission shall ensure that reasonable terms and conditions are in place to protect consumers.

(3) If the Commission authorizes a natural gas company to charge market-based rates under this subsection, the Commission shall review periodically whether the market-based rate is just, reasonable, and not unduly discriminatory or preferential.

15 U.S. Code § 717c–1—Prohibition on market manipulation

It shall be unlawful for any entity, directly or indirectly, to use or employ, in connection with the purchase or sale of natural gas or the purchase or sale of transportation services subject to the jurisdiction of the Commission, any manipulative or deceptive device or contrivance (as those terms are used in section 78j (b) of this title) in contravention of such rules and regulations as the Commission may prescribe as necessary in the public interest or for the protection of natural gas ratepayers. Nothing in this section shall be construed to create a private right of action.

15 U.S. Code § 717d—Fixing rates and charges; determination of cost of production or transportation

(a) Decreases in rates

Whenever the Commission, after a hearing had upon its own motion or upon complaint of any State, municipality, State commission, or gas distributing company, shall find that any rate, charge, or classification demanded, observed, charged, or collected by any natural-gas company in connection with any transportation or sale of natural gas, subject to the jurisdiction of the Commission, or that any rule, regulation, practice, or contract affecting such rate, charge, or classification is unjust, unreasonable, unduly discriminatory, or preferential, the Commission shall determine the just and reasonable rate, charge, classification, rule, regulation, practice, or contract to be thereafter observed and in force, and shall fix the same by order: Provided, however,

That the Commission shall have no power to order any increase in any rate contained in the currently effective schedule of such natural gas company on file with the Commission, unless such increase is in accordance with a new schedule filed by such natural gas company; but the Commission may order a decrease where existing rates are unjust, unduly discriminatory, preferential, otherwise unlawful, or are not the lowest reasonable rates.

(b) Costs of production and transportation

The Commission upon its own motion, or upon the request of any State commission, whenever it can do so without prejudice to the efficient and proper conduct of its affairs, may investigate and determine the cost of the production or transportation of natural gas by a natural-gas company in cases where the Commission has no authority to establish a rate governing the transportation or sale of such natural gas.

15 U.S. Code § 717e—Ascertainment of cost of property

(a) Cost of property

The Commission may investigate and ascertain the actual legitimate cost of the property of every natural-gas company, the depreciation therein, and, when found necessary for rate-making purposes, other facts which bear on the determination of such cost or depreciation and the fair value of such property.

(b) Inventory of property; statements of costs

Every natural-gas company upon request shall file with the Commission an inventory of all or any part of its property and a statement of the original cost thereof, and shall keep the Commission informed regarding the cost of all additions, betterments, extensions, and new construction.

15 U.S. Code § 717f—Construction, extension, or abandonment of facilities

(a) Extension or improvement of facilities on order of court; notice and hearing

Whenever the Commission, after notice and opportunity for hearing, finds such action necessary or desirable in the public interest, it may by order direct a natural-gas company to extend or improve its transportation facilities, to establish physical connection of its transportation facilities with the facilities of, and sell natural gas to, any person or municipality engaged or legally authorized to engage in the local distribution of natural or artificial gas to the public, and for such purpose to extend its transportation facilities to communities immediately adjacent to such facilities or to territory served by such natural-gas company, if the Commission finds that no undue burden will be placed upon such natural-gas company thereby: Provided, That the Commission shall have no authority to compel the enlargement of transportation facilities for such purposes, or to compel such natural-gas company to establish physical connection or sell natural gas when to do so would impair its ability to render adequate service to its customers.

(b) Abandonment of facilities or services; approval of Commission

No natural-gas company shall abandon all or any portion of its facilities subject to the jurisdiction of the Commission, or any service rendered by means of such facilities, without the permission and approval of the Commission first had and obtained, after due hearing, and a finding by the Commission that the available supply of natural gas is depleted to the extent that the continuance of service is unwarranted, or that the present or future public convenience or necessity permit such abandonment.

(c) Certificate of public convenience and necessity

(1) (A) No natural-gas company or person which will be a natural-gas company upon completion of any proposed construction or extension shall engage in the transportation or sale of natural gas, subject to the jurisdiction of the Commission, or undertake the construction or extension of any facilities therefor, or acquire or operate any such facilities or extensions thereof, unless there is in force with respect to such natural-gas company a certificate of public convenience and necessity issued by the Commission authorizing such acts or operations: Provided, however, That if any such natural-gas company or predecessor in interest was bona fide engaged in transportation or sale of natural gas, subject to the jurisdiction of the Commission, on February 7, 1942, over the route or routes or within the area for which application is made and has so operated since that time, the Commission shall issue such certificate without requiring further proof that public convenience and necessity will be served by such operation, and without further proceedings, if application for such certificate is made to the Commission within ninety days after February 7, 1942. Pending the determination of any such application, the continuance of such operation shall be lawful.

(B) In all other cases the Commission shall set the matter for hearing and shall give such reasonable notice of the hearing thereon to all interested persons as in its judgment may be necessary under rules and regulations to be prescribed by the Commission; and the application shall be decided in accordance with the procedure provided in subsection (e) of this section and such certificate shall be issued or denied accordingly: Provided, however, That the Commission may issue a temporary certificate in cases of emergency, to assure maintenance of adequate service or to serve particular customers, without notice or hearing, pending the determination of an application for a certificate, and may by regulation exempt from the requirements of this section temporary acts or operations for which the issuance of a certificate will not be required in the public interest.

(2) The Commission may issue a certificate of public convenience and necessity to a natural-gas company for the transportation in interstate commerce of natural gas used by any person for one or more high-priority uses, as defined, by rule, by the Commission, in the case of—

(A) natural gas sold by the producer to such person; and

(B) natural gas produced by such person.

(d) Application for certificate of public convenience and necessity

Application for certificates shall be made in writing to the Commission, be verified under oath, and shall be in such form, contain such information, and notice thereof shall be served upon such interested parties and in such manner as the Commission shall, by regulation, require.

(e) Granting of certificate of public convenience and necessity

Except in the cases governed by the provisos contained in subsection (c)(1) of this section, a certificate shall be issued to any qualified applicant therefor, authorizing the whole or any part of the operation, sale, service, construction, extension, or acquisition covered by the application, if it is found that the applicant is able and willing properly to do the acts and to perform the service proposed and to conform to the provisions of this chapter and the requirements, rules, and regulations of the Commission thereunder, and that the proposed service, sale, operation, construction, extension, or acquisition, to the extent authorized by the certificate, is or will be required by the present or future public convenience and necessity; otherwise such application shall be denied. The Commission shall have the power to attach to the issuance of the certificate and to the exercise of the rights granted thereunder such reasonable terms and conditions as the public convenience and necessity may require.

(f) Determination of service area; jurisdiction of transportation to ultimate consumers

(1) The Commission, after a hearing had upon its own motion or upon application, may determine the service area to which each authorization under this section is to be limited. Within such service area as determined by the Commission a natural-gas company may enlarge or extend its facilities for the purpose of supplying increased market demands in such service area without further authorization; and

(2) If the Commission has determined a service area pursuant to this subsection, transportation to ultimate consumers in such service area by the holder of such service area determination, even if across State lines, shall be subject to the exclusive jurisdiction of the State commission in the State in which the gas is consumed. This section shall not apply to the transportation of natural gas to another natural gas company.

(g) Certificate of public convenience and necessity for service of area already being served

Nothing contained in this section shall be construed as a limitation upon the power of the Commission to grant certificates of public convenience and necessity for service of an area already being served by another natural-gas company.

(h) Right of eminent domain for construction of pipelines, etc.

When any holder of a certificate of public convenience and necessity cannot acquire by contract, or is unable to agree with the owner of property to the compensation to be paid for, the necessary right-of-way to construct, operate, and maintain a pipe line or pipe lines for the transportation of natural gas, and the necessary land or other property, in addition to right-of-way, for the location of compressor stations, pressure apparatus, or other stations or equipment necessary to the proper operation of such pipe line or pipe lines, it may acquire the same by the exercise of the right of eminent domain in the district court of the United States for the district in which such property may be located, or in the State courts. The practice and procedure in any action or proceeding for that purpose in the district court of the United States shall conform as nearly as may be with the practice and procedure in similar action or proceeding in the courts of the State where the property is situated: Provided, That the United States district courts shall only have jurisdiction of cases when the amount claimed by the owner of the property to be condemned exceeds $3,000.

15 U.S. Code § 717g—Accounts; records; memoranda

(a) Rules and regulations for keeping and preserving accounts, records, etc.

Every natural-gas company shall make, keep, and preserve for such periods, such accounts, records of cost-accounting procedures, correspondence, memoranda, papers, books, and other records as the Commission may by rules and regulations prescribe as necessary or appropriate for purposes of the administration of this chapter: Provided, however, That nothing in this chapter shall relieve any such natural-gas company from keeping any accounts, memoranda, or records which such natural-gas company may be required to keep by or under authority of the laws of any State. The Commission may prescribe a system of accounts to be kept by such natural-gas companies, and may classify such natural-gas companies and prescribe a system of accounts for each class. The Commission, after notice and opportunity for hearing, may determine by order the accounts in which particular outlays or receipts shall be entered, charged, or credited. The burden of proof to justify every accounting entry questioned by the Commission shall be on the person making, authorizing, or requiring such entry, and the Commission may suspend a charge or credit pending submission of satisfactory proof in support thereof.

(b) Access to and inspection of accounts and records

The Commission shall at all times have access to and the right to inspect and examine all accounts, records, and memoranda of natural-gas companies; and it shall be the duty of such natural-gas companies to furnish to the Commission, within such reasonable time as the Commission may order, any information with respect thereto which the Commission may by order require, including copies of maps, contracts, reports of engineers, and other data, records, and papers, and to grant to all agents of the Commission free access to its property and its accounts, records, and memoranda when requested so to do. No member, officer, or employee of the Commission shall divulge any fact or information which may come to his knowledge during the course of examination of books, records, data, or accounts, except insofar as he may be directed by the Commission or by a court.

(c) Books, accounts, etc., of the person controlling gas company subject to examination

The books, accounts, memoranda, and records of any person who controls directly or indirectly a natural-gas company subject to the jurisdiction of the Commission and of any other company controlled by such person, insofar as they relate to transactions with or the business of such natural-gas company, shall be subject to examination on the order of the Commission.

15 U.S. Code § 717h—Rates of depreciation

(a) Depreciation and amortization

The Commission may, after hearing, require natural-gas companies to carry proper and adequate depreciation and amortization accounts in accordance with such rules, regulations, and forms of account as the Commission may prescribe. The Commission may from time to time ascertain and determine, and by order fix, the proper and adequate rates of depreciation and amortization of the several classes of property of each natural-gas company used or useful in the production, transportation, or sale of natural gas. Each natural-gas company shall conform its depreciation and amortization accounts to the rates so ascertained, determined, and fixed. No natural-gas company subject to the jurisdiction of the Commission shall charge to operating expenses any depreciation or amortization charges on classes of property other than those prescribed by the Commission, or charge with respect to any class of property a percentage of depreciation or amortization other than that prescribed therefor by the Commission. No such natural-gas company shall in any case include in any form under its operating or other expenses any depreciation, amortization, or other charge or expenditure included elsewhere as a depreciation or amortization charge or otherwise under its operating or other expenses. Nothing in this section shall limit the power of a State commission to determine in the exercise of its jurisdiction, with respect to any natural-gas company, the percentage rates of depreciation or amortization to be allowed, as to any class of property of such natural-gas company, or the composite depreciation or amortization rate, for the purpose of determining rates or charges.

(b) Rules

The Commission, before prescribing any rules or requirements as to accounts, records, or memoranda, or as to depreciation or amortization rates, shall notify each State commission having jurisdiction with respect to any natural-gas company involved and shall give reasonable opportunity to each such commission to present its views and shall receive and consider such views and recommendations.

15 U.S. Code § 717i—Periodic and special reports

(a) Form and contents of reports

Every natural-gas company shall file with the Commission such annual and other periodic or special reports as the Commission may by rules and regulations or order prescribe as necessary or appropriate to assist the Commission in the proper administration of this chapter. The Commission may prescribe the manner and form in which such reports shall be made, and require from such natural-gas companies specific answers to all questions upon which the Commission may need information. The Commission may require that such reports shall include, among other things, full information as to assets and liabilities, capitalization, investment and reduction thereof, gross receipts, interest due and paid, depreciation, amortization, and other reserves, cost of facilities, cost of maintenance and operation of facilities for the production, transportation, or sale of natural gas, cost of renewal and replacement of such facilities, transportation, delivery, use, and sale of natural gas. The Commission may require any such natural-gas company to make adequate provision for currently determining such costs and other facts. Such reports shall be made under oath unless the Commission otherwise specifies.

(b) Unlawful conduct

It shall be unlawful for any natural-gas company willfully to hinder, delay, or obstruct the making, filing, or keeping of any information, document, report, memorandum, record, or account required to be made, filed, or kept under this chapter or any rule, regulation, or order thereunder.

15 U.S. Code § 717j—State compacts for conservation, transportation, etc., of natural gas

(a) Assembly of pertinent information; report to Congress

In case two or more States propose to the Congress compacts dealing with the conservation, production, transportation, or distribution of natural gas it shall be the duty of the Commission to assemble pertinent information relative to the matters covered in any such proposed compact, to make public and to report to the Congress information so obtained, together with such recommendations for further legislation as may appear to be appropriate or necessary to carry out the purposes of such proposed compact and to aid in the conservation of natural-gas resources within the United States and in the orderly, equitable, and economic production, transportation, and distribution of natural gas.

(b) Assembly of information relative to operation of compact; report to Congress

It shall be the duty of the Commission to assemble and keep current pertinent information relative to the effect and operation of any compact between two or more States heretofore or hereafter approved by the Congress, to make such information public, and to report to the Congress, from time to time, the information so obtained, together with such recommendations as may appear to be appropriate or necessary to promote the purposes of such compact.

(c) Availability of services, etc., of other agencies

In carrying out the purposes of this chapter, the Commission shall, so far as practicable, avail itself of the services, records, reports, and information of the executive departments and other agencies of the Government, and the President may, from time to time, direct that such services and facilities be made available to the Commission.

15 U.S. Code § 717k—Officials dealing in securities

It shall be unlawful for any officer or director of any natural-gas company to receive for his own benefit, directly or indirectly, any money or thing of value in respect to the negotiation, hypothecation, or sale by such natural-gas company of any security issued, or to be issued, by such natural-gas company, or to share in any of the proceeds thereof, or to participate in the making or paying of any dividends, other than liquidating dividends, of such natural-gas company from any funds properly included in capital account.

15 U.S. Code § 717*l*—Complaints

Any State, municipality, or State commission complaining of anything done or omitted to be done by any natural-gas company in contravention of the provisions of this chapter may apply to the Commission by petition, which shall briefly state the facts, whereupon a statement of the complaint thus made shall be forwarded by the Commission to such natural-gas company, which shall be called upon to satisfy the complaint or to answer the same in writing within a reasonable time to be specified by the Commission.

15 U.S. Code § 717n—Process coordination; hearings; rules of procedure

(a) **Definition**

In this section, the term "Federal authorization"—

(1) means any authorization required under Federal law with respect to an application for authorization under section 717b of this title or a certificate of public convenience and necessity under section 717f of this title; and

(2) includes any permits, special use authorizations, certifications, opinions, or other approvals as may be required under Federal law with respect to an application for authorization under section 717b of this title or a certificate of public convenience and necessity under section 717f of this title.

(b) **Designation as lead agency**

(1) **In general**

The Commission shall act as the lead agency for the purposes of coordinating all applicable Federal authorizations and for the purposes of complying with the National Environmental Policy Act of 1969 (42 U.S.C. 4321 et seq.).

(2) **Other agencies**

Each Federal and State agency considering an aspect of an application for Federal authorization shall cooperate with the Commission and comply with the deadlines established by the Commission.

(c) **Schedule**

(1) **Commission authority to set schedule**

The Commission shall establish a schedule for all Federal authorizations. In establishing the schedule, the Commission shall—

(A) ensure expeditious completion of all such proceedings; and

(B) comply with applicable schedules established by Federal law.

(2) **Failure to meet schedule**

If a Federal or State administrative agency does not complete a proceeding for an approval that is required for a Federal authorization in accordance with the schedule established by the Commission, the applicant may pursue remedies under section 717r(d) of this title.

(d) Consolidated record

The Commission shall, with the cooperation of Federal and State administrative agencies and officials, maintain a complete consolidated record of all decisions made or actions taken by the Commission or by a Federal administrative agency or officer (or State administrative agency or officer acting under delegated Federal authority) with respect to any Federal authorization. Such record shall be the record for—

(1) appeals or reviews under the Coastal Zone Management Act of 1972 (16 U.S.C.1451 et seq.), provided that the record may be supplemented as expressly provided pursuant to section 319 of that Act [16 U.S.C. 1465]; or

(2) judicial review under section 717r (d) of this title of decisions made or actions taken of Federal and State administrative agencies and officials, provided that, if the Court determines that the record does not contain sufficient information, the Court may remand the proceeding to the Commission for further development of the consolidated record.

(e) Hearings; parties

Hearings under this chapter may be held before the Commission, any member or members thereof, or any representative of the Commission designated by it, and appropriate records thereof shall be kept. In any proceeding before it, the Commission in accordance with such rules and regulations as it may prescribe, may admit as a party any interested State, State commission, municipality or any representative of interested consumers or security holders, or any competitor of a party to such proceeding, or any other person whose participation in the proceeding may be in the public interest.

(f) Procedure

All hearings, investigations, and proceedings under this chapter shall be governed by rules of practice and procedure to be adopted by the Commission, and in the conduct thereof the technical rules of evidence need not be applied. No informality in any hearing, investigation, or proceeding or in the manner of taking testimony shall invalidate any order, decision, rule, or regulation issued under the authority of this chapter.

§ 717*o*. Administrative powers of Commission; rules, regulations, and orders

The Commission shall have power to perform any and all acts, and to prescribe, issue, make, amend, and rescind such orders, rules, and regulations as it may find necessary or appropriate to carry out the provisions of this chapter. Among other things, such rules and regulations may define accounting, technical, and trade terms used in this chapter; and may prescribe the form or forms of all statements, declarations, applications, and reports to be filed with the Commission, the information which they shall contain, and the time within which they shall be filed. Unless a different date is specified therein, rules and regulations of the Commission shall be effective thirty days after publication in the manner which the Commission shall prescribe. Orders of the Commission shall be effective on the date and in the manner which the Commission shall prescribe. For the purposes of its rules and regulations, the Commission may classify persons and matters within its jurisdiction and prescribe different requirements for different classes of persons or matters. All rules and regulations of the Commission shall be filed with its secretary and shall be kept open in convenient form for public inspection and examination during reasonable business hours.

15 U.S. Code § 717p—Joint boards

(a) Reference of matters to joint boards; composition and power

The Commission may refer any matter arising in the administration of this chapter to a board to be composed of a member or members, as determined by the Commission, from the State or each of the States affected or to be affected by such matter. Any such board shall be vested with the same power and be subject to the same duties and liabilities as in the case of a member of the Commission when designated by the Commission to hold any hearings. The action of such board shall have such force and effect and its proceedings shall be conducted in such manner as the Commission shall by regulations prescribe. The Board shall be appointed by the Commission from persons nominated by the State commission of each State affected, or by the Governor of such State if there is no State commission. Each State affected shall be entitled to the same number of representatives on the board unless the nominating power of such State waives such right. The Commission shall have discretion to reject the nominee from any State, but shall thereupon invite a new nomination from that State. The members of a board shall receive such allowances for expenses as the Commission shall provide. The Commission may, when in its discretion sufficient reason exists therefor, revoke any reference to such a board.

(b) Conference with State commissions regarding rate structure, costs, etc.

The Commission may confer with any State commission regarding rate structures, costs, accounts, charges, practices, classifications, and regulations of natural-gas companies; and the Commission is authorized, under such rules and regulations as it shall prescribe, to hold joint hearings with any State commission in connection with any matter with respect to which the Commission is authorized to act. The Commission is authorized in the administration of this chapter to avail itself of such cooperation, services, records, and facilities as may be afforded by any State commission.

(c) Information and reports available to State commissions

The Commission shall make available to the several State commissions such information and reports as may be of assistance in State regulation of natural-gas companies. Whenever the Commission can do so without prejudice to the efficient and proper conduct of its affairs, it may, upon request from a State commission, make available to such State commission as witnesses any of its trained rate, valuation, or other experts, subject to reimbursement of the compensation and traveling expenses of such witnesses. All sums collected hereunder shall be credited to the appropriation from which the amounts were expended in carrying out the provisions of this subsection.

15 U.S. Code § 717q—Appointment of officers and employees

The Commission is authorized to appoint and fix the compensation of such officers, attorneys, examiners, and experts as may be necessary for carrying out its functions under this chapter; and the Commission may, subject to civil-service laws, appoint such other officers and employees as are necessary for carrying out such functions and fix their salaries in accordance with chapter 51 and subchapter III of chapter 53 of title 5.

15 U.S. Code § 717r—Rehearing and review

(a) Application for rehearing; time

Any person, State, municipality, or State commission aggrieved by an order issued by the Commission in a proceeding under this chapter to which such person, State, municipality, or State commission is a party may apply for a rehearing within thirty days after the issuance of such order. The application for rehearing shall set forth specifically the ground or grounds upon which such application is based. Upon such application the Commission shall have power to grant or deny rehearing or to abrogate or modify its order without further hearing. Unless the Commission acts upon the application for rehearing within thirty days after it is filed, such application may be deemed to have been denied. No proceeding to review any order of the Commission shall be brought by any person unless such person shall have made application to the Commission for a rehearing thereon. Until the record in a proceeding shall have been filed in a court of appeals, as provided in subsection (b) of this section, the Commission may at any time, upon reasonable notice and in such manner as it shall deem proper, modify or set aside, in whole or in part, any finding or order made or issued by it under the provisions of this chapter.

(b) Review of Commission order

Any party to a proceeding under this chapter aggrieved by an order issued by the Commission in such proceeding may obtain a review of such order in the court of appeals of the United States for any circuit wherein the natural-gas company to which the order relates is located or has its principal place of business, or in the United States Court of Appeals for the District of Columbia, by filing in such court, within sixty days after the order of the Commission upon the application for rehearing, a written petition praying that the order of the Commission be modified or set aside in whole or in part. A copy of such petition shall forthwith be transmitted by the clerk of the court to any member of the Commission and thereupon the Commission shall file with the court the record upon which the order complained of was entered, as provided in section 2112 of title 28. Upon the filing of such petition such court shall have jurisdiction, which upon the filing of the record with it shall be exclusive, to affirm, modify, or set aside such order in whole or in part. No objection to the order of the Commission shall be considered by the court unless such objection shall have been urged before the Commission in the application for rehearing unless there is reasonable ground for failure so to do. The finding of the Commission as to the facts, if supported by substantial evidence, shall be conclusive. If any party shall apply to the court for leave to adduce additional evidence, and shall show to the satisfaction of the court that such additional evidence is material and that there were reasonable grounds for failure to adduce such evidence in the proceedings before the Commission, the court may order such additional evidence to be taken before the Commission and to be adduced upon the hearing in such manner and upon such terms and conditions as to the court may seem proper. The Commission may modify its findings as to the facts by reason of the additional evidence so taken, and it shall file with the court such modified or new findings, which is supported by substantial evidence, shall be conclusive, and its recommendation, if any, for the modification or setting aside of the original order. The judgment and decree of the court, affirming, modifying, or setting aside, in whole or in part, any such order of the Commission, shall be final, subject to review by the Supreme Court of the United States upon certiorari or certification as provided in section 1254 of title 28.

(c) Stay of Commission order

The filing of an application for rehearing under subsection (a) of this section shall not, unless specifically ordered by the Commission, operate as a stay of the Commission's order. The commencement of proceedings under subsection (b) of this section shall not, unless specifically ordered by the court, operate as a stay of the Commission's order.

(d) Judicial review

(1) In general

The United States Court of Appeals for the circuit in which a facility subject to section 717b of this title or section 717f of this title is proposed to be constructed, expanded, or operated shall have original and exclusive jurisdiction over any civil action for the review of an order or action of a Federal agency (other than the Commission) or State administrative agency acting pursuant to Federal law to issue, condition, or deny any permit, license, concurrence, or approval (hereinafter collectively referred to as "permit") required under Federal law, other than the Coastal Zone Management Act of 1972 (16 U.S.C. 1451 et seq.).

(2) Agency delay

The United States Court of Appeals for the District of Columbia shall have original and exclusive jurisdiction over any civil action for the review of an alleged failure to act by a Federal agency (other than the Commission) or State administrative agency acting pursuant to Federal law to issue, condition, or deny any permit required under Federal law, other than the Coastal Zone Management Act of 1972 (16 U.S.C. 1451 et seq.), for a facility subject to section 717b of this title or section 717f of this title. The failure of an agency to take action on a permit required under Federal law, other than the Coastal Zone Management Act of 1972, in accordance with the Commission schedule established pursuant to section 717n (c) of this title shall be considered inconsistent with Federal law for the purposes of paragraph (3).

(3) Court action

If the Court finds that such order or action is inconsistent with the Federal law governing such permit and would prevent the construction, expansion, or operation of the facility subject to section 717b of this title or section 717f of this title, the Court shall remand the proceeding to the agency to take appropriate action consistent with the order of the Court. If the Court remands the order or action to the Federal or State agency, the Court shall set a reasonable schedule and deadline for the agency to act on remand.

(4) Commission action

For any action described in this subsection, the Commission shall file with the Court the consolidated record of such order or action to which the appeal hereunder relates.

(5) Expedited review

The Court shall set any action brought under this subsection for expedited consideration.

15 U.S. Code § 717s—Enforcement of chapter

(a) Action in district court for injunction

Whenever it shall appear to the Commission that any person is engaged or about to engage in any acts or practices which constitute or will constitute a violation of the provisions of this chapter, or of any rule, regulation, or order thereunder, it may in its discretion bring an action in the proper district court of the United States, or the United States courts of any Territory or other place subject to the jurisdiction of the United States, to enjoin such acts or practices and to enforce compliance with this chapter or any rule, regulation, or order thereunder, and upon a proper showing a permanent or temporary injunction or decree or restraining order shall be granted without bond. The Commission may transmit such evidence as may be available concerning such acts or practices or concerning apparent violations of the Federal antitrust laws to the Attorney General, who, in his discretion, may institute the necessary criminal proceedings.

(b) Mandamus

Upon application of the Commission the district courts of the United States and the United States courts of any Territory or other place subject to the jurisdiction of the United States shall have jurisdiction to issue writs of mandamus commanding any person to comply with the provisions of this chapter or any rule, regulation, or order of the Commission thereunder.

(c) Employment of attorneys by Commission

The Commission may employ such attorneys as it finds necessary for proper legal aid and service of the Commission or its members in the conduct of their work, or for proper representation of the public interest in investigations made by it, or cases or proceedings pending before it, whether at the Commission's own instance or upon complaint, or to appear for or represent the Commission in any case in court; and the expenses of such employment shall be paid out of the appropriation for the Commission.

(d) Violation of market manipulation provisions

In any proceedings under subsection (a) of this section, the court may prohibit, conditionally or unconditionally, and permanently or for such period of time as the court determines, any individual who is engaged or has engaged in practices constituting a violation of section 717c–1 of this title (including related rules and regulations) from—

(1) acting as an officer or director of a natural gas company; or

(2) engaging in the business of—

(A) the purchasing or selling of natural gas; or

(B) the purchasing or selling of transmission services subject to the jurisdiction of the Commission.

15 U.S. Code §717t—General penalties

(a) Any person who willfully and knowingly does or causes or suffers to be done any act, matter, or thing in this chapter prohibited or declared to be unlawful, or who willfully and knowingly omits or fails to do any act, matter, or thing in this chapter required to be done, or willfully and knowingly causes or suffers such omission or failure, shall, upon conviction thereof, be punished by a fine of not more than $1,000,000 or by imprisonment for not more than 5 years, or both.

(b) Any person who willfully and knowingly violates any rule, regulation, restriction, condition, or order made or imposed by the Commission under authority of this chapter, shall, in addition to any other penalties provided by law, be punished upon conviction thereof by a fine of not exceeding $50,000 for each and every day during which such offense occurs.

15 U.S. Code §717t–1—Civil penalty authority

(a) In general

Any person that violates this chapter, or any rule, regulation, restriction, condition, or order made or imposed by the Commission under authority of this chapter, shall be subject to a civil penalty of not more than $1,000,000 per day per violation for as long as the violation continues.

(b) Notice

The penalty shall be assessed by the Commission after notice and opportunity for public hearing.

(c) Amount

In determining the amount of a proposed penalty, the Commission shall take into consideration the nature and seriousness of the violation and the efforts to remedy the violation.

15 U.S. Code § 717t–2—Natural gas market transparency rules

(a) In general

(1) The Commission is directed to facilitate price transparency in markets for the sale or transportation of physical natural gas in interstate commerce, having due regard for the public interest, the integrity of those markets, fair competition, and the protection of consumers.

(2) The Commission may prescribe such rules as the Commission determines necessary and appropriate to carry out the purposes of this section. The rules shall provide for the dissemination, on a timely basis, of information about the availability and prices of natural gas sold at wholesale and in interstate commerce to the Commission, State commissions, buyers and sellers of wholesale natural gas, and the public.

(3) The Commission may—

(A) obtain the information described in paragraph (2) from any market participant; and

(B) rely on entities other than the Commission to receive and make public the information, subject to the disclosure rules in subsection (b) of this section.

(4) In carrying out this section, the Commission shall consider the degree of price transparency provided by existing price publishers and providers of trade processing services, and shall rely on such publishers and services to the maximum extent possible. The Commission may establish an electronic information system if it determines that existing price publications are not adequately providing price discovery or market transparency.

(b) Information exempted from disclosure

(1) Rules described in subsection (a)(2) of this section, if adopted, shall exempt from disclosure information the Commission determines would, if disclosed, be detrimental to the operation of an effective market or jeopardize system security.

(2) In determining the information to be made available under this section and the time to make the information available, the Commission shall seek to ensure that consumers and competitive markets are protected from the adverse effects of potential collusion or other anticompetitive behaviors that can be facilitated by untimely public disclosure of transaction-specific information.

(c) Information sharing

(1) Within 180 days of August 8, 2005, the Commission shall conclude a memorandum of understanding with the Commodity Futures Trading Commission relating to information sharing, which shall include, among other things, provisions ensuring that information requests to markets within the respective jurisdiction of each agency are properly coordinated to minimize duplicative information requests, and provisions regarding the treatment of proprietary trading information.

(2) Nothing in this section may be construed to limit or affect the exclusive jurisdiction of the Commodity Futures Trading Commission under the Commodity Exchange Act (7U.S.C. 1 et seq.).

(d) Compliance with requirements

(1) The Commission shall not condition access to interstate pipeline transportation on the reporting requirements of this section.

(2) The Commission shall not require natural gas producers, processors, or users who have a de minimis market presence to comply with the reporting requirements of this section.

(e) Retroactive effect

(1) Except as provided in paragraph (2), no person shall be subject to any civil penalty under this section with respect to any violation occurring more than 3 years before the date on which the person is provided notice of the proposed penalty under section717t–1 (b) of this title.

(2) Paragraph (1) shall not apply in any case in which the Commission finds that a seller that has entered into a contract for the transportation or sale of natural gas subject to the jurisdiction of the Commission has engaged in fraudulent market manipulation activities materially affecting the contract in violation of section 717c–1 of this title.

15 U.S. Code § 717u—Jurisdiction of offenses; enforcement of liabilities and duties

The District Courts of the United States and the United States courts of any Territory or other place subject to the jurisdiction of the United States shall have exclusive jurisdiction of violations of this chapter or the rules, regulations, and orders thereunder, and of all suits in equity and actions at law brought to enforce any liability or duty created by, or to enjoin any violation of, this chapter or any rule, regulation, or order thereunder. Any criminal proceeding shall be brought in the district wherein any act or transaction constituting the violation occurred. Any suit or action to enforce any liability or duty created by, or to enjoin any violation of, this chapter or any rule, regulation, or order thereunder may be brought in any such district or in the district wherein the defendant is an inhabitant, and process in such cases may be served wherever the defendant may be found. Judgments and decrees so rendered shall be subject to review as provided in sections 1254, 1291, and 1292 of title 28. No costs shall be assessed against the Commission in any judicial proceeding by or against the Commission under this chapter.

15 U.S. Code § 717v — Separability

If any provision of this chapter, or the application of such provision to any person or circumstance, shall be held invalid, the remainder of the chapter, and the application of such provision to persons or circumstances other than those as to which it is held invalid, shall not be affected thereby.

15 U.S. Code § 717w—Short title

This chapter may be cited as the "Natural Gas Act."

15 U.S. Code § 717x—Conserved natural gas

(a) Determination of entitlement

(1) For purposes of determining the natural gas entitlement of any local distribution company under any curtailment plan, if the Commission revises any base period established under such plan, the volumes of natural gas which such local distribution company demonstrates —

(**A**) were sold by the local distribution company, for a priority use immediately before the implementation of conservation measures, and

(**B**) were conserved by reason of the implementation of such conservation measures,

shall be treated by the Commission following such revision as continuing to be used for the priority use referred to in subparagraph (A).

(**2**) The Commission shall, by rule, prescribe methods for measurement of volumes of natural gas to which subparagraphs (A) and (B) of paragraph (1) apply.

(**b**) **Conditions, limitations, etc.**

Subsection (a) of this section shall not limit or otherwise affect any provision of any curtailment plan, or any other provision of law or regulation, under which natural gas may be diverted or allocated to respond to emergency situations or to protect public health, safety, and welfare.

(**c**) **Definitions**

For purposes of this section —

(**1**) The term "conservation measures" means such energy conservation measures, as determined by the Commission, as were implemented after the base period established under the curtailment plan in effect on November 9, 1978.

(**2**) The term "local distribution company" means any person engaged in the transportation, or local distribution, of natural gas and the sale of natural gas for ultimate consumption.

(**3**) The term "curtailment plan" means a plan (including any modification of such plan required by the Natural Gas Policy Act of 1978 [15 U.S.C. 3301 et seq.]) in effect under the Natural Gas Act [15 U.S.C. 717 et seq.] which provides for recognizing and implementing priorities of service during periods of curtailed deliveries.

15 U.S. Code § 717y—Voluntary conversion of natural gas users to heavy fuel oil

(**a**) **Transfer of contractual interests**

(**1**) In order to facilitate voluntary conversion of facilities from the use of natural gas to the use of heavy petroleum fuel oil, the Commission shall, by rule, provide a procedure for the approval by the Commission of any transfer to any person described in paragraph 2(B)(i), (ii), or (iii) of contractual interests involving the receipt of natural gas described in paragraph 2(A).

(**2**)

(**A**) The rule required under paragraph (1) shall apply to —

(**i**) natural gas —

(**I**) received by the user pursuant to a contract entered into before September 1, 1977, not including any renewal or extension thereof entered into or on or after such date other than any such extension or renewal pursuant to the exercise by such user of an option to extend or renew such contract;

(**II**) other than natural gas the sale for resale or the transportation of which was subject to the jurisdiction of the Federal Power Commission under the Natural Gas Act [15 U.S.C. 717 et seq.] as of September 1, 1977;

(**III**) which was used as a fuel in any facility in existence on September 1, 1977.

(**ii**) natural gas subject to a prohibition order issued under section 717z of this title.

(**B**) The rule required under paragraph (1) shall permit the transfer of contractual interests—

(**i**) to any interstate pipeline;

(**ii**) to any local distribution company served by an interstate pipeline; and

(**iii**) to any person served by an interstate pipeline for a high priority use by such person.

(**3**) The rule required under paragraph (1) shall provide that any transfer of contractual interests pursuant to such rule shall be under such terms and conditions as the Commission may prescribe. Such rule shall include a requirement for refund of any consideration, received by the person transferring contractual interests pursuant to such rule, to the extent such consideration exceeds the amount by which the costs actually incurred, during the remainder of the period of the contract with respect to which such contractual interests are transferred, in direct association with the use of heavy petroleum fuel oil as a fuel in the applicable facility exceeds the price under such contract for natural gas, subject to such contract, delivered during such period.

(**4**) In prescribing the rule required under paragraph (1), and in determining whether to approve any transfer of contractual interests, the Commission shall consider whether such transfer of contractual interests is likely to increase demand for imported refined petroleum products.

(b) Commission approval

(**1**) No transfer of contractual interests authorized by the rule required under subsection (a)(1) of this section may take effect unless the Commission issues a certificate of public convenience and necessity for such transfer if such natural gas is to be resold by the person to whom such contractual interests are to be transferred. Such certificate shall be issued by the Commission in accordance with the requirements of this subsection and those of section 7 of the Natural Gas Act [15 U.S.C. 717f], and the provisions of such Act [15 U.S.C. 717 et seq.] applicable to the determination of satisfaction of the public convenience and necessity requirements of such section.

(**2**) The rule required under subsection (a)(1) of this section shall set forth guidelines for the application on a regional or national basis (as the Commission determines appropriate) of the criteria specified in subsection (e)(2) and (3) of this section to determine the maximum consideration permitted as just compensation under this section.

(c) Restrictions on transfers unenforceable

Any provision of any contract, which provision prohibits any transfer of any contractual interests thereunder, or any commingling or transportation of natural gas subject to such contract with natural gas the sale for resale or transportation of which is subject to the jurisdiction of the Commission under the Natural Gas Act [15 U.S.C. 717 et seq.], or terminates such contract on the basis of any such transfer, commingling, or transportation, shall be unenforceable in any court of the United States and in any court of any State if applied with respect to any transfer approved under the rule required under subsection (a)(1) of this section.

(d) Contractual obligations unaffected

The person acquiring contractual interests transferred pursuant to the rule required under subsection (a)(1) of this section shall assume the contractual obligations which the person transferring such contractual interests has under such contract. This section shall not relieve the person transferring such contractual interests from any contractual obligation of such person under such contract if such obligation is not performed by the person acquiring such contractual interests.

(e) Definitions

For purposes of this section—

(1) The term "natural gas" has the same meaning as provided by section 2(5) of the Natural Gas Act [15 U.S.C. 717a (5)].

(2) The term "just compensation", when used with respect to any contractual interests pursuant to the rule required under subsection (a)(1) of this section, means the maximum amount of, or method of determining, consideration which does not exceed the amount by which—

(A) the reasonable costs (not including capital costs) incurred, during the remainder of the period of the contract with respect to which contractual interests are transferred pursuant to the rule required under subsection (a)(1) of this section, in direct association with the use of heavy petroleum fuel oil as a fuel in the applicable facility, exceeds

(B) the price under such contract for natural gas, subject to such contract, delivered during such period.

For purposes of subparagraph (A), the reasonable costs directly associated with the use of heavy petroleum fuel oil as a fuel shall include an allowance for the amortization, over the remaining useful life, of the undepreciated value of depreciable assets located on the premises containing such facility, which assets were directly associated with the use of natural gas and are not usable in connection with the use of such heavy petroleum fuel oil.

(3) The term "just compensation", when used with respect to any intrastate pipeline which would have transported or distributed natural gas with respect to which contractual interests are transferred pursuant to the rule required under subsection (a)(1) of this section, means an amount equal to any loss of revenue, during the remaining period of the contract with respect to which contractual interests are transferred pursuant to the rule required under subsection (a)(1) of this section, to the extent such loss—

(A) is directly incurred by reason of the discontinuation of the transportation or distribution of natural gas resulting from the transfer of contractual interests pursuant to the rule required under subsection (a)(1) of this section; and

(B) is not offset by—

(i) a reduction in expenses associated with such discontinuation; and

(ii) revenues derived from other transportation or distribution which would not have occurred if such contractual interests had not been transferred.

(4) The term "contractual interests" means the right to receive natural gas under contract as affected by an applicable curtailment plan filed with the Commission or the appropriate State regulatory authority.

(5) The term "interstate pipeline" means any person engaged in natural gas transportation subject to the jurisdiction of the Commission under the Natural Gas Act [15 U.S.C. 717 et seq.].

(6) The term "high-priority use" means any use of natural gas (other than its use for the generation of steam for industrial purposes or electricity) identified by the Commission as a high priority use for which the Commission determines a substitute fuel is not reasonably available.

(7) The term "heavy petroleum fuel oil" means number 4, 5, or 6 fuel oil which is domestically refined.

(8) The term "local distribution company" means any person, other than any intrastate pipeline or any interstate pipeline, engaged in the transportation, or local distribution, of natural gas and the sale of natural gas for ultimate consumption.

(9) The term "intrastate pipeline" means any person engaged in natural gas transportation (not including gathering) which is not subject to the jurisdiction of the Commission under the Natural Gas Act.

(10) The term "facility" means any electric powerplant, or major fuel burning installation, as such terms are defined in the Powerplant and Industrial Fuel Use Act of 1978 [42 U.S.C. 8301 et seq.].

(11) The term "curtailment plan" means a plan (including any modification of such plan required by the Natural Gas Policy Act of 1978 [15 U.S.C. 3301 et seq.]), in effect under the Natural Gas Act or State law, which provides for recognizing and implementing priorities of service during periods of curtailed deliveries by any local distribution company, intrastate pipeline, or interstate pipeline.

(12) The term "interstate commerce" has the same meaning as such term has under the Natural Gas Act.

(f) Coordination with this chapter

(1) Consideration in any transfer of contractual interests pursuant to the rule required under subsection (a)(1) of this section shall be deemed just and reasonable for purposes of sections 4 and 5 of the Natural Gas Act [15 U.S.C. 717c, 717d] if such consideration does not exceed just compensation.

(2) No person shall be subject to the jurisdiction of the Commission under the Natural Gas Act [15 U.S.C. 717 et seq.] as a natural gas-company (within the meaning of such Act) or to regulation as a common carrier under any provision of Federal or State law solely by reason of making any sale, or engaging in any transportation, of natural gas with respect to which contractual interests are transferred pursuant to the rule required under subsection (a)(1) of this section.

(3) Nothing in this section shall exempt from the jurisdiction of the Commission under the Natural Gas Act [15 U.S.C. 717 et seq.] any transportation in interstate commerce of natural gas, any sale in interstate commerce for resale of natural gas, or any person engaged in such transportation or such sale to the extent such transportation, sale, or person is subject to the jurisdiction of the Commission under such Act without regard to the transfer of contractual interests pursuant to the rule required under subsection (a)(1) of this section.

(4) Nothing in this section shall exempt any person from any obligation to obtain a certificate of public convenience and necessity for the sale in interstate commerce for resale or the transportation in interstate commerce of natural gas with respect to which contractual interests are transferred pursuant to the rule required under subsection (a)(1) of this section.

(g) Volume limitation

No supplier of natural gas under any contract, with respect to which contractual interests have been transferred pursuant to the rule required under subsection (a)(1) of this section, shall be required to supply natural gas during any relevant period in volume amounts which exceed the lesser of—

(1) the volume determined by reference to the maximum delivery obligations specified in such contract;

(2) the volume which such supplier would have been required to supply, under the curtailment plan in effect for such supplier, to the person, who transferred contractual interests pursuant to the rule required under subsection (a)(1) of this section, if no such transfer had occurred; and

(3) the volume actually delivered or for which payment would have been made pursuant to such contract during the 12-calendar-month period ending immediately before such transfer of contractual interests.

15 U.S. Code § 717z—Emergency conversion of utilities and other facilities

(a) Presidential declaration

The President may declare a natural gas supply emergency (or extend a previously declared emergency) if he finds that—

(1) a severe natural gas shortage, endangering the supply of natural gas for high-priority uses, exists or is imminent in the United States or in any region thereof; and

(2) the exercise of authorities under this section is reasonably necessary, having exhausted other alternatives (not including section 3363 of this title) to the maximum extent practicable, to assist in meeting natural gas requirements for such high-priority uses.

(b) Limitation

(1) Any declaration of a natural gas supply emergency (or extension thereof) under subsection (a) of this section, shall terminate at the earlier of—

(A) the date on which the President finds that any shortage described in subsection (a) of this section does not exist or is not imminent; or

(B) 120 days after the date of such declaration of emergency (or extension thereof).

(2) Nothing in this subsection shall prohibit the President from extending, under subsection (a) of this section, any emergency (or extension thereof) previously declared under subsection (a) of this section, upon the expiration of such declaration of emergency (or extension thereof) under paragraph (1)(B).

(c) Prohibitions

During a natural gas emergency declared under this section, the President may, by order, prohibit the burning of natural gas by any electric powerplant or major fuel-burning installation if the President determines that—

(1) such powerplant or installation had on September 1, 1977 (or at any time thereafter) the capability to burn petroleum products without damage to its facilities or equipment and without interference with operational requirements;

(2) significant quantities of natural gas which would otherwise be burned by such powerplant or installation could be made available before the termination of such emergency to any person served by an interstate pipeline for use by such person in a high-priority use; and

(3) petroleum products will be available for use by such powerplant or installation throughout the period the order is in effect.

(d) Limitations

The President may specify in any order issued under this section the periods of time during which such order will be in effect and the quantity (or rate of use) of natural gas that may be burned by an electric powerplant or major fuel-burning installation during such period, including the burning of natural gas by an electric powerplant to meet peak load requirements. No such order may continue in effect after the termination or expiration of such natural gas supply emergency.

(e) **Exemption for secondary uses**

The President shall exempt from any order issued under this section the burning of natural gas for the necessary processes of ignition, startup, testing, and flame stabilization by an electric powerplant or major fuel-burning installation.

(f) **Exemption for air-quality emergencies**

The President shall exempt any electric powerplant or major fuel-burning installation in whole or in part, from any order issued under this section for such period and to such extent as the President determines necessary to alleviate any imminent and substantial endangerment to the health of persons within the meaning of section 7603 of title 42.

(g) **Limitation on injunctive relief**

(1) Except as provided in paragraph (2), no court shall have jurisdiction to grant any injunctive relief to stay or defer the implementation of any order issued under this section unless such relief is in connection with a final judgment entered with respect to such order.

(2)

(A) On the petition of any person aggrieved by an order issued under this section, the United States District Court for the District of Columbia may, after an opportunity for a hearing before such court and on an appropriate showing, issue a preliminary injunction temporarily enjoining, in whole or in part, the implementation of such order.

(B) For purposes of this paragraph, subpenas for witnesses who are required to attend the District Court for the District of Columbia may be served in any judicial district of the United States, except that no writ of subpena under the authority of this section shall issue for witnesses outside of the District of Columbia at a greater distance than 100 miles from the place of holding court unless the permission of the District Court for the District of Columbia has been granted after proper application and cause shown.

(h) **Definitions**

For purposes of this section—

(1) The terms "electric powerplant", "powerplant", "major fuel-burning installation", and "installation" shall have the same meanings as such terms have under section 8302 of title 42.

(2) The term "petroleum products" means crude oil, or any product derived from crude oil other than propane.

(3) The term "high priority use" means any—

(A) use of natural gas in a residence;

(B) use of natural gas in a commercial establishment in amounts less than 50 Mcf on a peak day; or

(C) any use of natural gas the curtailment of which the President determines would endanger life, health, or maintenance of physical property.

(4) The term "Mcf", when used with respect to natural gas, means 1,000 cubic feet of natural gas measured at a pressure of 14.73 pounds per square inch (absolute) and a temperature of 60 degrees Fahrenheit.

(i) Use of general terms

In applying the provisions of this section in the case of natural gas subject to a prohibition order issued under this section, the term "petroleum products" (as defined in subsection (h)(2) of this section) shall be substituted for the term "heavy petroleum fuel oil" (as defined in section 717y (e)(7) of this title) if the person subject to any order under this section demonstrates to the Commission that the acquisition and use of heavy petroleum fuel oil is not technically or economically feasible.

Appendix E

Climate Change

A. Maine Revised Statutes: RGGI

Title 38: WATERS AND NAVIGATION
Chapter 3-B: REGIONAL GREENHOUSE GAS INITIATIVE

§ 580. Short title

This chapter may be known and cited as "the Regional Greenhouse Gas Initiative Act of 2007." [2007, c. 317, § 17 (NEW).]

§ 580-A. Definitions

As used in this chapter, unless the context otherwise indicates, the following terms have the following meanings. [2007, c. 317, § 17 (NEW).]

1. Allocation. "Allocation" means the number of carbon dioxide allowances to be credited to a carbon dioxide budget unit or to the general account of the sponsor of an approved carbon dioxide emissions offset project.

[2007, c. 317, § 17 (NEW) .]

1-A. Account. "Account" means a general account or a compliance account.

[2009, c. 200, § 3 (NEW) .]

2. Carbon dioxide allowance. "Carbon dioxide allowance" or "carbon dioxide emissions allowance" means a limited authorization by the department for the emission of up to one ton of carbon dioxide.

[2007, c. 317, § 17 (NEW) .]

3. Carbon dioxide budget unit. "Carbon dioxide budget unit" means any single fossil fuel fired unit that serves a generator with a nameplate capacity equal to or greater than 25 megawatts of electrical output.

[2007, c. 608, § 4 (AMD) .]

4. Carbon dioxide budget unit compliance account or compliance account. "Carbon dioxide budget unit compliance account" or "compliance account" means the account established by the department for a carbon dioxide budget unit wherein carbon dioxide

531

emissions allowances and carbon dioxide offset allowances are held and available for compliance purposes under the carbon dioxide cap-and-trade program.

[2009, c. 200, §4 (AMD) .]

5. Carbon dioxide emissions budget. "Carbon dioxide emissions budget" means the total amount of carbon dioxide emissions allowances allocated by the State on an annual basis.

[2007, c. 317, §17 (NEW) .]

6. Carbon dioxide emissions offset project. "Carbon dioxide emissions offset project" means a project that reduces or avoids loading of carbon dioxide and other greenhouse gases in the atmosphere and is demonstrated to qualify as real, additional, verifiable, enforceable and permanent as those terms are defined in rules adopted by the department. "Carbon dioxide emissions offset project" includes, but is not limited to, landfill and agricultural methane capture and destruction, reduction in emissions of sulfur hexafluoride, sequestration of carbon due to forestry practices and reduction or avoidance of carbon dioxide emissions from natural gas, oil or propane end-use combustion due to end-use energy efficiency and other categories established by the department by rule.

[2013, c. 369, Pt. D, §2 (AMD) .]

6-A. Carbon dioxide general account or general account. "Carbon dioxide general account" or "general account" means the account established by the department upon the request of an entity wherein the entity may hold carbon dioxide allowances and carbon dioxide offset allowances. The general account is separate from the compliance account.

[2009, c. 200, §5 (NEW) .]

7. Carbon dioxide offset allowance. "Carbon dioxide offset allowance" means a carbon dioxide allowance awarded to the sponsor of a carbon dioxide emissions offset project.

[2007, c. 317, §17 (NEW) .]

8. Combined cycle system. "Combined cycle system" means a system composed of one or more combustion turbines, heat recovery system generators and steam turbines configured to improve overall efficiency of electrical generation or steam production.

[2007, c. 317, §17 (NEW) .]

9. Combined heat and power unit. "Combined heat and power unit" means a device that simultaneously generates electricity and thermal power and operates at a high level of output efficiency by utilizing the waste heat created as a by-product of electricity generation for domestic, commercial or industrial heating or cooling purposes, and whose useful thermal output equals at least 10% of the fossil fuel energy input of the unit.

[2007, c. 317, §17 (NEW) .]

10. Electrical generating unit. "Electrical generating unit" means a fossil fuel fired combustion device that serves a generator.

[2007, c. 317, §17 (NEW) .]

11. Fossil fuel. "Fossil fuel" means natural gas, petroleum, coal or any form of solid, liquid or gaseous fuel derived from such a material.

[2007, c. 317, §17 (NEW) .]

12. Fossil fuel fired unit. "Fossil fuel fired unit" means:

A. With regard to a unit that commenced operation prior to January 1, 2005, a unit fueled by the combustion of fossil fuel, alone or in combination with any other fuel, where the fossil fuel combusted constitutes, or is projected to comprise, more than 50% of the annual heat input on a British Thermal Unit basis during any calendar year; or [2007, c. 608, §5(NEW).]

B. With regard to a unit that commences operation on or after January 1, 2005, a unit fueled by the combustion of fossil fuel, alone or in combination with any other fuel, where the fossil fuel combusted constitutes, or is projected to comprise, more than 5% of the annual heat input on a British Thermal Unit basis during any calendar year. [2007, c. 608, §5(NEW).]

[2007, c. 608, §5 (AMD) .]

13. Generator. "Generator" means a device that produces electricity and is required to be reported as a generating unit pursuant to the United States Department of Energy Form 860.

[2007, c. 317, §17 (NEW) .]

14. Gross electrical generation. "Gross electrical generation" means the electrical output in megawatts at the terminals of the generator.

[2007, c. 317, §17 (NEW) .]

15. Integrated manufacturing facility. "Integrated manufacturing facility" means a facility that:

A. Received an air emissions license from the department prior to the effective date of this subsection; [2007, c. 317, §17 (NEW).]

B. Produces electricity from one or more carbon dioxide budget units, including one or more combined heat and power units, for transmission over the facilities of a transmission and distribution utility; and [2007, c. 317, §17 (NEW).]

C. Routinely produces one or more other products for sale. [2007, c. 317, §17 (NEW).]

[2007, c. 317, §17 (NEW) .]

16. Long-term electricity contract. "Long-term electricity contract" means a contract for a period of 3 years or more with a carbon dioxide budget unit for the purchase of electricity.

[2007, c. 317, §17 (NEW) .]

17. Memorandum of Understanding; memorandum. "Memorandum of Understanding" or "memorandum" means the Regional Greenhouse Gas Initiative Memorandum of Understanding dated December 20, 2005 that establishes an electric power sector carbon emissions cap-and-trade program within the northeast region of the United States.

[2007, c. 317, §17 (NEW) .]

17-A. Model rule. "Model rule" means the model rule, as amended, referenced in the memorandum of understanding.

[2013, c. 369, Pt. D, §3 (NEW) .]

18. Nameplate capacity. "Nameplate capacity" means the maximum electrical generating output, expressed in megawatts, that a generator can sustain over a specified period of time when not restricted by seasonal or other deratings.

[2007, c. 317, §17 (NEW) .]

18-A. Proprietary information. "Proprietary information" means production, commercial or financial information claimed as confidential on documents required to be submitted to participate in an auction, the disclosure of which would impair the competitive position of the account holder and would make available information that is not otherwise available.

[2009, c. 200, § 6 (NEW) .]

18-B. Other independent system operator participating states. "Other independent system operator participating states" means the following states participating in the regional greenhouse gas initiative as of January 1, 2011 that are located within the New England independent system operator control area: Connecticut, Massachusetts, New Hampshire, Rhode Island and Vermont.

[2011, c. 277, § 1 (NEW) .]

19. Regional greenhouse gas initiative. "Regional greenhouse gas initiative" means the initiative referred to in the Memorandum of Understanding and the corresponding model rule that memorializes the ongoing cooperative effort by the State and other states to design and implement a regional carbon dioxide cap-and-trade program covering carbon dioxide emissions from electrical generating units in the signatory states.

[2007, c. 317, § 17 (NEW) .]

20. Regional organization. "Regional organization" means the entity that will manage the regional greenhouse gas initiative on a regional basis and with which the State contracts for related service.

[2007, c. 317, § 17 (NEW) .]

21. Regional transmission organization. "Regional transmission organization" means the independent systems operator that administers and oversees the wholesale electricity markets in which the State participates.

[2007, c. 317, § 17 (NEW) .]

22. Ton. "Ton" means 2,000 pounds.

[2007, c. 317, § 17 (NEW) .]

23. Transmission and distribution utility. "Transmission and distribution utility" means a transmission and distribution utility as defined in Title 35-A, section 3201, subsection 6, 12 or 16.

[2007, c. 317, § 17 (NEW)]

SECTION HISTORY 2007, c. 317, § 17 (NEW). 2007, c. 608, §§ 4, 5 (AMD). 2009, c. 200, §§ 3-6 (AMD). 2011, c. 277, § 1 (AMD). 2013, c. 369, Pt. D, §§ 2, 3 (AMD).

§ 580-B. Cap-and-trade program established

A carbon dioxide cap-and-trade program, referred to in this section as "the program," is established in accordance with this section. [2007, c. 317, § 17 (NEW).]

1. Application. All carbon dioxide budget units are subject to the carbon dioxide cap-and-trade program, except that a carbon dioxide budget unit is exempt from the program if:

    A. It is incapable of producing enough energy to generate 25 megawatts or more of electrical output; [2007, c. 317, § 17 (NEW).]

    B. Its sale of electricity to any power distribution system is less than 10% of its gross electrical generation on an annual basis. In calculating this percentage, all electricity transmitted to the regional grid over the facilities of a transmission and distribution utility as a result of verifiable conservation and demand-side management initiatives or any emergency mandate of the regional transmission organization or lawful order of a governmental authority is not included in the calculation of annual sales; or [2007, c. 317, § 17 (NEW).]

C. Fifty percent or more of its annual heat input comes from the combustion of fuels other than fossil fuels. [2007, c. 317, § 17 (NEW).]

[2007, c. 317, § 17 (NEW).]

2. Contingent on initiation of comparable programs. The carbon dioxide cap-and-trade program commences no earlier than January 1, 2009 and only when other states that are participating in the regional greenhouse gas initiative that produce a minimum of 35,000,000 tons of annual carbon dioxide emissions budget and participate in a wholesale electricity market administered and overseen by the regional transmission organization have initiated a comparable carbon dioxide cap-and-trade program. Nothing in this section precludes the department from initiating air emissions licensing of carbon dioxide budget sources or from participating in auctions for the sale of carbon dioxide allowances.

[2007, c. 608, § 6 (AMD) .]

2-A. Condition for withdrawal. The State shall withdraw from the regional greenhouse gas initiative when a sufficient number of other independent system operator participating states have withdrawn such that the total carbon dioxide emissions budget for the calendar year 2009, as specified in the Memorandum of Understanding, of the remaining other independent system operator participating states is less than 35,000,000 tons. If the condition is met for withdrawal from the regional greenhouse gas initiative, the department shall:

A. Immediately take all necessary steps to withdraw the State from all memoranda of understanding and contracts with states participating in the regional greenhouse gas initiative relating to the regional greenhouse gas initiative; and [2011, c. 277, § 2 (NEW).]

B. Submit legislation to the Legislature to make the necessary changes in law to reflect the State's withdrawal from the regional greenhouse gas initiative. [2011, c. 277, § 2(NEW).]

[2011, c. 277, § 2 (NEW) .]

3. Base annual budget. Until January 1, 2014, the base annual carbon dioxide emissions budget is established at 5,948,902 tons of carbon dioxide. For the year 2014, the base annual carbon dioxide emissions budget is established at 3,277,250 tons of carbon dioxide. Beginning with the year 2015, the annual carbon dioxide emissions budget must decline by 2.5% each year through the year 2020.

[2013, c. 369, Pt. D, § 4 (AMD) .]

3-A. Interim adjustments for banked allowances. The 2014 base annual carbon dioxide emissions budget of 3,277,250 tons of carbon dioxide and base annual budgets for 2015 to 2020 must be reduced by an amount equivalent to the quantity of banked allowances in excess of the quantity of allowances required for compliance at the end of 2013. The State's interim adjustments for banked allowances must be made in proportion to the State's share of the total annual carbon dioxide emissions budget for all states participating in the regional greenhouse gas initiative.

[2013, c. 369, Pt. D, § 5 (NEW) .]

4. Rules implementing program. The department shall adopt rules to implement the program. Rules must be consistent with the model rule. The rules must include, but are not limited to:

A. Provisions for the establishment of a system for the annual assignment, sale and distribution of carbon dioxide emissions allowances consistent with the carbon dioxide emissions budget; [2007, c. 317, § 17 (NEW).]

B. Provisions for the establishment of carbon dioxide budget unit compliance obligation accounts; [2007, c. 317, § 17 (NEW).]

C. Provisions for the establishment of carbon dioxide offset project allowance categories and requirements; [2007, c. 317, § 17 (NEW).]

D. Provisions for the implementation of a licensing process for carbon dioxide budget units; [2007, c. 317, § 17 (NEW).]

E. Provisions for the establishment of a carbon dioxide emissions and carbon dioxide allowance tracking program; and [2007, c. 317, § 17 (NEW).]

F. Provisions to manage the carbon dioxide allowance auction developed in coordination with other states and jurisdictions in the regional greenhouse gas initiative and in a manner that is consistent with provisions adopted by those states and jurisdictions and, to the extent feasible, that:

(1) Ensure close monitoring of allowance transactions in a manner that guards against collusion and market manipulation;

(2) Ensure ongoing authentic price discovery and minimize price volatility;

(3) Facilitate open participation for bidding to all individuals or entities that meet the financial requirements jointly adopted by the participating states;

(4) Minimize administration and transaction costs and provide for an open and transparent user-friendly system;

(5) Provide that ongoing monitoring of market activity is undertaken by entities that have complete financial independence from any market participant;

(6) For purposes of civil and criminal enforcement authority under section 349, establish a contract term at the time an allowance is purchased at the regional auction for violations of market rules jointly adopted by the participating states and jurisdictions or through another method of ensuring state jurisdiction; and

(7) Guarantee that the Attorney General, the Public Utilities Commission and the commissioner have access to all auction information and information concerning allowance trading activity, including reports provided to the regional organization by a market monitor. [2007, c. 317, § 17 (NEW).]

Rules adopted pursuant to this subsection are routine technical rules as defined in Title 5, chapter 375, subchapter 2-A.

[2013, c. 369, Pt. D, § 6 (AMD) .]

5. Enforcement. Violations of this chapter are enforceable, and penalties may be imposed in accordance with sections 347-A, 348 and 349.

[2007, c. 317, § 17 (NEW) .]

6. Waiver of enforcement; suspension of compliance obligation. The commissioner has authority, under the exceptional circumstances set out in paragraphs A and B, to waive or suspend requirements of this chapter.

A. If the regional greenhouse gas initiative results in price levels for allowances that will result in immediate and irreparable harm to the operations of a carbon dioxide budget unit regulated under this chapter, including but not limited to the termination of business at that location, the commissioner may, in consultation with the Attorney General and the chair of the Public Utilities Commission, grant a temporary waiver of enforcement not to exceed one year for any violation by an individual regulated carbon dioxide budget unit of a requirement of this chapter. [2007, c. 317, § 17 (NEW).]

B. In cases of emergency events that are beyond the control of a carbon dioxide budget unit, the commissioner may temporarily suspend the compliance obligation under a particular permit until such time as the emergency no longer is in effect. [2007, c. 317, § 17 (NEW).]

The department shall adopt rules for the implementation of this subsection. Rules adopted pursuant to this subsection are major substantive rules as defined in Title 5, chapter 375, subchapter 2-A and must be submitted to the Legislature by January 15, 2008 for review by the Joint Standing Committee on Natural Resources during the Second Regular Session of the 123rd Legislature.

[2007, c. 317, § 17 (NEW) .]

7. Allocation of carbon dioxide emissions allowances. The department shall allocate 100% of the annual carbon dioxide emissions allowances for public benefit to produce funds for carbon reduction and energy conservation, as specified in Title 35-A, section 10109. Except as provided in subsections 7-A and 8, the department shall sell the carbon dioxide emissions allowances at public auction, in accordance with rules adopted under subsection 4. Revenue resulting from the sale of allowances must be deposited in the Regional Greenhouse Gas Initiative Trust Fund established under Title 35-A, section 10109.

[2009, c. 652, Pt. A, § 60 (RPR) .]

7-A. Voluntary renewable energy market set-aside. The department shall set aside a portion of the State's annual carbon dioxide emissions budget in a voluntary renewable market set-aside account. The allowances from this account must be retired in an amount equal to the amount of carbon dioxide emissions reduced by the voluntary purchase of eligible renewable energy credits by persons in the State up to the amount held in the set-aside account. For purposes of this subsection, "eligible renewable energy credits" means renewable energy credits generated within the states that are participating in the regional greenhouse gas initiative.

Before February 1, 2010, the portion of the State's annual carbon dioxide emissions budget that is set aside in a voluntary renewable market set-aside account pursuant to this subsection may not exceed 2% of that budget. The department shall report to the joint standing committee of the Legislature having jurisdiction over utilities and energy matters by January 15, 2010 as to whether that 2% cap is appropriate. By January 31, 2010, the Efficiency Maine Trust, established under Title 35-A, section 10103, in consultation with the department, shall establish the cap on the portion of the State's annual carbon dioxide emissions budget that is set aside in a set-aside account.

[2009, c. 372, Pt. B, § 5 (AMD) .]

8. Combined heat and power incentive; set aside. The department shall set aside a portion of the State's annual carbon dioxide emissions allowances in an allowance account for carbon dioxide budget units that are combined heat and power units and are located at integrated manufacturing facilities. The department shall use these allowances for existing carbon dioxide budget units to reflect only that portion of each unit's emissions related to electricity and thermal power generated at a carbon dioxide budget unit that is a combined heat and power unit, whether it is a combined cycle system or other energy generation configuration of which the carbon dioxide budget unit is a part, that are not transmitted across the facilities of a transmission and distribution utility.

The department shall adopt rules setting forth the proper treatment of combined heat and power units. The rules may distinguish between combined heat and power units that commence operation after July 1, 2007 and those that commence operation before July 1, 2007. Rules adopted pursuant to this subsection are routine technical rules as defined in Title 5, chapter 375, subchapter 2-A.

[2007, c. 317, § 17 (NEW) .]

9. Integrated manufacturing facilities. This subsection governs the treatment of integrated manufacturing facilities under this chapter.

A. The compliance obligation for a carbon dioxide budget unit at an integrated manufacturing facility is the carbon dioxide emissions associated with electricity resulting from the combustion of fossil fuels and transmitted over the facilities of a transmission and distribution utility. Absent any contractual arrangement to the contrary, the department shall presume that electricity from sources other than carbon dioxide budget units is transmitted first. The department shall adopt rules governing the compliance obligation for electricity generated at integrated manufacturing facilities and transmitted over the facilities of a transmission and distribution utility. [2007, c. 317, § 17 (NEW).]

B. The department shall establish the Integrated Manufacturing Facility Retirement Account to ensure proper accounting for carbon emissions from the generation of electricity and heat from fossil fuels at integrated manufacturing facilities. [2007, c. 317, § 17 (NEW).]

C. The purchase of electricity pursuant to a long-term electricity contract renders the purchaser an owner of a carbon dioxide budget unit for purposes of this chapter and obligates the owner to obtain the carbon dioxide emissions allowances applicable to the compliance obligation associated with the carbon dioxide budget unit. For purposes of this paragraph, "owner" means:

(1)   The holder of any portion of the legal or equitable title in a carbon dioxide budget unit;

(2)   The holder of a leasehold interest in a carbon dioxide budget unit, other than a passive lessor or a person who has an equitable interest through such lessor whose rental payments are not based, either directly or indirectly, upon the revenues or income from that unit; or

(3)   A purchaser of electricity from a carbon dioxide budget unit under a contractual arrangement for greater than a 3-year period.

If no person has title to the electricity under subparagraphs (1) to (3), the owner is any holder of any portion of the legal or equitable title to the output of a carbon dioxide budget unit or any holder of a leasehold interest in such a unit. [2007, c. 317, § 17 (NEW).]

Rules adopted pursuant to this subsection are routine technical rules as defined in Title 5, chapter 375, subchapter 2-A.

[2007, c. 317, § 17 (NEW) .]

10. Annual report. The department, the Public Utilities Commission and the trustees of the Efficiency Maine Trust established pursuant to Title 35-A, section 10103 shall submit a joint report to the joint standing committees of the Legislature having jurisdiction over natural resources matters and utilities and energy matters by March 15th annually. The report must assess and address:

A. The reductions of greenhouse gas emissions from carbon dioxide budget units, conservation programs funded by the Regional Greenhouse Gas Initiative Trust Fund pursuant to Title 35-A, section 10109 and carbon dioxide emissions offset projects; [2009, c. 652, Pt. A, §61 (RPR).]

B. The improvements in overall carbon dioxide emissions and energy efficiency from sources that emit greenhouse gases including electrical generation and fossil fuel fired units;[2009, c. 652, Pt. A, §61 (RPR).]

C. The maximization of savings through systemic energy improvements statewide; [2009, c. 652, Pt. A, §61 (RPR).]

D. Research and support of new carbon dioxide offset allowance categories for development in the State; [2009, c. 652, Pt. A, §61 (RPR).]

E. Management and cost-effectiveness of the State's energy conservation and carbon reduction programs and efforts funded by the Regional Greenhouse Gas Initiative Trust Fund, established pursuant to Title 35-A, section 10109; [2009, c. 652, Pt. A, §61 (RPR).]

F. The extent to which funds from the Regional Greenhouse Gas Initiative Trust Fund, established pursuant to Title 35-A, section 10109, serve customers from all classes of the State's transmission and distribution utilities; and [2009, c. 652, Pt. A, §61 (RPR).]

G. The revenues and expenditures of the Regional Greenhouse Gas Initiative Trust Fund, established pursuant to Title 35-A, section 10109. [2009, c. 652, Pt. A, §61 (RPR).]

The department, the Public Utilities Commission and the trustees of the Efficiency Maine Trust may include in the report any proposed changes to the program established under this chapter.

The joint standing committee of the Legislature having jurisdiction over natural resources matters may submit legislation relating to areas within the committee's jurisdiction in connection with the program. The joint standing committee of the Legislature having jurisdiction over utilities and energy matters may submit legislation relating to areas within the committee's jurisdiction in connection with the program.

[2013, c. 369, Pt. D, §7 (AMD) .]

11. Confidentiality. To protect the integrity of individual auctions administered under the carbon dioxide cap-and-trade program established in this section, the following records are confidential as provided in this subsection.

A. Except as provided in this paragraph, the following records are confidential for a period of 3 years beginning at the time of application, submission, award or record creation by the department or its agents:

(1)   Auction bid and award information specific to any one account holder;

(2)   Carbon dioxide allowance and carbon dioxide offset allowance account holdings; and

(3)   Carbon dioxide allowance and carbon dioxide offset allowance transactions.

This paragraph does not prohibit the release of carbon dioxide allowance and carbon dioxide offset allowance account holdings and transactions in an aggregated form that does not permit the identification of any person or entity.

The commissioner may release information described in subparagraph (1), (2) or (3) before the expiration of the 3-year period if the commissioner determines that confidentiality of that information is no longer required to protect the integrity of individual auctions administered under the carbon dioxide cap-and-trade program. [2009, c. 200, § 11 (NEW).]

B. The following records remain confidential and may not be disclosed except pursuant to a court order or upon the written consent of the account holder:

(1)   Proprietary information contained in documents required to be submitted to participate in an auction conducted under the carbon dioxide cap-and-trade program; and

(2)   Carbon dioxide allowance and carbon dioxide offset allowance transaction prices. This subparagraph does not prohibit the release of transaction prices calculated in an aggregated manner that does not permit the identification of any person or entity. [2009, c. 200, § 11 (NEW).]

Records containing any emission, offset or allowance tracking information submitted for the purpose of demonstrating compliance with the carbon dioxide cap-and-trade program and rules adopted to implement the program are public records subject to disclosure under Title 1, chapter 13.

[2009, c. 200, § 11 (NEW) .]

SECTION HISTORY

2007, c. 317, § 17 (NEW). 2007, c. 608, §§ 6, 7 (AMD). 2009, c. 200, §§ 7-11 (AMD). 2009, c. 372, Pt. B, §§ 4-6 (AMD). 2009, c. 652, Pt. A, §§ 60, 61(AMD). 2011, c. 277, § 2 (AMD). 2013, c. 369, Pt. D, §§ 4-7 (AMD).

§ 580-C. Construction; absence of limitation

Nothing in this chapter may be construed to limit: [2007, c. 317, § 17 (NEW).]

1. Withdrawal by State. The ability of this State to withdraw from the regional greenhouse gas initiative; or

[2007, c. 317, § 17 (NEW) .]

2. Categories of carbon dioxide emissions offset projects. The categories of carbon dioxide emissions offset projects that may qualify under agreements among the states and jurisdictions participating in the regional greenhouse gas initiative, particularly with respect to additional categories that take advantage of the geographical, economic or natural resources of this State.

[2007, c. 317, § 17 (NEW) .]

SECTION HISTORY

2007, c. 317, § 17 (NEW).

B. Maine Department of Environmental Protection Regulations

Chapter 156: CO_2 BUDGET TRADING PROGRAM

SUMMARY: This regulation establishes the Maine component of the CO_2 Budget Trading Program, which is designed to stabilize and then reduce anthropogenic emissions of CO_2, a greenhouse gas, from CO_2 budget sources in an economically efficient manner.

1. CO_2 Budget Trading Program General Provisions

A. Applicability

(1) This regulation applies statewide.

(2) The CO_2 Budget Trading Program will commence no earlier than January 1, 2009 and only when other states meeting the following criteria have initiated comparable CO_2 budget trading programs:

  (a) such states have wholesale electricity markets that are administered and overseen by the same Regional transmission organization as are Maine's; and

  (b) the combined CO_2 emissions budgets from such states total at least 35,000,000 tons per year.

  The Department may initiate air emissions licensing of CO_2 budget sources and participate in auctions for the sale of CO_2 allowances prior to commencement of the CO_2 Budget Trading Program.

(3) This regulation applies to any CO_2 budget unit except as provided for in subsection 1(A)(4) below.

(4) Limited Exemption. A unit that supplies less than or equal to ten percent (10%) of its gross electrical generation for transmission over the facilities of a transmission and distribution utility on an annual basis shall be exempt from the requirements of this regulation, with the exception of the following sections:

  (a) Section 1(B)—Definitions;

  (b) Section 1(G)—Computation of Time; and, as applicable

  (c) Section 4(H)—Monitoring, Recordkeeping, and Reporting Requirements as required by the Department to demonstrate that the unit is eligible for the limited exemption.

  In determining whether or not the 10% applicability trigger is exceeded, all electricity transmitted over the facilities of a transmission and distribution utility as result of verifiable conservation and demand-side management initiatives or as a result of any emergency mandate from the Regional transmission organization or a lawful order of a governmental authority, is excluded from the calculation.

B. Definitions

(1) **Account number.** "Account number" means the identification number given by the Department or its agent to each CO_2 Allowance Tracking System account.

(2) **Acid rain emissions limitation.** "Acid rain emissions limitation" as defined in 40 CFR 72.2, means a limitation on emissions of sulfur dioxide or nitrogen oxides under the Acid Rain Program under Title IV of the Clean Air Act.

(3) **Administrator.** "Administrator" means the Administrator of the United States Environmental Protection Agency or the Administrator's authorized representative.

(4) **Allocate or allocation.** "Allocate" or "allocation" means the determination by the Department of the number of CO_2 allowances to be credited to a CO_2 budget unit, any general account established by the Department, the Consumer benefit account, or the general account of the sponsor of an approved CO_2 emissions offset project.

(5) **Allocation year.** "Allocation year" means a calendar year for which the Department allocates CO_2 allowances pursuant to Sections 2 and 9 of this Chapter. The allocation year of each CO_2 allowance is reflected in the unique identification number given to the allowance pursuant to subsection 7(B)(3) of this Chapter.

(6) **Anaerobic digester.** "Anaerobic digester" means a device that promotes the decomposition of organic material to simple organics and gaseous biogas products, usually accomplished by means of controlling temperature and volume, and including a methane recovery system.

(7) **Anaerobic digestion.** "Anaerobic digestion" means the degradation of organic material including manure brought about through the action of microorganisms in the absence of elemental oxygen.

(8) **Anaerobic storage.** "Anaerobic storage" means storage of organic material in an oxygen-free environment, or under oxygen-free conditions, including but not limited to, holding tanks, ponds, and lagoons.

(9) **ANSI.** "ANSI" means American National Standards Institute.

(10) **ASHRAE.** "ASHRAE" means American Society of Heating, Refrigerating and Air-Conditioner Engineers.

(11) **Attribute.** "Attribute" means a characteristic associated with electricity generated using a particular renewable fuel, such as its generation date, facility geographic location, unit vintage, emissions output, fuel, state program eligibility, or other characteristic that can be identified, accounted, and tracked.

(12) **Attribute credit.** "Attribute credit" means the attributes related to one megawatt-hour of electricity generation.

(13) **Automated data acquisition and handling system or DAHS.** "Automated data acquisition and handling system" or "DAHS" means that component of the continuous emissions monitoring system, or other emissions monitoring system approved for use under Section 4 of this Chapter, designed to interpret and convert individual output signals from pollutant concentration monitors, flow monitors, diluent gas monitors, and other component parts of the monitoring system to produce a continuous record of the measured parameters in the measurement units required by Section 4 of this Chapter.

(14) **Award.** "Award" means the determination by the Department of the number of offset CO_2 allowances to be recorded in the general account of a project sponsor pursuant to subsection 9(F) of this Chapter. Award is a type of allocation.

(15) **Behind-the-meter CO_2 emissions.** "Behind-the-meter CO_2 emissions" means the difference between the total annual CO_2 emissions from a CO_2 budget unit that is a Combined heat and power unit at an Integrated manufacturing facility and the annual CO_2 emissions associated with the Net electricity that is transmitted over the facilities of a Transmission and distribution utility from such a unit.

(16) **Billing meter.** "Billing meter" means a measurement device used to measure electric or thermal output for commercial billing under a contract.

(17) **Biogas.** "Biogas" means gas resulting from the decomposition of organic matter under anaerobic conditions. The principle constituents are methane and CO_2.

(18) **Boiler.** "Boiler" means an enclosed fuel-fired combustion device used to produce heat and to transfer heat to recirculating water, steam, or other medium.

(19) **Boiler (commercial).** "Boiler (commercial)" means a self-contained, low-pressure appliance for supplying steam or hot water to a commercial building.

(20) **Boiler (residential).** "Boiler (residential)" means a self-contained, low-pressure appliance for supplying steam or hot water to a residential building.

(21) **British thermal unit or Btu.** "British thermal unit" or "Btu" is a measure of energy. One Btu means the amount of heat required to raise the temperature of one pound of water one degree Fahrenheit.

(22) **Building envelope.** "Building envelope" means the elements of a building that separate conditioned space from unconditioned space, or that enclose semi-heated space, through which thermal energy may be transferred to or from the exterior, unconditioned space, or conditioned space. Includes all elements that separate the interior of a building from the outdoor environment, including walls, windows, foundation, basement slab, ceiling, roof, and insulation.

(23) **Cost containment reserve trigger price or CCR trigger price.** "Cost containment reserve trigger price or CCR trigger price" means the minimum price at which CO_2 CCR allowances are offered for sale by the Department or its agent at an auction. The CCR trigger price shall be \$4.00 per CO_2 allowance for calendar year 2014, \$6.00 per CO_2 allowance in calendar year 2015, \$8.00 per CO_2 allowance in calendar year 2016 and \$10.00 per CO_2 allowance in calendar year 2017. Each calendar year thereafter, the CCR trigger price shall be 1.025 multiplied by the CCR trigger price from the previous calendar year, rounded to the nearest whole cent.

(24) **CO_2.** "CO_2" means carbon dioxide.

(25) **CO_2 allowance.** "CO_2 allowance" means a limited authorization by the Department under the CO_2 Budget Trading Program to emit up to one ton of CO_2, subject to all applicable limitations contained in this regulation. No provision of this regulation shall be construed to limit the authority of the Department to terminate or limit such authorization to emit. This limited authorization does not constitute a property right.

(26) **CO_2 allowance auction or auction.** "CO_2 allowance auction or auction" means an auction in which the Department or its agent offers CO_2 allowances for sale.

(27) **CO_2 allowance deduction or deduct CO_2 allowances.** "CO_2 allowance deduction or deduct CO_2 allowances" means the permanent withdrawal of CO_2 allowances by the Department or its agent from a CO_2 Allowance Tracking System compliance account to account for the number of tons of CO_2 emitted from a CO_2 budget source for a control period or an interim control period, determined in accordance with Section 4 of this Chapter, or for the forfeit or retirement of CO_2 allowances as provided by this regulation.

(28) **CO_2 allowances held or hold CO_2 allowances.** "CO_2 allowances held" or "hold CO_2 allowances" means the CO_2 allowances recorded by the Department or its agent, or submitted to the Department or its agent for recordation, in ac-

cordance with Sections 7 and 8 of this Chapter, in a CO_2 Allowance Tracking System account.

(29) **CO_2 allowance tracking system.** "CO_2 allowance tracking system" means the system by which the Department or its agent records allocations, deductions, and transfers of CO_2 allowances under the CO_2 Budget Trading Program. The tracking system may also be used to track CO_2 emissions offset projects, CO_2 allowance prices, and emissions from affected sources.

(30) **CO_2 allowance tracking system account.** "CO_2 allowance tracking system account" means an account in the CO_2 allowance tracking system established by the Department or its agent for purposes of recording the allocation, holding, transferring, retiring, or deducting of CO_2 allowances.

(31) **CO_2 allowance transfer deadline.** "CO_2 allowance transfer deadline" means midnight of the March 1 occurring after the end of the relevant control period and each relevant interim control period or, if that March 1 is not a business day, midnight of the first business day thereafter and is the deadline by which CO_2 allowances must be submitted for recordation in a CO_2 budget source's compliance account in order to meet the source's CO_2 budget emissions limitation for the control period and each interim control period immediately preceding such deadline.

(32) **CO_2 authorized account representative.** "CO_2 authorized account representative" means, for a CO_2 budget source and each CO_2 budget unit at the source, the natural person who is authorized by the owners and operators of the source and all CO_2 budget units at the source, in accordance with Section 6 of this Chapter, to represent and legally bind each owner and operator in matters pertaining to the CO_2 Budget Trading Program or, for a general account, the natural person who is authorized, under Section 7 of this Chapter, to transfer or otherwise dispose of CO_2 allowances held in the general account.

(33) **CO_2 budget emissions limitation.** "CO_2 budget emissions limitation" means the tonnage equivalent of the CO_2 allowances required in a control period or interim control period for compliance deduction in subsection 5(D)(3) of this Chapter for a CO_2 budget source for a control period or an interim control period.

(34) **CO_2 budget license.** "CO_2 budget license" means the portion of the legally binding license issued by the Department pursuant to *Major and Minor Source Air Emission License Regulations*, 06-096 CMR 115 (effective December 24, 2005) of the Department's Regulations to a CO_2 budget source.

(35) **CO_2 budget source.** "CO_2 budget source" means a source that includes one or more CO_2 budget units.

(36) **CO_2 budget source compliance account or Compliance account.** "CO_2 budget unit compliance account" or "Compliance account" means the account established by the Department for a CO_2 budget source wherein CO_2 allowances are held and available for use by the source for a control period and each interim control period for compliance purposes under this CO_2 Budget Trading Program.

(37) **CO_2 Budget Trading Program.** "CO_2 Budget Trading Program" means a multi-state CO_2 air pollution control and emissions reduction program established pursuant to this regulation and corresponding regulations in other states as a means of reducing emissions of CO_2 from CO_2 budget sources.

(38) **CO_2 Budget Trading Program Adjusted Budget.** "CO_2 Budget Trading Program Adjusted Budget" means the budget determined in accordance with Section 2 of this Chapter and is the annual amount of CO_2 in tons available in Maine for allocation in a given allocation year, in accordance with the CO_2 Budget Trading Program. CO_2 offset allowances allocated to project sponsors and CO_2 CCR allowances offered for sale at an auction are separate from and additional to CO_2 allowances allocated from the CO_2 Budget Trading Program adjusted budget.

(39) **CO_2 Budget Trading Program Base Budget.** "CO_2 Budget Trading Program Base Budget" means the budget specified in Section 2 of this Chapter. CO_2 offset allowances allocated to project sponsors and CO_2 CCR allowances offered for sale at an auction are separate from and additional to CO_2 allowances allocated from the CO_2 Budget Trading Program Base Budget.

(40) **CO_2 budget unit.** "CO_2 budget unit" means any single fossil fuel-fired unit that serves a generator with a nameplate capacity equal to or greater than 25 MW electrical output.

(41) **CO_2 cost containment reserve allowance or CO_2 CCR allowance.** "CO_2 cost containment reserve allowance or CO_2 CCR allowance" means a CO_2 allowance that is offered for sale at an auction by the Department for the purpose of containing the cost of CO_2 allowances. CO_2 CCR allowances offered for sale at an auction are separate from and additional to CO_2 allowances allocated from the CO_2 Budget Trading Program base and adjusted budgets. CO_2 CCR allowances are subject to all applicable limitations contained in this Chapter.

(42) **CO_2 emissions credit retirement(s).** "CO_2 emissions credit retirement(s)" means the permanent retirement of greenhouse gas allowances or credits issued pursuant to any governmental mandatory carbon constraining program outside the United Sates that places a specific tonnage limit on greenhouse gas emissions, or certified greenhouse gas emissions reduction credits issued pursuant to the United Nations Framework Convention on Climate Change (UNFCCC) or protocols adopted through the UNFCCC process.

(43) **CO_2 emissions offset project or Offset project.** "CO_2 emissions offset project" or "Offset project" means a project that reduces greenhouse gas emissions from a source that is not a CO_2 budget unit. "CO_2 emissions offset project" includes: landfill and agricultural methane capture and destruction, reduction in emissions of sulfur hexafluoride, sequestration of carbon due to afforestation, and reduction or avoidance of CO_2 emissions from natural gas, oil or propane end-use combustion due to end-use energy efficiency. A CO_2 offset project includes all equipment, materials, items, or actions directly related to the reduction of CO_2 equivalent emissions or the sequestration of carbon specified in a consistency application submitted pursuant to subsection 9(C)(3) of this Chapter. Equipment, materials, items, or actions unrelated to an offset project reduction of CO_2 equivalent emissions or the sequestration of carbon, but occurring at a location where an offset project occurs, shall not be considered part of a CO_2 offset project, unless specified at subsection 9(D) of this Chapter.

(44) **CO_2 equivalent or CO_2e.** "CO_2 equivalent" or "CO_2e" means the quantity, in tons, of a given greenhouse gas multiplied by its global warming potential (GWP).

(45) **CO_2 offset allowance(s).** "CO_2 offset allowance(s)" means a CO_2 allowance that is awarded to the sponsor of a CO_2 emissions offset project pursuant to subsection 9(F) of this Chapter and is subject to the relevant compliance deduction limitations of subsection 5(D)(1)(c) of this Chapter.

(46) **Combined cycle system.** "Combined cycle system" means a system comprised of one or more combustion turbines, heat recovery steam generators, and steam turbines configured to improve overall efficiency of electricity generation or steam production.

(47) **Combined heat and power unit.** "Combined heat and power unit" means a device that simultaneously generates electricity and thermal power and that operates at a high level of output efficiency by utilizing the waste heat created as a by-product of electricity generation for domestic, commercial or industrial heating or cooling purposes, and whose useful thermal output equals at least 10% of the fossil fuel energy input of the unit.

(48) **Combustion turbine.** "Combustion turbine" means an enclosed fossil or other fuel-fired device that is comprised of a compressor (if applicable), a combustor, and a turbine, and in which the flue gas resulting from the combustion of fuel in the combustor passes through the turbine, rotating the shaft to a generator.

(49) **Commence commercial operation.** "Commence commercial operation" means, with regard to a unit that serves a generator, the date the unit began to produce steam, gas, or other heated medium used to generate electricity for sale or use, including test generation. Such date shall remain the unit's date of commencement of operation even if the unit is subsequently modified, reconstructed, or repowered.

(50) **Commence operation.** "Commence operation" means the date a unit began any mechanical, chemical, or electronic process, including start-up of a unit's combustion chamber. Such date shall remain the unit's date of commencement of operation even if the unit is subsequently modified, reconstructed, or re-powered.

(51) **Commercial building.** "Commercial building" means a building to which the provisions of ANSI/ASHRAE/IESNA Standard 90.1 apply, which includes buildings except low-rise residential buildings. Low-rise residential buildings include single family homes, multifamily structures of three stories or fewer above grade, and manufactured homes (modular and mobile).

(52) **Condensing mode.** "Condensing mode" means the design and operation of furnaces or boilers in a mode that leads to the production of condensate in flue gases.

(53) **Conflict of Interest.** "Conflict of Interest" means a situation that may arise with respect to an individual in relation to any specific project sponsor, CO_2 emissions offset project or category of offset projects, such that the individual's other activities or relationships with other persons or organizations render or may render the individual incapable of providing an impartial certification opinion, or otherwise compromise the individual's objectivity in performing certification functions.

(54) **Consumer benefit account.** "Consumer benefit account" means a general account established by the Department or its agent from which CO_2 allowances

will be sold or distributed in order to provide funds to encourage and foster the following: promotion of energy efficiency measures, direct mitigation of electricity ratepayer impacts attributable to the implementation of the CO_2 Budget Trading Program, promotion of renewable or non-carbon- emitting energy technologies, stimulation or reward of investment in the development of innovative carbon emissions abatement technologies with significant carbon reduction potential, promotion and reward for combined heat and power projects, and/or the administration of Maine's component of the CO_2 Budget Trading Program.

(55) **Continuous emissions monitoring system or CEMS.** "Continuous emissions monitoring system or CEMS" means the equipment required under Section 4 of this Chapter to sample, analyze, measure, and provide, by means of readings recorded at least once every 15 minutes (using an automated DAHS), a permanent record of stack gas volumetric flow rate, stack gas moisture content, and oxygen or CO_2 concentration (as applicable), in a manner consistent with 40 CFR Part 75 and Section 4 of this Chapter. The following systems are the principal types of continuous emissions monitoring systems required under Section 4 of this Chapter.

(a) A flow monitoring system, consisting of a stack flow rate monitor and an automated data acquisition and handling system and providing a permanent, continuous record of stack gas volumetric flow rate, in standard cubic feet per hour (scfh);

(b) A nitrogen oxides emissions rate (or NOX-diluent) monitoring system, consisting of a NOx pollutant concentration monitor, a diluent gas (CO_2 or O_2) monitor, and an automated data acquisition and handling system and providing a permanent, continuous record of NOX concentration, in parts per million (ppm), diluent gas concentration, in percent CO_2 or O_2; and NOx emissions rate, in pounds per million British thermal units (lb/MMBtu);

(c) A moisture monitoring system, as defined in 40 CFR 75.11(b)(2) and providing a permanent, continuous record of the stack gas moisture content, in percent water;

(d) A CO_2 monitoring system, consisting of a CO_2 pollutant concentration monitor (or an oxygen monitor plus suitable mathematical equations from which the CO_2 concentration is derived) and an automated data acquisition and handling system and providing a permanent, continuous record of CO_2 emissions, in percent CO_2; and

(e) An oxygen monitoring system, consisting of an oxygen concentration monitor and an automated data acquisition and handling system and providing a permanent, continuous record of oxygen, in percent oxygen.

(56) **Control period.** "Control period" means a three-calendar-year time period. The first control period is from January 1, 2009 to December 31, 2011, inclusive. Each subsequent sequential three-calendar-year period is a separate control period. The first two calendar years of each control period are each defined as an interim control period, beginning on January 1, 2015.

(57) **Cooperating Regulatory Agency.** "Cooperating Regulatory Agency" means a regulatory agency in a state or United States jurisdiction that is not a Participating

State that has entered into a memorandum of understanding with the Department to carry out certain obligations relative to CO_2 emissions offset projects in that state or United States jurisdiction, including but not limited to the obligation to perform audits of offset project sites, and report violations of this Chapter.

(58) **DAHS.** "DAHS" means data acquisition and handling system.

(59) **Eligible Biomass.** [Reserved]

(60) **Energy conservation measure (ECM) or energy efficiency measure (EEM*).** "Energy conservation measure (ECM) or energy efficiency measure (EEM)" means a set of activities designed to increase the energy efficiency of a building or improve the management of energy demand. An ECM/EEM may involve one or more of the following: physical changes to facility equipment, modifications to a building, revisions to operating and maintenance procedures, software changes, or new means of training or managing users of the building or operations and maintenance staff.

(61) **Energy performance.** "Energy performance" means a measure of the relative energy efficiency of a building, building equipment, or building components, as measured by the amount of energy required to provide building services. For building equipment and components, a relative measure of the impact of equipment or components on building energy usage.

(62) **Energy services.** "Energy services" means provision of useful services to building occupants, such as heating and hot water, cooling, and lighting.

(63) **Excess emissions.** "Excess emissions" means any tonnage of CO_2 emitted by a CO_2 budget source during a control period that exceeds the CO_2 budget emissions limitation for the source.

(64) **Excess interim emissions.** "Excess interim emissions" means any tonnage of CO_2 emitted by a CO_2 budget source during an interim control period multiplied by 0.50 that exceeds the CO_2 budget emissions limitation for the source.

(65) **First control period interim adjustment for banked allowances.** "First control period interim adjustment for banked allowances" means an adjustment applied to the CO_2 Budget Trading Program base budget for allocation years 2014 through 2020 to address the surplus allocation year 2009, 2010 and 2011 allowances held in general and compliance accounts, including compliance accounts established pursuant to the CO_2 Budget Trading Program, but not including accounts opened by participating states.

(66) **Forest offset project.** "Forest offset project" means an offset project involving reforestation, improved forest management or avoided conversion.

(67) **Forest offset project data report.** "Forest offset project data report" means the report prepared by a project sponsor each year that provides the information and documentation required by this subsection or the forest offset protocol.

(68) **Forest offset protocol.** "Forest offset protocol" means the protocol titled "Regional Greenhouse Gas Initiative Offset Protocol U.S. Forest Projects", published by the participating states on June 13, 2013.

(69) **Fossil fuel.** "Fossil fuel" means natural gas, petroleum, coal, or any form of solid, liquid, or gaseous fuel derived from such material.

(70) **Fossil fuel-fired unit.** "Fossil fuel-fired unit" means:

    (a) With regard to a unit that commenced operation prior to January 1, 2005, a unit fueled by the combustion of fossil fuel, alone or in combination with any other fuel, where the fossil fuel combusted constitutes, or is projected to comprise, more than 50% of the annual heat input on a British Thermal Unit basis during any calendar year; or

    (b) With regard to a unit that commenced operation on or after January 1, 2005, a unit fueled by the combustion of fossil fuel, alone or in combination with any other fuel, where the fossil fuel combusted constitutes, or is projected to comprise, more than 5% of the annual heat input on a British Thermal Unit basis during any calendar year.

(71) **Furnace (residential).** "Furnace (residential)" means a self-contained, indirect-fired appliance that supplies heated air to a residential building through ducts to conditioned spaces.

(72) **General account.** "General account" means a CO_2 allowance tracking system account, established under Section 7 of this Chapter, that is not a compliance account.

(73) **Generator.** "Generator" means a device that produces electricity and is required to be reported as a generating unit pursuant to the United States Department of Energy's form 860.

(74) **Global warming potential (GWP).** "Global warming potential (GWP)" means a measure of the radiative efficiency (heat-absorbing ability) of a particular gas relative to that of CO_2 after taking into account the decay rate of each gas (the amount removed from the atmosphere over a given number of years) relative to that of CO_2. Global warming potentials used in this regulation are consistent with the values used in the Intergovernmental Panel on Climate Change, Fourth Assessment Report.

(75) **Gross electrical generation or Gross generation.** "Gross electrical generation" or "Gross generation" means the electrical output (in MW or MWe) at the terminals of the generator.

(76) **HVAC system.**"HVAC system" means the system or systems that provide, either collectively or individually, heating, ventilation, or air conditioning to a building, including the equipment, distribution network, and terminals.

(77) **IESNA.** "IESNA" means Illuminating Engineering Society of North America.

(78) **Independent verifier.** "Independent verifier" means an individual that has been approved by the Department or its agent to conduct verification activities with regard to CO_2 emissions offset projects.

(79) **Initiated.** "Initiated" with respect subsection 1(A)(2) of this Chapter means that a state has signed the Regional Greenhouse Gas Initiative Memorandum of Understanding and initiated rulemaking to implement the program.

(80) **Integrated manufacturing facility.** "Integrated manufacturing facility" means a facility that:

    (a) Received an air emissions license from the Department prior to July 1, 2007;

    (b) Produces electricity from one or more CO_2 budget units, including one or more combined heat and power units, for transmission over the facilities of a transmission and distribution utility; and

(c) Routinely produces one or more other products for sale.

(81) **Integrated manufacturing facility pre-retirement account.** "Integrated manufacturing facility pre-retirement account" means a general account that the Department opens and manages in accordance with the incentive program under this regulation for CO_2 budget units that are Combined heat and power units at Integrated manufacturing facilities.

(82) **Integrated manufacturing facility retirement account.** "Integrated manufacturing facility retirement account" means a general account that the Department opens and manages in order to permanently retire the CO_2 allowances associated with the incentive program under this regulation for CO_2 budget units that are Combined heat and power units at Integrated manufacturing facilities.

(83) **Intentional reversal.** "Intentional reversal" means any reversal caused by a forest owner's negligence, gross negligence or willful intent, including harvesting, development and harm to the area within the offset project boundary.

(84) **Interim control period.** "Interim control period" means a one-calendar-year time period, during each of the first and second calendar years of each three year control period. The first interim control period starts on January 1, 2015 and ends on December 31, 2015, inclusive. The second interim control period starts on January 1, 2016 and ends on December 31, 2016 inclusive. Each successive three year control period will have two interim control periods, comprised of each of the first two calendar years of that control period.

(85) **Life-of-the-unit contractual arrangement.** "Life-of-the-unit contractual arrangement" means a unit participation power sales agreement under which a customer reserves, or is entitled to receive, a specified amount or percentage of nameplate capacity and/or associated energy from any specified unit pursuant to a contract:

(a) for the life of the unit;

(b) for a cumulative term of no less than 25 years, including contracts that permit an election for early termination; or

(c) for a period equal to or greater than 20 years or 70 percent of the economic useful life of the unit determined as of the time the unit is built, with option rights to purchase or release some portion of the nameplate capacity and associated energy generated by the unit at the end of the period.

(86) **Long-term electricity contract.** "Long-term electricity contract" means, with regards to a CO_2 budget unit at an integrated manufacturing facility, a contract for a period of 3 years or more for the purchase of electricity from that CO_2 budget unit.

(87) **Market penetration rate.** "Market penetration rate" means a measure of the diffusion of a technology, product, or practice in a defined market, as represented by the percentage of annual sales for a product or practice, or as a percentage of the existing installed stock for a product or category of products, or as the percentage of existing installed stock that utilizes a practice. The Department may determine an appropriate market definition and market penetration metric for a category of technology, product or practice, and may issue guidance specifying the technologies, products or practices that meet a specified market penetration rate.

(88) **Maximum potential hourly heat input.** "Maximum potential hourly heat input" means an hourly heat input used for reporting purposes when a unit lacks certified monitors to report heat input. If the unit intends to use appendix D of 40 CFR Part 75 to report heat input, this value should be calculated, in accordance with 40 CFR Part 75, using the maximum fuel flow rate and the maximum gross calorific value. If the unit intends to use a flow monitor and a diluent gas monitor, this value should be reported, in accordance with 40 CFR Part 75, using the maximum potential flow rate and either the maximum CO_2 concentration (in percent CO_2) or the minimum oxygen concentration (in percent O_2).

(89) **Megawatt or MW.** "Megawatt" or "MW" means a unit of energy equal to 1000 kilowatts or 1,000,000 watts.

(90) **Memorandum of understanding or MOU.** "Memorandum of understanding" or "MOU" means the Regional Greenhouse Gas Initiative Memorandum of Understanding dated December 20, 2005 that establishes an electric power sector carbon emissions cap-and-trade program within the northeast region of the United States.

(91) **MMBtu.** "MMBtu" means one million British thermal units.

(92) **Minimum reserve price.** "Minimum reserve price" means the minimum reserve price in calendar year 2014 shall be $2.00. Each calendar year thereafter, the minimum reserve price shall be 1.025 multiplied by the minimum reserve price from the previous calendar year, rounded to the nearest whole cent.

(93) **Monitoring system.** "Monitoring system" means any monitoring system that meets the requirements of Section 4 of this Chapter, including a continuous emissions monitoring system, an excepted monitoring system, or an alternative monitoring system.

(94) **MWe.** "MWe" means megawatt electrical.

(95) **MWh or Megawatt-hour.** "MWh or "Megawatt-hour" means the amount of power (in megawatts) used or produced over a certain period of time (in hours).

(96) **Nameplate capacity.** "Nameplate capacity" means the maximum electrical generating output, expressed in megawatts, that a generator can sustain over a specified period of time when not restricted by seasonal or other de-ratings as measured in accordance with the United States Department of Energy standards.

(97) **Net electricity.** "Net electricity" means the difference between the electricity that is produced at an integrated manufacturing facility and transmitted over the facilities of a Transmission and distribution utility and the electricity that is purchased over the facilities of a Transmission and distribution utility and used at the Integrated manufacturing facility.

(98) **Non-CO_2 budget unit.** "Non-CO_2 budget unit" means a unit that does not meet the applicability criteria in subsection 1(A) of this Chapter.

(99) **On-site combustion.** "On-site combustion" means the combustion of fossil fuel at a building to provide building services, such as heating, hot water, or electricity.

(100) **Operator.** "Operator" means any person who operates, controls, or supervises a CO_2 budget unit or a CO_2 budget source and shall include, but not be

limited to, any holding company, utility system, or plant manager of such a unit or source.

(101) **Owner.** "Owner" means:

(a) The definition of "owner" associated with the licensing, monitoring, recordkeeping, reporting, and compliance related requirements except those under Section 5 of this Chapter means:

   (i) any holder of any portion of the legal or equitable title in a CO_2 budget unit;

   (ii) any holder of a leasehold interest in a CO_2 budget unit, other than a passive lessor, or a person who has an equitable interest through such lessor, whose rental payments are not based, either directly or indirectly, upon the revenues or income from the CO_2 budget unit; or

   (iii) if no person has title or interest in the CO_2 budget unit as described in subparagraphs (i) or (ii) above, the owner is any holder of any portion of the legal or equitable title to the electrical output of a CO_2 budget unit.

(b) The definition of "owner" for the purpose of obtaining and making available CO_2 allowances for compliance deduction purposes under sub-section 5of this Chapter means:

   (i) any purchaser of electricity transmitted for purposes of resale over the facilities of a transmission and distribution utility who purchases such electricity under a long-term electricity contract from a CO_2 budget unit located at an Integrated Manufacturing Facility;

   (ii) any purchaser of electricity transmitted for purposes of resale over the facilities of a transmission and distribution utility who purchases such electricity under a life-of-the-unit contractual arrangement in which the purchaser controls the dispatch of the unit from a CO_2 budget unit which is not located at an Integrated Manufacturing Facility; or

   (iii) if in the instance there exists no purchaser of electricity under a long-term electricity contract, and there exists no purchaser of electricity under a life-of-the-unit contractual arrangement, the "owner" for the purpose of obtaining and making available CO_2 allowances for compliance deduction purposes under section 5of this Chapter is defined as under subparagraphs (a)(i)-(iii) of this definition.

(c) The definition of "owner" associated with any general account means any person who has an ownership interest with respect to the CO_2 allowances held in the general account and who is subject to the binding agreement for the CO_2 authorized account representative to represent that person's ownership interest with respect to the CO_2 allowances.

(d) The definition of "owner" associated with any offset project means any person who has legal or rightful title to the equipment, building, property, or operations associated with the offset project.

(102) **Participating state.** "Participating state" means a state that has established a corresponding regulation as part of the CO_2 Budget Trading Program.

(103) **Passive solar.** "Passive solar" means a combination of building design features and building components that utilize solar energy to reduce or eliminate the need for mechanical heating and cooling and daytime artificial lighting.

(104) **Permanently retired.** "Permanently retired" means a greenhouse gas allowance or credit has been "permanently retired" if it has been placed in a retirement account controlled by the jurisdiction that generated the allowance or credit, or has been placed in an allowance retirement account controlled by the Department, or is otherwise deemed unusable by the Department.

(105) **Project commencement.** "Project commencement" means, for an offset project involving physical construction, other work at an offset project site, or installation of equipment or materials, the date of the beginning of such activity. For an offset project that involves the implementation of a management activity or protocol, the date on which such activity is first implemented or such protocol first utilized. For an offset project involving reforestation, improved forest management, or avoided conversion, the date specified in Section 3.2 of the forest offset protocol.

(106) **Receive** or **receipt of.** "Receive" or "receipt of" means, when referring to the Department or its agent, to come into possession of a document, information, or correspondence (whether sent in writing or by authorized electronic transmission), as indicated in an official correspondence log, or by a notation made on the document, information, or correspondence, by the Department or its agent in the regular course of business.

(107) **Recordation, record, or recorded.** "Recordation," "record," or "recorded" means, with regard to CO_2 allowances, the movement of CO_2 allowances by the Department or its agent from one CO_2 Allowance Tracking System account to another, for purposes of allocation, transfer, retirement, or deduction.

(108) **Regional Greenhouse Gas Initiative.** "Regional Greenhouse Gas Initiative" means the ongoing cooperative effort by the states of Maine, New Hampshire, Vermont, Connecticut, New York, New Jersey, Massachusetts, Rhode Island, Maryland and Delaware and such others states as may in the future become a part of the program to design and implement a regional CO_2 cap-and-trade program covering CO_2 emissions from CO_2 budget units in the signatory states.

(109) **Regional Transmission Organization or RTO.** "Regional Transmission Organization" or "RTO" means the independent systems operator that administers and oversees wholesale electricity markets.

(110) **Regional-type anaerobic digester**. "Regional-type anaerobic digester" means an anaerobic digester using feedstock from more than one agricultural operation, or importing feedstock from more than one agricultural operation. Also referred to as a "community digester" or "centralized digester."

(111) **Renewable energy.** "Renewable energy" means electricity generated from any resource that meets the resource type and vintage for Class I of the Maine Portfolio Requirement 65-407 CMR Chapter 311.

(112) **Renewable energy credits or RECs.** "Renewable energy credits" or "RECs" means the characteristics associated with the generation of one megawatt-hour of electricity from a renewable energy source, such as its generation date, facility geographic location, unit vintage, emissions output, fuel, state

program eligibility, or other characteristic that can be identified, accounted, and tracked.

(113) **Renewable portfolio standard or RPS.** "Renewable portfolio standard" or "RPS" means a statutory or regulatory requirement that a load-serving entity provide a certain portion of the electricity it supplies to its customers from renewable energy sources, or any other statutory or regulatory requirement that a certain portion of electricity supplied to the electricity grid be generated from renewable energy sources.

(114) **Reporting period.** "Reporting period" means the period of time covered by a forest offset project data report. The first reporting period for an offset project in an initial crediting period may consist of 6 to 24 consecutive months; all subsequent reporting periods in an initial crediting and all reporting periods in any renewed crediting period must consist of 12 consecutive months.

(115) **Reserve price.** "Reserve price" means the minimum acceptable price for each CO_2 allowance in a specific auction. The reserve price at an auction is either the minimum reserve price or the CCR trigger price, as specified in subsection 2(G) of this Chapter.

(116) **Residential building.** "Residential building" means a low-rise residential building to which the provisions of ANSI/ASHRAE/IESNA Standard 90.1 do not apply. Includes, *inter alia*, single family homes, multifamily structures of three stories or fewer above grade, and manufactured homes (modular and mobile).

(117) **RESNET.** "RESNET" means Residential Energy Services Network.

(118) **Reversal.** "Reversal" means a GHG emission reduction or GHG removal enhancement for which CO_2 offset allowances have been issued that is subsequently released or emitted back into the atmosphere due to any intentional or unintentional circumstances.

(119) **Second control period interim adjustment for banked allowances.** "Second control period interim adjustment for banked allowances" means an adjustment applied to the CO_2 Budget Trading Program base budget for allocation years 2015 through 2020 to address the allocation year 2012 and 2013 allowances held in general and compliance accounts, including compliance accounts established pursuant to the CO_2 Budget Trading Program, but not including accounts opened by participating states, that are in addition to the aggregate quantity of 2012 and 2013 emissions from all CO_2 budget sources in all of the participating states.

(120) **Serial number.** "Serial number" means, when referring to CO_2 allowances, the unique identification number assigned to each CO_2 allowance by the Department or its agent under subsection 7(B)(3) of this Chapter.

(121) **SF_6.** "SF_6" means sulfur hexafluoride.

(122) **SF_6-containing operating equipment.** "SF_6-containing operating equipment" means any equipment used for the transmission and distribution of electricity that contains SF_6.

(123) **Source.** "Source" means any governmental, institutional, commercial, or industrial structure, installation, plant, building, or facility that emits or has

the potential to emit any air pollutant. A "source," including a "source" with multiple units, shall be considered a single "facility."

(124) **Sponsor or Project sponsor.** "Sponsor" or "Project sponsor" means any person who meets the requirements of the CO_2 authorized account representative for the general account of an eligible CO_2 emissions offset project or CO_2 emissions credit retirement.

(125) **State.** "State" means a State, the District of Columbia, the Commonwealth of Puerto Rico, the Virgin Islands, Guam, and American Samoa and includes the Commonwealth of the Northern Mariana Islands.

(126) **Submit** or **serve.** "Submit" or "serve" means to send or transmit a document, information, or correspondence to the person specified in accordance with the applicable regulation:

(a) in person;

(b) by United States Postal Service; or

(c) by other means of dispatch or transmission and delivery.

Compliance with any "submission," "service," or "mailing" deadline shall be determined by the date of dispatch, transmission, or mailing and not the date of receipt.

(127) **System benefit fund.** "System benefit fund" means any fund collected directly from retail electricity or natural gas ratepayers.

(128) **Ton** or **tonnage.** "Ton" or "tonnage" means any "short ton," or 2,000 pounds. For the purpose of determining compliance with the CO_2 budget emissions limitation, total tons for a control period and each interim control period shall be calculated as the sum of all recorded hourly emissions (or the tonnage equivalent of the recorded hourly emissions rates) in accordance with Section 4 of this Chapter, with any remaining fraction of a ton equal to or greater than 0.50 ton deemed to equal one ton and any fraction of a ton less than 0.50 ton deemed to equal zero tons. A short ton is equal to 0.9072 metric tons.

(129) **Total solids.** "Total solids" means the total of all solids in a sample. They include the total suspended solids, total dissolved solids, and volatile suspended solids.

(130) **Transmission and distribution utility.** "Transmission and distribution utility" means a transmission and distribution utility as defined in 35-A MRSA § 3201, subsections 6, 12 or 16.

(131) **Undistributed CO_2 allowances.** "Undistributed CO_2 allowances" means CO_2 allowances originally allocated to a set aside account as pursuant to Section 2 of this Chapter that were not distributed.

(132) **Unintentional Reversal.** "Unintentional Reversal" means any reversal, including wildfires or disease that is not the result of the forest owner's negligence, gross negligence or willful intent.

(133) **Unit.** "Unit" means a stationary boiler, combustion turbine, or combined cycle system.

(134) **Unit operating day.** "Unit operating day" means a calendar day in which a unit combusts any fuel.

(135) **Unsold CO$_2$ allowances.** "Unsold CO$_2$ allowances" means CO$_2$ allowances that have been made available for sale in an auction conducted by the Department or its agent, but not sold.

(136) **Verification.** "Verification" means the determination by an independent verifier that certain parts of a CO$_2$ emissions offset project application and/or measurement, monitoring or verification report conforms to the requirements of Section 9 of this Chapter.

(137) **Volatile solids.** "Volatile solids" means the fraction of total solids that is comprised primarily of organic matter.

(138) **Voluntary renewable energy purchases.** "Voluntary renewable energy purchases" means the purchase of renewable energy credits (RECs) by a retail electricity customer on a voluntary basis. The renewable energy or RECs related to such purchases may not be used by the generator or purchaser to meet any regulatory mandate, such as a renewable portfolio standard (RPS).

(139) **Voluntary renewable energy retirement account.** "Voluntary renewable energy retirement account" means a general account that the Department opens and manages in order to permanently retire CO$_2$ allowances associated with the Voluntary renewable energy purchase provisions contained in subsection 2(F)(4) of this Chapter.

(140) **Voluntary renewable energy set-aside account.** "Voluntary renewable energy set-aside account" means a general account that the Department opens and manages in accordance with the Voluntary renewable energy purchase provisions contained in subsection 2(F)(4) of this Chapter.

(141) **Whole-building energy performance.** "Whole-building energy performance" means the overall energy performance of a building, taking into account the integrated impact on energy usage of all building components and systems.

(142) **Whole-building retrofit.** "Whole-building retrofit" means any building project that involves the replacement of more than one building system, or set of building components, and also requires a building permit.

(143) **Zero net energy building.** "Zero net energy building" means a building designed to produce as much energy as the building is projected to use, as measured on an annual basis.

C. Liability

(1) No license revision shall excuse any violation of the requirements of the CO$_2$ Budget Trading Program that occurs prior to the date that the revision takes effect.

(2) Any provision of the CO$_2$ Budget Trading Program that applies to a CO$_2$ budget source (including a provision applicable to the CO$_2$ authorized account representative of a CO$_2$ budget source) shall also apply to the owners and operators of such source and of the CO$_2$ budget units at the source.

(3) Any provision of the CO$_2$ Budget Trading Program that applies to a CO$_2$ budget unit (including a provision applicable to the CO$_2$ authorized account representative of a CO$_2$ budget unit) shall also apply to the owners and operators of such unit.

D. **Effect on other authorities.** No provision of the CO$_2$ Budget Trading Program, a CO$_2$ budget license application, or a CO$_2$ budget license, shall be construed as exempting or excluding the owners and operators and, to the extent applicable, the CO_2 authorized account representative of a CO_2 budget source or CO_2 budget unit from compliance with any other provisions of applicable State and federal law and regulations.

E. Severability. If any provision of this Regulation, or its application to any particular person or circumstances, is held invalid, the remainder of this Regulation, and the application thereof to other persons or circumstances, shall not be affected thereby.

F. Enforcement. Except as provided in CO_2 Budget Trading Program Waiver and Suspension, 06-096, Chapter 157, violations of this chapter are enforceable, and penalties may be imposed in accordance with 38 M.R.S.A. sections 347-A, 348, and 349.

G. Computation of time

(1) Unless otherwise stated, any time period scheduled, under the CO_2 Budget Trading Program, to begin on the occurrence of an act or event shall begin on the day the act or event occurs.

(2) Unless otherwise stated, any time period scheduled, under the CO_2 Budget Trading Program, to begin before the occurrence of an act or event shall be computed so that the period ends the day before the act or event occurs.

(3) Unless otherwise stated, if the final day of any time period, under the CO_2 Budget Trading Program, falls on a weekend or a State or Federal holiday, the time period shall be extended to the next business day.

CO_2 Allowance Allocation Provisions

A. CO_2 Budget Trading Program Base Budget

(1) For 2014 the CO_2 budget trading program base budget is 3,277,250 tons.

(2) For 2015 the CO_2 budget trading program base budget is 3,195,319 tons.

(3) For 2016 the CO_2 budget trading program base budget is 3,115,436 tons.

(4) For 2017 the CO_2 budget trading program base budget is 3,037,550 tons.

(5) For 2018 the CO_2 budget trading program base budget is 2,961,611 tons.

(6) For 2019 the CO_2 budget trading program base budget is 2,887,571 tons.

(7) For 2020 the CO_2 budget trading program base budget is 2,815,382 tons.

B. CO_2 Allowance Allocations

(1) CO_2 Allowances available for allocation. For allocation years 2014 through 2020, the CO_2 Budget Trading Program adjusted budget shall be the maximum number of allowances available for allocation in a given allocation year, except for CO_2 offset allowances and CO_2 CCR allowances.

(2) Cost Containment Reserve (CCR) allocation. The Department shall allocate CO_2 CCR allowances, separate from and additional to the CO_2 Budget Trading Program base budget set forth in subsection 2(A) of this Chapter to the auction account. The CCR allocation is for the purpose of containing the cost of CO_2 allowances. The Department shall allocate CO_2 CCR allowances in the following manner:

(a) The Department shall initially allocate 180,069 CO_2 CCR allowances for calendar year 2014.

(b) On or before January 1, 2015 and each calendar year thereafter, the Department shall allocate CO_2 CCR allowances in an amount equal to 360,137 minus the number of CO_2 CCR allowances that remain in the auction account at the end of the prior calendar year.

(3) First control period interim adjustment for banked allowances. By January 15, 2014, the Department shall determine the first control period interim adjustment for banked allowances quantity for allocation years 2014 through 2020 by the following formula:

FCPIABA = (FCPA/7) × RS%

Where:

FCPIABA is the first control period interim adjustment for banked allowances quantity in tons.

FCPA, the first control period adjustment, is the total quantity of allocation year 2009, 2010 and 2011 CO_2 allowances held in general and compliance accounts, including compliance accounts established pursuant to the CO_2 Budget Trading Program, but not including accounts opened by participating states, as reflected in the CO_2 Allowance Tracking System (COATS) on January 1, 2014.

RS% is Maine's 2013 Budget divided by the 2013 Regional Budget.

(4) Second control period interim adjustment for banked allowances. On March 17, 2014, the Department shall determine the second control period interim adjustment for banked allowances quantity the allocation years 2015 through 2020 by the following formula:

SCPIABA = ((SCPA − SCPE)/6) × RS%

Where:

SCPIABA is the second control period interim adjustment for banked allowances quantity in tons.

SCPA, second control period adjustment, is the total quantity of allocation year 2012 and 2013 CO_2 allowances held in general and compliance accounts, including compliance accounts established pursuant to the CO_2 Budget Trading Program, but not including accounts opened by participating states, as reflected in the CO_2 Allowance Tracking System (COATS) on March 17, 2014.

SCPE, second control period emissions, is the total quantity of 2012 and 2013 emissions from all CO_2 budget sources in all participating states, reported pursuant to CO_2 Budget Trading Program as reflected in the CO_2 Allowance Tracking System (COATS) on March 17, 2014.

RS% is Maine's 2013 Budget divided by the 2013 Regional Budget.

C. CO_2 Budget Trading Program Adjusted Budget 2014. The Department shall determine the CO_2 Budget Trading Program adjusted budget for the 2014 allocation year by the following formula:

AB = BB − FCPIABA

Where:

AB is the CO_2 Budget Trading Program 2014 adjusted budget.

BB is the CO_2 Budget Trading Program 2014 base budget.

FCPIABA is the first control period interim adjustment for banked allowances quantity.

D. CO_2 Budget Trading Program Adjusted Budgets for 2015 through 2020. On April 15, 2014 the Department shall determine the CO_2 Budget Trading Program adjusted budgets for the 2015 through 2020 allocation years by the following formula:

AB = BB−(FCPIABA + SCPIABA)

Where:

AB is the CO_2 Budget Trading Program adjusted budget.

BB is the CO_2 Budget Trading Program base budget.

FCPIABA is the first control period interim adjustment for banked allowances

SCPIABA is the second control interim adjustment for banked allowances.

E. Publishing the CO_2 Trading Program Adjusted Budgets. After making the determinations in subsections 2(C) and (D) of this Chapter the Department or its Agent will publish the CO2 Trading Program Adjusted Budgets for the 2014 through 2020 allocation years.

F. Consumer benefit account allocation. The Department will allocate one hundred percent (100%) of Maine's CO_2 Budget Trading Program base budget to the Consumer benefit account. A portion of the CO_2 allowances held in the Consumer benefit account will be transferred to an Integrated manufacturing facility pre-retirement account and handled as described in subsection 2(G)(1), (2), and (3) below. A portion, not to exceed 2% of the CO_2 Budget Trading Program base budget , of the CO_2 allowances held in the Consumer benefit account will be transferred to a Voluntary renewable energy set-aside account and handled as described in subsection 2(G)(4) below. CO_2 allowances remaining in the Consumer benefit account will be auctioned for sale by the Department or its agent.

(1) Incentive for CO_2 budget units that are Combined heat and power units at Integrated manufacturing facilities. Annually, the Department will transfer a portion of the CO_2 allowances allocated to the Consumer benefit account to an Integrated manufacturing facility pre-retirement account. Such CO_2 allowances are intended to promote and reward the operation of CO_2 budget units that are Combined heat and power units at Integrated manufacturing facilities by using the CO_2 allowances to offset the Behind-the-meter CO_2 emissions. The methods by which the number of CO_2 allowances will be distributed are described in subsections 2(F) (2), (3), and (4) of this Chapter.

(2) Reservation of CO_2 allowances for Integrated manufacturing facilities. Integrated manufacturing facilities will be responsible for submitting and the Department will be responsible for approving projections of each CO_2 budget unit's anticipated Behind-the-meter CO_2 emissions. The number of CO_2 allowances equal to the total approved projected amount of Behind-the-meter CO_2 emissions from the CO_2 budget units will be transferred from the Consumer benefit account to the Integrated manufacturing facility pre-retirement account.

(3) Balancing of the Integrated manufacturing facility pre-retirement account. Each calendar year the Department will compare the number of CO_2 allowances held in the Integrated manufacturing facility pre-retirement account with the total actual reported Behind-the-meter CO_2 emissions from each Integrated manufacturing facility. If there are fewer CO_2 allowances held in the Integrated manufacturing facility pre-retirement account than needed, additional CO_2 allowances will be added to the next year's predicted number of CO_2 allowances and transferred into the Integrated manufacturing facility pre-retirement account

to balance the account. If there are more CO_2 allowances held in the Integrated manufacturing facility pre-retirement account than needed, only as many CO_2 allowances will be transferred from next year's Consumer benefit account as needed to cover future Behind-the-meter CO_2 emissions.

(4) Voluntary renewable energy purchases. The Department will set aside and permanently retire CO_2 allowances to promote and reward the voluntary purchase by consumers in Maine of renewable energy credits generated from within any participating state. The handling of such CO_2 allowances shall be accomplished by the Department as follows:

   (a) Prior to the beginning of each control period the Department shall transfer 2% of the CO_2 Budget Trading Program base budget from each year of the control period from the Consumer benefit account into the Voluntary renewable energy set-aside account.

   (b) By August 31st of each year beginning in 2010, the Department shall permanently retire the number of CO_2 allowances equal to the amount of avoided CO_2 emissions from the previous calendar year, determined using the following equation, subject to the limitations in subparagraph (c) and requirements of subparagraphs (d) and (e) of this subsection:

$$AE = \sum_{i=1}^{n} (MWH_{REC})_i \times (MER)/2000$$

   Where,

   AE = the amount of avoided CO_2 emissions (in tons rounded to the nearest whole ton).

   MWH_{REC} = the number of renewable energy credits (RECs) voluntarily purchased by Maine consumers during each calendar year (in equivalent MWhrs on a state-by-state basis), which have been generated within a participating state.

   MER = the most recently published annual average marginal emission rate (in lbs of CO_2 per MWh) as reported by the corresponding participating state's regional transmission organization.

   i = each participating state from which RECs were purchased by Maine consumers.

   (c) If the total amount of avoided CO_2 emissions calculated pursuant to subparagraph (b) of this subsection exceeds the number of CO_2 allowances held in the Voluntary renewable energy set-aside account for an associated vintage year, then the number of CO_2 allowances to be retired shall be equal to the total number of CO_2 allowances contained in the Voluntary renewable energy set-aside account for that particular vintage year.

   (d) If the total amount of avoided CO_2 emissions calculated pursuant to subparagraph (b) of this subsection is less than the number of CO_2 allowances held in the Voluntary renewable energy set-aside account for an associated vintage year, then the number of CO_2 allowances in an amount equal to the calculated avoided CO_2 emissions shall be retired and any excess CO_2 allowances shall be transferred back into the Consumer benefit account and offered for sale at auction.

(e) By August 31, 2010 and August 31st of each year thereafter, the Department shall retire the number of CO_2 allowances determined pursuant to sub-paragraphs (c) and (d) of this subsection by transferring them into the Voluntary renewable energy retirement account.

(f) Data for the amount of renewable energy credits voluntarily purchased by Maine consumers and required for the equation specified in subparagraph (b) of this subsection will be obtained from renewable energy credit tracking systems associated with the regional transmission organizations operating in the states where the credits were generated. For credits that originate in areas with no credit tracking system, verifiable evidence of purchases by Maine consumers of renewable energy credits will be obtained from the entity that oversees the electricity transmission system in that area. Renewable energy credit data must be verifiable and document the following information:

   (i)   Number of renewable energy credits, in MWh, purchased by retail con-sumers, by customer class in Maine, during the previous calendar year;

   (ii) Documentation that the renewable energy credits were procured by the retail provider;

   (iii) State where the renewable energy credits were generated;

   (iv) Time period when the renewable energy credits were generated;

   (v)   Any additional information required by the Department necessary to demonstrate that such renewable energy credit purchase is eligible in Maine and not being credited in more than one participating state and is not being credited toward any renewable portfolio standard;

   (vi) Annual average marginal CO_2 emission rate for electricity generation, in pounds CO_2/MWh, as most recently reported by the regional trans-mission organization or the entity that oversees electricity transmission in areas with no RTO;

(5) Public notice of the number of CO_2 allowances to be auctioned. Each Calendar year the Department or its agent will make public the number of CO_2 allowances that are planned to be auctioned in the coming year and the number of CO_2 allowances that are planned to be transferred to the Integrated manufacturing facility pre-retirement account.

(6) Serial numbers for allocated CO_2 allowances. When allocating CO_2 allowances to and recording them in an account, the Department or its agent will assign each CO_2 allowance a unique identification number that will include digits identifying the year for which the CO_2 allowance is allocated.

G. Auction of CO_2 CCR Allowances

(1) Purpose. The following rules shall apply to each CO_2 allowance auction. The Department or its agent may specify additional information in the auction notice for each auction. Such additional information may include the time and location of the auction, auction rules, registration deadlines and any additional information deemed necessary or useful.

(2) General requirements

   (a) The Department or its agent shall include the following information in the auction notice for each auction:

(i)   The number of CO_2 allowances offered for sale at the auction, not including any CO_2 CCR allowances;

(ii) The number of CO_2 CCR allowances that will be offered for sale at the auction if the condition of subsection 2(G)(b)(i) of this Chapter is met;

(iii) The minimum reserve price for the auction; and

(iv) The CCR trigger price for the auction.

(b) The Department or its agent shall follow these rules for the sale of CO_2 CCR allowances:

(i) CO_2 CCR allowances shall only be sold at an auction in which total demand for allowances, above the CCR trigger price, exceeds the number of CO_2 allowances available for purchase at the auction, not including any CO_2 CCR allowances.

(ii) If the condition of subsection 2(G)(b)(i) of this Chapter is met at an auction, then the number of CO_2 CCR allowances offered for sale by the Department or its agent at the auction shall be equal to the number of CO_2 CCR allowances in the auction account at the time of the auction.

(iii) After all of the CO_2 CCR allowances in the auction account have been sold in a given calendar year, no additional CO_2 CCR allowances will be sold at any auction for the remainder of that calendar year, even if the condition of subsection 2(G)(b)(i) of this Chapter is met at an auction; and

(iv) At an auction in which CO_2 CCR allowances are sold, the reserve price for the auction shall be the CCR trigger price.

(v)   If the condition of subsection 2(G)(b)(i) of this Chapter is not satisfied, no CO_2 CCR allowances shall be offered for sale at the auction, and the reserve price for the auction shall be equal to the minimum reserve prices.

(c) The Department or its agent shall implement the reserve price in the following manner:

(i)   No allowances shall be sold at any auction for a price below the reserve price for that auction; and

(ii) If the total demand for the allowances at an auction is less than or equal to the total number of allowances made available for sale in that auction, then the auction clearing price for the auction shall be the reserve price.

H. Undistributed and Unsold CO_2 Allowances

(1) The Department may retire undistributed CO_2 allowances at the end of each control period.

(2) The Department may retire unsold CO_2 allowances at the end of each control period.

3. Licensing Requirements

A. General CO_2 budget source licensing requirements

(1) Each CO_2 budget source must obtain a CO_2 budget source license to be issued by the Department pursuant to *Major and Minor Source Air Emission License Regulations*, 06-096 CMR 115 (effective December 24, 2005).

(2) Each CO_2 budget source license shall contain all applicable CO_2 Budget Trading Program requirements and shall be a complete and distinguishable license under subsection 3(A)(1) of this Chapter.

B. Schedule for submission license applications. For any CO_2 budget source, the CO_2 authorized account representative shall submit a complete CO_2 budget source license application under subsection 3(C) of this Chapter covering such CO_2 budget source to the Department by the later of the effective date of this regulation based on the criteria listed in subsection 1(A)(2) of this Chapter or 12 months before the date on which the CO_2 budget source, or a new CO_2 budget unit at the source, commences operation.

C. Application information requirements. A complete CO_2 budget source license application shall include the following elements concerning the CO_2 budget source for which the application is submitted, in a format prescribed by the Department:

(1) Identification of the CO_2 budget source, including plant name and the ORIS (Office of Regulatory Information Systems) or facility code assigned to the source by the Energy Information Administration of the United States Department of Energy, if applicable;

(2) Identification of each CO_2 budget unit at the CO_2 budget source; and

(3) Any supplemental information that the Department determines is necessary in order to review the CO_2 budget source license application and issue or deny a CO_2 budget source license.

4. Monitoring, Recordkeeping, and Reporting Requirements

A. General requirements. The owners and operators, and to the extent applicable, the CO_2 authorized account representative of a CO_2 budget unit, shall comply with the monitoring, recordkeeping and reporting requirements as provided in this Chapter and all applicable sections of 40 CFR Part 75. For purposes of complying with such requirements, the definitions in subsection 1(B) of this Chapter and in 40 CFR 72.2 shall apply, and the terms "affected unit," "designated representative," and "continuous emissions monitoring system" (or "CEMS") in 40 CFR Part 75 shall be replaced by the terms "CO_2 budget unit," "CO_2 authorized account representative," and "continuous emissions monitoring system" (or "CEMS"), respectively, as defined in subsection 1(B) of this Chapter.

(1) Requirements for installation, certification, and data accounting. The owner or operator of each CO_2 budget unit must meet the following requirements.

(a) Install all monitoring systems required under this section for monitoring CO_2 mass emissions. This includes all systems required to monitor CO_2 concentration, stack gas flow rate, oxygen concentration, heat input, and fuel flow rate, as applicable, in accordance with 40 CFR 75.13, 75.71 and 75.72 and all portions of appendix G of 40 CFR Part 75.

(b) Successfully complete all certification tests required under subsection 4(B) of this Chapter and meet all other requirements of this section and 40 CFR Part 75 applicable to the monitoring systems under subsection 4(A)(1)(a) of this Chapter.

(c) Record, report and quality-assure the data from the monitoring systems under subsection 4(A)(1)(a) of this Chapter.

(2) Compliance dates. The owner or operator shall meet the monitoring system certification and other requirements of subsection (4)(A)(1)(a) through 4(A)(1)(c) of this Chapter on or before the following dates. The owner or operator shall record, report and quality-assure the data from the monitoring systems under subsection 4(A)(1)(a) of this Chapter on and after the following dates:

(a) The owner or operator of a CO_2 budget unit that commences commercial operation before July 1, 2008, must comply with the requirements of this section by the effective date of this regulation based on the criteria listed in subsection 1(A)(2) of this Chapter.

(b) The owner or operator of a CO_2 budget unit that commences commercial operation on or after July 1, 2008 must comply with the requirements of this section by the later of the following dates:

(i) The effective date of this regulation based on the criteria listed in subsection 1(A)(2) of this Chapter; or

(ii) The earlier of:

(A) 90 unit operating days after the date on which the unit commences commercial operation, or

(B) 180 calendar days after the date on which the unit commences commercial operation.

(c) For the owner or operator of a CO_2 budget unit for which construction of a new stack or flue installation is completed after the applicable deadline under subsection 4(A)(2)(a), 4(A)(2)(b) or 4(A)(2)(c) of this Chapter by the earlier of:

(i) 90 unit operating days after the date on which emissions first exit to the atmosphere through the new stack or flue; or

(ii) 180 calendar days after the date on which emissions first exit to the atmosphere through the new stack or flue.

(3) Reporting data

(a) Except as provided in subsection 4(A)(3)(b) of this Chapter, the owner or operator of a CO_2 budget unit that does not meet the applicable compliance date set forth in subsection 4(A)(2)(a), 4(A)(2)(b), and 4(A)(2)(c) of this Chapter for any monitoring system under subsection 4(A)(1)(a) of this Chapter shall, for each such monitoring system, determine, record, and report maximum potential (or as appropriate minimum potential) values for CO_2 concentration, CO_2 emissions rate, stack gas moisture content, fuel flow rate and any other parameter required to determine CO_2 mass emissions and heat input in accordance with 40 CFR 75.31(b)(2) or (c)(3), section 2.4 of appendix D of 40 CFR Part 75 or section 2.5 of appendix G of 40 CFR Part 75 as applicable.

(b) The owner or operator of a CO_2 budget unit that does not meet the applicable compliance date set forth in subsection 4(A)(2)(c) of this Chapter for any monitoring system under subsection 4(A)(1)(a) of this Chapter shall, for each such monitoring system, determine, record, and report substitute data using the applicable missing data procedures in Subpart D, or appendix D or appendix E of 40 CFR Part 75, in lieu of the maximum potential (or as appropriate minimum potential) values for a parameter if the owner or operator demonstrates that there is continuity between the data streams for that parameter before and after the construction or installation under subsection 4(A)(2)(c) of this Chapter.

(4) Prohibitions

   (a) No owner or operator of a CO_2 budget unit or a non-CO_2 budget unit monitored under 40 CFR 75.72(b)(2)(ii) shall use any alternative monitoring system, alternative reference method, or any other alternative for the required continuous emissions monitoring system without having obtained prior written approval in accordance with subsection 4(F) of this Chapter.

   (b) No owner or operator of a CO_2 budget unit or a non-CO_2 budget unit monitored under 40 CFR 75.72(b)(2)(ii) shall operate the unit so as to discharge, or allow to be discharged, CO_2 emissions to the atmosphere without accounting for all such emissions in accordance with the applicable provisions of this section and 40 CFR Part 75.

   (c) No owner or operator of a CO_2 budget unit or a non-CO_2 budget unit monitored under 40 CFR 75.72(b)(2)(ii) shall disrupt the continuous emissions monitoring system, any portion thereof, or any other approved emissions monitoring method, and thereby avoid monitoring and recording CO_2 mass emissions discharged into the atmosphere, except for periods of recertification or periods when calibration, quality assurance testing, or maintenance is performed in accordance with the applicable provisions of this section and 40 CFR Part 75.

   (d) No owner or operator of a CO_2 budget unit or a non-CO_2 budget unit monitored under 40 CFR 75.72(b)(2)(ii) shall retire or permanently discontinue use of the continuous emissions monitoring system, any component thereof, or any other approved emissions monitoring system under this section, except under any one of the following circumstances:

      (i) The owner or operator is monitoring emissions from the unit with another certified monitoring system approved, in accordance with the applicable provisions of this section and 40 CFR Part 75, by the Department for use at that unit that provides emissions data for the same pollutant or parameter as the retired or discontinued monitoring system; or

      (ii) The CO_2 authorized account representative submits notification of the date of certification testing of a replacement monitoring system in accordance with subsection 4(B)(4)(c)(i) of this Chapter.

B. Initial certification and recertification requirements

   (1) The owner or operator of a CO_2 budget unit shall be exempt from the initial certification requirements of this section for a monitoring system under subsection 4(A)(1)(a) of this Chapter if the following conditions are met:

      (a) The monitoring system has been previously certified in accordance with 40 CFR Part 75; and

      (b) The applicable quality-assurance and quality-control requirements of 40 CFR 75.21 and appendix B, appendix D and appendix E of 40 CFR Part

75 are fully met for the certified monitoring system described in subsection 4(B)(1)(a) of this Chapter.

(2) The recertification provisions of this section shall apply to a monitoring system under subsection 4(A)(1)(a) of this Chapter exempt from initial certification requirements under subsection 4(B)(1) of this Chapter.

(3) If the Administrator has previously approved a petition under 40 CFR 75.17(a) or (b) for apportioning the CO_2 emissions rate measured in a common stack or a petition under 40 CFR 75.66 for an alternative requirement in 40 CFR 75.12, 40 CFR 75.17 or Subpart H of 40 CFR Part 75, the CO_2 authorized account representative shall resubmit the petition to the Department under subsection 4(F)(1) of this Chapter to determine whether the approval applies under this program.

(4) Except as provided in subsection 4((B)(1) of this Chapter, the owner or operator of a CO_2 budget unit shall comply with the following initial certification and recertification procedures for a continuous emissions monitoring system and an excepted monitoring system under appendices D and E of 40 CFR Part 75 and under subsection 4(A)(1)(a) of this Chapter. The owner or operator of a unit that qualifies to use the low mass emissions excepted monitoring methodology in 40 CFR 75.19 or that qualifies to use an alternative monitoring system under Subpart E of 40 CFR Part 75 shall comply with the procedures in subsection 4(B)(5) or 4(B)(6) of this Chapter, respectively.

(a) Requirements for initial certification. The owner or operator shall ensure that each continuous emissions monitoring system required under subsection 4(A)(1)(a) of this Chapter (which includes the automated data acquisition and handling system) successfully completes all of the initial certification testing required under 40 CFR 75.20 by the applicable deadlines specified in subsection 4(A)(2) of this Chapter. In addition, whenever the owner or operator installs a monitoring system in order to meet the requirements of this section in a location where no such monitoring system was previously installed, initial certification in accordance with 40 CFR 75.20 is required.

(b) Requirements for recertification. Whenever the owner or operator makes a replacement, modification, or change in a certified continuous emissions monitoring system under subsection 4(A)(1)(a) of this Chapter that the Administrator or the Department determines significantly affects the ability of the system to accurately measure or record CO_2 mass emissions or heat input or to meet the quality-assurance and quality-control requirements of 40 CFR 75.21 or appendix B to 40 CFR Part 75, the owner or operator shall recertify the monitoring system according to 40 CFR 75.20(b). Furthermore, whenever the owner or operator makes a replacement, modification, or change to the flue gas handling system or the unit's operation that the Administrator or the Department determines to significantly change the flow or concentration profile, the owner or operator shall recertify the continuous emissions monitoring system according to 40 CFR 75.20(b). Examples of changes which require recertification include: replacement of the analyzer, change in location or orientation of the sampling probe or site, or changing of flow rate monitor polynomial coefficients.

(c) Approval process for initial certifications and recertification. Subsections 4(B)(4)(c)(i) through (iv) of this Chapter apply to both initial certification and recertification of a monitoring system under subsection 4(A)(1)(a) of this Chapter. For recertifications, replace the words "certification" and "initial certification" with the word "recertification," replace the word "certified" with "recertified," and follow the procedures in 40 CFR 75.20(b)(5) and (g)(7) in lieu of the procedures in subsection 4(B)(4)(c)(v) of this Chapter.

(i)   Notification of certification. The CO_2 authorized account representative shall submit to the Department or its agent, the appropriate EPA Regional Office and the Administrator a written notice of the dates of certification in accordance with subsection 4(D) of this Chapter.

(ii) Certification application. The CO_2 authorized account representative shall submit to the Department or its agent a certification application for each monitoring system. A complete certification application shall include the information specified in 40 CFR 75.63.

(iii) Provisional certification data. The provisional certification date for a monitor shall be determined in accordance with 40 CFR 75.20(a)(3). A provisionally certified monitor may be used under the CO_2 Budget Trading Program for a period not to exceed 120 days after receipt by the Department of the complete certification application for the monitoring system or component thereof under subsection 4(B)(4)(c)(ii) of this Chapter. Data measured and recorded by the provisionally certified monitoring system or component thereof, in accordance with the requirements of 40 CFR Part 75, will be considered valid quality-assured data (retroactive to the date and time of provisional certification), provided that the Department does not invalidate the provisional certification by issuing a notice of disapproval within 120 days of receipt of the complete certification application by the Department.

(iv) Certification application approval process. The Department will issue a written notice of approval or disapproval of the certification application to the owner or operator within 120 days of receipt of the complete certification application under subsection 4(B)(4)(c)(ii) of this Chapter. In the event the Department does not issue such a notice within such 120-day period, each monitoring system which meets the applicable performance requirements of 40 CFR Part 75 and is included in the certification application will be deemed certified for use under the CO_2 Budget Trading Program.

(A) Approval notice. If the certification application is complete and shows that each monitoring system meets the applicable performance requirements of 40 CFR Part 75, then the Department will issue a written notice of approval of the certification application within 120 days of receipt.

(B) Incomplete application notice. If the certification application is not complete, then the Department will issue a written notice of incompleteness that sets a reasonable date by which the CO_2 authorized account representative must submit the additional information required to complete the certification application. If the CO_2 authorized account representative does not comply with the notice of incompleteness by the specified date, then the Department may issue a notice of disapproval under subsection 4(B)(4)(c)(iv) of this Chapter. The 120 day review period shall not begin before receipt of a complete certification application.

(C) Disapproval notice. If the certification application shows that any monitoring system or component thereof does not meet the performance requirements of 40 CFR Part 75, or if the certification application is incomplete and the requirement for disapproval under subsection 4(B)(4)(c)(iv) of this Chapter is met, then the Department will issue a written notice of disapproval of the certification application. Upon issuance of such notice of disapproval, the provisional certification is invalidated by the Department and the data measured and recorded by each uncertified monitoring system or component thereof shall not be considered valid quality assured data beginning with the date and hour of provisional certification. The owner or operator shall follow the procedures for loss of certification in subsection 4(B)(4)(c)(v) of this Chapter for each monitoring system or component thereof, which is disapproved for initial certification.

(D) Audit decertification. The Department may issue a notice of disapproval of the certification status of a monitor in accordance with subsection 4(C)(2) of this Chapter.

(v) Procedures for loss of certification. If the Department issues a notice of disapproval of a certification application under subsection 4(B)(4)(c)(iv)(C) or a notice of disapproval of certification status under subsection 4(B)(4)(c)(iv)(D) of this Chapter, then:

(A) the owner or operator shall substitute the following values for each disapproved monitoring system, for each hour of unit operation during the period of invalid data beginning with the date and hour of provisional certification and continuing until the time, date, and hour specified under 40 CFR 75.20(a)(5)(i) or 40 CFR 75.20(g)(7):

(I) For units using or intending to monitor for CO_2 mass emissions using heat input or for units using the low mass emissions excepted methodology under 40 CFR 75.19, the maximum potential hourly heat input of the unit; or

(II) For units intending to monitor for CO_2 mass emissions using a CO_2 pollutant concentration monitor and a flow monitor, the maximum potential concentration of CO_2 and the maximum potential flow rate of the unit under section 2.1 of appendix A of 40 CFR Part 75.

(B) The CO_2 authorized account representative shall submit a notification of certification retest dates and a new certification application in accordance with subsections 4(B)(4)(c)(i) and (ii) of this Chapter; and

(C) The owner or operator shall repeat all certification tests or other requirements that were failed by the monitoring system, as indicated in the Department's notice of disapproval, no later than 30 unit operating days after the date of issuance of the notice of disapproval.

(5) Initial certification and recertification procedures for low mass emissions units using the excepted methodologies under 40 CFR 75.19. The owner or operator of a unit qualified to use the low mass emissions excepted methodology under 40 CFR 75.19 shall meet the applicable certification and recertification requirements of 40 CFR 75.19, 40 CFR 75.20(h) and subsection 4(B) of this Chapter. If the owner or operator of such a unit elects to certify a fuel flow meter system for heat input determinations, the owner or operator shall also meet the certification and recertification requirements in 40 CFR 75.20(g).

(6) Certification/recertification procedures for alternative monitoring systems. The CO_2 authorized account of each unit for which the owner or operator intends to use an alternative monitoring system approved by the Administrator and, if applicable, the Department under Subpart E of 40 CFR Part 75 shall comply with the applicable notification and application procedures of 40 CFR 75.20(f).

C. Out-of-control periods

(1) Whenever any monitoring system fails to meet the quality assurance and quality control requirements or data validation requirements of 40 CFR Part 75, data shall be substituted using the applicable procedures in Subpart D, appendix D, or appendix E of 40 CFR Part 75.

(2) Audit decertification. Whenever both an audit of a monitoring system and a review of the initial certification or recertification application reveal that any monitoring system should not have been certified or recertified because it did not meet a particular performance specification or other requirement under subsection 4(B) of this Chapter or the applicable provisions of 40 CFR Part 75, both at the time of the initial certification or recertification application submission and at the time of the audit, the Department or Administrator will issue a notice of disapproval of the certification status of such monitoring system. For the purposes of this paragraph, an audit shall be either a field audit or an audit of any information submitted to the Department or the Administrator. By issuing the notice of disapproval, the Department or Administrator revokes prospectively the certification status of the monitoring system. The data measured and recorded by the monitoring system shall not be considered valid quality-assured data from the date of issuance of the notification of the revoked certification status until the date and time that the owner or operator completes subsequently approved initial certification or recertification tests for the monitoring system. The owner or operator shall follow the initial certification or recertification procedures in subsection 4(B) of this Chapter for each disapproved monitoring system.

D. Notifications. The CO_2 authorized account representative for a CO_2 budget unit shall submit written notice to the Department and the Administrator in accordance with 40 CFR 75.61.

E. Recordkeeping and reporting

(1) General provisions. The CO_2 authorized account representative shall comply with all recordkeeping and reporting requirements in this section, the applicable record keeping and reporting requirements under 40 CFR 75.73 and with the requirements of subsection 6(A)(5) of this Chapter.

   (a) Unless otherwise provided, the owners and operators of the CO_2 budget source and each CO_2 budget unit at the source shall keep on site at the source each of the following documents for a period of 10 years from the date the document is created. This period may be extended for cause, at any time prior to the end of 10 years, in writing by the Department.

(i)   The account certificate of representation for the CO_2 authorized account representative for the source and each CO_2 budget unit at the source and all documents that demonstrate the truth of the statements in the account certificate of representation, in accordance with subsection 6(D) of this Chapter; provided that the certificate and documents shall be retained on site at the source beyond such 10-year period until such documents are superseded because of the submission of a new account certificate of representation.

(ii) All emissions monitoring information, in accordance with Section 4 of this Chapter.

(iii) Copies of all reports, compliance certifications, and other submissions and all records made or required under the CO_2 Budget Trading Program.

(iv) Copies of all documents used to complete a CO_2 budget license application, any other submission under the CO_2 Budget Trading Program, and all documents used to demonstrate compliance with the requirements of the CO_2 Budget Trading Program.

(b) The CO_2 authorized account representative of a CO_2 budget source and each CO_2 budget unit at the source shall submit the reports and compliance certifications required under the CO_2 Budget Trading Program, including those under Section 5 of this Chapter.

(2) Monitoring plans. The owner or operator of a CO_2 budget unit shall comply with requirements of 40 CFR 75.62.

(3) Certification applications. The CO_2 authorized account representative shall submit an application to the Department within 45 days after completing all initial certification or recertification tests required under subsection 4(B) of this Chapter including the information required under CFR 75.63 and 40 CFR 75.73 (c) and (e).

(4) Quarterly reports. The CO_2 authorized account representative shall submit quarterly reports, as follows:

(a) The CO_2 authorized account representative shall report the CO_2 mass emissions data and heat input data for the CO_2 budget unit, in an electronic format prescribed by the Department for each calendar quarter beginning with:

(i)   for a unit that commences commercial operation before July 1, 2008, the earlier of the calendar quarter covering January 1, 2009 through March 31, 2009 or the first full calendar quarter following the effective date of this regulation based on the criteria listed in subsection 1(A)(2) of this Chapter; or

(ii) for a unit commencing commercial operation on or after July 1, 2008, the calendar quarter corresponding to, the earlier of the date of provisional certification or the applicable deadline for initial certification under subsection 4(A)(2) of this Chapter or, unless that quarter is the third or fourth quarter of 2008, in which case reporting shall commence in the quarter covering January 1, 2009 through March 31, 2009 or the first full calendar quarter following the effective date of this regulation based on the criteria listed in subsection 1(A)(2) of this Chapter.

(b) The CO_2 authorized account representative shall submit each quarterly report to the Department or its agent within 30 days following the end of the calendar quarter covered by the report. Quarterly reports shall be submitted in the manner specified in Subpart H of 40 CFR Part 75 and 40 CFR 75.64. Quarterly reports shall include all of the data and information required in Subpart H of 40 CFR Part 75 for each CO_2 budget unit (or group of units using a common stack) as well as information required in Subpart G of 40 CFR Part 75, except for opacity and SO_2 provisions.

(c) Compliance certification. The CO_2 authorized account representative shall submit to the Department or its agent a compliance certification in support of each quarterly report based on reasonable inquiry of those persons with primary responsibility for ensuring that all of the unit's emissions are correctly and fully monitored. The certification shall state that:

  (i) the monitoring data submitted were recorded in accordance with the applicable requirements of this section and 40 CFR Part 75, including the quality assurance procedures and specifications; and

  (ii) for a unit with add-on CO_2 emissions controls and for all hours where data are substituted in accordance with 40 CFR 75.34(a)(1), the add-on emissions controls were operating within the range of parameters listed in the quality assurance/quality control program under appendix B of 40 CFR Part 75 and the substitute values do not systematically underestimate CO_2 emissions; and

  (iii) the CO_2 concentration values substituted for missing data under Subpart D of 40 CFR Part 75 do not systematically underestimate CO_2 emissions.

F. Petitions

(1) Except as provided in subsection 4(F)(3) of this Chapter, the CO_2 authorized account representative of a CO_2 budget unit that is subject to an Acid Rain emissions limitation may submit a petition under 40 CFR 75.66 to the Administrator requesting approval to apply an alternative to any requirement of this Chapter. Application of an alternative to any requirement of this Chapter is in accordance with this Chapter only to the extent that the petition is approved in writing by the Administrator, in consultation with the Department.

(2) The CO_2 authorized account representative of a CO_2 budget unit that is not subject to an Acid Rain emissions limitation may submit a petition under 40 CFR 75.66 to the Administrator requesting approval to apply an alternative to any requirement of this Chapter. Application of an alternative to any requirement of this Chapter is in accordance with this Chapter only to the extent that the petition is approved in writing by both the Department and the Administrator.

(3) The CO_2 authorized account representative of a CO_2 budget unit that is subject to an Acid Rain emissions limitation may submit a petition under 40 CFR 75.66 to the Administrator requesting approval to apply an alternative to a requirement concerning any additional CEMS required under the common stack provisions of 40 CFR 75.72 or a CO_2 concentration CEMS used under 40 CFR 75.71(a)(2). Application of an alternative to any requirement of this Chapter is in accordance

with this Chapter only to the extent the petition is approved in writing by both the Department and the Administrator.

G. CO$_2$ budget units that co-fire eligible biomass *[Reserved]*

H. Additional requirements to provide output data

(1) In a state that requires the use of information submitted to the Regional Transmission Organization (RTO) to document megawatt-hours (MWh) the CO$_2$ budget unit shall submit to the Department or its agent the same MWh value submitted to the RTO and a statement certifying that the MWh of electrical output reported reflects the total actual electrical output for all CO$_2$ budget units at the facility used by the RTO to determine settlement resources of energy market participants.

(2) A CO$_2$ budget unit in a state that requires gross output to be used that also reports gross hourly MW to the Administrator, shall use the same electronic data report (EDR) gross output (in MW), as submitted to the Administrator, for the hour times operating time in the hour, added for all hours in a year. A CO$_2$ budget unit that does not report gross hourly MW to the Administrator shall submit to the Department or its agent information in accordance with subsection 4(H)(5)(a) of this Chapter.

(3) A CO$_2$ budget unit in a state that requires net electrical output, shall submit to the Department or its agent information in accordance with subsection 4(H)(5)(a) of this Chapter. A CO$_2$ budget source whose electrical output is not used in RTO energy market settlement determinations shall propose to the Department a method for quantification of net electrical output.

(4) CO$_2$ budget sources selling steam should use billing meters to determine net steam output. A CO$_2$ budget source whose steam output is not measured by billing meters or whose steam output is combined with output from a non-CO$_2$ budget unit prior to measurement by the billing meter shall propose to the Department an alternative method for quantification of net steam output. If data for steam output is not available, the CO$_2$ budget source may report heat input providing useful steam output as a surrogate for steam output.

(5) Monitoring. The owner or operator of each CO$_2$ budget unit, in a state that requires the CO$_2$ budget unit's net output, must meet the following requirements. Each CO$_2$ budget source must provide a description of the net output monitoring approach in an output monitoring plan. The output monitoring plan application must include a description and diagram as stated below.

(a) Submit a diagram of the electrical and/or steam system for which output is being monitored, specifically including the following:

(i) If the CO$_2$ budget unit monitors net electric output, the diagram should contain all CO$_2$ budget units and all generators served by each CO$_2$ budget unit and the relationship between CO$_2$ budget units and generators. If a generator served by a CO$_2$ budget unit is also served by a non-affected unit, the non-affected unit and its relationship to each generator should be indicated on the diagram as well. The diagram should indicate where the net electric output is measured and should include all electrical inputs and outputs to and from the plant. If net electric output is determined using a billing meter, the diagram should show each billing meter used to determine net sales of electricity and should show that all electricity measured at the point of sale is generated by the CO_2 budget units.

(ii) If the CO_2 budget unit monitors net thermal output, the diagram should include all steam or hot water coming into the net steam system, including steam from CO_2 budget units and non-affected units, and all exit points of steam or hot water from the net steam system. In addition, each input and output stream will have an estimated temperature, pressure and phase indicator, and an enthalpy in Btu/lb. The diagram of the net steam system should identify all useful loads, house loads, parasitic loads, any other steam loads and all boiler feedwater returns. The diagram will represent all energy losses in the system as either usable or unusable losses. The diagram will also indicate all flow meters, temperature or pressure sensors or other equipment used to calculate gross thermal output. If a sales agreement is used to determine net thermal output, the diagram should show the monitoring equipment used to determine the sales of steam.

(b) Submit a description of each output monitoring system. The description of the output monitoring system should include a written description of the output system and the equations used to calculate output. For net thermal output systems descriptions and justifications of each useful load should be included.

(c) Submit a detailed description of all quality assurance/quality control activities that will be performed to maintain the output system in accordance with subsection 4(H)(7) of this Chapter.

(d) Submit documentation supporting any output value(s) to be used as a missing data value should there be periods of invalid output data. The missing data output value must be either zero or an output value that is likely to be lower than a measured value and that is approved as part of the monitoring plan required under this subsection.

(6) Initial Certification. A certification statement must be submitted by the CO_2 authorized account representative stating that either the output monitoring system consists entirely of billing meters or that the output monitoring system meets one of the accuracy requirements for non-billing meters listed in subsection 4(H)(6)(b) of this Chapter. This statement may be submitted with the certification application required under subsection 4(E)(3) of this Chapter.

(a) Billing Meters. The billing meter must record the electric or thermal output. Any electric or thermal output values that the facility reports must be the same as the values used in billing for the output. Any output measurement equipment used as a billing meter in commercial transactions requires no additional certification or testing requirements.

(b) Non-Billing Meters. For non-billing meters, the output monitoring system must either meet an accuracy of within 10% of the reference value, or each component monitor for the output system must meet an accuracy of within 3% of the full scale value, whichever is less stringent.

(i) The system approach to accuracy must include a determination of how the system accuracy of 10% is achieved using the individual components in the system and should include data loggers and any watt meters used to calculate the final net electric output data and/or any flow meters for steam or condensate, temperature measurement devices, absolute pressure measurement devices, and differential pressure devices used for measuring thermal energy.

(ii) A component approach to accuracy. If testing a piece of output measurement equipment shows that the output readings are not accurate to within 3.0 percent or less of the full scale value, then retest or replace the measurement equipment and meet that requirement. Data remain invalid until the output measurement equipment passes an accuracy test or is replaced with another piece of equipment that passes the accuracy test.

(7) Ongoing QA/QC. Ongoing quality assurance/quality control activities must be performed in order to maintain the output system.

(a) Billing Meters. In the case where billing meters are used to determine output, no QA/QC activities beyond what are already performed are required.

(b) Non-Billing Meters. Certain types of equipment such as potential transformers, current transformers, nozzle and venture type meters, and the primary element of an orifice plate only require an initial certification of calibration and do not require periodic recalibration unless the equipment is physically changed. However, the pressure and temperature transmitters accompanying an orifice plate will require periodic retesting. For other types of equipment, either recalibrate or re-verify the meter accuracy at least once every two years (i.e., every eight calendar quarters), unless a consensus standard allows for less frequent calibrations or accuracy tests. For non-billing meters, the output monitoring system must either meet an accuracy of within 10% of the reference value, or each component monitor for the output system must meet an accuracy of within 3% of the full scale value, whichever is less stringent. If testing a piece of output measurement equipment shows that the output readings are not accurate to within 3.0 percent of the full scale value, then the equipment should be repaired or replaced to meet that requirement.

(c) Out-of-control periods. If testing a piece of output measurement equipment shows that the output readings are not accurate to the certification value, data remain invalid until the output measurement equipment passes an accuracy test or is replaced with another piece of equipment that passes the accuracy test. Omit the invalid data and report either zero or an output value that is likely to be lower than a measured value and that is approved as part of the monitoring plan required under subsection 4(H)(5) of this Chapter.

(8) Recordkeeping and Reporting

(a) General provisions. The CO_2 authorized account representative shall comply with all recordkeeping and reporting requirements in subsection 4(H) of this Chapter and with the requirements of subsection 6(A)(5) of this Chapter.

(b) Recordkeeping. Facilities shall retain data used to monitor, determine, or calculate net generation for ten years.

(c) Annual reports. The CO_2 authorized account representative shall submit annual net output reports, as follows. The data must be sent both electronically and in hardcopy by March 1 for the immediately preceding control period to the Department or its agent. The annual report shall include unit level MWh, all useful steam output and a certification statement from the CO_2 authorized account representative stating the following, "I am authorized to make this submission on behalf of the owners and operators of the CO_2 budget sources or CO_2 budget units for which the submission is made. I certify under penalty of law that I have personally examined, and am familiar with, the statements and information submitted in this document and all its attachments. Based on my inquiry of those individuals with primary responsibility for obtaining the information, I certify that the statements and information are to the best of my knowledge and belief true, accurate, and complete. I am aware that there are significant penalties for submitting false statements and information or omitting required statements and information, including the possibility of fine or imprisonment."

5. Compliance Requirements

A. Compliance Certification Report

(1) Applicability and deadline. For each control period in which a CO_2 budget source is subject to the CO_2 budget emissions limitation, the CO_2 authorized account representative of the source shall submit to the Department by the March 1 following the relevant control period, a compliance certification report. A compliance certification report is not required as part of the compliance obligation during an interim control period.

(2) Contents of report. The CO_2 authorized account representative shall include in the compliance certification report under subsection 5(A)(1) of this Chapter the following elements, in a format prescribed by the Department:

(a) identification of the source and each CO_2 budget unit at the source;

(b) at the CO_2 authorized account representative's option, the serial numbers of the CO_2 allowances that are to be deducted from the source's compliance account under subsection 5(D) of this Chapter for the control period, including the serial numbers of any CO_2 offset allowances that are to be deducted subject to the limitations of subsection 5(D)(1)(c) of this Chapter; and

(c) the compliance certification under subsection 5(A)(3) of this Chapter.

(3) Compliance certification. In the compliance certification report under subsection 5(A)(1) of this Chapter, the CO_2 authorized account representative shall certify, based on reasonable inquiry of those persons with primary responsibility for operating the source and the CO_2 budget units at the source in compliance with the CO_2 Budget Trading Program, whether the source and each CO_2 budget unit at the source for which the compliance certification is submitted was operated during the calendar years covered by the report in compliance with the requirements of the CO_2 Budget Trading Program, including:

(a) whether the source was operated in compliance with the CO_2 budget emissions limitation;

(b) whether the monitoring plan applicable to each unit at the source has been maintained to reflect the actual operation and monitoring of the unit, and contains all information necessary to attribute CO_2 emissions to the unit, in accordance with Section 4;

(c) whether all the CO_2 emissions from the units at the source were monitored or accounted for through the missing data procedures and reported in the quarterly monitoring reports, including whether conditional data were reported in the quarterly reports in accordance with Section 4 of this Chapter. If conditional data were reported, the owner or operator shall indicate whether the status of all conditional data has been resolved and all necessary quarterly report resubmissions have been made;

(d) whether the facts that form the basis for certification under Section 4 of this Chapter of each monitor at each unit at the source, or for using an excepted monitoring method or alternative monitoring method approved under Section 4 of this Chapter, if any, have changed; and

(e) if a change is required to be reported under subsection 5(A)(3)(d) of this Chapter, specify the nature of the change, the reason for the change, when the change occurred, and how the unit's compliance status was determined subsequent to the change, including what method was used to determine emissions when a change mandated the need for monitor recertification.

B. Department Action on Compliance Certifications

(1) The Department or its agent may review and conduct independent audits concerning any compliance certification or any other submission under the CO_2 Budget Trading Program and make appropriate adjustments of the information in the compliance certifications or other submissions.

(2) The Department or its agent may deduct CO_2 allowances from or transfer CO_2 allowances to a source's compliance account based on the information in the compliance certifications or other submissions, as adjusted under subsection 5(B)(1) of this Chapter.

C. CO_2 Budget Unit Compliance Account Requirements

(1) The owners and operators of each CO_2 budget source and each CO_2 budget unit at the source shall hold CO_2 allowances available for compliance deductions under subsection 5(D) of this Chapter, as of the CO_2 allowance transfer deadline, in the source's compliance account in an amount not less than the total CO_2 emissions for the control period from all CO_2 budget units at the source less the CO_2 allowances deducted to meet the requirements of subsection 5(C)(2) of this Chapter, with respect to the previous two interim control periods, as determined in accordance with Sections 7 and 4 of this Chapter.

(2) The owners and operators of each CO_2 budget source and each CO_2 budget unit at the source shall hold CO_2 allowances available for compliance deductions under subsection 5(D) of this Chapter, as of the CO_2 allowance transfer deadline, in the source's compliance account in an amount not less than the total CO_2 emissions for the interim control period from all CO_2 budget units at the source multiplied by 0.50, as determined in accordance with Sections 7 and 4 of this Chapter.

(3) Each ton of CO_2 emitted in excess of the CO_2 budget emissions limitation for a control period shall constitute a separate violation of this Chapter and applicable state law.

(4) Each ton of excess interim emissions shall constitute a separate violation of this Chapter and applicable state law.

(5) A CO_2 budget unit shall be subject to the requirements under subsection 5(C)(1) of this Chapter starting on the later, of January 1, 2009, the first full calendar quarter following the effective date of this regulation based on the criteria listed in subsection 1(A)(2) of this Chapter, or the date on which the unit commences operation.

(6) CO_2 allowances shall be held in, deducted from, or transferred among CO_2 Allowance Tracking System accounts in accordance with Sections 2, 7, and 8, and with subsection 9(F) of this Chapter.

(7) A CO_2 allowance shall not be deducted, in order to comply with the requirements under subsection 5(C)(1) or (2) of this Chapter, for a control period or interim control period that ends prior to the year for which the CO_2 allowance was allocated. A CO_2 offset allowance shall not be deducted, in order to comply with the requirements under subsection 5(C)(1) or (2) of this Chapter, to cover emissions beyond the applicable percent limitations set out in subsection 5(D)(1)(c) of this Chapter.

(8) A CO_2 allowance under the CO_2 Budget Trading Program is a limited authorization to emit one ton of CO_2 in accordance with the CO_2 Budget Trading Program. No provision of the CO_2 Budget Trading Program, the CO_2 budget license application, or the CO_2 budget license or any provision of law shall be construed to limit the authority of the State to terminate or limit such authorization.

(9) A CO_2 allowance under the CO_2 Budget Trading Program does not constitute a property right.

D. Compliance Deductions

(1) Allowances available for compliance deduction. CO_2 allowances that meet the following criteria are available to be deducted for compliance with a CO_2 budget source's CO_2 budget emissions limitation for a control period or an interim control period.

    (a) The CO_2 allowances, other than CO_2 offset allowances, are of allocation years that fall within a prior control period, the same control period, or the same interim control period for which the allowances will be deducted.

    (b) The CO_2 allowances are held in the CO_2 budget source's compliance account as of the CO_2 allowance transfer deadline for that control period or interim control period or are transferred into the compliance account by a CO_2 allowance transfer correctly submitted for recordation under subsection 8(A) of this Chapter by the CO_2 allowance transfer deadline for that control period or interim control period.

    (c) For CO_2 offset allowances, the number of CO_2 offset allowances that are available to be deducted for compliance with a CO_2 budget source's CO_2 budget emissions limitation for a control period or interim control period may not exceed 3.3 percent of the CO_2 budget source's CO_2 emissions for that control period, or 0.50 times the CO_2 budget source's CO_2 emissions for an interim control period, as determined in accordance with Sections 7 and 4 of this Chapter.

    (d) The CO_2 allowances are not necessary for deductions for excess emissions for a prior control period under subsection 5(D)(4) of this Chapter.

(2) Deductions for compliance. Following the recordation, in accordance with subsection 8(B) of this Chapter, of CO_2 allowance transfers submitted for recordation in the CO_2 budget source's compliance account by the CO_2 allowance transfer deadline for a control period or interim control period, the Department or its agent will deduct CO_2 allowances available under subsection 5(D)(1) of this Chapter to cover the source's CO_2 emissions (as determined in accordance with Section 4 of this Chapter) for the control period or interim control period, as follows:

   (a) until the amount of CO_2 allowances deducted equals the number of tons of total CO_2 emissions (or 0.50 times the number of tons of total CO_2 emissions for an interim control period), determined in accordance with Section 4 of this Chapter, from all CO_2 budget units at the CO_2 budget source for the control period or interim control period; or

   (b) if there are insufficient CO_2 allowances to complete the deductions in subsection 5(D)(2)(a) of this Chapter, until no more CO_2 allowances available under subsection 5(D)(1) of this Chapter remain in the compliance account.

(3) Identification of available CO_2 allowances by serial number and default compliance deductions.

   (a) The CO_2 authorized account representative for a source's compliance account may request that specific CO_2 allowances, identified by serial number, in the compliance account be deducted for emissions or excess emissions for a control period or interim control period in accordance with either subsection 5(D)(2) or 5(D)(4) of this Chapter. Such identification shall be made in the compliance certification report submitted in accordance with subsection 5(A) of this Chapter.

   (b) The Department or its agent will deduct CO_2 allowances for a control period or interim control period from the CO_2 budget source's compliance account, in the absence of an identification or in the case of a partial identification of available CO_2 allowances by serial number under subsection 5(D)(3)(a) of this Chapter, in the following descending order:

      (i) any CO_2 allowances, other than CO_2 offset allowances, that are available for deduction under subsection 5(D)(1) of this Chapter and were allocated to the units at the source, in the order of recordation; and then

      (ii) any CO_2 allowances, other than CO_2 offset allowances, that are available for deduction under subsection 5(D)(1) of this Chapter and were allocated other than to units at the source and transferred and recorded in the compliance account pursuant to Section 8 of this Chapter, in the order of recordation; and then

      (iii) subject to the relevant compliance deduction limitations under subsection 5(D)(1)(c) of this Chapter, any CO_2 offset allowances transferred and recorded in the compliance account pursuant to Section 8 of this Chapter, in the order of recordation.

(4) Deductions for excess emissions

   (a) After making the deductions for compliance under subsection 5(D)(2) of this Chapter, the Department or its agent will deduct from the CO_2 budget source's compliance account a number of CO_2 allowances, allocated for allocation years that occur after the control period in which the source has excess emissions, equal to three times the number of the source's excess emissions. In the event that a source has insufficient CO_2 allowances to cover three times the number of the source's excess emissions, the source shall be required immediately to deposit sufficient allowances in its compliance account. No CO_2 offset allowances may be deducted to account for the source's excess emissions.

(b) Any CO_2 allowance deduction required under subsection 5(D)(4)(a) of this Chapter shall not affect the liability of the owners and operators of the CO_2 budget source or the CO_2 units at the source for any fine, penalty, or assessment, or their obligation to comply with any other remedy, for the same violation, as ordered under applicable State law. The following guidelines will be followed in assessing fines, penalties or other obligations.

  (i) For purposes of determining the number of days of violation, if a CO_2 budget source has excess emissions for a control period, each day in the control period constitutes a day in violation unless the owners and operators of the unit demonstrate that a lesser number of days should be considered.

  (ii) Each ton of excess emissions is a separate violation.

  (iii) For purposes of determining the number of days of violation, if a CO_2 budget source has excess interim emissions for an interim control period, each day in the interim control period constitutes a day in violation unless the owners and operators of the unit demonstrate that a lesser number of days should be considered.

  (iv) Each ton of excess interim emissions is a separate violation.

(c) The propriety of the Department's determination that a CO_2 budget source had excess emissions and the concomitant deduction of CO_2 allowances from that CO_2 budget source's account may be later challenged in the context of the initial administrative enforcement, or any civil or criminal judicial action arising from or encompassing that excess emissions violation. The commencement or pendency of any administrative enforcement, or civil or criminal judicial action arising from or encompassing that excess emissions violation will not act to prevent the Department or its agent from initially deducting the CO_2 allowances resulting from the Department's original determination that the relevant CO_2 budget source has had excess emissions. Should the Department's determination of the existence or extent of the CO_2 budget source's excess emissions be revised either by a settlement or final conclusion of any administrative or judicial action, the Department will act as follows.

  (i) In any instance where the Department's determination of the extent of excess emissions was too low, the Department will take further action under subsections 5(D)(4)(a) and (b) of this Chapter to address the expanded violation.

  (ii) In any instance where the Department's determination of the extent of excess emissions was too high, the Department will distribute to the relevant CO_2 budget source a number of CO_2 allowances equaling the number of CO_2 allowances deducted which are attributable to the difference between the original and final quantity of excess emissions. Should such CO_2 budget source's compliance account no longer exist, the CO_2 allowances will be provided to a general account selected by the owner or operator of the CO_2 budget source from which they were originally deducted.

E. Action by the Department on submissions

(1) The Department may review and conduct independent audits concerning any submission under the CO_2 Budget Trading Program and make appropriate adjustments of the information in the submissions.

(2) The Department may deduct CO_2 allowances from or transfer CO_2 allowances to a source's compliance account based on information in the submissions, as adjusted under subsection 5(D)(6)(a) of this Chapter.

6. CO_2 Authorized Account Representative Provisions

A. Authorization and responsibilities

(1) Except as provided under subsection 6(B) of this Chapter, each CO_2 budget source, including all CO_2 budget units at the source, shall have one and only one CO_2 authorized account representative, with regard to all matters under the CO_2 Budget Trading Program concerning the source or any CO_2 budget unit at the source.

(2) The CO_2 authorized account representative of the CO_2 budget source shall be selected by an agreement binding on the owners and operators of the source and all CO_2 budget units at the source.

(3) Upon receipt by the Department or its agent of a complete account certificate of representation under subsection 6(D) of this Chapter, the CO_2 authorized account representative of the source shall represent and, by his or her representations, actions, inactions, or submissions, legally bind each owner and operator of the CO_2 budget source represented and each CO_2 budget unit at the source in all matters pertaining to the CO_2 Budget Trading Program, notwithstanding any agreement between the CO_2 authorized account representative and such owners and operators. The owners and operators shall be bound by any decision or order issued to the CO_2 authorized account representative by the Department or a court regarding the source or unit.

(4) No CO_2 budget permit shall be issued, and no CO_2 Allowance Tracking System account shall be established for a CO_2 budget source, until the Department or its agent has received a complete account certificate of representation under subsection 6(D) of this Chapter for a CO_2 authorized account representative of the source and the CO_2 budget units at the source.

(5) Each submission under the CO_2 Budget Trading Program shall be submitted, signed, and certified by the CO_2 authorized account representative for each CO_2 budget source on behalf of which the submission is made. Each such submission shall include the following certification statement by the CO_2 authorized account representative: "I am authorized to make this submission on behalf of the owners and operators of the CO_2 budget sources or CO_2 budget units for which the submission is made. I certify under penalty of law that I have personally examined, and am familiar with, the statements and information submitted in this document and all its attachments. Based on my inquiry of those

individuals with primary responsibility for obtaining the information, I certify that the statements and information are to the best of my knowledge and belief true, accurate, and complete. I am aware that there are significant penalties for submitting false statements and information or omitting required statements and information, including the possibility of fine or imprisonment."

(6) The Department or its agent will accept or act on a submission made on behalf of owners or operators of a CO_2 budget source or a CO_2 budget unit only if the submission has been made, signed, and certified in accordance with subsection 6(A)(5) of this Chapter.

B. Alternate CO_2 authorized account representative

(1) An account certificate of representation may designate one and only one alternate CO_2 authorized account representative who may act on behalf of the CO_2 authorized account representative. The agreement by which the alternate CO_2 authorized account representative is selected shall include a procedure for authorizing the alternate CO_2 authorized account representative to act in lieu of the CO_2 authorized account representative.

(2) Upon receipt by the Department or its agent of a complete account certificate of representation under subsection 6(D) of this Chapter, any representation, action, inaction, or submission by the alternate CO_2 authorized account representative shall be deemed to be a representation, action, inaction, or submission by the CO_2 authorized account representative.

(3) Except in this section and subsections 6(A)(1), 6(C), 6(D), and 7(B) of this Chapter, whenever the term "CO_2 authorized account representative" is used in this Chapter, the term shall be construed to include the alternate CO_2 authorized account representative.

C. Changing the account certificate of representation

(1) Changing the CO_2 authorized account representative. The CO_2 authorized account representative may be changed at any time upon receipt by the Department or its agent of a superseding complete account certificate of representation under subsection 6(D) of this Chapter. Notwithstanding any such change, all representations, actions, inactions, and submissions by the previous CO_2 authorized account representative prior to the time and date when the Department or its agent receives the superseding account certificate of representation shall be binding on the new CO_2 authorized account representative and the owners and operators of the CO_2 budget source and the CO_2 budget units at the source.

(2) Changing the alternate CO_2 authorized account representative. The alternate CO_2 authorized account representative may be changed at any time upon receipt by the Department or its agent of a superseding complete account certificate of representation under subsection 6(D) of this Chapter. Notwithstanding any such change, all representations, actions, inactions, and submissions by the previous alternate CO_2 authorized account representative prior to the time and date when the Department or its agent receives the superseding account certificate of representation shall be binding on the new alternate CO_2 authorized account representative and the owners and operators of the CO_2 budget source and the CO_2 budget units at the source.

(3) Changes in the owners or operators

(a) In the event a new owner or operator of a CO_2 budget source or a CO_2 budget unit is not included in the list of owners and operators submitted in the account certificate of representation, such new owner or operator shall be deemed to be subject to and bound by the account certificate of representation, the representations, actions, inactions, and submissions of the CO_2 authorized account representative and any alternate CO_2 authorized account representative of the source or unit, and the decisions, orders, actions, and inactions of the Department, as if the new owner or operator were included in such list.

(b) Within 30 days following any change in the owners and operators of a CO_2 budget source or a CO_2 budget unit, including the addition of a new owner or operator, the CO_2 authorized account representative or alternate CO_2 authorized account representative shall submit a revision to the account certificate of representation amending the list of owners and operators to include the change.

D. Account certificate of representation

(1) A complete account certificate of representation for a CO_2 authorized account representative or an alternate CO_2 authorized account representative shall include the following elements in a format prescribed by the Department or its agent:

(a) identification of the CO_2 budget source and each CO_2 budget unit at the source for which the account certificate of representation is submitted;

(b) the name, address, e-mail address, telephone number, and facsimile transmission number of the CO_2 authorized account representative and any alternate CO_2 authorized account representative;

(c) a list of the owners and operators of the CO_2 budget source and of each CO_2 budget unit at the source;

(d) the following certification statement by the CO_2 authorized account representative and any alternate CO_2 authorized account representative: "I certify that I was selected as the CO_2 authorized account representative or alternate CO_2 authorized account representative, as applicable, by an agreement binding on the owners and operators of the CO_2 budget source and each CO_2 budget unit at the source. I certify that I have all the necessary authority to carry out my duties and responsibilities under the CO_2 Budget Trading Program on behalf of the owners and operators of the CO_2 budget source and of each CO_2 budget unit at the source and that each such owner and operator shall be fully bound by my representations, actions, inactions, or submissions and by any decision or order issued to me by the Department or a court regarding the source or unit."; and

(e) the signature of the CO_2 authorized account representative and any alternate CO_2 authorized account representative and the dates signed.

(2) Unless otherwise required by the Department or its agent, documents of agreement referred to in the account certificate of representation shall not be submitted to the Department or its agent. Neither the Department nor its agent shall be under any obligation to review or evaluate the sufficiency of such documents, if submitted.

E. Objections concerning the CO_2 authorized account representative

(1) Once a complete account certificate of representation under subsection 6(D) of this Chapter has been submitted and received, the Department and its agent will rely on the account certificate of representation unless and until the Department or its agent receives a superseding complete account certificate of representation under subsection 6(D) of this Chapter.

(2) Except as provided in subsections 6(C)(1) or (2) of this Chapter, no objection or other communication submitted to the Department or its agent concerning the authorization, or any representation, action, inaction, or submission of the CO_2 authorized account representative shall affect any representation, action, inaction, or submission of the CO_2 authorized account representative or the finality of any decision or order by the Department or its agent under the CO_2 Budget Trading Program.

(3) Neither the Department nor its agent will adjudicate any private legal dispute concerning the authorization or any representation, action, inaction, or submission of any CO_2 authorized account representative, including private legal disputes concerning the proceeds of CO_2 allowance transfers.

F. **Delegation of account representative responsibilities**

(1) A CO_2 authorized account representative may delegate, to one or more natural persons, his or her authority to make an electronic submission to the Department or its agent under this Chapter.

(2) An alternate CO_2 authorized account representative may delegate, to one or more natural persons, his or her authority to make an electronic submission to the Department or its agent under this section.

(3) In order to delegate authority to make an electronic submission to the Department or its agent in accordance with subsections 6(F)(1) and (2) of this Chapter, the CO_2 authorized account representative or alternate CO_2 authorized account representative, as appropriate, must submit to the Department or its agent a notice of delegation, in a format prescribed by the Department that includes the following elements:

(a) The name, address, e-mail address, telephone number, and facsimile transmission number of such CO_2 authorized account representative or alternate CO_2 authorized account representative;

(b) The name, address, e-mail address, telephone number and facsimile transmission number of each such natural person, herein referred to as the "electronic submission agent";

(c) For each such natural person, a list of the type of electronic submissions under either subsection 6(F)(1) or 6(F)(2) of this Chapter for which authority is delegated to him or her; and

(d) The following certification statements by such CO_2 authorized account representative or alternate CO_2 authorized account representative:

(i) "I agree that any electronic submission to the Department or its agent that is by a natural person identified in this notice of delegation and of a type listed for such electronic submission agent in this notice of delegation and that is made when I am a CO_2 authorized account representative or alternate CO_2 authorized account representative, as appropriate, and before this notice of delegation is superseded by another notice of delegation under CO_2 Budget Trading Program 06–096 Chapter XX(6)(F)(4) shall be deemed to be an electronic submission by me."

    (ii) "Until this notice of delegation is superseded by another notice of delegation under CO_2 Budget Trading Program 06–096 Chapter XX(6)(F)(4), I agree to maintain an e-mail account and to notify the Department or its agent immediately of any change in my e-mail address unless all delegation authority by me under CO_2 Budget Trading Program 06–096 Chapter XX(6)(F) of the is terminated."

(4) A notice of delegation submitted under subsection 6(F)(3) of this Chapter shall be effective, with regard to the CO_2 authorized account representative or alternate CO_2 authorized account representative identified in such notice, upon receipt of such notice by the Department or its agent and until receipt by the Department or its agent of a superseding notice of delegation by such CO_2 authorized account representative or alternate CO_2 authorized account representative as appropriate. The superseding notice of delegation may replace any previously identified electronic submission agent, add a new electronic submission agent, or eliminate entirely any delegation of authority.

(5) Any electronic submission covered by the certification in subsection 6(F)(3)(d)(i) of this Chapter and made in accordance with a notice of delegation effective under subsection 6(F)(4) of this Chapter shall be deemed to be an electronic submission by the CO_2 authorized account representative or alternate CO_2 authorized account representative submitting such notice of delegation.

7. CO_2 Allowance Tracking System

A. CO_2 Allowance Tracking System accounts

(1) Any person wishing to purchase or otherwise hold CO_2 allowances must open a compliance or general account.

(2) Nature and function of compliance accounts. Consistent with subsection 7(B)(1) of this Chapter, the Department or its agent will establish one compliance account for each CO_2 budget source. Allocations of CO_2 allowances pursuant to Section 2 of this Chapter and deductions or transfers of CO_2 allowances pursuant to subsections 5(B), 5(D), 7(F), or Section 8 of this Chapter will be recorded in the compliance accounts in accordance with this section.

(3) Nature and function of general accounts. Consistent with subsection 7(B)(2) of this Chapter, the Department or its agent will establish, upon request, a general account for any person. Transfers of CO_2 allowances pursuant to Section 8 of this Chapter will be recorded in the general account in accordance with this section.

B. Establishment of accounts

(1) Compliance accounts. Upon receipt of a complete account certificate of representation under subsection 6(D) of this Chapter, the Department or its agent will establish a compliance account for each CO_2 budget source for which the account certificate of representation was submitted.

(2) General accounts

    (a) Application for general account. Any person may apply to open a general account for the purpose of holding and transferring CO_2 allowances. An application for a general account may designate one and only one CO_2 authorized account representative and one and only one alternate CO_2 authorized account representative who may act on behalf of the CO_2 authorized account representative. The agreement by which the alternate CO_2 authorized account representative is selected shall include a procedure for authorizing the alternate CO_2 authorized account representative to act in lieu of the CO_2 authorized account representative. A complete application for a general account shall be submitted to the Department or its agent and may include, but not be limited to the following elements in a format prescribed by the Department or its agent:

(i) name, address, e-mail address, telephone number, and facsimile transmission number of the CO_2 authorized account representative and any alternate CO_2 authorized account representative;

(ii) at the option of the CO_2 authorized account representative, organization name and type of organization;

(iii) a list of all persons subject to a binding agreement for the CO_2 authorized account representative or any alternate CO_2 authorized account representative to represent their ownership interest with respect to the CO_2 allowances held in the general account;

(iv) the following certification statement by the CO_2 authorized account representative and any alternate CO_2 authorized account representative: "I certify that I was selected as the CO_2 authorized account representative or the CO_2 alternate authorized account representative, as applicable, by an agreement that is binding on all persons who have an ownership interest with respect to CO_2 allowances held in the general account. I certify that I have all the necessary authority to carry out my duties and responsibilities under the CO_2 Budget Trading Program on behalf of such persons and that each such person shall be fully bound by my representations, actions, inactions, or submissions and by any order or decision issued to me by the Department or its agent or a court regarding the general account.";

(v) the signature of the CO_2 authorized account representative and any alternate CO_2 authorized account representative and the dates signed; and

(vi) unless otherwise required by the Department or its agent, documents of agreement referred to in the application for a general account shall not be submitted to the Department or its agent. Neither the Department nor its agent shall be under any obligation to review or evaluate the sufficiency of such documents, if submitted.

(b) Authorization of CO_2 authorized account representative

(i) Upon receipt by the Department or its agent of a complete application for a general account under subsection 7(B)(2)(a) of this Chapter:

(A) The Department or its agent will establish a general account for the person or persons for whom the application is submitted.

(B) The CO_2 authorized account representative and any alternate CO_2 authorized account representative for the general account shall represent and, by his or her representations, actions, inactions, or submissions, legally bind each person who has an ownership interest with respect to CO_2 allowances held in the general account in all matters pertaining to the CO_2 Budget Trading Program, notwithstanding any agreement between the CO_2 authorized account representative or any alternate CO_2 authorized account representative and such person. Any such person shall be bound by any order or decision issued to the CO_2 authorized account representative or any alternate CO_2 authorized account representative by the Department or its agent or a court regarding the general account.

(C) Any representation, action, inaction, or submission by any alternate CO_2 authorized account representative shall be deemed to be a representation, action, inaction, or submission by the CO_2 authorized account representative.

(ii) Each submission concerning the general account shall be submitted, signed, and certified by the CO_2 authorized account representative or any alternate CO_2 authorized account representative for the persons having an ownership interest with respect to CO_2 allowances held in the general account. Each such submission shall include the following certification statement by the CO_2 authorized account representative or any alternate CO_2 authorized account representative: "I am authorized to make this submission on behalf of the persons having an ownership interest with respect to the CO_2 allowances held in the general account. I certify under penalty of law that I have personally examined, and am familiar with, the statements and information submitted in this document and all its attachments. Based on my inquiry of those individuals with primary responsibility for obtaining the information, I certify that the statements and information are to the best of my knowledge and belief true, accurate, and complete. I am aware that there are significant penalties for submitting false statements and information or omitting required statements and information, including the possibility of fine or imprisonment."

(iii) The Department or its agent will accept or act on a submission concerning the general account only if the submission has been made, signed, and certified in accordance with subsection 7(B)(2)(b)(ii) of this Chapter.

(c) Changing CO_2 authorized account representative and alternate CO_2 authorized account representative; changes in persons with ownership interest.

(i) The CO_2 authorized account representative for a general account may be changed at any time upon receipt by the Department or its agent of a superseding complete application for a general account under subsection 7(B)(2)(a) of this Chapter. Notwithstanding any such change, all representations, actions, inactions, and submissions by the previous CO_2 authorized account representative prior to the time and date when the Department or its agent receives the superseding application for a general account shall be binding on the new CO_2 authorized account representative and the persons with an ownership interest with respect to the CO_2 allowances in the general account.

(ii) The alternate CO_2 authorized account representative for a general account may be changed at any time upon receipt by the Department or its agent of a superseding complete application for a general account under subsection 7(B)(2)(a) of this Chapter. Notwithstanding any such change, all representations, actions, inactions, and submissions by the previous alternate CO_2 authorized account representative prior to the time and date when the Department or its agent receives the superseding application for a general account shall be binding on the new alternate CO_2 authorized account representative and the persons with an ownership interest with respect to the CO_2 allowances in the general account.

(iii) In the event a new person having an ownership interest with respect to CO_2 allowances in the general account is not included in the list of such persons in the application for a general account, such new person shall be deemed to be subject to and bound by the application for a general account, the representations, actions, inactions, and submissions of the CO_2 authorized account representative and any alternate CO_2 authorized account representative, and the decisions, orders, actions, and inactions of the Department or its agent, as if the new person were included in such list.

(iv) Within 30 days following any change in the persons having an ownership interest with respect to CO_2 allowances in the general account, including the addition of persons, the CO_2 authorized account representative or any alternate CO_2 authorized account representative shall submit a revision to the application for a general account amending the list of persons having an ownership interest with respect to the CO_2 allowances in the general account to include the change.

(d) Objections concerning CO_2 authorized account representative

(i) Once a complete application for a general account under subsection 7(B)(2)(a) of this Chapter has been submitted and received, the Department or its agent will rely on the application unless and until a superseding complete application for a general account under subsection 7(B)(2)(a) of this Chapter is received by the Department or its agent.

(ii) Except as provided in subsections 7(B)(2)(c)(i) and (ii) of this Chapter, no objection or other communication submitted to the Department or its agent concerning the authorization, or any representation, action, inaction, or submission of the CO_2 authorized account representative or any alternate CO_2 authorized account representative for a general account shall affect any representation, action, inaction, or submission of the CO_2 authorized account representative or any alternate CO_2 authorized account representative or the finality of any decision or order by the Department or its agent under the CO_2 Budget Trading Program.

(iii) Neither the Department nor its agent will adjudicate any private legal dispute concerning the authorization or any representation, action, inaction, or submission of the CO_2 authorized account representative or any alternate CO_2 authorized account representative for a general account, including private legal disputes concerning the proceeds of CO_2 allowance transfers.

(e) Delegation by CO_2 authorized account representative and alternate CO_2 authorized account representative.

   (i) A CO_2 authorized account representative may delegate, to one or more natural persons, his or her authority to make an electronic submission to the Department or its agent provided for under Sections 7 and 8 of this Chapter.

   (ii) An alternate CO_2 authorized account representative may delegate, to one or more natural persons, his or her authority to make an electronic submission to the Department or its agent provided for under Sections 7 and 8 of this Chapter.

   (iii) In order to delegate authority to make an electronic submission to the Department or its agent in accordance with subsections 7(B)(2)(d)(i) and (ii) of this Chapter, the CO_2 authorized account representative or alternate CO_2 authorized account representative, as appropriate must submit to the Department or its agent a notice of delegation, in a format prescribed by the Department that includes the following elements:

      (A) The name, address, e-mail address, telephone number, and facsimile transmission number of such CO_2 authorized account representative or alternate CO_2 authorized account representative;

      (B) The name, address, e-mail address, telephone number and facsimile transmission number of each such natural person, herein referred to as "electronic submission agent";

      (C) For each such natural person, a list of the type of electronic submissions under either subsection 7(B)(1) or 7(B)(2) of this Chapter for which authority is delegated to him or her; and

      (D) The following certification statements by such CO_2 authorized account representative or alternate CO_2 authorized account representative:

         (I) "I agree that any electronic submission to the Department or its agent that is by a natural person identified in this notice of delegation and of a type listed for such electronic submission agent in this notice of delegation and that is made when I am a CO_2 authorized account representative or alternate CO_2 authorized account representative, as appropriate, and before this notice of delegation is superseded by another notice of delegation under CO_2 Budget Trading Program 06–096 Chapter XX 6(B)(2)(e)(iv) shall be deemed to be an electronic submission by me."

         (II) "Until this notice of delegation is superseded by another notice of delegation under CO_2 Budget Trading Program 06–096 Chapter XX 7(B)(2)(e)(iv), I agree to maintain an e-mail account and to notify the Department or its agent immediately of any change in my e-mail address unless all delegation authority by me under CO_2 Budget Trading Program 06–096 Chapter XX 7(B)(2)(e) is terminated."

(iv) A notice of delegation submitted under subsection 7(B)(2)(e)(iii) of this Chapter shall be effective, with regard to the CO_2 authorized account representative or alternate CO_2 authorized account representative identified in such notice, upon receipt of such notice by the Department or its agent and until receipt by the Department or its agent of a superseding notice of delegation by such CO_2 authorized account representative or alternate CO_2 authorized account representative as appropriate. The superseding notice of delegation may replace any previously identified electronic submission agent, add a new electronic submission agent, or eliminate entirely any delegation of authority.

(v) Any electronic submission covered by the certification in subsection 7(B)(2)(e)(iii)(D)(I) of this Chapter and made in accordance with a notice of delegation effective under subsection 7(B)(2)(e)(iv) of this Chapter shall be deemed to be an electronic submission by the CO_2 authorized account representative or alternate CO_2 authorized account representative submitting such notice of delegation.

(3) Account identification. The Department or its agent will assign a unique identifying number to each account established under subsections 7(B)(1) or (2) of this Chapter.

C. CO_2 authorized account representative responsibilities. Following the establishment of a CO_2 Allowance Tracking System account, all submissions to the Department or its agent pertaining to the account, including, but not limited to, submissions concerning the deduction or transfer of CO_2 allowances in the account, shall be made only by the CO_2 authorized account representative for the account.

D. Banking. Each CO_2 allowance that is held in a compliance account or a general account will remain in such account unless and until the CO_2 allowance is deducted or transferred under subsections 5(B), 5(D), 7(F), or Section 8 of this Chapter. CO_2 allowances that are held in a compliance account or a general account may be used by a CO_2 budget unit to meet the requirements of this Chapter in any subsequent control period regardless of the year the CO_2 allowance originated.

E. Account error. The Department or its agent may, at its sole discretion and on his or her own motion, correct any error in any CO_2 Allowance Tracking System account. Within 10 business days of making such correction, the Department or its agent will notify the CO_2 authorized account representative for the account.

F. Closing of general accounts

(1) A CO_2 authorized account representative of a general account may instruct the Department or its agent to close the account by submitting a statement requesting deletion of the account from the CO_2 Allowance Tracking System and by correctly submitting for recordation under subsection 8(A) of this Chapter a CO_2 allowance transfer of all CO_2 allowances in the account to one or more other CO_2 Allowance Tracking System accounts.

(2) If a general account shows no activity for a period of six years or more and does not contain any CO_2 allowances, the Department or its agent may notify the CO_2 authorized account representative for the account that the account will be closed in the CO_2 Allowance Tracking System following 20 business days after the notice is sent. The account will be closed after the 20-day period unless

before the end of the 20-day period the Department or its agent receives a correctly submitted transfer of CO_2 allowances into the account under subsection 8(A) of this Chapter or a statement submitted by the CO_2 authorized account representative demonstrating to the satisfaction of the Department or its agent good cause as to why the account should not be closed.

8. CO_2 Allowance Transfer Provisions

A. Submission of CO_2 allowance transfers. The CO_2 authorized account representatives seeking recordation of a CO_2 allowance transfer shall submit the transfer to the Department or its agent. To be considered correctly submitted, the CO_2 allowance transfer shall include the following elements in a format specified by the Department or its agent:

(1) the numbers identifying both the transferor and transferee accounts;

(2) a specification by serial number of each CO_2 allowance to be transferred;

(3) the printed name and signature of the CO_2 authorized account representative of the transferor account and the date signed;

(4) the date of the completion of the last sale or purchase transaction for the allowance, if any; and

(5) the purchase or sale price of the allowance that is the subject of a sale or purchase transaction under subsection 8(A)(4) of this Chapter.

B. Recordation

(1) Within 5 business days of receiving a CO_2 allowance transfer, except as provided in subsection 8(B)(2) of this Chapter, the Department or its agent will record a CO_2 allowance transfer by moving each CO_2 allowance from the transferor account to the transferee account as specified by the request, provided that:

    (a) the transfer is correctly submitted under subsection 8(A) of this Chapter; and

    (b) the transferor account includes each CO_2 allowance identified by serial number in the transfer.

(2) A CO_2 allowance transfer that is submitted for recordation following the CO_2 allowance transfer deadline and that includes any CO_2 allowances that are of allocation years that fall within a control period or interim control period prior to or the same as the control period or interim control period to which the CO_2 allowance transfer deadline applies will not be recorded until after completion of the process of recordation of CO_2 allowance deductions for compliance in subsection 5(D)(2) of this Chapter.

(3) Where a CO_2 allowance transfer submitted for recordation fails to meet the requirements of subsection 8(B)(1) of this Chapter, the Department or its agent will not record such transfer.

C. Notification Requirements

(1) Notification of recordation. Within 5 business days of recordation of a CO_2 allowance transfer under subsection 8(B) of this Chapter, the Department or its agent will notify each party to the transfer. Notice will be given to the CO_2 authorized account representatives of both the transferor and transferee accounts.

(2) Notification of non-recordation. Within 10 business days of receipt of a CO_2 allowance transfer that fails to meet the requirements of subsection 8(B)(1) of

this Chapter, the Department or its agent will notify the CO_2 authorized account representatives of both accounts subject to the transfer of:

(a) a decision not to record the transfer, and

(b) the reasons for such non-recordation.

(3) Nothing in this section shall preclude the submission of a CO_2 allowance transfer for recordation following notification of non-recordation.

9. CO_2 Emissions Offset Projects

A. Purpose. The Department will provide for the award of CO_2 offset allowances to sponsors of CO_2 emissions offset projects that have reduced or avoided atmospheric loading of CO_2 equivalent or sequestered carbon as demonstrated in accordance with the applicable provisions of this section. The requirements of this section seek to ensure that CO_2 offset allowances awarded represent CO_2 equivalent emission reductions or carbon sequestration that are real, additional, verifiable, enforceable, and permanent within the framework of a standards-based approach. Subject to the relevant compliance deduction limitations of subsection 5(D)(1)(c) of this Chapter, CO_2 offset allowances may be used by any CO_2 budget source for compliance purposes.

B. General requirements

(1) Eligible CO_2 emissions offset projects. The Department may award CO_2 offset allowances to the sponsor of any of the following offset projects that have satisfied all the applicable requirements of this section.

(a) Offset project types. The following types of offset projects are eligible for the award of CO_2 offset allowances.

(i) Landfill methane capture and destruction;

(ii) Reduction in emissions of sulfur hexafluoride (SF_6);

(iii) Sequestration of carbon due to reforestation, improved forest management or avoided conversion;

(iv) Reduction or avoidance of CO_2 emissions from natural gas, oil, or propane end-use combustion due to end-use energy efficiency; and

(v) Avoided methane emissions from agricultural manure management operations.

(b) Offset project locations. Eligible offset projects may be located in any of the following locations:

(i) in any participating state; and

(ii) in any state or other United States jurisdiction in which a cooperating regulatory agency has entered into a memorandum of understanding with the Department to carry out certain obligations relative to CO_2 emissions offset projects in that state or U.S. jurisdiction, including but not limited to the obligation to perform audits of offset project sites, and report violations of this section.

(2) Project sponsor. Any person may act as the sponsor of an eligible CO_2 emissions offset project.

(3) General Additionality Requirements. Except as provided with respect to specific offset project standards in subsection 9(E) of this Chapter, the following general requirements shall apply.

(a) CO_2 offset allowances shall not be awarded to an offset project that is required pursuant to any local, state or federal law, regulation, or administrative or judicial order. If an offset project receives a consistency determination under subsection 9(D) of this Chapter and is later required by local, state or federal law, regulation, or administrative or judicial order, then the offset project shall remain eligible for the award of CO_2 offset allowances until the end of its current allocation period but its eligibility shall not be extended for an additional allocation period.

(b) CO_2 offset allowances shall not be awarded to an offset project that includes an electric generation component, unless the project sponsor transfers legal rights to any and all attribute credits (other than the CO_2 offset allowances awarded under subsection 9(F) of this Chapter generated from the operation of the offset project that may be used for compliance with a renewable portfolio standard or other regulatory requirement, to the Department or its agent.

(c) CO_2 offset allowances shall not be awarded to an offset project that receives funding or other incentives from any system benefit fund, or funds or other incentives provided through the consumer benefit or strategic energy purpose allocation required pursuant to subsection 2(F) of this Chapter.

(d) CO_2 offset allowances shall not be awarded to an offset project that is awarded credits or allowances under any other mandatory or voluntary greenhouse gas program, except for as described in subsection 9(D)(3)(j) of this Chapter.

(4) Maximum allocation periods for CO_2 emissions offset projects

(a) Maximum allocation periods. Except as provided in subsection 9(B)(4)(b) of this Chapter, the Department may award CO_2 offset allowances under subsection 9(F) of this Chapter for an initial 10-year allocation period. At the end of the initial 10-year allocation period, upon a showing by the project sponsor that the offset project continues to meet all applicable requirements of this section, the Department may award CO_2 offset allowances for a second 10-year allocation period. Prior to the expiration of the initial allocation period, the offset project sponsor must submit a consistency application pursuant to subsection 9(C) of this Chapter and receive a consistency determination from the Department pursuant to subsection 9(C)(5)(b) of this Chapter.

(b) Maximum allocation period. The Department may award CO_2 offset allowances under subsection 9(F) of this Chapter for any project involving reforestation, improved forest management or avoided conversion offset project for an initial 25-year allocation period. At the end of the initial 25-year allocation period or any subsequent crediting period, the Department may award CO_2 offset allowances for a subsequent 25-year allocation period, provided the offset sponsor has submitted a consistency application for the offset project pursuant to subsection 9(C) of this Chapter prior to the expiration of the initial allocation period, and the Department has issued a consistency determination pursuant to subsection 9(C)(5)(b) of this Chapter.

(5) Offset Project Audit. Project sponsors shall provide the Department or its agent access to the physical location of the offset project to inspect for compliance

with this section. For offset projects located in any state or other U.S. jurisdiction that is not a participating state, project sponsors shall also provide the cooperating Department with access to the physical location of the project to inspect for compliance with this section.

(6) Ineligibility due to noncompliance. If at any time the Department determines that a project sponsor has not complied with the requirements of this section, then the Department may revoke and retire any and all CO_2 offset allowances in the project sponsor's account. If at any time the Department determines that an offset project does not comply with the requirements of this section, then the Department may revoke any approvals it has issued relative to an offset project.

C. Application process

(1) Establishment of general account. The sponsor of an offset project must establish a general account under subsection 7(B)(2) of this Chapter. All submissions to the Department required for the award of CO_2 offset allowances under this section must be from the CO_2 authorized account representative for the general account of the sponsor of the relevant offset project, herein referred to as "project sponsor".

(2) Consistency application deadlines

(a) For offset projects not involving reforestation, improved forest management or avoided conversion the consistency application must be submitted by the date that is 6 months after the offset project is commenced..

(b) For offset projects involving reforestation, improved forest management or avoided conversion the consistency application must be submitted by the date that is one year after the offset project is commenced, except for as described in subsection 9(D)(3)(i) of this Chapter.

(c) Any consistency application that fails to meet the deadlines of subsection 9(C)(2) of this Chapter will result in the denial of the consistency application and the continued ineligibility of the subject offset project.

(3) Consistency application contents

(a) For an offset project, the consistency application must include the following information:

(i) The project's sponsor's name, address, e-mail address, telephone number, facsimile transmission number, and account number.

(ii) The offset project description as required by the relevant provisions of subsection 9(D) of this Chapter.

(iii) A demonstration that the offset project meets all applicable requirements set forth in this section.

(iv) The emissions baseline determination as required by the relevant provisions of subsection 9(D) of this Chapter.

(v) An explanation of how the projected reduction or avoidance of atmospheric loading of CO_2 or CO_2 equivalent or the sequestration of carbon is to be quantified, monitored, and verified as required by the relevant provisions of subsection 9(D) of this Chapter.

(vi) A completed consistency application agreement that reads as follows: "The undersigned project sponsor recognizes and accepts that the application for, and the receipt of, CO_2 offset allowances under the CO_2 Budget Trading Program is predicated on the project sponsor following all the requirements of Section 9 of this Chapter. The undersigned project sponsor holds the legal rights to the offset project, or has been granted the right to act on behalf of a party that holds the legal rights to the offset project. I understand that eligibility for the award of CO_2 offset allowances under Section 9 of this Chapter is contingent on meeting the requirements of Section 9 of this Chapter. I authorize the Department or its agent to audit this offset project for purposes of verifying that the offset project, including the monitoring and verification plan, has been implemented as described in this application. I understand that this right to audit shall include the right to enter the physical location of the offset project. I submit to the legal jurisdiction of Maine."

(vii) A statement and certification report signed by the offset project sponsor certifying that all offset projects for which the sponsor has received CO_2 offset allowances under this section (or similar provisions in the rules of other participating states), under the sponsor's ownership or control (or under the ownership or control of any entity which controls, is controlled by, or has common control with the sponsor) are in compliance with all applicable requirements of the CO_2 Budget Trading Program in all participating states.

(viii) A verification report and certification statement signed by an independent verifier accredited pursuant to subsection 9(E) of this Chapter that expresses that the independent verifier has reviewed the entire application and evaluated the following in relation to the applicable requirements at subsections 9(B) and 9(D) of this Chapter, and any applicable guidance issued by the Department.

    (A) The adequacy and validity of information supplied by the project sponsor to demonstrate that the offset project meets the applicable eligibility requirements of subsections 9(C) and 9(E) of this Chapter.

    (B) The adequacy and validity of information supplied by the project sponsor to demonstrate baseline emissions pursuant to the applicable requirements at subsection 9(D) of this Chapter.

    (C) The adequacy of the monitoring and verification plan submitted pursuant to the applicable requirements at subsection 9(D) of this Chapter.

    (D) Such other statements as may be required by the Department.

(ix) Disclosure of any voluntary or mandatory programs, other than the CO_2 Budget Trading Program, to which greenhouse gas emissions data related to the offset project has been, or will be reported.

(x) For offset projects located in a state or United States jurisdiction that is not a participating state, a demonstration that the project sponsor has complied with all requirements of the cooperating Department in the state or United States jurisdiction where the offset project is located.

(4) Place for filing consistency application

(a) For an offset project located in one participating state (in whole or in part), the consistency application must be filed with the appropriate Department in that State.

(b) For an offset project located wholly outside all participating states, the consistency application may be filed with the appropriate Department in any one participating state, provided a copy of the consistency application shall be filed with the cooperating Department in the state or United States jurisdiction where the offset project is located.

(c) For an offset project located in more than one participating state, the consistency application must be filed in the participating state where the larger part of the CO_2 equivalent emissions reduction or carbon sequestration due to the offset project is projected to occur.

(5) Department action on consistency applications

(a) Completeness determination. Within 30 days following receipt of the consistency application filed pursuant to subsection 9(C)(2) of this Chapter, the Department will notify the project sponsor whether the consistency application is complete. A complete consistency application is one that is in an approved form and is determined by the Department to be complete for the purpose of commencing review of the consistency application. In no event shall a completeness determination prevent the Department from requesting additional information in order to enable the Department to make a consistency determination under subsection 9(C)(5)(b) of this Chapter.

(b) Consistency determination. Within 90 days of making the completeness determination under subsection 9(C)(5)(a) of this Chapter, the Department will issue a determination as to whether the offset project is consistent with the requirements of subsections 9(B) and 9(C) of this Chapter and the requirements of the applicable offset project standard of subsection 9(D) of this Chapter. For any offset project found to lack consistency with these requirements, the Department will inform the project sponsor of the offset project's deficiencies.

D. CO_2 emissions offset project categories and associated standards

(1) Landfill methane capture and destruction. Offset projects that capture and destroy methane from landfills may qualify for the award of CO_2 offset allowances under this section, provided they meet the requirements of this subsection.

(a) Eligibility. Eligible landfill methane capture and destruction offset projects shall occur at landfills that are not subject to the New Source Performance Standards (NSPS) for municipal solid waste landfills, 40 CFR Part 60, Subpart Cc and Subpart WWW.

(b) Offset project description. The offset project sponsor shall provide a detailed narrative of the offset project actions to be taken, including documentation that the offset project meets the eligibility requirements of subsection 9(D)(1)(a) of this Chapter. The project narrative shall include the following information.

(i) Owner and operator of the offset project;

(ii) Location and specifications of the landfill where the offset project will occur, including waste in place;

(iii) Owner and operator of the landfill where the offset project will occur; and

(iv) Specifications of the equipment to be installed and a technical schematic of the offset project.

(c) Emissions baseline determination. The emissions baseline shall represent the potential fugitive landfill emissions of CH_4 (in tons of CO_2e), as represented by the CH_4 collected and metered for thermal destruction as part of the offset project. Baseline emissions of CH4 shall be calculated as follows:

Emissions (tons CO_2e) = $(V \times M \times (1 - OX) \times GWP)/2000$

where:

V = Volume of CH_4 collected (ft^3)

M = Mass of CH_4 per cubic foot (0.04246 lbs/ft^3 default value at 1 atmosphere and 20°C)

OX = Oxidation factor (0.10), representing estimated portion of collected CH_4 that would have eventually oxidized to CO_2 if not collected

GWP = CO_2e global warming potential of CH_4 (25)

(d) Calculating emissions reductions. Emissions reductions shall be determined based on potential fugitive CH_4 emissions that would have occurred at the landfill if metered CH_4 collected from the landfill for thermal destruction as part of the offset project was not collected and destroyed. CO_2e emissions reductions shall be calculated as follows:

Emissions Reductions (tons CO_2e) = $(V \times M \times (1 - OX) \times C_{ef} \times GWP)/2000$

where:

V = Volume of CH_4 collected (ft^3)

M = Mass of CH_4 per cubic foot (0.04246 lbs/ft^3 default value at 1 atmosphere and 20°C)

OX = Oxidation factor (0.10), representing estimated portion of collected CH_4 that would have eventually oxidized to CO_2 if not collected

C_{ef} = Combustion efficiency of methane control technology (0.98)

GWP = CO_2e global warming potential of CH_4 (25)

(e) Monitoring and verification requirements. Offset projects shall employ a landfill gas collection system that provides continuous metering and data computation of landfill gas volumetric flow rate and CH_4 concentration. Annual monitoring and verification reports shall include monthly volumetric flow rate and CH_4 concentration data, including documentation that the CH_4 was actually supplied to the combustion source. Monitoring and verification is also subject to the following requirements:

(i) The project sponsor shall submit a monitoring and verification plan as part of the consistency application that includes a quality assurance and quality control program associated with equipment used to determine landfill gas volumetric flow rate and CH_4 composition. The monitoring and verification plan shall also include provisions for ensuring that measuring and monitoring equipment is maintained, operated, and calibrated based on manufacturer recommendations, as well as provisions for the retention of maintenance records for audit purposes. The monitoring and verification plan shall be certified by an independent verifier accredited pursuant to subsection 9(E) of this Chapter.

(ii) The project sponsor shall annually verify landfill gas CH_4 composition through landfill gas sampling and independent laboratory analysis using applicable U.S. Environmental Protection Agency laboratory test methods.

(2) Reduction in emissions of sulfur hexafluoride (SF6). Offset projects that prevent emissions of sulfur hexafluoride to the atmosphere from equipment in the electricity transmission and distribution sector, through capture and storage, recycling, or destruction, may qualify for the award of CO_2 offset allowances under this section, provided they meet the requirements of this subsection.

(a) Eligibility

(i) Eligible offset projects shall consist of incremental actions beyond those taken during the baseline year to achieve a reduction in SF6 emissions relative to the baseline year. Eligible actions may include an expansion of existing actions. The identified actions to be taken shall be consistent with the guidance provided in High-voltage switchgear and control gear — Part 303: Use and handling of sulfur hexafluoride (SF_6) (IEC/TR 62271-303 ed1.) and Electric Power Research Institute (EPRI), SF6 Management for Substations (1020014 2010).

(ii) Except as provided in subsection 9(D)(2)(a)(iii) of this Chapter, eligible offset projects shall have an SF6 entity-wide emissions rate for the baseline year that is less than the applicable emissions rate in Table 1 [below]. The entity-wide SF6 emissions rate shall be calculated as follows:

SF_6 Emissions Rate (%) = (Total SF6 Emissions for Reporting Year) / (Total SF_6 Nameplate Capacity at End of Reporting Year)

where:

SF_6 Nameplate Capacity refers to all SF_6-containing equipment owned and/or operated by the entity, at full and proper SF_6 charge of the equipment rather than the actual charge of the equipment (which may reflect leakage).

(iii) An SF_6 offset project shall be eligible even if the SF_6 entity-wide emissions rate in the baseline year exceeds the applicable rate in subsection 9(D)(2)(a)(ii) of this Chapter, provided that the project sponsor demonstrates and the Department determines that the project is being implemented at a transmission and distribution utility serving a predominantly urban service territory and that at least two of the following factors prevent optimal management of SF_6.

(A) The entity is comprised of older than average installed transmission and distribution equipment in relation to the national average age of equipment.

(B) A majority of the entity's electricity load is served by equipment that is located underground, and poor accessibility of such un-

Table 1: SF$_6$ Emissions Rate Performance Standards

A. Emission Regions

Region A	Region B	Region C	Region D	Region E
Connecticut	Alabama	Colorado	Arkansas	Alaska
Delaware	District of Columbia	Illinois	Iowa	Arizona
Maine	Florida	Indiana	Kansas	California
Massachusetts	Georgia	Michigan	Louisiana	Hawaii
New Jersey	Kentucky	Minnesota	Missouri	Idaho
New York	Maryland	Montana	Nebraska	Nevada
New Hampshire	Mississippi	North Dakota	New Mexico	Oregon
Pennsylvania	North Carolina	Ohio	Oklahoma	Washington
Rhode Island	South Carolina	South Dakota	Texas	
Vermont	Tennessee	Utah		
	Virginia	Wisconsin		
	West Virginia	Wyoming		

B. Emissions Rate Performance Standards

Region	Emission Rate[a]
Region A	9.68%
Region B	5.22%
Region C	9.68%
Region D	5.77%
Region E	3.65%
U.S. (National)	9.68%

[a] Based on weighted average 2004 emissions rates for U.S. EPA SF6 Partnership utilities in 11 each region. If the weighted average emissions rate in a region is higher than the national weighted average, the default performance standard is the national weighted average emissions rate.

derground equipment precludes management of SF6 emissions through regular ongoing maintenance.

(C) The inability to take a substantial portion of equipment out of service, as such activity would impair system reliability.

(D) Required equipment purpose or design for a substantial portion of entity transmission and distribution equipment results in inherently leak-prone equipment.

(b) Offset project description. The offset project sponsor shall provide a detailed narrative of the offset project actions to be taken, including documentation that the offset project meets the eligibility requirements of subsection 9(D)(2)(a) of this Chapter. The offset project narrative shall include the following information.

(i) Description of the transmission and distribution utility suitable in detail to specify the service territory served by the entity.

(ii) Owner and operator of the transmission and distribution utility.

(c) Emissions baseline determination. If the consistency application is filed on or after January 1, 2009, baseline SF$_6$ emissions shall be determined based on annual entity-wide reporting of SF$_6$ emissions for the calendar year immediately preceding the calendar year in which the consistency application is filed (designated the baseline year). The reporting entity shall systematically track and account for all entity-wide uses of SF6 in order to determine entity-wide emissions of SF_6. The scope of such tracking and accounting shall include all electric transmission and distribution assets and all SF_6-containing and SF_6-handling equipment owned and/or operated by the reporting entity.

(i) Emissions (lbs.) shall be determined based on the following mass balance method:

SF_6 Emissions (lbs.) = (SF_6 Change in Inventory) + (SF_6 Purchases and Acquisitions) − (SF_6 Sales and Disbursements) − (Change in Total SF_6 Nameplate Capacity of Equipment)

where:

Change in Inventory is the difference between the quantity of SF6 gas in storage at the beginning of the reporting year and the quantity in storage at the end of the reporting year. The term "quantity in storage" includes all SF_6 gas contained in cylinders (such as 115-pound storage cylinders), gas carts, and other storage containers. It does not refer to SF_6 gas held in SF_6-using operating equipment. The change in inventory will be negative if the quantity of SF_6 gas in storage increases over the course of the year.

Purchases and Acquisitions of SF_6 is the sum of all the SF_6 gas acquired from other parties during the reporting year, as contained in storage containers or SF_6-using operating equipment.

Sales and disbursements of SF_6 is the sum of all the SF_6 gas sold or otherwise disbursed to other parties during the reporting year, as contained in storage containers and SF6-using operating equipment.

Change in Total SF_6 Nameplate Capacity of Equipment is the net change in the total volume of SF_6-containing operating equipment during the reporting year. The net change in nameplate capacity is equal to new equipment nameplate capacity, minus retired nameplate capacity. This quantity will be negative if the retired equipment has a total nameplate capacity larger than the total nameplate capacity of the new equipment. "Total nameplate capacity" refers to the full and proper SF_6 charge of the equipment rather than to the actual charge, which may reflect leakage.

(i) Emissions shall be calculated as follows:

Emissions (tons CO_2e) = $[(V_{iby} - V_{iey}) + (PA_{psd} + PA_e + PA_{rre}) - (SD_{op} + SD_{rs} + SD_{df} + SD_{sor}) - (CNP_{ne} - CNP_{rse})] \times GWP/2000$

where (all SF_6 values are in lbs.):

V_{iby} = SF_6 inventory in cylinders, gas carts, and other storage containers (not SF_6-containing operating equipment) at the beginning of the reporting year

V_{iey} = SF_6 inventory in cylinders, gas carts, and other storage containers (not SF_6-containing operating equipment) at the end of the reporting year

PA_{psd} = SF_6 purchased from suppliers or distributors in cylinders

PA_e = SF_6 provided by equipment manufacturers with or inside SF_6-containing operating equipment

PA_{rre} = SF_6 returned to the reporting entity after off-site recycling

SD_{op} = Sales of SF_6 to other parties, including gas left in SF_6-containing operating equipment that is sold

SD_{rs} = Returns of SF_6 to supplier (producer or distributor)

SD_{df} = SF_6 sent to destruction facilities

SD_{sor} = SF_6 sent off-site for recycling

CNP_{ne} = Total SF_6 nameplate capacity of new SF_6-containing operating

equipment at proper full charge CNP_{rse} = Total SF_6 nameplate capacity of retired or sold SF_6-containing operating equipment at proper full charge

GWP = CO_2e global warming potential of SF_6 (22,800)

(ii) As part of the consistency application required pursuant to subsections 9(C)(2) and (3) of this Chapter and in annual monitoring and verification reports required pursuant to subsections 9(F)(2) and (3) of this Chapter, the project sponsor shall provide the documentation required by subsections 9(D)(2)(e)(i) through (iii) of this Chapter to support emissions calculations.

(d) Calculating emissions reductions. Emissions reductions shall represent the annual entity-wide emissions reductions of SF6 for the reporting entity, relative to emissions in the baseline year. Emissions reductions shall be determined as follows, using the quantification method outlined in subsection 9(D)(2)(c)(ii) of this Chapter to determine emissions in both the baseline year and reporting year(s):

Emissions Reduction (tons CO_2e) = [(Total Pounds of SF_6 Emissions in Baseline Reporting Year) − (Total Pounds of SF_6 Emissions in Reporting Year)] × GWP/2000

where:

GWP = CO_2e global warming potential of SF_6 (22,800)

(e) Monitoring and verification requirements. The annual monitoring and verification report shall include supporting material detailing the calculations and data used to determine SF6 emissions reductions, and shall also provide the following documentation.

(i) The project sponsor shall identify a facility(ies) managed by the entity from which all SF_6 gas is procured and disbursed and maintain an entity-wide log of all SF_6 gas procurements and disbursals. The entity-wide log shall include the weight of each cylinder transported before shipment from the facility(ies) and the weight of each cylinder after return to the facility(ies). A specific cylinder log shall also be maintained for each cylinder that is used to fill equipment with SF_6 or reclaim SF_6 from equipment. The cylinder log shall be retained with the cylinder and indicate the location and specific identifying information of the equipment being filled, or from which SF$_6$ is reclaimed, and the weight of the cylinder before and after this activity. The cylinder log shall be returned with the cylinder to the facility when the activity is complete or the cylinder is empty.

(ii) A current entity-wide inventory of all SF$_6$-containing operating equipment and all other SF6-related items, including cylinders, gas carts, and other storage containers used by the entity. The inventory shall be reviewed by an independent verifier accredited pursuant to subsection 9(E) of this Chapter.

(iii) The project sponsor shall provide a monitoring and verification plan as part of the consistency application, which shall include an SF$_6$ inventory management and auditing protocol and a process for quality assurance and quality control of inventory data. The monitoring and verification plan shall be certified by an independent verifier accredited pursuant to subsection 9(E) of this Chapter.

(3) Sequestration of carbon due to reforestation, improved forest management or avoided conversion. Offset projects that involve reforestation, improved forest management or avoided conversion may qualify for the award of CO$_2$ offset allowances under this section, provided they meet all the requirements of this subsection and the forest offset protocol.

(a) Eligibility. Eligible forest offset projects shall satisfy all eligibility requirements of the forest protocol and this Subsection.

(b) Offset Project description. The offset project sponsor shall provide a detailed narrative of the offset project actions to be taken, including documentation that the offset project meets the eligibility requirements of subsection 9(D)(3)(a) of this Chapter. The offset project description must include all information identified in sections 8.1 and 9.1 of the forest offset protocol and any other information deemed necessary by the Department.

(c) Carbon sequestration baseline determination. Baseline onsite carbon stocks shall be determined as required by sections 6.1.1, 6.1.2, 6.2.1, 6.2.2, 6.2.3, 6.3.1 and 6.3.2 of the forest offset protocol, as applicable.

(d) Calculating carbon sequestered. Net GHG reductions and GHG removal enhancements shall be calculated as required by section 6 of the forest offset protocol. The project's risk reversal rating shall be calculated as required by Appendix D of the forest offset protocol.

(e) Monitoring and verification requirements. Monitoring and verification is subject to the following requirements:

(i) Monitoring and verification reports shall include all forest offset data reports submitted to the Department, including any additional data required by section 9.2.2 of the forest offset protocol.

(ii) The consistency application shall include a monitoring and verification plan certified by an independent verifier accredited pursuant to subsection 9(E) of this Chapter. The monitoring and verification plan shall consist of a forest carbon inventory program, as required by section 8.1 of the forest offset protocol.

(iii) Monitoring and verification shall be submitted not less than every six years, except that the first monitoring and verification report for reforestation projects must be submitted within twelve years of project commencement.

(iv) The applicant shall allow access to the offset project site to the accredited independent verifier, or as requested by the Department.

(f) Forest Offset Project Data Reports. A project sponsor shall submit a forest offset project data report to the Department for each reporting period. Each forest offset project data report must cover a single reporting period. Reporting periods must be contiguous; there must be no gaps in reporting once the first reporting period has commenced.

(g) Prior to the award of CO_2 offset allowances pursuant to subsection 9(F) of this Chapter, or to any surrender of allowances pursuant to subsection 9(D)(3)(h) of this Chapter, any quantity expressed in metric tons, or metric tons of CO_2 equivalent, shall be converted to tons using the conversion factor specified in definition of ton or tonnage in subsection 1(B) of this Chapter.

(h) Carbon Sequestration Permanence. The offset project shall meet the following requirements to address reversals of sequestered carbon:

(i) Unintentional reversals. Requirements for unintentional reversals are as follows:

(A) The project sponsor must notify the Department of the reversal and provide an explanation for the nature of the unintentional reversal within 30 calendar days of its discovery; and

(B) The project sponsor must submit to the Department a verified estimate of current carbon stocks within the offset project boundary within one year of the discovery of the unintentional reversal.

(ii) Intentional reversals. Requirements for intentional reversals are as follows:

(A) If an intentional reversal occurs, the project sponsor shall, within 30 calendar days of the intentional reversal:

I. Provide notice, in writing, to the Department of the intentional reversal; and

II. Provide a written description and explanation of the intentional reversal to the Department.

(B) Within one year of the occurrence of an intentional reversal, the project sponsor shall submit to the Department a verified estimate of current carbon stocks within the offset project boundary.

(C) If an intentional reversal occurs, and CO_2 offset allowances have been awarded to the offset project, the forest owner must surrender to the Department or its agent for retirement a quantity of CO_2 allowances corresponding to the quantity of CO_2 equivalent tons reversed within six months of notification by the Department.

I. Notification by the Department will occur after the verified estimate of carbon stocks has been submitted to the Department, or after one year has elapsed since the occurrence of the reversal if the project sponsor fails to submit the verified estimate of carbon stocks.

II. If the forest owner does not surrender valid CO_2 allowances to the Department within six months of notification by the Department, the forest owner will be subject to enforcement action and each CO_2 equivalent ton of carbon sequestration reversed will constitute a separate violation of this Chapter and applicable state law.

(D) Project Termination. Requirements for project termination are as follows:

I. The project sponsor must surrender to the Department or its agent for retirement a quantity of CO_2 Allowances in the amount calculated pursuant to project termination provisions in the forest offset protocol within six months of project termination.

II. If the project sponsor does not surrender to the Department or its agent a quantity of CO_2 Allowances in the amount calculated pursuant to project termination provisions in the forest offset protocol within six months of project termination, they will be subject to enforcement action and each CO_2 offset allowance not surrendered will constitute a separate violation of this Chapter and applicable state law.

(iii) Disposition of Forest Sequestration Projects After a Reversal. If a reversal lowers the forest offset project's actual standing live carbon stocks below its project baseline standing live carbon stocks, the forest offset project will be terminated by the Department.

(i) Timing of forest offset projects. The Department may award CO_2 offset allowances under subsection 9(F) of this Chapter only for forest offset projects that are initially commenced on or after January 1, 2014.

(j) Projects that Have Been Awarded Credits by a Voluntary Greenhouse Gas Reduction Program. The provisions of subsections 9(B)(3)(d) and 9(C)(2) of this Chapter shall not apply to forest projects that have been awarded credits under a voluntary greenhouse gas reduction program provided that the following conditions are satisfied. For such projects, the number of CO_2 offset allowances will be calculated pursuant to the requirements of subsection 9(D)(3) of this Chapter without regard to quantity of credits that were awarded to the project under the voluntary program.

(i) The project satisfies all other general requirements of Section 9 of this Chapter, including all specific requirements of subsection 9(D)(3), for all reporting periods for which the project has been awarded credits under a voluntary greenhouse gas program and also intends to be award CO_2 offset allowances pursuant to subsection 9(F) of this Chapter.

(ii) At the time of submittal of the consistency application for the project, the project submits forest offset data reports and a monitoring and verification report covering all reporting periods for which the project has been awarded credits under a voluntary greenhouse gas program and also intends to be awarded CO_2 offset allowances pursuant subsection 9(F) of this Chapter. Forest offset data reports and monitoring and verification reports must meet all requirements of subsection 9(D)(3)(f) of this Chapter.

(iii) The consistency application includes information sufficient to allow the Department to make the following determinations, and the voluntary greenhouse gas program has published information on its website to allow the Department to verify the information included in the consistency application.

(A) The offset project has met all legal and contractual requirements to allow it to terminate its relationship with the voluntary greenhouse gas program, and such termination has been completed.

(B) The project sponsor or voluntary greenhouse gas program has cancelled or retired all credits that were awarded for carbon sequestration that occurred during the time periods for which the project intends to be awarded CO_2 offset allowances pursuant to subsection 9(F) of this Chapter, and such credits were cancelled or required for the sole purpose of allowing the project to be awarded CO_2 offset allowances pursuant to subsection 9(F) of this Chapter.

(4) Reduction or avoidance of CO_2 emissions from natural gas, oil, or propane end-use combustion due to end-use energy efficiency. Offset projects that reduce CO_2 emissions by reducing on-site combustion of natural gas, oil, or propane for end-use in an existing or new commercial or residential building by improving the energy efficiency of fuel usage and/or the energy-efficient delivery of energy services may qualify for the award of CO_2 offset allowances under this section, provided they meet the requirements of this subsection. Eligible new buildings are limited to new buildings that are designed to replace an existing building on the offset project site, or new buildings designed to be zero net energy buildings.

(a) Eligibility

(i) Eligible offset projects shall reduce CO_2 emissions through one or more of the following energy conservation measures (ECMs):

(A) improvements in the energy efficiency of combustion equipment that provide space heating and hot water, including a reduction in fossil fuel consumption through the use of renewable energy;

(B) improvements in the efficiency of heating distribution systems, including proper sizing and commissioning of heating systems;

(C) installation or improvement of energy management systems;

(D) improvement in the efficiency of hot water distribution systems and reduction in demand for hot water;

(E) measures that improve the thermal performance of the building envelope and/or reduce building envelope air leakage;

(F) measures that improve the passive solar performance of buildings and utilization of active heating systems using renewable energy; and

(G) fuel switching to a less carbon-intensive fuel for use in combustion systems, including the use of liquid or gaseous renewable fuels, provided that conversions to electricity are not eligible.

(ii) Performance standards

(A) All end-use energy efficiency offset projects. All offset projects under this subsection shall meet the applicable performance criteria set forth in this clause.

I. Installation best practice. Any combustion equipment and related air handling equipment (HVAC systems) installed as part of an offset project shall be sized and installed in accordance with the applicable requirements and specifications outlined in this section.

1. Commercial HVAC systems shall meet the applicable sizing and installation requirements of ANSI/ASHRAE/IESNA Standard 90.1-(SI Edition)-2010: Energy Standard for Buildings Except Low-Rise Residential Buildings and ANSI/ASHRAE Standard 62.2-2010: Ventilation for Acceptable Indoor Air Quality.

2. Residential HVAC systems shall meet the applicable sizing specifications of Air Conditioner Contractors of America (ACCA) Manual J: Residential Load Calculation (Eight Edition-Full), and the applicable installation specifications ANSI/ACCA 5 QI—2007 "HVAC Quality Installation Specification".

II. Whole-building energy performance. New buildings or whole-building retrofits that are part of an offset project shall meet the requirements of this section.

1. Commercial buildings shall exceed the energy performance requirements of ANSI/ASHRAE/IESNA Standard 90.1(SI Edition)-2010: Energy Standard for Buildings except Low-Rise Residential Buildings by 30%, with the exception of multifamily residential buildings classified as commercial by ANSI/ASHRAE/IESNA Standard 90.1(SI Edition)-2010, which shall exceed these energy performance requirements by 20%.

2. Residential buildings shall exceed the energy performance requirements of the 2012 International Energy Conservation Code by 30%.

(B) Maximum market penetration rate for offset projects initiated on or after January 1, 2009. For offset projects initiated on or after January 1, 2009, the project sponsor shall demonstrate, to the satisfaction of the Department, that the energy conservation measures implemented as part of the offset project have a market penetration rate of less than 5%.

(b) Offset project description. The offset project sponsor shall provide a detailed narrative of the offset project actions to be taken, including documentation that the offset project meets the eligibility requirements of subsection

9(D)(4)(a) of this Chapter. The offset project narrative shall include the following information.

(i) Location and specifications of the building(s) where the offset project actions will occur;

(ii) Owner and operator of the building(s);

(iii) The parties implementing the offset project, including lead contractor(s), subcontractors, and consulting firms;

(iv) Specifications of equipment and materials to be installed as part of the offset project; and

(v) Building plans and offset project technical schematics, as applicable.

(c) Emissions baseline determination. The emissions baseline shall be determined in accordance with the requirements of this paragraph, based on energy usage (MMBtu) by fuel type for each energy conservation measure, derived using historic fuel use data from the most recent calendar year for which data is available, and multiplied by an emissions factor and oxidation factor for each respective fuel in Table 2 below.

Table 2 Emissions and Oxidation Factors

Fuel	Emissions Factor (lbs. CO_2/MMBtu)	Oxidation Factor
Natural Gas	116.98	0.995
Propane	139.04	0.995
Distillate Fuel Oil	161.27	0.99
Kerosene	159.41	0.99

(i) Isolation of applicable energy conservation measure baseline. The baseline energy usage of the application to be targeted by the energy conservation measure shall be isolated in a manner consistent with the guidance at subsection 9(D)(4)(e) of this Chapter.

(ii) Annual baseline energy usage shall be determined as follows:

Energy Usage (MMBtu) = $\text{BEU}_{\text{AECM}} \times A$

where:

BEU_{AECM} = Annual pre-installation baseline energy use by fuel type (MMBtu) attributable to the application(s) to be targeted by the energy conservation measure(s). If applicable building codes or equipment standards require that equipment or materials installed as part of the offset project meet certain minimum energy performance requirements, baseline energy usage for the application shall assume that equipment or materials are installed that meet such minimum requirements. For offset projects that replace existing combustion equipment, the assumed minimum energy performance required by applicable building codes or equipment standards shall be that which applies to new equipment that uses the same fuel type as the equipment being replaced. Baseline energy usage shall be determined in accordance with the applicable requirements at subsection 9(D)(4)(e) of this Chapter.

A = Adjustments to account for differing conditions during the two time periods (pre-installation and post-installation), such as weather, building occupancy, and changes in building use or function. Adjustments shall be determined in accordance with the applicable requirements of subsection 9(D)(4)(e) of this Chapter.

(iii) Annual baseline emissions shall be determined as follows:

$$\text{Emissions (lbs. } CO_2) = \sum_{i=1}^{n} BEU_i \times EF_i \times OF_i$$

where:

BEU_i = Annual baseline energy usage for fuel type i (MMBtu) demonstrated pursuant to the requirements of subsection 9(D)(4)(e)(i) through (iv) of this Chapter.

EF_i = Emissions factor (lbs. CO_2/MMBtu) for fuel type i listed at subsection 9(D)(4)(c), Table 2 of this Chapter.

OF_i = Oxidation factor for fuel type i listed at subsection 9(D)(4)(c), Table 2 of this Chapter.

(d) Calculating emissions reductions. Emissions reductions shall be determined based upon annual energy savings by fuel type (MMBtu) for each energy conservation measure, multiplied by the emissions factor and oxidation factor for the respective fuel type at subsection 9(D)(4)(c), Table 2 of this Chapter.

(i) Annual energy savings shall be determined as follows:

$$\text{Energy Savings (MMBtu)} = (BEU_{AECM} \times A) - (PIEU_{ECM} \times A)$$

where:

$BEUA_{ECM}$ = Annual pre-installation baseline energy use by fuel type (MMBtu) calculated pursuant to subsections 9(D)(4)(e)(i) through (iv) of this Chapter.

$PIEU_{ECM}$ = Annual post-installation energy use by fuel type (MMBtu) attributable to the energy conservation measure. Post-installation energy usage shall be determined in accordance with the applicable requirements at subsections 9(D)(4)(e)(i) through (iv) of this Chapter.

A = Adjustments to account for any differing conditions during the two time periods (pre-installation and post-installation), such as weather, building occupancy, and changes in building use or function. Adjustments shall be determined in accordance with the applicable requirements at subsection 9(D)(4)(e) of this Chapter.

(ii) Annual emissions reductions shall be determined as follows:

$$\text{Emissions (lbs. } CO_2) = \sum_{i=1}^{n} ES_i \times EF_i \times OF_i$$

where:

ES_i = Energy savings for fuel type i (MMBtu) demonstrated pursuant to the requirements at subsection 9(D)(4)(e) of this Chapter.

EF_i = Emissions factor (lbs. CO_2/MMBtu) for fuel type i listed at subsection 9(D)(4)(c), Table 2 of this Chapter.

OF_i = Oxidation factor for fuel type i listed at subsection 9(D)(4)(c), Table 2 of this Chapter.

(e) Monitoring and verification requirements. As part of the consistency application, the project sponsor shall provide a monitoring and verification plan certified by an independent verifier accredited pursuant to subsection 9(E) of this Chapter. Monitoring and verification reports shall be certified by an independent verifier accredited pursuant to subsection 9(E) of this Chapter. Independent verifiers must conduct a site audit when reviewing the first monitoring and verification report submitted by the project sponsor, except for offset projects that save less than 1,500 MMBtu per year. For offset projects that save less than 1,500 MMBtu per year, the project sponsor must provide the independent verifier with equipment specifications and copies of equipment invoices and other relevant offset project-related invoices. All offset project documentation, including the consistency application and monitoring and verification reports, shall be signed by a Professional Engineer, identified by license number. Monitoring and verification shall also meet the following requirements:

(i) General energy measurement and verification requirements. Monitoring and verification of energy usage shall be demonstrated through a documented process consistent with the following protocols and procedures, as applicable:

(A) For existing commercial buildings, determination of baseline energy usage shall be consistent with the International Performance Measurement & Verification Protocol, Volume I: Concepts and Options for Determining Energy and Water Savings (IPMVP), "Option B. Retrofit Isolation" and "Option D. Calibrated Simulation." If a building project involves only energy conservation measures implemented as part of a CO_2 emissions offset project, a process consistent with IPMVP "Option C. Whole Facility" may be used, as applicable. Application of the IPMVP general guidance shall be consistent with the applicable detailed specifications in ASHRAE Guideline 14-2002, Measurement of Energy and Demand Savings.

(B) For new commercial buildings, determination of baseline energy usage shall be consistent with the International Performance Measurement & Verification Protocol, Volume III: Concepts and Options for Determining Energy Savings in New Construction (IPMVP), "Option D. Calibrated Simulation." Application of the IPMVP general guidance shall be consistent with the applicable detailed specifications in ASHRAE Guideline 14-2002, Measurement of Energy and Demand Savings.

(C) For existing and new residential buildings, determination of baseline energy usage shall be consistent with the requirements of the RESNET National Energy Rating Technical Standards and National Home Energy Rating Technical Guidelines, 2013 (Chapter 3 and Appendix A of 2013 Mortgage Industry National Home Energy Rating System Standards).

(ii) Isolation of applicable energy conservation measure. In calculating both baseline energy usage and energy savings, the applicant shall isolate the impact of each eligible energy conservation measure (ECM), either through direct metering or energy simulation modeling. For offset projects with multiple ECMs, and where individual ECMs can affect the performance of others, the sum of energy savings due to individual ECMs shall be adjusted to account for the interaction of ECMs. For commercial buildings, this process shall be consistent with the requirements of ASHRAE Guideline 14-2002, Measurement of Energy and Demand Savings, and ANSI/ASHRAE/IESNA Standard 90.1-(SI Edition)-2010: Energy Standard for Buildings Except Low-Rise Residential Buildings. For residential buildings, this process shall be consistent with the re-quirements of RESNET National Home Energy Rating Technical Guidelines, 2006 (Chapter 3 and Appendix A of 2006 Mortgage Industry National Home Energy Rating System Standards) and adopted enhancements dated 2007-2012. Reductions in energy usage due to the energy conservation measure shall be based upon actual energy usage data. Energy simulation modeling shall only be used to determine the relative percentage contribution to total fuel usage (for each respective fuel type) of the application targeted by the energy conservation measure.

(iii) Calculation of energy savings. Annual energy savings are to be determined based on the following:

Energy Savings (MMBtu) = $(\text{BEU}_{\text{AECM}} \times \text{A}) - (\text{PIEU}_{\text{ECM}} \times \text{A})$

where:

BEU_{AECM} = Annual pre-installation baseline energy use by fuel type (MMBtu) attributable to the application(s) to be targeted by the en-ergy conservation measure(s), based upon annual fuel usage data for the most recent calendar year for which data is available. For new buildings, baseline energy use for a reference building equiva-lent in basic configuration, orientation, and location to the building in which the eligible energy conservation measure(s) is imple-mented shall be determined according to ASHRAE Guideline 14-2002, Measurement of Energy and Demand Savings and ANSI/ASHRAE/IESNA Standard 90.1- (SI Edition)-2010, Section 11 and Appendix G. Where energy simulation modeling is used to evaluate an existing building, modeling shall be conducted in accor-dance with ASHRAE Guideline 14-2002, Measurement of Energy and Demand Savings, and ANSI/ASHRAE/IESNA Standard 90.1-(SI Edition)-2010, Section 11 and Appendix G. For existing and new residential buildings, energy simulation modeling shall be con-ducted in accordance with the requirements of RESNET National Home Energy Rating Technical Guidelines, 2006 (Chapter 3 and Appendix A of 2006 Mortgage Industry National Home Energy Rat-ing System Standards and adopted enhancements dated 2007-2012).

PIEU_{ECM} = Annual post-installation energy use by fuel type (MMBtu) attributable to the energy conservation measure, to be verified based on annual energy use after installation of the energy conservation measure(s), consistent with the requirements of ASHRAE Guideline 14-2002, Measurement of Energy and Demand Savings. Where energy simulation modeling is used to evaluate a new or existing building, modeling shall be conducted in accordance with ASHRAE Guideline 14-2002, Measurement of Energy and Demand Savings, and ANSI/ASHRAE/IESNA Standard 90.1-(SI Edition)-2010, Section 11 and Appendix G. For existing and new residential buildings, energy simulation modeling shall be consistent with the requirements of RESNET National Home Energy Rating Technical Guidelines, 2006 (Chapter 3 and Appendix A of 2006 Mortgage Industry National Home Energy Rating System Standards and adopted enhancements dated 2007-2012).

A = Adjustments to account for any differing conditions during the two time periods (pre-installation and post-installation), such as weather (weather normalized energy usage based on heating and cooling degree days), building occupancy, and changes in building use or function. For commercial buildings, adjustments shall be consistent with the specifications of ASHRAE Guideline 14-2002, Measurement of Energy and Demand Savings, and ANSI/ASHRAE/IESNA Standard 90.1- (SI Edition)-2010, Section 11 and Appendix G. For residential buildings, adjustments shall be consistent with the specifications of RESNET National Home Energy Rating Technical Guidelines, 2006 (Chapter 3 and Appendix A of 2006 Mortgage Industry National Home Energy Rating System Standards and adopted enhancements dated 2007-2012).

(iv) Provision for sampling of multiple like offset projects in residential buildings. Offset projects that implement similar measures in multiple residential buildings may employ representative sampling of buildings to determine aggregate baseline energy usage and energy savings. Sampling protocols shall employ sound statistical methods. Any sampling plan shall be certified by an independent verifier, accredited pursuant to subsection 9(E) of this Chapter.

(5) Avoided methane emissions from agricultural manure management operations. Offset projects that capture and destroy methane from animal manure using anaerobic digesters may qualify for the award of CO_2 offset allowances under this section, provided they meet the requirements of this subsection.

(a) Eligibility

(i) CO_2 offset allowances may be awarded for the destruction of that portion of methane generated by the anaerobic digester that would have been generated in the absence of the offset project through the uncontrolled anaerobic storage of manure, or organic food wastes.

(ii) Eligible offset projects shall employ only manure-based anaerobic digester systems using livestock manure as the majority of digester feedstock, defined as more than 50% of the mass input into the digester on an annual basis. Organic food wastes used by an anaerobic digester shall only be that which would have been stored in anaerobic conditions in the absence of the offset project.

(iii) The provisions of subsections 9(B)(3)(b) and (c) of this Chapter shall not apply to agricultural manure methane offset projects provided either of the following requirements are met.

(A) The offset project is located in a state that has a market penetration for anaerobic digester projects of 5% or less. The market penetration determination shall utilize the most recent market data available at the time of submission of the consistency application pursuant to subsection 9(C) of this Chapter and shall be determined as follows:

$$MP\ (\%) = MG_{AD} / MG_{STATE}$$

where:

MG_{AD} = Average annual manure generation for the number of dairy cows and swine serving all anaerobic digester projects in the applicable state at the time of submission of a consistency application pursuant to subsection 9(C) of this Chapter.

MG_{STATE} = average annual manure production of all dairy cows and swine in the state at the time of submission of a consistency application pursuant to subsection 9(C) of this Chapter.

(B) The offset project is located at a farm with 4,000 or less head of dairy cows, or a farm with equivalent animal units, assuming an average live weight for dairy cows (lbs./cow) of 1,400 lbs., or, if the project is a regional-type digester, total annual manure input to the digester is designed to be less than the average annual manure produced by a farm with 4,000 or less head of dairy cows, or a farm with equivalent animal units, assuming an average live weight for dairy cows (lbs./cow) of 1,400 lbs.

(b) Offset project description. The offset project sponsor shall provide a detailed narrative of the offset project actions to be taken, including documentation that the offset project meets the eligibility requirements of subsection 9(D)(5)(a) of this Chapter. The offset project narrative shall include the following information.

(i) Owner and operator of the offset project;

(ii) Location and specifications of the facility where the offset project will occur;

(iii) Owner and operator of the facility where the offset project will occur;

(iv) Specifications of the equipment to be installed and a technical schematic of the offset project; and

(v) Location and specifications of the facilities from which anaerobic digester influent will be received, if different from the facility where the offset project will occur.

(c) Emissions baseline determination. The emissions baseline shall represent the potential emissions of the CH_4 that would have been produced in a baseline scenario under uncontrolled anaerobic storage conditions and released directly to the atmosphere in the absence of the offset project.

(vi)[sic] Baseline CH_4 emissions shall be calculated as follows:

$$CO_2e\ (tons) = (V_m \times M)/2000 \times GWP$$

where:

CO_2e = Potential CO_2e emissions due to calculated CH_4 production under site-specific anaerobic storage and weather conditions

V_m = Volume of CH_4 produced each month from degradation of volatile solids in a baseline uncontrolled anaerobic storage scenario under site-specific storage and weather conditions for the facility at which the manure is generated (ft^3)

M = Mass of CH_4 per cubic foot (0.04246 lb/ft^3 default value at one atmosphere and 20°C) GWP = Global warming potential of CH_4 (25)

(ii) The estimated amount of volatile solids degraded each month under the uncontrolled anaerobic storage baseline scenario (kg) shall be calculated as follows:

$$VS_{deg} = VS_{avail} * f$$

where:

VS = volatile solids as determined from the equation:

$$VS = M_m \times TS_\% \times VS_\%$$

where:

M_m = mass of manure produced per month (kg)

$TS_\%$ = concentration (percent) of total solids in manure as determined through EPA 160.3 testing method

$VS_\%$ = concentration (percent) of volatile solids in total solids as determined through EPA 160.4 testing method (USEPA Method Number 160.4, Methods for the Chemical Analysis of Water and Wastes (MCAWW) (EPA/600/4-79/020))

VS_{avail} = volatile solids available for degradation in manure storage each month as determined from the equation:

$$VS_{avail} = VS_p + 1/2\ VS_{in} - VS_{out}$$

where:

VS_p = volatile solids present in manure storage at beginning of month (left over from previous month) (kg)

VS_{in} = volatile solids added to manure storage during the course of the month (kg). The factor of 1/2 is multiplied by this number to represent the average mass of volatile solids available for degradation for the entire duration of the month.

VS_{out} = volatile solids removed from the manure storage for land application or export (assumed value based on standard farm practice)

f = van't Hoff-Arrhenius factor for the specific month as determined using the equation below. Using a base temperature of 30° C, the equation is as follows:

$$f = \exp[E * (T_2 - T_1)/(GC * T_1 * T_2)]$$

where:

f = conversion efficiency of VS to CH_4 per month

E = activation energy constant (15,175 cal/mol)

T_2 = average monthly ambient temperature for farm (converted from ° Celsius to ° Kelvin) as determined from the nearest National Weather Service certified weather station (if reported temperature ° C > 5 ° C; if reported temperature ° C < 5 ° C, then F = 0.104)

T1 = 303.15 (30° C converted to ° K)

GC = ideal gas constant (1.987 cal/K mol)

(iii) The volume of CH_4 produced (ft^3) from degradation of volatile solids shall be calculated as follows:

$$V_m = (VS_{deg} \times B_o) \times 35.3147$$

where:

V_m = volume of CH_4 (ft^3)

VS_{deg} = volatile solids degraded (kg)

B_o = manure type-specific maximum methane generation constant (m^3 CH_4/kg VS degraded). For dairy cow manure, B_o = 0.24 m^3 CH4/kg VS degraded. The methane generation constant for other types of manure shall be those cited at U.S. EPA, *Inventory of U.S. Greenhouse Gas Emissions and Sinks: 1990-2010*, Annex 3 Table A-162 (U.S. EPA, April 2012), unless the project sponsor proposes an alternate methane generation constant. If the project sponsor proposes to use a methane generation constant other than the one found in the above-cited reference, the project sponsor must provide justification and documentation to the Department.

(d) Calculating emissions reductions. Emissions reductions shall be determined based on the potential emissions (in tons of CO_2e) of the CH_4 that would have been produced in the absence of the offset project under a baseline scenario that represents uncontrolled anaerobic storage conditions, as calculated pursuant to subsections 9(D)(5)(c)(i) through (iii) of this Chapter, and released directly to the atmosphere. Emissions reductions may not exceed the potential emissions of the digester, as represented by the annual volume of CH_4 produced by the anaerobic digester, as monitored pursuant to subsection 9(D)(5)(e) of this Chapter. If the project is a regional-type digester, CO_2 emissions due to transportation of manure and organic food wastes from the site where the manure and organic food wastes were generated to the anaerobic digester shall be subtracted from the emissions reduction calculated pursuant to subsections 9(D)(5)(c)(i) through (iii) of this Chapter. Transport CO_2 emissions shall be determined through one of the following methods:

(i) Documentation of transport fuel use for all shipments of manure and organic food wastes from off-site to the anaerobic digester during each reporting year and a log of transport miles for each shipment. CO_2 emissions shall be determined through the application of an emissions factor for the fuel type used. If this option is chosen, the following emission factors shall be applied as appropriate.

(A) Diesel fuel: 22.912 lbs. CO_2/gallon.

(B) Gasoline: 19.878 lbs. CO_2/gallon.

(C) Other fuel: submitted emission factor approved by the Department.

(ii) Documentation of total tons of manure transported from off- site for input into the anaerobic digester during each reporting year, as monitored pursuant to subsection 9(D)(5)(e)(i) of this Chapter, and a log of transport miles and fuel type used for each shipment. CO_2 emissions shall be determined through the application of a ton-mile transport emission factor for the fuel type used. If this option is chosen, the following emission factors shall be applied as appropriate for each ton of manure delivered, and multiplied by the number of miles transported.

(A) Diesel fuel: 0.131 lbs. CO_2 per ton-mile.

(B) Gasoline: 0.133 lbs. CO_2 per ton-mile.

(C) Other fuel: submitted emission factor approved by the Department.

(e) Monitoring and verification requirements. Offset projects shall employ a system that provides metering of biogas volumetric flow rate and determination of CH_4 concentration. Monitoring and verification reports shall include monthly biogas volumetric flow rate and CH4 concentration determination. Monitoring and verification shall also meet the following requirements:

(i) If the offset project is a regional-type digester, manure and organic food waste from each distinct source supplying to the anaerobic digester shall be sampled monthly to determine the amount of volatile solids present. Any emissions reduction will be calculated according to mass of manure and organic food waste (kg) being digested and percentage of volatile solids present before digestion, consistent with the requirements at subsections 9(D)(5)(c) and 9(D)(5)(e)(iii) of this Chapter, and apportioned accordingly among sources. The project sponsor shall provide supporting material and receipts tracking the monthly receipt of manure and organic food waste (kg) used to supply the anaerobic digester from each manure supplier.

(ii) If the offset project includes the digestion of organic food wastes eligible pursuant to subsection 9(D)(5)(a)(ii) of this Chapter, organic food wastes shall be sampled monthly to determine the amount of volatile solids (VS) present before digestion, consistent with the requirements at subsections 9(D)(5)(c) and 9(D)(5)(e)(iii) of this Chapter, and apportioned accordingly.

(iii) The project sponsor shall submit a monitoring and verification plan as part of the consistency application that includes a quality assurance and quality control program associated with equipment used to determine biogas volumetric flow rate and CH_4 composition. The monitoring and verification plan shall be specified in accordance with the applicable monitoring requirements listed in Table 3 below. The monitoring and verification plan shall also include provisions for ensuring that measuring and monitoring equipment is maintained, operated, and calibrated based on manufacturer's recommendations, as well as provisions for the retention of maintenance records for audit purposes. The monitoring and verification plan shall be certified by an independent verifier accredited pursuant to subsection 9(E) of this Chapter.

Table 3. Input Monitoring Requirements

Input Parameter	Measurement Unit	Frequency of Sampling	Sampling Method(s)
Influent flow (mass) into the digester	Kilograms (kg) per month (wet weight)	Monthly total into the digester	Average herd population and American Society of Agricultural and Biological Engineers (ASABE) standard (ASAE D384.2, March 2005) Digester influent pump flow Recorded weight
Influent total solids concentration (TS)	Percent (of sample)	Monthly, depending upon recorded variations	U.S. EPA Method Number 160.3
Influent volatile solids (VS) content of manure	Percent (of TS)	Monthly, depending upon recorded variations	USEPA Method Number 160.4, Methods for the Chemical Analysis of Water and Wastes (MCAWW) (EPA/600/4-79/020)
Average monthly ambient temperature	Temperature °C	Monthly (based on farm averages)	Closest National Weather Service certified weather station

E. Accreditation of Independent verifiers

(1) Standards for Accreditation. Independent verifiers may be accredited by the Department to provide verification services as required of project sponsors under this section, provided that independent verifiers meet all of the requirements of this section.

    (a) Verifier minimum requirements. Each accredited independent verifier shall demonstrate knowledge of the following topics:

        (i) utilizing engineering principlesP

        (ii) quantifying greenhouse gas emissionsP

        (iii) developing and evaluating air emissions inventories:

        (iv) auditing and accounting principlesP

        (v) knowledge of information management systemsP

        (vi) knowledge of the requirements of this section and other applicable requirements of this ChapterP and

        (vii) such other qualifications as may be required by the Department to provide competent verification services as required for individual offset categories specified at subsection 9(D) of this Chapter.

    (b) Organizational qualifications. Accredited independent verifiers shall demonstrate that they meet the following requirements:

    (i)   verifiers shall have no direct or indirect financial relationship, beyond a contract for provision of verification services, with any offset project developer or project sponsorP

    (ii) verifiers shall employ staff with professional licenses, knowledge, and experience appropriate to the specific category(ies) of offset projects under subsection 9(D) of this Chapter that they seek to verifyP

    (iii) verifiers shall hold a minimum of one million U.S. dollars of professional liability insurance. If the insurance is in the name of a related entity, the verifier shall disclose the financial relationship between the verifier and the related entity, and provide documentation supporting the description of the relationshipP and

    (iv) verifiers shall demonstrate that they have implemented an adequate management protocol to identify potential conflicts of interest with regard to an offset project, offset project developer, or project sponsor, or any other party with a direct or indirect financial interest in an offset project that is seeking or has been granted approval of a consistency application pursuant to subsection 9(C)(5) of this Chapter, and remedy any such conflicts of interest prior to providing verification services.

  (c) Prequalification of verifiers. The Department may require prospective verifiers to successfully complete a training course, workshop, or test developed by the Department or its agent, prior to submitting an application for accreditation.

(2) Application for accreditation. An application for accreditation shall not contain any proprietary information, and shall include the following:

  (a) the applicant's name, address, email address, telephone number, and facsimile transmission numberP

  (b) documentation that the applicant has at least two years of experience in each of the knowledge areas specified at subsections 9(E)(1)(a)(i) through (v) of this Chapter, and as may be required pursuant to subsection 9(E)(1)(a)(vii) of this Chapter P

  (c) documentation that the applicant has successfully completed the requirements at subsection 9(E)(1)(c) of this Chapter, as applicableP

  (d) a sample of at least one work product that provides supporting evidence that the applicant meets the requirements at subsections 9(E)(1)(a) and (b) of this Chapter. The work product shall have been produced, in whole or in part, by the applicant and shall consist of a final report or other material provided to a client under contract in previous work. For a work product that was jointly produced by the applicant and another entity, the role of the applicant in the work product shall be clearly explainedP

  (e) documentation that the applicant holds professional liability insurance as required pursuant to subsection 9(E)(1)(b)(iii) of this Chapter.

  (f) documentation that the applicant has implemented an adequate management protocol to address and remedy any conflict of interest issues that may arise, as required pursuant to subsection 9(E)(1)(b)(iv) of this Chapter.

(3) Department action on applications for accreditation. The Department shall approve or deny a complete application for accreditation within 45 days after

submission. Upon approval of an application for accreditation, the independent verifier shall be accredited for a period of three years from the date of application approval.

(4) Reciprocity. Independent verifiers accredited in other participating states may be deemed to be accredited in Maine, at the discretion of the Department.

(5) Conduct of accredited verifiers

   (a) Prior to engaging in verification services for an offset project sponsor, the accredited verifier shall disclose all relevant information to the Department to allow for an evaluation of potential conflict of interest with respect to an offset project, offset project developer, or project sponsor. The accredited verifier shall disclose information concerning its ownership, past and current clients, related entities, as well as any other facts or circumstances that have the potential to create a conflict of interest.

   (b) Accredited verifiers shall have an ongoing obligation to disclose to the Department any facts or circumstances that may give rise to a conflict of interest with respect to an offset project, offset project developer, or project sponsor.

   (c) The Department may reject a verification report and certification statement from an accredited verifier, submitted as part of a consistency application required pursuant to subsection 9(C)(2) of this Chapter or submitted as part of a monitoring and verification report submitted pursuant to subsection 9(F)(2) of this Chapter, if the Department determines that the accredited verifier has a conflict of interest related to the offset project, offset project developer, or project sponsor.

   (d) The Department may revoke the accreditation of a verifier at any time given cause, for the following:

      (i) failure to fully disclose any issues that may lead to a conflict of interest situation with respect to an offset project, offset project developer, or project sponsorP

      (ii) the verifier is no longer qualified due to changes in staffing or other criteriaP

      (iii) negligence or neglect of responsibilities pursuant to the requirements of this sectionP and

      (iv) intentional misrepresentation of data or other intentional fraud.

F. **Award of CO_2 offset allowances**

   (1) Quantities of CO_2 offset allowances that may be awarded

      (a) CO_2 emissions offset projects. Following the issuance of a consistency determination under subsection 9(C)(5)(b) of this Chapter and the approval of a monitoring and verification report under the provisions of subsection 9(F)(5) of this Chapter, the Department will award one CO_2 offset allowance for each ton of demonstrated reduction in CO_2 or CO_2 equivalent emissions or sequestration of CO_2.

      Recordation of CO_2 offset allowances. After CO_2 offset allowances are awarded under subsection 9(F)(1)(a) of this Chapter, the Department shall record such CO_2 offset allowances in the project sponsor's general account.

(2) Deadlines for submittal of monitoring and verification reports

   (a) For CO_2 emissions offset projects undertaken prior to January 1, 2009, the project sponsor must submit the monitoring and verification report covering the pre-2009 period by June 30, 2009.

   (b) For CO_2 emissions offset projects undertaken on or after January 1, 2009, the monitoring and verification report must be submitted within 6 months following the completion of the last calendar year during which the offset project achieved CO_2 equivalent reductions or sequestration of CO_2 for which the project sponsor seeks the award of CO_2 offset allowances.

(3) Contents of monitoring and verification reports. For an offset project, the monitoring and verification report must include the following information:

   (a) The project's sponsor's name, address, email address, telephone number, facsimile transmission number, and account number.

   (b) The CO_2 emissions reduction or CO_2 sequestration determination as required by the relevant provisions of subsection 9(D) of this Chapter, including a demonstration that the project sponsor complied with the required quantification, monitoring, and verification procedures under subsection 9(D) of this Chapter, as well as those outlined in the consistency application approved pursuant to subsection 9(C)(5)(b) of this Chapter.

   (c) A signed statement that reads "The undersigned project sponsor hereby confirms and attests that the offset project upon which this monitoring and verification report is based is in full compliance with all of the requirements of Section 9 of this Chapter. The project sponsor holds the legal rights to the offset project, or has been granted the right to act on behalf of a party that holds the legal rights to the offset project. I understand that eligibility for the award of CO_2 offset allowances under Section 9 of this Chapter is contingent on meeting the requirements of Section 9 of this Chapter. I authorize the Department or its agent to audit this offset project for purposes of verifying that the offset project, including the monitoring and verification plan, has been implemented as described in the consistency application that was the subject of a consistency determination by the Department. I understand that this right to audit shall include the right to enter the physical location of the offset project. I submit to the legal jurisdiction of Maine."

   (d) A certification signed by the offset project sponsor certifying that all offset projects for which the sponsor has received offset allowances under this section (or similar provisions in the rules of other participating states), under the sponsor's ownership or control (or under the ownership or control of any entity which controls, is controlled by, or has common control with the sponsor) are in compliance with all applicable requirements of the CO_2 Budget Trading Program in all participating states.

   (e) A verification report and certification statement signed by an independent verifier accredited pursuant to subsection 9(E) of this Chapter that documents that the independent verifier has reviewed the monitoring and verification report and evaluated the following in relation to the applicable requirements at subsection 9(D) of this Chapter, and any applicable guidance issued by the Department.

(i) The adequacy and validity of information supplied by the project sponsor to determine CO_2 emissions reductions or CO_2 sequestration pursuant to the applicable requirements at subsection 9(D) of this Chapter.

(ii) The adequacy and consistency of methods used to quantify, monitor, and verify CO_2 emissions reductions and CO_2 sequestration in accordance with the applicable requirements at subsection 9(D) of this Chapter and as outlined in the consistency application approved pursuant to subsection 9(C)(5)(b) of this Chapter.

(iii) Such other evaluations and verification reviews as may be required by the Department. The adequacy and validity of information supplied by the project sponsor to demonstrate that the offset project meets the applicable eligibility requirements of subsection 9(D) of this Chapter.

(f) Disclosure of any voluntary or mandatory programs, other than the CO_2 Budget Trading Program, to which greenhouse gas emissions data related to the offset project has been, or will be reported.

(g) For offset projects located in a state or United States jurisdiction that is not a participating state, a demonstration that the project sponsor has complied with all requirements of the cooperating regulatory agency in the state or United States jurisdiction where the offset project is located.

(4) Place for filing monitoring and verification reports. The monitoring and verification report must be filed with the same Department that issued the consistency determination for the offset project pursuant to subsection 9(C)(5)(b) of this Chapter.

(5) Department action on monitoring and verification reports. The Department will approve or deny a complete monitoring and verification report within 45 days following receipt of a complete report.

———————

STATUTORY AUTHORITY: 38 MRSA, Sections 585-A, 580, 580-A, 580-B, and 580-C

EFFECTIVE DATE:

January 5, 2008, filing 2007-544

AMENDED:

July 22, 2008 — filing 2008-317

November 26, 2013 — filing 2013-290

Chapter 158: CO_2 BUDGET TRADING PROGRAM AUCTION PROVISIONS

SUMMARY: This regulation provides for the administration and implementation by the Department of CO_2 allowance auctions and programs to promote the purposes of the Consumer Benefit Account as provided by CO_2 Budget Trading Program, 06-096 CMR 156. This regulation complements the provisions of the CO_2 Budget Trading Program, which was established by the Department to stabilize and then reduce anthropogenic emissions of CO_2, a greenhouse gas, from CO_2 budget sources.

1. Applicability. This regulation applies to any person who participates in RGGI CO_2 allowance auctions.

2. **Definitions**

A. **Applicant.** "Applicant" means a party submitting an application.

B. **Ascending price, multiple round auction.** "Ascending price, multiple round auction" means a multiple-round auction starting with an opening price which increases each round by predetermined increments. In each round, bidders offer the quantity they are willing to purchase at the posted price. Rounds continue so long as demand exceeds the quantity offered for sale. At the completion of the final round, the Department or its agent may allocate allowances:

   (1) at the final price to remaining bidders and withhold unsold allowances for a future auction;

   (2) at the penultimate price, first to final round bidders and then to bidders in the penultimate round in chronological order of bid during the penultimate round for all remaining allowances; or

   (3) according to an alternative mechanism designed to effectuate the objectives of this Chapter.

C. **Beneficial interest.** "Beneficial interest" means profit, benefit, or advantage resulting from the ownership of a CO_2 allowance.

D. **Bidder.** "Bidder" means a party that has met the requirements of subsection 3(C) of this Chapter to participate in an auction.

E. **CO_2 allowance auction or auction.** "CO_2 allowance auction or auction" means an auction in which the Department or its agent offers CO_2 allowances for sale.

F. **CO_2 allowance auction website.** "CO_2 allowance auction website" means a website established by the Department or its agent that will contain information regarding the CO_2 Budget Trading Program and auctions to be conducted pursuant to this Chapter.

G. **CO_2 budget source.** "CO_2 budget source" means a source that includes one or more CO_2 budget units.

H. **CO_2 budget source compliance account or compliance account.** "CO_2 budget source compliance account" or "compliance account" means the account established by the Department or its agent for a CO_2 budget source wherein CO_2 allowances are held and available for compliance purposes under CO_2 Budget Trading Program, 06-096 CMR 156.

I. **CO_2 Budget Trading Program.** "CO_2 Budget Trading Program" means a multi-state CO_2 air pollution control and emissions reduction program established pursuant to this regulation and corresponding regulations in other states as a means of reducing emissions of CO_2 from CO_2 budget sources.

J. **CO_2 budget unit.** "CO_2 budget unit" means a fossil fuel-fired unit that serves a generator with a nameplate capacity equal to or greater than 25 MW electrical output.

K. **CO_2 cost containment reserve allowance or CO_2 CCR allowance.** "CO_2 cost containment reserve allowance or CO_2 CCR allowance" means a CO_2 allowance that is offered for sale at an auction by the Department for the purpose of containing the cost of CO_2 allowances. CO_2 CCR allowances offered for sale at an auction are separate from and additional to CO_2 allowances allocated from the

CO_2 Budget Trading Program base and adjusted budgets. CO_2 CCR allowances are subject to all applicable limitations contained in this Chapter.

L. **Consumer Benefit Account.** "Consumer Benefit Account" means a general account established by the Department or its agent from which CO_2 allowances will be sold or distributed in order to provide funds to encourage and foster the following: promotion of energy efficiency measures, direct mitigation of electricity ratepayer impacts attributable to the implementation of the CO_2 Budget Trading Program, promotion of renewable or non-carbon-emitting energy technologies, stimulation or reward of investment in the development of innovative carbon emissions abatement technologies with significant carbon reduction potential, promotion and reward for combined heat and power projects, and/or the administration of Maine's component of the CO_2 Budget Trading Program.

M. **Control period.** "Control period" means a three-calendar-year time period. The first control period is from January 1, 2009 to December 31, 2011, inclusive. Each subsequent sequential three-calendar-year period is a separate control period. The first two calendar years of each control period are each defined as an interim control period beginning on January 1, 2015.

N. **Cost containment reserve trigger price or CCR trigger price.** "Cost containment reserve trigger price or CCR trigger price" means the minimum price at which CO_2 CCR allowances are offered for sale by the Department or its agent at an auction. The CCR trigger price shall be $4.00 per CO_2 allowance for calendar year 2014, $6.00 per CO_2 allowance in calendar year 2015, $8.00 per CO_2 allowance in calendar year 2016 and $10.00 per CO_2 allowance in calendar year 2017. Each calendar year thereafter, the CCR trigger price shall be 1.025 multiplied by the CCR trigger price from the previous calendar year, rounded to the nearest whole cent.

O. **Current Market Price.** "Current Market Price" means the volume-weighted average of (1) transaction prices reported to the Department or its agent, (2) prices as reported publicly through reputable sources, (3) CO2 allowance award price(s) from preceding CO2 Allowance Auctions, or (4) any combination of these options.

P. **Efficiency Maine Trust.** "Efficiency Maine Trust" means the trust established by the Efficiency Maine Trust Act, 35-A MRSA § 10103 that is authorized to receive revenue resulting from the sale of CO_2 allowances, deposit those allowances in the Regional Greenhouse Gas Initiative Trust Fund and expend that revenue in accordance with 35-A MRSA § 10109.

Q. **General account.** "General account" means a CO_2 allowance tracking system account, established under 06-096 CMR 156 (7),, that is not a compliance account.

R. **Minimum Reserve Price or MRP.** "Minimum Reserve Price" or "MRP" means the minimum reserve price in calendar year 2014 shall be $2.00. Each calendar year thereafter, the minimum reserve price shall be 1.025 multiplied by the minimum reserve price from the previous calendar year, rounded to the nearest whole cent.

S. **Notice of CO_2 allowance auction.** "Notice of CO_2 allowance auction" means the notification prior to each CO_2 allowance auction that will inform potential bidders of the date, time and location of the auction.

T. **Participating state.** "Participating state" means a state that has established a corresponding regulation as part of the CO_2 Budget Trading Program.

U. **Reserve price.** "Reserve Price" means the minimum acceptable price for each CO_2 allowance in a specific auction. The reserve price at an auction is either the minimum reserve price or the CCR trigger price, as specified in CO_2 Budget Trading Program, 06-096 CMR 156(2)(G).

V. **Regional Greenhouse Gas Initiative or RGGI.** "Regional Greenhouse Gas Initiative" or "RGGI" means the ongoing cooperative effort by the states of Maine, New Hampshire, Vermont, Connecticut, New York, Massachusetts, Rhode Island, Maryland and Delaware and such others states as may in the future become a part of the program to design and implement, using each state's individual sovereign authority, a regional CO_2 cap-and-trade program covering CO_2 emissions from CO_2 budget units in the signatory states.

W. **Regional Greenhouse Gas Initiative Trust Fund.** "Regional Greenhouse Gas Initiative Trust Fund" means the non-lapsing fund established by The Efficiency Maine Trust Act 35-A MRSA § 10109(2) and administered by the Efficiency Maine Trust to support the goals and implementation of the CO_2 Budget Trading Program, into which revenue resulting from the sale of CO_2 allowances shall be deposited.

X. **Uniform-price, sealed-bid auction.** "Uniform-price, sealed-bid auction" means a single round sealed-bid auction in which bidders may submit multiple bids at different prices; the price paid by all awarded bidders with the highest bid for the available allowances is equal to the highest rejected bid.

3. **CO_2 Allowance Auction Provisions**

A. **The Consumer Benefit Account**

(1) The Department will establish and administer the Consumer Benefit Account in accordance with CO_2 Budget Trading Program 06-096 CMR 156 (2)(F)..

(2) CO_2 allowances allocated to the State will be held in the Consumer Benefit Account and made available for sale in CO_2 allowance auctions as described in this Chapter.

(3) The proceeds from the auctions of Maine's CO_2 allowances will be received by the Efficiency Maine Trust and deposited into the Regional Greenhouse Gas Initiative Trust Fund , in accordance with 35-A MRSA § 10109(2).

B. **Implementation and administration of CO_2 Allowance Auctions**

(1) The Department or its agent will conduct auctions to sell CO_2 allowances allocated into the Consumer Benefit Account, pursuant to this Chapter.

(2) The Department will design, implement and administer CO_2 Allowance Auctions, or contract for these services, in accordance with the objectives identified in CO_2 Budget Trading Program, 06-096 CMR 156, this Chapter and as provided by law.

(3) The Department or its agent intends to conduct or participate in any of the following, or a combination thereof:

(a) a multi-state CO_2 allowance auction or auctions;

(b) an auction or auctions coordinated with one or more participating states; or

(c) a Maine state auction.

(4) The Department or its agent intends to hold auctions at least annually; auctions may be held as often as practical and necessary to effectuate the objectives of the CO_2 Budget Trading Program, at the Department or its agent's discretion.

(5) Prior to the end of each control period, CO_2 allowances in a quantity equal to the number of CO_2 allowances allocated to the Consumer Benefit Account for such control period will be made available for sale. The Department or its agent may also make available for sale CO_2 allowances for future control periods.

(6) Prior to any auction, the Department or its agent may set a binding reserve price to be accepted for CO_2 allowances in such auction. The reserve price will be disclosed to prospective bidders prior to the auction.

(7) Any CO_2 allowances left unsold in any auction may be made available for sale in a subsequent auction or auctions, in quantities and in a manner determined by the Department or its agent.

(8) In conducting CO_2 allowance auctions, the Department or its agent may employ any of the following auction formats, or an auction format consisting of any or all of the components thereof:

(a) Uniform-price sealed-bid; or

(b) Ascending price, multiple-round.

(9) Notice of Auctions

(a) A notice of CO_2 allowance auction ("notice") will be published on the CO_2 Allowance Auction Website or the Department website at least 45 days prior to the date upon which each auction may be conducted. Such notices may be transmitted electronically to parties requesting such notification.

(b) Each notice will provide a specific description of the auction format for each auction, including all auction participation requirements, and will include but not be limited to the following information:

(i) date and time of the auction;

(ii) location and/or electronic address of auction;

(iii) number and vintage of CO_2 allowances to be auctioned;

(iv) bid format;

(v) pre-qualification instructions and application;

(vi) the terms and conditions that will govern auction transactions;

(vii) other pertinent rules of the auction; and

(viii) identification of a Department Contact Person.

C. **Participation Eligibility and Requirements**

(1) The auction or auctions will be open to participation by all individuals or entities that meet the financial requirements of this subsection.

(2) Any party wishing to participate in a CO_2 Allowance Auction shall first:

(a) open and maintain a compliance or general account in Maine or other participating state pursuant to the provisions in CO_2 Budget Trading Program 06-096 CMR 156 or comparable regulations in a participating state;

(b) submit a completed application in the format and manner provided in the notice to the Department or its agent on or before the application deadline date specified in the notice of CO_2 allowance auction; and

(i) Application information and forms will be made available electronically on the CO_2 allowance auction website or the Department website. As part of the application, bidders shall provide information and documentation, as specified in the application, relating to bidder's ability and authority to execute bids and honor contractual obligations. Information and documentation sought in the application may include but may not be limited to:

(A) information and documentation regarding the corporate identity, ownership, and capital structure of the bidder;

(B) declaration of any beneficial interest of any allowance that may be acquired through the auction;

(C) the identification of any indictment or felony conviction of the bidder, corporate officers, directors, principals or partners of the applicant. ; or

(D) the identification of any previous or pending investigation with respect to any alleged violation of any rule, regulation or law associated with any commodity market or exchange.

NOTE: *All information and data submitted in an application will be governed by the provisions of the Freedom of Access Law, Title 1 M.R.S. Section 401 et seq., as amended. If an applicant believes its application contains information exempt from the definition of "public records," 1 M.R.S. §402(3), it should put the Department on notice as to that claim by conspicuously marking such documents as "claimed confidential." The Department will handle such documents in accordance with its standard operating procedures governing potentially confidential records under the Freedom of Access law.*

(ii) Failure to provide any information required by the application may result in its being returned as incomplete. Prospective bidders whose applications have been determined to be incomplete will be given a reasonable opportunity, and in no event less than 10 business days, to provide additional information and to cure such deficiencies.

(iii) Prospective bidders that qualify for participation under this subsection will be qualified for all subsequent CO_2 allowance auctions, and may bid in such auctions provided that such party has complied with the financial security requirements of this subsection. The Department or its agent may require applicants previously found qualified to update and re-file applications on an annual basis.

(iv) Prior to each CO_2 allowance auction a prospective bidder that has qualified under this subsection must notify the Department or its agent of its intent to participate in the upcoming auction. This notification shall include either a signed statement that there has been no change to the information provided in the application, or a revised application if changes have occurred.

(v) The Department or its agent may suspend or revoke its approval of an application if the bidder fails to comply with this Chapter and/or the provisions of CO_2 Budget Trading Program, 06-096 CMR 156. A decision under this subsection is final agency action.

(c) provide financial security in the form of a bond, cash, certified funds, or an irrevocable stand-by letter of credit, in a form acceptable to the Department or its agent.

(i) Bids in any auction may be limited to the level of financial security provided by the bidder.

(ii) Financial security may be forfeited to and retained by the Department or its agent in the event the bidder's offer is accepted in a CO_2 allowance auction and the bidder fails to tender payment of the full amount when due.

(iii) Bidders may request return of their financial security at any time prior to or following any CO_2 allowance auction, and the Department or its agent shall return said financial security provided that the Department or its agent has no current or pending claim to such security as a result of a failure of the bidder to comply with these regulations or to pay the full amount of its accepted bid when due.

(d) If the Department or its agent determines that a bidder has provided false or misleading information, or has withheld pertinent information in its application, or has otherwise failed to comply with any material provision of this Chapter, the bidder may be prohibited from participating in any future CO_2 allowance auctions. A decision under this subsection is final agency action.

(e) Any applicant or bidder that has been found to have violated any rule, regulation, or law associated with any commodity market or exchange may be precluded from participation in CO_2 allowance auctions. A decision under this subsection is final agency action.

D. Auction Bids and Transfer of Allowances

(1) All bids shall be in a form prescribed by the Department or its agent, which shall be made available electronically on the CO_2 Allowance Auction Website, as appropriate. All bids submitted will be considered binding offers for the purchase of allowances under the rules of the auction.

(2) No bidder or combination of bidders that have related beneficial interests may bid on more than 25% of the allowances available for sale in any given auction.

(3) Successful bidders must submit payment in full to the Department or its agent in accordance with the deadline specified in each Auction Notice.

(4) Upon receipt of payment the Department or its agent shall transfer or have transferred the corresponding CO_2 allowances to the successful bidder's

compliance or general account in accordance with CO_2 Budget Trading Program, 06-096 CMR 156 (8)(B) and (C).

(5) Within 10 days of the auction certification the Department or its agent shall publish the auction clearing price and the total number of allowances sold in such auction on the CO_2 Allowance Auction Website.

STATUTORY AUTHORITY: 38 MRSA §§ 585-A, 580, 580-A, 580-B, and 580-C

EFFECTIVE DATE:

July 22, 2008 — filing 2008-318

AMENDED:

November 26, 2013 — filing 2013-291

Index